The American Pageant

Volume 2: Since 1865

120°W
110°W
100°W
90°W
49°N
42°N
40°N
30°N
Washington
1889
Columbia R.
Oregon Country
(By Agreement with Britain, 1846)
Oregon
1859
Idaho
1890
Montana
1889
Missouri R.
North Dakota
1889
South Dakota
1889
Wyoming
1890
Nebraska
1867
Louisiana Purchase
(From France, 180
Colorado
1876
Kansas
1861
Oklahom
1907
Great Salt Lake
Nevada
1864
Utah
1896
Mexican Cession
(1848)
Colorado R.
California
1850
Arizona
1912
New Mexico
1912
Pacific Ocean
Gadsden Purchase
(From Mexico, 1853)
Texas
(Independent Republic, Annexed 1845)
Texas
1845
Rio Grande
Nueces R.
Pacific Ocean
Hawai'i
1959
Hawai'i
(Annexed 1898)
20°N
0 50 100 Km.
0 50 100 Mi.
155°W
Russia
70°N
Alaska
1959
Canada
60°N
Alaska Purchase
(From Russia, 1867)
170°E
50°N
Pacific Ocean
0 200 400 Km.
0 250 400 Mi.
180°
170°W
160°W
150°W
140°W
Mexico

Territorial Growth of the United States
1820 Date of state's admission to the Union
Geographic center of population by decade
Canada
Lake Superior
Lake Michigan
Lake Huron
Lake Ontario
Lake Erie
St. Lawrence R.
Mississippi R.
90°W
80°W
70°W
60°W
Maine 1820
VT. 1791
N.H.
Mass.
Conn.
R.I.
New York
Pennsylvania
New Jersey
Delaware
Maryland
1790
Mason-Dixon Line
The Original Thirteen Colonies
Wisconsin 1848
nnesota 1858
Michigan 1837
Iowa 1846
Illinois 1818
Indiana 1816
Ohio 1803
West Virginia 1863
Virginia
Kentucky 1792
Missouri 1821
2020
36°30'N Missouri Compromise Line
The Original United States (By Treaty with Britain, 1783)
North Carolina
Tennessee 1796
Arkansas 1836
South Carolina
Georgia
Mississippi 1817
Alabama 1819
Louisiana 1812
(Seized from Spain, 1810, 1813)
Florida (By Treaty with Spain, 1819)
Florida 1845
Atlantic Ocean
Gulf of Mexico
Bahamas
Cuba
Haiti
Dominican Republic
0 150 300 Km.
0 150 300 Mi.
N
Puerto Rico (Acquired from Spain, 1898)
Virgin Is. (Acquired from Denmark, 1916–1917)
Puerto Rico
Virgin Islands
19°N
18°N
68°W
67°W
66°W
65°W
0 25 50 Km.
0 25 50 Mi.

Greenland
(Denmark)
80°N
Iceland
Alaska
(U.S.)
60°N
Canada
Ire
United States
40°N
Azores
(Port.)
Portu
Bermuda
(U.K.)
Atlantic Ocean
Midway Is.
(U.S.)
Bahamas
Dominican Rep.
Western
Sahara
(Morocco)
Hawaiian Is.
(U.S.)
Mexico
Virgin Is.
(U.S.)
Cuba
Jamaica
Haiti
St. Kitts and Nevis
Antigua and Barbuda
20°N
Maur
Belize
Puerto Rico
(U.S.)
Dominica
Cape
Verde
Honduras
Barbados
Senegal
Guatemala
St. Lucia
Gambia
El Salvador
Nicaragua
Grenada
St. Vincent and
the Grenadines
Guinea-bissau
Guine
Pacific Ocean
Costa Rica
Venezuela
Trinidad and Tobago
Sierra
Leone
Panama
Guyana
Liberia
Colombia
Fr. Guiana
(France)
Equator
Galapagos Is.
(Ecuador)
Ecuador
Surinam
0°
São To
Peru
Brazil
Samoa
Bolivia
French Polynesia
(France)
Tonga
20°S
Paraguay
Easter Is.
(Chile)
Chile
Uruguay
Argentina
40°S
0
1,000
2,000 Km.
0
1,000
2,000 Mi.
Falkland Is.
(U.K.)
160°W
140°W
120°W
100°W
80°W
60°W
40°W
20°W
60°S
80°S

ic Ocean
Russia
Finland
Estonia
Sweden
Latvia
Lithuania
Den.
Belarus
Poland
Germany
Ukraine
CZ.
Slk.
Aus.
Hung.
Moldova
Sln.
CR.
Romania
Italy
B. H.
SE.
K.
Bulgaria
MO.
Mac.
Albania
Greece
Georgia
Turkey
Armenia
Cyprus
Azerbaijan
Malta
Tunisia
Syria
Lebanon
Israel
Iraq
Iran
Kazakhstan
Uzbekistan
Turkmenistan
Kyrgyzstan
Tajikistan
Afghanistan
Pakistan
Mongolia
People's Republic of China
N. Korea
S. Korea
Japan
Pacific Ocean
Libya
Egypt
Jordan
Kuwait
Bahrain
Qatar
Saudi Arabia
United Arab Emirates
Oman
Nepal
Bhutan
Bangladesh
India
Myanmar (Burma)
Laos
Taiwan
Vietnam
Thailand
Cambodia (Kampuchea)
Philippines
Niger
Chad
Sudan
Eritrea
Yemen
Djibouti
Ethiopia
Benin
Nigeria
Central African Rep.
South Sudan
Cameroon
Somalia
Uganda
Kenya
Gabon
Rwanda
Dem. Rep. of Congo
Congo
Burundi
Tanzania
Seychelles
Sri Lanka
Maldives
Brunei Darussalam
Malaysia
Singapore
Palau
Mariana Islands (U.S.)
Guam (U.S.)
Federated States of Micronesia
Wake I. (U.S.)
Marshall Islands
Kiribati
Nauru
Indian Ocean
Indonesia
Papua New Guinea
Timor Leste
Solomon Is.
Tuvalu
Vanuatu
Fiji
New Caledonia (France)
Angola
Zambia
Malawi
Comoros
Namibia
Zimbabwe
Madagascar
Mauritius
Botswana
Mozambique
Swaziland
South Africa
Lesotho
Australia
New Zealand
Abbreviations
Aus. Austria
Bel. Belgium
B. H. Bosnia and Herzegovina
CR. Croatia
CZ. Czech Republic
Den. Denmark
Hung. Hungary
K. Kosovo
Lux. Luxembourg
Mac. Macedonia
MO. Montenegro
Neth. Netherlands
SE. Serbia
Slk. Slovakia
Sln. Slovenia
Switz. Switzerland
20°E
40°E
60°E
80°E
100°E
120°E
140°E
160°E

"Cengage Unlimited is a game changer.
When you think about everything it includes—all access to online textbooks, option for textbook rentals, etc.—all for a super reasonable price, who could say no to saving money?"
—Lindsey M., Student, El Paso Community College
Taking more than one class that requires Cengage course materials?
Visit cengage.com/unlimited to learn how you can save money.
Cengage Unlimited
MindTap | WebAssign | Cengage Infuse | OpenNOW | SAM | CNOWv2 | OWLv2 | eTextbooks

The American Pageant

A History of the American People

Volume 2: Since 1865

Eighteenth Edition

David M. Kennedy
Stanford University

Margaret O'Mara
University of Washington

Lizabeth Cohen
Harvard University

Cengage

Australia • Brazil • Canada • Mexico • Singapore • United Kingdom • United States

***The American Pageant: A History of the American People*, Eighteenth Edition, Volume 2: Since 1865**
David M. Kennedy/Margaret O'Mara/ Lizabeth Cohen

SVP, Product Management: Cheryl Costantini
VP, Product Management: Heather Bradley Cole
Portfolio Product Director: Laura Ross
Senior Portfolio Product Manager: Joseph Potvin
Product Assistant: Danny Rader
Learning Designer: Leslie Taggart
Content Creation Manager: Christina Battista
Senior Content Manager: Philip Lanza
Senior Subject Matter Expert: Robert Alper
Senior Digital Project Manager: Liz Newitt
Marketing Development Manager: Chris Walz
Manufacturing Planner: Rebecca Cross
Senior Manager, Content Acquisition Operations: Alex Ricciardi
Senior Content Acquisition Analyst: Deanna Ettinger
Production Service: MPS Limited
Compositor: MPS Limited
Art Director: Sarah Cole
Cover Designer: Sarah Cole
Cover Image: *Lift Up Thy Voice and Sing* (ca. 1942–1944), William H. Johnson. Smithsonian American Art Museum, Washington, DC/Art Resource, NY
Table of Contents Design Images:
The Granger Collection/Library of Congress Alamy Stock Photo
Library of Congress
Nebraska State Historical Society
Library of Congress Prints and Photographs Division [LC-USZ6-1222]
Library of Congress Prints and Photographs Division [LC-DIG-pga-00755]
The Granger Collection/Alamy Stock Photo
The Granger Collection, NYC
The Granger Collection, NYC
Science History Images/Alamy Stock Photo
The Library of Congress
Alpha Stock/Alamy Stock Photo
National Archives
U.S. Air Force Photo
NASA Photo/Alamy Stock Photo
Bettmann/Getty Images
mccool/Alamy Stock Photo
Courtesy Ronald Reagan Library
Everett Collection Inc./Alamy Stock Photo
Reuters/Bryan Woolston

Library of Congress Control Number: 2024933643

Student Edition:
ISBN: 978-0-357-89888-8

Cengage
5191 Natorp Boulevard
Mason, OH 45040
USA

Printed in the United States of America
Print Number: 01 Print Year: 2024

About the Authors

David M. Kennedy is the Donald J. McLachlan Professor of History Emeritus and Director Emeritus of The Bill Lane Center for the American West at Stanford University, where he has taught for more than five decades. Born and raised in Seattle, he received his undergraduate education at Stanford and did his graduate training at Yale in American Studies, combining the fields of history, economics, and literature. His first book, *Birth Control in America: The Career of Margaret Sanger* (1970), was honored with both the Bancroft Prize and the John Gilmary Shea Prize. His study of the World War I era, *Over Here: The First World War and American Society* (1980; rev. ed., 2005), was a Pulitzer Prize finalist. In 1999, he published *Freedom from Fear: The American People in Depression and War, 1929–1945*, which won the Pulitzer Prize for History, as well as the Francis Parkman Prize, the English-Speaking Union's Ambassador's Prize, and the Commonwealth Club of California's Gold Medal for Literature.

At Stanford, Kennedy has taught both undergraduate and graduate courses in American political, diplomatic, intellectual, and social history, as well as in American literature. He has received several teaching awards, including the Dean's Award for Distinguished Teaching and the Hoagland Prize for Excellence in Undergraduate Teaching. He has been a visiting professor at the University of Florence, Italy, and in 1995–1996 served as the Harmsworth Professor of American History at Oxford University. He has accepted invitations to speak about American History in many countries, including Germany, Denmark, Finland, France, Turkey, China, Canada, and Russia. He has also served on the Advisory Board for the PBS television series, *The American Experience*, and as a consultant to several documentary films, including *The Great War*, *Cadillac Desert*, and *Woodrow Wilson*. From 1990 to 1995, he chaired the Test Development Committee for the Advanced Placement United States History examination. He is an elected Fellow of the American Academy of Arts and Sciences and of the American Philosophical Society and served from 2002 to 2011 on the board of the Pulitzer Prizes. Since 2000, he has served as the Editor of the Oxford History of the United States. Secretary of Agriculture Tom Vilsack in 2015 appointed Kennedy to the Advisory Council for the Pacific Northwest National Scenic Trail, which will run from Glacier National Park in Montana to the Pacific shore in Washington State. In 2018, PBS released "American Creed," a film he made jointly with former Secretary of State Condoleezza Rice.

The father of two sons and a daughter, and grandfather of seven, in his leisure time he enjoys hiking, bicycling, river-rafting, flying, sea-kayaking, and fly-fishing. His most recent book is *World War II and the West It Wrought* (2020), co-edited with Mark Brilliant.

Margaret O'Mara is the Scott and Dorothy Bullitt Chair of American History at the University of Washington, where she has taught since 2007. Raised in Little Rock, Arkansas, where she attended Little Rock Central High School thirty years after its racial integration made headlines around the world, she received her undergraduate degree from Northwestern University, her doctorate in History from the University of Pennsylvania, and held a postdoctoral fellowship at Stanford's Bill Lane Center for the West. Between undergraduate and graduate study, she worked in Washington, DC, as a member of Bill Clinton's presidential administration, serving as an economic and social policy aide in the White House and in the U.S. Department of Health and Human Services. Her first book, *Cities of Knowledge: Cold War Science and the Search for the Next Silicon Valley* (2005), derived from her prizewinning doctoral dissertation. It traced the Cold War origins of America's modern technology industry and the role of research universities in the genesis and growth of high-tech regions nationwide. Her second book, *Pivotal Tuesdays: Four Elections That Shaped the Twentieth Century* (2015), explored the American presidential elections of 1912, 1932, 1968, and 1992 and the great cultural and political transformations that surrounded them. In 2019, she published *The Code: Silicon Valley and the Remaking of America*, named a best book of the year by the *Financial Times* and *Publishers Weekly* as well as one of *New York Magazine*'s best books on Silicon Valley.

At the University of Washington, O'Mara teaches a range of History courses to both undergraduate and graduate students, including survey courses on the American presidency and the history of the digital age. In 2013, she was the recipient of the university's inaugural Distinguished Teaching Award for teaching with technology. An active media commentator and public speaker, she has lectured about American politics, business, and the history of high technology across the United States and internationally. She was a contributing opinion writer at *The New York Times* from 2019 to 2021, and her writing has appeared in *The Washington Post, WIRED, MIT Technology Review, Foreign Affairs,* and other national and global outlets. She has also been a historical consultant for Mattel's *American Girl* dolls and books. O'Mara is an OAH Distinguished Lecturer and a past fellow of the Center for Advanced Study in the Behavioral Sciences, the American Council of Learned Societies, and the National Forum on the Future of Liberal Education. She is a series editor of the Politics and Society in Modern America series at Princeton University Press and serves on the editorial board of *Modern American History.*

An avid hiker and enthusiastic traveler, O'Mara lives in Mercer Island, Washington, with her husband, Jeff, and their two daughters.

Lizabeth Cohen is the Howard Mumford Jones Professor of American Studies and a Distinguished Service Professor in the history department at Harvard University. In 2007–2008 she was the Harmsworth Professor of American History at Oxford University. Born and raised in the New York metropolitan area, she received her AB from Princeton University and her MA and PhD from the University of California at Berkeley. Her first book, *Making a New Deal: Industrial Workers in Chicago, 1919–1939* (1990), won the Bancroft Prize in American History and the Philip Taft Labor History Award and was a finalist for the Pulitzer Prize. In 2014, it appeared in Cambridge University Press's Canto Classic Series. Her next book, *A Consumers' Republic: The Politics of Mass Consumption in Postwar America* (2003), explored how an economy and culture built around mass consumption shaped social life and politics in post–World War II America. An article related to this book, "From Town Center to Shopping Center: The Reconfiguration of Community Marketplaces in Postwar America" (1996), was honored as the best article in urban history by the Urban History Association and received the ABC-CLIO, America: History and Life Award for the journal article that most advances previously unconsidered topics. Her latest book, *Saving America's Cities: Ed Logue and the Struggle to Renew Urban America in the Suburban Age* (2019), probes the complexities of urban renewal in American cities after World War II. It won the Bancroft Prize in 2020. She currently is co-authoring a book on the impact and experience of deindustrialization in the United States and France beginning in the last third of the twentieth century.

From 2011 to 2018, Cohen served as the Dean of the Radcliffe Institute for Advanced Study at Harvard, a major center for scholarly research, creative arts, and public programs. Before attending graduate school, she taught history at the secondary level and worked in history and art museums.

Cohen is married to an historian of modern France, with whom she shares two daughters and four grandchildren.

Thomas A. Bailey (1903–1983) was the original author of *The American Pageant* and saw it through its first seven editions. He taught history for nearly forty years at Stanford University, his alma mater. Long regarded as one of the nation's leading historians of American diplomacy, he was honored by his colleagues in 1968 with election to the presidencies of both the Organization of American Historians and the Society for Historians of American Foreign Relations. He was the author, editor, or co-editor of some twenty books, but the work in which he took most pride was *The American Pageant*, through which, he liked to say, he had taught American history to several million students.

Brief Contents

Contents

Part Seven

UNCLE SAM'S
LATEST
GREATEST
SHORTEST
WAR
LESLIE'S WEEKLY

PEACE

Part Eight

Making an American Superpower 1945–1980 844

Maps

Tables

Figures

Preface

This eighteenth edition of *The American Pageant* reflects our continuing commitment to bring the most recent scholarship about American history to the broadest possible student audience, while preserving the lively readability that has long been the *Pageant*'s hallmark. We are often told that the *Pageant* stands out as the only American history text with a distinctive personality, an observation that brings us much satisfaction. We define the *Pageant*'s leading characteristics as clarity, concreteness, a strong emphasis on major themes, integration of a broad range of historical topics into a coherent and clutter-free narrative, attention to a variety of interpretive perspectives, and a colorful writing style leavened, as appropriate, with wit. That personality, we strongly believe, is what has made the *Pageant* both appealing and useful to countless students for more than six decades.

This edition of the *Pageant* introduces a new coauthor, Margaret O'Mara, who holds the Scott and Dorothy Bullitt Chair of American History in the History Department at the University of Washington. After graduating from Northwestern University and working in the White House, she went on to earn her PhD from the University of Pennsylvania, followed by a post-doctoral fellowship at Stanford's Bill Lane Center for the American West. She has authored several books, including *Cities of Knowledge: Cold War Science and the Search for the Next Silicon Valley* (2005) and *The Code: Silicon Valley and the Remaking of America* (2019).

Our collaboration on the *Pageant* reflects our respective scholarly interests, which are complementary to a remarkable degree. While we share broad interests in the evolving character of American society and in its global role, David Kennedy is primarily a political and economic historian, while Margaret O'Mara brings to the *Pageant* her deep interest in the history of technology, particularly the information and communications technologies that are revolutionizing the modern world. Together, we have strengthened the *Pageant*'s long tradition of integrating political, social, environmental, technological, cultural, and international history into an accessible and compelling narrative.

We have revised the *Pageant* chapter by chapter, even paragraph by paragraph, guided by our shared commitment to tell the story of the American past as vividly, clearly, and responsibly as possible, without sacrificing a sense of the often sobering seriousness of history and of its sometimes challenging complexity. Drawing on the insights of the latest historical scholarship, we have given special attention in this edition to issues of Black history and race relations, and we have substantially expanded our coverage of Native American and Asian American history. In accordance with modern scholarly usage, we use the Indigenous names of specific Native nations and individuals (along with, as appropriate, their Anglicized names) whenever possible. We use the term "Indian" only in the context of accepted historical terminology (e.g., "Indian Territory," or "Plains Indians").

Goals of *The American Pageant*

Like its predecessors, this edition of *The American Pageant* seeks to cultivate in its readers the critical thinking skills necessary for balanced judgment and informed understanding about American society by holding up to the present the mirror and measuring rod that is the past. This new edition continues to divide the narrative of American history into nine parts, to reflect the ways in which American history is being taught today. Each of the nine parts opens with an introductory essay highlighting major themes and perspectives, essentially posing the question, "What's the story?" in the chapters that follow. Those essays—and the Focus Questions that accompany them—are meant to help students to understand that the study of history is not just a matter of piling up mountains of facts but is principally concerned with discovering complex patterns of change over time and organizing seemingly disparate events, actions, and ideas into meaningful chains of cause and consequence. This edition also adds Chapter Outlines and Focus Questions at the beginning of each chapter, as well as Summaries at each chapter's conclusion, to aid students in comprehending and critically engaging with the material.

A strong narrative propels the story, reinforced by several special features, conspicuously including a prominent new feature in this edition, **The Presence of the Past**. The Presence of the Past essays are offered in the spirit of William Faulkner's famed declaration that "*the past is never dead, it's not even past.*" They demonstrate that long-ago events can cast both shadow and light far into the future, reminding us that we live in communities of time that connect us to the generations who have gone before us, as well as those who will follow. The seven essays in this feature address the Electoral College; judicial review; the Fourteenth Amendment to the Constitution; immigration policy; the myth of the "Lost Cause"; "redlining" and its impact on the Black community; and the practice of "filibustering" in the U.S. Senate. Importantly, in addition to nurturing a sense of the living past, these essays are also intended to serve as platforms for the teaching of Civics, a subject notoriously and regrettably underemphasized in many of our educational systems.

Other special features include the following:

- **Makers of America** showcases the diverse peoples and movements that have built the country and shaped its evolution, from various racial and ethnic communities to scientists, engineers, suburbanites, and environmental and civil rights activists.
- **Contending Voices** pairs conflicting quotations from original historical sources, accompanied by questions that encourage critical thinking by asking students to assess how people in the historical past understood hotly contested subjects. Still more highlighted quotes throughout the text help students hear the language of real people who shaped and experienced historical events. This edition incorporates many new, diverse voices into these features. They complement the historiographical debates covered in the **Varying Viewpoints** essays by highlighting how historical actors themselves debated the meaning of the events they experienced.
- **Examining the Evidence** enables students to deepen their understanding of the historical craft by conveying how historians develop interpretations of the past through research in many different kinds of primary sources. Here students learn to probe a wide range of historical documents and artifacts: correspondence between Abigail and John Adams in 1776, and what it reveals about women's place in the era of the American Revolution; the Gettysburg Address and the light it sheds not only on President Lincoln's brilliant oratory but also on his vision of the American nation; a letter from a black freedman to his former enslaver in 1865 that illuminates his family's experience in slavery as well as their hopes for a new life; the manuscript census of 1900 and what it teaches us about immigrant households on the Lower East Side of New York at the dawn of the twentieth century; and a Cold-War era national security document that yields deep insight into the foreign policy-making process.
- **Thinking Globally** essays present different aspects of the American experience contextualized within world history. Readers learn how developments in North America were part of worldwide phenomena, be it the challenge to empires in the eighteenth century, the rise of socialist ideology in the nineteenth century, or the globalization that followed World War II in the twentieth century. Students also see how key aspects of American history—such as participating in the slave trade and its abolition, making a revolution for independence, creating an integrated national state in the mid-nineteenth century, and struggling to survive the Great Depression and World War II—were encountered by other nations but resolved in distinctive ways according to each country's history, cultural traditions, and political and economic structures.

The *Pageant*'s paramount goal is not to teach the art of prophecy but the much subtler and more difficult arts of seeing historical developments in context, of understanding the roots and direction and pace of change, and of distinguishing what is truly new under the sun from what is not. The study of history, it has been rightly said, does not make one smart for the next time, but wise forever. Throughout the text, we believe that anchoring the narrative of events in a coherent interpretive framework facilitates readers' acquisition of important historical thinking skills, including periodization, synthetic reasoning, and contextual and comparative analysis.

We hope that the *Pageant* will help to develop the art of critical thinking in its readers and that those who use the book will take from it both a fresh appreciation of what has gone before and a seasoned perspective on what is to come. We hope, too, that readers will take as much pleasure in reading *The American Pageant* as we have had in writing it.

Changes in the Eighteenth Edition

As in past revisions, we have updated and streamlined the entire text narrative, focusing especially on three items: (1) the Black American experience, having thoroughly revised the discussion of Black history from colonial times to the twenty-first century, harvesting the rich body of new scholarship that has illuminated this long, complex, and consequential chapter in the national story; (2) the role of technological innovation in shaping the human experience, for both better and worse; and (3) connecting the dots between past and present to illuminate the deep roots of the republic's current circumstances. A new concluding chapter brings the story up through the first years of the Biden presidency, placing the tumultuous events of recent years into a comprehensible historical context.

The chapters in Part Six, examining the late nineteenth century, have been reordered and revised. We have also compressed the discussion of both the Civil War and World War II into single chapters for each episode, so that the text in its entirety now numbers thirty-eight chapters (previously forty). All tables and figures have been revised to include the latest available statistical data.

Global Context

Recognizing that we inhabit an increasingly interconnected planet, we have continued to deepen the *Pageant*'s treatment of the global context of American history. Today, political leaders, capital investment, consumer products, rock bands, the internet, and much else constantly traverse the globe. But even before sophisticated technology and mass communication, complex exchanges among peoples and nations around the world deeply shaped the course of American history. Students will frequently encounter in these pages the people, ideas, and events that crossed national borders to influence the experience of the United States. They will also be invited to compare salient aspects of American history with developments elsewhere in the world. We believe that a full understanding of what makes America exceptional requires knowing about other societies and knowing when and why America's path followed or departed from that taken by other nations.

Within each chapter, both text and graphics help students compare American developments to developments around the world. The frontier experience, railroad building, cotton production, city size and urban reform strategies, automobile ownership, the economic effects of the Great Depression, women's participation in voting and the workforce, the cultural upheavals of the 1960s, the controversies over immigration in many countries, and much more should be understood as parts of world trends, not just as isolated American phenomena. New boxed quotes bring more international voices to the events chronicled in the *Pageant*'s historical narrative. Updated "Varying Viewpoints" essays reflect new interpretations of significant trends and events, emphasizing, when appropriate, their global contexts.

This edition also gives renewed attention to teaching strategies and pedagogical materials aimed at helping students deepen their comprehension of American history. New visual materials—documentary images, graphs, and tables—illuminate complex and important historical ideas. Readers will also find redesigned maps with topographical detail and clear labeling to better communicate the text's analytical points. Key terms are printed in bold in each chapter and defined in a glossary at the end of the book. Every chapter begins with a **Chapter Outline** and concludes with a **Chapter Summary**, as well as a detailed chronology and a list of readable books to consult in order **To Learn More**. In addition, lists of **Key Terms** and **People to Know**—created to help students focus on the most significant people introduced in that chapter—appear at the end of each chapter to help students review chapter highlights. An Appendix contains annotated copies of the Declaration of Independence and Constitution and key historical events and dates, such as admission of the states and the outcomes of presidential elections.

Refer to the Supplements section that follows for a complete description of the many materials found online. It is our hope that readers will view online resources such as MindTap as an exploratory laboratory enhancing *The American Pageant*'s text.

Notes on Content Revisions

Part One—Peopling a Continent ca. 33,000 BCE–1700 CE

Chapter 1 New World Beginnings: 33,000 BCE–1680 CE

- Chapter substantially updated and expanded to more effectively address Native American history, particularly before European contact
- New discussion of alternative theories of First Peoples' arrival in North America
- Updated geological information in "The Shaping of North America" section
- Substantial update to material on pre-Columbian Native American economies and cultures in the "The Earliest Americans" section
- Further updates to post-contact Native American history throughout the chapter, with new material in "Exploration and Rivalry" section
- Fresh discussion of the Pueblo Revolt of 1680 and the resulting spread of horses throughout the continent
- Expanded discussion of Junipero Serra and California missions

Chapter 2 The Contest for North America: 1500–1664

- Chapter reorganized to incorporate more Native American history. More attention to the contest for North America among competing empires than assumption of British hegemony.
- Extended discussion of enslavement of Native peoples

Chapter 3 Settling the English Colonies: 1619–1700

- Chapter reorganized to discuss the seventeenth century English plantations together, with an emphasis on contingency
- Enlarged discussion of colonial slave trade
- Expanded treatment of settler relations with Native peoples in New England

Part Two—Building British North America: 1607–1775

Chapter 4 American Life in the Seventeenth Century: 1607–1692

- Added treatment of religion among enslaved people

Chapter 5 Colonial Society on the Eve of Revolution: 1700–1775

- New material to strengthen analysis of Native American history
- New treatment of slave resistance in colonial America
- Expanded focus on Phillis Wheatley

Chapter 6 The Road to Revolution: 1754–1775

- Deepened discussion of the Enlightenment context for American revolutionary thought

- New material on Native American history and the continental competition of European powers

Part Three—Founding a New Nation 1775–1800

Chapter 7 America Secedes from the Empire: 1775–1783
- New material on the role of Native Americans in the Revolutionary War era
- Extended discussion of slavery's role in shaping the U.S. Constitution
- Updated Varying Viewpoints on "Whose Revolution?"

Chapter 8 The Confederation and the Constitution: 1776–1790
- Expanded discussion of the three-fifths clause
- New material on the earliest abolitionist movements
- New discussion of slavery's role in the national economy

Chapter 9 Launching the New Ship of State: 1789–1800
- Much enlarged discussion of the role of the Caribbean, especially Haiti, in the life of the early republic

Part Four—Building the New Nation 1800–1860

Chapter 10 The Triumphs and Travails of the Jeffersonian Republic: 1800–1812
- Considerably new material on Native Americans in the Southwest and Old Northwest
- Expanded discussion of relation between Thomas Jefferson and Sally Hemings

Chapter 11 The War of 1812 and the Upsurge of Nationalism: 1812–1824
- Revised discussion of the financial crisis of 1819
- New discussion of early migration into the Deep South
- Revised treatment of the Compromise of 1820 ("Missouri Compromise")

Chapter 12 The Rise of a Mass Democracy: 1824–1840
- Expanded discussion of Andrew Jackson's Indian Removal policies
- New material on American colonization of Texas
- Varying Viewpoints on "What Was Jacksonian Democracy?" updated

Chapter 13 Forging the National Economy: 1790–1860
- Dilated discussion of George Caitlin and origins of National Parks
- Expanded analysis of cotton's role in the national economy

Chapter 14 The Ferment of Reform and Culture: 1790–1860
- Much more analysis of the several movements for the abolition of slavery
- Much expanded discussion of Brigham Young and the Mormon migration to the Salt Lake Valley
- Varying Viewpoints on "Reform: Who? What? How? and Why?" updated

Chapter 15 The South and Slavery: 1793–1860
- Significantly revised and reorganized chapter to emphasize the capitalist values of slavery, as well as African American agency and voices
- New quotations from Frederick Douglass
- New discussion of slavery in Northern states
- New discussion of enslaved peoples' resistance efforts
- Expanded treatment of abolitionism

Part Five—Testing the New Nation: 1841–1877

Chapter 16 Manifest Destiny and Its Legacy: 1841–1848
- New material on President Tyler's precedent-setting role as first vice-president to succeed a president who died in office, and first to have a veto over-ridden by Congress

Chapter 17 Renewing the Sectional Struggle: 1848–1854
- Broadened discussion of racial diversity—and friction—in California's mining camps

Chapter 18 Descending Toward Disunion: 1854–1861
- Sharpened focus on repeated failures to resolve the "slavery problem" throughout the troubled decade of the 1850s
- Deepened critical appraisal of the Dred Scott decision

Chapter 19 The Furnace of Civil War: 1861–1865
- This and following chapter from previous editions consolidated into a single chapter on the coming and waging of the Civil War

Chapter 20 The Ordeal of Reconstruction: 1865–1877
- Entire chapter extensively revised to emphasize white Southern resistance to Reconstruction, the extent of violence, Grant's efforts to suppress the Ku Klux Klan, and the origins of the Jim Crow system of legally sanctioned segregation and oppression

Part Six—Forging an Industrial Society: 1865–1900

Chapter 21 Political Upheaval in the Gilded Age: 1869–1896
- Chapter moved forward to immediately follow chapter on Reconstruction
- Expanded discussion of the end of Reconstruction and birth of Jim Crow, including latest data on extent of extra-legal violence and lynching
- Significantly revised "Makers of America" feature on Chinese Americans

Chapter 22 The Conquest of the West: 1865–1896
- Chapter revised to open with building of the transcontinental railroad and the Irish and Chinese immigrants responsible for its construction
- Native American leaders and key battles now referred to by Native as well as Anglicized names
- Revised and expanded discussion of Native American policy and the Dawes Severalty Act

Chapter 23 The Industrial Era Dawns: 1865–1900
- Expanded discussion of the technological and economic consequences of railroad expansion, including its role in the seizure and partitioning of Native lands
- More detailed discussion of technological innovation and industrialization, as well as the emergent financial system and its leaders

Chapter 24 America Moves to the City: 1865–1900
- Discussion of immigrant life revised, with key points from "Makers of America" feature on Italian Americans integrated into text as well as into the new "Presence of the Past" feature on immigration (appearing in Chapter 34)
- Expanded discussion of emergence of collegiate and professional sports, and new discussion of women's sports

Chapter 25 Rumbles of Discontent: 1865–1900
- Chapter opens with discussion of mechanization of agriculture previously in Chapter 22
- Revised and expanded discussion of Populism

Part Seven—Struggling for Justice at Home and Abroad: 1890–1945

Chapter 26 Empire and Expansion: 1890–1909
- Reframed and expanded discussion of American empire, drawing on the latest scholarship
- Further discussion of indigenous experience and perspectives on American empire

Chapter 27 Progressivism and the Republican Roosevelt: 1901–1912
- Revised "Makers of America" feature on the environmental movement, with fresh discussion of climate change and climate activism
- Updated "Why is there no Socialism in the United States?" essay with additional discussion of racial divisions as an obstacle to class solidarity

Chapter 28 Wilsonian Progressivism in Peace and War: 1913–1920
- New "Presence of the Past" feature on the U.S. Senate and the filibuster
- New section on the 1918–1920 influenza pandemic

Chapter 29 Prosperity and Its Perils: 1920–1932
- New material on Henry Ford
- New discussion of race and civil rights in the 1920s, including the rise of the second Ku Klux Klan, anti-lynching campaigns, and the Tulsa Race Massacre of 1921
- Expanded discussion of evangelical Christianity and its leaders
- New "Presence of the Past" feature on the myth of the Lost Cause

Chapter 30 The Great Depression and the New Deal: 1933–1939
- New "Presence of the Past" feature on redlining, replacing and greatly expanding earlier discussions of discrimination in the housing market

Chapter 31 The Cauldron of World War II: 1933–1945
- Major revisions to create new chapter that covers the darkening international politics of the 1930s, the events precipitating America's entry into the conflict, and the nation's wartime experience at home and overseas
- New opening epigram from Franklin D. Roosevelt, new box quote on the horrors of the concentration camps from General Dwight D. Eisenhower

Part Eight—Making an American Superpower: 1945–1980

Chapter 32 The Cold War Begins: 1945–1952
- New discussion of military spending and the growth of the electronics and early computer industries
- Extended discussion of Truman-era civil rights measures and postwar race relations
- Revised "Makers of America" feature on the suburbanites

Chapter 33 Affluence and Anxiety: 1952–1963
- Expanded discussion of the Korean War and its legacies
- Enhanced discussion of the bracero program, tribal termination policy, and postwar urban migration of Native Americans
- Significantly revised discussion of postwar art and culture, with fresh emphasis on the contributions of nonwhite artists, writers, and architects
- New discussion of voter registration drives in the civil rights-era Deep South

Chapter 34 The Stormy Sixties: 1963–1973
- Reframed discussion of urban rebellions and police violence, from 1965 Watts uprising forward
- New "The Presence of the Past" feature on immigration
- Expanded discussion of the decade's working-class movements for social change, including the campaigns of Cesar Chavez and the United Farm Workers
- New discussion of the space program

Chapter 35 A Sea of Troubles: 1973–1980
- Revised and updated discussion of economic globalization and the catalysts of economic stagnation and inflation in the 1970s

- Expanded discussion of feminist activist movements in text, incorporating prior "Makers of America" feature on feminism
- More discussion of women's activism on both left and right, including Shirley Chisholm, Pauli Murray, and Phyllis Schlafly

Part Nine—Sustaining Democracy in a Global Age: 1980 to the Present

Chapter 36 The Resurgence of Conservatism: 1980–1992

- Expanded discussion of conservative movements surrounding and beyond Ronald Reagan
- New discussion of the political significance of the South in Republican politics
- Expanded section on the rise of the personal computer industry and Silicon Valley
- New material on nuclear freeze movement and antiwar activism

Chapter 37 America Enters the Twenty-First Century: 1992–2008

- Chapter now includes the George W. Bush presidency, the 2008 financial crisis, and the election of Barack Obama
- New "Makers of America" feature on the increasingly diverse modern popular culture
- More discussion of the growth of the high-tech economy, liberalized global trade, and competition with China

Chapter 38 American Reckoning: 2009–2024

- Substantial new material on Trump's presidency, the COVID-19 pandemic, the 2020 election, the January 6 insurrectionist attack on the U.S. Capitol, and Biden's first three years in office
- Expanded discussion of global affairs, including the Russian invasion of Ukraine and the Israel-Hamas conflict
- New material on climate disruption and climate activism
- Discussion of the rise of social media and emergence of "Big Tech" platforms

MindTap

Create a unique learning experience and increase students' retention and confidence using MindTap for *The American Pageant: A History of the American People*, Eighteenth Edition, which gives students access to the eTextbook, videos, assessments, and study tools for your course. Built on proven learning research and theory, MindTap presents concepts by pairing assessment and content in a visually captivating side-by-side format.

Boost Comprehension with Improved Learning Design

Students build their understanding as they complete activities in Learn It, Practice It, and Apply It folders. Students focus first on recalling main ideas and key details from the textbook chapter, then they investigate primary sources to enrich their understanding of the period. Finally, students apply their new knowledge as they explore maps and write persuasive essays.

The Primary Source for Critical Thinking

Students flex their critical thinking muscles in auto-graded quizzes as they read and respond to primary source excerpts that link historical voices to larger political, economic, and social concerns. In addition to auto-graded activities, students are prompted to write about sources as they explore these diverse perspectives.

Adaptable to Suit the Needs of You and Your Students

For students who would benefit from sustained help with writing, each Apply It folder includes a short lesson and writing activity on one particular aspect of writing, such as framing a question for inquiry, crafting a thesis, and using historical evidence. For instructors, the placement of MindTap activities is entirely customizable to give you the ultimate decision-making power for your classroom. Activities can be used in the MindTap platform or within your institution's learning management system.

Inspire Curiosity, Apply Learning

Activities such as "Why Does This Topic Matter to Me?" tell compelling stories and are approachable in terms of length and language, motivating students and inspiring curiosity as they move through the material.

Acquaint Students with the Fundamentals from the Start

What's a primary source? How can a student write effective essays about history? Help students familiarize themselves with these and other all-important concepts and skills, such as how to read maps and how to evaluate historical arguments, with MindTap's assignable, auto-gradable history skills tutorials. New tutorials on "How to Analyze Primary Sources" and "How to Write in History" offer step-by-step directions to help students succeed in these essential skills.

In thirty-four new "Key Concept" videos, students also learn how historians use concepts to create historical knowledge that relate fundamental ideas such as the state, freedom, rights, and power to chapter topics and their own life experiences.

And There Are Additional Upgrades with This New Edition

The NEW downloadable Focus on the Chapter's Main Points helps students take notes on each textbook chapter as they read it. Students can check their knowledge of the chapter's key details with the NEW "Check Your Understanding of the Chapter Details" quiz before they take the NEW auto-graded "Test Your Knowledge of the Chapter" assessment.

Supplements

Instructor Resources

Additional instructor resources for this product are available online. Instructor assets include an Instructor's Manual, Educator's Guide, PowerPoint® slides, and a test bank powered by Cognero®. Sign up or sign in at www.cengage.com to search for and access this product and its online resources.

Instructor's Companion Website

The Instructor's Companion Website, accessed through the Instructor Resource Center (login.cengage.com), houses all of the supplemental materials you can use for your course. The Instructor's Manual includes chapter summaries, suggested lecture topics, discussion questions, descriptions of activities found in MindTap and PowerPoint Lecture slides, topics for student research, relevant websites, and suggestions for additional videos. The PowerPoint Lectures are ADA-compliant slides that collate the key takeaways from the chapter in concise visual formats perfect for in-class presentations or for student review. Finally, Cengage Learning Testing powered by Cognero® is a flexible online system that allows you to author, edit, and manage test bank content from multiple Cengage Learning solutions, create multiple test versions in an instant, and deliver tests from your LMS, your classroom, or wherever you want.

Cengage Unlimited

With Cengage Unlimited (cengage.com/unlimited/instructor), a student has access to our entire library of eBooks and online learning platforms, at least four free hardcopy rentals, and hundreds of skill-building activities to boost student success and career readiness. Cengage Unlimited is available to all higher education and career students in the United States, in bookstores and online. For customers outside the United States, contact your local sales partner.

Acknowledgments

Many people have contributed to this revision of *The American Pageant.* Foremost among them are the countless students and teachers who have sent us unsolicited comments or inquiries. We have learned from every one of them and encourage all readers to offer us suggestions for improving future editions.

Reviewers for the Eighteenth Edition

We are especially indebted to Professor Leslie Harris of Northwestern University, who responded with extraordinary alacrity and uncommon acumen to our request for a thorough review of the *Pageant*'s treatment of Black history.

In addition, we owe a special thanks to Serena Shah of Stanford University, Erik Baker of Harvard University, and Ethan Benson, Alika Bourgette, and Jess Cavalari of the University of Washington for their invaluable assistance throughout the revision process.

We also appreciate feedback for this revision from the following reviewers:

Robert Anderson, Penn State University
Jay Carriker, Wiley College
George Edgar, De Anza College
Dustin Gann, Midland University
Neil Greenwood, Cleveland State Community College
Jennifer Grohol, Bakersfield College
Timothy Hayburn, Rowan University
John Hilston, Eastern Florida State College
Kelli Yoshie Nakamura, Kapi'olani Community College
Chloe Northrop, Tarrant County College
Sarah Angela Pacelli, Siena College
David B. Raymond, Northern Maine Community College
Natalia Anatolyevna Starostina, Oklahoma City University

David M. Kennedy
Margaret O'Mara
Lizabeth Cohen

Critics say that America is a lie because its reality falls so far short of its ideals. They are wrong. America is not a lie; it is a disappointment. But it can be a disappointment only because it is also a hope.

Samuel P. Huntington
American Politics: The Promise of Disharmony, 1981

Chapter 20

The Ordeal of Reconstruction: 1865–1877

> With malice toward none, with charity for all, with firmness in the right as God gives us to see the right, let us strive on to finish the work we are in, to bind up the nation's wounds, to care for him who shall have borne the battle and for his widow and orphan, to do all which may achieve and cherish a just and lasting peace among ourselves and with all nations.
>
> Abraham Lincoln, Second Inaugural, March 4, 1865

Chapter Outline

- The defeated South
- Freed people after slavery
- President Andrew Johnson's Reconstruction policies
- The Black Codes
- Congressional Reconstruction policies
- Johnson clashes with Congress
- Military Reconstruction, 1867–1877
- Freed people enter politics
- "Black Reconstruction" and the Ku Klux Klan
- The Colfax Massacre and the limits of Reconstruction
- The impeachment of Andrew Johnson
- The legacy of Reconstruction

Examining the Evidence: Letter from a Freedman to His Old Master, 1865

The battle was done, the buglers silent. Bone-weary and bloodied, the American people, North and South, Black and white, now faced the staggering challenges of binding up the nation's wounds and fully redeeming the promise of emancipation. Four questions loomed large. How would liberated Black people fare as free men and women? How would the Southern states be reintegrated into the Union? Who would direct the process of Reconstruction—the Southern states themselves, the president, or Congress? And most vexing of all, how would the white South—militarily defeated but largely unreconciled to the abolition of slavery—adapt to the revolutionary post-emancipation social order?

Robert E. Lee chillingly foreshadowed much of what was to come when he and Ulysses Grant rendezvoused on horseback near Appomattox for a final conversation about what the future might hold. Lee "said to me that the South was a big country," Grant recalled, "and that we might have to march over it three or four times before the war entirely ended."

Focus Questions

1. What were the major problems facing the South and the nation after the Civil War?
2. How did Black and white Americans, Southerners and Northerners, each respond to the end of slavery and approach race relations under new conditions of freedom?
3. How did Andrew Johnson's policies enable the Radical Republicans to gain control of Reconstruction policy?
4. In what ways did the defeated South resist federal efforts to make racial equality a reality?
5. What were the primary successes and failures of Reconstruction, and what legacy did it leave for later generations of Americans?

20-1 The Problems of Peace

The Presence of the Past: The Fourteenth Amendment and the "Second Founding"

Varying Viewpoints: Did Reconstruction Fail?

Other questions also clamored for answers. What should be done with the captured Confederate ringleaders, all of whom were liable to charges of treason? During the war, a popular Northern song had been "Hang Jeff Davis to a Sour Apple Tree," and even innocent children had lisped it. Davis was clapped into irons during the early days of his two-year imprisonment. But the mood changed swiftly. Davis and his fellow rebel leaders were ultimately released, partly because the odds were that no Southern jury would convict them. Less than four years after Appomattox, President Andrew Johnson pardoned all Confederate leaders. Congress removed all remaining civil disabilities thirty years later and posthumously restored Davis's citizenship in 1978, as well as Lee's in 1975.

Dismal indeed was the picture presented by the war-racked South when the rattle of musketry faded. Handsome cities of yesteryear, such as Charleston and Richmond, were rubble-strewn and weed-choked (refer to Image 20.1). An Atlantan returned to his once-prosperous hometown and remarked, "Hell has laid her egg, and right here it hatched."

Southern economic life had creaked to a halt. Banks and businesses had locked their doors, ruined by runaway inflation. Factories were smokeless, silent, dismantled. The transportation system lay in shambles. Before the war, five different railroad lines had converged on Columbia, South Carolina; now the nearest connected track was twenty-nine miles away. Efforts to untwist the rails corkscrewed by Sherman's soldiers proved bumpily unsatisfactory.

Agriculture—the economic lifeblood of the South—was grotesquely crushed. Once-white-carpeted cotton fields now yielded a lush harvest of nothing but green weeds. A labor system dependent on human enslavement had utterly collapsed, and the devastation of war and its aftermath impoverished landowners large and small. Seed was scarce, and livestock had been driven off by victorious Yankees. Pathetic instances were reported of men hitching themselves to plows, while women and children gripped the handles. Not until 1870 did the seceded states produce as large a cotton crop as that of the fateful year 1860, and much of that yield came from new acreage in the southwest.

The princely planter aristocrats were humbled by the war—at least temporarily. Reduced to unaccustomed poverty, they faced charred and gutted mansions and almost worthless land. Their primary form of wealth had been enslaved human beings, valued at more than $2 billion, an "investment" that had evaporated with emancipation.

Beaten but unbent, many white Southerners remained stubbornly recalcitrant. They cursed the "damn Yankees" and spoke of "your government" in Washington instead of "our government."

Image 20.1 Charleston, South Carolina, in Ruins, April 1865 Rebel troops evacuating Charleston blew up military supplies to deny them to General William Tecumseh Sherman's forces. The explosions ignited fires that all but destroyed the city.

Strictly speaking, Lee had surrendered only his Army of Northern Virginia; other Confederate forces remained in the field, and sporadic clashes with Union forces continued in parts of the South for several weeks after Appomattox. Some die-hard rebels urged Jefferson Davis and the Confederate cabinet to seek refuge in Cuba, there to plot an eventual revival of the war of secession. Some five thousand Confederate troops, along with their families and slaves, fled to Maximilian's Mexico where they briefly established a "New Virginia Colony" with plans to one day march in strength back to old Virginia. Acknowledging no crime, these former Confederates continued to believe that their view of secession was correct and that the "Lost Cause" was still a just war. One popular anti-Union song ran,

> I'm glad I fought agin her, I only wish we'd won,
> And I ain't axed any pardon for anything I've done.

Attitudes like that boded ill for the prospects of true racial equality as well as painless sectional reconciliation.

20-2 Freedmen Define Freedom

Confusion abounded in the still-smoldering South about the precise meaning of "freedom" for Black people. Emancipation took effect haltingly and unevenly in different parts of the conquered Confederacy. As Union armies marched in and out of various localities, many Black Southerners found themselves emancipated and then re-enslaved. A formerly enslaved North Carolinian estimated that he had celebrated freedom about twelve times. Desperate refugees from one Texas county fleeing to the free soil of the liberated county next door were attacked by slave owners as they swam across the river that marked the county line. The next day, trees along the riverbank were bent with swinging corpses—a grisly warning to others dreaming of liberty. Other planters resisted emancipation more legalistically, stubbornly protesting that slavery was lawful until state legislatures or the Supreme Court declared otherwise. For most, the shackles of bondage were not struck off in a single mighty blow; those long-oppressed by slavery had to wrench free of their chains link by link.

Prodded by the bayonets of Union armies of occupation, all slaveholders were eventually forced to recognize the former slaves' permanent freedom. Though some freed people initially responded to Lincoln's proclamation with suspicion and uncertainty, they quickly found ways to embrace their newfound liberty. Many took new names in place of the ones given by their enslavers and adopted the formal honorifics of "Mr." or "Mrs." Those with means abandoned the coarse cottons that had been their only clothing when enslaved and donned the silks, satins, and fashions of genteel whites. Southern whites perceived such behavior as insubordinate, but they could not deny the reality of emancipation. "Never before had I a word of impudence from any of our black folk," wrote one nonplussed white Southerner, "but they are not ours any longer." (Refer to "Examining the Evidence: Letter from a Freedman to His Old Master, 1865," p. 498.)

Tens of thousands of emancipated Black Southerners took to the roads, some simply to test their freedom, others to search for long-lost spouses, parents, and children. Emancipation allowed the reunification and preservation of families, and many newly freed men and women were at last able to formalize "slave marriages" and make their children legal heirs. Many went to work for wages in towns and cities, where existing free Black communities provided protection and mutual assistance. Whole communities sometimes moved together in search of opportunity. From 1878 to 1880, some twenty-five thousand freedmen and freedwomen from Louisiana, Texas, and Mississippi surged in a mass exodus to Kansas. The westward flood of these "Exodusters" was stemmed only when steamboat captains refused to transport more Black migrants across the Mississippi River.

Under slavery, Black people had often worshiped alongside whites, but now they formed their own churches pastored by their own ministers. Black churches grew robustly. The 150,000-member Black Baptist Church of 1850 reached 500,000 by 1870, while the African

Houston H. Holloway, age twenty at the time of his emancipation, recalled his feelings upon hearing of his freedom:

"I felt like a bird out of a cage. Amen. Amen. Amen. I could hardly ask to feel any better than I did that day. . . . The week passed off in a blaze of glory."

The reunion of long-lost relatives also inspired joy; one Union officer wrote home,

"Men are taking their wives and children, families which had been for a long time broken up are united and oh! such happiness. I am glad I am here."

The Granger Collection, New York

Image 20.2 **Educating Young Freedmen and Freedwomen, ca. 1867** Newly freed Black people in the South regarded schooling as the key to improving their children's lives and the fulfillment of a long-sought right that had been denied them in slavery. These schoolchildren are lined up outside their rural North Carolina one-room schoolhouse alongside their teachers, both Black and white.

Methodist Episcopal Church quadrupled in size from 100,000 to 400,000 in the first decade after emancipation. These churches formed the bedrock of Black community life, and they soon gave rise to other benevolent, fraternal, and mutual aid societies. All these organizations helped Black people defend their newly won freedom.

Emancipation also meant education for many men and women for whom literacy had previously been forbidden. Freedmen wasted no time establishing societies for self-improvement. They undertook to raise funds to purchase land, build schoolhouses, and hire teachers (refer to Image 20.2). One member of a North Carolina education society asserted that "a schoolhouse would be the first proof of their *independence*." Harriet Jacobs, who had escaped to freedom in the North as a young woman and become a prominent abolitionist, courageously returned to the land of her servitude at the end of the war to found a school for freed Black men and women in Savannah, Georgia (refer to Image 20.3).

Harriet Jacobs

Image 20.3 **Harriet Jacobs (ca. 1813–1897)** Born into slavery in North Carolina, she spent seven years hiding in a cramped attic crawlspace before finally escaping to the North and to freedom. Responding to a defense of slavery penned by the widow of former President John Tyler, she published her own harrowing life-story in 1861: *Incidents in the Life of a Slave Girl*. She founded the Jacobs School for escaped "contrabands" in Alexandria, Virginia, during the Civil War. Her ambitious educational initiatives in Reconstruction-era Savannah were eventually frustrated by Ku Klux Klan violence.

Letter from a Freedman to His Old Master, 1865

What was it like to experience the transition from slavery to freedom? Four million Southern Black men, women, and children faced this exhilarating and formidable prospect with the end of the war. For historians, recovering the African American perspective on emancipation is challenging. Unlike their previous white masters, Black freedmen and women left few written records. But one formerly enslaved person captured in a letter to his "Old Master" (whose surname he bore) the heroic determination of many Black people to build new independent and dignified lives for themselves and their families.

During the war, Jourdon Anderson escaped slavery in Tennessee with his wife and two daughters. After relocating to the relative safety of Ohio, he received a communication from his former owner asking him to return. In his bold reply, reportedly "dictated by the old servant" himself, Anderson expressed his family's new expectations for life as free people and distrust of his former master's intentions. He made reference to his "comfortable home," his daughters' schooling, the church that he and his wife were free to attend regularly, and the peace of mind that came with knowing that "my girls [would not be] brought to shame by the violence and wickedness of their young masters." Countering the master's command, Anderson and his wife asked for full reparations of $11,680 in back wages from their decades as enslaved people. He closed by reiterating that "the great desire of my life is to give my children an education and have them form virtuous habits." While Anderson and most other enslaved people were forbidden from learning to read or write, this letter demonstrates how they asserted themselves as parents, workers, and citizens not only from the distance of a former free state like Ohio but also deep within the former slave states of the South. Was the tone of Anderson's letter (and postscript) serious or tongue-in-cheek? What did "freedom" mean for Anderson and other Black families in the months following emancipation? How did the eventual accomplishments of Reconstruction correspond with the initial expectations of people like Anderson and his former owner?

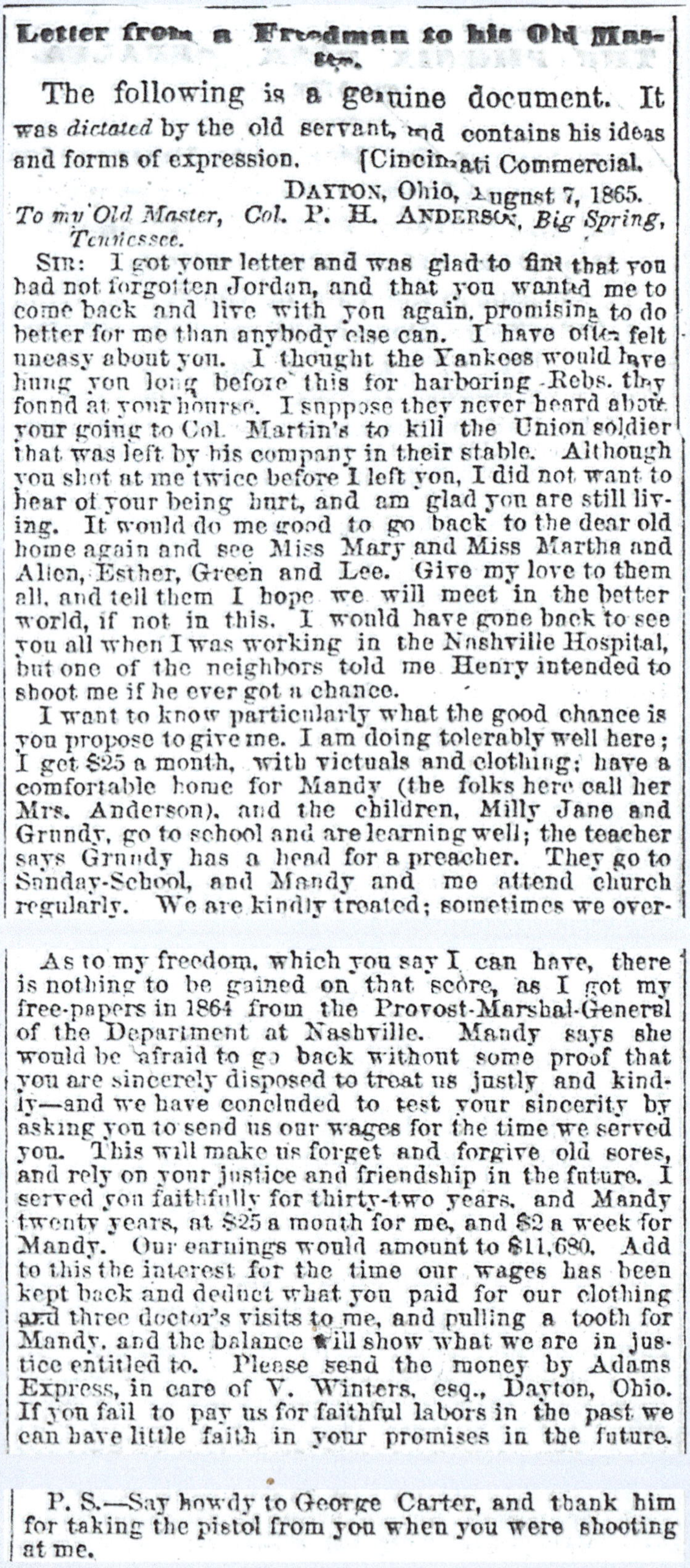

Letter from a Freedman to his Old Master.

The following is a genuine document. It was *dictated* by the old servant, and contains his ideas and forms of expression. [Cincinnati Commercial.

DAYTON, Ohio, August 7, 1865.

To my Old Master, Col. P. H. ANDERSON, *Big Spring, Tennessee.*

SIR: I got your letter and was glad to find that you had not forgotten Jordan, and that you wanted me to come back and live with you again, promising to do better for me than anybody else can. I have often felt uneasy about you. I thought the Yankees would have hung you long before this for harboring Rebs. they found at your house. I suppose they never heard about your going to Col. Martin's to kill the Union soldier that was left by his company in their stable. Although you shot at me twice before I left you, I did not want to hear of your being hurt, and am glad you are still living. It would do me good to go back to the dear old home again and see Miss Mary and Miss Martha and Allen, Esther, Green and Lee. Give my love to them all, and tell them I hope we will meet in the better world, if not in this. I would have gone back to see you all when I was working in the Nashville Hospital, but one of the neighbors told me Henry intended to shoot me if he ever got a chance.

I want to know particularly what the good chance is you propose to give me. I am doing tolerably well here; I get $25 a month, with victuals and clothing; have a comfortable home for Mandy (the folks here call her Mrs. Anderson), and the children, Milly Jane and Grundy, go to school and are learning well; the teacher says Grundy has a head for a preacher. They go to Sunday-School, and Mandy and me attend church regularly. We are kindly treated; sometimes we over-

As to my freedom, which you say I can have, there is nothing to be gained on that score, as I got my free-papers in 1864 from the Provost-Marshal-General of the Department at Nashville. Mandy says she would be afraid to go back without some proof that you are sincerely disposed to treat us justly and kindly—and we have concluded to test your sincerity by asking you to send us our wages for the time we served you. This will make us forget and forgive old sores, and rely on your justice and friendship in the future. I served you faithfully for thirty-two years, and Mandy twenty years, at $25 a month for me, and $2 a week for Mandy. Our earnings would amount to $11,680. Add to this the interest for the time our wages has been kept back and deduct what you paid for our clothing and three doctor's visits to me, and pulling a tooth for Mandy, and the balance will show what we are in justice entitled to. Please send the money by Adams Express, in care of V. Winters, esq., Dayton, Ohio. If you fail to pay us for faithful labors in the past we can have little faith in your promises in the future.

P. S.—Say howdy to George Carter, and thank him for taking the pistol from you when you were shooting at me.

New-York Tribune Tuesday, August 22, 1865

Image 20.4 Anderson's Letter, as Reprinted in the *New York Tribune*, August 22, 1865

But demand soon outstripped the supply of qualified Black teachers. The newly emancipated accepted the aid of Northern white women sent by the American Missionary Association, who volunteered their services as teachers. Black leaders also turned to the federal government for help for their communities. They were going to need all the friends—and power—they could muster in Washington.

Most provocatively to Southern whites, emancipation meant that Black males now had access to political power. Hundreds of thousands of formerly enslaved men cast ballots in the decade after 1865, and 320 were elected to state and federal offices. As events were to show, nothing proved more hotly intolerable to "unreconstructed" white people.

20-3 The Freedmen's Bureau

Abolitionists had long preached that slavery was a degrading institution. Now the emancipators were faced with the brutal reality that many freedmen were illiterate, without property or money, and with scant knowledge of how to prosper as free people. To cope with these issues throughout the conquered South, Congress created the **Freedmen's Bureau** on March 3, 1865.

On paper at least, the bureau was intended to be a kind of rudimentary welfare agency. It was to provide food, clothing, medical care, and especially, education—both to freedmen and white refugees. Heading the bureau was a warmly sympathetic friend to Black people, Union General Oliver O. Howard, who later founded and served as president of Howard University in Washington, DC.

The bureau achieved its greatest successes in education. It taught an estimated 200,000 Black men, women, and children how to read. Many formerly enslaved people had a passion for learning, partly because they wanted to close the gap between themselves and white people and partly because they longed to read the Word of God. In one elementary class in North Carolina sat four generations of the same family, ranging from a six-year-old child to a seventy-five-year-old grandmother.

But in other areas, the bureau's accomplishments fell tragically short of Black Americans' needs and expectations. Although the bureau was authorized to settle freed people on forty-acre tracts confiscated from the Confederates, little land actually made it into the hands of Black farmers. Instead, local administrators often collaborated with planters in expelling freedmen from towns and cajoling them into signing labor contracts to work for their former masters.

In reality, the Union army was a far more reliable guarantor of freedmen's civil rights in the occupied South than the beleaguered bureau. Still, the white South resented the bureau as a meddlesome federal interloper that threatened to upset white racial dominance. President Andrew Johnson, who shared the white supremacist views of most white Southerners, repeatedly tried to kill it, and it expired in 1872.

20-4 Johnson: The Tailor President

What manner of man was Andrew Johnson, the black-haired Tennessean who now inherited the martyred Lincoln's mantle?

No citizen, not even Lincoln, had ever reached the White House from humbler beginnings. Born to impoverished parents in North Carolina and orphaned early, Johnson never attended school but was apprenticed to a tailor at age ten. Ambitious to get ahead, he taught himself to read, and later his wife taught him to write and do simple arithmetic. Like many another self-made man, he was inclined to overpraise his maker.

Johnson early became active in politics in Tennessee, where he had moved when seventeen years old. He shone as an impassioned champion of poor whites against the planter aristocrats, although he himself had been a slaveholder. He excelled as a two-fisted stump speaker before angry and heckling crowds, who on occasion greeted his political oratory with cocked pistols, not just cocked ears. Elected to Congress, he attracted much favorable attention in the North (but not the South) when he refused to secede with his own state. After Tennessee was partially "redeemed" by Union armies, he was appointed war governor and served courageously in an atmosphere of danger.

Image 20.5 Crushed by the Constitution President Andrew Johnson revered the U.S. Constitution but eventually felt its awesome weight in his impeachment trial.

Political exigency next thrust Johnson into the vice presidency. Lincoln's Union party in 1864 needed to attract support from the War Democrats and other pro-Southern elements, and Johnson, a Democrat, seemed to be the ideal man. Unfortunately, he appeared at the vice-presidential inaugural ceremonies the following March in a scandalous condition. He had recently been afflicted with typhoid fever, and although not known as a heavy drinker, he was urged by his friends to take a stiff bracer of whiskey. This he did—with unfortunate results.

"Old Andy" Johnson was no doubt a man of parts—unpolished parts. He professed steadfast devotion to duty and to the people, and was a dogmatic champion both of states' rights and the U.S. Constitution. He would often present a copy of the document to visitors, and he was buried with one as a pillow.

Yet the man who had raised himself from the tailor's bench to the president's chair was a misfit. A Southerner who did not understand the North, a Tennessean who had earned the distrust of the South, a Democrat who had never been accepted by the Republicans, a president who had never been elected to the office, a white supremacist charged with managing the transition to freedom of millions of formerly enslaved Black people, he was not at home in a Republican White House. Hotheaded, contentious, and stubborn, he was the wrong man in the wrong place at the wrong time (refer to Image 20.5).

20-5 Presidential Reconstruction

Even before the shooting war had ended, the political war over Reconstruction had begun. Abraham Lincoln believed that the Southern states had never legally withdrawn from the Union. Their formal restoration to the Union would therefore be relatively simple. Accordingly, Lincoln in 1863 proclaimed his **"10 percent" Reconstruction plan**. It decreed that a state could be reintegrated into the Union when the equivalent of at least 10 percent of its total voters in the presidential election of 1860 had taken an oath of allegiance to the United States and pledged to abide by emancipation. The next step would be formal establishment of a state government. Lincoln would then recognize the purified regime.

Lincoln's proclamation provoked a sharp reaction in Congress, where many Republicans feared the restoration of the planter aristocracy to power and even the possible re-enslavement of Black people. Republicans therefore leveraged their considerable Congressional majority to pass the **Wade-Davis Bill** in 1864. The bill required that 50 percent of a state's voters take the oath of allegiance and demanded stronger safeguards for emancipation than Lincoln's as the price of readmission to the Union. Lincoln "pocket-vetoed" this bill by refusing to sign it after Congress had adjourned. His fellow Republicans were outraged. They refused to seat delegates from Louisiana after that state had reorganized its government in accordance with Lincoln's 10 percent plan in 1864.

Table 20.1 Principal Reconstruction Proposals and Plans

Year	Proposal or Plan
1864–1865	Lincoln's 10 percent proposal
1865–1866	Johnson's version of Lincoln's proposal, with Thirteenth Amendment
1866–1867	Congressional plan: 10 percent plan with Fourteenth Amendment
1867–1877	Congressional plan of military Reconstruction: Fourteenth Amendment plus Black suffrage, later established nationwide by Fifteenth Amendment

The controversy surrounding the Wade-Davis Bill had revealed deep differences between the president and Congress. Unlike Lincoln, many in Congress insisted that the seceders had indeed left the Union—had "committed suicide" as republican states—and had therefore forfeited all their rights. They could be readmitted only as "conquered provinces" on such conditions as Congress should decree.

This episode revealed further fissures within Republican ranks over sectional reconciliation, civil rights, and the balance of power between president and Congress. Two factions were emerging. The majority moderate group tended to agree with Lincoln that the seceded states should be restored to the Union as simply and swiftly as reasonable—though on Congress's terms, not the president's. The minority Radical group believed that the South should atone more painfully for its sins. Before the South should be restored, the Radicals wanted its racial hierarchies uprooted, the haughty planters punished, and the emancipated freedmen protected by federal power. Some of the Radicals were secretly pleased when the assassin's bullet felled Lincoln, for the martyred president had shown tenderness toward the South. Spiteful "Andy" Johnson, who shared their hatred for the planter aristocrats, would presumably also share their desire to reconstruct the South with a rod of iron.

Johnson soon disillusioned them. He agreed with Lincoln that the seceded states had never legally been outside the Union. Thus, he quickly recognized several of Lincoln's 10 percent governments, and on May 29, 1865, he issued his own Reconstruction proclamation (refer to Table 20.1). It disfranchised certain leading Confederates, including those with taxable property worth more than $20,000, though they might petition him for personal pardons. It called for special state conventions, which were required to repeal the ordinances of secession, repudiate all Confederate debts, and ratify the slave-freeing Thirteenth Amendment. States that complied with these conditions, Johnson declared, would be swiftly readmitted to the Union.

Johnson, savoring his dominance over the high-toned aristocrats who now begged for his favor, granted pardons in abundance. Bolstered by the political resurrection of the planter elite, the recently rebellious states moved rapidly in the second half of 1865 to organize governments. But as the pattern of the new governments became clear, Republicans of all stripes grew furious.

> In his third annual address in 1867, President Johnson unapologetically revealed his disdain for the Republican-sponsored Reconstruction governments:
>
> "But if anything can be proved by known facts, if all reasoning upon evidence is not abandoned, it must be acknowledged that in the progress of nations Negroes have shown less capacity for government than any other race of people. No independent government of any form has ever been successful in their hands. On the contrary, wherever they have been left to their own devices they have shown a constant tendency to relapse into barbarism. In the Southern states, however, Congress has undertaken to confer upon them the privilege of the ballot. Just released from slavery, it may be doubted whether as a class they know more than their ancestors how to organize and regulate civil society. Indeed, it is admitted that the blacks of the South are not only regardless of the rights of property, but so utterly ignorant of public affairs that their voting can consist in nothing more than carrying a ballot to the place where they are directed to deposit it."

20-6 The Baleful Black Codes

Among the first acts of the new Southern state regimes sanctioned by Johnson was the passage of the iron-toothed **Black Codes**. These laws were designed to control the lives of the emancipated Black Southerners, almost as severely as the slave statutes had done in pre–Civil War days. Mississippi passed the first such law in November 1865, and other Southern states soon followed suit. The Black Codes varied in severity from state to state (Mississippi's was the harshest and Georgia's the most lenient), but they had much in common. The Black Codes aimed, above all, to ensure a stable and subservient labor force. The crushed Cotton Kingdom could not rise from its weeds until the fields were once again put under hoe and plow—and many white plantation owners

Image 20.6 Sharecroppers Picking Cotton Although many freed people found themselves picking cotton on their former masters' plantations, they took comfort that they were at least paid wages and could work as a family unit. In time, however, they became ensnared in the web of debt that their planter bosses spun to keep a free labor force tightly bound to them.

wanted to make sure that they retained the authority they had exercised over Black field hands and plow drivers in the days of slavery.

The codes therefore imposed dire penalties on Black workers who "jumped" their labor contracts, which usually committed them to work for the same employer for one year, and generally at pittance wages. Violators could be made to forfeit back wages or could be forcibly dragged back to work by a paid "Negro-catcher." In Mississippi the captured freedmen could be fined and then hired out to pay their fines—an arrangement that closely resembled slavery itself.

The codes also sought to restore as nearly as possible the preemancipation system of Black disenfranchisement and economic oppression. Freedom was legally recognized, as were some other privileges, such as the right to marry. But all the codes forbade a Black man from serving on a jury; some even barred Black farmers from renting or leasing land. A Black person could be punished for "idleness" by being sentenced to work on a chain gang. All the codes sought to prohibit Black men from voting.

These oppressive laws testified to the depths of white supremacist sentiments in much of the still-rebellious South. They mocked the ideal of freedom so recently purchased by buckets of blood. The Black Codes imposed terrible burdens on the so-recently unfettered Black Southerners, who now faced a formidable struggle against mistreatment and poverty to make their way as free people. The worst features of the Black Codes would eventually be repealed, but their revocation could not by itself lift liberated Black citizens into economic independence. Lacking capital, and with little to offer but their labor, thousands of impoverished formerly enslaved people slipped into the status of sharecropper farmers (refer to Image 20.6). So did many landless white Southerners. Luckless sharecroppers gradually sank into a morass of virtual peonage and remained there for generations. Formerly slaves to masters, countless Black freedmen as well as poorer whites in effect became shackled to the soil and to their creditors. Yet the dethroned planter aristocracy resented even this pitiful concession to freedom. Sharecropping was the "wrong policy," said one planter. "It makes the laborer too independent; he becomes a partner, and has a right to be consulted."

The Black Codes made an ugly impression in the North. If the formerly enslaved people were being effectively re-enslaved, people asked, had not the Boys in Blue spilled their blood in vain? Had the North really won the war?

20-7 Congressional Reconstruction

These questions grew more insistent when the congressional delegations from the newly reconstituted Southern states presented themselves in the Capitol in December 1865. To the shock and disgust of the Republicans, many former Confederate leaders were on hand to claim their seats.

The appearance of these ex-rebels was a natural but costly blunder. White voters of the South, seeking able representatives, had turned instinctively to their experienced statesmen. But most of the Southern leaders were tainted by active association with the **"Lost Cause."** Among them were four former Confederate generals, five colonels, and various members of the Richmond cabinet and Congress. Most offensive to Northern sensibilities was the shrimpy but brainy Alexander Stephens, ex-vice president of the Confederacy, still under indictment for treason.

The presence of these "whitewashed rebels" infuriated the Republicans in Congress. The war had been fought to restore the Union, but not on these kinds of terms. The Republicans were in no hurry to embrace their former enemies—virtually all of them Democrats—in the chambers of the Capitol. While the South had been "out" from 1861 to 1865, the Republicans in Congress had enjoyed a relatively free hand. They had passed much legislation that favored the North, such as the Morrill Tariff, the Pacific Railroad Act, and the Homestead Act. Now many Republicans balked at giving up this political advantage. On the first day of the congressional session, December 4, 1865, they slammed the door in the face of the newly elected Southern delegations.

Looking to the future, the Republicans were alarmed to realize that a restored South would be stronger than ever in national politics. Before the war, only three-fifths of the Black population had been counted in apportioning congressional representation. Now all Black people were fully counted, substantially expanding the South's political power. Eleven Southern states had seceded and been subdued by force of arms. But now, owing to full counting of free Black Southerners, the rebel states were entitled to twelve more votes in Congress, and twelve more presidential electoral votes, than they had previously enjoyed. Again, angry voices in the North raised the cry, "Who won the war?"

Republicans had good reason to fear that ultimately they might be elbowed aside. Southerners might join hands with Democrats in the North and win control of Congress or maybe even the White House. If this happened, they could perpetuate the Black Codes, virtually re-enslaving Black freedmen. They could dismantle the economic program of the Republican party by lowering tariffs, rerouting the transcontinental railroad, repealing the free-farm Homestead Act, and possibly even repudiating the war-swollen national debt. President Johnson thus deeply disturbed the congressional Republicans when he announced on December 6, 1865, that the recently rebellious states had satisfied his conditions and that in his view the Union was now restored.

20-8 Johnson Clashes with Congress

A clash between president and Congress was now inevitable. It exploded into the open in February 1866, when the president vetoed a bill (later repassed) extending the life of the controversial Freedmen's Bureau.

Aroused, the Republicans swiftly struck back. In March 1866 they passed the **Civil Rights Bill**, a landmark in the history of civil rights legislation. The measure conferred American citizenship on Black people and struck directly at the Southern states' Black Codes. President Johnson saw the bill as an unconstitutional trampling of states' rights, and resolutely vetoed the measure. Congress steamrollered its passage over his veto—something that happened repeatedly thereafter. The friendless president, dubbed "Sir Veto" and "Andy Veto," had his presidential wings clipped, as Congress increasingly assumed the dominant role in running the government. One critic called Johnson "the dead dog of the White House."

Republicans now increasingly feared that the Southerners might one day win control of Congress and repeal the hated civil rights law. So the lawmakers undertook to rivet the principles of the Civil Rights Bill into the Constitution as the **Fourteenth Amendment**. Approved by Congress and sent to the states in June 1866 and ratified in 1868, the Fourteenth Amendment was among the most sweeping constitutional revisions ever passed and proved to be a major pillar of constitutional law ever after. It (1) conferred civil rights on the freedmen, including an explicit recognition of *national* citizenship, while guaranteeing "equal protection of the laws" to all citizens, even while excluding a specific guarantee of the franchise; (2) reduced proportionately the representation of a state in Congress and in the Electoral College if it denied Black men the ballot, thereby abolishing the original Constitution's notorious "three-fifths" clause but stopping short of a constitutional guarantee of the right to vote; (3) disqualified from federal and state office former Confederates who as federal officeholders had once sworn "to support the Constitution of the United States"; and (4) guaranteed the federal debt, while repudiating all Confederate debts. (Refer to the text of the Fourteenth Amendment in the Appendix.) Its equal protection clause, while designed to meet the needs of the moment, became the foundation for later civil rights expansions—for Black Americans and others—in later centuries (refer to "The Presence of the Past: The Fourteenth Amendment and the 'Second Founding'," pp. 504–506).

The Presence of the Past

The Fourteenth Amendment and the "Second Founding"

"*While the Union survived the civil war, the Constitution did not.*" — Thurgood Marshall, 1987.

Marshall, the first Black Justice to serve on the Supreme Court, was describing the epochal impact of the three Reconstruction-era constitutional amendments: the Thirteenth, abolishing slavery; the Fourteenth, guaranteeing national citizenship and protecting against wrongful treatment by the states; and the Fifteenth, prohibiting racial qualifications for voting.

Though it took several generations for the story fully to unfold, taken together, those amendments eventually nurtured a judicial and social revolution so sweeping that many historians have appraised their combined effect as nothing less than a "Second Founding." All three have become pillars of the nation's very identity and its solemn commitment to principles of freedom, equality, and fair play.

The most complicated, controversial, and consequential of those three post–Civil War revisions to the Constitution has been the Fourteenth Amendment. The Amendment's 439 words made it nearly ten times longer than either of its two Reconstruction-era companions, a clue to the complexity of the matters it addressed. The long history of its impact traces the sometimes halting but steadily advancing evolution of some of American society's most cherished—though still contested—democratic ideals.

Crafted in response to post–Civil War circumstances, the far-reaching Fourteenth Amendment has been applied in more modern court cases than any other constitutional provision.

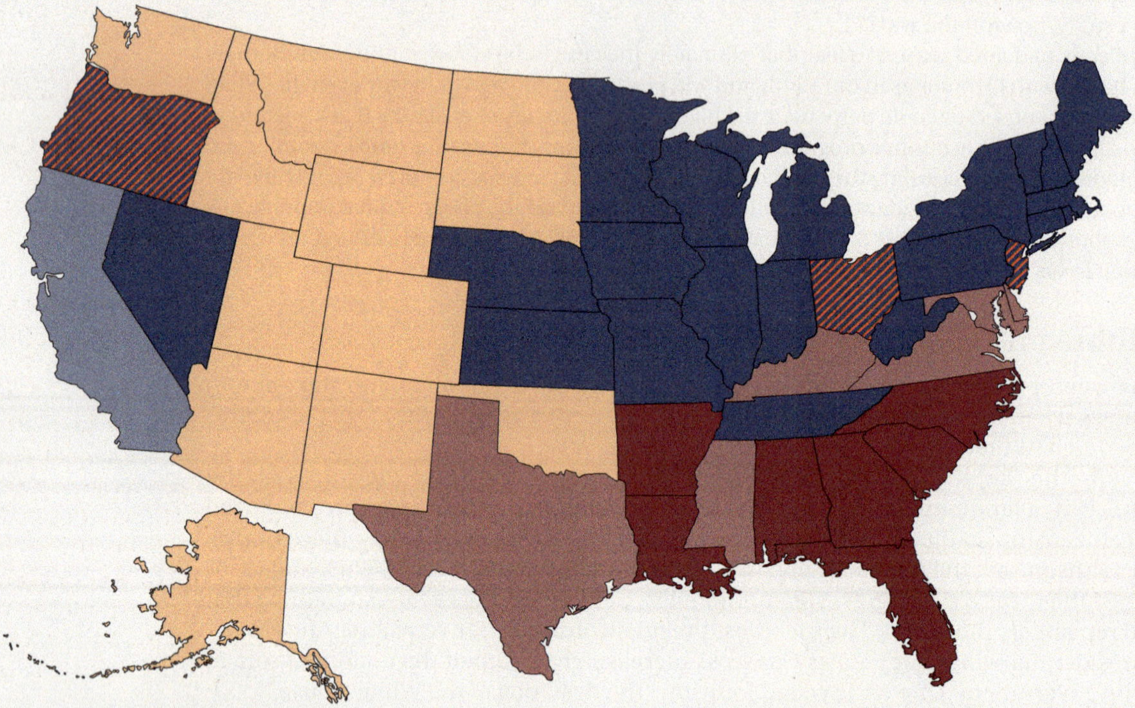

- Ratified the Fourteenth Amendment prior to national certification, 1866–1868
- First rejected, then ratified prior to national certification, 1868
- First rejected, then ratified following national certification, 1869–1976
- Ratified following national certification, 1959
- Ratified, then ratification withdrawn, then re-ratified. (Oregon rescinded ratification following national certification, though was included in the official count that allowed for passage and certification of the amendment.)
- U.S. Territories in 1868 (not yet states)

Map 20.1 The Rocky Road to Ratification Many Northern states readily ratified the Fourteenth Amendment. Most Southern states did so only as a condition for readmission to the Union. Though the requisite three-quarters of states had approved by 1868, making the Amendment the law of the land, a few held out until well into the twentieth century.

Ratified in 1868, the Amendment constitutionalized the protections for Black people encoded in the Civil Rights Act of 1866, which bestowed birthright citizenship and other rights on all non-Native inhabitants, conspicuously including the formerly enslaved. Congressional Republicans feared the Act could be repealed when Southern delegates returned to the Capitol. Accordingly, they made ratification of the Amendment a precondition for readmittance to the Union.

From that measure to safeguard particular Black rights in the immediate aftermath of Emancipation flowed a lengthy stream of federal efforts to secure a broad spectrum of rights for many people, of many different races, creeds, and conditions.

Two words—*citizen* and *person*—and one phrase—*equal protection of the laws*—capture the Amendment's essence, and its impressive legacies in the realms of civil liberties and individual rights.

AP Photo/David Zalubowski

Image 20.7 The Living Fourteenth Amendment Protesters in 2008 invoked the Fourteenth Amendment to oppose California's Proposition 8, a ballot initiative that banned same-sex marriage. The courts agreed, ruling that "Prop 8" violated both the "due process" and "equal protection" clauses of the Amendment.

The Constitution of 1787 made mention of "citizen of the United States" (Art. II, Sec. 1), but left it to the individual states to define the specific attributes of citizenship, including qualifications for voting. Some states conferred various degrees of citizenship on free Black persons, and some did not. In his inflammatory decision in the 1857 *Dred Scott* case (refer to "18-7 The Dred Scott Bombshell," pp. 442–443), Chief Justice Roger Taney made a distinction between state and national citizenship and infamously declared that Black people were not eligible for national citizenship because they had "no rights which the white man was bound to respect."

That noxious ruling the Fourteenth Amendment now once and for all exploded with its ringing affirmation that "All persons born or naturalized in the United States, and subject to the jurisdiction thereof, are *citizens of the United States* (emphasis added) and of the State wherein they reside."* The Amendment further stipulated that "No State shall make or enforce any law which shall abridge the privileges or immunities of citizens of the United States; nor shall any State deprive any person of life, liberty, or property, without due process of law."**

The "Privileges and Immunities" clause in the original Constitution had been intended to prevent states from discriminating against citizens from other states. But the incorporation of that language into the Fourteenth Amendment now theoretically opened the door for the *federal* government to compel states to honor the rights of all—now decidedly *national*—citizens. That door was soon slammed shut in the still highly controversial 1873 *Slaughter-House* and 1876 *Cruikshank* cases (refer to "20-14, The Ku Klux Klan," pp. 512–513) when the Supreme Court severely limited the definition of rights that fell under the protection of federal power. Those rulings effectively opened the era of Jim Crow disenfranchisement and denial of Black civil rights in the South.

Jurists and scholars continue to debate the intended scope of the Constitution's "privileges and immunities" language. But in the twentieth century, activists looked to other clauses of the Fourteenth Amendment to secure civil rights, notably its protections for liberty and equal protection of the law.

(*continued*)

*The careful wording of the Amendment deliberately excluded supposedly self-governing Native Americans. Indigenous peoples had to wait until the 1924 Indian Citizenship Act for recognition as citizens, though some states still attempted to restrict their right to vote.

**The Amendment went on to penalize states that attempted to revive the original Constitution's notorious "three-fifths" clause, though in a gesture of lingering loyalty to the doctrine of states' rights it did not outright prohibit that practice. That defect was imperfectly addressed by the soon-to-be passed Fifteenth Amendment, and more effectively remedied nearly a century later by the Voting Rights Act of 1965. (Refer to "34-4 Reclaiming the Right to Vote," pp. 912, 915–916.)

Moreover, twentieth-century courts increasingly ruled that the Bill of Rights was applicable to the states as well. Known as "incorporation," this legal doctrine has effectively undermined the *Slaughter-House* ruling. And as time went on, the list of federally secured rights expanded to include such matters as the right to have equal access to education, to be protected from hate crimes, to practice contraception, to marry whom one chose and—from 1973 until 2022—to have an abortion in the first trimester of pregnancy. The Amendment thus provided the leverage for a post-WWII "rights revolution" and a substantial amplification of federal power—as well as an expansion of the judiciary's role.

No less importantly, the Amendment declared that no state could "deny to any *person* (emphasis added) within its jurisdiction the equal protection of the laws." That simple two-syllable word has had enormous consequences, not least for the millions of immigrants who entered the country in the century and a half after the Civil War (refer to "The Presence of the Past: Immigration—Legal, Illegal, and Otherwise," pp. 913–915). When in the 1970s the state of Texas attempted to block undocumented immigrant children from attending public schools, the Supreme Court slapped down the Texas law as repugnant to the Fourteenth Amendment's guarantees of protection to all "persons"—whether citizens or not—within the state's jurisdiction (*Plyer v. Doe,* 1982). A comparable California ballot initiative (Proposition 187) met a similar fate a decade later. Argument continues over what constitutes "personhood," as anti-abortion advocates define the fetus as a person whose life and liberty the government is obliged to protect.

As Thurgood Marshall sagely noted—and as the twentieth-century civil rights champion Martin Luther King Jr. shrewdly understood—those words inscribed on nineteenth-century constitutional parchment could be mobilized lifetimes later in the never-ending struggle for all people to grasp the full promise of American life. And as King repeatedly insisted (echoing antebellum abolitionists): "The arc of the moral universe is long, but it bends towards justice." The Fourteenth Amendment has been the mighty tool that has done a lot of that bending.

The Radical faction was disappointed that the Fourteenth Amendment did not grant the right to vote, but all Republicans were agreed that no state should be welcomed back into the Union fold without first ratifying the Fourteenth Amendment. Yet President Johnson advised the Southern states to reject it, and all of the "sinful eleven," except Tennessee, defiantly spurned the amendment. Their spirit was reflected in a Southern song:

And I don't want no pardon for what I was or am,
I won't be reconstructed and I don't give a damn.

20-9 Swinging 'Round the Circle with Johnson

As 1866 lengthened, the battle intensified between the Congress and the president. The root of the controversy was Johnson's "10 percent" governments that had passed the most stringent Black Codes. Congress had tried to temper the worst features of the codes by extending the life of the embattled Freedmen's Bureau and passing the Civil Rights Bill. Both were measures Johnson had vetoed. Now the issue was Southern acceptance of the principles enshrined in the Fourteenth Amendment. The Republicans would settle for nothing less. Indeed, they soon insisted on even more.

The crucial congressional elections of 1866—more crucial than some presidential elections—were fast approaching. Johnson was naturally eager to escape from the clutch of Congress by securing a majority favorable to his soft-on-the-South policy. Invited to dedicate a Chicago monument to Stephen A. Douglas, he undertook to speak at various cities en route in support of his views.

Johnson's notorious "swing 'round the circle," beginning in the late summer of 1866, was a seriocomedy of errors. The president delivered a series of "give 'em hell" speeches, in which he accused the Radicals in Congress of having planned large-scale anti-Black riots and murder in the South. As he spoke, hecklers hurled insults at him. Reverting to his stump-speaking days in Tennessee, he shouted back angry retorts, amid cries of "You be damned" and "Don't get mad, Andy." The dignity of his high office sank to a new low, as the old charges of drunkenness were revived.

As a vote-getter, Johnson was highly successful—for the opposition. His inept speechmaking heightened the cry "Stand by Congress" against the "Tailor of the Potomac." When the ballots were counted, the Republicans had rolled up more than a two-thirds majority in both houses of Congress.

20-10 Republican Principles and Programs

The Republicans now had a veto-proof Congress and virtually unlimited control of Reconstruction policy. But they still disagreed sharply among themselves over the best course to pursue in the South.

The Radicals in the Senate were led by the courtly and principled idealist Charles Sumner, still convalescing from his prewar caning on the Senate floor. Sumner tirelessly labored not only for Black freedom but for racial equality. In the House the most powerful Radical was Thaddeus Stevens, a crusty and vindictive congressman from Pennsylvania. Seventy-four years old in 1866, he was a curious figure, with a protruding lower lip, a heavy black wig covering his bald head, and a congenitally disfigured foot. An unswerving ally of Black Americans, he had defended runaway enslaved people in court without fee. Long rumored to be carrying on an affair with his Black housekeeper, he insisted on burial in a Black cemetery. His fierce support of Black freedom was matched by his vitriolic hatred of rebellious white Southerners. A masterly parliamentarian with a razor-sharp mind and withering wit, Stevens was a leading figure on the Joint (House-Senate) Committee on Reconstruction.

Still opposed to rapid restoration of the Southern states, the Radicals wanted to keep them out as long as possible and apply federal power to bring about a drastic social and economic transformation in the South. But moderate Republicans, invoking the principles of states' rights and self-government, recoiled from the full implications of the Radical program. They preferred policies that restrained the states from abridging citizens' rights, rather than policies that directly involved the federal government in individual lives. The actual policies adopted by Congress showed the influence of both these schools of thought, though the moderates, as the majority faction, had the upper hand. And one thing both groups had come to agree on by 1867 was the necessity to enfranchise Black voters, even if it took federal troops to do it (refer to Image 20.8).

Reading Room 2020/Alamy Stock Photo

Image 20.8 Republicans Campaigning in Baton Rouge, Louisiana, 1868 The soldiers' caps and regimental flags demonstrate the continuing federal military presence in the Reconstruction South. Radical Republican congressman Thaddeus Stevens said that Reconstruction must "revolutionize Southern institutions, habits, and manners. . . . The foundation of their institutions . . . must be broken up and relaid, or all our blood and treasure have been spent in vain."

20-11 Military Reconstruction

An explosion of vicious and bloody race riots erupted in several Southern cities, providing the background and stimulus for congressional action. In Memphis, Tennessee, for example, a white mob in the spring of 1866 burned twelve Black schools, four churches, and more than fifty homes, and murdered forty-six Black people. Congress at last passed the **Reconstruction Act** on March 2, 1867 (refer to Map 20.2). Supplemented by later measures, this drastic legislation divided the South into five military districts, each commanded by a Union general and policed by blue-clad soldiers, about twenty thousand all told. The act also temporarily disfranchised tens of thousands of former Confederates.

Congress additionally laid down stringent conditions for the readmission of the seceded states. The wayward states were required to ratify the Fourteenth Amendment, the constitutional enshrinement of the 1866 Civil Rights Bill that gave the formerly enslaved people their rights as citizens. The bitterest pill of all to white Southerners was the stipulation that they guarantee in their state constitutions full suffrage for their former adult male slaves. Yet the act, reflecting moderate sentiment, stopped short of giving the freedmen land or education at federal expense. The overriding purpose of the moderates was to create an electorate in Southern states that would vote those states back into the Union on acceptable terms and thus free the federal government from direct responsibility for the protection of Black rights. As later events would demonstrate, this approach proved woefully inadequate to the cause of justice for Black Americans.

The Radical Republicans were still worried. The danger loomed that once the unrepentant states were readmitted, they would amend their constitutions so as to withdraw the ballot from their Black citizens. The only ironclad safeguard was to incorporate Black male suffrage in the federal Constitution. A pattern was emerging: Just as the Fourteenth Amendment had constitutionalized the principles of the Civil Rights Bill, now Congress sought to provide constitutional protection for the suffrage provisions in the Reconstruction Act. This goal was finally achieved by the **Fifteenth Amendment**, passed by Congress in 1869 and ratified by the required number of states in 1870 (refer to the Appendix).*

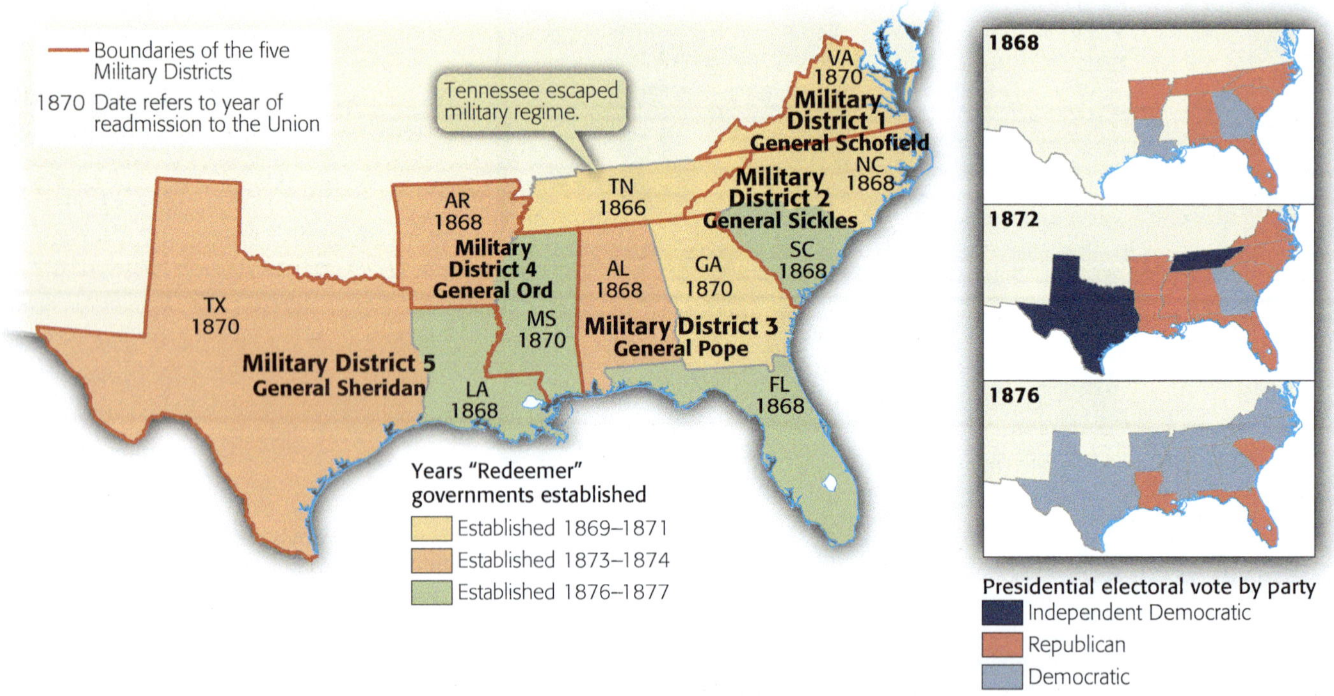

Map 20.2 Military Reconstruction, 1867 (five districts and commanding generals) For many white Southerners, military Reconstruction amounted to turning the knife in the wound of defeat. An often-repeated story of later years had a Southerner remark, "I was sixteen years old before I discovered that damnyankee was two words."

*Strikingly, the "free" states of California and Oregon rejected the amendment, fearing it would enfranchise their large Chinese populations. Oregon finally ratified only in 1960, California in 1962.

Table 20.2 Southern Reconstruction by State

State	Readmitted to Representation in Congress	Home Rule (Democratic or "Redeemer" Regime) Reestablished	Comments
Tennessee	July 24, 1866		Ratified Fourteenth Amendment in 1866 and hence avoided military Reconstruction*
Arkansas	June 22, 1868	1874	
North Carolina	June 25, 1868	1870	
Alabama	June 25, 1868	1874	
Florida	June 25, 1868	1877	Federal troops restationed in 1877, as result of Hayes-Tilden electoral bargain
Louisiana	June 25, 1868	1877	Same as Florida
South Carolina	June 25, 1868	1877	Same as Florida
Virginia	January 26, 1870	1869	
Mississippi	February 23, 1870	1876	
Texas	March 30, 1870	1874	
Georgia	[June 25, 1868] July 15, 1870	1872	Readmitted June 25, 1868, but returned to military control after expulsion of Black lawmakers from legislature

*For many years, Tennessee was the only state of the secession to observe Lincoln's birthday as a legal holiday. Many states in the South still observe the birthdays of Jefferson Davis and Robert E. Lee.

Military Reconstruction of the South not only usurped certain functions of the president as commander in chief but set up martial regimes of shaky legality. The Supreme Court had already ruled, in the case ***Ex parte Milligan*** (1866), that military tribunals could not try civilians, even during wartime, in areas where the civil courts were open. Military rule in peacetime seemed starkly contrary to the spirit of the Constitution. But the circumstances were extraordinary in the Republic's history, and for the time being the Supreme Court avoided offending the Republican Congress.

Prodded into line by federal bayonets, the Southern states got on with the task of constitution making. By 1870 all of them had reorganized their governments and had been accorded full rights (refer to Table 20.2). Federal troops—the South's hated "bluebellies"—remained until the new Republican regimes appeared to be firmly entrenched. Yet the South's Reconstruction proved as fleeting as anxious proponents of civil rights had feared. When troops finally left a former Confederate state, its government swiftly passed back into the hands of white **Redeemers**, or "Home Rule" regimes, which were inevitably Democratic. Finally, in 1877, the last federal muskets were removed from state politics, and the "solid" Democratic South congealed (refer to "21-7 The Compromise of 1877 and the End of Reconstruction," pp. 529–530).

At a constitutional convention in Alabama, freed people affirmed their rights in the following declaration:

"We claim exactly the same rights, privileges and immunities as are enjoyed by white men—we ask nothing more and will be content with nothing less. . . . The law no longer knows white nor black, but simply men, and consequently we are entitled to ride in public conveyances, hold office, sit on juries and do everything else which we have in the past been prevented from doing solely on the ground of color."

20-12 No Women Voters

The passage of the three Reconstruction-era Amendments—the Thirteenth, Fourteenth, and Fifteenth—delighted former abolitionists but deeply disappointed advocates of women's rights. Women had played a prominent part in the prewar abolitionist movement and had often pointed out that both white women and all Black people lacked basic civil rights, especially the crucial right to vote. The struggle for Black freedom and the crusade for women's rights, therefore, were one and the same in the eyes of many white women. During the war, feminist leaders such as Elizabeth Cady Stanton and Susan B. Anthony had temporarily suspended their own demands and worked wholeheartedly for the cause of Black emancipation. The **Woman's Loyal League** had gathered nearly 400,000 signatures on petitions asking Congress to pass a constitutional amendment prohibiting slavery.

Now, with the war ended and the Thirteenth Amendment passed, feminist leaders believed that their time had come. They reeled with shock, however, when the wording of the Fourteenth Amendment, which defined equal national citizenship, for the first time inserted the word *male* into the Constitution in referring to a citizen's right to vote. Both Stanton and Anthony campaigned actively against the Fourteenth Amendment despite the pleas of Frederick Douglass, who had long supported woman suffrage but believed that this was "the Negro's hour." When the Fifteenth Amendment proposed to prohibit denial of the vote on the basis of "race, color, or previous condition of servitude," Stanton and Anthony wanted the word *sex* added to the list. They lost this battle, too. Fifty years would pass before the Constitution granted women the right to vote.

The prominent suffragist and abolitionist Susan B. Anthony (1820–1906) was outraged over the proposed exclusion of women from the Fourteenth Amendment. In a conversation with her former male allies Wendell Phillips and Theodore Tilton, she reportedly held out her arm and declared,

> "Look at this, all of you. And hear me swear that I will cut off this right arm of mine before I will ever work for or demand the ballot for the Negro and not the woman."

20-13 Black Rights and Freedoms in the Reconstruction South

Black Americans now had secured at least a measure of formal freedom. But their white allies in Congress had only haltingly and somewhat belatedly secured the franchise for them. Both Presidents Lincoln and Johnson had proposed to give the ballot gradually to selected Black men who qualified for it through education, property ownership, or military service. Moderate Republicans and even many Radicals at first hesitated to bestow suffrage on the freedmen. The Fourteenth Amendment, in many ways the heart of the Republican program for Reconstruction, had fallen short of guaranteeing the right to vote. (It envisioned for Black men the same status as that of white women—citizenship without voting rights.) But by 1867, Congressional hesitation had given way to a hard determination to enfranchise the former enslaved people wholesale and immediately. By glaring contrast, most of the Northern states, before ratification of the Fifteenth Amendment in 1870, withheld the ballot from their tiny free-Black minorities. White Southerners naturally concluded that the Republicans were hypocritical in insisting on Black enfranchisement in the South (refer to Image 20.9).

Image 20.9 Freedmen Voting, Richmond, Virginia, 1871 The exercise of democratic rights by former enslaved people constituted a political and social revolution in the South and was bitterly resented by white citizens.

The Granger Collection/Alamy Stock Photo

Having gained their right to suffrage, Southern Black men seized the initiative and began to organize politically. Their primary vehicle became the **Union League**, originally a pro-Union organization based in the North. Assisted by Northern Black activists, freedmen turned the league into a network of political clubs that educated members in their civic duties and campaigned for Republican candidates. The league's mission soon expanded to include building Black churches and schools, representing Black grievances before local employers and government, and recruiting militias to protect Black communities from white retaliation.

Though African American women did not obtain the right to vote, their leadership and activism advanced the political cause. Black women mobilized for the parades and rallies common in Black communities during the early years of Reconstruction and helped assemble mass meetings in the newly constructed Black churches. They swelled the crowd at the constitutional conventions held throughout the South in 1867, monitoring the proceedings and participating in informal votes outside the convention halls.

But Black men elected as delegates to the state constitutional conventions held the greater political authority. They formed the backbone of the Black political community. At the conventions, they sat down with whites to hammer out new state constitutions, which most importantly provided for universal male suffrage. Though the subsequent elections produced no Black governors or majorities in state senates, Black political participation expanded exponentially during Reconstruction. Between 1868 and 1876, fourteen Black congressmen and two Black senators, Hiram Revels and Blanche K. Bruce, both of Mississippi, served in Washington, DC (refer to Image 20.10). Hundreds of Black men also served in state governments as lieutenant governors and representatives, and in local governments as mayors, magistrates, sheriffs, and justices of the peace.

The sight of formerly enslaved people holding office deeply offended their onetime enslavers, who lashed out with particular fury at the freedmen's white allies, labeling them **scalawags** and **carpetbaggers**. The scalawags were Southerners, often former Unionists and Whigs. The former Confederates accused them, with wild exaggeration and outright falsehood, of plundering the treasuries of the Southern states through their political influence in the Radical governments. The carpetbaggers, on the other hand, were supposedly sleazy Northerners who had packed all their worldly goods into a carpetbag suitcase at war's end and had come south to seek personal power and profit. In fact, most were former Union soldiers and Northern businessmen and professionals who wanted to play a role in modernizing the "New South."

How well or badly did the Reconstruction regimes rule? The legislatures passed much desirable legislation and introduced many sorely needed reforms benefiting Southerners of all races. For the first time in Southern history, steps were taken toward establishing adequate public schools. Tax systems were streamlined; public works were launched; and property rights were guaranteed to women. Many reforms were retained by the all-white "Redeemer" governments that later returned to power. Those that enlarged and protected the rights of Black people, however, were not.

Image 20.10 Congressman John R. Lynch of Mississippi After John Lynch was freed by the Union army, he got an education at a freedmen's school in Natchez, Mississippi. At age twenty-four, he became speaker of the Mississippi House. In 1872, Lynch joined six other African Americans in Congress, where he made his greatest mark in the long debate over the Civil Rights Act of 1875, barring discrimination in public accommodations. Lynch drew on his own humiliating experiences as a Black man in the South to argue for a law prohibiting discrimination on public transportation like trains and at places like inns, restaurants, and theaters. The law passed but was not enforced. It was ruled unconstitutional in 1883.

In 1895, Thomas E. Miller, a Black South Carolina legislator, defended the record of his state's Reconstruction-era government:

"The gentleman . . . speaks of the piling up of the state debt; of jobbery and peculation during the period between 1869 and 1873 in South Carolina, but he has not found voice eloquent enough, nor pen exact enough, to mention those imperishable gifts bestowed upon South Carolina between 1873 and 1876 by Negro legislators – the laws relative to finance, the building of penal and charitable institutions, and, greatest of all, the establishment of the public school system. Starting as infants in legislation in 1869, many wise measures were not thought of, many injudicious acts were passed. But in the administration of affairs for the next four years, having learned by experience the result of bad acts, we immediately passed reformatory laws touching every department of state, county, municipal, and town governments. These enactments are today upon the statute books of South Carolina. They stand as living witnesses of the Negro's fitness to vote and legislate upon the rights of mankind."

". . . We were eight years in power. We had built schoolhouses, established charitable institutions, built and maintained the penitentiary system, provided for the education of the deaf and dumb, rebuilt the jails and courthouses, rebuilt the bridges and reestablished the ferries. In short, we had reconstructed the State and placed it upon the road to prosperity . . . ."

As in the postwar North, no small measure of corruption and graft flourished amid this rapid and wholesale political refashioning of the South. One "thrifty" governor in a single year "saved" $100,000 from a salary of $8,000. Yet the crimes of the Southern governments were no more outrageous than the scams and felonies being perpetrated in the North at the same time, especially in Boss Tweed's New York (refer to "21-2 The Era of Good Stealings," p. 524).

20-14 The Ku Klux Klan

Deeply resentful and enraged by the new racial order, some white people resorted to savage measures against federal rule. A number of secret organizations mushroomed forth, the most notorious of which was the "Invisible Empire of the South," or **Ku Klux Klan**, founded in Tennessee in 1866 (refer to Image 20.11). Besheeted nightriders, their horses' hooves muffled, would approach the cabin of any they considered an "upstart" Black family and hammer on the door. In ghoulish tones, one thirsty horseman would demand a bucket of water. Then, under pretense of drinking, he would pour it into a rubber attachment concealed beneath his mask and gown, smack his lips, and declare that this was the first water he had tasted since he was killed at the Battle of Shiloh. If fright did not produce the desired effect, violent force was employed.

Terror and brutality proved effective. Many ex-bondsmen and white Northern transplants, quick to take a hint, shunned the polls. Those brave souls who resisted were flogged, mutilated, or murdered. (Such horrors marked the beginning of decades of vigilante violence against Black communities and other minorities in the South and beyond.) In one Louisiana parish in 1868, white assailants in two days killed or wounded two hundred victims; a pile of twenty-five bodies was found half-buried in the woods. By such atrocious practices were Black people "kept in their place"—that is, down. The Klan became a refuge for numerous bandits and cutthroats. Any scoundrel could don a sheet.

Congress, outraged by this night-riding lawlessness, passed the harsh **Force Acts** of 1870 and 1871. President Grant then ordered federal troops, including Black soldiers, into the South to stamp out the "lash law." Frederick Douglass later said that Grant was "the shelter and savior of my people in the hour of supreme danger." Attorneys from the Department of Justice, created in 1870 to address the swelling postwar obligations of federal law enforcement, indicted some three thousand Klansmen, and achieved more than a thousand convictions. The KKK was momentarily suppressed, but the Invisible Empire continued its tactics in the guise of "dancing clubs," "missionary societies," and "rifle clubs." When a white mob killed some 150 Black men in Colfax, Louisiana, on Easter Sunday, 1873, federal officials invoked the Force Acts to bring the perpetrators of the **Colfax Massacre** to justice. But the Supreme Court, in the notorious 1876 case of ***United States v. Cruikshank***, overturned their convictions. The Court held that the protections for civil liberties guaranteed in the Fourteenth Amendment applied only to *state* actions, not to actions undertaken by individuals, no matter how heinous.

The *Cruikshank* ruling came three years after the Supreme Court had narrowed the scope of federal authority to protect individual rights in its first major Fourteenth Amendment decision, ***The Slaughter-House Cases***. Ruling against a group of New Orleans butchers who had sued the city after being required to practice their trade in a city-owned slaughterhouse, the Court majority found that it had not been Congress' intent for the federal government to protect *all* rights nor to infringe on states' ability to impose certain restrictions on their citizens. Reinforcing this more restrictive interpretation of the Amendment, the wretched *Cruikshank* decision effectively blocked federal safeguards for civil rights for nearly a century thereafter.

White resistance undermined attempts to empower Black people politically. The white South, for many decades, openly flouted the Fourteenth and Fifteenth Amendments. Wholesale disfranchisement of Black Southerners, starting conspicuously about 1890, was achieved by intimidation, fraud, and trickery as well as brute terror. Among various underhanded schemes were literacy tests, unfairly administered by white election workers to the advantage of illiterate white voters. In the eyes of white Southerners, the goal of white supremacy fully justified these dishonorable devices.

20-15 Johnson Walks the Impeachment Plank

Radical Republicans meanwhile had been sharpening their hatchets for President Johnson. Annoyed by the obstruction of the "drunken tailor" in the White House, they falsely accused him of maintaining there a clutch of "dissolute women." As the president continued to thwart federal Reconstruction and do little to defend Black freedom, Johnson's Congressional adversaries decided to remove him altogether by constitutional processes.*

As an initial step, Congress in 1867 passed the **Tenure of Office Act**—as usual, over Johnson's veto. Contrary to precedent, the new law required the president to secure the consent of the Senate before he could remove his appointees once they had been approved by that body. One purpose was to freeze into the cabinet the secretary of war, Edwin M. Stanton, a holdover from the Lincoln administration. Although outwardly loyal to Johnson, he was secretly serving as a spy and informer for the Radicals.

Johnson provided the Radicals with a pretext to begin impeachment proceedings when he abruptly dismissed Stanton early in 1868. The House of Representatives immediately voted 126 to 47 to impeach Johnson for "high crimes and misdemeanors," charging him with various violations of the Tenure of Office Act. Two additional articles related to Johnson's verbal assaults on the Congress, involving "disgrace, ridicule, hatred, contempt, and reproach."

Dallas Historical Society, Texas, USA/The Bridgeman Art Library

Image 20.11 Klansmen in Costume Members of the Ku Klux Klan like these two garbed men utilized terrorist violence on behalf of a political agenda: the disenfranchisement of African Americans and their Republican allies and the reinstatement of white supremacist rule by "Redeemer" governments.

20-16 A Not-Guilty Verdict for Johnson

With unrestrained zeal the Radical-led Senate now sat as a court to try Johnson—the first impeachment trial of an American president. In accordance with constitutional procedure, the House conducted the prosecution. The trial aroused intense public interest and, with one thousand tickets printed, proved to be the biggest show of 1868. Johnson kept what was left of his dignity and sobriety and maintained a discreet silence. His battery of attorneys argued that the president, convinced that the Tenure of Office Act was unconstitutional, had fired Stanton merely to put a test case before the Supreme Court. (That slow-moving tribunal finally ruled indirectly in Johnson's favor fifty-eight years later.) House prosecutors, including smooth-talking Benjamin F. Butler and age-enfeebled Thaddeus Stevens, had a harder time building a compelling case for impeachment.

On May 16, 1868, the day for the first voting in the Senate, the tension was electric, and heavy breathing could be heard in the galleries. By a margin of only one vote (possibly the result of outright bribery), the Radicals failed to muster the two-thirds majority for Johnson's removal. Seven resistant Republican senators, mainly moderates, voted "not guilty."

Several factors shaped the outcome. Fears of creating a destabilizing precedent played a role, as did principled opposition to abusing the constitutional mechanism of checks and balances. Political considerations also figured conspicuously. As the vice presidency remained vacant

*For impeachment, refer to Art. I, Sec. II, para. 5; Art. I, Sec. III, paras. 6, 7; Art. II, Sec. IV, in the Appendix.

under Johnson, his successor would have been Radical Republican Benjamin Wade, co-author of the war-time Wade-Davis Bill and president pro tempore of the Senate. Wade was fiercely disliked by many members of the business community for his soft-money, pro-labor views and was distrusted by moderate Republicans. Meanwhile, Johnson indicated through his attorney that he would stop obstructing Republican policies in return for remaining in office.

Diehard Radicals were infuriated by their failure to muster a two-thirds majority for Johnson's removal. "The Country is going to the Devil!" cried the ailing Stevens as he was carried from the hall. But the nation, though violently aroused, accepted the verdict with a good temper that did credit to its political maturity. In a less stable republic, an armed uprising might have erupted against the president.

The nation thus narrowly avoided a dangerous precedent that would have gravely weakened one of the three branches of the federal government. Johnson was clearly guilty of bad speeches, bad judgment, and bad temper. It was less clear that his behavior rose to the Constitution's vaguely defined standard of "high crimes and misdemeanors." From the standpoint of his political opponents, his greatest crime had been to stand inflexibly in Reconstruction's path.

The following excerpt is part of a heartrending appeal to Congress in 1871 by a group of Black citizens from Kentucky:

"We believe you are not familiar with the description of the Ku Klux Klans riding nightly over the country, going from county to county, and in the county towns, spreading terror wherever they go by robbing, whipping, ravishing, and killing our people without provocation, compelling colored people to break the ice and bathe in the chilly waters of the Kentucky River."

"The [state] legislature has adjourned. They refused to enact any laws to suppress Ku-Klux disorder. We regard them [the Ku-Kluxers] as now being licensed to continue their dark and bloody deeds under cover of the dark night. They refuse to allow us to testify in the state courts where a white man is concerned. We find their deeds are perpetrated only upon colored men and white Republicans. We also find that for our services to the government and our race we have become the special object of hatred and persecution at the hands of the Democratic Party. Our people are driven from their homes in great numbers, having no redress only [except] the United States court, which is in many cases unable to reach them."

A Black leader protested to white readers in 1868,

"It is extraordinary that a race such as yours, professing gallantry, chivalry, education, and superiority, living in a land where ringing chimes call child and sire to the Gospel of God—that with all these advantages on your side, you can make war upon the poor defenseless black man."

20-17 The Purchase of Alaska

Johnson's administration, though ineffective at home, achieved its most enduring success in the field of foreign relations.

The Russians by 1867 were in a mood to renew their offer, previously tendered in the 1850s, to sell the vast and chilly expanse of land now known as Alaska. They had overextended themselves in North America and feared that in the likely event of another war with Britain, they would lose their defenseless northern province to the sea-dominant British. Alaska, moreover, had been ruthlessly "furred out" and was a growing economic liability. Eager to unload their "frozen asset" on the Americans, the Russians put out seductive feelers in Washington. They preferred the United States to any other purchaser, primarily because they wanted to strengthen the American Republic as a barrier against their ancient British enemy.

In 1867, Secretary of State William Seward, an ardent expansionist, signed a treaty with Russia that transferred Alaska to the United States for the bargain price of $7.2 million. But Seward's enthusiasm for these frigid wastes was not shared by his ignorant or uninformed countrymen, who jeered at **Seward's Folly**, "Seward's Icebox," "Frigidia," and "Walrussia."

Then why did Congress and the American public sanction the purchase? For one thing, Russia, alone among the powers, had been conspicuously friendly to the North during the recent Civil War. Americans did not feel that they could offend their great and good friend, the tsar, by hurling his walrus-covered icebergs back into his face. Besides, the territory was rumored to be teeming with furs, fish, and gold, and it might yet "pan out" profitably—as it later did with natural resources, including oil and gas. So Congress and the country accepted "Seward's Polar Bear Garden," somewhat derisively but nevertheless hopefully.

20-18 The Legacy of Reconstruction

Many white Southerners regarded Reconstruction as a more grievous wound than the war itself. Their resentment continued to fester in the generations that followed. Southern elites deplored the upending of the slave-labor economy and the great power and wealth that it once had bestowed. They saw Black political empowerment as white *dis*empowerment. Many Southern whites came to remember military Reconstruction's enforcement of Black civil rights as an outrageous, unconstitutional intrusion into their state and local affairs. Yet few rebellions have ended with the victors sitting down to a love feast with the vanquished. Given the explosiveness of the issues that had caused the war, and the immense human loss of the fighting, the wonder is that Reconstruction was not even harsher than it was. The fact is that Lincoln, Johnson, and most Republicans had no clear picture at war's end of what federal policy toward the South should be. Policymakers groped for the right policies, influenced as much by Southern responses to defeat and emancipation as by any plans of their own to impose a specific program on the South.

The Republicans acted from a mixture of idealism and political expediency. They wanted both to protect the freedmen and freedwomen and to promote the fortunes of the Republican party, as well as advance the bold programs of national state-building begun during the war. Black Americans in North and South mobilized mightily to assert their rights not simply as a freed people, but as enfranchised, educated American citizens. When Reconstruction had robust support from both ends of Pennsylvania Avenue during the presidency of Ulysses S. Grant, a more perfect union briefly seemed possible. But it was not to be. The light of liberty that had fitfully and briefly shone on Black Southerners was quickly and violently extinguished after the last U.S. troops withdrew. It would not reignite in the South for nearly one hundred years.

Moderate Republicans never fully appreciated the extensive effort necessary to make the formerly enslaved people completely independent citizens, nor the lengths to which white Southerners would go to preserve their system of racial dominance. Had Thaddeus Stevens's ambitious program of drastic economic reforms and heftier protection of political rights been enacted, things might well have been different. But deep-seated racism, ingrained American resistance to tampering with property rights, and unbending loyalty to the principle of local self-government, combined with spreading indifference in the North to the plight of freedmen and freedwomen, proved to be insuperable obstacles. Perhaps the greatest regret is that the nation could not muster the political will to make good on its profession that all men and women are created equal (refer to Image 20.12). Despite good intentions by Republicans, the Old South was in many ways more resurrected than reconstructed, which spelled continuing woe for generations of Black Southerners.

The remarkable ex-slave Frederick Douglass (1817?–1895) wrote in 1882,

> "Though slavery was abolished, the wrongs of my people were not ended. Though they were not enslaved people, they were not yet quite free. No man can be truly free whose liberty is dependent upon the thought, feeling, and action of others, and who has himself no means in his own hands for guarding, protecting, defending, and maintaining that liberty. Yet the Negro after his emancipation was precisely in this state of destitution. . . . He was free from the individual master, but the slave of society. He had neither money, property, nor friends. He was free from the old plantation, but he had nothing but the dusty road under his feet. He was free from the old quarter that once gave him shelter, but a slave to the rains of summer and the frosts of winter. He was, in a word, literally turned loose, naked, hungry, and destitute, to the open sky."

Fotosearch/Getty Images

Image 20.12 Is This a Republican Form of Government? by Thomas Nast, Harper's Weekly, 1876 The nation's most prominent political cartoonist expressed his despair at the tragic way that Reconstruction had ended—with few real gains for the former enslaved people.

Varying Viewpoints

Did Reconstruction Fail?

Few topics have triggered as much intellectual warfare as the "dark and bloody ground" of Reconstruction. The period provoked questions—sectional, racial, and constitutional—about which people felt deeply and remain deeply divided even today. Scholarly argument goes back conspicuously to a Columbia University historian, William A. Dunning, whose students in the early 1900s published a series of histories of the Reconstruction South. Dunning and his disciples were influenced by the turn-of-the-century spirit of sectional reconciliation as well as by current theories about Black racial inferiority. Sympathizing with the white South, they wrote about the Reconstruction period as a kind of national disgrace, foisted upon a prostrate region by vindictive and self-seeking Radical Republican politicians. If the South had wronged the North by seceding, the North had wronged the South by reconstructing.

A second cycle of scholarship in the 1920s was impelled by a widespread suspicion that the Civil War itself had been a tragic and unnecessary blunder. Attention now shifted to Northern politicians. Scholars like Howard Beale further questioned the motives of the Radical Republicans. To Beale and others, the Radicals had masked a ruthless desire to exploit Southern labor and resources behind a false front of "concern" for the freed enslaved people. Moreover, Northern advocacy of Black voting rights was merely a calculated attempt to ensure a Republican political presence in the defeated South. The unfortunate Andrew Johnson, in this view, had valiantly tried to uphold constitutional principles in the face of this cynical Northern onslaught.

Although ignored by his contemporaries, scholar, Black nationalist, and founder of the National Association for the Advancement of Colored People W. E. B. Du Bois wrote a sympathetic history of Reconstruction in 1935 that became the basis for historians' interpretations ever since. Following World War II, Kenneth Stampp and others, influenced by the modern civil rights movement, built on Du Bois's argument and claimed that Reconstruction had been a noble though ultimately failed attempt to extend American principles of equity and justice. The Radical Republicans and the carpetbaggers were now heroes, whereas Andrew Johnson was castigated for his obstinate racism. By the early 1970s, this view had become orthodoxy, and it generally holds sway today. Yet some scholars, such as Michael Benedict and Leon Litwack, disillusioned with the inability to achieve full racial justice in the 1960s and 1970s, began once more to scrutinize the motives of Northern politicians immediately after the Civil War. They claimed to discover that Reconstruction had never been very radical and that the Freedmen's Bureau and other agencies had merely allowed white planters to maintain their dominance over local politics as well as over the local economy.

More recently, Eric Foner has powerfully reasserted the argument that Reconstruction was a truly radical and noble attempt to establish an interracial democracy. Drawing on the work of Du Bois, Foner has emphasized the comparative approach to American Reconstruction. Clearly, Foner has admitted, Reconstruction did not create full equality, but it did allow Black Southerners to form political organizations and churches, to vote, and to establish some measure of economic independence. In South Africa, the Caribbean, and other areas once marked by slavery, these opportunities were much harder to come by. Many of the benefits of Reconstruction were erased by whites in the South during the Gilded Age, but in the twentieth century, the constitutional principles and organizations developed during Reconstruction provided the focus and foundation for the post–World War II civil rights movement—which some have called the second Reconstruction. Steven Hahn's *A Nation Under Our Feet: Black Political Struggles in the Rural South from Slavery to the Great Migration* (2003) emphasizes the assertiveness and ingenuity of African Americans in creating new political opportunities for themselves after emancipation.

Chapter Summary

With the Civil War over, the nation faced the difficult challenges of rebuilding the South, assisting the freed people, reintegrating the Southern states into the Union, and deciding who would direct the Reconstruction process.

The South was economically devastated and socially revolutionized by emancipation. As plantation owners reluctantly confronted the end of enslaved labor, Black people took their first steps in freedom. Black churches and the Freedmen's Bureau enabled freed people to begin to shape their own destinies, though the bureau was limited and fiercely opposed.

The new president, Andrew Johnson, was politically inept and personally contentious. His attempt to implement a moderate plan of Reconstruction, along the lines originally suggested by Lincoln, fell victim to white Southerners' severe treatment of Black people, his pro-Southern sympathies, and his own political blunders.

Republicans imposed harsh military Reconstruction on the South after their gains in the 1866 congressional elections. The Southern states reentered the Union with new Radical governments, which rested partly on the newly enfranchised Black population, but also had support from some white

Southerners, called "scalawags" by their critics. These governments were sometimes corrupt, but they also implemented important reforms, especially in education and social welfare. For a time, acting from a mixture of idealism and political expediency, Republicans tried seriously to build a new Republican Party in the South to guarantee Black rights. But the divisions between moderate and Radical Republicans meant that Reconstruction's aims were often limited and confused, despite successful passage of the important Fourteenth and Fifteenth Amendments guaranteeing Black civil rights and Black male voting rights.

Embittered white Southerners hated the Radical governments and mobilized reactionary terrorist organizations such as the Ku Klux Klan to restore white supremacy. The Radical Republican House of Representatives impeached Johnson, but the Senate failed narrowly to convict him. In the end, the inadequate Reconstruction policy, which never fully addressed the deep economic and social legacy of slavery and the Civil War, failed disastrously and left a legacy of bitterness on all sides.

Key Terms

- Freedmen's Bureau (499)
- "10 percent" Reconstruction plan (500)
- Wade-Davis Bill (500)
- Black Codes (501)
- "Lost Cause" (503)
- Civil Rights Bill (503)
- Fourteenth Amendment (503)
- Reconstruction Act (508)
- Fifteenth Amendment (508)
- *Ex parte Milligan* (509)
- Redeemers (509)
- Woman's Loyal League (509)
- Union League (511)
- scalawags (511)
- carpetbaggers (511)
- Ku Klux Klan (512)
- Force Acts (512)
- Colfax Massacre (512)
- *United States v. Cruikshank* (512)
- *The Slaughter-House Cases* (512)
- Tenure of Office Act (513)
- Seward's Folly (514)

People to Know

- Oliver O. Howard
- Harriet Jacobs
- Andrew Johnson
- Thaddeus Stevens
- Hiram Revels
- Blanche Bruce
- Edwin M. Stanton
- Benjamin Wade
- William Seward

Chronology

1863	• Lincoln announces "10 percent" Reconstruction plan	
1864	• Lincoln vetoes Wade-Davis Bill	
1865	• Lincoln assassinated • Johnson issues Reconstruction proclamation • Congress refuses to seat Southern congressmen	• Freedmen's Bureau established • Southern states pass Black Codes
1866	• Congress passes Civil Rights Bill over Johnson's veto • Congress passes Fourteenth Amendment • Johnson-backed candidates lose congressional election	• *Ex parte Milligan* case • Murderous race riots in Memphis, Tennessee • Ku Klux Klan founded

(*continued*)

1867	• Reconstruction Act • Tenure of Office Act	• United States purchases Alaska from Russia
1868	• Johnson impeached and acquitted • Johnson pardons Confederate leaders	
1870	• Fifteenth Amendment ratified • Department of Justice created	
1870–1871	• Force Acts to suppress Ku Klux Klan	
1872	• Freedmen's Bureau ended • 1873 Colfax Massacre	
1873	• *The Slaughter-House Cases*	
1875	• *United States v. Cruikshank*	
1877	• Reconstruction ends	

To Learn More

Ron Chernow, *Grant* (2017)

Richard N. Current, *Those Terrible Carpetbaggers: A Reinterpretation* (1988)

Gregory M. Downs, *After Appomattox: Military Occupation and the Ends of War* (2015)

W. E. B. Du Bois, *Black Reconstruction in America* (1935)

Douglas R. Egerton, *The Wars of Reconstruction* (2014)

Carole Emberton, *Beyond Redemption: Race, Violence, and the American South After the Civil War* (2015)

Eric Foner, *Reconstruction: America's Unfinished Revolution, 1863–1877* (1988)

__________, *Forever Free: The Story of Emancipation and Reconstruction* (2005)

Henry Louis Gates, *Stony the Road: Reconstruction, White Supremacy, and the Rise of Jim Crow* (2019)

Steven Hahn, *A Nation Under Our Feet: Black Political Struggles in the Rural South from Slavery to the Great Migration* (2003)

Kate Masur, *An Example for All the Land: Emancipation and the Struggle over Equality in Washington, D.C.* (2010)

Peggy Pascoe, *What Comes Naturally: Miscegenation Law and the Making of Race in America* (2009)

Michael Perman, *Emancipation and Reconstruction* (rev. ed., 2003)

Lawrence Powell, *New Masters: Northern Planters During the Civil War and Reconstruction* (1980)

Julie Saville, *The Work of Reconstruction: From Slave to Wage Laborer in South Carolina, 1860–1870* (1994)

David O. Stewart, *Impeached: The Trial of President Andrew Johnson and the Fight for Lincoln's Legacy* (2009)

Jeremi Suri, *Civil War by Other Means: America's Long and Unfinished Fight for Democracy* (2022)

Booker T. Washington, *Up from Slavery* (1901)

Heather Andrea Williams, *Self-Taught: African American Education in Slavery and Freedom* (2005)

Part 6

Forging an Industrial Society 1865–1900

A nation of farmers fought the Civil War in the 1860s. By the close of the century, America was an industrial superpower. For generations, Americans had plunged into the wilderness and plowed their fields. Now they settled in explosively growing cities and toiled in smoke-belching factories. Yet the nation still was a land divided. Industrial wealth and new streams of foreign immigration reshaped an increasingly urban North. Racial repression and often gruesome violence suffused the mostly rural South. Repeated clashes with Indigenous peoples convulsed the far West as white settlement pushed relentlessly across Native American lands. Economic, technological, and political change came so swiftly and massively that it seemed to many Americans that a whole new civilization had emerged.

In some ways it had. The sheer scale of the new industrial society was dazzling. Transcontinental railroads knitted the country together from sea to sea. New industries like oil and steel grew to staggering size—and made megamillionaires out of entrepreneurs like oilman John D. Rockefeller and steel maker Andrew Carnegie. The great trusts dwarfed the federal government in size and might. Partisan infighting, political corruption, and weak leadership too often rendered the government in Washington feeble and ineffective.

Drawn by the allure of industrial employment, Americans moved to the city, much like their counterparts in industrializing Europe, Russia, and Japan. Rural Americans and European immigrants alike flocked to mill town and metropolis in search of steady jobs. Migration was a global phenomenon, as millions of people uprooted by wars and economic disruptions crossed continents and oceans in search of better lives—not all of them to America.

For a nation founded in opposition to big institutions and distant rulers, the sudden scaling up of American life sowed fear and bewilderment among many. Even on the western frontier, that legendary bastion of rugged loners, the hand of government was increasingly felt, as army battalions waged war on the Indigenous peoples of the Plains and federal authority was invoked to regulate the use of natural

Science & Society Picture Library/Getty Images

Image VI.1 Corliss Engine The towering, 1400-horsepower steam engine awed the millions visiting the Centennial Exposition in Philadelphia in 1876, its mighty pistons generating enough energy to power 800 other machines on display at the fair. More efficient than water power and freeing factories from having to locate near a water source, the spread of steam engines like the Corliss amplified the scale and speed of industrial growth.

resources. The rise of powerful monopolies called into question the government's traditional hands-off policy toward business, and a growing band of reformers increasingly clamored for government regulation of private enterprise. The mushrooming cities, with their need for transport systems, schools, hospitals, sanitation, and fire and police protection, required bigger governments and budgets than an earlier generation could have imagined. As never before, Americans struggled to adapt old ideals of individual autonomy to the new realities of industrial civilization.

With economic change came social and political turmoil. Labor violence brought bloodshed to places such as Chicago and Homestead, Pennsylvania. Small farmers, squeezed by debt and foreign competition, rallied behind the People's, or "Populist," Party, a radical movement of the 1880s and 1890s that attacked the power of Wall Street, big business, and the banks. Anti-immigrant sentiment swelled. Bitter disputes over tariffs and monetary policy deeply divided the country, setting debtors against lenders, farmers against manufacturers, the West and South against the Northeast, Main Street against Wall Street. And in this unfamiliar era of big money and expanding government, corruption flourished, from town hall to Congress, fueling loud cries for political reform.

As railroads drove their iron arrows through the heart of the West, Native Americans lost their land and life-sustaining buffalo herds. By the 1890s, after three decades of fierce fighting with the U.S. Army, those who had once roamed across the vast rolling prairies struggled to preserve their shattered cultures within the confinement of reservations, while the U.S. government continued its decades-long push to "civilize" nomadic societies by forcing families onto meager homesteads and their children into distant boarding schools.

The South remained the one region largely untouched by the Industrial Revolution sweeping the rest of America. Even before the last federal troops marched out in 1877, the post-emancipation era had inflicted violent new forms of racial injustice on African Americans, the vast majority of whom continued to live in the Old South. State legislatures systematically deprived Black Americans of their constitutionally mandated political rights, including the right to vote. Strict segregation of schools, housing, and all kinds of public facilities—a system known as "Jim Crow"—made a mockery of African Americans' Reconstruction-era hopes for equality before the law. As "scientific" ideas about racial inferiority gained credibility, the rest of America looked the other way. Black Southerners endured relentless discrimination, violence, and—all too often—death at the hands of hate-filled mobs.

Focus Questions

1. How did urbanization alter the economy, politics, and culture of the United States?
2. How, if at all, were the institutions of the American presidency and Congress different in the late nineteenth century from what they are today?

Chronicle/Alamy Stock Photo

Image VI.2 Dearborn Street, Chicago Loop, Around 1900 "America is energetic, but Chicago is in a fever," marveled a visiting Englishman about turn-of-the-century Chicago. Street scenes like this were common in America's booming new cities, especially in the "Lord of the Midwest."

Chapter 21

Political Upheaval in the Gilded Age: 1869–1896

[I]n a free country likes ours, where any man can run for Congress and anybody can vote for him, you can't expect immortal purity all the time—it ain't in nature.

Mark Twain, *The Gilded Age* (1873)

Chapter Outline

- Ulysses S. Grant, soldier-president
- Corruption and reform in the post–Civil War era
- The depression of the 1870s
- Political parties and partisans
- The Compromise of 1877 and the end of Reconstruction
- The emergence of Jim Crow
- Class conflict and ethnic clashes

Contending Voices: The Spoils System

Makers of America: From China to America

Fueled by robust if chaotic economic dynamism, the population of the post–Civil War Republic continued to vault upward by vigorous leaps. Census takers reported over 39 million people in 1870, a gain of 26.6 percent over the preceding decade, as the immigrant tide surged again. The United States became the third-most populous nation in the Western world, ranking behind Russia and France.

But the political institutions of the United States did not keep pace with its physical and industrial growth. Disillusionment ran deep in the postwar era among idealistic Northerners who had spilled their blood for union and emancipation. Support among white Americans for the cause of Black civil rights was weakening. Instead of Lincoln's promise of "a new birth of freedom," the postwar era spawned a new birth of racism in the former Confederate States, as well as pervasive corruption, widening inequality, and a string of presidents unable or unwilling to turn the tide.

Focus Questions

1. Why was the Gilded Age a period of political patronage, corruption, and stalemate between the two major parties? Given these negative factors, why did political participation achieve such high levels?
2. How did the disputed Hayes-Tilden election of 1876 contribute to the end of Reconstruction?
3. Why did the end of Reconstruction lead to the "Jim Crow" system of segregation in the South, and how did racial segregation and the sharecropping system trap both Black people and disadvantaged white people in poverty?
4. What caused the rise of class and ethnic conflict in the 1870s, and why were Chinese immigrants singled out for hostility and exclusion?
5. Why did the political system and the heated political partisanship of the Gilded Age yield so little attention to the major social and economic issues of the time—except the tariff?

21-1 The "Bloody Shirt" Elects Grant

The notion still prevailed that good generals would make good presidents. Stubble-bearded General Ulysses S. Grant was by far the most popular Northern hero to emerge from the war. Grateful citizens of Philadelphia, Washington, and his hometown of Galena, Illinois, passed the hat and in each place presented him with a house. New Yorkers tendered him a check for $105,000. The general, silently puffing on his cigar, unapologetically accepted these gifts as his just deserts for having rescued the Union.

Scovill, Inc./Smithsonian National Museum of American History

Image 21.1 Grant & Colfax Campaign Medal Three tumultuous years after war's end, Ulysses S. Grant's plea to "let us have peace" became a slogan of his 1868 presidential campaign. Political parties used mass-produced memorabilia like this medal to build voter support in an era when political custom still discouraged candidates from actively campaigning.

Grant was a victorious general but a political rookie. His one presidential vote had been cast for the Democratic ticket in 1856, and he had spent his adulthood in barracks and on battlefields rather than venturing into the electoral rough-and-tumble. A better judge of horseflesh than of humans, his cultural background was breathtakingly narrow. He once reportedly remarked that Venice (Italy) would be a fine city if only it were drained. The Republicans, eager to move on from the maddening and mercurial Andrew Johnson, enthusiastically nominated Grant for the presidency in 1868. The party's platform sounded a clarion call for continued Reconstruction of the South and defense of Black freedom under the glinting steel of federal bayonets. Grant, always a man of few words, struck a highly popular note in his letter accepting the nomination when he said, "Let us have peace." This noble sentiment became a leading campaign slogan (refer to Image 21.1) and was later engraved on his tomb beside the Hudson River.

Expectant Democrats, meeting in their own nominating convention, denounced military Reconstruction but could agree on little else. Wealthy Eastern delegates demanded a plank promising that federal war bonds be redeemed in gold—even though many of the bonds had been purchased with badly depreciated paper greenbacks. Poorer Midwestern delegates answered with the "Ohio Idea," which called for redemption in greenbacks. Debt-burdened agrarian Democrats thus hoped to keep more money in circulation and keep interest rates lower. This dispute introduced a bitter contest over monetary policy that continued to convulse the Republic until the century's end.

Midwestern delegates got the platform but not the candidate. The nominee, former New York governor Horatio Seymour, scuttled the Democrats' faint hope for success by repudiating the Ohio Idea. Republicans whipped up enthusiasm for Grant by energetically **"waving the bloody shirt"**—that is, reviving gory memories of the Civil War—which became for the first time a prominent feature of a presidential campaign.* "Vote as You Shot" was a powerful Republican slogan aimed at Union army veterans.

Grant won the 1868 contest, with 214 electoral votes to 80 for Seymour. But the former general scored a majority of only 300,000 in the popular vote (3,013,421 to 2,706,829). Most white voters apparently supported Seymour, and the ballots of three still-unreconstructed Southern states (Mississippi, Texas, and Virginia) were not counted at all. An estimated 500,000 formerly enslaved people gave Grant his margin of victory. With near-equal support for both parties among the white electorate, keeping the ballot in the hands of Black freedmen became politically essential to the Republicans (refer to Image 21.2). Lincoln's party could not take future victories "for Granted."

The Granger Collection

Image 21.2 Freedman Electioneering The votes of formerly enslaved people provided the margin of victory for Ulysses S. Grant and the Republicans in 1868. This wood engraving depicts newly enfranchised Black men casting their first presidential votes.

*The expression is said to have derived from a speech by Representative Benjamin F. Butler of Massachusetts, who allegedly waved before the House the bloodstained nightshirt of a Northern visitor assaulted by the Klan.

21-2 The Era of Good Stealings

Grant came into office as a rapidly expanding postwar state created bounteous opportunities for the unscrupulous. Unfortunately, the rot began at the top. Grant too often valued loyalty over experience in making senior appointments. Favor seekers haunted the White House, plying the president with cigars, wines, and horses. His election was a godsend to his in-laws of the Dent family, several dozen of whom attached themselves to the public payroll.

Soon after Grant's inauguration, he became ensnared in a scheme concocted by two millionaire financiers, "Jubilee Jim" Fisk and Jay Gould. The extravagant and corpulent Fisk provided the "brass," while the undersized and cunning Gould provided the brains. The pair concocted a plot in 1869 to corner the gold market, a slippery game that would work only if the federal Treasury refrained from selling gold. The conspirators believed they had an easy mark in new President Grant, lobbying him directly and through his brother-in-law, who received $25,000 for his complicity. For weeks Fisk and Gould madly bid the price of gold skyward, so they could later profit from its heightened value. But on "Black Friday" (September 24, 1869), the bubble broke when the Treasury, contrary to Grant's supposed assurances, was compelled to release gold. The price of gold plunged, and scores of honest businesspeople were driven to the wall. A congressional probe concluded that Grant had done nothing illegal, though he had acted stupidly and indiscreetly.

The easygoing Grant was most thoroughly tarred by the **Crédit Mobilier scandal**, which erupted as he readied for reelection in 1872. Union Pacific Railroad insiders had formed the Crédit Mobilier construction company and then cleverly hired themselves at inflated prices to build the railroad line, earning dividends as high as 348 percent. Fearing that Congress might blow the whistle, the company furtively distributed shares of its valuable stock to key congressmen. A newspaper exposé and congressional investigation of the scandal led to the formal censure of two congressmen and the revelation that the vice president of the United States had accepted payments from Crédit Mobilier.

The breath of scandal in Washington also reeked of alcohol. In 1874–1875, the sprawling Whiskey Ring robbed the Treasury of millions in excise-tax revenues. "Let no guilty man escape," declared President Grant. But when his own private secretary turned up among the culprits, he volunteered a written statement to the jury that helped exonerate the thief. Further rottenness in the Grant administration came to light in 1876, forcing Secretary of War William Belknap to resign after pocketing bribes from suppliers to the Indian reservations. Grant, loyal to a fault, accepted Belknap's resignation "with great regret."

21-3 The Liberal Republican Revolt of 1872

A few skunks can pollute a large area. Although the great majority of businesspeople and government officials continued to conduct their affairs with decency and honor, the whole postwar atmosphere stank of corruption. The Man in the Moon, it was said, had to hold his nose when passing over America. Freewheeling railroad promoters like the Crédit Mobilier scoundrels too often left gullible bond buyers with only "two streaks of rust and a right of way." Unethical stock-market manipulators like Fisk and Gould were a cinder in the public eye. Too many judges and legislators put their power up for hire. Cynics defined an honest politician as one who, when bought, would stay bought.

By 1872, a powerful wave of disgust with this corruption provided a political opening for those who also disliked Grant's continued support of military Reconstruction. A small group of elite citizens banded together to form the Liberal Republican party. Voicing the slogan "Turn the Rascals Out," they urged a major house-cleaning of the executive branch as well as an end to military Reconstruction, which they considered a dangerous case of government overreach.

The Liberal Republicans muffed their chance when their Cincinnati nominating convention astounded the country by nominating the brilliant but erratic Horace Greeley for the presidency. Although Greeley was the fearless editor of the *New York Tribune*, he was dogmatic, emotional, petulant, and notoriously unsound in his political judgments.

More astonishing still was the action of the office-hungry Democrats, who foolishly proceeded to endorse Greeley's candidacy. In swallowing Greeley, the Democrats "ate crow" in large gulps, for the eccentric editor had long blasted them as traitors, slave shippers, saloon keepers, horse thieves, and idiots (refer to Image 21.3). Yet Greeley pleased the Democrats, North and South, when he pleaded for clasping hands across "the bloody chasm."

In the mud-spattered campaign that followed, regular Republicans denounced Greeley as an atheist, a communist, a free-lover, a vegetarian, and a cosigner of Jefferson Davis's bail bond. Democrats derided Grant as an ignoramus, a drunkard, and a swindler. But the regular Republicans, chanting "Grant us another term," pulled the president through. The count in the electoral column was 286 to 66, in the popular column 3,596,745 to 2,843,446. Grant edged Greeley by 750,000 votes, well more than double his 1868 margin.

Liberal Republican agitation frightened the regular Republicans into cleaning their own house before they were thrown out of it. In the wake of the intraparty turmoil, Congressional support for Reconstruction became shakier. Sympathy for the former Southern rebels increased. The Republican Congress in 1872 passed a general amnesty act, exempting all but some five hundred former Confederate leaders from the Fourteenth Amendment's restrictions on their eligibility for political office. Congress also moved to reduce high tariffs imposed during the war and to fumigate the Grant administration by taking the first steps to create a permanent civil service. Like many American third parties, the Liberal Republicans left some enduring footprints, even in defeat.

Image 21.3 Can Greeley and the Democrats "Swallow" Each Other? 1872 This cartoon by Thomas Nast is a Republican gibe at the forced alliance between these former foes. General William Tecumseh Sherman wrote from Paris to his brother, "I feel amazed to see the turn things have taken. Grant who never was a Republican is your candidate; and Greeley who never was a Democrat, but quite the reverse, is the Democratic candidate."

21-4 Depression, Deflation, and Inflation

Grant's woes deepened in the paralyzing economic **panic of 1873**. Bursting with startling rapidity, the crash was one of many that rollercoastered the economy in this age of unbridled capitalist expansion. Overreaching promoters deluded themselves that war-fueled boom times would go on forever. They laid more railroad track, sank more mines, erected more factories, and sowed more grainfields than peacetime markets could bear. Bankers, in turn, had made too many imprudent loans to finance those enterprises. When profits failed to materialize, loans went unpaid, and the whole credit-based house of cards fluttered down. The United States did not suffer alone. Nations worldwide underwent a similar economic collapse in 1873.

Boom times became gloom times as more than fifteen thousand American businesses went bankrupt. In New York City, an army of unemployed riotously battled police. Black Americans were especially hard hit. The Freedman's Savings and Trust Company had made unsecured loans to several companies that went under. Black depositors who had entrusted over $7 million to the bank lost their savings, and Black economic development and Black confidence in savings institutions went down with it.

Hard times inflicted the worst punishment on debtors, including almost all farmers, who clamored ever more loudly for inflationary policies. Proponents of inflation breathed new life into the issue of greenbacks. During the war, $450 million of the "folding money" had been issued, but it had depreciated under a cloud of popular mistrust and dubious legality.* By 1868, the Treasury had already withdrawn $100 million of the "battle-born currency" from circulation, and "hard-money" people everywhere looked forward to its complete disappearance. But now afflicted agrarian and debtor groups—"cheap-money" supporters—clamored for a reissuance of the greenbacks. With a crude but essentially accurate grasp of monetary theory, they reasoned that more money meant cheaper money and, hence, rising prices and easier-to-pay debts. Creditors, of course, reasoning from the same premises, advocated precisely the opposite policy. They had no desire to see the money they had loaned repaid in depreciated dollars. They wanted deflation, not inflation.

The "hard-money" advocates carried the day. In 1874 they persuaded a confused Grant to veto a bill to print more paper money. They scored another victory in the Resumption Act of 1875, which pledged the government to the further withdrawal of greenbacks from

*The Supreme Court in 1870 declared the Civil War Legal Tender Act (legalizing paper currency) unconstitutional. With the concurrence of the Senate, Grant thereupon added to the bench two justices who could be counted on to help reverse that decision, which happened in 1871. This is how the Court grew to its current size of nine justices.

David A. Wells (1828–1898), a leading economist of the era, described the global dimensions of the depression that struck the United States in 1873:

"Its most noteworthy peculiarity has been its universality; affecting nations that have been involved in war as well as those which have maintained peace; those which have a stable currency, based on gold, and those which have an unstable currency, based on promises which have not been kept; those which live under systems of free exchange of commodities, and those whose exchanges are more or less restricted. It has been grievous in old communities like England and Germany, and equally so in Australia, South Africa, and California, which represent the new; it has been a calamity exceeding[ly] heavy to be borne, alike by the inhabitants of sterile Newfoundland and Labrador, and of the sunny, fruitful sugar-islands of the East and West Indies."

circulation and to the redemption of all paper currency in gold at face value, beginning in 1879.

Down but not out, debtors now looked for relief to another precious metal, silver. The "sacred white metal," they claimed, had received a raw deal. In the early 1870s, the Treasury stubbornly and unrealistically maintained that an ounce of silver was worth only one-sixteenth as much as an ounce of gold, though open-market prices for silver were higher. Silver miners thus stopped offering their shiny product for sale to the federal mints. With no silver flowing into the federal coffers, Congress formally dropped the coinage of silver dollars in 1873. Fate then played a sly joke when new silver discoveries later in the 1870s shot production up and forced silver prices down. Westerners from silver-mining states joined with debtors in assailing the "Crime of '73," demanding a return to the "Dollar of Our Daddies." Like the demand for more greenbacks, the demand for the coinage of more silver was nothing more nor less than another scheme to promote inflation.

Hard-money Republicans resisted this scheme and counted on Grant to hold the line against it. He did not disappoint them. The Treasury began to accumulate gold stocks against the appointed day for resumption of metallic-money payments. Coupled with the reduction of greenbacks, this policy was called "contraction." It had a noticeable deflationary effect—the amount of money per capita in circulation actually *decreased* between 1870 and 1880, from $19.42 to $19.37. Contraction probably worsened the impact of the depression. But the new policy did restore the government's credit rating, and it brought the embattled greenbacks up to their full face value. When Redemption Day came in 1879, few greenback holders bothered to exchange the lighter and more convenient bills for gold.

Republican hard-money policy had a political backlash. It helped elect a Democratic House of Representatives in 1874, and in 1878 it spawned the Greenback Labor party, which polled over a million votes and elected fourteen members of Congress. The contest over monetary policy was far from over.

21-5 Pallid Politics in the Gilded Age

The political seesaw was delicately balanced throughout most of the **Gilded Age** (a sarcastic name given by Mark Twain in 1873 to the three-decade-long post–Civil War era). Even a slight nudge could tip the teeter-totter to the advantage of the opposition party. Every presidential election was a squeaker, and the majority party in the House of Representatives switched six times in the eleven sessions between 1869 and 1891. In only three sessions did the same party control the House, the Senate, and the White House. Wobbling in such shaky equilibrium, politicians tiptoed timidly, producing a political record that was often trivial and petty.

Few significant economic issues separated the major parties. Democrats and Republicans saw very nearly eye-to-eye on questions like the tariff and civil-service reform, and majorities in both parties substantially agreed even on the much-debated currency question. Yet despite their rough agreement on these national matters, the two parties were ferociously competitive with each other. They were tightly and efficiently organized, and they commanded fierce loyalty from their members. Voter turnouts reached heights unmatched before or since. Nearly 80 percent of eligible voters cast their ballots in presidential elections in the three decades after the Civil War. On election days, droves of the party faithful tramped behind marching bands to the polling places, and "ticket splitting," or failing to vote the straight party line, was as rare as a silver dollar.

How can this apparent paradox of political consensus and partisan fervor be explained? The answer lies in the sharp ethnic and cultural differences in the membership of the two parties—in distinctions of style and tone, and especially of religious sentiment. Republican voters tended to adhere to those creeds that traced their lineage to Puritanism. They stressed strict codes of personal morality and believed that government should play a role in regulating both the economic and the moral affairs of society. Democrats, among whom immigrant Lutherans and Roman Catholics figured heavily, were more likely to adhere to faiths that took a less stern view of human weakness. Their religions professed toleration of differences in an imperfect world, and

A

B

Image 21.4A and B The Political Legacy of the Civil War Union veterans of the Civil War supported Republican candidate Rutherford B. Hayes in 1876. The Grand Army of the Republic (GAR), the Union veterans' organization, voted heavily for the GOP (Grand Old Party) in the post–Civil War years.

they spurned government efforts to impose a single moral standard on the entire society. These differences in temperament and religious values often produced raucous political contests at the local level, where issues like prohibition and education loomed large.

Democrats had a solid electoral base in the South and in the northern industrial cities, teeming with immigrants and controlled by well-oiled political machines (refer to "24-3 Machines and Reformers Compete and Clash," pp. 599–602). Republican strength lay largely in the Midwest and the rural and small-town Northeast. Black Southerners continued to vote Republican in significant numbers. Another important bloc of Republican ballots came from the members of the Grand Army of the Republic (GAR)—a politically potent fraternal organization of several hundred thousand Union veterans of the Civil War (refer to Image 21.4).

The lifeblood of both parties was **patronage**—disbursing jobs by the bucketful in return for votes, kickbacks, and party service. Boisterous infighting over patronage beset the Republican Party in the 1870s and 1880s. A "Stalwart" faction, led by the handsome and imperious Roscoe ("Lord Roscoe") Conkling, U.S. senator from New York, unblushingly embraced the time-honored system of swapping civil-service jobs for votes. Opposed to the Conklingites were the so-called Half-Breeds, who flirted coyly with civil-service reform, but whose real quarrel with the Stalwarts was over who should grasp the ladle that dished out the spoils. The champion of the Half-Breeds was James G. Blaine of Maine, a radiantly personable congressman with an elastic conscience. But despite the color of their personalities, Conkling and Blaine succeeded only in stalemating each other and deadlocking their party.

21-6 The Hayes-Tilden Standoff, 1876

Hangers-on around President Grant, like fleas urging their ailing dog to live, begged the "Old Man" to try for a third term in 1876. Grant believed in the continued necessity of Reconstruction and worried that a successor might not stay the course. But he was no longer the political

Library of Congress

Image 21.5 Grant as Acrobat Scandal-wracked President Ulysses S. Grant vowed not to seek a third term in 1876, but he unsuccessfully sought the Republican nomination four years later (losing to James A. Garfield). This 1880 cartoon by *Puck*'s Joseph Keppler mockingly portrays Grant on a "third term" trapeze with a strap of "corruption" dangling the major scandals of his presidency.

innocent of 1868, and it was obvious that a third-term bid would meet with ferocious political opposition (refer to Image 21.5). Grant ended the speculation by issuing a public letter in 1875 announcing that he would abide by the two-term tradition.

With Grant out of the running and with the Conklingites and Blaineites neutralizing each other, the Republicans turned to a compromise candidate, Rutherford B. Hayes, who was obscure enough to be dubbed "The Great Unknown." His foremost qualification was the fact that he hailed from the electorally fickle but potent state of Ohio, where he had served three terms as governor. So crucial were the "swing" votes of Ohio in the cliffhanging presidential contests of the day that the state produced more than its share of presidential candidates. A political saying of the 1870s paraphrased Shakespeare:

> Some are born great,
> Some achieve greatness,
> And some are born in Ohio.

Pitted against the humdrum Hayes was the Democratic nominee, Samuel J. Tilden, who had risen to fame as an anticorruption crusader in New York. The election was one of the closest in American history. Campaigning against Republican scandal, Tilden racked up 184 electoral votes of the needed 185, with 20 votes in four states—three of them in the South—doubtful because of irregular returns (refer to Map 21.1). Surely Tilden could pick up at least one of these, especially in view of the fact that he had narrowly bested Hayes in the popular vote, 4,284,020 to 4,036,572.

Both parties scurried to send "visiting statesmen" to the contested Southern states of Louisiana, South Carolina, and Florida. All three disputed states submitted two sets of returns, one Democratic and one Republican. As the weeks drifted by, the paralysis tightened, generating a dramatic constitutional crisis. The Constitution merely specifies that the electoral returns from the states shall be sent to Congress, and in the presence of the House and Senate, they shall be opened by the president of the Senate (refer to the Twelfth Amendment in the Appendix). But who should count them? On this point the Constitution was silent. If counted by the president of the Senate (a Republican), the Republican returns would be selected. If counted by the Speaker of the House (a Democrat), the Democratic returns would be chosen. How could the impasse be resolved?

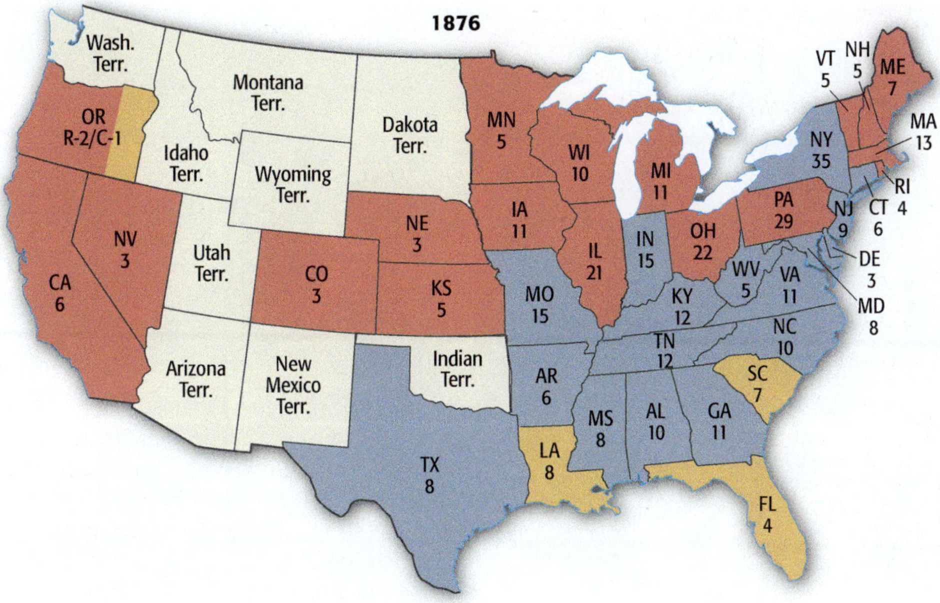

Candidate (Party)	Uncontested Electoral Vote	Electoral Vote		Popular Vote	
Hayes (Republican)	165	185	50%	4,034,311	48.0%
Tilden (Democrat)	184	184	50%	4,288,546	51.0%
Contested					
Territories					

Map 21.1 Hayes-Tilden Disputed Election of 1876 (with electoral vote by state) Nineteen of the twenty disputed votes composed the total electoral count of Louisiana, South Carolina, and Florida. The twentieth was one of Oregon's three votes, cast by an elector who turned out to be ineligible because he was a federal officeholder (a postmaster), contrary to the Constitution (refer to Art. II, Sec. I, para. 2).

21-7 The Compromise of 1877 and the End of Reconstruction

The danger loomed that there would be no president on Inauguration Day, March 4, 1877. "Tilden or Blood!" cried Democratic hotheads, and some of their "Minute Men" began to drill with arms. To break the election deadlock, Congress set up an electoral commission consisting of fifteen men selected from the Senate, the House, and the Supreme Court (refer to Table 21.1). The Senate and House were nearly evenly split between the two parties, but Republican appointees were the majority of the Court. The result was that Republicans had a one-vote majority on the commission.

In February 1877, about a month before Inauguration Day, the Senate and House met together in an electric atmosphere to settle the dispute. The roll of the states was tolled off alphabetically. When Florida was reached—the first of the three Southern states with two sets of returns—the disputed documents were referred to the electoral commission, which sat in a nearby chamber. After prolonged discussion the members agreed, by the partisan vote of eight Republicans to seven Democrats, to accept the Republican returns. Outraged Democrats in Congress, smelling defeat, undertook to launch a filibuster "until hell froze over." So close was the margin of safety that the explosive issue was settled only three days before the new president was officially sworn into office. The nation breathed a collective sigh of relief.

The chaos and closed-door negotiations made it difficult to pinpoint exactly how the electoral crisis was at last resolved. The prevailing interpretation has been that the "**Compromise of 1877**"

Table 21.1 Composition of the Electoral Commission, 1877

Members	Republicans	Democrats
Senate (Republican majority)	3	2
House (Democratic majority)	2	3
Supreme Court	3	2
Total	8	7

Image 21.6 **The End of Reconstruction, 1877** President Hayes's "Let 'em Alone" policy replaces the carpetbags and bayonets of the Grant administration, signifying the end of federal efforts to promote racial equality in the South—until the "second Reconstruction" of the civil rights era nearly a century later.

compelled the Democrats to concede the White House to Hayes in return for his agreement to withdraw federal troops from the two states in which they remained, Louisiana and South Carolina.

Whatever the backroom deals, it was clear by 1877 that the grand experiment of Reconstruction was effectively finished. Only about 3,200 U.S. soldiers remained in the former Confederacy by 1876. The Southern Democrats, self-styled as "Redeemers," were back in control of eight of the eleven rebel states. Violent campaigns of Black voter suppression convulsed the 1876 campaign in the South. The compromise bought peace at a steep price. Partisan violence was averted by sacrificing the civil rights of Black Southerners. With the Hayes-Tilden deal, the Republican Party of Sumner and Stevens and Lincoln quietly abandoned its commitment to racial equality (refer to Image 21.6).

The **Civil Rights Act of 1875** was in a sense the last feeble gasp of the congressional "radical" Republicans. The act supposedly guaranteed equal accommodations in public places and prohibited racial discrimination in jury selection, but the law was born toothless and stayed that way for nearly a century. The Supreme Court pronounced much of the act unconstitutional in the *Civil Rights Cases* (1883). The Court declared that the Fourteenth Amendment prohibited only *government* violations of civil rights, not the denial of civil rights by *individuals*. When President Hayes withdrew the last blue-clad federal troops that were propping up Reconstruction governments, Black Southerners were left to fight for their freedoms mostly on their own (refer to "20-14 The Ku Klux Klan," pp. 512–513).

21-8 The Birth of Jim Crow in the Post-Reconstruction South

Shamelessly relying on fraud and intimidation, white "Redeemer" governments assumed political power in the South and exercised it ruthlessly. Black men and women now asserted their rights at great personal cost, risking jobs, homes, health, and their very lives. Thousands violently perished at the hands of white mobs.

Poor farmers, both Black and white, were forced into **sharecropping** and tenant farming. Through the "crop-lien" system, storekeepers extended credit to small farmers for food and supplies and in return took a lien on their harvests. Shrewd merchants manipulated the system so that farmers remained perpetually in debt to them. For generations to come, Southern Black farm families were condemned to eke out a threadbare living under conditions scarcely better than slavery (refer to Map 21.2).

With white Southerners back in the political saddle, daily discrimination against Black citizens grew increasingly oppressive. What had started as the informal separation of the races in the immediate postwar years developed by the 1890s into systematic state-level legal codes of

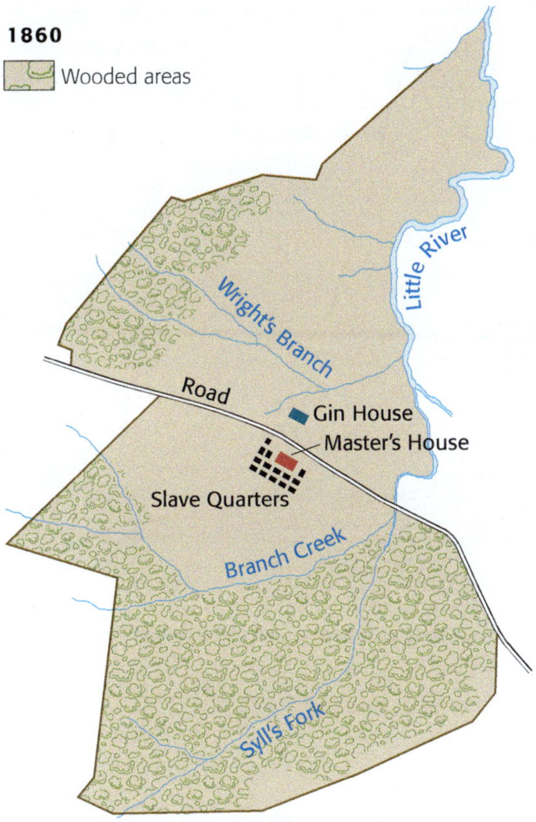

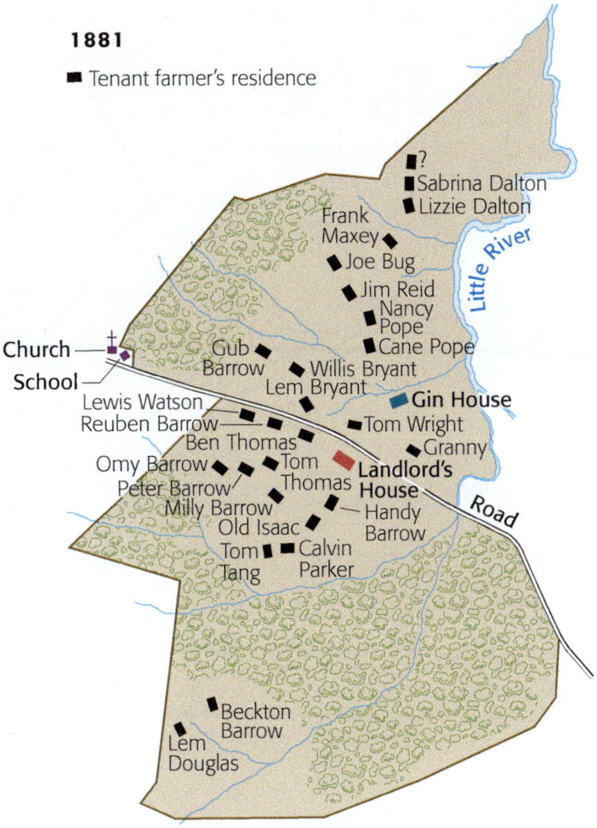

Map 21.2 A Southern Plantation, Before and After the Civil War The emancipated freedpeople moved out of the slave quarters and into humble cabins dispersed around the plantation. The master had now become the landlord and the employer, and the formerly enslaved had become tenant farmers and sharecroppers, an economic subordination often little better than enslavement.

segregation known as **Jim Crow** laws. Southern states enacted literacy requirements, voter-registration laws, and poll taxes—and tolerated violent intimidation of Black voters—to enforce wholesale disfranchisement of Black Southerners.

The Supreme Court validated the South's segregationist social order in the case of ***Plessy v. Ferguson*** (1896). It ruled that "separate but equal" facilities were constitutional under the "equal protection" clause of the Fourteenth Amendment. That declaration belied the grotesquely unequal reality. Segregated in barely funded schools and separated from whites in nearly all public facilities, including railroad cars, theaters, and even restrooms, Black people were assaulted daily by galling reminders of their second-class citizenship. To ensure the stability of this political and economic "new order," Southern whites dealt harshly with those who dared to violate the region's code of racial conduct. As federal courts looked the other way, a record number of Black people were killed by mob violence—lynched—during the 1890s, most often for the "crime" of asserting themselves as equals (refer to Table 21.2, Figure 21.1, and Image 21.7). Thousands of Black people were cruelly sentenced, often for minor offenses, to forced labor prison camps, where they were virtually re-enslaved. It would take a second Reconstruction, nearly a century later, to redress the racist imbalance of Southern society.

Table 21.2 Black American Lynching Victims by Southern State, 1877–1950

Alabama	361
Arkansas	492
Florida	311
Georgia	589
Kentucky	168
Louisiana	549
Mississippi	654
North Carolina	123
South Carolina	185
Tennessee	233
Texas	335
Virginia	84
Total	**4,084**

Source: EJI, *Lynching in America* (3rd ed), p. 40: https://eji.org/wpcontent/uploads/2005/11/lynching-in-america-3d-ed-110121.pdf

21-9 Class Conflicts and Ethnic Clashes

The year 1877 marked more than the formal end of Reconstruction. As the curtains officially closed on regional warfare, they opened on scenes of class struggle. The explosive atmosphere was largely a by-product of the long years of "great depression" and deflation

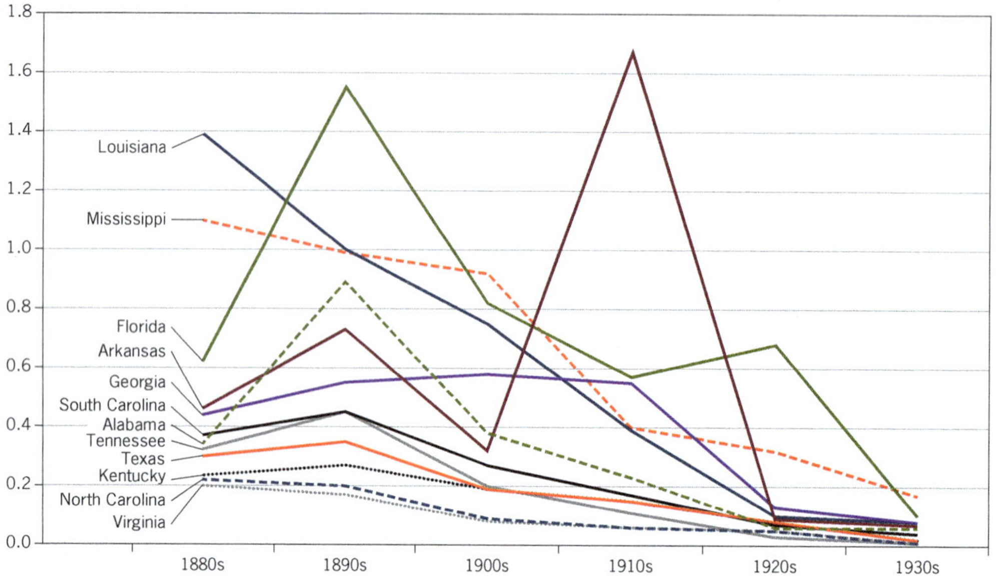

Figure 21.1 Racial Terror Lynching in the Jim Crow South, 1880–1940. This chart from the Equal Justice Initiative shows the number of Black people lynched annually per 100,000 residents in Southern states from the end of Reconstruction to World War II.

Source: EJI Lynching in America (3rd ed), p. 44: https://eji.org/wp-content/uploads/2005/11/lynching-in-america-3d-ed-110121.pdf

following the panic of 1873. Railroad workers faced particularly hard times and grew ever more bitter as they watched the railroad owners continue to rake in huge profits. When the presidents of the nation's four largest railroads collectively decided in 1877 to cut employees' wages by 10 percent, the workers struck back—touching off the first nationwide confrontation between capital and labor.

The **Great Strike of 1877** quickly descended into bloody violence. Railroad lines and telegraph wires facilitated networks of people and information that allowed work stoppages to spread like wildfire from the eastern seaboard to the deep Midwest. President Hayes's decision to

Image 21.7 Jim Crow Justice In 1893, a Black man named Henry Smith was burned at the stake in Paris, Texas, accused of sexually assaulting a four-year-old white girl. Hundreds of gawkers poured into the city from the surrounding county to watch the gruesome spectacle. Public executions like this one, or the more common lynching of Black men, were aimed at intimidating African Americans into accepting second-class status in the Jim Crow South.

call in federal troops to quell the unrest brought the striking laborers an outpouring of working-class support. The battles between workers and soldiers lasted several weeks and left over one hundred people dead.

The failure of the great railroad strike exposed the weakness of the labor movement in the face of massive government intervention on the side of the railroads. The federal courts, U.S. Army, state militias, and local police all lent their muscle to keeping the engines of big business operating at full throttle, and the workers be damned.

Meanwhile, racial and ethnic fissures among workers fractured labor unity. Divisions were particularly acute between the Irish and the Chinese in California. By 1880, the Golden State counted seventy-five thousand Asian newcomers, about 9 percent of its entire population. Mostly single males with little money or education, they hailed predominantly from the Taishan district of K'uang-t'ung (Guangdong) province in southern China. The men had first come to America to dig in the goldfields and to sledgehammer the tracks of the transcontinental railroads across the West. When the gold supply petered out and the tracks were laid, many—perhaps half of those who arrived before the 1880s—returned home to China with their meager savings, in a pattern of **circular migration** followed by many European newcomers as well (refer to "Makers of America: From China to America," pp. 534–535).

Those who remained in America faced extraordinary hardships. They worked at the most menial jobs, often as cooks, laundrymen, or domestic servants. Without women or families, they were deprived of the children who in other immigrant communities eased their parents' assimilation through their exposure to the English language and American customs in school.

In San Francisco Irish-born demagogue Denis Kearney incited his followers to violent abuse of the hapless Chinese newcomers. The Kearneyites, many of whom were themselves recently arrived immigrants from Europe, hotly resented the competition of cheap labor from the still more recently arrived Chinese, "the meanest slave on earth," Kearney viciously declared. The present tens of thousands of Chinese "coolies" were regarded as a menace, the prospective millions as a calamity (refer to Image 21.8). Taking to the streets, gangs of Kearneyites terrorized the Chinese by shearing off their long braided "queues" of hair. A Kearneyite riot in San Francisco in 1877 left four Chinese dead.

Congress slammed the door on Chinese immigrant laborers when it passed the **Chinese Exclusion Act** in 1882, prohibiting nearly all further immigration from China. The door stayed shut until 1943. Some exclusionists even tried to strip native-born Chinese Americans of their citizenship, but the Supreme Court ruled in *U.S. v. Wong Kim Ark* in 1898 that the Fourteenth Amendment guaranteed citizenship to all persons born in the United States. This doctrine of "birthright citizenship" (or *jus soli*, the "right of the soil," as contrasted with *jus sanguinis*, the "right of blood-tie," which based citizenship on the parents' nationality) provided important protections to Chinese Americans as well as to other immigrant communities.

21-10 Garfield and Arthur

As the presidential campaign of 1880 approached, "Rutherfraud" Hayes was a man without a party, denounced and repudiated by the Republican Old Guard. The Republican Party sought a new standard-bearer for 1880 and finally settled on a dark-horse candidate, James A. Garfield, from the electorally powerful state of Ohio. His vice-presidential running mate was a notorious Stalwart operative, Chester A. Arthur of New York.

Garfield barely squeaked out a victory over the Democratic candidate and Civil War hero, Winfield Scott Hancock. He polled only 39,213 more votes than Hancock—4,453,295 to 4,414,082—but his margin in the electoral column was a comfortable 214 to 155.

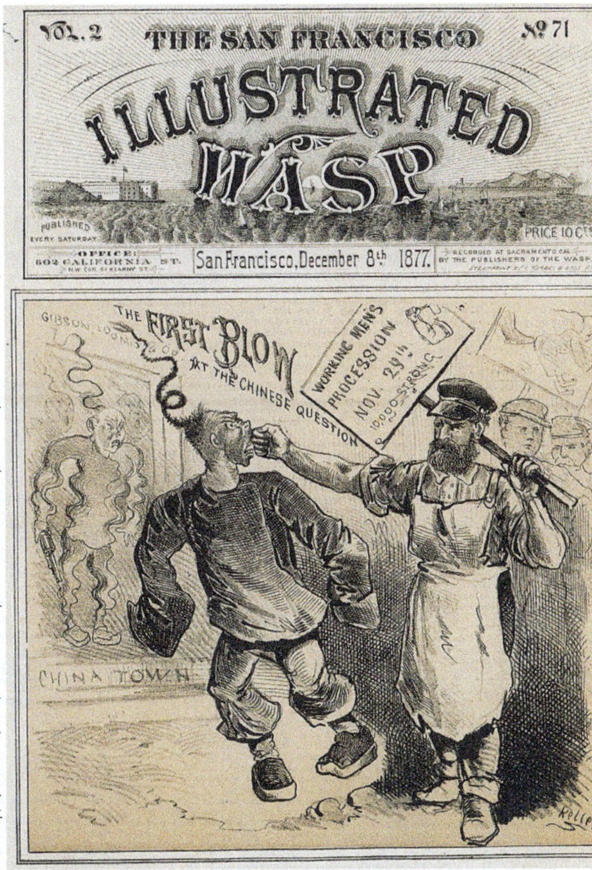

The Wasp, x(F850.W18, vol.2, no.71. Courtesy of The Bancroft Library, University of California, Berkeley

Image 21.8 The First Blow at the Chinese Question, 1877 White workers, seething with economic anxiety and ethnic prejudice, savagely mistreated Chinese immigrants in California in the 1870s.

From China to America

Between 1800 and 1925, at least 3 million Chinese people left their homeland to labor around the globe. The once-great Chinese Empire was disintegrating at the same time that its population was exploding, creating severe land shortages and opening up the unstable country to European imperial powers bent on unlocking the riches of a nation closed to outsiders for centuries. Chinese men, faced with economic hardship and violent turmoil in their homeland and lured by labor shortages as far afield as Southeast Asia, Australia, and the Americas, migrated by the tens of thousands to work the plantations and dig the mines that fueled a burgeoning global economy. By the 1880s, more than 100,000 Chinese immigrants had entered the United States to contribute their muscle to building the West, wrenching minerals from stubborn rock and helping to lay the transcontinental railroads that stitched together the American nation (refer to Table 21.3).

Although those who set off from China for destinations as diverse as Vietnam, Cuba, Peru, and the United States included a few merchants and artisans, most were unskilled country folk. In some cases, families pooled their money to send out a son, but most travelers, desperately poor, obtained their passage through Chinese middlemen, who advanced them ship fare in return for their promise to work off their debts after they landed. This contracting sometimes led to conditions so cruel that the practice was ignominiously called "pig selling."

The first Chinese people arrived in Spanish America as early as 1565, but few followed those earliest pioneers. Until the 1848 discovery of gold in California, there were fewer than 50 people of Chinese descent living in the United States. But by 1852, at least 25,000 had arrived in California, which they dubbed the "golden mountain." At that decade's end, Chinese workers made up nearly a quarter of the state's manual laborers, even though they were only a tenth of the population. Employers nationwide viewed the Chinese as cheap labor, recruiting them to cut sugar cane in the South and break strikes in New England shoe factories. A treaty negotiated with China in 1868 by the American diplomat Anson Burlingame guaranteed important civil rights to Chinese immigrants.

The Chinese America of the late nineteenth century was overwhelmingly a bachelor society. Although about half of the Chinese migrants during this period returned to their homeland, many stayed. "Chinatowns" sprang up wherever economic opportunities presented themselves—in railroad towns, farming villages, and cities. Excluded by white racism and persecuted by incidents of horrific racist violence, Chinese Americans found safety in community.

Table 21.3 Population of Chinese Ancestry in the United States, 1850–2010

Year	Population	Males per One Female	Percentage U.S.-Born	Persons Achieving Legal Permanent Resident Status in Preceding Decade*
1850	4,018†	—	—	32
1860	34,933	19	—	35,933
1870	64,199	13	1	54,028
1880	105,465	21	1	133,139
1890	107,488	27	3	65,797
1900	89,863	19	10	15,268
1970††	436,062	N.A.	N.A.	81,107
1980	806,040	N.A.	N.A.	134,977
1990	1,505,229	N.A.	N.A.	283,029
2000	2,271,562	0.94^	29	458,952
2010	3,347,229	0.89	33.5	649,294

*Includes Chinese immigrants in Hawaii after 1898; includes immigrants from Hong Kong beginning in 1970.

†Estimated.

††The passage of the Chinese Exclusion Act in 1882 sharply reduced the Chinese population in the United States. Liberalization of American immigration laws and Chinese policies beginning in the 1970s, however, has led to a great increase in population of Chinese ancestry in the United States.

^This gender ratio is for all Asian Americans, not only persons of Chinese descent.

Sources: U.S. Census Bureau, relevant years; U.S. Department of Homeland Security, *Statistical Yearbook of the Immigration and Naturalization Service*, 2010.

Mounting anti-Chinese agitation forced the repudiation of the Burlingame Treaty in 1880, and in 1882 the Chinese Exclusion Act barred nearly all Chinese from the United States for six decades. Those men and the few women who remained raised families and reared a new generation of Chinese Americans. They were joined by thousands more immigrants who made the journey illegally or took advantage of the few exceptions permissible under the Exclusion Act. This second generation still suffered from great discrimination, often left with the lowest-paying and most dangerous work. Yet a great many did manage to open their own restaurants, laundries, and other small businesses. The enterprises formed a solid economic foundation for their small community and the much larger one that would emerge by the late twentieth century with a huge influx of new immigrants arriving from China.

Roy D. Graves pictorial collection [graphic], BANC PIC 1905.17500 v.29:33-ALB. Courtesy of The Bancroft Library, University of California, Berkeley

Image 21.9 Chinese Butcher Shop, San Francisco, ca. 1890

The new president was energetic and able, but he was immediately ensnared in a political conflict between his secretary of state, James G. Blaine, and Blaine's Stalwart nemesis, Senator Roscoe Conkling. Then, as the Republican factions dueled, tragedy struck. A disappointed and mentally deranged office seeker, Charles Guiteau, shot President Garfield in the back in a Washington railroad station. Garfield lingered in agony for eleven weeks and died on September 19, 1881. Guiteau, when seized, reportedly cried, "I am a Stalwart. Arthur is now President of the United States." The implication was that now the Conklingites would all get good jobs. Guiteau's attorneys argued that he was not guilty because of his incapacity to distinguish right from wrong—an early instance of the "insanity defense." The defendant himself demonstrated his weak grip on reality when he asked all those who had benefited politically from the assassination to contribute to his defense fund. These tactics availed little. Guiteau was found guilty of murder and hanged.

Garfield's death had one positive outcome: It shocked politicians into reforming the shameful spoils system. The unlikely instrument of reform was Chester Arthur. Observers at first underestimated him. His record of cronyism and his fondness for fine wines and elegant clothing (including eighty pairs of trousers) suggested that he was little more than a foppish dandy. But Arthur surprised his critics by prosecuting several fraud cases and giving his former Stalwart pals the cold shoulder (refer to Image 21.10).

Disgust with Garfield's murder gave the Republican party itself a previously undetected taste for reform. The medicine finally applied to the long-suffering federal government was the **Pendleton Act** of 1883—the so-called Magna Carta of civil-service reform. It made compulsory campaign contributions from federal employees illegal, and it established the Civil Service Commission to make appointments to federal jobs on the basis of competitive examinations rather than "pull."

Although at first covering only about 10 percent of federal jobs, civil-service reform did rein in the most blatant abuses. Yet like many well-intentioned reforms, it bred unintended problems of its own. With the "plum" federal posts now beyond their reach, politicians were forced to look elsewhere for money, "the mother's milk of politics." Increasingly, they turned to the bulging coffers of the big corporations. A new breed of "boss" emerged—less skilled at mobilizing small armies of immigrants and other voters on election day, but more adept at milking dollars from manufacturers and lobbyists. The Pendleton Act partially divorced politics from

Image 21.10 The Balloon in Distress—Throwing out Ballast, 1882 President Arthur surprised many by showing a reformist streak in office. This cartoon depicts him chucking Republican cronies overboard to help unsnag the GOP balloon from the tree of "public indignation."

Buyenlarge/Superstock

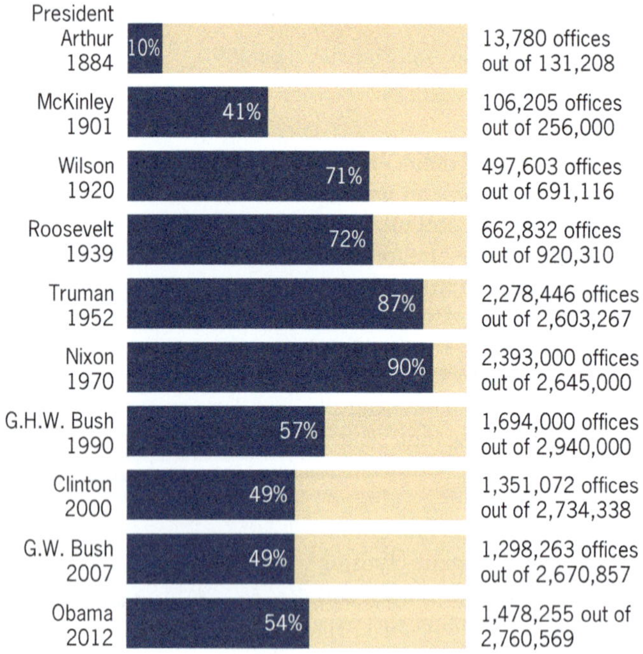

Figure 21.2 Civil-Service Employment The proportion of federal jobs that are classified, or subject to rigid civil-service laws and competitive requirements, has greatly increased since Arthur's presidency. The total number of civil-service jobs has remained relatively stable since the 1950s, even as the government has expanded in size and budget. The decline in classified civil-service jobs in recent decades reflects the changes mandated by the Postal Reorganization Act of 1971, which moved U.S. Postal Service employees from competitive to excepted service. Excepted jobs are not subject to rigid civil-service laws passed by Congress.

Sources: U.S. Office of Personnel Management, Federal Civilian Workforce Statistics—Employment and Trends, http://www.opm.gov/feddata; and unpublished data.

patronage, but it helped drive politicians into "marriages of convenience" with big-business leaders (refer to Figure 21.2).

President Arthur's surprising display of integrity offended too many powerful Republicans. His ungrateful party turned him out to pasture, and in 1886 he died of a cerebral hemorrhage.

21-11 The Blaine-Cleveland Mudslingers of 1884

James G. Blaine's persistence in pursuit of his party's presidential nomination finally paid off in 1884. The dashing Maine politician, blessed with almost every political asset except a reputation for honesty, was the clear choice of the Republican convention in Chicago. But many reform-minded Republicans gagged on Blaine's candidacy. Blaine's enemies publicized the fishy-smelling "Mulligan letters," written by Blaine to a Boston businessman and linking the powerful politician to a corrupt deal involving federal favors to a southern railroad. At least one of the damning documents ended with the furtive warning "Burn this letter." Some reformers, unable to swallow Blaine, bolted to the Democrats. They were sneeringly dubbed Mugwumps, a word of Algonquian derivation meant to suggest that they were "sanctimonious" or "holier-than-thou."*

Victory-starved Democrats turned enthusiastically to a noted reformer, Grover Cleveland. A burly bachelor with a soup-straining mustache and a taste for chewing tobacco, Cleveland was a solid but not brilliant lawyer of forty-seven. He had rocketed from the mayor's office in Buffalo to the governorship of New York and the presidential nomination in three short years. Known as "Grover the Good," he enjoyed a well-deserved reputation for probity in office.

*Latter-day punsters gibed that the Mugwumps were priggish politicians who sat on the fence with their "mugs" on one side and their "wumps" on the other.

Contending Voices

The Spoils System

In a famous series of newspaper interviews in 1905, George Washington Plunkitt (1842–1924), a political "boss" in the same Tammany Hall Democratic political "machine" that had spawned William Marcy ("Boss") Tweed, candidly described his ethical and political principles, which included a distinction between "honest graft and dishonest graft." Here he condemns civil-service reform while defending the efficacy of the patronage system.

"This civil service law is the biggest fraud of the age. It is the curse of the nation. There can't be no real patriotism while it lasts. How are you goin' to interest our young men in their country if you have no offices to give them when they work for their party? . . . First, this great and glorious country was built up by political parties; second, parties can't hold together if their workers don't get the offices when they win; third, if the parties go to pieces, the government they built up must go to pieces, too; fourth, then there'll be h– to pay."

Future U.S. president Theodore Roosevelt (1858–1919), by contrast, served as a civil-service commissioner from 1889 to 1895 and charged the patronage system with "tending to degrade American politics."

"The men who are in office only for what they can make out of it are thoroughly unwholesome citizens, and their activity in politics is simply noxious. . . . Decent private citizens must inevitably be driven out of politics if it is suffered to become a mere selfish scramble for plunder, where victory rests with the most greedy, the most cunning, the most brazen. The whole patronage system is inimical to American institutions; it forms one of the gravest problems with which democratic and republican government has to grapple."

Consider This:

Who benefited and who lost out in the process of reforming the civil service and curbing political patronage?

But Cleveland's admirers soon got a shock. Resolute Republicans, digging for dirt in the past of bachelor Cleveland, unearthed the report that he had been involved in an amorous affair with a Buffalo widow. She had an illegitimate son, now eight years old, for whom Cleveland had made financial provision (refer to Image 21.11). Democratic elders were demoralized. They hurried to Cleveland and urged him to lie like a gentleman, but their ruggedly honest candidate insisted, "Tell the truth."

The campaign of 1884 sank to perhaps the lowest level thus far seen in American experience, as the two parties grunted and shoved for the hog trough of office. Few fundamental differences separated them. Even the bloody shirt had faded to a pale pink.* Personalities, not principles, claimed the headlines. Crowds of Democrats surged through city streets, chanting—to the rhythm of left, left, left, right, left—"Burn, burn, burn this letter!" Republicans taunted in return, "Ma, ma, where's my pa?" Defiant Democrats shouted back, "Gone to the White House, ha, ha, ha!"

The contest hinged on the state of New York, where Blaine blundered badly in the closing days of the campaign. A witless Republican clergyman damned the Democrats in a speech as the party of "Rum, Romanism, and Rebellion"—insulting with one swift stroke the culture, the faith, and the patriotism of New York's

Library of Congress

Image 21.11 "I Want My Pa!" Malicious anti-Cleveland cartoon.

*Neither candidate had served in the Civil War. Cleveland had hired a substitute to go in his stead while he supported his widowed mother and two sisters. Blaine was the only Republican presidential candidate from Grant through McKinley (1868–1900) who had not been a Civil War officer.

numerous Irish American voters. Blaine was present at the time but lacked the presence of mind to repudiate the statement immediately. The pungent phrase, shortened to "RRR," stung and stuck. Blaine's silence seemed to give assent, and the wavering Irishmen who deserted his camp helped account for Cleveland's paper-thin plurality of about a thousand votes in New York State, enough to give him the presidency. Cleveland swept the solid South and squeaked into office with 219 to 182 electoral votes and a skinny popular vote margin of 4,879,507 to 4,850,293.

21-12 "Old Grover" Takes Over

Bull-necked Cleveland in 1885 was the first Democrat to take the oath of presidential office since Buchanan, twenty-eight years earlier. Huge question marks hung over his ample frame. Could the "party of disunion" be trusted to govern the Union? Would desperate Democrats, ravenously hungry after twenty-four years of exile, trample the frail sprouts of civil-service reform in a stampede to the patronage trough? Could Cleveland restore a measure of respect and power to the maligned and enfeebled presidency?

Cleveland was a man of principles, most of them safely orthodox by the standards of his day. A staunch apostle of the hands-off creed of laissez-faire, the new president caused the hearts of businesspeople and bankers to throb with contentment. He summed up his political philosophy in 1887 when he vetoed a bill to provide seeds for drought-ravaged Texas farmers. "Though the people support the government," he declared, "the government should not support the people." As tactless as a mirror and as direct as a bulldozer, he was outspoken, unbending, and profanely hot-tempered.

At the outset Cleveland narrowed the North–South chasm by naming to his cabinet two former Confederates. As for the civil service, Cleveland was whipsawed between the demands of the Democratic faithful for jobs and the demands of the Mugwumps, who had helped elect him, for reform. Believing in the merit system, Cleveland at first favored the cause of the reformers, but he eventually caved in to the carpings of Democratic bosses and fired almost two-thirds of the 120,000 federal employees, including 40,000 incumbent (Republican) postmasters, to make room for "deserving Democrats."

Niday Picture Library/Alamy Stock Photo

Image 21.12 Tariff Wars The cartoonist lambasts Republicans, including Jay Gould, William Vanderbilt, and Ulysses S. Grant, for their high-tariff policies that raised prices for working people.

21-13 Cleveland Battles for a Lower Tariff

Cleveland also risked his political neck by prodding the hornet's nest of the tariff issue. During the Civil War, tariff schedules had been jacked up to new high levels, partly to raise revenues for the insatiable military machine. American industry, which was preponderantly in Republican hands, had profited from this protection and hated to see the sheltering benefits reduced in peacetime. But the high duties continued to pile up revenue at the customs-houses, and by 1881 the Treasury was running an annual surplus amounting to an embarrassing $145 million. Most of the government's income, in those pre–income tax days, came from the tariff.

Congress could reduce the vexatious surplus in two ways. One was to squander it on pensions and "pork-barrel" bills and thus win support of veterans and other self-seeking groups. The other was to lower the tariff—something the big industrialists vehemently opposed. Grover Cleveland, the rustic Buffalo attorney, had known little and cared less about the tariff before entering the White House. But as he studied the subject, he was much impressed by the arguments for downward revision of the tariff schedules. Lower barriers would mean lower prices for consumers and less protection for monopolies (refer to Image 21.12). Most important, they would mean an end to the Treasury surplus, a standing mockery of Cleveland's professed belief in fiscal orthodoxy and small-government frugality. After much hesitation Cleveland saw his duty and overdid it.

With his characteristic bluntness, Cleveland tossed an appeal for lower tariffs like a bombshell into the lap of Congress in late 1887. The response was electric. Cleveland succeeded admirably in smoking the issue out into the open. Democrats were deeply frustrated by the obstinacy of their chief. Republicans rejoiced at his apparent recklessness, bellowing loudly that lower tariffs would mean higher taxes, lower wages, and increased unemployment. The old warrior Blaine gloated, "There's one more President for us in [tariff] protection." For the first time in years, a real issue divided the two parties as the 1888 presidential election loomed.

Collection of Janice L. and David J. Frent

Image 21.13 Weighing the Candidates, 1888 Novelties like this were widely distributed in late-nineteenth-century political campaigns. This miniature scale could be adjusted in either candidate's favor. Here the Republican Harrison rather improbably outweighs the corpulent Democratic candidate, Grover Cleveland.

Dismayed Democrats, seeing no alternative, somewhat dejectedly renominated Grover Cleveland in their St. Louis convention. Eager Republicans turned to Benjamin Harrison, whose grandfather was former president William Henry ("Tippecanoe") Harrison. The tariff was the prime issue. The two parties flooded the country with some 10 million pamphlets on the subject.

The specter of a lowered tariff spurred the Republicans to frantic action. In an impressive demonstration of the post–Pendleton Act politics of alliances with big business, they raised a war chest of some $3 million—the heftiest yet—largely by "frying the fat" out of nervous industrialists. The money was widely used to line up corrupt "voting cattle" known as "repeaters" and "floaters." In Indiana, always a crucial "swing" state, votes were shamelessly purchased for as much as $20 each.

On election day Harrison nosed out Cleveland, 233 to 168 electoral votes. A change of about 7,000 ballots in New York would have reversed the outcome. Cleveland actually polled more popular votes, 5,537,857 to 5,447,129, but he nevertheless became the first sitting president to be voted out of his chair since Martin Van Buren in 1840 (refer to Image 21.13).

21-14 The Billion-Dollar Congress

After a four-year famine, the Republicans under Harrison licked their lips hungrily for the bounty of federal offices. They yearned to lavish upon the party faithful the fat surpluses produced by the high tariffs. But in the House of Representatives, they had only three more votes than the necessary quorum of 163 members, and the Democrats were preparing to obstruct all House business by refusing to answer roll calls, demanding roll calls to determine the presence of a quorum, and employing other delaying tactics.

Into this tense cockpit stepped the new Republican Speaker of the House, Thomas B. Reed of Maine. A hulking figure who towered six feet three inches, he was renowned as a master debater. He spoke with a harsh nasal drawl and wielded a verbal harpoon of sarcasm. To one congressman who quoted Henry Clay that he would "rather be right than be president," Reed caustically retorted that he "would never be either." Opponents cringed at the crack of his quip.

Reed soon bent the intimidated House to his imperious will. He counted as present Democrats who had not answered the roll and who, rule book in hand, furiously denied that they were legally there. By such tactics "Czar" Reed utterly dominated the "Billion-Dollar" Congress—the first in history to appropriate that sum. Congress showered pensions on Civil War veterans and increased government purchases of silver. To keep the revenues flowing in—and to protect Republican industrialists from foreign competition—the Billion-Dollar Congress also passed the McKinley Tariff Act of 1890, boosting rates to their highest peacetime level ever (an average of 48.4 percent on dutiable goods).

Sponsored in the House by rising Republican star William McKinley of Ohio, the new tariff act brought fresh woes to farmers (refer to Image 21.14). Debt-burdened farmers had no choice but to buy manufactured goods from high-priced protected American industrialists and were compelled

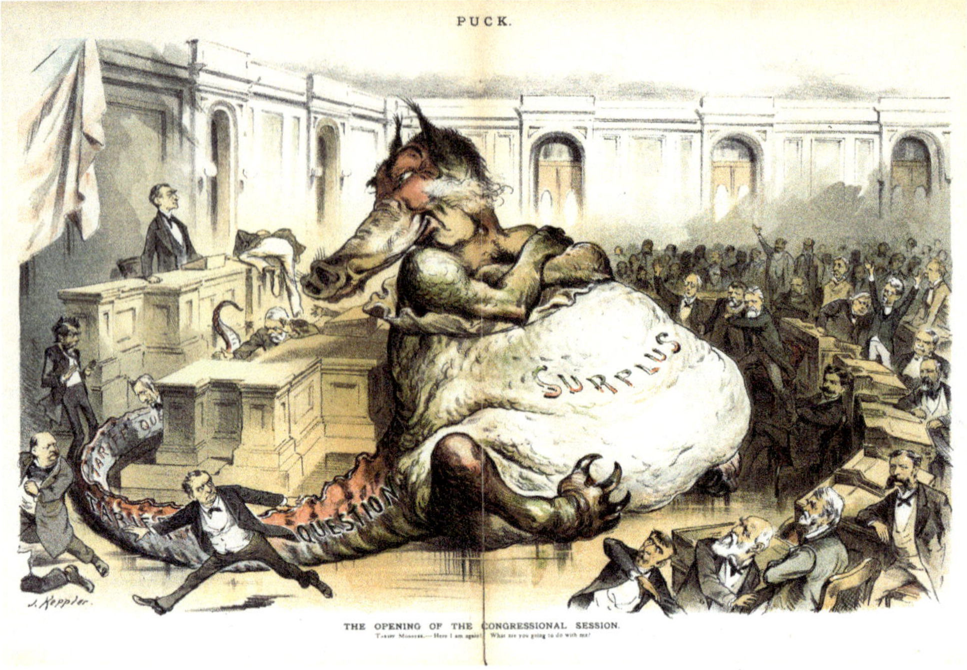

Image 21.14 **The High-Tariff Monster** Republican tariff policies punished farmers and working people with higher prices, but poured rivers of revenue into federal coffers, leading to the "Billion-Dollar Congress" that was seated in 1889.

The New York Historical Society/Getty Images

to sell their own agricultural products into highly competitive, unprotected world markets. Mounting discontent against the McKinley Tariff caused many rural voters to rise in wrath. In the congressional elections of 1890, the Republicans lost their precarious majority and were reduced to just 88 seats, as compared with 235 Democrats. Even the much-touted McKinley went down to defeat. Ominously for conservatives, the new Congress also included nine members of the Farmers' Alliance, a militant organization of Southern and Western farmers. The ascendancy of the Alliance climaxed decades of indebted farmers' distress and working-people's woes, and it heralded a volcanic eruption of political protest that was soon to engulf the entire land.

Chapter Summary

After the soaring ideals and tremendous sacrifices of the Civil War, the post–Civil War era was generally one of political disillusionment and even cynicism. Politicians from the White House to the courthouse were deeply enmeshed in corruption and scandal, while the actual economic, ethnic, and racial problems afflicting industrializing America festered beneath the surface without being seriously addressed.

The popular war hero Grant was a poor politician, and his administration was rife with corruption. Despite occasional futile reform efforts by high-minded Liberal Republicans and "Mugwumps," politics in the Gilded Age was monopolized by the two patronage-fattened parties, which competed vigorously for spoils while essentially agreeing on most national policies. Cultural and religious differences, different ethnic and regional bases, and deeply felt local issues like prohibition and education fueled intense party competition and unprecedented voter participation. Periodic complaints by political reformers and "soft-money" farmers' advocates failed to make much of a dent on politics or the laissez-faire business economics of the time.

The deadlocked and bitterly contested 1876 election led to the crass Compromise of 1877, which contributed to the end of Reconstruction, abandoning the Southern Black population to white "Redeemer" regimes. An oppressive economic system that combined tenant farming and sharecropping with racial segregation and oppression was thereafter fastened on the South, enforced by sometimes lethal violence. Racial prejudice against Chinese immigrants was also linked with labor unrest in the 1870s and 1880s.

Garfield's assassination by a disappointed office seeker spurred the beginnings of civil service reform but made politics more dependent on big business. Cleveland, the first Democratic president since the Civil War, proposed a lower tariff, creating the first real issue in national politics for some time. Republicans regained power under Harrison in the election of 1888, but their high-tariff policies sparked a voter backlash that in 1890 elected both a Democratic congressional majority and some members of the radical group Farmers' Alliance.

Key Terms

- "waving the bloody shirt" (523)
- Crédit Mobilier scandal (524)
- panic of 1873 (525)
- Gilded Age (526)
- patronage (527)
- Compromise of 1877 (529)
- Civil Rights Act of 1875 (530)
- sharecropping (530)
- Jim Crow (531)
- *Plessy v. Ferguson* (531)
- Great Strike of 1877 (532)
- circular migration (533)
- Chinese Exclusion Act (533)
- Pendleton Act (535)

People to Know

- Jay Gould
- Horace Greeley
- Rutherford B. Hayes
- James A. Garfield
- Chester Arthur
- Grover Cleveland
- Thomas B. Reed

Chronology

1868	• Grant defeats Seymour for presidency	
1869	• Fisk and Gould corner gold market	
1872	• Crédit Mobilier scandal exposed • Liberal Republicans break with Grant	• Grant defeats Greeley for presidency
1873	• Panic of 1873	
1875	• Whiskey Ring scandal • Civil Rights Act of 1875	• Resumption Act
1876	• Hayes-Tilden election standoff and crisis	
1877	• Compromise of 1877 • Reconstruction ends	• Railroad strikes paralyze nation
1880	• Garfield defeats Hancock for presidency	
1881	• Garfield assassinated; Arthur assumes presidency	
1882	• Chinese Exclusion Act	
1883	• *Civil Rights Cases* • Pendleton Act sets up Civil Service Commission	
1884	• Cleveland defeats Blaine for presidency	
1888	• Harrison defeats Cleveland for presidency	
1890	• "Billion-Dollar" Congress • McKinley Tariff Act	• Sherman Silver Purchase Act (repealed 1893)

To Learn More

Stephen Cresswell, *Rednecks, Redeemers, and Race: Mississippi after Reconstruction, 1877–1917* (2006)

William Gillette, *Retreat from Reconstruction, 1869–1879* (1979)

Steven Hahn, *A Nation Under Our Feet: Black Political Struggles in the Rural South from Slavery to the Great Migration* (2003)

Michael F. Holt, *By One Vote: The Disputed Presidential Election of 1876* (2008)

Paul Krause, *The Battle for Homestead, 1880–1892: Politics, Culture, and Steel* (1992)

Jackson Lears, *Rebirth of a Nation: The Making of Modern America, 1877–1920* (2009)

Heather Cox Richardson, *The Death of Reconstruction: Race, Labor, and Politics in the Post-Civil War North, 1865–1901* (2001)

C. Vann Woodward, *Origins of the New South, 1877–1913* (1951)

________, *The Strange Career of Jim Crow* (rev. ed., 1974)

Chapter 22

The Conquest of the West: 1865–1896

Up to our own day American history has been in a large degree the history of the colonization of the Great West. The existence of an area of free land, its continuous recession, and the advance of American settlement westward, explain American development.

Frederick Jackson Turner, 1893

The White Man, who possesses this whole vast country from sea to sea, who roams over it at pleasure, and lives where he likes, cannot know the cramp we feel in this little spot, with the undying remembrance of the fact, which you know as well as we, that every foot of what you proudly call America, not very long ago belonged to the red man.

Washakie (Shoshone), 1878

Chapter Outline

- The coming of the transcontinental railroad
- Native Americans and white settlers on the Plains
- Contradictions and betrayals in U.S. policy toward Native Americans
- The mining and cattle frontiers
- Free lands and fraud
- The great thirst in the arid West

When the Civil War crashed to a close, the frontier line was still wavering westward toward the fabled "100th Meridian," which defines the eastern boundary of the West, America's most arid region (refer to Map 22.4). A long north-south fringe of settlement, bulging outward here and there, stretched roughly from the Canadian border to central Texas. Between this jagged line and the settled areas on the Pacific slope, virtually no white people dwelled. The few exceptions were the islands of Mormons in Utah, occasional trading posts and gold camps, and several formerly Mexican enclaves scattered throughout the Southwest.

The Great West was a rough square sprawling about a thousand miles on each side. Embracing mountains, plateaus, deserts, and plains, it was the largely parched habitat of several powerful Indigenous peoples, their enormous horse herds, and countless bison, prairie dogs, and coyotes. Pioneers flung themselves greedily on this enormous prize, as if to ravish it. As the century drew toward a close, they had displaced its original inhabitants and declared the frontier "closed." The former domain of the native peoples had been carved into states and the four territories of Utah, Arizona, New Mexico, and "Indian Territory," or Oklahoma. Probably never before in human experience had so huge an area been transformed so rapidly.

Focus Questions

1. Who built the transcontinental railroad, how was it financed, and why was connecting the continent by rail a priority of the federal government?
2. What was the way of life of Native Americans of the West in the 1860s and 1870s, and how did they resist the white encroachment on their lands in those decades?
3. What policies and practices regarding Native Americans did the federal government develop after the end of the Plains wars?
4. How did miners and cattlemen develop their profitable economic activities throughout the West, and how were their original enterprises transformed in later decades?
5. What led farmers to push out onto the Great Plains in the 1870s and 1880s, and why was their type of grain-growing agriculture both so initially profitable and environmentally fragile in the region?
6. What made the American West a genuinely unique region of the country, and how have those features retained their distinctiveness?

22-1 Binding the Union with Railroad Ties

The locomotive's piercing whistle heralded the onslaught of the westward-streaming settlers. The ink on the Oregon and Mexican treaties of the 1840s was barely dry before Congress began discussing a transcontinental railroad. Sectional disagreement over the proposed line's location stalled the project, but when the South seceded, Congress wasted little time authorizing a northern route for the long-awaited line. One weighty argument for action was the urgency of bolstering the Union, already disrupted, by binding the Pacific Coast—especially gold-rich California—more securely to the rest of the Republic.

President Lincoln signed the Pacific Railway Act on July 1, 1862. The law was a landmark in its generosity and a model for infrastructure programs to come. Rather than building the railroad itself, the government induced private companies to build the line, and allowed them to profit from it.

Two railroad companies—the Union Pacific and the Central Pacific—received liberal loans and generous donations of acreage paralleling the tracks. Railroad placement meant further Native *dis*placement, as most government "grants" were made from tribal lands. All told, Washington rewarded the railroads with 174 million acres, and the western states contributed 49 million more—a total area larger than Texas (refer to Map 22.1).

The United States was not alone in its subsidization of transcontinental railroad building. Across an industrializing Europe and its empires, the construction of railway systems drove economic growth and reinforced colonial power. The extension of rails into thinly populated regions was unprofitable until the areas could be built up. Government subsidies encouraged private promoters who were unwilling to suffer heavy initial losses. In the early years, the bounty of public subsidies triggered a frenzy of rail construction that far exceeded demand.

Noisy criticism, especially in later years, was leveled at the giveaway of so valuable a birthright to greedy corporations. But the government did receive beneficial returns, including long-term preferential rates for postal service and military traffic. Granting land was also a "cheap" way to subsidize a much-desired transportation system because it avoided new taxes for direct cash grants. The railroads could turn the land into gold by using it as collateral for loans from private bankers or, later, by selling it. This they often did, at an average price of $3 an acre. Critics were also prone to overlook the fact that the land did not have even that relatively modest value until the railroads had ribboned it with steel.

Frontier villages touched by the magic wand of the iron rail became flourishing cities; those that were bypassed often withered away and became "ghost towns." Little wonder that communities fought one another for the privilege of playing host to the railroads. Ambitious towns customarily held out monetary and other attractions to the builders, who sometimes blackmailed them into contributing more generously.

22-2 The Railroad Builders

Congress commissioned the Union Pacific Railroad—note the word *Union*—to thrust westward from Omaha, Nebraska. For each mile of track constructed, the company was granted 20 square miles of land, alternating in 640-acre sections on either side of the track. For each mile,

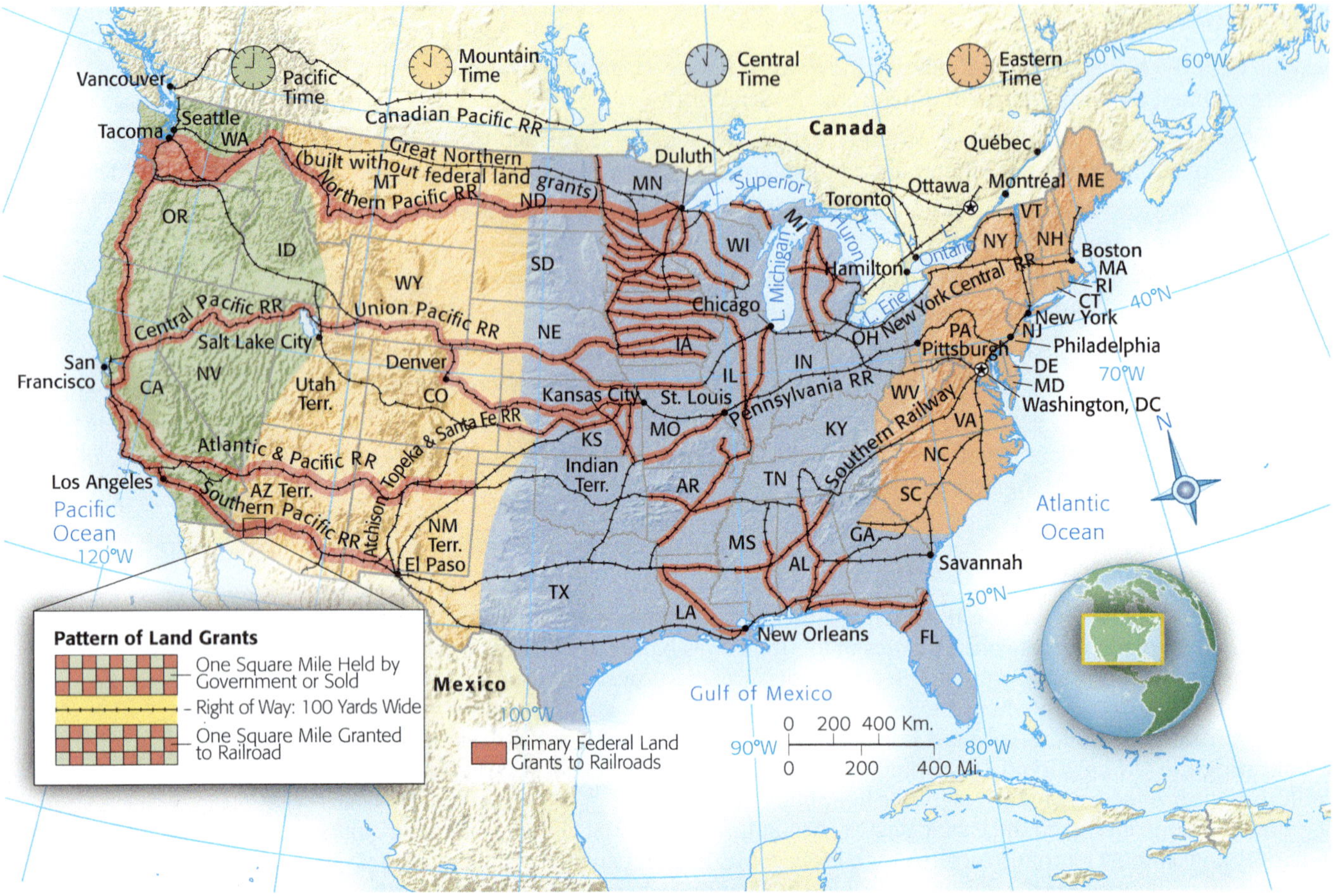

Map 22.1 Federal Land Grants to Railroads Just over 30,000 miles of railroad tracks laced the United States when the guns first spoke at Fort Sumter in 1861, mostly in the Northeast. By 1900 the nation had over 190,000 railroad miles mostly west of the Mississippi, more than that for all of Europe combined. The heavy red lines indicate areas within which the railroads might be given specific parcels of land, reserved in belts of various widths on either side of a railroad's right of way. Until the railroad selected the individual mile-square sections it chose to possess, *all* such sections within the belt were withdrawn from eligibility for settlement.

the builders were also to receive a generous federal loan, ranging from $16,000 on the flat prairie land to $48,000 for mountainous country. The laying of rails began in earnest after the Civil War ended in 1865, and with juicy loans and land grants available, the "groundhog" promoters made all possible haste.

The brutal work of railroad construction demanded workers who were cheap, efficient, and expendable. Whether driving rails across the rainless prairies or blasting tunnels through towering western mountains, hundreds lost their lives in premature explosions and other mishaps. Nearly all were immigrants.

Sweating construction gangs of mostly Irish "Paddies" (Patricks), many of them Union Army veterans, sledge-hammered westward at a frantic pace. At day's end, workers tried their best to find relaxation and conviviality in their tented towns, known as "hells on wheels," often teeming with as many as ten thousand men and a sprinkling of sex workers and performers. A favorite drinking song went like this:

> Then drill, my Paddies, drill;
> Drill, my heroes, drill;
> Drill all day,
> No sugar in your tay [tea]
> Workin' on the U.P. Railway.

Rail laying at the California end was undertaken by the Central Pacific Railroad. This line pushed boldly eastward from boomtown Sacramento, over and through the massive,

Image 22.1 Snow Sheds on the Central Pacific Railroad in the Sierra Nevada Mountains, by Joseph H. Becker, ca. 1869 Formidable obstacles of climate and terrain confronted the builders of the Central Pacific Railroad in the mountainous heights of California. Note the Chinese laborers in the foreground.

snow-clogged Sierra Nevada range (refer to Image 22.1). The railroad's owners were four self-made men—the so-called Big Four. The quartet included the enterprising ex-governor Leland Stanford of California, whose talents lay less in business than in skillful leveraging of political connections, and the burly, energetic Collis P. Huntington, an adept lobbyist and unrepentantly competitive entrepreneur. The Big Four cleverly operated through two construction companies, and although they walked away with tens of millions in profits, they kept their hands relatively clean by not becoming involved in the bribing of congressmen.

The Central Pacific, which received the same princely subsidies as the Union Pacific, had the same incentive to haste. The nerves of the Big Four were strained when their workers could chip only a few inches a day tunneling through solid rock. The Central Pacific's fifteen thousand Chinese workers toiled under even more daunting conditions than their Union Pacific counterparts, and for one-half to one-third of the pay (refer to Image 22.2). On one record-breaking day, a pick-and-shovel army of some five thousand mostly Chinese workers laid ten miles of track in twelve hours. When the Chinese went on strike for better pay and working conditions, the Big Four cut off their food supplies and warned that any disruptors would be shot. The strikers relented, but the shaken railroad barons raised pay and awarded a bonus when the line was complete.

That "wedding of the rails" was finally celebrated near Ogden, Utah, in 1869, as two locomotives—"facing on a single track, half a world behind each back"—gently touched cowcatchers. The colorful ceremony included the breaking of champagne bottles and the driving of a last ceremonial (golden) spike, with Leland Stanford clumsily wielding a silver maul. In all, the Union Pacific built 1086 miles, the Central Pacific 689 miles.

The screeching iron horse altered the western landscape and economy. It took farmers out to their land, carried the fruits of their toil to market, and brought them their manufactured necessities. Clusters of farm settlements paralleled the railroads, just as earlier they had followed the rivers. Cattle could no longer roam free, lest the herds wander into the

Image 22.2 Chinese Railroad Workers Laying Track for the Union Pacific Railroad Near Promontory, Utah Chinese people made up as much as ninety percent of the workforce responsible for building the western portion of the transcontinental railroad, the largest and most difficult engineering project of its time. Working eleven hours a day, six days a week, Chinese laborers were paid far less than their white counterparts.

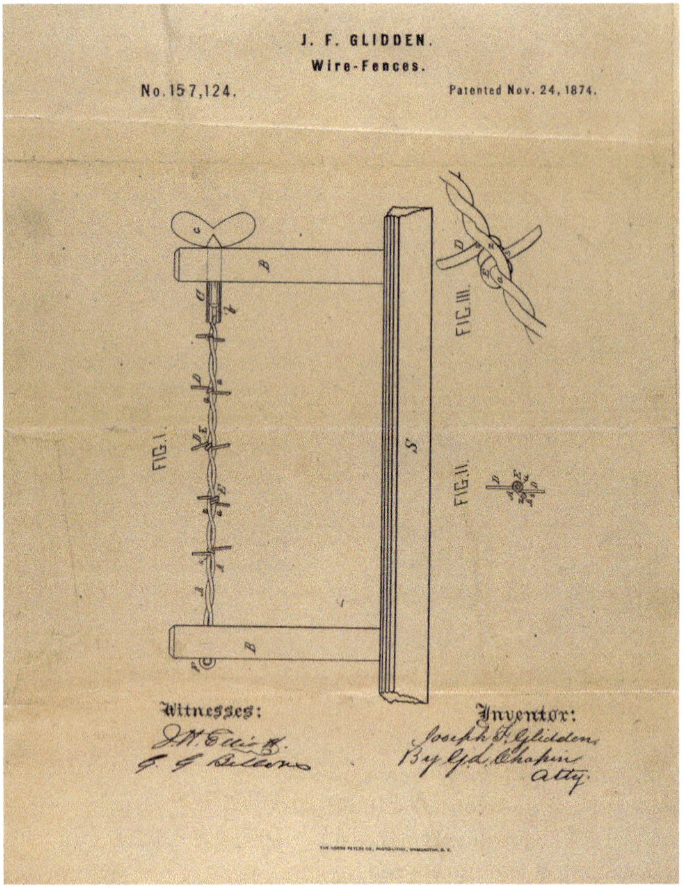

Image 22.3 **Joseph Glidden's Improvement to Barbed Wire, 1874.** The push to settle the West led to a number of Americans filing patents for barbed wire—a cheap and efficient means of enclosing large expanses of prairie land for livestock grazing. The most enduring of these was invented by Joseph Glidden, an Illinois farmer, in 1874. Here is the illustration from his original patent application for this now-familiar design.

path of an oncoming locomotive. A new invention—barbed wire fencing—allowed ranchers to cheaply enclose the once wide-open plains (refer to Image 22.3).

The land also felt the impact of the railroad—especially the broad, ecologically fragile midsection of the continent that Thomas Jefferson had purchased from France in 1803. Settlers following the railroads plowed up the tallgrass prairies of Iowa, Illinois, Kansas, and Nebraska and planted well-drained, rectangular cornfields. On the shortgrass prairies of the high plains in the Dakotas and Montana, range-fed cattle rapidly displaced the buffalo. The white pine forests of Michigan, Wisconsin, and Minnesota disappeared into lumber that was rushed by rail to prairie farmers, who used it to build houses and fences.

The completion of the railroads transformed the lives of millions of people across the continent. But the western lines shot an iron arrow through the hearts of the region's Indigenous peoples, whose traditional ways of life were utterly upended.

22-3 Native Americans and White Settlers on the Plains

Native Americans numbered about 340,000 in 1860, many of them living in tightly organized mobile societies that traversed the vast grasslands of the trans-Missouri West. But to their eternal misfortune, these Western Indigenous peoples lived in the path of the relentlessly advancing transcontinentals and the white settlers following in their wake. Conflict loomed between demands of an acquisitive, industrializing nation and Native American lifeways that had evolved over centuries to adapt to the challenging environment of the sparsely watered western plains (refer to "Makers of America: The Plains Indians," pp. 548–549).

Migration and conflict—and sometimes dramatic cultural change—were no strangers in the water-poor West, even before settlers began to arrive. The Comanches had driven the Apaches off the central plains into the upper Rio Grande valley in the eighteenth century. By mid-nineteenth century, a vast livestock-trading Comanche empire dominated the heart of the continent, including large parts of present-day New Mexico, Colorado, Kansas, Oklahoma, and Texas. Farther north, harried by the Mandans and Chippewas, the Cheyenne in the century before the Civil War had abandoned their villages along the upper reaches of the Mississippi and Missouri Rivers, and moved into what are now the Dakotas. The Sioux displaced from the Great Lakes woodlands in the late eighteenth century, emerged onto the plains to prey upon the Crows, Kiowas, and Pawnees (refer to Image 22.4). Mounted on horses whose ancestors had been loosed during the Pueblo Revolt of the late seventeenth century, peoples like the Cheyenne and the Sioux transformed themselves within just a few generations from foot-traveling, crop-growing villagers to wide-ranging traders and prodigiously efficient buffalo hunters. Ironically, grazing competition from their own horses and the very efficiency of mounted hunting threatened to extinguish the vast bison herds that had lured them onto the Plains in the first place.

When white soldiers and settlers edged onto the Great Plains in the decades just before the Civil War, they exacerbated already fierce enmities among Indigenous groups and ultimately undermined the foundations of Native American culture. White intruders also spread cholera, typhoid, and smallpox among the peoples of the Plains, with devastating results. Equally harmful, white settlers put further pressure on the steadily shrinking bison population by hunting and by grazing their livestock on the prairie grasses. As the once-mammoth buffalo

William Henry Jackson/Getty Images

Image 22.4 Pawnee in Front of Their Lodge, ca. 1868
The Pawnees of central Nebraska never made war on the United States, which they regarded as an ally in their own struggles against the marauding Sioux.

herds dwindled, warfare intensified among the Plains tribes for ever-scarcer prey and ever-shrinking hunting grounds. "I am traveling all over this country, and am cutting the trees of my brothers," an Arikara leader told a U.S. Army officer along the Platte River in 1835. "I am killing their buffalo before my friends arrive so that when they come up, they can find no buffalo."

United States officials tried to control the Plains Indians, as they had done with the once-mighty Native nations east of the Mississippi, by signing treaties with the "chiefs" of various "tribes" at Fort Laramie in 1851 and at Fort Atkinson in 1853. The treaties marked the beginnings of the **reservation system** in the West. They established boundaries for the territory of each tribe and attempted to separate the Native Americans into two great "colonies" to the north and south of a corridor of intended white settlement.

But the white treaty makers misunderstood both Native American government and Native American society. *Tribes* and *chiefs* were often fictions of the white imagination, which could not grasp the fact that many Native Americans recognized only the authority of their immediate families or perhaps a band elder. And the mobile culture of the Plains Indians was utterly alien to the concept of living out one's life in the confinement of a defined territory.

In the 1860s, the federal government herded the Plains Indians into still-smaller confines, principally the "Great Sioux Reservation" in Dakota Territory and Indian Territory in present-day Oklahoma, into which dozens of southern Plains tribes were forced.

These Native peoples had surrendered their ancestral lands only when they had received solemn promises from Washington that they would be left undisturbed and provided with food, clothing, and other supplies. Regrettably, the federal agents were often corrupt. They palmed off moth-eaten blankets, spoiled beef, and other defective provisions on the hapless recipients. One of these cheating officials, on an annual salary of $1,500, returned home after four years with an estimated "savings" of $50,000.

As early as the Coronado expedition in 1541, Spanish explorers marveled at the Plains Indians' reliance on the buffalo:

"With the skins [the Indians] build their houses; with the skins they clothe and shoe themselves; from the skins they make ropes and also obtain wool. From the sinews they make thread, with which they sew their clothing and likewise their tents. From the bones they shape awls, and the dung they use for firewood, since there is no fuel in all that land. The bladders serve as jugs and drinking vessels. They sustain themselves on the flesh of the animals, eating it slightly roasted and sometimes uncooked. Taking it in their teeth, they pull with one hand; with the other they hold a large flint knife and cut off mouthfuls, swallowing it half chewed, like birds. They eat raw fat, without warming it."

One disheartened Indian complained to the white Sioux Commission created by Congress,

"Tell your people that since the Great Father promised that we should never be removed we have been moved five times. . . . I think you had better put the Indians on wheels and you can run them about wherever you wish."

Makers of America

The Plains Indians

The last of the Native peoples of North America to bow before the military might of the whites, the Indigenous peoples of the northern Great Plains long defended their lands and their ways of life against the American cavalry. After the end of the Indian wars, toward the close of the nineteenth century, the Plains tribes struggled on, jealously guarding their communities against white encroachment. Crowded onto reservations, subject to ever-changing federal policies, assailed by corrupt settlers and Indian agents, the Plains Indians have nonetheless preserved much of their ancestral culture to this day.

Before Europeans first appeared in North America in the sixteenth century, the vast plains from northern Texas to Saskatchewan were home to some thirty different tribes. There was no typical Plains Indian; each tribe spoke a distinct language, practiced its own religion, and formed its own government. When members of different bands met on the prairies, communication depended on a special sign language.

Native Americans had first trod the arid plains to pursue sprawling herds of antelope, elk, and especially buffalo—all important sources of protein. But these early peoples of the plains were not exclusively hunters: the women were expert farmers, coaxing lush gardens of pumpkins, squash, corn, and beans from the dry but fertile soil. Still, the shaggy pelt and heavy flesh of the buffalo constituted the staff of life on the plains. Hunted by men, the great bison were butchered by women, who used every part of the beast. They fashioned horns and hooves into spoons, and intestines into containers. They stretched sinews into strong bowstrings and wove buffalo hair into ropes. Meat not immediately eaten was pounded into pemmican—thin strips of smoked or sun-dried buffalo flesh mixed with berries and stuffed into rawhide bags.

The wide-roaming Plains Indians sought what shelter they could in small bands throughout the winter, gathering together in summer for religious ceremonies, socializing, and communal buffalo hunts. At first these seasonal migrations required arduous loading and carting. The Native Americans carried all their possessions or heaped them on wheelless carts called travois, which were dragged by dogs—their only beasts of burden.

Then in the sixteenth century, the mounted Spanish *conquistadores* ventured into the New World. The Pueblo Revolt of 1680 resulted in the release of countless Spanish steeds onto the plains. Those feral horses revolutionized societies, turning the Plains tribes into efficient hunting machines that promised to banish hunger from the prairies. But horse-mounted hunters turned out to be too efficient: overhunting made buffalo ever harder to find. The plains ponies also ignited furious competition for grazing lands, for trade goods, and for ever more horses, making wars of aggression and of revenge increasingly bitter and frequent.

A

Gift of Mrs. Joseph Harrison, Jr./Smithsonian American Art Museum

B

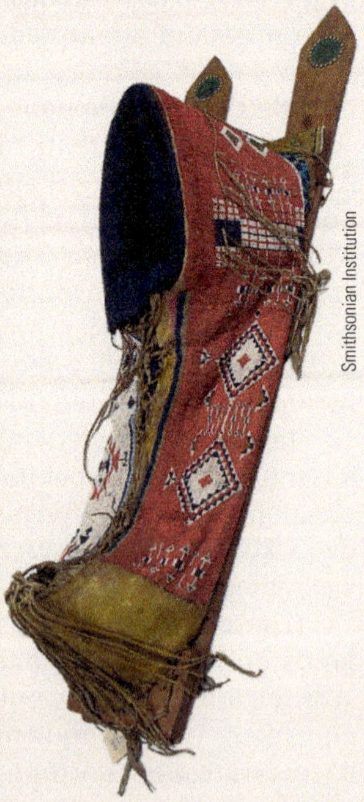

Smithsonian Institution

Image 22.5A and B (A) A Comanche Village, by George Catlin, 1834, (B) A Comanche Cradleboard for Carrying a Baby

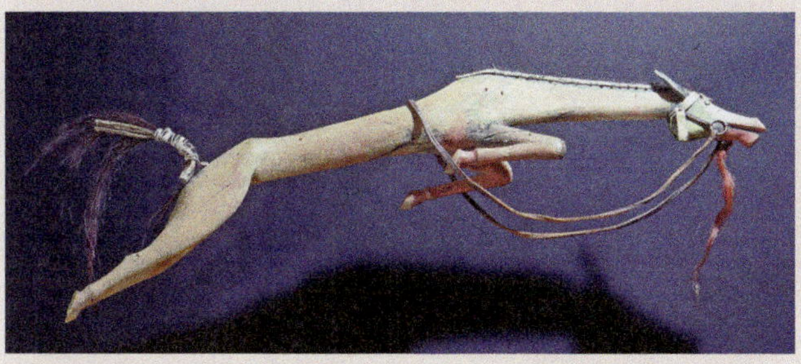

Werner Forman/Getty Images

Image 22.6 A Sioux Carving Horses were essential to the culture of the Plains Indians, and they often carved likenesses of horses killed in battle. Note the red-stained holes depicting this horse's wounds.

The European invasion soon eclipsed the Native Americans' short-lived era of the horse. After many battles, the Plains Indians found themselves crammed together on tiny reservations, clinging with tired but determined fingers to their traditions. Although much of Plains Indian culture persists to this day, the Native Americans' free-ranging way of life has passed into memory. As Black Elk, an Oglala Sioux, put it, "Once we were happy in our own country and we were seldom hungry, for then the two-leggeds and the four-leggeds lived together like relatives, and there was plenty for them and for us. But then the Wasichus [white people] came, and they made little islands for us. . .and always these islands are becoming smaller, for around them surges the gnawing flood of Wasichus."

Library of Congress

Image 22.7 Red Deer, a Sioux Woman, Poses with Her Baby, ca. 1900

For more than a decade after the Civil War, fierce warfare between Native nations and the U.S. Army raged in various parts of the West (refer to Map 22.2). Army troops, Union and Confederate veterans alike—many of them recent immigrants who had, ironically, fled Europe to avoid military service—met formidable adversaries in the Plains Indians, whose superb horsemanship gave them baffling mobility. Fully one-fifth of all U.S. Army personnel on the western frontier were African American—dubbed *Buffalo Soldiers* by their Native adversaries, supposedly because of the resemblance of their hair to the bison's furry coat.

22-4 The American Indians Fight Back

The United States' determination to "close" and settle the western frontier led to ferocious clashes. Aggressive whites sometimes shot peaceful natives on sight, without provocation or compunction. At the **Sand Creek Massacre**, in 1864, Colonel J. M. Chivington's Colorado militia butchered more than two hundred Cheyenne, who apparently thought they had been promised immunity. Chivington's troopers cold-bloodedly shot women praying for mercy, rifled-butted the brains out of bawling babies, and tortured, scalped, and unspeakably mutilated countless Cheyenne warriors.

A young lieutenant told Colonel Chivington that to attack the Indians would be a violation of pledges:

"His reply was, bringing his fist down close to my face, 'Damn any man who sympathizes with Indians.' I told him what pledges were given the Indians. He replied that he 'had come to kill Indians, and believed it to be honorable to kill Indians under any and all circumstances.'"

Map 22.2 Indian Wars, 1860–1890 Surrendering in 1877, Chief Joseph of the Nez Perce declared, "Our chiefs are killed. . . . The old men are all dead. . . . The little children are freezing to death. . . . I want to have time to look for my children. . . . Hear me, my chiefs. My heart is sick and sad. From where the sun now stands I will fight no more forever."

Atrocity begot atrocity. In 1866, Lakota warriors moved to block construction of the Bozeman Trail, being built to the Montana goldfields in violation of the 1851 Fort Laramie Treaty. A war party led by the famed Oglala Lakota strategist Mahpíya Lúta (Red Cloud) ambushed Captain William J. Fetterman's command of eighty-one soldiers and civilians in Wyoming's Bighorn Mountains. They left not a single survivor and grotesquely disfigured the corpses. One trooper's face was spitted with 105 arrows. George Armstrong Custer, the buckskin-clad "boy general" of Civil War fame, now demoted to colonel and turned Indian fighter, wrote that Fetterman's annihilation "awakened a bitter feeling toward the savage perpetrators." The cycle of vicious warfare intensified.

The Fetterman massacre eventually led to one of the few—though short-lived—Indigenous victories in the Plains wars, the **Battle of the Greasy Grass** (also known as the Battle of Little Bighorn). In another Treaty of Fort Laramie, signed in 1868, the U.S. government grudgingly abandoned the Bozeman Trail. The sprawling "Great Sioux Reservation" was guaranteed to the Dakota, Lakota, and Nakota peoples. But in 1874 a new round of warfare with the Plains peoples began when Custer led a "scientific" expedition—once again in violation of solemn treaties—into the Black Hills of South Dakota (part of the reservation) and announced that he had discovered gold. Hordes of greedy gold-seekers swarmed into the Sioux lands. The aggrieved Lakota, led by Tasunke Witco (Crazy Horse) aided by their Cheyenne and Arapahoallies, once again rose up in arms, inspired by their political and spiritual leader Tatanka-Iyotanka (Sitting Bull).

Colonel Custer's 7th Cavalry, nearly half of them immigrants, set out to suppress the uprising and push the Native fighters back to reservation lands. Attacking Sitting Bull's camp of approximately eight thousand along the Little Bighorn River in present-day eastern Montana, the "White Chief with Yellow Hair" and about 250 officers and men were completely wiped out in 1876—ironically, the nation's Centennial year (refer to Image 22.8). But the Native Americans' hour of triumph was brief. In a series of battles across the northern plains in the ensuing months, the U.S. Army relentlessly hunted down those who had humiliated Custer.

One band of Nez Perce peoples in northeastern Oregon were goaded into daring flight in 1877 when U.S. authorities tried to push them onto a reservation. Chief Joseph—whose Nez Perce name, Heinmot Tooyalakekt, signified "Thunder Rising to Loftier Mountain Heights"—finally surrendered his band of some seven hundred men, women, and children after a tortuous, seventeen-hundred-mile, three-month-long trek across the Continental Divide toward Canada. There Joseph had hoped to rendezvous with Sitting Bull, who had taken refuge north of the border after Custer's defeat. Betrayed into believing they would be returned to their ancestral lands in Idaho, the Nez Perce instead were sent to a dusty reservation in Kansas, where 40 percent of them perished from disease. The survivors were eventually allowed to return to Idaho.

Powerful Apache tribes of Arizona and New Mexico were among the most difficult for U.S. troops to overcome. Led by the famously fearless Goyaałé (Geronimo), the Apache raided U.S. encampments and spent years evading their pursuers on both sides of the U.S.-Mexico border (refer to Image 22.9).

History and Art Collection/Alamy Stock Photo

Image 22.8 Battle of the Greasy Grass (Little Bighorn), by Amos Bad Heart Bull This depiction of the battle by an Oglala Sioux tribal historian and artist shows Crazy Horse (in spotted war paint, center) firing on a trooper of Custer's 7th Cavalry. The ground is littered with the bodies of dead soldiers.

Civil War veteran and long-time Indian fighter General Philip Sheridan (1831–1888) reflected on the wars against the Native peoples:

"We took away their country and their means of support, broke up their mode of living, their habits of life, introduced disease and decay among them, and it was for this and against this they made war. Could anyone expect less?"

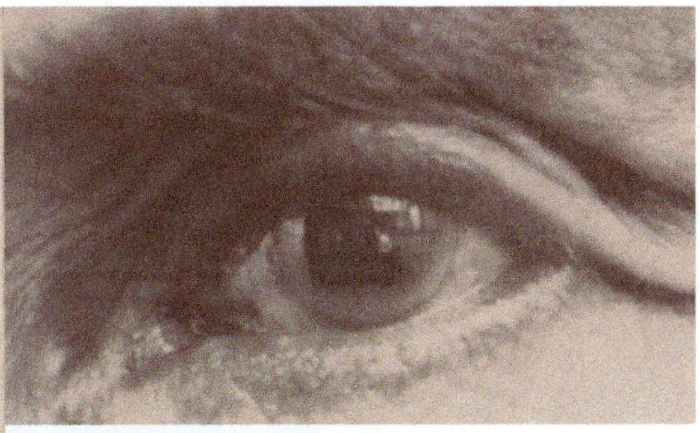
Library of Congress

Image 22.9 Geronimo (ca. 1823–1909), Also Known by His Apache Name, Goyaałé (One Who Yawns) In 1851, Mexican troops killed Geronimo's family, initiating his lifelong hatred of Mexicans. Ironically, in later life, when he repeatedly fled the intolerable confinement of reservations in the United States, he sought refuge—and freedom—in Mexico. Persuaded at last to surrender to American authorities in 1886, he spent the remainder of his life on reservations in Florida, Alabama, and Oklahoma. In 1904, the aging warrior posed for this portrait at the St. Louis studio of sisters Emme and Mayme Gerhard. The close-up view of his left eye reflects the female photographer.

Scattered remnants of the warriors were finally persuaded to surrender after the Apache women had been exiled to Florida. Geronimo remained a revered leader and later gained fame through appearances at international expositions and Theodore Roosevelt's 1905 inauguration parade. The Apache ultimately were relocated to reservations in Arizona and New Mexico.

22-5 Bellowing Herds of Bison

Deeply disrupted by the relentless fire-and-sword policy of the U.S. Army and the transcontinentals' screeching locomotives, the Plains Indians' wide-ranging ways of life were ultimately dealt a fatal blow by the near-extermination of the buffalo. Tens of millions of bison—described by early Spaniards as "hunchback cows"—carpeted the western prairies when white Americans first arrived. These shaggy, lumbering animals were the staff of life for Native Americans (refer to "Makers of America: The Plains Indians," pp. 548–549). Their flesh provided food; their dried dung (*buffalo chips*) provided fuel; their hides provided clothing, lariats, and harnesses.

When the Civil War ended, some 15 million of these meaty beasts grazed across the western plains. In 1868, a Kansas Pacific locomotive had to wait eight hours for a herd to amble across the tracks. Much of the food supply of the railroad construction crews came from leathery buffalo steaks. William "Buffalo Bill" Cody—a telescope-eyed crack shot—earned his nickname by killing over four thousand animals in eighteen months while employed as a buffalo hunter by the Kansas Pacific railroad.

With the completion of the railroad, the massacre of the herds escalated sharply. The creatures were slain for their hides (which among other uses could be turned into commercial leather for machine belting), for their tongues or a few other choice cuts, or for sheer amusement. "Sportsmen" on lurching railroad trains would lean out the windows and blaze away at the animals to satisfy their lust for slaughter or excitement. Such wholesale butchery left fewer than a thousand buffalo alive by 1885, and the once-prolific beasts were in danger of complete extinction (refer to Image 22.10). The whole story is a gut-wrenching example of the greed and waste that accompanied the conquest of the continent.

Image 22.10 The Wages of Slaughter This pile of skulls testifies to scale of bison destruction on the nineteenth-century plains.

Image 22.11 Hydraulic Mining, Idaho, 1901 Once miners had panned and dredged the most accessible gold from streambeds, they ripped open the earth itself in search of other deposits. High-pressure streams of water, delivered through huge nozzles called "monitors," washed away entire hillsides and created the nightmarish, debris-strewn landscapes that still scar western mountains and foothills.

22-6 Mining: From Dishpan to Ore Breaker

The conquest of Indigenous territories and the coming of the railroad fueled the growth of the mining frontier. The golden gravel of California continued to yield "pay dirt" for a lucky few, and in 1858, an electrifying gold discovery convulsed Colorado. Avid "fifty-niners" or "Pikes Peakers" rushed west to rip at the ramparts of the Rockies. But again there were more miners than minerals. Many gold-grubbers, with "Pikes Peak or Bust" inscribed on the canvas of their covered wagons, creaked wearily back eastward with the added inscription, "Busted, by Gosh."

Fifty-niners also poured feverishly into Nevada in 1859, after the fabulous Comstock Lode had been uncovered. The "Kings of the Comstock" extracted a fantastic amount of gold and silver, worth more than $340 million, from 1860 to 1890. The scantily populated state of Nevada, "child of the Comstock Lode," was prematurely railroaded into the Union in 1864, partly to provide three electoral votes for President Lincoln.

Smaller lucky strikes drew frantic gold- and silver-seekers into Montana, Idaho, and other western states, as well as to the Fraser River district in Canada's British Columbia. Boomtowns, known as *Helldorados,* sprouted from the desert sands. Sweat-stained miners swilled adulterated liquor "rotgut" in smoky saloons, accompanied by accommodating women. Lynch law and vigilante justice, as in gold-rush California, preserved a crude semblance of order. When the diggings petered out, the gold-seekers decamped, leaving eerily picturesque "ghost towns," such as Virginia City, Nevada, as mute testimony to the West's tumultuous past.

Once the loose surface gold was gobbled up, resourceful miners imported ore-breaking machinery to smash the gold-bearing quartz. This operation was so expensive that it could ordinarily be undertaken only by corporations pooling the wealth of stockholders.

Gradually the age of big business came to the **mining industry**. Impersonal and imperious corporations, with their costly machinery and trained engineers, replaced dishpan-wielding, bewhiskered miners (refer to Image 22.11). Yet the mining frontier had played a vital role in settling the continent. Magnetlike, it attracted population and wealth, while advertising the wonders of the Wild West. Single or widowed white women, far outnumbered by men, found economic independence running boardinghouses as well as through sex work. The boost that women gave the small settler population on the rough frontier earned them the vote in Wyoming (1869), Utah (1870), Colorado (1893), and Idaho (1896) long before their sisters in the East could cast a ballot.

The amassing of precious metals facilitated the building of railroads and intensified the already bitter conflict between settlers and Native Americans. The outpouring of silver and gold

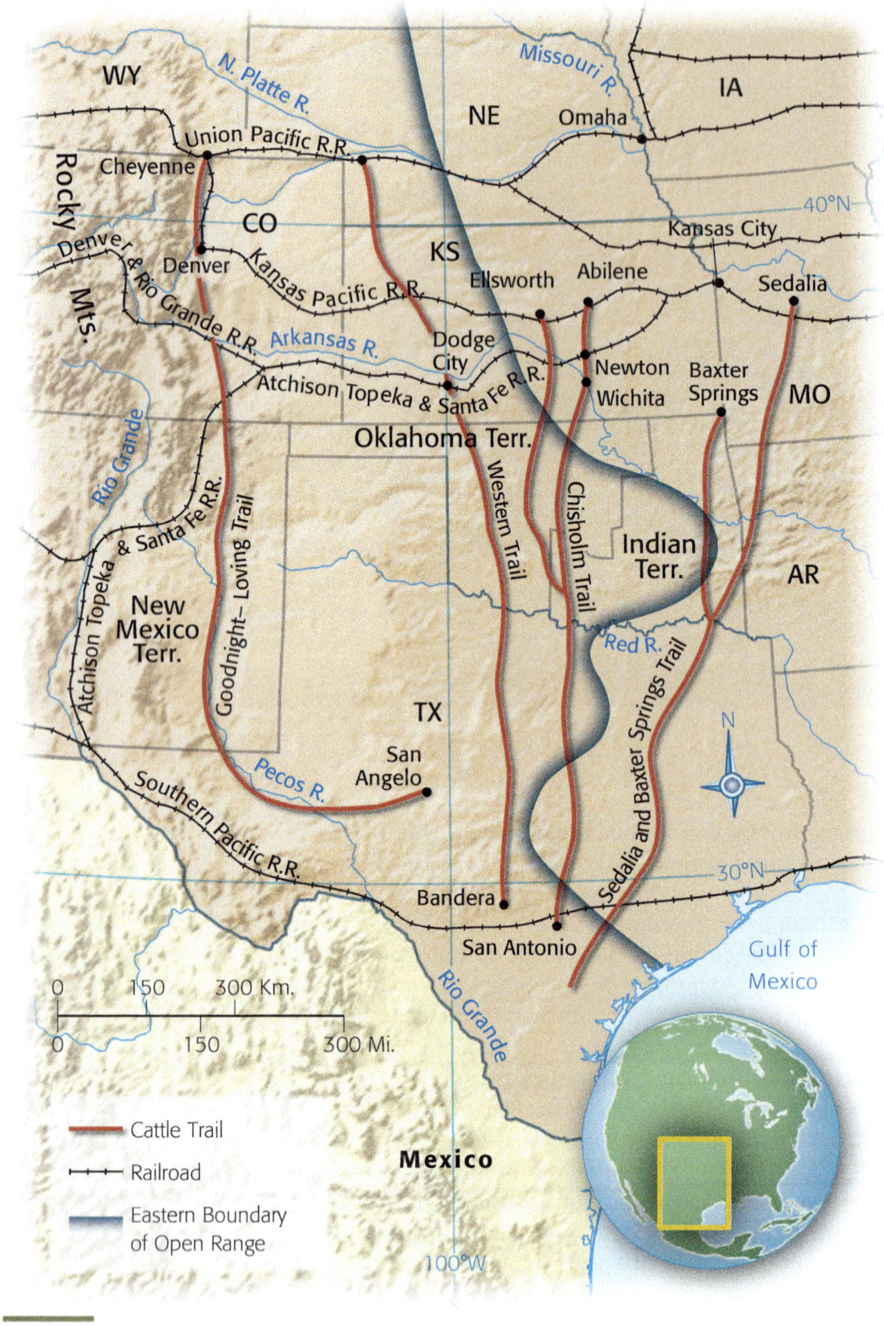

Map 22.3 Cattle Trails

enabled the Treasury to resume specie payments in 1879 and injected the silver issue into U.S. politics. "Silver Senators," representing the thinly peopled "acreage states" of the West, used their disproportionate influence to promote the interests of the silver miners. The mining frontier also added to American folklore and literature, as the writings of Bret Harte and Mark Twain so colorfully attest.

22-7 Beef Bonanzas and the Long Drive

When the Civil War ended, the grassy plains of Texas supported several million tough, long-horned cattle. These scrawny beasts, whose horns could measure eight feet from tip to tip, were killed primarily for their hides. There was no way of getting their stringy meat profitably to market.

But inventive stockmen soon introduced new breeds of beef cattle onto the Great Plains, and new ways of getting to market. Their giant herds moved with the seasons on the "Long Drive" (refer to Map 22.3). Texas cowboys—Black, white, and Mexican—drove herds numbering from one thousand to ten thousand head slowly over the unfenced and unpeopled plains. The bawling beasts grazed en route on free government grass, until they reached a railroad terminal at a flyspecked cow town like Dodge City—"the Bibulous Babylon of the Frontier"—or Abilene (Kansas), where order was maintained by Marshal James B. ("Wild Bill") Hickok, a formidable gunman who reputedly killed only in self-defense or in the line of duty. He was fatally shot in the back of the head in 1876 while playing poker (and legendarily holding what became known as the "dead man's hand" of two pair, black aces and black eights).

As long as the grazing was free, the Long Drive proved profitable—that is, to the luckier cattlemen who escaped Native American attacks, stampedes, cattle fever, and other hazards. From 1866 to 1888, bellowing herds, totaling over 4 million steers, were driven northward from the beef bowl of Texas. The steer was king in a Cattle Kingdom richly carpeted with grass.

This was the heyday of the cowboy. The cowhand's equipment—from "shooting irons" and ten-gallon hat to chaps and spurs—served a useful, not an ornamental, function (refer to Image 22.12). A "genuwine" gun-toting cowpuncher, riding where men were men and smelled like horses, could justifiably boast of his toughness.

These bowlegged Knights of the Saddle, with their colorful trappings and cattle-lulling songs, became part of American folklore. Many of them, perhaps five thousand, were Black migrants, who especially enjoyed the new-found freedom of the open range.

But what the Lord giveth, the Lord also can taketh away. The classic cowboy era lasted scarcely a quarter-century. The railroad made the Long Drive, and the railroad unmade the Long Drive, primarily because the locomotives ran both ways. The same rails that bore the cattle from the open range to the kitchen range brought out the homesteader and the sheep-herder. Both of these intruders, sometimes amid flying bullets, built the barbed-wire fences that spelled the end of the free-grazers on the open range. Then the ghastly winter of 1886–1887, with blinding blizzards reaching 68 degrees below zero, left thousands of dazed cattle starving and freezing. Overexpansion and overgrazing likewise took their toll, as the cowboys slowly gave way to plowboys.

The only escape for the stockmen was to make cattle-raising a big business and avoid the perils of overproduction. Breeders learned to fence their ranches, lay in winter feed, import blooded bulls, and produce fewer and meatier animals. They also learned to organize. The Wyoming Stock-Growers' Association, especially in the 1880s, virtually controlled the state and its legislature. Meanwhile new business models and new technologies rewrote the rules of the range. From the sprawling and stinking stockyards at Kansas City and Chicago, "beef barons" like the Swifts and Armours consolidated the cattle industry, shipping their fresh products to the East Coast in the newly perfected refrigerator cars.

Bettmann/Getty Images

Image 22.12 Dressed to Kill Cowboys came in all varieties and sizes in the wild and woolly frontier West—and in all kinds of garb as well.

22-8 Sodbusters and Homesteaders

Miners and cattlemen created the romantic legend of the West, but it was the sober sodbuster who wrote the most indelible chapter of frontier history. A fresh day dawned for Western settlers with the Homestead Act of 1862. The new law, born during the Civil War, allowed settlers—provided they had "never borne arms against the government of the United States"—to acquire as much as 160 acres of land (a quarter-section) for a filing fee of $10. By living on it for five years, improving it, and paying a nominal fee of $1.25 an acre, a homesteader could take possession of permanent title.

The Homestead Act marked a drastic departure from previous policy. Before the act, public land had been sold primarily for revenue. Now it was to be given away to encourage a rapid filling of what were considered to be empty spaces and to provide a stimulus to the family farm, still considered "the backbone of democracy." The new law was a godsend to farmers who could not afford to buy large holdings. During the forty years after its passage, about half a million families took advantage of the Homestead Act to carve out new homes in the vast stretches of open frontier. Yet five times that many *purchased* their land from the railroads, the land companies, or the states (refer to Figure 22.1).

The Homestead Act often turned out to be a cruel hoax. The standard 160 acres, quite adequate in the humid East and the well-watered Mississippi basin, frequently proved pitifully inadequate on the rain-starved, sun-blistered side of the continent. Thousands of homesteaders, perhaps two out of three, were forced to give up the one-sided struggle against drought. Uncle Sam, it was said, bet 160 acres against ten dollars that the settlers could not live on their homesteads for five

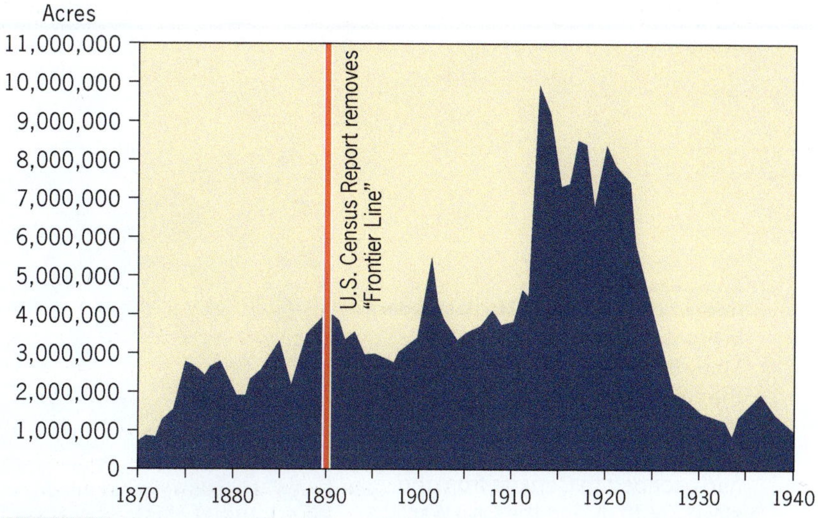

Figure 22.1 Homesteads from Public Lands This chart illustrates acreage legally transferred to individual ownership. By 1890, white homesteads and settlements had pushed so far westward that the Census Bureau no longer referenced a "frontier line" in its reporting.

In making the arduous journey across the western prairies, many women settlers discovered new confidence in their abilities. Early on in her trek, Mary Richardson Walker (1811–1897) confided in her diary that

"my circumstances are rather trying. So much danger attends me on every hand. A long journey before me, going I know not whither, without mother or sister to attend me, can I expect to survive it all?"

Only a month later, she recorded that

"in the afternoon we rode thirty-five miles without stopping. Pretty well tired out, all of us. Stood it pretty well myself."

years. One of these unsuccessful gambles in Greer County, western Oklahoma, inspired a folk song:

> Hurrah for Greer County! The land of the free,
> The land of the bedbug, grasshopper, and flea;
> I'll sing of its praises, I'll tell of its fame,
> While starving to death on my government claim.

Naked fraud was the unwanted offspring of the Homestead Act. Perhaps ten times more of the public domain wound up in the clutches of land-grabbing promoters than in the hands of bona fide small farmers. Unscrupulous corporations would use dummy homesteaders—often their employees or unwitting immigrants bribed with cash or a bottle of beer—to grab the best properties containing timber, minerals, and oil. Settlers would later swear that they had "improved" the property by erecting a "twelve by fourteen" dwelling, which turned out to measure twelve by fourteen *inches*.

The railways also played a major role in driving enthusiasm for Western settlement (refer to "Examining the Evidence: Robert Louis Stevenson's Transcontinental Journey, 1879," p. 557). Some railroad companies induced Americans as well as European immigrants to buy the cheap land earlier granted to the railroads by the government. The Northern Pacific Railroad at one time had nearly a thousand paid agents in Europe distributing roseate leaflets in various languages.

Early settler successes on windswept "tall-grass" prairies of the Midwest opened the gateways to the agricultural West even wider. These eastern reaches of the Plains were for the most part treeless, and the tough sod had been pounded solid by millions of buffalo hooves. Early European explorers and trappers had assumed that the soil must be sterile, simply because it was not heavily watered and did not support immense forests. But once the prairie sod was broken with heavy iron plows pulled by four yokes of oxen—the "plow that broke the plains"—the earth proved astonishingly fruitful. *Sodbusters* poured onto the land. Lacking trees for lumber and fuel, they built homes from the very sod they dug from the ground and burned corncobs for warmth (refer to Image 22.13). But farther westward, on the short-grass prairies in the "rain-shadow" of the Rocky Mountains, conditions proved considerably more challenging.

Lured by higher wheat prices resulting from crop failures elsewhere in the world, settlers in the 1870s rashly pushed yet farther toward the sunset, onto the poor, marginal lands beyond the **100th meridian**. That imaginary line, running north to south from the Dakotas through west Texas, separated two climatological regions—a well-watered area to the east, and a semiarid area to the

Image 22.13 Nebraska Homesteaders in Front of Their Sod House, 1887 Many Black Americans joined in the westward migration of the late nineteenth century. These two brothers and their families had escaped to Canada from the slave South during the Civil War. Returning to the United States in the 1880s, they took advantage of the Homestead Act to stake out farms in Custer County, Nebraska.

Nebraska State Historical Society

Examining the Evidence

Robert Louis Stevenson's Transcontinental Journey, 1879

The celebrated Scottish writer Robert Louis Stevenson, author of such enduring classics as *Treasure Island, Kidnapped*, and *The Strange Case of Dr. Jekyll and Mr. Hyde*, journeyed from Scotland to California in 1879 to rendezvous with his American fiancée, Frances Osbourne. Between New York and San Francisco, Stevenson traveled on the transcontinental railroad line completed just ten years earlier, and he dutifully recorded his impressions of America, the West in particular, as he made his way toward California. Stevenson's account of his trip provides an unusually gifted writer's vivid portrait of the trans-Mississippi West at the close of the era of the Indian wars. Like all travelogues, Stevenson's colorful tale may reveal as much about the traveler as it does about the things he saw. Yet historians frequently make use of such documents to reconstruct the original appearance and texture of places that were once the exotic destinations of adventurous travelers, before they were transformed by the onrush of modernity. In the passages reproduced here, inspired by the view as Stevenson's train passed through Nebraska and Wyoming, what features of the landscape does the author find most remarkable? How does he portray the railroad?

Source: Robert Louis Stevenson, *Across the Plains* (New York: Charles Scribner's Sons, 1897).

The Plains of Nebraska

. . .We were at sea—there is no other adequate expression—on the plains of Nebraska. . . . It was a world almost without a feature; an empty sky, an empty earth; front and back, the line of railway stretched from horizon to horizon, like a cue across a billiard-board; on either hand, the green plain ran till it touched the skirts of heaven. . . . [G]razing beasts were seen upon the prairie at all degrees of distance and diminution; and now and again we might perceive a few dots beside the railroad which grew more and more distinct as we drew nearer till they turned into wooden cabins, and then dwindled and dwindled in our wake until they melted into their surroundings, and we were once more alone upon the billiard-board. The train toiled over this infinity like a snail; and being the one thing moving, it was wonderful what huge proportions it began to assume in our regard. . . .

[That] evening we left Laramie [Wyoming]. . . . And yet when day came, it was to shine upon the same broken and unsightly quarter of the world. Mile upon mile, and not a tree, a bird, or a river. Only down the long, sterile cañons, the train shot hooting and awoke the resting echo. That train was the one piece of life in all the deadly land; it was the one actor, the one spectacle fit to be observed in this paralysis of man and nature. And when I think how the railroad has been pushed through this unwatered wilderness and haunt of savage tribes, and now will bear an emigrant for some £12 from the Atlantic to the Golden Gates; how at each stage of the construction, roaring, impromptu cities, full of gold and lust and death, sprang up and then died away again, and are now but wayside stations in the desert; how in these uncouth places pig-tailed Chinese pirates worked side by side with border ruffians and broken men from Europe, talking together in a mixed dialect, mostly oaths, gambling, drinking, quarrelling and murdering like wolves; how the plumed hereditary lord of all America heard, in this last fastness, the scream of the 'bad medicine waggon' charioting his foes; and then when I go on to remember that all this epical turmoil was conducted by gentlemen in frock coats, and with a view to nothing more extraordinary than a fortune and a subsequent visit to Paris, it seems to me, I own, as if this railway were the one typical achievement of the age in which we live, as if it brought together into one plot all the ends of the world and all the degrees of social rank, and offered to some great writer the busiest, the most extended, and the most varied subject for an enduring literary work. . . .

west (refer to Map 22.4). Bewhiskered and one-armed geologist John Wesley Powell, explorer of the Colorado River's Grand Canyon and later director of the U.S. Geological Survey, warned in his seminal 1878 ***Report on the Lands of the Arid Region of the United States*** that beyond the 100th meridian so little rain fell that agriculture was impossible without massive irrigation.

Ignoring Powell's advice, farmers embraced the delusion that "rain follows the plow," and heedlessly chewed up the crusty earth in western Kansas, eastern Colorado, and Montana. They quickly went broke as a six-year drought in the 1880s further desiccated the already dusty region. Western Kansas lost half its population between 1888 and 1892. "There is no God west of Salina," one hapless homesteader declared.

In the wake of the devastating drought, the new technique of "dry farming" took root on the Great Plains. Its methods of frequent shallow cultivation supposedly were adapted to the arid western environment, but over time, dry farming created a finely pulverized surface soil that contributed to the notorious "Dust Bowl" several decades later (refer to "30-11 Dust Bowls and Black Blizzards," pp. 794–796).

Map 22.4 Average Annual Precipitation, with Major Agricultural Products, 1900 Northern Hemisphere storms typically circle the globe in a west-to-east direction. Much of the life-nourishing water in these storms is dumped as rainfall on the western slopes of the Pacific coastal ranges and the Rocky Mountains, casting huge "rain shadows" in the Great Basin and in the western Great Plains, up to the line of the 100th meridian. Westward-faring pioneers had to learn new agricultural techniques when they pushed settlement into the drought-prone regions west of the 100th meridian, as reflected in the patterns of crop distribution by 1900.

Other adaptations to the western environment were more successful. Tough strains of wheat, resistant to cold and drought, were imported from Russia and blossomed into billowing yellow carpets. Wise farmers abandoned corn in favor of sorghum and other drought-resistant grains. Barbed wire solved the problem of how to build fences on the treeless prairies. But much of the water-scarce West remained idle and thinly peopled until well into the twentieth century.

Eventually federally financed irrigation projects—on a colossal scale, beyond even what John Wesley Powell had dreamed—caused the Great American Desert to bloom. A century after Powell's predictions, arching dams had tamed the Missouri and Columbia Rivers and had so penned up and diverted the canyon-gnawing Colorado that its mouth in the Gulf of California was dry. More than 45 million acres were irrigated in seventeen western states. In the long run, the hydraulic engineers had more to do with shaping the modern West than all the trappers, miners, cavalrymen, and cowboys there ever were (refer to Map 22.5). As one engineer boasted, "We enjoy pushing rivers around."

22-9 "Kill the Indian and Save the Man"

Sickened by the violent clashes between westward settlers and Indigenous groups, and disgusted with the corruption of unscrupulous federal agents tasked with managing the unruly frontier, President Grant announced a new "**Peace Policy**" in 1869. He appointed pious church-people, mostly Quakers, as Indian agents, with instructions to encourage Native people to "walk the white man's road." He also forbade military expeditions onto reservations. But Grant's well-meaning policy produced precious little peace. Indigenous peoples who had spent centuries developing mobile societies suitable to the Plains' ecology had little interest in settling down as farmers and attempting to eke a living from its windswept and arid soil. Confined to ever-shrinking territories, bands of Native Americans often "went off the reservation," inflaming white settlers, who then called for military assistance—or took matters into their own well-armed hands.

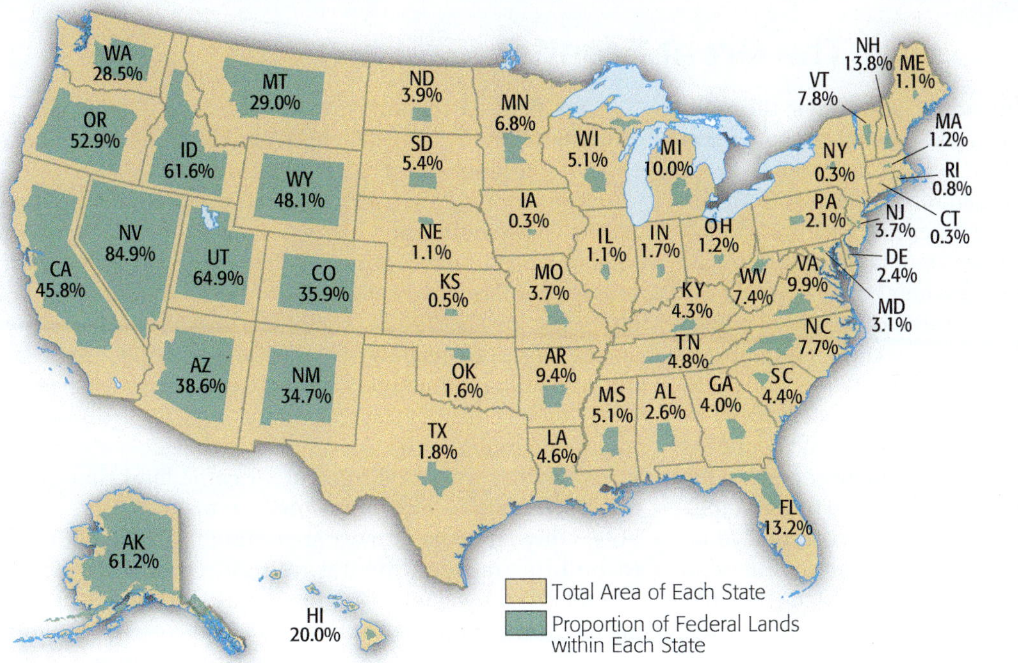

Map 22.5 Myth and Reality in the West: Percentage of Federal Lands Within Each State, 2013 American folklore pictures the western United States as a land of rugged individualists who tamed the wild region with grit and brawn. The reality is that the federal government has long been by far the West's largest landowner—and that federal projects, especially dam building, have done more to shape the region than all the cowboys and sodbusters ever did. (Source: Bill Lane Center for the American West, Stanford University.)

Congress at last declared in 1871 that the United States would no longer recognize tribes as sovereign nations and would cease to make treaties with them. There ensued a long period of debate about Indian policy. Opinions differed sharply. Hard-liners continued to insist on forced containment and brutal suppression. Humanitarian reformers wanted to treat the first peoples kindly and encourage them to assimilate into white society. Neither side showed much respect for Native American cultures.

But the national conscience was beginning to stir uneasily over the plight of American Indians. Helen Hunt Jackson, a Massachusetts writer of children's literature, pricked the moral sense of Americans in 1881 when she published *A Century of Dishonor*. The book chronicled the sorry record of government ruthlessness and chicanery in dealing with Native Americans. Her later novel *Ramona* (1884), a love story about American discrimination against California Indians that idealized the supposedly kinder and gentler era of the Spanish missions, sold some 600,000 copies and further inspired sympathy for Native Americans.

The misbegotten offspring of the movement to reform Indian policy was the **Dawes Severalty Act** of 1887. Reflecting the assimilationist views of the reformers, the act dissolved many tribes as legal entities, wiped out tribal ownership of land, and offered land grants to individual family heads of 160 free acres—mirroring the provisions of the Homestead Act from a quarter-century earlier. The bar for success was set higher, however. If the grantees behaved themselves like "good" white settlers, they would get full title to their holdings, as well as U.S. citizenship, in twenty-five years, a probationary period that was later extended. Full citizenship was at last granted to all Native Americans only in 1924.

Former reservation land not allotted under the Dawes Act was to be sold to railroads and white settlers, with the proceeds used by the federal government to educate and "civilize" the Native peoples. This arrangement boosted a preexisting push to educate Native American children in boarding schools, separate from their parents and their tribes.

In 1879, the government had already funded the Carlisle Indian School in Pennsylvania, where Native American children were taught English and inculcated with white values and customs. "Kill the Indian and save the man" was the school founder's motto. Christian reformers, who often administered educational facilities on the reservations, sometimes withheld food to force Native people to give up their tribal religions and assimilate to white society. Learning and speaking Indigenous languages was prohibited. In the 1890s the federal government expanded its network of Indian boarding schools and sent "field matrons" to the reservations to teach Native American women the art of sewing and to preach the virtues of chastity and hygiene.

These measures aimed at creating "rugged individualists" struck directly at traditional tribal organization. The Dawes Act ignored the inherent reliance of Native culture on tribally held

Thinking Globally

The Great Frontiers

The American pioneers who surged westward in the nineteenth century were part of a great global land grab that changed lives and landscapes on several continents. From the Australian Outback to the Canadian prairies, from the Argentine pampas to the Russian steppes and the African savannas, millions of mostly white settlers poured into vast new territories and claimed them as their own.

Everywhere, the settlers encountered Indigenous peoples who had lived on those lands since time immemorial. With their superiority in weaponry, transportation, and political organization, everywhere the newcomers prevailed. By the century's close, they had displaced or destroyed countless native peoples and extended their dominion over parts of the planet once considered too remote or rugged to be habitable.

The American frontier soon became the stuff of legend, and even the subject of a scholarly explanation of American uniqueness—Frederick Jackson Turner's fabled "frontier thesis," which hailed the gumption and moxie of the pioneers and commended them as the agents of civilization and democracy. Yet far from being unique, those westering Americans had much in common with settlers in sister societies abroad. Argentina had its cowboys (gauchos), and Australia had its colorful backcountry outlaws, such as Ned Kelly, whose exploits rivaled those of Billy the Kid. The Russians and South Africans had their own versions of "Manifest Destiny," and like the Americans they often cloaked them in the language of racial superiority.

The world's various frontiers also reflected the particularities of geography and history. Australians soon conceded that much of their continent—the world's driest—was too arid for traditional farming. Most of the Outback proved suitable only for enormous "sheep stations," sometimes measuring tens of thousands of acres. Consequently, small-farm homesteading of the American and Canadian type never took root, nor did cities of any consequence emerge in the parched Australian interior.

Canada's westward movement came later than that in the United States and proceeded somewhat more peaceably. Only after the Ottawa government promised in 1871 to build a transcontinental railroad connecting eastern Canada to its western provinces did settlement begin in earnest. And unlike in America, where restless pioneers typically struck out on their own and made much mischief among themselves and with the Indigenous peoples they encountered, in Canada settlers were generally preceded by government authorities—usually the red-jacketed North-West Mounted Police, or "Mounties"—who established at least a semblance of order before large numbers of

Library and Archives Canada/Royal Canadian Mounted Police fonds/a202180

Image 22.14 The Northwest Mounted Police on Parade, Calgary, Alberta, ca. 1901 Empowered by an act of Parliament in 1873 to establish Canadian authority and order in the Northwest Territories, this force made frontier settlement somewhat more peaceful in Canada than in the United States. In 1920 the North-West Mounted Police absorbed the Dominion Police and became the famed Royal Canadian Mounted Police, or "Mounties."

Image 22.15 Russian Peasants in Siberia, 1910

pioneers appeared on the scene. As a result, though friction between Canada's "First Nations" and white settlers was hardly unknown, and sometimes violent, Canada's frontier was markedly less turbulent than America's. Canada, then and now a more law-abiding society than the United States, never had a "Wild West" like that of its southern neighbor.

In Argentina and Russia, inherited patterns of landholding and politics shaped their nineteenth-century frontiers. When Argentina's General Julio Roca vanquished the native Araucanians in 1879, he flung open the horizonless pampas to white settlement. But he also retained the venerable custom, handed down from Spanish colonial times, of apportioning the land in gigantic *estancias* (ranches) to a few favored fellow soldiers and friends. These lordly landowners then employed wage workers, mostly Italian immigrants, who turned the fertile Argentine interior into a beef bowl and breadbasket to the world. The immigrants themselves, however, had little hope of ever possessing land of their own.

Russia's frontier lay to the east and long felt the heavy hand of the tsar. For centuries autocratic rulers had strong-armed landowning nobles to move their serfs onto the "virgin lands" beyond the settled edge of European Russia. By the nineteenth century, imperial Russia had pushed its frontier onto the rolling steppes of central Asia, home to Tartars, Kalmyks, Kazakhs, and myriad other Indigenous peoples. Only military conquest and a strengthened state bureaucracy made possible European settlement in those regions. Between 1867 and 1897, more than a million of the tsar's subjects left for the hinterland. As elsewhere, the railroad proved essential to the growth of the tsarist empire, especially after the government began construction of the Trans-Siberian line in 1891.

The Dutch-descended Afrikaners, or Boers, in southern Africa found their frontier to the north, and unlike their American counterparts, they made scant claim to be spreading democracy. Rather, they sought to escape British rule in the Cape Colony—in particular, to escape from the threat of racial equality for Black people after Britain abolished slavery in the 1830s. The Afrikaners' "Great Trek" took them into the land of the Zulus, who ferociously resisted the oncoming Boers but eventually, like Indigenous peoples everywhere, were forced to submit to white rule.

In the Americas, Australia, Asia, and Africa, the great frontier of the nineteenth century was the companion of conquest. The frontier brought opportunity to some and oppression to others. In many places it nurtured democracy; elsewhere it invigorated autocracy. And everywhere it expanded the domains of European civilization—for better or worse.

Image 22.16 Lakotas Receiving Rations at Standing Rock Reservation, ca. 1881 Once the scourge of the plains, the Lakota (part of the Sioux tribes) were reduced by the 1890s to the humiliation of living on government handouts.

resources, literally pulling the land out from under them (refer to Image 22.16). By 1900, Indigenous Americans had lost 50 percent of the 156 million acres they had held just two decades earlier (refer to Map 22.6). The forced-assimilation doctrine remained the cornerstone of the government's policy for nearly half a century, until the Indian Reorganization Act (the "Indian New Deal") of 1934 partially reversed the individualistic approach and belatedly tried to restore the tribal basis of Indigenous life (refer to "30-11 Dust Bowls and Black Blizzards," pp. 794–796).

Paternalistic reformers, convinced that they knew better than the Native people themselves what was good for them, also moved aggressively to suppress the "Ghost Dance," a religious movement that swept through the western tribes beginning in 1889. When it spread to the Lakota people in 1890, the U.S. Army bloodily stamped it out at the **Wounded Knee Massacre**. Soldiers killed an estimated two hundred mostly defenseless Lakota men, women, and children. Some thirty troopers also died. At least twenty of them were awarded the Congressional Medal of Honor, recognition hotly contested at the time and controversial ever since.

The violence, disease, and social upheaval of the era reduced the Native population by 1890 to about 248,000, or 0.004 percent of the U.S. population. Yet efforts to assimilate if not annihilate American Indian culture and identity did not succeed. The 2020 U.S. Census counted 9.7 million persons who identified as Native American alone or in combination, nearly 3 percent of the total.

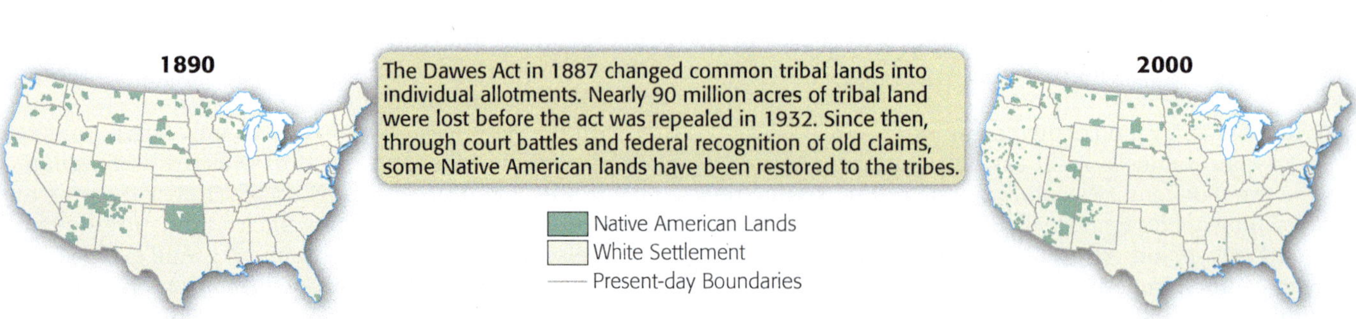

Map 22.6 Vanishing Lands Once masters of the continent, Native Americans have been squeezed into just 2 percent of U.S. territory.

Contending Voices

The Ghost Dance and the Wounded Knee Massacre

James McLaughlin (1842–1923), a U.S. Indian Service agent involved in events precipitating the bloody 1890 confrontation at Wounded Knee, depicted the Sioux's "Ghost Dance" as a dangerous practice hindering their assimilation and progress:

"The [Ghost Dance] doctrine was artfully framed to appeal to the cupidity of the Indian and to inflame him against the whites, carrying with it promise of return to the free life, with plenty of buffalo and no prospect of work. . . . A more pernicious system of religion could not have been offered to a people who stood on the threshold of civilization, and who hungered for a realization of dreams that would free them from present poverty, probable hunger, and the prospect of toil."

The Cheyenne Indian Porcupine described the Ghost Dance in the following terms:

"If we dance, our gardens will grow nice and we will never get sick or crazy. We must not quarrel or scold each other. We must not hate each other. Must love each other. We must love all the world. . . . I must not tell lies. We must work; if the white man asks us to work we must say yes and not no. . . . [We] must not quarrel with the whites or kill them. We must dance. If we don't dance we will get crazy and poor."

Consider This:

What alternative paths might U.S.-Indian relations have followed during the era of America's intensive westward expansion?

22-10 The Far West Comes of Age

The territories of the Great West experienced a remarkable surge to statehood as the nineteenth century came to a close. Booming Colorado, offspring of the Pikes Peak gold rush, proudly joined the Union in 1876 as "the Centennial State." In 1889–1890, a Republican Congress, eagerly seeking more Republican electoral and congressional votes, admitted in a wholesale lot six new states: North Dakota, South Dakota, Montana, Washington, Idaho, and Wyoming. The Mormon Church formally banned polygamy in 1890, paving the way for Utah's admission to statehood in 1896. Only Oklahoma, New Mexico, and Arizona remained to be lifted into statehood from contiguous territory on the mainland of North America.

In a last grand gesture, heedless of prior promises to Native American peoples, the federal government made available to settlers vast stretches of fertile plains in the district of Oklahoma (Choctaw for "red people"). This terminus of the Trail of Tears had been promised decades earlier to the Cherokee, Muscogee, Seminole, Chickasaw and Choctaw peoples removed from the Southeast. Scores of overeager and well-armed "sooners," illegally jumping the gun, entered Oklahoma Territory soon after the announcement that Oklahoma would now become settler land. They had to be evicted repeatedly by federal troops, who on occasion would shoot the intruders' horses.

On April 22, 1889, all was in readiness for the legal opening, and some fifty thousand "boomers" were poised expectantly on the boundary line. At high noon the bugle shrilled, and a horde of "eighty-niners" poured in on lathered horses or careening vehicles. That night a lonely spot on the prairie had mushroomed into the tent city of Guthrie, with over 10,000 people. By the end of the year, Oklahoma boasted more than 65,000 non-Native inhabitants, and Congress made it a territory. Native Americans, now less than 20 percent of the territory's population, tried and failed to carve out their own separate state of Sequoyah, but in 1907 Oklahoma became the "Sooner State."

The Native spokesman Plenty Coups (1848–1932) said in 1909,

"I see no longer the curling smoke rising from our lodge poles. I hear no longer the songs of the women as they prepare the meal. The antelope have gone; the buffalo wallows are empty. Only the wail of the coyote is heard. The white man's medicine is stronger than ours. . . . We are like birds with a broken wing."

Image 22.17 Working Women of the West Women as well as men toiled daily in the Great Plains, serving as homestead farmers and teachers in addition to performing domestic duties. This woman is gathering buffalo chips in a wheelbarrow, to be used for fuel.

22-11 The Fading Frontier

In 1890, the superintendent of the census announced that for the first time in America's experience, a frontier line was no longer discernible. All the unsettled areas were now broken into by isolated bodies of American settlement (refer to Image 22.17). This "closing" of the frontier inspired one of the most influential and hotly debated essays ever written about American history—Frederick Jackson Turner's "The Significance of the Frontier in American History" in 1893 (refer to "Thinking Globally: The Great Frontier," pp. 560–561).

The secretary of war had prophesied in 1827 that five hundred years would be needed to fill the West. But as the westward-tramping nation finally recognized that the continent's land was not inexhaustible, seeds were planted to preserve the vanishing resource. The government set aside land for national parks—first Yellowstone in 1872, followed by Yosemite and Sequoia in 1890, and several more in the decades to follow.

Throughout the nineteenth century, the western frontier had been touted—by politicians and presidents, writers and artists, journalists and promoters—as a symbol of opportunity, and as something essential to American identity. Its supposed passing was declared by some of the same tastemakers to mark the end of a romantic phase of the nation's internal development and the arrival of vexing economic and psychological problems.

For many white Americans of the nineteenth century, the frontier allegedly functioned as a safety valve for a growing nation with a surging, diverse population and a boom-and-bust capitalist economy. The theory was that when hard times came, the unemployed who cluttered the city pavements merely moved west, took up farming, and prospered. In truth, relatively few city dwellers, at least in the populous eastern centers, migrated to the frontier during depressions. Most of them did not know how to farm; few of them could raise enough money to transport themselves westward and then pay for livestock and expensive machinery.

Yet free acreage did lure to the West a host of immigrant farmers who otherwise might have remained in the eastern cities to clog the job markets and to crowd the festering and already overpopulated slums. And the very *possibility* of westward migration may have induced urban employers to maintain wage rates high enough to discourage workers from leaving.

By the late nineteenth century, however, the real safety valve was not the rural homestead but in western cities like Chicago, Denver, and San Francisco. There, failed farmers, busted miners, and displaced Easterners found ways to seek their fortunes. Indeed, after about 1880 the area from the Rocky Mountains to the Pacific Coast was the most urbanized region in America, measured by the percentage of people living in cities—and has remained so ever since.

Varying Viewpoints

Was the West Really "Won"?

For more than half a century, the Turner thesis dominated historical writing about the West. In his famous essay of 1893, "The Significance of the Frontier in American History," historian Frederick Jackson Turner argued that the frontier experience molded both region and nation. Not only the West, Turner insisted, but the national character had been uniquely shaped by the westward movement. Pioneers had brought the raw West into the embrace of civilization. And the struggle to overcome the challenges of the western wilderness—including distance, deserts, drought, and Indians—had transformed *Europeans* into tough, inventive, and self-reliant *Americans*.

Turner's thesis raised a question that Americans found especially intriguing in 1893. Just three years earlier, the superintendent of the census declared that the frontier, defined as the boundary of a zone with little or no settled population, had closed forever. What new forces, Turner asked, would shape a distinctive American national character, now that the testing ground of the frontier had been plowed and tamed?

Turner's hypothesis that the American character was forged in the western wilderness is surely among the most provocative statements ever made about the formative influences on the nation's development. But as the frontier era recedes ever further into the past, scholars are less persuaded that Turner's thesis adequately explains the national character. American society is still conspicuously different from European and other cultures, even though Turner's frontier disappeared more than a century ago.

Modern scholars charge that Turner based his thesis on several questionable assumptions. Historian David J. Weber, for example, suggests that the line of the frontier did not define the quavering edge of "civilization" but marked the boundary between diverse cultures, each with its own claims to legitimacy and, indeed, to legitimate possession of the land. The frontier should therefore be understood not as the place where "civilization" triumphed over "savagery," but as the principal site of interaction between those cultures.

Several so-called New Western historians take this argument still further. Scholars such as Patricia Nelson Limerick, Richard White, and Donald Worster suggest that the cultural and ecological damage inflicted by advancing "civilization" must be reckoned with in any final accounting of what the pioneers accomplished. These same scholars insist that the West did not lose its regional identity after the frontier line was no longer recognizable in 1890. The West, they argue, is still a unique part of the national mosaic, a region whose history, culture, and identity remain every bit as distinctive as those of New England or the Old South.

But where Turner saw the frontier as the principal shaper of the region's character, the New Western historians emphasize the effects of ethnic and racial confrontation, topography, climate, and the roles of government and big business as the factors that have made the modern West. They thus reject Turner's east-to-west, Anglocentric narrative on the triumphal civilizing of the wilderness. As they see the matter, European and American settlers did not tame the West, but rather conquered it through suppressing the Native American and Hispanic peoples who had preceded them into the region. But those conquests were less than complete, so the argument goes, and the West therefore remains, uniquely among American regions, a perpetual **borderland**, an unsettled arena of commingling and competition among those groups. Moreover, in these accounts the West's distinctively challenging climate and geography yielded to human habitation not through the efforts of heroic individual pioneers, but only through massive corporate and federal investments in transportation systems (like the transcontinental railroad and the Interstate Highway System) and irrigation projects (like the watering of California's Central Valley). Such developments still give western life its special character today.

Frederick Jackson Turner declared, "American history has been in a large degree the history of the colonization of the Great West." Indeed, the seizing and settling the trans-Mississippi West in the late nineteenth century was but the last chapter in a saga of westward movement by European-Americans since Columbus's landing—from the West Indies to the Chesapeake shore, from the valleys of the Hudson and Connecticut Rivers to the valleys of the Tennessee and Ohio Rivers.

And yet the movement of white Americans into the trans-Mississippi West stands apart. There, Native American peoples and U.S. soldiers waged exceptionally bitter and violent battles over control of territory, and there most Native Americans live today. There "Anglo" culture connected and collided most directly with "Hispanic" culture—the historic rival of the Anglo-Americans for dominance in the New World. The Southwest remains the most Hispanicized region in America. There America faced across the Pacific to Asia, and the West has long been home to the nation's largest and most deeply rooted communities of Asian Americans. There the scale and severity of the environment posed their largest challenges to human ambitions to "tame" it with farming, mining, logging, and ranching. There the environment, with its aridity and still-magical emptiness, continues to mold social and political life, its droughts and wildfires among the most dramatic harbingers of a changing climate. And although the popular mythos of the Great West revolves around rugged individualism—of lone cowboys, swashbuckling outlaws, heroic homesteaders—in no other region has the federal government been such a consequential engine of development. With its territorial wars against Native American peoples and the vast landholdings that resulted, with its subsidies to the railroads and later massive irrigation projects, the U.S. government shaped the West's economic and social landscape to a degree unmatched in any other region, far more than many Americans recognize.

The westward-moving pioneers and the country they confronted assumed mythic proportions in the American mind. They were immortalized by such writers as Bret Harte, Mark Twain, Helen Hunt Jackson, and Francis Parkman, and by such painters as George Catlin, Frederic Remington, and Albert Bierstadt. Hollywood westerns popularized a mythic frontier where lone cowboys and rugged homesteaders were the heroes, and Indigenous peoples the villains or victims. The terms *pioneer* and *frontier* still connote dreaming big and daring greatly—whether launching rockets into space or conquering a deadly disease.

Turner's "frontier thesis" long ago lost its hold among historians. The environmental and human costs of the relentless push across the continent, especially those borne by Native people, are now more broadly acknowledged. Some of these harms are beginning to be remedied. For better or worse, the past planting of American civilization in the immense western wilderness continues to shape America's present.

Chapter Summary

At the close of the Civil War, the Great Plains and Mountain West were still controlled by Native Americans who hunted buffalo on horseback and fiercely resisted white encroachment on their land and way of life. But the coming of the transcontinental railroad and white settlers' farming, mining, and grazing gradually broke up the Native Americans' land, while disease and the destruction of the buffalo reduced their numbers and ended their way of life. After a series of sharp military clashes, the federal government eventually forced Native Americans onto largely barren reservations.

Attempting to coerce Native Americans into adopting white ways, Congress passed the Dawes Act, which eliminated tribal ownership of land, while often insensitive "humanitarians" created a network of Native American boarding schools that further assaulted traditional culture.

The mining and cattle frontiers created colorful chapters in the history of the American West, but small operators in these fields eventually gave way to large-scale corporate businesses. Farmers carried out the final phase of settlement, lured by free homesteads, railroads, and irrigation. Beginning in the 1870s, farmers began pushing onto the treeless prairies beyond the 100th meridian, using techniques of dry farming that gradually contributed to soil erosion. Irrigation projects, later financed by the federal government, allowed specialized forms of farming in some areas of the arid West to flourish.

The census declared the end of the frontier in 1890, concluding a formative phase of American history. The frontier was less of a safety valve for American class conflict than many believed, but it did have some impact on keeping American wage rates relatively high. The newest western frontier was actually in western cities, which helped make the West the most urbanized (by percentage) region of the United States by the 1890s. Though the frontier's closing signified the end of traditional westward expansion, the Great West remained a distinctively diverse demographic, social, and environmental region of the nation.

Key Terms

- reservation system (547)
- Sand Creek Massacre (549)
- Greasy Grass (Little Bighorn), Battle of the (550)
- mining industry (553)
- 100th meridian (556)
- *Report on the Lands of the Arid Region of the United States* (557)
- Peace Policy (558)
- Dawes Severalty Act (559)
- Wounded Knee Massacre (562)
- borderland (565)

People to Know

- Leland Stanford
- Collis P. Huntington
- Frederick Jackson Turner
- Red Cloud (Mahpíya Lúta)
- Sitting Bull (Tatanka-Iyotanka)
- Chief Joseph (Heinmot Tooyalakekt)
- Geronimo (Goyaałé)
- George Armstrong Custer
- John Wesley Powell

Chronology

ca. 1700–1800	• New Indigenous peoples move onto Great Plains
1858	• Pikes Peak gold rush
1859	• Nevada Comstock Lode discovered
1862	• Homestead Act
1864	• Sand Creek massacre • Nevada admitted to Union
1876	• Battle of the Little Bighorn • Colorado admitted to Union
1877	• Nez Perce war
1881	• Helen Hunt Jackson publishes *A Century of Dishonor*
1884	• Federal government outlaws Native American Sun Dance
1885	• Canadian Pacific Railway, first transcontinental rail line, completed across Canada
1887	• Dawes Severalty Act
1889	• Oklahoma opened to U.S. citizen settlement
1889–1890	• North Dakota, South Dakota, Montana, Washington, Idaho, and Wyoming admitted to Union
1890	• Census Bureau declares frontier line ended • Battle of Wounded Knee
1891	• Construction of Trans-Siberian Railroad begins
1893	• Frederick Jackson Turner publishes "The Significance of the Frontier in American History"
1907	• Oklahoma admitted to Union
1924	• Native Americans granted U.S. citizenship
1934	• Indian Reorganization Act

To Learn More

Dee Brown, *Bury My Heart at Wounded Knee: An Indian History of the American West* (1970)

William Cronon, *Nature's Metropolis: Chicago and the Great West* (1991)

Jared Farmer, *On Zion's Mount: Mormons, Indians, and the American Landscape* (2008)

Manu Karuka, *Empire's Tracks: Indigenous Nations, Chinese Workers, and the Transcontinental Railroad* (2019)

Ari Kelman, *Misplaced Massacre* (2013)

Patricia Nelson Limerick, *Legacy of Conquest: The Unbroken Past of the American West* (1987)

John Wesley Powell, *Report on the Lands of the Arid Region of the United States* (1879)

Daniel Sharfstein, *Thunder in the Mountains: Chief Joseph, Oliver Otis Howard, and the Nez Perce War* (2017)

Frederick Jackson Turner, "The Significance of the Frontier in American History" (1893)

Louis S. Warren, *Buffalo Bill's America: William Cody and the Wild West Show* (2006)

________, *God's Red Son: The Ghost Dance Religion and the Making of Modern America* (2017)

Elliott West, *The Contested Plains: Indians, Goldseekers, and the Rush to Colorado* (1998)

________, *The Last Indian War* (2009)

Richard White, *"It's Your Misfortune and None of My Own": A New History of the American West* (1991)

________, *Railroaded: The Transcontinentals and the Making of Modern America* (2011)

Chapter 23

The Industrial Era Dawns: 1865–1900

The wealthy class is becoming more wealthy; but the poorer class is becoming more dependent. The gulf between the employed and the employer is growing wider; social contrasts are becoming sharper; as liveried carriages appear; so do barefooted children.

Henry George, 1879

Chapter Outline

- The railroad boom
- Speculators and financiers
- Early efforts at government regulation
- The rise of mass production
- Lords of industry
- The gospel of wealth
- Reining in the trusts
- Industry in the South
- Widening inequality
- The laboring classes
- The rise of trade unions

Examining the Evidence: The Photography of Lewis W. Hine

Makers of America: The Knights of Labor

Varying Viewpoints: Industrialization: Boon or Blight?

In the post–Civil War decades, America's Industrial Revolution roared into high gear. Generous government subsidies and transformative new technologies brought forth a unified, continent-size domestic market. With change on a scale that amounted to nothing less than an economic revolution came a widening wealth and income gap, as well as new challenges to traditional ways of life, political institutions, and constitutional norms.

As late as 1870, agriculture remained the nation's biggest business. But by 1900, it accounted for less than half of the national economy, as manufacturing industries boomed. Until the end of the Civil War, the United States imported more merchandise than it exported. By 1900, U.S. factories annually delivered more than $600 million worth of manufactured goods to the world's marketplaces.

A nation of farmers and independent producers was becoming a nation of wage earners. In 1860, half of all workers were self-employed. By the century's end, two of every three working Americans depended on an employer to pay their wages. Workers formed unions to fight for better pay and working conditions, but faced stiff corporate and government opposition. Organized labor embraced only about 3 percent of working people by 1900.

Americans did not achieve economic transformation in isolation. Foreign investment, immigrant labor, international trade, and imported technologies helped to make it possible. By century's end, the lives of millions of Americans had been forever altered—and the United States was about to stand up before the world as an industrial colossus.

Focus Questions

1. How did the transcontinental railroad network promote the post–Civil War transformation of American society?
2. How did the American economy come to be dominated by monopolistic corporations in industries such as steel and oil, and what was the public and governmental response to these huge combinations?
3. Why was the South generally excluded from industrial development, and how did racial and class conflict shape the still largely rural region?

4. How did industrialization alter American society, particularly the role of the working class and of women?
5. What obstacles did late-nineteenth-century American labor unions face in mobilizing American workers?

23-1 The Iron Horse Spans the Continent

The rise of the railroad was central to the nation's propulsive economic expansion (refer to Figure 23.1). Completion of the transcontinental line—a magnificent engineering feat for that day—was one of America's most impressive peacetime undertakings. It welded the West Coast

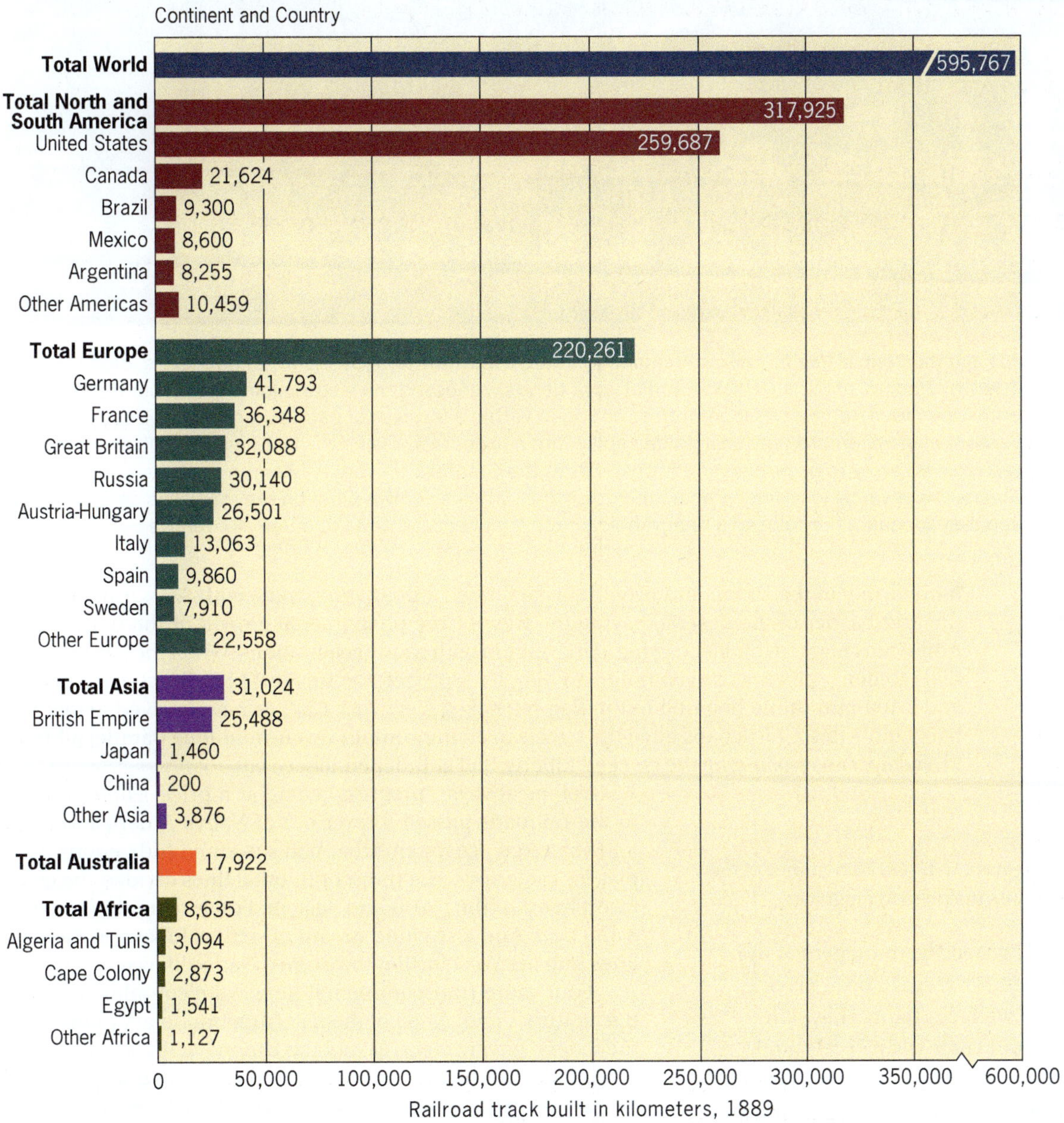

Figure 23.1 Railroads Worldwide, 1889 By the close of the nineteenth century, the United States had more miles of railroad track than all of Europe combined, and much of the new trackage ran west of the Mississippi. This trend continued into the new century. A 1904 calculation of railway track per 10,000 inhabitants in 1904 found that the United States had 26.4 miles of track compared to 15.2 miles for the second-place country, Sweden. Much further behind were the major western European nations of France (7.3), Germany (6.1), and Great Britain and Ireland (5.4).

Sources: Henry Poor, *Poor's Manual of the Railroads of the United States for 1891* (1891); Slason Thompson, *Railway Statistics of the United States of America for the Year Ending June 30, 1906, Compared with the Official Reports of 1905 and Recent Statistics of Foreign Railways (1907).*

Image 23.1 **The Union Pacific and the Central Pacific Link at Promontory Point, Utah, May 10, 1869** Railroad financiers, dignitaries, spectators, and Chinese (Central Pacific) and Irish (Union Pacific) work gangs witnessed the historic joining that created the nation's first transcontinental railroad. After the two locomotives chugged within a few feet of each other, Central Pacific chief and former California governor Leland Stanford tapped a golden spike into a prepared hole on the last tie with a silver-plated maul. The golden spike was whisked away to be preserved for posterity at the Stanford University Museum, but the iron one that replaced it was hardly ordinary. It was wired to a Union Pacific telegraph line, while a copper plate on the maul was connected to a Central Pacific wire. When they touched, they closed a telegraphic circuit that sent the news to cities all over the country.

more firmly to the Union and eventually facilitated a flourishing trade with Asia. It penetrated the arid barrier of the deserts, paving the way for the phenomenal growth of the Great West. Americans marked this electrifying achievement with gaudy celebrations. When the last ceremonial (golden) spike was driven home on May 10, 1869 (refer to Image 23.1), church bells pealed and a 100-gun salute boomed out in flag-bedecked New York City, as news arrived across the telegraph wires. Chicagoans filled the streets in an impromptu seven-mile-long parade; jubilant Philadelphians again rang the cracked Liberty Bell at Independence Hall.

Yet, as always, "progress" came at a price. Land granted to the railroads passed forever out of Native American hands and shattered ecosystems that had sustained Indigenous peoples for millennia. The transcontinental lines divided the great bison herds of the plains and hastened their reduction to near-extinction. And a swelling stream of settlers following the raillines into the West further threatened Native lifeways.

Four more transcontinental lines were completed before the century's end. None of them secured monetary loans from the federal government, as had the Union Pacific and the Central Pacific. Still, all but the last received generous grants of land.

The Northern Pacific Railroad, stretching from Lake Superior to Puget Sound, reached its terminus in 1883. The Atchison, Topeka, and Santa Fe, snaking through the southwestern deserts to California, was completed in 1884. The Southern Pacific linked New Orleans to San Francisco. The Great Northern, which reached Seattle from Duluth in 1893, was the creation of a far-visioned Canadian American, "Empire Builder"

In 1892 James Baird Weaver (1833–1912), nominee of the Populists, wrote regarding the railroad magnates,

"In their delirium of greed the managers of our transportation systems disregard both private right and the public welfare. Today they will combine and bankrupt their weak rivals, and by the expenditure of a trifling sum possess themselves of properties which cost the outlay of millions. Tomorrow they will capitalize their booty for five times the cost, issue their bonds, and proceed to levy tariffs upon the people to pay dividends upon the fraud."

World History Archive/Alamy Stock Photo

Image 23.2 "Let 'em Rip, Commodore!" Millionaire magnates Cornelius Vanderbilt and James Fisk battled throughout 1868 and 1869 for control of the lucrative Erie Railroad, which ran between New York City and Chicago. Vanderbilt ultimately won the prize.

James J. Hill, a blunt, bearlike man who was probably the greatest railroad builder of all. Constructing multiple lines and diversifying into cattle ranching, factories, and finance, Hill amassed a great fortune and spurred the economic development of the Pacific Northwest. Unlike his rivals, Hill rode through later financial storms with flying colors.

As the western lines grew, older eastern networks combined and expanded. The largest was the New York Central, captained by burly, boisterous, and bewhiskered "Commodore" Cornelius Vanderbilt. Having made millions in steamboating, he cannily turned, in his late sixties, to a new career in railroading. The vast fortune produced by Vanderbilt's heavily traveled lines, including the first route between New York and Chicago, at one point made him the richest person in both America and Europe (refer to Image 23.2).

23-2 Technological Transformations

Technological improvements proved a boon to the railroads. Especially significant was the steel rail produced using the **Bessemer-Kelly Process**. This method was developed in the 1850s by British inventor Henry Bessemer, although Kentucky kettle manufacturer William Kelly had stumbled on it a few years earlier. Both men discovered that cold air blown on red-hot iron caused the metal to become white-hot by igniting the carbon and thus eliminating impurities. Converting iron to steel had long been a slow, expensive process. But the new "air boiling" technique was faster and cheaper, and it rolled out stronger steel. Vanderbilt helped popularize the method when he replaced the old iron tracks of the New York Central with the tougher metal. Other railroad barons followed. A standard gauge of track width further enabled a unified, national network during the postwar years, thus eliminating the expense and inconvenience of numerous changes from one line to another.

Other refinements played vital roles in railroading. The Westinghouse air brake enhanced both efficiency and safety. The Pullman Palace Cars, advertised as "gorgeous traveling hotels," began to carry well-heeled travelers in the 1860s. Alarmists condemned them as "wheeled torture chambers" and potential funeral pyres, however, for the wooden cars were equipped with swaying kerosene lamps. Appalling accidents continued to be almost daily tragedies, despite safety improvements.

The railroads emerged as the nation's biggest businesses, employing more people than any other industry. By 1891, the Pennsylvania Railroad alone had 110,000 employees—over three times the number of soldiers then enlisted in the U.S. Army.

Time itself was bent to the railroads' needs. Until the 1880s, every town in the United States had its own "local" time, dictated by the sun's position. When it was noon in Chicago, it was

11:50 A.M. in St. Louis and 12:18 P.M. in Detroit. For railroad operators worried about keeping schedules and avoiding wrecks, this patchwork of local times was a nightmare. Thus on November 18, 1883, the major rail lines decreed that the continent would henceforth be divided into four "time zones." Baffled Americans, dutifully resetting their clocks and watches, called it "the day of two noons."

23-3 Lords of the Rail

Some of the nation's richest men prior to the Civil War were slaveholding Southern planters. A raw new aristocracy of railroad men now replaced them. Their multiwebbed lines became the playthings of Wall Street, and financiers and stock speculators also amassed colossal wealth.

The public interest was frequently trampled underfoot as the railroad titans waged brutal wars for control of rails and markets. Vanderbilt, when told that the law stood in his way, reportedly exclaimed, "Law! What do I care about the law? Hain't I got the power?" On another occasion he supposedly threatened some associates: "I won't sue you, for the law is too slow. I'll ruin you." His son, William H. Vanderbilt, when asked in 1883 about the discontinuance of a fast mail train, reportedly snorted, "The public be damned!"

While dismissing the public, the railroaders blandly bought and sold people in public life. They bribed judges and legislatures, employed arm-twisting lobbyists, and elected their own "creatures" to high office. They showered free passes on journalists and politicians in profusion. One railroad man noted in 1885 that in the West "no man who has money, or official position, or influence thinks he ought to pay anything for riding on a railroad."

Railroad kings were, for a time, virtual industrial monarchs. As manipulators of a huge natural monopoly, they exercised more direct control over the lives of more people than did the president of the United States—and their terms were not limited to four years. They increasingly shunned the crude bloodletting of cutthroat competition and began to cooperate with one another to rule the railroad dominion. Sorely pressed to show at least some returns on their bloated investments, they entered into defensive alliances to protect precious profits.

The earliest form of combination was the "pool"—an agreement to divide the business in a given area and share the profits. Other rail barons granted secret rebates or kickbacks to powerful shippers in return for steady and assured traffic. Often they slashed their rates on routes where they faced competition, but they more than made up the difference on noncompeting ones, where they might actually charge more for a short haul than for a long one. As a result, small farmers usually paid the highest rates, while large customers got the best deals.

23-4 Government Bridles the Iron Horse

It was neither healthy nor politically acceptable that so many people should be at the mercy of so few. Impoverished farmers, especially in the Midwest, began to wonder if the nation had not escaped from the Slavery Power only to fall into the hands of the money power, as represented by the railroad plutocracy (refer to Image 23.3).

A jarring economic depression in the 1870s goaded some farmers into protesting against being "railroaded" into bankruptcy. Under pressure from organized agrarian groups like the Grange (Patrons of Husbandry), many midwestern legislatures tried to regulate the railroad monopoly. The scattered state efforts screeched to a halt in 1886. The Supreme Court, in the famed case of *Wabash, St. Louis & Pacific Railroad Company v. Illinois,* decreed that individual states had no power to regulate *inter*state commerce. If the mechanical monster were to be corralled, the federal government would have to do the job.

Congress therefore passed the epochal **Interstate Commerce Act** in 1887. It prohibited rebates and pools and required the railroads to publish their rates openly. It also forbade unfair discrimination against shippers and outlawed charging more for a short haul than for a long one over the same line. Most important, it set up the Interstate Commerce Commission (ICC) to administer and enforce the new legislation.

Despite acclaim, the Interstate Commerce Act emphatically did not represent a popular victory over corporate wealth. One of the leading corporation lawyers of the day, Richard Olney, shrewdly noted that the new commission "can be made of great use to the railroads. It satisfies the popular clamor for a government supervision of railroads, at the same time that such

Image 23.3 Robber Barons Cyrus Field, Jay Gould, Cornelius Vanderbilt, and Russell Sage Kept Afloat on the Broken Backs of America's Workingmen, 1883. Cheap and abundant labor fueled the enormous Gilded Age fortunes of financiers like Gould and Sage and shipping and railroad titans like Field and Vanderbilt. This 1883 cartoon reflects the growing public outcry at America's widening wealth inequality.

supervision is almost entirely nominal. . . . The part of wisdom is not to destroy the Commission, but to utilize it."

What the new legislation did do was to provide an orderly forum where competing business interests could resolve their conflicts in peaceable ways. The country could now avoid ruinous rate wars among the railroads and outraged, "confiscatory" attacks on the lines by pitchfork-prodded state legislatures. This was a modest accomplishment but by no means an unimportant one. The Interstate Commerce Act tended to stabilize, not revolutionize, the existing business system.

Yet the act still ranks as a red-letter law. It was the first large-scale attempt by Washington to regulate business in the interest of society at large. It reflected the rising dominance of federal authority over that of individual states. It heralded the arrival of a series of independent regulatory commissions in the next century, which would irrevocably commit the government to the daunting task of monitoring and guiding the private economy. It foreshadowed the doom of freewheeling, buccaneering business practices and served full notice that there was a public interest in private enterprise that government was bound to protect.

23-5 Miracles of Mechanization

Postwar industrial expansion, partly a result of the railroad network, rapidly began to assume mammoth proportions. When Lincoln was elected in 1860, the Republic ranked only fourth among the manufacturing nations of the world. By 1894, it had bounded into first place. Why the sudden upsurge?

Liquid capital, previously scarce, was now becoming abundant. The word *millionaire* had not been coined until the 1840s, and in 1861 only a handful of individuals were eligible for this class. But the Civil War, partly through profiteering, created immense fortunes. Foreign investors, chiefly British, contributed still more capital. Unlike in other countries, in America investor dollars flowed mostly into private hands, not public coffers.

Innovations in transportation fueled growth, too, by bringing the nation's amazingly abundant natural resources—particularly coal, oil, and iron—to the factory door. A shipping system through the Great Lakes carried rich iron ore from Minnesota's Mesabi Range to Chicago and Cleveland for refining. This priceless bonanza, where mountains of red-rusted ore could be scooped up by steam shovels, ultimately became a cornerstone of a vast steel empire. Copper, bauxite, and zinc made similar journeys from mine to manufacture.

The sheer size of the American market encouraged innovators to invent mass-production methods. With cheap transportation crisscrossing the nation and an ever-larger population able

Ralph Waldo Emerson (1803-1882) writing in 1860, reflected frequently expressed sentiments of the era's white reformers in equating immigrant experience with that of enslaved Africans:

"The German and Irish millions, like the Negro, have a great deal of guano in their destiny. They are ferried over the Atlantic, and carted over America, to ditch and to drudge, to make corn cheap, and then to lie down prematurely to make a spot of green grass on the prairie."

and eager to consume, anyone who could make an appealing new product available for a good price in large quantities—and figure out how to market it—thrived. Industrialists continued to refine the pre-Civil War "American System" of using specialized machinery to make interchangeable parts, culminating in 1913 with Henry Ford's fully developed moving assembly line for his Model T (refer to "11-7 'The American System'," pp. 258–259, and "29-1 Putting America on Rubber Tires," pp. 740–741).

The captains of industry had a major incentive to invent machines: they made it possible to replace expensive skilled labor with unskilled workers, now cheap and plentiful as a result of massive immigration. Steel, the keystone industry, was built largely on the sweat of low-wage immigrant labor from eastern and southern Europe, working in two 12-hour shifts, seven days a week.

Just as existing industries served as hothouses of innovation, other inventions gave rise to whole new lines of business. Between 1860 and 1890, some 440,000 patents were issued. Women claimed many patents, often related to household life: a tablecloth protector, an improved milk pail spout, patterns for making children's clothing. Business operations were facilitated by machines such as the cash register, the stock ticker, and the typewriter, while the refrigerator car, the electric dynamo, and the electric railway speeded urbanization.

One of the most consequential inventions was the telephone, introduced by Alexander Graham Bell in 1876. America was suddenly turned into a nation of "telephoniacs," as his invention spawned a gigantic communications network. Teenaged "telephone boys" were at first employed as operators, but their on-the-job beer drinking, prank calling, and profanity shocked patrons. Young men's bad manners created opportunity for young women, who took over the fast-paced work of the switchboards, further expanding the social impact of the telephone.

The most prolific and celebrated inventor of the era was Thomas Alva Edison (1847–1931). Edison had lost nearly all his hearing at the age of twelve, most likely from scarlet fever. He later maintained that his disability enabled him to concentrate without distraction, a claim buttressed by his extraordinary productivity (refer to Image 23.4). Over his lifetime, Edison acquired more patents—1,093—than any other American during this furiously inventive age. "Genius," he said, "is one percent inspiration and ninety-nine percent perspiration." Wondrous devices poured out of the New Jersey "invention factory" of Edison and his 200-man team—the phonograph, the mimeograph, the dictaphone, and the moving picture. Edison is probably best known for his perfection in 1879 of the electric light bulb, which turned night into day and transformed ancient human habits as well. People had previously slept an average of nine hours a night; now they slept just a bit more than seven.

Library of Congress Prints and Photographs Division [LC-USZ62-35005]

Image 23.4 Thomas Alva Edison in His Lab, 1888. Edison was dubbed the "Wizard of Menlo Park," New Jersey, where he lived and established the first major industrial research laboratory. Edison was not only an ingenious inventor but he also figured out how to apply the principles of mass production to his inventions. Phonographs, telephones, telegraphs, incandescent electric lighting, fluoroscopes, kinetoscopes, and many more technological wonders spread throughout the world following their development in Edison's lab.

23-6 Carnegie, Man of Steel

"Steel is king!" might well have been the exultant war cry of the new industrialized generation. Cheap, abundant steel made using the Bessemer-Kelly method poured forth from American mills, employing tens of thousands of workers in the hard, hot labor. The mighty metal ultimately held together the new steel society, from skyscrapers to coal scuttles, fueling national economic growth and building enormous fortunes.

Steel was a scarce commodity in the wood-and-brick America of Abraham Lincoln. Considerable iron went into railroad rails and bridges, but steel was expensive and was used largely for products like cutlery. The early iron horse snorted exclusively (and dangerously) over iron rails. When in the 1870s "Commodore" Vanderbilt of the New York Central began to use steel rails, he was forced to import them from Britain. Yet thanks to new production methods and intense domestic demand, within a mere twenty years the United States had outdistanced all foreign competitors and was pouring out more than one-third of the world's supply of steel. By 1900, America was producing as much as Britain and Germany combined.

Andrew Carnegie (1835–1919) wrote in 1889,

"The man who dies leaving behind him millions of available wealth, which was his to administer during life, will pass away 'unwept, unhonored, and unsung,' no matter to what uses he leaves the dross which he cannot take with him. Of such as these the public verdict will then be: 'The man who dies thus rich dies disgraced.'"

Kingpin among steelmasters was Andrew Carnegie, an undersized, charming Scotsman. As a towheaded lad of thirteen, he was brought to America by his impoverished parents in 1848 and got a job as a bobbin boy at $1.20 a week. Mounting the ladder of success so fast that he was said to have scorched the rungs, he forged ahead by working hard, doing the extra chore, cheerfully assuming responsibility, and smoothly cultivating influential people.

After accumulating some capital, Carnegie entered the steel business in the Pittsburgh area. A gifted organizer and administrator, he succeeded by growing a network of well-connected associates and by eliminating many middlemen. Although inclined to be tough-fisted in business, he was not a monopolist and disliked monopolistic trusts. His remarkable organization was a partnership that involved, at its maximum, about forty "Pittsburgh millionaires." By 1900, he was producing one-fourth of the nation's Bessemer-Kelly steel. He and his partners in these pre–income tax days were dividing profits of $40 million a year as their take-home pay, with the "Napoleon of the Smokestacks" himself receiving a cool $25 million.

Carnegie left a lasting mark on American business enterprise by controlling every phase of his steel-making operation. His miners scratched the ore from the earth in the Mesabi Range; Carnegie ships floated it across the Great Lakes; Carnegie railroads delivered it to the blast furnaces at Pittsburgh. When the molten metal finally poured from the glowing crucibles into the waiting ingot molds, no other hands but those in Carnegie's employ had touched the product. Carnegie thus pioneered the tactic of **vertical integration**, combining into one organization all phases of manufacturing from mining to marketing. His goal was to improve efficiency by making supplies more reliable, controlling the quality of the product at all stages of production, and eliminating middlemen's fees. This system became the prevailing model for large-scale American manufacturing for the better part of a century.

23-7 Morgan, Lord of Finance

Standing astride virtually the entire economy was the financial giant of the age, J. Pierpont Morgan. "Jupiter" Morgan had made a legendary reputation for himself and his Wall Street banking house by financing the reorganization of railroads, insurance companies, and banks (refer to Image 23.5). An impressive figure of a man, with massive shoulders, shaggy brows, piercing eyes, and a bulbous, acne-cursed red nose, he had established an enviable reputation for integrity. He did not believe that "money power" was dangerous, except when in dangerous hands—and he did not regard his own hands as dangerous.

The imperious Morgan devised a variety of schemes for eliminating "wasteful" competition and consolidating wealth. Catastrophic depressions in the 1870s and 1890s drove into his welcoming arms many bleeding businesspeople, wounded by cutthroat competition. His prescribed remedy was to consolidate rival enterprises and to ensure future harmony by placing officers of his own banking syndicate on their various boards of directors. These came to be known as **interlocking directorates**.

Library of Congress Prints and Photographs Division [LC-USZ62-20579]

Image 23.5 **J. P. Morgan (1837–1913)** As the most influential banker of his day, Morgan symbolized to many people the power and arrogance of "finance capitalism." The chronic skin disorder on his nose inspired the taunt "Johnny Morgan's nasal organ has a purple hue."

The force of circumstances brought Morgan and Carnegie into collision. By 1900, the canny little Scotsman, weary of turning steel into gold, was eager to sell his holdings. Morgan had meanwhile plunged heavily into the manufacture of steel pipe tubing. Carnegie, cleverly threatening to invade the same business, was ready to ruin his rival if he did not receive his price. The steelmaster's agents haggled with the imperious Morgan for eight agonizing hours, and the financier finally agreed to buy out Carnegie for over $400 million.

Morgan moved rapidly to expand his new industrial empire. He took the Carnegie holdings, added others, "watered" the stock liberally, and in 1901 launched the enlarged United States Steel Corporation. Capitalized at $1.4 billion, it was America's first billion-dollar corporation—a larger sum than the total estimated wealth of the nation in 1800. The Industrial Revolution, with its hot Bessemer-Kelly breath, had come into its own.

23-8 Rockefeller, Titan of the Trusts

The sudden emergence of the oil industry was one of the most striking developments of the years during and after the Civil War. Traces of oil found on streams had earlier been bottled for back-rub and other patent medicines, but not until 1859 did the first well in Pennsylvania—"Drake's Folly"—pour out its liquid "black gold." Almost overnight an industry was born that was to take more wealth from the earth than all of the gold extracted by California's forty-niners and their western successors. Kerosene, derived from petroleum, was the first major product of the infant oil industry. Burned from a cotton wick in a glass chimney lamp, kerosene produced a much brighter flame than whale oil. The oil business boomed; by the 1870s, kerosene was America's fourth most valuable export. Whaling, in contrast, the lifeblood of ocean-roaming New Englanders since before the days of *Moby Dick*, swiftly became a sick industry.

But what technology gives, technology takes away. By 1885, 250,000 of Thomas Edison's electric lightbulbs were in use; fifteen years later, perhaps 15 million. The new electric industry rendered kerosene obsolete, just as kerosene had rendered whale oil obsolete. Only in rural America and overseas did a market continue for oil-fired lamps.

Oil might thus have remained a modest, even a shrinking, industry but for yet another turn of the technological tide—the invention of the automobile. By 1900, the gasoline-burning internal combustion engine had clearly bested its rivals, steam and electricity, as the superior means of automobile propulsion. As the century of the automobile dawned, the oil business got a new, long-lasting, and hugely profitable lease on life.

John D. Rockefeller—lanky, shrewd, ambitious, and abstemious (he neither drank, smoked, nor swore)—came to dominate the oil industry. Born to a family of precarious income, he became a successful businessman at age nineteen. One upward stride led to another, and in 1870 he organized the **Standard Oil Company**. Locating his refineries in Cleveland, he sought to eliminate the middlemen and squeeze out competitors.

Rockefeller bolstered the efficiency of the vertically integrated supply chain with the market-gobbling technique of **horizontal integration**, which simply meant absorbing or allying with competitors to monopolize a given market. Rockefeller perfected a device for controlling bothersome rivals—the **trust**. Stockholders in various smaller oil companies assigned their stock to the board of directors of the Standard Oil Company. Rockefeller's firm then consolidated and concerted the operations of the previously competing enterprises. Critics of the pious titan lamented that "let us prey" was Rockefeller's unwritten motto. Wielding vast power, Standard Oil soon cornered virtually the entire world petroleum market. Weaker competitors, left out of the trust agreement, were forced to the wall. Rockefeller's stunning success inspired many imitators, and the word *trust* came to be generally used to describe any large-scale business combination.

Pious and parsimonious, Rockefeller flourished in an era of completely free enterprise. Meaningful government regulations were absent, and businesses wrote their own ethical rules (refer to Image 23.6). Operating "just to the windward of the law," Rockefeller pursued a policy of rule or ruin. "Sell all the oil that is sold in your district" was the hard-boiled order that went out to his local agents. By 1877, Rockefeller controlled 95 percent of all the oil refineries in the country.

Rockefeller—"Reckafellow," as Carnegie had once called him—showed little mercy. Employing spies and extorting secret rebates from the railroads, he even forced the lines to pay him rebates on the freight bills of his competitors. "The time was ripe" for aggressive consolidation, he later reflected. "It had to come, though all we saw at the moment was the need to save ourselves from wasteful conditions. . . . The day of combination is here to stay. Individualism has gone, never to return."

Image 23.6 The Octopus, 1904 This cartoon visually captures a feeling of widespread resentment against Standard Oil as a powerful, sprawling "octopus" whose tentacles controlled all branches of government.

On the other side of the ledger, Rockefeller's oil monopoly did turn out a superior product at a relatively cheap price. It achieved important economies, both at home and abroad, by its large-scale methods of production and distribution. This, in truth, was the tale of the other trusts as well. The efficient use of expensive machinery called for bigness, and consolidation proved more profitable than ruinous price wars.

Other trusts blossomed along with oil. These included the sugar trust, the tobacco trust, the leather trust, and the harvester trust, which amalgamated some two hundred competitors. The meat industry arose on the backs of bawling western herds, and meat kings like Gustavus F. Swift and Philip Armour took their place among the new royalty.

Patrician families looked on in horror as those they considered to be an arrogant class of "new rich" elbowed the old guard aside. Not surprisingly, the ranks of the later antitrust crusaders were frequently spearheaded by the "best men"—genteel old-family do-gooders who were not radicals but conservative defenders of their own vanishing influence.

23-9 The Gospel of Wealth

Monarchs of yore invoked the divine right of kings, and America's industrial plutocrats took a somewhat similar stance. Some candidly credited heavenly help. "Godliness is in league with riches," preached the Episcopal bishop of Massachusetts, and hardfisted John D. Rockefeller piously acknowledged that "the good Lord gave me my money." Steel baron Andrew Carnegie codified the new doctrine in 1889 in a famous article entitled, simply, "Wealth," later republished as "The Gospel of Wealth." He preached that the wealthy were only the temporary stewards of society's riches. They were therefore obliged to assume moral responsibility for the uplift of the less fortunate. "The man who dies rich," Carnegie concluded, "dies disgraced."

Self-justification by the wealthy inevitably involved contempt for the poor. Many of the rich, especially the newly rich, were self-made millionaires; not acknowledging the advantages of their gender, race, or professional connections, they concluded that those who stayed poor must be lazy and lacking in enterprise. The Reverend Russell Conwell of Philadelphia became rich by delivering his lecture "Acres of Diamonds" thousands of times. In it he charged, "There is not a poor person in the United States who was not made poor by his own shortcomings." Such attitudes pervaded the era's campaigns of social reform.

Plutocracy, like the earlier slavocracy, took its stand firmly on the Constitution. The clause that gave Congress sole jurisdiction over interstate commerce was a godsend to the monopolists; their high-priced lawyers used it time and again to thwart controls by the state legislatures. Giant trusts likewise sought refuge behind the Fourteenth Amendment, which had been originally designed to protect the rights of the formerly enslaved as persons (refer to "The Presence of the Past: The Fourteenth Amendment," pp. 504–506). The courts ingeniously interpreted a corporation to be a legal "person" and decreed that, as such, it could not be deprived of its property by a state without "due process of law" (refer to Amendment XIV, para. 1 in the Appendix). Great industrialists sought to incorporate in "easy states," like New Jersey, where the restrictions on big business were mild or nonexistent. For example, the Southern Pacific Railroad, with much of its trackage in California, was incorporated in Kentucky.

23-10 Government Tackles the Trusts

At long last, activist citizens and lawmakers began to catch up with the runaway train of monopoly power. Reformers first tried to control the trusts through state legislation, as they had earlier attempted to curb the railroads. But state regulation had little effect on continent-spanning corporations. Congress needed to act. After prolonged pulling and hauling, the **Sherman Anti-Trust Act** of 1890 passed nearly unanimously.

The Sherman Act flatly forbade combinations in restraint of trade, but it was so loosely worded that it proved ineffective. Clever corporation lawyers wriggled easily through its legal loopholes, and the Justice Department lost seven of its first eight antitrust cases. But it was unexpectedly effective in one respect. Contrary to its original intent, it was used to curb labor unions or labor combinations that were deemed to be restraining trade.

More new trusts were formed in the 1890s than during any other like period. Not until 1914 were the paper jaws of the Sherman Act fitted with reasonably sharp teeth. Until then, there was some question whether the government would control the trusts or the trusts the government (refer to Image 23.7).

Still, the reformers and labor leaders who decried the iron grip of monopolistic corporations had reason to hope. A revolutionary new principle had been written into the law books by the Sherman Anti-Trust Act of 1890, as well as by the Interstate Commerce Act of 1887. Private greed should henceforth be subordinated to public need.

23-11 The South in the Age of Industry

The industrial tidal wave that washed over the North after the Civil War caused only feeble ripples in the economic backwater of the South. As late as 1900, the South still produced a smaller percentage of the nation's manufactured goods than it had before the Civil War. The plantation system had degenerated into a pattern of absentee landownership. White and Black sharecroppers now tilled the soil for a share of the crop or became tenants, in economic bondage to landlords who controlled needed credit and supplies (refer to "21-8 The Birth of Jim Crow in the

Image 23.7 Washington as Seen by the Trusts, 1900 "What a funny little government," John D. Rockefeller observes in this satirical cartoon. His own wealth and power are presumed to dwarf the resources of the federal government.

Image 23.8 Virginia Tobacco Workers, 1887 Men and women are making "twists" for tobacco chewers.

Post-Reconstruction South," pp. 530–531). By exploiting labor of poor Southerners both Black and white—all while tightening the vise of Jim Crow segregation—the South's planter class began to rebuild fortunes that the Civil War had blasted away.

King Tobacco dethroned King Cotton in parts of the South (refer to Image 23.8). The region's agriculture received a technological boost in the 1880s, when machine-made cigarettes replaced the roll-your-own variety and tobacco consumption shot up. James Buchanan Duke took full advantage of the new technology to mass-produce the addictive "coffin nails." The business innovations of the industrial North—conspicuously including vertical and horizontal—came South. In 1890, in what was becoming a familiar pattern, Duke absorbed his main competitors into the American Tobacco Company. The tobacco giant's most successful brand, Lucky Strike, later popularized smoking among women with memorable slogans like "Reach for a Lucky Instead of a Sweet." The cigarette czar later showed such generosity to Trinity College, near his birthplace in Durham, North Carolina, that the trustees gratefully changed its name to Duke University.

Industrialists tried to coax the agricultural South out of the fields and into the factories. Prominent among the boosters of a "new South" was silver-tongued Henry W. Grady, editor of the *Atlanta Constitution*. He tirelessly exhorted the ex-Confederates to become "Georgia Yankees" able to outplay the North at the industrial game because of the South's large and "willing" Black labor force who could be paid little to work hard without complaint.

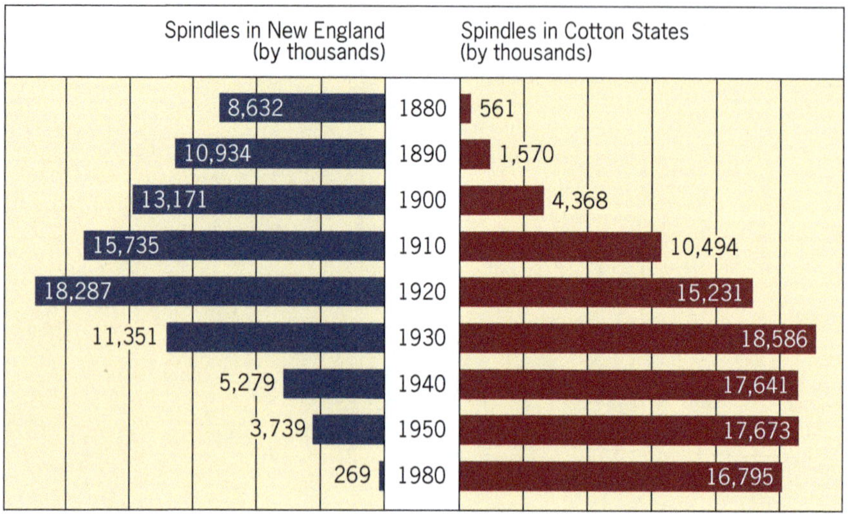

Figure 23.2 Cotton Manufacturing Moves South, 1880–1980 Textile manufacturing usually looms large in the early stages of industrial development. In the later stages, it gives way to higher technology businesses. This trend can be seen here, both in the migration of textile manufacturing to the southern United States and in the decline in the number of spindles in the United States as a whole since the 1930s, as developing Third World countries became major textile producers.

Sources: *Historical Statistics of the United States* and *Statistical Abstract of the United States*, relevant years.

Saturated with such racist assumptions, this industrial vision not only aimed to expand Southern enterprise but uphold elite white rule.

Yet formidable obstacles lay in the path of Southern industrialization. One came from Northern-dominated railroads. Bending to pressure from captains of industry, the lines gave preferential rates to manufactured goods moving southward from the North and to raw materials moving northward from the South. The net effect was to keep the South a supplier of raw materials to the manufacturing metropolis, unable to develop a substantial industrial base of its own.

A bitter example of this economic discrimination against the South was the "Pittsburgh plus" pricing system in the steel industry. Rich deposits of coal and iron ore near Birmingham, Alabama, worked by low-wage Southern labor, should have given steel manufacturers there a competitive edge, especially in Southern markets. But the steel lords of Pittsburgh brought pressure to bear on the compliant railroads. As a result, Birmingham steel, no matter where it was delivered, was charged a fictional fee, as if it had been shipped from Pittsburgh. This stunting of the South's natural economic advantages throttled the growth of the Birmingham steel industry. The region remained predominantly rural.

One exception was in textile manufacturing, where the South fared considerably better. Southerners had long resented shipping their fiber to New England, and now their cry was "Bring the mills to the cotton." Beginning about 1880, Northern capitalists began to erect cotton mills in the South, largely in response to tax benefits and the prospect of cheap and nonunionized labor (refer to Figures 23.2 and 23.3).

The textile mills slowly wove an industrial thread into the fabric of Southern life, but at a considerable human cost. The mills took root in the chronically depressed and mostly white Piedmont region of southern Appalachia and came to utterly dominate the communities in which they were located. Black workers were excluded from all but the most menial jobs in the mills, while rural whites poured out of the hills and hollows to seek employment in the hastily erected company mill towns. Whether white or Black, keeping labor cheap and nonunionized became almost a religion among Southern industrialists. Entire families—often derided as "hillbillies" or "lintheads"—worked from dawn to dusk amid the whirring spindles. They were paid at half the rate of their Northern counterparts and often received their compensation in the form of credit at a company store, to which—by design of the company ownership—they were habitually in debt.

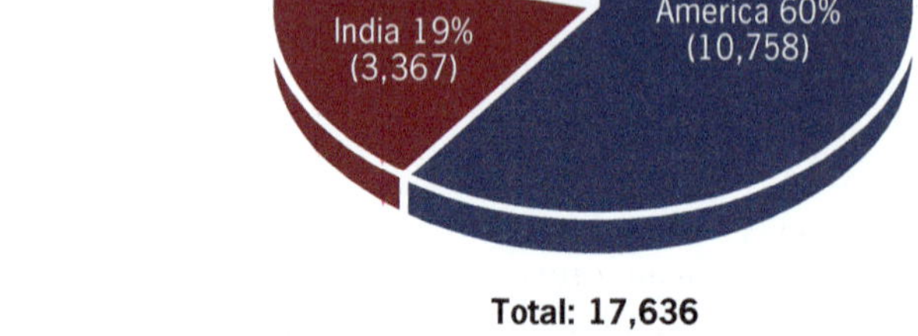

Figure 23.3 World Cotton Production, 1903 Cotton manufacturing grew in the United States in the early twentieth century, and raw cotton production reached higher levels than anywhere else in the world.

Source: John A. Todd, *The World's Cotton Crops* (1915), 395–396.

But despite their depressed working conditions and poor pay, many Southerners saw employment in the mills as a salvation, the first steady jobs and wages they had ever known. With many mills and factories eager to tap the cheap labor of women and children, mill work often offered destitute farm-fugitive families their only chance to remain together (refer to Image 23.9 and "Examining the Evidence: The Photography of Lewis W. Hine," p. 583).

Library of Congress Prints and Photographs Division [LC-USZ62-73866]

Image 23.9 **Women Canning Shrimp, 1893** Long hours, low pay, and wretched working conditions were the common fate of women who labored not for "pin money," but to help support their families. The "family wage" for the workingman was more a hope than a reality.

23-12 The American People in the Age of Industry

Economic miracles wrought during the decades after the Civil War enormously increased the wealth of the Republic and changed how Americans lived, worked, traveled, and communicated. Though life expectancy declined somewhat in the turbulent earliest decades of industrialization, by century's end the American standard of living was rising sharply. American workers then enjoyed more physical comforts than their counterparts in any other industrial nation. Urban centers mushroomed as the insatiable factories demanded more American labor and as immigrants swarmed like honeybees to the new jobs (refer to Map 23.1).

Early Jeffersonian ideals, bred in a nation of farmers, withered before the smudgy blasts from the big-city smokestacks. As agriculture declined in relation to manufacturing, America could no longer aspire to be a nation of small freehold farms. Jefferson's concepts of free enterprise, with neither help nor hindrance from Washington, were being thrown out the factory window.

Older ways of life wilted in the heat of the factory furnaces. The very concept of time was revolutionized. Rural American migrants and peasant European immigrants, used to living by the languid clock of nature, now had to regiment their lives by the factory whistle. The seemingly arbitrary discipline of industrial labor did not come easily and sometimes had to be forcibly taught. One large corporation simultaneously instructed its Polish immigrant workers in the English language and in the obligations of factory work schedules:

> I hear the whistle. I must hurry.
> I hear the five-minute whistle.
> It is time to go into the shop. . . .
> I change my clothes and get ready to work.
> The starting whistle blows.
> I eat my lunch.
> It is forbidden to eat until then. . . .
> I work until the whistle blows to quit.
> I leave my place nice and clean.
> I put all my clothes in the locker.
> I must go home.

Probably no single group was more profoundly affected by the new industrial age than women. Propelled into industry by recent inventions, chiefly the typewriter and the telephone switchboard, millions of stenographers and "hello girls" discovered new economic and social opportunities. The "Gibson Girl," a magazine image of an independent and athletic "new woman" created in the 1890s by the artist Charles Dana Gibson, became the romantic ideal of the age (refer to Image 23.10). For middle-class women, careers often meant delayed marriages and smaller families. Most women workers, however, toiled neither for independence nor for glamour, but out of economic necessity. They faced the same long hours and dangerous working conditions as did their mates and brothers, and they earned less, as wages for "women's jobs" were usually set below those for men's.

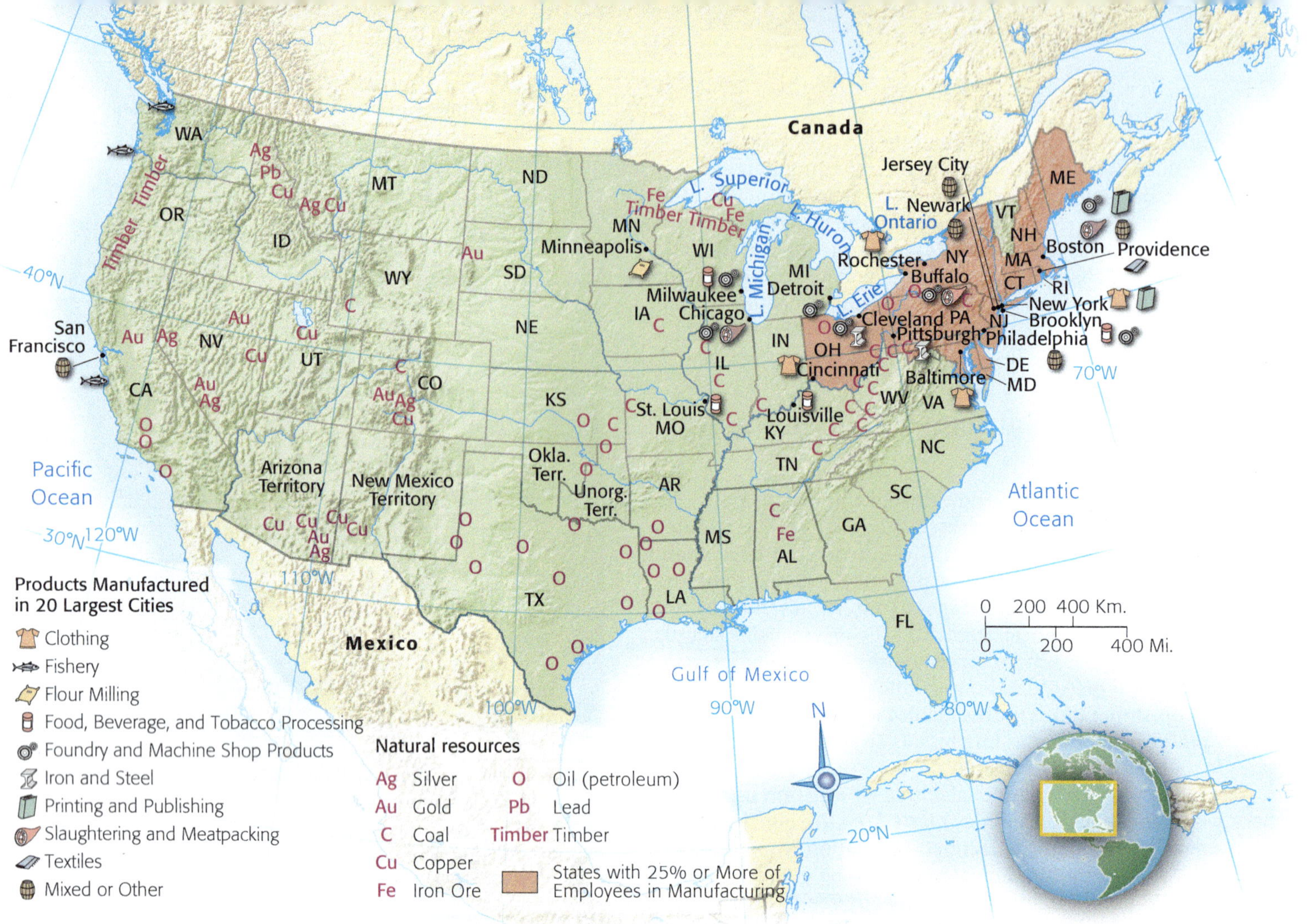

Map 23.1 American Industry in 1900 By the end of the nineteenth century, once-rural America boasted the world's largest industrial output—a development with enormous consequences for politics, diplomacy, and family life.

Golfing Foursome, ca. 1900 (gouache and w/c on board), Granville-Smith, Walter (1870–1938)/© American Illustrators Gallery, NYC/www.asapworldwide.com/The Bridgeman Art Library

Image 23.10 Golfing Gibson Girls The image of the so-called Gibson Girl—healthy, athletic, and confident—was hardly confined to the pen of its creator, illustrator Charles Dana Gibson. Other turn-of-the-century artists also depicted such modern women, including Walter Granville-Smith in this 1900 painting of a golf outing. The Gibson Girl ideal inspired new standards of female fashion as the twentieth century opened and came to symbolize women's growing independence and assertiveness.

Examining the Evidence

The Photography of Lewis W. Hine

The pell-mell onrush of industrialization after the Civil War spawned countless human abuses, few more objectionable than the employment of children, often in hazardous jobs. For decades reformers tried to arouse public outrage against child labor, and they made significant headway at last with the help of photography—especially the photographs of Lewis W. Hine (1874–1940). A native of Wisconsin, Hine in 1908 became the staff photographer for the National Child Labor Committee, an organization committed to ending child labor. These two images are typical of Hine's work. A 1909 photo depicts young "doffers," whose job it was to remove fully wound bobbins from textile spinning machines. He shows the boys climbing dangerously on the whirling mechanism, and his own caption for the photo names the mill—"Bibb Mill No. 1, Macon, Georgia"—but not the boys, as if to underline the impersonal, dehumanizing nature of their work and the specific responsibilities of their employer. His 1911 portrait of "breaker boys" in a Pennsylvania coal mine captures similarly grim and perilous working conditions. Hine's other subjects included child workers on Colorado beet farms, in Gulf Coast fish canneries, and in the glass, tobacco, and garment trades. Hine's images contributed heavily to the eventual success of the campaign to end child labor in the New Deal era. He is also celebrated as one of the fathers of documentary photography. Why might Hine's graphic images have succeeded in stirring public opinion more powerfully than factual and statistical demonstrations of the evil of child labor? Given Hine's own reform objectives, can his photographs—or any so-called documentary images—be taken at face value as literal, accurate information about the past?

Library of Congress Prints and Photographs Division [LC-USZ6-1222]

Image 23.11 Young "Doffers" at Bibb Mill, Macon, Georgia, 1909

Library of Congress Prints and Photographs Division [LC-DIG-nclc-01133]

Image 23.12 Breaker Boys at South Pittson, Pennsylvania, 1911 Photographer Lewis W. Hine captured the grimness of these mine helpers' lives. For hours they sat on benches abo ve a moving belt, breathing coal dust deep into their lungs and kicking large pieces of coal with their feet, breaking the lumps to uniform size for shipment. Photographs like this one became icons of the reform crusade against child labor, a campaign that succeeded only with the passage of the Fair Labor Standards Act in 1938.

The clattering machine age likewise accentuated class division. "Industrial buccaneers" flaunted bloated fortunes, and their rags-to-riches spouses displayed glittering diamonds. Such extravagances evoked bitter criticism. Some of it was envious, but much of it rose from a small but increasingly vocal group of socialists and other radicals, many of whom were recent European immigrants. The existence of an oligarchy of money was amply demonstrated by the fact that in 1900 about one-tenth of the people owned nine-tenths of the nation's wealth (refer to Image 23.13).

Real wages were rising, and times were good for workers who were working. But with dependence on wages came vulnerability to the swings of the economy and the whims of the employer. The fear of unemployment was never distant. A breadwinner's illness could mean catastrophe

A

B

Image 23.13A and B **The New Rich and the New Immigrants** A well-to-do family plays chess at its parlor table (refer to 23.13A), while a tenement family does "piecework" around its kitchen table—shelling nuts for commercial use (refer to 23.13B). The young working girl seems to be "snitching" some nuts for herself. The apparently growing gulf between the rich and the poor deeply worried reformers in the late nineteenth century. They feared that democracy could not survive in the face of such gross inequality.

for an entire family. Nothing more sharply defined the growing difference between working-class and middle-class conditions of life than the precariousness of the laborer's lot. Reformers struggled, mostly in vain, to introduce a measure of security—job and wage protection, and provision for temporary unemployment—into the lives of the working class.

Strong pressures for foreign trade also developed as the tireless industrial machine threatened to saturate the domestic market. Aided by developments like the laying of a transatlantic telegraph in 1866 and the opening of the Suez Canal in 1869, international trade became ever faster, cheaper, and easier. American products radiated out all over the world—notably the five-gallon kerosene can of the Standard Oil Company. The flag follows trade, and empire tends to follow the flag—a harsh lesson that America was soon to learn.

23-13 In Unions There Is Strength

The sweat of the laborer lubricated the vast new industrial machine. Yet the wage workers did not share proportionately with their employers in the benefits of the age of big business.

The worker was becoming a tiny cog in the giant engine of industry. Before the Civil War, the worker might have toiled in a small plant whose owner hailed the employee in the morning by first name and inquired after the family's health. But now the factory laborer was employed by a corporation whose priorities were efficiency, scale, and delivering maximum returns to stockholders.

New machines displaced employees. Though in the long run more jobs were created than destroyed by automation, in the short run the manual worker was often hard hit. A glutted labor market limited workers' ability to negotiate higher pay or benefits. Employers could take advantage of the vast new railroad network and bring in lower-cost workers from the four corners of the country and across oceans. During the 1880s and 1890s, several hundred thousand unskilled workers a year poured into the country from Europe, creating a labor market more favorable to the boss than the worker.

Whether native-born or immigrant, individual workers were powerless to battle single-handedly against giant industry. Employers could pool vast wealth through thousands of stockholders, retain high-priced lawyers, buy up the local press, and put pressure on the politicians. They could import strikebreakers ("scabs") and employ thugs to beat up labor organizers. In 1886, the cunning financier Jay Gould reputedly boasted, "I can hire one-half of the working class to kill the other half."

Employers could lock their doors against rebellious workers—a procedure called the "lockout"—and then starve them into submission. They could compel them to sign "ironclad oaths" or "yellow-dog contracts," both of which were solemn agreements not to join a labor union. They could put the

age fotostock/SuperStock

Image 23.14 The Strike, by Robert Koehler, 1886 Scenes like this were becoming more typical of American life in the late nineteenth century as industrialism advanced spectacularly and sometimes ruthlessly. Here Koehler (1850–1917) shows an entire community of men, women, and children—many of them apparently immigrant newcomers—challenging the power of the "boss." The scene is tense but orderly, though violence seems to be imminent as one striker reaches for a rock.

names of agitators on a "black list" and circulate it among fellow employers. A corporation might even own the company town, with its high-priced grocery stores and "easy" credit. Often the worker sank into perpetual debt. Countless thousands of blackened coal miners were born in a company house, nurtured by a (high-priced) company store, and buried in a company graveyard—prematurely dead.

Corporations also counted on the government as a faithful ally. They could call on the federal courts—presided over by well-fed and conservative judges—to issue injunctions ordering the strikers to cease striking. If defiance and disorder ensued, the company could request the state and federal authorities to bring in troops.

The middle-class public, annoyed by recurrent strikes, grew deaf to the outcry of the worker. American wages were perhaps the highest in the world: a princely dollar a day for pick-and-shovel labor. Carnegie and Rockefeller had battled their way to the top, and the view was common that the laborer could do likewise. Somehow the strike seemed like a foreign importation—socialistic and hence unpatriotic (refer to Image 23.14). Big business might combine into trusts to raise prices, but the worker must not combine into unions to raise wages. Unemployment seemed to be an act of God, who somehow would take care of the laborer.

23-14 Labor Gains Strength

Unable to improve their lot individually, workers banded together. Labor unions had been few and disorganized in 1861, but were given a boost by the Civil War. This bloody conflict, with its drain on human resources, put more of a premium on labor and the mounting cost of living provided an urgent incentive to unionization. By 1872, several hundred thousand workers had joined thirty-two national unions, representing such crafts as bricklayers, typesetters, and shoemakers.

The **National Labor Union**, organized in 1866, represented a giant bootstride by workers. One of the earliest national-scale unions to organize in the Americas or Europe, it aimed to unify workers across locales and trades to challenge their ever more powerful bosses. The union lasted six years and attracted the impressive total of some 600,000 members, including the skilled, unskilled, and farmers. In keeping with the times, it was composed almost entirely of native-born white men, excluding Chinese workers and making only nominal efforts to include women and African Americans. Black workers organized their own Colored National Labor Union as an adjunct, but the persistent racism of white unionists prevented the two national unions from working together. The National Labor Union agitated for the arbitration of industrial disputes and the eight-hour workday, winning the latter for federal government workers in 1868. But the devastating depression of the 1870s left labor reeling. Wage reductions in 1877 touched off such disruptive strikes on the railroads (refer to The Great Strike of 1877 in "21-9 Class Conflicts and Ethnic Clashes," pp. 531–533) that nothing short of federal troops could restore order.

A new organization—the **Knights of Labor**—seized the torch dropped by the defunct National Labor Union (refer to "Makers of America: The Knights of Labor," pp. 588–589). The Knights of Labor sought to include workers—skilled and unskilled, male and female, Catholic and Protestant—in "one big union," with the ugly exception of barring workers of Chinese descent. The Knights thrust their lance into campaigns for economic and social reform, including producers' cooperatives and codes for safety and health and sustaining a determined campaign the eight-hour workday.

Despite their outward success, the Knights were riding for a fall. They became involved in a number of May Day strikes in 1886, about half of which failed. A focal point was Chicago, home to about eighty thousand Knights. The city was also honeycombed with a few hundred anarchists, many of them foreign-born, who were advocating a violent overthrow of the American government. Tensions rapidly built up to the bloody **Haymarket Square** episode. In the wake of a spate of unruly labor demonstrations, on May 4, 1886, the Chicago police advanced on a meeting called to protest alleged brutalities by the authorities. Suddenly a dynamite bomb was thrown that killed or injured several dozen people, including police.

Hysteria swept the Windy City. Police rounded up eight anarchists, although nobody proved that they had anything to do directly with the bomb. But the judge and jury held that since they had preached incendiary doctrines, they could be charged with conspiracy. Five were sentenced to death, one of whom committed suicide, and the other three were given stiff prison terms.

Agitation for clemency mounted. In 1892, some six years later, John P. Altgeld, a German-born Democrat of strong liberal tendencies, was elected governor of Illinois. After studying the Haymarket case exhaustively, he pardoned the three survivors—leading to his defeat for reelection. He died a few years later in relative obscurity, "The Eagle Forgotten." Whatever the merits of the case, Altgeld displayed courage in opposing what he regarded as a gross injustice.

The Haymarket Square bomb helped blow the props from under the Knights of Labor. They were associated in the public mind, though mistakenly, with the anarchists. The eight-hour movement suffered correspondingly, and subsequent strikes by the Knights met with scant success.

But it was the Knights' big tent that ultimately proved its fatal flaw. Unskilled labor could easily be replaced by strikebreaking "scabs." Higher-skilled craft unionists could not readily be supplanted and hence enjoyed a superior bargaining position. They finally wearied of sacrificing this advantage on the altar of solidarity with their unskilled coworkers. They sought refuge in a federation of exclusively skilled craft unions—the American Federation of Labor. The desertion of the skilled craft unionists dealt the Knights a body blow. By the 1890s they had melted away to 100,000 members.

23-15 The AF of L to the Fore

The **American Federation of Labor**, born in 1886, soon took the spotlight, led by the charismatic, square-jawed Samuel Gompers. Born in a London tenement to a Jewish family of cigar makers, Gompers arrived in New York City aged thirteen, and quickly took up his father's trade. Taking his turn at reading works of political theory aloud to fellow cigar makers, he was pressed into overtime service because of his strong voice. Rising spectacularly in the labor ranks, he was elected president of the American Federation of Labor every year except one from 1886 to 1924.

Significantly, the American *Federation* of Labor was just what it called itself—a federation. It consisted of an association of self-governing national unions, each of which kept its independence, with the AF of L unifying overall strategy. No individual laborer could join the central organization.

Gompers adopted a down-to-earth approach, soft-pedaling attempts to engineer sweeping social reform. A bitter foe of socialism, he shunned politics for economic strategies and goals. Gompers had no quarrel with capitalism, but he demanded a fairer share for labor. All he wanted, he said, was "more." Promoting what he called a "pure and simple" unionism, he sought better wages, hours, and working conditions.

Unlike the somewhat utopian Knights of Labor, Gompers was not concerned with the sweet by-and-by but with the bitter here and now. He advocated the "trade agreement" authorizing the **closed shop**—or all-union labor. His chief weapons were the walkout and the boycott, enforced by "We don't patronize" signs. The stronger craft unions of the federation, by pooling funds, were able to amass a war chest that would enable them to ride out prolonged strikes (refer to Image 23.15).

The AF of L thus established itself on solid but narrow foundations. Although attempting to speak for all workers, it fell far short of being representative of them. Composed of skilled craftsmen, like the carpenters and the bricklayers, it was willing to let unskilled laborers, including women and especially Black laborers, fend for themselves. Though hard-pressed by big industry, the federation was basically nonpolitical. But it did attempt to persuade members to reward friends and punish foes at the polls. The AF of L weathered the panic of 1893 reasonably well, and by 1900 it could boast a membership of 500,000. Critics referred to it, with questionable accuracy, as "the labor trust."

Labor disorders continued, peppering the years from 1881 to 1900 with a total of over 23,000 strikes. These disturbances involved 6,610,000 workers, with a total loss to both employers and employees of $450 million. The strikers lost about half their strikes and won or compromised the remainder.

But attitudes toward labor had begun to change perceptibly by 1900. The public was beginning to concede the right of workers to organize, to bargain collectively, and to strike. As a sign of the times, Congress in 1894 made Labor Day a legal holiday. A few industrialists had come to perceive the wisdom of avoiding costly economic warfare by bargaining with the unions and signing agreements. But the vast majority of employers continued to fight organized labor, which achieved its grudging gains only after recurrent strikes and frequent reverses.

Management still held the whip hand. Only about 3 percent of workers were union members in 1900. Several trouble-fraught decades were to pass before labor was to gain the numbers and the solidarity to stand up effectively to capital. If the age of big business had dawned, the age of big labor was still some distance over the horizon.

Library of Congress

Image 23.15 Samuel Gompers (1850–1924) Gompers (second from the right in the first row), shown here marching in a labor demonstration in Washington, DC, in 1919, once declared, "Show me the country in which there are no strikes and I'll show you that country in which there is no liberty."

Makers of America

The Knights of Labor

It was 1875. The young worker was guided into a room, where his blindfold was removed. Surrounding him were a dozen men, their faces covered by hoods. One of the masked figures solemnly asked three questions: "Do you believe in God?" "Do you gain your bread by the sweat of your brow?" "Are you willing to take a solemn vow, binding you to secrecy, obedience, and mutual assistance?" Yes, came the reply. The men doffed their hoods and joined hands in a circle. Their leader, the Master Workman, declared, "On behalf of the toiling millions of earth, I welcome you to this Sanctuary, dedicated to the service of God, by serving humanity." Then the entire group burst into song:

> Storm the fort, ye Knights of Labor,
> Battle for your cause;
> Equal rights for every neighbor,
> Down with tyrant laws!

The carefully staged pageantry then drew to a close. The worker was now a full-fledged member of the Knights of Labor.

He had just joined a loose-knit organization of some 100,000 workingpeople, soon to swell to nearly a million after the Knights led several successful strikes in the 1880s. The first women Knights joined in 1881, when an all-female local was established in the shoe trade in Philadelphia, and one in ten members was a woman by 1885. Women were organizers, too. Fiery Mary Harris ("Mother") Jones got her start agitating for the Knights in the Illinois coalfields. The first all-Black local was founded among coal miners in Ottumwa, Iowa. The Knights preached tolerance and the solidarity of all working men and women, and they meant it, but even their inclusionary spirit had its limits. Chinese workers were barred from joining, and the Knights vigorously supported the Chinese Exclusion Act of 1882. They also championed the Contract Labor Law of 1885, which aimed to restrain competition from low-wage immigrant workers—though immigrants, especially the Irish, were themselves disproportionately represented among the Knights' membership.

Terence V. Powderly, born to Irish immigrant parents in Carbondale, Pennsylvania, in 1849, became the Grand Master Workman of the Knights in 1879. Slightly built, with mild blue eyes behind glasses, he had dropped out of school at age thirteen to take a job guarding railroad track switches and rose to mayor of Scranton, Pennsylvania, in the 1870s. In 1894, he became a lawyer—despite the fact that the Knights excluded lawyers from membership. A complex, colorful, and sometimes cynical man, he denounced the "multimillionaires [for] laying the foundation for their colossal fortunes on the bodies and souls of living men." In the eyes of Powderly and his Knights, only the economic and political independence of American workers could preserve republican traditions and institutions from corruption by monopolists and other "parasites."

Powderly denounced "wage-slavery" and dedicated the Knights to achieving the "cooperative commonwealth." Shunning socialism, which advocated government ownership of the means of production, Powderly urged laborers to save enough from their wages to purchase mines, factories, railroads, and stores. They would thereby create a kind of toilers' utopia; because labor would own and operate those enterprises, workers themselves would be owner-producers, and the conflict between labor and capital would evaporate. The Knights actually did operate a few businesses, including coal mines in Indiana, but all eventually failed.

Powderly's vision of the cooperative commonwealth reflected the persistent dream of many nineteenth-century American workers that they would all one day become producers. As expectant capitalists, they lacked "class consciousness"—that is, a sense of themselves as a permanent working class that must organize to overhaul the capitalist system. Samuel Gompers, by contrast, accepted the framework of American capitalism, and his American Federation

Bain News Service

Image 23.16 **"Mother Jones"**

of Labor sought to work within that framework, not to overturn it. Gompers's conservative strategy, not Powderly's utopian dream, eventually carried the day. The swift decline of the Knights in the 1890s underscored the obsolescence of their unrealistic, even naive, view that a bygone age of independent producers could be restored. Yet the Knights' commitment to unifying all workers in one union—regardless of race (excepting the Chinese), gender, ethnicity, or skill level—provided a blueprint for the eventual success of similarly committed unions like the Congress of Industrial Organizations in the 1930s.

The Granger Collection, NYC

Image 23.17 Machinist Frank J. Ferrell, Black Delegate of District Assembly No. 49, Introducing General Master Workman Terence Powderly to the Tenth Annual Convention of the Knights of Labor, Held in Richmond, Virginia, 1886

The Library of Congress

Image 23.18 Women Delegates to the 1886 Convention of the Knights of Labor

Varying Viewpoints

Industrialization: Boon or Blight?

The capitalists who forged an industrial America in the late nineteenth century were once called captains of industry—a respectful title that bespoke the awe due their wondrous material accomplishments. But these economic innovators have never been universally admired. During the Great Depression of the 1930s, when the entire industrial order they had created seemed to have collapsed utterly, it was fashionable to speak of them as *robber barons*—a term implying scorn for their high-handed methods. This sneer often issued from the lips and pens of leftist critics like Matthew Josephson, who sympathized with the working classes that were allegedly brutalized by the factory system.

Criticism has also come from writers nostalgic for a preindustrial past. These critics believe that industrialization stripped away the traditions, values, and independence of native farmers and immigrant craftspeople. Conceding that economic development elevated the material standard of living for working Americans, this interpretation contends that the Industrial Revolution diminished their spiritual "quality of life." Accordingly, historians like Herbert Gutman and David Montgomery portray labor's struggle for control of the workplace as the central drama of industrial expansion.

Nevertheless, even these historians concede that class-based protest has never been as powerful a force in the United States as in several European countries. Many historians believed that this is so because greater social mobility in America dampened class tensions. The French observer Alexis de Tocqueville noted in the 1830s that America had few huge inherited fortunes and that most of its wealthy men were self-made. For two centuries, a majority of Americans believed that greater opportunity distinguished the New World from the Old.

In the 1960s, historians led by Stephan Thernstrom began to test this long-standing belief. Looking at such factors as occupation, wealth, and geographic mobility, they tried to gauge the nature and extent of social mobility in the United States. Most of these historians concluded that although relatively few Americans made rags-to-riches leaps like those heralded in the Horatio Alger stories, large numbers experienced small improvements in their economic and social status. Few sons of laborers became corporate tycoons, but many more became line bosses and white-collar clerks.

Unlike in Europe, the American working class was racially, ethnically, and linguistically diverse, even though many settled in communities that reflected their cultural and ethnic backgrounds. Historians found, however, that race and ethnicity often affected one's chances for success. For instance, the children and grandchildren of Jewish immigrants tended to rise faster in the professions than Americans of Italian and Irish descent, even though they also faced prejudice, especially in the South. And well into the twentieth century, punishing segregation in the Jim Crow South choked off avenues for Black upward mobility, as did persistent racial discrimination in the cities of the North. There, anti-Black and anti-Asian racism as well as prejudice against Catholics and Jews often posed insurmountable barriers to social solidarity.

Meanwhile, several historians, conspicuously including Richard White, have argued that the degree of social mobility in Gilded-Age America has been overstated. Although most Americans took small steps upward, they generally remained within the class in which they began. Thus, White and others argue, the inequality of a capitalistic class system persisted in America's seemingly fluid society.

Chapter Summary

Aided by government land grant subsidies and loans, the first transcontinental rail line was completed in 1869, soon followed by others. This rail network opened vast new markets and prompted industrial growth. The power and corruption of the railroads led to public demands for regulation. State regulation was declared unconstitutional, but in 1887 the federal government took a small step with the Interstate Commerce Act.

New technologies like the Bessemer steel process and new forms of business organization led to the growth of huge corporate trusts, which often employed ruthless anticompetitive practices. Andrew Carnegie in the steel industry and John D. Rockefeller in oil led the way. Many sectors of the economy came to be dominated by monopolistic trusts that used "interlocking directorates" and other pressure tactics to control competitors. Business-oriented ideologies like the religious "gospel of wealth" and naturalistic Social Darwinism celebrated the wealthy as "fittest" to survive and denigrated poverty as a sign of laziness or moral failure.

While industrialization did raise the general economy and standard of living, its benefits were very unevenly distributed. The South remained largely rural and dependent on Northern industry, despite "New South" proclamations and the growth of low-wage textile factories in the region. The industrial working class struggled at the bottom of the growing class divisions of American society. Increasingly transformed from independent producers and farmers to dependent wage earners, America's workers became vulnerable to illness, industrial accidents, and unemployment.

Workers' early attempts at labor organization were generally ineffective, hindered by corporate and governmental opposition and their own limited ideologies. The National Labor Union enjoyed brief success but then collapsed. The secretive Knights of Labor attracted many workers in the 1880s, but faded after the Haymarket bombing. Gompers's American Federation of Labor successfully organized skilled craft laborers but completely ignored most industrial workers, women, and Black people. Middle class public attitudes toward organized labor slowly became more positive after 1900, but business retained the upper hand and only a small minority of workers were unionized.

Key Terms

- Bessemer-Kelly Process (571)
- Interstate Commerce Act (572)
- vertical integration (575)
- interlocking directorates (575)
- Standard Oil Company (576)
- horizontal integration (576)
- trust (576)
- Sherman Anti-Trust Act (578)
- National Labor Union (585)
- Knights of Labor (586)
- Haymarket Square (586)
- American Federation of Labor (586)
- closed shop (587)

People to Know

- Cornelius Vanderbilt
- Alexander Graham Bell
- Thomas Alva Edison
- Andrew Carnegie
- J.P. Morgan
- John D. Rockefeller
- Mary Harris "Mother" Jones
- Terence V. Powderly
- Samuel Gompers

Chronology

1862	• Congress authorizes transcontinental railroad	
1866	• National Labor Union organized • First working transatlantic telegraph cable	
1869	• Transcontinental railroad joined near Ogden, Utah • Knights of Labor organized	• Suez Canal completed
1870	• Standard Oil Company organized	
1876	• Bell invents telephone	
1879	• Edison invents electric light	
1886	• Haymarket Square bombing • *Wabash* case	• American Federation of Labor formed
1887	• Interstate Commerce Act	
1890	• Sherman Anti-Trust Act	
1901	• United States Steel Corporation formed	

To Learn More

Sven Beckert, *The Monied Metropolis: New York City and the Consolidation of the American Bourgeoisie, 1850–1896* (2001)

James Green, *Death in the Haymarket: A Story of Chicago, the First Labor Movement, and the Bombing That Divided Gilded Age America* (2006)

Tera W. Hunter, *To 'Joy My Freedom: Southern Black Women's Lives and Labors After the Civil War* (1997)

Alice Kessler-Harris, *Out to Work: A History of Wage-Earning Women in the United States* (1982)

David Montgomery, *The Fall of the House of Labor: The Workplace, the State, and American Labor Activism, 1865–1925* (1987)

Richard White, *The Republic for Which It Stands: The United States during Reconstruction and the Gilded Age, 1865–1896* (2017)

Chapter 24

America Moves to the City: 1865–1900

America is Great and Chicago is Her Prophet.

Julian Ralph, *Harper's* 1893

Chapter Outline

- The rise of the city
- The "New Immigrants"
- Settlement houses, social workers, and political machines
- Nativists and immigration restriction
- Churches in the city
- Evolution and education
- Booker T. Washington and W. E. B. Du Bois
- The growth of higher education
- The reading public
- The "New Woman" and the new morality
- Realism reshapes American literature, art, and architecture
- The commercialization of popular entertainment

Examining the Evidence: Manuscript Census Data, 1900

Contending Voices: The New Immigration

Born in the country, America moved to the city in the decades following the Civil War. By the year 1900, the United States' upsurging population nearly doubled from its level of some 40 million souls enumerated in the census of 1870. Yet in the same period, the population of American cities *tripled.* By the end of the nineteenth century, four out of ten Americans were city dwellers, in striking contrast to the rustic population of stagecoach days.

This cityward drift affected not only the United States but the entire industrializing world. European peasants, pushed off the land in part by competition from cheap American foodstuffs, were pulled into cities—in both Europe and America—by the new lure of industrial jobs. A revolution in American agriculture thus fed the industrial and urban revolutions in Europe, as well as in the United States.

Focus Questions

1. What features characterized the new industrial city, and what was its impact on American society?
2. Why did the massive "New Immigration" from southern and eastern Europe stir opposition from many native-born Americans, and how did political machines, social reformers, and women adapt to the new urban and immigrant era?
3. What were the major challenges facing American religious life in the late nineteenth century? How did the growth of Catholic and Jewish populations as well as new religious movements alter the character of an historically Protestant America?
4. What were the major changes in American educational and cultural life in the late nineteenth century, and how did the intellectual and artistic turn toward "realism" reflect the new conditions of an urban and scientific civilization?
5. Why were there such fierce moral debates in the late nineteenth century, especially over issues concerning sex, women, and the family, and how did feminist activists work to alter ingrained cultural attitudes?

24-1 The Urban Frontier

The growth of American metropolises was spectacular. In 1860, no city in the United States could boast a million inhabitants; by 1890, New York, Chicago, and Philadelphia had vaulted past the million mark. By 1900, New York, with some 3.5 million people, was the second-largest city in the world, outranked only by London. (Refer to "Examining the Evidence: Manuscript Census Data, 1900," p. 595). Chicago, a modest town of barely 100,000 residents on the eve of the Civil War, was by century's end teeming with nearly two million souls—a majority of them either immigrants or the children of immigrants. Throughout the world, cities were exploding. London, Paris, Berlin, Tokyo, Moscow, Mexico City, Calcutta, and Shanghai all doubled or tripled in size between 1850 and 1900.

American cities grew both up and out. The cloud-brushing skyscraper allowed more people and workplaces to be packed onto a parcel of land. Appearing first as a ten-story building in Chicago in 1885, the skyscraper, supported by its skeleton of steel, was made viable thanks to the electric elevator. An opinionated Chicago architect, Louis Sullivan (1856–1924), contributed formidably to the further development of the skyscraper with his famous principle that "form follows function." Nesting loftily above city streets in the high-rises that Sullivan helped to make popular, prosperous urbanites looked down serenely at the clamorous streets below.

Americans were also becoming commuters, carted daily between home and job on the mass-transit lines that radiated from city centers to outlying neighborhoods. Electric trolleys, powered by wagging antennae from overhead wires, propelled city limits explosively outward. By the end of the century, the nation's first subway opened in Boston; London had led the way by building a subway as early as 1863. The compact and communal "walking city," its boundaries fixed by the limits of leg-power, gave way to the immense and impersonal megalopolis, carved into distinctly different districts for business, industry, and residential neighborhoods—which were in turn segregated by race, ethnicity, and social class.

Rural life could not compete with the siren song of the city (refer to Figure 24.1). Industrial jobs, above all, drew people off American and European farms and into factory centers. The urban lifestyle also held powerful attractions. The predawn milking of cows had little appeal when compared with the late-night glitter of city lights, particularly alluring to young adults yearning for independence. Electricity, indoor plumbing, and telephones—whose numbers dialed upward from some 50,000 in 1880 to over 1 million in 1900—all made life in the big city more enticing. Engineering marvels like New York's awesome Brooklyn Bridge, a harplike suspension span dedicated in 1883, further added to the seductive glamour of the gleaming cities (refer to Image 24.1).

Cavernous department stores such as Macy's in New York and Marshall Field's in Chicago attracted urban middle-class shoppers and provided urban working-class jobs, many of them for women. The bustling emporiums also heralded a dawning era of consumerism and accentuated widening class divisions. When Carrie Meeber, novelist Theodore Dreiser's fictional heroine in *Sister Carrie* (1900), escapes from rural boredom to Chicago just before the turn of the century, it is the spectacle of the city's dazzling department stores that awakens her fateful yearning for a richer, more elegant way of life—for entry into the privileged urban middle class, whose existence she had scarcely imagined in the sleepy countryside.

The move to the city introduced Americans to new ways of consuming. Country dwellers produced little household waste, and domestic animals or scavenging pigs ate cast-off food scraps on the farm. Rural women mended and darned worn clothing rather than discarding it. Household products were sold in bulk at the local store, without wrapping. Mail-order houses such as Sears and Montgomery Ward, which increasingly displaced the rural "general store" in the late nineteenth century, at first did not list trash barrels or garbage cans in their catalogues. In the city, however, goods came in throwaway bottles, boxes, bags, and cans. Apartment houses had no adjoining barnyards where residents might toss garbage to the hogs. Cheap, ready-to-wear clothing and swiftly changing fashions pushed old suits and dresses out of

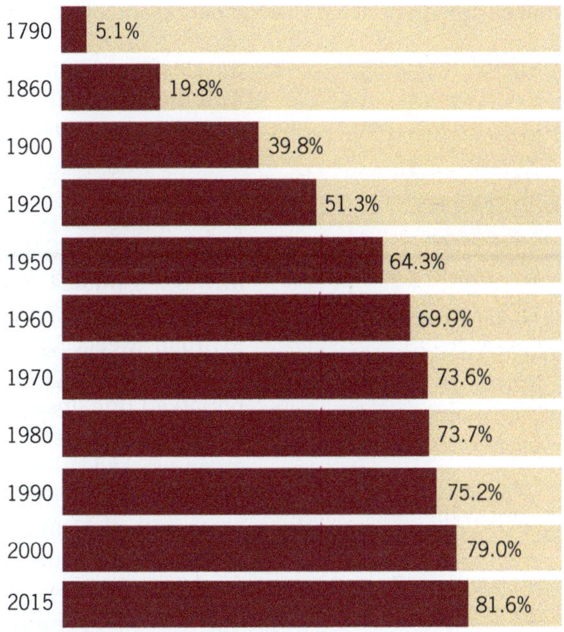

Figure 24.1 The Shift to the American City This chart shows the percentage of total population living in locales with a population of twenty-five hundred or more. Note the slowing of the cityward trend from 1970 on.

Sources: *Historical Statistics of the United States*; U.S. Census Bureau.

Library of Congress Prints and Photographs Division [LC-DIG-pga-00755]

Image 24.1 The Brooklyn Bridge The Brooklyn Bridge opened on May 24, 1883. It had taken thirteen years to build and was the largest suspension bridge in the world, as well as the first made of steel wire. On opening day, an astonishing 1,800 vehicles and 150,300 people made the short but breathtaking trek between the New York City boroughs of Manhattan and Brooklyn. The first person to cross was Emily Warren Roebling, the daughter-in-law of the original designer, John Augustus Roebling, and the wife of his son, Washington Roebling, who had taken over the job when his father died suddenly in 1869. When Washington fell ill himself, Emily learned civil engineering and oversaw much of the remaining work on the bridge.

the closet and onto the trash heap. Waste disposal, in short, was an issue new to the urban age. And the mountains of waste that urbanites generated further testified to a cultural shift away from the virtues of thrift to the conveniences of consumerism.

The jagged skyline of America's perpendicular civilization could not fully conceal the human costs of a feverish growth. Crime surged on the city's newly paved streets, from the petty thievery of quick-fingered pickpockets to the violent mayhem of organized gangs. Sanitary facilities could not keep pace with the mushrooming population explosion. Impure water, uncollected garbage, unwashed bodies, and droppings from draft animals enveloped many cities in a suffocating stench. A horse daily emitted up to fifty pounds of manure and a gallon of urine, liberally applied to urban streets. Small wonder that Baltimore was described as smelling like a billion polecats.

The cities were monuments of contradiction. They represented "humanity compressed," remarked one observer, "the best and the worst combined, in a strangely composite community." They harbored merchant princes and miserable paupers, stately banks and sooty factories, green-grassed suburbs and treeless slums, towering skyscrapers and stinking tenements. The glaring contrasts that assaulted the eye in New York reminded one visitor of "a lady in ball costume, with diamonds in her ears, and her toes out at the boots."

The city's poorest residents crammed into filthy and rat-infested neighborhoods that grew ever more crowded, especially after the appearance in 1879 of the "dumbbell" tenement (refer to Figure 24.2). So named because of the outline of its floor plan, the dumbbell was usually seven or eight stories high, with shallow, sunless, and foul-smelling air shafts providing minimal ventilation. Several families were sardined onto each floor of the barracks like structures, and they shared a malodorous toilet in the hall. In these fetid warrens, conspicuously in New York's "Lung Block," hundreds of unfortunate urbanites coughed away their lives. "Flophouses" abounded where the half-starved and unemployed might sleep for a few cents on verminous mattresses. Slum dwellers strove mightily to earn enough to escape their wretched surroundings. Many found success as shopkeepers, selling to neighbors in their immigrant communities. Others left the swarming cities altogether, headed to the wide-open expanses of the Great West.

Examining the Evidence

Manuscript Census Data, 1900

Article I of the Constitution requires that a census of the American people be taken every ten years, in order to provide a reliable basis for congressional apportionment. Early censuses gathered little more than basic population numbers, but over the years the census takers have collected information on other matters as well—including occupational categories, educational levels, and citizenship status—yielding copious raw data for historical analysis. The census of 1890 was the first to use punch cards and electric tabulating machines, which greatly expanded the range of data that could be assembled and correlated—though the basic information was still hand-recorded by individual canvassers who went door-to-door to question household members and fill out the census forms. Those handwritten forms, as much as the aggregate numbers printed in the final census tally, can furnish invaluable insights to the historian. Despite its apparent bureaucratic formality, the form shown here richly details the lives of the residents of a tenement house on New York's Lower East Side in 1900. See in particular the entries for the Goldberg family at the bottom of Image 24.2 (husband Jacob [listed as head of house], his wife Sarah, three daughters, and two sons). In what ways does this document reflect the great demographic changes that swept late-nineteenth-century America? What light does it shed on the character of immigrant "ghettos"? What further use might historians make of information like this?

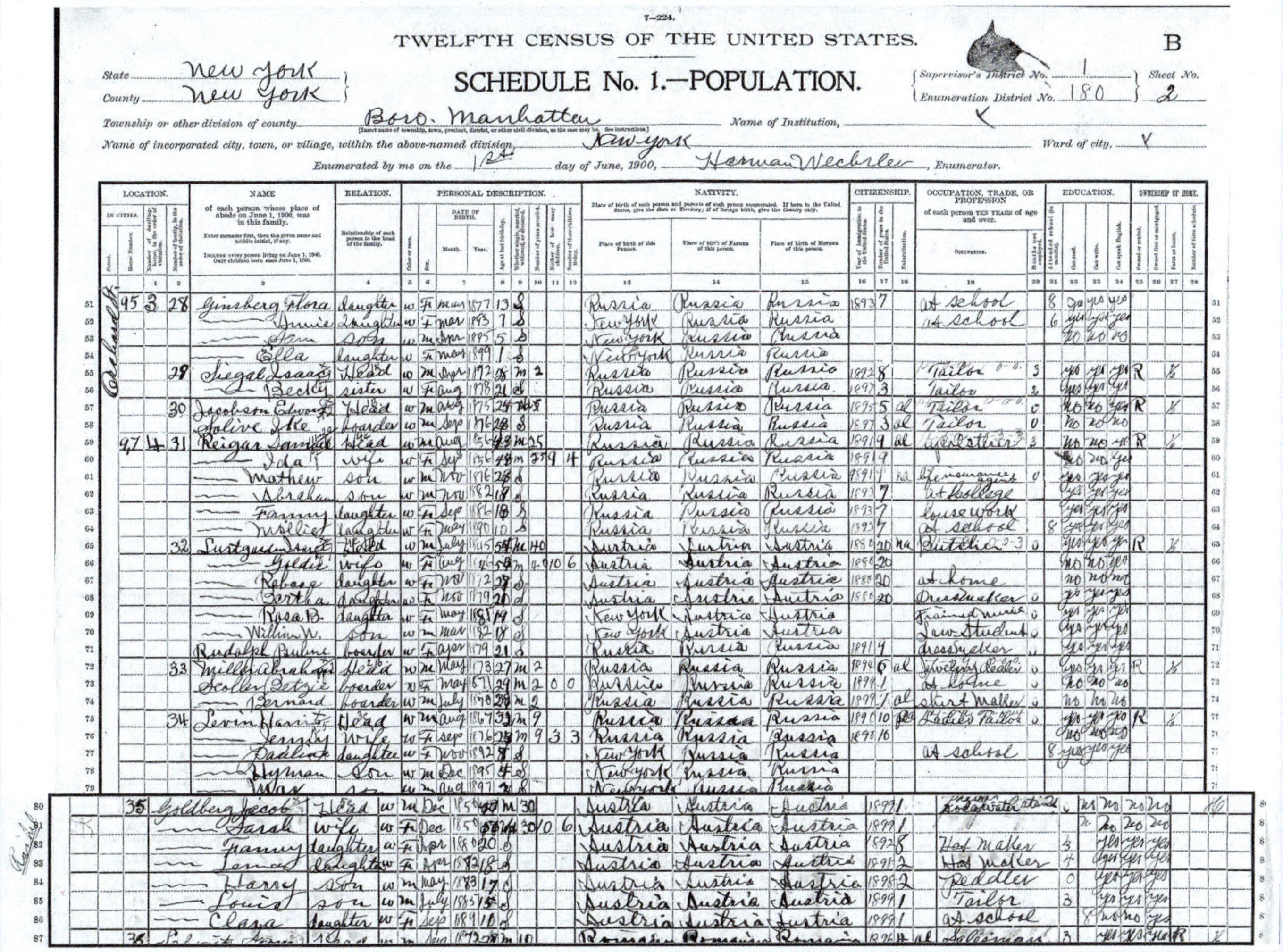

7–224.

TWELFTH CENSUS OF THE UNITED STATES. B

SCHEDULE No. 1.—POPULATION.

State: New York
County: New York
Supervisor's District No. 1
Enumeration District No. 180
Sheet No. 2

Township or other division of county: Boro. Manhattan [Insert name of township, town, precinct, district, or other civil division, as the case may be. See instructions.]
Name of Institution: X
Name of incorporated city, town, or village, within the above-named division: New York
Ward of city: X
Enumerated by me on the 1st day of June, 1900, Herman Wechsler, Enumerator.

Line	Street	House No. (1)	Dwelling (2)	Family (3)	Name (3)	Relation (4)	Color (5)	Sex (6)	Month (7)	Year (7)	Age (8)	Marital (9)	Yrs married (10)	Mother of (11)	Living (12)	Birthplace of person (13)	of father (14)	of mother (15)	Year of immigration (16)	Years in U.S. (17)	Naturalization (18)	Occupation (19)	Months not employed (20)	Attended school (21)	Can read (22)	Can write (23)	Speak English (24)	Owned or rented (25)	Free or mortgaged (26)	Farm or house (27)	Farm schedule (28)
51	Orchard St.	95	3	28	Ginsberg Flora	daughter	w	F	may	1877	13	S				Russia	Russia	Russia	1893	7		at school		8	yes	yes	yes				
52					Annie	daughter	w	F	mar	1893	7	S				New York	Russia	Russia				at school		6	yes	yes	yes				
53					Sam	son	w	M	Apr	1895	5	S				New York	Russia	Russia							no	no	no				
54					Ella	daughter	w	F	may	1899	1	S				New York	Russia	Russia													
55				29	Siegal Isaac	Head	w	M	Apr	1872	28	M	2			Russia	Russia	Russia	1892	8		Tailor	3		yes	yes	yes	R		H	
56					Becky	sister	w	F	aug	1878	21	S				Russia	Russia	Russia	1897	3		Tailor	2		yes	yes	yes				
57				30	Jacobson Edward	Head	w	M	aug	1875	24	[illegible]				Russia	Russia	Russia	1895	5	al	Tailor	0		no	no	yes	R		H	
58					Solive Ike	boarder	w	M	Sep	1876	23	S				Russia	Russia	Russia	1897	3	al	Tailor	0		no	no	no				
59		97	4	31	Reigar Samuel	Head	w	M	aug	1856	43	M	25			Russia	Russia	Russia	1891	9	al	[illegible]	3		no	no	no	R		H	
60					Ida	wife	w	F	Sep	1856	43	M	25	9	4	Russia	Russia	Russia	1891	9					no	no	yes				
61					Mathew	son	w	M	Nov	1876	23	S				Russia	Russia	Russia	1891	9	na	life insurance agent	0		yes	yes	yes				
62					Abraham	son	w	M	Nov	1882	18	S				Russia	Russia	Russia	1893	7		at college			yes	yes	yes				
63					Fanny	daughter	w	F	Sep	1886	13	S				Russia	Russia	Russia	1893	7		house work			yes	yes	yes				
64					Mollie	daughter	w	F	May	1890	10	S				Russia	Russia	Russia	1893	7		at school		8	yes	yes	yes				
65				32	Lustgarden Isaac	Head	w	M	July	1845	54	M	40			Austria	Austria	Austria	1880	20	na	Butcher	0		yes	yes	yes	R		H	
66					Goldie	wife	w	F	aug	[illegible]	53	M	40	10	6	Austria	Austria	Austria	1880	20					no	no	yes				
67					Rebecca	daughter	w	F	Nov	1872	27	S				Austria	Austria	Austria	1880	20		at home			no	no	no				
68					Bertha	daughter	w	F	Nov	1879	20	S				Austria	Austria	Austria	1880	20		Dressmaker	0		yes	yes	yes				
69					Rosa B.	daughter	w	F	May	1881	19	S				New York	Austria	Austria				Trained nurse	0		yes	yes	yes				
70					William W.	son	w	M	mar	1882	18	S				New York	Austria	Austria				Law student	0		yes	yes	yes				
71					Rudalph Pauline	boarder	w	F	Apr	1879	21	S				Russia	Russia	Russia	1891	4		dressmaker	0		yes	yes	yes				
72				33	Miller Abraham	Head	w	M	May	1873	27	M	2			Russia	Russia	Russia	1894	6	al	Jewelry peddler	0		yes	yes	yes	R		H	
73					Scoller Betzie	boarder	w	F	May	1871	29	M	2	0	0	Russia	Russia	Russia	1899	1		at home	0		no	no	no				
74					Bernard	boarder	w	M	July	1870	29	M	2			Russia	Russia	Russia	1899	1	al	Skirt maker	0		no	no	no				
75				34	Levin Harris	Head	w	M	aug	1867	33	M	9			Russia	Russia	Russia	1890	10	pa	Ladies Tailor	0		yes	yes	no	R		H	
76					Jenny	wife	w	F	Sep	1876	23	M	9	3	3	Russia	Russia	Russia	1890	10					no	no	no				
77					Badlick	daughter	w	F	Nov	1892	8	S				New York	Russia	Russia				at school		8	yes	yes	yes				
78					Hyman	son	w	M	Dec	1895	4	S				New York	Russia	Russia													
79					Max	son	w	M	aug	1897	2	S				New York	Russia	Russia													
80				35	Goldberg Jacob	Head	w	M	Dec	1850	49	M	30			Austria	Austria	Austria	1899	1		[illegible] soda water	0		no	no	no				
81					Sarah	wife	w	F	Dec	1850	49	M	30	10	6	Austria	Austria	Austria	1899	1					no	no	no				
82					Fanny	daughter	w	F	Apr	1880	20	S				Austria	Austria	Austria	1892	8		Hat maker	3		yes	yes	yes				
83					Lena	daughter	w	F	Apr	1882	18	S				Austria	Austria	Austria	1898	2		Hat maker	4		yes	yes	yes				
84					Harry	son	w	M	May	1883	17	S				Austria	Austria	Austria	1898	2		Peddler	0		yes	yes	yes				
85					Louis	son	w	M	July	1885	15	S				Austria	Austria	Austria	1899	1		Tailor	3		yes	yes	yes				
86					Clara	daughter	w	F	Sep	1891	10	S				Austria	Austria	Austria	1899	1		at school		8	no	no	yes				
87				36	[illegible]	Head	w	M	Nov	1872	27	M	10			Roumania	Roumania	Roumania	1896	4	al	Salesman	3		yes	yes	yes	R		H	

Image 24.2 Page from 1900 U.S. Census Canvasser Manuscript, Manhattan, New York

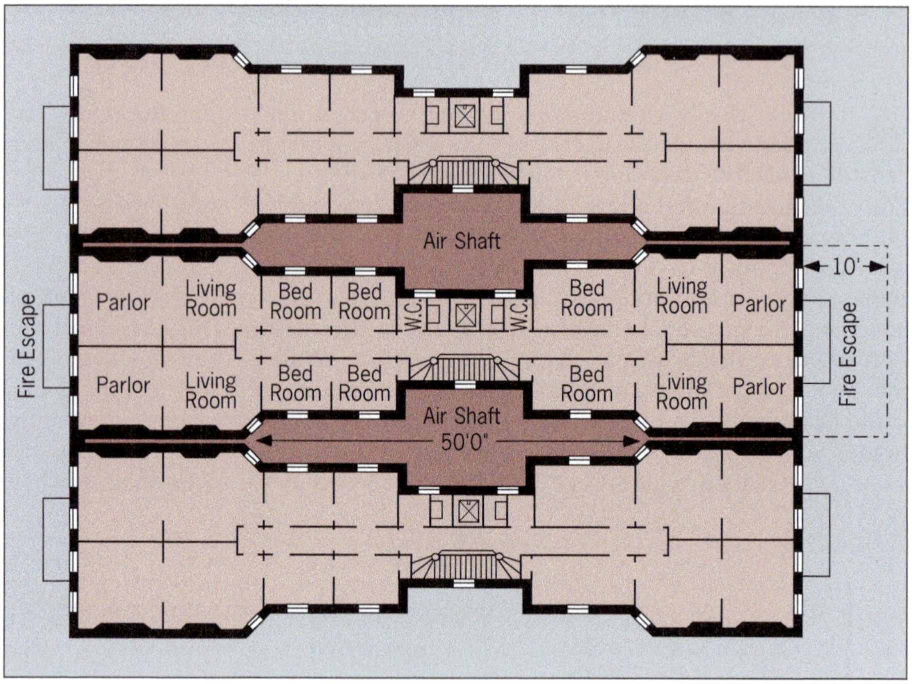

Figure 24.2 **Dumbbell Tenement** This was the standard architectural plan for the human warehouses on New York's Lower East Side. Despite the innovation of an air shaft to bring light and ventilation to the middle of the building, only one room in each of the apartments was directly exposed to sunlight and open air. All families on a floor shared the toilet ("W.C.") in the hallway.

Built hurriedly and haphazardly, America's industrial boomtowns were vulnerable to both natural and man-made disasters. In 1871, two-thirds of downtown Chicago burned in a raging fire that left ninety thousand people homeless and destroyed more than fifteen thousand buildings. Closely packed wooden structures fed the insatiable flames, prompting Chicago and other wary cities to require stone and iron buildings downtown. Clean water and sewage systems were slow to develop. Cholera and typhoid epidemics swept neighborhoods with alarming regularity. Tuberculosis—debilitating, highly contagious, and ultimately fatal—plagued the densely packed poor. The wealthiest began to leave the risky central cities behind and head for semirural suburbs. These leafy "bedroom communities" eventually ringed the brick-and-concrete cities with greenbelts of relative affluence.

24-2 The New Immigration

The massive disruptions of the Industrial Revolution, as well as the powerful pull of the American urban magnet, were felt even in faraway Europe. A seemingly endless stream of immigrants continued to pour in from the old "mother continent." In each of the three decades from the 1850s through the 1870s, more than 2 million migrants had stepped onto America's shores. By the 1880s, the stream had swelled to a rushing torrent, as more than 5 million cascaded into the country. A new high for a single year was reached in 1882, when 788,992 arrived—or more than 2,100 a day (refer to Figure 24.3).

Until the 1880s, most immigrants had come from the British Isles and western Europe, chiefly Germany and Ireland, as well as the many Chinese newcomers who settled in the cities and towns of the Far West. Many of these earlier immigrants had faced virulent nativism, especially the Irish and the Chinese (the latter being legally excluded in 1882). By the last decades of the century, however, the "old" European immigrants had adjusted well to American life by building supportive ethnic organizations and melding into established communities. Although anti-Catholic sentiment remained strong and many still lived, worked, and worshiped among their own, they had come to be largely accepted as "American" by the native-born.

In the last decades of the nineteenth century, the character of the immigrant stream changed drastically (refer to Figure 24.4). The so-called **New Immigrants** came from southern and eastern Europe. Among them were Italians, Jews, Croats, Slovaks, Greeks, and Poles. They came from countries with little history of democratic government, where people had grown accustomed to cringing before despotism and where opportunities for advancement were few. These newcomers totaled only 19 percent of the inpouring immigrants in the 1880s; by the first decade of the

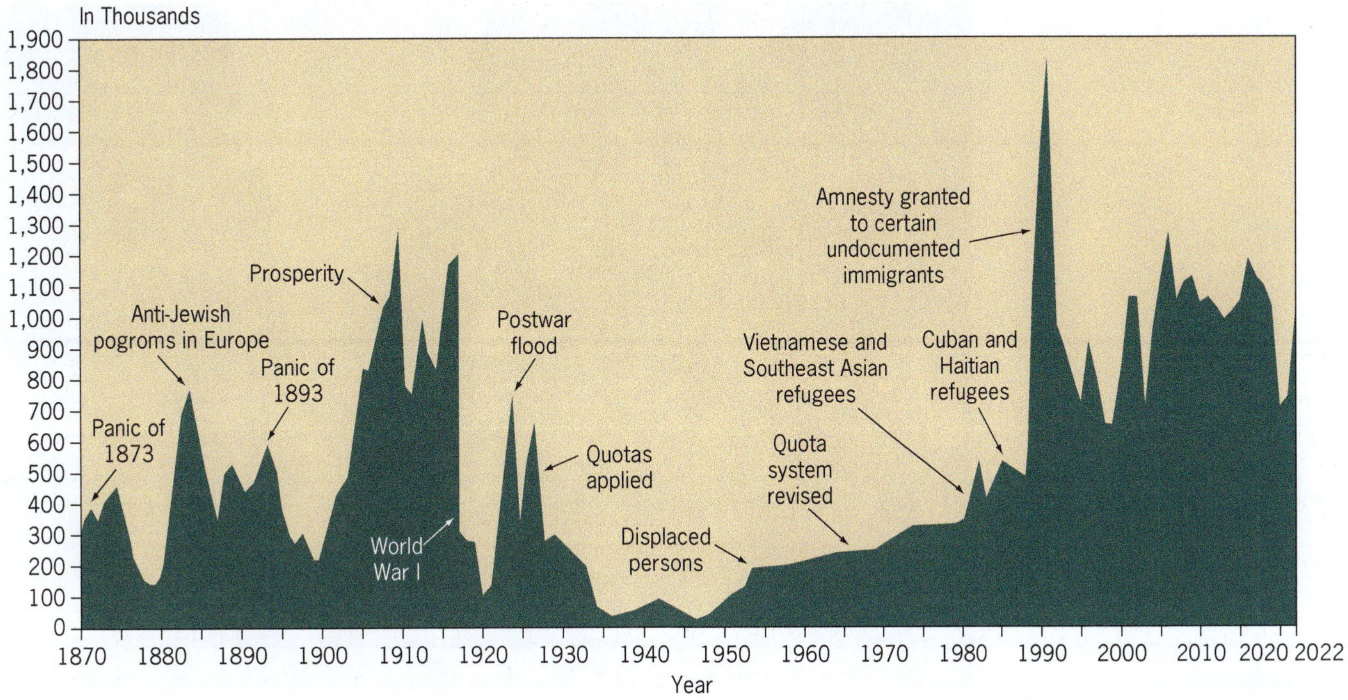

Figure 24.3 Annual Immigration, 1870–2022 After 1924, these numbers include only legal, documented immigrants. The 1989 total includes 478,814 people granted permanent residence status under the "amnesty" provisions of the 1986 Immigration Reform and Control Act. The 1990 total includes 880,372 people granted permanent residence under these provisions. The peak came in 1991, when 1,123,162 people were affected by amnesty. The COVID-19 pandemic significantly limited the number of legal entries in 2020 and 2021.

Sources: *Statistical Abstract of the United States*, relevant years; Department of Homeland Security, *Yearbook of Immigration Statistics*, 2015.

twentieth century, they constituted an astonishing 66 percent of the total. They clung together in cities like New York and Chicago, where the "Little Italys" and "Little Polands" soon claimed more inhabitants than many of the largest cities of the same nationality in the Old World (refer to Image 24.3).

Why were these quaintly garbed strangers hammering on the gates? In part, they left their native countries because Europe seemed to have no room for them. The population of the Old World was growing vigorously. It nearly doubled in the century after 1800, thanks in part to

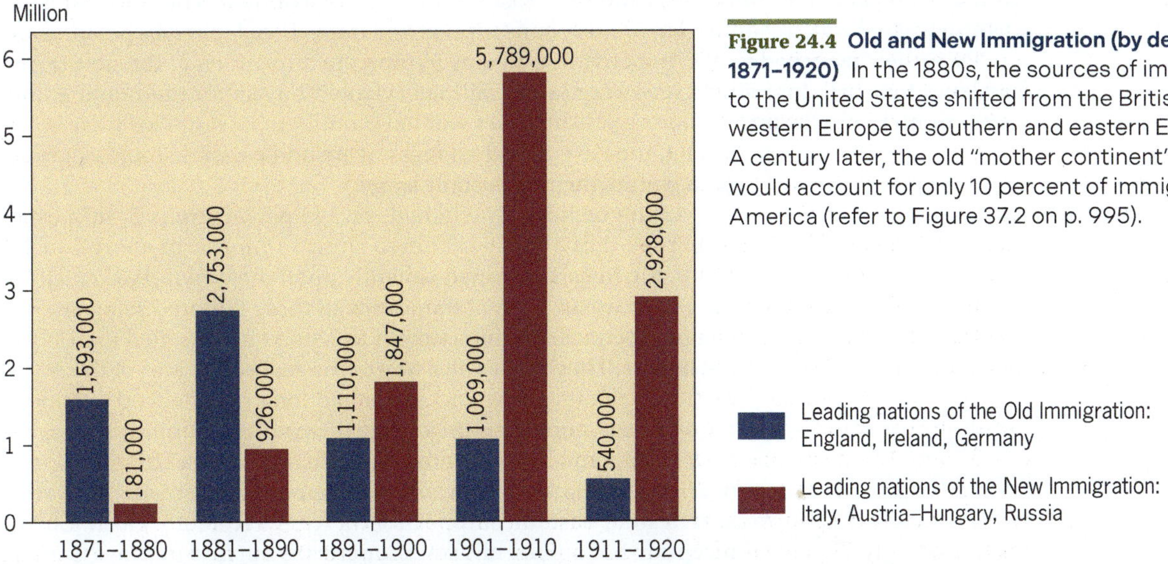

Figure 24.4 Old and New Immigration (by decade, 1871–1920) In the 1880s, the sources of immigration to the United States shifted from the British Isles and western Europe to southern and eastern Europe. A century later, the old "mother continent" of Europe would account for only 10 percent of immigrants to America (refer to Figure 37.2 on p. 995).

Image 24.3 Mulberry Street on New York City's Lower East Side, ca. 1900 Population densities in early twentieth-century American cities were among the highest in the world. Mulberry Street, shown in this photo, was at the heart of New York's "Little Italy" neighborhood.

abundant supplies of fish and grain from America and to the widespread cultivation in Europe of that humble New World transplant, the potato.

American food imports and the galloping pace of European industrialization shook the peasantry loose from its ancient habitats and customary occupations, creating a vast, footloose army of the unemployed. Europeans by the millions drained out of the countryside and into European cities. Most stayed there, but some kept moving and left Europe altogether.

About 60 million Europeans abandoned the Old Continent in the nineteenth and early twentieth centuries. Roughly half of them moved to the United States, while their compatriots spread out across the globe to South America, Canada, Africa, and Australia. Masses of people were already in motion in Europe before they felt the tug of the American magnet. This European diaspora, though dominated by immigration to the United States, was, in many ways, simply a by-product of the urbanization of Europe.

"America fever" proved highly contagious in Europe. The United States was often painted as a land of fabulous opportunity in the "America letters" sent by friends and relatives already transplanted—letters that were soiled by the hands of many readers. "We eat here every day," wrote one jubilant Pole, "what we get only for Easter in our [native] country." The land of the free was also blessed with freedom from military conscription and from official religious persecution.

Profit-seeking Americans trumpeted throughout Europe the attractions of the new promised land. Industrialists wanted low-wage labor, railroads wanted buyers for their land grants, states wanted more taxpayers, and steamship lines wanted more human cargo for their holds. In fact, the ease and cheapness of steam-powered shipping greatly accelerated the transoceanic surge.

As the century lengthened, savage persecutions of minorities in Europe drove many shattered souls to American shores. In the 1880s, the Russians turned violently upon their own Jews, chiefly in the Polish areas. Tens of thousands of these battered refugees, survivors of centuries of harassment as hated outcasts, fled their burning homes. They made their way to the seaboard cities of the Atlantic Coast, notably New York. Jews had long experienced city life in Europe—a circumstance that made them virtually unique among the New Immigrants. Many of them brought their urban skills of tailoring or shopkeeping to American cities (refer to Image 24.4). Destitute and devout, eastern European Jews were frequently given a frosty reception not only by old-stock Americans but also by those German

Mary Antin (1881–1949), who came to America from Russian Poland in 1894 when thirteen years of age, later wrote in *The Promised Land* (1912),

"So at last I was going to America! Really, really going, at last! The boundaries burst. The arch of heaven soared. A million suns shone out for every star. The winds rushed in from outer space, roaring in my ears, 'America! America!'"

Image 24.4 Jewish Women Working in a Sweatshop, ca. 1910 Countless immigrant women found their first American employment in shops like this.

Jews who had arrived decades earlier and prospered in the United States, some as garment manufacturers who now employed their coreligionists as cheap labor.

Many of the immigrants never intended to become Americans in any case. A large number of them were single men who worked in the United States for several months or years and then returned home with their hard-earned roll of American dollars. Some 25 percent of the nearly 20 million people who arrived between 1820 and 1900 were "birds of passage" who eventually returned to their country of origin. For them the attraction of the American magnet was never strong.

Even those who stayed in America struggled heroically to preserve their traditional culture. Catholics expanded their parochial-school systems, and Jews established Hebrew schools. Foreign-language newspapers abounded. Yiddish theaters, kosher-food stores, Polish parishes, Greek restaurants, and Italian social clubs all attested to the desire to keep old ways alive. Yet time took its toll on these efforts to conserve the customs of the Old World in the New. The children of the immigrants grew up speaking fluent English, sometimes mocking the broken grammar of their parents. They often rejected the Old Country manners of their mothers and fathers in their desire to plunge headlong into the mainstream of American life.

24-3 Machines and Reformers Compete and Clash

America's government system, nurtured in wide-open spaces, was ill-suited to the cement forests of the great cities. Beyond minimal checking to identify criminals and the mentally ill, the federal government did virtually nothing to ease the assimilation of immigrants into American society. State governments, usually dominated by rural representatives, did even less. City governments, overwhelmed by the sheer scale of rampant urban growth, proved woefully inadequate.

By default, the business of ministering to the immigrants' needs fell to the unofficial "governments" of the urban **political machines**, exemplified by New York's notorious Tammany Hall, long

Image 24.5 "That's What's the Matter." Cartoonist Thomas Nast attacked New York City's "Boss" Tweed in a series of cartoons like this one that appeared in *Harper's Weekly* in 1871. Here Nast depicts the corrupt Tweed as a figure both menacing and comic, towering over the ballot box to ensure the vote count would go in his favor.

led by the flamboyantly corrupt William Marcy "Boss" Tweed. Trading jobs and services for votes, machines like the **Tweed Ring** claimed the political loyalty of thousands of followers (refer to Image 24.5). In return for their support at the polls, the machine boss provided jobs on the city's payroll, found housing for new arrivals, tided over the destitute with gifts of food and clothing, patched up minor scrapes with the law, and helped get schools, parks, and hospitals built in immigrant neighborhoods.

Reformers gagged at this cynical exploitation of the immigrant vote, and the Tweed Ring became synonymous with sleazy political shenanigans as well as the growing electoral power of a foreign-born working class. Cries of voter fraud and stolen elections grew louder among aghast elites, as more of New York's immigrants flocked to the polls.

Tweed's luck finally ran out. The *New York Times* published damning evidence of corruption in 1871, though offered $5 million not to do so. The pro-Republican and rabidly anti-immigrant cartoonist Thomas Nast pilloried Tweed mercilessly. The burly "Boss"—240 pounds of rascality—reportedly complained that his followers could not help seeing "them damn pictures." New York attorney Samuel J. Tilden headed the prosecution of Tweed, gaining fame that later paved the path to his presidential nomination. Having pushed the boundaries of "honest graft" far beyond what even this money-hungry age would bear. Unwept and unbailed, Tweed died behind bars.

The urban machines were fairly decried for their corruption. Yet they also provided invaluable assistance to struggling people that was forthcoming from no other source. Fortunately, the nation's social conscience, slumbering since the antislavery crusade, was gradually awakening to the plight of the urban masses.

One pathbreaking reformer was Jane Addams (1860–1935). Born into a prosperous Illinois family, Addams was one of the first generation of college-educated women. Upon graduation, she sought other outlets for her large talents than could be found in teaching or charitable volunteer work, then the only permissible occupations for a young woman of her social class. Inspired by a visit to England, she acquired the decaying Hull mansion in Chicago in 1889. There she established Hull House, the most prominent (though not the first) American **settlement house**.

Soft-spoken but tenacious, Addams became a kind of urban American saint in the eyes of many admirers. The philosopher William James told her, "You utter instinctively the truth we others vainly seek." She was a broad-gauge reformer who courageously condemned war as well as poverty, and she eventually won the Nobel Peace Prize in 1931. But her pacifism also earned her the enmity of some Americans, including the Daughters of the American Revolution, who choked on her antiwar views and expelled her from membership in their august organization.

Located in a poor immigrant neighborhood of Greeks, Italians, Russians, and Germans, Hull House offered instruction in English, counseling to help newcomers cope with American big-city life, child-care services for working mothers, and cultural activities for neighborhood residents (refer to Image 24.6). Following Jane Addams's lead, women founded settlement houses in other cities as well. Conspicuous among the houses was Lillian Wald's Henry Street Settlement in New York, which opened its doors in 1893.

The settlement houses became centers of women's activism and of social reform. The women of Hull House successfully lobbied in 1893 for an Illinois anti-sweatshop law that protected women workers and prohibited child labor. They were led in this case by the black-clad Florence Kelley, a ferocious fighter in the urban jungle. Armed with the insights of socialism and endowed with the voice of an actress, Kelley was a lifelong battler for the welfare of women and children, both Black and white. She later moved to the Henry Street Settlement in New York and served for three decades as general secretary of the National Consumers League.

Image 24.6 Hull House Choir, ca. 1910 The settlement house that Jane Addams founded in Chicago not only provided social services and education to poor immigrants but also sponsored cultural activities like this choir, whose members ranged from children to senior citizens.

The pioneering work of Addams, Wald, and Kelley helped blaze the trail that many women—and some men—later followed into careers in urban reform and the new profession of social work. For these female reformers, and for many other women, the city offered a new kind of frontier opportunity.

24-4 Narrowing the Welcome Mat

Antiforeignism, or "nativism," earlier had raged against Irish and German arrivals in the 1840s and 1850s. It bared its ugly face in the 1880s with fresh ferocity, given sharper bite by the racist pseudoscience of eugenics, which falsely contended that skin color and ethnic origin determined human intelligence and "fitness."

The New Immigrants had come for much the same reasons as the Old—to escape the poverty and squalor of Europe and to seek new opportunities in America. But nativists worried that America was becoming not a melting pot but a dumping ground. They viewed the eastern and southern Europeans as culturally and religiously alien hordes and often gave them an ugly reception. The high birthrate of these young and mobile people raised worries among the native-born that they would soon be outnumbered and outvoted. Still more horrifying to some was the prospect that the nation would be "mongrelized" by a mixture of "inferior" southern European blood and that the fairer Anglo-Saxon types would disappear. One New England writer cried out in anguish,

> O Liberty, white Goddess! is it well
> To leave the gates unguarded?

Some native-born Americans blamed the immigrants and the political machines they spawned for the degradation of urban government. Some trade unionists assailed the alien arrivals for their willingness to work for "starvation" wages that seemed to the newcomers like princely sums, and for importing in their intellectual baggage such seemingly dangerous doctrines as socialism, communism, and anarchism. Many business leaders, who had welcomed the flood of cheap manual labor, began to fear that they had embraced a Frankenstein's monster.

Antiforeign organizations, reminiscent of the "Know-Nothings" of pre–Civil War days, were now revived in a different guise. Notorious among them was the American Protective Association (APA), which was created in 1887 and soon claimed a million members. In pursuing its nativist goals, the APA urged voting against Roman Catholic candidates for office and sponsored the publication of lustful fantasies about runaway nuns.

Organized labor was quick to throw its growing weight behind the move to choke off the rising tide of foreigners. Frequently used as strikebreakers, the wage-depressing immigrants were hard to unionize because of the language and cultural barriers that divided them. Labor leaders argued, not illogically, that if American industry was entitled to protection from foreign goods, American workers were entitled to protection from foreign laborers.

Congress finally nailed up partial bars against the inpouring immigrants. The first national immigration restriction law, barring admission to "lunatics" and "those likely to become a public charge," was passed in 1882, the same year as the infamous Chinese Exclusion Act (refer to "21-9 Class Conflicts and Ethnic Clashes," pp. 531–533). Congress further responded to pained outcries from organized labor when in 1885 it prohibited the importation of foreign workers under contract—usually for substandard wages. In later years other federal laws lengthened the list of undesirables to include the mentally ill, polygamists, prostitutes, alcoholics, anarchists, and people carrying contagious diseases (refer to Image 24.7).

A proposed literacy test, long a favorite of nativists because it favored the Old Immigrants over the New, met vigorous opposition on the grounds that literacy was more a measure of opportunity than of intelligence. It was finally enacted in 1917, after three presidents had vetoed it.

In response to nativists who condemned the New Immigrants as despicable human specimens threatening to drag down the American race, the Jewish immigrant playwright Israel Zangwill (1864–1926) celebrated the new superior American emerging out of what he called "the great melting pot" of European races:

"America is God's crucible, the great melting pot, where all the races of Europe are melting and re-forming! . . . Germans and Frenchmen, Irishmen and Englishmen, Jews and Russians—into the Crucible with you all! God is making the American!"

Image 24.7 Looking Backward Older immigrants, trying to keep their own humble arrival in America "in the shadows," sought to close the bridge that had carried them and their ancestors across the Atlantic.

In 1886, the Statue of Liberty arose in New York harbor, a gift from the people of France (refer to Image 24.8). On its base were inscribed the words of Emma Lazarus:

> Give me your tired, your poor
> Your huddled masses yearning to breathe free,
> The wretched refuse of your teeming shore.

To many nativists, that noble language described only too accurately the "scum" washed up by the New Immigrant tides. Yet the uprooted immigrants, unlike "natives" lucky enough to have had parents who caught an earlier ship, became American citizens the hard way. They stepped off the boat, often penniless but ready to put their shoulders to the nation's industrial wheels and to reinvent their lives, build new communities, and remake a nation.

24-5 Churches Confront the Urban Challenge

The Christian churchgoing population of the United States swelled in the industrial era, growing from 34 percent of the population in 1850 to 45 percent in 1890. The bulging size and changing character of the urban population created new pressures for Protestant churches, which long had taken a leading role in providing aid to the urban poor. For these denominations, many traditional doctrines and pastoral approaches seemed irrelevant amid explosive and diverse urban growth. Reflecting the wealth of their prosperous parishioners, many of the old-line churches in large cities like New York were distressingly slow to raise their voices against social and economic inequities. Trinity Episcopal Church in New York actually owned some of the city's worst slum properties.

The Library of Congress

Image 24.8 The Statue of Liberty's Head on Display in a Park in Paris, 1883 She was a centennial "birthday present" from the French to the American people.

Contending Voices

The New Immigration

Writing in 1891 in support of a literacy test for immigrants, Massachusetts Republican Henry Cabot Lodge (1850–1924) emphasized a distinction between the recent stream of immigrants from southern and eastern Europe and earlier arrivals from Great Britain and Germany:

"Thus it is proved, first, that immigration to this country is increasing, and, second, that it is making its greatest relative increase from races most alien to the body of the American people and from the lowest and most illiterate classes among those races."

Six years later, Democratic president Grover Cleveland (1837–1908) disputed the merits of just such a distinction:

"It is said . . . that the quality of recent immigration is undesirable. The time is quite within recent memory when the same thing was said of immigrants who, with their descendants, are now numbered among our best citizens."

Consider This:

What political factors might account for the contrasting positions taken by these two public officials?

Concerned about what they saw as a spreading moral vacuum, a new generation of **liberal Protestants** rose to the fore. With roots in the Unitarian revolt against orthodox Calvinism, liberal ideals and a fresh emphasis on social justice came into the mainstream of American Protestantism between 1875 and 1925.

Prominent in this awakening were several Protestant clergymen, who sought to apply the lessons of Christianity to the slums and factories. Noteworthy among them was Walter Rauschenbusch, who in 1886 became pastor of a German Baptist church in New York City. Also conspicuous was Washington Gladden, who took over a Congregational church in Columbus, Ohio, in 1882. Preaching the "social gospel," they both insisted that the churches tackle the burning social issues of the day. The Sermon on the Mount, they declared, was the science of society, and many social gospelers predicted that socialism would be the logical outcome of Christianity. These "Christian socialists" did much to prick callous middle-class consciences, preparing the path for the progressive reform movement after the turn of the century.

These believers rejected biblical literalism, urging Christians to view biblical stories not as dogma but as models for Christian behavior. Evangelicalism still ran strong, however, as urban revivalists like Dwight Lyman Moody, a former shoe salesman, captivated audiences with his message of forgiveness (refer to Image 24.9). In cities filled with transplanted and often lonely migrants, the churches' emphasis on community fellowship and earthly salvation attracted many followers.

Simultaneously, the Roman Catholic and Jewish faiths were gaining enormous strength from the New Immigration. By 1900, Roman Catholics had become the largest single Christian denomination in the United States, numbering nearly 9 million communicants—well more than double the number of thirty years earlier. Growing numbers of Catholics slightly eased the social prejudice against them. Cardinal James Gibbons (1834–1921), an urban Catholic leader devoted to American unity, was immensely popular with Roman Catholics and Protestants alike. Acquainted with every president from Andrew Johnson to Warren Harding, he employed his liberal sympathies to assist the American labor movement.

By 1890, Americans could choose from 150 religious denominations as well as new faith-based social movements. One was the band-playing Salvation Army, whose soldiers without swords invaded America from England in 1879 and established an evangelical beachhead on the country's street corners, preaching to the most destitute urban dwellers.

MPI/Archive Photos/Getty Images

Image 24.9 Dwight Lyman Moody
In top hat, Moody poses ca. 1870 with a group of orphans at one of his Chicago missions.

Another American-born new faith rising up in response to the changes of modern life was the Church of Christ, Scientist (Christian Science), founded by New Englander Mary Baker Eddy in 1879 after she had suffered much ill health. Rejecting modern medicine and preaching that the true practice of Christianity heals sickness, she set forth her views in a blockbuster book titled *Science and Health with Key to the Scriptures* (1875), which sold 400,000 copies before her death and millions of copies thereafter. Hurried, anxious, and increasingly urbanized America proved a fertile field for converts to the Christian Scientist doctrine of relief from discord and disease through prayer. By the time she died in 1910, Eddy had founded an influential new church that embraced several hundred thousand devoted worshipers.

Urbanites also participated in a new kind of religious-affiliated organization, the Young Men's and Women's Christian Associations. The YMCA and the YWCA, established in the United States before the Civil War, grew by leaps and bounds. Combining physical and other kinds of education with religious instruction, the "Y's"—along with the Young Men's and Women's Hebrew Associations, which eventually merged into Jewish Community Centers—appeared in virtually every major American city by the end of the nineteenth century.

24-6 Darwin Disrupts the Churches

Old-time religion received many blows from modern trends, including a booming sale of books on comparative religion and on historical criticism as applied to the Bible. Most unsettling of all were the writings of the English naturalist Charles Darwin. In lucid prose he set forth the sensational theory that higher forms of life had slowly evolved from lower forms, through a process of random biological mutation and adaptation.

Though not the first scientist to propose an evolutionary hypothesis, Darwin broke new ground with his idea of "natural selection." Nature, in his view, blindly selected organisms for survival or death based on random, inheritable variations that they happened to possess. Some traits conferred advantages in the struggle for life, and hence better odds of passing them along to offspring. By providing a material explanation for the evolutionary process, Darwin's theory explicitly rejected the "dogma of special creations," which ascribed the design of each fixed species to divine agency.

Darwin's radical ideas evoked the wrath of scientists and laymen alike. Many zoologists, like Harvard's Louis Agassiz, held fast to the old doctrine of "special creations." By 1875, however, the majority of scientists in America and elsewhere had embraced the theory of organic evolution, though not all endorsed natural selection as its agent. Clergymen and theologians responded to Darwin's theory in several ways. At first most believers joined scientists in rejecting his ideas outright. After 1875, by which time most natural scientists had embraced evolution, the religious community split into two camps. A conservative minority stood firmly behind the Scripture as the infallible Word of God, and they condemned what they thought was the "bestial hypothesis" of the Darwinians. Their rejection of scientific consensus spawned a muscular view of biblical literalism that eventually gave rise to fundamentalism in the twentieth century.

Most religious thinkers parted company with the conservatives and flatly refused to accept the Bible in its entirety as either history or science. They feared that hostility toward evolution would alienate educated believers. Over time, an increasing number of liberal thinkers were able to reconcile Darwinism with Christianity. They heralded the revolutionary theory as a newer and grander revelation of the ways of the Almighty. As one commentator observed,

> Some call it Evolution,
> And others call it God.

Darwinism also provided the seed for the pernicious, and pseudo-scientific doctrine of eugenics, or "social Darwinism." Applying Darwin's principles of natural selection *within* one species—human beings—social Darwinists contended that different racial and ethnic groups also followed an evolutionary hierarchy, and that white Anglo-Saxons were at the top. The "science" of eugenics was accepted as a legitimate field of academic study for decades.

The rise of scientific thinking, Darwinian and otherwise, undoubtedly did much to loosen religious moorings and to promote skepticism among the gospel-glutted. While the liberal efforts at compromise did succeed in keeping many Americans in the pews, those compromises also tended to relegate religious teaching to matters of personal faith, private conduct, and family life. As science began to explain more of the external world, commentators on nature and society increasingly refrained from adding religious perspectives to the discussion.

24-7 The Lust for Learning

Public education continued its upward climb. The ideal of tax-supported elementary schools, adopted on a nationwide basis before the Civil War, was still gathering strength. Americans were accepting the truism that a free government cannot function successfully if the people are shackled by ignorance. Beginning about 1870, more and more states were making at least a grade-school education compulsory. This gain, incidentally, helped check the frightful abuses of child labor.

Spectacular indeed was the spread of high schools, especially by the 1880s and 1890s. Before the Civil War, fewer than 10 percent of Americans could boast of a high-school degree. But the concept that education through high school was the birthright of every citizen was now gaining impressive support. By 1900, some six thousand high schools graced the land. The illiteracy rate fell from 20 percent in 1870 to 10.7 percent in 1900.

Other trends were noteworthy. Teacher-training schools, then called "normal schools," experienced a striking expansion after the Civil War. In 1860 there were only twelve of them, in 1910 over three hundred. Kindergartens, earlier borrowed from Germany, began to gain strong support. The New Immigration in the 1880s and 1890s also invigorated private Catholic parochial schools, which fast became a major pillar of the nation's educational structure (and testified both to the reluctance of immigrants to abandon their cultural patrimony, and the discrimination Catholics faced outside their communities). In the realm of adult education, the Chautauqua movement, launched in 1874 on the shores of Lake Chautauqua in New York, sponsored public lectures and home study courses nationwide that reached hundreds of thousands of knowledge-hungry men and women.

24-8 Washington, Du Bois, and Education for Black People

War-torn and impoverished, the South lagged far behind other regions in public education, and African Americans suffered most severely. A staggering 44 percent of nonwhite citizens were illiterate in 1900. Some help came from Northern philanthropists, but those most dedicated to educational uplift were Black leaders themselves.

The most celebrated champion of Black education was Booker T. Washington. The once-enslaved Washington's classic autobiography, *Up from Slavery* (1900), tells how he slept under a board sidewalk to save for his schooling. Called in 1881 to head the **Tuskegee Normal and Industrial School** (later Tuskegee University) in Alabama, he began with forty Black students in a tumbledown shanty. Undaunted, he taught trades useful for gaining gain self-respect and economic security. Washington's self-help approach to solving the nation's racial problems was labeled "accommodationist" because it stopped short of directly challenging white supremacy (refer to Image 24.10). Recognizing the depths of Southern white racism, Washington avoided the issue of *social* equality. Instead, he grudgingly acquiesced in segregation in return for the right to develop—however modestly and painstakingly—the economic and educational resources of the Black community. Economic independence would ultimately be the ticket, Washington believed, to Black political and civil rights.

Washington's commitment to training young Black students in agriculture and the trades guided the curriculum at Tuskegee Institute and made it an ideal place for slave-born George Washington Carver to teach and research. After Carver joined the faculty in 1896, he became an internationally famous agricultural chemist who provided a much-needed boost to the Southern economy by discovering hundreds of new uses for the lowly peanut (shampoo, axle grease), sweet potato (vinegar), and soybean (paint).

Library of Congress Prints and Photographs Division [LC-DIG-ppmsca-13491]

Image 24.10 Booker T. Washington (1856–1915) In a famous speech in New Orleans in 1895, Washington grudgingly acquiesced in social separateness for Black people. On that occasion, he told his largely white audience, "In all things that are purely social, we can be as separate as the fingers, yet one as the hand in all things essential to mutual progress."

Other Black leaders, notably Dr. W. E. B. Du Bois, assailed Booker T. Washington as an "Uncle Tom" who was condemning their race to manual labor and perpetual inferiority. Instead, Du Bois argued, the goal must be complete equality for Black people, both social and economic. Born free in Massachusetts, Du Bois was of mixed African, French, Dutch, and Native American descent ("Thank God, no Anglo-Saxon," he would add). After a determined struggle, he earned a PhD at Harvard, the first Black person to achieve that goal. ("The honor, I assure you, was Harvard's," he later quipped). Calling for the comparably privileged and educated "talented tenth" of the Black community to take on leadership in the struggle for racial equality, Du Bois helped found the National Association for the Advancement of Colored People (NAACP) in 1909 and became editor of its influential journal, *The Crisis*. An exceptionally gifted historian, sociologist, and poet, he wrote landmark studies of urban racial and economic segregation, Black identity, and the shortchanged struggle for racial freedom during and after Reconstruction. He died in self-exile in Africa in 1963, at the age of ninety-five (refer to Image 24.11). Many of Du Bois's differences with Washington reflected the contrasting life experiences of Black Southerners and Black Northerners.

W. E. B. Du Bois (1868–1963) wrote in his 1903 classic, *The Souls of Black Folk*,

"It is a peculiar sensation, this double consciousness, this sense of always looking at one's self through the eyes of others, of measuring one's self through the eyes of others. . . . One ever feels his two-ness—an American, a Negro; two souls, two thoughts, two unreconciled strivings; two warring ideals in one dark body, whose dogged strength alone keeps it from being torn asunder."

24-9 The Hallowed Halls of Ivy

Colleges and universities also shot up like vigorous young saplings in the decades after the Civil War. A college education increasingly seemed indispensable in the scramble for the golden apple of success (refer to Table 24.1). Women's colleges were gaining ground, including the so-called "Seven Sisters" colleges of the Northeast (Barnard, Bryn Mawr, Mount Holyoke, Radcliffe, Smith, Vassar, and Wellesley). Universities open to both genders were blossoming, notably in the Midwest. By 1880, every third college graduate was a woman.

Image 24.11 **W. E. B. Du Bois (1868–1963)** In 1961, at the end of a long lifetime of struggle for racial justice in the United States, Du Bois renounced his American citizenship at the age of ninety-three and took up residence in the newly independent African state of Ghana.

So too were Black Americans finding new opportunities for higher education. By the turn of the century, the Black institutes and academies sowed during Reconstruction had blossomed into a crop of southern Black colleges. Howard University in Washington, DC, Hampton Institute in Virginia, Atlanta University, and numerous others nurtured higher education for Blacks until the civil rights gains of the 1960s made widespread attendance at white institutions possible.

The truly phenomenal growth of higher education owed much to the Morrill Act of 1862. This enlightened law provided generous grants of public lands to the states for support of education. **Land-grant colleges,** most of which became state universities, in turn bound themselves to provide certain services, such as military training. The Hatch Act of 1887, extending the Morrill Act, provided federal funds for the establishment of agricultural experiment stations in connection with the land-grant colleges. These two pieces of legislation spawned over a hundred colleges and universities, including such institutions as the University of California (1868), the Ohio State University (1870), and Texas A&M (1876).

Private philanthropy richly supplemented government grants to higher education. Many of the new industrial millionaires, moved both by educational commitment as well as a desire to transcend their rapacious reputations, donated immense fortunes to educational enterprises. A philanthropist was cynically described as "one who steals privately and gives publicly." In the twenty years from 1878 to 1898, these money barons gave away about $150 million. Noteworthy among the new private universities of high quality were Cornell (1865) and Leland Stanford Junior (1891), the latter founded in memory of the deceased fifteen-year-old only child of a builder of the Central Pacific Railroad (refer to Image 24.12). The University of Chicago, opened in 1892, speedily forged into a front-rank position, lubricated by John D. Rockefeller's oil millions. Rockefeller died at ninety-seven, after having donated some $550 million to various philanthropies.

Significant also was the sharp increase in professional and technical schools, where hands-on modern laboratories were replacing the virtuoso demonstrations performed by instructors in front of their passive students. Towering among the specialized institutions was Johns Hopkins University, opened in 1876, which maintained the nation's first high-grade graduate school. Several generations of American scholars, repelled by snobbish English cousins and attracted by painstaking Continental methods, had attended German universities. Johns Hopkins ably carried on the Germanic tradition of profusely footnoted tomes. Reputable scholars no longer had to go abroad for a gilt-edged graduate degree. Dr. Woodrow Wilson, among others, received his PhD (in American History) from Johns Hopkins.

Homegrown influences shaped the modern American university as much as German models. Antebellum colleges had stressed the "unity of truth," or the idea that knowledge and morality existed in a single system. Religious instruction in moral philosophy and natural theology served as pillars of the old classical curriculum. In the wake of the Darwinian challenge, when religion and science seemed less compatible, university reformers struggled to reconcile scientific education and religion to preserve the unity of moral and intellectual purpose. When that effort faltered, university educators abandoned moral instruction and divorced "facts" from "values."

Other pressures also helped doom the traditional curriculum. The new industrialization brought insistent demands for "practical" courses and specialized vocational training in engineering and the physical sciences. The elective system, where students selected courses, was gaining popularity. Reformers also emphasized fields of concentration to prepare students for entry into a profession. Specialization, not synthesis, became the primary goal of a university education. The reform spirit received a powerful boost in the 1870s when Dr. Charles W. Eliot, a vigorous young chemist, became president of Harvard College and embarked upon a lengthy career of educational statesmanship. As a sign of the secularizing times, Eliot changed Harvard's motto from *Christo et Ecclesiae* (For Christ and Church) to *Veritas* (Truth).

Table 24.1 Educational Levels, 1870–2020

Year	Percentage of Population with High School Degree or Higher*	Percentage of Population with Bachelor's Degree or Higher	Percentage of Men over 25 with College Degrees	Percentage of Women over 25 with College Degrees
1870	2.0			
1880	2.5			
1890	3.5			
1900	6.4			
1910	13.5	2.7		
1920	16.4	3.3		
1930	19.1	3.9		
1940	24.5	4.6	5.5	3.8
1950	34.3	6.2	7.3	5.2
1960	41.1	7.7	9.7	5.8
1970	55.2	11.0	14.1	8.2
1980	68.6	17.0	20.9	13.6
1990	77.6	21.3	24.4	18.4
2000	84.1	25.6	27.8	23.6
2010	87.1	29.9	30.3	29.6
2020	90.9	37.5	36.7	38.3

*Years 1870 to 1890 refer to high school graduates as percentage of 17-year-old population. Subsequent years refer to high school graduates as percentage of population 25 and older.

Sources: Digest of Education Statistics, 2022, a publication of the National Center for Education Statistics, https://nces.ed.gov/programs/digest/d21/tables/dt21_104.10.asp; Statistical Abstract of the United States, relevant years.

Courtesy of the Department of Special Collections, Stanford University Libraries

Image 24.12 Stanford University Under Construction, Late Nineteenth Century Gilded Age fortunes endowed new private universities like Stanford, founded by Californian railroad magnate Leland Stanford and his wife Jane in memory of their only son Leland Jr., who died of typhoid fever at age fifteen.

Chicago Daily News

Image 24.13 The "Penny Press" The *Chicago Daily News* was but one of several cheap, mass-circulation newspapers that flourished in the new urban environment of Gilded Age America.

Medical schools and medical science after the Civil War also prospered. Despite the enormous sale of patent medicines and so-called Indian remedies—"good for man or beast"—the new scientific gains led to markedly improved public health. Revolutionary discoveries abroad, such as the germ theory of the French scientist Louis Pasteur and the antiseptic surgery of English physician Joseph Lister, left their imprint on America.*

The popularity of heavy whiskers waned as the century ended; such hairy adornments were now coming to be regarded as germ traps. New health-promoting precautions ranged from campaigns against public spitting to construction of modern water and sewage systems. As medical science improved and once-common diseases ebbed, American life expectancy measurably increased.

24-10 The Appeal of the Press

Well-stocked public libraries served as poor peoples' universities. The magnificent Library of Congress building, which opened its doors in 1897, provided thirteen acres of floor space in the largest and costliest edifice of its kind in the world. A new era was inaugurated by the philanthropy of steel baron Andrew Carnegie. This openhanded Scotsman, book-starved in his youth, contributed $60 million for the construction of nearly 1,700 public libraries all over the country, with an additional 750 scattered around the English-speaking world from Great Britain to New Zealand. By 1900, there were about nine thousand free circulating libraries in America, each with at least three hundred books.

Roaring newspaper presses, spurred by the invention of the Linotype in 1885, more than kept pace with the demands of a word-hungry public. But the heavy investment in machinery and plant was accompanied by a growing fear of offending advertisers and subscribers. Bare-knuckle editorials were, to an increasing degree, being supplanted by feature articles and noncontroversial syndicated material. The day of slashing journalistic giants like Horace Greeley was passing.

Sensationalism, at the same time, was capturing the public taste. Non-English-speaking immigrants, along with strap-hanging urban commuters, created a profitable market for news that was vividly illustrated and punchily written (refer to Image 24.13). Sex, scandal, and other human-interest stories burst into the headlines, as a vulgarization of the press accompanied the growth of circulation. Critics now complained in vain of these "presstitutes."

Two new journalistic tycoons emerged. Joseph Pulitzer, Hungarian-born and near-blind, was a leader in the techniques of sensationalism through his ownership of the *St. Louis Post-Dispatch* and *New York World*. His use of colored comic supplements featuring the "Yellow Kid" gave the name **yellow journalism** to his lurid sheets. A close and ruthless competitor was the youthful William Randolph Hearst. Expelled from Harvard College for a crude prank, he drew on his California father's mining millions to build a powerful chain of newspapers, beginning with the *San Francisco Examiner* in 1887.

Unfortunately, the overall influence of Pulitzer and Hearst was not altogether wholesome. Although both championed many worthy causes, their ultimate pursuit was not truth, but increased circulation: both "stooped, snooped, and scooped to conquer." The extremes to which newspapers of the day trafficked in scandal and sensational rumor was happily somewhat offset by the introduction of syndicated material and by the strengthening of the news-gathering Associated Press, which had been founded in the 1840s.

*From Pasteur came the word *pasteurize*; from Lister came *Listerine*.

24-11 Apostles of Reform

Magazines partially satisfied the public appetite for good reading, notably old East Coast standbys like *Harper's*, the *Atlantic Monthly*, and *Scribner's Monthly* and new western entrants such as the California-based *Overland Monthly*. Possibly the most influential journal of all was the liberal and highly intellectual New York *Nation*, which was read largely by professors, preachers, and publicists as "the weekly Day of Judgment." Launched in 1865 by the Irish-born Edwin L.Godkin, a merciless critic, it crusaded militantly for civil-service reform, honesty in government, and a moderate tariff. The *Nation* attained only a modest circulation—about ten thousand in the nineteenth century—but Godkin believed that if he could reach the right ten thousand leaders, his ideas through them might reach tens of millions.

Henry George (1839–1897) wrote in *Progress and Poverty* (1879),

"Our boasted freedom necessarily involves slavery, so long as we recognize private property in land. Until that is abolished, Declarations of Independence and Acts of Emancipation are in vain. So long as one man can claim the exclusive ownership of the land from which other men must live, slavery will exist, and as material progresses on, must grow and deepen!"

Another journalist-author, Henry George, was an original thinker who left an enduring mark. Poor in formal schooling, he was rich in idealism. After seeing poverty at its worst in India and land-grabbing at its greediest in California, he took pen in hand. His classic treatise *Progress and Poverty* undertook to solve "the great enigma of our times"—"the association of progress with poverty." According to George, the pressure of a growing population on a fixed supply of land unjustifiably pushed up property values, showering unearned profits on owners of land. A single 100 percent tax on those windfall profits would eliminate unfair inequalities and restore the United States to its more equitable republican origins.

George soon became a most controversial figure. His single-tax idea was so horrifying to the propertied classes that his manuscript was rejected by numerous publishers. Finally brought out in 1879, the book gradually broke into the best-seller lists and ultimately sold some 3 million copies. George lectured widely in America and Britain, and his proposals resounded for decades. As late as 1903, a young female follower applied for a patent for the George-inspired "The Landlord's Game," which bore a striking resemblance to Parker Brothers' later "Monopoly," released in 1935. In the earlier game, the point was not to amass property but to expose the unfair advantage enjoyed by the landlord and to show "how the single tax would discourage speculation."

Edward Bellamy, a quiet Massachusetts Yankee, was another journalist-reformer of remarkable power. In 1888 he published a socialistic novel, *Looking Backward*, in which the hero, falling into a hypnotic sleep, awakens in the year 2000. He "looks backward" and finds that the social and economic injustices of 1887 have melted away under an idyllic government, which has nationalized big business to serve the public interest. To a nation already alarmed by the trust evil, the book had a magnetic appeal and sold over a million copies. Scores of Bellamy Clubs sprang up to discuss this utopian socialist vision, and they heavily influenced American reform movements near the end of the century. Edward was not the only Bellamy to leave a mark: his cousin Francis, a clergyman and journalist with similarly reformist beliefs, is credited with writing the original Pledge of Allegiance in 1893.

24-12 The New Morality

Nineteenth-century American society could be oppressively conventional in its social and sexual expectations, especially for women. Iconoclastic New Yorker Victoria Woodhull thus shook the pillars of prevailing morality when in 1871 she divorced her husband and publicly proclaimed her belief in free love (refer to Image 24.14). Woodhull had already gained

Pictorial Press Ltd/Alamy Stock Photo

Image 24.14 "Get Thee Behind Me, (Mrs.) Satan!" A colorful and charismatic figure, Victoria Claflin Woodhull was the first woman to run for the presidency, in 1872. That same year, noted cartoonist Thomas Nast viciously attacked her for advocating free love.

Table 24.2 Marriages and Divorces, 1890–2021*

Year	Marriages	Divorces	Ratio of Divorces to Marriages
1890	570,000	33,461	1:17
1900	709,000	55,751	1:12
1910	948,166	83,045	1:11
1920	1,274,476	170,505	1:7
1930	1,126,856	195,961	1:5
1940	1,595,879	264,000	1:6
1950	1,667,231	385,144	1:4.3
1960	1,523,381	393,000	1:3.8
1970	2,159,000	708,000	1:3
1980	2,390,000	1,189,000	1:2
1990	2,443,000	1,182,000	1:2
2000	2,329,000	NA	NA
2010	2,096,000	NA	NA
2015	2,221,579	NA	NA
2021	1,985,072	NA	NA

*Divorce data have not been collected by the federal government since 1998. Beginning with Massachusetts' legalization in 2004, same-sex marriages in the states where legal are included in the national totals for marriages.

Sources: *Statistical Abstract of the United States,* relevant years; National Center for Health Statistics, *National Vital Statistics Report,* relevant years.

celebrity as a feminist and suffragist, the first female Wall Street stockbroker, and a spiritual medium who claimed she could communicate with the dead. With her sister Tennessee Claflin she published a periodical, *Woodhull and Claflin's Weekly,* which further shocked "respectable" society in 1872 by charging that Henry Ward Beecher, the most famous preacher of his day, had for years been carrying on an adulterous affair.

Beyond the feminist free-lovers, the raucous popular culture of urban America tested the moral principles of America's prim and proper middle class. The moralists' foremost champion was a floridly bewhiskered crusader, Anthony Comstock, who waged lifelong war on the "immoral" as an urban activist and U.S. postal inspector. He persuaded Congress to pass a federal statute—the notorious "Comstock Law" of 1873—prohibiting the delivery of "obscene" material (including promotions for birth control) by mail. This self-appointed defender of sexual purity boasted that he had confiscated no fewer than 202,679 "obscene pictures and photos"; 4,185 "boxes of pills, powders, etc., used by abortionists"; and 26 "obscene pictures, framed on walls of saloons." His proud claim was that he had driven at least fifteen people to suicide.

The activism of the Woodhull sisters and Comstock exposed to daylight the battle in late-nineteenth-century America over sexual attitudes and the place of women. Switchboards and typewriters in the booming cities became increasingly the tools of women's independence. Young workingwomen headed to dance halls and nightclubs when the day was done, enjoying a new sense of freedom in the cities. This "new morality" began to be reflected in mounting divorce rates, the spreading practice of birth control, and increasingly frank discussion of sexual topics. From the late nineteenth century dates the beginning of the "divorce revolution" that transformed the United States' social landscape in the twentieth century (refer to Table 24.2). By 1913, said one popular magazine, the chimes had struck "sex o'clock in America."

24-13 Families and Women in the City

Paradoxically, the crowded cities were emotionally isolating places. Uprooted parents and their children had to go it alone, separated from clan, kin, and village. Not only fathers but mothers and even children as young as ten years old often worked, and usually in widely dispersed locations. On the farm, having many children meant having more hands to help with hoeing and harvesting; but in the city, more children meant more mouths to feed, more crowding in sardine-tin tenements, and more human baggage to carry in the uphill struggle for social mobility.

Not surprisingly, birthrates continued to decline, as young people delayed marriage and more couples learned the techniques of birth control. The drop in family size in fact affected rural Americans as well as urban dwellers, and old-stock "natives" as well as new immigrants.

Women's growing independence in the urban environment brought to the fore some notable women writers, conspicuously including Charlotte Perkins Gilman. A distant relative of Harriet Beecher Stowe, the free-thinking Gilman shunned traditional feminine frills and instead devoted herself to a vigorous regimen of physical exercise and philosophical meditation.

In 1898, Gilman published *Women and Economics*, which called on women to abandon their dependent status and contribute to the larger life of the community through productive involvement in the economy. Rejecting all claims that biology gave women a fundamentally different character from men, she argued that "our highly specialized motherhood is not so advantageous as believed." She advocated centralized nurseries and cooperative kitchens to facilitate women's participation in the workforce—anticipating by more than half a century the day-care centers and convenience-food services of a later day.

> In 1906 progressive reformer Jane Addams (1860–1935) argued that granting women the vote would improve the social and political condition of American cities:
>
> "City housekeeping has failed partly because women, the traditional housekeepers, have not been consulted as to its multiform activities. The men have been carelessly indifferent to much of the civic housekeeping, as they have been indifferent to the details of the household. . . . City government demands the help of minds accustomed to detail and a variety of work, to a sense of obligation to the health and welfare of young children, and to a responsibility for the cleanliness and comfort of other people."

Gilman's call for female participation in the world of wage labor reflected epochal changes already underway, as more than a million women joined the workforce in the single decade of the 1890s. But strict social codes prescribed which women might work and what jobs they might hold. Because employment for wives and mothers was considered taboo, the vast majority of working women were single. Their jobs also depended on their race, ethnicity, and class. Black women had few opportunities beyond domestic service.

White-collar jobs as social workers, secretaries, department store clerks, and telephone operators were largely reserved for native-born women, while immigrant women tended to cluster in particular industries, as Jewish women did in the garment trades. Although hours were often long, pay low, and advancement limited, a job still bought workingwomen some economic and social independence. After contributing a large share of their earnings to their families, many women still had enough money in their pocketbooks to enter a new urban world of sociability—excursions to amusement parks with friends on days off and Saturday night dances with the "fellas."

24-14 Women Fight for the Franchise

Beyond addressing the world of work, fiery feminists also continued to insist on the ballot. They had been demanding the vote since before the Civil War, but many high-minded female reformers had temporarily shelved the cause of women to battle for the rights of Black Americans. In 1890, militant suffragists formed the **National American Woman Suffrage Association (NAWSA).** Its founders included aging pioneers like Elizabeth Cady Stanton, who had helped organize the first women's rights convention in 1848, and her long-time comrade Susan B. Anthony, the radical Quaker spitfire who had courted jail by trying to cast a ballot in the 1872 presidential election.

By 1900, a new generation of women had taken command of the suffrage battle. Their most effective leader was Carrie Chapman Catt, a pragmatic and businesslike reformer of relentless dedication. Significantly, under Catt's leadership, the suffragists deemphasized the argument that women deserved the vote as a matter of right because they were in all respects the equals of men. Instead, Catt stressed the desirability of giving women the vote if they were to continue to discharge their traditional duties as homemakers and mothers in the increasingly public world of the city. Women had special responsibility for the health of the family and the education of children, the argument ran. On the farm, women might discharge these responsibilities in the separate sphere of the isolated homestead. But in the city, they needed a voice on boards of public health, police commissions, and school boards.

By thus linking the ballot to a traditional definition of women's role, suffragists registered encouraging gains as the new century opened, despite continuing showers of rotten eggs and the jeers of male critics who insisted that women were made for loving, not voting. Women were

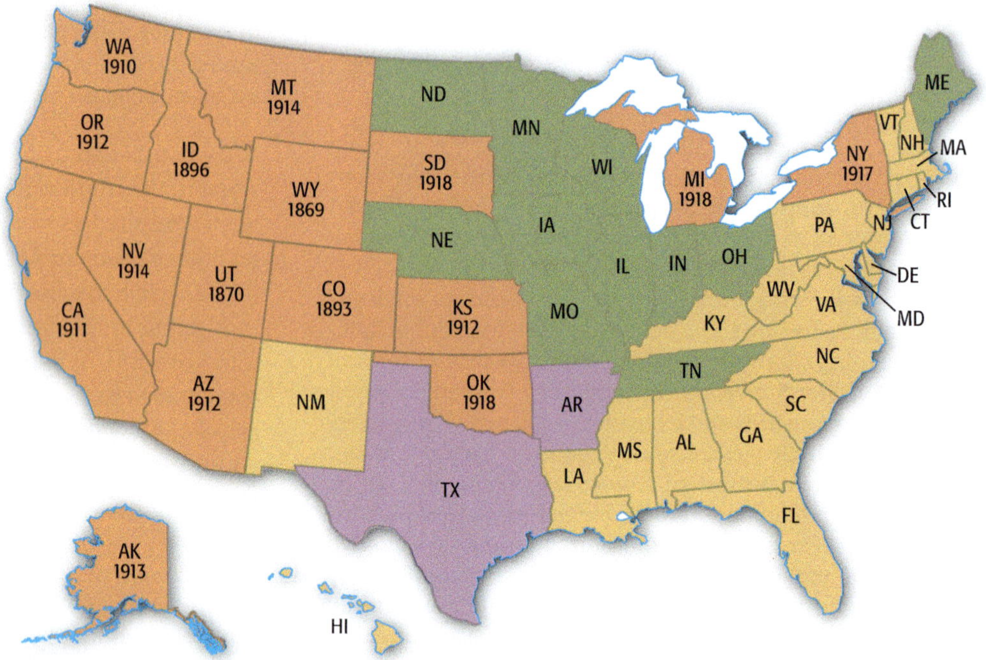

Map 24.1 Woman Suffrage Before the Nineteenth Amendment Dates show when a state or territory adopted woman suffrage. Note the concentration of woman suffrage states in the West.

increasingly permitted to vote in local elections, particularly on issues related to the schools. Wyoming Territory—later called "the Equality State"—granted the first unrestricted suffrage to women in 1869. Many western states soon followed Wyoming's example (refer to Map 24.1). Paralleling these triumphs, most of the states by 1890 had passed laws to permit wives to own or control their property after marriage. City life also fostered the growth of a spate of women's organizations, including the General Federation of Women's Clubs, which counted some 200,000 members in 1900. Meanwhile, in 1893 New Zealand became the first nation to grant women equal suffrage rights, further inspiring American reformers.

The reborn suffrage movement and other women's organizations largely excluded Black women from their ranks. Fearful that an integrated campaign would compromise its efforts to get the vote, the National American Woman Suffrage Association limited membership to whites. Black women, however, created their own associations. Especially notable was journalist and teacher Ida B. Wells. Outraged when a white mob lynched three of her friends in Memphis, Tennessee, in 1892, Wells bravely and doggedly launched her life-long campaign against lynching (refer to Image 24.15). Threats against her life forced her to move from Memphis to Chicago, where she continued to publicize the extralegal violence when white-owned newspapers did not, and in 1896 she helped found the National Association of Colored Women. In 2020, Wells received a posthumous Pulitzer Prize for her courageous reporting.

24-15 Prohibiting Alcohol and Promoting Reform

Urban culture remained a drinking culture, and alarming gains by "Demon Rum" spurred the temperance reformers to redoubled zeal. Especially loathsome to them was the shutter-doored corner saloon, "the poor man's club," that was the worker's refuge from a day of hard labor and the demands of a needy family. Temperance crusaders tut-tutted that the barroom helped keep both the man and his family poor. The tipplers retorted that temperance reform amounted to a middle-class assault on working-class lifestyles.

The National Prohibition party, organized in 1869, polled a sprinkling of votes in some of the ensuing presidential elections. Among the favorite songs these sober souls belted out were "I'll Marry No Man If He Drinks," and "The Drunkard's Doom." The Protestant faith of many reformers infused the tunes with evangelical zeal:

> Now, all young men, a warning take,
> And shun the poisoned bowl;
> 'Twill lead you down to hell's dark gate,
> And ruin your own soul.

Women figured prominently in the battle against booze. They organized the **Woman's Christian Temperance Union (WCTU)** in 1874. The white ribbon was its symbol of purity; the saintly Frances E. Willard—cousin of educator Emma Willard and also a champion of birth control—was its leading spirit. Less saintly was the raging "Kansas Cyclone," Carrie A. Nation, whose first husband had died of alcoholism. With her hatchet she boldly smashed saloon bottles and bars. Her "hatchetations" brought considerable disrepute to the prohibition movement because of the violence of her one-woman crusade (refer to Image 24.16).

But rum was now on the run. The potent Anti-Saloon League was formed in 1893, with its members singing "The Saloon Must Go" and "Vote for Cold Water, Boys." Female supporters sang "The Lips That Touch Liquor Must Never Touch Mine." Statewide prohibition, which had made surprising gains in Maine and elsewhere before the Civil War, was sweeping new states into the "dry" column (refer to Image 24.17). The great triumph—but only a temporary one—came in 1919, when the national prohibition amendment (Eighteenth) was bolted into the Constitution (refer to "29-9 The Prohibition 'Experiment,'" pp. 753–754).

Banners of other social crusaders were aloft. The American Society for the Prevention of Cruelty to Animals (ASPCA) was created in 1866 after its founder had witnessed brutality to horses in Russia. The American Red Cross was launched in 1881, with the dynamic and diminutive five-foot-tall Clara Barton, the "angel" of Civil War battlefields, at the helm.

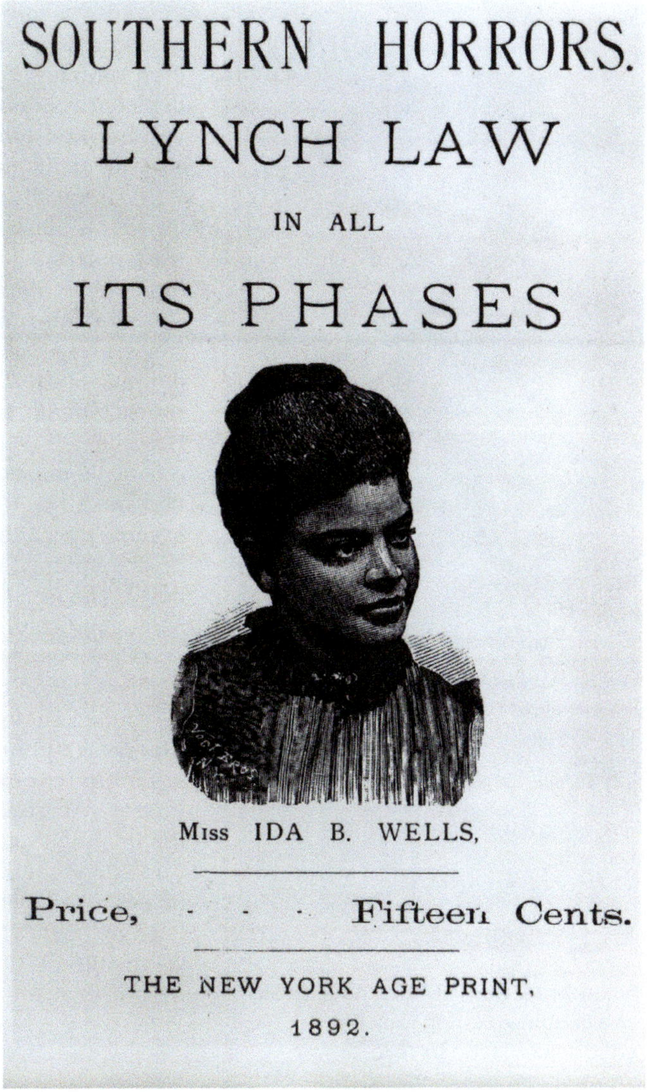

Schomburg Center, NYPL/Art Resource, NY

Image 24.15 **Ida B. Wells (1862–1931)** Ida B. Wells courageously and tirelessly crusaded against the lynching of African Americans. Her sensational pamphlet of 1892 summoned Black people to defend themselves against white violence, declaring that "a Winchester rifle should have a place of honor in every Black home."

24-16 Postwar Culture, Lowbrow and High

Not all social activity proved so serious. Post–Civil War Americans devoured millions of "dime novels" featuring fantastical descriptions of a wild and woolly West. In these tales, paint-bedaubed Native Americans and quick-triggered gunmen like "Deadwood Dick" shot off vast quantities of powder, and virtue invariably triumphed. Parents frowned upon these lurid paperbacks, but goggle-eyed youths read them in haylofts or in schools behind the broad covers of geography books. The mystique of the Old West enchanted many Europeans as well. The German writer Karl May (1842–1912) delighted millions of readers with his extravagantly romanticized tales of characters like the noble Apache, Winnetou, and his stalwart white brother, Old Shatterhand. From such fabulations countless foreigners formed lasting impressions of American history and culture. Among May's enraptured fans were Albert Einstein and Adolf Hitler.

General Lew Wallace was another influential writer of the day. He sought to combat the prevailing wave of Darwinian skepticism with his novel *Ben-Hur: A Tale of the Christ* (1880). A phenomenal success, the book sold an estimated 2 million copies in many languages, including Arabic and Chinese, and later appeared on stage and screen. It was the *Uncle Tom's Cabin* of the anti-Darwinists, who found in it support for the Holy Scriptures.

AP Images/Bill Haber, File

Image 24.16 Carrie Nation Advertised as a Lecturer Nation took her antidrink crusade to several universities, including Harvard and Yale, which she denounced as "hellholes." Predictably, the students greeted her with wild burlesque. "All Nations Welcome but Carrie" became a standard saying in saloons throughout the land.

An even more popular writer was Horatio Alger, a Puritan-reared New Englander who in 1866 forsook the pulpit for the pen. "Holy Horatio" wrote more than a hundred volumes of juvenile fiction that sold over 17 million copies. His stock formula depicted a poor boy new to the city who, through a combination of virtue, hard work, and bravery, achieved success, honor, and middle-class respectability—a kind of survival of the purest, especially nonsmokers, nondrinkers, nonswearers, and nonliars. (Ironically, accusations of sexual impropriety haunted Alger throughout his life.) With "Ragged Dick," his poor-boy character made good, Alger implanted in his readers a lasting and peculiarly American conviction that there is always room at the top for those of pure heart and unrelenting hustle.

Literature and the arts were not immune to the era's sweeping changes. American writers forsook the romantic sentimentality of an earlier age as **Realism** came to dominate post–Civil War literature. Authors increasingly found their subjects in the coarse human comedy and material drama of the world around them. William Dean Howells (1837–1920) emerged as the era's preeminent advocate of such unsentimental literature. A printer's son from Ohio, Howells had scant schoolhouse education, but his busy pen carried him high into the literary circles of the East. In 1871, he became the editor in chief of the prestigious Boston-based *Atlantic Monthly*, where he championed the careers of several young American writers. His most famous novel, *The Rise of Silas Lapham* (1885), describes the moral trials of a newly rich paint manufacturer caught up in the caste system of Brahmin Boston.

Two recipients of Howells's patronage and friendship—Mark Twain and Henry James—carried literary realism to new heights. With his meager formal schooling in frontier Missouri, the mustachioed Twain (1835–1910) typified a new breed of American authors in revolt against the elegant refinements of the old New England school of writing. Christened Samuel Langhorne Clemens, he had served for a time as a Mississippi riverboat pilot and later took his pen name, Mark Twain, from the boatman's cry that meant "two fathoms." After a two-week stint in the local Confederate militia, Twain journeyed westward to Nevada and California, a trip he described, with a mixture of truth and tall tales, in *Roughing It* (1872). One year later, he teamed up with Charles Dudley Warner to write *The Gilded Age*. An acid satire on post–Civil War political corruption and speculative greed, the book gave a name to an era.

Anoka County Historical Society

Image 24.17 Doused for the Cause, Minnesota, 1878 These umbrella-toting temperance crusaders stood their ground, despite the water poured on them by the indignant wife of the billiard-hall owner.

Many other books flowed from Twain's busy pen. *The Adventures of Tom Sawyer* (1876) preceded *The Adventures of Huckleberry Finn* (1884), an American masterpiece that defied Twain's own definition of a classic as "a book which people praise and don't read." Over the decades, countless readers have been captivated by Huck's and Jim's search for freedom and friendship across the colorful (and often racist) backdrop of the antebellum Mississippi River valley. Journalist, humorist, satirist, and foe of social injustice, he made his most enduring contribution in capturing frontier realism and colloquial humor in the authentic American dialect (refer to Image 24.18).

Culture Club/Getty Images

Image 24.18 **Mark Twain (1835–1910)** Born Samuel Langhorne Clemens, he was not only America's most popular author but also a renowned platform lecturer. This photograph was taken in Dublin, New Hampshire, in August 1906 by Albert Bigelow Paine, Mark Twain's biographer.

Twain's homegrown vernacular met its match in Henry James's elegantly filigreed prose. James (1843–1916) was a well-born New Yorker who turned from law to literature and spent most of his life in Europe. Taking as his dominant theme the confrontation of innocent Americans with crafty Europeans, James penned a remarkable number of brilliant realist novels, including *The Portrait of a Lady* (1881) and *The Wings of the Dove* (1902). His book *The Bostonians* (1886) was one of the first novels about the rising feminist movement. James's fiction experimented with point of view and interior monologue. He frequently cast women as his central characters, exploring their inner reactions to complex situations with a deftness that marked him as a master of "psychological realism."

James's good friend Edith Wharton (1862–1937) took a magnifying glass to the inner psychological turmoil and moral shortcomings of post–Civil War high society. Born into wealth, Wharton spent her years in the blue-blooded social circles of New York, Newport, and Paris. In 1885, she married well but not happily, and she increasingly turned her energies to writing. Wharton's many novels, including *The House of Mirth* (1905) and *The Age of Innocence* (1920), exposed the futile struggles and interior costs of striving characters stuck on the social ladder.

Wharton's portrayal of upper-crust social strife verged on **naturalism**, a more intense literary response than mainstream realism to the social dislocations and scientific tumult of late-nineteenth-century America. Emphasizing the determinative influence of heredity and social environments in shaping character, naturalistic writers sought to apply detached scientific objectivity to the study of human beings—or "human beasts," in French novelist Émile Zola's famous phrase. While realist authors often treated middle- and upper-class characters in everyday settings, naturalistic novelists often focused on lower-class, marginal characters in extreme or sordid environments.

Stephen Crane (1871–1900), the fourteenth child of a Methodist minister, rose quickly to prominence with *The Red Badge of Courage* (1895), the stirring story of a bloodied young Civil War recruit ("fresh fish") under the extreme stress of fire. Crane himself had never seen a battle and wrote entirely from printed Civil War records. Sharing the misfortune of his many characters, he died of tuberculosis in 1900 when only twenty-eight.

Gritty, naturalistic portrayals of contemporary life and social problems were the literary order of the day by the turn of the century. Jack London (1876–1916), famous as a nature writer in such books as *The Call of the Wild* (1903), depicted a future fascistic revolution in *The Iron Heel* (1907), a book that displayed London's socialist leanings. Frank Norris (1870–1902), like London a Californian, wrote *The Octopus* (1901), an earthy saga of the stranglehold in which railroad and corrupt politicians held California wheat ranchers.

In 1935 Ernest Hemingway (1899–1961) wrote,

"All modern American literature comes from one book by Mark Twain called *Huckleberry Finn*. . . . All American writing comes from that. There was nothing before. There has been nothing as good since."

Conspicuous among the new naturalistic "social novelists" rising in the literary firmament was Theodore Dreiser

In "The Art of Fiction" (1884), Henry James (1843–1916) articulated the technical goals of realist literature:

"[T]he air of reality . . . seems to me to be the supreme virtue of a novel. . . . [I]t is here that he [the novelist] competes with his brother the painter in *his* attempt to render the look of things, the look that conveys their meaning, to catch the colour, the relief, the expression, the surface, the substance of the human spectacle."

(1871–1945), who burst upon the literary scene in 1900 with *Sister Carrie*, a daringly candid story about a poor working girl adapting to urban life in Chicago and New York. She becomes one man's mistress, then elopes with another, and finally strikes out on her own career on the stage. The fictional Carrie's disregard for prevailing moral standards so offended Dreiser's publisher that the book was soon withdrawn from circulation, though it later reemerged as an acclaimed American classic.

Sharing a common documentary impulse with realist and naturalistic fiction, **regionalism** as a movement sought to chronicle the peculiarities of local ways of life before the coming wave of industrial standardization. Twain, London, and Bret Harte, among other Western writers, popularized legends of the Old West. A foppishly dressed New Yorker, Harte (1836–1902) struck it rich in California with gold-rush stories, especially "The Luck of Roaring Camp" (1868) and "The Outcasts of Poker Flat" (1869).

Black writers also reached national audiences, notably Paul Laurence Dunbar (1872–1906) and Charles W. Chesnutt (1858–1932). Dunbar's poetry—particularly his acclaimed *Lyrics of Lowly Life* (1896)—and Chesnutt's fiction—short stories in Howells's *Atlantic Monthly* and *The Conjure Woman* (1899)—embraced the use of Black dialect and folklore to capture the spontaneity and richness of Black culture.

Southern white women writers shaped the era's literary legacy as well. Drawing from her experiences as a young bride and businesswoman in Louisiana, the daring feminist Kate Chopin (1851–1904) wrote candidly about adultery, suicide, and women's ambitions in *The Awakening* (1899). Largely ignored after her death, Chopin was rediscovered by later readers who embraced her lyrical meditation on the female restlessness beneath the surface of "respectability" in the Gilded Age.

Some important authors, of course, defied categorization. The gifted Henry Adams (1838–1918)—son of Charles Francis, grandson of John Quincy, and great-grandson of John—turned unrivaled family connections into a prolific career as a historian, novelist, and critic. In his nine-volume *History of the United States During the Administrations of Jefferson and Madison* (1889–1891), Adams defended his patrician heritage from posthumous attack. He channeled his alarm at modern trends into his best-known work, *The Education of Henry Adams* (1907), an autobiographical account of his own failure to come to grips with the chaotic forces of turn-of-the-century life.

24-17 Artistic Triumphs

Realism and regionalism also energized the American art world, much as they did the literary sphere. Philadelphia's native son Thomas Eakins (1844–1916) created a veritable artistic catalog of his hometown's social, scientific, and sporting life at the end of the nineteenth century. Boston-born Winslow Homer (1836–1910), who as a youth had secretly drawn sketches in school, brought a similar mastery to the pastoral farms and tossing seas of the Northeast (refer to Image 24.19).

Following in the footsteps of the expatriate writers Henry James and Edith Wharton, prominent American painters working in the realist style made their living abroad. James Whistler (1834–1903) did much of his work, including the celebrated portrait of his mother, in England. This eccentric and quarrelsome Massachusetts Yankee had earlier dropped out of West Point after failing chemistry. "Had silicon been a gas," he later jested, "I would have been a major general." Another gifted portrait painter, likewise self-exiled in England, was John Singer Sargent (1856–1925). His flattering but somewhat superficial likenesses of the British nobility and America's nouveau riche were highly prized. Mary Cassatt (1844–1926), an American in exile in Paris, painted sensitive portrayals of modern women and children that earned her a place in the pantheon of the French impressionist painters, whose work revolutionized the European art world after their 1874 debut.

The most gifted sculptor yet produced by America was Augustus Saint-Gaudens (1848–1907). Born in Ireland of an Irish mother and a French father, he became an adopted American. The national urge to commemorate the Civil War brought him a number of famous commissions, including the stirring Robert Gould Shaw Memorial, erected on Boston Common in 1897. It

Image 24.19 ***Snap the Whip*, by Winslow Homer, 1872** Among Homer's most famous and controversial paintings, it has been interpreted both as an homage to the innocence of youth and the simplicity of rural life and as a somber allegory about the fragility of human relationships.

depicts Colonel Shaw, a young white "Boston Brahmin" officer, leading his Black troops into battle in the Civil War (refer to Image 19.12, "The Fabled 54th Massachusetts Infantry Regiment," p. 477).

Music, too, was gaining popularity. America of the 1880s and 1890s was assembling high-quality symphony orchestras, notably in Boston, Chicago, and Philadelphia. The famed Metropolitan Opera House of New York was erected in 1883. In its fabled "Diamond Horseshoe," the newly rich, often under the pretense of enjoying the imported singers, would flaunt their jewels, gowns, and furs.

While symphonies and operas were devoted to bringing European music to elite American audiences, new strains of homegrown American music were sprouting in the South, another outgrowth of the regionalist trend. Black folk traditions like spirituals and "ragged music" were evolving into the blues, ragtime, and jazz, which would transform American popular music in the twentieth century.

A marvelous invention was the reproduction of music by mechanical means. The phonograph, though a squeakily imperfect instrument when invented in 1877 by the deaf Edison, had by 1900 reached over 150,000 homes. Americans were rapidly being dosed with "canned music," as the "sitting room" piano increasingly gathered dust.

24-18 The White City

Wrenching changes to the nation's cities inspired a new generation of architects and planners to reshape American urban space with the **City Beautiful movement**. Its proponents wanted the new American city not just to look beautiful but also to convey a confident sense of harmony, order, and monumentality. To achieve these effects, they copied European styles of beaux arts classicism and planning ideas from the master builder of Paris, Baron Georges-Eugène Haussmann, who in the 1860s had recast the City of Light with grand boulevards, parks, and public buildings. Aiming to assert America's prominence among the greatest urban cultures of the Western world, architects constructed grandiose urban landmarks such as New York's

Image 24.20 **World's Columbian Exposition, Chicago, 1893** Lagoons helped make the exposition's main buildings, dubbed the "White City," shimmer as the "City Beautiful," in stark contrast to the blocks of dull gray buildings that dominated the real Chicago.

GL Archive/Alamy Stock Photo

Hamlin Garland (1860–1940), the well-known Midwestern novelist and writer of short stories, was immensely impressed by the cultural value of Chicago's Columbian Exposition. He wrote to his aged parents on their Dakota farm,

"Sell the cook stove if necessary and come. You must see this fair."

Grand Central Terminal (1913). City planners like Calvert Vaux and Daniel Burnham redesigned Chicago, Washington, DC, and other cities, aiming to create communities that would inspire civic virtue in their inhabitants. To this end, they joined contemporary landscape architects and park builders like Frederick Law Olmsted, who sought to foster virtue and egalitarian values with his designs for New York's Central Park (1873) and Boston's "Emerald Necklace" (1896), as well as the campus of Stanford University, which opened in 1891.

Burnham's first major project, which came to symbolize the City Beautiful movement, was his design for the great **World's Columbian Exposition**, being held in Chicago in 1893 (refer to Image 24.20). His imposing landscape of pavilions and fountains honored the four hundredth anniversary of Columbus's first voyage. This so-called dream of loveliness was visited by 27 million people (roughly equivalent to two-fifths of the nation's population). The Chicago exposition did much to raise American artistic standards and promote city planning. Most fairgoers, however, proved more interested in lowbrow and decidedly more entertaining delights of the fair's carnival Midway, which debuted new inventions like bubble gum and the Ferris Wheel, as well as the contortions of a "hootchy-kootchy" dancer named "Little Egypt."

24-19 The Business of Amusement

Fun and frolic were not neglected by the workaday American. The pursuit of happiness, heralded in the Declaration of Independence, had by century's end become a frenzied scramble. Varied diversions beckoned. The legitimate stage still flourished, as appreciative audiences responded to the lure of the footlights. Vaudeville, with its coarse jokes and graceful acrobats, continued to be immensely popular during the 1880s and 1890s, as were minstrel shows in the South, now performed by Black singers and dancers rather than by whites wearing blackface as in the North before the Civil War. The circus—high-tented and multiringed—finally emerged full-blown. Phineas T. Barnum, the master showman who had early discovered that "the public likes to be humbugged," joined hands with James A. Bailey in 1881 to stage the "Greatest Show on Earth."*

Colorful "Wild West" shows, first performed in 1883, were even more distinctively American (refer to Image 24.21). Headed by the knightly, goateed, and free-drinking William F.

*It became Ringling Bros. and Barnum & Bailey Circus and ended its 146-year run in 2017.

Buffalo Bill Center of the West/REX/Shutterstock.com

Image 24.21 Buffalo Bill's Wild West Show, ca. 1907 By the late 1800s, the "Wild West" was already passing into the realm of myth—and popular entertainment. Famed frontiersman William F. ("Buffalo Bill") Cody (1846–1917) made his fortune showing off Western cowboys and Native Americans to enthusiastic urban audiences at his traveling performances in the United States as well as in Europe—where the popularity of writers like Karl May had already primed audiences to lap up representations of the American West that were far more fanciful than factual.

("Buffalo Bill") Cody, the troupe included "war-whooping Indians," live buffalo, and deadeye marksmen as well as markswomen, notably the girlish Annie Oakley. Rifle in hand, she could at thirty paces perforate a tossed-up card half a dozen times before it fluttered to the ground.

Baseball emerged as a national mania (refer to Image 24.22). Crowds as large as forty thousand swarmed into big-city ballparks. A league of professional players formed in the 1870s, and in 1888 an all-star baseball team toured the world, using the pyramids as a backstop while in Egypt. While early baseball clubs had racially integrated teams, baseball segregated as it professionalized, with Black players banished to "Negro Leagues." The early stars of the white baseball

Granger

Image 24.22 William Howard Taft Begins a Presidential Tradition, 1910 By the early twentieth century, baseball was well on its way to becoming "America's National Pastime." Taft's ceremonial first pitch at a Washington, DC, Senators game on April 14, 1910, began the tradition of a U.S. president making a season-opening toss in the professional leagues.

Image 24.23 The Origin of Women's College Basketball Nineteenth-century women's colleges provided opportunities both academic and athletic and played a major role in the emergence of women's team sports. Smith College instructor Senda Berenson adapted the new sport of "Basket Ball" for her students, refereeing what is considered to be the first official women's basketball game at the college in 1893. Here, the players of Smith's sophomore class of 1895 pose for their team portrait.

leagues included many first- and second-generation European immigrants, and the appeal of the game crossed boundaries of ethnicity and class. In a working-class world of hard labor and limited leisure, a day at the ballpark became an affordable escape.

Basketball was invented in 1891 by James Naismith, a YMCA instructor in Springfield, Massachusetts. The next year, Smith College's Senda Berenson founded the first women's team (refer to Image 24.23). Bicycling was another activity enjoyed by men and women alike by the turn of the twentieth century. City parks and boulevards filled with pedaling young men in boater hats and women in shirtwaists, enjoying the freedom of life on two wheels.

A gladiatorial trend toward spectator sports, rather than participative sports, was exemplified by football. This rugged game, with its dangerous flying wedge, had become popular well before 1889, when Yale man Walter C. Camp chose his first "All American" team. The Yale–Princeton game of 1893 drew fifty thousand cheering fans, while foreigners jeered that the nation was getting sports "on the brain."

Even pugilism, with its long background of bare-knuckle brutality, gained a new and gloved respectability in 1892. Agile "Gentleman Jim" Corbett, a scientifically professional boxer, wrestled the world championship from the aging and alcoholic John L. Sullivan, the fabulous "Boston Strong Boy."

The land of the skyscraper was plainly becoming more standardized, owing largely to the new industrialization. Although race and ethnicity assigned urban Americans to distinctive neighborhoods and workplaces, to an increasing degree they shared a common popular culture—playing, reading, shopping, and talking alike. As the century drew to a close, the explosion of cities paradoxically made Americans more diverse and more similar at the same time.

Chapter Summary

The United States moved from the country to the city in the post–Civil War decades. Mushrooming urban development created new opportunity for many who migrated from farms and small towns and across the Atlantic from Europe, but it also created severe social problems, including overcrowded, unhealthy living conditions and a sharp economic divide between rich and poor.

Especially after the 1880s, city populations swelled with "New Immigrants" from southern and eastern Europe. With their culturally different customs and non-Protestant religions, the newcomers often met with nativist hostility and discrimination. Congress began to throw up barriers to immigration, including a complete ban on the Chinese.

Religion had to adjust to social, cultural, and intellectual changes. The immigrant faiths of Roman Catholicism and Judaism gained considerable strength, while conflicts over evolution and biblical interpretation divided American Protestantism into fundamentalist and modernist wings.

American education expanded rapidly, especially at the secondary and collegiate levels. Major new research universities were founded, both by state governments and by wealthy industrialists. Women's opportunities for education advanced in both separate institutions and coeducation. Black leaders Washington and Du Bois fought for economic advancement but divided over integration and the question of manual education versus development of an elite "talented tenth."

Significant conflicts over moral values, especially relating to sexuality and the role of women, became heated in the late nineteenth century. The new urban environment provided expanded opportunities for young, unmarried women but families grew more isolated as migration separated men and women from their birthplaces and extended families. The divorce rate rose, multigenerational households became rarer, and average family size shrank.

American literature and the arts reflected the social and moral issues of the new urban, industrial age. The major literary and artistic movements of realism, naturalism, and regionalism reflected the new energy and sophistication of American culture, which gained national acclaim and increasing international respect. Leisure-time amusements and sports became enormously popular but more standardized, in keeping with the new industrial nation.

Key Terms

- New Immigrants (596)
- political machines (599)
- Tweed Ring (600)
- settlement house (601)
- liberal Protestants (604)
- Tuskegee Normal and Industrial School (607)
- land-grant colleges (608)
- yellow journalism (610)
- National American Woman Suffrage Association (NAWSA) (613)
- Woman's Christian Temperance Union (WCTU) (615)
- Realism (616)
- naturalism (617)
- regionalism (618)
- City Beautiful movement (619)
- World's Columbian Exposition (620)

People to Know

- Jane Addams
- Charles Darwin
- Booker T. Washington
- W. E. B. Du Bois
- Joseph Pulitzer
- William Randolph Hearst
- Carrie Chapman Catt
- Horatio Alger
- Mark Twain
- Henry James
- Theodore Dreiser
- Winslow Homer
- Augustus Saint-Gaudens
- Frederick Law Olmsted
- Karl May

Chronology

1859	• Charles Darwin publishes *On the Origin of Species*	
1862	• Morrill Act provides public land for higher education	
1863	• World's first subway system opens in London	
1866	• American Society for the Prevention of Cruelty to Animals (ASPCA) created	
1869	• Wyoming Territory grants women right to vote	
1871	• *Woodhull and Claflin's Weekly* published	
1873	• Comstock Law • Construction of New York's Central Park officially completed	
1874	• Woman's Christian Temperance Union (WCTU) organized • Chautauqua education movement launched	
1876	• Johns Hopkins University graduate school established	
1879	• Henry George publishes *Progress and Poverty* • Dumbbell tenement introduced	• Mary Baker Eddy establishes Christian Science • Salvation Army begins work in America
1881	• Booker T. Washington becomes head of Tuskegee Institute • American Red Cross founded	• Henry James publishes *The Portrait of a Lady* • Barnum and Bailey first join to stage "Greatest Show on Earth"

(*continued*)

1882	• First immigration-restriction laws passed	
1883	• Brooklyn Bridge completed • Metropolitan Opera House built in New York	
1884	• Mark Twain publishes *The Adventures of Huckleberry Finn*	
1885	• Chicago's Home Insurance Building built, the world's first skyscraper	
1886	• Statue of Liberty erected in New York harbor	
1887	• American Protective Association (APA) formed • Hatch Act supplements Morrill Act	
1888	• Edward Bellamy publishes *Looking Backward* • American all-star baseball team tours world	
1889	• Jane Addams founds Hull House in Chicago	
1890	• William James publishes *The Principles of Psychology* • National American Woman Suffrage Association (NAWSA) formed	
1891	• Basketball invented • Stanford University opens	
1893	• Lillian Wald opens Henry Street Settlement in New York • Anti-Saloon League formed	• World's Columbian Exposition held in Chicago • New Zealand grants women right to vote
1895	• Stephen Crane publishes *The Red Badge of Courage*	
1897	• Library of Congress opens • Robert Gould Shaw Memorial erected on Boston Common	
1898	• Charlotte Perkins Gilman publishes *Women and Economics*	
1899	• Kate Chopin publishes *The Awakening*	
1900	• Theodore Dreiser publishes *Sister Carrie*	
1907	• Henry Adams privately publishes *The Education of Henry Adams*	
1909	• National Association for the Advancement of Colored People (NAACP) founded	

To Learn More

Irving Howe, *World of Our Fathers* (1976)

Kenneth T. Jackson, *Crabgrass Frontier: The Suburbanization of America* (1985)

David Levering Lewis, *W. E. B. Du Bois: Biography of a Race, 1868–1919* (1993)

__________, *W. E. B. Du Bois: The Fight for Equality and the American Century, 1919–1963* (2000)

Louis Menand, *The Metaphysical Club: A Story of Ideas in America* (2001)

Kathy Peiss, *Cheap Amusements: Working Women and Leisure in Turn-of-the-Century New York* (1986)

Jacob Riis, *How the Other Half Lives* (1890)

Daniel Rodgers, *Atlantic Crossings: Social Politics in a Progressive Age* (1998)

Roy Rosenzweig and Elizabeth Blackmar, *The Park and the People: A History of Central Park* (1992)

Carroll Smith-Rosenberg, *Disorderly Conduct: Visions of Gender in Victorian America* (1985)

Ronald Takaki, *Strangers from a Different Shore: A History of Asian Americans* (1989)

Alan Trachtenberg, *The Incorporation of America: Culture and Society in the Gilded Age* (1982)

Aristide R. Zolberg, *A Nation by Design: Immigration Policy in the Fashioning of America* (2006)

Chapter 25

Rumbles of Discontent: 1865–1900

> You come to us and tell us that the great cities are in favor of the gold standard. We reply that the great cities rest upon our broad and fertile prairies. Burn down your cities and leave our farms, and your cities will spring up again as if by magic. But destroy our farms and the grass will grow in the streets of every city in the country.
>
> William Jennings Bryan, "Cross of Gold" Speech, 1896

Chapter Outline

- The industrialization of agriculture
- Farmers protest
- Benjamin Harrison and the "Billion Dollar Congress"
- Grover Cleveland, depression and discontent
- Workers in revolt
- Strikes at Homestead and Pullman
- The Populists
- Bryan versus McKinley, 1896

Contending Voices: Populism and Anti-Populism

Varying Viewpoints: The Populists: Radicals or Reactionaries?

Once the backbone of the republic, farmers were increasingly beleaguered in the sunset decades of the nineteenth century. Burdened by debt and beset by foreign competition, they sought sometimes radical political remedies to their ever-more urgent economic predicament. Meanwhile, the masses of factory workers newly recruited from American fields and foreign countries accumulated their own list of grievances suffered at the hands of often heedless and grasping bosses. For a fleeting moment the prospect loomed of a farmer-labor alliance that might upend Gilded Age capitalism. But by century's end, the conservative guardians of order had gained the upper hand. Truly meaningful reform lay in the lap of the future.

Focus Questions

1. How did the agricultural revolution change Great Plains farming, and what were the consequences for ordinary farmers?
2. What were the causes of Western and Southern farmers' protests, and how did those grievances eventually find organized expression in the radical Populist Party?
3. How did the deep depression that began in 1893 deepen rural and labor unrest in the country, and why was President Cleveland so ineffectual in addressing the crisis?
4. Why was the Bryan–McKinley campaign of 1896 the most momentous election since that of 1860, and how were McKinley and the Republicans finally able to turn back Bryan and the populist silver crusade?

25-1 The Farm Becomes a Factory

The rapid **mechanization of agriculture** in the late nineteenth century was almost as striking as the mechanization of industry. As in the cities, technological and economic change had dramatic social and political consequences.

American farmers had once been self-reliant jacks-and-jills-of-all-trades. They had raised their own food, fashioned their own clothing, and bartered for other necessities with neighbors. As America industrialized and urbanized, the demands of new markets drove farmers to concentrate on growing single "cash" crops, such as wheat or corn. The self-sufficient yeoman farmer was rapidly becoming a country businessman, transporting his crops by rail and ship to far-flung markets around the world. Profits, if any, went to buy foodstuffs at the general store and manufactured goods in town or by mail order. The Chicago firm of Aaron Montgomery Ward sent out its first catalog—a single sheet—in 1872. By 1900, the catalog swelled to hundreds of pages and was an essential source of supplies for thousands of rural households.

Farmers' prosperity no longer depended on America alone. The nation's growers, especially in the immense grain-producing areas of the Mississippi Valley, had become cogs in a global market system. Burdens of debt and the challenges of foreign competition bound them to vast banking, transportation, and marketing networks. When the rolling fields of Argentina, Russia, and other foreign countries flourished, the price of American grain fell and sodbusters faced ruin.

New technology accelerated this transition. A powerful steam engine, for example, could drag behind it simultaneously the plow, seeder, and harrow. The "combine" (combined reaper-thresher), invented in the 1880s, drawn by twenty to forty horses, both reaped and bagged the grain, dramatically increasing the speed and volume of wheat harvesting (refer to Image 25.1). Widespread use of such costly equipment demanded sophisticated management. But many farmers, who had borrowed heavily to buy this expensive machinery, were unskilled businesspeople and struggled to adapt.

Agricultural modernization thus drove many small farmers off the land, swelling the ranks of the new industrial workforce and consolidating small family farms into large-scale "agribusinesses." The rural population steadily decreased, but those farmers who remained became astoundingly productive, making America the world's breadbasket and butcher shop. The farm was attaining the status of a factory—an outdoor grain factory. Some "bonanza" wheat farms in the Minnesota-North Dakota area were larger than fifteen thousand acres, with communication by telephone from one part to another. These "factories in the fields" foreshadowed the thoroughgoing commercialization of the nation's food system in the next century.

In California's phenomenally productive (and phenomenally irrigated) Central Valley, agriculture was a big business from its earliest days. California farms and ranches, carved out of giant Spanish Mexican land grants and the railroads' huge holdings, were from the outset more than

Image 25.1 Grain Harvesting in Washington State Humans, horses, and machines join forces in this turn-of-the-century scene.

Library of Congress, Prints & Photographs Division, Reproduction number LC-USZ62-71468 (b&w film copy neg. of half stereo)

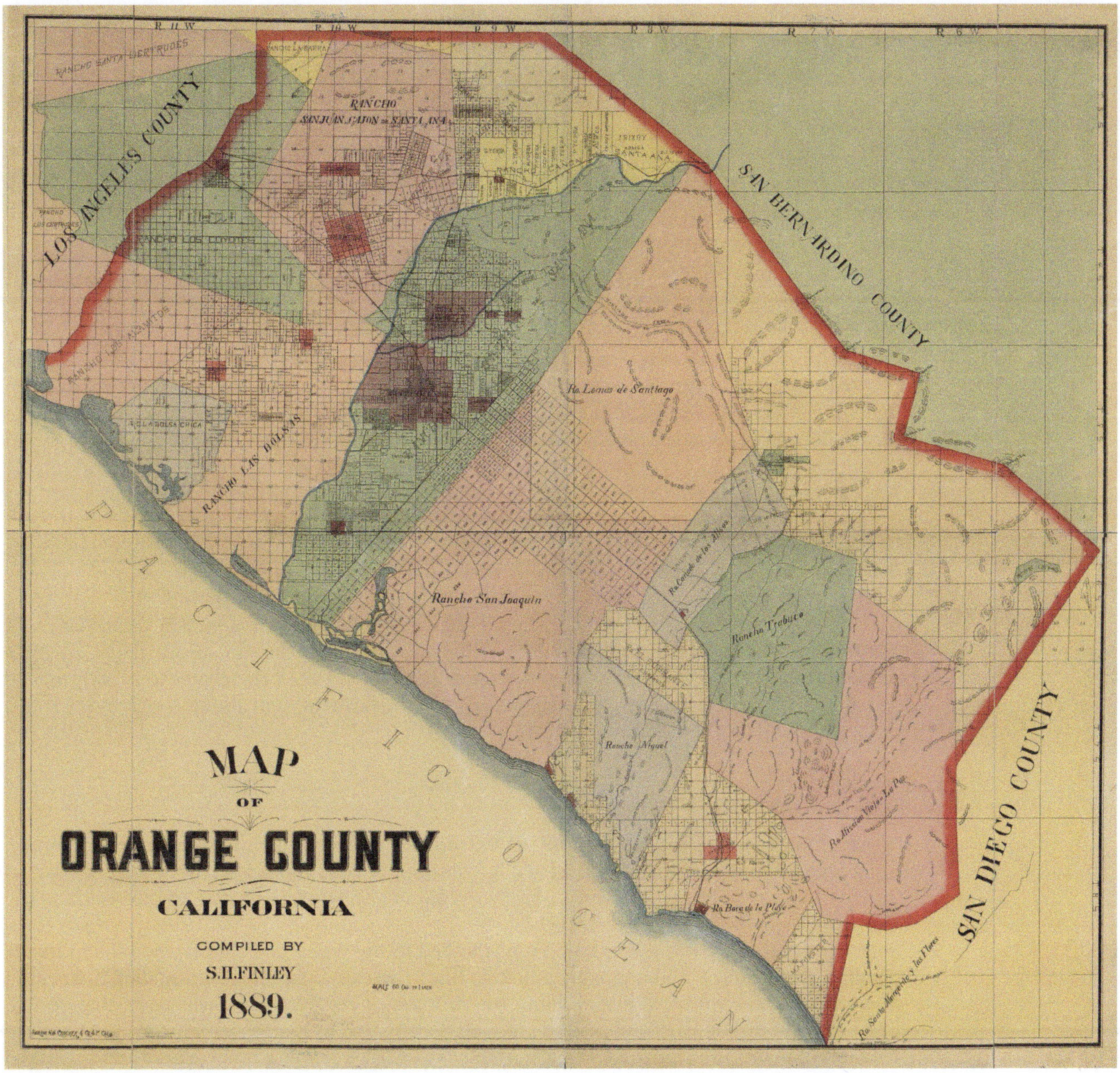

Library of Congress

Image 25.2 Ranchos of Orange County, California, 1889 California's large landholdings, or *ranchos*, were a legacy of Spanish and Mexican rule. Concentrating land ownership in a few hands, they enabled industrial-scale farming and cattle ranching operations to emerge in the state in the late nineteenth century.

three times larger than the national average (refer to Image 25.2). The reformer Henry George in 1871 described the Golden State as "not a country of farms but a country of plantations and estates." With the advent of the railroad refrigerator car in the 1880s, California fruit and vegetable crops, raised on sprawling tracts by ill-paid migrant Mexican and Asian farmhands, sold at a handsome profit in the affluent urban markets of the East.

25-2 Deflation Dooms the Debtor

Once midwestern farmers hopped aboard the one-crop economy—wheat or corn—they were in the same leaky boat with the Southern cotton growers. As long as prices stayed high, all went well. But when they skidded in the 1880s, bankruptcy fell like a blight on the farm belts.

Low prices and a deflated currency became twinned worries for the frustrated farmers—North, South, and West. If a farm family had borrowed a thousand dollars in 1855, when wheat

A contemporary farm protest song, "The Kansas Fool," ran,

The bankers followed us out west;
And did in mortgages invest;
They looked ahead and shrewdly planned,
And soon they'll have our Kansas land.

was worth about a dollar a bushel, they expected to pay back the equivalent of one thousand bushels, plus interest, when the mortgage fell due. But if they let their debt run to 1890, when wheat had fallen to about fifty cents a bushel, they would have to pay back the price of two thousand bushels for the thousand dollars they had borrowed, plus interest. This unexpected burden struck them as unjust, though their steely-eyed creditors often branded the complaining farmers as slippery and dishonest rascals.

The deflationary pinch on the debtor was exacerbated by the static money supply. Scarce dollars pushed prices downward. In 1870, the currency in circulation for each person was $19.42; in 1890, it was only $22.67. Yet during those twenty years, population as well as the volume of business and industrial activity had increased manyfold, intensifying the scramble for available currency.

The forgotten farmers were caught on a treadmill. In a vicious circle, their costly farm machinery increased their output of grain, lowered the price, and drove them even deeper into debt. Mortgages engulfed homesteads at an alarming rate; by 1890, Nebraska alone reported more than 100,000 farms blanketed with mortgages. In this age of freewheeling and largely unregulated capitalism, agents of far-off eastern loan companies charged powerless farmers ruinous rates of mortgage interest, sometimes as high as 40 percent. The threat of bankruptcy and foreclosure perpetually shadowed the family farm. The repeated thud of the sheriff-auctioneer's hammer kept announcing to the world that another sturdy American farmer had become landless in a richly landed nation.

Farm tenancy was displacing farm ownership like spreading stinkweed. The trend was especially marked in the sharecropping South, where cotton prices also sank dismayingly. By 1880, one-fourth of all American farms were operated by tenants. The United States was ready to feed the world, but under the new industrial feudalism, the farmers were about to sink into a status suggesting Old World serfdom.

25-3 Unhappy Farmers

Even Mother Nature ceased smiling, as her powerful forces conspired against agriculture. Mile-wide clouds of grasshoppers, leaving "nothing but the mortgage," periodically ravaged heartland farms. The terrible cotton-boll weevil was also wreaking havoc in the South by the early 1890s.

The good earth was going sour. Floods added to the waste of erosion, which had already washed the topsoil off millions of once-lush southern acres. A long succession of droughts seared the trans-Mississippi West, beginning in the summer of 1887. Whole towns were abandoned. "Going home to the wife's folks" and "In God we trusted, in Kansas we busted" were typical laments of many impoverished farmers, as they fled their weather-beaten shacks and sunbaked sod houses. One irate "poet" snarled,

Fifty miles to water,
A hundred miles to wood,
To hell with this damned country,
I'm going home for good.

To add to their miseries, the soil-tillers were gouged by their governments—local, state, and national. Their land was often overassessed, and they paid painful local property taxes, whereas wealthy Easterners could conceal their stocks and bonds in safe-deposit boxes. High protective tariffs in these years poured profits into the pockets of manufacturers. Farmers, on the other hand, had no choice but to sell their low-priced products in a fiercely competitive, unprotected world market, while buying high-priced manufactured goods in a protected home market.

The farmers were also "farmed" by increasingly monopolistic corporations and processors. They were at the mercy of the harvester trust, the barbed-wire trust, and the fertilizer trust, all of which could control output and raise prices to sometimes extortionate levels. Middlemen took a juicy "cut" from the selling price of the goods that the farmers bought. Operators pushed storage rates to the ceiling at grain warehouses and elevators.

In addition, the railroad "octopus" held the grain growers tightly in its grip. Freight rates could be so high that the farmers sometimes lost less if they burned their corn for fuel than if they shipped it. If they raised their voices in protest, ruthless railroad operators might let their grain spoil in damp places or refuse to provide them with cars when needed.

The windburned sons and daughters of the sod felt that they deserved honor, not hardship, for their role in developing the country. They cried out angrily against those powerful and distant forces that seemed to hold the heartland's economic future so tightly in their grip: the loan sharks and railway agents, the tariff-happy lawmakers, and money-drunk Wall Street financiers.

Farmers still made up nearly one-half the population in 1890, but they were far less powerful on the national political scene than numbers might imply. The manufacturers and the railroad barons knew how to combine to promote their interests, and so, increasingly, did industrial workers. But farmers stubbornly remained by nature and circumstance independent and individualistic—dead set against consolidation or regimentation. They were geographically isolated, often lightly educated, with little in common other than their shared economic plight. They never did organize successfully to restrict production until forced by the federal government nearly half a century later, in Franklin Roosevelt's New Deal days. What they did manage to organize was a monumental political uprising.

25-4 Farmers Take Their Stand

Agrarian unrest had flared forth earlier, in the Greenback movement shortly after the Civil War. Sagging prices in the late 1860s prompted a host of farmers to seek relief from low prices and high indebtedness by demanding an inflation of the currency with paper money ("greenbacks"). They thus put the "money question" at the center of the nation's political agenda, where it remained for the following three decades.

Meanwhile, farmers tried in vain to build organizations that would effectively safeguard their interests. Prominent among them was the National Grange of the Patrons of Husbandry—better known as the Grange—organized in 1867. Its leading spirit was Oliver H. Kelley, a shrewd and energetic Minnesota farmer then working as a clerk in Washington. Kelley's first objective was to enhance the lives of isolated farmers through social, educational, and fraternal activities. Farm men and women, cursed with loneliness in widely separated farmhouses, found the Grange's picnics, concerts, and lectures a godsend. Kelley, a Mason, even found farmers receptive to his mumbo-jumbo of passwords and secret rituals, as well as his four-ply hierarchy, ranging (for men) from Laborer to Husbandman and (for women) from Maid to Matron. The Grange spread like an old-time prairie fire and by 1875 claimed 800,000 members, chiefly in the Midwest and South. Buzzing with gossip, these calicoed and calloused folk often met in red schoolhouses around potbellied stoves.

The Grangers gradually raised their goals from individual self-improvement to improvement of the farmers' collective plight (refer to Image 25.3). In a determined effort to escape the clutches of the trusts, they established cooperatively owned stores for consumers and cooperatively owned grain elevators and warehouses for producers.

Embattled Grangers also went into politics, enjoying their most gratifying success in the grain-growing regions of the upper Mississippi Valley, chiefly in Illinois, Wisconsin, Iowa, and Minnesota. There, through state legislation, they strove to regulate railway rates and the storage fees charged by railroads and by the operators of warehouses and grain elevators. Many of the state courts, notably in Illinois, were disposed to recognize the principle of public control of private business for the general welfare.

A number of the so-called Granger Laws, however, were badly drawn, and they were bitterly fought through the high courts by the well-paid lawyers of the "interests." Following judicial restraints on legislation by individual states, most severely at the hands of the Supreme Court in the famous *Wabash* decision of 1886 (refer to "23-4 Government Bridles the Iron Horse," pp. 572–573), the Grangers' influence faded. But their organization lived on as a social organization, brightening rural life with a variety of community activities.

Farmers' grievances likewise found a vent in the Greenback Labor Party, which combined the inflationary appeal of the earlier Greenbackers with a program for improving the lot of long-suffering labor. In 1878, the high-water mark of the movement, the Greenback Laborites polled over a million votes and elected fourteen members of Congress. In the presidential election of 1880, the Greenbackers ran General James B. Weaver, an old Granger who was a favorite of Civil War veterans and who possessed a remarkable voice and bearing. He spoke to perhaps half a million citizens in a hundred or so speeches but polled only 3 percent of the total popular vote.

Image 25.3 The Farmers' Grievances This poster from 1875 expresses one of the agrarian radicals' fundamental premises: that all other walks of life were dependent—or even parasitic—on the indispensable work of farmers. In his famous "Cross of Gold" speech in 1896 (refer to "25-10 Golden McKinley and Silver Bryan," pp. 637–639), Populist presidential candidate William Jennings Bryan put it this way: "Burn down your cities and leave our farms, and your cities will spring up again as if by magic; but destroy our farms and the grass will grow in the streets of every city in the country."

The most consequential manifestation of rural discontent was the Farmers' Alliance, founded in Texas in the late 1870s (refer to "21-14 The Billion-Dollar Congress," pp. 539–540). As in the Grange, Alliance farmers came together to socialize, but more importantly to break the strangling grip of the railroads and manufacturers through cooperative buying and selling. Local chapters spread throughout the South and the Great Plains during the 1880s, until by 1890 members numbered more than a million hard-bitten souls.

The Alliance weakened itself by ignoring the plight of landless tenant farmers, sharecroppers, and farmworkers. Even more debilitating was the Alliance's exclusion of African Americans, who made up nearly half the agricultural workers of the South. In the 1880s a separate Colored Farmers' National Alliance emerged to attract Black farmers, and by 1890 membership numbered more than 250,000. Initial hopes that white and Black farmers might work together in the same organization soon faded as Jim Crow segregation intensified.

25-5 Power to the People

As farm misery spread, momentum mounted for a political movement that could rally against the powerful, remote interests that seemed to control the countryside's destiny. Out of the Farmers' Alliances a new political party emerged in the early 1890s: the People's Party. Better known as the **Populists**, these frustrated farmers attacked Wall Street and the "money trust." On the stump and on the pages of rural newspapers, fiery prophets leapt forward to trumpet the Populist cause.

The free coinage of silver struck many Populists as a cure-all, especially after the circulation of an enormously popular pamphlet titled *Coin's Financial School* (1894). Written by William Hope Harvey, it was illustrated by clever woodcuts, one of which depicted a gold ogre beheading a beautiful silver maiden. In fiction parading as fact, the booklet showed how the "little professor"—"Coin" Harvey—overwhelmed the bankers and professors of economics with his brilliant arguments on behalf of free silver.

Another notorious spellbinder was red-haired Ignatius Donnelly of Minnesota, three times elected to Congress. The queen of the Populist "calamity howlers" was Mary Elizabeth ("Mary Yellin'") Lease, a daughter of Irish immigrants and suffragist known as the "Kansas Pythoness" (refer to Image 25.4). She reportedly demanded that Kansans should raise "less corn and more hell." The big-city *New York Evening Post* snarled, "We don't want any more states until we can civilize Kansas." To many easterners, complaint, not corn, was rural America's staple crop.

Underneath cries for economic justice often rang another, ominously familiar note: blaming a foreign "other" for the farmers' woes. Populist condemnations of "Wall Street" subtly—and sometimes not so subtly—pointed fingers at the Jewish families who were among the world's most powerful financiers. Mary Lease warned of politicians who were allowing the nation's commercial system to fall under "a company of Jews" and accused President Grover Cleveland of being "the agent of Jewish bankers." Instances of such unvarnished anti-Semitism were few, but they reflected deeply rooted social prejudices that even the most radical of reformers could not escape.

Yet the Populists were leading not a culture war but a deadly earnest and impassioned campaign to relieve the farmers' material miseries, and they hoped to make common cause with sorely abused working people as well. Smiles faded from Republican and Democratic faces alike as countless thousands of Populists began to sing "Good-bye, My Party, Good-bye." In 1892, the Populists met in Omaha and adopted a scorching platform that denounced "the prolific womb of governmental injustice." They demanded inflation through free and unlimited coinage of silver at the rate of sixteen ounces of silver to one ounce of gold. They further called for a graduated income tax; government ownership of the railroads, telegraph, and telephone; the direct election of U.S. senators; a one-term limit on the presidency; the adoption of the initiative and referendum to allow citizens to shape legislation more directly; a shorter workday; and immigration restriction. As their presidential candidate, the Populists uproariously nominated the eloquent old Greenbacker, General James B. Weaver.

Racial divisions continued to hobble the Populists in the South, but in the West their ranks were swelling. Could the People's Party now reach beyond its regional bases in agrarian America, join hands with restless urban workers, and mount a successful attack on the northeastern citadels of power?

An epidemic of nationwide strikes in the summer of 1892 raised the prospect that the Populists could weld together just such a coalition of abused workers and indebted farmers in a revolutionary joint assault on the capitalist order. At Andrew Carnegie's Homestead steel plant near Pittsburgh, Pennsylvania, company officials called in three hundred armed Pinkerton detectives in July to crush the defiant **Homestead strike** by steelworkers angry over pay cuts (refer to Image 25.5). Strikers,

Historical/Getty Images

Image 25.4 Mary E. Lease (1853–1933) "Wall Street owns the country," this Populist firebrand declared in 1890. "The great common people of this country are slaves, and monopoly is the master."

Granger, NYC

Image 25.5 The Homestead Strike, 1892 Three hundred armed Pinkerton detectives floated on barges down the Monongahela River to the site of the Carnegie steel plant at Homestead, Pennsylvania. Met by a defiant and disciplined force of strikers, they were compelled to surrender. Here the Pinkerton men are shown disembarking from their barges after their capitulation, while the jeering strikers ashore exult in their victory.

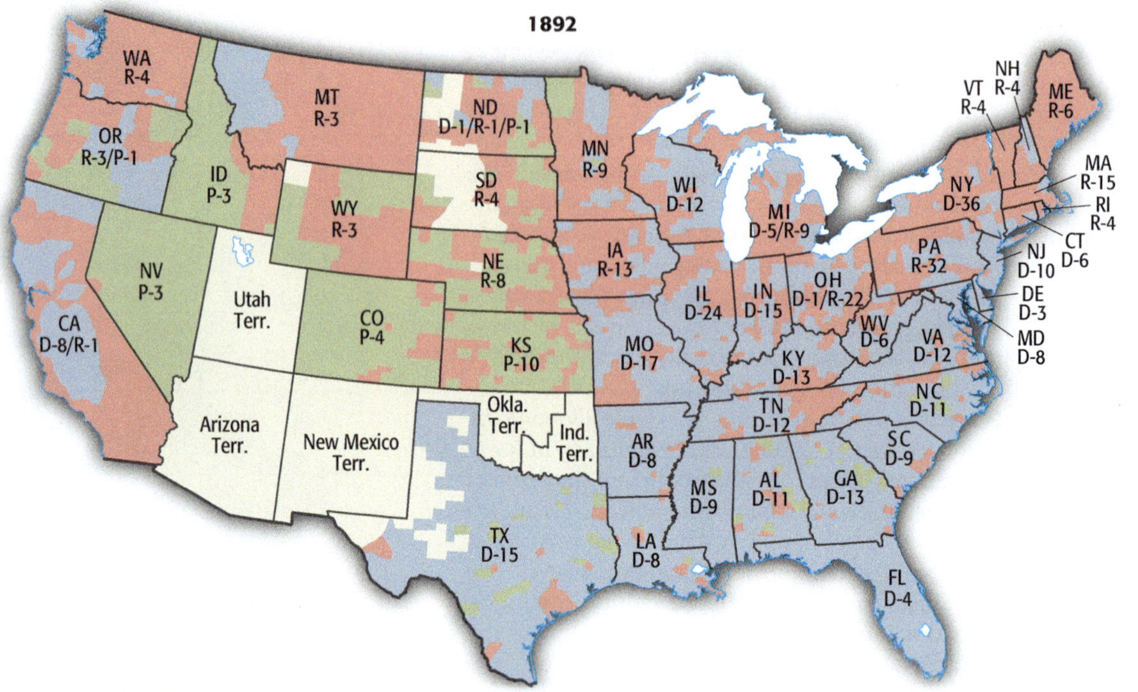

Candidate (Party)	Electoral Vote		Popular Vote	
Cleveland (Democrat)	277	62%	5,555,426	46.1%
Harrison (Republican)	145	33%	5,182,690	43.0%
Weaver (People's)	22	5%	1,029,846	8.5%

Territories, Indian Reservations, Unsettled, etc.

Map 25.1 Presidential Election of 1892 (showing vote by county) Note the concentration of Populist strength in the semiarid farming regions of the western half of the country. (Compare this with Map 22.4, showing average annual precipitation with major agricultural products as of 1900, on p. 558.)

armed with rifles and dynamite, forced their assailants to surrender after a vicious battle that left ten people dead and some sixty wounded. Government troops were eventually summoned, and both the strike and the union were broken. That same month, federal troops bloodily smashed a strike among silver miners in Idaho's booming Coeur d'Alene district.

The Populists made a remarkable showing in the 1892 presidential election (refer to Map 25.1). They rolled up 1,029,846 popular votes and 22 electoral votes for General Weaver. They thus became one of the few third parties in U.S. history to break into the electoral column. But they fell far short of an electoral majority. Populist electoral votes came from only six midwestern and western states, four of which (Kansas, Colorado, Idaho, and Nevada) fell completely into the Populist basket (refer to Image 25.6).

25-6 Racism Undermines a Movement

The South, although a hotbed of agrarian agitation, proved especially unwilling to throw in its lot with the new party. Race was the reason. The more than 1 million Southern Black farmers organized in the Colored Farmers' National Alliance shared a host of complaints with poor white farmers, and for a time their common economic goals promised to overcome their racial differences. Recognizing the crucial edge that Black votes could give them in the South, Populist leaders like Georgia's Tom Watson reached out to the Black community. Watson, a wiry redhead who could "talk like the thrust of a Bowie knife," declared: "There is no reason why the black man should not understand that the law that hurts me, as a farmer, hurts him, as a farmer." Many Black people were disillusioned enough with the party of Lincoln to respond. Alarmed, the conservative white "Bourbon" elite in the South played cynically upon historic racial antagonisms to counter the Populists' appeal for interracial solidarity and to woo back poor white voters.

Image 25.6 The Kansas Legislature, 1893 Rifle-bearing Populists seized the Kansas capitol after the election of 1892 to make good their claim that they had won at the polls. Republicans disagreed and eventually prevailed when sergeants at arms, shown here, restored order.

Black Southerners were heavy losers. The Populist-inspired reminder of potential Black political strength led to the near-total extinction of what little African American suffrage remained in the South. White Southerners more aggressively than ever used literacy tests and poll taxes to deny Black voters the ballot. The notorious **grandfather clause** exempted from those requirements anyone whose forebear had voted in 1860—when, of course, enslaved Black people had not voted at all. More than half a century would pass before Black Southerners could again vote in appreciable numbers. Accompanying this disfranchisement were more severe Jim Crow laws, designed to enforce racial segregation in public places, including hotels and restaurants, and backed up by lynchings and other atrocities.

The conservative crusade to eliminate the Black vote in the South suppressed a potentially large Populist constituency and thereby dealt the national Populist movement a crippling blow. Even Tom Watson abandoned his interracial appeals and, in time, became a vociferous racist himself (refer to Image 25.7). After 1896, the Populist Party lapsed increasingly into vile racism and staunchly advocated Black disfranchisement. Such were the bitterly ironic fruits of the Populist campaign in the South.

Image 25.7 Thomas Edward Watson (1865–1922) Populist leader Tom Watson of Georgia began his public career promoting interracial political cooperation, though he sometimes despaired that many poor white farmers preferred to "hug the chains of . . . wretchedness rather than do any experimenting on [the race] question." Watson himself eventually succumbed to racism. In 1913, he proclaimed that "the Negro has no comprehension of virtue, honesty, truth, gratitude, and principle. The South has to lynch him occasionally, and flog him, now and then, to keep him from blaspheming the Almighty by his conduct . . . and color."

25-7 Cleveland Copes with a Catastrophic Depression

Grover Cleveland took office once again in 1893, the only president ever reelected after defeat. He was the same old bull-necked and bullheaded Cleveland. But though it was the same old Cleveland, it was not the same old country. Farmers choking on debt were up in arms, exploited workers were stirring, and now the advance shadows of economic panic were falling darkly.

Hardly had Cleveland settled into the presidential chair when the devastating depression of 1893 burst about his burly frame. Lasting nearly four years, it was the most punishing economic downturn of the nineteenth century. The splurge of overbuilding and speculation, increasingly disruptive labor disorders, tight-money policies, and the deepening agricultural depression created a near-perfect storm of economic distress. Free-silver agitation—the cry to expand the money supply with unlimited coinage of silver—had also damaged American credit abroad, and the usual pinch on American finances had come when European banking houses began to call in loans to the United States.

The gathering calamity spread deep and far. About eight thousand American businesses collapsed in six months. Dozens of bankrupted railroad lines went into the hands of receivers. Soup kitchens fed the unemployed, while jobless "tramps" wandered hungrily around the country. Local charities did their feeble best, but the federal government, bound by the let-nature-take-its-course philosophy of the times, saw no legitimate way to relieve the suffering masses.

Cleveland, who had earlier been bothered by a surplus, was now saddled with a deepening deficit. The Treasury was required to issue legal tender notes for the silver bullion that it bought. Owners of the paper currency would then present it for gold, and by law the notes had to be reissued. New holders would repeat the process, thus draining away precious gold in an "endless-chain" operation.

Alarmingly, the gold reserve in the Treasury dropped below $100 million, which was popularly regarded as the safe minimum for supporting about $350 million in outstanding paper money. Cleveland saw no alternative but to halt the bleeding away of gold by engineering a repeal of the Sherman Silver Purchase Act of 1890. For this purpose, he summoned Congress into an extra session in the summer of 1893.

Unknown to the country, complications threatened from another quarter. A malignant growth had developed on the roof of Cleveland's mouth, and it had to be removed on a private yacht with extreme secrecy. If the president had died under the surgeon's knife, his place would have been taken by the "soft-money" vice president, Illinois' Adlai E. Stevenson—an eventuality that would have exponentially intensified the crisis.

Repeal of the Sherman Silver Purchase Act only partially stopped the hemorrhaging of gold from the Treasury. In February 1894, the gold reserve sank to a dismaying $41 million. The United States was now in grave danger of going off the gold standard—a move that would render the nation's currency volatile and unreliable as a measure of value and that would also mortally cripple America's international trade. Cleveland floated two Treasury bond issues in 1894, totaling over $100 million, but the "endless-chain" operations continued relentlessly.

Early in 1895, Cleveland turned in desperation to J. P. Morgan, "the bankers' banker" and the head of a Wall Street syndicate. After tense negotiations at the White House, the bankers agreed to lend the government $65 million in gold. The loan temporarily restored confidence in the nation's finances. But relief was brief.

25-8 Cleveland Breeds a Backlash

The bond deal stirred up a storm. The Wall Street ogre, especially in the eyes of the silverites and other debtors, symbolized all that was wicked and rotten in American politics. Protesters savagely condemned President Cleveland's secretive dealings with the mighty "Jupiter" Morgan as a "sellout" of the national government.

Cleveland suffered further embarrassment with the passage of the protectionist Wilson-Gorman Tariff in 1894. An outraged Cleveland grudgingly allowed the bill, which also contained a 2 percent tax on incomes over $4,000, to become law without his signature. When the Supreme Court struck down the income-tax provision in 1895,* the Populists and other disaffected groups assailed the move as further proof that the courts were only the tools of the plutocrats.

The revitalized Republicans, singing "Times Are Mighty Hard," won the congressional elections of 1894 in a landslide—244 seats to 105 for the Democrats. Republicans began to look forward to the presidential race of 1896 with unconcealed glee.

*It violated the "direct tax" clause. Refer to Art. I, Sec. IX, para. 4 in the Appendix. The Sixteenth Amendment to the Constitution, adopted in 1913, permitted an income tax.

Despite his gruff integrity and occasional courage, Grover Cleveland failed utterly to cope with the serious economic crisis that befell the country in 1893. He was tied down in office by the same threads that held all the politicians of the day to Lilliputian levels. Grant, Hayes, Garfield, Arthur, Harrison, and Cleveland are often referred to as the "forgettable presidents." Bewhiskered and bland in person, they left mostly blanks—or blots—on the nation's political record, as issues like the tariff, the money question, the plight of the farmers, and the rights of labor continued to fester. What little political vitality existed in Gilded Age America was to be found in local settings or in Congress, which overshadowed the White House for most of this period. But before the century ended, down-and-out debtors and disgruntled workers would make one last titanic effort to wring reform out of the torpid political system—in the momentous election of 1896.

25-9 Coxey's Army and the Pullman Strike

The panic of 1893 and the severe ensuing depression strengthened the Populists' argument that farmers and laborers alike were being victimized by an oppressive economic and political system. Ragged armies of the unemployed began marching to protest their plight. In the growing hordes of displaced industrial toilers, the Populists saw potential political allies.

The most famous marcher was "General" Jacob S. Coxey, a wealthy Ohio quarry owner. He set out for Washington in 1894 with a few score of supporters and a swarm of newspaper reporters (refer to Image 25.8). His platform included a demand that the government relieve unemployment with an inflationary public works program, supported by some $500 million in legal tender notes to be issued by the Treasury. Coxey himself rode in a carriage with his wife and infant son, appropriately named Legal Tender Coxey, while his tiny "army" tramped along behind, singing,

> We're coming, Grover Cleveland,
> 500,000 strong,
> We're marching on to Washington
> to right the nation's wrong.

Library of Congress/Getty Images

Image 25.8 Coxey's Army on the March, 1894 Large throngs joined Coxey for parts of his "march," but relatively few made it all the way to his destination of Washington, DC.

After the Pullman strike collapsed, Eugene Debs (1855–1926) said,

"No strike has ever been lost."

In 1897 he declared,

"The issue is Socialism versus Capitalism. I am for Socialism because I am for humanity."

The "Commonweal Army" of Coxeyites finally straggled into the nation's capital, but the invasion took on the aspects of a comic opera when "General" Coxey and his "lieutenants" were arrested for walking on the grass.

Elsewhere, labor protests erupted once again into violent flare-ups, notably in Chicago. Most dramatic was the crippling **Pullman strike** of 1894. Eugene V. Debs, a charismatic labor leader, had helped organize the American Railway Union of about 150,000 members. The Pullman Palace Car Company had constructed a model "company town" near Chicago with housing, shops, and other amenities intended to contain worker unrest and reduce turnover. Pullman was hit hard by the depression and cut wages by about one-third, while refusing to lower rent for the company houses. Infuriated workers lashed out. They overturned Pullman cars and paralyzed railway traffic from Chicago to the Pacific coast. The American Federation of Labor conspicuously declined to support the Pullman strikers, thus enhancing the AF of L's reputation for "respectability" even while weakening labor's cause by driving a large wedge into the workers' ranks.

The turmoil in Chicago was menacing but not yet completely out of hand. At least this was the judgment of Governor John Peter Altgeld of Illinois, a friend of the downtrodden, who had pardoned the Haymarket Square anarchists the year before (refer to "23-14 Labor Gains Strength," pp. 585–586). But U.S. attorney general Richard Olney, an archconservative and an ex-railroad attorney, urged the dispatch of federal troops. His legal grounds were that the strikers were interfering with the transit of the U.S. mail. President Cleveland supported Olney with the ringing declaration, "If it takes the entire army and navy to deliver a postal card in Chicago, that card will be delivered."

To the delight of conservatives, federal troops, bayonets fixed, crushed the Pullman strike (refer to Image 25.9). Debs was sentenced to six months' imprisonment for contempt of court because he had defied a federal injunction to cease striking. Ironically, the lean labor agitator spent much of his enforced leisure reading radical literature, which led to his later leadership of the socialist movement in America.

Embittered cries of "government by injunction" now burst from worker's mouths. Washington had never before used such a legal weapon to break a strike. It was all the more hurtful because defiant workers who were held in contempt could be imprisoned without a jury trial, as employers tried to smash labor unions by court action. Populists and other debtors were likewise incensed. They saw in the brutal Pullman episode further proof of an unholy alliance between business and the courts.

Image 25.9 The Pullman Strike, 1894
Illinois National Guardsmen fire on Pullman Company strikers on July 7, 1894. Police clubs and U.S. Army rifles and bayonets finally broke the back of the strike, which halted railroads throughout the country.

25-10 Golden McKinley and Silver Bryan

The smoldering grievances of the long-suffering farmers and the depression-plagued laborers gave ominous significance to the forthcoming election of 1896. Conservatives of all stripes trembled at the prospect of an impending smash-up, while down-and-out husbandmen and discontented workers cast about desperately for political salvation. Increasingly, monetary policy—whether to maintain the gold standard or inflate the currency by monetizing silver—loomed as the issue on which the election would turn.

The leading candidate for the Republican presidential nomination in 1896 was former congressman William McKinley of Ohio, sponsor of the ill-starred tariff bill of 1890 (refer to "21-14 The Billion-Dollar Congress," pp. 539–540). He had established a creditable Civil War record, having risen to the rank of major; he hailed from the electorally potent state of Ohio; and he could point to long years of honorable service in Congress, where he had made many friends with his kindly and conciliatory manner.

As a presidential candidate, McKinley was largely the creature of a fellow Ohioan, Marcus Alonzo Hanna, who had made his fortune in the iron business and now coveted the role of president-maker. "I love McKinley," he once said. As a wholehearted Hamiltonian, Hanna believed that a prime function of government was to aid business. Earnest and forceful, he became the personification of big industry in politics. He was often caricatured in cartoons, quite unfairly, as a bloated bully in a loud checkered suit with a dollar sign in each square. He honestly believed that in some measure prosperity "trickled down" to the laborer, whose dinner pail was full when business flourished. Critics assailed this idea as equivalent to feeding the horses in order to feed the sparrows.

The hardheaded Hanna organized his preconvention campaign for McKinley with consummate skill and with a liberal outpouring of his own money. The convention steamroller, well lubricated with Hanna's dollars, nominated McKinley on the first ballot in St. Louis in June 1896 and launched into the work of the national campaign (refer to Image 25.10). The Republican platform cleverly straddled the money question but leaned toward hard-money policies. It declared for the gold standard, even though McKinley's voting record in Congress had been embarrassingly friendly to silver. The platform also condemned hard times and Democratic incapacity, while pouring praise on the protective tariff (refer to Image 25.11).

Dissension riddled the Democratic camp. Cleveland no longer led his party. The depression had driven the last nail into his political coffin. Dubbed "the Stuffed Prophet," he was undeniably the most unpopular man in the country. Labor-debtor groups remembered too vividly his intervention in the Pullman strike, the backstairs Morgan bond deal, and especially his stubborn hard-money policies. Ultraconservative in finance, Cleveland now looked more like a Republican than a Democrat on the money issue.

Rudderless, the Democratic convention met in Chicago in July 1896, with the silverites lusting for victory. Shouting insults at the absent Cleveland, the delegates refused, by a suicidal vote of 564 to 357, to endorse their own administration. They had the enthusiasm and the numbers; all they lacked was a leader.

Image 25.10 McKinley Campaign Headquarters, Chicago, 1896 Those few Black Americans who could exercise their right to vote in the 1890s still remained faithful to "the party of Lincoln."

Image 25.11 Crying for Protection, 1896 Uncle Sam is called on in this cartoon to nurse so-called infant industries—some of which had in fact long since grown into vigorous adulthood.

Contending Voices

Populism and Anti-Populism

William Jennings Bryan (1860–1925) electrified the Democratic convention in Chicago in 1896 with his "Cross of Gold" speech. He succinctly described the differences in governing philosophies that divided his Populist supporters from their opponents:

> "There are two ideas of government. There are those who believe that, if you will only legislate to make the well-to-do prosperous, their prosperity will leak through on those below. The Democratic [and Populist] idea, however, has been that if you legislate to make the masses prosperous, their prosperity will find its way up through every class which rests upon them."

Famed Kansas journalist William Allen White (1868–1944), editor of *The Emporia Gazette* and nationally known as the "Sage of Emporia," lambasted the populists as "gibbering idiots" in a fiery editorial ("What's the Matter with Kansas") published on August 15, 1896. Citing the passage from Bryan's "Cross of Gold" speech quoted immediately above, he wrote:

> "That's the stuff! Give the prosperous man the dickens! Legislate the thriftless man into ease, whack the stuffing out of the creditors and tell the debtors who borrowed the money five years ago when money 'per capita' was greater than it is now, that the contraction of currency gives him a right to repudiate.
>
> Whoop it up for the ragged trousers; put the lazy, greasy fizzle, who can't pay his debts, on the altar, and bow down and worship him. Let the state ideal be high. What we need is not the respect of our fellow men but the chance to get something for nothing."

Consider This:

How did these different attitudes about government and the economy continue to shape public policy in the century that followed?

A new Moses suddenly appeared in the person of William Jennings Bryan of Nebraska. Then only thirty-six years of age and known as "the Boy Orator of the Platte,"* the former congressman strode confidently onto the platform before fifteen thousand people. His masterful presence was set off by a peninsular jaw and raven-black hair. He radiated authenticity and energy.

The convention-hall setting was made to order for a magnificent oratorical effort. A hush fell over the delegates as Bryan rose to speak. His organlike voice rolled into the outer corners of the huge hall, fervently pleading for silver. Rising to supreme heights of eloquence, he thundered, "We will answer their demands for a gold standard by saying to them: 'You shall not press down upon the brow of labor this crown of thorns, you shall not crucify mankind upon a cross of gold.'"

The Cross of Gold speech was a sensation. Swept off its feet in a tumultuous scene, the Democratic convention nominated Bryan the next day. The platform demanded inflation through the unlimited coinage of silver at the ratio of 16 ounces of silver to 1 ounce of gold, though the market ratio was about 32 to 1. This meant that the silver in a dollar would be worth about fifty cents.

Democratic "Gold Bugs," unable to swallow Bryan, bolted their party over the silver issue. A conservative senator from New York, when asked if he was a Democrat still, reportedly replied, "Yes, I am a Democrat still—very still." The Democratic minority, including Cleveland, charged that the Populist-silverites had stolen both the name and the clothes of their party. They nominated a lost-cause ticket of their own, and many of them, including Cleveland, not too secretly hoped for a McKinley victory.

The Populists now faced a dilemma; the Democratic majority had appropriated their main plank—"16 to 1," that "heaven-born ratio." The bulk of the Populists, fearing a hard-money McKinley victory, endorsed both "fusion" with the Democrats and Bryan for president, sacrificing their identity in the mix. Singing "The Jolly Silver Dollar of the Dads," they became in effect

*One contemporary sneered that Bryan, like the Platte River in his home state of Nebraska, was "six inches deep and six miles wide at the mouth."

the "Demo-Pop" party, though a handful of the original Populists refused to support Bryan and went down with their colors nailed to the mast.

25-11 Plowholders Versus Bondholders

Mark Hanna smugly assumed that he could make the tariff the focus of the campaign. But Bryan, a dynamo of energy, forced the free-trade issue into the backseat when he took to the stump on behalf of free silver. Sweeping through twenty-seven states and traveling 18,000 miles, he made nearly six hundred speeches—thirty-six in one day—and even invaded the East, "the enemy's country." The poet Vachel Lindsay caught the spirit of his oratorical orgy:

> Prairie avenger, mountain lion,
> Bryan, Bryan, Bryan, Bryan,
> Gigantic troubadour, speaking like a siege gun,
> Smashing Plymouth Rock with his boulders
> from the West.*

Free silver became almost as much a religious as a financial issue. Hordes of fanatical free-silverites hailed Bryan as the messiah to lead them out of the wilderness of debt. They sang, "We'll All Have Our Pockets Lined with Silver" and "No Crown of Thorns, No Cross of Gold."

Bryan created panic among eastern conservatives with his threat of converting their holdings overnight into fifty-cent dollars. The "Gold Bugs" responded with their own free and unlimited coinage of verbiage. They vented their alarm in abusive epithets, ranging from "fanatic" and "madman" to "traitor" and "murderer." "In God We Trust, with Bryan We Bust," the Republicans sneered, while one Eastern clergyman cried, "That platform was made in Hell."

McKinley, recognizing that few mortals could compete with Bryan's bombastic barnstorming, chose to campaign from the front porch of his home in Canton, Ohio, inviting supporters from across the nation to attend a series of carefully choreographed campaign events capped with a pithy speech by the candidate himself. Scribbling reporters on McKinley's front lawn relayed the proceedings to far-off readers, and visitors returned home flush with excitement with all they had seen in Canton. The clever orchestration of McKinley's **front porch campaign** and the magnetic oratory of Bryan marked the start of a new era in presidential campaigning in which the personality, charisma, and communication skills of the candidate came to the fore.

The campaign also set new standards for election-year spending. Widespread fear of Bryan and the "silver lunacy" enabled "Dollar Mark" Hanna, now chairman of the Republican National Committee, to shine as a money-raiser. He "shook down" the trusts and plutocrats and piled up an enormous "slush fund" for a "campaign of education"—or of propaganda, depending on one's point of view. Reminding the voters of Cleveland's "Democratic panic," Republicans appealed to the "belly vote" with their prize slogan, "McKinley and the Full Dinner Pail."

The McKinleyites thus amassed the most formidable political campaign chest thus far in American history. At all levels—national, state, and local—it amounted to about $16 million, as contrasted with about $1 million for the poorer Democrats (ironically, roughly "16 to 1"). With some justification, the Bryanites accused Hanna of buying the election and of floating McKinley into the White House on a tidal wave of mud and money.

Bryan's cyclonic campaign began to lose steam as the weeks passed. Fear was probably Hanna's strongest ally, as it was Bryan's worst enemy. Republican businesspeople placed contracts with manufacturers—contingent on the election of McKinley. A few factory owners, with thinly veiled intimidation, paid off their workers and told them not to come to work on Wednesday morning if Bryan won. Reports also circulated that employers were threatening to pay their employees in fifty-cent pieces, instead of in dollars, if Bryan triumphed. Such were some of the "dirty tricks" of the "Stop Bryan, Save America" crusade (refer to Image 25.12).

Hanna's campaign methods paid off. On election day McKinley triumphed decisively. The vote was 271 to 176 in the Electoral College and 7,102,246 to 6,492,559 in the popular election. Driven by fear and excitement, an unprecedented outpouring of voters flocked to the polls. McKinley ran strongly in the populous urban East, where he carried every county of New England, and in the upper Mississippi Valley. Bryan's states, concentrated in the debt-bedeviled South and

---

*Reprinted from *Collected Poems of Vachel Lindsay: Revised Edition* by Vachel Lindsay. New York: Macmillan, 1948.

Library of Congress Prints and Photographs Division [LC-USZC4-9712]

Image 25.12 The Sacrilegious Candidate A hostile cartoonist makes sport of Bryan's notorious Cross of Gold speech in 1896.

the arid trans-Mississippi West, boasted more acreage than McKinley's but less population (refer to Map 25.2).

The free-silver election of 1896 was arguably the most significant political turning point since Lincoln's victories in 1860 and 1864. Despite Bryan's strength in the South and West, the results vividly demonstrated his lack of appeal to the unmortgaged farmer and especially to the eastern urban laborer. Many wage earners in the East voted for their jobs and full dinner pails, threatened as they were by free silver, free trade, and fireless factories. Living precariously on a fixed wage, the factory workers had no reason to favor inflation, which was the heart of the Bryanites' program. Thus the dream of an electorally successful coalition of farmers and workers failed to materialize.

The Bryan-McKinley battle heralded the advent of a new era in American politics. At first glance, the election seemed to be the age-old story of the underprivileged many against the privileged few, of the indebted backcountry against the wealthier seaboard, the country against the city, agrarians against industrialists, workers against bosses, labor against capital, Main Street against Wall Street, the nobodies against the somebodies. Yet when Bryan made his evangelical appeal to all those supposed foes of the existing social order, they fell pathetically short of a political majority.

The outcome was instead a resounding victory for big business, the big cities, middle-class values, and financial

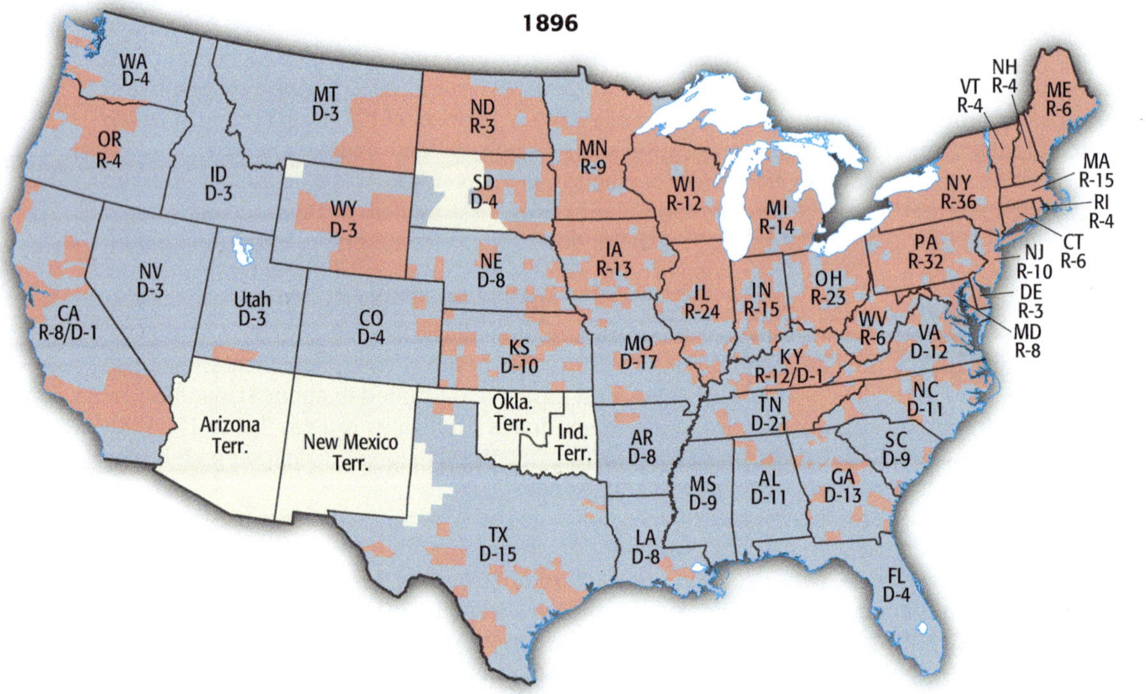

Candidate (Party)	Electoral Vote		Popular Vote	
McKinley (Republican)	271	61%	7,102,246	51.1%
Bryan (Democrat)	176	39%	6,492,559	47.7%

Territories, Indian Reservations, unsettled, etc.

Map 25.2 Presidential Election of 1896 (showing vote by county) This election tolled the death knell of the Gilded Age political party system, with its razor-close elections, strong party loyalties, and high voter turnouts. It also revealed distinct regional voting patterns. William Jennings Bryan's sweep of the southern and western states could not match McKinley's strong showing in the more populous North and East. For years after 1896, Republicans predominated, and citizens showed a declining interest in joining parties and voting.

Varying Viewpoints

The Populists: Radicals or Reactionaries?

Taking their cue from contemporary satirical commentaries like Mark Twain and Charles Dudley Warner's *The Gilded Age* (1873), the first historians who wrote about the post–Civil War era judged it harshly. They condemned its politicians as petty and corrupt, lamented the emergence of a new plutocratic class, and railed against the arrogance of corporate power. Such a view is conspicuous in Charles and Mary Beard's *The Rise of American Civilization* (4 vols., 1927–1942), perhaps the most influential American history textbook ever written.

The Beards were leaders of the so-called progressive school of historical writing that flourished in the early years of the twentieth century. Progressive historians, many of whom grew up in the Gilded Age, shared in a widespread disillusionment that the Civil War had failed to generate a rebirth of American idealism. Their political sympathies were chillingly antibusiness and warmly pro-labor, pro-farmer, and pro-reform.

Historians of the progressive persuasion identified Populism as virtually the only organized opposition to the social, economic, and political order that took shape in the last decades of the nineteenth century. The Populists thus became heroes to several generations of writers who bemoaned that order and looked back longingly at Americans' agrarian past. John D. Hicks, *The Populist Revolt* (1931), is the classic portrayal of the Populists as embattled farmers hurling defiance at Wall Street and the robber barons in a last-ditch defense of their simple, honest way of life. Bowed but unbroken by the defeat of their great champion, William Jennings Bryan, in the presidential election of 1896, the Populists, Hicks claimed, left a reforming legacy that flourished again in the progressive era and the New Deal.

Hicks's point of view was the dominant one until the 1950s, when it was sharply criticized by Richard Hofstadter in *The Age of Reform* (1955). Hofstadter charged that the progressive historians had romanticized the Populists, who were best understood not as picturesque protesters but as "harassed little country businessmen" bristling with provincial prejudices. The city-born-and-bred Hofstadter argued that the Populist revolt was aimed not just at big business and the money power but also somewhat irrationally at urbanism, immigrants, the East, and modernity itself. Hofstadter thus exposed a "dark side" of Populism, which contained elements of backwoods anti-intellectualism, paranoia, and anti-Semitism.

In the 1960s several scholars, inspired by the work of C. Vann Woodward, as well as by sympathy with the protest movements of that turbulent decade, began to rehabilitate the Populists as authentic reformers with genuine grievances. Especially notable in this vein was Lawrence Goodwyn's *Democratic Promise: The Populist Movement in America* (1976). Goodwyn depicted the Populists as reasonable radicals who were justifiably resentful of their eclipse by urban industrialism and finance capitalism. He also portrayed Populism as the last gasp of popular political participation, a democratic "moment" in American history that expired with the Populists' absorption into the Democratic party.

Two subsequent works, Edward L. Ayers's *Promise of the New South* (1992) and Robert C. McMath's *American Populism* (1993), synthesized many of the older perspectives and presented a balanced view of the Populists as radical in many ways but also limited by their nostalgia for a lost agrarian past. Charles Postel's *The Populist Vision* (2007) made the strongest argument yet for the movement's forward-looking, modernizing elements, while Eric Rauchway's *Blessed Among Nations* (2006) argued that Populism was a reaction to America's increased reliance on foreign investment. And in his magisterial work, *The Republic for Which it Stands* (2017), Richard White largely rehabilitates the Populists as expressing the only plausible—though eventually doomed—alternative to the juggernaut of industrial capitalism that utterly transformed late-nineteenth-century American society.

conservatism. Bryan's defeat marked the last serious effort to win the White House with mostly agrarian votes. The future of presidential politics lay not on the farms, with their dwindling population, but in the mushrooming cities, with their growing hordes of freshly arriving immigrants.

The Grand Old Party's smashing victory of 1896 also heralded a Republican grip on the White House for sixteen consecutive years—indeed, for all but eight of the next thirty-six years. McKinley's election also imparted a new character to the American political system. The long reign of Republican political dominance that it ushered in was accompanied by diminishing voter participation in elections, the weakening of party organizations, and the fading away of issues like the money question and civil-service reform, which came to be replaced by concern for industrial regulation and the welfare of labor. Scholars have dubbed this new political era the period of the **fourth party system**, signaling a break with the previous "third party system," in place since 1860 and characterized by remarkably high voter turnouts and close contests between Democrats and Republicans.

In gold-standard Britain, there was much relief over McKinley's victory. *The London Standard* commented,

"The hopelessly ignorant and savagely covetous waifs and strays of American civilization voted for Bryan, but the bulk of the solid sense, business integrity, and social stability sided with McKinley. The nation is to be heartily congratulated."

25-12 Business Conservatism Enthroned

An eminently "safe" McKinley took the inaugural oath in 1897. With his impeccable white vest, he seemed never to perspire, even in oppressively muggy Washington. Though a man of considerable ability, he was an ear-to-the-ground politician who seldom got far out of line with majority opinion. His cautious, conservative nature caused him to shy away from the flaming banner of reform. Business was given a free rein, and the trusts, which had trusted him in 1896, were allowed to develop more mighty muscles without serious restraints.

Almost as soon as McKinley took office, the tariff issue, which had played second fiddle to silver in the "Battle of '96," quickly forced itself to the fore. The current Wilson-Gorman law was not raising enough revenue to cover the annual Treasury deficits, and the Republican trusts thought that they had purchased the right to additional tariff protection by their lush contributions to Hanna's war chest. In due course, supporters rammed the Dingley Tariff Bill through the House in 1897, under the pounding gavel of the rethroned Speaker of the House, "Czar" Reed. The proposed new rates were high, but not high enough to satisfy the paunchy lobbyists, who once again descended on the Senate. Over 850 amendments were tacked onto the overburdened bill. The resulting piece of patchwork finally established the average rates at 46.5 percent, substantially higher than the Democratic Wilson-Gorman Act of 1894 and in some categories even higher than the McKinley Act of 1890.

Prosperity, long lurking around the corner, began to return with a rush in 1897, the first year of McKinley's term. The depression of 1893 had run its course. Farm prices rose. Paint-thirsty midwestern barns blossomed in new colors. The wheels of industry resumed their hum. Republican politicians, like crowing roosters believing they caused the sun to rise, claimed credit for attracting the sunlight of prosperity (refer to Image 25.13).

With the return of growth, the money issue that had overshadowed politics since the Civil War gradually faded away. The **Gold Standard Act** of 1900, passed over last-ditch silverite opposition, provided that the paper currency be redeemed freely in gold. Nature and science gradually provided an inflation that the "Gold Bug" East had fought so frantically to prevent. Electrifying discoveries of new gold deposits in Canada's fabled Klondike, as well as in Alaska, South Africa, and Australia, brought huge quantities of gold onto world markets, as did the perfecting of the cheap cyanide process for extracting gold from low-grade ore. Moderate inflation thus took care of the currency needs of an explosively expanding nation, as its circulatory system greatly improved. The tide of "silver heresy" rapidly receded, and the "Popocratic" fish were left gasping high and dry on a golden-sanded beach.

A

The Granger Collection, NYC

B

The Granger Collection, NYC

Image 25.13A and B Campaign Gimcracks, 1896 These mechanical cards predicted Republican prosperity with McKinley and economic ruin with William Jennings Bryan.

Chapter Summary

Post–Civil War industrialization had a disturbing effect on American farmers. As the farmers opened vast new lands to cultivation, agriculture was becoming a mechanized business dependent on specialized production and international markets. Once declining prices and other woes doomed the farmers to permanent debt and dependency, they began to protest their lot, first through the Grange and then through the Farmers' Alliances, the prelude to the People's (Populist) Party. The Populists made spectacular gains in the West and the South, but racial divisions eventually undermined Southern Populism. The Populists' initial attempts to form an interracial farmers' coalition failed and threatened conservative white people, who then used the occasion to virtually end Black voting and reinforce segregation.

The major depression that began in 1893 accelerated farmer protest as well as labor unrest and strikes, leading to a growing class conflict. In both factories and mines, bitter strikes erupted. Some were broken with military force, including the bitter Pullman strike of 1894. President Grover Cleveland's use of anti-labor court injunctions and his turn to J. P. Morgan to uphold the gold standard made him deeply unpopular in his own party.

In 1896 pro-silver hero William Jennings Bryan captured the Democratic Party's nomination, and with Populist support led a fervent campaign against the "Gold Bug" Republicans and their candidate William McKinley. McKinley's success in winning urban workers away from Bryan proved a turning point in American politics, signaling the triumph of the city, the middle class, and a new party system. The return of prosperity in McKinley's first term ended the late-nineteenth-century preoccupation with monetary issues and made Republicans the dominant party for two generations.

Key Terms

- mechanization of agriculture (626)
- Populists (630)
- Homestead strike (631)
- grandfather clause (633)
- Pullman strike (636)
- front porch campaign (639)
- fourth party system (641)
- Gold Standard Act (642)

People to Know

- Oliver H. Kelley
- William Hope "Coin" Harvey
- Mary Elizabeth Lease
- James B. Weaver
- Eugene Victor Debs
- John Peter Altgeld
- Grover Cleveland
- Jacob S. Coxey
- Tom Watson
- William McKinley
- Marcus Alonzo Hanna

Chronology

1867	• Oliver H. Kelley founds the Grange	
1892	• Homestead steel strike • Coeur d'Alene (Idaho) silver miners' strike • People's party candidate James B. Weaver wins twenty-two electoral votes	• Cleveland defeats Harrison and Weaver to regain presidency
1893	• Depression of 1890s begins	
1894	• "Coxey's Army" marches on Washington • Pullman strike	
1895	• J. P. Morgan's banking syndicate loans $65 million in gold to federal government	
1896	• Utah admitted to Union • McKinley defeats Bryan for presidency	
1897	• Dingley Tariff Act	
1900	• Gold Standard Act	

To Learn More

Paul Krause, *The Battle for Homestead, 1880–1892: Politics, Culture, and Steel* (1992)

Jackson Lears, *Rebirth of a Nation: The Making of Modern America, 1877–1920* (2009)

Robert W. Merry, *President McKinley: Architect of the American Century* (2017)

Charles Postel, *The Populist Vision* (2007)

Heather Cox Richardson, *The Death of Reconstruction: Race, Labor, and Politics in the Post-Civil War North, 1865–1901* (2001)

Mark W. Summers, *The Era of Good Stealings* (1993)

Richard White, *The Republic for Which It Stands: The United States During Reconstruction and the Gilded Age, 1865–1896* (2017)

R. Hal Williams, *Realigning America: McKinley, Bryan, and the Remarkable Election of 1896* (2010)

C. Vann Woodward, *Origins of the New South, 1877–1913* (1951)

________, *The Strange Career of Jim Crow* (rev. ed., 1974)

Part 7

Struggling for Justice at Home and Abroad 1890–1945

The new century brought astonishing changes and bestowed upon the United States new prominence and power on the world stage. After a brief war against Spain in 1898, a nation born in a revolutionary war of independence and long the champion of national self-determination itself became an imperial power, seizing control of the Philippines, Puerto Rico, and Guam. Uncle Sam's venture into empire touched off a bitter national debate about America's role in the world and ushered in a long period of argument over the responsibilities, at home as well as abroad, of a modern industrial nation.

Industrialization continued apace. The massive trusts of the nineteenth century became behemoths in the first part of the twentieth. The most transformative technology of the age was the automobile, a high-tech marvel turned ubiquitous consumer product. A huge wave of immigration continued to alter the face of the nation, especially the cities, where most Americans lived by 1920. Black Southerners, seeking opportunity and escape from Jim Crow's oppression, also migrated to the mostly northern cities, reshaping urban culture and national politics.

Changes of such magnitude raised vexing questions. What role should the United States play in the world? How could the enormous power of industry be guided to the benefit of society as a whole? How would the millions of new immigrants make their way in America? What should the country

Bettmann/Getty Images

Image VII.1 Anti-lynching Campaigners Protest in Washington, DC, December 1934 An epidemic of racial violence and extrajudicial killings swept through the nation in the early twentieth century, becoming one catalyst of the civil rights movement.

do about poverty, disease, and the continuing plague of racial inequality? All these issues turned on a fundamental point: Should government remain narrowly limited in its powers, or did the times require a more potent government that would actively shape society and secure American interests abroad?

The progressive movement represented an ambitious attempt to answer those questions. Reform-minded men and women from all walks of life and from both major parties shared in the progressive crusade for greater government activism. Buoyed by this outlook, Presidents Theodore Roosevelt, William Howard Taft, and Woodrow Wilson enlarged the capacity of government to "bust" business trusts, regulate corporations, and promote fair labor practices, child welfare, conservation, and consumer protection. The progressive-era presidents also challenged America's tradition of isolationism in foreign policy, launching diplomatic and economic initiatives in the Caribbean, Central America, and East Asia. Wilson aspired to "make the world safe for democracy" by rallying support for American intervention in the First World War.

The progressive spirit waned, however, as the United States retreated during the 1920s into what President Harding called "normalcy." Isolationist sentiment revived with a vengeance. Blessed with a booming economy, Americans turned their gaze inward to baseball heroes, radio, jazz, movies, and the first mass-produced American automobile, the Model T Ford. Presidents Harding, Coolidge, and Hoover backed off from the economic regulatory zeal of their predecessors.

"Normalcy" also had a brutal side. Thousands of suspected radicals were jailed or deported in the Red Scare of 1919 and 1920. Anti-immigrant passions flared until immigration quotas in 1924 squeezed the flow of newcomers to a trickle. Race riots scorched several northern cities in the summer of 1919, a sign of how embittered race relations had become in the wake of the Great Migration of Black Southerners to wartime jobs in northern industry. A reborn Ku Klux Klan staged a comeback, not just in the South but in the North and West as well.

"Normalcy" itself soon proved short-lived, a casualty of the stock-market crash of 1929 and the Great Depression that followed. As Americans watched banks fail, businesses collapse, and millions of people lose their jobs, they asked with renewed urgency what role the government should play in rescuing the nation. President Franklin D. Roosevelt's answer was the "New Deal"—an ambitious array of relief programs, public works, and economic regulations that failed to cure the Depression but left an impressive legacy of government-directed social reforms.

Even as most Americans came to accept an expanded federal government role at home under FDR's leadership in the 1930s, they still clung stubbornly to isolationism. The United States did little in the 1930s to check the rising military aggression of Japan and Germany. By the early 1940s, events forced Americans to reconsider. Once Hitler's Germany had seized control of most of Europe, Roosevelt, who had long opposed the isolationists, found ways to aid a beleaguered Britain. When Japan attacked the American naval base at Pearl Harbor, Hawai'i, in December 1941, isolationists at last fell silent. Roosevelt led a stunned but determined nation into the Second World War, and victory in 1945 positioned the United States to assume a commanding position in the postwar world order.

National Archives

Image VII.2 **Bound for Guadalcanal, 1942** These troops were headed for one of the bloodiest battles of World War II, in the southwest Pacific's Solomon Islands. America threw some 15 million men and the full weight of its enormous economy into the struggle against German and Japanese aggression.

Focus Questions

1. How did the role of the United States in world affairs change over the course of the first half of the twentieth century?
2. How did reform movements and increased government activism alter the relationship between American citizens and their government?

Chapter 26

Empire and Expansion: 1890–1909

We assert that no nation can long endure half republic and half empire, and we warn the American people that imperialism abroad will lead quickly and inevitably to despotism at home.

Democratic National Platform, 1900

Chapter Outline

- The sources of American expansionism
- The Hawai'i question
- The Spanish-American War, 1898
- The invasion of Cuba
- Acquiring Puerto Rico (1898) and the Philippines (1899)
- Crushing the Filipino insurrection
- The Open Door in China
- William McKinley's assassination makes Theodore Roosevelt president (1901)
- The Panama Canal
- Theodore Roosevelt on the world stage

Contending Voices: Debating Imperialism

Makers of America: The Puerto Ricans

Makers of America: The Filipinos

Thinking Globally: The Age of Empire

Varying Viewpoints: Why Did America Become a Colonial Power?

In the years immediately following the Civil War, Americans remained astonishingly indifferent to the outside world. Enmeshed in struggles over Reconstruction and absorbed in efforts to heal the wounds of civil war, build an industrial economy, make their cities habitable, and settle the sprawling West, most citizens took little interest in international affairs. But the sunset decades of the nineteenth century witnessed a momentous shift in U.S. foreign policy. America's new diplomacy reflected the far-reaching changes that were reshaping agriculture, industry, and the social structure. American statesmen also responded to the intensifying scramble of several other nations for international advantage in a modern age of empire. By the beginning of the twentieth century, America had acquired its own overseas territories, an astonishing departure from its venerable anticolonial traditions. The world now had to reckon with a new great power, potentially powerful but with diplomatic ambitions and principles that remained to be defined.

Focus Questions

1. Why did the United States abandon its historic isolationism and turn outward to develop imperial great power ambitions at the end of the nineteenth century?
2. What were the causes of the Spanish-American War, and how did the war lead to the acquisition of an American empire in the Philippines, Guam, and Puerto Rico?
3. Why was there such a vigorous national debate over imperialism, and how did the Filipino rebellion against U.S. rule contribute to doubts about America's overseas role?
4. How did the United States become increasingly involved in China and elsewhere in East Asia, and what were the Open Door policy toward China and Theodore Roosevelt's diplomacy with Japan intended to achieve?
5. How did Theodore Roosevelt vigorously assert American power in Panama and elsewhere in Latin America, and why did the "Roosevelt Corollary" to the Monroe Doctrine stir controversy?

26-1 America Turns Outward

Several developments fed the nation's ambition for overseas expansion. Owners of great industrial and agricultural enterprises began to look for markets beyond American shores as production boomed. Leaders also fretted that if the United States could not expand, it might explode. Their country was bursting with new people, wealth, and productive capacity—and it was trembling from the hammer blows of labor violence and agrarian unrest. Overseas markets might provide a safety valve to relieve those pressures.

Popular culture whetted the people's appetite for overseas involvement. The lurid "yellow press" of Joseph Pulitzer and William Randolph Hearst described foreign exploits as manly adventures, the kind of dashing derring-do that was the stuff of young boys' dreams. Pious missionaries, inspired by books like the Reverend Josiah Strong's *Our Country: Its Possible Future and Its Present Crisis,* looked overseas for new souls to harvest. Echoing John O'Sullivan's long-ago call of "manifest destiny," Strong trumpeted the superiority of Anglo-Saxon civilization and summoned Americans to spread their religion and their values to the "backward" peoples. He cast his seed on fertile ground.

At the same time, expansionist Americans like Theodore Roosevelt and Congressman (later Senator) Henry Cabot Lodge invoked Social Darwinism to argue that the earth rightfully belonged to the strong and the fit—that is, to Uncle Sam. Their convictions strengthened as latecomers to the colonial scramble scooped up leavings from the banquet table of earlier diners (refer to Image 26.1). The continent of Africa, its interior largely unexplored, was partitioned by the Europeans in the 1880s in a pell-mell rush of colonial conquest. In the 1890s, Japan, Germany, and Russia all extorted concessions from the anemic Chinese Empire. If America was to survive in the competition of modern nation-states, expansionists argued, it also must become an imperial power.

The development of a new steel navy also focused attention overseas. Naval officer and historian Alfred Thayer Mahan's book of 1890, *The Influence of Sea Power upon History, 1660–1783,* argued that control of the sea was the key to world dominance. Mahan helped stimulate the naval race among the great powers that gained momentum around the turn of the century. Seizing on Mahan's argument, internationalists like Roosevelt pushed for a mightier navy as well as an American-built isthmian canal between the Atlantic and the Pacific.

In 1896 *The Washington Post* editorialized,

> "A new consciousness seems to have come upon us—the consciousness of strength—and with it a new appetite, the yearning to show our strength. . . . Ambition, interest, land hunger, pride, the mere joy of fighting, whatever it may be, we are animated by a new sensation. We are face to face with a strange destiny. The taste of Empire is in the mouth of the people even as the taste of blood is in the jungle. It means an Imperial policy, the Republic, renascent, taking her place with the armed nations."

Image 26.1 The Imperial Menu A pleased Uncle Sam gets ready to place his order with headwaiter William McKinley. Swallowing some of these possessions eventually produced political indigestion.

The undiplomatic 1895 note to Britain by Secretary of State Richard Olney (1835–1917) read,

"To-day the United States is practically sovereign on this continent, and its fiat is law upon the subjects to which it confines its interposition. . . . Its infinite resources combined with its isolated position render it master of the situation and practically invulnerable as against any or all other powers."

America's new international interest manifested itself in several ways. Two-time Secretary of State James G. Blaine pushed his **Big Sister policy**, aimed at rallying the Latin American nations behind Uncle Sam's leadership and opening Latin American markets to Yankee traders. Blaine's efforts bore some fruit in 1889, when he presided over the first Pan-American Conference, held in Washington, DC, the modest beginnings of an increasingly important series of inter-American assemblages.

Several international crises or near-wars also marked the path of American diplomacy in the late 1880s and early 1890s. The American and German navies nearly came to blows in 1889 over the faraway Samoan Islands in the South Pacific, which were formally divided between the two nations in 1899. (German Samoa eventually became an independent republic; American Samoa remains an American possession.) The lynching of eleven Italian immigrants in New Orleans in 1891 brought America and Italy to the brink of war, until the United States agreed to pay compensation. In another ugly affair, American demands on Chile after the deaths of two American sailors in the port of Valparaiso in 1892 made hostility between the two countries seem inevitable. The threat of attack by Chile's modern navy spread alarm on the Pacific Coast, until the Chileans finally agreed to pay an indemnity. A simmering argument between the United States and Canada over seal hunting near the Pribilof Islands off the coast of Alaska was resolved by arbitration in 1893. The willingness of Americans to risk war over such distant and minor disputes demonstrated the aggressive new national mood.

America's new belligerence combined with old-time anti-British feeling to generate a crisis between the United States and Britain in 1895–1896. The jungle boundary between British Guiana and Venezuela had long been in dispute, but the discovery of gold in the contested area brought the conflict between Britain and Venezuela to a head.

President Cleveland and Secretary of State Richard Olney waded into the affair with a combative note to Britain invoking the Monroe Doctrine. Not content to stop there, the pugnacious Olney haughtily informed the world's number one naval power that the United States was now calling the tune in the Western Hemisphere.

Unimpressed British officials shrugged off Olney's salvo as just another twist of the lion's tail and replied that the affair was none of Uncle Sam's business. President Cleveland—"mad clear through," as he put it—sent a bristling special message to Congress. He urged an appropriation for a commission of experts, who would run the line where it ought to go. If the British would not accept this rightful boundary, he implied, the United States would fight for it.

The entire country, irrespective of political party, was swept off its feet in an outburst of hysteria. War seemed inevitable. Fortunately, sober second thoughts prevailed on both sides of the Atlantic. A rising challenge from Kaiser Wilhelm's Germany, as well as a looming war with the Dutch-descended Boers in South Africa, left Britain in no mood for war with America. London backed off and consented to arbitration.

The chastened British, their eyes fully opened to the European peril, were now determined to cultivate Yankee friendship. The British inaugurated an era of "patting the eagle's head," which replaced a century or so of America's "twisting the lion's tail." Sometimes called the **Great Rapprochement**—or reconciliation—between the United States and Britain, the new Anglo-American cordiality became a cornerstone of both nations' foreign policies as the twentieth century opened (refer to Image 26.2).

Image 26.2 They Can't Fight Britain and America waged a war of words during the Venezuelan boundary dispute, but cooler heads prevailed. A new era of diplomatic cooperation between the two former foes dawned, as they saw themselves bound together by ties of language, culture, and mutual economic interest. As the German chancellor Otto von Bismarck reportedly remarked, "The supreme geopolitical fact of the modern era is that the Americans speak English."

26-2 Spurning the Hawaiian Pear

The Pacific island kingdom of Hawai'i had early attracted the attention of Americans. In the morning years of the nineteenth century, the breeze-brushed islands were a way station and provisioning point for Yankee shippers, sailors, and whalers. In 1820 the first New England missionaries arrived, uninvited, preaching the twin blessings of Protestant Christianity and protective calico to the Native Hawaiian population. White Americans came intending to "do good"—and did well, as Hawai'i became an increasingly important center for sugar production.

Americans gradually came to regard the Hawaiian Islands as a virtual extension of their own coastline—despite the fact that Hawai'i was a constitutional monarchy whose sovereign status was widely recognized by other nations. The State Department, beginning in the 1840s, repeatedly warned other powers to keep their grasping hands off. America further tightened its grip in 1887 when it signed a treaty with the Hawaiian government guaranteeing priceless naval-base rights at spacious Pearl Harbor.

But trouble was brewing in the insular paradise. Old World pathogens had scythed the Indigenous Hawaiian population down to one-sixth of its size at the time of the first contact with Europeans, leading the American sugar lords to import large numbers of Asian laborers to work the canefields and sugar mills. By century's end, Chinese and Japanese immigrants outnumbered both whites and Native Hawaiians, amid mounting worries that Tokyo might be tempted to intervene on behalf of its often-abused nationals.

The Granger Collection/Alamy Stock Photo

Image 26.3 Queen Liliuokalani (1838–1917) Liliuokalani was the last reigning queen of Hawai'i, whose defense of native Hawaiian self-rule led to a revolt by white settlers and to her dethronement. She wrote many songs, the most famous of which was "Aloha Oe," or "Farewell to Thee," played countless times by Hawaiian bands for departing tourists.

Then sugar markets went sour in 1890 when the **McKinley Tariff** raised barriers against the Hawaiian product. White American planters thereupon renewed their efforts to secure the annexation of Hawai'i to the United States. They were blocked by the resolute Queen Liliuokalani, a constitutional monarch who insisted that Native Hawaiians should retain their lawful control of the islands (refer to Image 26.3). American sugar planters had other ideas, orchestrating an illegal revolt early in 1893, establishing the short-lived Republic of Hawai'i. They were openly assisted by American troops, who landed under the unauthorized orders of the expansionist American minister in Honolulu. "The Hawaiian pear is now fully ripe," he wrote exultantly to his superiors in Washington, "and this is the golden hour for the United States to pluck it."

A treaty of annexation was rushed to Washington, but before it could be railroaded through the Senate, Republican president Harrison's term expired and Democratic president Cleveland came in. Suspecting that his powerful nation had gravely wronged the deposed Queen Liliuokalani and her people, "Old Grover" abruptly withdrew the treaty. A subsequent investigation determined that a majority of the Hawaiian natives opposed annexation. Although Queen Liliuokalani could not be reinstated, the sugarcoated move for annexation had to be temporarily abandoned. The Hawaiian pear continued to ripen until the fateful year of 1898, when the United States acquired its overseas empire (refer to Map 26.1).

26-3 Cubans Rise in Revolt

The once-mighty Spanish empire had shrunk to only a few territories by the end of the nineteenth century. The stirrings for self-determination among those still ruled from Madrid erupted into open revolt in Cuba in 1895. The roots of the Cuban war for independence were partly economic. Sugar production—the backbone of the island's prosperity—was crippled after Spain abolished slavery in Cuba in 1886, raising labor costs for plantation owners. Sugar was further damaged when the American tariff of 1894 restored high duties on the toothsome product.

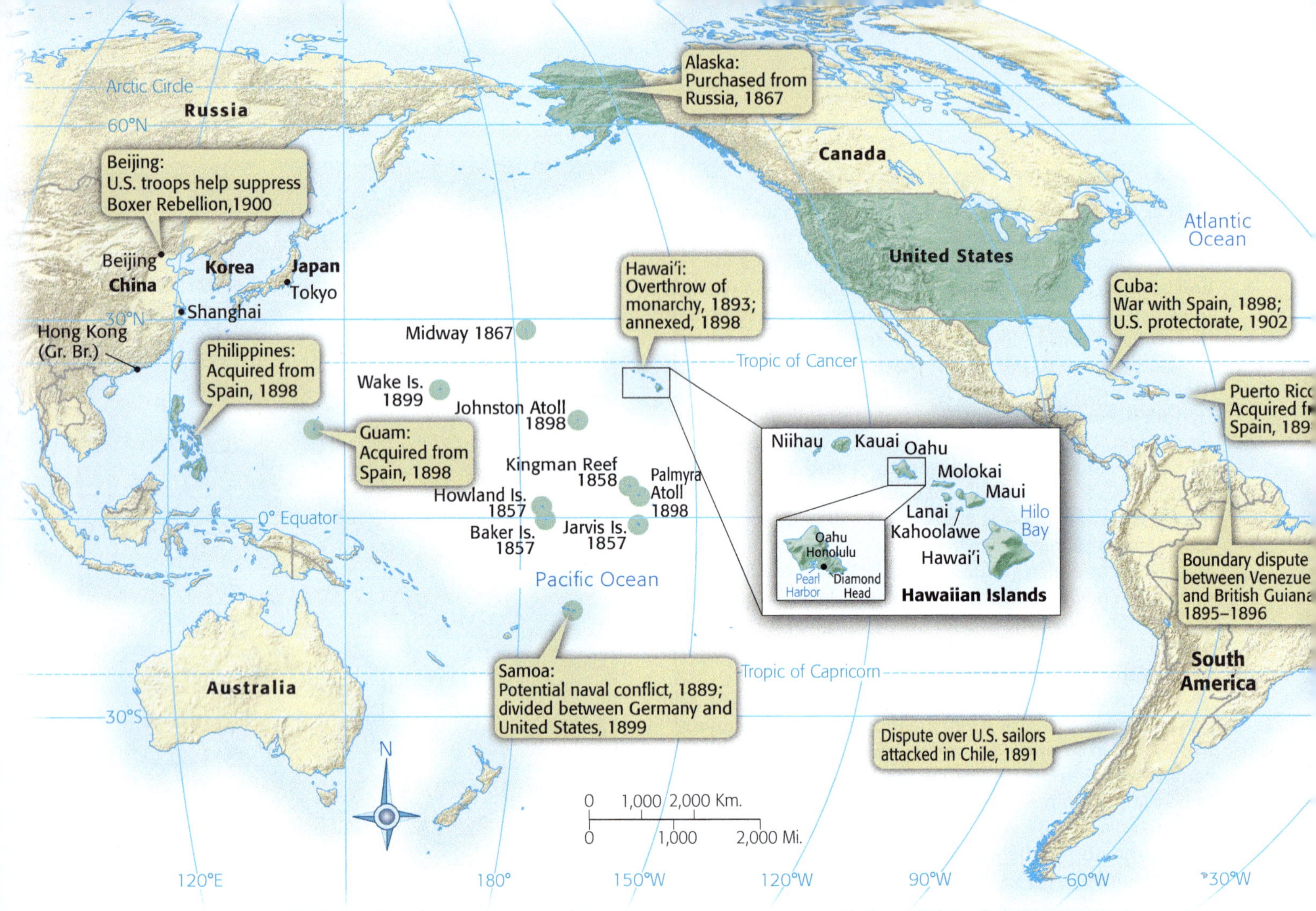

Map 26.1 **United States Expansion, 1857–1917** With the annexation of the Philippines, Hawai'i, and Puerto Rico in 1898, the United States became an imperial power.

The desperate insurgents had failed to secure Cuban independence in two earlier uprisings. This time, however, the conflict between Spanish forces and the badly outgunned ***insurrectos*** (revolutionaries) menaced American interests on the island, including an investment stake of about $50 million and annual trade of about $100 million.

The conflict also aroused American sympathies for the Cuban underdogs. Strategic considerations came into play as well. As the calculating Senator Lodge put it, Cuba lay "right athwart the line" that led to the much-anticipated Panama Canal. Whoever controlled Cuba, said Lodge, "controls the Gulf [of Mexico]." Much was riding on the outcome of events in troubled Cuba.

Fuel was added to the Cuban conflagration in 1896 with the arrival of the Spanish general "Butcher" Weyler. He undertook to crush the rebellion by herding many civilians into barbed-wire reconcentration camps, where they could not give assistance to the armed *insurrectos*. Lacking proper sanitation, these enclosures turned into deadly pestholes; the victims died like dogs.

Atrocities in Cuba were red meat for the sensational new "yellow journalism" of William Randolph Hearst and Joseph Pulitzer. Engaged in a titanic duel for circulation, each attempted to outdo the other with screeching headlines and hair-raising "scoops." Where atrocity stories did not exist, they were invented. Hearst sent the gifted artist Frederic Remington to Cuba to draw sketches, allegedly with the pointed admonition, "You furnish the pictures and I'll furnish the war." Among other outrages, Remington depicted Spanish customs officials brutally disrobing and searching an American woman. Most readers of Hearst's *Journal*, their indignation soaring, had no way of knowing that such tasks were performed by female attendants. Hearst also sensationally publicized a private letter from the Spanish minister in Washington, Dupuy de Lôme. The indiscreet epistle, stolen from the mails, described President McKinley in decidedly unflattering terms. The resulting uproar forced Dupuy de Lôme's resignation and further infuriated the American public.

Then early in 1898, Washington sent the battleship *Maine* to Cuba, ostensibly for a "friendly visit" but actually to protect and evacuate Americans if a dangerous flare-up should occur and

Fouquet

Image 26.4 The Explosion of the *Maine*, February 15, 1898 Encouraged and amplified by the "yellow press," the outcry over the tragedy of the *Maine* helped drive the country into an impulsive war against Spain.

to demonstrate Washington's concern for the island's stability. Tragedy struck on February 15, 1898, when the ***Maine*** mysteriously blew up in Havana harbor, with a loss of 260 sailors (refer to Image 26.4).

Two investigations of the iron coffin ensued, one by U.S. naval officers and the other by Spanish officials. The Spaniards concluded that the explosion had been internal and presumably accidental; the Americans argued that the blast had been caused by a submarine mine. The explosion's causes remain somewhat mysterious even today, but the leading theory favors Spain's interpretation. In 1976, U.S. Navy Admiral H. G. Rickover confirmed the original Spanish finding with compelling evidence that the initial explosion had resulted from spontaneous combustion in one of the coal bunkers adjacent to a powder magazine.

But Americans in 1898, now mad for war, blindly embraced the less likely explanation. Lashed to fury by the yellow press, they leapt to the inaccurate conclusion that the Spanish government had been guilty of intolerable treachery. The battle cry of the hour became

> Remember the Maine!
> To hell with Spain!

Nothing would do but to hurl the "dirty" Spanish flag from the hemisphere.

The national war fever burned ever higher, even though American diplomats had already gained Madrid's agreement to Washington's two basic demands: an end to the reconcentration camps and an armistice with Cuban rebels. The cautious McKinley found himself in a jam. He did not want hostilities, but neither did he want Spain to remain in possession of Cuba. Nor,

Many Spaniards felt that accusations about their blowing up the *Maine* reflected on Spanish honor. One Madrid newspaper spoke up:

"The American jingoes . . . imagine us capable of the most foul villainies and cowardly actions. Scoundrels by nature, the American jingoes believe that all men are made like themselves. What do they know about noble and generous feelings? . . . We should not in any way heed the jingoes: they are not even worth our contempt, or the saliva with which we might honor them in spitting at their faces."

for that matter, did he want a fully independent Cuba, over which the United States could exercise no control. More impetuous souls denounced the circumspect president as "Wobbly Willie" McKinley. Fight-hungry Theodore Roosevelt reportedly snarled that the "white-livered" occupant of the White House did not have "the backbone of a chocolate éclair." The president, whose shaken nerves required sleeping pills, was even being hanged in effigy.

McKinley, recognizing the inevitable, eventually yielded and gave the people what they wanted. But public pressure did not fully explain McKinley's course. He had little faith in Spain's oft-broken promises. He worried about Democratic reprisals in the upcoming presidential election of 1900 if he continued to appear indecisive in a time of crisis. He also acknowledged America's commercial and strategic interests in Cuba.

On April 11, 1898, McKinley sent his war message to Congress, urging armed intervention to free the oppressed Cubans. The legislators responded uproariously with what was essentially a declaration of war. In a burst of self-righteousness, they likewise adopted the hand-tying **Teller Amendment**. This proviso proclaimed to the world that when the United States had overthrown Spanish misrule, it would give the Cubans their freedom—a declaration that caused imperialistic Europeans to smile skeptically.

26-4 Dewey's May Day Victory at Manila

The American people plunged into the war lightheartedly, like schoolchildren off to a picnic. Bands blared incessantly "There'll Be a Hot Time in the Old Town Tonight" and "Hail, Hail, the Gang's All Here," leading some foreigners to believe that those were national anthems.

The war got off to a giddy start for American forces. Even before the declaration of war, on February 25, 1898, while Navy Secretary John D. Long was away from the office, his hot-blooded assistant secretary, Theodore Roosevelt, took matters into his own hands. Roosevelt cabled Commodore George Dewey, commanding the American Asiatic Squadron at Hong Kong, to descend upon Spain's Philippines in the event of war. "The very devil seemed to possess him," Long later wrote of Roosevelt's actions. But President McKinley subsequently confirmed Roosevelt's instructions, even though an attack in the distant Far East seemed like a strange way to free nearby Cuba.

Dewey carried out his orders magnificently on May 1, 1898 (refer to Map 26.2). Sailing boldly with his six warships at night into the fortified harbor of Manila, he trained his guns the next morning on the moldy ten-ship Spanish fleet. The entire collection of antiquated and overmatched vessels was quickly destroyed, with a loss of nearly four hundred Spaniards killed and wounded, and without the loss of a single American life.

Taciturn George Dewey became a national hero overnight. An amateur poet blossomed forth with this:

Oh, dewy was the morning
Upon the first of May,
And Dewey was the Admiral,
Down in Manila Bay.
And dewy were the Spaniards' eyes,
Them orbs of black and blue;
And dew we feel discouraged?
I dew not think we dew!

Yet Dewey was in a perilous position. He had destroyed the enemy fleet, but he could not storm the forts of Manila with his sailors. His nerves frayed, he was forced to wait in the sweltering bay while troop reinforcements were slowly assembled in America. The appearance of German warships in Manila harbor deepened the tension.

Long-awaited American troops, finally arriving in force, captured Manila on August 13, 1898, in collaboration with Filipino revolutionaries commanded by their well-educated leader, Emilio Aguinaldo (refer to Image 26.5).

Map 26.2 Dewey's Route in the Philippines, 1898

Image 26.5 **Emilio Aguinaldo (ca. 1869–1964) and Followers, 1900** Aguinaldo had a colorfully checkered career. Exiled from the Philippines by the Spanish in 1897, he was brought back in 1898 to assist the American invasion. A year later, he led the Filipino insurrection against the new American rulers. Captured in 1901, he declared his loyalty to the United States. During World War II, he collaborated with the Japanese when they occupied the Philippines. After a lifetime of political intrigue and armed struggle, Aguinaldo died peacefully in Manila in 1964 in his ninety-fifth year.

Dewey, to his later regret, had brought this shrewd and magnetic revolutionary from exile in Asia so that he might weaken Spanish resistance.

These thrilling events in the Philippines had meanwhile focused attention on Hawai'i. An impression spread that America needed the archipelago as a coaling and provisioning way station, in order to send supplies and reinforcements to Dewey. McKinley also worried that Japan might grab the Hawaiian Islands while America was distracted elsewhere. A joint resolution of annexation was rushed through Congress and approved by McKinley on July 7, 1898. It granted Hawaiian residents U.S. citizenship; Hawai'i received full territorial status in 1900.*

26-5 The Confused Invasion of Cuba

Shortly after the outbreak of war, the Spanish government ordered a fleet of decrepit warships to Cuba. Panic seized the eastern seaboard of the United States. American vacationers abandoned their seashore cottages, while nervous investors moved their securities to inland depositories. The Spanish "armada" eventually wheezed into bottle-shaped Santiago harbor, Cuba, where it was easily blockaded by the much more powerful American fleet.

Sound strategy seemed to dictate that an American army be sent in from the rear to drive out the Spanish ships. Leading the invading force was the grossly overweight General William R. Shafter, a would-be warrior so blubbery and gout-stricken that he had to be carried about on a door. His troops were woefully unequipped for war in the tropics; they had been amply provided with heavy woolen underwear and uniforms designed for subzero operations against the Plains Indians in the American West.

The **Rough Riders**, a part of the invading army, now charged onto the stage of history. This colorful regiment of volunteers, short on discipline but long on dash, consisted largely of Western cowboys and other hardy characters, with a sprinkling of ex-polo players and ex-convicts. Commanded by Colonel Leonard Wood, the group was organized principally by the glory-chasing

*To this day, no formal treaty of annexation has been signed between Hawai'i and the United States.

Everett Historical/Shutterstock.com

Image 26.6 **Colonel Theodore Roosevelt with Some of the "Rough Riders"** Roosevelt later described his first encounter with the Spanish enemy: "Soon we came to the brink of a deep valley. There was a good deal of cracking of rifles way off in front of us, but as they used smokeless powder, we had no idea as to exactly where they were, or who they were shooting at. Then it dawned on us that we were the target. The bullets began to come overhead, making a sound like the ripping of a silk dress, with sometimes a kind of pop. . . . We advanced, firing at them, and drove them off."

Theodore Roosevelt, who had resigned from the Navy Department to serve as lieutenant colonel (refer to Image 26.6). He was so nearsighted that as a safeguard he took along a dozen pairs of spectacles, cached in handy spots on his person or nearby.

About the middle of June, a bewildered American army of seventeen thousand men finally embarked at congested Tampa, Florida, amid scenes of indescribable confusion. Shafter's landing near Santiago, thanks to the diversionary tactics of Cuban *insurrectos*, met little opposition. Brisk fighting broke out on July 1 at El Caney and Kettle Hill, up which Colonel Roosevelt and his horseless Rough Riders charged, with strong support from two crack Black regiments. They suffered heavy casualties, but the colorful colonel, having the time of his life, shot a Spaniard with his revolver and rejoiced to see his victim double up like a jackrabbit. He later wrote a book on his exploits, which the famed satirist Finley Peter Dunne's character "Mr. Dooley" remarked ought to have been titled *Alone in Cubia* [*sic*].

The American army, fast closing in on Santiago, spelled doom for the badly outgunned Spanish fleet. On July 3, the Spaniards dutifully steamed out of the harbor and into the teeth of the waiting American warships. "Don't cheer, men," Captain Philip of the *Texas* admonished his seamen. "The poor devils are dying." Shortly thereafter Santiago surrendered (refer to Map 26.3).

Hasty preparations were now made for a descent upon Puerto Rico before the war should end. There the American army met even less resistance than in Cuba. By this time, Spain had satisfied its honor. On August 12, 1898, it signed an armistice.

If the Spaniards had held out a few months longer in Cuba, the American army might have melted away. The inroads of malaria, typhoid fever, dysentery, and yellow fever became so severe that hundreds were incapacitated—"an army of convalescents." Others suffered from fetid canned meat known as "embalmed beef." All told, nearly four hundred men lost their lives to bullets; over five thousand succumbed to bacteria and other causes.

With a mixture of modesty and immodesty, Colonel Theodore Roosevelt (1858–1919) wrote privately in 1903 of his "Rough Riders,"

"In my regiment nine-tenths of the men were better horsemen than I was, and probably two-thirds of them better shots than I was, while on the average they were certainly hardier and more enduring. Yet after I had had them a very short while they all knew, and I knew too, that nobody else could command them as I could."

26-6 America's Course (Curse?) of Empire

Late in 1898 Spanish and American negotiators met in Paris. War-racked Cuba, as expected, was freed from its Spanish overlords. The Americans had little difficulty in securing the remote Pacific island of Guam, which they had captured early in the conflict from the astonished Spaniards, who, lacking a cable, had not known that a war was on. Spain also ceded Puerto Rico to the United States as payment for war costs. Ironically, the last remnant of Spain's vast New World empire thus became the first territory ever annexed to the United States without the express promise of eventual statehood. In the decades to come, American investment in the island and Puerto Rican migration to the United States would make this acquisition one of the weightier consequences of this somewhat carefree war (refer to "Makers of America: The Puerto Ricans," pp. 658–659).

Knottiest of all was the problem of the Philippines, a veritable apple of discord. These lush islands not only embraced an area larger than the British Isles but also contained an ethnically diverse population of some 7 million souls. McKinley was confronted with a devil's dilemma. He did not feel that America could honorably give the islands back to Spanish misrule, especially after it had fought a war to free Cuba. And America would be turning its back upon its responsibilities in a cowardly fashion, he believed, if it simply pulled up anchor and sailed away.

McKinley viewed virtually all the choices open to him as trouble-fraught. He believed that the Filipinos, if left to govern themselves, might fall into anarchy. One of the major powers, possibly aggressive Germany or Japan, might then try to seize them. The result could be a major war into which the United States would be sucked. Seemingly the least of the evils consistent with national honor and safety was to acquire all the Philippines and then perhaps give the Filipinos their freedom later.

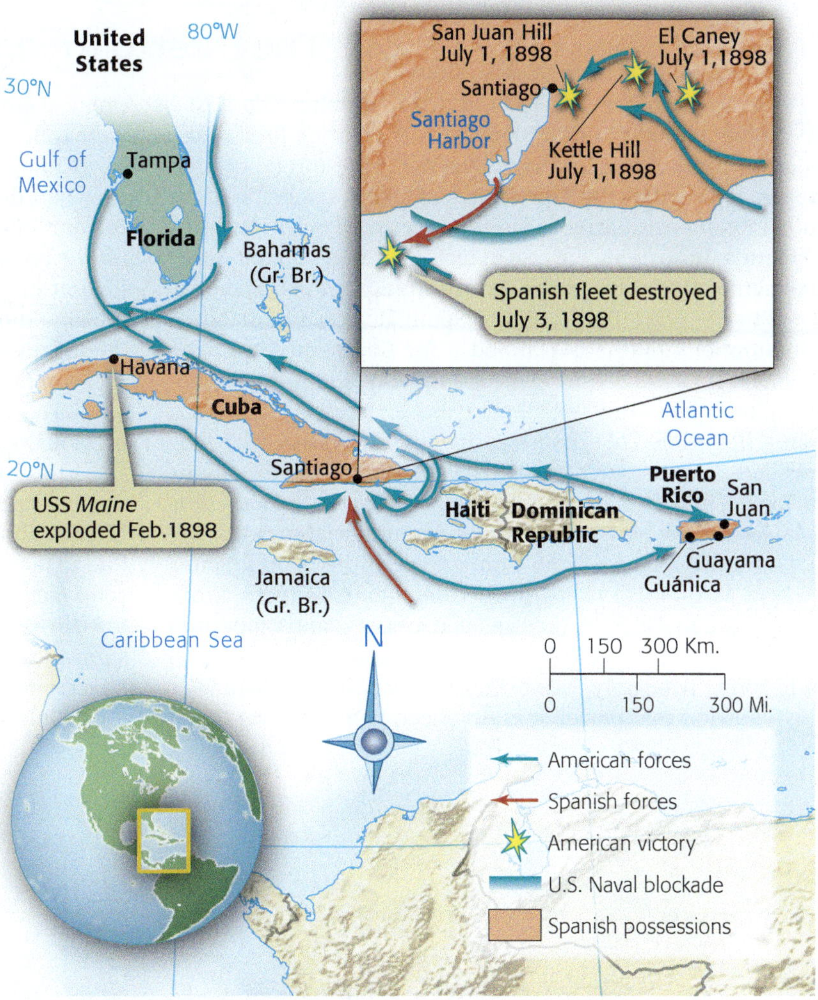

Map 26.3 **The Cuban Campaign, 1898**

President McKinley, ever sensitive to public opinion, kept a carefully attuned ear to the ground. The rumble that he heard seemed to call for the entire group of islands. Zealous Protestant missionaries were eager for new converts from Spanish Catholicism,* and the invalid Mrs. McKinley, to whom her husband was devoted, expressed deep concern about the welfare of the Filipinos. Wall Street had generally opposed the war, but awakened by the booming of Dewey's guns, it was clamoring for profits in the Philippines.

A tormented McKinley later claimed that he went down on his knees seeking divine guidance and heard an inner voice telling him to take all the Philippines and Christianize and "civilize" them. Accordingly, he decided for outright annexation of the islands. Manila remained a sticking point with the Spaniards because it had been captured the day *after* the armistice was signed, and the city could not therefore properly be claimed among the spoils of war. But the Americans broke the deadlock by agreeing to pay Spain $20 million for the Philippine Islands—the last great Spanish haul from the New World.

The signing of the pact of Paris touched off one of the most impassioned foreign-policy debates in American history. The issue of what to do with the Philippines confronted Americans with fundamental questions about their national identity. Except for glacial Alaska, coral-reefed Hawai'i, and a handful of Pacific atolls acquired mostly for whaling stations and guano fertilizer needed to replenish southern soil exhausted by overcultivation, the Republic had hitherto absorbed only contiguous territory on the continent. With the exception of Hawai'i, where Native peoples were both numerous and resistant to American annexation, all previous non-continental accessions had been thinly peopled. All, including Hawai'i, were eligible for ultimate statehood. But in the Philippines, the nation had on its hands a distant tropical archipelago populated by

*The Philippines had been substantially Christianized by Catholics before the founding of Jamestown in 1607.

Makers of America

The Puerto Ricans

At dawn on July 26, 1898, the U.S. warship *Gloucester* steamed into Puerto Rico's Guánica harbor, fired at the Spanish blockhouse, and landed some thirty-three hundred troops. Within days the Americans had taken possession of the militarily strategic Caribbean island a thousand miles southeast of Florida. In so doing they set in motion changes on the island that ultimately brought a new wave of immigrants to U.S. shores.

Puerto Rico had been a Spanish possession since Christopher Columbus claimed it for Castile in 1493. The Spaniards enslaved many of the island's forty thousand Indigenous Taino people and set them to work on farms and in mines. Many Tainos died of exhaustion and disease, and in 1511 they rebelled. The Spaniards crushed the uprising, killed thousands of Tainos, and then began importing enslaved Africans—thus establishing the basis for Puerto Rico's multiracial society.

The first Puerto Rican immigrants to the United States arrived as political exiles in the nineteenth century. From their haven in America, they agitated for the island's independence from Spain. In 1897 Spain finally granted the island local autonomy; ironically, however, the Spanish-American War the following year placed it in American hands. Puerto Rican political émigrés in the United States returned home, but they were soon replaced by poor islanders looking for work.

Changing conditions in Puerto Rico after the U.S. takeover had driven these new immigrants north. Although slow to grant Puerto Ricans U.S. citizenship, the Americans quickly improved health and sanitation on the island, triggering a population surge in the early twentieth century. At the same time, growing monopoly control of Puerto Rico's sugar cane plantations undermined the island's subsistence economy, and a series of hurricanes devastated the coffee plantations that had employed large numbers of people. With almost no industry to provide wage labor, Puerto Rico's unemployment rate soared.

Thus when Congress finally granted Puerto Ricans U.S. citizenship in 1917, thereby eliminating immigration hurdles, many islanders hurried north to find jobs. Over the ensuing decades, Puerto Ricans went to work in Arizona cotton fields, New Jersey soup factories, and Utah mines. The majority, however, clustered in New York City and found work in the city's cigar factories, shipyards, and garment industry. Migration slowed somewhat after the 1920s as the Great Depression shrank the job market on the mainland and as World War II made travel hazardous.

BPK, Berlin/Art Resource, NY

Image 26.7 The First Puerto Ricans The Spanish *conquistadores* treated the native Taino people in Puerto Rico with extreme cruelty, and these Indigenous inhabitants were virtually extinct by the mid-1500s.

AP Images/Tina Fineberg

Image 26.8 Protesting in New York Puerto Ricans demonstrate in April 2001 against U.S. Navy bombing exercises on the Puerto Rican island of Vieques.

Dave G. Houser/The Image Bank Unreleased/Getty Images

Image 26.9 Preparing for Carnaval (Carnival) This mask maker displays an elaborate *máscara de carton* (paper maché mask) made for the annual Puerto Rican festival. Masked figures at *Carnaval* have been part of Puerto Rican culture for more than two hundred years.

When World War II ended in 1945, the sudden advent of cheap air travel sparked an immigration explosion (and set the stage for Leonard Bernstein's great musical production, *West Side Story*, which adapted the story of Romeo and Juliet to the clash of white and Puerto Rican gangs in New York City). As late as the 1930s, the tab for a boat trip to the mainland exceeded the average Puerto Rican's yearly earnings. But with an airplane surplus after World War II, the six-hour flight from Puerto Rico to New York cost under fifty dollars. The Puerto Rican population on the mainland quadrupled between 1940 and 1950 and tripled again by 1960. In 1970, 1.5 million Puerto Ricans lived in the United States, one-third of the island's total population.

U.S. citizenship and affordable air travel made it easy for Puerto Ricans to return home. Thus to a far greater degree than most immigrant groups, Puerto Ricans kept one foot in the United States and the other on their native island. By some estimates 2 million people a year journeyed to and from the island during the postwar period. Puerto Rico's gubernatorial candidates sometimes campaigned in New York for the thousands of voters who were expected to return to the island in time for the election.

This transience worked to keep Puerto Ricans' educational attainment and English proficiency far below the national average. At the same time, the immigrants encountered a deep-seated racism in America unlike anything on their multiracial island. For several decades after the Second World War, Puerto Ricans remained one of the poorest groups in the United States, with a median family income below that of African Americans and Mexican Americans.

Still, Puerto Ricans have fared better economically in the United States than on the island, where, in 1970, 60 percent of all inhabitants lived below the poverty line. In recent years Puerto Ricans have attained more schooling, and many have attended college. Invigorated by the civil rights movement of the 1960s, Puerto Ricans also became more politically active, electing growing numbers of congressmen and state and city officials.

over 8 million inhabitants comprising a dizzying array of languages, cultures, and ethnicities (refer to Image 26.10).

Opponents of annexation argued that such a step would dishonor and ultimately destroy America's venerable commitments to self-determination and anticolonialism. "Goddamn the United States for its vile conduct in the Philippine Isles!" burst out the usually mild-mannered Professor William James. The Harvard philosopher could not believe that the United States could "puke up its ancient soul in five minutes without a wink of squeamishness." Speaker of the House

Bettmann/Getty Images

Image 26.10 **Uncle Sam and People from His Colonies, Postcard, ca. 1900** The acquisition of Puerto Rico, the Philippines, Hawai'i, and other Pacific islands brought millions of people of color under the American flag and, as depicted here, the paternal watch of "Uncle Sam." Whether they would eventually become citizens or remain colonial subjects was hotly debated in the United States. Many anti-imperialists opposed colonial expansion precisely because they regarded the exotic new peoples as "unassimilable."

Thomas "Czar" Reed resigned in protest against America's new imperial adventure—an unfortunately rare display of political conscience and courage.

The **Anti-Imperialist League** sprang into being to fight the McKinley administration's expansionist moves. The organization counted among its members some of the most prominent people in the United States, including the presidents of Stanford and Harvard Universities and the novelist Mark Twain. The anti-imperialist blanket even stretched over such strange bedfellows as the labor leader Samuel Gompers and the steel titan Andrew Carnegie.

Anti-imperialists raised many objections. The Filipinos thirsted for freedom; to annex them would violate the "consent of the governed" philosophy in the Declaration of Independence and the Constitution. Despotism abroad might well beget despotism at home. Imperialism was costly and unlikely ever to turn a profit. Annexation would inject the United States into the seething political and military cauldron of East Asia. Annexationists also stoked racial fears when they suggested that the accession of the Philippines might make more nonwhite peoples eligible for American citizenship.

Imperialist proponents countered that Philippine annexation would simply continue a glorious history of expansion that had pushed American civilization to the shores of the Pacific and now beyond. If Americans were "morally bound to abandon the Philippines," thundered Theodore Roosevelt, "we were also morally bound to abandon Arizona to the Apaches." Imperialists could sing a seductive song. They appealed to patriotism, invoked America's "civilizing mission," and played up possible trade profits. Manila, they claimed, might become another Hong Kong, the fabulously successful commercial

President William McKinley (1843–1901) later described his decision to annex the Philippines:

"When next I realized that the Philippines had dropped into our laps, I confess I did not know what to do with them. . . . I went down on my knees and prayed Almighty God for light and guidance. . . . And one night late it came to me this way. . . . That there was nothing left for us to do but to take them all, and to educate the Filipinos, and uplift and civilize and Christianize them and by God's grace do the very best we could by them, as our fellow men, for whom Christ also died. And then I went to bed and went to sleep, and slept soundly."

Contending Voices

Debating Imperialism

The contest over American imperialism took place on the Senate floor as well as around the globe. In 1900 Senator Albert J. Beveridge (1862–1927), Republican from Indiana, returned from an investigative trip to the Philippines to defend its annexation:

"The Philippines are ours forever. . . . And just beyond the Philippines are China's illimitable markets. We will not retreat from either. We will not abandon our opportunity in the Orient. We will not renounce our part in the mission of our race: trustee, under God, of the civilization of the world."

Two years later Senator George F. Hoar (1826–1904), Republican from Massachusetts, broke with his party to denounce American annexation of the Philippines and other territories:

"You cannot maintain despotism in Asia and a republic in America. If you try to deprive even a savage or a barbarian of his just rights you can never do it without becoming a savage or a barbarian yourself."

Consider This:

Was the alleged conflict between American power and American democratic ideals a fundamentally new problem at the turn of the twentieth century, or a new variation on a recurring tension in the country's history?

entrepôt that so richly served British interests in Asia. Rudyard Kipling, the British poet laureate of imperialism, urged America down the slippery path with a quotable poem that he had circulated before publication to Theodore Roosevelt and Henry Cabot Lodge (Roosevelt found it "good sense" but "poor poetry"):

> Take up the White Man's burden—
> Ye dare not stoop to less—
> Nor call too loud on Freedom
> To cloak your weariness.

In short, the wealthy Americans must help to uplift (and exploit) the underprivileged, underfed, and underclad of the world.

Over heated protests, the Senate approved the treaty with Spain with just one vote to spare on February 6, 1899. America was now officially an empire.

26-7 Perplexities in Puerto Rico and Cuba

From the outset, the status of Puerto Rico was anomalous—neither a state nor a territory, and with little prospect of eventual independence. The **Foraker Act** of 1900 accorded the Puerto Ricans a limited degree of popular government (and outlawed cockfighting, a favorite island pastime). Congress granted U.S. citizenship to Puerto Ricans in 1917 but withheld full self-rule. Although the American regime worked wondrous improvements in education, sanitation, and transportation, many of the inhabitants still aspired to independence. Great numbers of Puerto Ricans ultimately moved to New York City, profoundly shaping its culture and politics.

The annexation of Puerto Rico (and the Philippines) posed a thorny legal problem: Did the Constitution follow the flag? Did American laws, including tariff laws and the Bill of Rights, apply with full force to the newly acquired possessions? "Who are we?" a group of Puerto Rican

Three years after the Spanish-American War ended, a foreign diplomat in Washington remarked,

"I have seen two Americas, the America before the Spanish American War and the America since."

petitioners asked Congress in 1900. "Are we citizens or are we subjects?" Beginning in 1901 with the ***Insular Cases***, a badly divided Supreme Court decreed, in effect, that the flag did outrun the Constitution, and that the outdistanced document did not necessarily extend with full force to the new windfall. Puerto Ricans (and Filipinos) might be subject to American rule, but they did not enjoy all American rights.

Cuba, scorched and chaotic, presented another headache. An American military government, set up under the able management of General Leonard Wood of Rough Rider fame, rapidly expanded the capacities of Cuban government, finance, education, agriculture, and public health. A frontal attack was launched on yellow fever. Spectacular experiments were performed by Dr. Walter Reed and others using American soldiers as test subjects, and the stegomyia mosquito was proved to be the lethal carrier. Cleaning up breeding places for mosquitoes wiped out yellow fever in Havana, while dampening the fear of recurrent epidemics in cities of the South and Atlantic seaboard.

The United States, honoring its self-denying Teller Amendment of 1898, withdrew from Cuba in 1902. Old World imperialists could scarcely believe their eyes. But the Washington government could not turn this rich and strategic island completely loose on the international sea; a grasping power like Germany might secure dangerous lodgment near America's soft underbelly. The Cubans were therefore forced to write into their own constitution of 1901 the so-called **Platt Amendment**.

The Cubans loathed the amendment, which served McKinley's ultimate purpose of bringing Cuba under American control. ("Plattism" survives as a colloquial term of derision even in modern-day Cuba.) The newly "liberated" Cubans were forced to agree not to conclude treaties that might compromise their independence (as Uncle Sam saw it) and not to take on debt beyond their resources (as Uncle Sam measured them). They further agreed that the United States might intervene with troops to restore order when it saw fit. Finally, the Cubans promised to sell or lease needed coaling or naval stations, ultimately two and then only one (Guantánamo), to their powerful "benefactor." The United States finally abrogated the amendment in 1934, although Uncle Sam still occupies a 28,000-acre Cuban beachhead at Guantánamo under an agreement that can be revoked only by the consent of both parties.

The Granger Collection, NYC

Image 26.11 The New Jingoism An enthusiastic Uncle Sam cheers the U.S. Navy in the "splendid little war" of 1898. Many Americans, however, were less than enthused about America's new imperial adventure.

26-8 New Horizons in Two Hemispheres

In essence, the Spanish-American War was a kind of colossal coming-out party. Dewey's thundering guns merely advertised the fact that the nation was already a world power. The war itself was short (113 days), low in casualties, and theatrically successful—despite the bungling. Secretary of State John Hay called it a "splendid little war" (refer to Image 26.11). American prestige rose sharply, and the Europeans grudgingly accorded the Republic more respect. Britain, France, Russia, and other great powers pointedly upgraded their legations in Washington, DC, which had previously been regarded as a diplomatic backwater.

An exhilarating new martial spirit thrilled America, buoyed along by the newly popular military marching-band music of John Philip Sousa. Most Americans did not start the war with consciously imperialistic motives, but after falling through the cellar door of imperialism in a drunken fit of idealism, they wound up with imperialistic and colonial fruits in their grasp. Captain Mahan's big-navyism seemed vindicated, energizing popular support for more and better battleships. A masterly organizer, Secretary of War Elihu Root established a general staff for the army and founded the War College in Washington.

One of the most significant results of the conflict was the further closing of the "bloody chasm" between North and South (refer to Image 26.12). Thousands of patriotic white Southerners had flocked to the Stars and Stripes, and the gray-bearded General Joseph ("Fighting Joe") Wheeler—a Confederate cavalry hero of about a thousand Civil War skirmishes and battles—was given a command in Cuba. He allegedly cried, in the heat of battle, "To hell with the Yankees! Dammit, I mean the Spaniards."

Even so, the newly imperial nation was not yet prepared to pay the full bill for its new status. By taking on the Philippine Islands, the United States became a full-fledged Far Eastern power. But the distant islands eventually became a "heel of Achilles"—a kind of indefensible hostage given to Japan, as events proved in World War II. Here and elsewhere, the Americans had shortsightedly assumed burdensome commitments that they proved unwilling to defend with appropriate naval and military outlays.

Image 26.12 Cuba Libre, 1898 Supporters of the Spanish-American War celebrated it as aiding the reconciliation of North and South under a common flag and emancipatory cause. This photographic tableau portrays veterans of the Union and Confederate armies shaking hands before a young, fair-skinned girl personifying the "liberated" Cuba.

26-9 "Little Brown Brothers" in the Philippines

The liberty-loving Filipinos assumed that they, like the Cubans, would be granted their freedom after the Spanish-American War. They were tragically deceived. Washington excluded them from the peace negotiations with Spain and made clear its intention to stay in the Philippines indefinitely. Bitterness toward the occupying American troops erupted into open insurrection on February 4, 1899, led by the revolutionary and onetime American ally Emilio Aguinaldo. Having plunged into war with Spain to free Cuba, the United States was now driven to deploy some 126,000 troops ten thousand miles away to rivet shackles onto a people who asked for nothing but freedom—in the American tradition.

Outmanned and outgunned, the Filipino troops soon melted into the jungle to wage guerrilla warfare against the American occupiers. Only months earlier, American soldiers believed they were rescuing helpless victims of Spanish tyranny. Now they viewed the Filipinos as dangerous racial "others" and enemies of the United States. This shift drove an increasingly sordid, atrocity-filled conflict. Uncle Sam's soldiers adopted the "water cure"—forcing water down victims' throats until they yielded information or died. American-built reconcentration camps rivaled those of "Butcher" Weyler in Cuba. Having begun the Spanish war with noble ideals, America now dirtied its hands. One New York newspaper published a reply to Rudyard Kipling's famous poem:

> We've taken up the white man's burden
> Of ebony and brown;
> Now will you kindly tell us, Rudyard,
> How we may put it down?

Image 26.13 Filipino Women Seek Help from American Soldiers For three years after its annexation of the Philippine Islands in 1898, the United States fought a savage war to suppress a Filipino rebellion against American rule. More than 200,000 Filipinos perished. There was bitter irony in this clash, as the Americans had claimed to be "liberating" the Filipinos from their oppressive Spanish masters, but the Yankee liberators were sometimes no less oppressive than the Spaniards they had ousted.

The Americans broke the back of the Filipino insurrection in 1901, when they cleverly infiltrated a guerrilla camp and captured Aguinaldo. But sporadic fighting dragged on for many dreary months, eventually claiming the lives of 4,234 Americans and more than 200,000 Filipinos (refer to Image 26.13).

Future president William H. Taft, an able, amiable, and famously portly Ohioan, became civil governor of the Philippines in 1901. Forming a strong yet patronizing attachment to the Filipinos, he called them his "little brown brothers" and danced light-footedly with the Filipino women. But McKinley's "benevolent assimilation" of the Philippines proceeded with painful slowness. Washington poured millions of dollars into the islands to improve roads, sanitation, and public health. Important economic ties, including trade in sugar, developed between the two peoples. American teachers set up an unusually good school system and helped make English a second language. But all this vast expenditure was no compensation for true freedom. The Filipinos hated compulsory Americanization and pined for liberty. They had to wait nearly half a century for it, not obtaining their independence until the Fourth of July 1946. In the meantime, thousands of Filipinos emigrated to the United States (refer to "Makers of America: The Filipinos," pp. 666–667).

26-10 Hinging the Open Door in China

Ominous events had meanwhile been brewing in faraway and enfeebled China. After China's defeat by Japan in 1894–1895, the imperialistic European powers, notably Russia and Germany, moved in. Like vultures descending upon a wounded animal, they began to tear away valuable leaseholds and economic spheres of influence from the Manchu government.

A growing group of Americans viewed the vivisection of China with alarm. Churches worried about their missionary strongholds (refer to Image 26.14). Merchants feared that Europeans would monopolize Chinese markets. An anxious American public, openly prodded by the press and slyly nudged by certain free-trade Britons, demanded that Washington do something.

Image 26.14 American Missionary Grace Roberts Teaching in China, 1903 By the turn of the twentieth century, thousands of American men and women had established Christian missions in faraway places such as Hawai'i, China, Africa, and Turkey. Missionaries' educational and religious work helped build sentimental, political, and economic ties between Americans and distant nations. At times, however, these close connections led to violent confrontations, such as when the nationalist Boxer rebels attacked missionaries in China in 1900 as symbols of foreign encroachment. Protestant women justified their missionary activities as a logical extension of their traditional female duty to nurture and uplift, but in reality, these foreign assignments often propelled them to undertake responsibilities that their stateside mothers and sisters rarely encountered.

Secretary of State John Hay, a quiet but witty poet-novelist-diplomat with a flair for capturing the popular imagination, finally decided on a dramatic move.

In the summer of 1899, Hay dispatched to all the great powers a communication soon known as the **Open Door note.** He urged them to announce that in their leaseholds or spheres of influence they would respect certain Chinese rights and the ideal of fair competition. Tellingly, Hay had not bothered to consult the Chinese themselves.

The phrase *Open Door* quickly caught the American public's fancy. But Hay's proposal caused much squirming in the leading capitals of the world, though all the great powers save Russia, with covetous designs on Manchuria, eventually agreed to it.

Open Door or not, patriotic Chinese did not care to be used as a doormat by the Western powers. In 1900 a superpatriotic group, known as the "Boxers" for their training in the martial arts, broke loose with the cry "Kill Foreign Devils." In what became known as the **Boxer Rebellion**, they murdered more than two hundred foreigners and thousands of Chinese Christians and besieged the foreign diplomatic community in the capital, Beijing (Peking).

A multinational rescue force of some 18,000 soldiers arrived in the nick of time and quelled the rebellion. They included several thousand American troops dispatched from the Philippines to protect U.S. rights under the 1844 Treaty of Wanghia (refer to "17-11 The Allure of Asia," pp. 427–428) and to keep the Open Door propped open.

The victorious allied invaders acted angrily and vindictively. They assessed prostrate China an excessive indemnity of $333 million, of which America's share was to be $24.5 million. When Washington discovered that this sum was much more than enough to pay damages and expenses, it remitted about $18 million, to be used for the education of a selected group of Chinese students in the United States—a not-so-subtle initiative to further the westernization of Asia.

Secretary Hay let fly another paper broadside in 1900, announcing that henceforth the Open Door would embrace the territorial integrity of China, in addition to its commercial integrity. Those principles helped spare China from possible partition in those troubled years and were formally incorporated into the Nine-Power Treaty of 1922, only to be callously violated by Japan's takeover of Manchuria a decade later (refer to "29-16 America Seeks Benefits Without Burdens," pp. 761–762).

26-11 Imperialism or Bryanism in 1900?

President McKinley's renomination by the Republicans in 1900 was a foregone conclusion. He had won a war and acquired rich, though burdensome, real estate; he had safeguarded the gold standard; and he had brought the promised prosperity of the full dinner pail. An irresistible vice-presidential boom developed for Theodore ("Teddy") Roosevelt (TR), the cowboy-hero of the Cuban campaign. Capitalizing on his war-born popularity, he had been elected governor of New York, where the local political bosses had found him headstrong and difficult to manage. They therefore devised a scheme to kick the colorful colonel upstairs into the vice presidency.

This plot to railroad Roosevelt worked beautifully. Gesticulating wildly, he sported a Western-style cowboy hat that made him stand out like a white crow at the Republican convention. To cries of "We want Teddy!" he was handily nominated. A wary Mark Hanna reportedly moaned that there would now be only one heartbeat between "that damned cowboy" and the presidency of the United States.

William Jennings Bryan was the odds-on choice of the Democrats, meeting at Kansas City. Their platform proclaimed that the paramount issue was Republican overseas imperialism (refer to Image 26.15).

McKinley once more campaigned cannily from his front porch. Bryan once again took to the stump in a cyclonic campaign. The intervening "splendid little war" had changed

Image 26.15 Columbia's Easter Bonnet Many Americans felt a surge of pride as the United States became an imperial power at the dawn of the twentieth century. But then and later, America's world role proved hotly controversial, at home as well as abroad.

Makers of America

The Filipinos

At the beginning of the twentieth century, the United States, its imperial muscles just flexed in the war with Spain, found itself in possession of the Philippines. Uncertain of how to manage this empire, which seethed resentfully against its new masters, the United States promised to build democracy in the Philippines and to ready the islanders for home rule. Almost immediately after annexation, the American governor of the archipelago sent a corps of Filipino students to the United States, hoping to forge future leaders steeped in American ways who would someday govern an independent Philippines. Yet this small student group found little favor in their adopted country, although in their native land many went on to become respected citizens and leaders.

Most Filipino immigrants to the United States in these years, however, came not to study but to toil. With Chinese immigration banned, Hawai'i and the Pacific Coast states turned to the Philippines for cheap agricultural labor. Beginning in 1906 the Hawaiian Sugar Planters Association aggressively recruited Filipino workers. Enlistments grew slowly at first, but by the 1920s thousands of young Filipino men had reached the Hawaiian Islands and been assigned to sugar plantations or pineapple fields.

Typically a young Filipino wishing to emigrate first made his way to Manila, where he signed a contract with the growers that promised three years' labor in return for transportation to Hawai'i, wages, free housing and fuel, and return passage at the end of the contract. Not all the emigrants returned; there remain in Hawai'i today some former field workers still theoretically eligible for free transport back to their native land.

Those Filipinos venturing as far as the American mainland found work less arduous but also less certain than did their countrymen on Hawaiian plantations. Many mainlanders worked seasonally—in winter as domestic servants, busboys, or bellhops; in summer journeying to the fields to harvest lettuce, strawberries, sugar beets, and potatoes. Eventually Filipinos, along with Mexican immigrants, shared the dubious honor of making up California's agricultural workforce.

A mobile society, Filipino Americans also were overwhelmingly male; there was only one Filipino woman for every fourteen Filipino men in California in 1930. Thus the issue of intermarriage became acutely sensitive. California and many other states prohibited the marriage of Asians and Caucasians in demeaning laws that remained on the books until 1948. And if a Filipino so much as approached a Caucasian woman, he could expect reprisals—sometimes violent. For example, white vigilante groups roamed the Yakima Valley in Washington and the San Joaquin and Salinas Valleys in California, intimidating and even attacking Filipinos whom they accused of improperly accosting white women. In 1930 one Filipino was murdered and others wounded after

Library of Congress Prints and Photographs Division

Image 26.16 Filipino Laborers at Work on a Hawaiian Pineapple Plantation, Between 1910 and 1925

they invited some Caucasian women to a dance. Undeterred, the Filipinos challenged the restrictive state laws and the hooligans who found in them an excuse for mayhem. But Filipinos, who did not become eligible for American citizenship until 1946, long lacked political leverage.

After World War II, Filipino immigration accelerated. Between 1950 and 1970, the number of Filipinos in the United States nearly doubled, with women and men stepping aboard the new transpacific airliners in roughly equal numbers. Many of these recent arrivals sprang from sturdy middle-class stock and sought in America a better life for their children than the Philippines seemed able to offer. Today the war-torn and perpetually depressed archipelago sends more immigrants to American shores than does any other Asian nation.

Museum of History & Industry, Seattle

Image 26.17 **Filipino-American "Little Royalty," 1958** West Coast cities became home to vibrant Filipino communities before and after the islands gained their 1946 independence from American rule. These boys and girls were named to the "Little Royalty" court presiding over "Fiesta Filipina," an annual commemoration of Philippines Independence in Seattle.

the stakes, however. Lincoln, Bryan charged, had abolished slavery for 3.5 million Africans; McKinley had reestablished it for 7 million Filipinos. Roosevelt out-Bryaned Bryan, touring the country with revolver-shooting cowboys. Flashing his monumental teeth and pounding his fist into his palm, Roosevelt denounced all dastards who would haul down Old Glory.

McKinley handily triumphed by a much wider margin than in 1896: 7,218,491 to 6,356,734 popular votes, and 292 to 155 electoral votes. But victory for the Republicans was not a mandate for or against imperialism. If there was any mandate at all it was for the two Ps: prosperity and protectionism. Meanwhile, the New York bosses gleefully looked forward to watching the nettlesome Roosevelt "take the veil" as vice president.

26-12 TR: Brandisher of the Big Stick

Kindly William McKinley had scarcely served another six months when, in September 1901, he was murdered by a deranged anarchist in Buffalo, New York. Roosevelt rode a buckboard out of his campsite in the Adirondacks to take the oath of office, becoming, at age forty-two, the youngest president thus far in American history.

Born into a wealthy and distinguished New York family, Roosevelt, a red-blooded blue blood, had fiercely built up his spindly, asthmatic body by a stern and self-imposed routine of exercise. Educated partly in Europe, he graduated from Harvard with Phi Beta Kappa honors and published, at the age of twenty-four, the first of some thirty volumes of muscular prose. He worked as a ranch owner and cowboy in the Dakotas before pursuing his political career full-time. Barrel-chested, bespectacled, and five feet ten inches tall, with mulelike molars, squinty eyes, droopy mustache, and piercing voice, he was ever the delight of cartoonists (refer to Image 26.18).

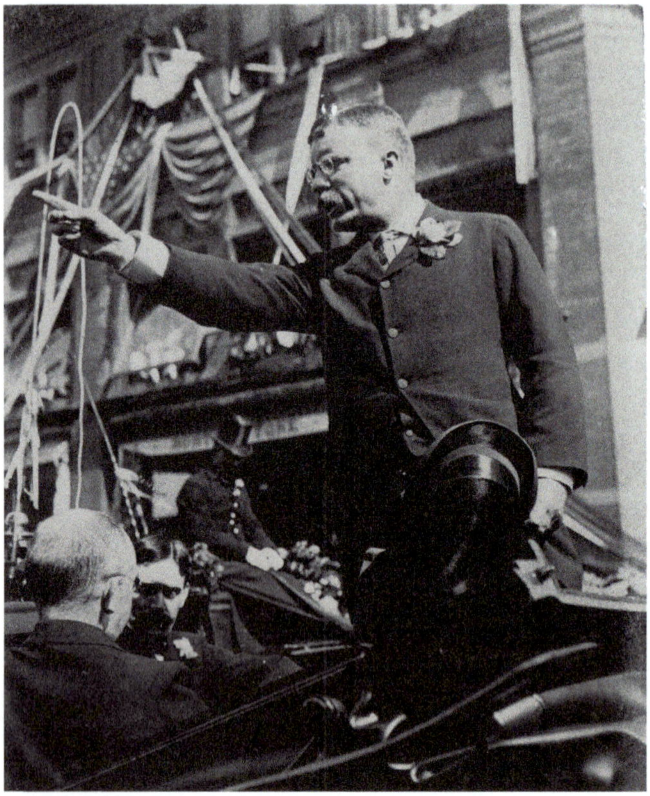

Bob Thomas/Popperfoto/Getty Images

Image 26.18 Theodore Roosevelt Roosevelt gives a speech with both voice and body language in Willimantic, Connecticut, in 1902.

The Rough Rider's high-voltage energy was electrifying. Believing that it was better to wear out than to rust out, he would shake the hands of some six thousand people at one stretch or ride horseback many miles in a day as an example for portly cavalry officers. Incurably boyish and bellicose, Roosevelt ceaselessly preached the virile virtues and denounced pacifistic "flubdubs" and "mollycoddles." An ardent champion of military and naval preparedness, he adopted as his pet proverb, "Speak softly and carry a big stick, [and] you will go far."

His outsized ego caused it to be said of him that he wanted to be the bride at every wedding and the corpse at every funeral. He loved people and mingled with those of all ranks, from Catholic cardinals to professional prizefighters, one of whom partially blinded Roosevelt's left eye in a White House bout. "TR" commanded an idolatrous personal following. After visiting him, a journalist wrote, "You go home and wring the personality out of your clothes."

Above all, TR believed that the president should lead, boldly. He had no real respect for the delicate checks and balances among the three branches of the government. The president, he felt, may take any action in the general interest that is not specifically forbidden by the laws of the Constitution.

26-13 Building the Panama Canal

Roosevelt soon applied his bullish energy to foreign affairs. The Spanish-American War had reinvigorated interest in the long-talked-about canal across the Central American isthmus, through which only printer's ink had ever flowed. Americans had learned a sobering lesson when the battleship *Oregon*, stationed on the Pacific Coast at the outbreak of war in 1898, took weeks to steam all the way around South America to join the U.S. fleet in Cuban waters. An

Image 26.19 Cutting Through the Continental Divide in Panama The Culebra Cut, the southeastern section of the Panama Canal that extends through the Continental Divide, was later renamed the Gaillard Cut in honor of the U.S. Army Corps of Engineers officer who oversaw this excavation but died shortly before the canal opened in 1914. The cut was one of the greatest engineering feats of its time. Hundreds of drills prepared holes for tons of dynamite, which twice daily blasted the rock so that it could be excavated by steam shovels. Dirt trains, shown in the foreground, then hauled loads of debris to dumps twelve miles away. The summit of Culebra Mountain, through which the cut was made, was lowered from 193 feet to 40 feet above sea level and widened considerably.

Library of Congress Prints and Photographs Division [LC-USZ62-121883]

isthmian canal would plainly augment the strength of the navy by increasing its mobility. Such a waterway would also make easier the defense of such recent acquisitions as Puerto Rico, Hawai'i, and the Philippines, while facilitating the operations of the U.S. merchant marine.

Theodore Roosevelt wrote to a correspondent in February 1904,

"I have been hoping and praying for three months that the Santo Domingans would behave so that I would not have to act in any way. I want to do nothing but what a policeman has to do. . . . As for annexing the island, I have about the same desire to annex it as a gorged boa-constrictor might have to swallow a porcupine wrong-end-to."

Initial obstacles in the path of the canal builders were legal rather than geographical. By the terms of the ancient Clayton-Bulwer Treaty, concluded with Britain in 1850, the United States could not secure exclusive control over an isthmian route. But by 1901, America's British cousins were willing to yield ground. Confronted with an unfriendly Europe and bogged down in the South African Boer War, they consented to the **Hay-Pauncefote Treaty** in 1901. It not only gave the United States a free hand to build the canal but conceded the right to fortify it as well.

But where exactly should the canal be dug? Many American experts favored a route across Nicaragua, but agents of the old French Canal Company were eager to salvage something from their costly failure at S-shaped Panama. Represented by a young, energetic, and unscrupulous engineer, Philippe Bunau-Varilla, the New Panama Canal Company suddenly dropped the price of its holdings from $109 million to the fire-sale price of $40 million.

Congress in June 1902 finally decided on the Panama route (refer to Image 26.19). The scene now shifted to Colombia, of which Panama was a restive part. The Colombian senate rejected an American offer of $10 million and annual payment of $250,000 for a six-mile-wide zone across Panama. Roosevelt railed against "those dagoes" who were frustrating his ambitions. Meanwhile, impatient Panamanians, who had rebelled numerous times, were ripe for another revolt. They had counted on a wave of prosperity to follow construction of the canal, and they feared that the United States would now turn to the Nicaraguan route. Scheming Bunau-Varilla was no less disturbed by the prospect of losing the company's $40 million. Working hand in glove with the revolutionists, he helped incite a rebellion on November 3, 1903. U.S. naval forces prevented Colombian troops from crossing the isthmus to quell the uprising.

Roosevelt moved rapidly to make steamy Panama a virtual outpost of the United States. Just three days after the insurrection, he hastily extended the right hand of recognition. Fifteen days later, Bunau-Varilla, who was now the Panamanian minister despite his French citizenship, signed the Hay–Bunau-Varilla Treaty in Washington. The price of the canal strip was left the same, but the zone was widened from six to ten miles. The French company gladly pocketed its $40 million from the U.S. Treasury.

Roosevelt, it seems clear, did not actively plot to tear Panama from the side of Colombia. But the conspirators knew of his angrily expressed views, and they counted on his using the big stick to hold Colombia at bay. The Rough Rider became so indiscreetly involved in the Panama affair as to create the impression that he had been a secret party to the intrigue, and the so-called rape of Panama marked an ugly downward lurch in U.S. relations with Latin America.

Canal construction began in 1904, in the face of daunting difficulties ranging from labor troubles to landslides and lethal tropical diseases. Colonel William C. Gorgas, the quiet and determined

Library of Congress Prints and Photographs Division [LC-USZ62-121883]

exterminator of yellow fever in Havana, ultimately made the Canal Zone "as safe as a health resort." At a cost of some $400 million, an autocratic West Point engineer, Colonel George Washington Goethals, ultimately brought the project to completion in 1914, just as World War I was breaking out.

26-14 TR Magnifies Monroe's Doctrine

Prompted by repeated Latin American debt defaults, Roosevelt soon intruded further into the affairs of America's New World neighbors. Nations such as Venezuela and the Dominican Republic were chronically in arrears in their payments to European creditors. Germany actually bombarded a town in delinquent Venezuela in 1903.

Roosevelt feared that if the Germans or British got their foot in the door as bill collectors, they might remain in Latin America, in flagrant violation of the Monroe Doctrine. He therefore declared a brazen policy of "preventive intervention," better known as the **Roosevelt Corollary** to the Monroe Doctrine. He announced that in the event of future financial malfeasance by the Latin American nations, the United States itself would intervene, take over the customshouses, pay off the debts, and keep the troublesome Europeans on the other side of the Atlantic. In short, no outsiders could push around the Latin nations except Uncle Sam, Policeman of the Caribbean (refer to Image 26.20). This new brandishing of the big stick in the Caribbean became effective in 1905, when the United States took over the management of tariff collections in the Dominican Republic, an arrangement formalized in a treaty with the Dominicans two years later.

TR's rewriting of the Monroe Doctrine probably did more than any other single step to promote the "Bad Neighbor" policy begun in these years. As time wore on, the new corollary was used to justify wholesale interventions and repeated landings of the marines, all of which helped turn the Caribbean into a "Yankee lake." To Latin Americans it seemed as though the revised Monroe Doctrine, far from providing a shield, was a cloak behind which the United States sought to strangle them.

The shadow of the big stick likewise fell again on Cuba in 1906. Revolutionary disorders brought an appeal from the Cuban president, and "necessity being the mother of intervention," U.S. Marines landed. These police forces were withdrawn temporarily in 1909, but in Latin American eyes the episode was but another example of the creeping power of the Colossus of the North.

William Allen Rogers

Image 26.20 Theodore Roosevelt and His Big Stick in the Caribbean, 1904 Roosevelt's policies seemed to be turning the Caribbean into a Yankee pond.

26-15 Roosevelt on the World Stage

Booted and spurred, Roosevelt charged into international matters far beyond Latin America. The outbreak of war between Russia and Japan in 1904 gave him a chance to perform as a global statesman. The Russian bear, having lumbered across Asia, was seeking to bathe its frostbitten paws in the ice-free ports of China's Manchuria, particularly Port Arthur. In Japanese eyes, Manchuria and Korea in tsarist hands were pistols pointed at Japan's strategic heart. The Japanese responded in 1904 with a devastating surprise pounce on the Russian fleet at Port Arthur. They proceeded to administer a humiliating series of beatings to the inept Russians—the first serious military setback to a major European power by a non-European force since the Turkish invasions of the sixteenth century. But as the war dragged on, Japan began to run short of men and yen—a weakness it did not want to betray to the enemy. Tokyo officials therefore approached Roosevelt in the deepest secrecy and asked him to help sponsor peace negotiations.

Roosevelt was happy to oblige, as he wanted to avoid a complete Russian collapse so that the tsar's empire could remain a counterweight to Japan's growing power. At Portsmouth, New Hampshire, in 1905, TR guided the warring parties to a settlement that satisfied neither side and left the Japanese, who felt they had won the war, especially resentful. Japan was forced to drop its demands for a cash indemnity and Russian evacuation of Sakhalin Island, though it received some compensation in the form of effective control over Korea, which it formally annexed in 1910.

For achieving this agreement, as well as for helping arrange an international conference at Algeciras, Spain, in 1906 to mediate North African disputes, TR received the Nobel Peace Prize in 1906. But the price of his diplomatic glory was high for U.S. foreign relations. Two historic friendships withered on the windswept plains of Manchuria. U.S. relations with Russia, once friendly, soured as the Russians implausibly accused Roosevelt of robbing them of military victory. Revelations about savage massacres of Russian Jews further poisoned American feeling against Russia. Japan, once America's protégé, felt cheated out of its due compensation. Both newly powerful, Japan and America now became rivals in Asia, as fear and jealousy between them grew. "A subjick race is on'y funny whin it's raalysubjek," said newspaper humorist Finley Peter Dunne's beloved character Mr. Dooley. "About three years ago I stopped laughin' at Japanese jokes." (Refer to "Thinking Globally: The Age of Empire," pp. 672–673.)

26-16 Japanese Laborers in California

America's Pacific Coast soon felt the effects of the Russo-Japanese War. A new restlessness swept over the rice paddies of Japan, occasioned by the recent conflict's dislocations and tax burdens. A new wave of Japanese immigrants began pouring into the fertile valleys of California, toiling in its fields and canneries and over time becoming farmers themselves (refer to Image 26.21).

Hum Images/Alamy Stock Photo

Image 26.21 Japanese Workers on a Fruit Farm in California, ca. 1910

Thinking Globally

The Age of Empire

The closing years of the nineteenth century witnessed an unprecedented explosion of imperialism, roughly defined as the forcible imposition of one country's rule on the unwilling inhabitants of another. Between 1870 and the outbreak of World War I in 1914, a handful of European states extended their sway over nearly one-quarter of the earth's surface. Other countries followed suit, notably Japan and eventually the United States.

All the imperial powers had in common a heritage of nationalism and a high degree of industrialization. They commanded the elaborate administrative apparatus of large, unified states, along with quantities of wealth, technology, and murderous firepower utterly beyond the capacity of the so-called backward peoples they sought to dominate. As a result, imperialism was, from the start, a lopsided game. As one English wit mordantly noted in 1898,

> Whatever happens, we have got
> The Maxim gun, and they have not.

Yet ultimately, even with their enormously disproportionate advantages, the imperial states were unable to sustain the age of imperialism for much more than a century.

In many ways, modern imperialism resembled eighteenth-century mercantilism, as economically advanced states backed away from the free-trade doctrines that had energized the early stages of the Industrial Revolution and sought instead to create what one British imperialist called "a great self-sustaining and self-protecting empire." The new imperialism also differed from older colonialism in that the imperial powers sought not merely to exploit but also to transform, modernize, and "westernize" the "backward" societies under their control.

Imperialists often justified their dominion over less developed societies with high-toned slogans. The British professed to be nobly shouldering "the white man's burden." The French piously invoked their *mission civilisatrice* (civilizing mission). The Germans touted the benefits of spreading their vaunted *Kultur* (culture). The Americans prated about the superiority of the Anglo-Saxons, as the Japanese did about their own "Yamato" race.

These protestations may have been sincere, but other motives more powerfully propelled the imperial enterprise. Prominent among them was the quest for new markets, as maturing industrial economies appeared to be exhausting the possibilities for economic growth at home. The need for reliable sources of products such as cotton, sugar, copper, coffee, and tea also figured conspicuously. An even more compelling incentive was the need to protect the huge investments of capital that built the railroads, highways, bridges, ports, mills, foundries, mines, smelters, and telegraphs of the developing world. By the eve of the First World War, fully one-quarter of Britain's accumulated wealth was invested overseas.

But perhaps the most important factor driving the imperialist venture was simply the competitive nature of the international system itself. In an unstable, unpredictable world inhabited by ambitious and wary powers, no state thought it could afford to cede an advantage, however ill-defined, to any real or imagined rival. Indeed, quite independently of their hard economic value, colonies came to be considered the necessary symbols of great-power status. This perverse logic proved to be a powerful dynamic: once the imperial race began, it was difficult to stop. As Cecil Rhodes, the fabled British colonizer in southern Africa, once said, "I would annex the planets, if I could. I often think of that."

Image 26.22 **A Young Ho Chi Minh** Ho Chi Minh (1890–1969), the father of Vietnamese independence, is shown here attending the Congress of the Socialist Party in Tours, France, where the French Communist party was created in late December 1920. He had earlier tried to persuade Woodrow Wilson and other world leaders at the Paris Peace Conference in 1919 that they should support an independent Vietnam, freed from French colonial domination.

Library of Congress Prints and Photographs Division [LC-USZ62-62808]

So when Belgium's King Leopold took an interest in Africa's Congo basin in the 1870s, he touched off a mad imperial scramble that eventually involved Belgium, Britain, Germany, France, Italy, and Portugal. Less than two decades later, with the exceptions of Ethiopia and Liberia, the entire continent, much of it unexplored and of dubious economic value, lay under European domination (refer to Map 26.4).

In Asia, Germany annexed part of New Guinea in 1884. France completed its annexation of Indochina (present-day Vietnam, Laos, and Cambodia) that same year. Britain acquired Burma (now Myanmar) in 1885 and parts of Borneo and the Malay Peninsula soon after. Japan closed its grip on Okinawa in 1872, Formosa (Taiwan) in 1895, Port Arthur in 1905, and Korea in 1910. All those powers, in addition to Russia, also had designs on China, which despite its venerable history seemed a poor match for the energetic "nations on the make." In the Open Door notes of 1899 and 1900 (refer to "26-10 Hinging the Open Door in China," pp. 664–665), the United States tried to temper the imperialists' appetites for Chinese territory and concessions, while at the same time America was becoming an imperial power itself with the takeover of the Philippines and Puerto Rico.

The imperialists brought not only their might and their majesty, their capital and their Maxim guns. They also brought their ideas, including concepts of nationalism, self-determination, and democracy. In 1919 a young Vietnamese nationalist named Nguyen Sinh Cung unsuccessfully petitioned the post–World War I peacemakers at Versailles for his country's right to self-determination. A little more than half a century later, under the name Ho Chi Minh, he secured Vietnam's independence by prevailing in a war first against the French and then against the Americans. By that time the United States had long since voluntarily relinquished the Philippines (in 1946, though Puerto Rico remains an American possession), and virtually all of Africa and Asia had been decolonized. With the handover of Hong Kong (1997) and Macao (1999) to the People's Republic of China, the age of empire effectively ended.

Map 26.4 The Great Powers and Their Colonial Possessions, 1913

Varying Viewpoints

Why Did America Become a Colonial Power?

American imperialism has long been an embarrassing topic for students of American history, who remember the Republic's own revolutionary origins and anticolonial tradition. Perhaps for that reason, many historians have tried to explain the dramatic overseas expansionism of the 1890s as some kind of aberration—a sudden, singular, and short-lived departure from time-honored American principles and practices. Various explanations have been offered to account for this spasmodic lapse. Scholars such as Julius Pratt pointed to the irresponsible behavior of the yellow press. Richard Hofstadter ascribed America's imperial fling to the "psychic crisis of the 1890s," a crisis brought on, he argued, by the strains of the decade's economic depression and the Populist upheaval. More recently, scholars such as Kristin Hoganson have emphasized the interplay between the decade's gendered ideals and the sudden lurch for overseas territory. Worried that American society had grown "feminine" since the closing of the frontier, jingoes successfully urged William McKinley to see the Philippines as a tropical tonic to restore the nation's virility.

Howard K. Beale emphasized the contagious scramble for imperial possessions by the European powers, as well as Japan, in these years. In Beale's argument, the United States—and Theodore Roosevelt in particular—succumbed to a kind of international peer pressure: if other countries were expanding their international roles and even establishing colonies around the globe, could the United States safely refrain from doing the same? According to Beale, Theodore Roosevelt was no simpleminded imperial swashbuckler, but a coolly calculating diplomatic realist who perceived that if the United States did not hold its own against other powers, it would soon risk being pushed around, even in its own hemisphere, despite the Monroe Doctrine.

Others dismiss the 1890s as no kind of aberration at all. Drawing a through-line from the Louisiana Purchase to the acquisition of the Philippines, Walter Nugent argues that the United States was imperialistic from its inception, a nation that merely continued its "habit of empire-building" from the earliest days of Western settlement to the wars of the twentieth century. Other scholars contend that, like its European colonial forebears, the United States was a "settler" society that pursued race-fueled expansion in the Pacific just as it had in Indian territory. For many Americans at the time, the conquest of "primitive" peoples by a superior "Christian" civilization was welcomed as a natural, foreordained outcome.

More recent scholarship by Paul Kramer and others has stressed the degree to which American imperialists turned to European precedents for guidance and inspiration. U.S. colonial officials in the Philippines and Puerto Rico circulated widely in the British colonial world, selectively adapting elements of British imperial policy.

Perhaps the most controversial interpretation of American imperialism has come from a so-called New Left school of writers, inspired by William Appleman Williams (and before him by V. I. Lenin's 1916 book *Imperialism: The Highest Stage of Capitalism*). Historians such as Williams and Walter LaFeber argue that the explanation for political and military expansion abroad is to be found in economic expansion at home. Increasing industrial output, so the argument goes, required ever more raw materials and, especially, overseas markets. To meet those needs, the nation adopted a strategy of "informal empire," shunning formal territorial possessions (with the conspicuous exceptions of Puerto Rico and the Philippines), but seeking economic dominance over foreign markets, materials, and investment outlets. That "revisionist" interpretation, in turn, has been sharply criticized by scholars who point out that foreign trade accounted for only a tiny share of American output and that the diplomacy of this period was far too complex to be reduced to "economic need."

Although Japanese residents never amounted to more than 3 percent of the state's population, white Californians ranted about a new "yellow peril" and feared being drowned in an Asian sea.

A showdown on the influx came in 1906, when San Francisco's school board, coping with the aftermath of a frightful earthquake and fire, ordered the segregation of Chinese, Japanese, and Korean students in a special school to free more space for white schoolchildren. Instantly the incident boiled into an international crisis. The people of Japan, understandably sensitive on questions of race, regarded this discrimination as an insult to them and their beloved children. On both sides of the Pacific, irresponsible war talk sizzled in the yellow press—the real "yellow peril." Roosevelt, who as a Rough Rider had relished shooting, was less happy over the prospect that California might stir up a war that all the other states would have to wage. He therefore invited the entire San Francisco Board of Education, headed by a bassoon-playing mayor under indictment for graft, to come to the White House.

TR finally broke the deadlock, but not until he had brandished his big stick and bared his big teeth. The Californians were induced to repeal the offensive school order and to accept what came to be known as the **"Gentlemen's Agreement."** By this secret understanding, worked out during 1907–1908, Tokyo agreed to stop the flow of laborers to the American mainland by withholding passports.

Worried that his intercession might be interpreted in Tokyo as prompted by fear, Roosevelt hit upon a dramatic scheme to impress and intimidate the Japanese. He daringly decided to send the entire battleship fleet on a highly visible voyage around the world. Late in 1907, sixteen sparkling-white, smoke-belching battleships started from Virginia waters. Their commander pointedly declared that he was ready for "a feast, a frolic, or a fight." The **Great White Fleet**—saluted by cannonading champagne corks—received tumultuous welcomes in Latin America, Hawai'i, New Zealand, and Australia (though it ended up having to borrow coal from the British to complete the voyage).

As events turned out, an overwhelming reception in Japan was the high point of the trip. Tens of thousands of kimonoed schoolchildren, trained to wave tiny American flags, movingly sang "The Star-Spangled Banner." In the warm diplomatic atmosphere created by the visit of the fleet, the United States signed the **Root-Takahira agreement** with Japan in 1908. It pledged both powers to respect each other's territorial possessions in the Pacific and to uphold the Open Door in China. For the moment, at least, the two rising rival powers had found a means to maintain the peace.

Chapter Summary

The previously isolated United States dramatically turned its attention overseas in the 1890s, leading to a sudden burst of imperialism. Among the stimuli for the new imperialism were the desire for new economic markets, the sensationalistic "yellow press," Protestant missionary fervor, "Social Darwinist" ideology, great-power rivalry, and naval competition.

American intervention in the Venezuelan boundary dispute of 1895–1896 demonstrated an aggressive new assertion of the Monroe Doctrine. After a severe war scare, the event led to an American–British rapprochement. Longtime American involvement in Hawai'i climaxed in 1893 with a revolt against the Hawaiian government by white American planters. The new government sought annexation by the United States, but President Cleveland blocked the effort.

The Spanish–American War began in 1898 over American outrage about Spanish oppression of its Cuban colony. American support for the Cuban rebellion was whipped into intense popular fervor by the "yellow press." After the *Maine* explosion in February 1898, outraged public opinion pushed a reluctant President McKinley into war, even though Spain was ready to concede on the major issues.

An astounding first development of the war was Admiral Dewey's naval victory in May 1898 in the rich Spanish islands of the Philippines in the Pacific. American troops, assisted by Filipino rebels, captured the Philippine capital of Manila. Despite military confusion and many deaths from disease, American forces also easily and quickly overwhelmed the Spanish in Cuba and Puerto Rico.

McKinley's decision to take the Philippines precipitated a long and bitter debate in Congress and the country over the wisdom and justice of American imperialism. The narrow proimperialist victory in the Senate made the Philippines, Guam, and Puerto Rico American colonial possessions. Despite continuing doubts about the wisdom of imperialism, the United States had asserted itself as a new international power, including in East Asia.

America's decision to take the Philippines stirred violent resistance from the Filipinos, who had expected independence. The brutal war to defeat the Filipino rebels was longer and costlier than the Spanish–American conflict.

Economic interests, missionary efforts, and European imperialistic intrusion led to growing American involvement in China and elsewhere in East Asia. Hay's Open Door policy helped prevent the European great powers from dismembering and colonizing China. The United States joined an international expedition to suppress the nationalistic, antiforeign Boxer Rebellion.

McKinley readily defeated Bryan's anti-imperialist campaign in 1900 to win reelection. Assuming the presidency after McKinley's assassination, Theodore Roosevelt developed an assertive American foreign policy. When his plans to build a canal in Panama were frustrated by the Colombian Senate, he supported a Panamanian revolt that enabled the strategically important canal to be built. He also revised the Monroe Doctrine by adding a Roosevelt Corollary that declared an American right to intervene in Latin America, stirring considerable resentment south of the U.S. border.

Roosevelt successfully negotiated a compromise end to the Russo-Japanese War but angered both parties in the process. The United States and Japan became competitors in the Pacific. Japanese immigration and Pacific Coast residents' fears of a "yellow peril" added to tensions, but Roosevelt's diplomacy enabled the two countries to maintain a fragile peace.

Key Terms

- Big Sister policy (650)
- Great Rapprochement (650)
- McKinley Tariff (651)
- *insurrectos* (652)
- *Maine* (653)
- Teller Amendment (654)
- Rough Riders (655)
- Anti-Imperialist League (660)
- Foraker Act (661)
- *Insular Cases* (662)
- Platt Amendment (662)
- Open Door note (665)
- Boxer Rebellion (665)
- Hay-Pauncefote Treaty (669)
- Roosevelt Corollary (670)
- Gentlemen's Agreement (674)
- Great White Fleet (675)
- Root-Takahira agreement (675)

People to Know

- Josiah Strong
- Alfred Thayer Mahan
- James G. Blaine
- Richard Olney
- Liliuokalani
- "Butcher" Weyler
- Dupuy de Lôme
- George Dewey
- Emilio Aguinaldo
- William H. Taft
- John Hay
- Theodore ("Teddy") Roosevelt

Chronology

1820	• New England missionaries arrive in Hawai'i	
1889	• Samoa crisis with Germany • Pan-American Conference	
1890	• Mahan publishes *The Influence of Sea Power upon History*	
1891	• New Orleans crisis with Italy	
1892	• Valparaiso crisis with Chile	
1893	• Pribilof Islands dispute with Canada • White planter revolt in Hawai'i	• Cleveland refuses Hawai'i annexation
1895	• Cubans revolt against Spain	
1895–1896	• Venezuelan boundary crisis with Britain	
1898	• *Maine* explosion in Havana harbor • Spanish-American War • Teller Amendment	• Dewey's victory at Manila Bay • Hawai'i annexed
1899	• Senate ratifies treaty acquiring Philippines • Aguinaldo launches rebellion against United States in Philippines	• First American Open Door note
1900	• Hawai'i receives full territorial status • Foraker Act for Puerto Rico • Boxer Rebellion and U.S. military expedition to China	• Second Open Door note • McKinley defeats Bryan for presidency
1901	• Supreme Court *Insular Cases* • Platt Amendment • McKinley assassinated; Roosevelt becomes president	• Filipino rebellion suppressed • Hay-Pauncefote Treaty with Britain gives United States exclusive right to build Panama Canal
1902	• U.S. troops leave Cuba • Colombian senate rejects U.S. proposal for canal across Panama	
1903	• Panamanian revolution against Colombia • Hay-Bunau-Varilla Treaty gives United States control of Canal Zone in newly independent Panama	
1904	• Roosevelt Corollary to Monroe Doctrine	
1904–1914	• Construction of Panama Canal	
1905	• United States takes over Dominican Republic customs service • Roosevelt mediates Russo-Japanese peace treaty	
1906	• San Francisco Japanese education crisis • Roosevelt arranges Algeciras Conference	
1906–1909	• U.S. Marines occupy Cuba	
1907	• Great White Fleet makes world voyage	
1907–1908	• "Gentlemen's Agreement" with Japan	
1908	• Root-Takahira agreement	
1917	• Puerto Ricans granted U.S. citizenship	

To Learn More

Gail Bederman, *Manliness and Civilization: A Cultural History of Gender and Race in the United States, 1880–1917* (1995)

Robert L. Beisner, *Twelve Against Empire: The Anti-Imperialists, 1898–1900* (1968)

Ada Ferrer, *Insurgent Cuba: Race, Nation, and Revolution, 1868–1898* (2005)

Julia Greene, *The Canal Builders: Making America's Empire at the Panama Canal* (2009)

George C. Herring, *From Colony to Superpower: U.S. Foreign Relations Since 1776* (2008)

Kristin L. Hoganson, *Fighting for American Manhood* (1998)

William R. Hutchison, *Errand to the World: American Protestant Thought and Foreign Missions* (1987)

Daniel Immerwahr, *How to Hide an Empire* (2018)

Matthew Frye Jacobson, *Barbarian Virtues: The United States Encounters Foreign Peoples at Home and Abroad, 1876–1917* (2000)

Lilikalā Kame'elehiwa, *Native Lands and Foreign Desires* (1992)

Paul A. Kramer, *The Blood of Government: Race, Empire, the United States, and the Philippines* (2006)

Walter LaFeber, *The Cambridge History of American Foreign Relations*, vol. 2: *The American Search for Opportunity, 1865–1913* (1993)

Eric Love, *Race Over Empire* (2004)

Ernest R. May, *Imperial Democracy: The Emergence of America as a Great Power* (1961)

Robert W. Merry, *President McKinley, Architect of the American Century* (2017)

Walter Nugent, *Habits of Empire* (2008)

Louis A. Perez, Jr., *The War of 1898: The United States and Cuba in History and Historiography* (1998)

Ileana Rodríguez-Silva, *Silencing Race: Disentangling Blackness, Colonialism, and National Identities in Puerto Rico* (2012)

Emily S. Rosenberg, *Spreading the American Dream: American Economic and Cultural Expansion, 1890–1945* (1982)

Chapter 27

Progressivism and the Republican Roosevelt: 1901–1912

When I say I believe in a square deal I do not mean . . . to give every man the best hand. If the cards do not come to any man, or if they do come, and he has not got the power to play them, that is his affair. All I mean is that there shall be no crookedness in the dealing.

Theodore Roosevelt, 1905

Chapter Outline

- Campaigning against social injustice
- The muckrakers
- Women battle for reforms and against the saloon
- Roosevelt, labor, and the trusts
- Racial tensions
- Safeguarding consumers and protecting the environment
- The troubled presidency of William Howard Taft
- Taft's "dollar diplomacy"
- Roosevelt breaks with Taft
- The election of 1912: The New Freedom versus the New Nationalism

Contending Voices: Debating the Muckrakers

Nearly 76 million Americans greeted the new century in 1900. Almost one in seven of them was foreign-born. In the fourteen years of peace that remained before the Great War of 1914–1918 engulfed the globe, 13 million more migrants would carry their bundles down the gangplanks to the land of promise.

Hardly had the twentieth century dawned on the ethnically and racially mixed American people than they were convulsed by a reform movement, the likes of which the nation had not seen since the 1840s. The new crusaders, who called themselves "progressives," waged war on many evils, notably monopoly, corruption, inefficiency, and social injustice. The progressive army was large, diverse, and widely deployed, but it had a single battle cry: "Strengthen the State." The "real heart of the movement," explained one of the progressive reformers, was "to use government as an agency of human welfare."

Focus Questions

1. What were the origins and central principles of the progressive movement?
2. What were the primary achievements of progressivism at the local, state, and national levels, and why were female reformers so important to its success?
3. How did President Theodore Roosevelt apply progressive principles to the American economy, and why were consumer protection and conservation such important progressive causes for Roosevelt?
4. How did William Howard Taft's policies split the Republican Party and inspire Theodore Roosevelt's progressive revolt?
5. What made the election of 1912 a genuine contest of ideologies as well as of the three candidates, Roosevelt, Taft, and Wilson? Why did Wilson win the election?

27-1 Progressive Roots

Thinking Globally: "Why Is There No Socialism in the United States?"
Examining the Evidence: *Muller v. Oregon*, 1908
Makers of America: The Environmentalists
Varying Viewpoints: Who Were the Progressives?

The groundswell of the new reformist wave went far back—to the Greenback Labor Party of the 1870s and the Populists of the 1890s, to the mounting unrest throughout the land as grasping industrialists concentrated more and more power in fewer and fewer hands. An outworn philosophy of hands-off individualism seemed increasingly out of place in the modern machine age. Social and economic problems were now too complex for the intentionally feeble Jeffersonian organs of government. Progressive theorists were insisting that society could no longer afford the luxury of a limitless "let-alone" (laissez-faire) policy. The people, through government, must substitute mastery for drift.

Well before 1900, perceptive politicians and writers had begun to pinpoint targets for the progressive attack. Bryan, Altgeld, and the Populists loudly branded the "bloated trusts" with the stigma of corruption and wrongdoing. In 1894, Henry Demarest Lloyd charged headlong into the Standard Oil Company with his book *Wealth Against Commonwealth*. Iconoclastic Thorstein Veblen assailed the new rich with his prickly pen in *The Theory of the Leisure Class* (1899), a savage attack on "predatory wealth" and "conspicuous consumption." In Veblen's view, the parasitic leisure class engaged in wasteful "business" (or making money for money's sake) rather than productive "industry" (or making goods to satisfy real needs). He urged that social leadership pass from these superfluous financial finaglers to truly useful engineers.

Other pen-wielding knights likewise entered the fray. The keen-eyed and keen-nosed Danish immigrant Jacob A. Riis (refer to Images 27.1 and 27.2), a reporter for the *New York Sun*,

Image 27.1 Immigrant Children at Mott Street Industrial School, New York City, 1889 In classrooms like this one, captured here by famed photographer Jacob Riis, educators tried to respect their immigrant students' ancestral cultures while also cultivating loyalty to their adopted country by teaching civics and appreciation for American patriotic symbols and rituals.

Image 27.2 Room in a Tenement Flat, 1910 Tenement life on the Lower East Side of New York City was exposed by the camera of Jacob Riis, who compiled a large photographic archive of turn-of-the-century urban life. Many families counted themselves lucky to share a single room, no matter how squalid.

shocked middle-class Americans in 1890 with *How the Other Half Lives*. His account was a damning indictment of the dirt, disease, vice, and misery of the rat-gnawed human rookeries known as New York slums. The book deeply influenced a future New York City police commissioner, Theodore Roosevelt. Novelist Theodore Dreiser used his blunt prose to batter promoters and profiteers in *The Financier* (1912) and *The Titan* (1914).

Caustic critics of social injustice issued from several other corners. Socialists, many of whom were European immigrants inspired by the strong movement for state socialism in the Old World, began to register appreciable strength at the ballot box (refer to "Thinking Globally: 'Why Is There No Socialism in the United States?'" pp. 682–683). High-minded messengers of the **social gospel** promoted a brand of progressivism based on Christian teachings. They used religious doctrine to demand better housing and living conditions for the urban poor. University-based economists urged new reforms modeled on European examples, importing policy ideas from Berlin to Baltimore. Feminists in multiplying numbers added social justice to suffrage on their list of needed reforms. With urban pioneers like Jane Addams in Chicago and Lillian Wald in New York blazing the way, women entered the fight to improve the lot of families living and working in the festering cities.

27-2 Raking Muck with the Muckrakers

Beginning about 1902, the exposing of evil became a flourishing industry among American publishers. A group of aggressive ten- and fifteen-cent popular magazines surged to the front, notably *McClure's*, *Cosmopolitan*, *Collier's*, and *Everybody's*. Waging fierce circulation wars, they dug deep for the dirt that the public loved to hate. Enterprising editors financed extensive research and encouraged pugnacious writing by their bright young reporters, whom President Roosevelt branded as **muckrakers** in 1906. Annoyed by their excess of zeal, he compared the mudslinging magazine dirt-diggers to the figure in Bunyan's *Pilgrim's Progress* who was so intent on raking manure that he could not see the celestial crown dangling overhead.

Despite presidential scolding, these muckrakers boomed circulation, and some of their most scandalous exposures were published as best-selling books. The reformer-writers ranged far, wide, and deep in their crusade to lay bare the muck of iniquity in American society. In 1902 a brilliant New York reporter, Lincoln Steffens, launched a series of articles in *McClure's* titled "The Shame of the Cities." He fearlessly unmasked the corrupt alliance

Contending Voices

Debating the Muckrakers

In his muckraker speech (1906), Theodore Roosevelt (1858–1919) chastised the new investigative journalists for being excessively negative and sensational:

> "Now, it is very necessary that we should not flinch from seeing what is vile and debasing. There is filth on the floor and it must be scraped up with the muck-rake; and there are times and places where this service is the most needed of all the services that can be performed. But the man who never does anything else, who never thinks or speaks or writes, save of his feats with the muck-rake, speedily becomes, not a help to society, not an incitement to good, but one of the most potent forces for evil."

Years later, leading muckraker Ida Tarbell (1857–1944) offered her own take on Roosevelt's consternation:

> "I felt at the time that Mr. Roosevelt had a good deal of the usual conviction of the powerful man in public life that correction should be left to him, a little resentment that a profession outside his own should be stealing his thunder."

Consider This:

Were the muckrakers ultimately a help or a hindrance to reform?

between big business and municipal government. Steffens was followed in the same magazine by Ida M. Tarbell (refer to Image 27.3), a pioneering journalist who published a devastating but factual exposé of the Standard Oil Company. (Her father had been ruined by the oil interests.)

Plucky muckrakers fearlessly tilted their pen-lances at varied targets. They assailed the malpractices of life insurance companies and tariff lobbies. They roasted the beef trust, the "money trust," the railroad barons, and the corrupt amassing of American fortunes. Thomas W. Lawson, an erratic speculator who had himself made $50 million on the stock market, laid bare the practices of his accomplices in "Frenzied Finance," a series of articles that appeared in *Everybody's*. Lawson, by fouling his own nest, made many enemies among his rich associates, and he died a poor man.

David G. Phillips shocked an already startled nation by his series in *Cosmopolitan* titled "The Treason of the Senate" (1906). He boldly charged that seventy-five of the ninety senators did not represent the people at all but the railroads and trusts. This withering indictment, buttressed by facts, impressed President Roosevelt. Phillips continued his attacks through novels and was fatally shot in 1911 by a disturbed young man who was convinced one of Phillips' novels had maligned his family.

Some of the most effective fire of the muckrakers was directed at social evils. The ugly list included the immoral "white slave" traffic in women, the rickety slums, and the appalling number of industrial accidents. The sorry subjugation of America's nine million Black citizens—of whom 90 percent still lived in the South and one-third were illiterate—was spotlighted in Ray Stannard Baker's *Following the Color Line* (1908). The abuses of child labor were brought luridly to light by John Spargo's *The Bitter Cry of the Children* (1906).

Vendors of potent patent medicines (often heavily spiked with alcohol) likewise came in for bitter criticism. These conscienceless vultures sold incredible quantities of adulterated or habit-forming drugs, while "doping" the press with lavish advertising. Muckraking attacks in *Collier's* were ably reinforced by Dr. Harvey W. Wiley, chief chemist of the Department of Agriculture, who with his famous "Poison Squad" performed experiments on himself.

Pictorial Press Ltd./Alamy Stock Photo

Image 27.3 Ida Tarbell (1857–1944) in Her Office Tarbell was the most eminent woman in the muckraking movement and one of the most respected business historians of her generation. In 1904, she earned a national reputation for publishing a scathing history of the Standard Oil Company, the "Mother of Trusts." Two years later she joined Ray Stannard Baker, William Allen White, and other muckrakers in purchasing the *American* magazine, which became a journalistic podium in their campaign for honest government and an end to business abuses.

Thinking Globally

"Why Is There No Socialism in the United States?"

The Industrial Revolution that began in Britain in the late eighteenth century had by 1900 utterly transformed life in the Western world and beyond. It also had spawned a powerful theory of history, grounded in the writings of Karl Marx. Marxists believed that history's driving engine was class conflict; that in the industrial era that conflict had been starkly reduced to the contest between capitalists and workers (the *bourgeoisie* and the *proletariat*); and that an inevitable socialist revolution would result in the triumph of the proletariat and the emergence of a classless society. Its organizing principle would be "From each according to his ability, to each according to his needs."

Improbable as it might seem today, many nineteenth-century Marxists expected the first socialist revolution to occur in the United States. Marx himself saw America as the country where capitalism had developed more "shamelessly" than elsewhere, thus setting the stage for the "final conflict" that would yield the socialist utopia. Violent labor upheavals like those at Homestead (refer to "25-5 Power to the People," pp. 630–632), Haymarket Square (refer to "23-14 Labor Gains Strength," pp. 585–586), and Pullman (refer to "25-9 Coxey's Army and the Pullman Strike," pp. 635–636) seemed to confirm that analysis, and a chorus of European Marxists stepped up their prophecies. Marx's collaborator Friedrich Engels wrote in the aftermath of the Haymarket eruption in May 1886 that in Europe it had taken workers decades to evolve a common "class consciousness," but "on the more favored soil of America, where no medieval ruins bar the way . . . the working class" would do so "within 10 months."

But it was not to be. Twenty years later, the head of the German Social Democratic party lamented that "we are waiting for you Americans to do something."

The Americans had done a little something, but amid all the ferment of reform in the progressive era, they remained a sore disappointment to European radicals. Eugene V. Debs organized the Socialist Party in 1901 and won 6 percent of the vote in the presidential election of 1912. But the Socialist Party remained a tiny, marginal group. It never posed a serious challenge to the major American parties and never remotely approached the stature of Old-World working-class parties such as the French Socialists, the Italian Communists, the German Social Democrats, and the British Labour Party. At one time or another, most of these European organizations became ruling parties that implemented socialist ideas such as national ownership of core industries, robust support for labor unions, and lavish welfare programs—developments that to this day have had only feeble if any counterparts in the United States.

The failure of Marx's predictions about America occasioned much soul-searching about the plausibility of his entire theory of history. In 1904, a young German scholar named Werner Sombart traveled to the United States—much as Alexis de Tocqueville had done nearly seventy-five years earlier—to examine America's puzzling reality firsthand (refer to "Thinking Globally: Alexis de Tocqueville on Democracy in America and Europe," Chapter 12, pp. 280–281). Two years later he published the notable book *Why Is There No Socialism in the United States?* "If Socialism follows as a necessary reaction to capitalism," he asked, why was there no socialist movement worthy of the name in "the country with the most advanced capitalist development, namely the United States?" Sombart gave several answers:

1. The strikingly egalitarian social manners of all Americans. "The bowing and scraping before the 'upper classes,' which produces such an unpleasant impression in Europe, is completely unknown," he noted, reflecting the workers' refusal or inability to consider themselves a class apart.
2. The "safety valve" of the western frontier, which allowed workers to walk away from oppressive employers and strike out on their own. Sombart exaggerated the effects of the frontier (refer to "22-11 The Fading Frontier," pp. 564–566), but he did call attention to the remarkable geographic mobility of American workers, which worked to inhibit their sense of class permanence and class solidarity.

Ian Dagnall Computing/Alamy Stock Photo

Image 27.4 The Prophet of the Class Struggle, Karl Marx (1818–1883)

3. An accident of historical timing—perhaps Sombart's shrewdest observation. Sombart shared with Tocqueville a deep insight into the American experience. Unlike Europe, where the struggles for political and economic rights went forward in tandem, in America, beginning in the Jacksonian era, workers had largely achieved a significant measure of political equality well before the onset of America's own Industrial Revolution. They had a stake in the existing political order from the outset and little incentive to overturn it. As another German socialist put it, for the purposes of building class consciousness, "the *struggle* for freedom is very much superior to the effortless possession of a freedom that others have won before." That observation echoed Tocqueville's celebrated dictum that because the United States never had a feudal phase, it was *born* free, instead of *becoming* so, and was "reaping the fruits of the democratic revolution without having had the revolution itself."
4. The American workers' remarkably high standard of living. "On roast beef and apple pie," Sombart concluded in a famous sentence, "all socialist utopias have gone to pot."

For all his brilliance, Sombart gave scant attention to yet another circumstance that impeded working-class solidarity in the United States: the remarkable ethnic, religious, and even linguistic diversity of American workers—and, most conspicuously, often bitter divisions between Black and white workers. Well after Emancipation, Black workers confronted ugly discrimination in labor markets as well as exclusion from membership in craft unions. Employers often cynically recruited Black hires as strike breakers (or "scabs"), further inflaming racial hostility. W. E. B. Du Bois pointed out these inequities in work published in Europe around the same time as Sombart. Written in French and German, Du Bois's findings went largely unnoticed in the United States. Nearly a century later, historians of race and labor came to similar conclusions.

Since the collapse of Soviet communism in the 1990s, Marxism stands largely discredited, and some Western European societies are edging away from socialist ideas such as national ownership of industries. As one historian has suggested, "One might well ask not 'Why is there no socialism in the United States?' but 'Why has there been no socialist transformation in any advanced capitalist society?'"

The International Pub. Co., Cleveland, OH

Image 27.5 The IWW Seeks Subscribers, 1911 This poster aimed to attract subscribers to *Industrial Worker*, the newspaper of the Industrial Workers of the World (IWW). The IWW was a small but vocal radical labor union that hoped to unify American workers in "one big union," irrespective of their jobs, gender, or race. Its motto was "An injury to one is an injury to all." At its peak in 1923, the union claimed 100,000 members, commonly known as Wobblies, and could marshal the support of some 300,000 more, mostly workers on the docks and in mines, lumbering, and textiles.

In his muckraking classic "The Shame of the Cities" (1904), Lincoln Steffens (1866–1936) decried the great threat posed by New York City's Tammany machine:

"Bribery is no ordinary felony, but treason; . . . 'corruption which breaks out here and there and now and then' is not an occasional offense, but a common practice, and . . . the effect of it is literally to change the form of our government from one that is representative of the people to an oligarchy, representative of special interests."

Full of sound and fury, the muckrakers signified much about the nature of the progressive reform movement. They were long on lamentation but stopped short of revolutionary remedies. To right social wrongs, they counted on publicity and an aroused public conscience, not drastic political change. They sought not to overthrow capitalism but to cleanse it. The cure for the ills of American democracy, they earnestly believed, was more democracy.

27-3 Political Progressivism

The question "Who were the progressives?" evokes contradictory answers. Progressive reformers included militarists such as Theodore Roosevelt, who thrilled at the strenuous life, as well as pacifists such as Jane Addams, whose loftiest goals included the abolition of war (refer to Image 27.6). Female settlement workers hoping to "Americanize" recent immigrants mobilized alongside labor unionists and enlightened businessmen to strengthen the helping hand of government. In diverse ways, and sometimes with divergent aims, the progressives sought to modernize American institutions to achieve two chief goals: to use the state to curb monopoly power and to improve the common person's conditions of life and labor. Progressives emerged in both major parties, in all regions, and at all levels of government. The truth is that progressivism was less a monolithic minority movement and more a broadly dispersed majority mood (refer to "Varying Viewpoints: Who Were the Progressives?" p. 701).

One of the first objectives of progressives was to regain the power that had slipped from the hands of the people into those of the "interests." These ardent reformers pushed for direct primary elections so as to undercut power-hungry party bosses. They favored the **initiative** so that voters could directly propose legislation themselves, thus bypassing the boss-bought state legislatures. Progressives also agitated for the **referendum.** This device would place laws on the ballot for final approval by the people, especially laws that had been railroaded through a compliant legislature by free-spending agents of big business. The **recall** would enable the voters to remove faithless elected officials, particularly those who had been bribed by bosses or lobbyists.

Rooting out graft also became a prime goal of earnest progressives. A number of state legislatures passed corrupt-practices acts, which limited the amount of money that candidates could spend for their election. Such legislation also restricted huge gifts from corporations, for which the donors would expect special favors. The secret **Australian ballot** was likewise being introduced more widely in the states to counteract boss rule. Bribery was less feasible when bribers could not tell if they were getting their money's worth from the bribed.

Direct election of U.S. senators became a favorite goal of progressives, especially after the muckrakers had exposed the scandalous intimacy between greedy corporations and Congress. By 1900, the Senate had so many rich men that it was often sneered at as the "Millionaires' Club." Too many of these prosperous solons, elected as they then were by trust-dominated legislatures, heeded the voice of their "masters" rather than the voice of the masses.

A constitutional amendment to bring about the popular election of senators had rough sledding in Congress, for the plutocratic members of the Senate were happy with existing methods. But several states established primary elections in which the voters expressed their preferences for the Senate. The local legislatures, when choosing senators, found it politically wise to heed the voice of the people. Partly as a result of such pressures, the Seventeenth Amendment to the Constitution, approved in 1913, established the direct election of U.S. senators (refer to the Appendix). But the expected improvement in caliber was slow in coming.

Woman suffrage, the goal of female reformers for many decades, likewise received powerful new support from the progressives early in the 1900s. The political reformers believed that women's votes would elevate the political tone, and the foes of the saloon felt that they could count on the support of enfranchised females. The suffragists, with their cry of "Votes for Women" and "Equal Suffrage for Men and Women," protested bitterly against "Taxation Without

Image 27.6 Jane Addams and Fellow Pacifists, 1915 Addams cofounded the Women's Peace Party in 1915. Its pacifist platform was said to represent the views of the "mother half of humanity." Although the party initially attracted twenty-five thousand members, America's entry into the war two years later eroded popular support because pacifist internationalism became suspect as anti-American.

Representation." Many of the states, especially the more liberal ones in the West, such as Washington, California, and Oregon, gradually extended the vote to women. But by 1910, nationwide female suffrage was still a decade away, and a suffragist could still be sneeringly defined as "one who has ceased to be a lady and has not yet become a gentleman."

> The suffrage campaign of the early twentieth century benefited from a new generation of women who considered themselves feminists. At a mass meeting in New York in 1914, Marie Jenny Howe (1870–1934), a minister by training as well as a prominent early feminist, proclaimed,
>
> "We intend simply to be ourselves, not just our little female selves, but our whole big human selves."

27-4 Progressivism in the Cities and States

Progressives scored some of their most impressive gains in the cities. Frustrated by the inefficiency and corruption of machine-oiled city government, many localities followed the pioneering example of Galveston, Texas. In 1901, it had appointed expert-staffed commissions to manage urban affairs. Other communities adopted the city-manager system, also designed to take politics out of municipal administration. Some of these "reforms" obviously valued efficiency—the paramount concern of many progressives—more highly than democracy, as control of civic affairs was further removed from the people's hands.

Urban reformers likewise attacked "slumlords," juvenile delinquency, and wide-open prostitution (vice-at-a-price), which flourished in red-light districts unchallenged by bribed police. Public-spirited Americans looked to English and German cities for lessons on how to clean up their water supplies, light their streets, and run their trolley cars. The vogue of public ownership of utilities swept the nation as local governments tried to halt the corrupt sale of franchises.

Progressivism naturally bubbled up to the state level, notably in Wisconsin, which became a yeasty laboratory of reform. The governor of the state, pompadoured Robert M. ("Fighting Bob") La Follette, was an undersized but overbearing crusader who emerged as the most militant of the progressive Republican leaders. After a desperate fight with entrenched monopoly, he reached the governor's chair in 1901. Routing the lumber and railroad interests, he wrested considerable control from the crooked corporations and returned it to the people. He also perfected a scheme for regulating public utilities, while laboring in close association with experts on the faculty of the state university at Madison.

Other states marched steadily toward the progressive camp, as they undertook to regulate railroads and trusts, chiefly through public utility commissions. Oregon was not far behind Wisconsin, and California made giant bootstrides under the stocky Hiram W. Johnson. Elected Republican governor in 1910, this dynamic prosecutor of grafters helped break the dominant grip of the Southern Pacific Railroad on California politics and then, like La Follette, set up a political machine of his own. Heavily whiskered Charles Evans Hughes, the able and audacious reformist Republican governor of New York, had earlier gained national fame as an investigator of malpractices by gas and insurance companies and by the coal trust.

27-5 Progressive Women

Women proved themselves an indispensable part of the progressive army. A crucial focus for women's activism was the settlement house movement (refer to "24-3 Machines and Reformers Compete and Clash," pp. 599–602). At a time when women could neither vote nor hold political office, settlement houses offered a side door to public life. They exposed middle-class women to the problems plaguing America's cities, including poverty, political corruption, and intolerable working and living conditions. They also gave them the skills and confidence to attack those evils. The women's club movement provided an even broader civic entryway for many middle-class women. Literary clubs, where educated women met to improve themselves with poetry and prose, had existed for decades. But in the late nineteenth and early twentieth centuries, many of these clubs set aside Shakespeare and Henry James for social issues and current events. "Dante has been dead for several centuries," observed the president of the General Federation of Women's Clubs in 1904. "I think it is time that we dropped the study of his *Inferno* and turned our attention to our own."

Nineteenth-century notions of "separate spheres" dictated that a woman's place was in the home, so most female progressives defended their new activities as an extension—not a rejection—of the traditional roles of wife and mother. Thus, they were often drawn to moral and "maternal" issues like keeping children out of smudgy mills and sweltering sweatshops, attacking the scourge of tuberculosis bred in airless tenements, winning pensions for mothers with dependent children, and ensuring that only safe food products found their way to the family table. Female activists agitated through organizations like the National Consumers League (1899) and the Women's Trade Union League (1903), as well as through two new federal agencies, the Children's Bureau (1912) and the Women's Bureau (1920), both in the Department of Labor. These wedges into the federal bureaucracy, however small, gave female reformers a national stage for social investigation and advocacy.

Campaigns for factory reform and temperance particularly attracted women foot soldiers. Unsafe and unsanitary sweatshops—factories where workers toiled long hours for low wages—were a public scandal in many cities. Florence Kelley, a former resident of Jane Addams's Hull House, became the state of Illinois's first chief factory inspector and one of the nation's leading advocates for improved factory conditions. In 1899, Kelley took control of the newly founded National Consumers League, which mobilized female consumers to pressure for laws safeguarding women and children in the workplace. In the landmark case ***Muller v. Oregon*** (1908), crusading attorney Louis D. Brandeis persuaded the Supreme Court to accept the constitutionality of laws protecting women workers by presenting evidence of the harmful effects of factory labor on women's weaker bodies. Although this argument calling for special protection for women seemed discriminatory by later standards and closed many "male" jobs to women, progressives at the time hailed Brandeis's achievement as a triumph over existing legal doctrine, which afforded employers total control over the workplace

Examining the Evidence

Muller v. Oregon, 1908

Court records provide notably fruitful sources for historians. They not only tell often-colorful stories about the lives of ordinary men and women caught up in the legal system, they also by their very nature testify to the norms and values that lawyers employ to make their cases and that judges invoke to explain their decisions. The case of *Muller v. Oregon* (refer to "27-5 Progressive Women," pp. 686–689) is especially instructive on both counts. The official Supreme Court records tell how on September 4, 1905, Joe Haselbock, a supervisor in Curt Muller's Grand Laundry in Portland, Oregon, asked an employee, Mrs. E. Gotcher, to remain after hours to do an extra load of laundry. That request violated Oregon's law prohibiting women from working more than ten hours per day. Mrs. Gotcher later complained to the authorities, and Muller was fined $10. Muller refused to pay and took his case all the way to the U.S. Supreme Court. In its landmark decision (below), the Court upheld the constitutionality of the Oregon statute, and Muller at last had to cough up his fine. On what grounds did the Court justify its ruling? What does Justice David J. Brewer's argument on behalf of the Court's decision suggest about the cultural identity and social role of women in early-twentieth-century American society?

(208 U.S. 412)
CURT MULLER, Plff. in Err.,
v.
STATE OF OREGON.

. . . That woman's physical structure and the performance of material functions place her at a disadvantage in the struggle for subsistence is obvious. This is especially true when the burdens of motherhood are upon her . . . and as healthy mothers are essential to vigorous offspring, the physical well-being of woman becomes an object of public interest and care in order to preserve the strength and vigor of the race.

Still again, history discloses the fact that woman has always been dependent upon man. He established his control at the outset by superior physical strength, and this control in various forms, with diminishing intensity, has continued to the present. . . . It is still true that in the struggle for subsistence she is not an equal competitor with her brother. . . . Differentiated by these matters from the other sex, she is properly placed in a class by herself, and legislation designed for her protection may be sustained, even when like legislation is not necessary for men, and could not be sustained. It is impossible to close one's eyes to the fact that she still looks to her brother and depends upon him. . . . The two sexes differ in structure of body, in the functions to be performed by each, in the amount of physical strength, in the capacity for long continued labor, particularly when done standing, the influence of vigorous health upon the future well-being of the race, the self-reliance which enables one to assert full rights, and in the capacity to maintain the struggle for subsistence. This difference justifies a difference in legislation, and upholds that which is designed to compensate for some of the burdens which rest upon her.

We have not referred in this discussion to the denial of the elective franchise in the state of Oregon, for while that may disclose a lack of political equality in all things with her brother, that is not of itself decisive. The reason runs deeper, and rests in the inherent difference between the two sexes, and in the different functions in life which they perform. . . .

(refer to "Examining the Evidence: *Muller v. Oregon*, 1908," above). The American welfare state that emerged from female activism focused more on protecting women and children than on granting benefits to everyone, as was the case in much of Western Europe, with its stronger labor movements.

Crusaders for these humane measures did not always have smooth sailing. One dismaying setback came in 1905, when the Supreme Court, in ***Lochner v. New York***, invalidated a New York law establishing a ten-hour day for bakers. Yet the reformist progressive wave finally washed up into the judiciary, and in 1917 the Court upheld a ten-hour law for factory workers.

Laws regulating factories were worthless if not enforced, a truth horribly demonstrated in 1911 by the lethal **Triangle Shirtwaist Company fire** in New York City. Locked doors and other flagrant violations of the fire code turned the factory into a death trap. One hundred forty-six workers, most of them young immigrant women, were incinerated or leapt from eighth- and ninth-story windows to their deaths. Lashed by the public outcry, including a massive strike by women in the needle trades, the New York legislature passed much stronger laws regulating the hours and conditions of sweatshop toil (refer to Image 27.7). Other legislatures followed, and by 1917 thirty states had put

Bettmann/Getty Images

Image 27.7 The Wages of Negligence Family members arrive at the morgue to identify the bodies of victims of the Triangle Shirtwaist Company fire in 1911. Outrage over this calamity galvanized a generation of reformers to fight for better workplace safety rules.

workers' compensation laws on the books, providing insurance to workers injured in industrial accidents. Gradually, the concept of the employer's responsibility to society was replacing the old dog-eat-dog philosophy of unregulated free enterprise.

Corner saloons, with their shutter doors, naturally attracted the ire and fire of progressives. Alcohol was intimately connected with prostitution in red-light districts, with the drunken voter, with crooked city officials dominated by "booze" interests, and with the blowsy "boss" who counted poker chips by night and miscounted ballots by day (including the "cemetery vote"). By 1900, cities like New York and San Francisco had one saloon for about every two hundred people.

Antiliquor campaigners received powerful support from several militant organizations, notably the Woman's Christian Temperance Union (WCTU). Founder Frances E. Willard, who would fall to her knees in prayer on saloon floors, mobilized nearly 1 million women to "make the world homelike" and built the WCTU into the largest organization of women in the world. She found a vigorous ally in the Anti-Saloon League, which was aggressive, well organized, and well financed.

Caught up in the crusade, some states and numerous counties passed "dry" laws, which controlled, restricted, or

Fotosearch/Archive Photos/Getty Images

Image 27.8 Temperance Propaganda This Women's Christian Temperance Union cartoon illustrates the influential role of women in the temperance movement. Alcohol abuse—then and later—threatened the stability and economic well-being of the family, still predominantly considered the "woman's sphere" in the early twentieth century.

abolished alcohol (refer to Image 27.8). The big cities were generally "wet," for they had a large immigrant vote accustomed in the Old Country to the free flow of wine and beer. When World War I erupted in 1914, nearly one-half of the population lived in "dry" territory, and nearly three-fourths of the total area had outlawed saloons. Demon Rum was groggy and about to be floored—temporarily—by the Eighteenth Amendment in 1919.

Roosevelt was a charismatic figure who made a powerful impression on his contemporaries. The journalist William Allen White (1868–1944) later wrote of his first meeting with TR in 1897,

"He sounded in my heart the first trumpet call of the new time that was to be. . . . I had never known such a man as he, and never shall again. He overcame me. And in the hour or two we spent that day at lunch, and in a walk down F Street, he poured into my heart such visions, such ideals, such hopes, such a new attitude toward life and patriotism and the meaning of things, as I had never dreamed men had. . . . After that I was his man."

27-6 TR's Square Deal for Labor

Theodore Roosevelt, although something of an imperialistic busybody abroad, was touched by the progressive wave at home. Like other reformers, he feared that the "public interest" was being submerged in the drifting seas of indifference. Everybody's interest was nobody's interest. Roosevelt decided to make it his. His sportsman's instincts spurred him into demanding a "Square Deal" for capital, labor, and the public at large. Broadly speaking, the president's program embraced three C's: control of the corporations, consumer protection, and conservation of natural resources.

The Square Deal for labor received its acid test in 1902, when a crippling strike broke out in the anthracite coal mines of Pennsylvania. Some 140,000 besooted workers, many of them illiterate immigrants, had long been frightfully exploited and accident-plagued. They demanded, among other improvements, a 20 percent increase in pay and a reduction of the working day from ten to nine hours.

Unsympathetic mine owners, confident that a chilled public would react against the miners, refused to arbitrate or even negotiate. One of their spokesmen, multimillionaire George F. Baer, reflected the high-and-mighty attitude of certain ungenerous employers. Workers, he wrote, would be cared for "not by the labor agitators, but by the Christian men to whom God in His infinite wisdom has given the control of the property interests of this country."

As coal supplies dwindled, factories and schools were forced to shut down, and even hospitals felt the icy grip of winter. Desperately seeking a solution, Roosevelt summoned representatives of the striking miners and the mine owners to the White House. He was profoundly annoyed by the "extraordinary stupidity and bad temper" of the "wooden-headed gentry" who operated the mines. As he later confessed, if it had not been for the dignity of his high office, he would have taken one of them "by the seat of the breeches" and "chucked him out of the window."

Roosevelt finally resorted to his trusty big stick when he threatened to seize the mines and operate them with federal troops. Faced with this first-time-ever threat to use federal bayonets against capital, rather than labor, the owners grudgingly consented to arbitration. A compromise decision ultimately gave the miners a 10 percent pay boost and a working day of nine hours. But their union was not officially recognized as a bargaining agent.

Keenly aware of the mounting antagonisms between capital and labor, Roosevelt urged Congress to create the new Department of Commerce and Labor. This goal was achieved in 1903. (Ten years later, the agency was split in two.) An important arm of the newborn cabinet body was the Bureau of Corporations, which was authorized to probe businesses engaged in interstate commerce. The bureau was highly useful in helping to break the stranglehold of monopoly and in clearing the road for the era of "trust-busting."

27-7 TR Corrals the Corporations

The sprawling railroad octopus sorely needed restraint. The Interstate Commerce Commission (ICC), created in 1887 as a feeble sop to the public, had proved woefully inadequate. Railroad barons could simply appeal the commission's decisions on rates to the federal courts—a process that might take ten years.

Spurred by the former-cowboy president, Congress passed effective railroad legislation, beginning with the **Elkins Act** of 1903. This curb was aimed primarily at the rebates that sharply favored the railroads' largest and wealthiest shippers. Heavy fines could now be imposed both on the railroads that gave rebates and on the firms that accepted them.

Library of Congress

Image 27.9 Roosevelt Tames the Trusts Legend to the contrary, Roosevelt did not attack all trusts indiscriminately. Rather, he pursued a few high-profile cases against a handful of corporate giants in order to "tame" other businesses into accepting government regulation.

Still more effective was the Hepburn Act of 1906. Free passes for favored shippers and politicians, with their odor of bribery, were severely restricted. The once-infantile ICC now grew real teeth, with new authority to set limits on freight rates and require the firms to submit annual reports of their dealings. After decades of galloping growth, the iron horse at last had a regulatory bridle.

Railroads also provided Roosevelt with an opportunity to brandish his antitrust bludgeon. *Trusts* had come to be a fighting word in the progressive era. Roosevelt believed that these industrial behemoths, with their efficient means of production, had arrived to stay. He concluded that there were "good" trusts, with public consciences, and "bad" trusts, which lusted greedily for power. He was determined to respond to the popular outcry against the trusts but was also determined not to throw out the baby with the bathwater by indiscriminately smashing all large businesses (refer to Image 27.9).

Roosevelt as a trustbuster first burst into the headlines in 1902 with an attack on the Northern Securities Company, a railroad holding company organized by financial titan J. P. Morgan and empire builder James J. Hill. These Napoleonic moguls of money sought to achieve a virtual monopoly of the railroads in the Northwest. Roosevelt was therefore challenging the most regal potentates of the industrial aristocracy.

The railway promoters appealed to the Supreme Court, which in 1904 upheld Roosevelt's antitrust suit and ordered the Northern Securities Company to be dissolved. The *Northern Securities* decision jolted Wall Street and angered big business but greatly enhanced Roosevelt's reputation as a trust smasher.

Roosevelt's big stick crashed down on other giant monopolies, as he initiated over forty legal proceedings against them. The Supreme Court in 1905 declared the beef trust illegal, and the heavy fist of justice fell upon monopolists controlling sugar, fertilizer, harvesters, and other key products.

Much mythology has inflated Roosevelt's reputation as a trustbuster. The Rough Rider understood the political popularity of monopoly-smashing, but he did not consider it sound economic policy. Combination and integration, he felt, were the hallmarks of the age, and to try to stem the tide of economic progress by political means he considered the rankest folly. Bigness was not necessarily badness, so why punish success? Roosevelt's real purpose in assaulting the Goliaths of industry was symbolic: to prove conclusively that the government, not private business, ruled the country. He believed in regulating, not fragmenting, the big-business combines. The threat of dissolution, he felt, might make the sultans of the smokestacks more amenable to federal regulation—as it did.

In truth, Roosevelt never swung his trust-crushing stick with maximum force. In many ways, the huge industrial behemoths were healthier—though perhaps more "tame"—at the end of Roosevelt's reign than they had been before. His successor, William Howard Taft, actually "busted" more trusts than TR did. In one celebrated instance in 1907, Roosevelt even gave his personal blessing to J. P. Morgan's plan to have U.S. Steel absorb the Tennessee Coal and Iron Company, without fear of antitrust reprisals. When Taft then launched a suit against U.S. Steel in 1911, the political reaction from TR was explosive.

27-8 Caring for the Consumer

Roosevelt backed a noteworthy measure in 1906 that benefited both corporations and consumers. Big meatpackers were being shut out of certain European markets because some American meat—from the small packinghouses, claimed the giants—had been found to be tainted. Foreign governments were even threatening to ban all American meat imports by throwing out the good beef with the bad botulism.

At the same time, American consumers hungered for safer canned products. Their appetite for reform was whetted by Upton Sinclair's sensational novel *The Jungle*, published in 1906.

Sinclair, a dedicated Socialist, intended his revolting tract to focus attention on the plight of the workers in the big canning factories, but instead he appalled the public with his description of disgustingly unsanitary food products. (As he put it, he aimed for the nation's heart but hit its stomach.) The book described in noxious detail the filth, disease, and putrefaction in Chicago's damp, ill-ventilated slaughterhouses. Many readers, including Roosevelt, were so sickened that for a time they found meat unpalatable. The president was moved by the loathsome mess in Chicago to appoint a special investigating commission, whose cold-blooded report almost outdid Sinclair's novel. It related how piles of poisoned rats, rope ends, splinters, and other debris were scooped up and canned as potted ham. A cynical jingle of the time ran,

> Mary had a little lamb,
> And when she saw it sicken,
> She shipped it off to Packingtown,
> And now it's labeled chicken.

Backed by a nauseated public, Roosevelt induced Congress to pass the **Meat Inspection Act** of 1906. It decreed that the preparation of meat shipped over state lines would be subject to federal inspection from corral to can (refer to Image 27.10). Although the largest packers resisted certain features of the act, they accepted it as an opportunity to drive their smaller, fly-by-night competitors out of business. At the same time, they could receive the government's seal of approval on their exports. As a companion to the Meat Inspection Act, the **Pure Food and Drug Act** of 1906 was designed to prevent the adulteration and mislabeling of foods and pharmaceuticals.

Historical/Getty Images

Image 27.10 Minding the Meat White-jacketed inspectors examine the hogs in a Swift & Company packinghouse in Chicago. Agents like these made some progress in cleaning up America's septic slaughterhouses after the passage of the Meat Inspection Act of 1906.

27-9 Earth Control

Wasteful Americans, assuming that their natural resources were inexhaustible, had looted and polluted their incomparable domain with unparalleled speed and greed. Western ranchers and timbermen were especially eager to accelerate the destructive process, for they panted to build up the country, and the environmental consequences be hanged. But even before the end of the nineteenth century, far-visioned leaders saw that such a squandering of the nation's birthright would have to be halted, or America would sink from resource richness to despoiled dearth.

A first feeble step toward conservation had been taken with the Desert Land Act of 1877, under which the federal government sold arid land cheaply on the condition that the purchaser irrigate the thirsty soil within three years. More successful was the Forest Reserve Act of 1891, authorizing the president to set aside public forests as national parks and other reserves (refer to Image 27.11). Under this statute some 46 million acres of magnificent trees were rescued from the lumberman's saw in the 1890s and preserved for posterity. The Carey Act of 1894 distributed federal land to the states on the condition that it be irrigated and settled.

A new day in the history of conservation dawned with Roosevelt (refer to "Makers of America: The Environmentalists," pp. 694–695). Huntsman, naturalist, rancher, lover of the great outdoors, he was appalled by the pillaging of timber and mineral resources. Other dedicated conservationists, notably Gifford

The Yosemite Museum, Yosemite National Park

Image 27.11 High Point for Conservation Roosevelt and famed naturalist John Muir visit Glacier Point, on the rim of Yosemite Valley, California. In the distance is Yosemite Falls; a few feet behind Roosevelt is a sheer drop of 3,254 feet.

In his annual message to Congress in 1907, Roosevelt declared prophetically,

"We are prone to speak of the resources of this country as inexhaustible; this is not so. The mineral wealth of the country, the coal, iron, oil, gas, and the like, does not reproduce itself, and therefore is certain to be exhausted ultimately; and wastefulness in dealing with it to-day means that our descendants will feel the exhaustion a generation or two before they otherwise would."

Pinchot, head of the federal Division of Forestry, had broken important ground before him. But Roosevelt seized the banner of leadership and charged into the fray with all the weight of his prestige, his energy, his firsthand knowledge, and his slashing invective.

The thirst of the desert still unslaked, Congress responded to the whip of the Rough Rider by passing the landmark **Newlands Reclamation Act** of 1902. Washington was authorized to collect money from the sale of public lands in the sun-baked western states and then use these funds for the development of irrigation projects. Settlers repaid the cost of reclamation from their now-productive soil, and the money was put into a revolving fund to finance more such enterprises. The giant Roosevelt Dam, constructed on Arizona's Salt River, was appropriately dedicated by Roosevelt in 1911. Thanks to this epochal legislation, dozens of dams were thrown across virtually every major western river in the ensuing decades.

Roosevelt pined to preserve the nation's shrinking forests. By 1900, only about a quarter of the once-vast virgin timberlands remained standing. Lumbermen had already logged off most of the first-growth timber from Maine to Michigan, and the sharp thud of their axes was beginning to split the silence in the great fir forests of the Pacific slope (refer to Image 27.12). Roosevelt proceeded to set aside in federal reserves some 125 million acres, or almost three times the acreage thus saved from the saw by his three predecessors. He similarly earmarked millions of acres of coal deposits, as well as water resources useful for irrigation and power. To set a shining example, in 1902 he banned Christmas trees from the White House.

Library of Congress Prints and Photographs Division [LC-USZ62-57478]

Image 27.12 Loggers in the State of Washington, ca. 1901 It took the sweat and skill of many men to conquer a giant fir like this one. Once the tree was felled, a team of oxen driven by a "bullwhacker" would drag the log out of the woods along a "skid road." *Skid road* (sometimes corrupted as *skid row*) was also a name for the often-sleazy sections of logging towns, where loggers spent their time in the off-season.

Conservation, including reclamation, may have been Roosevelt's most enduring tangible achievement. He was buoyed in this effort by an upwelling national mood of concern about the disappearance of the frontier—believed to be the source of such national characteristics as individualism and democracy. An increasingly citified people worried that too much civilization might not be good for the national soul (refer to Image 27.13). City dwellers snapped up Jack London's *Call of the Wild* (1903) and other books about nature, and urban youngsters made the outdoor-oriented Boy Scouts of America the country's largest youth organization. Middle-class clubwomen raised money for nature preserves and organized the Massachusetts—and later National—Audubon Society to save wild native birds by banning the use of plumes to ornament fashionable ladies' hats. The Sierra Club, founded in 1892, dedicated itself to preserving the wildness of the western landscape.

The preservationists lost a major battle in 1913 when the federal government allowed the city of San Francisco to build a dam for its municipal water supply in the spectacular, high-walled **Hetch Hetchy Valley** in Yosemite National Park (refer to Image 27.14). The Hetch Hetchy controversy laid bare a deep division between conservationists that persists to the present day. To the preservationists of the Sierra Club, including famed naturalist John Muir, Hetch Hetchy was a "temple" of nature that should be held inviolable by the civilizing hand of humanity. But other conservationists, among them President Roosevelt's chief forester, Gifford Pinchot, believed that "wilderness was waste." Pinchot and Roosevelt wanted to *use* the nation's natural endowment intelligently. In their eyes they had to battle on two fronts: against greedy commercial interests that abused nature, as well as against romantic preservationists in thrall to simple "woodman-spare-that-tree" sentimentality.

Under Roosevelt professional foresters and engineers developed a policy of "multiple-use resource management."

They sought to combine recreation, sustained-yield logging, watershed protection, and summer stock grazing on the same expanse of federal land.

At first, many Westerners resisted the federal management of natural resources, but they soon learned how to take advantage of new agencies like the Forest Service and especially the Bureau of Reclamation. The largest ranches and timber companies, in particular, figured out how to work hand in glove with federal conservation programs devoted to the rational, large-scale, and long-term use of natural resources. The one-man-and-a-mule logger or the one-man-and-a-dog sheepherder had little clout in the new resources bureaucracy. Single-person enterprises were shouldered aside, in the interest of efficiency, by the combined bulk of big business and big government.

27-10 The "Roosevelt Panic" of 1907

Roosevelt was handily elected president "in his own right" in 1904 and entered his new term buoyed by his enormous personal popularity—the cuddly "teddy bear" honored one of his bear-hunting exploits (when he saved the life of a cub), and children piped vigorously on whistles modeled on his famous teeth. Yet the conservative Republican bosses considered him as dangerous and unpredictable as a rattlesnake. They grew increasingly restive as Roosevelt in his second term called ever more loudly for regulating corporations, taxing incomes, and protecting workers. Roosevelt, meanwhile, had partly defanged himself after his election in 1904 by announcing that under no circumstances would he be a candidate for a third term. This was a tactical blunder, for the power of the king wanes when the people know he will be dead in four years.

Roosevelt suffered a sharp setback in 1907 when a short but punishing panic descended on Wall Street. The financial flurry featured frightened "runs" on banks, suicides, and criminal indictments against speculators.

Image 27.13 **The Machine and Nature** These hardy sightseers at the Grand Canyon in 1911 ironically and probably unwittingly foreshadowed the mass tourism that arrived with the dawning automobile age. Soon millions of motorized Americans would regularly flee from the cities and suburbs to "get away from it all" in wilderness sites increasingly overrun by their fellow refugees from "civilization."

Image 27.14 **Flooding the Hetch Hetchy Valley to Quench San Francisco's Thirst** Preservationists led by John Muir battled for seven years—unsuccessfully—to prevent the building of a dam that would turn this spectacular glacial valley in Yosemite National Park into the Hetch Hetchy Reservoir, which would provide San Francisco with water. Muir observed, "Dam Hetch Hetchy! As well dam for water-tanks the people's cathedrals and churches, for no holier temple has ever been consecrated by the heart of man." Today environmentalists are campaigning to restore the Hetch Hetchy Valley by removing the dam.

Makers of America

The Environmentalists

Humans have long been awed by nature, but they have also yearned to be its masters. Native American peoples shaped the natural environment to serve their purposes—burning forests and grasslands, for example, to improve hunting habitats—but they lacked the technologies to make Mother Earth bow deeply to their will. The earliest European colonists saw North America as a "howling wilderness" and toiled mightily with ax and plow to tame it. By the mid-nineteenth century, Americans commanded powerful new technologies like the railroad and steam-powered dredges, which promised unbridled dominion over the natural world. Only then did voices begin to be heard in defense of the wounded earth—the faint first stirrings of what would come to be called "environmentalism."

In a pattern that would often be repeated, nature's earliest defenders tended to be well-off townsfolk and city dwellers, like Henry David Thoreau and Ralph Waldo Emerson. The Americans most likely to appreciate the value of the pristine wilderness, it seemed, were those who had ceased to struggle against it. ("Cities, not log cabins, produce Sierra Clubbers," one historian noted.) For the loggers, miners, and farmers who continued to sweat their living out of nature's grudging embrace, concern for environmental niceties often seemed like the sanctimonious piety of a privileged elite.

By the dawn of the twentieth century, many genteel, urban Americans had come to romanticize their pioneer forebears. They reinvented hunting and fishing as sports for the well-to-do, not simply as ways to put food on the table. Preservationists like John Muir waxed lyrical about the mystic allure of unspoiled nature. Seizing the popular mood, Theodore Roosevelt deliberately constructed a public image of himself as a manly outdoorsman—raising cattle in the Dakotas, shooting lions in Africa, rafting down wild rivers in the Amazon basin—and as president he greatly expanded the system of national forests. But Roosevelt was also a pioneer of another sort—as a prominent promoter of the progressive-era "conservation" movement, composed of a loose coalition of scientists, bureaucrats, and businesspeople dependent on stable access to America's rich endowment of natural resources. Progressive conservationists believed that nature must be neither uncritically reverenced nor wastefully exploited but must instead be efficiently utilized. Thus, the same TR who admired the wonders of Yosemite Valley in the company of John Muir also supported the professional forester Gifford Pinchot, declaring in a 1903 speech at Pinchot's home that "the object of our forest policy is not to preserve the forests because they are refuges for the wild creatures of the wilderness, but the making of prosperous homes. . . . Use must be the test by which the forester tries himself."

Pinchot's "rational use" philosophy guided America's natural resource policy until the mid-twentieth century. It justified the systematic harvesting of millions of trees in the sprawling national forests whose boundaries Roosevelt had expanded, and the drowning of vast river valleys behind massive dams that Roosevelt's Reclamation Service helped to build. This attitude toward nature triumphed in the New Deal era of the 1930s, when the federal government initiated colossal projects that undertook nothing less than reengineering the face of the continent—including the Tennessee Valley Authority, the Soil Conservation Service, and the Shelterbelt tree-planting project on the Great Plains. The huge reach of these New Deal projects also introduced millions of Americans to the concept that nature had to be treated with respect, helping to stimulate the post–World War II grassroots environmental movement.

USDA Forest Service, Grey Towers NHS

Image 27.15 The Father of the Forest Service An outdoorsman and accomplished fly fisherman, Gifford Pinchot helps his son cast a line on the Delaware River near his Pennsylvania home, ca. 1930.

Ron Chapple/Corbis

Image 27.16 Lake Powell, Utah Named for the famed explorer John Wesley Powell and formed by one of the several dams on the Colorado River, Lake Powell has been a focus of intense controversy. It drowned the spectacularly beautiful Glen Canyon but created recreational facilities for countless Americans.

ZUMA Press, Inc./Alamy Stock Photo

Image 27.17 Protesting on Capitol Hill, 2018 As climate disruption intensified, young people across the globe rallied for robust policies to protect the planet. Here, members of the youth-focused "Sunrise Movement" urge the U.S. Congress to adopt the climate-protecting "Green New Deal."

The rise of ecological science in the post–World War II era fundamentally changed the debate about the relation of nature to civilization. Ecologists charged that the apparent "rationality" of the earlier conservationists dangerously neglected the fateful intricacies of biological systems. They called attention to the stunningly complex webs of interrelationships that linked together seemingly unrelated organisms—and to the perils of tampering even slightly with the delicate biological fabrics that nature had taken millennia to weave. Rachel Carson helped to popularize the new outlook in her sensational 1962 exposé, *Silent Spring*, about the far-reaching effects of pesticides on birds, plants, and animals—including humans.

The advent of ecological studies coincided with a revival of preservationist sentiment, especially in the suburbs, where Americans increasingly dwelled. Hordes of affluent baby boomers took to America's trails, slopes, and waterways—often on public lands like Arizona's wondrous Grand Canyon National Park, or public waters like Utah's shimmering (and man-made) Lake Powell. Membership in environmental organizations such as the Sierra Club and the Audubon Society soared, as a generation infatuated with nature demanded a clean and green world. The first celebration of Earth Day, on April 22, 1970, marked the political maturation of modern-day environmentalism, which wedded scientific analysis with respect for nature's majesty. That same year saw the creation of the federal Environmental Protection Agency (EPA), soon followed by the Endangered Species Act and other legislation designed to regulate the relationship between humans and nature.

At the outset of the twenty-first century, global warming served dramatic notice that planet Earth was the biggest ecological system of them all—and one that did not recognize national boundaries. Scientific evidence confirmed that the world's climate was changing, thanks to the cumulative atmospheric residues of carbon-based fossil fuels (coal, oil, and gas) burned since the beginning of the Industrial Revolution. Planetary warming was wreaking global havoc, including extreme weather events, shifts in growing seasons for staple crops like wheat, corn, and rice, shrinking fresh-water supplies, and rising ocean temperatures that severely stressed already diminished fisheries. The world's peoples struggled to come to grips with these challenges, even as some Americans questioned whether humans had any responsibility for them. Yet climate skepticism gradually receded, as an ever-growing number of Americans—especially in flood- and hurricane-threatened coastal cities and the parched, wildfire-scorched West—came to acknowledge the potentially catastrophic consequences of human-driven climate change. Newly energetic environmental activists—conspicuously including young people whose futures are most at risk—pushed for Washington lawmakers to enact a "Green New Deal," a new chapter in the long struggle to sustain a healthy planet.

The financial world hastened to blame Roosevelt for the storm. It cried that this "quack" had unsettled industry with his boat-rocking tactics. Conservatives damned him as "Theodore the Meddler" and branded the current distress the "Roosevelt panic." The hot-tempered president angrily lashed back at his critics when he accused "certain malefactors of great wealth" of having deliberately engineered the monetary crisis to force the government to relax its assaults on trusts. Ironically, it was domineering financier J. P. Morgan, one of the most notorious of those so-called malefactors, who orchestrated a consortium of New York bankers to put an end to the panic.

Fortunately, the **panic of 1907** paved the way for long-overdue monetary reforms. Precipitating a currency shortage, the flurry laid bare the need for a more elastic medium of exchange. In a crisis of this sort, the hard-pressed banks were unable to increase the volume of money in circulation, and those with ample reserves were reluctant to lend to their less fortunate competitors. Congress in 1908 responded by passing the Aldrich-Vreeland Act, which authorized national banks to issue emergency currency backed by various kinds of collateral. The path was thus smoothed for the momentous Federal Reserve Act of 1913 (refer to "28-3 Wilson Battles the Bankers," p. 707).

27-11 The Rough Rider Thunders Out

Still warmly popular in 1908, Roosevelt could easily have won a second presidential nomination and almost certainly the election. But he felt bound by his impulsive postelection promise after his victory in 1904.

The departing president thus naturally sought a successor who would carry out "my policies." The man of his choice was amiable, ample-girthed, and huge-framed William Howard Taft, secretary of war and a mild progressive (refer to Image 27.18). As an heir apparent, he had often been called upon in Roosevelt's absence to "sit on the lid"—all 350 pounds of him. At the Republican convention of 1908 in Chicago, Roosevelt used his control of the party machinery—the "steamroller"—to push through Taft's nomination on the first ballot. Three weeks later, in mile-high Denver, in the heart of silver country, the Democrats nominated twice-beaten William Jennings Bryan.

The dull campaign of 1908 featured the rotund Taft and the now-balding "Boy Orator" both trying to don the progressive Roosevelt mantle. The solid Judge Taft read cut-and-dried speeches, while Bryan griped that Roosevelt had stolen his policies from the Bryanite camp. A majority of voters chose stability with Roosevelt-endorsed Taft, who polled 321 electoral votes to 162 for Bryan. The victor's popular count was 7,675,320 to 6,412,294. The election's only surprise came from the Socialists, who amassed 420,793 votes for Eugene V. Debs, the hero of the Pullman strike of 1894 (refer to "25-9 Coxey's Army and the Pullman Strike," pp. 635–636).

Roosevelt, ever in the limelight, left soon after the election for a lion hunt in Africa. His numerous enemies clinked glasses while toasting "Health to the lions," and a few irreverently prayed that some big cat would "do its duty." But TR survived, still bursting with energy at the age of fifty-one in 1909.

Roosevelt was branded by his adversaries as a wild-eyed radical, but his reputation as an eater of errant industrialists now seems inflated. He fought many a sham battle, and the number of laws he inspired was certainly not in proportion to the amount of noise he emitted. He was often under attack from the reigning business lords, but the more enlightened of them knew that they had a friend in the White House. Roosevelt should be remembered first and foremost as the cowboy who started to tame the bucking bronco of adolescent capitalism, thus ensuring it a long adult life.

TR's enthusiasm and perpetual youthfulness, like an overgrown Boy Scout's, appealed to the young of all ages. "You must always remember," a British diplomat cautioned his colleagues, "that the president is about six." He served as a political lightning rod to protect capitalists against popular

Image 27.18 Baby, Kiss Papa Good-bye Theodore Roosevelt leaves his baby, "My Policies," in the hands of his chosen successor, William Howard Taft. Friction between Taft and Roosevelt would soon erupt, however, prompting Roosevelt to return to politics and challenge Taft for the presidency.

indignation—and against socialism, which Roosevelt regarded as "ominous." He strenuously sought the middle road between unbridled individualism and paternalistic collectivism. His conservation crusade, which tried to mediate between the romantic wilderness-preservationists and the rapacious resource-predators, was probably his most typical and his most lasting achievement.

Yet, as with many reformers of his generation, TR's progressivism often wavered at the color line. He did speak out against lynching and boldly defied Southern segregationist sentiment in 1901 when he invited the Black leader Booker T. Washington to dine with his family at the White House. But five years later he also summarily ordered dishonorable discharges for more than 150 Black "buffalo soldiers" accused on trumped-up charges of inciting violence in Brownsville, Texas. The **Brownsville Affair** outraged the Black community. Only in 1972 did Congress at last pardon the unfairly accused men—only one of whom was then living—and retroactively grant them honorable discharges.

Several other contributions of Roosevelt lasted beyond his presidency. First, he greatly enlarged the power and prestige of the presidential office—and masterfully developed the technique of using the big stick of publicity as a political bludgeon. Second, he helped shape the progressive movement and beyond it the liberal reform campaigns later in the century. His Square Deal, in a sense, was the grandfather of the New Deal later launched by his fifth cousin, Franklin D. Roosevelt. Finally, to a greater degree than any of his predecessors, TR opened the eyes of Americans to the fact that they shared the world with other nations. As a great power, they had fallen heir to responsibilities—and had been seized by ambitions—from which there was no escaping.

27-12 Taft: A Round Peg in a Square Hole

William Howard Taft, with his ruddy complexion and upturned mustache, at first inspired widespread confidence. "Everybody loves a fat man," the saying went in a time when obesity was rarer and less stigmatized. The jovial 350-pound Taft, with "mirthquakes" of laughter bubbling up from his abundant abdomen, was personally popular. He had graduated second in his class at Yale and had established a sterling reputation as a lawyer and judge, though he was widely regarded as hostile to labor unions. He had been a trusted administrator under Roosevelt—in the Philippines, at home, and in Cuba, where he had served capably as a troubleshooter.

But "good old Will" suffered from lethal political handicaps. Roosevelt had led the conflicting elements of the Republican party by the sheer force of his personality. Taft, in contrast, had none of the arts of a dashing political leader and none of Roosevelt's zest for the fray (refer to Image 27.19). Recoiling from the clamor of controversy, he generally adopted an attitude of passivity toward

Image 27.19 **Ex-President Theodore Roosevelt Watches President Taft Struggle with the Demands of Government, 1910**

Congress. He was a poor judge of public opinion, and his candor made him a chronic victim of "foot-in-mouth" disease.

Taft was no doubt a mild progressive, but at heart he was more wedded to the status quo than to change. Significantly, his cabinet did not contain a single representative of the party's "insurgent" wing, which was on fire for reform of current abuses, especially the tariff.

27-13 The Dollar Goes Abroad as a Diplomat

Though ordinarily lethargic, Taft bestirred himself to use the lever of American investments to boost American political interests abroad, an approach to foreign policy that his critics denounced as **dollar diplomacy**. Washington warmly encouraged Wall Street bankers to sluice their surplus dollars into foreign areas of strategic concern to the United States, especially in the Far East and in the regions critical to the security of the Panama Canal. By preempting investors from rival powers, such as Germany, New York bankers would thus strengthen American defenses and foreign policies, while bringing further prosperity to their homeland—and to themselves. The almighty dollar thereby supplanted the big stick.

China's Manchuria was the object of Taft's most spectacular effort to inject the reluctant dollar into the Far Eastern theater. Newly ambitious Japan and imperialistic Russia, recent foes, controlled the railroads of this strategic province. President Taft saw in the Manchurian railway monopoly a possible strangulation of Chinese economic interests and a consequent slamming of the Open Door in the faces of U.S. merchants. In 1909, Secretary of State Philander C. Knox blunderingly proposed that a group of American and foreign bankers buy the Manchurian railroads and then turn them over to China under a self-liquidating arrangement. Both Japan and Russia, unwilling to be jockeyed out of their dominant position, bluntly rejected Knox's overtures. Taft was showered with ridicule.

Another dangerous new trouble spot was the revolution-riddled Caribbean—now virtually a Yankee lake. Hoping to head off trouble, Washington urged Wall Street bankers to pump dollars into the financial vacuums in Honduras and Haiti to keep out foreign funds. The United States, under the Monroe Doctrine, would not permit foreign nations to intervene, and consequently felt obligated to put its money where its mouth was to prevent economic and political instability.

Again, necessity was the mother of armed Caribbean intervention. Sporadic disorders in palm-fronded Cuba, Honduras, and the Dominican Republic brought American forces to these countries to restore order and protect American investment. A revolutionary upheaval in Nicaragua, partly fomented by American interests, resulted in the landing of twenty-five hundred marines in 1912. The marines remained in Nicaragua for thirteen years (refer to Map 28.1, p. 710).

27-14 Taft the Trustbuster

Taft managed to gain some fame as a crusher of monopolies. The ironic truth is that the placid Taft brought ninety suits against the trusts during his 4 years in office, as compared with some forty-four for Roosevelt in 7½ years.

By fateful happenstance, the most sensational judicial actions during the Taft regime came in 1911. In that year, the Supreme Court ordered the dissolution of the mighty Standard Oil Company, which was judged to be a combination in restraint of trade in violation of the Sherman Anti-Trust Act of 1890. At the same time, the Court handed down its famous "rule of reason." This doctrine held that only those combinations that "unreasonably" restrained trade were illegal. This fine-print proviso ripped a huge hole in the government's antitrust net.

Even more explosively, in 1911 Taft decided to press an antitrust suit against the U.S. Steel Corporation. This initiative infuriated Roosevelt, who had personally been involved in one of the mergers that prompted the suit. Once Roosevelt's protégé, President Taft was increasingly taking on the role of his antagonist. The stage was being set for a bruising confrontation.

27-15 Taft Splits the Republican Party

Lowering the barriers of the formidable protective tariff—the "Mother of Trusts"—was high on the agenda of the progressive members of the Republican party, and they at first thought they had a friend and ally in Taft. True to his campaign promises to reduce tariffs, Taft called Congress into special session in March 1909. The House proceeded to pass a moderately reductive bill, but senatorial reactionaries tacked on hundreds of upward tariff revisions. Only items such as hides, sea moss, and canary seed were left on the duty-free list. Much to the dismay of his supporters,

Taft signed the **Payne-Aldrich Bill**, rubbing salt in their wounds by proclaiming it "the best bill that the Republican party ever passed."

Taft revealed a further knack for shooting himself in the foot in his handling of conservation. The portly president was a dedicated conservationist, and his contributions—like the establishment of the Bureau of Mines to control mineral resources—actually equaled or surpassed those of Roosevelt. But his praiseworthy accomplishments were largely erased in the public mind by the noisy Ballinger-Pinchot quarrel that erupted in 1910.

When Secretary of the Interior Richard Ballinger opened public lands in Wyoming, Montana, and Alaska to corporate development, he was sharply criticized by Gifford Pinchot, chief of the Agriculture Department's Division of Forestry and a stalwart Rooseveltian. When Taft dismissed Pinchot on the narrow grounds of insubordination, a storm of protest arose from conservationists and from Roosevelt's friends, who were legion. The whole unsavory episode further widened the growing rift between the president and the former president, onetime bosom political partners.

The reformist wing of the Republican party was now up in arms, while Taft was being pushed increasingly into the embrace of the stand-pat Old Guard. By the spring of 1910, the Grand Old Party was split wide open, owing largely to the clumsiness of Taft. A suspicious Roosevelt returned triumphantly to New York in June 1910 and shortly thereafter stirred up a tempest. Unable to keep silent, he took to the stump at Osawatomie, Kansas, and shocked the Old Guard with a flaming speech. The doctrine that he proclaimed—popularly known as the **"New Nationalism"**—urged the national government to increase its power to remedy economic and social abuses.

Weakened by these internal divisions, the Republicans lost badly in the congressional elections of 1910. In a victory of landslide proportions, the Democrats emerged with 228 seats, leaving the once-dominant Republicans with only 161. In a further symptom of the reforming temper of the times, a Socialist representative, Austrian-born Victor L. Berger, was elected from Milwaukee.* The Republicans, by virtue of holdovers, retained the Senate, 51 to 41, but the insurgents in their midst were numerous enough to make that hold precarious.

27-16 The Taft-Roosevelt Rupture

The sputtering uprising in Republican ranks had now blossomed into a full-fledged revolt. Early in 1911 the National Progressive Republican League was formed, with the fiery, white-maned Senator La Follette of Wisconsin its leading candidate for the Republican presidential nomination. The assumption was that Roosevelt, an anti–third termer, would not permit himself to be "drafted."

But the restless Rough Rider began to change his views about third terms as he saw Taft, hand in glove with the hated Old Guard, discard "my policies." In February 1912, Roosevelt formally wrote to seven state governors that he was willing to accept the Republican nomination. His reasoning was that the third-term tradition applied to three *consecutive elective* terms. Exuberantly he cried, "My hat is in the ring!" and "The fight is on and I am stripped to the buff!"

Roosevelt forthwith seized the Progressive banner, while La Follette, who had served as a convenient pathbreaker, was awkwardly elbowed aside. Girded for battle, the Rough Rider came clattering into the presidential primaries then being held in many states. He shouted through half-clenched teeth that the president had fallen under the thumb of the reactionary bosses and that although Taft "means well, he means well feebly." The once-genial Taft, now in a fighting mood, retorted by branding Roosevelt supporters "emotionalists and neurotics."

A Taft-Roosevelt explosion was near in June 1912, when the Republican convention met in Chicago. The Rooseveltites, who were about 100 delegates short of winning the nomination, challenged the right of some 250 Taft delegates to be seated. Most of these contests were arbitrarily settled in favor of Taft, whose supporters held the throttle of the convention steamroller. The Roosevelt adherents, crying "fraud" and "naked theft," in the end refused to vote, and Taft triumphed.

Roosevelt, the supposedly good sportsman, refused to quit the game. Having tasted for the first time the bitter cup of defeat, he was now on fire to lead a third-party crusade.

27-17 The "Bull Moose" Campaign of 1912

Office-hungry Democrats—who had held the White House for only eight of the previous fifty-two years—were jubilant over the disruptive Republican brawl at the convention in Chicago. If they could come up with an outstanding reformist leader, they had an excellent chance to win the

*He was eventually denied his seat in 1919, during a wave of anti-communist hysteria.

White House. Such a leader appeared in Dr. Woodrow Wilson, once a mild conservative but now a militant progressive. The Virginia-born and Georgia-raised historian had made his name as a brilliant scholar of American government before rising in 1902 to the presidency of Princeton University, where he had achieved sweeping educational reforms.

Wilson entered politics in 1910 when New Jersey bosses, needing a respectable "front" candidate for the governorship, offered him the nomination. They expected to lead the academic novice by the nose, but to their surprise, Wilson waged a passionate reform campaign in which he assailed the "predatory" trusts and promised to return state government to the people. Riding the crest of the progressive wave, the "Schoolmaster in Politics" was swept into office. Once in the governor's chair, Wilson drove through the legislature a sheaf of forward-looking measures that made reactionary New Jersey one of the more liberal states—and its zealous chief executive a leading contender for the presidency.

When the Democrats met at Baltimore in 1912, Wilson was nominated on the forty-sixth ballot, aided by William Jennings Bryan's switch to his side. The Democrats gave Wilson a strong progressive platform to run on, dubbed the **New Freedom** program.

Surging events had meanwhile been thrusting Roosevelt to the fore as a candidate for the presidency on a third-party Progressive Republican ticket. The fighting ex-cowboy, angered by his recent rebuff, was eager to lead the charge. A pro-Roosevelt Progressive convention assembled in Chicago in August 1912. Dramatically symbolizing the rising political status of women, as well as Progressive support for the cause of social justice, settlement-house pioneer Jane Addams placed Roosevelt's name in nomination for the presidency. Thunderous applause erupted when Roosevelt declared, "We stand at Armageddon, and we battle for the Lord!" William Allen White, the caustic Kansas journalist, later wrote, "Roosevelt bit me and I went mad."

Roosevelt boasted that he felt "as strong as a bull moose," and the bull moose took its place with the donkey and the elephant in the American political zoo (refer to Image 27.20). As one poet whimsically put it,

> I want to be a Bull Moose,
> And with the Bull Moose stand
> With antlers on my forehead
> And a Big Stick in my hand.

Image 27.20 The Raging Bull, 1912 When Theodore Roosevelt bolted the Republican Party in 1912 to run as the candidate for the Progressive, or "Bull Moose" Party, he scrambled the political calculations of both the traditional parties—but in the end his candidacy split the Republican vote and helped to elect Woodrow Wilson.

Varying Viewpoints

Who Were the Progressives?

Debate about progressivism has revolved mainly around a question that is simple to ask but devilishly difficult to answer: Who were the progressives? It was once taken for granted that progressive reformers were simply the heirs of the Jeffersonian-Jacksonian-Populist reform crusades. They were the oppressed and downtrodden common folk who finally erupted in wrath and demanded their due.

But in his influential *Age of Reform* (1955), Richard Hofstadter astutely challenged that view. Progressive leaders, he argued, were not drawn from the ranks of society's poor and marginalized. Rather, they were middle-class people threatened from above by the emerging power of new corporate elites and from below by a restless working class. It was not economic deprivation but "status anxiety," Hofstadter insisted, that prompted these people to become reformers. Their psychological motivation, Hofstadter concluded, rendered many of their reform efforts quirky and ineffectual.

By contrast, "New Left" historians, notably Gabriel Kolko, argued that progressivism was dominated by established business leaders who successfully directed "reform" to their own conservative ends. In this view government regulation (as embodied in new agencies like the Federal Reserve Board and the Federal Tariff Commission, and in legislation like the Meat Inspection Act) simply accomplished what two generations of private efforts had failed to do: dampen cutthroat competition, stabilize markets, and make America safe for monopoly capitalism.

Still other scholars, notably Robert H. Wiebe and Samuel P. Hays, argued that the progressives were neither the psychologically or economically disadvantaged nor the old capitalist elite, but were, rather, members of a rapidly emerging, self-confident social class possessed of the new techniques of scientific management, technological expertise, and organizational know-how. This "organizational school" of historians did not see progressivism as a struggle of the "people" against the "interests," as a confused and nostalgic campaign by status-threatened reformers, or as a conservative coup d'état. The progressive movement, in this view, was by and large an effort to rationalize and modernize many social institutions by introducing the wise and impartial hand of government regulation.

This view had much to recommend it. Yet despite its widespread acceptance among historians, it could not adequately account for the titanic political struggles of the progressive era that the "organizational school" regarded as simple adjustments to modernity. It brushed over the deep philosophical differences that divided progressives themselves—such as between Roosevelt's New Nationalism and Wilson's New Freedom. Furthermore, as David Southern, Michael McGerr, and Thomas Leonard have shown, the "organizational school" often overlooked the racist assumptions that undergirded much progressive thinking. Many progressives, for example, supported segregation and eugenics even as they campaigned for fairer wages, cleaner cities, and better schools. In addition, the organizational approach did not account for the important role of women in advocating progressive reforms, as demonstrated by Robyn Muncy, Linda Gordon, and Theda Skocpol. Building the American welfare state in the early twentieth century, they have argued, was fundamentally a gendered activity inspired by a "female dominion" of social workers and "social feminists." Finally, scholars such as Daniel T. Rodgers have added that essential inspiration also came from across the Atlantic. Looking to their peers in Europe, American reformers adopted ideas and policies from London, Paris, and Berlin, though many of these programs would only bear fruit during the New Deal.

The overshadowing question of the 1912 campaign was which of two varieties of progressivism would prevail—Roosevelt's New Nationalism or Wilson's New Freedom. Both men favored a more active government role in economic and social affairs, but they disagreed sharply over specific strategies. Roosevelt preached the theories spun out by the progressive thinker Herbert Croly in his book *The Promise of American Life* (1910). Croly and TR both favored continued consolidation of trusts and labor unions, paralleled by the growth of powerful regulatory agencies in Washington. Roosevelt and his "bull moosers" also campaigned for woman suffrage and a broad program of social welfare, including minimum wage laws and publicly supported health care. Clearly, the bull moose Progressives looked forward to the kind of comprehensive welfare state that Franklin Roosevelt's New Deal would one day make a reality.

Wilson's New Freedom, by contrast, favored small enterprise, entrepreneurship, and the free functioning of minimally regulated and unmonopolized markets. The Democrats shunned social-welfare proposals and pinned their economic faith on competition—on the "man on the make," as Wilson put it. The New Freedom program called for banking reform and tariff reductions, but its keynote was not regulation but fragmentation of the big industrial combines, chiefly by means of vigorous enforcement of the antitrust laws. The election of 1912 thus offered the voters a choice not merely of policies but of political and economic philosophies—a rarity in U.S. history.

Former professor Wilson won handily, with 435 electoral votes and 6,296,547 popular votes, or 41 percent of the total. The "third-party" candidate, Roosevelt, finished second, receiving 88 electoral votes and 4,118,571 popular votes. Taft won only 8 electoral votes and 3,486,720 popular votes (refer to Map 27.1). To the impressive tally for both progressive candidates must be added some support for the Socialist candidate, the persistent Eugene V. Debs, who rolled up 900,672 votes, 6 percent of the total cast. Starry-eyed Socialists dreamed of being in the White House within eight years.

Taft went on to a fruitful old age. He taught law for eight pleasant years at Yale University and in 1921 became chief justice of the Supreme Court—a job for which he was far more happily suited than the presidency.

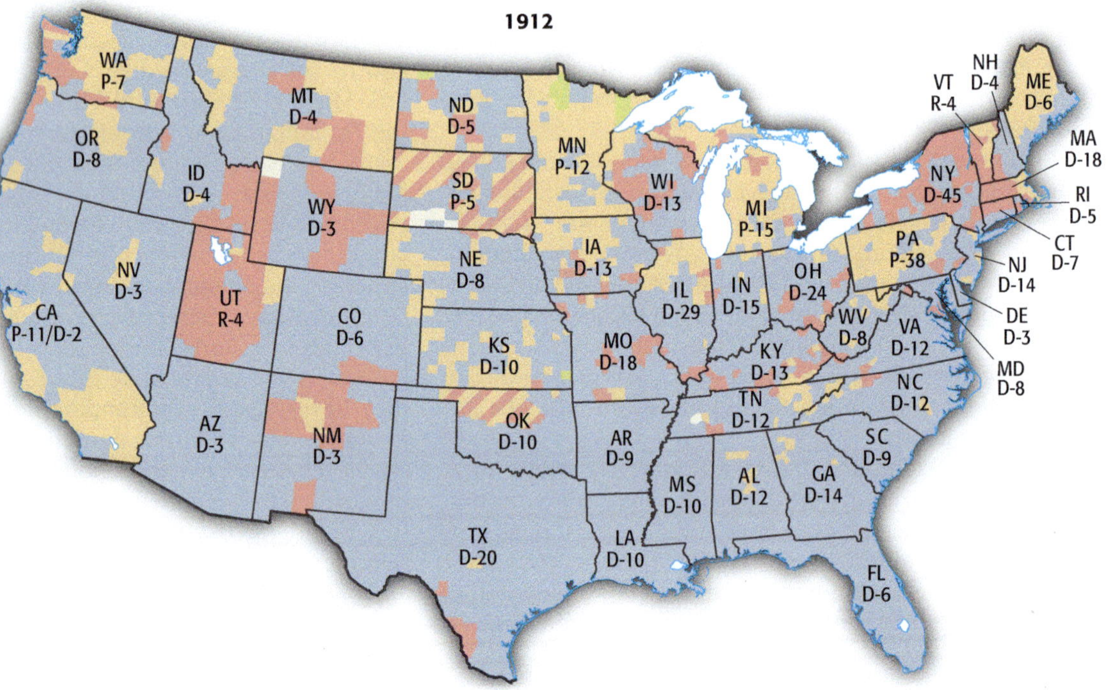

Candidate (Party)	Electoral Vote		Popular Vote	
Wilson (Democrat)	435	82.0%	6,296,547	41.9%
Roosevelt (Progressive)	88	16.5%	4,118,571	27.4%
Taft (Republican)	8	1.5%	3,486,720	23.2%
Debs (Socialist)	0	0.0%	900,672	6.0%

No returns, unsettled, etc.

Map 27.1 Presidential Election of 1912 (showing votes by county, with electoral vote by state) The Republican split surely boosted Wilson to victory, as he failed to win a clear majority in any state outside the old Confederacy. The election gave the Democrats solid control of the White House and both houses of Congress for the first time since the Civil War.

Chapter Summary

The progressive movement of the early twentieth century became the greatest American reform crusade since abolitionism. Inaugurated by old Populists, socialists, social gospelers, female reformers, and muckraking journalists, progressivism became a widely popular effort to strengthen government's power to address the many social and economic problems associated with industrialization and urbanization.

Progressivism began at the city and state levels, where it initially focused on "good government" political reforms to corral corrupt bosses. It then turned to correcting a host of social and economic evils that seemed to require national action by the federal government. Women played an especially critical role in galvanizing progressive social concern. Seeing such issues as child labor, poor tenement housing, and consumer causes as a natural extension of their traditional roles as wives and mothers, female activists brought significant changes in both law and public attitudes in these areas.

At the national level, Roosevelt's Square Deal vigorously deployed the federal government to promote the public interest and mediate conflicts between labor interests and the corporate trusts. Rooseveltian progressivism also focused attention on consumer and environmental concerns. Conservation became an important public crusade under Roosevelt, although sharp disagreements divided wilderness preservationists like John Muir from moderate conservationists like Roosevelt and his chief forester Gifford Pinchot, who favored the "multiple use" of nature.

Roosevelt personally selected his longtime subordinate Taft as his political successor, expecting him to carry out "my policies." But Taft proved to be a poor politician who fell under the thumb of the conservative Republican Old Guard and rapidly lost public support. The progressives' hostility to Taft split the Republican party, and when Roosevelt failed to win the nomination, he launched a fiery third-party crusade in the 1912 election under the banner of his new Progressive ("Bull Moose") Party. Delighted at the Republican split, Democrats nominated New Jersey governor Woodrow Wilson, a strong reformer. Roosevelt and Wilson offered competing progressive visions in the campaign. Roosevelt's New Nationalism stressed regulation of business and labor along with developing a comprehensive welfare state, while Wilson's New Freedom promoted economic fairness and competition. Wilson won the fiercely contested election, with Roosevelt second, Taft third, and Socialist Eugene Debs fourth.

Key Terms

- social gospel (680)
- muckrakers (680)
- initiative (684)
- referendum (684)
- recall (684)
- Australian ballot (684)
- *Muller v. Oregon* (686)
- *Lochner v. New York* (687)
- Triangle Shirtwaist Company fire (687)
- Elkins Act (689)
- Meat Inspection Act (691)
- Pure Food and Drug Act (691)
- Newlands Reclamation Act (692)
- Hetch Hetchy Valley (692)
- panic of 1907 (696)
- Brownsville Affair (697)
- dollar diplomacy (698)
- Payne-Aldrich Bill (699)
- New Nationalism (699)
- New Freedom (700)

People to Know

- Ida Tarbell
- Henry Demarest Lloyd
- Thorstein Veblen
- Eugene Debs
- Jacob A. Riis
- Robert M. ("Fighting Bob") La Follette
- Hiram W. Johnson
- Florence Kelley
- Frances E. Willard
- Gifford Pinchot
- John Muir
- Herbert Croly

Chronology

1892	• Sierra Club founded	
1899	• National Consumers League founded	
1901	• Commission system established in Galveston, Texas • Progressive Robert La Follette elected governor of Wisconsin	• American Socialist Party of America formed
1902	• Lincoln Steffens and Ida Tarbell publish muckraking exposés • Anthracite coal strike	• Newlands Act
1903	• Department of Commerce and Labor established • Elkins Act	• Women's Trade Union League founded
1904	• *Northern Securities* case • Roosevelt wins election to first full term as president	
1905	• *Lochner v. New York*	
1906	• Hepburn Act • Upton Sinclair publishes *The Jungle*	• Meat Inspection Act • Pure Food and Drug Act
1907	• "Roosevelt panic"	
1908	• *Muller v. Oregon* • Taft defeats Bryan for presidency	• Aldrich-Vreeland Act
1909	• Payne-Aldrich tariff	
1910	• Ballinger-Pinchot affair • Washington State grants woman suffrage	
1911	• Triangle Shirtwaist Company fire • Standard Oil antitrust case	• U.S. Steel Corporation antitrust suit • California grants woman suffrage
1912	• Taft wins Republican nomination over Roosevelt • Wilson defeats Taft and Roosevelt for presidency	• Arizona, Kansas, and Oregon grant woman suffrage • Children's Bureau established in Department of Labor
1913	• Seventeenth Amendment passed (direct election of U.S. senators) • Federal Reserve Act	• San Francisco decides to build Hetch Hetchy Reservoir
1920	• Women's Bureau established in Department of Labor	

To Learn More

Peri E. Arnold, *Remaking the Presidency: Roosevelt, Taft, and Wilson, 1901–1916* (2009)

John Morton Blum, *The Republican Roosevelt* (1954)

Nancy Cott, *The Grounding of Modern Feminism* (1987)

Glenda Gilmore, *Gender and Jim Crow: Women and the Politics of White Supremacy in North Carolina, 1896–1920* (1996)

Doris Kearns Goodwin, *The Bully Pulpit: Theodore Roosevelt, William Howard Taft, and the Golden Age of Journalism* (2013)

Samuel P. Hays, *Conservation and the Gospel of Efficiency* (1959)

Richard Hofstadter, *The Age of Reform* (1955)

T. J. Jackson Lears, *No Place of Grace: Antimodernism and the Transformation of American Culture* (1981)

_________, *Rebirth of a Nation: The Making of Modern America, 1877–1920* (2009)

Thomas Leonard, *Illiberal Reformers: Race, Eugenics & American Economics in the Progressive Era* (2017)

Robyn Muncy, *Creating a Female Dominion in American Reform* (1991)

Kevin P. Murphy, *Political Manhood: Red Bloods, Mollycoddles, and the Politics of Progressive Era Reform* (2008)

Daniel T. Rodgers, *Atlantic Crossings: Social Politics in a Progressive Age* (1998)

Nick Salvatore, *Eugene V. Debs: Citizen and Socialist* (1982)

Kathryn Kish Sklar, *Florence Kelley and the Nation's Work* (1995)

Chapter 28

Wilsonian Progressivism in Peace and War: 1913–1920

American enterprise is not free; the man with only a little capital is finding it harder and harder to get into the field, more and more impossible to compete with the big fellow. Why? Because the laws of this country do not prevent the strong from crushing the weak.

Woodrow Wilson, The New Freedom, 1913

Chapter Outline

- Wilson the idealist
- Tackling the tariff, the banks, and the trusts
- Wilson's diplomacy in the Western Hemisphere
- War in Europe and American neutrality
- The reelection of Wilson, 1916
- America goes to war, 1917
- Wilsonian idealism and the Fourteen Points
- Propaganda and civil liberties
- Workers, African Americans, and women on the home front
- The United States fights in France
- The influenza pandemic
- Peacemaking at Paris and the League of Nations
- The Senate rejects the Versailles Treaty

Woodrow Wilson's two tumultuous presidential terms saw the apex of progressive achievements, as well as entanglement in a global war that helped snuff out the reform fires at home. That outcome was ironic, as America entered the conflict buoyed by the same crusading idealism and confidence that had driven domestic progressivism.

Focus Questions

1. How did Wilsonian progressivism overcome the "triple wall of privilege"?
2. What were the central features of Wilson's moralistic foreign policy? How did he apply those principles to Latin America and then to Europe in World War I?
3. What was America's response to the outbreak of World War I? Why did the United States finally enter the war against Germany?
4. Why did Woodrow Wilson proclaim America's entry into the war as an ideological crusade for universal democracy and freedom, rather than simply an attempt to curb German military power?
5. How did America mobilize for war, and what was the war's impact on workers, women, and African Americans?
6. Why was Wilson forced to compromise his idealistic Fourteen Points peace plan at the Versailles Conference? What made the battle over ratifying the Treaty of Versailles so bitter, and why was the Treaty defeated?

28-1 Wilson: The Idealist in Politics

(Thomas) Woodrow Wilson, the second Democratic president since 1861, looked like the ascetic intellectual he was, with his clean-cut features, pinch-nose eyeglasses, and trim figure. Born in Virginia shortly before the Civil War and reared in Georgia and the

The Presence of the Past: The Senate: "Beautiful Machine" or Cemetery of Democracy?

Contending Voices: Battle of the Ballot

Varying Viewpoints: Woodrow Wilson: Realist or Idealist?

Carolinas, the professor-politician was the first man from a former Confederate state to reach the White House since Zachary Taylor, sixty-four years earlier (refer to Image 28.1). He brought with him the corrosive racial attitudes of the post-Reconstruction white South. In an essay on Reconstruction, he called the newly emancipated freedmen a "host of dusky children untimely put out of school." "The only place in the world, where nothing has to be explained to me," he once said, "is the South." Yet he fiercely identified with the unified nation. "Because I love the South," he wrote, "I rejoice in the failure of the Confederacy."

Son of a Presbyterian minister, Wilson was reared in an atmosphere of fervent piety, and he deftly used the presidential pulpit to preach his inspirational political sermons. "The President is at liberty, both in law and in conscience," he declared, "to be as big a man as he can." Convinced that Congress could not function properly unless the president got out in front and provided leadership, Wilson repeatedly relied on his eloquence to appeal over the heads of legislators to the sovereign people.

Splendid though Wilson's intellectual equipment was, he suffered from serious defects of personality. Incapable of acting the showman like "Teddy" Roosevelt, he lacked the common touch and knew it. Roosevelt "appeals to [the voters'] imagination; I do not," Wilson reflected. "He is a real, vivid person, whom they have seen and shouted themselves hoarse over and voted for, millions strong. I am a vague, conjectural personality, more made up of opinions and academic prepossessions than of human traits and red corpuscles."

ClassicStock/Alamy Stock Photo

Image 28.1 Woodrow Wilson (1856–1924), cover of *Life*, 1912 Before his election to the presidency of the United States in 1912, Wilson served as president of Princeton University (1902–1910) and governor of New Jersey (1910–1912). In all three offices, he earned a reputation as a moral idealist and reformer. In this *Life* magazine cover, he is depicted as a stern Roman consul. Wilson's academic background is represented by the scholarly owl at his side.

28-2 Wilson Tackles the Tariff

Leading with vigorous, methodical executive action, Wilson redefined the American presidency for the modern age. Few presidents have arrived at the White House with a clearer program than Wilson's or one destined to be so fully achieved. The new president called for an all-out assault on what he called "the triple wall of privilege": the tariff, the banks, and the trusts.

He tackled the tariff first, summoning Congress into special session in early 1913. In a precedent-shattering move, he did not send his presidential message over to the Capitol to be read loudly by a bored clerk, as had been the custom since Jefferson's day. Instead, he appeared in person before a joint session of Congress and presented his appeal with stunning clarity and force.

The House swiftly passed the **Underwood Tariff**, which provided for a substantial reduction of rates. When a swarm of lobbyists descended on the Senate seeking to disembowel the bill, Wilson promptly issued a combative message to the people, urging them to hold their elected representatives in line. The tactic worked. The force of public opinion, aroused by the president's oratory, secured late in 1913 final approval of the bill Wilson wanted.

The new Underwood Tariff substantially reduced import fees. It also was a landmark in tax legislation. Under authority granted by the recently ratified Sixteenth Amendment, Congress enacted a graduated income tax, beginning with a modest levy on incomes over $3,000 (then considerably higher than the average wage worker's annual income of $740). (Refer to the text of the Sixteenth Amendment in the Appendix.) By 1917, revenue from the income tax shot ahead of receipts from the tariff, helping to finance American intervention in World War I (refer to "28-11 War by Act of Germany," pp. 715–717). The income tax has since become the chief source of federal revenue.

28-3 Wilson Battles the Bankers

A second bastion of the "triple wall of privilege" was the antiquated and inadequate banking and currency system, long since outgrown by the Republic's lusty economic expansion. The country's financial structure, still creaking along under the Civil War National Banking Act, revealed glaring defects. Its most serious shortcoming, as exposed by the panic of 1907, was the inelasticity of the currency. Banking reserves were heavily concentrated in New York and a handful of other large cities and could not be mobilized in times of financial stress into areas that were badly pinched.

A House committee chaired by Congressman Arséne Pujo, a Louisiana Democrat, influenced reformers by tracing the tentacles of the "money monster" into the hidden vaults of American banking and business. President Wilson's confidant, progressive-minded Massachusetts attorney Louis D. Brandeis, further fanned the flames of reform with his incendiary though scholarly book *Other People's Money and How the Bankers Use It* (1914).

In June 1913, in a second dramatic personal appearance before both houses of Congress, the president delivered a stirring plea for sweeping reform of the banking system. He ringingly endorsed Democratic proposals for a decentralized bank in government hands, as opposed to Republican demands for a huge private bank with fifteen branches. Again appealing to the sovereign people, Wilson scored another triumph. In 1913, he signed the epochal **Federal Reserve Act**, the most important piece of economic legislation between the Civil War and the New Deal (refer to Image 28.2).

The Granger Collection, NYC

Image 28.2 Reading the Death Warrant This cartoon appeared in a New York newspaper soon after Woodrow Wilson called for dramatic reform of the banking system before both houses of Congress. With the "money trust" of bankers and businessmen cowed, Wilson was able to win popular and congressional support for the Federal Reserve Act of 1913.

The new Federal Reserve Board, appointed by the president, oversaw a nationwide system of twelve regional reserve districts, each with its own central bank. Although these regional banks were owned by member financial institutions, the final authority of the Federal Reserve Board guaranteed a substantial measure of public control. The board was also empowered to issue paper money—"Federal Reserve Notes"—backed by commercial paper, such as promissory notes of businesspeople. Thus, the amount of money in circulation could be swiftly increased as needed for the legitimate requirements of business.

28-4 The President Tames the Trusts

Without pausing for breath, Wilson pushed toward the last remaining rampart in the "triple wall of privilege"—the trusts. His third personal appearance before Congress led to passage of the **Federal Trade Commission Act** of 1914. The new law empowered a presidentially appointed commission to turn a searchlight on industries engaged in interstate commerce, such as the meatpackers. The commissioners were expected to crush monopoly at the source by rooting out unfair trade practices, including unlawful competition, false advertising, mislabeling, adulteration, and bribery.

The knot of monopoly was further cut by the **Clayton Anti-Trust Act** of 1914. It lengthened the shopworn Sherman Act's list of business practices that were deemed objectionable, including price discrimination and interlocking directorates (whereby the same individuals served as directors of supposedly competing firms), an end often achieved through **holding companies** (refer to Figure 28.1).

The Clayton Act also conferred long-overdue benefits on labor. Conservative courts had unexpectedly been ruling that trade unions, such as striking hatmakers in Danbury, Connecticut,

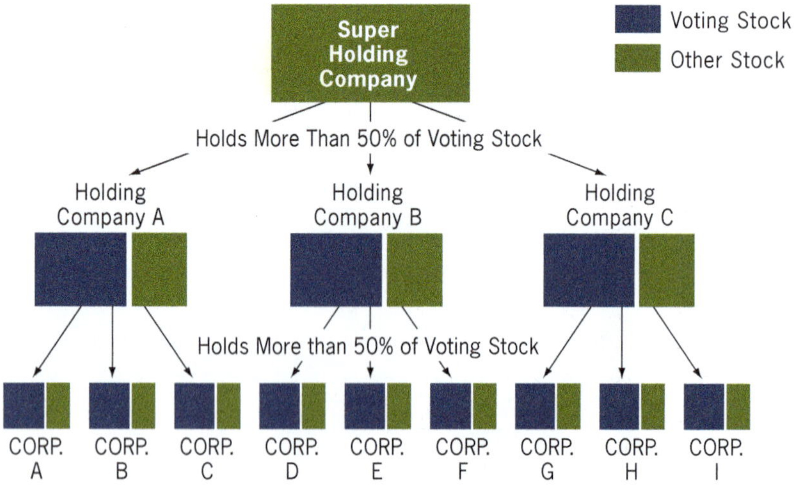

Figure 28.1 Organization of Holding Companies Keep in mind that the voting stock of a corporation is often only a fraction of the total stock.

fell under the antimonopoly restraints of the Sherman Act. The new law exempted labor and agricultural organizations from antitrust prosecution, while explicitly legalizing strikes and peaceful picketing. Union leader Samuel Gompers hailed the act as the Magna Carta of labor because it legally lifted human labor out of the category of "a commodity or article of commerce." But the rejoicing was premature, as conservative judges in later years continued to clip the wings of the union movement.

28-5 Wilson at the Peak

Having treated the nation to a dazzling demonstration of vigorous presidential leadership, Wilson pressed ahead with further reforms. The Federal Farm Loan Act of 1916 made credit available to farmers at low rates of interest—as long demanded by the Populists. The Warehouse Act of 1916 authorized loans on the security of staple crops—another Populist idea. Other laws benefited rural America by providing for highway construction and the establishment of agricultural extension work in the state colleges.

Sweaty laborers also made gains as the progressive wave foamed forward. Sailors, treated brutally from cat-o'-nine-tails days onward, were given relief by the La Follette Seaman's Act of 1915 requiring decent treatment and a living wage on American merchant ships. Wilson further helped workers with the **Workingmen's Compensation Act** of 1916, granting assistance to federal civil-service employees during periods of disability, as well as an act restricting child labor on products flowing into interstate commerce. (The stand-pat Supreme Court soon invalidated the latter law, however.) The **Adamson Act** of 1916 established an eight-hour day for all 1.7 million employees on trains in interstate commerce—with extra pay for overtime.

Wilson earned the enmity of businesspeople and bigots but endeared himself to progressives when in 1916 he nominated for the Supreme Court the prominent reformer Louis D. Brandeis—the first Jew to be called to the high bench. Yet Wilson's progressivism had its limits, and it clearly stopped short of better treatment for Black citizens.

Since the civil service reforms of the 1880s, thousands of African Americans had secured jobs in the federal government, where pay and promotion in racially integrated offices fueled the growth of Washington, DC's Black middle class. The Southern-bred Wilson reinstituted segregation in the federal bureaucracy, curtailing Black workers' opportunities for advancement. When a delegation of Black leaders personally protested to him, the schoolmasterish president declared himself offended and had them removed from the White House.

28-6 New Directions in Foreign Policy

In one important area, Wilson chose not to answer the trumpet call of the bull moosers. In contrast to Roosevelt and even Taft, Wilson recoiled at first from an aggressive foreign policy. Hating imperialism, he was repelled by TR's big stickism. Suspicious of Wall Street, he detested the so-called dollar diplomacy of Taft.

In office only a week, Wilson declared war on dollar diplomacy. He proclaimed that the government would no longer offer special support to American investors in Latin America and China. Shivering from this Wilsonian bucket of cold water, American bankers pulled out of the Taft-engineered six-nation loan to China the next day.

In a similarly self-denying vein, Wilson persuaded Congress in early 1914 to repeal the Panama Canal Tolls Act of 1912, which had exempted American coastwise shipping from tolls and thereby provoked sharp protests from injured Britain. The president further chimed in with the anti-imperial song of Bryan and other Democrats when he signed the **Jones Act** in 1916. It granted to the Philippines the boon of territorial status and promised independence as soon as a "stable government" could be established. Wilson's racial prejudices, however, made

Historical/Getty Images

Image 28.3 U.S. Marines in Haiti, 1919 The United States sent the marines to Haiti in 1915 to protect American economic interests. They remained for nineteen years.

it difficult for him to anticipate anything other than a long political tutelage for the Filipinos. Indeed, not until July 4, 1946—thirty years later—did the United States accept Philippine independence.

Political turmoil in Haiti soon forced Wilson to eat some of his anti-imperialist words. The climax of disorder came in 1914–1915, when an outraged populace literally tore to pieces the brutal Haitian president. In 1915, Wilson reluctantly dispatched marines to protect American lives and property. They remained for nineteen years, making Haiti an American protectorate (refer to Image 28.3). In 1916, he stole a page from Roosevelt's corollary to the Monroe Doctrine and concluded a treaty with Haiti providing for U.S. supervision of finances and the police.

In the same year, Wilson sent the leathernecked marines to quell riots in the Dominican Republic, and that debt-cursed land came under the shadow of the American eagle's wings for the next eight years. In 1917, the United States purchased from Denmark the Virgin Islands, in the West Indies, tightening the grip of Uncle Sam in these shark-infested waters. Increasingly, the Caribbean Sea, with its vital approaches to the now-navigable Panama Canal, was becoming a Yankee moat (refer to Map 28.1).

28-7 Moralistic Diplomacy in Mexico

Rifle bullets whining across the southern border served as a constant reminder that all was not quiet in Mexico. For decades, Mexico had been sorely exploited by foreign investors in oil, railroads, and mines. By 1913, American capitalists had sunk about a billion dollars into the underdeveloped but generously endowed country.

But if Mexico was rich, the Mexicans were poor. Fed up with their miserable lot, they at last revolted. Their revolution took an ugly turn in early 1913, when a conscienceless clique (with the support of President Taft's ambassador to Mexico) murdered the popular new revolutionary president and installed General Victoriano Huerta, a Huichol Indian, in the president's chair. All this chaos accelerated a massive migration of Mexicans to the United States. More than a million Spanish-speaking newcomers tramped across the southern border in the first three decades of the twentieth century. Settling mostly in Texas, New Mexico, Arizona, and California, they swung

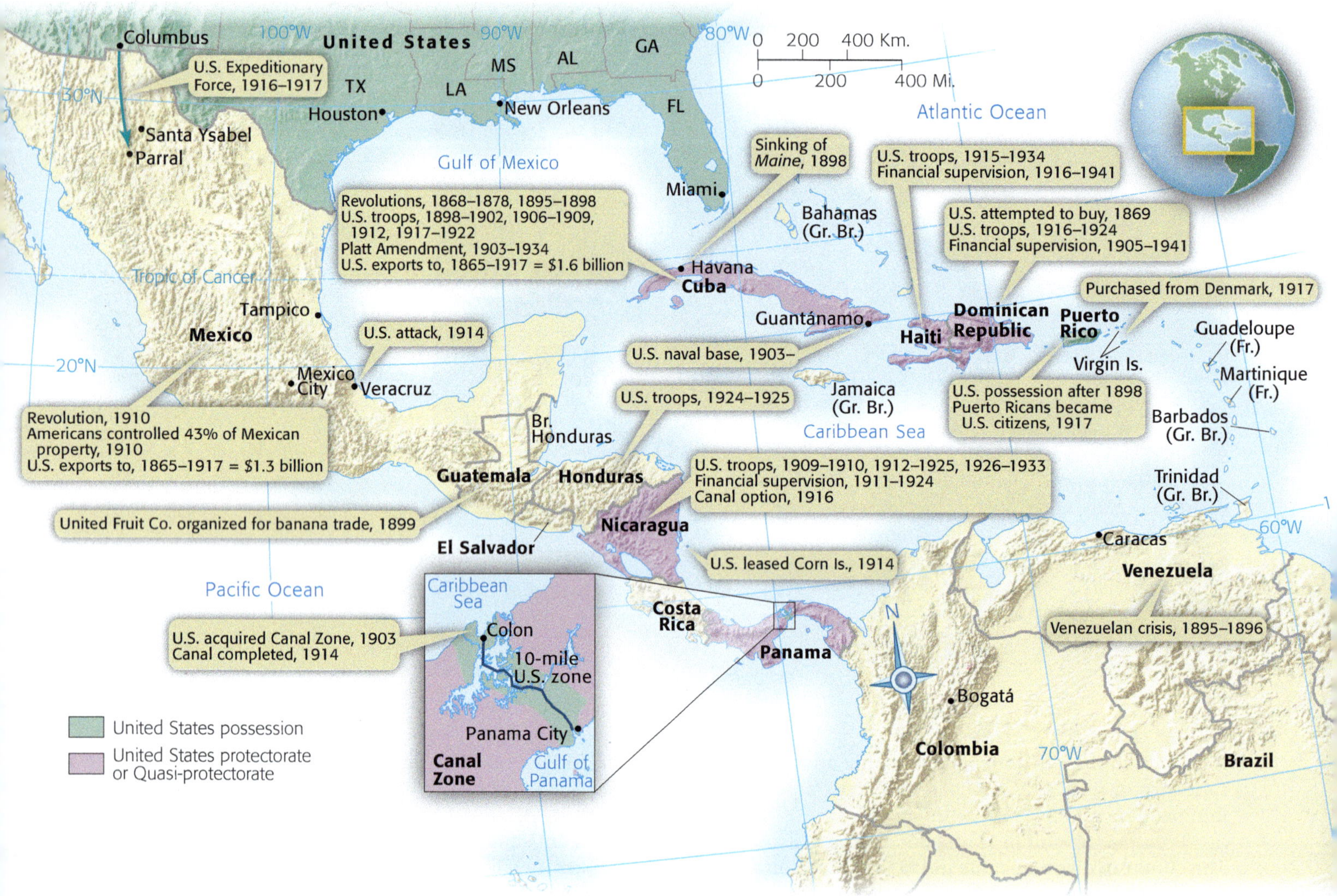

Map 28.1 The United States in the Caribbean, 1898–1941 This map explains why many Latin Americans accused the United States of turning the Caribbean Sea into a "Yankee lake." It also suggests that Uncle Sam was much less "isolationist" in his own backyard than he was in faraway Europe or Asia.

picks building highways and railroads or followed the fruit harvests as pickers. Though often segregated in Spanish-speaking enclaves, they helped to create a unique borderland culture that blended Mexican and American folkways.

The revolutionary bloodshed also menaced American lives and property in Mexico. Cries for intervention burst from the lips of American jingoes. Prominent among those chanting for war was the influential chain newspaper publisher William Randolph Hearst, whose views presumably were colored by his ownership of a Mexican ranch larger than Rhode Island. Yet once again, President Wilson refused to practice the same old dollar diplomacy of his predecessors, deeming it "perilous" to determine foreign policy "in the terms of material interest."

Wilson strove as best he could to steer a moral course in Mexico. He sent his aggressive ambassador packing, imposed an arms embargo, and refused to recognize officially the murderous government of "that brute" Huerta, even though most foreign powers acknowledged Huerta's bloody-handed regime. "I am going to teach the South American republics to elect good men," the former professor declared (refer to Image 28.4). He put his munitions where his mouth was in 1914, when he allowed American arms to flow to Huerta's principal rivals, white-bearded Venustiano Carranza and the firebrand Francisco ("Pancho") Villa.

The Mexican volcano erupted at the Atlantic seaport of Tampico in April 1914, when a small party of American sailors was arrested. The Mexicans promptly released the captives and apologized, but they refused the affronted American admiral's demand for a salute of twenty-one guns. Wilson, determined to eliminate Huerta, asked Congress for authority to use force against Mexico. Before Congress could act, Wilson ordered the navy to seize the Mexican port of Veracruz to thwart the arrival of a German steamer carrying Huerta-bound guns and ammunition.

Just as a full-dress shooting conflict seemed inevitable, Wilson was rescued by an offer of mediation from the ABC Powers—Argentina, Brazil, and Chile. Huerta collapsed in July 1914 under pressure from within and without. He was succeeded by his archrival, Venustiano Carranza, who hotly resented Wilson's military meddling. The whole sorry **Tampico Incident** did not augur well for the future of United States–Mexican relations.

"Pancho" Villa, a combination of bandit and Robin Hood, had meanwhile stolen the spotlight (refer to Image 28.5). He emerged as the chief rival to President Carranza, whom Wilson now reluctantly supported. Challenging Carranza's authority while also punishing the "gringos," in January 1916, Villa's men ruthlessly hauled sixteen young American mining engineers off a train traveling through northern Mexico and killed them. A month later, Villa and his followers, hoping to provoke a war between Wilson and Carranza, blazed across the border into Columbus, New Mexico, and murdered another nineteen Americans.

General John J. ("Black Jack")* Pershing, a grim-faced and ramrod-erect veteran of the Cuban and Philippine campaigns, was ordered to break up the bandit band. His hastily organized force of several thousand mounted troops penetrated deep into rugged Mexico with surprising speed. They clashed with Carranza's forces and mauled the Villistas but missed capturing Villa himself. As the threat of war with Germany loomed larger, the invading army was withdrawn in January 1917.

Image 28.4 Wilson Confronts Huerta A Mexican view of the tense standoff between Wilson and the Mexican president, Victoriano Huerta. The artist's rendering seems to reflect the famous observation of long-time Mexican leader Porfirio Diaz: "Poor Mexico! So far from God, so close to the United States."

Image 28.5 "Pancho" Villa with His Ragtag Army in Mexico, ca. 1916 His daring, impetuosity, and horsemanship made Villa a hero to the masses of northern Mexico. Yet he proved to be a violent and ineffective crusader against social abuses, and he was assassinated in 1923.

*So called from his earlier service as an officer with the crack Black 10th Cavalry.

28-8 Thunder Across the Sea

Europe's powder magazine, long smoldering, blew up in the summer of 1914, when the flaming pistol of a Serb patriot killed the heir to the throne of Austria-Hungary in Sarajevo. An outraged Vienna government, backed by Germany, forthwith presented a stern ultimatum to neighboring Serbia.

An explosive chain reaction followed. Tiny Serbia, backed by its powerful Slav neighbor Russia, refused to bend the knee sufficiently. The Russian tsar began to mobilize his ponderous war machine, menacing Germany on the east, even as his ally, France, confronted Germany on the west. In alarm, the Germans struck suddenly at France through unoffending Belgium; their objective was to knock their ancient enemy out of action so that they would have two free hands to repel Russia. Great Britain, its coastline jeopardized by the assault on Belgium, was sucked into the conflagration on the side of France.

Almost overnight most of Europe was locked in a fight to the death. On one side were arrayed the **Central Powers:** Germany and Austria-Hungary, and later Turkey and Bulgaria. On the other side were the **Allies:** principally France, Britain, and Russia, and later Japan and Italy. Americans thanked God for the ocean moats and self-righteously congratulated themselves on having had ancestors wise enough to have abandoned the hell pits of Europe. America felt strong, snug, smug, and secure—but not for long.

President Wilson issued the routine neutrality proclamation and called on Americans to be neutral in thought as well as deed. But such scrupulous evenhandedness proved difficult. Both sides wooed the great neutral in the West. The British enjoyed the boon of close cultural, linguistic, and economic ties with America and had the added advantage of controlling most of the transatlantic cables. Their censors sheared away war stories harmful to the Allies and drenched the United States with tales of German bestiality. The Germans and the Austro-Hungarians counted on the natural sympathies of their transplanted countrymen in America. Those with blood ties to the Central Powers numbered some 11 million in 1914, and some of these recent immigrants expressed noisy sympathy for the fatherland. Most, however, were simply grateful to be so distant from the fray (refer to Table 28.1).

The majority of Americans were anti-German from the outset. With his villainous upturned mustache, Kaiser Wilhelm II seemed the embodiment of arrogant autocracy, an impression strengthened by Germany's ruthless strike at neutral Belgium. German and Austrian agents further tarnished the image of the Central Powers in American eyes when they resorted to violence in American factories and ports. When a German operative in 1915 absentmindedly left his briefcase on a New York elevated car, its documents detailing plans for industrial sabotage were quickly discovered and publicized, further inflaming American opinion against the kaiser. Still, most Americans earnestly hoped to stay out of the horrible war.

Table 28.1 Principal Immigrant Nationalities in the United States, Census of 1910

Country of Origin		Foreign-Born	Natives with Two Foreign-Born Parents	Natives with One Foreign-Born Parent	Total
Central Powers	Germany	2,501,181	3,911,847	1,869,590	8,282,618
	Austria-Hungary	1,670,524	900,129	131,133	2,701,786
Allied Powers	Great Britain	1,219,968	852,610	1,158,474	3,231,052
	(Ireland)*	1,352,155	2,141,577	1,010,628	4,504,360
	Russia	1,732,421	949,316	70,938	2,752,675
	Italy	1,343,070	695,187	60,103	2,098,360
TOTAL (for all foreign countries, including those not listed)		13,345,545	12,916,311	5,981,526	32,243,282
Percentage of total U.S. population (91,972,266)		14.5	14.0	6.5	35.0

*Ireland was not yet independent.

Table 28.2 U.S. Exports to Belligerents, 1914–1916

Belligerent	1914	1915	1916	1916 Figure as a Percentage of 1914 Figure
Britain	$594,271,863	$911,794,954	$1,526,685,102	257%
France	159,818,924	369,397,170	628,851,988	393
Italy*	74,235,012	184,819,688	269,246,105	363
Germany	344,794,276	28,863,354	288,899	0.08

*Italy joined the Allies in April 1915.

28-9 America Earns Blood Money

When Europe burst into flames in 1914, the United States was bogged down in a worrisome business recession. But as fate would have it, British and French war orders soon pulled American industry out of the morass of hard times and onto a peak of war-born prosperity (refer to Table 28.2). Part of this boom was financed by American bankers, notably the Wall Street firm of J. P. Morgan and Company, which advanced to the Allies the enormous sum of $2.3 billion during the period of American neutrality.

American trade with Germany could legally have rivaled that with the Allies, but the British controlled the sea-lanes, and they threw a noose-tight blockade of mines and ships across the North Sea, gateway to German ports. Over the unavailing protests of American shippers, farmers, and manufacturers, the British began forcing American vessels off the high seas and into their ports. This harassment of American shipping proved highly effective, as trade between Germany and the United States virtually ceased.

Hard-pressed Germany did not tamely consent to being starved out. In retaliation for the British blockade, in February 1915 Berlin announced a submarine war area around the British Isles (refer to Map 28.2). The submarine was a weapon so new that existing international law could not be made to fit it. The old rule that a warship must stop and board a merchantman could hardly apply to submarines, which could easily be rammed or sunk if they surfaced.

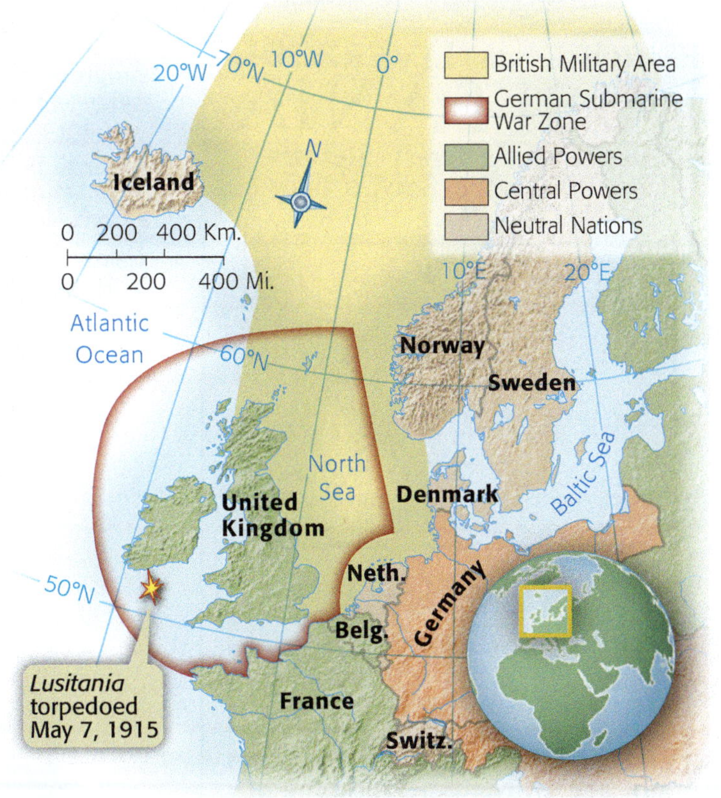

Map 28.2 British Military Area (declared November 3, 1914) and German Submarine War Zone (declared February 4, 1915)

The cigar-shaped marauders posed a dire threat to the United States—so long as Wilson insisted on maintaining America's neutral rights. Berlin officials declared that they would try not to sink *neutral* shipping, but they warned that mistakes would probably occur. Wilson now determined on a policy of calculated risk. He would continue to claim profitable neutral trading rights, while hoping that no high-seas incident would force his hand to grasp the sword of war.

The German submarines (known as **U-boats**, from the German *Unterseeboot*, or "undersea boat") meanwhile began their deadly work. In the first months of 1915, they sank about ninety ships in the war zone. Then the submarine issue became acute when the British passenger liner *Lusitania* was torpedoed and sank off the coast of Ireland on May 7, 1915, with the loss of 1,198 lives, including 128 Americans (refer to Images 28.6 and 28.7).

The Fatherland, the chief German-American propaganda newspaper in the United States, cried,

"We [Americans] prattle about humanity while we manufacture poisoned shrapnel and picric acid for profit. Ten thousand German widows, ten thousand orphans, ten thousand graves bear the legend 'Made in America.'"

The *Lusitania* was carrying 4,200 cases of small-arms ammunition, a fact the Germans used to justify the sinking. But Americans were swept by a wave of shock and anger at this act of "mass murder" and "piracy." The eastern United States, closer to the war, seethed with talk of fighting, but the rest of the country showed a strong distaste for hostilities. The peace-loving Wilson had no stomach for leading a disunited nation into war. Instead, by a series of increasingly strong condemnations, Wilson attempted to take the German warlords sharply to task. "There is such a thing," he declared, "as a man being too proud to fight." Even this measured approach proved too much for the strongly antiwar Secretary of State Bryan, who resigned in protest. But Wilson's policies incensed the war-thirsty Theodore Roosevelt. The Rough Rider assailed the spineless simperers who heeded the "weasel words" of the pacifistic professor in the White House.

Yet Wilson, sticking to his verbal guns, made some diplomatic progress. After another British liner, the *Arabic*, was sunk in August 1915, with the loss of two American lives, Berlin reluctantly agreed not to sink unarmed and unresisting passenger ships *without warning* (refer to Image 28.8). This pledge appeared to be violated in March 1916, when the Germans torpedoed a French passenger steamer, the *Sussex*. The infuriated Wilson informed the Germans that unless they renounced the inhuman practice of sinking merchant ships without warning, he would break diplomatic relations—an almost certain prelude to war.

Germany reluctantly knuckled under to President Wilson's *Sussex* ultimatum, agreeing not to sink passenger ships and merchant vessels

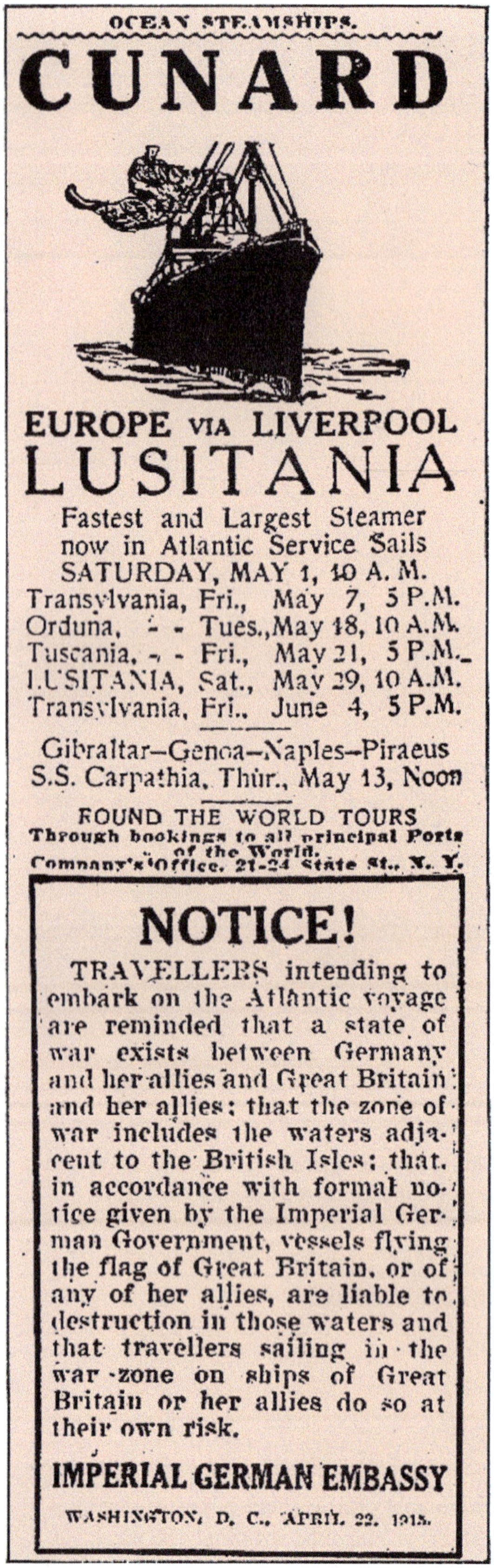

The Granger Collection, NYC

Image 28.6 Advertisement from the *New York Herald*, May 1, 1915 Six days later the *Lusitania* was sunk. Note the German warning.

Bettmann/Getty Images

Image 28.7 A German U-boat This deadly new weapon rendered useless existing rules of naval warfare, eventually pushing the United States to declare war against Germany in 1917.

without giving warning. But the Germans attached a long string to their *Sussex* pledge: the United States would have to persuade the Allies to modify what Berlin regarded as their illegal blockade. This, obviously, was something that Washington could not do. Wilson promptly accepted the German pledge, without accepting the "string." He thus won a temporary but precarious diplomatic victory—precarious because Germany could pull the string whenever it chose, and the president might suddenly find himself tugged over the cliff of war.

Image 28.8 "Here's Money for Your Americans. I May Drown Some More." Germany expressed "profound regret" for the deaths of 128 Americans aboard the torpedoed passenger liner *Lusitania* in 1915, but the incident helped feed a mounting anti-German sentiment in the United States.

28-10 Wilson Wins Reelection in 1916

Against this ominous backdrop, the presidential campaign of 1916 gathered speed. Both the bull moose Progressives and the Republicans met in Chicago. The Progressives uproariously renominated Theodore Roosevelt, but the Rough Rider, who loathed Wilson and all his works, had no stomach for splitting the Republicans again and ensuring the reelection of his hated rival. In refusing to run, he sounded the death knell of the Progressive party.

The Republicans drafted Supreme Court justice Charles Evans Hughes, a cold intellectual with a solid liberal record when he was governor of New York. The Republican platform condemned the Democratic tariff, assaults on the trusts, and Wilson's wishy-washiness in dealing with Mexico and Germany.

For his part, Wilson knew that his election in 1912 had been something of a fluke, owing largely to the Taft-Roosevelt split in the GOP Republican ranks. He had used his first term to identify himself as the candidate of progressivism and to woo the bull moose voters into the Democratic fold. The president, nominated by acclamation at the Democratic convention in St. Louis, now built his next campaign on the slogan "He Kept Us Out of War."

On election day, Hughes swept the East and looked like a surefire winner. Wilson went to bed that night prepared to accept defeat, while the New York newspapers displayed huge portraits of "The President-Elect—Charles Evans Hughes."

But the rest of the country turned the tide. Midwesterners and Westerners, attracted by Wilson's progressive reforms and antiwar policies, flocked to the polls for the president. The final result, in doubt for several days, hinged on California, which Wilson carried by some 3,800 votes out of about a million cast.

Wilson barely squeaked through, with a final vote of 277 to 254 in the Electoral College, and 9,127,695 to 8,533,507 in the popular column (refer to Map 28.3). The prolabor Wilson received strong support from the working class and from renegade bull moosers, whom Republicans failed to lure back into their camp. Wilson himself had not specifically promised to keep the country out of war, but probably enough voters relied on such implicit assurances to ensure his victory. Their hopeful expectations were soon rudely shattered.

During the 1916 campaign, J. A. O'Leary, the head of a pro-German and pro-Irish organization, sent a scorching telegram to Wilson condemning him for having been pro-British in approving war loans and ammunition traffic. Wilson shot back an answer:

"Your telegram received. I would feel deeply mortified to have you or anybody like you vote for me. Since you have access to many disloyal Americans and I have not, I will ask you to convey this message to them."

President Wilson's devastating and somewhat insulting response probably won him more votes than it lost.

28-11 War by Act of Germany

Destiny dealt cruelly with Woodrow Wilson. The lover of peace, as fate would have it, was forced to lead a hesitant and peace-loving nation into war. As the last days of 1916 slipped through the hourglass, the president made one final, futile attempt to mediate between the embattled belligerents. On January 22,

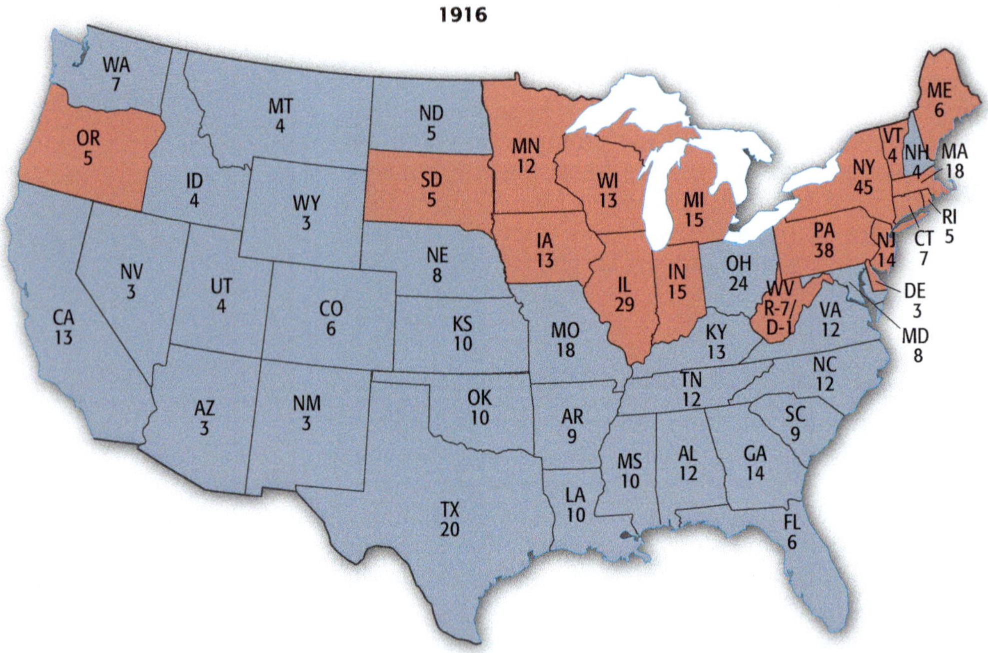

Candidate (Party)	Electoral Vote		Popular Vote	
Wilson (Democrat)	277	52.2%	9,127,695	51.7%
Hughes (Republican)	254	47.8%	8,533,507	48.3%

Map 28.3 Presidential Election of 1916 (with electoral vote by state) Wilson was so worried about being a lame duck president in a time of great international tensions that he drew up a plan whereby Hughes, if victorious, would be appointed secretary of state, Wilson and the vice president would resign, and Hughes would thus succeed immediately to the presidency.

1917, he delivered one of his most moving addresses, restating America's commitment to neutral rights and declaring that only a negotiated "peace without victory" would prove durable.

Germany's militarists responded with a blow of the armored fist. On January 31, 1917, they announced to an astonished world their decision to wage *unrestricted* submarine warfare, sinking *all* ships, including America's, in the war zone.

Why this rash act? War with America was the last thing Germany wanted. But after three ghastly years in the trenches, Germany's leaders decided the distinction between combatants and noncombatants was a luxury they could no longer afford. Thus, they jerked on the string they had attached to their *Sussex* pledge in 1916, desperately hoping to bring Britain to its knees before the United States entered the war. Wilson, his bluff called, broke diplomatic relations with Germany but refused to move closer to war unless the Germans undertook "overt" acts against American lives. To defend American interests short of war, the president asked Congress for authority to arm American merchant ships. When a band of Midwestern senators launched a filibuster to block the measure, Wilson denounced them as a "little group of willful men" who were rendering a great nation "helpless and contemptible." But their obstruction was a powerful reminder of the continuing strength of American isolationism (refer to "The Presence of the Past: The Senate: 'Beautiful Machine' or Cemetery of Democracy?" pp. 718–719).

Meanwhile, the sensational **Zimmermann note** was intercepted and published on March 1, 1917, infuriating Americans, especially Westerners. German foreign secretary Arthur Zimmermann had secretly proposed a German-Mexican alliance, tempting anti-Yankee Mexico with veiled promises of recovering Texas, New Mexico, and Arizona.

On the heels of this provocation came the long-dreaded "overt" acts in the Atlantic, where German U-boats sank four unarmed American merchant vessels in the first two weeks of March. As one Philadelphia newspaper observed, "The difference between war and what we have now is that now we aren't fighting back." Simultaneously came the extraordinary news that a revolution in Russia had toppled the cruel regime of the tsars. America could now fight foursquare for democracy on the side of the Allies, without the black sheep of Russian despotism in the Allied fold.

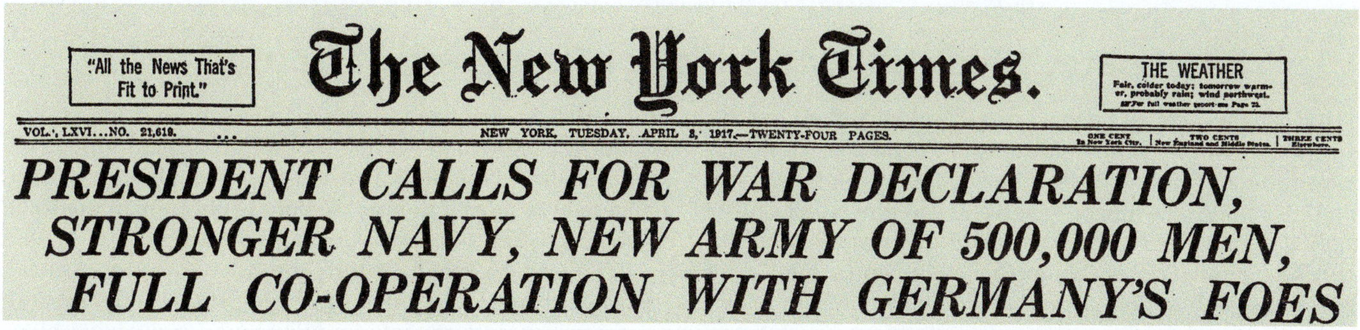
"All the News That's Fit to Print."

The New York Times.

THE WEATHER

VOL. LXVI...NO. 21,619. NEW YORK, TUESDAY, APRIL 3, 1917.—TWENTY-FOUR PAGES.

PRESIDENT CALLS FOR WAR DECLARATION, STRONGER NAVY, NEW ARMY OF 500,000 MEN, FULL CO-OPERATION WITH GERMANY'S FOES

NY Times

Image 28.9 WAR! Attacks by German submarines finally forced Wilson's hand, and he asked Congress for a declaration of war on April 2, 1917. Four days later, after considerable debate and with fifty-six dissenting votes, Congress obliged the president.

Subdued and solemn, Wilson at last stood before a hushed joint session of Congress on the evening of April 2, 1917, and asked for a declaration of war (refer to Image 28.9). He had lost his gamble that America could pursue the profits of neutral trade without being sucked into the ghastly maelstrom. A myth developed in later years that America was dragged unwittingly into war by munitions makers and Wall Street bankers, desperate to protect their profits and loans. Yet the weapons merchants and financiers were already thriving, unhampered by wartime government restrictions and heavy taxation. Their slogan might well have been "Neutrality Forever." The simple truth is that British harassment of American commerce had been galling but endurable; Germany had resorted to the mass killing of civilians. The difference was like that between a gang of thieves and a gang of murderers. President Wilson had drawn a clear, if risky, line against the depredations of the submarine. The German high command, in a last desperate throw of the dice, chose to cross it. In a figurative sense, America's war declaration of April 6, 1917, bore the unambiguous trademark "Made in Germany."

28-12 Wilsonian Idealism Enthroned

"It is a fearful thing to lead this great peaceful people into war," Wilson said in his war message. It proved fearful indeed. How could the president arouse the American people to shoulder this unprecedented burden? For more than a century, they had prided themselves on their isolation from the periodic outbursts of militarized violence that afflicted the Old World. Since 1914, their pride had been reinforced by the bountiful profits gained through neutrality. German U-boats had now roughly shoved a wavering America into the abyss, but ominously, no fewer than six senators and fifty representatives (including the first congresswoman, Jeannette Rankin of Montana) had voted against the war resolution. Wilson could whip up no enthusiasm, especially in the landlocked Midwest, by calling on the nation to fight to make the world safe from the submarine.

To galvanize the country, Wilson would have to proclaim more glorified aims. Radiating the spiritual fervor of his Presbyterian ancestors, he declared the supremely ambitious goal of a crusade "to make the world safe for democracy." Brandishing the sword of righteousness, Wilson hypnotized the nation with his lofty ideals. He contrasted the selfish war aims of the other belligerents, Allied and enemy alike, with America's shining altruism. America, he preached, did not fight like other belligerents for the sake of riches or territorial conquest. The Republic sought only to shape an international order in which democracy could flourish without fear of power-crazed autocrats and militarists.

In Wilsonian idealism the personality of the president and the exigencies of the moment were perfectly matched. The high-minded Wilson genuinely believed in the principles he so eloquently intoned—especially his prophetic insight that the modern world could not afford the kind of hyper-destructive war that advanced industrial states were now capable of waging. In any case, probably no other argument could have successfully converted the American people from their historic

> Woodrow Wilson's (1856–1924) War Message to Congress on April 2, 1917, evoked the soaring idealism and ambition of the era when it declared:
>
> "The world must be made safe for democracy. Its peace must be planted upon the tested foundations of political liberty. We have no selfish ends to serve. We desire no conquest, no dominion. We seek no indemnities for ourselves, no material compensation for the sacrifices we shall freely make."

The Presence of the Past

The Senate: "Beautiful Machine" or Cemetery of Democracy?

"[The] senate . . . must be in all cases a salutary check on the government," wrote James Madison in *Federalist 62*. In both its constitutional construction and its deliberative procedures, the U.S. Senate was meant to serve as the proverbial saucer cooling the hot legislative tea.* Each state, regardless of the size of its population, was to receive equal representation by two senators. Unlimited debate would allow roiling passions to give way to calm deliberation over contentious issues. Yet in practice, the Senate has at times impeded the very democratic process it was designed to uphold.

Unlike in the House of Representatives, Senate rules made no provision for ending discussion and bringing a bill to a vote. An unintended outcome of that commitment to unlimited debate was the "filibuster," a long speech designed to delay a vote or—by running out the clock on a legislative session—occasionally block a bill entirely.

"Talking a bill to death" became a familiar senatorial tactic as sectional debates over slavery and federal power intensified in the nineteenth century. The figure most closely associated with early filibustering was South Carolinian John C. Calhoun, who tried to stall a bill banning slavery in Oregon Territory in 1848. Responding to accusations of undemocratic obstruction of the majority's will, Calhoun declared that "action, action, action means nothing but plunder, plunder, plunder!" By the 1850s, the term *filibuster*, derived from the Dutch and Spanish words for pirate, had entered the political lexicon.

Filibustering persisted after the Civil War. The work of government had enlarged and new issues—the tariff, Black civil rights, monetary policy—became political flashpoints. Yet filibustering remained a relatively unusual occurrence, and most bills made it to a vote.

Then in March 1917, a small group of antiwar senators filibustered President Woodrow Wilson's request to arm American merchant ships on the perilous wartime seas of the North Atlantic (Refer to "28-11 War by Act of Germany," pp. 715–717). Wilson scorned them as "a little group of willful men" and berated the Senate as "the only legislative body in the world which cannot act when its majority is ready for action." Clergy denounced the obstructionist senators from their pulpits, several state legislatures formally condemned them, and one received a forty-pound iron cross inscribed "Lest the Kaiser Forget."

In response, the chamber at long last amended its procedures to close off debate when a supermajority of two-thirds of senators voted for "cloture," or a motion limiting further discussion. Supporters hoped that this new Senate Rule 22 would relegate the much-maligned filibuster to the dustbin of Senate history. Instead, the modern Senate became increasingly ensnarled in the procedural gridlock that cloture was intended to avert.

The high supermajority threshold made successful cloture motions rare. In the four decades following the adoption of Rule 22, cloture was invoked only five times. In the 1930s, Senator Huey Long (D-LA) infamously filibustered New Deal legislation by dictating recipes for fried oysters and "potlikker," and in 1935 he delivered a more than fifteen-hour-long stemwinder during which he recited the full Constitution. The tactic received a heroic Hollywood gloss when Jimmy Stewart delivered the most famous of fictional filibusters in the 1939 Frank Capra film, *Mr. Smith Goes to Washington*.

The mid-twentieth-century filibuster became a crucial instrument to protect Jim Crow segregation. Long-winded southern senators repeatedly filibustered civil rights bills. South Carolina Senator Strom Thurmond turned in one epic performance with the longest speech ever recorded in the Senate—a 1957 talkathon against a civil rights bill that clocked in at 24 hours and 18 minutes. A series of filibusters against the Civil Rights Act of 1964 tied up the Senate for 74 days.

Cloture was achieved more often after 1975, when the supermajority threshold was dropped from two-thirds to three-fifths, or sixty senators. Yet at the same time, the Senate made it possible for legislators to delay debate without actually delivering a speech. Senators could now simply register their intent to filibuster without having to take to the Senate floor for a dilatory stemwinder. This became known as the "silent" or "stealth" filibuster.

HLG/AP Photo

Image 28.10 The Filibustering Robert C. Byrd, Democrat of West Virginia Segregationist Southerners notoriously deployed the "talking filibuster" to delay Senate consideration of civil rights legislation in the 1950s and 1960s. Here, Byrd packs his briefcase after delivering an all-night filibuster of 14 hours, 13 minutes in June 1964. The landmark civil rights bill opposed by Byrd passed a few weeks later with bipartisan support.

The "talking filibuster" had been attention-getting and sometimes quite consequential, but it was rare, deployed amid debates over unusually controversial issues, and usually as a last resort. The silent filibuster, largely invisible to the media and the public, became ubiquitous, a potent partisan wrench to throw into the legislative gears to block action on immigration reform, gun control, and health care reform, among other issues.

Reflecting bipartisan frustration with the procedural snarl, some efforts to lower the cloture threshold have succeeded, though with controversial results. The stone-walling of Obama-era presidential appointments prompted a Democratic-led Senate in 2013 to allow federal judgeships and executive-branch confirmations to pass with a simple majority. U.S. Supreme Court nominations were initially excluded from this so-called "nuclear option," but in 2017 a Republican-dominated Senate reinterpreted Rule 22 to include them—enabling President Donald Trump to appoint three justices on simple-majority, mostly party-line votes. No longer the platform it had once been for dispassionate deliberation and careful consensus-building, the Senate was increasingly afflicted with the same partisan paralysis that hobbled the other branches of government.

The rules of the Senate "are more even than a beautiful machine," declared Massachusetts Senator Charles Sumner in 1866, "they are the very temple of constitutional liberty." Yet the rules of the Senate, combined with a two-senator-per-state constitutional architecture that bestows disproportionate influence on less-populous states,[†] has led modern critics to condemn the Senate as an anti-democratic institution badly in need of reform.

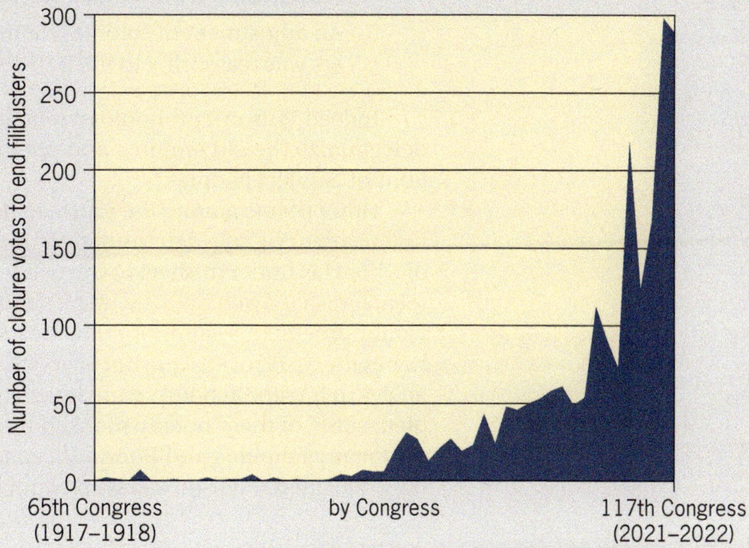

Figure 28.2 **The Rise of the Filibuster** From the 65th Congress (convened 1917–1918) to the 117th Congress (convened 2021–2022), this chart shows the increased use of the Senate filibuster in the upper chamber, evidenced by the number of votes on cloture taken to end filibuster activity.

*The analogy of the "senatorial saucer" long has been credited to President George Washington, although historians have found no evidence that he actually said it.

[†]The 26 least populous states elect half the members of the U.S. Senate, but they are home to just 17 percent of the U.S. population.

hostility to involvement in European squabbles. Americans, it seemed, could be either isolationists or crusaders, but nothing in between.

Wilson's appeal worked—perhaps too well. Holding aloft the torch of idealism, the president fired up the public mind to a fever pitch. "Force, force to the utmost, force without stint or limit," he cried, while the country responded less elegantly with "Hang the kaiser." Lost in the gale was Wilson's earlier plea for "peace without victory."

28-13 Wilson's Fourteen Potent Points

Wilson quickly came to be recognized as the moral leader of the Allied cause. He scaled a summit of inspiring oratory on January 8, 1918, when he delivered his famed **Fourteen Points** Address to an enthusiastic Congress. Although one of his primary purposes was to keep a reeling Russia in the war, Wilson's vision inspired all the drooping Allies to make mightier efforts and demoralized the enemy governments by holding out alluring promises to their dissatisfied minorities.

The first five of the Fourteen Points were broad in scope:

1. A proposal to abolish secret treaties pleased liberals of all countries.
2. Freedom of the seas appealed to the Germans, as well as to Americans who distrusted British sea power.

3. A removal of economic barriers among nations had long been the goal of liberal internationalists everywhere.
4. A reduction of armament burdens was gratifying to taxpayers in all countries.
5. An adjustment of colonial claims in the interests of both native peoples and the colonizers was reassuring to the anti-imperialists.

Indeed Wilson's pronouncement about colonies was potentially revolutionary. It helped to delegitimize the old empires and opened the road to eventual national independence for millions of "subject peoples."

Other points among the fourteen proved to be no less seductive. They held out the hope of independence ("self-determination") to oppressed minority groups, such as the Poles, millions of whom lay under the heel of Germany and Austria-Hungary. The capstone point, number fourteen, foreshadowed the League of Nations—an international organization that Wilson dreamed would provide a system of collective security. Yet Wilson's appealing points, though raising hopes the world over, were not everywhere applauded. Certain leaders of the Allied nations, with an eye to territorial booty, were less than enthusiastic. Hard-nosed Republicans at home grumbled; some of them openly mocked the "fourteen commandments" of "God Almighty Wilson." And many Filipinos and Puerto Ricans, their countries still under American imperial domination, considered Wilson a craven hypocrite.

Image 28.11 Anti-German Propaganda The government relied extensively on emotional appeals and hate propaganda to rally support for the First World War, which most Americans regarded as a distant "European" affair. This poster used gendered imagery to evoke the brutal German violation of Belgian neutrality in August 1914.

28-14 Manipulating Minds and Stifling Dissent

Mobilizing people's minds for war, both in America and abroad, was an urgent task facing the Washington authorities. The **Committee on Public Information**, headed by a brash journalist, George Creel, took on the job (refer to Image 28.11). Creel was a pioneer in the emerging businesses of public relations and advertising, which aspired to create positive images for "brands" and arouse in consumers desires that they never knew they had. His wartime job was to sell America on the war and sell the world on Wilsonian war aims. Creel employed some 150,000 workers at home and overseas. He sent out an army of 75,000 "four-minute men"—often longer-winded than that—who delivered countless speeches with "patriotic pep."

Creel's propaganda took varied forms. Posters were splashed on billboards in the "Battle of the Fences," as artists "rallied to the colors." Millions of leaflets and pamphlets, which contained the most pungent Wilson-isms, were showered like confetti upon the world. Hang-the-kaiser movies, carrying such titles as *The Kaiser, The Beast of Berlin* and *To Hell with the Kaiser*, revealed the helmeted "Hun" at his bloodiest. Arm-waving conductors by the thousands led huge audiences in songs that poured scorn on the enemy and glorified the "boys" in uniform.

The entire nation, catching the frenzied spirit of a religious revival, burst into song. This was undoubtedly America's singingest war. Most memorable was George M. Cohan's spine-tingling "Over There":

> Over there, over there
> Send the word, send the word over there,
> That the Yanks are coming, the Yanks are coming
> The drums rum-tumming ev'rywhere.

Creel typified American war mobilization, which relied more on aroused passion and voluntary compliance than on formal laws (refer to Image 28.12). But he oversold the ideals of Wilson and led the world to expect too much. When the president proved to be a mortal and not a god, the resulting disillusionment both at home and abroad was disastrous.

Patriotic fervor also had a darker side. German Americans numbered over 8 million, counting those with at least one parent foreign-born, out of a total population of 100 million. Most proved to be dependably loyal to the United States. Yet rumormongers were quick to spread tales of spying and sabotage; even trifling epidemics of diarrhea were blamed on German agents. A few German Americans were tarred, feathered, and beaten; in one extreme case a German Socialist in Illinois was lynched by a drunken mob.

As emotion mounted, hysterical hatred of Germans and things Germanic swept the nation. Orchestras found it unsafe to present German-composed music, like that of Wagner or Beethoven. German books were removed from library shelves, and German classes were canceled in high schools and colleges. Sauerkraut became "liberty cabbage," hamburger "liberty steak." Even beer became suspect, as patriotic Americans fretted over the loyalty of breweries with names like Schlitz and Pabst.

Both the **Espionage Act** of 1917 and the Sedition Act of 1918 reflected current fears about Germans and antiwar Americans. Especially visible among the nineteen hundred prosecutions pursued under these laws were antiwar Socialists and members of the radical Industrial Workers of the World (IWW). Kingpin Socialist Eugene V. Debs was tried under the Espionage Act in 1918 and sentenced to ten years in a federal penitentiary (refer to Image 28.13). IWW leader William D. ("Big Bill") Haywood and ninety-nine associates were similarly convicted. Virtually any criticism of the government could be censored and punished. Some critics claimed the new laws were bending, if not breaking, the First Amendment. But in ***Schenck v. United States*** (1919), the Supreme Court affirmed their legality, arguing that freedom of speech could be revoked when such speech posed a "clear and present danger" to the nation.

These prosecutions form an ugly chapter in the history of American civil liberty. With the dawn of peace, presidential pardons were rather freely granted, including President Harding's to Eugene Debs in 1921. Yet a few victims lingered behind bars into the 1930s.

Brey, Laura/Library of Congress Prints and Photographs Division [LC-USZC4-9659]

Image 28.12 Patriotic Persuasion Worried about the public's enthusiasm for the war, the government employed all the arts of psychology and propaganda to sustain the martial spirit. The prewar song "I Didn't Raise My Boy to Be a Soldier" was changed to "I Didn't Raise My Boy to Be a Slacker," which in turn inspired the cruel parody "I Didn't Raise My Boy to Be a Sausage."

28-15 Forging a War Economy

Victory was no foregone conclusion, especially since the Republic, despite ample warning, was caught flat-footedly unready for its leap into global war. The pacifistic Wilson had only belatedly backed some mild preparedness measures beginning in 1915. It would take a herculean effort to marshal America's daunting but disorganized resources and throw them into the field quickly enough to bolster the Allied war effort.

Towering obstacles confronted economic mobilizers. Sheer ignorance was among the biggest roadblocks. No one knew precisely how much steel or explosive powder the country was capable of producing. Old ideas also proved to be liabilities, as traditional fears of big government hamstrung efforts to orchestrate the economy from Washington. The largely voluntary character of economic war organization testified to ocean-insulated America's safe distance from the fighting—as well as to the still-modest scale of government powers in the progressive-era Republic.

Late in the war, after some bruising political battles, Wilson succeeded in imposing some order on this economic confusion. In March 1918 he appointed lone-eagle stock speculator Bernard Baruch to head the **War Industries Board**. Although the board had only feeble formal

Bettmann/Getty Images

Image 28.13 **Socialist Leader Eugene V. Debs Addresses an Antiwar Rally in 1918** For his denunciation of World War I, Debs was convicted under the Espionage Act of 1917 and sent to federal prison. In his courtroom speech defending himself against charges of disloyalty, he passionately declared, "While there is a lower class, I am in it; while there is a criminal element, I am of it; while there is a soul in prison, I am not free." He ran as a presidential candidate in 1920 while still incarcerated in his cell and received nearly a million votes.

powers and was disbanded just days after armistice, it set a precedent for the federal government to take a central role in economic planning in moments of crisis.

As the larder of democracy, America had to feed itself and its allies. Wilson tapped an American mining-company executive then living in London, Herbert Hoover, as head of the Food Administration. A Quaker by faith and engineer by training, Hoover shared his fellow war administrators' preference for relying on voluntary compliance rather than compulsory edicts. He deliberately rejected issuing ration cards, a practice used in Europe. Instead, he waged a whirlwind propaganda campaign through posters, billboards, newspapers, pulpits, and movies (refer to Image 28.14). To save food for export, Hoover proclaimed wheatless Wednesdays and meatless Tuesdays—all on a voluntary basis. Even children, when eating apples, were urged to be "patriotic to the core." The country soon broke out in a rash of vegetable "victory gardens." Thanks to the fervent patriotic wartime spirit, Hoover's voluntary approach worked. Farm production increased by one-fourth, and food exports to the Allies tripled in volume. Hoover's methods were widely imitated in other war agencies.

Congress severely restricted the use of foodstuffs for manufacturing alcoholic beverages, and the war-spawned mood of self-denial helped accelerate the wave of prohibition that was sweeping the country. Many leading brewers were German-descended, and this taint made the drive against alcohol all the more popular. The reformers' dream of a saloon-free nation was finally achieved—temporarily—in 1919 with the passage of the Eighteenth Amendment, prohibiting all alcoholic drinks. (Refer to the text of the Eighteenth Amendment in the Appendix.)

As prohibition indicated, despite the Wilson administration's preference for voluntary means of mobilizing the economy, over the course of the war the federal government expanded in size and power. The War Industries Board eventually issued production quotas, allocated raw materials, and set prices for government purchases. Following indescribable traffic snarls in late 1917, Washington took over the railroads. Time itself came under Uncle Sam's control when the entire country was ordered to observe daylight saving time to extend the workday and save on fuel.

Image 28.14 Food for Thought Wartime agencies flooded the country with posters like this in 1917–1918, exhorting women on the home front to "grow their own" and thus ease the pressure on food supplies.

28-16 Workers in Wartime

Spurred by the slogan "Labor Will Win the War," American workers sweated their way to victory. The War Department's 1918 "work or fight" rule threatened any unemployed male with being immediately drafted—a powerful discouragement to go on strike. But for the most part, government tried to treat labor fairly. Samuel Gompers and his American Federation of Labor (AFL) loyally supported the war and were rewarded for it. At war's end, the AFL had more than doubled its membership, to over three million, and in the most heavily unionized sectors—coal mining, manufacturing, and transportation—real wages had risen more than 20 percent over prewar levels.

Yet labor still harbored grievances and provoked unrest. Federal recognition of the right to organize eluded labor's grasp, while wartime inflation threatened to eclipse wage gains. Six thousand strikes, several bloody, broke out in the war years. The radical, antiwar **Industrial Workers of the World**, known as the "Wobblies" and sometimes derided as the "I Won't Works," engineered some of the most damaging industrial sabotage, and not without reason. As transient laborers in such industries as fruit and lumber, the Wobblies were victims of some of the shabbiest working conditions in the country.

The year 1919 began with the nation's first city-wide labor stoppage to be proclaimed a **"general strike."** Some 35,000 Seattle shipyard workers struck for higher wages. They were soon joined by another 25,000 sympathetic laborers, as the city came to a virtual stand-still for six days.

Before year's end, the greatest strike in American history rocked the steel industry. More than a quarter of a million steelworkers walked off their jobs to force employers to recognize their right to bargain collectively. The steel companies refused to negotiate and brought in thirty thousand Black strikebreakers to keep the mills running. After bitter confrontations that left more than a dozen workers dead, the strike collapsed, a grievous setback that crippled the union movement for more than a decade (refer to Image 28.15).

The Black workers who entered the steel mills in 1919 were but a fraction of the tens of thousands of Black Southerners drawn to the North by the magnet of war-industry employment and by the chance to escape the oppressive and violent Jim Crow South. These migrants made up the small-scale beginnings of the **Great Migration**, a northward trek that would eventually grow to massive proportions. Their sudden appearance in previously all-white neighborhoods sometimes sparked interracial violence. An explosive riot in East St. Louis, Illinois, in July 1917 resulted in the deaths of nine white and at least forty Black citizens. An equally gruesome race riot ripped through Chicago in July 1919 (refer to Image 28.16), triggered by an incident at a bathing beach that followed years of tension between white working-class residents and African Americans toiling as strikebreakers in meatpacking plants. Fifteen white and twenty-three Black people were killed during nearly two weeks of terror, a sober reminder that racial bigotry afflicted the whole nation, North as well as South.

Image 28.15 Suppressing the Steel Strike, Pittsburgh, 1919 The big steel producers ferociously resisted the unionization of their industry. In Pittsburgh compliant local officials bent to the steel makers' will and banned all outdoor meetings. Here billy-club wielding police arrest a suspected striker. Such strong-arm tactics ensured that the strike eventually failed, leaving the steel industry un-unionized until the New Deal championed labor's cause in the Depression decade of the 1930s.

28-17 Suffering Until Suffrage

Women also heeded the call of patriotism and opportunity. Thousands of female workers flooded into factories and fields, taking up jobs vacated by men who left the assembly line for the frontline. But the war split the women's movement deeply. Many progressive-era feminists were pacifists, inclined to oppose the participation both of America in the war and women in the war effort. This group found a voice in the National Woman's Party, led by Quaker activist Alice Paul, which demonstrated against "Kaiser Wilson" with marches and hunger strikes.

But the larger part of the suffrage movement, represented by the National American Woman Suffrage Association, supported Wilson's war. Leaders echoed Wilson's justification for fighting by arguing that women must take part in the war effort to earn a role in shaping the peace. The fight for democracy abroad was women's best hope for winning true democracy at home (refer to Image 28.17).

War mobilization gave new momentum to the suffrage fight. Impressed by women's war work, President Wilson endorsed woman suffrage as "a vitally necessary war measure." In 1917, New York voted for suffrage at the state level; Michigan, Oklahoma, and South Dakota followed. The next year, governments in Great Britain, Austria, Hungary, and Germany extended the suffrage to women. Not long after, the United States followed suit. In 1920, more than seventy years after the first calls for suffrage at Seneca Falls, the **Nineteenth Amendment** was ratified, giving all American women the right to vote. (Refer to the Appendix and Table 28.3.)

Despite political victory, women's wartime economic gains proved fleeting. Although a permanent Women's Bureau did emerge after the war in the Department of Labor, most women workers soon gave up their war jobs. Congress affirmed its support for women in their traditional role as mothers when it passed the **Sheppard-Towner Maternity Act** of 1921, providing federally financed instruction in maternal

Image 28.16 Chicago Race Riot, 1919 The policeman apparently arrived too late to spare this victim from being pelted by stones from an angry mob.

Contending Voices

Battle of the Ballot

In an open address to Congress in 1917, suffragist Carrie Chapman Catt (1859–1947) capitalized on the idealism of the day and invoked the founding principles of American democracy in arguing the case for women's right to vote:

"How can our nation escape the logic it has never failed to follow, when its last unenfranchised class calls for the vote? Behold our Uncle Sam floating the banner with one hand, 'Taxation without representation is tyranny,' and with the other seizing the billions of dollars paid in taxes by women to whom he refuses 'representation.' . . . Is there a single man who can justify such inequality of treatment, such outrageous discrimination? Not one."

Female anti-suffrage activists, for their part, often depicted their opposition to the ballot as a means to protect women's unique role in promoting reform free of corrupt politics, as Mrs. Barclay Hazard (1861–1938) explained in a 1907 speech:

"[We] must accept partisanship, political trickery, and office-seeking as necessary evils inseparable from modern conditions, and the question arises what can be done to palliate the situation. To our minds, the solution has been found by the entrance of women into public life. Standing in an absolutely independent political position, freed from all partisan affiliations, untrammeled by any political obligations, the intelligent, self-sacrificing women of today are . . . a third party whose disinterestedness none can doubt."

Consider This:

How did progressive-era notions inform the debate over suffrage?

and infant health care. In doing so, it also expanded the responsibility of the federal government for family welfare. Partial though feminist victories were, the developments during the World War I era foreshadowed a future when women's wage-labor and political power would reshape the American way of life.

A

National Archives

B

The Frent Collection/Getty Images

Image 28.17A and B **In the Trenches and to the Polls** Wars often bring opportunities and innovations as well as danger and destruction. As U.S. Army nurses went into harm's way at the fighting front in France, the century-long struggle for women's suffrage intensified on the home front, culminating in the Nineteenth Amendment in 1920.

Table 28.3 A Chronology of Women's Right to Vote in National Elections in Selected Nations

1893	New Zealand
1902	Australia (white women only until Aborigines included in 1962)
1906	Finland
1915	Denmark, Iceland
1918	Austria, Canada (women of British and French extraction only until 1950), Germany, Hungary, Poland, Russian Federation, United Kingdom (only women who were married, householders, or university graduates age 30 or over until 1928)
1919	Netherlands, Sweden
1920	United States, Czechoslovakia
1924	Mongolia
1930	South Africa (whites only until 1994), Turkey
1931	Spain (but women lost the vote under the dictator Francisco Franco, 1936–1976)
1934	Brazil, Cuba
1944	France
1945	Italy, Japan
1946	Yugoslavia
1947	Argentina, Mexico, Pakistan
1948	Israel, South Korea
1949	China, Syrian Arab Republic
1950	Haiti, India
1952	Greece, Lebanon
1956	Egypt
1963	Iran
1965	Afghanistan (revoked under Taliban rule, 1996–2001)
1971	Switzerland
1974	Jordan
2005	Kuwait
2015	Saudi Arabia (local elections only)

Sources: *Caroline Daley and Melanie Nolan, eds.,* Suffrage and Beyond: International Feminist Perspectives *(1994); http://www.ipu.org/english/issues/wmndocs/suffrage.htm; About.com, Women's History, International Woman Suffrage Timeline, http://womenshistory.about.com/od/suffrage/a/intl_timeline.htm.*

28-18 Making Plowboys into Doughboys*

Most citizens, at the outset, did not dream of sending a mighty force to France, assuming American naval power and material support would suffice. But in April and May of 1917, the European associates confessed that they were scraping the bottom not only of their money chests but, more ominously, of their manpower barrels. A huge American army would have to be raised, trained, and transported, or the whole western front would collapse. And America's army was hardly huge. With 100,000 regulars at the war's eve, it ranked only fifteenth among the armies of the world.

Conscription was the only answer to the need for raising an immense force with all possible speed. Wilson disliked a draft, as did many other Americans with Civil War memories, but he eventually accepted conscription as a disagreeable and temporary necessity. The proposed draft bill

*It is unclear why U.S. troops in World War I were called "doughboys," but this kind of nicknaming was common among other armies as well. French troops were called "poilus" ("hairy ones"); a British soldier was a "Tommy," an abbreviation of Tommy Atkins, a generic name (like "John Doe" in the United States) often used on British official forms.

immediately ran into a barrage of criticism in Congress, where one member declared that there was "precious little difference between a conscript and a convict." Six weeks after declaring war, Congress grudgingly passed conscription to supply the manpower for the **American Expeditionary Forces (AEF)** in Europe.

The draft machinery, on the whole, worked effectively. Within a few frantic months, the army grew to over 4 million men. For the first time, women were admitted to the armed forces: some 11,000 to the navy and 269 to the marines. (The army refused to enlist them.) African Americans also served in the AEF, though in strictly segregated units and usually under white officers. Military authorities hesitated to train Black men for combat, and the majority of African American soldiers were assigned to "construction battalions" or put to work unloading ships.

Ignoring grisly tales of the agonies of trench warfare, many young American men saw an opportunity for adventure and seized it. Author John Dos Passos (1896–1970) recollected how he felt going off to war in 1917:

"We had spent our boyhood in the afterglow of the peaceful nineteenth century. . . . What was war like? We wanted to see with our own eyes. We flocked into the volunteer services. I respected the conscientious objectors, and occasionally felt I should take that course myself, but hell, I wanted to see the show."

Recruits were supposed to receive six months of training in America and two more months overseas. But so great was the urgency that many doughboys were swept swiftly into battle scarcely knowing how to handle a rifle, much less a bayonet.

28-19 The Great Pandemic

American doughboys may have unwittingly brought something else to a world at war: a deadly **influenza pandemic** that swept the globe between 1918 and 1920, likely killing up to 50 million people. Theories abound about the pandemic's origins, but evidence points most strongly to a U.S. Army camp in Kansas, where over a thousand doughboys were sickened in February 1918—shortly before shipping off to European battlefields.

Consumed with ending the war, world leaders downplayed the lethality of the virus. President Wilson, concerned about distracting attention from the war effort, never spoke publicly about the so-called "Spanish flu." Congress allocated a mere $1 million to combat the pandemic. As the death toll soared, states and cities scrambled to close schools, cafes, and saloons. Health authorities urged citizens to stay home and don white muslin facemasks when in public (refer to Image 28.18). Many of those who scoffed at the flu's dangers paid dearly. In September 1918, a Liberty Loan parade in Philadelphia fueled an outbreak that killed 12,000 of the 200,000 people who attended.

Other nations experienced far higher death tolls. Yet few American households were left untouched by suffering. Sickening millions, the flu proved particularly lethal to children and young adults. Half of the American dead were between the ages of twenty and forty. The impact was so severe that the average life expectancy in the United States in 1918 was nearly twelve years lower than it had been in 1917. Overall, approximately 675,000 Americans perished.

GL Archive/Alamy Stock Photo

Image 28.18 The Great Influenza Pandemic As the contagious and deadly flu tore through America and the world in 1918 and 1919, shutdowns and other measures to control the virus altered many aspects of everyday life. In this 1918 image, a Seattle streetcar conductor refuses to let a rider aboard who is not wearing a protective face mask.

28-20 America Helps Hammer the Hun

Russia's collapse underscored the need for haste in ending the war. The communistic Bolsheviks, after seizing power late in 1917, ultimately withdrew their beaten country from the "capitalistic" war early in 1918. This sudden defection released hundreds of thousands of battle-tested Germans

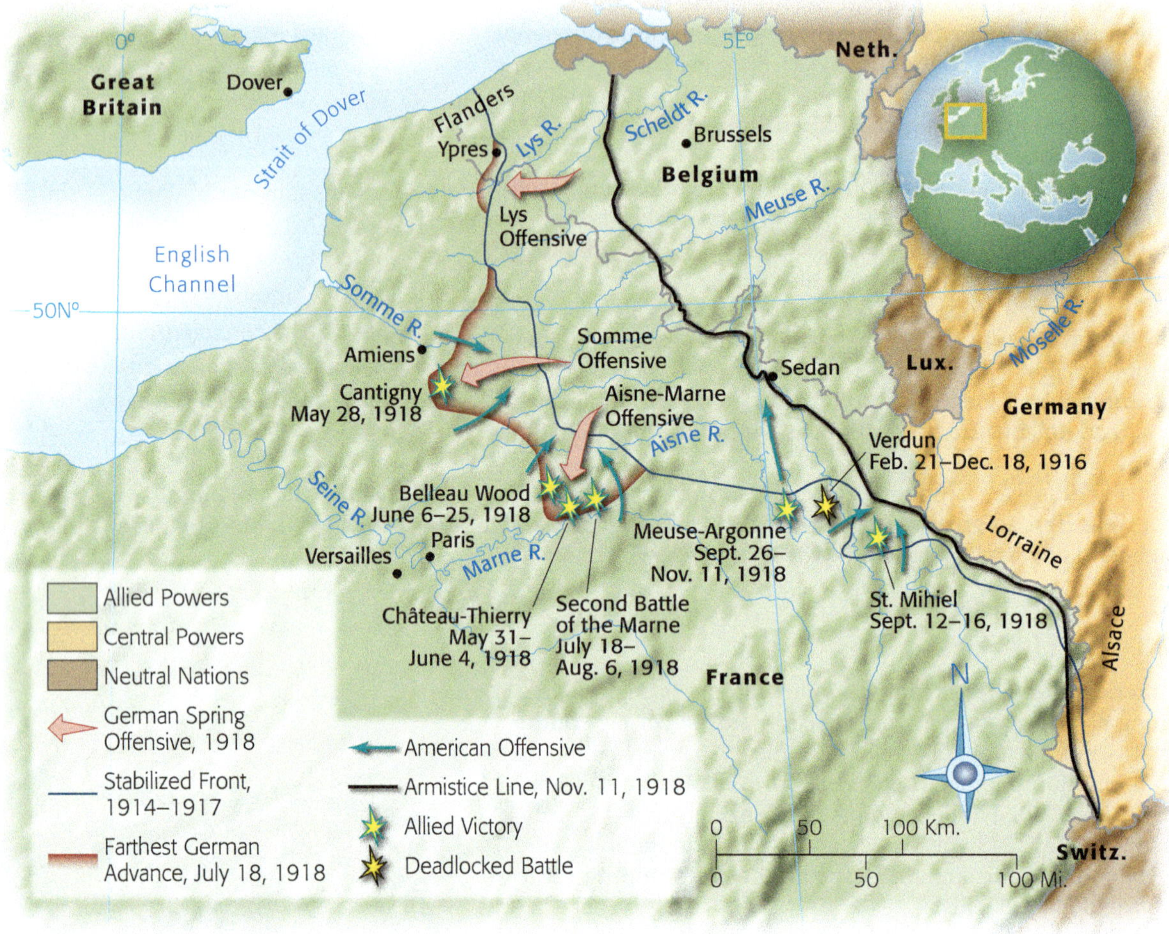

Map 28.4 Major U.S. Operations in France, 1918 One AEF soldier recorded in his diary his baptism of fire at St. Mihiel: "Hiked through dark woods. No lights allowed, guided by holding on the pack of the man ahead. Stumbled through underbrush for about half mile into an open field where we waited in soaking rain until about 10:00 P.M. We then started on our hike to the St. Mihiel front, arriving on the crest of a hill at 1:00 A.M. I saw a sight which I shall never forget. It was the zero hour and in one instant the entire front as far as the eye could reach in either direction was a sheet of flame, while the heavy artillery made the earth quake."

from the eastern front facing Russia to the western front in France, where, for the first time in the war, they were developing a dangerous superiority in manpower—and the Yanks were yet to arrive.

France gradually began to bustle with American doughboys (refer to Map 28.4).* The first trainees to reach the front were used as replacements in the Allied armies and were generally deployed in quiet sectors with the British and French. The newcomers soon made friends with the French girls—or tried to. One of the most sung-about women in history was the fabled "Mademoiselle from Armentières." A printable stanza ran,

She was true to me, she was true to you,
She was true to the whole damn army, too.

*American operations were not confined solely to France; small detachments fought in Belgium, Italy, and notably Russia. The United States, hoping to keep stores of munitions from falling into German hands when Bolshevik Russia quit fighting, contributed some five thousand troops to an Allied invasion of northern Russia. Wilson likewise sent nearly ten thousand troops to Siberia as part of an Allied expedition. The Bolsheviks long resented these "capitalistic" interventions, which they regarded as high-handed efforts to suffocate their infant communist revolution in its cradle.

ArteSi/Alamy Stock Photo

Image 28.19 Gassed, by John Singer Sargent The noted artist captures the horror of trench warfare in World War I. The enemy was often distant and unseen, and death came impersonally from gas or artillery fire. The large-scale and novel use of chemical weapons such as mustard gas killed and maimed thousands who fought in the conflict and psychologically traumatized many more, leading to the prohibition of such gases by the Geneva Protocol of 1925.

Not surprisingly, American soldiers suffered from high rates of venereal disease.

The dreaded German drive on the western front exploded in the spring of 1918. Spearheaded by about half a million troops, the enemy rolled forward with terrifying momentum. So dire was the peril that the Allied nations for the first time united under a supreme commander, the quiet French marshal Foch, whose axiom was "To make war is to attack."

At last the ill-trained "Yanks" were coming—and not a moment too soon. Late in May 1918, the German juggernaut, smashing to within forty miles of Paris, threatened to knock out France. Newly arrived American troops, numbering fewer than thirty thousand, were thrown into the breach at **Château-Thierry**, right in the teeth of the German advance. This was a historic moment—the first significant engagement of American troops in a European war (refer to Image 28.19). Battle-fatigued French soldiers gaped as the roads filled with endless truckloads of American doughboys, singing New World songs at the top of their voices, a seemingly inexhaustible flood of fresh and gleaming youth. It was clear that a new American giant had arisen in the West to replace the dying Russian titan in the East.

America had now put decisive military weight on the scales (refer to Figure 28.3). By July 1918, the awesome German drive had spent its force, and the AEF joined a Foch counteroffensive in the Second Battle of the Marne. This engagement marked the beginning of a German withdrawal that was never effectively reversed. In September 1918, nine American divisions (about 243,000 men) joined four French divisions to push the Germans from the St. Mihiel salient, a German dagger in France's flank.

The Americans meanwhile demanded and got a separate army under their own command. General John J. Pershing was assigned a front of eighty-five miles, stretching northwestward from the Swiss border to meet the French lines. As part of the last mighty Allied assault, Pershing's army undertook the **Meuse-Argonne offensive**, from September 26 to November 11, 1918. This battle, the most gargantuan thus far in American history, lasted forty-seven days and engaged 1.2 million American troops. With especially heavy fighting in the rugged Argonne Forest, the killed and wounded mounted to 120,000.

Victory was in sight—and fortunately so. The slowly advancing American armies in France were eating up their supplies so rapidly that they were in grave danger of running short. But the battered Germans were ready to stagger out of the trenches and cry "*Kamerad*" (Comrade). Their allies were deserting them, the

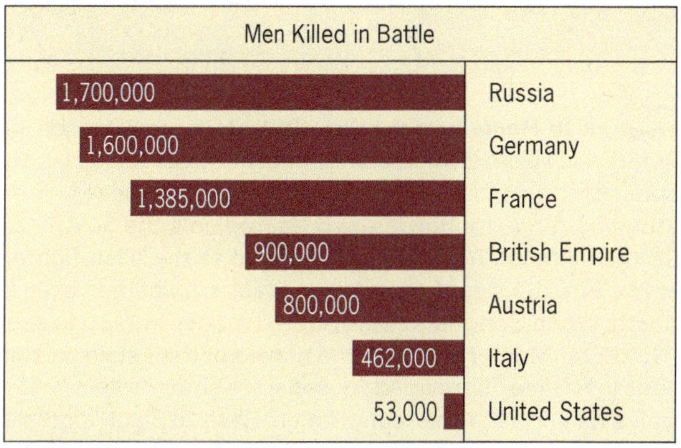

Figure 28.3 Approximate Comparative Losses in World War I

Theodore Roosevelt (1858–1919) favored the Germans' unconditional surrender. Referring to Wilson's practice of drafting diplomatic notes on his own typewriter, Roosevelt telegraphed several senators (October 24, 1918),

"Let us dictate peace by the hammering guns and not chat about peace to the accompaniment of clicking typewriters. The language of the fourteen points and the subsequent statements explaining or qualifying them are thoroughly mischievous."

British blockade was causing critical food shortages, and the sledgehammer blows of the Allies pummeled them relentlessly. Propaganda leaflets, containing seductive Wilsonian promises, rained down on their crumbling lines from balloons, shells, and rockets.

Berlin was now ready to hoist the white flag. In October 1918, the Germans sought from Wilson a peace based on the Fourteen Points. But the president made it clear that the kaiser must be thrown overboard before any armistice could be negotiated. War-weary Germans took the hint and forced the kaiser to flee to Holland, where he lived out his remaining twenty-three years, "unwept, unhonored, and unhung."

The exhausted Germans laid down their arms at eleven o'clock on the eleventh day of the eleventh month of 1918, and an eerie, numbing silence fell over the western front. War-taut America burst into a delirium of around-the-clock rejoicing, as the war to end wars had ended. But the costs to the world exceeded comprehension: nearly 9 million soldiers had died, and more than 20 million had suffered grievous wounds. The stunning toll of the still-raging influenza pandemic made matters even worse. Ultimately more than twelve times as many Americans died from the flu (675,000) than from wartime combat (53,402).

The United States' main contributions to the ultimate victory had been foodstuffs, munitions, credits, oil for this first mechanized war, and manpower—but not battlefield victories. The AEF fought only two major battles, at St. Mihiel and the Meuse-Argonne, both in the last two months of the four-year war, and they were still grinding away in the Meuse-Argonne, well short of their objectives, when the war ended. It was the *prospect* of endless U.S. troop reserves, rather than America's actual military performance, that eventually demoralized the Germans.

General Pershing's army itself, meanwhile, purchased more of its supplies in Europe than it shipped from the United States, including most of its artillery and nearly all of its aircraft. America was no arsenal of democracy in this war; that role awaited it in the next global conflict, two decades later.

Bettmann/Getty Images

Image 28.20 Home from the War, 1919 Most Black troops in World War I were denied combat duty and served as laborers and stevedores, but this wounded veteran had seen some tough fighting—though in a segregated unit, the 369th Colored Infantry Regiment, also known as the "Hell-fighters of Harlem." Segregation followed Black servicemen even into death. When Congress appropriated money in 1930 to send "Gold Star Mothers" to visit the graves of their slain soldier-sons in France, it provided for separate ships, hotels, and trains for African American women. Several Black mothers, preferring "to remain at home and retain our honor and self-respect," reluctantly refused to make the trip.

28-21 Wilson Steps Down from Olympus

Woodrow Wilson had helped to win the war. What part would he now play in shaping the peace? Expectations ran extravagantly high. As the fighting in Europe crashed to a close, the American president towered at the summit of his popularity and power. In lonely huts in the mountains of Italy, candles burned before poster-portraits of the revered American prophet. In Poland, starry-eyed university students would meet in the streets, clasp hands, and utter only one word: "Wilson." No other man had ever occupied so dizzy a pinnacle as moral leader of the world. But at this fateful moment, his sureness of touch deserted him, and he began to make a series of tragic fumbles.

Hoping to strengthen his hand at the Paris peace table, Wilson personally appealed for a Democratic victory in the congressional elections of November 1918. But as Americans grieved over the dead and tallied the many returning wounded (refer to Image 28.20), the maneuver backfired. War-weary voters instead returned a narrow Republican majority to Congress. Having staked his reputation on the outcome, Wilson went to Paris as a diminished leader. Unlike all the parliamentary statesmen at the table, he did not command a legislative majority at home.

Wilson's decision to go in person to Paris to help make the peace infuriated Republicans. At that time no president had traveled to Europe, and Wilson's journey looked to his critics like flamboyant grandstanding. He further ruffled Republican feathers when he snubbed the Senate in assembling his peace delegation and neglected to include a single Republican senator in his official party. The logical choice was the new chairman of the Senate Committee on Foreign Relations, aristocratically bewhiskered Henry Cabot Lodge of Massachusetts. But Wilson loathed him, and the feeling was hotly reciprocated. An accomplished author with a Harvard PhD, Lodge had been known as the "scholar in politics" until Wilson came on the scene. The two men were at daggers drawn, personally and politically.

28-22 An Idealist amid the Imperialists

Idealist Woodrow Wilson received tumultuous welcomes from the masses of France, England, and Italy, even as their wary statesmen tried to keep the new messiah at arm's length from worshipful crowds (refer to Image 28.21). When it came to negotiating the shape of the postwar world at the Paris Conference of great and small nations, begun on January 18, 1919, the Allies formed an inner clique, known as the Big Four, with Wilson representing the richest and freshest

Science History Images/Alamy Stock Photo

Image 28.21 Wilson in Dover, England, 1919 Hailed by many Europeans in early 1919 as the savior of the Western world, Wilson was a fallen idol only a few months later, when Americans repudiated the peace treaty he had helped to craft.

The English science fiction writer H. G. Wells (1866–1946), soon a strong proponent of the League of Nations, spoke for many Europeans when he praised Woodrow Wilson in 1917:

"In all the world there is no outstanding figure to which the world will listen, there is no man audible in all the world, in Japan as well as Germany and Rome as well as Boston—except the President of the United States."

great power, more or less in charge. He was joined by genial Premier Vittorio Orlando of Italy and brilliant Prime Minister David Lloyd George of Britain. Perhaps the most realistic of the quartet was cynical, hard-bitten Premier Georges Clemenceau of France, known as "the Tiger."

Wilson first bent his energies to preventing any vengeful parceling out of the former colonies and protectorates of the vanquished powers. (He was less attentive to the fate of colonies belonging to the victorious French and English.) Wilson tried to force through a compromise between naked imperialism and high-minded idealism. The victors would not take possession of the conquered territory outright but would receive it as trustees of the **League of Nations**. Strategic Syria, for example, was awarded to France, and oil-rich Iraq went to Britain. In practice, this half-loaf solution was little more than the old prewar colonialism, thinly disguised, although in the decades to come, anticolonial independence movements would wield the Wilsonian ideal of self-determination against their imperial occupiers.

Meanwhile, Wilson had been serving as midwife for a world parliament known as the League of Nations, which he envisioned as containing an assembly with seats for all nations and a council to be controlled by the great powers. To his great satisfaction, in February 1919 his fellow treatymakers agreed to make the League Covenant, Wilson's brainchild, an integral part of the final peace treaty. But tough bargains and grinding compromises loomed ahead in Paris.

The hardheaded Clemenceau pressed French demands for the German-inhabited Rhineland and the Saar Valley, a rich coal area. Faced with fierce Wilsonian opposition to this violation of self-determination, France settled for a compromise whereby the Saar basin would remain under the League of Nations for fifteen years, and then a popular vote would determine its fate.* Wilson's next battle was with Italy over Fiume, a valuable seaport inhabited by both Italians and Yugoslavs. When Italy demanded Fiume, Wilson insisted that the seaport go to Yugoslavia and appealed over the heads of Italy's leaders to the country's masses. The maneuver fell flat. The Italian delegates went home in a huff, while the Italian masses turned savagely against Wilson.

Another crucial struggle was with Japan over China's Shandong (Shantung) Peninsula and the German islands in the Pacific, which the Japanese had seized during the war. Japan received the strategic Pacific islands under a League of Nations mandate,† but Wilson staunchly opposed Japanese control of Shandong as a violation of self-determination for its 30 million Chinese residents. When the Japanese threatened to walk out, however, Wilson reluctantly accepted a compromise whereby Japan kept Germany's economic holdings on China's Shandong Peninsula and pledged to return the peninsula to China at a later date. The Chinese were outraged by this imperialistic solution, while Clemenceau jeered that Wilson "talked like Jesus Christ and acted like Lloyd George."

A completed **Treaty of Versailles**, after more weeks of wrangling, was handed to the Germans in June 1919—almost literally on the point of a bayonet. Excluded from the settlement negotiations at Paris, Germany had capitulated in the hope that it would be granted a peace based on the Fourteen Points. A careful analysis of the treaty shows that only about four of the twenty-three original Wilsonian points and subsequent principles were fully honored. Vengeance, not reconciliation, was the treaty's dominant tone. Loud and bitter cries of betrayal burst from German throats—charges that Adolf Hitler would soon reiterate during his meteoric rise to power.

Wilson was guilty of no conscious betrayal. But the Allied powers were torn by conflicting aims, many of them sanctioned by secret treaties. There had to be compromise at Paris or there would be no agreement. Faced with hard realities, Wilson was forced to abandon some of his less cherished Fourteen Points in order to salvage the more precious League of Nations. All the same, the loudly condemned treaty actually had much to commend it. Not least among its merits was the liberation of millions of minority peoples, such as the Poles, from the yoke of despotic dynasties.

---

*The Saar population voted overwhelmingly to rejoin Germany in 1935.

†In due time, the Japanese illegally fortified these islands—the Marshalls, Marianas, and Carolines—and used them as bases against the United States in World War II.

28-23 Wilson's Battle for Ratification

Returning to America, Wilson sailed straight into a political typhoon. Isolationists raised a whirlwind of protest against the treaty, especially against Wilson's commitment to ushering the United States into his newfangled League of Nations, which they regarded either as a useless "sewing circle" or an overpotent "superstate." The opposition's hard core was composed of a dozen or so militants led by Senators William Borah of Idaho and Hiram Johnson of California, known as **irreconcilables.** Invoking the revered advice of Washington and Jefferson, they wanted no part of any "entangling alliance."

Nor were the isolationists Wilson's only problem. Critics showered the Treaty of Versailles with abuse from all sides. Rabid Hun-haters regarded the pact as not harsh enough. Principled liberals thought it too punitive. German Americans, Italian Americans, and others whom Wilson had termed "hyphenated Americans" were aroused because the peace settlement was not sufficiently favorable to their native lands. Irish Americans in particular feared that the League would empower Britain in the face of any movement for Irish independence.

Despite mounting discontent, a strong majority of the people still seemed favorable to the treaty, with the "Wilson League" firmly riveted in it as Part I. At this time—early July 1919—Senator Lodge had no real hope of defeating the Treaty of Versailles. His strategy was merely to amend it in such a way as to "Americanize," "Republicanize," or "senatorialize" it. Lodge effectively used delay to muddle and divide public opinion. He read the entire 264-page treaty aloud in the Senate Foreign Relations Committee and held protracted hearings in which people of various nationalities aired their grievances.

Wilson fretted increasingly as the hot summer of 1919 wore on. The bulky pact was bogged down in the Senate, while the nation was drifting into confusion and apathy. He therefore decided to take his case to the country in a spectacular speechmaking tour. Wilson undertook his strenuous barnstorming campaign despite protests from physicians and friends. The president had never been robust; he had entered the White House nearly seven years before with a stomach pump and with headache pills for his neuritis. His frail body had begun to sag under the strain of his first wife's death in 1914, partisan strife, a global war, and a stressful peace conference. But he declared that he was willing to die, like the soldiers he had sent into battle, for the sake of the new world order.

The presidential tour, begun in September 1919, started off shakily in the isolationist strongholds of the Midwest, but the reception improved in the Rocky Mountain region and on the Pacific Coast. The high point—and the breaking point—of the return trip came in Pueblo, Colorado, September 25, 1919. With tears coursing down his cheeks, Wilson pleaded for the League of Nations as the only real hope of preventing future wars. That night he collapsed from physical and nervous exhaustion. A "funeral train" whisked him back to Washington, where several days later a stroke paralyzed one side of his body. During the next few weeks, he lay in a darkened room in the White House. For more than seven months, he did not meet with his cabinet.

The president's second wife, Edith Bolling Galt Wilson, a vivacious widow he had married four years earlier, was adamant that Wilson not resign despite the seriousness of his condition. Concealing the extent of the president's incapacitation from both cabinet and Congress, Edith Wilson prevented bedside visitors and screened all presidential correspondence. The First Lady denied that she was trying to usurp power. "I am not thinking of the country now, I am thinking of my husband," she declared. Her protectiveness nonetheless had political consequences.

Senator Lodge was now at the helm. After failing to amend the treaty outright, he finally came up with fourteen formal reservations to it—a sardonic slap at Wilson's Fourteen Points (refer to Image 28.22). These safeguards reserved the rights of the United States under the Monroe Doctrine and the Constitution and otherwise sought to protect American sovereignty. Wilson, hating Lodge, saw red at the mere suggestion of the Lodge reservations.

Image 28.22 Senator Henry Cabot Lodge and the Badly Battered Versailles Treaty Led by Massachusetts Senator Lodge, powerful chairman of the Senate Foreign Relations Committee, traditional isolationists refused to ratify the treaty, burying Woodrow Wilson's visionary dream of ending America's aloofness from world affairs.

Too feeble to lead, Wilson remained strong enough to obstruct. When the day finally came for the Senate vote, he sent word to all true Democrats to vote *against* the treaty with the odious Lodge reservations attached. Wilson hoped that when these were cleared away, the path would be open for ratification without reservations or with only some mild Democratic ones. On November 19, 1919, loyal Democrats in the Senate did Wilson's bidding, helping to reject the treaty. All told, about four-fifths of senators professed to favor the treaty, with or without reservations, yet a simple majority could not agree on a single proposition. It went down 55 to 39.

So strong was public indignation at the vote that the Senate was forced to act a second time. In March 1920, the treaty was brought up again, with the Lodge reservations tacked on. There was only one possible path to success—passing the pact with the reservations included. But the sickly Wilson, still sheltered behind drawn curtains, again sent word to all loyal Democrats to vote down the treaty with the obnoxious reservations. He thus signed the death warrant of the treaty as far as America was concerned. On March 19, 1920, the treaty netted a simple majority but failed to get the necessary two-thirds majority, by a count of 49 yeas to 35 nays.

Who defeated the treaty? The Lodge-Wilson personal feud, traditionalism, isolationism, disillusionment, and partisanship all contributed to the confused picture. But Wilson himself must bear a substantial share of the responsibility. He asked for all or nothing—and got nothing.

28-24 The "Solemn Referendum" of 1920

Wilson proposed to settle the treaty issue in the forthcoming presidential campaign of 1920 by appealing to the people for a "solemn referendum." This was sheer folly, for a true mandate on the League in the noisy arena of politics was clearly impossible.

Jubilant Republicans gathered in Chicago in June 1920 with wayward bull moosers back in the corral (after Theodore Roosevelt's death in 1919) and the senatorial Old Guard back in the saddle. A group of Senate bosses, meeting in the historic "smoke-filled" Room 404 of the Hotel Blackstone, informally decided on the affable and malleable Senator Warren G. Harding of Ohio as the party's presidential nominee. To run with the "folksy," backslapping former newspaper editor, the party nominated for vice president frugal, grim-faced Governor Calvin ("Silent Cal") Coolidge of Massachusetts. Meeting in San Francisco, Democrats nominated earnest Governor James M. Cox of Ohio, who strongly supported the League. His running mate was Assistant Navy Secretary Franklin D. Roosevelt, a young, handsome, vibrant New Yorker.

Democratic attempts to make the campaign a referendum on the League were thwarted by Senator Harding, who offered muddled and contradictory statements on the issue from his front porch. With newly enfranchised women swelling the vote totals, Harding was swept into power with a prodigious plurality of over 7 million votes—16,143,407 to 9,130,328 for Cox, the largest victory margin to that date in a presidential election. The electoral count was 404 to 127. Eugene V. Debs, federal prisoner number 9653 at the Atlanta Penitentiary, rolled up the largest vote ever for the left-wing Socialist Party—919,799.

Public desire for a change found vent in a resounding repudiation of "high-and-mighty" Wilsonianism. Tired of star-reaching idealism and soothed by Harding's promise of a "return to normalcy," voters were willing to accept a second-rate president—and they got a third-rate one.

Republican isolationists successfully turned Harding's victory into a death sentence for the League. Politicians increasingly shunned the League as they would a leper. When the legendary Wilson died in 1924, admirers knelt in the snow outside his Washington home. His "great vision" of a league for peace had perished long before.

28-25 The Betrayal of Great Expectations

America's spurning of the League was tragically shortsighted. The Republic had helped to win a costly war, but it foolishly kicked the fruits of victory under the table. Whether a strong international organization would have averted World War II in 1939 will always be a matter of dispute. But there can be no doubt that the orphaned League of Nations was undercut at the start by the refusal of the mightiest power on the globe to join it.

The ultimate collapse of the Treaty of Versailles must be laid, at least in some degree, at America's doorstep. This complicated pact, tied in with the four other peace treaties through the League Covenant, was a top-heavy structure designed to rest on a four-legged table. When the fourth leg, the United States, was never put into place, the rickety contraption teetered for over

Varying Viewpoints

Woodrow Wilson: Realist or Idealist?

As the first president to embroil the United States in a foreign war, Woodrow Wilson was obliged to make a systematic case to the American people to justify his unprecedented European intervention. His ideas have largely defined the character of American foreign policy ever since—for better or worse.

"Wilsonianism" comprised three closely related principles: (1) the era of American isolation from world affairs had irrevocably ended; (2) the United States must infuse its own founding ideals—including democracy, the rule of law, free trade, and national self-determination (or anticolonialism)—into the international order; and (3) American influence should be actively employed to steer the world away from rivalry and warfare and toward a cooperative and peaceful international system, maintained by the League of Nations or, later, the United Nations.

Whether that Wilsonian vision constituted hard-nosed realism or starry-eyed idealism has excited scholarly debate for nearly a century. "Realists," such as George F. Kennan and Henry Kissinger, have insisted that Wilson was anything but a realist. They criticized the president as a naive, impractical dreamer who failed to understand that the international order was, and always will be, an anarchic, unruly arena, outside the rule of law, where only military force can effectively protect the nation's security. In a sharp critique in his 1950 study, *American Diplomacy*, Kennan condemned Wilson's vision as "moralism-legalism." In this view Wilson dangerously threatened to sacrifice American self-interests on the altar of his admirable but ultimately unworkable ideas.

Wilson's defenders, including his biographers Arthur S. Link and Thomas J. Knock, argue that Wilson's idealism was in fact a kind of higher realism, recognizing as it did that armed conflict on the scale of World War I could never again be tolerated and that some framework of peaceful international relations simply had to be found. The development of nuclear weapons in a later generation gave this argument more force. This "liberal" defense of Wilsonianism derives from the centuries-old liberal faith that, given sufficient intelligence and willpower, the world can be made a better place. Realists have rejected this notion of moral and political progress as hopelessly innocent, especially as applied to international affairs.

Some leftist scholars, such as William Appleman Williams, have argued that Wilson was in fact a realist of another kind: a subtle and wily imperialist whose stirring rhetoric cloaked a grasping ambition to make the United States the world's dominant economic power. Sometimes called "the imperialism of free trade," this strategy allegedly sought not to decolonialize the world and open up international commerce for the good of peoples elsewhere but to create a system in which American economic might would irresistibly prevail. Wilson's defenders, however, counter that in a Wilsonian world, *all* parties would be better off because of free trade and international competition.

Still other scholars, especially John Milton Cooper Jr., have emphasized the absence of economic factors in shaping Wilson's diplomacy. Isolationism, claims Cooper, held such sway over American thinking precisely because the United States had such a puny financial stake abroad. No hard American economic interests were mortally threatened in 1917, nor for a long time thereafter. In these circumstances, Wilson and his political descendants, such as Franklin D. Roosevelt, had no choice but to appeal to abstract ideals and high principles. The "idealistic" Wilsonian strain in American diplomacy, in this view, may have been an unavoidable heritage of America's historically isolated situation. If so, it was Wilson's genius to make practical use of those ideas in his bid for popular support of his diplomacy.

Finally, a new generation of scholars has begun to explore the influence of Wilsonian ideals on social movements outside the United States and Europe. Erez Manela has argued that emerging anticolonial and nationalist movements appropriated Wilsonian ideals and adapted them to their own political ends, challenging forms of colonialism that Wilson himself failed to criticize. In this view, Wilsonianism's most enduring legacy, ironically, took root outside of the United States.

a decade and then crashed in ruins—a debacle that played into the hands of the German demagogue Adolf Hitler. The Senate's rejection of a Security Treaty with France pledging American support in the event of another German invasion likewise proved disastrous. That spurning compelled France to begin rearming aggressively—which drove the Germans, illegally, to do the same.

The United States hurt its own cause when it buried its head in the sand. Granted that the conduct of its Allies had been disillusioning, carrying through the Wilsonian program would have served its own interests. Had it forthrightly assumed its war-born responsibilities and resolutely embraced the role of global leader, the United States could have used its enormous strength to shape the world's future. Instead, it permitted the warring nations of World War I blithely to drift toward the abyss of a second and even more bloody international disaster.

Chapter Summary

As soon as he assumed the presidency, the eloquent, idealistic, but often ideologically self-righteous Woodrow Wilson successfully carried out a sweeping progressive program of economic reform of the tariff, money and banking, and the trusts—what Wilson called the "triple wall of privilege." He also achieved substantial social reforms that benefited women and the working classes, but he actually furthered Black segregation.

Wilson's attempt to implement similar progressive moral goals in foreign policy was less successful, as he stumbled into military involvements in the Caribbean and revolutionary Mexico. The outbreak of World War I in Europe brought growing risks of American involvement, especially because of the threat to neutral shipping from German submarine warfare. Led by President Wilson, most Americans sought to stay out of the war, though most sympathized more with the Allies than with the Germans.

Wilson temporarily avoided war by extracting the precarious *Sussex* pledge from Germany. His progressive campaign of 1916, appealing to workers and former bull moose supporters, narrowly won him reelection over Charles Evans Hughes and the Republicans. While Wilson never directly promised to stay out of war, his campaign slogan led many to believe so.

Germany's declaration of unlimited submarine warfare in January 1917, as well as the Zimmermann note proposing a German alliance with Mexico, finally caused the United States to declare war. Wilson aroused the country to patriotic heights by declaring the war an idealistic crusade for democracy and a just peace, based on his sweeping Fourteen Points.

Vigorous wartime propaganda stirred voluntary commitment to the war effort, but at the cost of stifling dissent and curtailing civil liberties. American voluntary mobilization worked wonders in organizing industry, producing food, and financing the war. Labor, including women, made substantial wartime gains, though numerous strikes and the radical IWW caused disruptions. Some progressive women opposed the war, but the majority of women's wartime efforts helped spur passage of the Nineteenth (Suffrage) Amendment. The beginnings of the Great Migration of Black people from the South to northern cities, sometimes as strikebreakers, led to racial tensions and riots. Against this backdrop of war and domestic turmoil, a two-year-long influenza pandemic killed 675,000 Americans and sickened many more.

To assemble the vast AEF in a brief time Congress enacted a military draft. America's soldiers took nearly a year to arrive in Europe, and they fought in only two major battles at the end of the war. America's main contribution to the Allied victory was the threat of endless supplies of men and matériel to follow. Wilson's immense prestige created high expectations for an idealistic peace based on his Fourteen Points. But his own political blunders and the opposition of European statesmen forced him to compromise his lofty aims and made the Versailles Treaty considerably harsher than he intended.

Opposition to Wilson and the League of Nations arose not only from traditional isolationists but from militant anti-Germans, liberals, and diverse ethnic groups. As Henry Cabot Lodge stalled the treaty in the U.S. Senate, Wilson tried to rouse the country on behalf of his cherished League. A stroke ended Wilson's pro-League speaking tour, and his stubborn refusal to compromise with Lodge and the Republicans finally killed the treaty and the League. Wilson sought a "solemn referendum" on the League in the election of 1920, but the public delivered a harsh repudiation of Wilsonianism. Republican isolationists turned Harding's victory into a death sentence for the League. America thus turned its back on international affairs and attempted to return to its isolationist traditions.

Key Terms

- Underwood Tariff (706)
- Federal Reserve Act (707)
- Federal Trade Commission Act (707)
- Clayton Anti-Trust Act (707)
- holding companies (707)
- Workingmen's Compensation Act (708)
- Adamson Act (708)
- Jones Act (708)
- Tampico Incident (711)
- Central Powers (712)
- Allies (712)
- U-boats (713)
- *Lusitania* (713)
- Zimmermann note (716)
- Fourteen Points (719)
- Committee on Public Information (720)
- Espionage Act (721)
- *Schenck v. United States* (721)
- War Industries Board (722)
- Industrial Workers of the World (723)
- general strike (723)
- Great Migration (723)

- Nineteenth Amendment (724)
- Sheppard-Towner Maternity Act (724)
- American Expeditionary Forces (AEF) (727)
- influenza pandemic, 1918–1920 (727)
- Battle of Château-Thierry (729)
- Meuse-Argonne offensive (729)
- League of Nations (732)
- Versailles, Treaty of (732)
- irreconcilables (733)

People to Know

- Louis D. Brandeis
- Victoriano Huerta
- Francisco ("Pancho") Villa
- Arthur Zimmermann
- George Creel
- Eugene V. Debs
- William D. ("Big Bill") Haywood
- Herbert C. Hoover
- Alice Paul
- Henry Cabot Lodge
- Edith Bolling Galt Wilson

Chronology

1913	• Underwood Tariff Act • Sixteenth Amendment (income tax)	• Federal Reserve Act • Huerta takes power in Mexico
1914	• Clayton Anti-Trust Act • Federal Trade Commission established	• U.S. seizes port of Veracruz, Mexico • World War I begins in Europe
1915	• La Follette Seaman's Act • *Lusitania* torpedoed and sunk by German U-boat	• Germany declares submarine war area around British Isles
1916	• *Sussex* ultimatum and pledge • U.S. exports to European belligerents skyrocket • Workingmen's Compensation Act • Federal Farm Loan Act • Warehouse Act	• Adamson Act • Pancho Villa raids New Mexico • Brandeis appointed to Supreme Court • Jones Act • Wilson defeats Hughes for presidency
1917	• Germany resumes unrestricted submarine warfare • Zimmermann note • Railroads placed under federal control • United States enters World War I	• Espionage Act of 1917 • Wilson calls for "peace without victory" • Bolshevik Revolution
1918	• Wilson proposes Fourteen Points • Sedition Act of 1918 • Battle of Château-Thierry	• Second Battle of the Marne • Meuse-Argonne offensive
1918–1919	• Armistice ends World War I • Worldwide influenza pandemic	
1919	• Paris Peace Conference and Treaty of Versailles • Wilson's pro-League tour and collapse	• Eighteenth Amendment (prohibition of alcohol) passed • First Senate defeat of Versailles Treaty
1920	• Final Senate defeat of Versailles Treaty after reconsideration • Nineteenth Amendment (woman suffrage) passed	• Harding defeats Cox for presidency

To Learn More

Nancy Bristow, *American Pandemic: The Lost Worlds of the 1918 Influenza Epidemic* (2017)

Christopher Capozzola, *Uncle Sam Wants You: World War I and the Making of the Modern American Citizen* (2008)

John Milton Cooper, Jr., *The Warrior and the Priest: Woodrow Wilson and Theodore Roosevelt* (1983)

__________, *Woodrow Wilson, A Biography* (2009)

Ernest Freeberg, *Democracy's Prisoners: Eugene V. Debs, the Great War, and the Right to Dissent* (2008)

Lewis L. Gould, *Four Hats in the Ring: The 1912 Election and the Birth of Modern Politics* (2008)

Maurine W. Greenwald, *Women, War, and Work: The Impact of World War I on Women Workers in the United States* (1980)

Adam Hochschild, *American Midnight: The Great War, a Violent Peace, and Democracy's Forgotten Crisis* (2022)

David M. Kennedy, *Over Here: The First World War and American Society* (rev. ed., 2005)

Thomas J. Knock, *To End All Wars: Woodrow Wilson and the Quest for a New World Order* (1992)

Erez Manela, *The Wilsonian Moment: Self-Determination and the International Origins of Anticolonial Nationalism* (2007)

Cameron McWhirter, *Red Summer: The Summer of 1919 and the Awakening of Black America* (2011)

Edward Stettner, *Shaping Modern Liberalism: Herbert Croly and Progressive Thought* (1993)

Trygve Throntveit, *Power Without Victory: Woodrow Wilson and the American Internationalist Experiment* (2017)

Robert W. Tucker, *Woodrow Wilson and the Great War: Reconsidering America's Neutrality, 1914–1917* (2007)

Chapter 29

Prosperity and Its Perils: 1920–1932

> We in America today are nearer to the final triumph over poverty than ever before in the history of any land. We have not yet reached the goal—but . . . we shall soon, with the help of God, be in sight of the day when poverty will be banished from this nation.
>
> Herbert Hoover, 1928

Chapter Outline

- The emergence of a mass-consumption economy
- The automobile era
- Radio and the movies
- Women's rights and sexual liberation
- The KKK returns
- Racial terror lynching in the Jim Crow South
- Immigration restriction, 1921–1924
- Prohibition and gangsterism
- Modernism and the Harlem Renaissance
- Religious fundamentalism and the Scopes trial
- Probusiness Republicans in the White House
- The Great Crash of 1929
- Hoover battles the Great Depression
- Instability abroad and growing aggression in Asia

The Presence of the Past: "The Lost Cause"

Bloodied by the war and disillusioned by the peace, Americans turned inward in the 1920s. They partly sealed off the domestic economy from the rest of the world and plunged headlong into a dizzying decade of startling technological innovation and unprecedented prosperity—at least in the booming cities where a majority of Americans now lived. Yet just beneath the glittering surface lurked nagging worries about the future, as new inventions, new consumer products, and new forms of leisure and entertainment deeply disrupted familiar ways of life. Awash in both affluence and anxiety, Americans denounced "radical" foreign ideas, condemned "un-American" lifestyles, and clanged shut the immigration gates against foreign peoples.

Three conservative Republican presidents—Warren G. Harding, Calvin Coolidge, and Herbert Hoover—steered the nation on the roller-coaster ride of the 1920s, a thrilling ascent from the depths of post–World War I recession to breathtaking economic heights, followed by a terrifying crash into the Great Depression.

Meanwhile, the United States retreated from its brief internationalist fling during World War I and resumed with a vengeance its traditional foreign policy of military unpreparedness and political isolationism.

Focus Questions

1. How did technological developments like the automobile, the motion picture, radio, and birth control contribute to American affluence and alter American culture in the 1920s?
2. Why did the United States turn so completely inward in the 1920s, and what public fears generated such developments as the red scare, the Ku Klux Klan, and severe immigration restrictions?
3. What were the causes and consequences of racial terror violence in the Jim Crow South, and how did Black Americans mobilize against this violence?
4. How and why did the conservative Republican administrations of Harding, Coolidge, and Hoover slow the pace of progressive reform and regulation?

Examining the Evidence: *The Jazz Singer*, 1927

Contending Voices: All That Jazz

Examining the Evidence: Lampooning Hoover, 1932

5. What regions, people, and industries benefited from the economic prosperity of the 1920s? Who did not, and why? What caused the Crash of 1929, and how did Hoover attempt to address the early Great Depression?

29-1 Putting America on Rubber Tires

A new industrial revolution slipped into high gear in America in the 1920s. Machinery was the new messiah—and the automobile was its principal prophet.

Of all the inventions of the era, the automobile cut the deepest track. It heralded an amazing new industrial system based on standardized parts, assembly-line fabrication, and mass-production techniques.

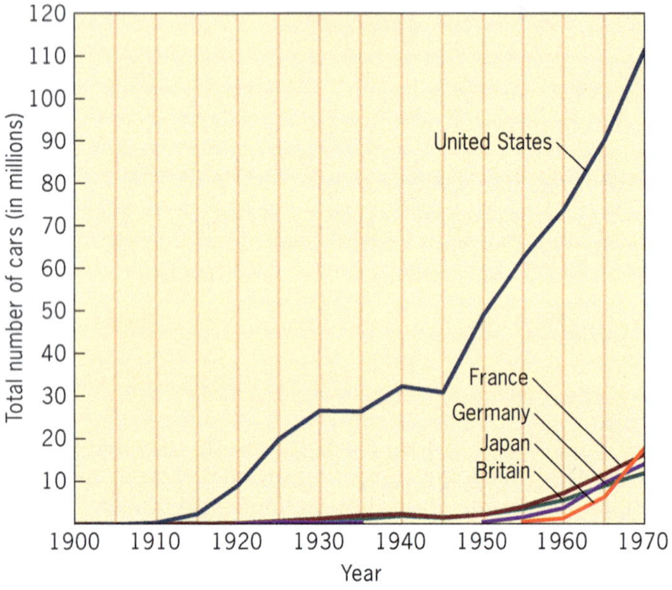

Figure 29.1 International Comparison of Number of Automobiles

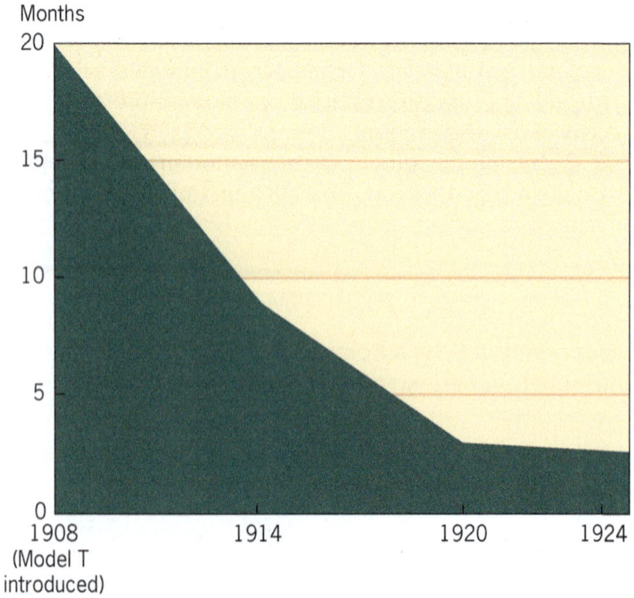

Figure 29.2 The Cost of a Model T Ford, 1908–1924 Henry Ford's mass-production techniques scaled up production while cutting costs and put the automobile within reach of the workingperson's wallet. (Cost is shown in months of labor for an employee at the average national wage.)

Americans adapted rather than invented the internal-combustion, gasoline-fueled engine; Europeans can claim the original honor. But as the twentieth century dawned, a few ingenious American entrepreneurs, conspicuously including Henry Ford, were rapidly accelerating the automobile industry from infancy to full-throttle adulthood.

Ford's high and hideous Model T ("Tin Lizzie"), first produced in 1908, was cheap, rugged, and reasonably reliable, though rough and clattering. By 1920, some 8 million passenger vehicles were chugging along the nation's roads. By decade's end, Americans owned 23 million cars, more than the rest of the world combined (refer to Figure 29.1).

Lean and silent Henry Ford, who was said to have wheels in his head, erected an immense motorcar empire, with Detroit as its capital. Ill-educated, this multimillionaire mechanic was socially and culturally narrow. "History is bunk," he once declared. But he dedicated himself with one-track devotion to building a car for what he called "the great multitude." He wanted it to be "large enough for the family, but small enough for the individual to run and care for." So economical were his methods that in the mid-1920s he was selling the Ford roadster for $260—well within the purse of a thrifty worker (refer to Figure 29.2). He is supposed to have remarked that a customer could buy an automobile of any color—just as long as it was black.

Ford's mechanized colossus owed much to the stopwatch efficiency techniques of Frederick W. Taylor, a prominent inventor and engineer who sought to eliminate wasted motion. His epitaph reads "Father of **Scientific Management**." Inspired by Taylor, Ford championed the technique of the moving assembly line, where semi-skilled or even unskilled workers endlessly performed simple repetitive tasks, a process that has been called **Fordism** (and was brilliantly mocked in Charlie Chaplin's classic 1936 film, *Modern Times*).

Ford made his vast River Rouge complex near Detroit into the world's largest integrated factory. His assembly-line construction eventually reached such perfection that a finished vehicle rolled off the line every ten seconds. The repetitive drudgery and punishing pace contributed to high labor turnover, so to retain workers, Ford introduced the "five-dollar day" in 1914, more than doubling wages.

Ford's pay boost came with strings attached. Workers had to comply with a rigorous code of conduct both at work and at home, enforced by a network of company spies. Immigrant employees had to participate in "Americanization" programs. The viciously antisemitic Ford, who peddled conspiracy theories about Jews in his personal newspaper, sought to make

The Granger Collection, NYC

Image 29.1 Gas Station, 1923 Gas stations like this one began to appear about 1913. Before that the nation's handful of automobile owners bought fuel from their local oil companies and stored it in tanks in their own yards.

his company a model for the kind of society he envisioned: homogenous, free of class conflict, and uncomplainingly committed to traditional Christian values.

29-2 The Advent of the Gasoline Age

The "horseless carriage" had a sweeping impact on American life. Employing directly or indirectly about 6 million people by 1930, the automobile industry was a major wellspring of the nation's prosperity. Thousands of new jobs emerged in supporting industries, including rubber, glass, fabrics, oil production and refining, as well as highway construction and thousands of service stations and garages (refer to Image 29.1). America's standard of living, energized by this infectious vitality, rose to an enviable level.

At first a luxury, the automobile quickly became a necessity. The geometry of commerce as well as the rhythms of work and family life were reorganized around cars and highways. Diets improved as perishable fresh fruits and vegetables could now be speedily brought from farm to table on the newly paved roads that ribboned across the land, often paid for by taxes on gasoline. Lured by sophisticated advertising (refer to Image 29.2), and encouraged by tempting installment-plan buying, countless Americans with modest paychecks acquired the habit of riding as they paid. By the late 1920s, Americans owned more automobiles than bathtubs. "I can't go to town in a bathtub," one homemaker explained.

Suburbs sprawled out still farther from urban cores, as motoring Americans gave birth to what soon became a nation of commuters. Meanwhile, the morals of flaming youth sagged correspondingly—at least in the judgment of their elders. What might young people get up to in the privacy of a closed-top Model T? An Indiana juvenile court judge voiced parents' worst fears when he condemned the automobile as "a house of prostitution on wheels." Even the decade's infamous crime waves were aided and abetted by the automobile, for gangsters could now make quick motorized getaways.

MPI/Getty Images

Image 29.2 A Window on the Future This image from 1924 captured a future that was just beginning to emerge in a world where cars, telephones—and women in business roles—would eventually be commonplace.

Everett Collection Historical/Alamy Stock Photo

Image 29.3 Lucky Lindy Charles A. Lindbergh (1902–1974) stands in front of the aircraft that made him famous. The first person to fly solo across the Atlantic, Lindbergh became an acclaimed celebrity—perhaps the first media-made "hero" of the twentieth century. His shining reputation later lost some of its luster when he voiced anti-Semitic sentiments and opposed American entry into World War II, though he went on to fly several combat missions in the war against Japan.

A lifelong resident of Muncie, Indiana, disguised as "Middletown" in Robert and Helen Lynd's exhaustive investigation of American life in a typical medium-size community during the 1920s, pooh-poohed their scientific sociological methods:

"Why on earth do you need to study what's changing this country? I can tell you what's happening in just four letters: A-U-T-O!"

Gasoline engines also provided the power that enabled humans to fulfill the age-old dream of sprouting wings. The Wright brothers, Orville and Wilbur, had performed "the miracle at Kitty Hawk," North Carolina, on December 17, 1903, when Orville took aloft a feebly engined plane that stayed airborne for 12 seconds and 120 feet. Thus two obscure Ohio bicycle repairmen launched the air age.

As aviation got off the ground, the world shrank. Private companies began to operate passenger lines with airmail contracts, which were in effect a subsidy from Washington. The first transcontinental airmail route connected New York and San Francisco in 1920.

In 1927, modest and skillful Charles A. Lindbergh, the so-called Flyin' Fool, electrified the world with the first solo west-to-east conquest of the Atlantic. Seeking a prize of $25,000, the lanky stunt flier courageously piloted his single-engine plane, the *Spirit of St. Louis*, from New York to Paris in a grueling thirty-three hours and thirty-nine minutes (refer to Image 29.3).

Lindbergh's exploit swept Americans off their feet. They clasped the soaring "Lone Eagle" to their hearts, as the bashful young man who had pioneered long-distance air travel also reluctantly pioneered the dubious terrain of an emerging celebrity culture. "Lucky Lindy" received an uproarious welcome in the "hero canyon" of lower Broadway, as eighteen hundred tons of ticker tape showered upon him.

Humanity's new wings increased the tempo of an already breathless civilization. The gods of war also eagerly embraced the lethal new aerial weapon. It had played a colorful but minor role in the Great War recently concluded, and would revolutionize warfare in the even greater conflict of World War II that erupted in the following decade. The Atlantic Ocean was shriveling to about the size of the Aegean Sea in the days of Socrates, while America's isolation behind ocean moats was becoming a bygone dream.

29-3 Radio Waves and Filmland Fantasies

The speed of the airplane was far eclipsed by the speed of radio waves. Guglielmo Marconi, an Italian, invented wireless telegraphy in the 1890s, and his brainchild was used for long-range communication during World War I.

Next came the voice-carrying radio. A red-letter day was posted on November 2, 1920, when the Pittsburgh radio station KDKA broadcast the results of the presidential election. Listeners heard the news in "real time," well before reading it in the next day's newspaper. Just four years later, more than 600 stations were beaming news and entertainment to millions of listeners, in a stunning demonstration of the impressive speed with which transformative technological innovations could be commercialized and broadly disseminated. In 1926, RCA (Radio Corporation of America) joined several local stations together in the first national radio network, NBC (National Broadcasting Company). Its first nationwide broadcast was the 1927 Rose Bowl football game from Pasadena, California. The airwaves were becoming so crowded that the government in 1927 created the Federal Radio Commission (FRC, later FCC, Federal Communications Commission) to license broadcasters and assign them designated frequencies. In contrast to the government-owned communications systems of Europe, radio in American remained in the domain of private enterprise, though under government regulation.

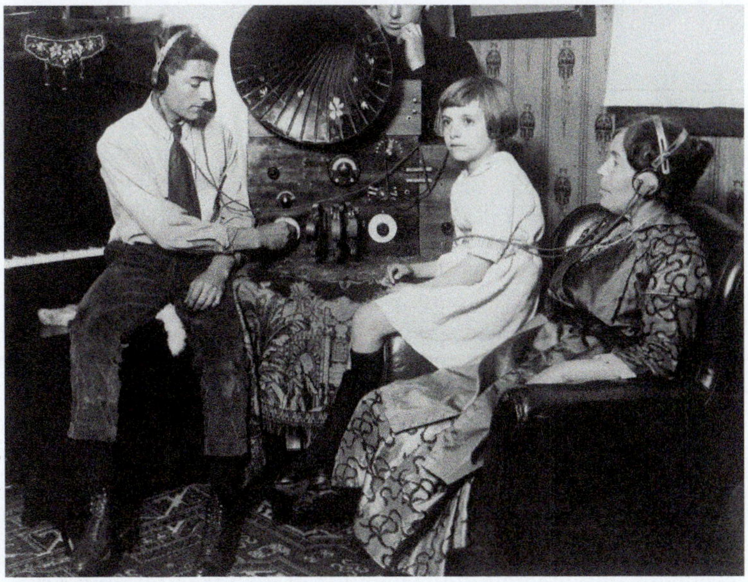
Bettmann/Getty Images

Image 29.4 Family "Listening In" to the Radio, 1922 The Lacambanne family of San Francisco gathered in their parlor to listen to a concert broadcast over the radio. In the early years, when only a handful of households could afford a radio, listening brought family and neighbors together to share a common experience.

While other marvels of the era—like the automobile—were luring Americans away from home, the radio was drawing them back. For much of the decade, family and neighbors gathered around a household's sole radio as they once had around the toasty hearth (refer to Image 29.4). At the same time, radio knitted the nation together. Listeners in diverse regions heard voices with standardized accents, while countless millions from coast to coast "tuned in" to the same perennial comedy favorites like "Amos 'n' Andy."

Movies proved yet another contributor to the growing industries of mass entertainment and the relentless homogenization of culture. The flickering movie was the fruit of numerous geniuses, including Thomas A. Edison. As early as the 1890s, penny arcades featured naughty one-minute "peep shows." The real birth of the modern movie came in 1903, when the first story sequence reached the screen. This breathless twelve-minute melodrama, *The Great Train Robbery*, a "western" filmed in New Jersey, was shown in five-cent theaters, popularly called "nickelodeons." Spectacular among the first full-length classics was D. W. Griffith's three-hour, twelve-reel *Birth of a Nation* (1915). Infamously racist, the film glorified the Ku Klux Klan of Reconstruction days and defamed both Black people and Northern "carpetbaggers." White Southerners reputedly fired guns at the screen during the attempted "rape" scene. After screening the film at the White House, President Wilson was said to have remarked, "It is like writing history with lightning." Black leaders angrily organized protest marches, petition campaigns, and public hearings. But *Birth of a Nation* became a blockbuster, drawing crowds nationwide and helping popularize a mythic, pro-Southern narrative of slavery and Reconstruction (refer to "The Presence of the Past: 'The Lost Cause'," pp. 744–746).

An enormous industry was thus launched. Sun-blessed Hollywood, in southern California, quickly became the movie capital of the world. A new era for film began in 1927 with the success of the first "talkie"—*The Jazz Singer*. Starring the white performer Al Jolson in blackface, the "sentimental melodrama" was a hit among both white and Black audiences (refer to "Examining the Evidence: *The Jazz Singer*, 1927," p. 747).

Movies eclipsed all other new forms of amusement in the phenomenal growth of their popularity. By the end of the decade, 80 million Americans went to the movies weekly, about 65 percent of the population. Movie "stars" of the first pulchritude commanded larger salaries than the president of the United States, in some cases as much as $100,000 for a single picture.

Critics bemoaned the vulgarization of popular tastes and the commercialization of culture wrought by the new technologies of radio and motion pictures. But the effects of the new mass media were not all negative. The insularity of ethnic communities eroded as the immigrants' children forsook the neighborhood vaudeville theater for the downtown movie palace or turned away from Grandma's Yiddish storytelling to tune in "The Goldbergs." If some of the rich diversity of the immigrants' Old Country cultures was lost, the standardization of tastes and of language hastened entry into the American mainstream—and set the stage for the emergence of a working-class political coalition that, for a time, would overcome the divisive ethnic differences of the past.

The Presence of the Past

"The Lost Cause"

"The Lost Cause" is a term used to describe a flagrantly spurious version of Southern history embraced by many white Southerners after the Civil War. It presented an extravagantly romanticized picture of the pre-war South as a benign society where contented slaves toiled faithfully for their revered masters, who in turn presided over a "moonlight-and-magnolias" commonwealth that was cruelly extinguished by aggressive "Yankees."

Cresting in popularity in the late nineteenth century, the myth of the Lost Cause fed on the national yearning for post-Civil War sectional reconciliation even as it helped to justify the suppression of Black rights in the Jim Crow South (refer to "21-9 Class Conflicts and Ethnic Clashes," pp. 531–533). Although many Americans contested its transparently false claims, the fable of the Lost Cause grotesquely distorted both academic and popular understanding of the Civil War and Reconstruction. It also inspired neo-Confederate and white supremacist movements well into the twenty-first century.

The mythology's name and core claims originated with Edward A. Pollard's *The Lost Cause* (1866), the first of several postwar polemics by Southern writers who traded sword for pen to refight the Civil War. Pollard and others argued that the Confederacy had legitimately seceded to defend constitutionally protected states' rights; that the slave system was benevolent and necessary to preserve a "natural" racial order; and that the rebels were not traitors but valiant defenders of the purest American ideals and a cherished way of life.

Black Americans strenuously pushed back against those fictions. Frederick Douglass condemned the "nauseating flatteries of Robert E. Lee" that proliferated after the Confederate General's death in 1870. Black leaders also strongly denounced the Lost Cause's depictions of "happy slaves" with no interest in freedom.

Despite its pro-Confederate claims, the myth of the Lost Cause captured the imaginations of many white Northerners with its message of shared grief and sectional rapprochement.

Library of Congress Prints and Photographs Division Washington, DC, 20540 USA

Image 29.5 **United Daughters of the Confederacy Wreath-Laying Ceremony, Arlington National Cemetery, 1922** Eight years after its dedication, members of the UDC gather before the towering bronze monument that stood at the center of the "Confederate section" of the national cemetery. Unlike the rest of the Arlington graves, the surrounding Confederate markers were arranged in concentric circles, not rows, and had distinctive pointed tops.

Proponents of the Lost Cause literally cemented the myth into the national consciousness by erecting over six hundred monuments between the 1890s and 1930s—the height of the Jim Crow era when racial violence and Black disenfranchisement reached their peaks (refer to "29-8 Terror Lynching and Racial Violence," p. 752). Statues commemorating Confederate heroes were erected across the South, delivering a clear, intimidating message to Black Southerners about their subservient place in the racial order.

Although Robert E. Lee had objected to glorifying the Confederacy, he became the monuments' most popular individual subject. In 1890, an estimated 100,000 citizens gathered in Richmond to dedicate an enormous equestrian statue of Lee. Monuments to the Confederacy appeared outside the South as well. In 1900, Congress authorized the reinternment of Confederate remains in a special section of Arlington National Cemetery. A Confederate Memorial statue featuring benignly sanitized depictions of slavery was installed there in 1914.

Women played leading roles in monument-building and the broader project of rewriting Southern history. The United Daughters of the Confederacy (UDC) was founded in 1894 with a mission to "collect and preserve the material for a truthful history of the war between the Confederate States and the United States of America." The UDC claimed nearly 100,000 members by the early twentieth century. UDC chapters took root throughout the South as well as in Seattle, Salt Lake City, New York, and other far-flung cities.

The UDC installed Confederate battle flags in Southern classrooms, and rewrote textbooks in terms favorable to the white South. Prominent academic historians reinforced the myth, including William A. Dunning of Columbia University and Princeton professor (and future U.S. president) Woodrow Wilson. Their well-received histories of the period downplayed the horrors of slavery and heaped scorn upon Reconstruction. What became known as "the Dunning School" long influenced historical interpretations of Reconstruction (refer to Chapter 20, "Varying Viewpoints: Did Reconstruction Fail?" p. 516).

Popular culture further amplified the message of the Lost Cause. Bestselling novels by Southern authors like Thomas F. Dixon and Margaret Mitchell spun memorable tales of gallant white Southerners, conniving Northern interlopers, and vengeful ex-slaves. Dixon persuaded Kentucky-born filmmaker D. W. Griffith to adapt his 1905 novel *The Clansman* into Hollywood's first feature-length film. Spectacular in scope and unvarnished in its racism, *The Birth of a Nation* (1915) drew sharp criticism from Black leaders for its warmly sympathetic portrayal of the Ku Klux Klan (refer to "29-3 Radio Waves and Filmland Fantasies," pp. 742–743).

The Birth of a Nation contributed to the modern revival of the Klan and inspired the largest and most famous of all Confederate monuments: a towering group portrait of Robert E. Lee, Jefferson Davis, and Thomas "Stonewall" Jackson carved into the 1,700-foot-high granite face of Stone Mountain, Georgia. Begun in 1916, the monument took over fifty years to complete.

Two decades after *The Birth of a Nation*, the film adaptation of Mitchell's sentimental pro-Southern saga *Gone with the Wind* (1939) broke box-office records and snagged eight Academy Awards (including, ironically enough, the first won by a Black performer). *Gone with the Wind* remains the highest-grossing film of all time—despite critical condemnation for its skewed portrayals of plantation slavery and Reconstruction.

(continued)

Saul Loeb/Getty Images

Image 29.6 Confederate Flag Carried Through the U.S. Capitol, January 6, 2021 In the modern era, white nationalists and hard-right adherents adopted the Confederate battle flag as a potent and controversial political symbol. Here a pro–Trump rioter carries the flag past portraits of two famous Civil War-era lawmakers: pro-slavery Senator John C. Calhoun (D-South Carolina) and abolitionist Senator Charles Sumner (R-Massachusetts).

Surging civil rights activism in the post-WWII South spurred a resurgence of Lost Cause activism as Confederate iconography was employed to stiffen segregationist resistance. White Southerners scoffed at court-ordered integration by renaming schools, highways, and parks after Jefferson Davis and Robert E. Lee. Nearly fifty new Confederate monuments were erected in the South between 1950 and 1970. Georgia added the Confederacy's "Stars and Bars" to the state flag in 1956, and South Carolina began flying the Confederate battle flag over its statehouse in 1961.

Civil rights legislation in the 1960s at last brought a legal end to Jim Crow but did not fully extinguish the flame of the Lost Cause. Well into the twenty-first century, some Southerners continued to defend the Confederate battle flag as a symbol of "heritage," as well as an expression of their continuing antipathy to the federal government. Over forty Confederate monuments have been built since 2000.

But as the twenty-first century unfolded, citizens both Black and white agitated for dismantling the Confederate monuments that dominated town squares and public parks. In 2020, Mississippi became the last state to remove elements of the Confederate banner from its state flag. In 2022, a government commission recommended the removal of the Confederate Memorial from Arlington National Cemetery.

Yet the enduring myth of the Lost Cause and its Confederate symbols continue to provoke controversy. When white supremacists descended on Charlottesville, Virginia, in 2017 to protest the planned removal of a statue of Robert E. Lee, a violent clash erupted, ending in one death and dozens of injuries. Mass protests following the 2020 murder of George Floyd led to the removal, relocation, or renaming of over 250 such memorials. Yet more than two thousand Confederate symbols and statues still stand, and seven Southern states have enacted laws to block their removal.

The Lost Cause myth is a notorious example of what might be called weaponized history. It won widespread acceptance at the turn of the twentieth century by promising national reconciliation after decades of sectional strife and a devastating civil war. Yet it conspicuously excluded Black Americans and served to perpetuate racial inequality. More than 150 years after the Confederacy's defeat, the struggle to comprehend its history and its symbols continues—illustrating once again the great Southern novelist William Faulkner's declaration that "the past is never dead. It's not even past."

29-4 The Mass-Consumption Economy

The automobile and radio revolutions heralded some momentous shifts in the character of the economy. Car-makers and other manufacturers seemed to have mastered the problems of production; their worries now focused on consumption. Could they find the mass markets for the goods they had contrived to spew forth in such profusion? Similarly, radio broadcasters needed reliable sources of revenue to pay for performers and for upgrading equipment.

Responding to these needs, yet another new industry emerged: advertising. By persuasion and ploy, seduction and sexual suggestion, advertisers sought to make Americans chronically discontented with their paltry possessions and want more, more, more. In August 1922 a New York City station aired the first radio advertisement, for a real estate developer. A founder of this new "profession" was Bruce Barton, prominent New York partner in a Madison Avenue firm. In 1925, Barton published a best seller, *The Man Nobody Knows*, setting forth the provocative thesis that Jesus Christ was the greatest adman of all time. "Every advertising man ought to study the parables of Jesus," Barton preached. "They are marvelously condensed, as all good advertising should be." Barton even had a good word to say for Christ's executive ability: "He picked up twelve men from the bottom ranks of business and forged them into an organization that conquered the world."

Buying on credit was another feature of the postwar economy. Incomes were growing, but not as fast as the dazzling array of consumer goods American manufacturers could now produce. "Possess today and pay tomorrow" became the message directed at buyers. Once-frugal descendants of Puritans went ever deeper into debt to own all kinds of newfangled marvels—refrigerators, vacuum cleaners, and especially cars and radios—that poured out of American factories. Prosperity thus accumulated an overhanging cloud of debt, and the economy became increasingly vulnerable to disruptions of the credit structure.

29-5 Sluggers, Flappers, and "Race Men"

Far-reaching changes in lifestyles and values paralleled the dramatic upsurge of the economy. Sports became big business. Ballyhooed by the "image makers," home-run heroes like George H. ("Babe") Ruth were far better known than most statesmen. The fans bought tickets in such

Examining the Evidence

The Jazz Singer, 1927

The Jazz Singer was the first feature-length "talkie," a motion picture in which the characters actually spoke, and its arrival spelled the end for "silent" films, where the audience read subtitles with live or recorded music as background. Although moviegoers flocked to *The Jazz Singer* to hear recorded sound, when they got there they found a movie concerned with themes of great interest to the urban, first- or second-generation immigrant audiences who were Hollywood's major patrons. *The Jazz Singer* told the story of a poor, assimilating Jewish immigrant torn between following his father's wish that he train as an Orthodox cantor and his own ambition to make a success of himself as a jazz singer, performing in the then-popular blackface style. The movie's star, Al Jolson, was himself an immigrant Jew who had made his name as a blackface performer.

The minstrel shows that had so electrified white American audiences in the nineteenth century remained popular in the early twentieth. By this time, Jewish entertainers had entirely monopolized these roles. Jolson, like other Jewish blackface performers, used his ability to impersonate a Black person to force his acceptance into mainstream white American society. This use of blackface seems ironic, since Black Americans in the 1920s were struggling with their own real-life battles against Jim Crow–era segregation and white racial violence.

Later critics condemned *The Jazz Singer* as insensitive. Yet Jolson's progressive racial attitudes and promotion of Black performers made him a favorite star among 1920s Black audiences, who embraced the film.

Besides the novelty of being a "talkie," what may have made *The Jazz Singer* a box office hit in 1927? How might different types of viewers in the audience have responded to the story? What does the continued acceptance of blackface reveal about racial attitudes at the time?

Sunset Boulevard/Getty Images

Image 29.7 **Al Jolson Performs in Blackface in *The Jazz Singer*, 1927.**

numbers that Babe's hometown park, Yankee Stadium, became known as "the house that Ruth built." In 1921, the hard-slugging heavyweight champion, Jack Dempsey, knocked out the dapper French light heavyweight Georges Carpentier. The Jersey City crowd in attendance had paid more than a million dollars—the first in a series of million-dollar "gates" in the golden 1920s. Ruth and Dempsey thus took their places alongside Charles Lindbergh and movie stars in the pantheon of media-made celebrities who were most famous simply for being famous.

Women found expanding opportunities for employment in the cities, though clustered in a few low-paying fields (such as retail clerking and office typing) that became classified as "women's work." An organized birth-control movement, led by the fiery feminist Margaret

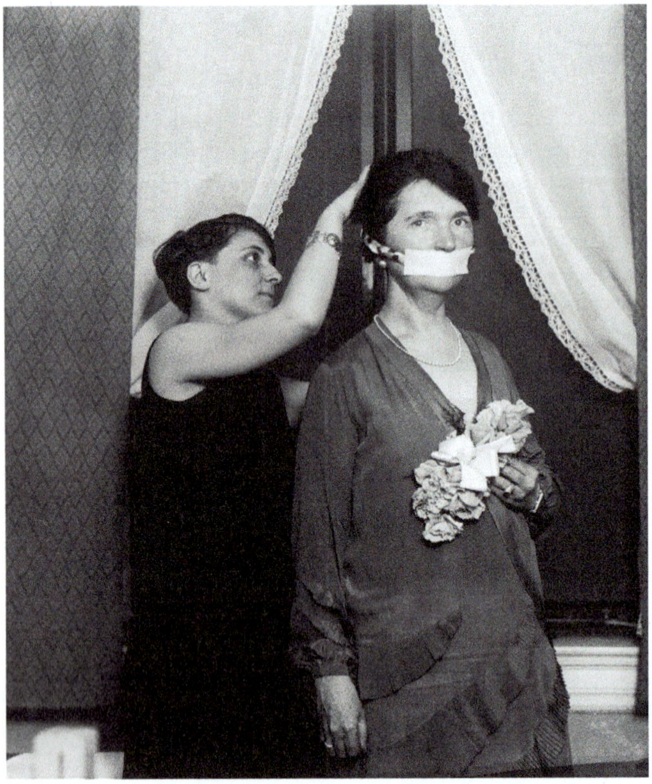

Bettmann/Getty Images

Image 29.8 Margaret Sanger (1879–1966) in Boston, 1929 Forbidden to speak on the inflammatory topic of birth control, a defiant Sanger covered her mouth and "lectured" in Boston by writing on a blackboard. Since 1912, Sanger had devoted herself to promoting birth control and establishing contraceptive clinics throughout the United States.

Everett Historical/Shutterstock.com

Image 29.9 The Guardian of Morality Women's new one-piece bathing suits were a sensation in the 1920s. Here a check is carefully made to ensure that not too much leg is showing.

Sanger, openly championed the use of contraceptives (refer to Image 29.8). Alice Paul's National Woman's Party began in 1923 to campaign for an Equal Rights Amendment to the Constitution. (The campaign was still stalled short of success more than a century later.) To some defenders of traditional ways, it seemed that the world had suddenly gone mad.

Organized religion remained an important part of modern life. Despite persistent stereotypes of cities as places of sin and moral dissolution, the rate of regular churchgoing in the mid-1920s was higher in the cities than the countryside. But the Fundamentalist champions of the old-time religion lost ground to the Modernists, who liked to think that God was a "good guy" and the universe a pretty chummy place.

In Los Angeles, charismatic Aimee Semple McPherson held packed auditoriums spellbound as she preached her "four-square gospel." Raising over $1 million from her faithful converts, "Sister Aimee" built an enormous, crystal-doored temple and a radio station that broadcast her sermons nationwide. McPherson became one of the most famous figures of the decade, although her popularity ebbed after she was accused of staging her own 1926 kidnapping, possibly to cover up an extramarital affair.

Even before the war, one observer thought the chimes had "struck sex o'clock in America," and the 1920s witnessed what many old-timers regarded as a veritable erotic eruption. Advertisers exploited sexual allure to sell everything from soap to car tires. Once-corseted maidens now proclaimed their new freedom as "flappers" in bobbed tresses and dresses. Young women swanned about with hemlines elevated, stockings rolled, breasts taped flat, cheeks rouged, and lips a "crimson gash" that held a dangling cigarette. Thus did the flapper symbolize a yearned-for and devil-may-care independence (some said wild abandon) in some American women. Still more adventuresome females shocked their elders when they sported the new one-piece bathing suits (refer to Image 29.9).

Justification for this new sexual frankness could be found in the recently translated writings of Dr. Sigmund Freud. This bearded Viennese physician argued that sexual repression was responsible for a variety of nervous and emotional ills. Thus not pleasure alone but also health demanded sexual gratification and liberation.

Many taboos flew out the window as sex-conscious Americans let themselves go. As unknowing Freudians, teenagers pioneered the sexual frontiers. In an earlier day, a kiss had been the near-equivalent of a proposal of marriage. But in the new era, young folk smooched in darkened movie houses or took to their parents' automobiles to explore the exotic territory of each other's bodies.

If the flapper was the goddess of the "era of wonderful nonsense," jazz was its sacred music. With its virtuoso wanderings and tricky syncopation, jazz moved northward from New Orleans along with Black migrants during World War I. Tunes like W. C. Handy's "St. Louis Blues" (1914) became instant classics, as the wailing saxophone became the trumpet of the new era. Black performers such as Handy, "Jelly Roll" Morton, Louis Armstrong, and Joe "King" Oliver gave birth to jazz, but all-white bands and white impresarios cornered a good deal of the profits.

Contending Voices

All That Jazz

Not all Americans welcomed the rising popularity of jazz music. For some stuffy traditionalists, including clergyman and writer Henry van Dyke (1852–1933), jazz symbolized the excessive liberation and dangerous exuberance of modern society.

"As I understand it, [jazz] is not music at all. It is merely an irritation of the nerves of hearing, a sensual teasing of the strings of physical passion. . . . '[J]azz' is an unmitigated cacophony, a combination of disagreeable sounds in complicated discords, a willful ugliness and a deliberate vulgarity."

But for a musical innovator like Duke Ellington (1899–1974), jazz's connection to the modern temper was the key to its authenticity and importance.

"I am trying to play the natural feelings of a people. . . . Beethoven, Wagner, and Bach are geniuses; no one can rob their work of the merit that is due it, but these men have not portrayed the people who are about us today, and the interpretation of these people is our future music."

Consider This:

How do music and other artistic genres reflect "the people who are about us today"?

A new racial consciousness blossomed in the northern Black communities that burgeoned during and after the war. Pride, solidarity, and social awareness animated the work and activism of the era's "race men" and "race women," bringing new visibility to Black art and politics. New York City's Harlem neighborhood counted some 150,000 African American residents in the 1920s. They sustained a vibrant, creative culture that nourished poets like Langston Hughes, whose first volume of verses, *The Weary Blues*, appeared in 1926. Harlem in the 1920s also spawned a charismatic political leader, Marcus Garvey (refer to Image 29.10). The Jamaican-born Garvey founded the **United Negro Improvement Association (UNIA)** to promote the resettlement of African Americans in their own "African homeland." Within the United States, the UNIA sponsored stores and other businesses, like the Black Star Line Steamship Company, to keep the Black community's dollars in Black pockets. Most of Garvey's enterprises failed

Library of Congress Prints and Photographs Division

Image 29.10 Marcus Garvey (1887–1940) In 1920, Garvey, the Jamaican-born founder of the United Negro Improvement Association, advocated a constitution to protect the rights of Black Americans. By that year his nationalist self-help organization boasted eleven hundred branches in forty countries in the Americas and Africa. Most of those branches were located in the United States, his base of operations until 1927.

financially, and Garvey himself was convicted in 1927 for alleged mail fraud and deported by a nervous U.S. government. But the pride that Garvey inspired among the 4 million people who counted themselves UNIA followers paved the way for other Black thinkers and activists, and proved important to the later founding of the Nation of Islam (Black Muslim) movement.

29-6 Seeing Red

Hysterical fears of Soviet Russia continued to color American thinking for several years after the Communists came to power in the **Bolshevik Revolution** of 1917. Even though the Communist Party in America remained tiny, when an epidemic of strikes convulsed the Republic at war's end, many upstanding Americans jumped to the conclusion that labor troubles were fomented by bomb-and-whisker Bolsheviks. Fire-and-brimstone evangelist Billy Sunday struck a responsive chord when he described a Bolshevik as "a guy with a face like a porcupine and a breath that would scare a pole cat. . . . If I had my way, I'd fill the jails so full of them that their feet would stick out the window."

The big **red scare** of 1919–1920 resulted in a nationwide crusade against left-wingers whose Americanism was suspect. Attorney General A. Mitchell Palmer earned the title of the "Fighting Quaker" by his excess of zeal in rounding up some six thousand suspects. When a bomb shattered both the nerves and the Washington home of Palmer in June 1919, the "Fighting Quaker" was thereupon dubbed the "Quaking Fighter."

Late in December 1919, a shipload of 249 alleged alien radicals was deported on the *Buford* (the "Soviet Ark") to the "workers' paradise" of Russia. One zealot cried, "My motto for the Reds is S.O.S.—ship or shoot." Hysteria got another boost in September 1920 when a still-unexplained bomb blast on Wall Street killed thirty-eight people and wounded more than a hundred others.

During 1919–1920 several nervous state legislatures passed **criminal syndicalism laws** outlawing the mere *advocacy* of violence to secure social change. Critics protested that mere words were not criminal deeds, that there was a great gulf between throwing fits and throwing bombs, and that "free screech" was for the nasty as well as the nice. The hysteria went so far that in 1920, five members of the New York legislature, all lawfully elected, were denied their seats simply because they were Socialists.

The red scare was a godsend to conservative businesspeople, who used it to break the backs of the fledgling unions. Labor's call for the "closed," or all-union, shop was denounced as "Sovietism in disguise." Employers, in turn, hailed their own antiunion campaign for the "open" shop as the **American plan**.

Anti-radicalism and antiforeignism were reflected in a notorious case regarded by liberals as a "judicial lynching." Nicola Sacco, a shoe-factory worker, and Bartolomeo Vanzetti, a fish peddler, were convicted in 1921 of the murder of a Massachusetts paymaster and his guard. The jury and judge were prejudiced in some degree against the defendants because they were Italians, atheists, anarchists, and draft dodgers.

Liberals and radicals the world over rallied to the defense of the two aliens doomed to die. The case dragged on for six years until 1927, when the condemned men were electrocuted. Communists and other radicals were thus presented with two martyrs in the "class struggle," while many American liberals hung their heads. The evidence against the accused, though damaging, betrayed serious weaknesses. If the trial had been held in a less-charged atmosphere, the outcome might well have been only a prison term.

29-7 The Second Coming of the KKK

Further evidence of the toxic mood of postwar America was the appearance of a new Ku Klux Klan, which mushroomed fearsomely in the early 1920s. Despite the familiar sheets and hoods, it more closely resembled the nativist movements of the 1850s than the nightriders of the 1860s. It was anti-Black, but also antiforeign, anti-Catholic, anti-Jewish, antipacifist, anti-Communist, anti-internationalist, anti-evolutionist, antibootlegger, antigambling, anti-adultery, and anti–birth control. It was also pro-Anglo-Saxon, pro-"native" American, and pro-Protestant. In short, the besheeted Klan betokened an extremist, ultraconservative uprising against many of the forces of diversity and modernity that were transforming American culture.

As reconstituted, the Klan spread with astonishing rapidity, appealing everywhere to white Protestants alarmed by immigration, labor radicalism, and the dizzying pace of social change.

Image 29.11 Klanswomen on Parade, 1928 Founded in the Reconstruction era, the Ku Klux Klan enjoyed a remarkable resurgence in the 1920s. Here women members, unmasked and unapologetic, march down Pennsylvania Avenue under the shadow of the Capitol dome.

Its largest strongholds were not in the South but the Midwest and Far West. The Klan was so powerful in Southern California that Anaheim (the future site of Disneyland) was nicknamed "Klanaheim."

At its peak in the mid-1920s, the Klan claimed about 5 million dues-paying members and wielded potent political influence. The "Knights of the Invisible Empire" capitalized on adolescent ardor for secret ritual, including among their officials Imperial Wizards, Grand Goblins, King Kleagles, and other "kreatures." The most impressive displays were "konclaves" and huge flag-waving parades. The most ominous symbol was the blazing cross. Although membership was semi-secret, Klansmen and Klanswomen proudly rallied in public with their faces uncovered (refer to Image 29.11). The Klan spread its message through modern tactics of advertising and marketing, including popular jingles and catchphrases. Klan songs included "The Fiery Cross on High," "One Hundred Percent American," and "The Ku Klux Klan and the Pope" (against kissing the Pope's toe). One brutal slogan was "Kill the Kikes, Koons, and Katholics."

This reign of hooded horror, so repulsive to the best American ideals, collapsed rather suddenly in the late 1920s, after scandalous embezzling by Klan officials launched a congressional investigation. The movement ultimately was exposed as a vicious racket based on a \$10 initiation fee, \$4 of which was kicked back to local organizers as an incentive to recruit. The KKK was an alarming manifestation of the stubborn intolerance and prejudice that that infected so much of the American body politic.

Hiram Wesley Evans (1881–1966), imperial wizard of the Ku Klux Klan, in 1926 plaintively described the white cultural grievances that fueled the 1920s Klan and lay behind much of the Fundamentalist revolt against "modernism":

"Nordic Americans for the last generation have found themselves increasingly uncomfortable and finally deeply distressed. . . . One by one all our traditional moral standards went by the boards, or were so disregarded that they ceased to be binding. The sacredness of our Sabbath, of our homes, of chastity, and finally even of our right to teach our own children in our own schools fundamental facts and truths were torn away from us. Those who maintained the old standards did so only in the face of constant ridicule. . . . We found our great cities and the control of much of our industry and commerce taken over by strangers. . . . We are a movement of the plain people, very weak in the matter of culture, intellectual support, and trained leadership. . . . This is undoubtedly a weakness. It lays us open to the charge of being 'hicks' and 'rubes' and 'drivers of second-hand Fords.'"

The Library of Congress

Image 29.12 Publicizing Racial Terror Between 1920 and 1938, the NAACP flew this flag outside its headquarters on Fifth Avenue in New York City, drawing attention to Southern lynching deaths and acts of racial violence often ignored by the national press of the time.

29-8 Terror Lynching and Racial Violence

Black Americans continued to battle the racial violence and extrajudicial lynching that had terrorized the South since Reconstruction. In twelve Southern states between 1877 and 1950, white mobs murdered 4,084 Black people. Another 341 Black people were lynched outside the South. These grisly spectacles were often photographed and witnessed by large crowds. The victims' corpses were left to dangle from nooses or dragged through Black neighborhoods. Yet few perpetrators were arrested, much less convicted, for these gruesome crimes.

Black journalists such as Ida B. Wells and groups like the newly founded (1909) National Association for the Advancement of Colored People (NAACP)—leveraging the growing readership of Black newspapers and the NAACP's monthly magazine, *The Crisis*, edited by W. E. B. Du Bois—struggled to bring the ugly truths of lynching to the attention of an apparently uncaring nation (refer to Image 29.12). Black leaders pressed in vain for Congress to pass federal anti-lynching legislation, but were repeatedly stymied by segregationist Southern lawmakers.

The increased prosperity and self-sufficiency of some Black communities triggered horrific incidents of mass violence. When Black sharecroppers in Elaine, Arkansas tried to meet with union organizers in 1919, an armed mob of nearly a thousand white locals and five hundred U.S. soldiers descended on the town to quell the "insurrection." Black residents were chased from their homes and hunted down over three bloody days. The exact death toll of the Elaine Massacre remains unknown, but is estimated to be in the hundreds.

In 1921, white rioters attacked the Tulsa, Oklahoma, district known as "Black Wall Street." Twenty-four hours of looting and burning later, a thriving African American community of ten thousand lay devastated, its thirty-five city blocks charred and smoking. As many as three hundred people may have died in the **Tulsa Race Massacre**. Deeper South, vigilantes targeted independent Black towns like Rosewood, Florida, which was burned to the ground in 1923. Its residents were hounded off their land and never compensated for their losses.

29-9 Stemming the Foreign Flood

Isolationist America of the 1920s, ingrown and provincial, had little use for the immigrants who began to stream into the country again as peace settled soothingly on the war-torn world. Some 800,000 stepped ashore in 1920–1921, about two-thirds of them from southern and eastern Europe. The "one-hundred-percent Americans," recoiling at the sight of this resumed "New Immigration," once again cried that the famed poem at the base of the Statue of Liberty was all too literally true: they claimed that a sickly Europe was indeed vomiting on America "the wretched refuse of its teeming shore."

Congress moved to plug the breach with the **Immigration Act of 1924**. It restricted immigration from Europe to 2 percent of persons of their nationality who had been living in the United States as recorded in the census of 1890, before which date comparatively few southern Europeans had arrived.* Great Britain and Northern Ireland, for example, could send 65,721 a year as against 5,802 for Italy. Southern Europeans bitterly denounced the device as unfair and discriminatory—a triumph for the "nativist" belief that blue-eyed and fair-haired northern

*Five years later, the Immigration Act of 1929, using 1920 as the quota base, virtually cut immigration in half by limiting the total to 152,574 a year. In 1965, Congress abolished the national-origins quota system.

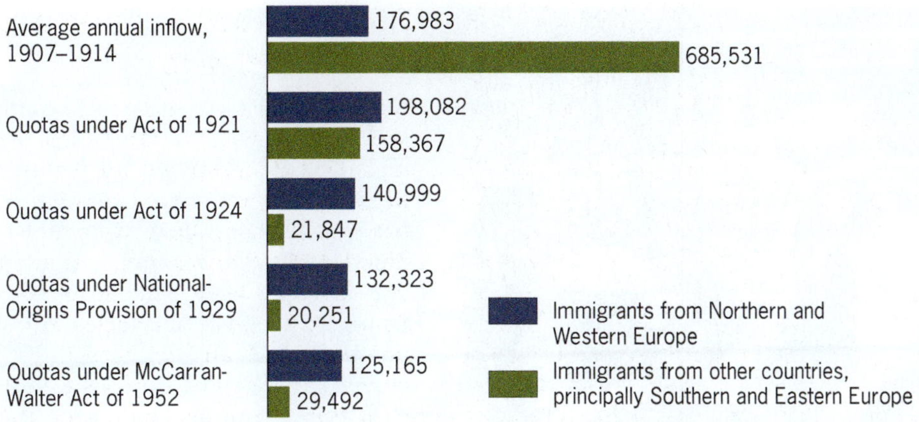

Figure 29.3 Annual Immigration and the Quota Laws Isolationists and nativists succeeded in damming up the flow of immigrants to the United States in the early 1920s. The Immigration Act of 1924 placed strict quotas on European immigrants and completely shut out the Japanese. Later laws continued the pattern. (Refer to "The Presence of the Past: Immigration—Legal, Illegal, and Otherwise," pp. 913–915.)

Europeans were of better blood. The purpose was clearly to freeze America's existing racial composition, which was largely northern European.

A flagrantly discriminatory section of the Immigration Act of 1924 effectively slammed the door against virtually all Asians and Arabs. Mass "Hate America" rallies erupted in Japan. One Japanese superpatriot expressed his outrage by committing suicide near the American embassy in Tokyo. Exempt from the quota system were Canadians and Latin Americans. Meanwhile, the **Indian Citizenship Act of 1924** granted citizenship to all Native Americans born in the United States—though some states illegally continued to deny voting rights to Native Americans for another quarter-century.

Immigration dwindled to a mere trickle. By 1931, probably for the first time in the American experience, more foreigners left than arrived. Quotas thus caused America to sacrifice something of its tradition of freedom and opportunity, as well as its future ethnic diversity (refer to Figure 29.3).

The Immigration Act of 1924 marked the end of an era—a period of virtually unrestricted immigration that in the preceding century had brought some 35 million newcomers to the United States, mostly from Europe. The immigrant tide was now cut off, but it left on American shores by the 1920s a patchwork of ethnic communities separated from each other and from the larger society by language, religion, and customs. Many of the most recent arrivals, including the Italians, Jews, and Poles, lived in isolated enclaves with their own houses of worship, newspapers, and theaters. Efforts to organize labor unions repeatedly foundered on the rocks of ethnic differences. Immigrant workers on the same shop floor might share a common interest in wages and working conditions, but they often had no common language with which to forge common cause. Indeed, cynical employers often played upon ethnic rivalries to keep their workers divided and powerless. Ethnic variety thus undermined class and political solidarity. It was an old American story, but one that some reformers hoped would not go on forever.

29-10 The Prohibition "Experiment"

One of the last spasms of the progressive reform movement was prohibition, loudly supported by crusading churches and by many women. The arid new order was authorized in 1919 by the **Eighteenth Amendment** (refer to the Appendix), as implemented by the **Volstead Act** passed by Congress later that year. Together these laws made the world "safe for hypocrisy."

Like the later "war on drugs," the "war on alcohol" represented in part an effort by self-righteous elites to improve the behavior of those they considered the unruly lower orders of society. White Southerners were eager to keep stimulants out of the hands of Black people, lest they burst out of "their place." In the West, prohibition represented an attack on all the vices associated with the ubiquitous Western saloon: public drunkenness, prostitution, corruption, and crime. Eastern "drys" saw prohibition as a way to upgrade the morals and make better workers out of bibulous immigrants (refer to Image 29.13). Unsurprisingly, strong opposition persisted among many "wet" foreign-born communities. Old World styles of sociability were

Image 29.13 No More Booze New York policemen look on in 1921 as workers empty a liquor barrel into the sewer.

built around drinking in beer gardens and corner taverns. Yet most Americans tried to reconcile themselves to the no-booze era. Everywhere carousers indulged in last wild flings, as the nation prepared to enter upon a seemingly permanent "alcoholiday."

But prohibitionists were naive in the extreme. They overlooked the tenacious American tradition of strong drink and of weak control by the central government, especially over private lives. They forgot that the federal authorities had never satisfactorily enforced a law where the majority of the people—or a strong minority—were hostile to it. They ignored the fact that one cannot make a crime overnight out of something that millions of people have never regarded as a crime. Lawmakers could not legislate away a thirst.

Slaking thirst now became a cherished personal liberty. Many ardent wets believed that the way to bring about repeal was to violate the law on a large enough scale. Hypocritical, hip-flasked legislators spoke or voted dry while privately drinking wet. ("Let us strike a blow for liberty" was an ironic toast.) Frustrated soldiers, returning from France, complained that prohibition had been "put over" on them while they were "over there." Grimy workers bemoaned the loss of their cheap beer, while pointing out that the idle rich could buy all the illicit alcohol they wanted. Flaming youth of the jazz age considered it cool to swill "liquid tonsillectomies" made from bathtub-brewed gin.

Prohibition simply did not prohibit. The old-time "men only" corner saloons were replaced by thousands of "speakeasies," each with its tiny grilled window through which the thirsty spoke softly before the barred door was opened. Foreign rum-runners, often from the West Indies, had their inning, and countless cases of liquor leaked down from Canada. Yet the "noble experiment" was not entirely a failure. Bank savings increased, and absenteeism in industry decreased, presumably because of the newly sober ways of formerly soused barflies. Death rates from alcoholism and cirrhosis declined, and on the whole, less alcohol was consumed than in the days before prohibition. But strong drink continued to be available. As one legendary tippler remarked, prohibition was "a darn sight better than no liquor at all."

Automaker Henry Ford (1863–1947), an ardent prohibitionist, posted this notice in his Detroit factory in 1922:

"From now on it will cost a man his job . . . to have the odor of beer, wine or liquor on his breath, or to have any of these intoxicants on his person or in his home. The Eighteenth Amendment is a part of the fundamental laws of this country. It was meant to be enforced. Politics has interfered with the enforcement of this law, but so far as our organization is concerned, it is going to be enforced to the letter."

29-11 The Golden Age of Gangsterism

Prohibition spawned shocking crimes. The lush profits of illegal alcohol led to bribery of the police, many of whom were induced to see and smell no evil. Violent wars broke out in the big cities between rival gangs—often rooted in immigrant neighborhoods—who sought to corner the rich market in booze. Rival triggermen used their sawed-off shotguns and chattering "typewriters" (machine guns) to "erase" bootlegging competitors who were trying to "muscle in" on their "racket." Arrests were few and convictions even fewer, as button-lipped gangsters covered for one another with the underworld's code of silence.

Chicago was by far the most spectacular example of lawlessness. Gang wars in the Windy City claimed nearly five hundred murdered mobsters. In 1925, "Scarface" Al Capone, a grasping and murderous booze distributor, began six years of gang warfare that netted him millions of blood-spattered dollars (refer to Image 29.14). He zoomed through the streets in an armor-plated car with bulletproof windows. A Brooklyn newspaper quipped,

> And the pistols' red glare,
> Bombs bursting in air
> Give proof through the night
> That Chicago's still there.

AP Images

Image 29.14 Gangster Al Capone Fishing in Florida Capone may have looked like any Chicago businessman on vacation, but his business was bigger and nastier than most, as he often eliminated his competition by murder. He was reported as saying, "Everybody calls me a racketeer. I call myself a businessman. When I sell liquor, it's bootlegging. When my patrons serve it on a silver tray on Lake Shore Drive, it's hospitality." He was finally jailed in 1932 for falsifying his income-tax returns.

Capone, though branded "Public Enemy Number One," could not be convicted of the cold-blooded massacre, on St. Valentine's Day in 1929, of seven disarmed members of a rival gang. But after serving most of an eleven-year sentence in a federal penitentiary for income-tax evasion, he was released as a syphilitic wreck.

Gangsters rapidly moved into other profitable and illicit activities: prostitution, gambling, and narcotics. Honest merchants were forced to pay "protection money" to the organized thugs; otherwise, their windows would be smashed, their trucks overturned, or their employees or themselves beaten up. **Racketeers** even invaded the ranks of local labor unions as organizers and promoters. Organized crime had come to be one of the nation's most gigantic businesses. By 1930, the annual "take" of the underworld was estimated to be from \$12 billion to \$18 billion—several times the income of the Washington government.

Criminal callousness sank to new depths in 1932 with the kidnapping for ransom, and eventual murder, of the infant son of aviator-hero Charles A. Lindbergh. The entire nation grieved with the Lindbergh family, causing Congress in 1932 to pass the so-called Lindbergh Law, making interstate abduction in certain circumstances a death-penalty offense.

29-12 Monkey Business in Tennessee

Education in the 1920s continued to make giant bootstrides. The proportion of seventeen-year-olds who finished high school almost doubled in the 1920s, to more than one in four.

The most revolutionary contribution to educational theory during these yeasty years was made by mild-mannered Professor John Dewey, who served on the faculty of Columbia University from 1904 to 1930. By common consent one of America's few front-rank philosophers, he set forth the principles of "learning by doing" that formed the foundation of so-called progressive education, with its greater "permissiveness." He believed that the workbench was as essential as the blackboard and that "education for life" should be a primary goal of the teacher.

Science also scored wondrous advances in these years. A massive public-health program, launched by the oil magnate John D. Rockefeller's richly endowed foundation in the South in 1909, had virtually wiped out the ancient affliction of hookworm by the 1920s. Better nutrition and health care helped to increase the life expectancy of a newborn infant from fifty years in 1901 to fifty-nine years in 1929.

Topical Press Agency/Getty Images

Image 29.15 The Battle over Evolution Opponents of Darwin's theories set up shop at the opening of the famed "Scopes Monkey Trial" in Dayton, Tennessee, in 1925. The trial was an early battle in an American culture war that was still being waged a century later.

> The bombastic Fundamentalist evangelist W. A. (Billy) Sunday (1862–1935) declared in 1925,
>
> "If a minister believes and teaches evolution, he is a stinking skunk, a hypocrite, and a liar."

Yet even though increasing numbers of Christians were coming to reconcile the revelations of religion with the findings of modern science, **Fundamentalism**, with its emphasis on a literal reading of the Bible, remained a vibrant force in American spiritual life. It was especially strong in the Baptist Church and in the rapidly growing Churches of Christ, organized in 1906. In the 1920s, Fundamentalists subjected both science and progressive education to unfriendly fire.

These devoted religionists charged that the teaching of Darwinian evolution was destroying faith in God and the Bible, while contributing to the moral breakdown of youth in the jazz age. In the heart of the so-called **Bible Belt** South, where the spirit of evangelical religion was especially robust, three Southern states, including Tennessee, prohibited the teaching of evolution, "the bestial hypothesis," in the public schools.

The stage was set for the memorable "Monkey Trial" at the hamlet of Dayton, in eastern Tennessee, in 1925 (refer to Image 29.15). Authorities indicted a likable high-school biology teacher, John T. Scopes, for teaching evolution. Batteries of newspaper reporters, armed with notebooks and cameras, descended on the quiet town to witness the **Scopes Trial**. Scopes was defended by nationally known attorneys, while former presidential candidate William Jennings Bryan, an ardent Presbyterian Fundamentalist, joined the prosecution. Taking the stand as an expert on the Bible, Bryan was made to appear foolish by the famed criminal lawyer Clarence Darrow. Five days after the trial was over, Bryan died of a stroke, no doubt brought on by the wilting heat and witness-stand strain.

This historic clash between theology and biology proved inconclusive. Scopes, the forgotten man of the drama, was found guilty and fined $100. But the supreme court of Tennessee, while upholding the law, set aside the fine on a technicality.* The Fundamentalists at best won only a hollow victory, for the absurdities of the trial cast ridicule on their cause.

29-13 Cultural Liberation

Literature and the arts were hardly immune to the infectiously disruptive spirit of the age. By the dawn of the 1920s, most of the custodians of an aging genteel culture had died—Henry James in 1916,

*The Tennessee law was not formally repealed until 1967.

Henry Adams in 1918, and William Dean Howells ("the Dean of American literature") in 1920. A few novelists who had been popular in the previous decades continued to thrive, notably the well-to-do, cosmopolitan New Yorker Edith Wharton and the Virginia-born Willa Cather, esteemed for her stark but sympathetic portrayals of pioneering on the prairies.

But in the decade after the war, a new generation of writers and artists burst upon the scene. Many of them hailed from ethnic and regional backgrounds different from that of the Protestant New Englanders who traditionally had dominated American cultural life. The newcomers exhibited the energy of youth, the ambition of excluded outsiders, and in many cases the smoldering resentment of ideals betrayed. Animated by the spark of the international modernist movement, they bestowed on American culture a new vitality, imaginativeness, and artistic daring.

Central to **modernism** was its questioning of social conventions and traditional authorities, considered outmoded by the accelerating changes of twentieth-century life. No one personified this iconoclasm better than H. L. Mencken, the "Bad Boy of Baltimore." As the era's most influential critic, Mencken promoted modernist causes in politics and literature. Little escaped his acidic wit. In his columns for the *Baltimore Sun*, he assailed marriage, patriotism, democracy, prohibition, Rotarians, and other sacred icons of the middle-class American "booboisie." The provincial South he contemptuously dismissed as "the Sahara of the Bozart" (a bastardization of *beaux arts*, French for the "fine arts"), and he scathingly attacked hypocritical do-gooders as "Puritans." Puritanism, he jibed, was "the haunting fear that someone, somewhere, might be happy."

H. L. Mencken's (1880–1956) obituary of his old nemesis, William Jennings Bryan, seethed with contempt for the American heartland:

"Out where the grass grows high, and the horned cattle dream away the lazy days, and men still fear the powers and principalities of the air—out there between the corn-rows he held his old puissance to the end. There was no need of beaters to drive in his game. The news that he was coming was enough. For miles the flivver dust would choke the roads."

The war had jolted many young writers out of their complacency about traditional values and literary standards. With their pens they probed for new codes of morals and understanding, as well as fresh forms of expression. F. Scott Fitzgerald, a handsome Minnesota-born Princetonian then only twenty-four years old, won instant acclaim when he published *This Side of Paradise* in 1920. Catching the spirit of the hour (often about 4 A.M.), Fitzgerald found "all gods dead, all wars fought, all faiths in man shaken." He followed this melancholy success with *The Great Gatsby* (1925), a brilliant commentary on the illusory American ideal of the self-made man. Midwesterner James Gatz reinvented himself as tycoon Jay Gatsby, only to be destroyed by the power of those with established wealth and social standing. Theodore Dreiser's masterpiece of 1925, *An American Tragedy*, similarly explored the pitfalls of social striving, as it dealt with the murder of a pregnant working girl by her socially ambitious young lover.

Ernest Hemingway, who had seen action on the Italian front in 1917, was among the writers most affected by the war. He responded to pernicious propaganda and the overblown appeal to patriotism by devising his own lean, word-sparing but word-perfect style. Hemingway wrote on the "iceberg" principle: "There is seven-eighths of it under water for every part that shows." His hard-boiled realism typified postwar writing. In *The Sun Also Rises* (1926), he told of disillusioned, spiritually numb American expatriates in Europe. In *A Farewell to Arms* (1929), he turned his own war story into one of the finest novels in any language about the war experience. Hemingway's literary successes and flamboyant personal life made him one of the most famous writers in the world, although he never escaped his demons. He won the Nobel Prize in literature in 1954—and brutally ended his own life with a shotgun blast in 1961.

Hemingway, Fitzgerald, and many other American writers and painters formed an artistic **"Lost Generation"** as expatriates in postwar Europe. They found shelter and inspiration in the Paris salon of their brainy and eccentric countrywoman, Gertrude Stein. Hobnobbing in Paris with the iconoclastic artists Pablo Picasso and Henri Matisse, Stein wrote radically experimental poetry and prose, including *Three Lives* (1909), *Tender Buttons* (1914), and, most famously, *The Autobiography of Alice B. Toklas* (1933), named for her lifelong partner.

Stein joined fellow American poets Ezra Pound and T. S. Eliot in the vanguard of modernist literary innovation. These "high modernists" experimented with the breakdown of traditional literary forms and exposed the losses associated with modernity. They wrote in a self-consciously internationalist mode, haughtily rejecting the parochialism they found at home. Pound, a brilliantly erratic Idahoan who permanently deserted America for Europe, rejected what he called "an old bitch civilization, gone in the teeth" and proclaimed his doctrine: "Make It New." Pound strongly influenced the Missouri-born and Harvard-educated Eliot, who took

In a score of novels, William Faulkner (1897–1962) explored the collective psychology of his native South, where the pressures of historical memory continually reverberated in the present. As he wrote in *Requiem for a Nun* (1951),

"The past is never dead. It's not even past."

up residence (and eventual citizenship) in England. In *The Waste Land* (1922), Eliot produced one of the most impenetrable but influential poems of the century. Composed of discontinuous segments, multiple perspectives, and arcane allusions, the poem depicts the fragmentation and frightening desolation of postwar society. Much more accessible was the poetry of fellow Harvard graduate e.e. cummings, who relied on unorthodox diction and peculiar typesetting to produce startling poetical effects.

Not all literary efforts of the era proved so radical. Many American writers continued to employ a familiar regionalist style that was by turns celebratory and critical. Poet Robert Frost, born in San Francisco, wrote hauntingly about the nature and folkways of his adopted New England. Ever-popular Carl Sandburg extolled the working classes of Chicago in strong, simple cadences. Other regionalist writers caustically probed Middle American small-town life. Sherwood Anderson dissected various fictional personalities in *Winesburg, Ohio* (1919), finding them all in some way warped by their cramped psychological surroundings. Sinclair Lewis, a hotheaded, heavy-drinking journalist from Sauk Centre, Minnesota, sprang into prominence in 1920 with *Main Street*, the best-selling story of one woman's unsuccessful revolt against provincialism. In *Babbitt* (1922) he affectionately pilloried George F. Babbitt, a prosperous, vulgar, middle-class real estate broker who slavishly conforms to the respectable materialism of his group. The word *Babbittry* was quickly coined to describe his all-too-familiar lifestyle.

William Faulkner, a dark-eyed, pensive Mississippian, focused on the displacement of the agrarian Old South by a rising industrial order. His life's work offered a fictional chronicle of an imaginary, history-rich Deep South county he named "Yoknapatawpha." In powerful books like *The Sound and the Fury* (1929) and *As I Lay Dying* (1930), Faulkner peeled back layers of time and consciousness from the constricted souls of his ingrown Southern characters. In contrast to Hemingway's spare prose, Faulkner experimented with multiple narrators, complex structure, and "stream of consciousness" techniques. His extended meditation on "the rag-tag and bob-ends of old tales and talkings" culminated in what some readers consider his greatest work, *Absalom, Absalom!* (1936).

The Granger Collection, NYC

Image 29.16 **Langston Hughes (1902–1967)** Raised in the Midwest, Hughes arrived in New York City in 1921 to attend Columbia University. He spent most of his life in Harlem, making it so much the center of his prolific and versatile literary career that he was often introduced as "the Poet Laureate of Harlem."

Though novelists and poets dominated modernist literary output in the 1920s, American composers and playwrights also made important contributions on the stage. Jerome Kern and Oscar Hammerstein's *Show Boat* debuted on Broadway in 1927 as the first true American "musical play." Eugene O'Neill, a restless Princeton dropout, emerged as America's first world-class playwright. In plays like *Strange Interlude* (1928), O'Neill laid bare Freudian notions of sex and the subconscious in a succession of dramatic soliloquies.

O'Neill arose from New York's Greenwich Village, which before and after the war was a seething cauldron of writers, painters, musicians, actors, and other would-be artists. After the war a Black cultural renaissance also took root uptown in Harlem, led by such gifted writers as Claude McKay, Langston Hughes (refer to Image 29.16), and Zora Neale Hurston, and by jazz artists like Louis Armstrong and Eubie Blake. In an outpouring of creative expression called the **Harlem Renaissance**, they proudly exulted in Black culture and argued for a "New Negro" who was a full citizen and a social equal to whites. Adopting modernist techniques, Hughes and Hurston captured the oral and improvisational traditions of contemporary Black Americans in poetry and prose.

29-14 The Republican "Old Guard" Returns

While young people shook loose from convention and artists and writers pushed creative boundaries, in Washington, DC, a politically conservative old order settled back into place with a heavy thud at war's end, crushing the reform seedlings that had sprouted in the progressive era.

The "return to normalcy" began with Warren G. Harding, inaugurated as president in 1921. Harding *looked* presidential. With erect figure, broad shoulders, high forehead, bushy eyebrows, and graying hair, he was one of the best-liked men of his generation. Yet the charming, smiling exterior concealed a weak, inept interior. With a mediocre mind, Harding quickly found himself beyond his depth in the presidency. "God! What a job!" was his anguished cry on one occasion.

Harding, like Grant, was unable to detect moral halitosis in his associates, and he was soon surrounded by his poker-playing, shirt-sleeved cronies of the "Ohio Gang." The difference between George Washington and Warren Harding, ran a current quip, was that while Washington could not tell a lie, Harding could not tell a liar. He "was not a bad man," said one observer. "He was just a slob."

Candidate Harding, who admitted his scanty mental furnishings, had promised to gather about him the "best minds" of the party. In addition to wealthy banker Andrew Mellon at Treasury, they included the brilliantly incisive Secretary of State Charles Evans Hughes, and "Great Engineer" Secretary of Commerce Herbert Hoover. But the "best minds" of the cabinet were largely offset by two of the worst: Senator Albert B. Fall of New Mexico, at the Department of the Interior and Harding's fellow Ohioan Harry M. Daugherty as attorney general.

29-15 A Government That Means Business

The economy kicked off its war harness in 1919, faltered a few steps in the recession of 1920–1921, and then sprinted forward for nearly seven years. Wartime government controls on the economy were swiftly dismantled. The War Industries Board disappeared with almost indecent haste. With its passing, progressive hopes for more government regulation of big business evaporated. A nest-feathering crowd moved into Washington and proceeded to hoodwink Harding, whom many regarded as an "amiable boob."

Meanwhile, the federal government moved to spend more soberly and tax wealth more lightly. In 1921, a Republican Congress created the **Bureau of the Budget**. The bureau's director was to assist the president in preparing careful estimates of receipts and expenditures for submission to Congress as the annual budget.

Burdensome taxes inherited from the war were especially distasteful to Secretary of the Treasury Mellon, as well as to his fellow millionaires. Consequently, Mellon helped engineer a series of dramatic tax reductions. In 1921, a wealthy person with an income of $1 million had paid $663,000 in income taxes; by 1926, thanks to Mellon's reforms, the same person paid about $200,000. Secretary Mellon's spare-the-rich policies thus shifted much of the tax burden from the wealthy to the middle-income groups.

Mellon, lionized by conservatives as the "greatest secretary of the Treasury since Hamilton," remains a controversial figure. True, he reduced the national debt by $10 billion—from about $26 billion to $16 billion. But foes of the emaciated multimillionaire also accused him of indirectly encouraging the bull market. If he had absorbed more of the national income in taxes, there would have been less money left for frenzied speculation. His refusal to do so typified the single-mindedly probusiness regime that dominated the political scene throughout the postwar decade.

This new Old Guard hoped to improve on the old business doctrine of laissez-faire. Their plea was not simply for government to keep its hands off business, but for government to help guide business along the path to profits. They subtly and effectively achieved their ends by putting the courts and the administrative bureaus into the safekeeping of fellow stand-patters for the duration of the decade (refer to Image 29.17).

The Supreme Court was a striking example of this trend. Harding lived less than three years as president, but he appointed four of the nine justices. Several of his choices were or became deep-dyed reactionaries, and they buttressed the dike against popular currents for nearly two decades. Harding's fortunate choice for chief justice was William Howard Taft. The ex-president at last had the job he had always wanted, and he not only performed his duties ably but surprisingly was more liberal than some of his cautious associates.

In the first years of the 1920s, the Supreme Court repeatedly axed progressive legislation. It killed a federal child-labor law, stripped away many of labor's hard-won gains,

The Granger Collection

Image 29.17 The Cash Register Chorus Business leaders loved Calvin Coolidge's capitalist-friendly policies.

and rigidly restricted government intervention in the economy. In the landmark case of ***Adkins v. Children's Hospital*** (1923), the Court reversed its own reasoning in *Muller v. Oregon* (refer to "27-5 Progressive Women," pp. 686–689), which had declared women to be deserving of special protection in the workplace, and invalidated a minimum-wage law for women. Its strained ruling was that because women now had the vote (Nineteenth Amendment), they were the legal equals of men and could no longer be protected by special legislation. The contradictory premises of the *Muller* and *Adkins* cases framed a debate over gender differences that would continue into the next century: Were women sufficiently different from men that they merited special legal and social treatment, or were they effectively equal in the eyes of the law and therefore undeserving of special protections and preferences?

Organized labor, buffeted by the era's pro-corporate, anti-radical mood, limped along badly in the postwar decade. Employers broke the bloody steel strike of 1919 by exploiting ethnic and racial divisions among the steelworkers and branding the strikers as dangerous "reds." A two-month railway strike in 1922 so disrupted interstate commerce that Congress passed a law requiring future disputes to be resolved by swift arbitration. Unions wilted in this hostile political environment, and membership shriveled by nearly 30 percent between 1920 and 1930.

Fierce suppression of the labor movement contributed to the stagnation of workers' wages even as employers' profits soared. By the end of the 1920s, the top 0.1 percent of families owned over 20 percent of American wealth, while the share of wealth owned by the bottom 90 percent of families declined considerably.

Justice Oliver Wendell Holmes (1841–1935), wryly dissenting in the Adkins case, said,

"It would need more than the Nineteenth Amendment to convince me that there are no differences between men and women, or that legislation cannot take those differences into account."

29-16 America Seeks Benefits Without Burdens

The United States' rejection of the Treaty of Versailles opened a decade when isolationism was enthroned in Washington (refer to Image 29.18). Harding regarded the League of Nations as a thing unclean, though he reluctantly dispatched "unofficial observers" to its seat in Geneva, Switzerland, to hang around like detectives shadowing a suspected criminal.

Disarmament was one international issue on which Harding finally seized the initiative, prodded by businesspeople unwilling to dig deeper into their pockets to finance the ambitious naval building program started during the war. A deadly contest was shaping up with Britain and Japan, which watched with alarm as the oceans filled with American vessels. Britain still commanded the world's largest navy, but the clatter of American riveters proclaimed that the United States would soon overtake it.

These worries brought about the headline-making Washington "Disarmament" Conference in 1921–1922. Invitations went to all the major naval powers—except Bolshevik Russia, whose government the United States refused officially to recognize. At the outset, Secretary Hughes startled the delegates with a comprehensive, concrete plan for declaring a ten-year "holiday" on the construction of battleships and even for scrapping some of the huge dreadnoughts already built. He proposed that the scaled-down navies of America and Britain should enjoy parity in battleships and aircraft carriers, with Japan on the small end of a 5:5:3 ratio. This arrangement sounded to the sensitive Japanese ambassador like "Rolls-Royce, Rolls-Royce, Ford."

The Granger Collection, NYC

Image 29.18 "I Sympathize Deeply with You, Madam, but I Cannot Associate with You," 1923 President Harding's secretary of state, Charles Evans Hughes, broke the news to a desperate, war-tattered Europe that America was going, and staying, home.

Complex bargaining, including face-saving compensation for Japan, yielded the Five-Power Naval Treaty of 1922 (refer to Figure 29.4). The British and Americans both conceded that they would refrain from fortifying their Far Eastern possessions, including the Philippines. The Japanese were not subjected to such restraints. An additional Four-Power Treaty bound Britain, Japan, France, and the United States to preserve the status quo in the Pacific—another concession to the jumpy Japanese. Finally, the Washington Conference gave chaotic China—"the Sick Man of the Far East"—a shot in the arm with the **Nine-Power Treaty** of 1922, whose signatories agreed to nail wide-open the Open Door in China.

When the final gavel banged, the Hardingites boasted loudly of their globe-shaking achievement in disarmament. But their satisfaction was somewhat illusory. No restrictions had been placed on small warships, and the other powers churned ahead with the construction of cruisers, destroyers, and submarines, while penny-pinching Uncle Sam lagged dangerously behind.

	Battleships	Battleship Tonnage	Aircraft Carrier Tonnage
U.S.	18	525,000	135,000
Britain	22	525,000	135,000
Japan	10	315,000	81,000
France	7	175,000	60,000
Italy	6	175,000	60,000

Figure 29.4 Limits Imposed by Washington Conference, 1921–1922 The pledge of the British and Americans to refrain from fortifying their Far Eastern possessions, while Japan was allowed to fortify its possessions, was the key to the naval-limitation treaty. The United States and Great Britain thus won a temporary victory but later paid a horrendous price when they had to dislodge the well-entrenched Japanese from the Pacific in World War II.

Congress also pointedly declared that it was making no commitment to the use of armed force or any kind of joint action when it ratified the Four-Power Treaty. These reservations, in effect, rendered the treaty a dead letter. Ominously, the American people seemed content to rely for their security on words and wishful thinking.

A similar sentimentalism welled up later in the decade, when Americans clamored for the "outlawry of war." The conviction spread that if quarreling nations would only take the pledge to foreswear war as an instrument of national policy, swords could be beaten into plowshares. Under President Calvin Coolidge, Secretary of State Frank B. Kellogg, who later won the Nobel Peace Prize for his role, signed the famed **Kellogg-Briand Pact** with the French foreign minister in 1928, ultimately ratified by sixty-two nations.

This new parchment peace was delusory in the extreme. Defensive wars were still permitted, and what scheming aggressor could not cook up an excuse of self-defense? Lacking both muscles and teeth, the pact was a diplomatic derelict—and virtually useless in a showdown. Yet it accurately—and dangerously—reflected the American mind in the 1920s, which was all too willing to be lulled into a false sense of security. This mood took even deeper hold in the ostrich-like neutralism of the 1930s.

29-17 Hiking the Tariff Higher

A comparable lack of realism afflicted foreign economic policy in the 1920s. Businesspeople, dazzled by a prosperous home market, sought to keep that market to themselves by flinging up insurmountable tariff walls around the United States.

In 1922, Congress passed the comprehensive **Fordney-McCumber Tariff Law**, raising rates to a trade-throttling level averaging 38.5 percent. The high-tariff course thus charted by the Republican regimes set off an ominous chain reaction. An impoverished Europe needed to sell its manufactured goods to the United States, particularly if it hoped to achieve economic recovery and to pay its huge war debt to Washington. America needed to give foreign nations a chance to make a profit from it so that they could buy its manufactured articles and repay debts. International trade, Americans were slow to learn, is a two-way street. In general, they could not sell to others in quantity unless they bought from them in quantity—or lent them more U.S. dollars.

Erecting tariff walls was a game that two could play. The American example spurred European nations, throughout the feverish 1920s, to pile up higher barriers themselves. These artificial obstacles were doubly bad. They hurt not only American-made goods but the products of European countries as well. The whole vicious circle further deepened the international economic distress, providing one more rung on the ladder by which Adolf Hitler scrambled to power.

The Granger Collection, NYC

Image 29.19 **Washington Officials Trying to Outpace the Teapot Dome Scandal, ca. 1922**

29-18 The Stench of Scandal, then "Silent Cal"

The loose morality and get-rich-quickism of the Harding era manifested themselves spectacularly in a series of scandals. Most shocking of all was the **Teapot Dome scandal**, an affair that involved priceless naval oil reserves at Teapot Dome (Wyoming) and Elk Hills (California). In 1921, slippery Secretary of the Interior Albert B. Fall induced his careless colleague, the secretary of the navy, to transfer these valuable properties to the Interior Department. Harding indiscreetly signed the secret order. Fall then quietly leased the lands to oilmen Harry F. Sinclair and Edward L. Doheny, but not until he had received a bribe ("loan") of $100,000 from Doheny and about three times that amount in all from Sinclair.

Teapot Dome, no tempest in a teapot, finally came to a whistling boil (refer to Image 29.19). Details of the crooked transaction gradually began to leak out in March 1923, two years after Harding took office. Fall, Sinclair, and Doheny were indicted the next year, but the case dragged through the courts until 1929. Finally Fall was found guilty of taking a bribe and was sentenced to one year in jail.

AP Images

Image 29.20 Calvin Coolidge, Gentleman Angler Coolidge "was a real conservative, a fundamentalist in religion, in the economic and social order, and in fishing," said his successor, Herbert Hoover, who had a fly fisherman's disdain for Coolidge's bait-fishing tactics—and for his predecessor's laissez-faire politics as well.

Still more scandals erupted. Persistent reports as to the underhanded doings of Attorney General Daugherty prompted a Senate investigation in 1924 of the illegal sale of pardons and liquor permits. Daugherty—described by Herbert Hoover as a man who "should never have been in any government"—was eventually forced to resign by Harding's successor, Calvin Coolidge.

Harding was spared the full revelation of these iniquities. While news of the scandals was beginning to break, he embarked on a speechmaking tour across the country. He died in San Francisco, on August 2, 1923, of pneumonia and thrombosis.

News of Harding's death was sped to Vice President Coolidge, then visiting at his father's New England farmhouse. By the light of two kerosene lamps, the elder Coolidge, a justice of the peace, used the old family Bible to administer the presidential oath to his son.

This homespun setting was symbolic of Coolidge (refer to Image 29.20). Quite unlike Harding, the stern-faced Vermonter, said to have been "weaned on a pickle," with his thin nose and tightly set lips, embodied the New England virtues of honesty and frugality. A man of vanishingly few words, "Silent Cal" believed that "the things I don't say can't get me into trouble." True to Republican philosophy, he became the "high priest of the great god Business." He believed that "the man who builds a factory builds a temple" and that "the man who works there worships there." No foe of industrial bigness, he let business have its head. "Coolidge luck" held during his five and a half prosperity-blessed years. But a catastrophic economic storm was slowly gathering momentum.

29-19 A Fragile Prosperity

Signals abounded that the economic joyride might end in a crash. Even in the best years of the 1920s, several hundred banks failed annually. Farmers were buffeted throughout the decade by boom-and-bust crop prices, slumping land values, and natural disasters. Much of the boom was built on borrowed money, making a market that seemed as mighty as a steel-girded skyscraper potentially as fragile as a house of cards.

This something-for-nothing craze was well illustrated by real estate speculation, especially the fantastic Florida boom that peaked in 1925 (refer to Image 29.21). Numerous underwater lots were sold to eager purchasers for preposterous sums. The whole wildcat scheme collapsed when the peninsula was devastated by a hurricane, which belied advertisements of a "soothing tropical wind."

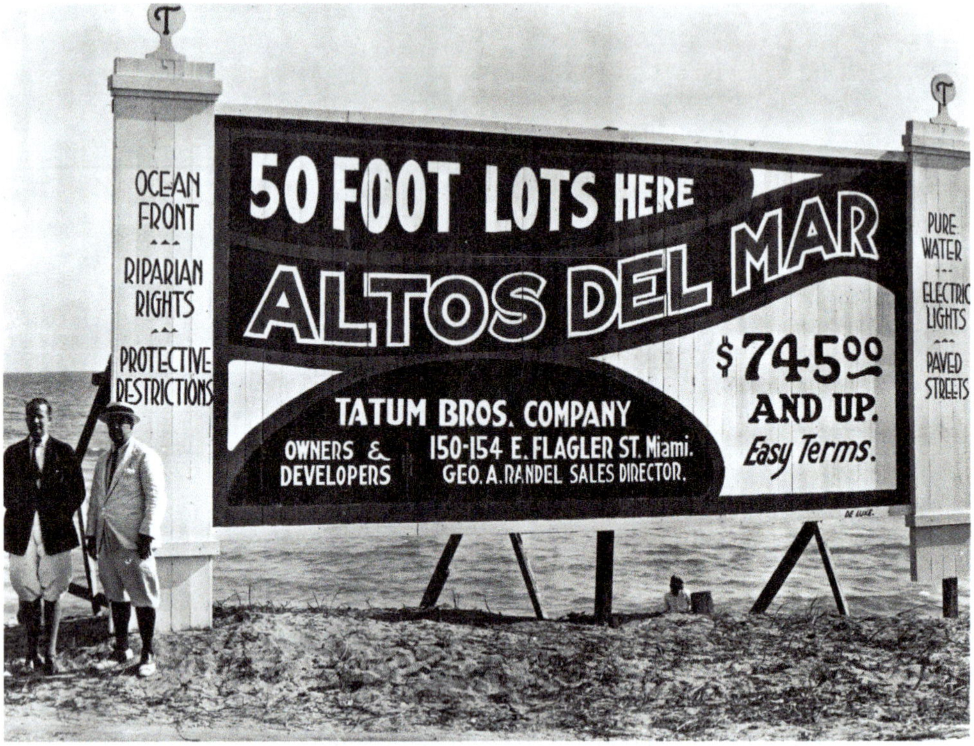

The Library of Congress

Image 29.21 Swampland Speculation, 1922 Lured by slick marketing and hopes of a quick profit, real estate investors rushed to sunny Florida in the early 1920s. The pop of this speculative real estate bubble in 1925 was an ominous (and unheeded) early sign of the economic precarity underneath the decade's roaring prosperity.

The stock exchange provided even greater sensations. Speculation ran wild, and an orgy of boom-or-bust trading pushed the market up to dizzy heights. "Never sell America short" and "Be a bull on America" were favorite catchwords, as Wall Street bulls gored one another and fleeced greedy lambs. Main Street met Wall Street as ordinary men and women began to invest in stocks and bonds. But most portfolios were small, and only 2.5 percent of Americans owned stock at the decade's end.

Sun-bronzed farmers were caught squarely in a boom-or-bust cycle in the postwar decade. While the fighting had raged, they had raked in money hand over gnarled fist; by the spring of 1920, the price of wheat had shot up to an incredible $3 a bushel. But peace brought an end to government-guaranteed high prices and to massive purchases by other nations, as foreign production reentered the stream of world commerce.

Machines also threatened to plow the farmers under an avalanche of their own overabundant crops. The gasoline-engine tractor was working a revolution on American farms (refer to Image 29.22). This steel mule was to cultivation and sowing what the McCormick reaper had been to harvesting. Blue-denimed farmers no longer had to plod after the horse-drawn

Hind Sight Media/Alamy Stock Photo

Image 29.22 Mechanizing Agriculture Just as the automobile replaced the horse on city streets, so did the gas-engine tractor replace horses and mules on the nation's farms in the 1920s. American farmers owned ten times more tractors in 1930 than they did in 1920. The smoke-belching tractors bolstered productivity but also increased the farmers' debt burden, as the Great Depression made tragically clear.

plow with high-footed gait. They could sit erect on their chugging mechanized chariots and turn under and harrow many acres in a single day. They could grow bigger crops on larger areas, using fewer horses and hired hands. The wartime boom had encouraged them to bring vast new tracts under cultivation, especially in the "wheat belt" of the upper Midwest. But such improved efficiency and expanded agricultural acreage helped to pile up more price-dampening surpluses.

Years before Wall Street faltered, a withering depression swept through agricultural districts in the 1920s, when one farm in four was sold for debt or taxes. As a plaintive song of the period ran,

There's no use talkin,' any man's beat,
With five-cent cotton and forty-cent meat.

Natural disaster compounded the economic pain. In 1927, the Great Mississippi Flood inundated 27,000 square miles of the richly fertile farmland in Arkansas, Louisiana, and Mississippi. Property losses reached $400 million. At least 246 people died of flood-related causes, and an estimated 700,000 others were left homeless.

Schemes abounded for bringing relief to the hard-pressed farmers. But farm prices stayed down, farmers' political temperatures stayed high, and the chasm between city and countryside grew wider.

29-20 A Three-Way Race for the White House in 1924

Self-satisfied Republicans, chanting "Keep Cool and Keep Coolidge," nominated "Silent Cal" for the presidency at their convention in Cleveland in the simmering summer of 1924. Squabbling Democrats had more difficulty choosing a candidate. Reflecting many of the cultural tensions of the decade, the party was hopelessly split between "wets" and "drys," urbanites and farmers, Fundamentalists and modernists, Northern liberals and Southern stand-patters, immigrants and old-stock Americans. In one symptomatic spasm of discord, the conventioneers failed by just one vote to pass a resolution condemning the Ku Klux Klan.

Deadlocked for an unprecedented 102 ballots, the convention at last turned wearily, sweatily, and unenthusiastically to John W. Davis. A wealthy corporation lawyer connected with the Wall Street banking house of J. P. Morgan and Company, the polished nominee was no less conservative than cautious Calvin Coolidge.

The field was now wide-open for a liberal candidate. The white-pompadoured Senator Robert ("Fighting Bob") La Follette from Wisconsin, perennial aspirant to the presidency and now sixty-nine years of age, sprang forward to lead a new Progressive Party. He gained the endorsement of the American Federation of Labor and enjoyed the support of the shrinking Socialist Party, but his major constituency was made up of the price-pinched farmers. La Follette's new Progressive Party, fielding only a presidential ticket, with no candidates for local office, proved to be only a shadow of the robust Progressive coalition of prewar days. Its platform called for government ownership of railroads and relief for farmers, lashed out at monopoly and antilabor injunctions, and urged a constitutional amendment to limit the Supreme Court's power to invalidate laws passed by Congress.

La Follette turned in a respectable showing, polling nearly 5 million votes. But "Cautious Cal" and the oil-smeared Republicans slipped easily back into office, overwhelming Davis, 15,718,211 to 8,385,283. The electoral count stood at 382 for Coolidge, 136 for Davis, and 13 for La Follette, all from his home state of Wisconsin (refer to Map 29.1).

29-21 Foreign-Policy Flounderings

Overshadowing all other foreign-policy problems in the 1920s was the knotty issue of international debts, a complicated tangle of private loans, inter-government war debts, and German reparations payments (refer to Figure 29.5). Almost overnight, World War I had reversed the international financial position of the United States. In 1914, America had been a debtor nation to the sum of about $4 billion; by 1922, it had become a creditor nation to the sum of about $16 billion. The newly almighty dollar rivaled the pound sterling as the financial giant of the world. American investors loaned some $10 billion to foreigners in the 1920s, though even this huge river of money could not fully refloat the war-shelled world economy.

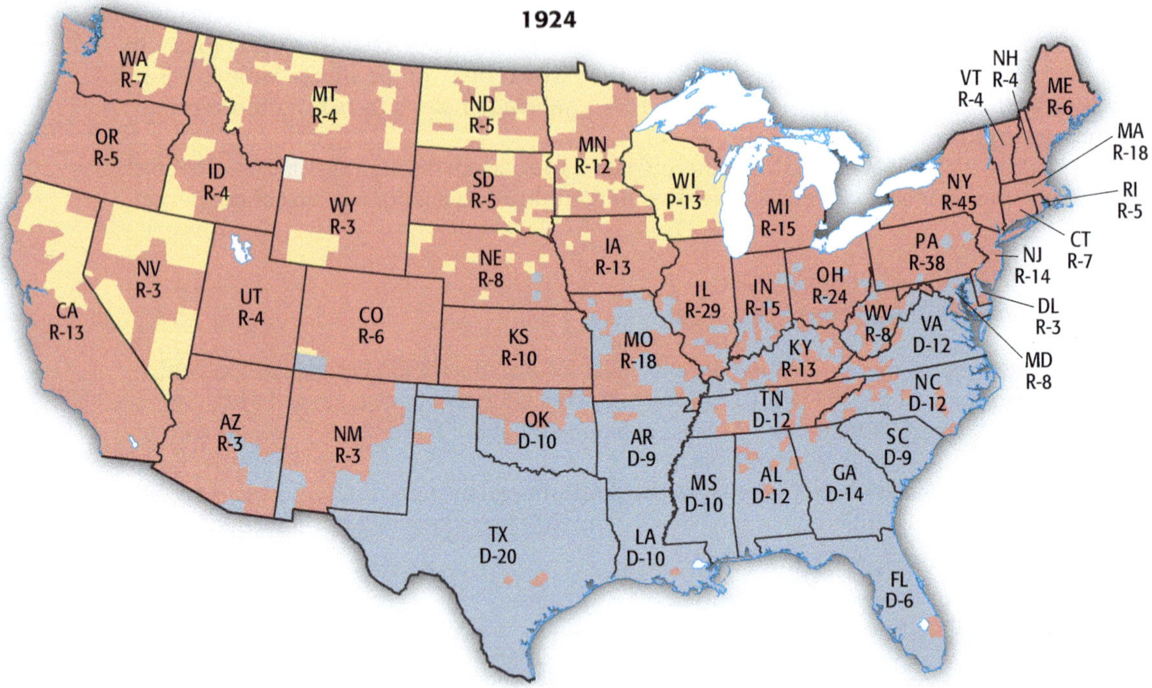

Candidate (Party)	Electoral Vote		Popular Vote	
Coolidge (Republican)	382	72%	15,718,211	54.0%
Davis (Democrat)	136	26%	8,385,283	28.8%
La Follette (Progressive)	13	2%	4,831,289	16.6%

No returns, unsettled, etc.

Map 29.1 Presidential Election of 1924 (showing popular vote by county) Note the concentration of La Follette's votes in the old Populist strongholds of the Midwest and the mountain states. His ticket did especially well in the grain-growing districts battered by the postwar slump in agricultural prices.

The key knot in the debt tangle was the $10 billion that the U.S. Treasury had loaned to the Allies during and immediately after the war. Uncle Sam held their IOUs—and he wanted to be paid. The Allies, in turn, protested that the demand for repayment was grossly unfair. The French and the British pointed out, with much justice, that they had held up a wall of flesh and bone against the common foe until America the Unready had finally entered the fray. America, they argued, should write off its loans as war costs, just as the Allies had been tragically forced to write off the lives of millions of young men. The debtors also complained that the real effect of their borrowed dollars had been to fuel the boom in the already roaring wartime economy in America, where nearly all their purchases had been made. And the final straw, protested the Europeans,

Figure 29.5 Aspects of the Financial Merry-go-round, 1921–1933 Great Britain, with a debt of over $4 billion owed to the U.S. Treasury, had a huge stake in proposals for inter-Allied debt cancellation, but France's stake was even larger. Less prosperous than Britain in the 1920s and more battered by the war, which had been fought on its soil, France owed nearly $3.5 billion to the United States and additional billions to Britain.

was that America's postwar tariff walls made it almost impossible for them to sell their goods to earn the dollars to pay their debts.

America's tightfisted insistence on getting its money back helped to harden the hearts of the Allies against conquered Germany. The French and the British demanded that the Germans make enormous reparations payments, totaling some $32 billion, as compensation for war-inflicted damages. The Allies hoped to settle their debts to the United States with the money received from Germany. The French, seeking to extort lagging reparations payments, sent troops into Germany's industrialized Ruhr Valley in 1923. Berlin responded by permitting its currency to inflate astronomically. At one point in October 1923, a loaf of bread cost 480 million marks, or about $120 million in preinflation money. German society teetered on the brink of mad anarchy, and the whole international house of financial cards threatened to flutter down in colossal chaos.

Sensible statesmen now urged that war debts and reparations alike be drastically scaled down or even canceled outright. Scroogelike, Calvin Coolidge turned aside suggestions of debt cancellation with a typically terse question: "They hired the money, didn't they?" The Washington administration proved especially unrealistic in its dogged insistence that there was no connection whatever between debts and reparations.

Reality finally dawned in the **Dawes Plan** of 1924. Negotiated largely by Charles Dawes, about to be nominated as Coolidge's running mate, it rescheduled German reparations payments and opened the way for further American private loans to Germany. The whole financial cycle now became still more complicated, as U.S. bankers loaned money to Germany, Germany paid reparations to France and Britain, and the former Allies paid war debts to the United States. Clearly the source of this monetary merry-go-round was the flowing well of American credit. When that well dried up after the great financial crash in 1929, the jungle of international finance quickly turned into a desert. President Herbert Hoover declared a one-year debt moratorium in 1931, and before long all the debtors had defaulted—except "honest little Finland," which struggled along making payments until the last of its debt was discharged in 1976.

The United States never did get its money, but it harvested a bumper crop of ill will. Irate French crowds on occasion attacked American tourists. European cartoonists caricatured Uncle Sam as Uncle Shylock, greedily whetting his knife for the last pound of Allied flesh. The bad taste left in American mouths by the whole sorry episode contributed powerfully to the storm-cellar neutrality legislation passed by Congress in the 1930s.

Glaring exceptions to the United States' inward-looking indifference to the outside world were several armed interventions in the Caribbean and Central America. American troops were withdrawn (after an eight-year stay) from the Dominican Republic in 1924, but they remained in Haiti from 1914 to 1934. President Coolidge in 1925 briefly removed American bayonets from troubled Nicaragua, where they had glinted intermittently since 1909, but in 1926 he sent them back, five thousand strong, and they stayed until 1933. American oil companies clamored for a military expedition to Mexico in 1926 when the Mexican government began to assert its sovereignty over oil resources. Coolidge kept cool and defused the Mexican crisis with some skillful diplomatic negotiating. But his mailed-fist tactics elsewhere bred sore resentments south of the Rio Grande, where angry citizens loudly assailed "*yanqui* imperialism."

29-22 The Triumph of Herbert Hoover, 1928

Poker-faced Calvin Coolidge, the tight-lipped "Sphinx of the Potomac," bowed out of the 1928 presidential race when he announced, "I do not choose to run." His logical successor was super-Secretary (of Commerce) Herbert Hoover, unpopular with the political bosses but the much-admired darling of the masses, who asked, "Hoo but Hoover?" He was nominated on a platform that clucked contentedly over both prosperity and prohibition (refer to Image 29.23).

Still-squabbling Democrats nominated Alfred E. "Al" Smith, four-time governor of New York and a wisecracking, glad-handing liberal who suffered from several fatal political handicaps. "Al(cohol)" Smith was soakingly and drippingly "wet" at a time when the country was still devoted to the "noble experiment" of prohibition. To a nation born in the country that had only recently moved to the city, native New Yorker Smith seemed too abrasively urban. He was a Roman Catholic in an overwhelmingly Protestant—and profoundly prejudiced—land. Many dry, rural, and Fundamentalist Democrats gagged on his candidacy, and they saddled the wet

Image 29.23 Herbert Hoover on the Road "Whistle-stop" campaigns, with candidates speaking from the rear platforms of trains, were a standard feature of American politics before the advent of television. Herbert Hoover here greets a crowd in McKeesport, Pennsylvania, during the 1932 campaign.

Bettmann/Getty Images

Smith with a dry running mate and a dry platform. Jauntily sporting a brown derby and a big cigar, Smith, "the Happy Warrior," tried to carry alcohol on one shoulder and water on the other. But his effort was doomed from the start.

Radio figured prominently in this campaign for the first time, and it helped Hoover more than Smith. The New Yorker had more personal sparkle, but he could not project it through the radio (which in his Lower East Side twang he pronounced "radd-dee-o," grating on the ears of many listeners). Iowa-born Hoover came out of the microphone better than he went in. Decrying un-American "socialism" and preaching "rugged individualism," he sounded both grassrootish and statesmanlike.

Hoover, with his double-breasted dignity, was a living example of the American success story and an intriguing mixture of two centuries. As a poor orphan boy reared in rural Iowa and Oregon, he had absorbed the nineteenth-century copybook maxims of industry, thrift, and self-reliance. After working his way through Stanford University, he became a fabulously successful mining engineer and a globally famous businessman, honing to a high degree the efficiency doctrines of the progressive era.

Long years of self-imposed exile had deepened his determination, abundantly supported by national tradition, to avoid foreign entanglements. His experiences abroad had further strengthened his faith in American individualism, private enterprise, and small government.

Though a citizen of the world and laden with international honors, he was quite shy, standoffish, and stiff. Never before elected to public office, he was thin-skinned in the face of criticism, and he did not adapt readily to the forced camaraderie and necessary give-and-take of political accommodation. His real power lay in his integrity, his humanitarianism, his passion for assembling the facts, his efficiency, his talents for administration, and his ability to inspire loyalty in close associates. They fondly called him "the Chief."

As secretary of commerce, Hoover had exhibited some progressive instincts. He endorsed labor unions and supported federal regulation of the new radio broadcasting industry. He even flirted for a time with the idea of government-owned radio, similar to the British Broadcasting Corporation (BBC).

As bands blared Smith's theme song, "The Sidewalks of New York," the campaign sank into the sewers beneath the sidewalks. Despite the best efforts of Hoover and Smith, religious bigotry raised its hideous head over Smith's Catholicism. An irresponsible whispering campaign claimed that "A Vote for Al Smith Is a Vote for the Pope."

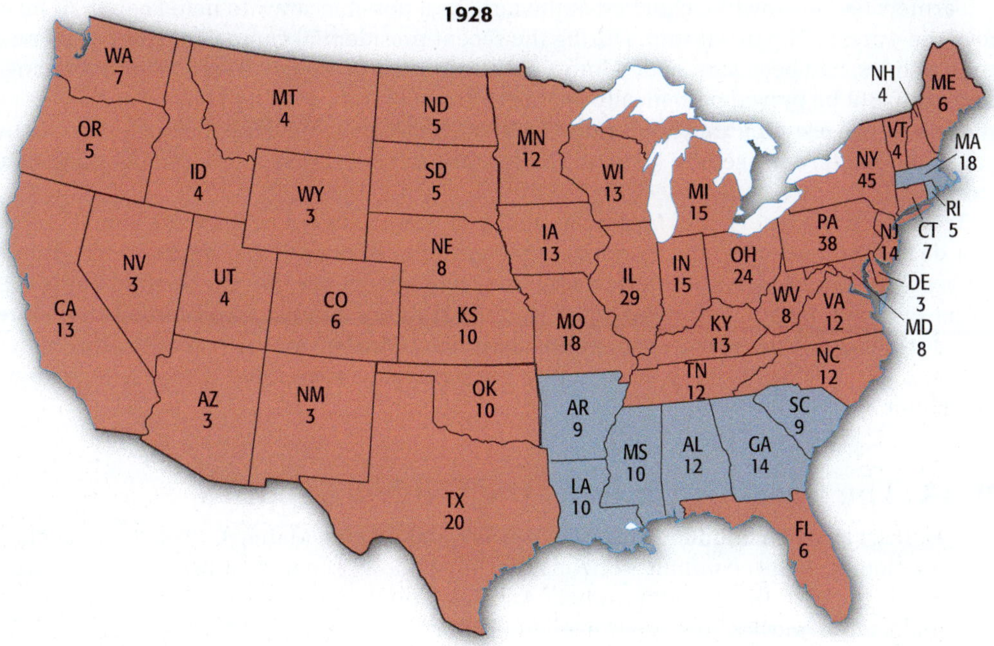

Candidate (Party)	Electoral Vote		Popular Vote	
Hoover (Republican)	444	83.6%	21,391,381	58.7%
Smith (Democrat)	87	16.4%	15,016,443	41.2%

Map 29.2 Presidential Election of 1928 (with electoral vote by state) Smith, despite his defeat, managed to poll almost as many votes as the victorious Coolidge had in 1924. By attracting to the party an immense urban or "sidewalk" vote, the breezy New Yorker foreshadowed Roosevelt's New Deal victory in 1932, when the Democrats patched together the solid South and the urban North. A cruel joke had the Catholic Smith cabling the Pope a single word after the election: "Unpack."

Hoover won in a landslide that cracked the proverbially Democratic "Solid South." He bagged 21,391,993 popular votes to 15,016,169 for his embittered opponent, while rolling up an electoral count of 444 to 87. A huge Republican majority was returned to the House of Representatives (refer to Map 29.2). The Bible Belt could not stomach "city slicker" Al Smith. It might have accepted a Catholic, or a wet, or the descendant of Irish grandparents, or an urbanite. But a concoction of Catholicism, wettism, foreignism, and liberalism brewed on the sidewalks of New York proved too bitter a dose to swallow. Smith's theme song was a constant and rasping reminder to small-town traditionalists that his upbringing had not been convincingly American.

29-23 President Hoover's First Moves

Prosperity in the late 1920s smiled broadly as the Hoover years began. Soaring stocks on the bull market continued to defy the laws of financial gravitation. But two immense groups of citizens were not getting their share of the riches flowing from the national cornucopia: the unorganized wage earners and especially the disorganized farmers.

Energetically calling Congress into an extraordinary special session, Hoover secured passage of the **Agricultural Marketing Act** in June 1929. It was designed to help the farmers help themselves, largely through producers' cooperatives. It set up the Federal Farm Board, with a revolving fund of half a billion dollars at its disposal. Money was lent generously to farm organizations seeking to buy, sell, and store agricultural surpluses. But the Board was soon suffocated by an avalanche of farm produce, as wheat dropped to fifty-seven cents a bushel and cotton to five cents a pound.

Farmers had meanwhile clutched at the tariff as a possible straw to help keep their heads above the waters of financial ruin. During the recent presidential campaign, Hoover, an amateur in politics, had been stampeded into a politically unwise pledge to seek "limited" changes in the tariff. But he proved pathetically unable to control tariff legislation once Congress got its hands on it. The resulting **Hawley-Smoot Tariff** of 1930 turned out to be the highest protective tariff in the nation's peacetime history. The average duty was raised to a trade-strangling 60 percent.

To angered foreigners, the Hawley-Smoot Tariff was a blow below the trade belt. It seemed like a declaration of economic warfare on the entire outside world. It became notorious in later years for plunging both America and other nations deeper into the terrible depression that had already begun. It increased international financial chaos and forced the United States further into the bog of economic isolationism. And economic isolationism, both at home and abroad, was playing directly into the hands of a hate-filled German demagogue, Adolf Hitler.

29-24 The Great Crash Ends the Golden Twenties

When Herbert Hoover confidently took the presidential oath on March 4, 1929, there had been few black clouds on the economic horizon. The "long boom" seemed endless, with the painful exception of the debt-blanketed farm belt. America's productive colossus—stimulated by the automobile, radio, movies, and other new industries—was roaring along at a dizzy speed that suggested a permanent plateau of prosperity. Few people sensed that it might smother its own fires by pouring out too much.

The speculative bubble was actually near the bursting point. Prices on the stock exchange continued to spiral upward and create a fool's paradise of paper profits. A few prophets of disaster were bold enough to sound warnings but were drowned out by the mad chatter of the ticker-tape machine.

A catastrophic crash came in October 1929. It was partially triggered by the British, who raised their interest rates in an effort to bring back capital lured abroad by American investments. Foreign investors and wary domestic speculators began to dump their "insecurities," and an orgy of selling followed. Tension built up to the panicky **Black Tuesday** of October 29, 1929, when 16,410,030 shares of stocks were sold in a save-who-may scramble. Wall Street became a wailing wall as gloom and doom replaced boom. A "sick joke" of the time had hotel room clerks ask registrants, "For sleeping or jumping?"

Losses, even in blue-chip securities, were unbelievable. By the end of 1929—two months after the initial crash—stockholders had lost $40 billion in paper values, or more than the total cost of World War I to the United States (refer to Figure 29.6 and Image 29.24). Worse was yet to come. Not until 1954, a quarter-century later, did stock values regain their 1929 levels.

The stock-market collapse heralded—but, contrary to much mythology, did not "cause"—the most prolonged and prostrating depression in American or world experience. By the end of 1930, more than 4 million workers in the United States were jobless; two years later the figure had about tripled. Hungry and despairing workers pounded pavements in search of nonexistent jobs ("We're firing, not hiring"). Where employees were not discharged, wages and salaries were often slashed. A current jingle ran,

> Mellon pulled the whistle,
> Hoover rang the bell
> Wall Street gave the signal
> And the country went to hell.

The misery and gloom were incalculable, as forests of dead chimneys stood stark against the sky. Over five thousand banks collapsed in the first three years of the depression, carrying down with

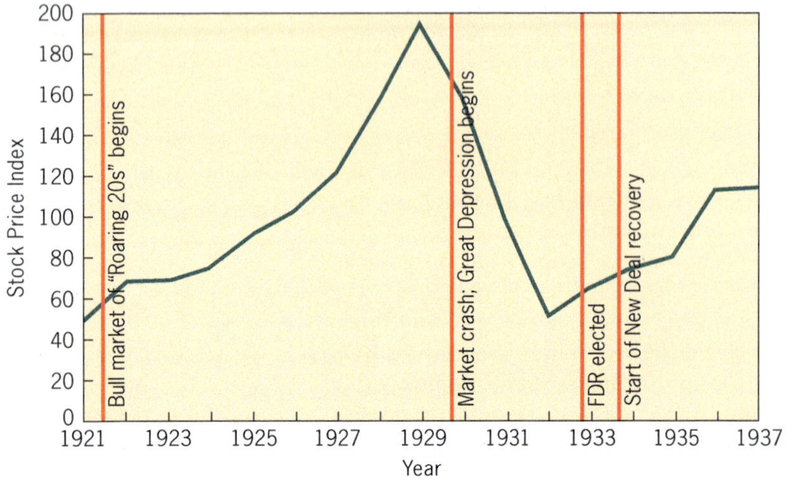

Figure 29.6 Index of Common Stock Prices (1926 = 100)

Shawshots/Alamy Stock Photo

Image 29.24 Pride Goes Before a Fall The great crash of 1929 humbled many a high-flying investor. The desperate curbside seller of this brand-new Chrysler Model 75 paid $1,550 for it just months before.

them the life savings of tens of thousands of ordinary citizens. Countless thousands of honest, hard-working people lost their homes and farms to the forecloser's hammer. Families felt the stress, as jobless fathers nursed their guilt and shame at not being able to provide for their households. Breadless breadwinners often blamed themselves for their plight, despite abundant evidence that the economic system, not individual initiative, had broken down (refer to Image 29.25). Mothers meanwhile nursed fewer babies, as hard times reached even into the nation's bedrooms, precipitating a decade-long dearth of births. As cash registers gathered cobwebs, the song "My God, How the Money Rolls In" was replaced with "Brother, Can You Spare a Dime?"

29-25 Hooked on the Horn of Plenty

What caused the Great Depression? After the heady binge of the 1920s, some kind of business-cycle downturn seemed all but inevitable. But why was the Great Depression so deep and so long? Part of the reason was the heedless confidence that preceded it. With so many newfangled products within the reach of middle-class wallets, manufacturers and politicians assured Americans that the credit-fueled opulence of the 1920s heralded a new state of affairs. "There will be no interruption of our permanent prosperity," announced Myron Forbes, president of Pierce-Arrow Motor Car Company, in 1928. (Pierce-Arrow went bankrupt a decade later.)

The market's iron law of gravity did not cause the depression. The stock market zigged up and plunged down several times after October 1929. Officials at the Federal Reserve, fearful of stoking another speculative bubble, kept interest rates high and made borrowing prohibitively expensive. By doing so, they unwittingly turned the crash of 1929 into a financial conflagration that squeezed the money supply and crushed hopes for an early recovery.

Yet despite these contributing factors, the Great Depression was not simply or even primarily an American affair. Rather, it was a global phenomenon. After World War I, the United States, Britain, France, and Germany returned

Art Directors & TRIP/Alamy Stock Photo

Image 29.25 Detail from California Industrial Scenes, by John Langley Howard, 1934 Howard used a social realist style to depict the large number of dispirited, unemployed workingmen in depression-era California, emphasizing their racial and ethnic diversity. Howard's work appears alongside twenty-six other fresco murals adorning the interior of the Coit Tower in San Francisco (refer to Image 30.8, p. 789 for another). These murals were sponsored by the Public Works of Art Project, the first of the New Deal's federal employment programs for artists.

The depression spectacle of want in the shadow of surplus moved an observer to write in *Current History* (1932),

"We still pray to be given each day our daily bread. Yet there is too much bread, too much wheat and corn, meat and oil and almost every commodity required by man for his subsistence and material happiness. We are not able to purchase the abundance that modern methods of agriculture, mining and manufacture make available in such bountiful quantities. Why is mankind being asked to go hungry and cold and poverty stricken in the midst of plenty?"

to using the gold standard, which stabilized currencies but meant that their powerful but troubled economies would sink or swim in the same boat. So when a prominent Vienna banking house failed in 1931, it triggered a chain-reaction in Europe that eventually rattled America's already shaky banking system to its rickety core. The ongoing tangle over war debts and reparations further prolonged their agony. And finally, the ill-conceived Hawley-Smoot Tariff of 1930 threw more sand into the gears of international commerce. A perfect storm resulted—war damage, economic miscalculation, the straitjacket of the gold standard, and shortsighted policies had brewed the greatest economic calamity in modern times, leaving the United States among the hardest-hit societies of all.

By 1931 the depression had become a national crisis. Through no fault of their own, a host of industrious citizens had lost everything. They wanted to work—but there was no work. The insidious effect of all this dazed despair on the nation's spirit was incalculable and long-lasting. America's "uniqueness" no longer seemed so unique or its Manifest Destiny so manifest. Hitherto the people had grappled with storms, trees, stones, and other physical obstacles. But the depression was a baffling wraith they could not grasp. Once-prosperous businessmen became panhandlers begging for food or "charity soup." In extreme cases "ragged individualists" slept under "Hoover blankets" (old newspapers), fought over the contents of garbage cans, or cooked their findings in old oil drums in tin-and-paper shantytowns cynically named **Hoovervilles** (refer to Image 29.26). The very foundations of America's social and political structure trembled.

Bettmann/Getty Images

Image 29.26 "Hooverville" in Seattle, 1934 In the early years of the depression, desperate, homeless people constructed shacks out of scavenged materials. These shantytowns sprang up in cities across the country.

29-26 Rugged Times for Rugged Individualists

Hoover's exalted reputation as a wonder-worker and efficiency engineer crashed about as dismally as the stock market. He doubtless would have shone in the prosperity-drenched Coolidge years, when he had foreseen the abolition of poverty and poor-houses. But damming the Great Depression proved to be a task beyond his engineering talents.

The perplexed president was impaled on the horns of a cruel dilemma. As a deservedly famed humanitarian, he was profoundly distressed by the widespread misery about him. Yet as a "rugged individualist" with the rare distinction of being a truly self-made man, Hoover shrank from the heresy of government handouts. Convinced that industry, thrift, and self-reliance were the virtues that had made America great, the president feared that a government doling out doles would weaken, perhaps destroy, the national fiber (refer to Image 29.27).

As the depression nightmare steadily worsened, relief by local government agencies broke down. Hoover was finally forced to turn reluctantly from his doctrine of log-cabin individualism and accept the proposition that the welfare of the people in a nationwide catastrophe is a direct concern of the national government.

The president at last worked out a compromise between the old hands-off philosophy and the "soul-destroying" direct dole then being used in England. He would assist the hard-pressed railroads, banks, and rural credit corporations, in the hope that if financial health were restored at the top of the economic pyramid, unemployment would be relieved at the bottom on a trickle-down basis (refer to "Examining the Evidence: Lampooning Hoover, 1932," p. 774).

Partisan critics sneered at the "Great Humanitarian"—he who had fed the faraway Belgians but would not use federal funds to feed needy Americans. Much of this criticism was unfair. No precedent provided guidance for counter-punching to a disaster on this scale. Orthodox economic theory held that market plunges, panics, and depressions were unfortunate but regular occurrences in capitalist societies. Previous downturns had been righted, eventually, without significant government intervention.

> Chicago businessman Martin Devries, defending President Herbert Hoover's restraint in responding to the Great Depression, argued he was a good man stuck in the wrong place, at the wrong time:
>
> "Hoover happened to be in a bad spot. The depression came on, and there he was. If Jesus Christ had been there, he'd have had the same problem. It's too bad for poor old Herbie that he happened to be there. This was a world-wide Depression. It wasn't Hoover's fault. In 1932 . . . , a monkey could have been elected against him, no question about it."

> Hoover spoke approvingly in a campaign speech in 1928 of "the American system of Rugged Individualism." In 1930 he referred to Cleveland's 1887 veto of a bill to appropriate seed grain for the drought-stricken farmers of Texas:
>
> "I do not believe that the power and duty of the General Government ought to be extended to the relief of individual suffering. . . . The lesson should be constantly enforced that though the people support the Government, the Government should not support the people."

29-27 Hoover Battles the Great Depression

President Hoover, in line with his "trickle-down" philosophy, at last recommended that Congress vote immense sums for useful public works. Though at heart an antispender, he secured from Congress appropriations totaling $2.25 billion for such projects.

Most imposing of the public enterprises was the gigantic Hoover Dam on the Colorado River. Voted by Congress in the days of Coolidge, it was begun in 1930 under Hoover and completed in

American Stock/Getty Images

Image 29.27 Feeding the Unemployed in the Early Depression, 1930 In an era without many government relief programs, unemployed men depended on the good will of their neighbors to get a meal.

Examining the Evidence

Lampooning Hoover, 1932

The pages of *The American Pageant* are filled with political cartoons that provide pungent commentary on historical events. With one image rather than many words, a cartoonist can convey a point of view much the way an editorial writer does. This cartoon appeared in the *Washington Daily News* on July 25, 1932, three and a half months before Republican president Hoover lost the presidential election to his Democratic challenger, Franklin D. Roosevelt. The cartoonist foretells Hoover's defeat in November and departure from the White House the following March (not January, as at present) and expresses his support for the Home Loan Bank Bill. With this proposal Hoover sought to come to the aid of home mortgage lenders in order to forestall them from foreclosing on homeowners. The cartoonist jokes that Hoover supported this bill because he identified with homeowners about to lose their homes, but he also cleverly insinuates that Hoover's banking reform was motivated by electoral opportunism. Surely Hoover sought to win public support in return for his new banking program as he battled for reelection, but the Home Loan Bank Bill also reflected Hoover's growing recognition that the federal government had to take direct action to remedy flaws that had precipitated the crisis of the Great Depression. As Hoover later recorded in his memoirs, "All this seems dull economics, but the poignant American drama revolving around the loss of the old homestead had a million repetitions straight from life, not because of the designing villain but because of a fault in our financial system." How does the cartoonist use caricature to make his point? What accounts for the political cartoon's special power? Are there limitations to this genre? Find another cartoon in this book and subject it to similar analysis.

FDR Library

Image 29.28 No Sympathy for Herbert Hoover, 1932

1936 under Roosevelt. It succeeded in creating the huge man-made Lake Mead for purposes of irrigation, flood control, and electric power.

Early in 1932, Congress, responding to Hoover's belated appeal, established the **Reconstruction Finance Corporation (RFC)**. With an initial working capital of half a billion dollars, this agency became a government lending bank. It was designed to shore up insurance companies, banks, agricultural organizations, railroads, and even hard-pressed state and local governments. But to preserve individualism and character, there would be no loans to individuals from this "billion-dollar soup kitchen."

"Pump-priming" loans by the RFC were no doubt of widespread benefit, though the organization was established many months too late for maximum usefulness. Projects that it supported were largely self-liquidating, and the government as a banker actually profited to the tune of many millions of dollars. Giant corporations so obviously benefited from this assistance that the RFC was dubbed—rather unfairly—"the millionaires' dole."

The truth is that Herbert Hoover, despite criticism of his "heartlessness," did inaugurate some significant new policies. In previous panics the masses had been forced to "sweat it out." Hoover's efforts, while feeble and constrained, probably prevented an even more serious collapse. Slow though Hoover was to abandon this nineteenth-century bias, by the end of his term he had started down the road toward government assistance for needy citizens—a road that Franklin Roosevelt would travel much further.

29-28 Routing the Bonus Army in Washington

Many veterans of World War I were numbered among the hard-hit victims of the depression. Nearly twenty thousand impoverished veterans formed the **"Bonus Expeditionary Force" (BEF)** and marched on Washington in the summer of 1932 to demand premature payment of the deferred bonus voted by Congress in 1924 and payable in 1945 (refer to Image 29.29).

These supplicants promptly set up unsanitary public camps and erected shacks on vacant lots—a gigantic "Hooverville." They thus created a menace to the public health, while attempting to intimidate Congress by their presence in force. After the pending bonus bill had failed in Congress by a narrow margin, Hoover arranged to pay the return fare of about six thousand bonus marchers. The rest refused to decamp, though ordered to do so.

Following riots that cost two lives, Hoover responded to the demands of the Washington authorities by ordering the army to evacuate the unwanted guests. The eviction was carried out by General Douglas MacArthur with bayonets and tear gas—and with far more severity than Hoover had planned. A few of the former soldiers were injured as the torch was put to their pathetic shanties in the inglorious "Battle of Anacostia Flats." An eleven-month-old "bonus baby" allegedly died from exposure to tear gas.

This brutal episode brought down additional abuse on the once-popular Hoover, who by now was the most loudly booed man in the country. The Democrats, not content with Hoover's vulnerable record, employed professional "smear" artists to drive him from office. Cynics sneered that the "Great Engineer" had in a few months "ditched, drained, and damned the country." The existing panic was unfairly branded "the Hoover depression." In truth, Hoover had been oversold as a wizard, and the public grumbled when his magician's wand failed to produce rabbits. The time was ripening for the Democratic Party to cash in on Hoover's calamities.

Image 29.29 The Bonus Army in Washington, DC, 1932 The U.S. government promised World War I veterans a bonus for their service to be paid in 1945. As the Great Depression deepened, veterans from across the nation set up camp in the capital during the summer of 1932 to demand early payout of their bonuses.

The Granger Collection, NYC

Image 29.30 Japanese Aggression in Manchuria This American cartoon lambastes Japan for disregarding international treaty agreements when it seized Manchuria in 1931. The next year, the Japanese would set up the puppet state of Manchukuo.

29-29 Japanese Militarists Attack China

The Great Depression, which brewed enough distress at home, added immensely to difficulties abroad. In September 1931, Japanese imperialists lunged into the Chinese province of Manchuria and proceeded to bolt shut the Open Door in the conquered area (refer to Image 29.30).

America had a strong sentimental stake in China but few significant economic interests. In fact, American commercial ties with Japan far outweighed those with China. Yet most Americans were stunned by this act of naked aggression. Possibly a tight blockade by the League of Nations, backed by the United States, would bring Japan sharply to book.

But the United States was not a member of the League, and Washington flatly rebuffed its initial attempts to secure American cooperation in applying economic pressure on Japan. Instead, Secretary of State Henry L. Stimson fired only paper bullets at the Japanese aggressors. The so-called Stimson Doctrine, proclaimed in 1932, declared that the United States would not recognize any territorial acquisitions achieved by force. Undeterred by this verbal slap on the wrist, Japan continued its aggressive campaign in China, launching a full-scale invasion just five years later.

In a broad sense, collective security died and World War II was born in 1931 on the windswept plains of Manchuria. The League members had the economic and naval power to halt Japan but lacked the courage to act. One reason—though not the only one—was that they could not count on America's support.

29-30 The Arrival of the Good Neighbor

World depression softened an age-old aggressive attitude in the United States toward its Latin neighbors. Following the stock-market collapse of 1929, Americans had less money to invest abroad, and millions of dollars' worth of corporate investments in Latin America went sour. The protection of U.S. business interests had been a major driver of Uncle Sam's hemispheric interventions; now, those businesses had fewer interests to protect. As so-called economic imperialism lost its purpose, Hoover strove to abandon the interventionist twist given to the Monroe Doctrine by Theodore Roosevelt. In 1932, he negotiated a new treaty with the French-speaking Republic of Haiti that ultimately provided for the complete withdrawal of American platoons within two years. Early in 1933, the last marine "leathernecks" sailed away from Nicaragua after an almost continuous stay of some twenty years.

Herbert Hoover, the engineer in politics, engineered the foundation stones of what his successor, Franklin Roosevelt, later christened "the policy of the good neighbor." Instead of dollar diplomacy and "banana wars," the United States promised mutual defense and nonintervention in the affairs of other nations. "Let us each and every one of us live and let live," Roosevelt declared. At home and abroad, the gathering storm clouds of the 1930s made that pledge a difficult one to keep.

Chapter Summary

A new mass-consumption economy fueled the spectacular prosperity of the 1920s. The automobile industry, led by Henry Ford, transformed the economy and altered American lifestyles. Charles Lindbergh's transatlantic flight symbolized the new era of air travel, while he became one of the first to bask in the new culture of celebrity.

The pervasive media of radio and film dramatically altered popular culture and values. The mass-consumption economy produced a profusion of new consumer goods, often purchased on credit and promoted by pervasive and often sexually suggestive advertising. Birth control and Freudian psychology overturned traditional sexual standards, especially for women. A surge of racial terror lynchings and violence in the Jim Crow South mobilized national movements for Black civil rights. Racial pride blossomed among Black people in the northern cities, where many had migrated from the South. Marcus Garvey's "back to Africa" movement failed but inspired a new spirit of Black self-assertion.

After the crusading idealism of World War I, America sharply turned inward, as many citizens became hostile to anything foreign or different. Radicals and immigrants were targeted in the red scare and the Sacco-Vanzetti case, while the resurgent Ku Klux Klan reflected some Protestant Americans' fears of ethnic and cultural change. New restrictions on immigration also reflected prejudice against "non-Anglo-Saxon" groups. Sharp cultural and religious conflicts also occurred over evolution and prohibition. The attempt to prohibit alcohol spurred widespread law-breaking and gangster violence.

Young literary rebels, many originally from the Midwest, scorned genteel culture and searched for new values, sometimes as expatriates in Europe. Black artists, musicians, and writers sparked a "Harlem Renaissance." An international modernist movement in the arts and culture self-consciously broke from the past by breaking with traditional literary genres, authorities, and social conventions.

After a brief postwar recession, the economy boomed in the 1920s, as exemplified by the soaring stock market. The Republican governments of the 1920s carried out active, probusiness policies while undermining much of the progressive legacy through repeal or lack of enforcement. Labor organizations fell into decline, while World War I veterans became a powerful lobbying group.

The Washington Naval Conference indicated America's strong desire in the 1920s to withdraw from international involvements. Sky-high tariffs protected America's booming industry but caused severe economic troubles elsewhere in the world while deepening the plight of farmers, who failed to share in the decade's prosperity.

As Teapot Dome and other scandals broke, Harding died and the puritanical Calvin Coolidge took office, thus avoiding political repercussions for the Republicans. Bitterly feuding Democrats—divided by region, religion, and culture—as well as the third-party La Follette Progressives fell easy victims to Coolidge and Republican prosperity in the election of 1924.

American demands for strict repayment of war debts created international economic difficulties and resentment of the United States. The Dawes Plan provided temporary relief, but the sky-high Hawley-Smoot Tariff proved another devastating blow to international trade. Herbert Hoover, a renowned businessman and humanitarian, won a landslide victory over the urban, "wet" Catholic Al Smith in 1928.

In the aftermath of the stock-market crash and international financial crises, the economy collapsed and America plunged into a horrible depression. Herbert Hoover's reputation declined sharply as he failed to relieve the acute national suffering, although he did make unprecedented but limited efforts to revive the economy through federal assistance. The global depression and American isolationism encouraged Japanese aggression in China's Manchuria province, which neither the United States nor the feeble League of Nations could thwart.

Key Terms

- Scientific Management (740)
- Fordism (740)
- United Negro Improvement Association (UNIA) (749)
- Bolshevik Revolution (750)
- red scare (750)
- criminal syndicalism laws (750)
- American plan (750)
- Tulsa Race Massacre (752)
- Immigration Act of 1924 (752)
- Indian Citizenship Act of 1924 (753)
- Eighteenth Amendment (753)
- Volstead Act (753)

- racketeers (755)
- Fundamentalism (756)
- Bible Belt (756)
- Scopes Trial (756)
- modernism (757)
- "Lost Generation" (757)
- Harlem Renaissance (758)
- Bureau of the Budget (759)
- *Adkins v. Children's Hospital* (760)
- Nine-Power Treaty (761)
- Kellogg-Briand Pact (762)
- Fordney-McCumber Tariff Law (762)
- Teapot Dome scandal (762)
- Dawes Plan (767)
- Agricultural Marketing Act (769)
- Hawley-Smoot Tariff (770)
- Black Tuesday (770)
- Hoovervilles (772)
- Reconstruction Finance Corporation (RFC) (774)
- Bonus Expeditionary Force (BEF) (775)

People to Know

- A. Mitchell Palmer
- Nicola Sacco
- Bartolomeo Vanzetti
- Al Capone
- John T. Scopes
- Frederick W. Taylor
- Henry Ford
- Charles A. Lindbergh
- Margaret Sanger
- Sigmund Freud
- H. L. Mencken
- F. Scott Fitzgerald
- Ernest Hemingway
- T. S. Eliot
- William Faulkner
- Langston Hughes
- Warren G. Harding
- Albert B. Fall
- Calvin Coolidge
- John W. Davis
- Alfred E. ("Al") Smith
- Herbert Hoover

Chronology

1903	• Wright brothers fly first airplane	• First story-sequence motion picture
1908	• Henry Ford introduces Model T	
1914	• W. C. Handy's "St. Louis Blues" debuts	
1917	• Bolshevik Revolution in Russia	
1919	• Eighteenth Amendment (Prohibition) • Volstead Act • Elaine Race Massacre	• Seattle general strike • Anderson publishes *Winesburg, Ohio* • American Legion founded
1919–1920	• "Red scare"	
1920	• Radio broadcasting begins • Fitzgerald publishes *This Side of Paradise* • Lewis publishes *Main Street*	• Esch-Cummins Transportation Act • Merchant Marine Act
1921	• Capper-Volstead Act • Tulsa Race Massacre • Sacco-Vanzetti trial	• Emergency Quota Act • Bureau of the Budget created
1922	• Five-Power Naval Treaty signed • Four-Power and Nine-Power Treaties on the Far East • Fordney-McCumber Tariff Law	• Lewis publishes *Babbitt* • Eliot publishes *The Waste Land*
1923	• Equal Rights Amendment (ERA) proposed • *Adkins v. Children's Hospital*	• Teapot Dome scandal • Harding dies; Coolidge assumes presidency
1924	• Immigration Act of 1924 • Adjusted Compensation Act for veterans • Dawes Plan for international finance	• U.S. troops leave Dominican Republic • Coolidge wins three-way presidential election

1925	• Scopes trial • Florida real estate boom	• Fitzgerald publishes *The Great Gatsby* • Dreiser publishes *An American Tragedy*
1926	• U.S. troops occupy Nicaragua • Hughes publishes *The Weary Blues*	• Hemingway publishes *The Sun Also Rises*
1927	• Lindbergh flies solo across Atlantic • First talking motion picture, *The Jazz Singer*	• The Great Mississippi Flood • Sacco and Vanzetti executed
1928	• Kellogg-Briand Pact • Hoover defeats Smith for presidency	• Hoover makes goodwill tour of Latin America • Eugene O'Neill's *Strange Interlude* debuts on Broadway
1929	• Agricultural Marketing Act sets up Federal Farm Board • Stock-market crash	• Faulkner publishes *The Sound and the Fury* • Hemingway publishes *A Farewell to Arms*
1930	• Hawley-Smoot Tariff	
1931	• Japanese invade Manchuria	
1932	• Reconstruction Finance Corporation (RFC) established • "Bonus Army" dispersed from Washington, DC • Al Capone imprisoned	• Stimson Doctrine • Treaty of withdrawal from Haiti

To Learn More

Liaquat Ahamed, *Lords of Finance: The Bankers Who Broke the World* (2009)

John Barry, *Rising Tide: The Great Mississippi Flood and How It Changed America* (1997)

Clare Corbould, *Becoming African Americans: Black Public Life in Harlem, 1919–1939* (2009)

Nancy Cott, *The Grounding of Modern Feminism* (1987)

Lynn Dumenil, *The Modern Temper: American Culture and Society in the 1920s* (1995)

Barry Eichengreen, *Golden Fetters: The Gold Standard and the Great Depression* (1992)

Megan Ming Francis, *Civil Rights and the Making of the Modern American State* (2014)

Linda Gordon, *The Second Coming of the KKK: The Ku Klux Klan of the 1920s and the American Political Tradition* (2017)

Robert Kanigel, *The One Best Way: Frederick Winslow Taylor and the Enigma of Efficiency* (1997)

David Levering Lewis, *When Harlem Was in Vogue* (1981)

Nelson Lichtenstein, *State of the Unions* (2013)

Michael Lienesch, *In the Beginning: Fundamentalism, the Scopes Trial, and the Making of the Antievolution Movement* (2007)

Nancy MacLean, *Behind the Mask of Chivalry: The Making of the Second Ku Klux Klan* (1993)

Roland Marchand, *Advertising the American Dream: Making Way for Modernity, 1920–1940* (1985)

Lisa McGirr, *The War on Alcohol: Prohibition and the Rise of the American State* (2015)

Mae M. Ngai, *Impossible Subjects: Illegal Aliens and the Making of Modern America* (2004)

Christine Stansell, *American Moderns: Bohemian New York and the Creation of a New Century* (1999)

Jan Voogd, *Race Riots and Resistance: The Red Summer of 1919* (2008)

Kenneth Whyte, *Hoover* (2017)

Joan Hoff Wilson, *Herbert Hoover, Forgotten Progressive* (1975)

Chapter 30

The Great Depression and the New Deal: 1933–1939

The country needs and . . . demands bold, persistent experimentation. It is common sense to take a method and try it. If it fails, admit it frankly and try another. But above all, try something.

Franklin D. Roosevelt, Campaign Speech, 1932

Chapter Outline

- Franklin D. Roosevelt as president
- The Hundred Days Congress, 1933
- Relief, recovery, and reform
- Depression demagogues
- Women in public life
- The National Recovery Administration
- Aid for agriculture
- The Dust Bowl and the Tennessee Valley Authority
- Housing and Social Security
- A new deal for labor
- The election of 1936
- The Supreme Court fight, 1937
- The New Deal assessed

The Presence of the Past: "Redlining," Residential Racial Segregation, and Homeownership

Contending Voices: The New Deal at High Tide

Varying Viewpoints: How Radical Was the New Deal?

Voters were in an ugly mood as the presidential campaign of 1932 neared. Countless factory chimneys remained ominously cold, while more than 11 million unemployed workers and their families sank ever deeper into the pit of poverty. Herbert Hoover may have won the 1928 election by promising "a chicken in every pot," but three years later that chicken seemed to have laid a discharge slip in every pay envelope.

Hoover, sick at heart, was renominated by the Republican convention in Chicago without great enthusiasm. The rising star of the Democratic firmament was Governor Franklin Delano Roosevelt of New York, a fifth cousin of Theodore Roosevelt. Like the Rough Rider, he had been born to a wealthy New York family, had graduated from Harvard, had been elected as a kid-gloved politician to the New York legislature, had served as governor of the Empire State, had been nominated for the vice presidency (though not elected), and had served capably as assistant secretary of the navy. Although both men were master politicians, adept with the colorful phrase, TR was pugnacious and confrontational, while FDR was suave and conciliatory—qualities that appealed strongly to a people traumatized by one of the greatest crises in American history.

Focus Questions

1. What personal qualities did Franklin Roosevelt bring to the presidency, and how did these shape both public attitudes and the New Deal policies designed to combat the Great Depression?
2. What were the primary New Deal efforts to achieve relief, recovery, and reform? Which were most successful and enduring, and which largely failed?
3. How did the early New Deal affect business, agriculture, and labor? Why did it meet with such strong opposition from some quarters, including the Supreme Court?
4. How did Roosevelt politically mobilize the "New Deal coalition" of Southerners, Catholics, Jews, Black people, and women to achieve his goals and lay the foundations for two generations of Democratic party dominance?
5. What did the New Deal truly accomplish? Is the idea of a large federal government role in the economy best understood as a response to a unique emergency, or a necessary feature of modern industrial life?

30-1 FDR: Politician in a Wheelchair

Polio, while putting steel braces on Franklin Roosevelt's legs, put additional steel into his soul. Until 1921, when the dread disease also known as infantile paralysis permanently disabled him at age 39, young Roosevelt—tall (six feet two inches), athletic, handsome, and rich—had impressed observers as charming and witty, yet something of a superficial and arrogant "lightweight." But illness humbled Roosevelt to the level of common clay. In courageously fighting his way back from complete helplessness to a hobbling partial mobility, he schooled himself in patience, tolerance, compassion, and strength of will. He once remarked that after trying for two years to wiggle one big toe, all else seemed easy.

Another of Roosevelt's great personal and political assets was his wife, Eleanor. The niece of Theodore Roosevelt, she was Franklin Roosevelt's distant cousin as well as his spouse. Tall and toothy, she overcame the misery of an unhappy childhood and emerged as a champion of the dispossessed—and, ultimately, as the "conscience of the New Deal." FDR's political career was as much hers as it was his own. She traveled countless miles either with him or on his behalf in all his campaigns, considering herself "his legs" after paralysis had struck. But Mrs. Roosevelt also marched to her own drummer. As a young woman, she had worked in a New York settlement house, and she later joined the Women's Trade Union League (refer to "27-5 Progressive Women," pp. 686–689) and the League of Women Voters. When she and Franklin moved into the White House, she brought an unprecedented number of women activists with her to Washington. This network of reformers helped make her the most active First Lady in history (refer to Image 30.1).

Through her lobbying on behalf of her husband, her speeches, and her syndicated newspaper column, Eleanor Roosevelt powerfully influenced the policies of the national government. Always she battled for the impoverished and the oppressed. At one meeting in Birmingham, Alabama, she confounded local authorities and flouted the segregation statutes by deliberately straddling the aisle separating the Black and white seating sections. Sadly, her personal relationship with her husband was often rocky due to his infidelities. Condemned by conservatives and loved by liberals, she was one of the most controversial—and consequential—public figures of the twentieth century.

Franklin Roosevelt's political appeal was amazing. His commanding presence and his golden speaking voice, despite an upper-crust accent, combined to make him the premier American orator of his generation. He could turn on his charm in private conversations as one would turn on a faucet. As a popular Depression-era governor of New York, he had sponsored heavy state spending to relieve human suffering. Though favoring frugality, he believed that money, rather than humanity, was expendable. He revealed a deep concern for the plight of the "forgotten man"—a phrase he used in a 1932 speech—although he was assailed by the rich as a "traitor to his class."

Exuberant Democrats met in Chicago in June 1932 and speedily nominated Roosevelt, even as other, more senior contenders crowded the field. Fellow New Yorker Al Smith felt entitled to a second chance, and a beautiful friendship wilted when he was elbowed aside for Roosevelt. The Democratic platform promised not only a balanced budget but sweeping social and economic reforms. Roosevelt flew daringly through stormy weather to Chicago, where he shattered precedent by accepting the nomination in person (previous nominees in both parties had decorously accepted nomination, often by letter or telegram, well after their conventions had adjourned). He electrified the delegates and the public with these words: "I pledge you, I pledge myself to a new deal for the American people."

AP Images

Image 30.1 Eleanor Roosevelt (1884–1962) Roosevelt was America's most active First Lady and commanded enormous popularity and influence during FDR's presidency. Here she emerges, miner's cap in hand, from an Ohio coal mine.

30-2 Presidential Hopefuls of 1932

In the campaign that followed, Roosevelt was especially eager to prove that he was not an invalid. Though his polio was no secret, he contrived to give the impression that he was substantially recovered. Braced on the arm of a son or an aide, he could manage a few lurching steps. In keeping with the journalistic standards of the day, the media obligingly refrained from reporting on his physical limitations (refer to Image 30.2). Prevailing prejudices about people with disabilities might have ended Roosevelt's political career had the public known the full extent of his infirmity.

Roosevelt consistently preached a New Deal for the "forgotten man," but he was annoyingly vague and somewhat contradictory. Many of his speeches were ghostwritten by the "Brains Trust" (popularly the **Brain Trust**), a small group of reform-minded intellectuals. They were predominantly youngish college professors who, as a kind of kitchen cabinet, later authored much of the **New Deal** legislation. Roosevelt rashly promised a balanced budget and berated heavy Hooverian deficits, amid cries of "Throw the Spenders Out!" and "Out of the Red with Roosevelt." All of this was to make ironic reading in later months.

In his successful campaign for the governorship of New York in 1928, Franklin Roosevelt (1882–1945) had played down alleged Democratic "socialism":

"We often hear it said that government operation of anything under the sun is socialistic. If that is so, our postal service is socialistic, so is the parcel post, which has largely taken the place of the old express companies; so are the public highways which took the place of the toll roads."

The high spirits of the Democrats found expression in the catchy tune "Happy Days Are Here Again." This theme song fit FDR's incandescent smile, his jauntily angled cigarette holder, his breezy optimism, and his promises to run the risk of bold experimentation.

Grim-faced Herbert Hoover remained in the White House, conscientiously battling the Depression through short lunches and long hours. Weary and despondent, Hoover unconvincingly repeated his faith in American private enterprise and individual initiative. His down-at-the-mouthism contrasted sharply with Roosevelt's tooth-flashing optimism and sparkling spirit. An embittered Hoover never

Franklin D. Roosevelt Presidential Library

Image 30.2 The Polio Survivor This rare candid photograph of President Roosevelt in his specially designed wheelchair was taken aboard the heavy cruiser USS *Indianapolis* in 1933. Though Roosevelt's illness was no secret, the media of the day generally acceded to the president's wishes and refrained from publishing images of him in his chair or wearing his ten-pound steel leg braces. Twelve years after this photograph was taken, the *Indianapolis* was sunk by a Japanese submarine just days after delivering components of the Hiroshima atomic bomb to the U.S. air base in the Marshall Islands. Nearly a thousand sailors perished, the worst loss of life from a single ship in the history of the U.S. Navy.

ceased to insist that the uncertainty and fear produced by Roosevelt's impending victory had plunged the nation more deeply into the Great Depression.

30-3 Hoover's Humiliation in 1932

A rising tide of prosperity had swept Hoover into office; the receding tide of economic depression now swept him out—along with the Republican Party—for a generation to follow. Democrats had only to harness the national grudge and let it pull them to victory. The flood of votes totaled 22,809,638 for Roosevelt and 15,758,901 for Hoover; the electoral count stood at 472 to 59. In all, only six rock-ribbed Republican states went for the loser.

One striking feature of the election was the beginning of a distinct shift of Black voters, traditionally grateful to the Republican Party of Lincoln, over to the Roosevelt camp. As the "last hired and first fired," Black Americans had been among the worst sufferers from the Depression. Beginning with the election of 1932, they became, notably in the great urban centers of the North, a vital element in the Democratic Party.

Hoover, though defeated and repudiated, continued to be president for four long months, until March 4, 1933 (refer to Image 30.3).* But it made little sense to embark on any long-range policies without the cooperation of Roosevelt—and an increasingly bitter Hoover had little desire to work with a man whose agenda he detested. Roosevelt's "so-called new deals," said Hoover, "would destroy the very foundations of the American system of life."

The victorious president-elect, in turn, proved no less uncooperative. Hoover at length succeeded in arranging two meetings with him to discuss the war-debt muddle. But Roosevelt, who airily remarked to the press, "It's not my baby," fought against assuming responsibility without authority. As Hoover privately confessed, he was trying to bind his successor to an anti-inflationary policy that would have made impossible many of the later New Deal experiments.

The stubborn refusal of two consummate politicians to put politics aside had grievous consequences for the country. With Washington deadlocked, the vast and vaunted American economic machine clanked to a virtual halt. One worker in four tramped the streets, feet weary and hands idle. Banks locked their doors all over the nation, as people nervously stuffed what meager money they had under their mattresses.

30-4 FDR and the Three Rs: Relief, Recovery, Reform

Great crises often call forth gifted leaders, and the hand of destiny tapped Roosevelt on the shoulder. On a dreary Inauguration Day, March 4, 1933, his vibrant voice, broadcast nationally from a bulletproof stand, provided the American people with inspirational new hope (refer to Image 30.4). He denounced the "money changers" who had brought on the calamity and declared that the government must wage war on the Great Depression as it would wage war on an armed foe. His clarion note was, "Let me assert my firm belief that the only thing we have to fear is fear itself."

Roosevelt moved decisively. Now that he had full responsibility, he boldly declared a nationwide banking holiday, March 6–10, as a prelude to opening the banks on a sounder basis. He then summoned the overwhelmingly Democratic Congress into special session to confront the

FDR Library

Image 30.3 The Vanquished and the Victor A dour Hoover and an ebullient Roosevelt ride to the inauguration ceremonies on March 4, 1933. This magazine cover was never published, presumably because of the editors' sensitivity about the attempted assassination of Roosevelt when he was riding in an open car in Florida on February 15, 1933, less than three weeks earlier. The attempt on Roosevelt's life ended in the death of Chicago mayor Anton J. Cermak.

*The Twentieth Amendment to the Constitution, ratified in 1933, moved the presidential inauguration date to January 20 and the annual date for the opening of Congress to January 3.

Bridgeman Images

Image 30.4 Unemployed and Frustrated Democratic candidate Franklin Roosevelt offered hope, if few concrete plans, to the millions struggling to cope with the Great Depression.

national emergency. During the so-called **Hundred Days** (March 9–June 16, 1933), members hastily cranked out an unprecedented basketful of remedial legislation (refer to Table 30.1).

Roosevelt's New Deal programs aimed at three Rs—relief, recovery, and reform. Short-range goals were relief and immediate recovery, especially in the first two years. Long-range goals were permanent recovery and reform of current abuses, particularly those that had produced the boom-or-bust catastrophe. The three-R objectives often overlapped and got in one another's way. But amid all the topsy-turvy haste, the gigantic New Deal program lurched forward.

Firmly ensconced in the driver's seat, President Roosevelt cracked the whip. A green Congress so fully shared the panicky feeling of the country that it was ready to rubber-stamp bills drafted by White House advisers. More than that, Congress gave the president extraordinary blank-check powers. Some of the laws it passed expressly delegated legislative authority to the chief executive. One senator complained that if FDR asked Congress "to commit suicide tomorrow, they'd do it."

Roosevelt delighted in exerting bold executive leadership. He was like the quarterback, as he put it, whose next play depends on the outcome of the previous play. So desperate was the mood of an action-starved public that any movement, even in the wrong direction, seemed better than no movement at all.

The frantic Hundred Days Congress passed many essentials of the New Deal "three Rs," though the sheer drama of this period has often exaggerated its importance, compared to the more lasting New Deal achievements that came later. (Refer to Table 30.2, p. 786). These early reforms owed much to the legacy of the pre–World War I progressive movement. Many of them were long overdue, sidetracked by the war in Europe and the Old Guard reaction of the 1920s. In an explosive burst of pent-up energy, New Dealers raided file cabinets full of old pamphlets on German social insurance, English housing and garden cities, Danish agricultural recovery, and American World War I collectivization. In time, they embraced progressive ideas such as unemployment insurance, old-age insurance, minimum-wage regulations, the conservation and development of natural resources, and restrictions on child labor. They also invented some new schemes, such as the Tennessee Valley Authority (refer to "30-13 The TVA Harnesses the Tennessee," pp. 796–797).

One Chinese observer of America, No-Yong Park (1899–1976), born in Manchuria and educated in the United States, remained optimistic about America even in the depths of the Great Depression. He wrote in *An Oriental View of American Civilization* (1934),

"Of all the peoples of the world, Americans, to my mind, are the most progressive. They are the ones who live in the future tense. Their mind and soul are always bent for the future. They never move backward and always march forward."

30-5 Roosevelt Manages the Money

Banking chaos cried aloud for immediate action. Congress pulled itself together and in an incredible eight hours had the Emergency Banking Relief Act of 1933 ready for Roosevelt's busy pen. The legislation was so speedily drafted that printed copies were not available for members to review. A rolled-up newspaper symbolically served. The new law invested the president with the power to regulate banking transactions and foreign exchange and to reopen solvent banks.

Roosevelt, the master showman, next turned to the radio to deliver the first of his thirty famous "fireside chats." As some 35 million people hung on his soothing words, he gave assurances that it was now safer to keep money in a reopened bank than "under the mattress." Confidence returned with a gush, and the banks began to unlock their doors.

Table 30.1 **Principal New Deal Acts During the Hundred Days Congress, 1933† (items in parentheses indicate secondary purposes)**

Recovery	Relief	Reform
FDR closes banks, March 6, 1933		
Emergency Banking Relief Act, March 9, 1933		
(Beer Act)	(Beer Act)	Beer and Wine Revenue Act, March 22, 1933
(CCC)	Unemployment Relief Act, March 31, 1933, creates Civilian Conservation Corps (CCC)	
FDR orders gold surrender, April 5, 1933		
FDR abandons gold standard, April 19, 1933		
(FERA)	Federal Emergency Relief Act, May 12, 1933, creates Federal Emergency Relief Administration (FERA)	
(AAA)	Agricultural Adjustment Act (AAA), May 12, 1933	
(TVA)	(TVA)	Tennessee Valley Authority Act (TVA), May 18, 1933
		Federal Securities Act, May 27, 1933
Gold-payment clause repealed, June 5, 1933		
(HOLC)	Home Owners' Refinancing Act, June 13, 1933, creates Home Owners' Loan Corporation (HOLC)	
National Industrial Recovery Act, June 16, 1933, creates National Recovery Administration (NRA), Public Works Administration (PWA)	(NRA, PWA)	(NRA)
(Glass-Steagall Act)	(Glass-Steagall Act)	Glass-Steagall Banking Reform Act, June 16, 1933, creates Federal Deposit Insurance Corporation

†For later New Deal measures, refer to Table 30.2, p. 786.

The Hundred Days, or Emergency, Congress buttressed public reliance on the banking system by enacting the **Glass-Steagall Banking Reform Act**. This measure created the Federal Deposit Insurance Corporation, which insured individual deposits up to $5,000 (later raised). Thus ended the disgraceful epidemic of bank failures, which dated back to the "wildcat" days of Andrew Jackson (refer to Figure 30.1).*

Roosevelt moved swiftly elsewhere on the financial front, seeking to protect the melting gold reserves and to prevent panicky hoarding. He ordered all private holdings of gold to be surrendered to the Treasury in exchange for paper currency and then took the nation off the gold standard. The Emergency Congress responded to his recommendation by canceling the gold-payment clause in all contracts and authorizing repayment in paper money. A "managed currency" was well on its way.

The goal of Roosevelt's managed currency was to promote inflation, which he believed would relieve debtors' burdens and stimulate new production. Roosevelt's principal instrument for achieving inflation was gold buying. He instructed the Treasury to purchase gold at increasing prices, ratcheting the dollar price of gold up from $21 an ounce in 1933 to $35 an ounce in early 1934,

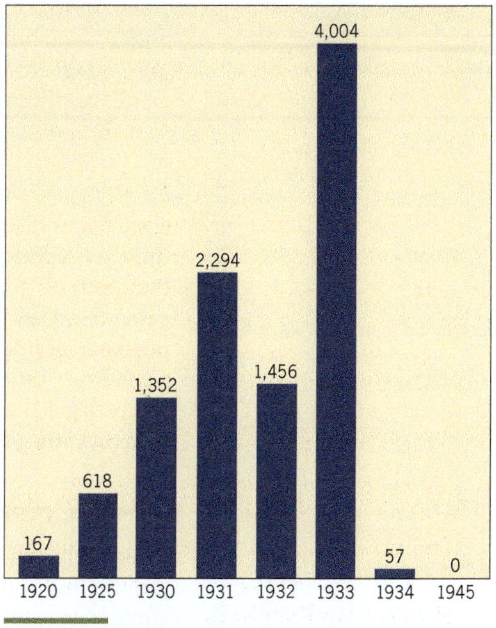

Figure 30.1 **Bank Failures Before and After the Glass-Steagall Banking Reform Act of 1933**

*When FDR was inaugurated in 1933, not a single Canadian bank had failed.

Table 30.2 Later Major New Deal Measures, 1933–1939 (items in parentheses indicate secondary purposes)

Recovery	Relief	Reform
(CWA)	FDR establishes Civil Works Administration (CWA), November 9, 1933	
Gold Reserve Act, January 30, 1934, authorizes FDR's devaluation, January 31, 1934		
		Securities and Exchange Commission (SEC) authorized by Congress, June 6, 1934
(Reciprocal Trade Agreements Act)	(Reciprocal Trade Agreements Act)	Reciprocal Trade Agreements Act, June 12, 1934 (refer to Section 32-4, pp. 851–852)
		Indian Reorganization Act, June 18, 1934
(FHA)	National Housing Act, June 28, 1934, authorizes Federal Housing Administration (FHA)	(FHA)
(Frazier-Lemke Act)	Frazier-Lemke Farm Bankruptcy Act, June 28, 1934	
(Resettlement Administration)	FDR creates Resettlement Administration, April 30, 1935	
(WPA)	FDR creates Works Progress Administration (WPA), May 6, 1935, under act of April 8, 1935	
(Wagner Act)	(Wagner Act)	Wagner Act (National Labor Relations Act), July 5, 1935
		Social Security Act, August 14, 1935
		Public Utility Holding Company Act, August 26, 1935
(Soil Conservation Act)	Soil Conservation and Domestic Allotment Act, February 29, 1936	
(USHA)	(USHA)	United States Housing Authority (USHA) established by Congress, September 1, 1937
(Second AAA)	Second Agricultural Adjustment Act, February 16, 1938	
(Fair Labor Standards Act)	(Fair Labor Standards Act)	Fair Labor Standards Act (Wages and Hours Bill), June 25, 1938
		Reorganization Act, April 3, 1939
		Hatch Act, August 2, 1939

a price that held for nearly four decades. This policy did increase the amount of dollars in circulation, as holders of gold cashed it in at the elevated prices. But this inflationary result also provoked the wrath of "sound-money" critics, who gagged on the "baloney dollar." The gold-buying scheme came to an end in February 1934, when FDR returned the nation to a limited gold standard for purposes of international trade only. Thereafter (until 1971—refer to "34-16 The Economy Shifts," pp. 935–936), the United States pledged itself to pay foreign bills, if requested, in gold at the rate of one ounce of gold for every $35 due. But domestic circulation of gold continued to be prohibited, and gold coins became collectors' items.

30-6 Creating Jobs for the Jobless

Overwhelming unemployment, even more than banking, clamored for prompt remedial action and the full force of Roosevelt's persuasive charm (refer to Image 30.5). One out of every four workers was jobless when FDR took his inaugural oath—the highest level of unemployment in

Image 30.5 The Champ: FDR Chatting with Reporters Roosevelt mastered the press as few presidents before or since have been able to do. He was also ingenious in finding opportunities to converse with reporters in situations where he could conceal his physical limitations.

Image 30.6 CCC Workers in Alaska, 1939 These Tlingit carvers in Alaska's southeastern panhandle were part of a CCC project to restore totem poles. Here they stand with a pole carved in the likeness of Abraham Lincoln.

the nation's history, before or since. The raw numbers understated the underlying misery, since the demography of the preponderantly male labor force at that time meant that nearly one in four *households* lost its sole breadwinner. Roosevelt had no hesitancy about using federal money to assist the unemployed and at the same time to "prime the pump" of industrial recovery. (A farmer has to pour a little water into a dry pump—that is, "prime it"—to start the flow.)

The Hundred Days Congress responded to Roosevelt's spurs when it created the **Civilian Conservation Corps (CCC)**, which proved to be perhaps the most popular of all the New Deal "alphabet agencies" (refer to Image 30.6). This law provided employment in fresh-air government camps for about 3 million uniformed young men, many of whom might otherwise have been driven by desperation into criminal habits. They did much lastingly useful work—including reforestation, firefighting (forty-seven lost their lives), flood control, and swamp drainage. The recruits were required to help their parents by sending home most of their pay. Both human resources and natural resources were thus conserved, though there were minor complaints of "militarizing" the nation's youth. Critics charged that CCC "soldiers" would later claim pensions for exposure to poisonivy.

One desperate Black man wrote to a newspaper in 1932,

"I am forty-eight; married twenty-one years; four children, three in school. For the last eight years I was employed as a Pullman conductor. Since September, 1930, they have given me seven months part-time work. Today I am an object of charity. . . . My small, weak, and frail wife and two small children are suffering and I have come to that terrible place where I could easily resort to violence in my desperation."

The first major effort of the new Congress to grapple with the millions of adult unemployed was the Federal Emergency Relief Act. Its chief aim was immediate relief rather than long-range recovery. The resulting Federal Emergency Relief Administration (FERA) was handed over to zealous Harry L. Hopkins, a wire-thin, chain-smoking New York social worker who had earlier won Roosevelt's friendship and who became one of his most influential advisers. Hopkins's agency in all granted about $3 billion to the states for direct dole payments or preferably for wages on work projects.

Immediate relief was also given to two large and hard-pressed special groups by the Hundred Days Congress. One section of the Agricultural Adjustment Act (AAA) made available many millions of dollars to help farmers meet their mortgages. Another law created the Home Owners' Loan Corporation (HOLC). Designed to refinance mortgages on nonfarm homes, it ultimately assisted about a million badly pinched households (refer to "The Presence of the Past: 'Redlining,' Residential Racial Segregation, and Homeownership," pp. 790–791). The agency not only bailed out mortgage-holding banks but also bolted the political loyalties of relieved middle-class homeowners securely to the Democratic Party.

Harassed by the continuing plague of unemployment, FDR himself established the Civil Works Administration (CWA) late in 1933 (refer to Table 30.2). As a branch of the FERA, it also fell under the direction of Hopkins. Designed to provide purely temporary jobs during the cruel winter emergency, it served a useful purpose. Tens of thousands of jobless were employed at leaf raking and other make-work tasks, which were dubbed "boondoggling." As this kind of labor put a premium on shovel-leaning slow motion, the scheme was widely criticized. "The only thing we have to fear," scoffers remarked, "is work itself."

Library of Congress Prints and Photographs Division [LC-USZ62-111013]

Image 30.7 Huey Long (1893–1935) Long pursued progressive policies as governor of Louisiana, even while he ruled the state with a dictatorial hand. A flamboyant and unpredictable populist, he set the orthodox political establishment on its ear, especially after he became a U.S. senator in 1930. Long's admirers called him the "Kingfish"; Franklin Roosevelt called him "one of the two most dangerous men in the country." (The other, said Roosevelt, was General Douglas MacArthur.)

30-7 A Day for Every Demagogue

Direct relief from Washington to needy families helped pull the nation through the ghastly winter of 1933–1934. But the disheartening persistence of unemployment and suffering demonstrated that emergency relief measures had to be not only continued but supplemented. One danger signal was the appearance of various demagogues, notably a magnetic "microphone messiah," Father Charles Coughlin, a Catholic priest in Michigan. He began broadcasting in 1930, preaching the slogan "Social Justice." His anti–New Deal harangues reached some 40 million fans and ultimately became so anti-Semitic, fascistic, and demagogic that he was silenced in 1942 by his ecclesiastical superiors.

Also notorious among the new brood of agitators were those who capitalized on popular discontent to make pie-in-the-sky promises. Most conspicuous were Dr. Francis E. Townsend, a retired California physician who promised everyone over sixty years of age $200 a month, and Senator Huey P. ("Kingfish") Long of Louisiana (refer to Image 30.7), who was said to have more brass than a government mule. He used his abundant rabble-rousing talents to publicize his "Share Our Wealth" program, which promised to make "Every Man a King." Every family was to receive $5,000, supposedly at the expense of the prosperous.

H. L. Mencken called Long's chief lieutenant, former clergyman Gerald L. K. Smith, "the gutsiest, goriest, loudest and lustiest, the deadliest and damndest orator ever heard on this or any other earth, the champion boob-bumper of all time." Fear of Long becoming a fascist dictator ended when an assassin murdered him in the Louisiana state capitol in 1935.

Father Coughlin and Huey Long frightened many Americans because they raised troubling questions about the link between fascism and economic crisis. Danger seemed to be lurking ominously in many corners of the world. Authoritarian rule was strengthening in Japan, while Adolf Hitler was acquiring absolute authority in Germany. Some even worried that Franklin Roosevelt himself would turn into a dictator.

Partly to quiet the groundswell of unrest that might lead to a political explosion, Congress authorized the Works Progress Administration (WPA) in 1935. The objective was employment on useful projects. Launched under the supervision of the ailing but energetic Hopkins, this remarkable agency ultimately spent about $11 billion on thousands of public buildings, bridges, and hard-surfaced roads. Not every WPA project strengthened the infrastructure—for instance, one controlled crickets in Wyoming, while another built a monkey pen in Oklahoma City. John Steinbeck, future Nobel Prize novelist, counted dogs in his California county. One of the most well-loved WPA programs was the Federal Art Project, which hired artists to create posters and murals—many still adorning post office walls (refer to Image 30.8). Critics sneered that WPA meant "We Provide

In 1935, Father Charles Coughlin (1891–1979) single-handedly defeated President Roosevelt's effort to win Senate ratification of a treaty providing for American membership in the World Court, a judicial body of limited authority established by the League of Nations. What FDR saw as a symbolic embrace of international responsibility Coughlin convinced his radio listeners was a conspiracy of international moneyed interests against American sovereignty:

"Our thanks are due to Almighty God in that America retains her sovereignty. Congratulations to the aroused people of the United States who, by more than 200,000 telegrams containing at least 1,000,000 names, demanded that the principles established by Washington and Jefferson shall keep us clear from foreign entanglements and European hatreds."

Alpha Stock/Alamy Stock Photo

Image 30.8 Public Art Mural by Victor Arnautoff (1896–1979), 1934 *The Pedestrian Scene*, painted on a wall of Coit Tower in San Francisco, was one of many murals commissioned by the federal government to employ artists during the Great Depression.

The Presence of the Past

"Redlining," Residential Racial Segregation, and Homeownership

"Redlining" describes home-financing policies that for decades limited minority peoples' ability to purchase the kinds of homes that are for most Americans their principal source of wealth. Ironically, redlining originated with an agency that was long considered one of the most successful innovations of the New Deal.

The New Dealers deliberately chose to avoid the massive public-housing projects fashionable in Europe. They sought instead to encourage private capital to invest in individual homeownership. To that end, they established the Home Owners' Loan Corporation (HOLC) in 1933 and the Federal Housing Administration (FHA) the following year to reduce the risks that had historically limited home-purchase financing. The two agencies standardized appraisal practices, made mortgage-lending safer by providing back-up insurance to lenders, and popularized the low-interest, long-term (typically 30 years), fixed-rate mortgage as the standard for home buyers. Together these policies saved 800,000 Depression-era homeowners from foreclosure, and eventually turned a nation of renters into a nation of homeowners. Homeownership rates rose from 47.8 percent in 1930 to 61.9 percent in 1960.

Consistent with those risk-reducing initiatives, HOLC asked local lenders and real estate appraisers to rate the credit-worthiness of various neighborhoods. The resulting reports, produced between 1935 and 1940, featured color-coded maps and accompanying "area descriptions" that assessed whether a neighborhood was "best," "definitely declining," or "hazardous." The racial and ethnic composition of an area figured prominently in its rating (refer to Image 30.9).

The HOLC maps placed the government's stamp of approval on an assumption already widely held by real estate professionals as well as many white homeowners: that racial integration of a neighborhood depressed property values. Despite evidence that nonwhite borrowers often had excellent credit histories, nearly every Black neighborhood in the nation was deemed a "hazardous" lending area by HOLC, making credit financing in those zones very difficult to come by.

"Redlining" worked in concert with other laws and practices to severely limit Black homeownership and maintain neighborhood racial segregation. While the U.S. Supreme Court's 1917 ruling in *Buchanan v. Warley* overturned explicitly race-exclusionary zoning laws, states and localities found other means to discriminate. Local planners limited multifamily housing and imposed lot-size standards to keep less affluent buyers out. Racial restrictions on property deeds often prohibited the sale or rental of a home to "any person not of the Caucasian race." (The presence of such covenants was a factor in HOLC's designation of a neighborhood as "best.") The Supreme Court ruled racially restrictive covenants unenforceable in *Shelley v. Kraemer* in 1948, but state and local governments continued to permit such restrictions for nearly two decades more.

After World War II, buying a home became Americans' most important path to building financial security and savings. The FHA vastly expanded its mortgage insurance programs, and the GI Bill provided veterans with even more generous home financing (refer to "32-14 Postwar Economic Anxieties," pp. 864–865). While some of the groups once "redlined" out of housing opportunity—such as Jews and Southern Europeans—met less discrimination in the postwar period, Black families continued to confront racially discriminatory real estate practices.

As thousands of suburban homes sprang from the raw earth of burgeoning postwar subdivisions, nonwhite mortgage applicants battled not only bank discrimination and racial covenants but the fierce resistance of developers as well as white residents. Of 120,000 new homes built in metropolitan Philadelphia between 1946 and 1953, for example, only 347 were open to Black buyers. William Levitt, whose "Levittowns" made him one of the most prolific suburban homebuilders of the postwar era (refer to "32-19 The Rush to the Suburbs," pp. 869–871), outright prohibited Black buyers and renters in his subdivisions. Across the nation, Black families who moved into majority-white neighborhoods endured rocks through their picture windows and burning crosses on their front lawns.

Homeownership among white people reached 65 percent by 1960, while only 38 percent of Black people owned their own homes. "Redlined" neighborhoods in central cities deteriorated further as white residents—many the children and grandchildren of once "undesirable" ethnic minorities—fled to the leafy suburbs.

The Fair Housing Act of 1968, passed in the wake of the assassination of Martin Luther King Jr., explicitly prohibited housing discrimination on the basis of race, religion, national origin, and, as amended, disability, sex (including gender identity), or family status. Yet the law proved notoriously hard to enforce.

With the Community Reinvestment Act (CRA) of 1977, Congress determined to put an end to "redlining" once and for all. The Act confirmed that financial institutions must extend capital and credit to *all* parts of the communities in which they are federally chartered, actively encouraged banks to lend to property owners in low-income areas, and monitored banks on their compliance. These measures substantially increased the flow of capital to once-excluded neighborhoods.

The CRA and subsequent federal measures catalyzed billions of dollars of fresh investment, but the many decades of limited access to mortgage credit bore heavy responsibility for the stubbornly persistent wealth gap between white and Black Americans. Nonwhites continued to live in neighborhoods with lower home values, encounter discrimination in home appraisals, and held disproportionate numbers of the most burdensome kinds of mortgage loans. About 4.5 percent of white American borrowers lost their homes to foreclosure during the global financial crisis of 2008–2009. Black and Latino borrowers had foreclosure rates of 7.9 percent and 7.7 percent, respectively.

Nine decades after the creation of HOLC, the racial disparities its maps so rigidly reinforced stubbornly persist. In 2022, 74.6 percent of white Americans owned their own homes. Only 45.3 percent of Black Americans were homeowners—a more than 29-point gap that is two points greater than that of 1960. The long-celebrated "American dream" of homeownership, and the inter-generational wealth that has flowed from it, remain out of reach for many Americans of color.

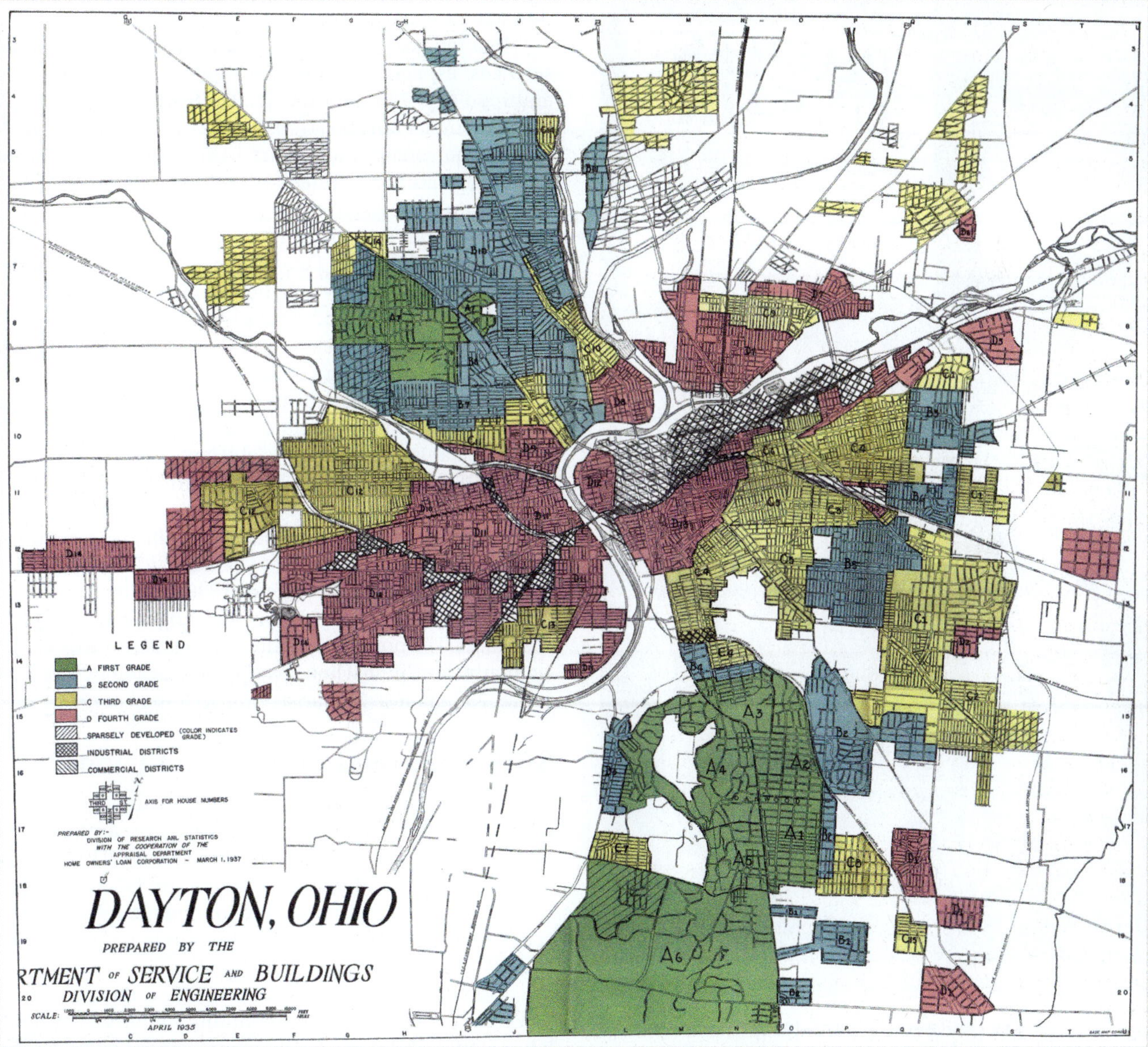

Image 30.9 Mapping Inequality, 1937 This map of Dayton, Ohio, was one of hundreds of "residential security maps" commissioned by the federal Home Owners' Loan Corporation (HOLC) to encourage private mortgage lending. Maps often were accompanied by narrative descriptions that detailed the racial and ethnic composition of each neighborhood.

Alms." But the fact is that over a period of eight years, nearly 9 million people were given jobs, not handouts. The WPA built long-lived public facilities, preserved workers' self-respect, nourished much precious talent, and sponsored more than a million works of art.

30-8 New Visibility for Women

Just over a decade after the ratification of the Nineteenth Amendment, American women began to carve a larger space for themselves in the nation's political and intellectual life. First Lady Eleanor Roosevelt may have been the most visible woman in the Roosevelt White House, but she was hardly the only female voice. Secretary of Labor Frances Perkins (1880–1965) burst through the gender barrier when she became America's first woman cabinet member. Mary McLeod Bethune (1875–1955), director of the Office of Minority Affairs in the National Youth Administration, served as the highest-ranking African American in the Roosevelt administration (refer to Image 30.10).

Moorland-Spingarn Research Center, Howard University, Washington, DC

Image 30.10 **Mary McLeod Bethune (1875–1955)** The daughter of ex-slaves and founder of a college in Florida, Bethune became the highest-ranking African American in the Roosevelt administration when she was appointed director of the Office of Minority Affairs in the National Youth Administration (NYA). From this base she organized the "Black Cabinet" to make sure Black people benefited from the New Deal programs along with whites. Here she is picketing against segregated hiring practices at the Peoples Drug Store chain, one of the earliest targets of the Black civil rights movement.

Women also made important contributions in the social sciences, especially in the relatively new and open field of anthropology. Ruth Benedict (1887–1948) carried on the work of her mentor, Franz Boas (1858–1942), by developing the "culture and personality movement" in the 1930s and 1940s. Benedict's landmark work, *Patterns of Culture* (1934), established the study of cultures as collective personalities. Each culture, like each individual, had its own "more or less consistent pattern of thought and action." One of Benedict's students, Margaret Mead (1901–1978), drew from her own scholarly studies of adolescence among Pacific island peoples to advance bold new ideas about sexuality, gender roles, and intergenerational relationships. With thirty-four books and a curatorship at the American Museum of Natural History in New York City to her credit, Mead helped popularize cultural anthropology and achieved a celebrity status rare among social scientists.

Pearl S. Buck (1892–1973) won similar acclaim as a novelist. Raised in China by Presbyterian missionary parents, Buck introduced American readers to Chinese peasant society. Her best-selling novel, *The Good Earth* (1931), earned her the Nobel Prize for literature in 1938, making her the third American (after Sinclair Lewis and Eugene O'Neill) to win the award. The popularity of her writings also nurtured public sympathy for China when it was later attacked by Japan (refer to "29-29 Japanese Militarists Attack China," p. 776).

30-9 Helping Industry and Labor

A daring attempt to stimulate a nationwide comeback was initiated when the Emergency Congress authorized the **National Recovery Administration (NRA).** This ingenious scheme was by far the most complex and far-reaching effort by the New Dealers to combine immediate relief with long-range recovery and reform. Triple-barreled, it was designed to assist industry, labor, and the unemployed.

Individual industries—over two hundred in all—were to work out codes of "fair competition," under which hours of labor would be reduced so that employment could be spread over more people. The law also included minimum-wage and maximum-hour provisions. Labor, under the NRA, gained additional benefits. Workers were formally guaranteed the right to organize and bargain collectively through representatives *of their own choosing*—not through handpicked agents of the company's choosing. The hated "yellow-dog," or anti-union, contract was expressly forbidden, and certain safeguarding restrictions were placed on the use of child labor.

Industrial recovery through the NRA's "fair competition" codes would at best be painful, for these called for self-denial by both management and labor. Mass meetings and monster parades, which included 200,000 marchers on New York City's Fifth Avenue, mobilized patriotic sentiment behind the new law. A handsome blue eagle became the symbol of the NRA. Merchants subscribing to a code displayed it in their windows with the slogan "We Do Our Part." A newly formed professional football team was christened the Philadelphia Eagles. Such was the enthusiasm for the NRA that for a brief period, there was a marked upswing in business activity, although Roosevelt had warned, "We cannot ballyhoo our way to prosperity."

But the high-flying eagle soon tumbled to earth. Too much self-sacrifice was expected of labor, industry, and the public for such a scheme to work. Critics began to brand the NRA "National Run Around" and "Nuts Running America," symbolized by what Henry Ford called "that damn Roosevelt buzzard." Some unscrupulous businesspeople publicly displayed the blue bird in their windows but secretly violated the codes. Then the Supreme Court shot down the dying eagle in 1935 in the famed *Schechter* "sick chicken" decision. The justices unanimously held that Congress could not "delegate legislative powers" to the executive. They further declared that congressional control of interstate commerce could not properly apply to a local fowl business, like that of the Schechter brothers in Brooklyn, New York. Roosevelt was incensed by this "horse and buggy" interpretation of the Constitution, but actually the Court helped him out of a bad jam.

The same act of Congress that hatched the NRA eagle also authorized the Public Works Administration (PWA), likewise intended both for industrial recovery and for unemployment relief. The agency was headed by the secretary of the interior, acid-tongued Harold L. Ickes, a free-swinging former Bull Mooser. Long-range recovery was the primary purpose of the new agency, and in time over $4 billion was spent on some 34,000 projects, which included public buildings, highways, and parkways. One spectacular achievement was the Grand Coulee Dam on the Columbia River in Washington State—the largest structure erected by humans since the Great Wall of China (refer to Image 30.11). In the depths of the Depression, the grand dam

Image 30.11 Grand Coulee Dam on the Columbia River, Washington State The Grand Coulee Dam was one of the most ambitious projects of the New Deal's Public Works Administration. It is one of the few man-made constructions visible from outer space, the largest concrete structure in the United States, and the central facility in the Columbia Basin Project, which generates electricity for the Pacific Northwest and provides irrigation for half a million acres of Columbia Valley farmland—services that have transformed the life of the region.

seemed the height of folly. It made possible the irrigation of millions of acres of new farmland—at a time when the government was desperately trying to reduce farm surpluses. It created more electrical power than the entire Tennessee Valley Authority—in a region with little industry and virtually no market for additional power. It erased Native fishing grounds and blocked salmon from reaching their historic spawning habitats. But with the outbreak of World War II and then postwar prosperity, the dam would come to seem a stroke of genius, transforming the entire region with abundant water and power.

Special stimulants aided the recovery of one segment of business—the liquor industry. Seeking new federal revenues, the Hundred Days Congress legalized light wine and beer with an alcoholic content not exceeding 3.2 percent by weight, and levied a tax of $5 on every barrel so manufactured. Disgruntled drys, unwilling to acknowledge the breakdown of law and order begotten by bootlegging, damned Roosevelt as "a 3.2 percent American." Saloon doors swung open again when the Twenty-First Amendment officially repealed Prohibition late in 1933 (refer to the Appendix).

30-10 Paying Farmers Not to Farm

The economic crisis that gripped the nation as the 1930s began was already old news in the American countryside. Ever since the end of war-boom days in 1918, farmers had been suffering from sinking prices and overproduction, especially in grain. The Great Depression only deepened their agony. Mortgages were foreclosed at increasing rates, embattled farmers burned corn for fuel, and some of them desperately tried to prevent the shipment of surplus crops to glutted markets. Rattled authorities clamped martial law on several volatile Iowa counties.

A radical new approach to farm recovery was embraced when the Emergency Congress established the **Agricultural Adjustment Administration (AAA)**. Through "artificial scarcity" this agency was to establish "parity prices" for basic commodities. "Parity" was the price set for a product that gave it the same real value, in purchasing power, that it had enjoyed during the period from 1909 to 1914. The AAA would eliminate price-depressing surpluses by paying growers to reduce their crop acreage. The millions of dollars needed for these payments were to be raised by taxing processors of farm products, such as flour millers, who in turn would shift the burden to consumers.

Unhappily, the AAA got off to a wobbly start. It began after much of the cotton crop for 1933 had been planted, and balky mules, trained otherwise, were forced to plow under countless young plants. Several million squealing pigs were purchased and slaughtered. Much of their meat was distributed to people on relief, but some of it was used for fertilizer. This "sinful" destruction of food, at a time when thousands of citizens were hungry, increased condemnation of the American economic system by many on the outraged left.

"Subsidized scarcity" did have the effect of raising farm income, but the whole confused enterprise met with acid criticism. Farmers, food processors, consumers, and taxpayers were all to some degree unhappy. Paying the farmers not to farm actually increased unemployment, at a time when other New Deal agencies were striving to decrease it. When the Supreme Court finally killed the AAA in 1936 by declaring its regulatory taxation provisions unconstitutional, foes of the plow-under program rejoiced loudly.

The New Deal Congress wasted no time finding other ways to prop up the nation's growers. The Soil Conservation and Domestic Allotment Act of 1936, along with the Second Agricultural Adjustment Act of 1938, transformed agriculture, once the realm of proudly independent yeoman farmers, into one of the nation's most tenderly government-coddled industries. Farm subsidies have ever since shaped what Americans grow and eat.

30-11 Dust Bowls and Black Blizzards

Nature meanwhile had been providing some unplanned scarcity. Late in 1933, a prolonged drought struck the states of the trans-Mississippi Great Plains. Rainless weeks were followed by furious, whining winds. Millions of tons of powdery topsoil torn from devastated homesteads blotted the sun from the sky from eastern Colorado to western Missouri—soon to be dubbed the **Dust Bowl**. Despondent citizens sat on front porches with protective masks on their faces, watching their farms swirl by. A seven-year-old boy in Kansas suffocated. Overawed victims of the Dust Bowl disaster predicted the end of the world or the second coming of Christ.

Drought and wind triggered the dust storms, but they were not the only culprits. The human hand had also worked its mischief. High grain prices during World War I had enticed farmers to bring countless acres of marginal land under cultivation. Worse, dry-farming techniques and mechanization had revolutionized Great Plains agriculture. The steam tractor and the disk plow tore up infinitely more sod than a team of oxen ever could, leaving the powdery topsoil to be swept away at nature's whim (refer to Map 30.1).

Burned and blown out of the Dust Bowl, tens of thousands of refugees fled their ruined acres. In five years, about 350,000 Oklahomans and Arkansans—"Okies" and "Arkies"—trekked to southern California in "junkyards on wheels" (refer to Image 30.12). Undeterred by signs saying "KEEP OUT," many found a new home in the San Joaquin Valley, which shared much in common with the southern plains—arid climate, cotton growing, newfound oil deposits, and abundant land. Yet the transition was cruel. Food, shelter, and clothing were scarce; the winter months, without work and heat, proved nearly unendurable for the migrants. The dismal story of these human tumbleweeds was realistically portrayed in John Steinbeck's best-selling novel *The Grapes of Wrath* (1939), which proved to be the *Uncle Tom's Cabin* of the Dust Bowl.

Zealous New Dealers, sympathetic toward the soil-tillers, made various other efforts to relieve their burdens. In 1935, the president set up the Resettlement Administration, charged

Map 30.1 The Extent of Erosion in the 1930s Note the extensive wind erosion in the western Oklahoma panhandle region, which was dubbed the "Dust Bowl" in the 1930s. Note also the fabled Route 66, along which families like Steinbeck's Joads made their way both to California and to the industrial cities of the Midwest. Mechanized farmers had "busted" the sod of the southern plains so thoroughly that they literally broke the back of the land. Tons of dust blew out of the Dust Bowl in the 1930s and darkened skies as far away as New York. A Kansas newspaperman reported in 1935 that in his dust-blanketed town, "Lady Godiva could ride through streets without even the horse seeing her."

with removing near-farmless farmers to better land. And more than 200 million young trees were successfully planted on the bare prairies as windbreaks by the young men of the Civilian Conservation Corps, even though one governor jeered at trying to "grow hair on a bald head."

Native Americans also felt the far-reaching hand of New Deal reform. Commissioner of Indian Affairs John Collier ardently sought to reverse the forced-assimilation policies in place since the Dawes Act of 1887 (refer to "22-9 'Kill the Indian and Save the Man,'" pp. 558–559). Inspired by a sojourn among the Pueblo Indians in Taos, New Mexico, Collier promoted the **Indian Reorganization Act of 1934** (the "Indian New Deal"). Its goals were to restore American Indian autonomy, revive tribes' interest in their identity and culture, preserve Native crafts and traditions, and stop the loss of Native lands. Encouraged by the new law, nearly two hundred tribes established local self-government. But many Native Americans derided the legislation as yet another example of government deciding what was best for them. Some condemned it as a "back-to-the-blanket" measure that sought to make museum pieces out of Indigenous peoples. Seventy-seven tribes refused to organize under the law's provisions, including the Navajos (*Dineh*) who were especially aggrieved by federal policies that had shifted vast tracts of their traditional grazing lands to white stockmen.

Library of Congress Prints and Photographs Division [USF34-018227]

Image 30.12 An Okie Family Hits the Road in the 1930s to Escape the Dust Bowl

Novelist John Steinbeck (1902–1968) relates in his novel *The Grapes of Wrath* (1939) that when the "Okies" and "Arkies" reached California, they found the big growers unwilling to pay more than twenty-five cents an hour for work in the fields. One owner mutters,

"A Red is any son-of-a-bitch that wants thirty cents an hour when we're paying twenty-five!"

30-12 Battling Bankers and Big Business

Reformist New Dealers were determined from the outset to curb the "money changers" who had played fast and loose with gullible investors before the Wall Street crash of 1929. The Hundred Days Congress passed the "Truth in Securities Act" (Federal Securities Act), which required promoters to provide potential investors with independently audited information regarding the soundness of their stocks and bonds. An old saying was thus reversed to read "Let the seller beware," although the buyer might never read the fine print.

In 1934, Congress took further steps to protect the public against fraud, deception, and inside manipulation. It created the Securities and Exchange Commission (SEC) as a badly needed watchdog over the risk-prone financial sector. These important New Deal reforms actually improved the efficiency of financial markets by furnishing buyers and sellers alike with reliable information on the basis of which reasonable prices could be determined.

New Dealers likewise directed their fire at public utility holding companies, those supercorporations. Citizens had seen one of these incredible colossi collapse during the spring of 1932, when Chicagoan Samuel Insull's multibillion-dollar financial empire crashed. Possibilities of controlling, with a minimum of capital, a half-dozen pyramided layers of big business suggested to Roosevelt "a ninety-six-inch dog being wagged by a four-inch tail." The Public Utility Holding Company Act of 1935 finally delivered a "death sentence" to this type of bloated growth, except where it might be deemed economically needful.

30-13 The TVA Harnesses the Tennessee

The sprawling electric-power industry also attracted the fire of New Deal reformers. Within a few decades, it had risen from nothingness to a behemoth with an investment of $13 billion. As public utilities, electric companies reached directly and regularly into the pocketbooks of millions of consumers for vitally needed services. Ardent New Dealers accused them of gouging the public with excessive rates, especially since they owed their profitability to having secured, often for a song, priceless waterpower sites from the public domain.

The tempestuous Tennessee River provided New Dealers with a rare opportunity. With its tributaries, the river drained a badly eroded area about the size of England, and one containing some 2.5 million of the most poverty-stricken communities in America. The federal government already owned valuable properties at Muscle Shoals, where it had erected plants for needed nitrates in World War I. By developing the hydroelectric potential of the entire area, Washington could combine the immediate advantage of putting thousands of people to work and a long-term project for reforming the power monopoly.

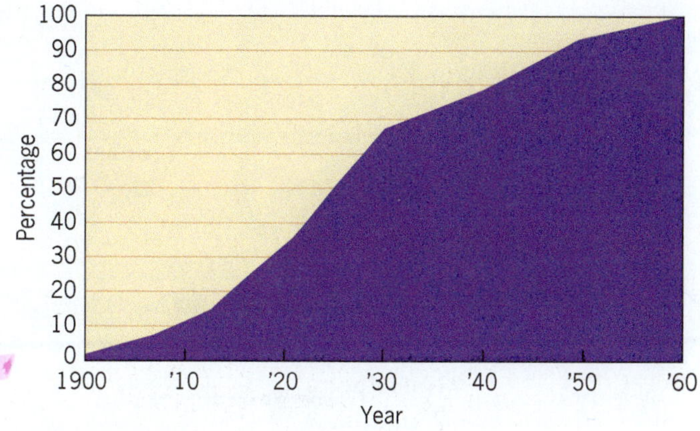

Figure 30.2 Occupied Households with Electric Service, 1900–1960 Well into the twentieth century, a majority of American households had no electrical service. The New Deal's Rural Electrification Agency and projects like the Tennessee Valley Authority (TVA) helped make electricity available to almost all Americans by 1960. African American leader Andrew Young later claimed that the TVA created the economic underpinnings of the civil rights movement: "It was the presence of the cheap electricity, lower interest rates, water projects, that laid the foundation for the New South."

An act creating the **Tennessee Valley Authority (TVA)** was passed in 1933 by the Hundred Days Congress. This far-ranging enterprise was largely a result of the steadfast vision and unflagging zeal of Senator George W. Norris of Nebraska, after whom one of the mighty dams was named. From the standpoint of "planned economy," the TVA was by far the most revolutionary of all the New Deal schemes.

This new agency was determined to discover precisely how much the production and distribution of electricity cost, so that a "yardstick" could be set up to test the fairness of rates charged by private companies. Utility corporations lashed back at this entering wedge of government control, charging that the low cost of TVA power was due to dishonest bookkeeping and the absence of taxes. Critics complained that the whole dream was "creeping socialism in concrete."

But the New Dealers, shrugging off such outcries, pointed a prideful finger at the amazing achievements of the TVA. The gigantic project brought to the area not only full employment and the blessings of cheap electric power (refer to Figure 30.2), but low-cost housing, abundant cheap nitrates for fertilizer, the restoration of eroded soil, reforestation, improved navigation, and flood control. Rivers ran blue instead of brown, and a once-poverty-cursed area was on its way to being transformed into one of the most flourishing regions in the United States.

Ambitious New Dealers agitated for similar enterprises in the valleys of the Columbia, Colorado, and Missouri Rivers. Federally built dams one day would span all those waterways, impounding more than 30 percent of the total annual runoff from the "roof of America" in the Rocky Mountains. Hydroelectric power from those dams would drive the growth of the urban West, and the waters they diverted would nurture agriculture in the previously bone-dry western deserts. But conservative reaction against the "socialistic" New Deal would confine the TVA's brand of federally guided resource management and comprehensive regional development to the Tennessee Valley (refer to Map 30.2).

30-14 Housing and Social Security

The New Deal had meanwhile framed sturdy new policies for housing construction. To speed recovery and better homes, Roosevelt set up the Federal Housing Administration (FHA) as early as 1934. The building industry was to be stimulated by small loans to householders, both for improving their dwellings and for completing new ones. So popular did the FHA prove to be that it was one of the few "alphabet agencies" to outlast the age of Roosevelt.

Congress bolstered the program in 1937 by authorizing the United States Housing Authority (USHA), an agency designed to lend money to states or communities for low-cost construction. Although units for about 650,000 low-income people were started, new building fell tragically short of needs. New Deal efforts to expand the project collided with brick-wall opposition from real estate promoters, builders, and landlords ("slumlords"), to say nothing of anti-New

Map 30.2 TVA Area More than twenty dams were constructed on the river's tributaries as part of a massive project to control flooding, generate hydroelectric power, and revitalize the Tennessee Valley region, while also creating jobs for the unemployed. The shaded area represents the area served by TVA electric power.

Dealers who attacked what they considered down-the-rathole spending. Nonetheless, for the first time in a century, the slum areas in America ceased growing and even shrank.

Incomparably more important was the success of New Dealers in the field of unemployment insurance and old-age pensions. Their greatest victory was the epochal **Social Security Act** of 1935—one of the most far-reaching laws ever to pass Congress. To cushion against future depressions, the measure provided for federal-state unemployment insurance. To provide security for old age, specified categories of retired workers were to receive regular payments from Washington. These payments ranged from $10 to $85 a month (later substantially increased) and were financed by a payroll tax on both employers and employees. Provision was also made for blind people, those with physical disabilities, at-risk youth, and others in need.

Republican opposition to the sweeping new legislation was bitter. "Social Security," insisted ex-president Hoover, "must be built upon a cult of work, not a cult of leisure." The GOP national chairman falsely charged that every worker would have to wear a metal dog tag for life. Yet security-starved citizens embraced the new system. Some went so far as to tattoo their new, nine-digit Social Security numbers onto their skin.

Social Security was largely inspired by the example of some of the more highly industrialized nations of Europe. In the agricultural America of an earlier day, there had always been farm chores for all ages, and the large family had cared for its own dependents. But in an urbanized economy, at the mercy of boom-or-bust cycles, the government was now recognizing its responsibility for the welfare of its citizens. By 1939, over 45 million elderly people were eligible for Social Security old-age benefits. In subsequent years, further categories of workers were added, including, belatedly, farm and domestic workers. Most Black workers fell into one of those two job categories, and their omission from Social Security's original version reflected the power that Southern Democrats in Congress wielded to block Roosevelt's most ambitious goals. To secure Southern votes, he was often compelled to limit how much his programs might benefit—and politically empower—Black Americans. For similar reasons, FDR consistently declined to support several anti-lynching bills introduced in Congress.

In contrast to Europe, where welfare programs generally were universal, Americans had to be employed and to hold certain kinds of jobs to qualify for coverage. But Social Security came closer to universal coverage than any U.S. program before it. Over time, the benefit came to be so cherished that any attempt to change the program was deemed "the third rail of American politics" (a reference to the dangerously high-voltage power supply of most urban railways). Means-tested programs for poor people, in contrast, were perpetually vulnerable to budget cuts or elimination. This two-tiered welfare state was one distinctively American contribution of the New Deal.

30-15 A New Deal for Labor

The NRA blue eagles, with their call for collective bargaining, had been a godsend to organized labor. As New Deal expenditures brought some slackening of unemployment, labor began to feel more secure and hence more self-assertive. A rash of walkouts occurred in the summer of 1934, including a paralyzing general strike in San Francisco (following a "Bloody Thursday"), which was broken only when outraged citizens resorted to vigilante tactics.

When the Supreme Court shot down the blue eagle, a Congress sympathetic to labor unions undertook to fill the vacuum. The fruit of its deliberations was the National Labor Relations Act of 1935, more commonly known as the **Wagner Act**, after its congressional sponsor, New York senator Robert F. Wagner. This trail-blazing law, considered the Magna Carta of American labor, created a powerful new National Labor Relations Board to protect the right of workers to engage in self-organization and to bargain collectively through representatives of their own choice.

Under the encouragement of a highly sympathetic National Labor Relations Board, a host of unskilled workers began to organize themselves into effective unions. The leader of this drive was beetle-browed, domineering, and melodramatic John L. Lewis, boss of the United Mine Workers. In 1935 he succeeded in forming the Committee for Industrial Organization (CIO) within the ranks of the skilled-craft American Federation of Labor (AFL). But skilled workers, ever since the days of the ill-fated Knights of Labor in the 1880s, had shown only lukewarm sympathy for the cause of unskilled labor, especially by Black workers. In 1936, following inevitable friction with the CIO, the older federation suspended the upstart unions associated with the newer organization.

Undaunted, the rebellious CIO moved on a concerted scale into the huge automobile industry. Late in 1936, the workers resorted to a revolutionary technique (earlier used in both Europe and America) known as the sit-down strike: they refused to leave the factory building of General Motors at Flint, Michigan, and thus prevented the importation of strikebreakers (refer to Image 30.13). Conservative defenders of private property were scandalized. The CIO

Bettmann/Getty Images

Image 30.13 General Motors Sit-Down Strikers, Flint, Michigan, 1937 Strikers like these sometimes kept their spirits up with the song "Sit Down":

When the boss won't talk
Don't take a walk;
Sit down, sit down

Image 30.14 Labor Triumphant After generations of struggle, organized labor made dramatic gains in membership and bargaining power during the New Deal years.

A worker at a Chevrolet plant in Flint, Michigan, wrote after the United Auto Workers–CIO victory in 1937,

> "The inhuman high speed is *no more*. We now have a voice, and have slowed up the speed of the line. And [we] are now treated as human beings, and not as part of the machinery. The high pressure is taken off. . . . It proves clearly that united we stand, divided or alone we fall."

finally won a resounding victory when its union, after heated negotiations, was recognized by General Motors as the sole bargaining agency for its employees.

Unskilled workers now pressed their advantage. The United States Steel Company, hitherto an impossible nut for labor to crack, averted a costly strike when it voluntarily granted rights of unionization to its CIO-organized employees. But the "little steel" companies fought back savagely. Citizens were shocked in 1937 by the Memorial Day massacre at the plant of the Republic Steel Company in South Chicago. In a bloody fracas, police fired on pickets and workers, leaving the area strewn with several score dead and wounded.

A better deal for labor continued when Congress, in 1938, passed the **Fair Labor Standards Act** (Wages and Hours Bill). It required industries involved in interstate commerce to adhere to minimum-wage and maximum-hour standards. The eventual goals were forty cents an hour (later raised) and a forty-hour week. Labor by children under sixteen (under eighteen if the occupation was dangerous) was forbidden. These reforms were bitterly though futilely opposed by many industrialists, especially by those southern textile manufacturers who had profited from low-wage labor. But the exclusion of agricultural, service, and domestic workers meant that Black Americans, Mexican Americans, and many women—who were concentrated in these fields—did not benefit from the act.

In later New Deal days, labor unionization thrived (refer to Image 30.14 and Figure 30.3). "Roosevelt wants you to join a union" was the rallying cry of professional organizers. The patrician president received valuable support at ballot-box time from labor leaders and many appreciative

Figure 30.3 Labor Union Membership in Selected Countries, 1913–2020 In the United States, the percentage of the labor force that was unionized increased until 1954, when it began a long-term decline. In the 1990s it had a brief rise with the organization of service and government workers, only to decline again thereafter, reaching a low of 10.3 percent in 2020. Note the different fortunes of organized labor in other countries in the face of the Great Depression, World War II, postwar prosperity, and deindustrialization.

Sources: James C. Docherty, *Historical Dictionary of Organized Labor*, 2nd ed., pp. 408–415 and 420–421. Copyright © 2004. Reprinted from Scarecrow Press; Organisation for Economic Co-Operation and Development, online OECD Employment database.

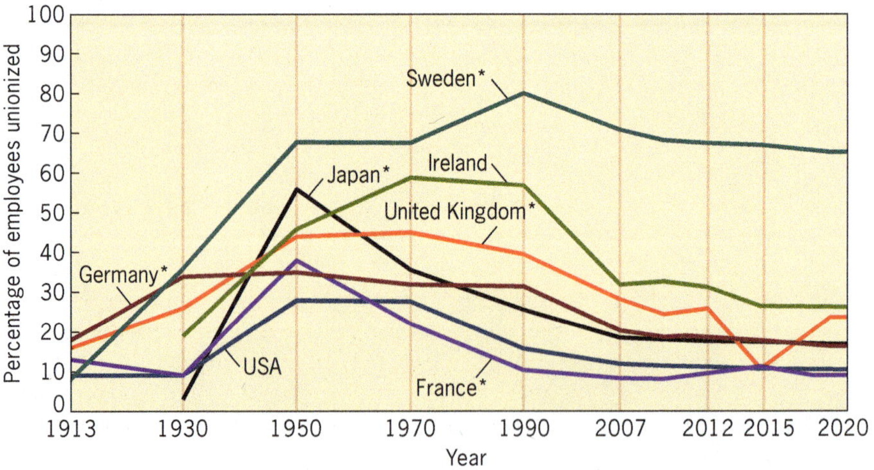

*For France, latest data available is 2018. For Germany, UK, Japan, and Sweden, latest data available is 2019.

working people. One mill worker remarked that Roosevelt was "the only man we ever had in the White House who would know that my boss is a s.o.b."

The CIO surged forward, breaking completely with the AFL in 1938. On that occasion the *Committee* for Industrial Organization was formally reconstituted as the **Congress of Industrial Organizations** (the new CIO), under the visionary though high-handed presidency of John L. Lewis. By 1940, the CIO could claim about 4 million members in its constituent unions, including some 200,000 Black workers. Nevertheless, bitter and annoying jurisdictional feuding involving strikes continued with the AFL. At times labor seemed more bent on costly civil war than on its age-old war with management.

30-16 Landon Challenges "the Champ"

As the presidential campaign of 1936 neared, the New Dealers were on top of the world. Unemployment was down (though not out), and millions of "reliefers" were grateful to their bountiful government. The exultant Democrats renominated Roosevelt on a platform squarely endorsing the New Deal.

The Republicans were hard-pressed to find someone to feed to "the Champ." They finally settled on the colorless but homespun and honest governor of the Sunflower State of Kansas, Alfred M. Landon. Landon himself was a moderate who accepted some New Deal reforms, although not the popular Social Security Act. But the Republican platform vigorously condemned the New Deal of Franklin "Deficit" Roosevelt for its radicalism, experimentation, confusion, and "frightful waste." Backing Landon, ex-president Hoover called for a "holy crusade for liberty," echoing the cry of the American Liberty League, a group of wealthy conservatives who had organized in 1934 to fight "socialistic" New Deal schemes. Roosevelt gave as good as he got. Angry enough to stretch sheet iron, the president took to the stump and denounced the "economic royalists" who sought to "hide behind the flag and the Constitution."

A landslide overwhelmed Landon, as the demoralized Republicans carried only two states, Maine and Vermont. This dismal showing caused political wiseacres to make the old adage read, "As Maine goes, so goes Vermont."* The popular vote was 27,752,869 to 16,674,665; the electoral count was 523 to 8—the most lopsided in 116 years. A good-humored newspaper columnist quipped, "If Landon had given one more speech, Roosevelt would have carried Canada, too." Democratic majorities, riding in on Roosevelt's magic coattails, were again returned to Congress. Jubilant Democrats could now claim more than two-thirds of the seats in the House and a like proportion in the Senate.

The battle of 1936, perhaps the most bitterly partisan since Bryan's defeat in 1896, partially bore out Republican charges of class warfare. Even more than in 1932, the needy economic groups were lined up against the so-called greedy economic groups. CIO units contributed generously to FDR's campaign chest. Many left-wingers turned to Roosevelt, as the customary third-party protest vote sharply declined. Black voters, several million of whom had also appreciated welcome relief checks, had by now largely shaken off their traditional allegiance to the Republican Party. To them, Lincoln was "finally dead."

FDR won primarily because he appealed to the "forgotten man," whom he never forgot. Some of the president's support was only pocketbook-deep: "Reliefers" were not going to bite the hand that doled out the government checks. No one, as Al Smith remarked, "shoots at Santa Claus." But Roosevelt in fact had forged an unlikely but powerful and enduring coalition of white Southerners, Black Northerners, urbanites, and poor people. He proved especially effective in marshaling the support of the multitudes of "New Immigrants"—mostly the Catholics and Jews who had swarmed into the great cities since the turn of the century. These once-scorned newcomers, with their now-numerous sons and daughters, had at last come politically of age. In the 1920s, one out of every twenty-five federal judgeships went to a Catholic; Roosevelt appointed Catholics to one out of every four.

30-17 Nine Old Men on the Bench

Bowing his head to the sleety blasts, Roosevelt took the presidential oath on January 20, 1937, instead of the traditional March 4. The Twentieth Amendment to the Constitution had been ratified in 1933 (refer to the Appendix). It swept away the postelection lame duck session of Congress and shortened by six weeks the awkward interregnum between election and inauguration.

---

*Maine, which traditionally held its state elections in September, was long regarded as a political weathervane, hence the expression "As Maine goes, so goes the nation."

Contending Voices

The New Deal at High Tide

Three days before the 1936 election, President Franklin Roosevelt (1882–1945) took the moral high ground in his fiery speech at New York's Madison Square Garden:

"I should like to have it said of my first Administration that in it the forces of selfishness and of lust for power met their match. I should like to have it said of my second Administration that in it these forces met their master. They are unanimous in their hate for me—*and I welcome their hatred.*"

One day prior to that, his predecessor Herbert Hoover (1874–1964) voiced the sentiments of many conservatives when he depicted the New Deal as a dangerous power grab:

"Through four years of experience this New Deal attack upon free institutions has emerged as the transcendent issue in America. All the men who are seeking for mastery in the world today are using the same weapons. They sing the same songs. They all promise the joys of Elysium without effort. But their philosophy is founded on the coercion and compulsory organization of men."

Consider This:

What ideologies about the nature of government lay behind Roosevelt's and Hoover's very different opinions of the New Deal? In what ways have their respective views persisted in American political life?

Flushed with victory, Roosevelt interpreted his reelection as a mandate to continue New Deal reforms. But in his eyes, the cloistered old men on the supreme bench, like fossilized stumbling blocks, stood stubbornly in the pathway of progress. In nine major cases involving the New Deal, the Roosevelt administration had been thwarted seven times. The Court was ultraconservative, and six of the nine oldsters in black were over seventy. As luck would have it, not a single member had been appointed by FDR in his first term.

Roosevelt, his "Dutch up," viewed with mounting impatience what he regarded as the obstructive conservatism of the Court. Some of these Old-Guard appointees were hanging on with a senile grip, partly because they felt it their patriotic duty to curb the "socialistic" tendencies of that radical in the White House. Roosevelt believed that the voters in three successive elections—the presidential elections of 1932 and 1936 and the midterm congressional elections of 1934—had returned a smashing verdict in favor of his program of reform. Democracy, in his view, meant rule by the people. If the American way of life was to be preserved, Roosevelt argued, the Supreme Court ought to get in line with the supreme court of public opinion.

Roosevelt finally hit upon a Court scheme that he regarded as "the answer to a maiden's prayer." In fact, it proved to be one of the more costly political misjudgments of his career. When he sprang his brainstorm on a shocked nation early in 1937, he caught the country and Congress completely by surprise. Roosevelt bluntly asked Congress for legislation to permit him to add a new justice to the Supreme Court for every member over seventy who would not retire. The maximum membership could then be fifteen. Roosevelt pointed to the necessity of injecting vigorous new blood, for the Court, he alleged, was far behind in its work. This charge, which turned out to be false, brought heated accusations of dishonesty. At best Roosevelt was headstrong and not fully attentive to the fact that the Court, in popular thinking, had become something of a sacred cow.

30-18 The Court Changes Course

Congress and the nation were promptly convulsed over Roosevelt's **Court-packing plan** to expand the Supreme Court. Critics vilified Franklin "Double-crossing" Roosevelt for attempting to break down the delicate checks and balances among the three branches of the government.

The Granger Collection, NYC

Image 30.15 The Response to Roosevelt's "Court-Packing" Plan, 1937 Even the Democratic donkey kicked up a storm in opposition to President Roosevelt's plan to expand the Supreme Court to as many as fifteen judges.

His enemies accused him of grooming himself as a dictator by trying to browbeat the judiciary. In the eyes of countless citizens, mostly Republicans but including many Democrats, basic liberties seemed to be in jeopardy. "God Bless the Supreme Court" was a fervent prayer.

The Court had meanwhile seen the ax hanging over its head. Whatever his motives, Justice Owen J. Roberts, formerly regarded as a conservative, began to vote on the side of his liberal colleagues. "The switch in time that saved nine" was the classic witticism inspired by this ideological change. By a five-to-four decision, the Court, in March 1937, upheld the principle of a state minimum wage for women, thereby reversing its stand on a different case a year earlier. In succeeding decisions, a Court more sympathetic to the New Deal upheld the National Labor Relations Act (Wagner Act) and the Social Security Act. Congress finally passed a court reform bill, but this watered-down version applied only to lower courts. Roosevelt, the master politician, thus suffered his first major legislative defeat at the hands of his own party in Congress. Americans have never viewed lightly a president's tampering with the Supreme Court, no matter how popular their chief executive may be (refer to Image 30.15).

Yet in losing this battle, Roosevelt incidentally won his campaign. The Court, as he had hoped, became markedly more friendly to New Deal reforms. Furthermore, a succession of deaths and resignations enabled him in time to make nine appointments to the tribunal—more than any of his predecessors since George Washington. The clock "unpacked" the Court.

In a sense, however, FDR lost both the Court battle and the wider policy war. He so aroused conservatives of both parties in Congress that few New Deal reforms were passed after 1937, the year of the fight to "pack" the bench. With this catastrophic miscalculation, Roosevelt squandered much of the political goodwill that had carried him to such a resounding victory in the 1936 election.

30-19 Twilight of the New Deal

Roosevelt's first term, from 1933 to 1937, did not banish the Depression from the land. Unemployment stubbornly persisted in 1936 at about 15 percent, down from the grim 25 percent of 1933 but still miserably high (refer to Figure 30.4). Despite the inventiveness of New Deal programs and the billions of dollars in "pump priming," recovery had been dishearteningly modest, though the country seemed to be inching its way back to economic health.

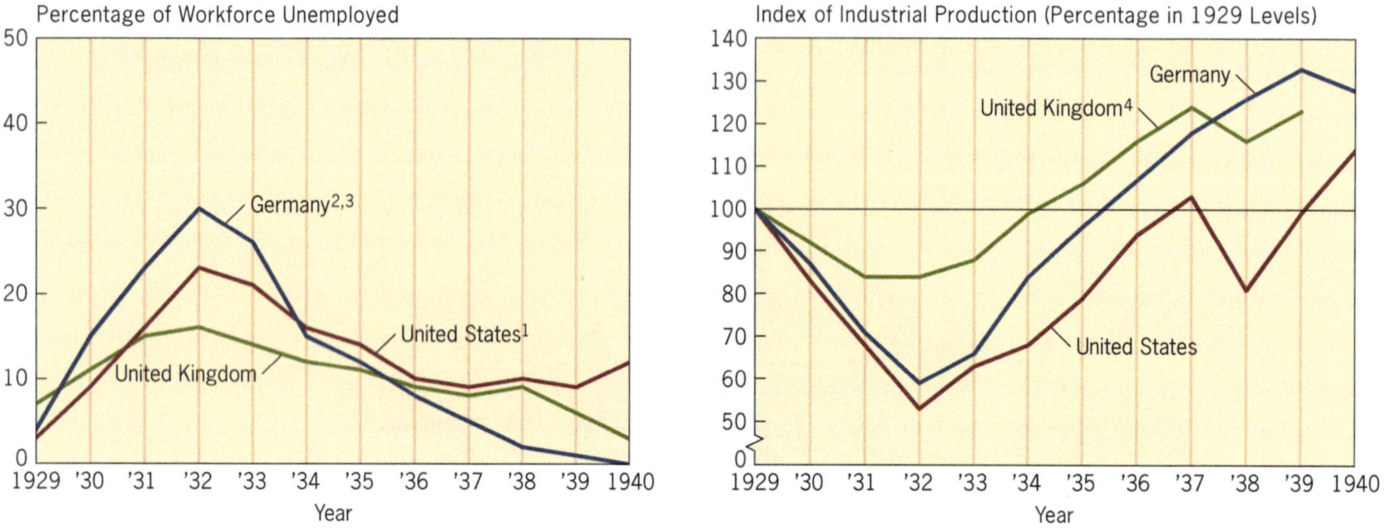

Figure 30.4 Economic Impact of the Great Depression on the United States, the United Kingdom, and Germany, 1929–1940

[1]Federal Emergency Relief Administration workers are counted as employed.

[2]Figure shows registered unemployment in Germany in 1929; industrial unemployment, as reported by unions, was 13.1 percent.

[3]Unemployment ceased to be an issue in Germany by 1939 with the mobilization for war. The labor force was actually augmented by the often-forced importation of foreign workers and the use of prison labor. Those who were unemployed suffered from a disability of some kind.

[4]This is an average of the industrial indexes in the United Kingdom for the first six months of 1939 only. Thereafter, no figures are available until 1946.

Sources: United States Historical Statistics, vol. 2; Statistical Yearbook of the League of Nations (1938–1939 and 1941–1942); International Historical Statistics, 1750–2005: Europe; State, Economy, and Society in Western Europe, 1815–1975, vol. 2.

Then, in 1937, the economy took another sharp downturn, a surprisingly severe depression-within-the-depression that the president's critics quickly dubbed the "Roosevelt recession." In fact, government policies had caused the nosedive, as new Social Security taxes began to bite into payrolls and as the administration cut back on spending out of continuing reverence for the orthodox economic doctrine of the balanced budget.

Only at this late date did Roosevelt at last frankly and deliberately embrace the recommendations of the British economist John Maynard Keynes. The New Deal had run deficits for several years, but all of them had been rather small and none was intended. Now, in April 1937, Roosevelt announced a bold program to stimulate the economy by planned deficit spending. Although the deficits were still undersized for the herculean task of conquering the Depression, this abrupt policy reversal marked a major turning point in the government's relation to the economy. **Keynesianism**—the use of government spending and fiscal policy to "prime the pump" of the economy and encourage consumer spending—became the new economic orthodoxy and remained so for decades.

Roosevelt had meanwhile been pushing some remaining reforms. Notably, he persuaded Congress to pass the Reorganization Act of 1939, the first major overhaul of the federal government's executive branch since George Washington's day. It created the Executive Office of the President, giving the chief executive limited but substantial power to structure his office and hire staff. Congress also adopted the much-heralded Hatch Act of 1939, prohibiting federal administrative officials, except the highest policy-making officers, from active political campaigning and soliciting. It proved to be an important but eventually inadequate measure to keep partisan politicking out of the work of government.

A basic objective of the New Deal was featured in Roosevelt's second inaugural address (1937):

"I see one-third of a nation ill-housed, ill-clad, ill-nourished. . . . The test of our progress is not whether we add more to the abundance of those who have much; it is whether we provide enough for those who have too little."

By 1938, the New Deal had clearly lost most of its early momentum. Magician Roosevelt could find few dazzling new reform rabbits to pull out of his tall silk hat. In the congressional elections of 1938, the Republicans, for the first time, cut heavily into the New Deal majorities in Congress, though failing to gain control of either house. The international crisis that came to a boil in 1938–1939 shifted public attention away from domestic reform and shored up Roosevelt's shaky political fortunes. But the New Deal, for all practical purposes, had shot its bolt.

30-20 New Deal or Raw Deal?

Roosevelt's agenda, though drawing on decades-old reform ideas, was a dramatic departure from the status quo, executed by a charismatic, singularly skillful president. It is not surprising that it attracted unrelenting criticism. Foes of the New Deal condemned its alleged waste, incompetence, confusion, contradictions, and cross-purposes, as well as the chiseling and graft in the alphabet agencies—"alphabet soup," sneered Al Smith. Roosevelt had done nothing, cynics said, that an earthquake could not have done better. The suspicion of radicalism still simmered in middle America's soul, and critics deplored the employment of "crackpot" college professors, leftist "pinkos," and outright Communists. Such subversives, it was charged, were trying to make America over in the Bolshevik-Marxist image under "Rooseveltski." The virulently anti-Roosevelt Hearst newspapers lambasted,

> The Red New Deal with a Soviet seal
> Endorsed by a Moscow hand,
> The strange result of an alien cult
> In a liberty-loving land.

Roosevelt was further accused by conservatives of being Jewish ("Rosenfield") and of tapping too many bright young Jewish leftists ("The Jew Deal") for his "Drain Trust."

Hardheaded businesspeople, who "had met a payroll," were shocked by the leap-before-you-look, try-anything-once spirit of Roosevelt, the jolly improviser. They accused him of confusing noise and movement with progress. Others appreciated the president's do-something approach. Humorist Will Rogers, the rope-twirling "poet lariat" of the era, remarked that if Roosevelt were to burn down the Capitol, people would say, "Well, we at least got a fire started, anyhow."

"Bureaucratic meddling" and "regimentation" were also bitter complaints of anti-New Dealers; in truth, bureaucracy did blossom. The federal government, with its hundreds of thousands of employees, became incomparably the largest single business in the country, as the states faded further into the background.

Promises of budget balancing, to say nothing of other promises, had flown out the window—so foes of the New Deal pointed out. The national debt had stood at the already enormous figure of $19.5 billion in 1932 and skyrocketed to $40.4 billion by 1939. America was becoming, its critics charged, a "handout state" trying to squander itself into prosperity—U.S. stood for "unlimited spending." Such lavish benefactions were undermining the old virtues of thrift and initiative. Ordinary Americans, once self-reliant citizens, were getting a bad case of the "gimmies": their wishbones were becoming larger than their backbones. In the nineteenth century, hard-pressed workers went West; now they went on relief.

Business was bitter. Accusing the New Deal of fomenting class strife, conservatives insisted that the laborer and the farmer—especially the big operator—were being pampered. Why "soak the successful"? Countless businesspeople, especially Republicans, declared that they could pull themselves out of the economic depression if they could only get the federal government—an interventionist big government—off their backs. Private enterprise, they charged, was being stifled by "planned economy," "planned bankruptcy," "creeping socialism," and the philosophy "Washington can do it better," with a federal pill for every ill. States' rights were being ignored, while the government was competing in business with its own citizens, under a "dictatorship of do-gooders."

The aggressive leadership of Roosevelt—"one-man supergovernment"—also came in for denunciation. Heavy fire was especially directed at his attempts to browbeat the Supreme Court and to create a "dummy Congress." Roosevelt had even tried in the 1938 elections, with backfiring results, to "purge" Democratic members of Congress who would not march in lockstep with him by supporting their primary challengers. The three senators whom he publicly opposed were all triumphantly reelected.

The most damning indictment of the New Deal was that it had failed to cure the Great Depression. Afloat in a sea of red ink, some argued, it had merely administered aspirin, sedatives, and Band-Aids. Many economists came to believe that better results would have been achieved by much greater deficit spending. Despite some $20 billion poured out in six years of deficit spending and lending, of leaf raking and pump priming, the gap between production and consumption did not wholly close. There were even more mountainous farm surpluses under Roosevelt than under Hoover. Millions of dispirited men and women were still unemployed in 1939, after six years of drain, strain, and pain. Not until World War II erupted in Europe and Asia was the unemployment headache solved.

30-21 FDR's Balance Sheet

New Dealers staunchly defended their record. Admitting that there had been some waste, they pointed out that relief—not economy—had been the primary object of their multifront war on the Depression. Conceding also that there had been some waste, they argued that it had been trivial in view of the immense sums spent and the obvious need for haste.

Champions of Roosevelt further declared that the New Deal had relieved the worst of the crisis in 1933. It promoted the philosophy of "balancing the human budget" and accepted the principle that the federal government was morally bound to prevent mass hunger and starvation by "managing" the economy. Government was to be used for the public good, not feared as the public's enemy. The collapse of America's economic system was averted, a fairer distribution of the national income was achieved, and the citizens were enabled to regain and retain their self-respect. And in retrospect, FDR's economic record looked better still. Substantial government investment in crucial infrastructure, including improved highways and waterways and the immense hydroelectricity-generating dams in the West, helped pave the way for the spectacular post–World War II economic boom (refer to Image 30.16).

Though hated by business tycoons, FDR should have been their patron saint, so his admirers claimed. He deflected popular resentments against business and may have saved the American system of free enterprise. Roosevelt's quarrel was not with capitalism but with capitalists; he purged American capitalism of some of its worst abuses so that it might be saved from itself. He may even have headed off a more radical swing to the left by a mild dose of what was mistakenly reviled as "socialism." The head of the American Socialist Party, when once asked if the New Deal had carried out the Socialist program, reportedly replied that it had indeed—on a stretcher. Nor, Roosevelt's later defenders claimed, did the New Deal bankrupt the United States: The sensational increase in the national debt was caused by World War II, not the New Deal. The national debt was only $40 billion in 1939 but $258 billion in 1945.

Image 30.16 **Our Skipper** This pro-FDR cartoon depicts a confident Roosevelt ignoring his critics while heading cheerily toward economic recovery. In fact, FDR's New Deal brought neither the recovery he promised nor the ruin his detractors prophesied. The Depression dragged on with only periodic improvement for nearly eight years under his leadership, until the cataclysmic emergency of World War II finally banished unemployment from the land.

Varying Viewpoints

How Radical Was the New Deal?

The Great Depression was both a great calamity and a great opportunity. How effectively Franklin Roosevelt responded to the calamity and what use he made of the opportunity are the two great questions that have animated historical debate about the New Deal.

Some historians have actually denied that there was much of a connection between the Depression and the New Deal. Arthur M. Schlesinger, Jr., for example, who believed in "cycles" of reform and reaction in American history, wrote that "there would very likely have been some sort of New Deal in the 1930s even without the Depression." But most of the first generation of historians who wrote about the New Deal (in the 1940s, 1950s, and early 1960s) agreed with Carl Degler's judgment that the New Deal was "a revolutionary response to a revolutionary situation." In this view, though Roosevelt never found a means short of war to bring about economic recovery, he shrewdly utilized the stubborn economic crisis as a means to enact sweeping reforms.

Some leftist scholars writing in the 1960s, however, notably Barton J. Bernstein, charged that the New Deal did not reach far enough. This criticism echoed the socialist complaint in the 1930s that the Depression represented the total collapse of American capitalism and that the New Deal had muffed the chance truly to remake American society. Roosevelt had the chance, these historians argued, to redistribute wealth, improve race relations, and bring the giant corporations to heel. Instead, said these critics, the New Deal simply represented a conservative holding action to shore up a sagging and corrupt capitalist order.

Those charges against the New Deal stimulated another generation of scholars in the 1970s, 1980s, and 1990s to look closely at the concrete institutional, attitudinal, and economic circumstances in which the New Deal unfolded. Historians such as James Patterson, Alan Brinkley, Kenneth Jackson, Harvard Sitkoff, and Lizabeth Cohen—sometimes loosely referred to as the "constraints school"—concluded that the New Deal offered just about as much reform as circumstances allowed and as the majority of Americans wanted. The findings of these historians are impressive: the system of checks and balances limited presidential power; the disproportionate influence of southern Democrats in Congress stalled attempts to move toward racial justice; the federal system, in fact, inhibited all efforts to initiate change from Washington.

Most important, a majority of the American people at the time wanted to reform capitalism, not overthrow it. Industrial workers, for example, were not hapless pawns upon whom the New Deal was foisted, frustrating their yearning for more radical change. Instead, as David Kennedy has argued, they sought security and self-determination in ways quite compatible with the New Deal's programs for unemployment insurance, old-age pensions, and guarantees of labor's right to organize.

Scholars including Alice Kessler-Harris, Linda Gordon, and Suzanne Mettler have argued that the New Deal had a more radical effect on men than on women. Social Security, for example, was designed to assist male breadwinners, who were then expected to share their benefits with their dependent wives and children. In addition, married women were rarely favored for government jobs in agencies such as the WPA. As a result, many women found themselves cast ever more firmly in the traditional role of wife and mother. Ira Katznelson, meanwhile, has re-centered scholarly attention on the key role of southern Democrats in Congress in shaping and constricting the New Deal along racial lines.

Perhaps William Leuchtenburg summed it up best when he described the New Deal as a "half-way revolution," neither radical nor conservative, but accurately reflecting the American people's needs and desires in the 1930s—and for a long time thereafter. The great "New Deal coalition" that dominated American politics for nearly four decades after Roosevelt's election in 1932 represented a broad consensus in American society about the opportunities and legitimate limits of government efforts to shape the social and economic order.

Roosevelt, like Jefferson, provided bold reform without a bloody revolution—at a time in history when some foreign nations were suffering armed uprisings and when many Europeans were predicting either communism or fascism for America. He was upbraided by the left-wing radicals for not going far enough, by the right-wing radicals for going too far. Choosing the middle road, he has been called the greatest American conservative since Hamilton. He was in fact Hamiltonian in his espousal of big government, but Jeffersonian in his concern for the "forgotten man."

Demonstrating anew the value of powerful presidential leadership, he exercised that power to relieve the erosion of the nation's greatest physical resource—its people. He helped preserve democracy in America in a time when democracies abroad were disappearing down the sinkhole of dictatorship. And in playing this role, he unwittingly girded the nation for its part in the titanic war that loomed on the horizon—a war in which democracy the world over would be at stake.

Chapter Summary

Franklin Roosevelt, a confident aristocrat with a common touch, swept into office with an urgent mandate to cope with the Depression emergency. His bank holiday and frantic Hundred Days legislation lifted America's spirits and created a host of new agencies to provide relief to the unemployed, economic recovery, and permanent reform of a largely unregulated capitalist system.

Roosevelt's early programs put millions of the unemployed back on the job through federal action, but failed to achieve the full economic recovery he sought. As popular demagogues like Senator Huey Long and Father Charles Coughlin gained followings among the suffering population, Roosevelt developed further ambitious programs to reform American industry, labor, and agriculture. The Supreme Court declared unconstitutional the most sweeping effort, the National Recovery Administration, and farmers continued to suffer from the Dust Bowl. But the TVA, Social Security, and the Wagner Act brought far-reaching social changes that especially benefited the economically disadvantaged.

Conservatives furiously denounced the New Deal, but Roosevelt formed a powerful coalition of urbanites, labor, "new immigrants," Black people, and southerners that swept him to victory in 1936. FDR and especially his vigorously reformist wife, Eleanor, brought new visibility to women in his administration and the country.

Roosevelt's overreaching court-packing plan failed, but the Supreme Court finally began approving New Deal legislation. The later New Deal encountered mounting conservative opposition and the stubborn persistence of unemployment. Although the New Deal was highly controversial, it steered a middle course between unregulated capitalism and socialism that prevented America from turning toward the extreme right-wing or left-wing dictatorships that were then taking hold in Europe.

Key Terms

- Brain Trust (782)
- New Deal (782)
- Hundred Days (784)
- Glass-Steagall Banking Reform Act (785)
- Civilian Conservation Corps (CCC) (787)
- National Recovery Administration (NRA) (792)
- Agricultural Adjustment Administration (AAA) (794)
- Dust Bowl (795)
- Indian Reorganization Act of 1934 (796)
- Tennessee Valley Authority (TVA) (797)
- Social Security Act (798)
- Wagner Act (799)
- Fair Labor Standards Act (800)
- Congress of Industrial Organizations (CIO) (801)
- Court-packing plan (802)
- Keynesianism (804)

People to Know

- Franklin Delano Roosevelt
- Eleanor Roosevelt
- Harry L. Hopkins
- Father Charles Coughlin
- Francis E. Townsend
- Huey P. ("Kingfish") Long
- John Steinbeck
- Frances Perkins
- Mary McLeod Bethune
- Robert F. Wagner

Chronology

1932	• Roosevelt defeats Hoover for presidency	
1933	• Bank holiday • Emergency Banking Relief Act • Beer and Wine Revenue Act • Hundred Days Congress enacts AAA, TVA, HOLC, NRA, and PWA • Federal Securities Act	• Glass-Steagall Banking Reform Act • CWA established • Twentieth Amendment (changed calendar of congressional sessions and date of presidential inauguration) • Twenty-first Amendment (prohibition repealed)
1934	• Gold Reserve Act • Securities and Exchange Commission authorized • Indian Reorganization Act	• FHA established • Frazier-Lemke Farm Bankruptcy Act
1935	• WPA established • Wagner Act • Resettlement Administration • Social Security Act	• Public Utility Holding Company Act • *Schechter* "sick chicken" case • CIO organized
1936	• Soil Conservation and Domestic Allotment Act • Roosevelt defeats Landon for presidency	
1937	• USHA established • Roosevelt announces "Court-packing" plan	
1938	• Second AAA • Fair Labor Standards Act	
1939	• Reorganization Act • Hatch Act	

To Learn More

Alan Brinkley, *Voices of Protest: Huey Long, Father Coughlin, and the Great Depression* (1982)

______, *The End of Reform: New Deal Liberalism in Depression and War* (1995)

Lizabeth Cohen, *Making a New Deal: Industrial Workers in Chicago, 1919–1939* (rev. ed., 2008)

Blanche Wiesen Cook, *Eleanor Roosevelt: A Life* (1992)

James N. Gregory, *American Exodus: The Dustbowl Migration and Okie Culture in California* (1989)

Ira Katznelson, *Fear Itself: The New Deal and the Origins of Our Time* (2013)

Robin D. G. Kelley, *Hammer and Hoe: Alabama Communists During the Great Depression* (1990)

David M. Kennedy, *Freedom from Fear: The American People in Depression and War* (1999)

Alice Kessler-Harris, *In Pursuit of Equity: Men, Women, and the Quest for Economic Citizenship in Twentieth-Century America* (2001)

Neil M. Maher, *Nature's New Deal: The Civilian Conservation Corps and the Roots of the American Environmental Movement* (2008)

Lois Scharf, *Eleanor Roosevelt: First Lady of American Liberalism* (1987)

Jeff Shesol, *Supreme Power: Franklin Roosevelt vs. the Supreme Court* (2010)

Nick Taylor, *American-Made: The Enduring Legacy of the WPA: When FDR Put the Nation to Work* (2008)

Studs Terkel, *Hard Times: An Oral History of the Great Depression* (1970)

Wendy Wall, *Inventing the "American Way": The Politics of Consensus from the New Deal to the Civil Rights Movement* (2008)

Chapter 31 The Cauldron of World War II: 1933–1945

Almighty God: Our sons, pride of our Nation, this day have set upon a mighty endeavor, a struggle to preserve our Republic, our religion, and our civilization, and to set free a suffering humanity. Lead them straight and true; give strength to their arms, stoutness to their hearts, steadfastness in their faith. . . . They will be sore tried, by night and by day, without rest—until the victory is won. The darkness will be rent by noise and flame. Men's souls will be shaken with the violences of war. For these men are lately drawn from the ways of peace. They fight not for the lust of conquest. They fight to end conquest. They fight to liberate. They fight to let justice arise, and tolerance and good will among all Thy people. They yearn but for the end of battle, for their return to the haven of home.

Franklin Roosevelt, "D-Day Prayer," June 6, 1944

Chapter Outline

- Roosevelt's early foreign policies
- German, Japanese, and Italian aggression
- The Neutrality Acts
- The horrors of the Holocaust
- The Lend-Lease Act and the Atlantic Charter, 1941
- Japanese attack on Pearl Harbor, December 7, 1941
- Internment of Japanese Americans
- Women in wartime
- Race relations during the war
- The wartime economy

Americans in the 1930s were slow to recognize just how the Great War of 1914–1918 and the unprecedented shock of the globe-spanning Great Depression had made the world a dangerous place.

But as the clouds of war gathered over Europe and Asia, President Roosevelt increasingly resolved to persuade the American people that no nation was safe in an era of naked aggression, which eventually erupted into the cataclysmic catastrophe of World War II.

Focus Questions

1. How and why did isolationism dominate American public opinion and foreign policy in the 1930s?
2. What issues and conflicts between America and Japan led up to the surprise Japanese attack on Pearl Harbor?
3. What was the war's impact on American society, including changing gender roles, regional migration, and race relations?
4. What were the principal war aims of the United States in WWII, and what strategy did it adopt in pursuit of those aims?
5. How did the United States develop the atomic bomb, and why was the dropping of two bombs on Japan so controversial?

- Turning the Japanese tide in the Pacific
- "D-Day" in Normandy (France), June 6, 1944
- U.S. drops the atomic bombs, August 1945

Examining the Evidence: Public-Opinion Polling in the 1930s

Contending Voices: To Intervene or Not to Intervene

Makers of America: The Japanese

Thinking Globally: America and the World in Depression and War: A Study in Contrasts

Varying Viewpoints: Atomic Bombs: Were They Justified?

31-1 Storm-Cellar Isolationism

The sixty-six-nation **London Economic Conference**, meeting in the summer of 1933, revealed how thoroughly Roosevelt's earliest foreign policy took a back seat to his strategy for domestic economic recovery. After first agreeing to participate in good faith, Roosevelt abruptly ordered the American delegates to withdraw, effectively scuttling the last opportunity for an internationally coordinated response to the Great Depression. Ambitious dictators—notably Germany's Adolf Hitler—took note of America's go-it-alone attitude.

Roosevelt matched isolationism from Europe with withdrawal from Asia. Congress provided in 1934 for the independence of the Philippines after a twelve-year period of further economic and political oversight—that is, by 1946. American isolationists rejoiced. Yet in Tokyo as in Berlin, cunning aggressors were calculating that they had little to fear from an inward-looking, isolationist America.

Closer to home, Roosevelt inaugurated a promising new era in relations with Latin America. He proclaimed in his inaugural address, "I would dedicate this nation to the policy of the Good Neighbor" (refer to Image 31.1). Deeds followed words, as Washington pulled the remaining Marines out of Haiti, released Cuba from some of the worst hobbles of the Platt Amendment, and acquiesced in Mexico's nationalization of its oil properties. Taken together, Roosevelt's noninvolvement in Europe and withdrawal from Asia, along with this fresh embrace of his New World neighbors, suggested that the United States would content itself with being merely a regional power, its interests confined exclusively to the Western Hemisphere.

At the same time, Roosevelt made at least one internationalist gesture in 1933 when he extended diplomatic recognition to the Soviet Union, whose communist government America and many other nations had shunned since its revolutionary birth more than a decade earlier.

31-2 The World Descends into Darkness

Post-1918 chaos in Europe, followed by the Great Depression, spawned the ominous spread of totalitarianism. The communist Union of Soviet Socialist Republics (USSR) led the way, as the Soviet Union's crafty and callous dictator Joseph Stalin purged his communist state of all suspected dissidents, ultimately executing hundreds of thousands and banishing millions to remote Siberian forced-labor camps. Blustery Benito Mussolini, a swaggering Fascist, seized the reins of power in Italy in 1922. Seeking empire in Africa, he brutally attacked Ethiopia in 1935 with bombers and tanks. And demonically fanatical Adolf Hitler plotted and harangued his way into power in Germany in 1933 at the head of the Nazi (National Socialist) Party.

Hitler was the most dangerous of the dictators because he combined the tremendous power of the German nation with unapologetic racism and extravagant dreams of imperial glory (refer to Image 31.2). A frustrated Austrian painter with a toothbrush mustache, a hypnotic orator and ruthless ruler, he had secured control of the Nazi Party by making political capital of the Treaty of Versailles and Germany's depression-spawned unemployment. He was thus a misbegotten child of the shortsighted postwar policies of the victorious Allies, including the United States. Hitler withdrew Germany from the League of Nations in 1933 and began clandestinely (and illegally) rearming. In 1936, the Nazi Hitler and the Fascist Mussolini allied themselves in the **Rome-Berlin Axis**.

International gangsterism was likewise spreading in the Far East, where imperial Japan was on the make. Like

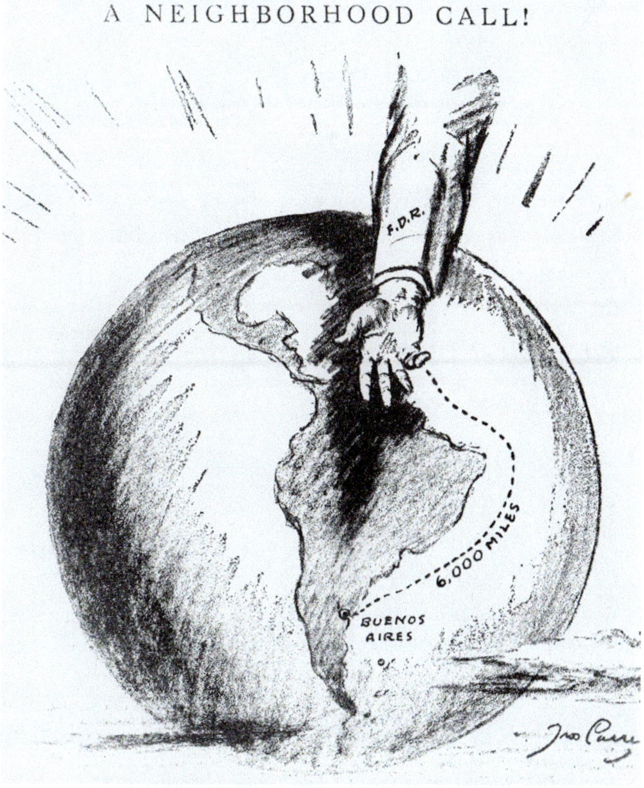

Image 31.1 FDR The Good Neighbor, 1936 Roosevelt used the occasion of the Inter-American Conference for the Maintenance of Peace in Buenos Aires to embark on a "good neighbor tour" of South America. With storm clouds gathering in Europe, he set hemispheric unity above American dominance and sought to turn the U.S. neighbors to the south into friends.

The thirst of Benito Mussolini (1883–1945) for national glory in Ethiopia is indicated by his remark in 1940:

"To make a people great it is necessary to send them to battle even if you have to kick them in the pants." (The Italians were notoriously unwarlike.)

In 1934 Mussolini proclaimed in a public speech,

"We have buried the putrid corpse of liberty."

Germany and Italy, Japan was a so-called have-not power. Like them, it resented the ungenerous Treaty of Versailles. Like them, it demanded additional space for its swelling population, especially in the resource-rich and strategically located northerly Chinese province of Manchuria. In 1940, Japan joined Germany and Italy in the **Tripartite Pact**, pledging mutual assistance in their respective imperial ambitions.

Mired down in the Great Depression, most Americans had little appreciation of the revolutionary forces being unleashed by the dictators. Many still believed that their encircling seas conferred a kind of magical immunity. They continued to suffer the disillusionment born of their participation in World War I, which they now regarded as a colossal blunder. Strong nationwide sentiment welled up for a constitutional amendment to forbid a declaration of war by Congress—except in case of invasion—unless there was a favorable popular referendum. It was a preposterously impractical idea, likened by one senator to requiring "a town meeting before permitting the fire department to face a blaze."

ugo Jaeger/The LIFE Picture Collection/Shutterstock.com

Image 31.2 **Adolf Hitler Reviewing Troops, Berlin, 1939**
Egging his people on with theatrical displays of pomp and ceremony, Hitler had created a vast military machine by 1939, when he started World War II with a brutal attack against Poland.

31-3 Isolationism at High Tide

Responding to overwhelming popular pressure, Congress tried to legislate the nation out of war. The **Neutrality Acts of 1935, 1936, and 1937**, taken together, stipulated that *when the president proclaimed* the existence of a foreign war, certain restrictions would automatically go into effect (refer to Image 31.3). No American could legally sail on a belligerent ship, sell or transport munitions to a belligerent, or make loans to a belligerent. This head-in-the-sand legislation in effect marked an abandonment of the traditional policy of freedom of the seas—a policy for which America had professedly fought two full-fledged wars and several undeclared wars.

The Spanish Civil War of 1936–1939 provided an early test of the neutrality policy. And as a kind of proving ground and dress rehearsal for World War II, the conflict in Spain furnished a painful object lesson in the folly of neutrality-by-legislation. Spanish rebels, headed by General Francisco Franco, generously backed by his fellow fascists Hitler and Mussolini, rose up against the duly elected republican government in Madrid, which in turn enjoyed the support of the Soviet Union. Left-leaning and other adventure-seeking Americans burned with passion to defend the struggling republic against Franco's fascist coup. Some three thousand young men and women headed to Spain to fight alongside the Loyalist republicans in the **Abraham Lincoln Brigade**.

Congress amended the existing neutrality legislation so as to apply an arms embargo to both Loyalists and rebels. Uncle Sam thus sat on the sidelines while Franco strangled the republican government of Spain. The democracies, including the United States, were so determined to stay out of war that they had helped to condemn a fellow democracy to death.

Sulfurous war clouds had meanwhile been gathering in the tension-taut Far East. In 1937, Japanese militarists, at the Marco Polo Bridge near Beijing (Peking), touched off the explosion that led to an all-out invasion of China. In a sense this attack was the curtain-raiser of World War II.

In Chicago—unofficial isolationist capital of America—President Roosevelt delivered his sensational **Quarantine Speech** in the autumn of 1937. Alarmed by the recent aggressions of Italy and Japan, he called for "positive endeavors" to "quarantine" the aggressors—presumably by economic embargoes.

The speech unleashed a cyclone of protest from isolationists. Startled by this angry response, Roosevelt retreated. "It's a terrible thing," he allegedly remarked, "to look over your shoulder when you are trying to lead—and find no one there." A British observer acidly noted that the Americans were "hardly a people to go tiger shooting with."

America's isolationist mood continued to intensify, especially in regard to China. In December 1937, Japanese aviators bombed and sank an American gunboat, the *Panay*, in Chinese waters, with a loss of two killed and thirty wounded. Tokyo hastened to make the necessary apologies and pay a proper indemnity, whereupon Americans breathed a deep sigh of relief that the *Panay* incident had not exploded into full-blown war.

Granger/Bridgeman Images

Image 31.3 "The Only Way We Can Save Her," 1939 Even as war broke out in Europe, many Americans continued to insist on the morality of U.S. neutrality.

Adolf Hitler meanwhile grew ever-bolder in Europe. In 1936, he brazenly marched into the demilitarized German Rhineland, contrary to the detested Treaty of Versailles. France and Britain looked on in an agony of indecision. Lashing his followers to a frenzy, Hitler undertook to persecute and then eliminate the Jewish population in the areas under his control. Calling upon his people to sacrifice butter for guns, he whipped the new German air force and mechanized ground divisions into the most devastating military machine the world had yet seen.

Suddenly, in March 1938, Hitler bloodlessly occupied German-speaking Austria, his birthplace. The democratic powers, wringing their hands in despair, prayed that this last grab would satisfy his passion for conquest. But like a drunken reveler calling for madder music and stronger wine, Hitler would not stop. Intoxicated by his recent gains, he demanded the cession of the German-inhabited Sudetenland in neighboring Czechoslovakia, "the last territorial claim I have to make in Europe." The leaders of Britain and France, badly unprepared for war, betrayed Czechoslovakia to Germany at a notorious conference in Munich when they consented to the shearing away of the Sudetenland.

Appeasement of the dictators, summarized by the word *Munich*, turned out to be merely surrender on the installment plan. It was like giving a cannibal a finger in the hope of saving an arm. In March 1939, scarcely six months later, Hitler suddenly erased the rest of Czechoslovakia from the map, contrary to his solemn vows. The democratic world was again stunned but still paralyzed.

31-4 Hitler's Belligerency and U.S. Neutrality

Joseph Stalin, the sphinx of the Kremlin, next astounded the world on August 23, 1939, by signing a nonaggression treaty with Hitler. With the signing of the Nazi-Soviet pact, World War II was only hours away. Hitler sent his mechanized divisions crashing into Poland at dawn on September 1, 1939 (refer to Image 31.4). Sixteen days later, Stalin's Red Army invaded Poland from the east.

> Canute Frankson (1890–ca. 1940), an African American member of the Abraham Lincoln Brigade, explained why he went to Spain to fight against the fascist Franco in 1937:
>
> "Since this is a war between whites who for centuries have held us in slavery, and have heaped every kind of insult and abuse upon us, segregated and Jim-crowed us; why [am] I, a Negro . . . in Spain today? Because we are no longer an isolated minority group fighting hopelessly against an immense giant. . . . Because if we crush Fascism here we'll save our people in America, and in other parts of the world from the vicious persecution, wholesale imprisonment, and slaughter which the Jewish people . . . are suffering under Hitler's Fascist heels. . . . We will build us a new society—a society of peace and plenty. There will be no color line, no Jim-Crow trains, no lynching. That is why, my dear, I'm here in Spain."

Britain and France, honoring their commitments to Poland, were finally moved to declare war. "It has come at last," Roosevelt said to a friend. "God help us all." Roosevelt speedily issued the routine proclamations of neutrality, but neutrality promptly became a heated issue in the United States. Ill-prepared Britain and France urgently needed American airplanes and other weapons, but the Neutrality Acts raised a sternly forbidding hand. Roosevelt induced Congress to pass the **Neutrality Act of 1939** allowing the European democracies to purchase war materials in America, but only on a "cash-and-carry basis." This meant that they would have to transport the munitions in their own ships, after paying for them in cash. America would thus avoid loans, war debts, and the torpedoing of American arms-carriers.

This unneutral neutrality law unfortunately hurt China, which was effectively blockaded by the Imperial Japanese Navy. But despite its defects, in Europe it clearly favored the democracies against the dictators. As the British and French navies controlled the Atlantic, the European aggressors could not send their ships to buy America's munitions. The United States not only improved its moral position but simultaneously helped its economic position. Overseas demand for war goods ultimately solved the decade-long unemployment crisis (refer to Figure 30.4 on p. 804).

31-5 The Fall of France

The months following the collapse of Poland, while France and Britain marked time, were known as the "phony war," which ended abruptly in April 1940 when Hitler's forces overran his weaker neighbors Denmark and Norway. Hardly pausing for breath, the next month he attacked the Netherlands and Belgium, followed by a paralyzing blow at France. By late June, France was forced to surrender (refer to Image 31.5). In a pell-mell

The Granger Collection, NYC

Image 31.4 Poland Falls to the Nazi Juggernaut, 1939 After swallowing Austria and Czechoslovakia in 1938, Hitler launched all-out war on Poland in September 1939, and the Nazi war machine seemed unstoppable.

Hulton Deutsch/Getty Images

Image 31.5 Hitler Swaggers into Paris, 1940 The fall of France to German forces in June 1940 was a galling blow to French pride and convinced many Americans that their country must mobilize to defeat the Nazi menace.

Examining the Evidence

Public-Opinion Polling in the 1930s

In 1936, the prominent news publication *Literary Digest* made a monumental gaffe when it relied on public-opinion polling data to forecast a victory for the Republican candidate, Alf Landon, over the incumbent, Franklin D. Roosevelt. As it happened, Roosevelt racked up a monstrous majority, winning the electoral votes of all but two states. The *Digest*'s error had been to compile its polling lists from records of automobile registration and telephone directories—unwittingly skewing its sample toward relatively well-off voters in an era when fewer than half of American families owned either a car or a telephone.

The *Digest*'s embarrassing mistake ended an era of informal polling techniques, as new, scientifically sophisticated polling organizations founded by George Gallup and Elmo Roper forged to the fore. From this date forward, polling became a standard tool for marketers and advertisers—as well as for political strategists and historians.

Yet controversy has long clouded the relationship between pollsters and politicians, who are often accused of abdicating their roles as leaders and slavishly deferring to public opinion, rather than trying to shape it. Franklin Roosevelt confronted this issue in the 1930s, as polls seemed to confirm the stubborn isolationism of the American people, even as the president grew increasingly convinced that the United States must play a more active international role.

What do the poll results below suggest about Roosevelt's handling of this issue? About the reliability of polling data? What are the legitimate political uses of public-opinion polls? How valuable are they to the historian?

[1.] (U.S. Oct 3 '39) Do you think the United States should do everything possible to help England and France win the war, except go to war ourselves?

Yes 62% No 38%

[2.] (U.S. Oct 3 '39) If it appears that Germany is defeating England and France, should the United States declare war on Germany and send our army and navy to Europe to fight?

	Yes	No
National total	29%	71%
BY GEOGRAPHICAL SECTION		
New England	33%	67%
Middle Atlantic	27	73
East central	25	75
West central	26	74
South	47	53
West	28	72
(Jan 30 '40) National total	23%	77%

[3.] (U.S. May 29 '40) If the question of the United States going to war against Germany came up for a national vote within the next two or three weeks, would you vote to go to war (go into the war or stay out of the war)?

Yes 16% No 84%

(June 11 '40) ....Go in 19% Stay out 81%

[4.] (U.S. Aug 5 '41) Should the United States go to war now against Japan?

	Yes	No	No opinion
	22%	78% = 100%	11%
(Oct 22 '41)	13	74	13

[5.] (U.S. Sept 17 '41) Should the United States go into the war now and send an army to Europe to fight?

Yes 9% No 87% No opinion 4%

[6.] (U.S. Nov 5 '41) If, in trying to defeat Germany, it becomes necessary to send a large American army to Europe, would you favor this step?

Yes 47% No 46% No opinion 7%

Source: From Hadley Cantril, ed., *Public Opinion, 1935–1946* (Princeton, N.J.: Princeton University Press, 1951).

Adolf Hitler (1889–1945) promised to win his fellow Germans Lebensraum, or "living space," and to win it by war if necessary. In his eyes, his nationalist and racist crusade justified every violent means at hand. As he told his commanders,

"When you start a war, what matters is not who is right, but who wins. Close your hearts to pity. Act with brutality. Eighty million Germans must get what is their due. Their existence must be made secure. The stronger man is in the right."

evacuation from the French port of Dunkirk, the British managed to salvage the bulk of their shattered army. The crisis providentially brought forth an inspired leader in Prime Minister Winston Churchill, the bulldog-jawed orator who nerved his people to stand up to Nazi aggression.

France's collapse shocked Americans out of their isolationist daydreams. Roosevelt now moved with electrifying energy and dispatch. He called upon his nation to build huge air fleets and a two-ocean navy. Congress, jarred out of its apathy, appropriated the astounding sum of $37 billion for the military buildup—more than the total cost of fighting World War I and about five times larger than any New Deal annual budget. Congress also passed a conscription law, approved September 6, 1940, America's first peacetime draft. It originally provided for annually training 1.2 million troops and 800,000 reserves.

31-6 Refugees from the Holocaust

Aroused by Adolf Hitler, the ancient demon of antisemitism brutally bared its fangs. The Nazi Party mobilized systematic violence against Jews with all the efficiency of the modern industrial state. On the night of November 9, 1938, state-sanctioned mobs ransacked more than seven thousand Jewish shops and synagogues throughout Germany. At least ninety-one Jews lost their lives, and about thirty thousand were sent to concentration camps in the turbulent wake of ***Kristallnacht***, the "night of broken glass" (refer to Image 31.6).

bpk, Berlin/Art Resource, NY

Image 31.6 Shattered Jewish Storefronts in Berlin This photo was taken after the attacks of Kristallnacht on November 9, 1938.

Many Jews attempted to escape from Hitler's racist juggernaut. In one poignant case, in May 1939, 937 passengers, almost all of them Jewish refugees, boarded the ship *St. Louis* in Hamburg and departed for Havana. When they reached Cuba, however, most were denied entry for lack of a valid Cuban visa. The *St. Louis* then sailed up the Atlantic coast of the United States, which proved no more hospitable, thanks to restrictive immigration laws as well as studied indifference from antisemitic State Department officials. The *St. Louis* eventually deposited its passengers in England, France, Belgium, and the Netherlands, where many of them subsequently perished under the Nazi heel.

Reports of the Nazi genocide began to be verified in 1942, and in early 1944 Roosevelt created the **War Refugee Board**, which eventually saved thousands of Hungarian Jews from deportation to the notorious death camp at Auschwitz. All told, 150,000 Jews, mostly Germans and Austrians, sought safe haven in the United States, which took in more refugees than any other country. But that was hardly enough. By the end of the war, some 6 million European Jews had been murdered in the Holocaust.

31-7 Half-Way to War

Hitler launched air attacks against Britain in August 1940, preparatory to an invasion scheduled for September. For months, the Battle of Britain raged in the air over the British Isles. The Royal Air Force's tenacious defense of its native islands eventually led Hitler to postpone his planned invasion indefinitely.

During the precarious months of the Battle of Britain, debate intensified in the United States over what foreign policy to embrace. Radio broadcasts from London brought the drama of the nightly German air raids directly into millions of American homes. Sympathy for Britain grew, but it was not yet sufficient to push the United States into war. Roosevelt faced a historic decision: whether to hunker down in the Western Hemisphere, assume a defensive "Fortress America" posture, and let the rest of the world go it alone; or to bolster beleaguered Britain by all means short of war itself. Both sides had their advocates.

Supporters of aid to Britain formed lobbying groups, the most potent of which was the Committee to Defend America by Aiding the Allies. Isolationists, determined to avoid American bloodshed at all costs, organized the **America First Committee** (refer to Image 31.7). Their most effective speechmaker was the famed aviator Colonel Charles A. Lindbergh, whose daring solo flight, ironically, had narrowed the Atlantic in 1927.

Roosevelt moved boldly when, on September 2, 1940, he agreed to transfer to Great Britain fifty antiquated, four-funnel destroyers left over from World War I. In return, the British promised to hand over to the United States eight valuable defensive base sites, stretching from Newfoundland to South America. These strategically located outposts were to remain under the Stars and Stripes for ninety-nine years.

Irving Haberman/IH Images/Getty Images

Image 31.7 Rallying for America First Formed in 1940 to lobby against American involvement in foreign wars, the "America First Committee" boasted 800,000 members at its peak. This 1941 rally in New York City was one of many large gatherings the group held around the nation.

Contending Voices

To Intervene or Not to Intervene

Chicago industrialist Sterling Morton (1885–1961), a backer of the isolationist America First Committee, emphasized the American tradition of nonintervention in an August 1940 speech:

"We should follow the advice of [George] Washington: We should maintain friendly relations with all nations, grant special favors to none. We should remember that the Monroe Doctrine was just as emphatic against American interference in Europe as against European interference in the Americas. We should not meddle in the affairs of other nations. . . . We have no mission to impose our ideas of government on others."

That same summer President Franklin Roosevelt (1882–1945) made a compelling case against the isolationists in a speech at the University of Virginia:

"Some indeed still hold to the now somewhat obvious delusion that we of the United States can safely permit the United States to become a lone island, a lone island in a world dominated by the philosophy of force. Such an island may be the dream of those who still talk and vote as isolationists. Such an island represents to me and to the overwhelming majority of Americans today a helpless nightmare of a people without freedom—the nightmare of a people lodged in prison, handcuffed, hungry, and fed through the bars from day to day by the contemptuous, unpitying masters of other continents."

Consider This:

What factors might explain the intense divisions in American opinion about intervening in the war?

31-8 Shattering the Two-Term Tradition

A distracting presidential election, as fate decreed, came in the midst of this crisis. Roosevelt readily accepted his Democratic party's nomination for an unprecedented third term. The 1940 Republican convention was swept off its feet by a colorful latecomer, Wendell L. Willkie, a son of Hoosier Indiana. A complete novice in politics, mocked by adversaries as a "simple barefoot Wall Street lawyer," he had rocketed from political obscurity in a few short weeks.

Willkie might have exploited the isolationist-interventionist breach with a muscular attack on Roosevelt's aid-to-Britain policies. But seeing eye-to-eye with FDR on the necessity of bolstering the beleaguered democracies, he refrained from assailing the president's pro-British position. Stung by taunts that he was leading the nation by the back door into the European slaughterhouse, Roosevelt declared, "Your boys are not going to be sent into any foreign wars"—a pledge that later came back to plague him.

The time-honored wisdom that one should not change horses in the middle of a stream was strong. Roosevelt might not have won—or even run—if there had not been a war crisis. But he triumphed overwhelmingly, beating Willkie by nearly five million votes and securing an Electoral College landslide of 449 to 82.

31-9 A Landmark Lend-Lease Law

By late 1940, embattled Britain was nearing the end of its financial tether, its credits in America rapidly consumed by enormous war orders. But Roosevelt found a way to lend or lease American arms to Britain and eventually to the Soviet Union and China as well. When the shooting was over, he explained, the guns and tanks could be returned, just as one's next-door neighbor would return a garden hose when a threatening fire was put out. The **Lend-Lease Bill**, patriotically numbered 1776, was approved in March 1941 by sweeping majorities in both houses of Congress.

Adolf Hitler called Lend-Lease tantamount to a declaration of war. For all practical purposes, he was right. The bill put American resources clearly into the scales on behalf of the victims of aggression (refer to Image 31.8). Yet the final legislation contained a controversial concession to isolationists that "Nothing in this Act shall be construed to authorize ... convoying [merchant] vessels by naval vessels of the United States." That self-denying provision prohibited U.S. Navy vessels from escorting ("convoying") American commercial ships across the Atlantic Ocean, leaving American commercial ships unprotected. This policy was soon to create a monumental headache for President Roosevelt.

Lend-lease was nevertheless a challenge hurled squarely into the teeth of the Axis dictators. By war's end in 1945, America had sent about $50 billion worth of arms and equipment to the nations fighting aggressors (refer to Map 31.1).

31-10 Edging Toward War

Out of a clear sky, on June 22, 1941, Hitler treacherously launched a devastating attack on the Soviet Union, his supposed partner in the nonaggression pact of 1939. Roosevelt quickly extended $1 billion in lend-lease aid to the suffering Russians—the first installment on an ultimate total of $11 billion. Meanwhile, the valor of Russia's Red Army, combined with the white paralysis of an early Russian winter, halted Hitler's invaders at the gates of Moscow.

With the surrender of the Soviet Union still a dread possibility, Churchill and Roosevelt met for a drama-charged meeting on the deck of a warship off the foggy coast of Newfoundland in August 1941. There the two leaders announced the **Atlantic Charter**. Echoing Wilson's Fourteen Points, the charter served as a semi-official statement of British and especially American war aims: self-determination for all peoples, free trade and freedom of the seas, and effective disarmament, pending a "permanent system of general security" (a new League of Nations). It also

Image 31.8 Pro-British Propaganda This patriotic poster was put out by the Committee to Defend America by Aiding the Allies.

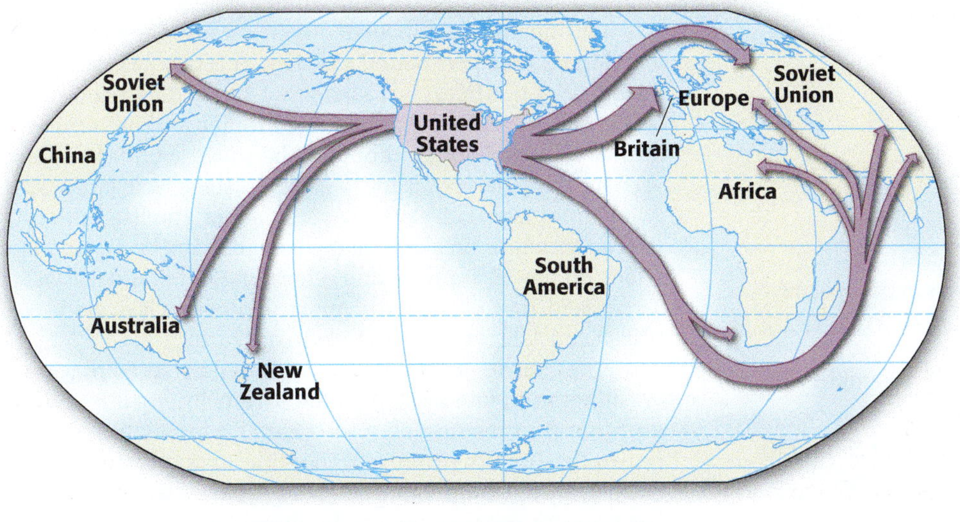

Map 31.1 Main Flow of Lend-Lease Aid (width of arrows indicates relative amount) The proud but desperate British prime minister, Winston Churchill, declared in early 1941, "Give us the tools and we will finish the job." Lend-lease eventually provided the British and other Allies with $50 billion worth of "tools."

Library of Congress

Image 31.9 ***The Four Freedoms*, by Norman Rockwell** In his January 6, 1941, speech to Congress requesting lend-lease aid to the Allies, President Roosevelt spoke eloquently of the "four freedoms" then under worldwide threat from Nazi and Japanese aggression. They are here given pictorial representation by Norman Rockwell, probably the most popular and best-loved American illustrator of the time. Though Roosevelt originally proclaimed the four freedoms as foreign policy aims—the pillars of what he hoped would be a new international order—Rockwell, perhaps unconsciously reflecting persistent isolationist sentiment, rendered them instead as domestic American values that needed to be safeguarded.

> Senator (later president) Harry S. Truman (1884–1972) expressed a common reaction to Hitler's invasion of the Soviet Union in 1941:
>
> "If we see that Germany is winning, we ought to help Russia, and if we see Russia is winning, we ought to help Germany, and that way let them kill as many as possible."

signaled Roosevelt's intent to end the long era of isolationism and permanently redefine America's relation to the rest of the world (refer to Image 31.9).

Meanwhile, lend-lease shipments of arms to Britain were being routinely sunk on the high seas by German submarine "wolf-packs." An obvious solution was for American warships to escort (or "convoy") the vulnerable vessels, but the sop to the isolationists in the enabling legislation explicitly prohibited such action. Risking the wrath of the America-First alarmists and invoking his authority as commander in chief, Roosevelt made the fateful decision to convoy in July 1941. He issued orders to the U.S. Navy to escort lend-lease shipments as far as Iceland. The British would then shepherd them the rest of the way.

Armed clashes inevitably followed. In September 1941 the U.S. destroyer *Greer*, provocatively trailing a German U-boat, was attacked by the undersea craft, without damage to either side. Roosevelt then proclaimed a shoot-on-sight policy. On October 17 the escorting destroyer *Kearny*, while engaged in a battle with U-boats, lost eleven men when it was crippled but not sent to the bottom. Two weeks later the destroyer *Reuben James* was torpedoed and sunk off southwestern Iceland, with the loss of more than a hundred officers and enlisted men.

Neutrality was still inscribed on the statute books, but American hearts and minds were changing. Congress, responding to public pressures and confronted with a shooting war, voted in mid-November 1941 to pull the teeth from the now-defunct Neutrality Act of 1939. Merchant ships could henceforth be legally armed, and they could enter the combat zones with munitions for Britain. Americans braced themselves for wholesale attacks by Hitler's submarines.

31-11 Surprise Assault on Pearl Harbor

But the blowup came not in the Atlantic but in the far-away Pacific.

Japan's position in the Far East had grown more perilous by the hour. It was still mired down in the costly and exhausting "China incident," from which it could extract neither honor nor victory. Its war machine was fatally dependent on immense shipments of steel, scrap iron, oil, and aviation gasoline from the United States.

Washington, late in 1940, finally imposed the first of its embargoes on Japan-bound supplies. This blow was followed in mid-1941 by a freezing of Japanese assets in the United States and a cessation of all shipments of gasoline and other sinews of war. As the oil gauge dropped, the squeeze on Japan grew steadily more nerve-racking. Japanese leaders were faced with two painful alternatives. They could either knuckle under to the Americans or break out of the embargo ring by a desperate attack on the oil supplies and other riches of Southeast Asia. To succeed, they needed to eliminate or drastically degrade the British and American naval forces in the Pacific.

Final tense negotiations with Japan took place in Washington in late 1941. The Americans briefly flirted with a proposal to resume oil and other shipments to Japan in return for Tokyo's promise to confine its future aggression exclusively to China. But that idea gained no traction, as the last hope for peace in the Pacific slipped away.

Misled by Japanese ship movements in the Far East, American leaders evidently expected the hammer to fall on British Malaya or on the Philippines. No one in Washington seemed to believe that the Japanese were either strong enough or foolhardy enough to strike Hawai'i.

But the shattering blow struck **Pearl Harbor**, on the Hawaiian island of Oahu, while Tokyo was deliberately prolonging negotiations in Washington. Japanese bombers, winging in from distant aircraft carriers, attacked without warning on the "Black Sunday" morning of December 7, 1941. It was a date, as Roosevelt told Congress, "which will live in infamy." Over 2,400 American service members and civilians died. A thousand more were wounded. The Americans lost many aircraft as well as almost the entirety of their battleship fleet (refer to Image 31.10). The nation's only stroke of fortune on this terrible day was that the three priceless aircraft carriers happened to be outside the harbor.

An angered Congress the next day officially recognized the war that had been "thrust" upon the United States. The roll call in the Senate and House fell only one vote short of unanimity. Germany and Italy, allies of Japan, spared Congress the indecision of debate by declaring war on December 11, 1941.

Roosevelt's war message to Congress began with these famous words:

"Yesterday, December 7, 1941—a date which will live in infamy—the United States of America was suddenly and deliberately attacked by naval and air forces of the Empire of Japan."

U.S. Army

Image 31.10 The Battleship *West Virginia* The shocking Japanese attack on Pearl Harbor on December 7, 1941, propelled the United States into World War II. One of the first ships to be hit, the USS *West Virginia* quickly sank at its mooring, taking at least seventy sailors down with it. By September 1944 the *West Virginia* had been repaired and was back in service.

American song titles after Pearl Harbor combined nationalism with unabashed racism: "We Are the Sons of the Rising Guns," "Oh, You Little Son of an Oriental," "To Be Specific, It's Our Pacific," "The Sun Will Soon Be Setting on the Land of the Rising Sun," "The Japs Don't Stand a Chinaman's Chance," and "We're Gonna Find a Fellow Who Is Yellow and Beat Him Red, White, and Blue."

Monica Sone (1919–2011), a college-age Japanese American woman in Seattle, recorded the shock she and her brother felt when they learned of Executive Order No. 9066, which authorized the War Department to remove Japanese—aliens and citizens alike—from their homes:

"In anger, Henry and I read and reread the Executive Order. Henry crumbled the newspaper in his hand and threw it against the wall. 'Doesn't my citizenship mean a single blessed thing to anyone? Why doesn't somebody make up my mind for me? First they want me in the army. Now they're going to slap an alien 4-C on me because of my ancestry. . . . ' Once more I felt like a despised, pathetic two-headed freak, a Japanese and an American, neither of which seemed to be doing me any good."

Image 31.11 Anti-Japanese Poster, World War II Government propaganda during the war exploited racial stereotypes, often depicting Japanese people with big teeth and poor vision.

31-12 The Shock of War

The United States was plunged into the inferno of World War II with the most stupefying and humiliating military defeat in its history. Inflamed Americans, especially on the Pacific Coast, cried out to "Avenge Pearl Harbor." But President Roosevelt steadfastly insisted that "defeat of Japan does not defeat Germany," while "defeat of Germany means defeat of Japan." Europe would be America's main battleground; America would fight only a defensive war in the Pacific. National unity was no worry, thanks to the electrifying Japanese blow at Pearl Harbor (refer to Image 31.11).

In contrast to World War I, when the patriotism of millions of immigrants was hotly questioned, World War II actually speeded the assimilation of many ethnic groups of European origin into American society. Immigration had been choked off for almost two decades before 1941, and America's ethnic communities were now composed of well-settled members, whose votes were crucial to Franklin Roosevelt's Democratic party. Americans of Southern and Eastern European descent, once decried as dangerously "alien," gradually were becoming understood as "white." Consequently, there was virtually no government witch-hunting of these groups, as had happened in World War I.

A painful exception was the plight of some 110,000 Japanese Americans, concentrated on the Pacific Coast (refer to "Makers of America: The Japanese," pp. 824–825). Nervous West Coast military commanders, fearing sabotage and espionage, forcibly herded them into internment camps, though about two-thirds of them were American-born U.S. citizens. "It will make a tremendous hole in our constitutional system," Secretary of War Henry Stimson confided to his diary. This brutal precaution, authorized under **Executive Order No. 9066**, was both unnecessary and unfair, as the loyalty and combat record of Japanese Americans proved to be admirable. But a wave of post–Pearl Harbor hysteria, backed by the long and ugly record of anti-Japanese prejudice on the West Coast, overwhelmed Americans' good sense—and their sense of justice. The internment camps deprived these uprooted Americans of dignity and basic rights, incarcerating men, women, and children who had committed no crimes. The internees also lost hundreds of millions of dollars in property and forgone earnings. The wartime Supreme Court in 1944 upheld the constitutionality of the Japanese removal in *Korematsu v. U.S.* But more than four decades later, in 1988, the U.S. government officially apologized for its actions and approved the payment of reparations of $20,000 to each camp survivor.

The war prompted other changes in the American mood. Many programs of the once-popular New Deal—including the Civilian Conservation Corps, the Works Progress Administration, and the National Youth Administration—were wiped out by the conservative Congress elected in 1942. Roosevelt declared in 1943 that "Dr. New Deal" was going into retirement, to be replaced by "Dr. Win-the-War." The era of New Deal reform was over, though the war eventually generated its own notable reforms, conspicuously including the **GI Bill** that financed the education and home-purchasing of a generation of veterans, thus helping to underwrite a quarter-century of phenomenal postwar prosperity.

31-13 Building the War Machine

The war crisis caused the drooping American economy to snap to attention. Massive military orders—over $100 billion in 1942 alone—almost instantly soaked up the idle industrial capacity of the still-lingering Great Depression. Orchestrated by the **War Production Board (WPB)**, American factories poured forth an avalanche of weaponry: 40 billion bullets, 300,000 aircraft, 76,000 ships, 86,000 tanks, and 2.6 million machine guns. The War Production Board halted the manufacture of nonessential items such as passenger cars. It assigned priorities for transportation and access to raw materials. When the Japanese invasion of British Malaya and the Dutch East Indies ruptured America's lifeline of natural rubber, the government imposed a national speed limit and gasoline rationing in order to conserve rubber and built fifty-one synthetic-rubber plants. By war's end, they were far outproducing the prewar supply.

These wonders of production also fueled a sharp inflationary surge in 1942. The **Office of Price Administration (OPA)** eventually brought ascending prices under control with extensive regulations. Rationing held down the consumption of critical goods such as meat and butter, though some "black marketeers" and "meatleggers" cheated the system. The **National War Labor Board (NWLB)** imposed ceilings on wage increases, while American workers, on the whole, were commendably committed to the war effort. Farmers, too, rolled up their sleeves and hauled in record-breaking billion-bushel wheat harvests. The **Office of Scientific Research and Development (OSRD)** channeled hundreds of millions of federal dollars into university-based scientific research, establishing the partnership between the government and universities that underwrote America's technological and economic leadership in the postwar era.

The armed services enlisted nearly 15 million men in World War II as well as some 216,000 women in noncombat roles (refer to Image 31.12). Best known of these

U.S. Army Center of Military History

Image 31.12 U.S. Army WACs Leaving England for France, 1944 Over 200,000 American women served in noncombat roles during World War II as members of the Women's Auxiliary Army Corps (WAAC) and Women's Army Corps (WAC), including during and after D-Day and the Allied liberation of France.

Makers of America

The Japanese

In 1853, the American commodore Matthew Perry sailed four gunboats into Japan's Uraga Bay and demanded that the nation open itself to diplomatic and commercial exchange with the United States. Perry's arrival ended two centuries of Japan's self-imposed isolation and eventually led to the overthrow of the last Japanese shogun (military ruler) and the restoration of the emperor. Within two decades of Perry's arrival, Japan's new "Meiji" government had launched the nation on an ambitious program of industrialization and militarization designed to make it the economic and political equal of the Western powers.

As Japan rapidly modernized, its citizens increasingly fled to America. A steep land tax imposed by the Meiji government to pay for its reforms drove more than 300,000 Japanese farmers off their land. In 1884, the Meiji government permitted Hawaiian planters to recruit contract laborers from among this displaced population. By the 1890s, many Japanese were sailing beyond Hawai'i to the ports of Long Beach, San Francisco, and Seattle.

Between 1885 and 1924, roughly 200,000 Japanese migrated to Hawai'i and around 180,000 more ventured to the U.S. mainland. They were a select group: Because the Meiji government saw overseas Japanese as representatives of their homeland, it strictly regulated emigration. Thus, Japanese immigrants to America arrived with more money than their European counterparts. Also, because of Japan's system of compulsory education, Japanese immigrants on average were better educated and more literate than European immigrants.

Women as well as men migrated. The Japanese government, wanting to avoid the problems of an itinerant bachelor society that it observed among the Chinese in the United States, actively promoted women's migration. Although most Japanese immigrants were young men in their twenties and thirties, thousands of women also ventured to Hawai'i and the mainland as contract laborers or as "picture brides," so called because their courtship had consisted exclusively of an exchange of photographs with their prospective husbands.

Like many Chinese and European immigrants, most Japanese who came to America expected to stay only temporarily. They planned to work hard for wages that were high by Japanese standards and then to return home and buy land. In Hawai'i most Japanese labored on the vast sugar cane plantations. On the mainland they initially found migratory work on the railroads or in fish, fruit, or vegetable canneries. A separate Japanese economy of restaurants, stores, and boardinghouses soon sprang up in cities to serve the immigrants' needs.

From such humble beginnings, many Japanese—particularly those on the Pacific Coast—quickly moved into farming. In the late nineteenth century, the spread of

Bettmann/Getty Images

Image 31.13 **Campaign Against the Japanese, Hollywood, California, 1923** Long before Japanese Americans were interned during World War II as a security risk, they faced intense discrimination throughout the United States.

irrigation shifted California agriculture from grain to fruits and vegetables, and the invention of the refrigerated railcar opened hungry new markets in the East. The Japanese, with centuries of experience in intensive farming, arrived just in time to take advantage of these developments. As early as 1910, Japanese farmers produced 70 percent of California's strawberries, and by 1940 they grew 95 percent of the state's snap beans and more than half of its tomatoes. One Japanese farmer, known as the Potato King, sent his children to Harvard and Stanford and died in 1926 with an estate valued at $15 million.

But the very success of the Japanese proved a lightning rod for trouble. On the West Coast, Japanese immigrants had long endured racist barbs and social segregation. Increasingly, white workers and farmers, jealous of Japanese success, pushed for immigration restrictions. Bowing to this pressure, President Theodore Roosevelt in 1908 negotiated the "Gentlemen's Agreement," under which the Japanese government voluntarily agreed to limit emigration. In 1913, the California legislature denied Japanese immigrants already living in the United States the right to own land.

Legally barred from becoming citizens, Japanese immigrants (the "Issei," from the Japanese word for *first*) became more determined than ever that their American-born children (the "Nissei," from the Japanese word for *second*) would reap the full benefits of their birthright. Japanese parents encouraged their children to learn English, to excel in school, and to get a college education. Many Nissei grew up in two worlds, a fact they often recognized by Americanizing their Japanese names. Although education and acculturation did not protect the Nissei from the hysteria of World War II, those assets did give them a springboard to success in the postwar era.

Library of Congress Prints and Photographs Division

Image 31.14 Japanese American Internees, 1942 After the U.S. Army's Western Defense Command ordered the forced removal of all Japanese and Japanese Americans living on the Pacific Coast, families had no choice but to pack up whatever they could carry and move to the "relocation centers" hastily erected farther inland.

The Denver Post/Getty Images

Image 31.15 Three Boys at Manzanar, by Toyo Miyatake (1895–1979) Miyatake was an acclaimed Japanese American photographer with his own studio in Los Angeles before he and his family were evacuated to the Manzanar internment camp. He was determined to pursue his craft there, at first working secretly and then with the knowledge of the authorities. His pictures are the only photographic records of daily camp life taken by an internee. The guards allowed him to step outside the barbed-wire fence to take this photograph.

Poster appeals and slogans urging women to enlist in the WACs (Women's Army Corps) were "Speed Them Back, Join the WAC," "I'd Rather Be with Them—Than Waiting for Them," "Back the Attack, Be a WAC! For America Is Calling," and (a song throwback to World War I) "The WACs and WAVES Will Win the War, Parlez Vous."

"women in arms" were the **WACs (Women's Army Corps)**, **WAVES (Women Accepted for Volunteer Emergency Service)** (navy), and **SPARs (U.S. Coast Guard Women's Reserve)**. As the arsenal of democracy, the United States exempted certain key categories of industrial and agricultural workers from the draft in order to keep its mighty industrial and food-producing machines humming.

But even with these exemptions, the draft left the nation's farms and factories so short of personnel that new workers had to be found. The internment program intensified the shortage, as many of Americans of Japanese ancestry worked in agriculture. An agreement with Mexico in 1942 brought thousands of short-term Mexican agricultural workers, called *braceros*, across the border to harvest the fruit and grain crops of the West. The ***Bracero* Program** outlived the war by some twenty years, ultimately bringing over 4 million Mexicans to work temporarily in the United States. It became a fixed feature of the agricultural economy in many western states until the program was terminated in 1964.

Even more dramatic was the march of women onto the factory floor. More than 6 million women of all races took up wartime jobs outside the home. Over half of them had never before worked for wages. Many of them were mothers, and the government was obliged to set up some three thousand day-care centers to care for "Rosie the Riveter's" children while she drilled the fuselage of a heavy bomber or joined the links of a tank track (refer to Image 31.16). When the war ended, Rosie and many of her sisters were in no hurry to put down their tools. They wanted to keep on working, and often they did. The war thus foreshadowed an eventual revolution in the roles of women in American society.

A

National Archives

B

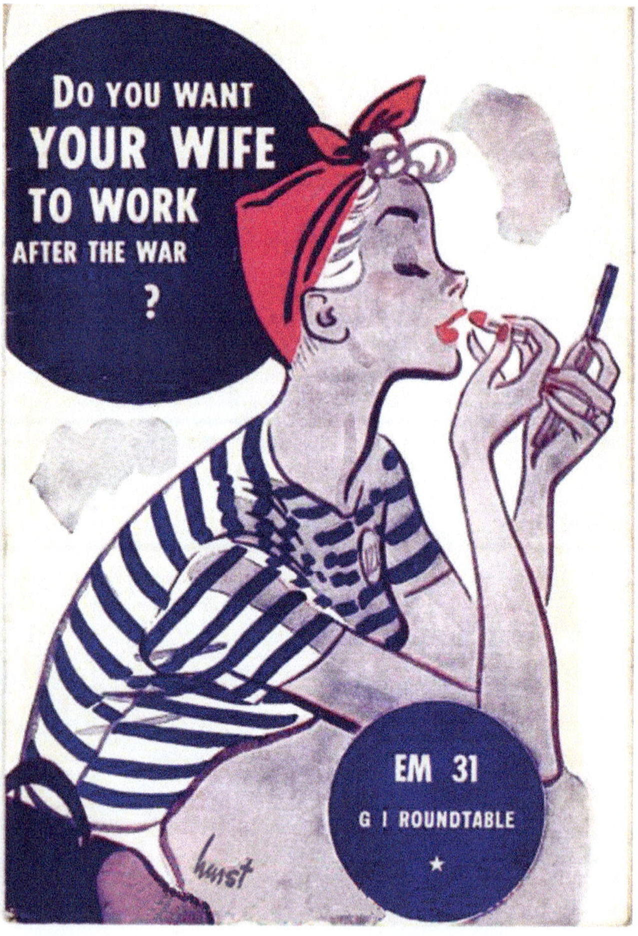

American Historical Association

Image 31.16A and B **Workers in Wartime—and Beyond?** More than 6 million women—more than 3 million of them homemakers who had never before worked for wages—entered the workforce during World War II. That work was valued and encouraged during the war years. But, as indicated by the pamphlet (Image 31.16B) intended for discussion groups among returning soldiers, the war's impending conclusion sparked male anxiety about women remaining in the workforce in peacetime.

Yet the war's immediate impact on women's lives has frequently been exaggerated. The great majority of American women—especially those with husbands present in the home or with small children to care for—did not work for wages in the wartime economy but continued in their traditional roles. In both Britain and the Soviet Union, a far greater percentage of women, including mothers, were pressed into industrial employment as the gods of war laid a much heavier hand on those societies than they did on the United States. A poll in 1943 revealed that a majority of American women would not take a job in a war plant if it were offered.

At war's end, two-thirds of women war workers left the labor force. Many of them were forced out of their jobs by employers and unions eager to reemploy returning servicemen. But half of them told census takers that they quit their jobs voluntarily because of family obligations. The immediate postwar period witnessed not a permanent widening of women's employment opportunities but a widespread rush into suburban domesticity and the mothering of the "baby boomers," who were born by the tens of millions in the decade and a half after 1945. America was destined to experience a thoroughgoing revolution in women's status later in the postwar period, but that epochal change was only beginning to gather momentum in the war years.

31-14 Wartime Migrations

The war also proved to be a demographic cauldron, churning and shifting the American population. War industries sucked people into boomtowns like Los Angeles, Detroit, Seattle, and Baton Rouge. California's population grew by nearly 2 million. The South experienced especially dramatic changes. The states of the old Confederacy received a disproportionate share of defense contracts, including nearly $6 billion of federally financed industrial facilities. Here were the seeds of the postwar blossoming of the "Sunbelt" (refer to Map 31.2 and Map 32.4, p. 868).

Despite this economic stimulus in the South, some 1.6 million Black migrants left the land of their once-enslaved ancestors to seek jobs in the war plants of the West and North. Now more than ever, anti-Black racism constituted a national, not a regional, issue. Explosive tensions developed over employment, housing, and segregated facilities. Black leader A. Philip Randolph

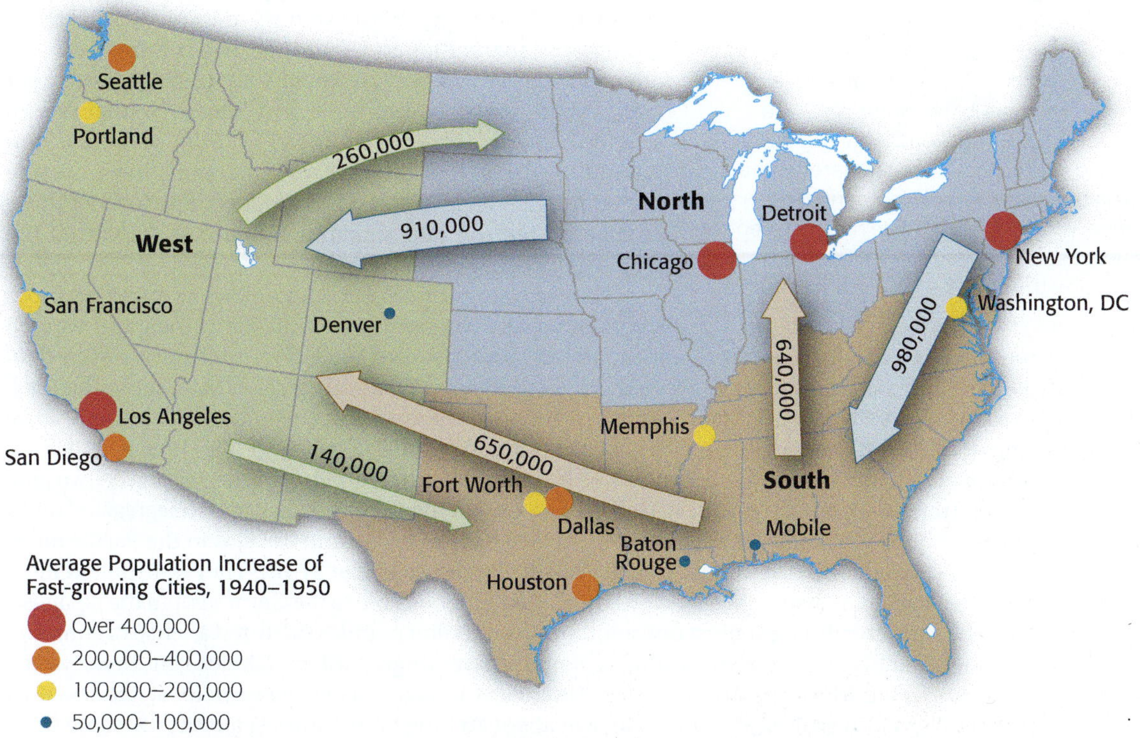

Map 31.2 Internal Migration in the United States During World War II Few events in American history have moved the American people about so massively as World War II. The West and the South boomed, and several war-industry cities grew explosively. A majority of migrants from the South were Black; 1.6 million African Americans left the region in the 1940s.

Sources: United States Department of Labor, Bureau of Labor Statistics and U.S. Census Bureau.

John Vachon/Getty Images

Image 31.17 Demanding the "Double V," 1941 This Chicago man pickets discriminatory hiring at a local dairy supplier. His protest—and the connection drawn in his sign between the fight abroad and the struggle at home—was part of a wave of rights activism by African Americans in the World War II era. A Black soldier asked: "Why is it we Negro soldiers . . . cannot be treated with equality and the respect due us? There is great need for drastic change in this man's Army! How can we be trained to protect America, which is called a *free* nation, when all around us rears the ugly head of segregation?" The wartime experience helped to energize the struggle for Black freedom in the postwar years.

threatened a massive "Negro March on Washington" in 1941 to demand equal opportunities for Black people in war jobs and in the armed forces. Roosevelt responded with an executive order forbidding discrimination in defense industries. In addition, the president established the **Fair Employment Practices Commission (FEPC)** to monitor compliance with his edict. He declared, "The American people are resolved that when our men and women return home from this war, they shall come back to a place where all persons, regardless of race, color, creed or place of birth, can live in peace, honor and human dignity."

Black men were also drafted into the armed forces, though they were still generally assigned to service branches rather than combat units and subjected to petty degradations such as segregated blood banks for the wounded. But in general, the war helped to embolden Black Americans in their long struggle for equality. They rallied behind the slogan **"Double V"**—victory over the dictators abroad and over racism at home (refer to Image 31.17). Membership in the National Association for the Advancement of Colored People (NAACP) shot up almost to the half-million mark, and a new organization committed to nonviolent "direct action," the **Congress of Racial Equality (CORE)**, was founded in 1942.

The northward migration of African Americans accelerated after the war, thanks to the advent of the mechanical cotton picker—an invention whose impact rivaled that of Eli Whitney's cotton gin. Introduced in 1944, this new mechanical marvel did the work of fifty people at about one-eighth the cost. Overnight, the Cotton South's historic need for cheap labor disappeared. Seeking a better life in the North and West, some 5 million Black tenant farmers and sharecroppers left the South in the three decades after the war. World War II brought about a second, larger Great Migration than during World War I, comparable in size to the earlier immigrant floods from Ireland, Italy, and Poland. By 1970, half of all Black Americans lived outside the South, almost all in cities. The speed and scale of these changes jolted the migrants and sometimes convulsed the communities that received them.

The war also prompted an exodus of Native Americans from the reservations. Thousands of Indigenous men and women found war work in the major cities, and thousands more answered Uncle Sam's call to arms. More than 90 percent of Native Americans resided on reservations in 1940; six decades later, more than half lived in cities, with a large concentration in southern California. Some twenty-five thousand Native American men served in the armed forces, including an Akimel O'odham (Pima) Indian, Ira Hayes, who was one of the six Marines immortalized in the famous photograph of the flag raising on Iwo Jima in 1945 (refer to Image 31.24, p. 836). Unlike Black troops, they were not placed into segregated units, and were often given special assignments. Comanches in Europe and Navajos in the Pacific made especially valuable contributions as **"code talkers"** (refer to Image 31.18). They transmitted radio messages in their native languages, which were incomprehensible to the Germans and the Japanese.

The sudden rubbing against one another of unfamiliar peoples nurtured a sense of common national identity, but it also produced some distressingly violent friction. In 1943, young "zoot-suit"-clad Mexicans and Mexican Americans in Los Angeles were viciously attacked by Anglo sailors who cruised the streets in taxicabs searching for victims. At almost the same time, an even more brutal race riot killed twenty-five Black and nine white people in Detroit.

31-15 Holding the Home Front

Despite these ugly episodes, Americans on the home front suffered little from the war, compared to the peoples of the other fighting nations. By war's end much of the planet was a smoking ruin, while America's heartland remained unscarred. Truth be told, the war enormously invigorated the American economy and lifted the country out of a decade-long Great Depression. The gross national product vaulted from less than $100 billion in 1940 to more than $200 billion in 1945. Corporate profits rose from about $6 billion in 1940 to almost twice that amount four years later. ("If you are going to try to go to war in a capitalist country," said Secretary of War Henry Stimson, "you have to let business make money out of the process, or business won't work.") Disposable personal income more than doubled. Americans had never had it so good—and they wanted it a lot better. When price controls were finally lifted in 1946, America's pent-up urge to consume pushed prices up 33 percent in less than two years. The rest of the world, meanwhile, was still clawing its way out from under the rubble of war.

The flood of war dollars—not the relatively modest rivulet of New Deal spending—at last swept the plague of unemployment from the land. War, not targeted economic policies, cured the Depression. The conflict was phenomenally expensive. The wartime bill amounted to more than $330 billion—twice as much as *all* previous federal spending since 1776. The national debt skyrocketed from $49 billion in 1941 to $259 billion in 1945. When production finally slipped into high gear, the war was costing about $10 million an hour.

National Archives

Image 31.18 Navajo Code Talkers, 1943 One of the best-kept secrets of World War II was the use of the Navajo language in a code designed to confuse the Japanese. These two Native Americans in a Marine unit from Arizona and New Mexico transmitted in code during the battle for Bougainville Island in the South Pacific in 1943.

31-16 War in the Pacific

Simultaneously with the assault on Pearl Harbor, the Japanese launched uniformly successful attacks across the Far East, including the American outposts of Guam, Wake, and the Philippines, as well as the Dutch East Indies (present-day Indonesia) and British bastions in Hong Kong and Singapore. Japanese warriors also seized the Solomon Islands, from which they threatened Australia. But Japanese leaders, afflicted with "victory disease," soon over-reached when they moved against Midway Island, more than a thousand miles northwest of Hawai'i. With this strategic base securely in hand, Tokyo could possibly even compel the United States to negotiate a cease-fire in the Pacific. But in the epochal **Battle of Midway**, the American defenders somewhat miraculously managed to sink four vitally important Japanese aircraft carriers.

Midway was a pivotal victory that halted Japan's juggernaut. The United States now partially revised the "Germany-first" strategy and went on the offensive in the Pacific. In August 1942, American ground forces gained a toehold on Guadalcanal Island, in the Solomons, and began a slow, grinding "island-hopping" advance toward the Japanese home islands (refer to Image 31.19). Japanese losses on Guadalcanal were 20,000, compared to 1,700 for the Americans. That casualty ratio of more than ten to one, Japanese to American, persisted throughout the Pacific war (refer to Map 31.3).

George Strock/The LIFE Picture Collection/Shutterstock.com

Image 31.19 Hell in the Pacific Assaulting Japanese island fortresses in the Pacific resulted in some of the most bloody and deadly battles of America's war. These American soldiers perished as they stepped ashore at Buna beach in New Guinea in 1942. Their damaged landing craft wallows in the surf behind them. Appearing in *Life* magazine on September 20, 1943, nearly two years after Pearl Harbor, this was the first photograph of dead GIs that the War Department allowed to be published.

31-17 The Allied Halting of Hitler

Hitler's Nazi Germany remained the primary enemy. Throughout 1942, German U-boats ("*Untersee*" or "under-sea" boats) inflicted horrendous losses on American supplies headed across the Atlantic to beleaguered Britain and Russia. More than 500 merchant ships were lost—111 in June alone—as ship destruction far outran construction. Hundreds of oil-begrimed merchant seamen perished

Map 31.3 United States Thrusts in the Pacific, 1942–1945 American strategists had to choose among four proposed plans for waging the war against Japan:

1. Defeating the Japanese in China by funneling supplies over the Himalayan "hump" from India.
2. Carrying the war into Southeast Asia (a proposal much favored by the British, who could thus regain Singapore).
3. Heavy bombing of Japan from Chinese air bases.
4. "Island hopping" from the South Pacific to within striking distance of the Japanese home islands.

The last strategy, favored by General Douglas Macarthur, was the one finally emphasized.

as unsung heroes in icy seas. The tide of subsea battle turned only when British code-breakers cracked the Germans' "Enigma" codes and began to pinpoint the locations of the U-boats lurking in the North Atlantic.

Elsewhere in 1942, a combined British-American force routed the invading Germans and Italians from North Africa; the Anglo-American Combined Bomber Offensive launched a round-the-clock strategic bombing campaign against Germany; and the Soviets' Red Army stalled the Nazi steamroller at Stalingrad and unleashed a crushing counteroffensive, which was never seriously reversed.

Soviet losses were already staggering in 1942: millions of soldiers and civilians lay dead, as Hitler's armies overran most of the western USSR. Anglo-American losses at this time could be counted only in the thousands. By war's end, the grave had closed over some 27 million Soviets, and a great swath of their country, equivalent in the United States to the area from Chicago to the Atlantic seaboard, had been laid waste. Small wonder that Kremlin leaders clamored for a second front to divert German strength westward (refer to Table 31.1, p. 839).

British prime minister Winston Churchill (1874–1965) observed in a speech in May 1943,

> "The proud German Army has by its sudden collapse, sudden crumbling and breaking up . . . once again proved the truth of the saying, 'The Hun [German] is always either at your throat or at your feet.'"

The campaign in North Africa, far away from Germany's heartland, did not satisfy the Russians' need for a second front in Europe. Then in January 1943, President Roosevelt met in a historic conference with Winston Churchill at Casablanca in French Morocco (refer to Image 31.20). The Big Two agreed to invade Sicily, and insist upon Italy's "unconditional surrender," a phrase deliberately echoing General Ulysses S. Grant during the Civil War. Such an unyielding policy would presumably hearten the ultra-suspicious Soviets, who professed to fear separate Allied peace negotiations. But Italy, like North Africa, was a long way from Germany and still not the kind of second front the Russians were demanding. Paradoxically, the tough-sounding unconditional surrender declaration was an admission of the continuing weakness of the Western Allies. Still unable in 1943 to mount the kind of second front their Soviet partner desperately wanted, the British and the Americans had little but words to offer Stalin.

"Unconditional surrender" proved to be one of the most controversial moves of the war. The main criticism was that it steeled the enemy to fight to a last-bunker resistance, while discouraging antiwar groups in Germany from revolting. Although there was some truth in these charges, no one can prove that "unconditional surrender" either shortened or lengthened the war. But this is known: By helping to destroy the German government utterly, the harsh policy forced a thorough postwar reconstruction.

The Allied forces, victorious in Africa, now turned against the not-so-soft underbelly of Europe. Sicily fell in August 1943. Shortly before the conquest of the island, Mussolini was deposed, and Italy surrendered unconditionally soon thereafter, in September 1943.

But if Italy dropped out of the war, the Germans did not drop out of Italy. Hitler's battle-hardened troops stubbornly resisted the Allied invaders now pouring onto the toe of the Italian boot. They also unleashed their fury against the Italians, who had turned their coats and declared war on Germany in October 1943. The Apennine mountains of Italy's elongated peninsula saw some of the bloodiest fighting of the war, even after Rome was taken on June 4, 1944. On May 2, 1945, only five days before Germany's official surrender, several hundred thousand Axis troops in Italy laid down their arms and became prisoners of war.

National Archives

Image 31.20 The Big Two British prime minister Winston Churchill and U.S. president Franklin D. Roosevelt meet at the Casablanca conference in Morocco, January 1943. The two leaders had a remarkable personal relationship that shaped the outcome of World War II and the course of history. They met in person nine times over the course of the war. "It is fun to be in the same decade with you," FDR cabled to Churchill after one of their meetings. As for Churchill, who was desperate for American aid in the struggle against Hitler, he once commented that "No lover ever studied the whims of his mistress as I did those of Franklin Roosevelt."

31-18 D-Day: June 6, 1944

The Soviets had never ceased their clamor for an all-out second front. In late 1943, the "Big Three"—Churchill, Roosevelt, and Stalin—met in person at the Iranian capital of Tehran to coordinate the long-promised effort. Prodigious preparation preceded the cross-channel invasion of France. Britain's fast-anchored isle virtually groaned with munitions, supplies, and nearly 3 million troops. Led by genial American General Dwight D. "Ike" Eisenhower, the massive Allied force landed on northwest France's Normandy coast on **D-Day** June 6, 1944 (refer to Image 31.21). They gradually enlarged their precarious beachhead, and finally broke out of the German iron ring that enclosed the landing zone. Most spectacular were the lunges

Library of Congress

Image 31.21 Allies Landing in Normandy, June 6, 1944 Nine-foot ocean swells on invasion day made loading the assault landing craft, such as the one pictured here, treacherous business. Many men were injured or tossed into the sea as the bathtublike amphibious vessels bobbed wildly up and down alongside the troop transports. As the vulnerable boats churned toward the beach, some officers led their tense, grim-faced troops in prayer. One major, recalling the remarkable Battle of Agincourt in 1415, quoted from Shakespeare's *Henry V*: "He that outlives this day, and comes safe home/Will stand a tip-toe when this day is named."

across France by American armored divisions, brilliantly commanded by blustery and profane General George S. ("Blood 'n' Guts") Patton. With the assistance of the French "underground," Paris was liberated in August 1944, amid exuberant manifestations of joy and gratitude (refer to Image 31.22). The first important German city (Aachen) fell to the Americans in October 1944, and the days of Hitler's "thousand-year Reich" were numbered.

31-19 FDR: The Fourth-Termite of 1944

The presidential campaign of 1944 came most awkwardly as the awful conflict roared to its climax in both Europe and Asia. Victory-starved Republicans nominated dapper Thomas E. Dewey, popular vote-getting governor of New York. His youth—he was only forty-two—prompted a prominent Democrat to sneer that the candidate had tossed his diaper into the ring. Democrats nominated FDR on the first ballot by acclamation. After much internal wrangling, the delegates settled on hitherto inconspicuous Senator Harry S. Truman of Missouri as his vice-presidential running mate. (Pundits cheekily called him "the second Missouri Compromise.") Roosevelt, as customary, won a sweeping victory: 432 to 99 in the Electoral College; 25,606,585 to 22,014,745 in the popular vote. Elated, he quipped that "the first twelve years are the hardest." But the exhausted president had only months to live.

31-20 The Last Days of Hitler

By late 1944, Germany seemed to be wobbling on its last legs. The Soviet surge had penetrated eastern Germany. Allied aerial "blockbuster" bombs, making the "rubble bounce" with around-the-clock attacks, were obliterating Germany's cities, factories, and transportation arteries.

Hitler then staked everything on one last throw of his reserves. Secretly concentrating a powerful force, he hurled it, on December 16, 1944, against the thinly held American lines in Belgium's befogged and snow-shrouded Ardennes Forest. His objective was the Belgian port

AGIP/Bridgeman Images

Image 31.22 Paris Is Liberated, August 1944 Celebration erupted onto the streets of Paris after its liberation by the American and French armies after four long years of German occupation. Here French women and American GIs pose jubilantly before the Eiffel Tower.

of Antwerp, key to the Allied supply operation. Caught off guard, the outmanned Americans were driven back, creating a deep "bulge" in the Allied line. The ten-day **Battle of the Bulge** (refer to Map 31.4) finally ended when the 101st Airborne Division stood firm at the vital bastion of Bastogne.

American troops reached the Elbe River, a short distance south of Berlin, in April 1945. American and Soviet advance guards dramatically clasped hands amid cries of "*Amerikanskie tovarishchi*" (American comrades). The liberators were horrified to find blood-spattered concentration camps, strewn with still-stinking corpses and starving, nearly dead prisoners. The Nazis had engaged in the scientific mass murder of an estimated 6 million Jews as well as other "undesirables": political opponents, racial minorities, gay men, and lesbian women (refer to Image 31.23). The Washington government had long been informed about Hitler's campaign of genocide against Jews and had been agonizingly slow to take steps against it. To this day the Holocaust stands out as the signature atrocity of World War II and a lasting reminder of humankind's capacity for evil.

The vengeful Soviets, clawing their way forward from the east, reached Berlin in April 1945. After desperate house-to-house fighting, followed by an orgy of pillage and rape, they captured the bomb-shattered city. Adolf Hitler, joined by the woman he had married less than two days earlier, committed suicide in an underground bunker on April 30, 1945.

Tragedy had meanwhile struck the United States. President Roosevelt, while relaxing at Warm Springs, Georgia, suddenly died from a massive cerebral hemorrhage on April 12, 1945. The crushing burden of twelve depression and war

General Dwight D. Eisenhower, in a letter to General George C. Marshall dated April 15, 1945 remarked:

"The things I saw beggar description… The visual evidence and the verbal testimony of starvation, cruelty and bestiality were… overpowering… I made the visit deliberately in order to be in a position to give first-hand evidence of these things if ever, in the future, there develops a tendency to charge these allegations merely to 'propaganda.'"

Map 31.4 World War II in Europe and North Africa, 1939–1945

Image 31.23 The Horror of the Holocaust Although the outside world had some knowledge of the Nazi death camps before the war's end, the full revelation of Hitler's atrocities as the Allies overran Germany in the spring of 1945 stunned and sickened the invading troops. At General Eisenhower's orders, German civilians were compelled to view the evidence of the Nazi regime's genocidal crimes—though these witnesses at Buchenwald tried to look the other way, as many had done during the war itself.

AP Images

years in the White House had finally taken its toll. Knots of confused, leaderless citizens gathered to discuss the future anxiously, as a bewildered, unbriefed Vice President Truman took the helm.

On May 7, 1945, what was left of the German government surrendered unconditionally. May 8 was officially proclaimed **V-E (Victory in Europe) Day** and was greeted with frenzied rejoicing in the Allied countries.

31-21 Japan Dies Hard

Japan's increasingly wobbly empire, meanwhile, was tottering to its fall.

Enormous American fire-bombing attacks, launched from the Mariana Islands, were reducing Japan's fragile wooden cities to cinders, nightly annihilating civilians by the tens of thousands. A massive raid on Tokyo, March 9–10, 1945, destroyed over 250,000 buildings and killed an estimated 83,000 people—a loss comparable to that later inflicted by the atomic bombs. America's steel vise was tightening mercilessly around Japan. The tiny island of Iwo Jima, needed as a haven for damaged American bombers returning from Japan, was captured in March 1945. This desperate twenty-five-day assault cost over four thousand American dead (refer to Image 31.24).

Okinawa, even closer to Japan, was next on the list. There the U.S. Navy suffered severe losses from Japanese suicide pilots ("kamikazes"), who crashed their bomb-laden planes onto the decks of the invading fleet. All told, the death squads sank over thirty ships and badly damaged scores more. The bloody and brutal battle for Okinawa dragged on from April to June of 1945. Over 12,000 Americans were killed and 37,000 were wounded. Japanese soldiers, fighting with stubborn courage from their caves, finally surrendered Okinawa after suffering far heavier losses of over 100,000 soldiers as well as 100,000 civilians.

National Archives

Image 31.24 The Flag Raising at Iwo Jima Atop Mount Suribachi, press photographer Joe Rosenthal snapped this dramatic picture of six American soldiers (one a Pima Indian from Arizona), probably the most famous of the war. The image became the inspiration for the United States Marine Corps War Memorial adjacent to Arlington National Cemetery just outside of Washington, DC.

31-22 The Atomic Bombs

Strategists in Washington were meanwhile planning an all-out invasion of the main islands of Japan—an invasion that presumably would cost hundreds of thousands of American (and even more Japanese) casualties. Tokyo, recognizing imminent defeat, secretly dispatched peace feelers to Moscow, which had not yet entered the Far Eastern war. But fire-bomb-scorched Japan still showed no outward willingness to surrender *unconditionally* to the Allies.

The **Potsdam conference**, held in a Berlin suburb in July 1945, sounded the death knell of the Japanese. There, President Truman, still new on his job, met in a seventeen-day parley with Joseph Stalin and the British leaders. The conferees issued a stern ultimatum to Japan: Surrender or be destroyed. American bombers showered the dire warning on Japan in tens of thousands of leaflets, but no encouraging response was forthcoming.

America had an extraordinary ace up its sleeve. Early in 1940, after Hitler's wanton assault on Poland, Roosevelt was persuaded by American and exiled scientists, notably German-born Albert Einstein, to push ahead with development of an atomic bomb. Fears that the Germans might first acquire such an awesome weapon provided a powerful spur to action. Ironically, Germany eventually abandoned its own atomic project as too costly. And as it happened, the war against Germany ended before the American weapon was ready. In a cruel twist, Japan—not Germany, the original target—suffered the fate of being the first nation subjected to atomic bombardment.

What was called the **Manhattan Project** pushed feverishly forward, fueled by American know-how and industrial power, along with the technical skills of British and other European scientists, many of them Jewish refugees. Finally, in the desert near Alamogordo, New Mexico, on July 16, 1945, the experts detonated the first awesome and devastating atomic device.

With Japan still refusing to surrender, on August 6, 1945, a lone American bomber dropped a single atomic bomb on the Japanese city of Hiroshima (refer to Image 31.25). The bomb wreaked havoc on a scale that stunned even its makers. In a blinding flash of death, heralded by a gigantic mushroom-shaped cloud, as many as 80,000 people perished instantaneously. Tens of thousands more later died hideously agonizing deaths from radiation disease. Two days later, on August 8, Stalin entered the war against Japan, determined to be in on the kill lest he lose a voice in the final division of Japan's possessions.

Image 31.25 Hiroshima, Japan, August 1945 The almost incomprehensibly destructive power of history's first atomic bomb is vividly evident in this photograph. The single bomb killed an estimated 130,000 Japanese, many of whom succumbed months after the blast to agonizing deaths from exposure to radiation.

Stubbornly resisting Japanese, though facing catastrophic devastation, still did not surrender. American aviators, on August 9, dropped a second atomic bomb on the city of Nagasaki (refer to "Varying Viewpoints: The Atomic Bombs: Were They Justified?" p. 840). The Japanese people could endure no more. On August 10, 1945, Tokyo sued for peace on one condition: that Hirohito, the bespectacled Son of Heaven, be allowed to remain on his ancestral throne as nominal emperor. Despite their "unconditional surrender" policy, the Allies accepted this condition on August 14, 1945. The Japanese, though losing face, were able to save both their exalted ruler and what was left of their native land.

The formal end came, with dramatic force, on September 2, 1945, when Japan officially surrendered on the deck of the American battleship *Missouri* in Tokyo Bay. Americans at home joyously celebrated **V-J (Victory over Japan) Day** (refer to Images 31.26 and 31.27).

The scientific director of the Manhattan Project, J. Robert Oppenheimer (1904–1967), later recalled his reaction as he witnessed the detonation of the first atomic bomb at the Trinity test site in Alamogordo, New Mexico, in July 1945. He was not only awed by the extraordinary force of this new weapon. He also feared the power to do harm that it gave to humans:

"I remembered the line from the Hindu scripture, the Bhagavad-Gita: 'Now I am become Death, the destroyer of Worlds.'"

AP Images

Image 31.26 The Japanese Surrender Representatives of the Japanese government arrived to sign the surrender document on the deck of the battleship *Missouri* in Tokyo harbor, September 2, 1945. General Douglas MacArthur then made a conciliatory address, expressing hope "that from this solemn occasion a better world shall emerge . . . a world founded on faith and understanding." A Japanese diplomat attending wondered "whether it would have been possible for us, had we been victorious, to embrace the vanquished with a similar magnanimity." Soon thereafter, General MacArthur took up his duties as director of the U.S. occupation of Japan.

Galerie Bilderwelt/Getty Images

Image 31.27 V-J Day (Victory over Japan Day) These workers at the Manhattan Project's top-secret facility in Oak Ridge, Tennessee, rejoiced at the war's end—and learned at last that what they had helped to build was an atomic bomb.

Thinking Globally

America and the World in Depression and War: A Study in Contrasts

The Great Depression of the 1930s was a monstrous, planetary-scale economic hurricane that wreaked havoc around the globe. All nations were walloped by its destructive force, but two were especially hard hit: the United States and Germany. In both countries, production of goods declined by nearly 50 percent and unemployment approached 25 percent. Also in both countries the Depression discredited existing political regimes and created opportunities for new leadership to emerge. Fatefully, Germany got Adolf Hitler, while the United States got Franklin D. Roosevelt.

Roosevelt and Hitler were of the same generation, both born in the 1880s. They came to power within weeks of each other—Hitler as Germany's chancellor on January 30, 1933, and Roosevelt as U.S. president on March 4, 1933. Both achieved office through democratic elections, though democracy soon withered under one's hand and flourished under the other's.

Roosevelt's entire presidency unfolded under the looming threat, and eventually the armed challenge, of Hitler's Nazi regime. FDR's record, as well as the very character of American democracy in the mid-twentieth century, can only be properly understood in that larger context.

Consider: In the spring of 1933, Roosevelt was coaxing legislation out of the Hundred Days Congress, forging labor unions and sundry ethnic and racial minorities into a long-lasting Democratic party coalition, and making innovative use of the radio to outflank the hostile media magnates who controlled the nation's newspapers. In those same months, Hitler was dissolving German labor unions and ruthlessly censoring the German press. Soon he declared the Nazis the only legal political party in Germany and proceeded to impose on the German people a reign of terror cruelly enforced by the Gestapo, the Nazis' grimly efficient secret police.

A year later, while Roosevelt worried about a possible political challenge from the swashbuckling Louisiana senator Huey P. Long, Hitler dispatched with his main Nazi rival, Ernst Röhm, by ordering his execution.

The following year, 1935, Roosevelt shepherded his sweeping reform program through Congress, notably including the Social Security Act, which helped to usher millions of Americans into the mainstream of American life, especially members of the great immigrant communities who had arrived a generation or so earlier. "We are going to make a country," Roosevelt said, "in which no one is left out." That same year, Hitler codified the Nazis' viciously anti-Semitic policies in the notorious Nuremberg Laws, stripping German Jews of their citizenship, barring them from the professions and military service, and prohibiting marriage between Jews and "Aryans" (defined by the Nazis as a master race of non-Jewish Caucasians, especially those having Nordic features)—all gruesome steps on the road to the genocidal wartime Holocaust, which would eventually murder some 6 million Jews.

Meanwhile, Hitler was relentlessly building his war machine, while FDR's America clung stubbornly to its traditional isolationism. And when the great conflict of World War II finally erupted, Hitler's Germany and Roosevelt's America fought decidedly different wars. Indeed, the United States' experience in the war stands in vivid contrast to the experience of all other combatants, including not only Germany but also America's allies in the "Grand Alliance."

Hitler's vaunted "thousand-year Reich" lay in smoldering ruins at war's end, his people dazed, demoralized, and starving. The strutting Führer had brewed a catastrophe so vast that its conclusion seemed to sunder the web of time itself. Germans remember the moment of their surrender on May 7, 1945, as the Stunde null, or "zero hour," when history's clock came to a fearful halt. Elsewhere, even America's main wartime partners, Great Britain and the Soviet Union, had paid a far greater price in blood and treasure than the United States. Uniquely among all the belligerents in World War II—perhaps uniquely in the history of warfare—the United States had managed to grow its civilian economy even while waging a hugely costly war. In Germany, Britain, and the Soviet Union, the civilian standard of living had gone down by approximately one-third. In the United States, the civilian economy had actually expanded by 15 percent, preparing the way for phenomenal prosperity in the postwar decades.

Image 31.28 **Franklin Delano Roosevelt, Thirty-second President of the United States**

Table 31.1 **The Comparative Costs of World War II**

Country	Military Deaths	Civilian Deaths	Government Expenditures	Damage to Civilian Property
China	2,000,000	7,750,000		
France	250,000	350,000		
Poland	123,000	6,000,000		
USSR	10,000,000	17,000,000	$192 billion	$128 billion
United Kingdom	300,000	60,600	$120 billion	$5 billion
United States	405,399	6*	$317 billion	
Germany (including Austria)	3,500,000	1,600,000	$272 billion	$50–$75 billion
Italy	242,000	60,000	$94 billion	
Japan	2,000,000	650,000		

*In the forty-eight states; additional civilian deaths occurred in Hawai'i, Alaska, and the Philippines.

Sources: World War II casualty estimates vary widely. The figures here are largely taken from David M. Kennedy, ed., *The Library of Congress World War II Companion;* I. C. B. Dear, ed., *The Oxford Companion to the Second World War;* Louis L. Snyder, *Historical Guide to World War II;* and John Ellis, *World War II: A Statistical Survey.*

And though 405,399 brave American service members died in World War II, proportionate to population, American losses were about one-third those of Britain and about one-sixtieth those of the Soviet Union, where some 10 million soldiers and a staggering 17 million civilians perished (see Table 31.1). By glaring contrast, in the forty-eight continental American states that had a star on the flag in 1945, the U.S. civilian death toll due to enemy action was just six persons, all of them the victims of a crude Japanese balloon-borne firebomb that exploded in their faces near the hamlet of Bly, Oregon, on May 5, 1945.

For all the misery that economic depression and war visited upon the United States, Americans could count their blessings that fortune had spared them the enormous deprivations and horrors that were all too common elsewhere. Yet some observers worried that America was now assuming leadership in a world where the depths of other peoples' wounds and woes could scarcely be imagined.

Hulton Archive/Getty Images

Image 31.29 **German Chancellor Adolf Hitler** Here, the German leader is greeted by crowds in the city of Nuremberg soon after his rise to power in 1933.

31-23 The Allies Triumphant

World War II proved to be terribly costly. American forces suffered some 1 million casualties, more than one-third of which were deaths. Compared with other wars, the proportion killed by wounds and disease was sharply reduced, owing in part to the use of blood plasma and "miracle" drugs, notably penicillin. Yet heavy though American losses were, the Soviet allies suffered casualties many times greater—more than 25 million people killed. In grim testimony to the nature of modern warfare, World War II was the first war that killed more civilians than armed combatants (refer to "Thinking Globally: America and the World in Depression and War: A Study in Contrasts," above).

Varying Viewpoints

The Atomic Bombs: Were They Justified?

No episode of the World War II era has provoked sharper controversy than the atomic bombings of Japan in August 1945. Lingering moral misgivings about the nuclear incineration of Hiroshima and Nagasaki have long threatened to tarnish America's crown of military victory. Some historians have argued that deeply embedded anti-Asian racism in the United States contributed to the decision to drop the bombs on a nonwhite people. Other commentators note that the Japanese were already reeling on the verge of collapse by 1945, and therefore history's most awful weapons—especially the second bomb, on Nagasaki—were unnecessary to bring the war to a conclusion. Still other scholars, notably Gar Alperovitz, have further charged that the atomic attacks on Hiroshima and Nagasaki were not the last shots of World War II, but the first salvos in the emerging Cold War. Alperovitz argues that President Truman willfully ignored Tokyo's attempts to negotiate a surrender in the summer of 1945 and rejected all alternatives to dropping the bomb because he wanted to intimidate and isolate the Soviet Union. He unleashed his horrible new weapons, so this argument goes, not simply to defeat Japan but to end the Far Eastern conflict before the Soviets could enter it, and thereby freeze them out of any role in formulating postwar reconstruction policy in Asia.

Each of these accusations has been vigorously rebutted. Richard Rhodes's exhaustive history of the making of the atomic bomb emphasizes that the Anglo-American atomic project began as a race against the Germans, who were known to be actively pursuing a nuclear weapons program. (Unknown to the Americans, Germany effectively terminated its effort in 1942, just as the Anglo-American project went into high gear.) From the outset, both British and American planners believed that the bomb, if successful, would be not just another weapon, but *the* ultimate instrument of destruction that would decisively deliver victory into the hands of whoever possessed it. They consequently assumed that it would be used at the earliest possible moment. There is, therefore, no credible reason to conclude that German cities would not have suffered the fate of Hiroshima and Nagasaki if nuclear weapons had become available sooner or if the European phase of the war had lasted longer.

It is true that American intelligence sources in the early summer of 1945 reported that some Japanese statesmen were trying to enlist the still-neutral Russians' good offices to negotiate a surrender. But as R. J. C. Butow's fine-grained study of Japan's decision to surrender demonstrated, and as later studies by Richard Frank and Waldo Heinrich have confirmed, it was unclear whether those initiatives had the full backing of the Japanese government. Moreover, the Japanese clung to several unacceptable conditions, including protection for their imperial system of government, the right to disarm and repatriate their own troops, no military occupation of the home islands, no international trials of alleged war criminals, and possible retention of some of their conquered territories. All this flew squarely in the face of America's repeatedly declared intention to settle for nothing less than *unconditional* surrender. As for the Nagasaki bomb (dropped on August 9), Butow and Frank also note that it conclusively dispelled the Japanese government's original assessment that the Hiroshima attack (on August 6) was a one-time-only stunt, with little likelihood of further nuclear strikes to follow. (Even then, some diehard military officers, refusing to acknowledge defeat, tried, on the night of August 14, to storm the Imperial Palace to seize the recording of the emperor's surrender announcement before it could be broadcast the following day.)

Could the use of the atomic bombs have been avoided? Studies by Martin J. Sherwin, Barton J. Bernstein, and McGeorge Bundy have shown that few policymakers at the time seriously asked that question. As Winston Churchill later wrote, "The decision whether or not to use the atomic bomb to compel the surrender of Japan was never even an issue. There was unanimous, automatic, unquestioned agreement around our table; nor did I ever hear the slightest suggestion that we should do otherwise." In fact, the "decision" to use the bomb was not made in 1945, but in 1942, when the United States committed itself to a crash program to build—and use—a nuclear weapon as swiftly as possible. Intimidating the Soviets might have been a "bonus" to using the bomb against Japan, but influencing Soviet behavior was never the *primary* reason for the fateful decision. American leaders wanted to end the war as soon as possible. To that end, they had always assumed the atomic bomb would be dropped as soon as it was available. That moment came on August 6, 1945.

Doubt and remorse about the atomic conclusion of World War II have plagued the American conscience ever since. Less often remarked on are the deaths of four times more Japanese noncombatants than died at Hiroshima and Nagasaki in the so-called conventional firebombing of some five dozen Japanese cities in 1945. Those deaths suggest that the deeper moral question should perhaps be addressed not to the particular technology of nuclear weaponry and the fate of those two unfortunate Japanese cities but to the quite deliberate decision, made by several combatants—including the Germans, the British, the Americans, and the Japanese themselves—to designate civilian populations as legitimate military targets.

America was fortunate in emerging with its mainland virtually unscathed. Two Japanese submarines had rather harmlessly attacked the California and Oregon coast, and a few Japanese fire-bomb balloons had drifted across the Pacific, killing six civilians in Oregon. But much of the rest of the industrial world was utterly demolished and destitute. America alone was untouched and healthy—oiled and muscled like a prize bull, standing astride the world's ruined landscape.

Assembly lines had proved as important as battle lines, and victory went again to the side with the most smokestacks. The enemy was almost literally smothered by bayonets, bullets, bazookas, and bombs. Hitler and his Axis co-conspirators had chosen to make war with machines, and the ingenious Yankees could ask for no more favorable terms of engagement. They demonstrated again, as they had in World War I, that the American way of war was simply more—more men, more weapons, more machines, more technology, and more money than any enemy could hope to match. From 1940 to 1945, the output of American factories was simply phenomenal. As Winston Churchill remarked, "Nothing succeeds like excess."

The internment of Japanese Americans and persistent racial segregation, even in the armed forces, did not prevent most Americans from remembering the conflict as the "good war." They basked proudly in the war's patriotic glow for the next two decades and more.

Chapter Summary

Roosevelt's early foreign policies, such as withdrawing from the London Economic Conference and establishing the Good Neighbor policy in Latin America, were governed by his determination to make domestic recovery the national priority. Depression-spawned chaos and war in Europe and Asia strengthened the isolationist impulse, as Congress passed a series of Neutrality Acts designed to prevent America from being drawn into foreign wars. The United States adhered to this policy for a time, despite the spreading aggression of Italy, Germany, and Japan. But after the outbreak of World War II in Europe, Roosevelt cautiously began to provide some aid to Britain.

After the fall of France in June 1940, Roosevelt provided greater assistance to desperate Britain and Congress passed the lend-lease program. Still-powerful isolationists protested these measures. Roosevelt won an unprecedented third term in 1940, but by a closer margin than his previous victories.

The fall of France and Hitler's invasion of the Soviet Union in June 1941 made apparent the threat to the survival of Western democracies. To help prevent a German victory over the USSR, Roosevelt extended lend-lease aid to Stalin. In August 1941, Roosevelt and Churchill issued the Atlantic Charter upholding shared democratic principles and outlining plans for future peace and security. By the summer of 1941, the United States was fighting an undeclared naval war with Nazi Germany in the North Atlantic.

Meanwhile, American economic embargoes against Japan made Japanese militarists desperate. With the United States insisting on Japanese withdrawal from China as a condition of resuming trade, the Japanese leaders decided that only a war with the United States would achieve their goals. The surprise attack on Pearl Harbor in December 1941 united the American people and plunged the United States into World War II.

America was badly wounded but roused to national unity and determination by Pearl Harbor. With the ugly exception of the Japanese American internment camps, World War II proceeded in the United States without the fanaticism and violations of civil liberties that occurred in World War I. The economy was effectively mobilized, using new sources of labor such as women and Mexican braceros. Numerous Black Americans and Native Americans also left their rural homelands and migrated to war-industry jobs in the cities of the North and West. The war brought full employment and prosperity, as well as enduring social changes, as millions of Americans were uprooted and thrown together in the military and in new communities across the country. The federal government became vastly more powerful and touched Americans' lives in numerous new ways.

The tide of Japanese conquest was stemmed at the Battles of Midway and the Coral Sea, and American forces then began a slow strategy of "island hopping" toward Tokyo. Allied troops first invaded North Africa and Italy in 1942–1943, providing a small, compromise "second front" to try to appease both the Soviet Union and Britain. The real second front came in June 1944 with the D-Day invasion of France. The Allies moved rapidly across France but faced a temporary setback in the Battle of the Bulge.

The seriously ill Roosevelt defeated Thomas Dewey and won a fourth term in 1944 just as Allied troops entered Germany. Soon after FDR's death in April 1945, American and Russian troops met in central Germany, bringing an end to Hitler's rule in May 1945. After a last round of brutal warfare on Okinawa and Iwo Jima, the dropping of two atomic bombs ended the war against Japan in August 1945.

Key Terms

- London Economic Conference (811)
- Rome-Berlin Axis (811)
- Tripartite Pact (812)
- Neutrality Acts of 1935, 1936, and 1937 (812)
- Abraham Lincoln Brigade (812)
- Quarantine Speech (813)
- Appeasement (813)
- Neutrality Act of 1939 (814)
- *Kristallnacht* (816)
- War Refugee Board (817)
- America First Committee (817)
- Lend-Lease Bill (818)
- Atlantic Charter (819)
- Pearl Harbor (821)
- Executive Order No. 9066 (822)
- GI Bill (823)
- War Production Board (WPB) (823)
- Office of Price Administration (OPA) (823)
- National War Labor Board (NWLB) (823)
- Office of Scientific Research and Development (OSRD) (823)
- WACs (Women's Army Corps) (826)
- WAVES (Women Accepted for Volunteer Emergency Service) (826)
- SPARs (U.S. Coast Guard Women's Reserve) (826)
- *Bracero* Program (826)
- Fair Employment Practices Commission (FEPC) (828)
- Double V (828)
- Congress of Racial Equality (CORE) (828)
- code talkers (828)
- Midway, Battle of (829)
- D-Day (831)
- Bulge, Battle of the (833)
- V-E (Victory in Europe) Day (835)
- Potsdam conference (836)
- Manhattan Project (836)
- V-J (Victory over Japan) Day (837)

People to Know

- Benito Mussolini
- Adolf Hitler
- Francisco Franco
- Wendell L. Willkie
- A. Philip Randolph
- Dwight D. "Ike" Eisenhower
- Harry S. Truman
- Albert Einstein

Chronology

1933	• FDR torpedoes London Economic Conference • United States recognizes Soviet Union • FDR declares Good Neighbor policy toward Latin America	• Hitler becomes German chancellor • Germany quits League of Nations
1934	• Tydings-McDuffie Act provides for Philippine independence on July 4, 1946	• U.S. Marines withdraw from Haiti
1935	• Mussolini invades Ethiopia • U.S. Neutrality Act of 1935	• Japan quits League of Nations
1936	• U.S. Neutrality Act of 1936 • Mussolini and Hitler form Rome-Berlin Axis	• German troops invade Rhineland
1936–1939	• Spanish Civil War	
1937	• U.S. Neutrality Act of 1937 • *Panay* incident	• Japan invades China
1938	• Hitler seizes Austria • Munich Conference	• *Kristallnacht* in Germany
1939	• Hitler seizes all of Czechoslovakia • Nazi-Soviet pact	• World War II begins in Europe with Hitler's invasion of Poland • U.S. Neutrality Act of 1939

1940	• Fall of France • Japan joins Tripartite Pact with Germany and Italy • Hitler invades Denmark, Norway, Netherlands, and Belgium • United States invokes first peacetime draft	• Battle of Britain • Bases-for-destroyers deal with Britain • FDR defeats Willkie for presidency
1941	• Lend-Lease Act • Hitler attacks Soviet Union	• Atlantic Charter • Japan attacks Pearl Harbor
1941	• United States declares war on Japan • Germany declares war on the United States • Randolph plans black march on Washington	• Fair Employment Practices Commission (FEPC) established • Roosevelt delivers "Four Freedoms" speech
1942	• Japanese Americans sent to internment camps • Japan conquers the Philippines • Battle of Midway	• United States invades North Africa • Congress of Racial Equality (CORE) founded
1943	• Allies hold Casablanca conference • Allies invade Italy • "Zoot-suit" riots in Los Angeles	• Race riot in Detroit • Japanese driven from Guadalcanal • Tehran conference
1944	• *Korematsu v. U.S.* • D-Day invasion of France	• Roosevelt defeats Dewey for presidency
1944–1945	• Battle of the Bulge	
1945	• Roosevelt dies; Truman assumes presidency • Germany surrenders • Battles of Iwo Jima and Okinawa	• Potsdam conference • Atomic bombs dropped on Hiroshima and Nagasaki • Japan surrenders

To Learn More

David M. Kennedy, *Freedom From Fear: The American People in Depression and War, 1929–1945* (1999)

David Reynolds, *From Munich to Pearl Harbor: Roosevelt's America and the Origins of the Second World War* (2001)

Deborah Cohen, *Braceros: Migrant Citizens and Transnational Subjects in the Postwar United States and Mexico* (2011)

Dominic Tierney, *FDR and the Spanish Civil War: Neutrality and Commitment in the Struggle That Divided America* (2007)

Gordon W. Prange, *At Dawn We Slept: The Untold Story of Pearl Harbor* (1981)

Irwin F. Gellman, *Good Neighbor Diplomacy: United States Policies in Latin America, 1933–1945* (1979)

Isabel Wilkerson, *The Warmth of Other Suns: The Epic Story of America's Great Migration* (2010)

James T. Sparrow, *Warfare State: World War II Americans and the Age of Big Government* (2011)

John M. Blum, *V Was for Victory: Politics and American Culture During World War II* (1976)

John W. Dower, *War Without Mercy: Race and Power in the Pacific War* (1986)

Justus D. Doenecke, *Storm on the Horizon: The Challenge to American Intervention, 1939–1941* (2000)

Kai Bird and Martin J. Sherwin, *American Prometheus: The Triumph and Tragedy of J. Robert Oppenheimer* (2005)

Kevin Allen Leonard, *The Battle for Los Angeles: Racial Ideology and World War II* (2006)

Lynne Olson, *Those Angry Days: Roosevelt, Lindbergh, and America's Fight over World War II, 1939–1941* (2013)

Primo Levi, *Survival in Auschwitz: The Nazi Assault on Humanity* (1961)

Richard Rhodes, *The Making of the Atomic Bomb* (1986)

Richard W. Frank, *Downfall: The End of the Imperial Japanese Empire* (1999)

Robert Dallek, *Franklin D. Roosevelt and American Foreign Policy, 1932–1945* (1995)

Roger Daniels, *Prisoners Without Trial: Japanese Americans in World War II* (1993)

Ronald H. Spector, *Eagle Against the Sun: The American War with Japan* (1985)

Ronald T. Takaki, *Double Victory: A Multicultural History of America in World War II* (2000)

Sean L. Malloy, *Atomic Tragedy: Henry L. Stimson and the Decision to Use the Bomb Against Japan* (2008)

Sherna Gluck, *Rosie the Riveter Revisited: Women, the War, and Social Change* (1988)

Part **8**

Making an American Superpower 1945–1980

World War II broke the back of the Great Depression in the United States and also ended the century-and-a-half-old American tradition of isolationism in foreign affairs. Alone among the warring powers, the United States emerged from the great conflict physically unscarred, economically healthy, and militarily muscled-up, especially with nuclear weapons. For more than two decades after 1945, Americans enjoyed an exceptional era of broadly shared prosperity at home and dominance abroad, challenged only by the Soviet Union in a protracted confrontation known as the Cold War. But setbacks both domestic and foreign began to bring that era to a close by the 1970s.

The lingering ravages of World War II abroad largely insulated American industries from foreign competition, while the Cold War conflict with the Soviet Union spurred huge public investments in infrastructure, scientific research, and education. Financed by this government spending, the digital computer beeped and whirred its way into American life, a fascinating and fearsome "electronic brain" that could do everything from calculating missile trajectories to forecasting the weather. Organized labor, thanks to gains made during the New Deal and World War II, claimed its own seat at the policy-making table.

The result was what economists term "The Great Compression"—a generation or more of rising living standards, impressive income equality, and a remarkable measure of social peace. A booming economy again put Americans on the move, heading by the millions to spanking-new suburbs and to the sunny climes of the Sunbelt. Interstate highways, military spending, and air conditioning opened up the long-somnolent South to industrialization and population growth on a scale unseen before, altering the region's politics and putting pressure on its separate and unequal racial order.

Invigorated by the prospect of endlessly spreading affluence, Americans in the postwar years had record numbers of babies, generously expanded the welfare state, widened opportunities for women, and even found the will to grapple at long last with the nation's ugliest legacy of injustice, its treatment of African Americans. Citizens

J. R. Eyerman/The LIFE Picture Collection/Shutterstock.com

Image VIII.1 A Suburban Society In the phenomenally affluent post-WWII years, newly prosperous Americans flocked to new suburban housing developments. By the twentieth century's end, a majority of Americans were suburbanites.

Image VIII.2 Burgers and the Ayatollah, 1980 Postwar prosperity gave way to postindustrial uncertainty in the 1970s. As war and revolution roiled the Middle East and growth slowed at home, Americans experienced gas shortages, spiking consumer prices, and a shift toward lower-paying, less secure jobs in a growing service sector.

Robert Landau/Alamy Stock Photo

trusted their government and had faith in the American dream that their children's lives would be more prosperous than their own.

The rising curve of expectations peaked in the 1960s, a stormy decade that saw great gains for civil rights and efforts to abolish poverty through President Lyndon Johnson's "Great Society" initiatives, but also brought turbulent social unrest driven by racial inequality, a rising generation's challenges to cultural mores, and protest against an increasingly unpopular and unwinnable Vietnam War. Disillusion with an already discredited political system deepened when the Watergate scandal forced Richard Nixon to become the first American president to resign from office.

Alongside government's loss of credibility, economic growth flattened in the 1970s, shrinking the horizon of hope for the future that had beckoned over the previous three decades. The seeds of America's economic predicament could be found in the very postwar international order that America had helped to build. Competition from reconstructed European and Japanese economies challenged domestic industries and their unionized workers. Technological breakthroughs in communications, information processing, and transportation spawned a new era of globalization that energized societies from Asia to Latin America and beyond.

As gains in productivity (output per worker-hour) slowed, a stubbornly sluggish economy undermined the social contract of the postwar era. Americans in the 1970s faced more fitful economic growth and stagnating incomes. Faith in government and other social institutions eroded, and free-market ideas took root.

Paradoxically, this era of escalating economic inequality also saw widening social inclusion. As "second-wave feminism" gathered steam in the 1970s, women burst through barriers that had long excluded them from traditional male domains—from the factory floor and the armed forces to the Ivy League. The historic successes of the civil rights movement in the 1960s reverberated for decades to come, as African Americans as well as other ethnic and cultural minorities (their numbers swelling in the wake of the landmark Immigration Act of 1965) demanded acceptance on their own terms in a multicultural America.

Turmoil in the economy and often acrid conflict over value-laden issues like abortion and affirmative action helped a resurgent conservative movement secure Ronald Reagan's election to the presidency in 1980. As booming industries like electronics and finance generated more and more of the nation's gross domestic product (GDP), economic opportunities shrank for Americans without a college degree. Intensified cultural, ideological, and political contestation redrew the electoral map, setting the stage for paralyzing partisan battles to come.

Focus Questions

1. What were the catalysts of postwar American prosperity? Who were its main beneficiaries, and who was excluded from it?
2. In what ways did the Cold War reshape American politics and society?

Chapter 32

The Cold War Begins: 1945–1952

> The United States stand at this moment at the summit of the world.
>
> Winston Churchill, 1945

Chapter Outline

- Harry S. Truman as president
- Origins of the Cold War
- The United Nations and the postwar world
- Communism and containment
- The Truman Doctrine, the Marshall Plan, and NATO
- Civil rights and the contentious 1948 election
- Domestic anticommunism and the menace of McCarthyism
- The Korean War, 1950–1953
- Military spending on science and technology
- The "Sunbelt" and the suburbs
- Homeowners and "redlining"
- Postwar prosperity and the baby boom

Contending Voices: Debating the Cold War

Makers of America: The Suburbanites

Varying Viewpoints: Who Was to Blame for the Cold War?

The American people, 140 million strong, cheered their nation's victories in Europe and Asia at the conclusion of World War II. But before the shouting had even faded, many Americans had begun to worry about their future. Four fiery years of global war had not entirely driven from their minds the painful memories of twelve desperate years of the Great Depression. Still more ominously, victory celebrations had barely ended before America's crumbling relations with its wartime ally, the Soviet Union, threatened a new and even more terrible international conflict.

Focus Questions

1. What were the primary causes of the Cold War between the United States and the Soviet Union, and how did the confrontation with communism spread to China and Korea?
2. How did the Cold War affect domestic American society, and what were the results of the widespread fear of both Soviet spying and communist subversion inside the United States?
3. What were the principal causes of the sustained period of postwar prosperity that began in the late 1940s?
4. How did the postwar "baby boom" and the mass migrations to the suburbs and the Sunbelt alter the character and concerns of American society?

32-1 Truman: The "Gutty" Man from Missouri

Presiding over the opening of the postwar period was an "accidental president"—Harry S. Truman. Trim and owlishly bespectacled, with his graying hair and friendly grin, Truman was called "the average man's average man." Even his height—five feet eight inches—was average. The first president in many years without a college education, he had farmed, served as an artillery officer in France during World War I, and failed as a haberdasher (a seller of men's clothing). He then tried his hand at precinct-level Missouri politics, through which he rose from county office to the U.S. Senate. Though a protégé of a notorious political machine in Kansas City, he had managed to keep his own hands clean.

The problems of the postwar period were staggering, and the suddenly burdened new president at first approached his tasks with humility. But gradually he evolved from a shrinking pipsqueak into a scrappy little cuss, gaining confidence to the point of cockiness. When the Soviet foreign minister complained, "I have never been talked to like that in my life," Truman shot back, "Carry out your agreements and you won't get talked to like that." Truman later boasted, "I gave him the one-two, right to the jaw."

A smallish man thrust into a super-sized job, Truman had down-home authenticity, few pretensions, rock-solid probity, and a lot of that old-fashioned character trait called moxie. Not one to dodge responsibility, he placed a sign on his White House desk that read, "The buck stops here." Among his favorite sayings was "If you can't stand the heat, get out of the kitchen." His mettle would soon be tested as tensions with Russia heated up.

32-2 Yalta: Bargain or Betrayal?

Vast and silent, the Soviet Union continued to be the great enigma. The conference at Tehran in 1943, where Roosevelt first met Joseph Stalin man to man, had cleared the air somewhat, but much remained unresolved—especially questions about the postwar fates of Germany, Eastern Europe, and Asia.

The **Yalta Conference**, the final fateful meeting of the Big Three, took place in February 1945 (refer to Image 32.1). At this former tsarist resort on the relatively warm shores of the Black Sea, Stalin, Churchill, and the fast-failing Roosevelt reached momentous agreements, after pledging their faith with vodka. Final plans were laid for smashing the buckling German lines and assigning occupation zones in Germany to the victorious powers. Stalin agreed that Poland, with revised boundaries, should have a representative government based on free elections—a pledge he soon broke. Bulgaria and Romania were likewise to have free elections—a promise also flouted. The Big Three further announced plans for fashioning a new international peacekeeping organization, the United Nations.

Of all the grave decisions at Yalta, the most controversial concerned the Far East. The atomic bomb had not yet been tested, and Washington strategists expected frightful American casualties in the projected assault on Japan. From Roosevelt's standpoint, it seemed highly desirable that Stalin should enter the Asian war, pin down Japanese troops in Manchuria and Korea, and lighten American losses. Stalin, striking a hard bargain, agreed to attack Japan within three months after the collapse of Germany. In return, the Soviets were promised the southern half of Sakhalin Island, lost to Japan in 1905; Japan's Kurile Islands; and control over the railroads and two key seaports in China's Manchuria.

As it turned out, Moscow's muscle was not necessary to knock out Japan. Critics charged that Roosevelt had betrayed Jiang Jieshi (Chiang Kai-shek) when he conceded control of Manchuria

Image 32.1 The Big Three From left to right, Churchill, Roosevelt, and Stalin sit somberly at their fateful meeting at Yalta in February 1945. Roosevelt was only weeks away from death.

to Stalin. The consequent undermining of Chinese morale, so the accusation ran, contributed powerfully to Jiang's overthrow by the communists four years later. The critics also assailed the "sellout" of Poland and other Eastern European countries.

Roosevelt's defenders countered that Stalin, with his mighty Red Army, could have secured much more of China if he wished and that the Yalta conference really set limits on his ambitions. Apologists for Roosevelt also contended that if Stalin had kept his promise to support free elections in Poland and the liberated Balkans, the future of U.S.-Soviet relations would have looked different. At the time of Yalta, Soviet troops occupied much of Eastern Europe, and a war to throw them out was unthinkable.

The fact is that America's grand strategy in World War II—leaving most of the fighting in Europe to the Russians on the eastern front, and delaying the second, or western, front until D-Day in mid-1944, when the war was nearly five years old—guaranteed that the Soviets would control much of eastern and central Europe at war's end. That was the price the United States paid for its relatively low casualty rates (refer to "Thinking Globally: America and the World in Depression and War: A Study in Contrasts," pp. 838–839). Later critics who howled about broken promises overlooked that fundamental point.

32-3 A Superpower Rivalry Takes Shape

History provided little hope that the United States and the Soviet Union would reach cordial understandings about the shape of the postwar world. Mutual suspicions were ancient, abundant, and abiding. Communism and capitalism were historically hostile social philosophies. The United States had refused officially to recognize the Bolshevik revolutionary government in Moscow until it was sixteen years old, in 1933. Soviet skepticism toward the West was nourished by the British and American delays in opening up a second front against Germany in Western Europe, while the Soviet army paid a grisly price on the Eastern Front. Britain and America had also frozen their Soviet "ally" out of the project to develop atomic weapons, further feeding Stalin's mistrust. The Washington government rubbed salt in Soviet wounds when it abruptly terminated vital lend-lease aid to a battered USSR in 1945 and spurned Moscow's plea for a $6 billion reconstruction loan—while approving a similar loan of $3.75 billion to Britain in 1946.

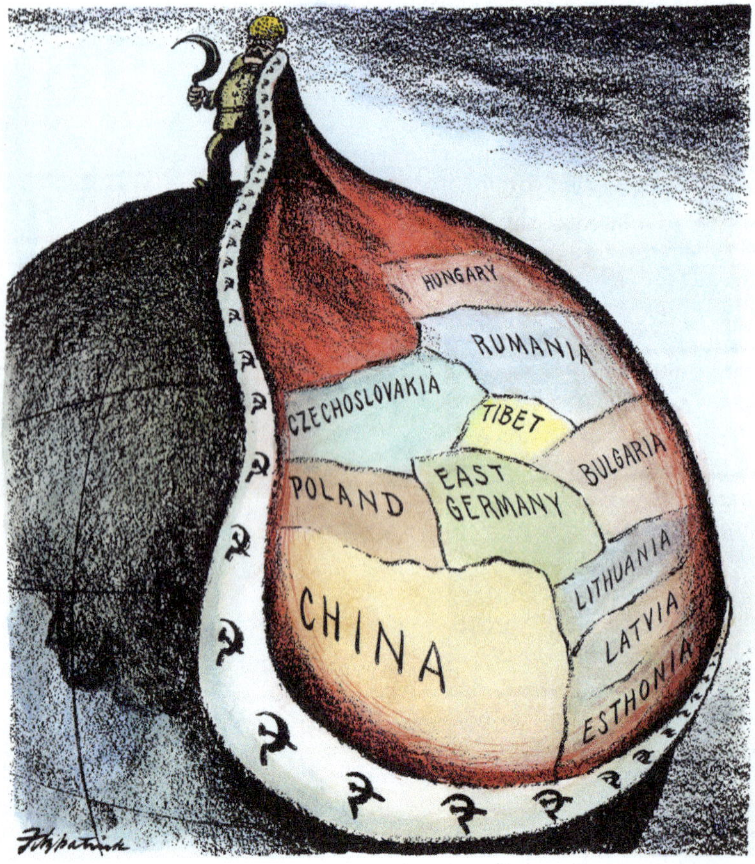

The Granger Collection, NYC

Image 32.2 The New Russian Empire, 1951 Anxiety beset Americans in the post–World War II years that Communist Russia was aggressively expanding its imperial reach.

Different visions of the postwar world also separated the two superpowers. Stalin aimed above all to guarantee the security of the Soviet Union. The USSR had twice in the twentieth century been stabbed in its heartland by attacks across the windswept plains of Eastern Europe. Stalin made it clear from the outset of the war that he was determined to have friendly governments along the Soviet western border, especially in Poland. By maintaining an extensive Soviet sphere of influence in Eastern and Central Europe, the USSR could protect itself and consolidate its revolutionary base as the world's leading communist country.

To many Americans, that "sphere of influence" looked like an ill-gained "empire" (refer to Image 32.2). Doubting that Soviet goals were purely defensive, they remembered the earlier Bolshevik call for world revolution. Stalin's emphasis on "spheres" also clashed with Franklin Roosevelt's Wilsonian dream of an "open world"—decolonized, demilitarized, and democratized, with a strong international organization to oversee global peace.

Even the ways in which the United States and the Soviet Union resembled each other were troublesome. Both countries had been largely isolated from world affairs before World War II—the United States through choice, the Soviet Union through rejection by the other powers. Both nations also had a history of conducting a kind of "missionary" diplomacy, trying to export to all the world the political doctrines precipitated out of their respective revolutionary origins.

Unaccustomed to their great-power roles, unfamiliar with or even antagonistic to each other, and each believing in the universal applicability of its own particular ideology, America and the USSR suddenly found themselves staring eyeball-to-eyeball over the prostrate body of a battered Europe. The wartime "Grand Alliance" of the United States, the Soviet Union, and Britain had been a misbegotten child of necessity. When the hated Hitler fell, long-simmering suspicion and rivalry between communistic, despotic Russia and capitalistic, democratic America rose to a boil. In a fateful progression of events, marked often by misperceptions as well as by genuine conflicts of interest, the two powers provoked each other into a tense standoff known as the **Cold War**. Enduring four and a half decades, the Cold War not only shaped Soviet-American relations but also overshadowed the entire postwar international order in every corner of the globe.

32-4 Shaping the Postwar World

Despite these obstacles, the United States did manage at war's end to erect some of the structures that would support Roosevelt's vision of an open world. The Atlantic Charter that he and Churchill had devised in 1941 proclaimed for all nations the rights to self-determination and free access to trade, while committing to a postwar international system designed to ensure the human rights to "freedom from fear and want" for all individuals, everywhere. As victory approached, the Western Allies worked to build the institutions that would embody those lofty goals.

At the **Bretton Woods Conference** in Bretton Woods, New Hampshire, in 1944, the Western Allies established the International Monetary Fund (IMF) to encourage world trade by regulating currency exchange rates. They also founded the International Bank for Reconstruction and Development (World Bank) to promote economic growth in war-ravaged and underdeveloped areas. Three years later, the General Agreement on Tariffs and Trade (GATT) reduced trade barriers among member nations and helped to form the basis for the transformative spread of economic globalization in the latter half of the century (refer to "Thinking Globally: The Era of Globalization," pp. 945–946).

In contrast to its behavior after World War I, the United States took the lead in creating these important international bodies and supplied most of their funding. Victorious and robust at the end of a conflict that had laid waste all the traditional great powers, America was uniquely positioned to shape the world order after World War II. The intensifying Cold War conflict, meanwhile, ensured that the Soviets and those within their sphere of influence would largely decline to participate in many of the new multilateral institutions.

The emerging global order extended international governance to realms beyond economics. As flags wept at half-mast, the United Nations Conference opened on schedule, April 25, 1945, despite Roosevelt's heart-breaking death thirteen days earlier. Unlike Woodrow Wilson with his League of Nations, Roosevelt had shrewdly moved to establish the new international body before the war's conclusion, so as to capitalize on the wartime spirit of cooperation and insulate planning for the United Nations from the potentially divisive issue of the peace settlement. Meeting at the San Francisco War Memorial Opera House, representatives from fifty nations fashioned the United Nations Charter. The United States took a leading role in shaping and funding the new organization. But, in contrast to its abstention from other postwar economic institutions, the Soviet Union expected to be a key participant in this body.

The **United Nations (UN)** was a successor to the old League of Nations, but it differed from its predecessor in significant ways. Born in a moment of idealism and designed to prevent another great-power war, the League had adopted rules denying the veto power to any party to a dispute. The UN, by contrast, more realistically provided that no member of the Security Council, dominated by the Big Five powers (the United States, Britain, the USSR, France, and China), could have action taken against it without its consent. The League, in short, presumed great-power conflict; the UN presumed great-power cooperation. Both approaches had their liabilities. The UN also featured the General Assembly, which could be controlled by smaller countries. In contrast to the chilly American reception of the League in 1919, the Senate overwhelmingly approved the UN Charter on July 28, 1945, by a vote of 89 to 2—not least because it provided safeguards for American sovereignty and freedom of action.

The United Nations, setting up its permanent glass home in New York City, had some gratifying initial successes. It played a large role in creating the new Jewish state of Israel. The UN

In June 1946 Bernard Baruch (1870–1965) presented a plan giving the United Nations worldwide authority over atomic energy, weapons, and research, saying,

"We are here to make a choice between the quick and the dead. That is our business. Behind the black portent of the new atomic age lies a hope which, seized upon with faith, can work our salvation. If we fail, then we have damned every man to be the slave of fear. Let us not deceive ourselves; we must elect world peace or world destruction."

Trusteeship Council guided former colonies to independence. The UN also issued a Universal Declaration of Human Rights, thanks to the leadership of former First Lady Eleanor Roosevelt. Through such arms as UNESCO (United Nations Educational, Scientific, and Cultural Organization), FAO (Food and Agricultural Organization), and WHO (World Health Organization), the UN brought benefits to peoples the world over.

The fearsome new technology of the atom, however, put to an early test the spirit of cooperation on which the UN had been founded. The new organization failed this test badly. U.S. delegate Bernard Baruch called in 1946 for a UN agency, free from the great-power veto, with worldwide authority over atomic energy, weapons, and research. The Soviet delegate countered that the possession of nuclear weapons should simply be outlawed by every nation. President Truman said that it would be folly to "throw away our gun until we are sure the rest of the world can't arm against us." The suspicious Soviets felt the same way and used their veto power to scuttle the proposals. A priceless opportunity to tame the nuclear monster in its infancy was lost.

32-5 The Problem of Germany

Hitler's ruined Reich posed especially thorny problems for all the wartime Allies. They agreed only that the cancer of Nazism had to be cut out of the German body politic, which involved punishing Nazi leaders for war crimes. The Allies joined in trying twenty-two top culprits at the **Nuremberg war crimes trial** during 1945–1946. Accusations included committing crimes against the laws of war and humanity and plotting aggressions contrary to solemn treaty pledges.

Justice, Nuremberg-style, was harsh. Twelve of the accused Nazis swung from the gallows, and seven were sentenced to long jail terms. "Foxy Hermann" Goering, whose blubbery chest had once blazed with ribbons, cheated the hangman a few hours before his scheduled execution by swallowing a hidden cyanide capsule. The trials of several small-fry Nazis continued for years, and the global pursuit of Nazi fugitives lasted for decades (refer to Image 32.3).

Beyond punishing the top Nazis, the Allies could agree on little about postwar Germany. Some American Hitler-haters, noting that an industrialized Germany had been a brutal aggressor, at first wanted to dismantle German factories and reduce the country to a potato patch. The Soviets were determined to rebuild their shattered land by extracting enormous reparations from the Germans. Both these desires clashed headlong with the reality that an industrial, healthy German economy was indispensable to the recovery of Europe.

Bettmann/Getty Images

Image 32.3 The Nuremberg War Crimes Trial, 1946 Of the Nazi defendants pictured here, from left to right in the first row, Hermann Goering committed suicide during the trial; Rudolf Hess was sentenced to life in prison and died of an apparent suicide in his cell in 1987; Joachim von Ribbentrop, Wilhelm Keitel, and Ernest Kaltenbrunner were executed; in the second row, Karl Doenitz was sentenced to ten years in prison; Erich Raeder was sentenced to life in prison but released in 1955; Baldur von Schirach was sentenced to twenty years in prison; and Fritz Sauckel was executed.

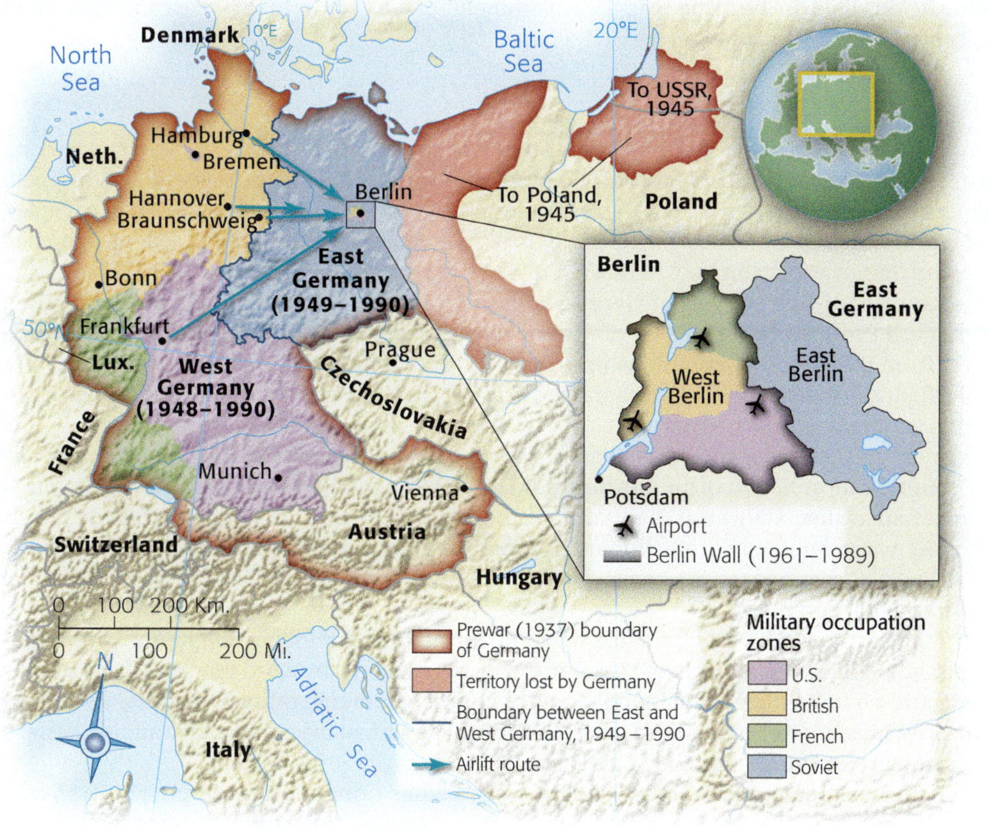

Map 32.1 Postwar Partition of Germany Germany lost much of its territory in the east to Poland and the Soviet Union. The military occupation zones were the bases for the formation of two separate countries in 1949, when the British, French, and American zones became West Germany, and the Soviet zone became East Germany. (The two Germanys were reunited in 1990.) Berlin remained under joint four-power occupation from 1945 to 1990 and became a focus and symbol of Cold War tensions.

Along with Austria, Germany had been divided at war's end into four military occupation zones, each assigned to one of the Big Four powers (France, Britain, America, and the USSR) (refer to Map 32.1). The Western Allies refused to allow Moscow to bleed their zones of the reparations that Stalin insisted he had been promised at Yalta. They also began to promote the idea of a reunited Germany. The communists responded by tightening their grip on their Eastern zone. Before long, it was apparent that Germany would remain indefinitely divided. West Germany eventually became an independent country, wedded to the West. East Germany, along with other Soviet-dominated Eastern European countries, such as Poland and Hungary, became nominally independent "satellite" states, bound to the Soviet Union. "From Stettin in the Baltic to Trieste in the Adriatic, an iron curtain has descended across the continent," declared Winston Churchill in May 1946 at the (then all-female) Westminster College, in Truman's home state of Missouri. The barrier of secrecy and isolation that Stalin clanged down across Europe would remain in place for more than four decades.

With Germany now split in two, there remained the problem of the rubble heap known as Berlin. Lying deep within the Soviet zone, this beleaguered isle in a red sea had been broken, like Germany as a whole, into sectors occupied by troops of each of the four victorious powers. In June 1948, the Soviets abruptly choked off all rail and highway access to Berlin. They evidently reasoned that the Allies would be starved out.

Berlin became a hugely symbolic issue for both sides. At stake was not only the fate of the city but a test of wills between Moscow and Washington. Amid hair-trigger tension, the Americans organized the gigantic **Berlin airlift** in 1948. Flying some of the very aircraft that had recently dropped bombs on the city, American pilots ferried thousands of tons of supplies a day to the grateful Berliners, their former enemies (refer to Image 32.4). Western Europeans took heart from this vivid demonstration of America's determination to honor its commitments in Europe. The Soviets, their bluff dramatically called, finally lifted their

Image 32.4 Berlin, 1948 Grateful city residents watch a U.S. airplane fly in much-needed supplies.

blockade in May 1949. In the same year, the governments of the two Germanys, East and West, were formally established. The Cold War had icily congealed.

32-6 Cold War Deepens

A crafty Stalin also probed the West's resolve at other sensitive points, including oil-rich Iran. Seeking to secure oil concessions similar to those held by the British and Americans, Stalin in 1946 broke an agreement to remove his troops from Iran's northernmost province, which the USSR had occupied during World War II. Instead, he used the troops to aid a rebel movement. Truman sent off a stinging protest, and the Soviet dictator backed down.

Moscow's hard-line policies in Germany, Eastern Europe, and the Middle East wrought a psychological Pearl Harbor. The eyes of Americans were jarred wide-open, and any remaining goodwill from the period of comradeship-in-arms evaporated in a cloud of dark distrust. "I'm tired of babying the Soviets," Truman remarked privately in 1946, as attitudes on both sides began to harden frostily.

Truman's piecemeal responses to various Soviet challenges took on intellectual coherence in 1947, with the formulation of the **containment doctrine**. Crafted by a brilliant young diplomat and Soviet specialist, George F. Kennan, this concept held that Russia, whether tsarist or communist, was relentlessly expansionary. But the Kremlin was also cautious, Kennan argued, and the flow of Soviet power into "every nook and cranny available to it" could be stemmed by "firm and vigilant containment."

Truman embraced Kennan's advice when he formally and publicly adopted a "get-tough-with-Russia" policy in 1947. His first dramatic move was triggered by word that heavily burdened Britain could no longer bear the financial and military load of defending Greece against communist pressures. If Greece fell, Turkey would presumably collapse, and the strategic eastern Mediterranean would pass into the Soviet orbit.

In a surprise appearance, the president went before Congress on March 12, 1947, and requested support for what came to be known as the **Truman Doctrine**. Specifically, he asked for $400 million to bolster Greece and Turkey, which Congress quickly granted. More generally, he declared that "it must be the policy of the United States to support free peoples who are resisting attempted subjugation by armed minorities or by outside pressures"—a sweeping and open-ended commitment of vast proportions. This was unambiguous internationalism on a scale unlike anything the United States had ever embraced, and it sparked vigorous debate then and since. Critics charged that Truman had overreacted by promising unlimited support to any tinhorn despot who claimed to be resisting "Communist aggression," and further complained that the Truman Doctrine needlessly polarized the world into pro-Soviet and pro-American camps, and unwisely defined the Soviet threat as primarily military in nature. Defenders of Truman have explained that it was the president's fear of a revived isolationism that led him to exaggerate the Soviet threat and deploy the charged language of a holy global war against godless communism.

The Granger Collection, NYC

Image 32.5 Where To? 1947 As this satirical view of the Truman Doctrine shows, not all Americans were sure where the country's new foreign policy was taking them.

Meanwhile, a threat of a different sort loomed in Western Europe—especially France, Italy, and Germany. Still suffering from the hunger and economic chaos spawned by war, these key nations were in grave danger of being taken over from the inside by Communist parties that could exploit these hardships.

The Truman administration concluded that bolder policy intervention—and more American money—would be necessary to realize its vision of a liberalized global economy. In a commencement address at Harvard University on June 5, 1947, Secretary of State George C. Marshall invited the Europeans to get together and work out a *joint* plan for their economic recovery. If they did so, then the United States would provide substantial financial assistance (refer to Image 32.5). This forced cooperation constituted a powerful nudge on the long road to the creation of the European Union (EU).

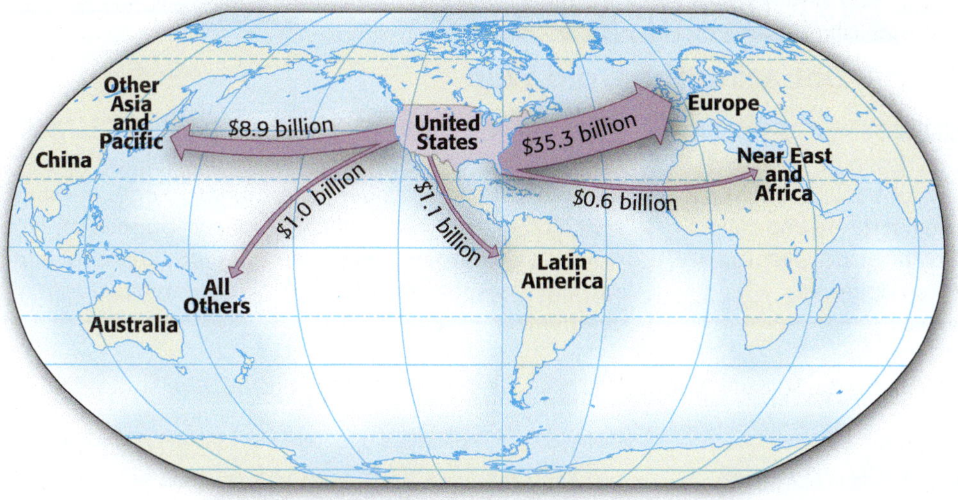

Map 32.2 United States Foreign Aid, Military and Economic, 1945–1954 Marshall Plan aid swelled the outlay for Europe. Note the emphasis on the "developed" world, with relatively little aid going to "developing."

The democratic nations of Europe rose enthusiastically to the life-giving promise of the so-called **Marshall Plan**. Worried that the Russian bear might hug the Marshall Plan to death, the Americans deliberately made the terms difficult for the USSR to accept. Nobody was surprised when the Soviets denounced the "Martial Plan" as one more capitalist trick.

The Marshall Plan called for spending $12.5 billion over four years in sixteen cooperating countries (refer to Map 32.2). Congress at first balked at this mammoth sum. But a Soviet-sponsored communist coup in Czechoslovakia jolted legislators into action, and they approved the first round of funding in April 1948. Congress evidently concluded that if Uncle Sam did not get the Europeans back on their feet, they would never get off his back.

Truman's Marshall Plan was a spectacular success. American dollars pumped reviving blood into the economic veins of the anemic Western European nations. Within a few years, most of them were exceeding their prewar outputs, as an "economic miracle" drenched Europe in prosperity (refer to Image 32.6). The Communist parties in Italy and France lost ground, and the "iron curtain" moved no farther westward.

A resolute Truman made another fateful decision in 1948. Access to Middle Eastern oil was crucial to the European recovery program and, increasingly, to the health of the U.S. economy, given finite American oil reserves. Yet the Arab oil countries adamantly opposed the creation of the Jewish state of Israel in the British mandate territory of Palestine. Should Israel be born, a Saudi Arabian leader warned Truman, the Arabs "will lay siege to it until it dies of famine."

Defying Arab wrath as well as the objections of his own State and Defense Departments and the European Allies, Truman officially recognized the state of Israel on the day of its birth, May 14, 1948. Humanitarian sympathy for the Jewish survivors of the Holocaust ranked high among his reasons. So did his wishes to preempt Soviet influence in the Jewish state and to retain the support of American Jewish voters. American policy of strong support for Israel would vastly complicate its relations with the Arab world in the decades ahead.

Bettmann/Getty Images

Image 32.6 The Marshall Plan Turns Enemies into Friends The poster in this 1950 photograph in Berlin reads, "Berlin Rebuilt with Help from the Marshall Plan."

Contending Voices

Debating the Cold War

In February 1946 Kremlin specialist George F. Kennan (1904–2005) sent his landmark "Long Telegram" to the State Department. In the eight-thousand-word message, Kennan assessed the Soviet threat and called for a new kind of response, which would eventually become known as the "containment doctrine."

"In summary, we have here a political force [Stalin's regime] committed fanatically to the belief that with [the] US there can be no permanent *modus vivendi*, that it is desirable and necessary that the internal harmony of our society be disrupted, our traditional way of life be destroyed, the international authority of our state be broken, if Soviet power is to be secure."

Six months later, former Vice President-turned-Secretary of Commerce Henry A. Wallace (1888–1965) wrote to President Truman to urge a more conciliatory policy. Wallace's lonely opposition to America's emerging Cold War policy would propel him into the top spot of a left-wing third-party presidential campaign in 1948.

"How do American actions since V-J Day appear to other nations? I mean by actions the concrete things like $13 billion for the War and Navy Departments, the Bikini tests of the atomic bomb, . . . and the effort to secure air bases spread over half the globe from which the other half of the globe can be bombed. . . . How would it look to us if Russia had the bomb and we did not, if Russia had 10,000-mile bombers and air bases within a thousand miles of our coast lines and we did not?"

Consider This:

How inevitable was the Cold War between the United States and the Soviet Union?

32-7 Girding for the Cold War

The Cold War—the struggle to contain Soviet communism—was not war, yet it was not peace. The standoff with the Kremlin banished the dreams of tax-fatigued Americans that tanks could be beaten into automobiles.

The Soviet menace spurred the unification of the armed services as well as the creation of a huge new national security apparatus. Congress in 1947 passed the National Security Act, creating the Department of Defense. The department was to be housed in the sprawling Pentagon building on the banks of the Potomac and to be headed by a new cabinet officer, the secretary of defense. Under the secretary, but without cabinet status, were the civilian secretaries of the navy, the army (replacing the old secretary of war), and the air force (a recognition of the rising importance of airpower). The uniformed heads of each service were brought together as the Joint Chiefs of Staff.

The National Security Act also established the National Security Council (NSC) to advise the president on security matters and the Central Intelligence Agency (CIA) to coordinate the government's foreign fact gathering. The "Voice of America," authorized by Congress in 1948, began beaming American radio broadcasts behind the iron curtain. In the same year, Congress resurrected the military draft, providing for the conscription of selected young men from nineteen to twenty-five years of age. The forbidding presence of the Selective Service System shaped millions of young people's educational, marital, and career plans in the following quarter-century. One shoe at a time, a war-weary America was reluctantly returning to a war footing.

The Soviet threat was forcing the democracies of Western Europe into an unforeseen degree of unity. In 1948, Britain, France, Belgium, the Netherlands, and Luxembourg signed a path-breaking treaty of defensive alliance at Brussels. They then invited the United States to join them. The proposal confronted the United States with a historic decision. America

Image 32.7 The View from Russia American views of Russian aggression in the early Cold War years were matched by Russian fears of American expansion. This Russian cartoon proclaims, "Phrases and Bases" (It rhymes in both Russian and English!), which could be loosely translated as "Words and War Preparation." The little capitalist stooge in the soldier's hip pocket is brandishing a withered olive branch in which is nested a tiny atomic bomb. He is broadcasting "Peace," "Defense," and "Disarmament" while standing next to an oversize sidearm burnished with a dollar sign, a motif echoed in the wad of cash in the soldier's front pocket. Meanwhile the soldier is planting an American base in Greece, a NATO member. U.S. bomber bases in Britain, Spain, France, and Italy are also shown.

had traditionally avoided entangling alliances, especially in peacetime (if the Cold War could be considered peacetime). Yet American participation in the emerging coalition could serve many purposes: It would strengthen the policy of containing the Soviet Union; it would provide a framework for the reintegration of Germany into the European family; and it would reassure jittery Europeans that a traditionally isolationist Uncle Sam was not about to abandon them to the marauding Russian bear—or to a resurgent and domineering Germany (refer to Image 32.7).

The Truman administration decided to join the European pact, called the **North Atlantic Treaty Organization (NATO)**, granting it a transatlantic character. With white-tie pageantry, the NATO treaty was signed in Washington on April 4, 1949. The twelve original signatories pledged to regard an attack on one as an attack on all and promised to respond with "armed force" if necessary. Despite last-ditch howls from immovable isolationists, the Senate approved the treaty on July 21, 1949, by a vote of 82 to 13. Membership was boosted to fourteen in 1952 with the inclusion of Greece and Turkey, to fifteen in 1955 with the addition of West Germany (refer to Image 32.8).

The NATO pact was epochal. It marked a dramatic departure from American diplomatic convention, a gigantic boost for European unification, and a significant step in the militarization of the Cold War. NATO became the cornerstone of all Cold War American policy toward Europe. With good reason pundits summed up NATO's threefold purpose: "to keep the Russians out, the Germans down, and the Americans in."

Image 32.8 Reaching Across the Atlantic in Peacetime, 1948 When the United States joined with the Western European powers in the North Atlantic Alliance, soon to be called the North Atlantic Treaty Organization, it overcame its historic isolationism in the wake of wars. By 1955, former enemy West Germany would be admitted to NATO to help defend Western Europe against Soviet aggression.

32-8 Reconstruction and Revolution in Asia

Reconstruction in Japan required less multilateral maneuvering—it was an all-American effort—but at the outset presented a staggeringly difficult task. Japan's major cities had been reduced to rubble. Its power grid was barely functional, and factories, railroads, and telephone lines didn't work at all. In charge of the occupying American army and the rebuilding effort was Supreme Allied Commander Douglas MacArthur, a five-star general of towering ego and forceful personality.

In the teeth of violent protests from Soviet officials, as well as from some in the United States who sought the harshest possible treatment of the Japanese, MacArthur pushed forward with democratization. With an imperiousness that exasperated Truman and impressed the Japanese, the general prosecuted Japan's war criminals (seven were hanged) and dictated a new national constitution that renounced militarism, bolstered women's equality, and introduced Western-style democratic government.

The six years of American occupation paved the way for a phenomenal economic recovery that within a few decades made Japan one of the world's mightiest industrial powers. Ironically, as with the U.S.-supported recovery of Western European economies, Japan's postwar ascendance eventually helped to end America's honeymoon as the unchallenged global economic kingpin. In a further irony, some of the Japanese management practices later envied by resentful U.S. firms were in fact seeded by American advisors during the occupation.

As Japan returned to capitalist democracy, China was on a much different trajectory. A bitter civil war had raged for years between Nationalists and communists. Washington had halfheartedly supported the Nationalist government of Generalissimo Jiang Jieshi (Chiang Kai-shek) in his struggle with the communists under Mao Zedong (Mao Tse-tung). But ineptitude and corruption within the generalissimo's regime gradually corroded the confidence of his people. Communist armies swept south, and late in 1949 Jiang was forced to flee with the remnants of his once-powerful force to the last-hope island of Formosa (Taiwan).

The collapse of Nationalist China was a depressing defeat for America and its allies in the Cold War—the worst to date. At one fell swoop, nearly one-fourth of the world's population—some 500 million people—was swept into the communist camp. The so-called fall of China became a bitterly partisan issue in the United States. Republicans, seeking out those who had "lost China," assailed President Truman and his bristly mustached secretary of state, Dean Acheson. They insisted that Democratic agencies, wormy with communists, had deliberately withheld aid from Jiang to trip him into his fall.

32-9 The Soviet Bomb

More bad news came in September 1949 when the Soviets shocked the world by exploding an atomic bomb—approximately three years earlier than many experts had thought possible. American strategists since 1945 had counted on keeping the Soviets in line by threats of a one-sided aerial attack with nuclear weapons. But atomic bombing was now a game that two could play.

To outpace the Soviets in nuclear weaponry, Truman ordered the development of the "H-bomb" (hydrogen bomb)—a city-smashing thermonuclear weapon that was a thousand times more powerful than the (uranium) atomic bomb. J. Robert Oppenheimer, former scientific director of the Manhattan Project and current chair of the Atomic Energy Commission, led a group of scientists in opposition to the program to design thermonuclear weapons on the grounds that they were instruments of genocide—or worse. Albert Einstein, the physicist whose theories had helped give birth to the atomic age and whose warnings to Roosevelt had helped set the Manhattan Project in motion, declared that "annihilation of any life on earth has been brought within the range of technical possibilities."

Disregarding such warnings, the United States exploded its first hydrogen device on a South Pacific atoll in 1952 (refer to Image 32.9). The Soviets countered with their first H-bomb explosion in 1953. Spurred on by massive government support in both countries for defense-related scientific research, the nuclear arms race entered a planet-menacing phase. The two sides were constrained only by the recognition that if the Cold War turned hot, it would leave no world for the communists to communize or the democracies to democratize. A perilously shaky peace of "mutual assured destruction" (MAD) brought an anxious stability to the superpower standoff.

Atomic scientist Edward Condon (1902–1974) warned as early as 1946—three years before the Soviets exploded their own atomic bomb—that Americans' confidence in their nuclear monopoly was a dangerous delusion that could unleash vicious accusations and scapegoating:

"The laws of nature, some seem to think, are ours exclusively.... Having created an air of suspicion and distrust, there will be persons among us who think our nations can know nothing except what is learned by espionage. So, when other countries make atom bombs, these persons will cry 'treason' at our scientists, for they will find it inconceivable that another country could make a bomb in any other way."

U.S. Air Force Photo

Image 32.9 The Hydrogen Bomb This test blast at Bikini Atoll in the Marshall Islands in 1954 was so powerful that one Japanese fisherman was killed and all twenty-two of his crewmates were seriously injured by radioactive ash that fell on their vessel some eighty miles away. Fishing boats a thousand miles from Bikini later brought in radioactively contaminated catches.

32-10 The Korean Volcano Erupts

Korea, the Land of the Morning Calm, heralded a new and more menacing phase of the Cold War—a shooting phase—in June 1950. When Japan collapsed in 1945, Soviet troops had accepted the Japanese surrender north of the thirty-eighth parallel on the Korean peninsula, and American troops had done likewise south of that line. Both superpowers professed to want the reunification and independence of Korea, a Japanese colony since 1910. But, as in Germany, each helped to set up rival regimes above and below the parallel.

By 1949, when the Soviets and Americans had both withdrawn their forces, the entire peninsula was a bristling armed camp, with two hostile regimes eyeing each other suspiciously. The explosion came on June 25, 1950. Spearheaded by Soviet-made tanks, North Korean army columns rumbled across the thirty-eighth parallel. Caught flat-footed, the South Korean forces were shoved back southward to a dangerously tiny defensive area around Pusan, their weary backs to the sea.

President Truman sprang quickly into the breach. The invasion seemed to provide devastating proof of a fundamental premise in the "containment doctrine" that shaped Washington's foreign policy: even a slight relaxation of America's guard was an invitation to communist aggression somewhere.

The Korean invasion prompted a massive expansion of the American military. A few months before, Truman's National Security Council had issued its famous **National Security Council Memorandum Number 68 (NSC-68)**, recommending that the United States quadruple its defense spending. Ignored at first because it seemed politically impossible to implement, NSC-68 got a new lease on life from the Korean crisis. "Korea saved us," Secretary of State Acheson later commented. Truman now ordered a massive military buildup, well beyond what was necessary for Korea. Soon the United States had 3.5 million men under arms and was spending $50 billion per year on the defense budget—some 13 percent of the GNP.

NSC-68 was a key document of the Cold War period, not only because it marked a major step in the militarization of American foreign policy, but also because it vividly reflected the sense of almost limitless possibility that pervaded postwar American society. NSC-68 rested on the assumption that the enormous American economy could bear without strain the huge costs of a gigantic rearmament program. Said one NSC-68 planner, "There was practically nothing the country could not do if it wanted to do it."

Truman took full advantage of a temporary Soviet absence from the United Nations Security Council on June 25, 1950, to obtain a unanimous condemnation of North Korea as an aggressor.

(Why the Soviets were absent remains controversial. Scholars once believed that the Soviets were just as surprised as the Americans by the attack. It now appears that Stalin had given his reluctant approval to North Korea's strike plan but believed that the fighting would be brief and that the United States would take little interest in it.) The Security Council also called upon all UN members, including the United States, to "render every assistance" to restore peace. Two days later, without consulting Congress, Truman ordered American air and naval units to support South Korea. Before the week was out, he also ordered General MacArthur's Japan-based occupation troops into action alongside the outflanked South Koreans. So began the ill-fated **Korean War**.

Officially, the United States was simply participating in a UN "police action." Participating nations, including Great Britain, Canada, and the Philippines, did make significant troop contributions. But the United States provided 88 percent of the UN contingents, and General MacArthur, UN commander of the entire operation, took his orders from Washington, not from the Security Council.

The Korean conflict spurred another policy move with long-term consequences when Truman signed the **Defense Production Act of 1950**. Modeled on the mobilization measures that built "an arsenal of democracy" during World War II, the statute empowered the president to order private companies to prioritize production deemed essential to national security. The Act unleashed an extraordinary surge of private-sector defense manufacturing that continued long after the fighting in Korea ceased. Later presidents used its muscle to respond to energy crises, natural disasters, and pandemics.

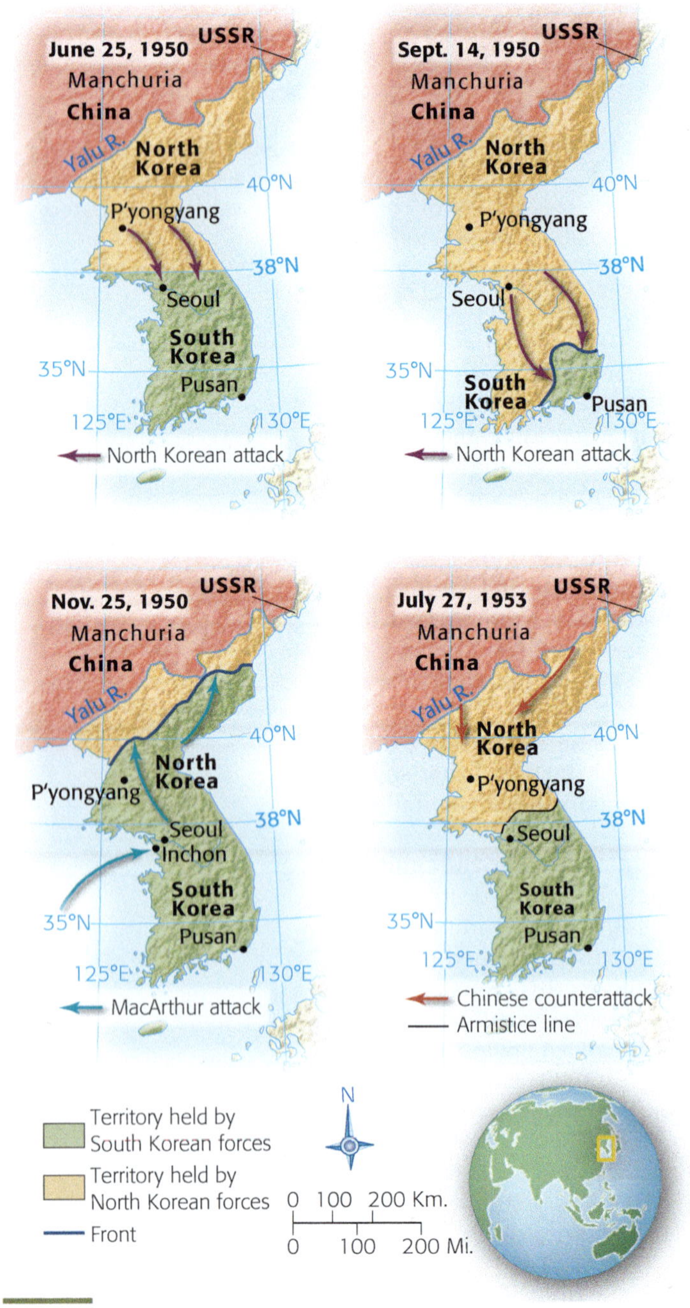

Map 32.3 The Shifting Front in Korea

32-11 The Military Seesaw in Korea

Rather than fight his way out of the southern Pusan perimeter, MacArthur launched a daring amphibious landing behind the enemy's lines at Inchon. This bold gamble on September 15, 1950, succeeded brilliantly; within two weeks the North Koreans had scrambled back behind the "sanctuary" of the thirty-eighth parallel. Truman's avowed intention was to restore South Korea to its former borders, but the pursuing South Koreans had already crossed the thirty-eighth parallel, and there seemed little point in permitting the North Koreans to regroup and come again. The UN General Assembly tacitly authorized a crossing by MacArthur, whom President Truman ordered northward, provided that there was no armed intervention by the Chinese or Soviets (refer to Map 32.3).

The Americans thus raised the stakes in Korea, and in so doing provoked another player to enter this dangerous game. In November 1950, tens of thousands of Chinese "volunteers" fell upon MacArthur's rashly overextended lines and hurled the UN forces reeling back down the peninsula. The fighting now sank into a frostbitten stalemate.

MacArthur, humiliated by this rout, pressed for drastic retaliation, including the use of nuclear weapons on the advancing Chinese and their supply lines. But Washington policymakers, with anxious eyes on Moscow, prudently refused to enlarge the already costly conflict. The chairman of the Joint Chiefs of Staff declared that a wider clash in Asia would be "the wrong war, at the wrong place, at the wrong time, and with the wrong enemy." Europe, not Asia, was the administration's first concern; and the USSR, not China, loomed as the more sinister foe.

Two-fisted General MacArthur felt that he was being asked to fight with one hand tied behind his back. He sneered at the concept of a "limited war" and insisted that "there is no substitute for victory." Truman resolutely resisted calls for nuclear escalation. When MacArthur began publicly criticizing the president's policies, Truman had no choice but to remove the insubordinate general from command—which he did on April 11, 1951. In July, truce discussions began in a rude field tent near the front line but were almost immediately snagged on the issue of prisoner exchange. Talks dragged on unproductively for nearly two years while men continued to die.

Meanwhile, MacArthur, a legend in his own mind, returned to an uproarious American welcome, whereas in many circles Truman was condemned as a "pig," an "imbecile," a "Judas," and an appeaser of communism (refer to Image 32.10). The Truman-MacArthur clash starkly exposed the depth of popular passions coursing through Cold War America.

Image 32.10 Truman Takes the Heat

32-12 The New Red Scare

As never before, international events deeply shaped American political and economic developments at home in the years after World War II. The solidifying Cold War with Russia fueled domestic political conflict and drew new boundaries for acceptable political opinion. Meanwhile, the postwar economic order that the United States helped to forge, combined with Cold War spending and investment, laid the foundations for a Long Boom that transformed the country over the next several decades.

A new anti-red chase accelerated within America's borders as U.S.-Soviet relations froze. Many nervous citizens feared that communist spies, paid with Moscow gold, were undermining the government and treacherously misdirecting foreign policy. In 1947, Truman launched a massive "loyalty" program. The attorney general drew up a list of ninety supposedly disloyal organizations, none of which was given the opportunity to prove its innocence. The Loyalty Review Board investigated more than 3 million federal employees, some 3,000 of whom either resigned or were dismissed, none under formal indictment.

Individual states likewise became intensely security-conscious. Loyalty oaths in increasing numbers were demanded of employees, especially teachers. The gnawing question for many earnest Americans was, Could the nation continue to enjoy traditional freedoms—especially freedom of speech, freedom of thought, and the right of political dissent—in a Cold War climate?

In 1949, eleven communists were brought before a New York jury for violating the Smith Act of 1940, the first peacetime antisedition law since 1798. Convicted of advocating the overthrow of the American government by force, the defendants were sent to prison. The Supreme Court upheld their convictions in *Dennis v. United States* (1951).

The House of Representatives in 1938 had established the **House Un-American Activities Committee (HUAC)** to investigate "subversion." In 1948, committee member Richard M. Nixon, a rising GOP star and ambitious red-catcher, led the chase after Alger Hiss, a prominent ex–New Dealer and a distinguished member of the "Eastern establishment" (refer to Image 32.11). Accused of being a communist agent in the 1930s, Hiss demanded the right to defend himself. He dramatically met his chief accuser before HUAC in August 1948. Hiss denied everything but was caught in embarrassing falsehoods, convicted of perjury in 1950, and sentenced to five years in prison.

The stunning success of the Soviet scientists in developing an atomic bomb was attributed by many to clever communist spies who stole American secrets. Notorious among those who had allegedly leaked atomic data to Moscow were two American citizens, Julius and Ethel Rosenberg. They were convicted in 1951 of espionage and sent to the electric chair in 1953—the only people in American history ever executed in peacetime for espionage. Though declassified evidence has subsequently strengthened the case against the Rosenbergs, at the time they enjoyed the support of many Americans who believed their claims of innocence. Their sensational trial and

Image 32.11 Richard Nixon, Red-Hunter Congressman Nixon (right) and another Congressional colleague tasked with investigating "un-American activities" examine the microfilm that figured as important evidence in Alger Hiss's conviction for perjury in 1950.

Some Republicans sharply criticized Joseph McCarthy. Maine's Senator Margaret Chase Smith, for example, declared,

"I don't want to see the Republican Party ride to political victory on the Four Horsemen of Calumny—Fear, Ignorance, Bigotry and Smear."

electrocution, combined with sympathy for their two orphaned children, began to sour some sober citizens on the excesses of the red-hunters.

Was America really riddled with Soviet spies? Soviet agents did infiltrate certain government agencies, though without severely damaging consequences, and espionage may have helped the Soviets to develop an atomic bomb somewhat sooner than they would have otherwise. But for some Americans, the hunt for communists was not just about fending off the military threat of the Soviet Union but about unsettling dangers that lurked closer to home. While men like Nixon led the search for communists in Washington, other politicians discovered that all manner of social changes—including increased sexual freedom and agitation for civil rights—could conveniently be tarred with a red brush. Anticommunist crusaders ransacked school libraries for "subversive" textbooks and drove debtors, drinkers, and homosexuals, all alleged to be security risks, from their jobs.

Some Americans, including President Truman, realized that the red hunt was turning into a witch hunt. In 1950, Truman vetoed the McCarran Internal Security Bill, which among other provisions authorized the president to arrest and detain suspicious people during an "internal security emergency." Critics protested that the bill smacked of police-state, concentration-camp tactics. But the congressional guardians of the Republic's liberties enacted the bill over Truman's veto.

The demagogic politics of anticommunism found its most dangerous practitioner in Joseph R. McCarthy, an obstreperous Republican senator from Wisconsin. Elected to the Senate on the basis of a trumped-up war-hero record, the swaggering senator crashed into the limelight in February 1950 when he accused Secretary of State Dean Acheson of knowingly employing 205 Communist Party members. Pressed to reveal the names, McCarthy later conceded that there were only 57 genuine communists and in the end failed to identify even one. Some of McCarthy's Republican colleagues nevertheless realized the partisan usefulness of this kind of attack on the Democratic administration. Ohio's Senator John Bricker reportedly said, "Joe, you're a dirty s.o.b., but there are times when you've got to have an s.o.b. around, and this is one of them."

McCarthy's rhetoric grew bolder and his accusations spread more wildly over the next several years. He saw the red hand of Moscow everywhere. The Democrats, he charged, "bent to whispered pleas from the lips of traitors." Incredibly, he even denounced General George Marshall, former army chief of staff and ex-secretary of state, as "part of a conspiracy so immense and an infamy so black as to dwarf any previous venture in the history of man."

McCarthy—and what became known as **McCarthyism**—flourished in the seething Cold War atmosphere of suspicion and fear. The senator was neither the first nor the most effective red-hunter, but he was surely the most ruthless, and he did the most damage to American traditions of fair play and free speech. The careers of countless officials, writers, and actors were ruined after "Low-Blow Joe" had "named" them, often unfairly, as communists or communist sympathizers. Weak-kneed politicians trembled in the face of such onslaughts, especially when opinion polls showed that a majority of the American people approved of McCarthy's crusade.

At the peak of his power, McCarthy effectively controlled personnel policy at the State Department inflicting severe damage on the morale and effectiveness of the professional foreign service. In particular, McCarthyite purges deprived the government of a number of Asian specialists who might have counseled a wiser course in Vietnam in the fateful decade that followed. McCarthy's antics also damaged America's international reputation for fair and open democracy at a moment when it was important to keep Western Europe on the United States' side.

McCarthy finally bent the bow too far when he accused members of the U.S. Army of subversion. The embattled military men fought back in thirty-five days of televised hearings in the spring of 1954. Television was in its infancy, making it all the more remarkable that up to 20 million Americans at a time watched the **Army-McCarthy hearings** in fascination

Bettmann/Getty Images

Image 32.12 McCarthy Maps a Menace The Wisconsin senator (standing) often made a mesmerizing spectacle out of his investigations into the allegedly wide-ranging domestic Communist conspiracy. But his recklessness got the better of him during the nationally televised Army-McCarthy hearings in 1954, where army counsel Joseph Welch (seated) proved a sympathetic and effective antagonist.

(refer to Image 32.12). Flickering on living-room screens, a boorish, surly McCarthy publicly cut his own throat by parading his essential meanness and irresponsibility. A few months later, the Senate formally condemned him for "conduct unbecoming a member." Three years later, unwept and unsung, McCarthy died of chronic alcoholism. But "McCarthyism" has passed into the English language as a label for the divisive fearmongering and unfair persecution that can so swiftly imperil democratic society.

In a moment of high drama during the Army-McCarthy hearings, attorney Joseph Welch (1890–1960) reproached McCarthy in front of a huge national television audience for threatening to slander a young lawyer on Welch's staff:

"Until this moment, Senator, I think I never really gauged your cruelty or your recklessness. Little did I dream you could be so cruel as to do an injury to that lad. . . . If it were in my power to forgive you for your reckless cruelty, I would do so. I like to think that I am a gentleman, but your forgiveness will have to come from someone other than me. . . . Have you no decency, sir, at long last? Have you left no sense of decency?"

32-13 Defining an American Creed

Beyond fights over security and civil liberties, the Cold War shaped American culture in profound ways. Many Americans interpreted the conflict between the capitalist West and the communist—and officially secular—East in religious terms. Truman found support for casting the Cold War as a battle between good and evil from theologians like the influential liberal Protestant clergyman Reinhold Niebuhr (1892–1971). A vocal enemy of fascism, communism, *and* pacifism in the 1940s and 1950s, Niebuhr divided the world into two polarized camps: the "children of light" and the "children of darkness." For Niebuhr, Christian justice, including force if necessary, required a "realist" response to "children of darkness" like Hitler and Stalin. But Niebuhr's realism also emphasized the dangers of fallibility and the limits of power, in contrast to the more crusading spirit of conservative Christian anticommunists. The postwar decades saw an emphasis on religious belief of any kind as a distinguishing feature of the "American Way," to be defended against atheistic communism. Congress's decision to insert the words "under God" into the Pledge of Allegiance in 1954 epitomized this Cold War impulse.

The Cold War had a chilling effect on the political left, muzzling more radical voices in institutions ranging from unions and universities to churches and civic organizations. Among those suppressed were some of the most forceful advocates for racial justice in the United States. Even moderate agitators for civil rights were often slandered as communists and fellow travelers.

But at the same time, competition with the Soviets for international support, like the earlier Allied fight against fascism during World War II, placed pressure on the United States to live up to its own stated democratic ideals. Northern white liberals became more troubled, and some more vocal, about the racial apartheid of the Jim Crow South. *An American Dilemma*, an influential two-volume examination of Southern race relations by Swedish economist Gunnar Myrdal, published in 1944, had stirred guilty white consciences while declaring that the "American creed" of equal opportunity would ultimately triumph over prejudice and injustice.

America's visibility in the world created new political opportunities and rhetorical tools for advocates to press civil rights claims. They successfully persuaded Truman to create a presidential committee on civil rights whose 1947 report, "To Secure These Rights," presented an unflinching portrait of the nation's civil rights failures and proposed a bold set of policy remedies on which "the national government must take the lead." The report shot like a thunderbolt through the Democratic Party, whose powerful Southern wing was further enraged when Truman took action on one of the report's recommendations by issuing the landmark **Executive Order 9981** in July 1948, which desegregated the armed forces.

32-14 Postwar Economic Anxieties

The communist menace was not the only specter haunting Americans after World War II. Economic uncertainty also loomed over the new peace. The decade of the 1930s had left deep scars. Joblessness and insecurity had pushed up the suicide rate and dampened the marriage rate. Babies went unborn as pinched budgets and sagging self-esteem wrought a sexual depression in American bedrooms. The war had banished the blight of depression, but would the respite last? Grim-faced observers were warning that the war had only temporarily lifted the pall of economic stagnation and that peace would bring the return of hard times. Homeward-bound GIs, so the gloomy predictions ran, would step out of the army's chow lines and back into the breadlines of the unemployed.

The faltering economy in the initial postwar years threatened to confirm the worst predictions of the doomsayers who foresaw another Great Depression. Real gross national product (GNP) slumped sickeningly in 1946 and 1947 from its wartime peak. With the removal of wartime price controls, prices levitated by 33 percent in 1946–1947. A wave of strikes swept the country. During 1946 alone, some 4.6 million laborers laid down their tools, fearful that soon they could barely afford the automobiles and other consumer goods their war-commandeered factories would soon manufacture. Workers also worried that belt-tightening employers might take advantage of the end of the war to roll back organized labor's wartime gains.

Labor's worst fears were soon realized. Drawing strength from middle-class frustration with the strike wave, conservatives and their business allies had their revenge against labor's New Deal gains with the **Taft-Hartley Act**. Passed in 1947 by a Republican-controlled Congress (the first in fourteen years) over President Truman's vigorous veto, the measure outlawed the "closed" (all-union) shop and banned a wide range of industrial activity. Reflecting the Cold War's chill, it prohibited strikes by federal workers, empowered the president to end strikes that threatened "national security," and required union leaders to take a noncommunist oath.

Taft-Hartley was only one of several obstacles that slowed the growth of organized labor in the years after World War II. In the heady days of the New Deal, unions had spread swiftly in the North, especially in huge manufacturing industries like steel and automobiles. But labor's postwar efforts to organize in the historically antiunion regions of the South and West proved frustrating. The CIO's **Operation Dixie**, aimed at unionizing Southern textile workers and steelworkers, failed miserably in 1948 to overcome white workers' lingering fears of racial mixing. Anticommunist purges removed from labor's ranks some of its most active organizers. Most importantly, workers in the rapidly growing service sector of the economy proved much more difficult to organize than the thousands of assembly-line workers who in the 1930s had poured into the auto and steel unions. Organized labor played a significant role in shaping the economic and political order in the United States for several decades after World War II. But the number of organized private-sector workers would peak in the 1950s and then begin a long, slow decline that persisted into the twenty-first century.

The Democratic administration, meanwhile, took some steps to forestall an economic downturn. It sold war factories and other government installations to private businesses at fire-sale prices. It secured passage of the **Employment Act of 1946**, making it government policy "to promote maximum employment, production, and purchasing power." The act created a three-member Council of Economic Advisers to provide the president with the data and the recommendations to make that policy a reality.

Most dramatic was the passage of the Servicemen's Readjustment Act of 1944—better known as the GI Bill of Rights, or the **GI Bill**. Enacted partly out of fear that the employment markets would never be able to absorb 15 million returning veterans at war's end, the GI Bill made generous provisions for sending the former soldiers to school. In the postwar decade, some 8 million veterans advanced their education at Uncle Sam's expense. The majority attended technical and vocational schools, but colleges and universities were crowded to the blackboards as more than 2 million ex-GIs stormed the halls of higher learning (refer to Image 32.13). The total eventually spent for education was some $14.5 billion in taxpayer dollars—$2 billion more than the Marshall Plan. The act also enabled the Veterans Administration (VA) to guarantee about $16 billion in loans for veterans to buy homes, farms, and small businesses. By raising educational levels and stimulating the construction industry, the GI Bill powerfully nurtured the robust and long-lived economic expansion that eventually took hold in the late 1940s.

The GI Bill's benefits were not equally shared, however. Pervasive racial discrimination meant that Black veterans in both North and South were routinely denied VA-guaranteed loans and admission to predominantly white colleges and universities, and often excluded from job training and placement in high-skilled fields. It was "as though the legislation were earmarked 'For White Veterans Only,'" noted a 1947 study, "Our Negro Veterans."

Bettmann/Getty Images

Image 32.13 Going to College on the GI Bill Financed by the federal government, thousands of World War II veterans crowded into college classrooms in the late 1940s. Universities struggled to house these older students, many of whom already had families. Pennsylvania State College resorted to setting up hundreds of trailers.

32-15 Democratic Divisions in 1948

Attacking high prices and "High-Tax Harry" Truman, the Republicans had won control of Congress in the congressional elections of 1946. Their prospects had seldom looked rosier as they gathered in Philadelphia to choose their 1948 presidential candidate. They noisily renominated warmed-over New York governor Thomas E. Dewey, still as debonair as if he had stepped out of a bandbox.

Also gathering in Philadelphia, Democratic politicos looked without enthusiasm on their hand-me-down president and sang, "I'm Just Mild About Harry." But a "dump Truman" movement collapsed when war hero Dwight D. Eisenhower declined to be drafted by Democrats. The peppery president, unwanted but undaunted, was then chosen in the face of vehement opposition by Southern delegates, alienated by his strong stand in favor of civil rights for Black Americans, especially his desegregation of the military.

Truman's nomination split the party wide-open. Embittered Southern Democrats from thirteen states, like their fire-eating forebears of 1860, met in their own convention, in Birmingham, Alabama, with Confederate flags brashly in evidence. Amid scenes of heated defiance, these "Dixiecrats" nominated arch-segregationist South Carolina Governor J. Strom Thurmond on a States' Rights party ticket.

To add to the confusion within Democratic ranks, former vice president Henry A. Wallace threw his hat into the ring. Having parted company with the administration over its get-tough-with-Russia policy, he was nominated by the new Progressive Party—a veritable menagerie of disgruntled former New Dealers, starry-eyed pacifists, well-meaning liberals, and communist-fronters. Wallace, a vigorous though perhaps unrealistic reformer, assailed Uncle Sam's "dollar imperialism" from the stump. Labeled by some as the "Pied Piper of the Politburo," he took a Soviet-friendly line that earned him drenchings with rotten eggs in hostile cities. But to his supporters, Wallace was a rare peace-loving voice in the deepening gloom of the Cold War.

Harry S. Truman Library

Image 32.14 The Harried Piano Player, 1948 Besieged by the left and right wings of his own party, and by a host of domestic and foreign problems, Truman was a long shot for reelection in 1948. But the scrappy president surprised his legions of critics by handily defeating his opponent, Thomas E. Dewey.

With the Democrats ruptured three ways and the Republican congressional victory of 1946 just past, Dewey's victory seemed assured (refer to Image 32.14). Overconfident

Bettmann/Getty Images

Image 32.15 **That Ain't the Way I Heard It!** Truman wins.

to the point of smugness, the Republican nominee confined himself to dispensing soothing-syrup trivialities like "Our future lies before us." The seemingly doomed Truman ("to err is Truman," his critics mocked) had to rely on his "gutfighter" instincts and folksy personality. Traveling the country by train to deliver some three hundred "give 'em hell" speeches, he lashed out at the Taft-Hartley "slave-labor" law and the "do-nothing" Republican Congress, while whipping up support for his program of civil rights, improved labor benefits, and health insurance.

On election night, the *Chicago Tribune* ran off an early edition with the headline "DEWEY DEFEATS TRUMAN." But in the morning, it turned out that "President" Dewey had embarrassingly managed to snatch defeat from the jaws of victory (refer to Image 32.15). Truman had swept to a stunning triumph, to the complete bewilderment of politicians, pollsters, prophets, and pundits. Even though Thurmond took away 39 electoral votes in the Deep South, Truman won 303 electoral votes, primarily from the South, Midwest, and West, besting Dewey's largely Eastern-based 189 total. To make the victory sweeter, the Democrats regained control of Congress as well, thanks especially to support from Republican-wary farmers, industrial workers, and African Americans.

Elected in his own right, Truman outlined a sweeping **Fair Deal** program in his 1949 message to Congress. Remarkable in scope and ambition, it called for improved housing, full employment, national health insurance, a higher minimum wage, better farm price supports, further rural electrification, an extension of Social Security, protection for civil rights (including support for anti-lynching legislation), and increased aid to developing countries. Most of the Fair Deal fell victim to vehement congressional opposition from Republicans and Southern Democrats. The only major successes came in raising the minimum wage, providing for public housing in the Housing Act of 1949, and extending old-age insurance to many more beneficiaries through the Social Security Act of 1950. Despite stiff legislative obstacles to broad reform, seismic shifts in the domestic economy were about to bring substantial improvements to many Americans' lives.

32-16 The Eruption of Affluence, 1950–1970

Gross national product began a halting climb in 1948. Then, beginning about 1950, the American economy surged onto an exceptional path of sustained growth that was to last virtually uninterrupted for two decades. America's economic performance became the envy of the world. National income nearly doubled in the 1950s and almost doubled again in the 1960s, shooting through the trillion-dollar mark in 1973. Americans, some 6 percent of the world's people, were enjoying about 40 percent of the planet's wealth.

This fantastic explosion of prosperity did not enrich all Americans and it did not touch all people evenly. But it transformed the lives of a majority of citizens and molded the agenda of politics and society for at least two generations. Prosperity underwrote social mobility; it paved the way for the eventual success of the civil rights movement; it eventually funded vast new social welfare programs, like Medicare; and it gave American leaders the resources and credibility to exercise unprecedented international leadership of the Cold War's "free world."

As the gusher of postwar prosperity poured forth its riches, Americans drank deeply from the gilded goblet. Millions of depression-pinched souls sought to make up for the sufferings of the 1930s. They determined to "get theirs" while the getting was good. A people who had once considered a chicken

In his inaugural address in January 1949, President Harry S. Truman (1884–1972) said,

"Communism is based on the belief that man is so weak and inadequate that he is unable to govern himself, and therefore requires the rule of strong masters. . . . Democracy is based on the conviction that man has the moral and intellectual capacity, as well as the inalienable right, to govern himself with reason and justice."

As Truman's Fair Deal was rebuffed by a hostile Congress, critics like the conservative *New York Daily News* gloated that the odious New Deal was finally vanquished:

"The New Deal is kaput like the Thirty Years' War or the Black Plague or other disasters. . . . [Its demise] is like coming out of the darkness into sunlight. Like feeling clean again after a long time in the muck."

in every pot the standard of comfort and security now could imagine two cars in every garage, swimming pools in their backyards, and family vacations to destinations near and far. The size of the "middle class," defined as households earning between $3,000 and $10,000 a year, doubled from pre–Great Depression days to include 60 percent of the American people by the mid-1950s.

Rising incomes gave American families money to buy new products. By 1960, nearly 90 percent of households owned a television set—a gadget invented in the 1920s but virtually unknown until the late 1940s. In another revolution of sweeping consequences, almost 60 percent of American families owned their own homes by 1960, compared with less than 40 percent in the 1920s.

Cheap energy helped to feed the economic boom. American and European companies controlled the flow of abundant petroleum from the sandy expanses of the Middle East and kept prices low. Anticipating a limitless future of low-cost fuels, the nation flung out endless ribbons of highways, installed air-conditioning in homes and offices, and engineered a sixfold increase in the country's electricity-generating capacity between 1945 and 1970. Spidery grids of electrical cables carried the pent-up power of oil, gas, coal, and falling water to run the tools of workers on the factory floor.

Workers, in turn, chalked up spectacular gains in productivity, which increased at an average rate of more than 3 percent per year in the two decades after the Korean War. Gains in productivity were also enhanced by the rising educational level of the workforce—thanks in large part to the GI Bill. By 1970, nearly 90 percent of the school-age population was enrolled in educational institutions—a dramatic contrast with the opening years of the century, when only half of this age group had attended school.

Better educated and better equipped, American workers in 1970 could produce nearly twice as much in an hour's labor as they had in 1950, and this rising productivity virtually doubled the average American's standard of living. When the link between productivity gains and income growth began to rupture in the 1970s, it signaled the beginning of the end of the postwar golden age (refer to Figure 38.5 on p. 1035).

Of all the beneficiaries of postwar prosperity, none reaped greater rewards than women. More than ever, urban offices and shops provided a bonanza of employment for female workers. The great majority of new jobs created in the postwar era went to women, as the service sector of the economy dramatically outgrew the old industrial and manufacturing sectors. Women accounted for a quarter of the American workforce at the end of World War II and for nearly half the labor pool five decades later.

Yet even as women continued their march into the workplace in the postwar years, popular culture glorified the traditional feminine roles of homemaker and mother. The clash between the prescriptive demands of suburban housewifery and the realities of employment eventually sparked a feminist revolt.

32-17 The Boost of Big Science

Wars both hot and cold also provided a powerful stimulus for this unprecedented economic explosion. While other industrialized nations had been bombed to rubble during World War II, the United States had used the war crisis to fire up its smokeless factories and rebuild its depression-plagued economy. Invigorated by battle but far removed from the fighting, then further boosted by postwar reconstruction initiatives, U.S. manufacturers had almost effortlessly come to dominate the ruined global landscape of the postwar period.

The glittering prosperity of the 1950s and 1960s also rested on the underpinnings of colossal Cold War military budgets, leading some critics to speak of a "permanent war economy" (refer to Figure 32.1). The economic upturn of 1950 was fueled by massive appropriations for the Korean War, and defense spending accounted for some 10 percent of the GNP throughout the ensuing decade. Pentagon dollars primed the pumps of high-technology industries such as aerospace, plastics, and electronics, becoming a financier and a deep-pocketed customer for new inventions like mainframe computers and microchips. The escalating arms race—as well as the accompanying need for sophisticated tools of surveillance and missile alert systems—drove advances in nuclear physics and telecommunication.

The equation was simple: National security depended on technological superiority, which entailed costly facilities for scientific research and ambitious efforts to recruit and train scientists. After the Soviets launched the world's first artificial satellite (*Sputnik I*) in 1957, the international space race became America's top scientific priority, unleashing a new wave of public spending on transistorized electronics and computer-aided communications.

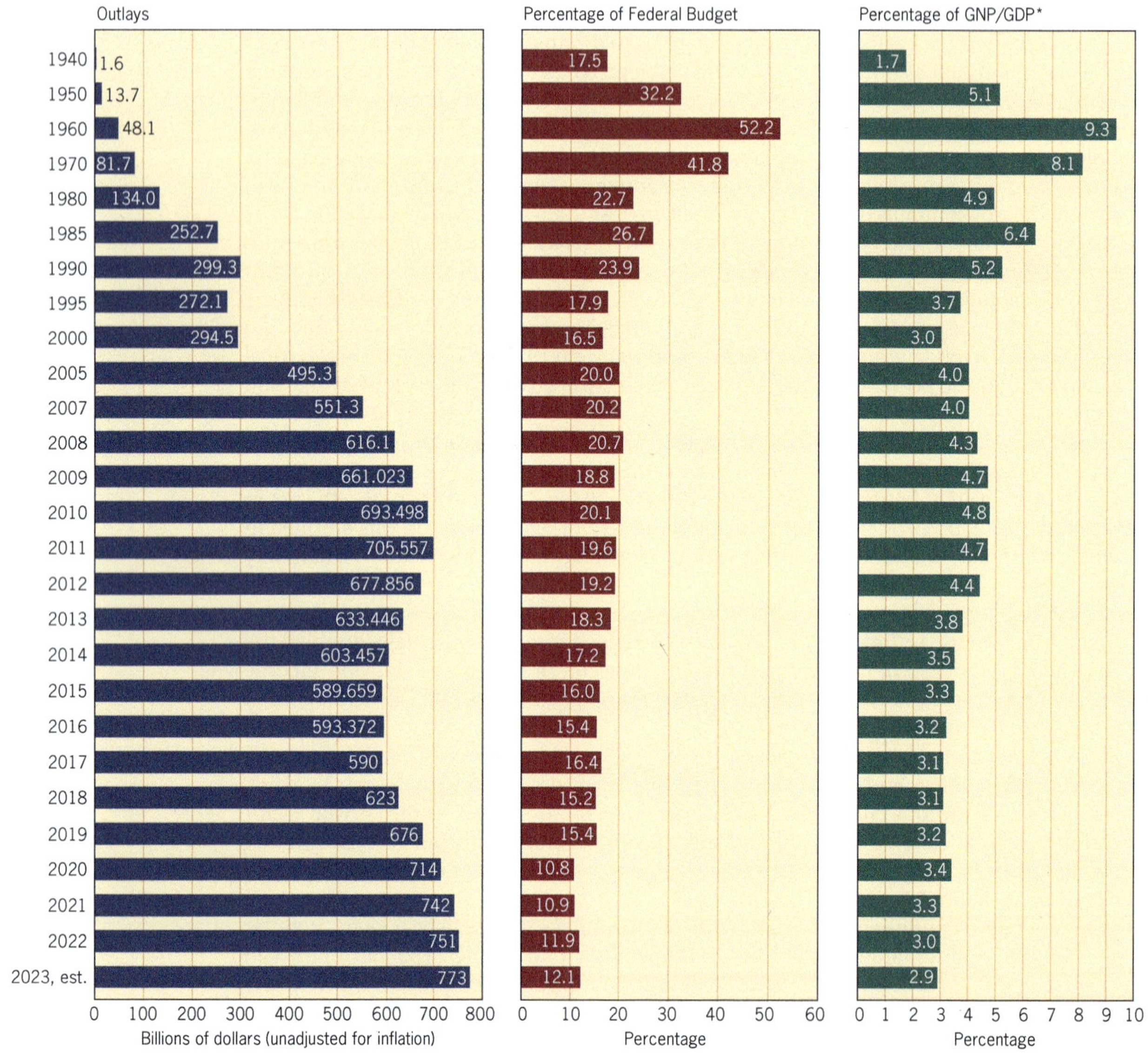

Figure 32.1 National Defense Budget, 1940–2023* Gross *national* product (GNP) was used before 1960. It includes income from overseas investment and excludes profits generated in the United States but accruing to foreign accounts. Gross *domestic* product (GDP), used thereafter, excludes overseas profits owed to American accounts but includes the value of all items originating in the United States, regardless of the destination of the profits. Until recent years those factors made for negligible differences in the calculation of *national* and *domestic* product, but most economists now prefer the latter approach.

Sources: *Statistical Abstract of the United States*, from US Office of Management and Budget [Congressional Budget Office], *Budget of the United States Government, Historical Tables*, annual. https://www.whitehouse.gov/omb/historical-tables/

In the 1950s, defense industries employed two-thirds of the nation's scientists and engineers. Laboratories, reactors, accelerators, and observatories proliferated. Some of these were government facilities. But, taking a cue from the mobilization of scientists during World War II—an "army of brains" spread across academic and industrial research laboratories as well as top-secret Manhattan Project outposts—postwar "Big Science" leaned heavily on universities and private-sector firms.

American universities, already swelling thanks to the GI Bill and a growing middle class, further expanded as federal money poured in. No longer ivory towers, they became "multiversities" with a significant economic impact on the regions around them. American aerospace and electronics manufacturers delivered a similar boost to regional productivity, vastly increasing productive capacities and payrolls. Concentrations of defense research and production emerged, notably along Route 128 outside Boston and in the agricultural Santa Clara Valley of Northern California—later rebranded "Silicon Valley."

32-18 The Smiling Sunbelt

Image 32.16 Agribusiness Expensive machinery of the sort shown here made most of American agriculture a capital-intensive, phenomenally productive big business by the twenty-first century—and sounded the death knell for many small-scale family farms.

The growth of the defense economy was among several momentous changes in the nation's basic economic structure. Also conspicuous was the accelerating shift of the workforce out of agriculture, which achieved productivity gains virtually unmatched by any other economic sector. Thanks largely to mechanization and to rich new fertilizers—as well as to government subsidies and price supports—one farmworker by the century's end could produce food for over fifty people, compared with about fifteen people in the 1940s.

The family farm nearly became an antique artifact as consolidation produced giant agribusinesses able to employ costly machinery (refer to Image 32.16). Farmers whose forebears had busted sod with oxen or horses now plowed their fields in air-conditioned tractor cabs, listening on their stereophonic radios to weather forecasts or the latest Chicago commodities market quotations. Once the mighty backbone of the agricultural Republic, and still some 15 percent of the labor force at the end of World War II, farmers made up a slim2 percent of working Americans by the turn of the twenty-first century—yet they fed much of the world.

These structural changes reflected—and in turn helped remake—the nation's economic geography. Especially striking was the growth of the **Sunbelt**—a fifteen-state area stretching in a smiling crescent from Virginia through Florida and Texas to Arizona and California. Within the Sunbelt was the "gunbelt" of defense manufacturing: the California electronics industry, the aerospace complexes of Florida and Texas, and the huge military installations that powerful Southern congressional representatives secured for their districts (refer to Map 32.4).

Drawn chiefly by jobs but also by warm climates made freshly livable by air conditioning, Americans increased the Sunbelt's population at a rate nearly double that of the old industrial zones of the Northeast (the "Frostbelt"). In the 1950s, California alone accounted for one-fifth of the entire nation's population growth and by 1963 had outdistanced New York as the most populous state—a position it still held in the twenty-first century with a 2020 population of almost 40 million, or close to one out of every eight Americans.

These dramatic shifts of population and wealth further broke the historic grip of the North on the nation's political life. Every elected occupant of the White House from 1964 to 2008 hailed from the Sunbelt, and the region's congressional representation (and weight in the Electoral College) rose as its population grew.

32-19 The Rush to the Suburbs

In all regions, another momentous population shift occurred in the postwar years: the mass movement of American families from cities to burgeoning suburbs (refer to "Makers of America: The Suburbanites," pp. 870–871). Suburbanization was not new. Americans with the means and mobility long had sought respite from the urban maelstrom by moving to the urban periphery. But in the post-WWII era, the suburban dream became much more widely attainable—and desirable—due largely to government policy.

The postwar suburban migration altered family life, consumption patterns, religious practices, and political allegiances. Yet it did little to alter deeply rooted patterns of residential segregation by race, nor discriminatory housing market practices. In the first decades of America's move to the suburbs, nonwhite citizens were conspicuously absent.

While other industrial countries struggled to rebuild their war-ravaged cities, policies in the United States encouraged movement away from urban centers. Federal Housing Administration (FHA) and Veterans Administration (VA) home-loan guarantees made it more economically attractive to own a home in the suburbs than to rent an apartment in the city. Tax deductions for

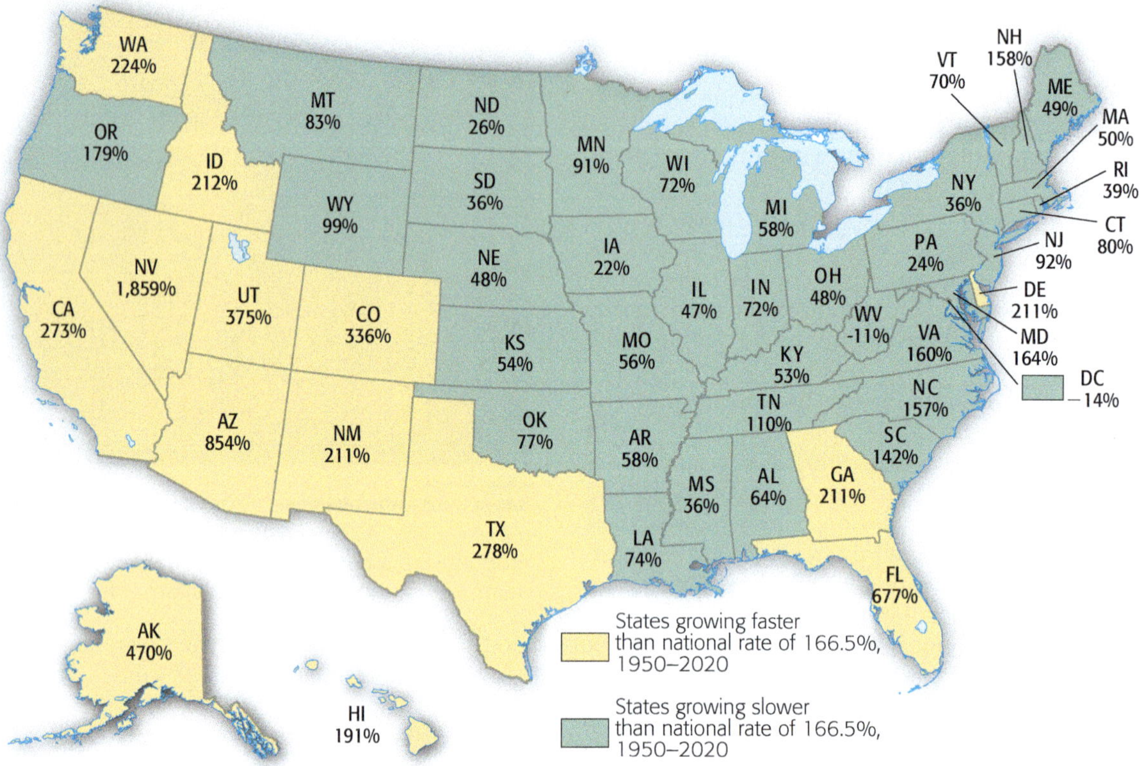

Map 32.4 Distribution of Population Increase, 1950–2020 States with figures higher than 166.5 percent were growing faster than the national average between 1950 and 2020. Note that much of the growth was in the "Sunbelt," a loose geographical concept, as some Deep South states had very little population growth, whereas the mountain and Pacific states were booming.

interest payments on home mortgages provided additional financial incentive. And government-built highways that sped commuters from suburban homes to city jobs further facilitated this mass migration. By 1960, one in every four Americans dwelt in suburbia, and a half-century later, more than half the nation's population did.

The construction industry boomed in the 1950s and 1960s to satisfy this demand. Pioneered by innovators like the Levitt brothers, whose first **Levittown** sprouted on New York's Long Island in the 1940s, builders revolutionized the techniques of home construction (refer to Image 32.17). Erecting hundreds or even thousands of dwellings in a single project, specialized crews working from standardized plans laid foundations, while others raised factory-assembled framing modules, put on roofs, strung wires, installed plumbing, and finished the walls in record time and with cost-cutting efficiency. Snooty critics wailed about the aesthetic monotony of the suburban "tract" developments, but eager homebuyers nevertheless moved into them by the millions.

The Supreme Court ruled in 1948 in *Shelley v. Kraemer* that racially restrictive covenants—a tool long deployed by realtors and homeowners to prevent racial and religious minorities from buying into all-white neighborhoods—could not be enforced. However, while white realtors and homeowners were prevented from using explicitly "racial" reasons to exclude Black buyers, they were able to pass zoning laws—specifying minimum lot and house sizes or population densities, for example—that discouraged low-income housing and maintained racially homogenous neighborhoods. "White flight" to the leafy green suburbs thus hollowed out the inner cities—especially those in the Northeast and Midwest—leaving them Black, brown, and broke as taxpaying businesses fled with their affluent customers from downtown shops to suburban shopping malls (another post–World War II invention). Black migrants from the South, blocked from settling in the suburbs, filled up the inner-city neighborhoods that were abandoned by the departing white middle class.

Government policies contributed to this pattern of deepening residential segregation. Supported by federal appraisal rules in which "risk" became a euphemism for "race" (refer to "The Presence of the Past: 'Redlining,' Residential Racial Segregation, and Homeownership," pp. 790–791), banks and other mortgage lenders often excluded entire neighborhoods from eligibility for home financing, making it difficult for Black and other nonwhite citizens to purchase homes. Known as **redlining**, this discriminatory practice further limited the mobility of Black Americans out of the central cities and made decent and affordable housing difficult to find. Redlining also had long-term, multi-generational effects, feeding the stubborn "wealth gap" between white and Black families. Because home values are most American families' principal financial asset, historical inequalities in real estate markets have impeded the ability of non-homeowners to generate wealth and pass it down from one generation to the next.

ClassicStock/Alamy Stock Photo

Image 32.17 A Model Home at Levittown Using mass-construction techniques and fueled by new home financing programs backed by the federal government, homebuilders William and Alfred Levitt built suburban homes by the thousands in New York, New Jersey, and Pennsylvania.

32-20 The Postwar Baby Boom

Alongside its economic boom, America experienced an equally dramatic **baby boom**—the huge leap in the birthrate in the decade and a half after 1945. Confident young men and women tied the nuptial knot in record numbers at war's end, and they began immediately to fill the nation's empty cradles. They thus touched off a demographic explosion that added more than 50 million bawling babies to the nation's population by the end of the 1950s.

The extraordinary mobility of the era added a further jolt to the baby boom's earthquake. For some three decades after 1945, an average of 30 million people changed residences every year. Families especially felt the strain, as distance divided parents from children, and brothers and sisters from one another. One sign of this sort of stress was the phenomenal popularity of advice books on child-rearing, especially Dr. Benjamin Spock's *The Common Sense Book of Baby and Child Care*. First published in 1945, it instructed millions of parents during the ensuing decades in the kind of homely wisdom that was once transmitted naturally from grandparent to parent.

As the oversize postwar generation grew to maturity, it was destined—like the fabled pig passing through the python—to strain and distort many aspects of American life. Elementary-school enrollments, for example, swelled to nearly 34 million pupils in 1970. Then began a steady decline, as the onward-marching age group left in its wake closed schools and unemployed teachers. The soaring birthrate crested in 1957 and was followed by a deepening birth dearth. By 1973, fertility rates had dropped below the point necessary to maintain existing population figures without further immigration.

Yet the maturing babies of the postwar era sent economic shock waves undulating through the decades. As tykes and toddlers in the 1940s and 1950s, "baby-boomers" made up a lucrative market for manufacturers of canned food and other baby products. As teenagers in the 1960s and 1970s, the same youngsters spent an estimated $20 billion a year for clothes and recorded rock music—and their sheer numbers laid the basis of the much-ballyhooed "youth culture" of that tumultuous decade.

In the 1980s, the horde of baby boomers bumped and jostled one another in the job market, struggling to get a foothold on the crowded ladder of social mobility. As the boomers entered middle age, a "secondary boom" of children peaked in the early 1990s—a faint demographic echo of the postwar population explosion. The impact of the huge postwar generation rippled through American society well into the twenty-first century, as its members passed into retirement and placed enormous strains on the Social Security and Medicare systems.

Makers of America

The Suburbanites

Few images evoke more vividly the prosperity of the postwar era than aerial photographs of sprawling suburbs. Neat rows of look-alike tract houses, each with a driveway and lawn and here and there a backyard swimming pool, came to symbolize the capacity of the economy to deliver the "American dream" to millions of families.

Suburbanization was hardly new. Well-off city dwellers had beaten paths to leafy outlying neighborhoods since the nineteenth century. But after 1945, the steady flow became a stampede. The baby boom, new highways, government guarantees for mortgage lending, and favorable tax policies all made suburbia blossom.

Who were the Americans racing to the new postwar suburbs? War veterans led the way in the late 1940s, aided by Veterans Administration mortgages that featured tiny down payments and low interest rates. The general public soon followed. The Federal Housing Administration (FHA) offered insured mortgages with low down payments and 2 to 3 percent interest rates on thirty-year loans. With deals like this, it was hardly surprising that American families flocked into "Levittowns," built by William and Alfred Levitt, and other similar suburban developments.

People of all kinds found their way to suburbia, heading for neighborhoods that varied from the posh to the plain. Yet for all this diversity, the overwhelming majority of suburbanites were white and middle-class. Racial discrimination by mortgage lenders made it difficult for the more than 1 million Black veterans of World War II to take advantage of the VA loans that allowed so many of their fellow soldiers to become first-time homebuyers. Convinced that the presence of minorities would depress property values, white homeowners sometimes violently intimidated prospective Black buyers. Some unscrupulous realtors capitalized on this racial animus to engage in "block-busting"—selling homes at inflated prices to one or two Black families, and buying up the remaining properties of panicked whites who fled and sold at distressed prices. As a result, postwar American metropolitan areas became ever more starkly segregated. Only 347 of the 120,000 units of housing built in metropolitan Philadelphia between 1946 and 1953 were open to Black occupants.

Image 32.18 "Average Americans" in Levittown Robert and Peggy Rehn, their young sons, and their family dog walk through the newly constructed suburb of Levittown, New York. With a mortgage, an annual income of about $3,000, and a wife who was a full-time homemaker, Robert Rehn "fit the 'average American' to a 't,'" declared the original caption to this 1951 photograph.

Life in the suburbs brought both opportunity and conformity. Men tended to work in either white-collar jobs or upper-level blue-collar positions such as foremen. Women usually worked in the home, so much so that suburbia came to symbolize the domestic confinement that feminists in the 1960s and 1970s decried in their campaign for women's rights.

The house itself became more important than ever as postwar suburbanites built their leisure lives around television, home improvement projects, and barbecues on the patio. The center of family life shifted to the fenced-in backyard, as neighborly city habits of visiting on the front stoop, gabbing on the sidewalk, and strolling to local stores disappeared. Institutions that had thrived as social centers in the city—churches, women's clubs, fraternal organizations, and taverns—had a tougher time attracting patrons in the privatized world of postwar suburbia.

The suburbs were a boon to the automobile, as parents jumped behind the wheel to shuttle children, groceries, and golf clubs to and fro. The second car, once an unheard-of luxury, became a practical "necessity" for suburban families constantly "on the go." A car culture sprang up with new destinations, like drive-through restaurants and drive-in movies. Roadside shopping centers edged out downtowns as places to shop. Meanwhile, the new interstate highway system enabled breadwinners to live farther and farther from their jobs and still commute to work daily.

Many suburbanites continued to depend on cities for jobs, though by the 1980s the suburbs themselves were becoming "edge cities" and important sites of

J. R. Eyerman/The LIFE Picture Collection/Shutterstock.com

Image 32.19 Drive-in Movie Theater, Utah, 1958 Going to the movies became one more thing Americans could do in their cars in the 1950s. Here moviegoers watch Charlton Heston as Moses in the Academy Award–winning motion picture *The Ten Commandments*. It was the last film made by famed director Cecil B. DeMille.

Harold M. Lambert/Getty Images

Image 32.20 Aerial View of the On-ramps to a Typical New Interstate Highway, 1950s

employment. Wherever they worked, suburbanites turned their backs on the city and its problems. They fought to maintain their communities as secluded retreats, independent municipalities with their own taxes, schools, and zoning restrictions designed to keep out public housing and the poor. Even the naming of towns and streets reflected a pastoral ideal. Poplar Terrace and Mountainview Drive were popular street names; East Paterson, New Jersey, was renamed Elmwood Park in 1973. With a majority of Americans living in suburbs by the 1980s, cities lost their political clout and much of the tax base that supported crucial public services. As local television news beamed out stories of "urban crisis" into suburban living rooms, the economic and social divides between city and suburb yawned even wider.

Middle-class African Americans began to move to the suburbs in substantial numbers by the 1980s, but even that migration failed to alter dramatically the racial divide of metropolitan America. Black suburbanites settled in towns like Rolling Oaks outside Miami or Brook Glen near Atlanta—Black middle-class towns in white-majority counties. Meanwhile, new immigrants from across the globe turned suburbs from California to Michigan into self-segregated "ethnoburbs." By the beginning of the twenty-first century, suburbia as a whole was more racially and economically diverse than at midcentury. But old patterns of residential segregation endured, and economic inequality increasingly separated older and poorer "inner-ring" suburbs from newer more affluent ones.

Varying Viewpoints

Who Was to Blame for the Cold War?

Whose fault was the Cold War? (And, for that matter, who should get credit for ending it?) For two decades after World War II, American historians generally agreed that the aggressive Soviets were solely responsible. This "orthodox" or "official" appraisal squared with the traditional view of the United States as a virtuous, innocent land with an idealistic foreign policy. This point of view also justified America's Cold War containment policy, which cast the Soviet Union as the aggressor that must be confined by an ever-vigilant United States. America supposedly had only defensive intentions, with no expansionary ambitions of its own.

In the 1960s, a vigorous revisionist interpretation flowered, powerfully influenced by disillusion over U.S. involvement in Vietnam. The revisionists stood the orthodox view on its head. The Soviets, they argued, had only defensive intentions at the end of World War II; it was the Americans who had behaved provocatively by brandishing their new atomic weaponry. Some of these critics pointed an accusing finger at President Truman, alleging that he abandoned Roosevelt's conciliatory approach to the Soviets and adopted a bullying attitude, emboldened by the American atomic monopoly.

More radical revisionists like Gabriel and Joyce Kolko even claimed to have found the roots of Truman's alleged belligerence in long-standing American policies of economic imperialism—policies that eventually resulted in the tragedy of Vietnam (refer to "33-8 A 'New Look' in Foreign Policy," p. 887). In this view, the Vietnam War followed logically from America's insatiable "need" for overseas markets and raw materials. Vietnam itself may have been economically unimportant, but, so the argument ran, a communist Vietnam represented an intolerable challenge to American hegemony. Revisionists cited their own version of the "domino theory," which war apologists used to defend America's military actions in Vietnam. According to the domino theory, if the United States declined to fight in Vietnam, other countries would lose their faith in America's will (or their fear of American power) and would tumble one after the other like "dominoes" into the Soviet camp. Revisionists stressed what they saw as the *economic necessity* behind the domino theory: losing in Vietnam, they claimed, would unravel the American economy.

In the 1970s, a "postrevisionist" interpretation emerged that is widely agreed upon today. Historians such as John Lewis Gaddis and Melvyn Leffler pooh-pooh the economic determinism of the revisionists, while frankly acknowledging that the United States did have vital security interests at stake in the post–World War II era. The postrevisionists analyze the ways in which inherited ideas (like isolationism) and the contentious nature of postwar domestic politics, as well as miscalculations by American leaders, led a nation in search of security into seeking not simply a sufficiency but a "preponderance" of power. The American *overreaction* to its security needs, these scholars suggest, exacerbated U.S.-Soviet relations and precipitated the four-decade-long nuclear arms race that formed the centerpiece of the Cold War.

In the case of Vietnam, the postrevisionist historians focus not on economic necessity but on a failure of political intelligence, induced by the stressful conditions of the Cold War, that made the dubious domino theory seem plausible. Misunderstanding Vietnamese intentions, exaggerating Soviet ambitions, and fearing to appear "soft on communism" in the eyes of their domestic political rivals, American leaders plunged into Vietnam, sadly misguided by their own Cold War obsessions.

Most postrevisionists, however, still lay the lion's share of the blame for the Cold War on the Soviet Union. By the same token, they credit the Soviets with ending the Cold War—a view hotly disputed by Ronald Reagan's champions, who claim that it was his anti-Soviet policies in the 1980s that brought the Russians to their knees (refer to "38-4 The Politics of Inequality," pp. 1033–1036). The great unknown, of course, is the precise nature of Soviet thinking in the Cold War years. Were Soviet aims predominantly defensive, or did the Kremlin incessantly plot world conquest? Was there an opportunity for reconciliation with the West following Stalin's death in 1953? Should Mikhail Gorbachev or Ronald Reagan be remembered as the leader who ended the Cold War? With the opening of Soviet archives, scholars are eagerly pursued answers to such questions, leading to a fresh wave of scholarship about the Soviet Union and the Communist bloc.

Chapter Summary

With the death of Franklin Roosevelt as World War II came to a close, Harry S. Truman suddenly was launched into the presidency. Regarded at first as a weak and fumbling figure, Truman evolved into a courageous statesman who boldly addressed unprecedented international and domestic challenges. The Yalta Conference near the end of World War II left major issues undecided and created growing controversy over postwar relations with the Soviet Union. The two new ideologically incompatible superpowers soon found themselves at odds over Eastern Europe, Germany, and the Middle East. A battered Europe, especially in Italy and France, threatened to succumb to powerful internal Communist parties.

The Truman Doctrine announced military aid to threatened noncommunist nations and an ideological crusade against international communism. The Marshall Plan provided economic assistance to starving and communist-threatened Europe, which soon joined the United States in the permanent NATO military alliance. But the triumph of communism in China created bitter divisions within the United States. Communist North Korea's unprovoked attack on pro-Western South Korea in 1950 led to the seesaw Korean War and a massive American military buildup. General MacArthur's insubordination and threats to expand the war to China led Truman to fire him.

Issues of the Cold War and civil rights fractured the Democratic party three ways in 1948, but a gutsy Truman campaign overcame the divisions to win a triumphant underdog victory over Dewey, Thurmond, and Wallace.

The Cold War and revelations of Soviet spying aroused deep fears of communist subversion at home, which spread into a general assault on alleged communist sympathizers as well as the socially marginal. Demagogic Wisconsin senator Joseph McCarthy gained immense power with his irresponsible attacks, but his influence finally collapsed after he attacked the U.S. Army.

In the immediate postwar years there were widespread fears of a return to depression. But fueled by cheap energy, increased worker productivity, and government programs like the GI Bill of Rights, the economy began a spectacular expansion that lasted from 1950 to 1970. This burst of affluence transformed American industry and society. More women joined the workforce even as popular culture glorified the roles of mother and homemaker.

Footloose Americans migrated to the Sunbelts of the South and West and to the growing suburbs. Government policies encouraged private-bank "redlining" that restricted home buying by ethnic minorities, leaving inner cities with a higher number of economically disadvantaged residents. Families grew rapidly, as the "baby boom" created a population bulge that would last for decades.

Key Terms

- Yalta Conference (847)
- Cold War (849)
- Bretton Woods Conference (849)
- United Nations (UN) (849)
- Nuremberg war crimes trial (850)
- Berlin airlift (851)
- containment doctrine (852)
- Truman Doctrine (852)
- Marshall Plan (853)
- North Atlantic Treaty Organization (NATO) (855)
- National Security Council Memorandum Number 68 (NSC-68) (857)
- Korean War (858)
- Defense Production Act of 1950 (858)
- House Un-American Activities Committee (HUAC) (859)
- McCarthyism (860)
- Army-McCarthy hearings (860)
- Executive Order 9981 (862)
- Taft-Hartley Act (862)
- Operation Dixie (862)
- Employment Act of 1946 (862)
- GI Bill (862)
- Fair Deal (864)
- Sunbelt (867)
- Levittown (868)
- redlining (869)
- baby boom (869)

People to Know

- Joseph Stalin
- Jiang Jieshi (Chiang Kai-shek)
- Alger Hiss
- George F. Kennan
- George C. Marshall
- Joseph McCarthy
- Reinhold Niebuhr
- Julius and Ethel Rosenberg
- Benjamin Spock

Chronology

1944	• Servicemen's Readjustment Act (GI Bill)	• Bretton Woods economic conference
1945	• Spock publishes *The Common Sense Book of Baby and Child Care* • Yalta Conference	• United States ends lend-lease to USSR • United Nations established
1945–1946	• Nuremberg war crimes trial in Germany	
1946	• Employment Act creates Council of Economic Advisers • Iran crisis	• Kennan's "Long Telegram" lays out "containment doctrine"
1946–1948	• Tokyo war crimes trials	
1947	• Truman Doctrine • Marshall Plan • Taft-Hartley Act	• National Security Act creates Department of Defense, National Security Council (NSC), and Central Intelligence Agency (CIA)
1948	• Israel founded; United States recognizes it • "Voice of America" begins radio broadcasts behind iron curtain	• Alger Hiss case begins • Truman defeats Dewey for presidency
1948–1949	• Berlin blockade	
1949	• NATO established • Communists defeat Nationalists in China	• Soviets explode their first atomic bomb
1950	• American economy begins postwar growth • McCarthy red hunt begins	• McCarran Internal Security Bill passed by Congress over Truman's veto
1950–1953	• Korean War	
1951	• Truman fires MacArthur	• Rosenbergs convicted of treason
1952	• United States explodes first hydrogen bomb	
1954	• Army-McCarthy hearings	
1957	• Postwar peak of U.S. birthrate	
1973	• U.S. birthrate falls below replacement level	

To Learn More

Dean Acheson, *Present at the Creation: My Years in the State Department* (1969)

Elizabeth Borgwardt, *A New Deal for the World: America's Vision for Human Rights* (2005)

Mark Brilliant and David M. Kennedy, eds., *World War II and the West It Wrought* (2020)

Lizabeth Cohen, *A Consumers' Republic: The Politics of Mass Consumption in Postwar America* (2003)

David M. P. Freund, *Colored Property* (2007)

John Lewis Gaddis, *The Cold War: A New History* (2005)

_______, *George F. Kennan: An American Life* (2011)

Herbert J. Gans, *The Levittowners* (1967)

David Halberstam, *The Coldest Winter: America and the Korean War* (2007)

Kenneth T. Jackson, *Crabgrass Frontier: The Suburbanization of the United States* (1985)

Jennifer Klein, *For All These Rights: Business, Labor, and the Shaping of America's Public-Private Welfare State* (2003)

Kevin Kruse and Thomas Sugrue, eds., *The New Suburban History* (2006)

Margaret O'Mara, *Cities of Knowledge: Cold War Science and the Search for the Next Silicon Valley* (2004)

Ellen Schrecker, *Many Are the Crimes: McCarthyism in America* (1998)

Bruce Schulman, *From Cotton Belt to Sunbelt: Federal Policy, Economic Development, and the Transformation of the South* (1991)

Chapter 33

Affluence and Anxiety: 1952–1963

Our soil is fertile, our agriculture productive. The air rings with the song of our industry—rolling mills and blast furnaces, dynamos, dams and assembly lines—the chorus of America the bountiful. . . . We live in a land of plenty, but rarely has this earth known such peril as today.

Dwight D. Eisenhower, January 21, 1957

Chapter Outline

- The postwar boom and new digital technologies
- Working women and feminism
- Consumer culture in the 1950s
- The election of Dwight D. Eisenhower
- Desegregation and the civil rights revolution
- Eisenhower Republicanism
- Cold War crises
- The space race and the arms race
- The election of John F. Kennedy, 1960
- Postwar writers, painters, and architect
- Kennedy's New Frontier
- "Flexible response" and the Vietnam quagmire
- Bay of Pigs invasion and the Cuban missile crisis
- The struggle for civil rights
- Kennedy assassinated, November 22, 1963

Unmatched in power or plenty, the United States bestrode the world like a colossus as the 1950s began to unfold. Broadly shared prosperity fueled confidence in the country's capacity to tackle major problems at home and abroad. But problems abounded nonetheless. Americans at midcentury were dug into the frontlines of the global Cold War while bitterly divided at home over the explosive issues of communist subversion and civil rights.

Focus Questions

1. What changes in the American economy and workforce fueled the rise of a mass, popular consumer culture in the 1950s?
2. What were the origins of the modern American civil rights movement, and what challenges did it face amid the generally conservative political and social environment of the 1950s? What enabled the movement to gain political momentum by the early 1960s?
3. What were the fundamental principles of "Eisenhower Republicanism" at home and abroad? How did Eisenhower manage to address numerous Cold War crises while avoiding war?
4. How did the American cultural "renaissance" of the 1950s and early 1960s reflect American affluence and prestige? Which writers and artists were more critical of America and the "American dream"?
5. Why did John F. Kennedy's "New Frontier" raise such high expectations, and to what extent were those expectations met at home and abroad?

Examining the Evidence: Advertising Prosperity, 1950s

Contending Voices: The "Kitchen Debate"

33-1 Affluence and Its Anxieties

The continuing post–World War II economic boom wrought wondrous changes in American society in the 1950s. Prosperity triggered an unprecedented surge in home construction, as a nation of renters became a nation of homeowners. One of every four homes standing in America in 1960 had been built during the 1950s, and 83 percent of those new homes were in suburbia.

Propelled by military spending and public investment in research, American science and technology fueled fabulous economic growth. The invention of the transistor in 1947 sparked a revolution in electronics, especially in computers. The first electronic computers assembled in the 1940s—called "electronic brains" by awed observers—were massive machines with hundreds of miles of wiring and thousands of fickle cathode ray tubes (refer to Image 33.1). Transistors and, later, printed circuits on silicon wafers made possible dramatic miniaturization and phenomenal computational speed. "Information processing" by computers transformed age-old business practices like billing and inventory control and incited further worries about automation's threat to American jobs. Enormous databases began to catalog American buying habits and personal information, soon raising alarms about computerized invasions of privacy that foreshadowed later and far greater debates over online privacy in the twenty-first century.

Few corporations epitomized America's postwar moment more vividly than the computer industry's market leader, **International Business Machines (IBM)**. From its nineteenth-century beginnings designing mechanical tabulators for the U.S. Census Bureau, the company known as "Big Blue" blossomed into a twentieth-century colossus of information processing. Its heavy investment in research yielded at least five Nobel Prizes among its employees. Emblazoned on every wall, desktop, company publication, and print ad was a one-word slogan: "THINK." The organizational discipline and market success of corporations like IBM energized the economy, even as it was sharply criticized in popular books like *The Man in the Gray Flannel Suit* (1955) and *The Organization Man* (1956).

Aerospace industries also grew fantastically in the 1950s, thanks both to the government's buildup of the Strategic Air Command (SAC) and to a robustly expanding passenger airline business—as well as to connections between military and civilian aircraft production. In 1957, the Seattle-based Boeing Company brought out the first large passenger jet, the "707," whose design owed much to the previous development of SAC's long-range strategic bomber, the B-52.

Bettmann/Getty Images

Image 33.1 An Early Computer, ca. 1950 Just a few decades later, technological improvements would bring the computing power of this bulky behemoth to the user's desktop.

The nature of the workforce was also changing. A crucial shift was marked in 1956 when "white-collar" workers for the first time outnumbered "blue-collar" workers, signaling the passage from an industrial to a postindustrial, or service-based, economy. Amid that fundamental transformation, organized labor slowly withered along with the smokestack industries that had sustained it. Union membership as a percentage of the labor force peaked at about 33 percent in 1954 and then went into steady decline (refer to Figure 30.3, p. 798).

The surge in white-collar employment eventually opened special opportunities for women (refer to Table 33.1). When World War II ended, many women, including those who had worked in war plants, left the wage-paying workforce. Swelling paychecks and affordable homes allowed many families to live well on only one income. A "cult of domesticity" in popular culture celebrated the conventionally feminine roles of mother and homemaker. When 1950s television programs like *Ozzie and Harriet* or *Leave It to Beaver* depicted idealized suburban families with a working husband, two children, and a homebound wife, they did so without irony; much of middle-class white America really did live that way. But as the 1950s progressed, a quiet revolution was gaining momentum that was destined to transform women's roles and even the character of the American family (refer to "Examining the Evidence: Advertising Prosperity, 1950s," p. 879).

Table 33.1 Occupational Distribution of Workingwomen, 1900–2020*

	1900	1920	1940	1960	1980	2016	2020
Total white-collar workers†	17.8%	38.8%	44.9%	52.5%	65.6%	72.1%	73.8%
Clerical workers	4.0	18.7	21.5	28.7	30.5	28.9	26.3
Manual workers	27.8	23.8	21.6	18.0	14.8	6.0	6.9
Farmworkers	18.9	13.5	4.0	1.8	1.0	0.3	0.4
Service workers††	33.5	23.9	29.4	21.9	18.1	21.4	18.8

*Major categories; percentage of all women workers in each category, calculated at fourteen and older until 1970 and then sixteen and older.

†Includes clerical, sales, professional, and technical workers, managers, and officials.

††Includes domestic servants.

Sources: *Historical Statistics of the United States*, *Statistical Abstract of the United States*, and Bureau of Labor Statistics, relevant years.

Of some 40 million new jobs created in the three decades after 1950, more than 30 million were in clerical and service work. Women filled the huge majority of these new positions. They were the principal employment beneficiaries of the postwar era, creating an extensive "pink-collar ghetto" of occupations that came to be dominated by women (refer to Image 33.2 and Figure 33.1).

Exploding employment opportunities for women in the 1950s kept pace with rising levels of female education. Only 26 percent of American women over 25 had completed high school in 1940; by 1970, over 55 percent had their diplomas. The number of women with college degrees more than doubled during that period as well, from 3.8 to 8.2 percent.

These trends unleashed a groundswell of social and psychological shocks that mounted to tidal-wave proportions in the decades that followed. Women's new dual roles as *both* workers *and* homemakers raised urgent questions about family life and traditional definitions of gender differences. Feminist Betty Friedan gave focus and fuel to women's feelings in 1963 when she published ***The Feminine Mystique***, a runaway best seller and a classic of feminist protest literature that helped to launch the modern women's movement. Friedan spoke in rousing accents to millions of able, educated women who applauded her indictment of the stifling boredom of suburban housewifery.

Underwood Photo Archives/SuperStock

Image 33.2 The Booming Service Sector Services displaced manufacturing as the most dynamic area of the economy in the post–World War II era, and women made up a majority of new workers in the nation's offices, dominating new, fast-growing fields like electronic data processing. Here, employees of the Erie Railroad in Cleveland enter data using tabulating machines and punch cards.

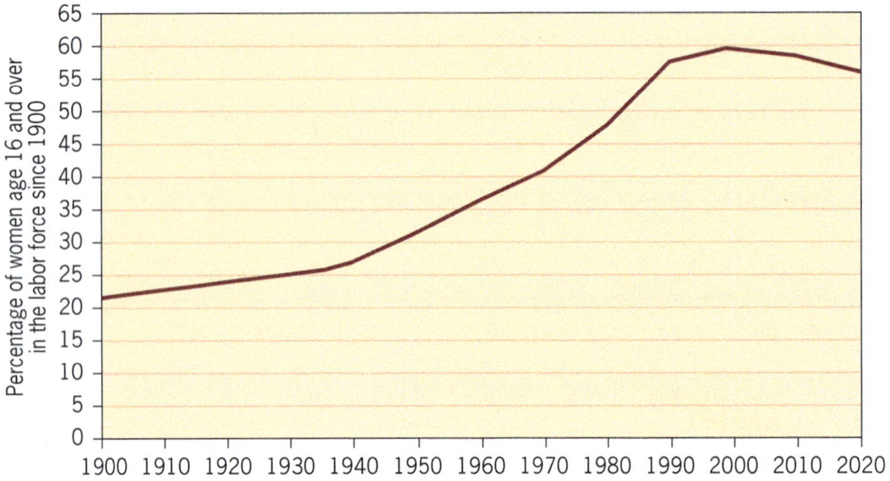

Figure 33.1 Women in the Labor Force, 1900–2020

Sources: *Historical Statistics of the United States* and *Statistical Abstract of the United States*, relevant years. BLS, Current Population Survey

33-2 Consumer Culture in the Fifties

The 1950s witnessed a huge expansion of the middle class and the blossoming of a consumer culture that defined a distinctive lifestyle. Diner's Club introduced the plastic credit card in 1949, just one year after the first "fast-food"–style McDonald's hamburger stand opened in San Bernardino, California (refer to Image 33.3). In 1955, Disneyland opened its doors in Anaheim, California. Easy credit, high-volume "fast-food" production, and new forms of leisure marked an emerging culture of consumption that soon moved beyond America's borders.

Everett Collection Historical/Alamy Stock Photo

Image 33.3 The Rise of the Golden Arches Maurice and Richard McDonald replaced their original drive-in hamburger stand in San Bernadino, California, with the iconic double-arched design in 1953. McDonald's soon became one of the largest franchised restaurant chains in the world and a global symbol of American consumerism. The chain's cultural importance is indicated by the fact that a detailed replica (shown here) of one of its first franchises, in Des Plaines, Illinois, serves as a historical museum for the company.

Examining the Evidence

Advertising Prosperity, 1950s

This Ford advertisement in a popular magazine encouraged readers to buy a second car. By the mid-1950s, once manufacturers had met the demand for cars, homes, appliances, and other consumer goods that a decade and a half of depression and world war had pent up, they worried about how to keep expanding their markets. "Planned obsolescence"—changing design frequently enough to necessitate replacement purchasing—was one strategy. Altering expectations about what consumers needed was another. This advertisement suggests that the up-to-date family, living in its modern-style suburban home, had no choice but to own two cars, one for the male breadwinner's business, the other for the wife's "ferrying the family." What kinds of gender role prescriptions are reinforced in this advertisement? What assumptions has Ford made about prospective buyers of its cars? How much can mass advertising tell us about the actual values of Americans living at a particular time?

Retro AdArchives/Alamy Stock Photo

Image 33.4 Promoting the "two-Ford family," 1950

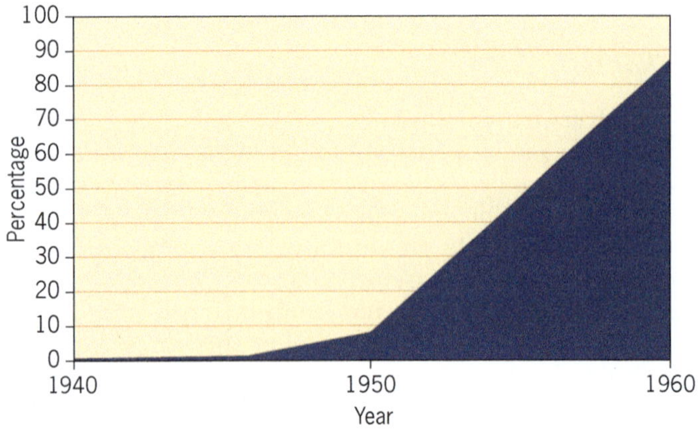

Figure 33.2 Percentage of Households with Television Sets, 1946–1960 Note the rapid adoption of this new device, a harbinger of the viral spread of technologies like cell phones and the Internet later in the century.

Crucial to the development of consumerism was the rapid rise of the new technology of television. Only 6 TV stations were broadcasting in 1946; a decade later, 442 stations were operating. TV sets were rich people's novelties in the 1940s, but 7 million sets were sold by 1951. By 1960, virtually every American home had one, in a stunning display of the speed with which new technologies can pervade and transform modern societies (refer to Figure 33.2).

Attendance at movies sank as the entertainment industry changed its focus from the silver screen to the picture tube. By the mid-1950s, advertisers annually spent $10 billion to hawk their wares on television, while critics fumed that the wildly popular new mass medium was degrading the public's aesthetic, social, moral, political, and educational standards. To the question "Why is television called a medium?" pundits replied, "Because it's never rare or well done."

Even religion capitalized on the powerful new electronic pulpit. Celebrity preachers and priests like the Baptist Billy Graham, the Pentecostal Holiness preacher Oral Roberts, and the Roman Catholic Fulton J. Sheen took to the airwaves to spread the Christian gospel. Television also catalyzed the commercialization of professional sports, as viewing audiences that once numbered in the stadium-capacity thousands could now be counted in the couch-potato millions.

Sports also reflected the shift in population toward the West and South. In 1958, baseball's New York Giants moved to San Francisco, and the Brooklyn Dodgers abandoned Flatbush for Los Angeles. Those moves touched off a new westward and southward movement of sports franchises. Shifting population and spreading affluence eventually led to substantial expansion of the major baseball leagues and the principal football and basketball leagues as well.

Image 33.5 The King With his fleshy face, pouting lips, and sexually suggestive gyrations, Elvis Presley became the high priest of rock 'n' roll in the 1950s, to the chagrin of parents everywhere. Bloated by fame, fortune, and drugs, he died in 1977 at the age of forty-two.

Popular music was dramatically transformed in the fifties with a new musical style known as **rock 'n' roll**. Born of a fusion of Southern Black rhythm and blues with white bluegrass and country, rock was "crossover" music, carrying its heavy beat and driving rhythms across America's racial divide.

No single artist can claim credit for its creation, although its earliest performers were mainly Black Southerners. However, it was Elvis Presley, a white singer born in 1935 in Tupelo, Mississippi, who became rock's first megastar (refer to Image 33.5). Listening and dancing to rock 'n' roll became a rite of passage for millions of young people around the world, from Japan to working-class Liverpool, England, where Elvis's fame inspired teenagers John Lennon and Paul McCartney to form a band that would become the Beatles.

Traditionalists were repelled by Presley and much else in the affluent fifties. Movie star Marilyn Monroe, with her ingenuous smile and dangerous curves, helped to popularize—and commercialize—new standards of sensuous sexuality. So did *Playboy* magazine, whose first issue Monroe graced in 1953. As the decade closed, Americans were well on their way to becoming free-spending consumers of mass-produced, standardized products, which were advertised on the electronic medium of television and often sold for their alleged sexual allure.

Many critics lamented the implications of this new consumerist lifestyle. Harvard sociologist David Riesman portrayed the postwar generation as a pack of conformists in *The Lonely Crowd* (1950). Harvard economist John Kenneth Galbraith bemoaned the spectacle of private opulence amidst public squalor in a series of books beginning with *The Affluent Society* (1958). But Galbraith's call to invest in the shared commons fell on mostly deaf ears in the giddily affluent 1950s.

33-3 The Advent of Eisenhower

Democratic prospects in the presidential election of 1952 were blighted by the military deadlock in Korea, Truman's clash with MacArthur, and war-bred inflation. Dispirited Democrats nominated a reluctant Adlai E. Stevenson, the eloquent and idealistic governor of Illinois. Republicans enthusiastically chose war hero General Dwight D. "Ike" Eisenhower on the first ballot. "Ike's" running mate was California senator and relentless red-hunter Richard M. Nixon (refer to Image 33.6).

Eisenhower was already the most popular American of his time, as "I Like Ike" buttons everywhere testified. Striking a grandfatherly, nonpartisan pose, Eisenhower left the rough campaigning to Nixon, who relished bare-knuckle political combat. The vice-presidential candidate lambasted his opponents with charges that they had cultivated corruption, caved in on Korea, and coddled communists. Nixon particularly blasted the cerebral Stevenson as "Adlai the appeaser," with a "Ph.D. from [Secretary of State] Dean Acheson's College of Cowardly Communist Containment."

Bettmann/Getty Images

Image 33.6 The Republicans' Choice, 1952 Nominee Eisenhower and his vice-presidential running mate, Nixon, greet the delegates.

Nixon himself faltered late in the campaign amid accusations that he had accepted illegal donations. Responding with a self-pitying live address on television, the vice-presidential nominee denied the charges and solemnly declared that the only campaign gift he had ever received was the family cocker spaniel, Checkers. The mawkish **Checkers Speech** saved Nixon's spot on the ticket and demonstrated the formidable political potential of the new medium. Much more than radio, television allowed candidates to bypass traditional party machinery and speak directly to voters. A future awaited, one critic observed, of "selling the president like toothpaste."

The outcome of the presidential election of 1952 was never really in doubt. Given an extra prod by Eisenhower's last-minute pledge to go personally to Korea to end the war, the voters overwhelmingly declared for Ike. He garnered 33,936,234 votes to Stevenson's 27,314,992, ringing up 442 electoral votes to 89 for his opponent (refer to Map 33.1). Ike also managed to pull enough Republican legislators into office on his military coattails to gain GOP control of both chambers of the new Congress by a hairbreadth.

True to his campaign pledge, president-elect Eisenhower flew to Korea for three days in December 1952. Seven bloody months later, an armistice was finally signed. The brutal and futile fighting had lasted three years. More than thirty thousand Americans lay dead, joined by perhaps more than a million Chinese, North Koreans, and South Koreans. Tens of billions of American dollars had been poured into the fight. Yet this terrible toll in blood and treasure bought only a return to the conditions of 1950: Korea remained divided at the thirty-eighth parallel, while the broader Cold War remained frigidly frozen.

Coming so soon after the much larger—and decisively triumphant—conflict of World War II and ending in inglorious stalemate, the Korean War became

1952

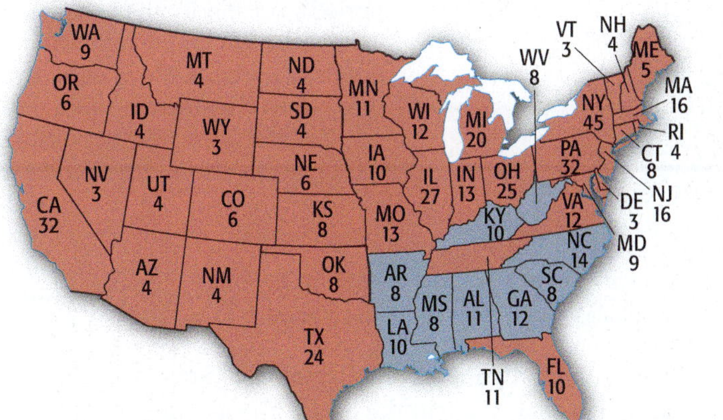

Candidate (Party)	Electoral Vote		Popular Vote	
Eisenhower (Republican)	442	83%	33,936,234	55.1%
Stevenson (Democrat)	89	17%	27,314,992	44.4%

Map 33.1 Presidential Election of 1952 (with electoral vote by state) A Democrat quipped, "If the voters liked the Republicans the way they liked Ike, the two-party system would be in bad shape." But Eisenhower scored a personal, not a party, victory. Republicans won minuscule majorities in Congress, which disappeared in the elections two years later. Eisenhower's victories in several Southern states, however, did signal the slow loosening of the Democratic lock on Dixie.

Image 33.7 An Integrated Unit in Korea Two years after President Truman's 1948 executive order desegregating the military, the Korean War marked the first time Black and white soldiers fought together in integrated units, as the Army filled losses in white units with Black recruits. The last all-Black Army battalion was abolished in 1954.

"The Forgotten War," in America's collective memory (refer to Image 33.7). The true number of U.S. war dead—36,516—was not confirmed until 2000. A wall memorializing the U.S. soldiers who died did not appear on Washington, DC's National Mall until 2022, and imprecision in Pentagon record-keeping left many names of the fallen misspelled or omitted altogether.

Both in the military and the civilian realms, Eisenhower had long cultivated a leadership style that self-consciously projected an image of sincerity, fairness, and optimism. In the White House, he now struck the pose of an "unpolitical" president, serenely above the petty partisan fray. He shrewdly knew that his greatest "asset" was his enjoyment of the "affection and respect of our citizenry," as he confided to his diary in 1949.

Ike thus seemed ideally suited to soothe the anxieties of Americans who yearned for a period of calm in which they could pursue their new ambitions for consumerist affluence. Ably playing this reassuring role, he presided over a decade of shaky peace and shining prosperity. Yet critics charged that he unwisely hoarded the "asset" of his immense popularity, rather than spend it for a good cause (especially civil rights). And his initial failure to stand up to the McCarthyist demagoguery bubbling up from within his own party showed either timidity or opportunism.

33-4 Desegregating American Society

America counted some 15 million Black citizens in 1950. They experienced far less of the postwar period's prosperity than their white fellow-citizens, thanks to pervasive racial discrimination. Those who had migrated to the cities of the North and West still encountered segregated public accommodations. Many banks would not lend them money to buy a home, and suburban developers and homeowners often outright refused to sell to them.

The harshest injustices afflicted the two-thirds of the Black population who still dwelled in the South. Every day of their lives, Black Southerners confronted an array of local laws and practices that kept them economically marginalized and electorally powerless. They not only attended segregated schools but were compelled to use separate public toilets, drinking fountains, restaurants, and waiting rooms (refer to Image 33.8). Trains and buses had "whites only" and "colored only" seating. Poll taxes, "grandfather clauses," and violent intimidation meant that about 20 percent of eligible Southern Black adults were registered to vote, and fewer than 5 percent were registered in some Deep South states like Mississippi and Alabama.

Where the law proved insufficient to enforce this Jim Crow regime, vigilante violence did the job. Six Black war veterans, claiming the rights for which they had fought overseas, were murdered in the summer of 1946—ghastly acts that helped persuade Harry Truman to embrace the cause of civil rights. A Mississippi mob murdered Black fourteen-year-old Emmett Till in 1955 for allegedly whistling at a white woman. His mother insisted on exposing his beaten and river-bloated body in an open casket to dramatize America's grotesque tolerance of racial violence. Till's killers were later acquitted by an all-white jury. His coffin is now an exhibit at the National Museum for African American History in Washington, DC.

A Black woman described the day-in, day-out humiliations of life in the Jim Crow South:

"You could not go to a white restaurant; you sat in a special place at the movie house; and Lord knows, you sat in the back of the bus. It didn't make any difference if you were rich or poor, if you were Black you were nothing. You might have a hundred dollars in your pocket, but if you went to the store you would wait at the side until all the clerks got through with all the white folks, no matter if they didn't have change for a dollar. Then the clerk would finally look at you and say, 'Oh, did you want something? I didn't see you there.'"

Segregation tarnished America's international image, much as McCarthyism did. Coverage of lynching and other racial abuses became staples of anti-American Soviet propaganda. International pressure combined with grassroots stirring of the national conscience as well as increasingly effective Black activism spurred some racial progress during and after World War II. In a growing number of northern cities and states, Black Americans battled for—and won—equal access to restaurants, hotels, theaters, and beaches. Jackie Robinson cracked baseball's color barrier when the Brooklyn Dodgers signed him in 1947. The National Association for the Advancement of Colored People (NAACP) pushed the Supreme Court in 1950 to rule in *Sweatt v. Painter* that separate professional schools for Black students failed to meet the test of equality. The repeal of the Chinese Exclusion Act in 1943, the Supreme Court's *Shelley v. Kraemer* decision in 1948 on the unenforceability of racially restrictive housing covenants, and a string of repeals of state-level anti-miscegenation laws signaled the decline of legal discrimination against not only Black Americans but other racial and ethnic minorities as well.

New York Times Co./Archive Photos/Getty Images

Image 33.8 The Face of Segregation These Black women in the segregated South of the 1950s were compelled to enter the movie theater through the "Colored Entrance." Once inside, they were restricted to a separate seating section, usually in the rear of the theater.

The South saw little of that progress in the early postwar years—but, increasingly, Black Southerners refused to suffer in silence. On a chilly day in December 1955, Rosa Parks, a college-educated Black seamstress who had long been active in the NAACP, made history in Montgomery, Alabama. She boarded a bus, took a seat in the "whites only" section, and refused to give it up. Her arrest for violating the city's Jim Crow statutes sparked a yearlong Black boycott of city buses and served notice throughout the South that Black people would no longer submit meekly to the absurdities and indignities of segregation.

The **Montgomery bus boycott** also catapulted to prominence a young pastor at Montgomery's Dexter Avenue Baptist Church, the Reverend Martin Luther King, Jr. The twenty-seven-year-old might have seemed an unlikely champion of the downtrodden and disfranchised, having been raised in a prominent Black family in Atlanta and educated partly in the North. But his oratorical skill, strategic savvy, commitment to both political and economic justice, and devotion to the nonviolent principles of India's Mohandas Gandhi all thrust him to the forefront of a new phase in the Black freedom struggle that soon pulsed across the South and the rest of the nation (refer to Image 33.9).

33-5 Seeds of the Civil Rights Revolution

While Truman desegregated the military in 1948 with a flourish of the presidential pen, the legislative recommendations of his civil rights commission proved a far harder sell. A conservative coalition of Republicans and Southern Democrats in Congress refused to pass civil rights legislation during Truman's second term. His White House successor, Eisenhower, showed no real interest in these issues—especially as most Black voters had shifted away from the party of Lincoln. By default, the Supreme Court assumed political leadership in the civil rights struggles of the 1950s.

Chief Justice Earl Warren, former Republican governor of California, shocked traditionalists with his active judicial intervention in previously taboo social issues. Publicly snubbed and privately scorned by Ike, Warren courageously led the Court to

Joseph E. Lowery (1921–2020), a Methodist minister and civil rights activist in Mobile, Alabama, reflected on the powerful message of the 1955 Montgomery bus boycott for Black riders:

"You see, what the bus thing did was simply more than withholding patronage from the bus; it was restoring a sense of dignity to the patrons, as best expressed by an oft-quoted Black woman in Montgomery who said, 'Since I've been walking, my feet are tired, but my soul's rested.' . . . [P]rior to the bus boycotts, the determination of our freedom rested with the courts. With the bus boycott, we determined it. . . . The court could say what it liked, we weren't gon' ride—in the back of the bus. We'd walk."

Image 33.9 Martin Luther King Jr. and His Wife, Coretta, Arrested King and his wife were arrested for the first time in Montgomery, Alabama, in 1955 while organizing the bus boycott.

address urgent issues that Congress and the president preferred to avoid, prompting "Impeach Earl Warren" signs to blossom along the nation's highways.

The unanimous decision of the Warren Court in ***Brown v. Board of Education of Topeka, Kansas*** in May 1954 was epochal. In a forceful opinion, the justices ruled that segregation in public schools was "inherently unequal" and thus unconstitutional. The uncompromising decision reversed the Court's earlier declaration of 1896 in *Plessy v. Ferguson* (refer to "21-8 The Birth of Jim Crow in the Post-Reconstruction South," p. 530–531) that "separate but equal" facilities were constitutional. Desegregation, the justices now insisted, must go ahead with "all deliberate speed."

The ruling sent the white South reeling, prompting organized campaigns of "massive resistance" against desegregation orders. More than a hundred Southern Congressional representatives and U.S. senators signed what they termed a "Declaration of Constitutional Principles" in 1956, pledging their undying resistance to federally mandated desegregation under the banner of "states' rights." Several states diverted public funds to hastily created private schools where the integration order was more difficult to apply. Many of these "segregation academies" remained in operation into the twenty-first century. "White citizens' councils," sometimes by the light of burning crosses, thwarted attempts to make integration a reality. Ten years after the Court's momentous ruling, fewer than 2 percent of the eligible Black students in the Deep South were sitting in classrooms with white peers (refer to Image 33.10).

President Eisenhower remained reluctant to promote integration. He shied away from employing his vast popularity and the prestige of his office to educate white Americans about the need for racial justice. His personal attitudes may have helped to restrain him. He had grown up in the all-white town of Abilene, Kansas, spent his career in a segregated army, and advised against integration of the armed forces in 1948. He complained that the Supreme Court's decision in *Brown v. Board of Education* had upset "the customs and convictions of at least two generations of Americans," and he steadfastly refused to issue a public statement endorsing the Court's conclusions. "I do not believe," he explained, "that prejudices, even palpably unjustifiable prejudices, will succumb to compulsion."

But in September 1957, Ike was forced to act. Orval Faubus, the governor of Arkansas, mobilized the National Guard to prevent nine Black students from enrolling in Little Rock's Central High School. Confronted with a direct challenge to federal authority, Eisenhower sent troops to escort the children to their classes. Heavy media coverage of "the crisis at Central High" made headlines around the world and gave further ammunition to Soviet propagandists.

In the same year, Congress passed the first Civil Rights Act since Reconstruction. Eisenhower characteristically reassured a Southern senator that the legislation represented "the mildest civil

Francis Miller/The LIFE Picture Collection/Shutterstock.com

Image 33.10 Integration in Little Rock, Arkansas, 1957 Fifteen-year-old Elizabeth Eckford endured scathing insults from white students and parents as she attempted to enter Little Rock's Central High School. The showdown at Little Rock was a replay of nineteenth-century confrontations over "states' rights," and forced a reluctant Eisenhower administration to assert the supremacy of federal power.

rights bill possible." It set up a permanent Civil Rights Commission to investigate violations of civil rights and authorized federal injunctions to protect voting rights.

Black activists increasingly took leadership of the civil rights movement into their own hands. Martin Luther King Jr. formed the Southern Christian Leadership Conference (SCLC) in 1957. It aimed to mobilize the vast power of Black churches on behalf of Black rights. This was an exceptionally shrewd strategy because the churches were the largest and best-organized Black institutions that had been allowed to flourish in a segregated society.

More spontaneous was the "sit-in" movement launched on February 1, 1960, by four Black college freshmen in Greensboro, North Carolina. Without a detailed plan or institutional support, they demanded service at a whites-only lunch counter (refer to Image 33.11). Observing that "fellows like you make our race look bad," even the Black waitress refused to serve them. But they kept their seats and returned the next day with nineteen classmates. The following day, eighty-five students joined in; by the end of the week, a thousand. The sit-in movement rolled swiftly across the South, swelling into a wave of wade-ins, lie-ins, and pray-ins to compel equal treatment in restaurants, transportation, employment, housing, and voter registration.

Library of Congress Prints and Photographs Division [LC-DIG-ppmsca-08095]

Image 33.11 Lunch Counter Sit-In, Greensboro, North Carolina, 1960 Black college students played critical roles in leading and building national support for the Southern civil rights movement in the early 1960s. This protest in Greensboro was the first of a wave of student-led lunch counter sit-ins across the segregated South.

In April 1960, Southern Black students formed the **Student Nonviolent Coordinating Committee** (SNCC, pronounced "snick") to give more focus and force to these efforts. Guided by the veteran civil rights activist Ella Baker, the SNCC's young and impassioned rank-and-file eventually departed from the more genteel tactics of the SCLC and the even more deliberate legalisms of the NAACP. Much of the increased visibility and leadership of young people was due to Baker's quiet but commanding influence. The granddaughter of a slave, the Virginia-born Baker assumed leadership positions at a time when most women were not empowered to be leaders—especially within a Southern civil rights movement dominated by magnetic male preachers like King. Perhaps paradoxically, the charismatic Baker advocated an anti-charismatic, grassroots-led approach to activism, convinced that "strong people don't need strong leaders."

33-6 Eisenhower Republicanism at Home

Eisenhower had entered the White House in 1953 pledging his administration to a philosophy of "dynamic conservatism." "In all those things which deal with people, be liberal, be human," he advised. But when it came to "people's money, or their economy, or their form of government, be conservative." This balanced, middle-of-the-road course harmonized with the depression-daunted and war-weary mood of the times. Some critics called Eisenhower's presidency a case of "the bland leading the bland." Importantly, such a cautious approach entailed no ambitious efforts to roll back the major achievements of the New Deal. As he told his brother, "Should any political party attempt to abolish Social Security, unemployment insurance, and eliminate labor and farm programs, you would not hear of that party again in our political history." Ike thus consolidated rather than destroyed the new social contract that had been forged during the Great Depression.

Eisenhower nonetheless sought to halt further expansions of government programs. He was determined to balance the federal budget and guard the Republic from what he called "creeping socialism." The former supreme Allied commander put the brakes on Truman's enormous military buildup, though defense spending still soaked up 10 percent of GDP. Eisenhower won Southern support by endorsing the transfer of control over offshore oil fields from the federal government to the states. He also tried to curb the TVA (refer to "30-13 The TVA Harnesses the Tennessee," pp. 796–797) by encouraging a private power company to compete with the massive public utility.

Ike also backed a public works project that dwarfed anything the New Dealers could have imagined. The **National Interstate and Defense Highways Act of 1956** authorized a $27 billion plan to build 42,000 miles of sleek, fast motorways. The act uncapped a gusher of federal road-building funds that paid for 90 percent of projects while states and localities contributed ten percent. As the act's title reflected, Eisenhower believed that such roads were essential to national defense, allowing U.S. troops to mobilize anywhere in the country in the event of a Soviet invasion. Laying down these modern, multilane roads created thousands of construction jobs and speeded the suburbanization of America.

The Highway Act boosted trucking, automobile, oil, and travel industries, while robbing the railroads, especially passenger trains, of business. The act also exacerbated problems of air quality and energy consumption, and its neighborhood-splitting freeways had disastrous consequences for many cities. Once-vibrant downtowns withered away while shopping malls and other sites of leisure and consumption flourished in the far-flung suburbs.

33-7 Immigration and Termination

Immigration bounded onto the presidential agenda soon after Eisenhower took office. A surge in illegal border crossings by Mexican job-seekers fueled concerns among both U.S. and Mexican officials that the influx would undercut the *Bracero* program of legally imported farmworkers (refer to "31-13 Building the War Machine," pp. 823–827). Eisenhower responded with a massive, military-style roundup of those who had entered illegally. The program's ill-chosen moniker was "**Operation Wetback**," a derogatory reference to the migrants' watery route across the Rio Grande. As many as 1 million Mexicans were apprehended and returned to Mexico in 1954 (refer to Image 33.12).

Native Americans, meanwhile, saw American lawmakers reverse the commitments to tribal preservation made by the "Indian New Deal" of 1934 (refer to "30-11 Dust Bowls and Black Blizzards," pp. 794–796). Instead, Eisenhower proposed to terminate the tribes as legal entities and sell off their land. Congressional leaders swiftly endorsed the measure. While framed as a step toward freeing the tribes from federal dictates, **termination policy** was in fact a return to the assimilationist goals of the Dawes Severalty Act of 1887 (refer to "22-9 'Kill the Indian and Save the Man'," pp. 558–562). Federal officials increased funding to—and oversight of—Native education. But few tribes agreed to termination. Similarly, a companion "urban relocation" program encouraged Native people to move to large cities for better economic opportunity. But promised jobs and social services often failed to materialize, and many migrants returned. Although western cities like Seattle became home to sizable communities of "urban Indians," 54 percent of Native people still lived in rural or small-town areas fifty years later. Termination had largely petered out by the time Eisenhower left office in 1961, although the program was not officially ended until 1970.

Bettmann/Getty Images

Image 33.12 Operation Wetback Thousands of Mexicans who had crossed the border illegally were forcibly repatriated in the federal government's 1954 military-style roundup, which was promoted in part by the Mexican government. The man in this photograph is being pulled across the border by a Mexican official, while an American spectator tries to pull him back into the United States.

33-8 A "New Look" in Foreign Policy

The 1952 Republican platform called for a "new look" in foreign policy. It condemned mere "containment" of communism as "negative, futile, and immoral." Incoming Secretary of State John Foster Dulles promised not merely to stem the red tide of Soviet communism but to "roll back" its gains and "liberate captive peoples." At the same time, the new administration promised to balance the budget by cutting military spending.

How were these two contradictory goals to be reached? Dulles answered with a **policy of boldness** in early 1954. Eisenhower would relegate the army and the navy to the backseat and build up the Strategic Air Command's air fleet of superbombers equipped with city-flattening nuclear bombs. These fearsome weapons would inflict "massive retaliation" on the Soviets or the Chinese in the event of hostilities. The advantages of this new policy were thought to lie in the power of nuclear intimidation and its relatively cheap price tag. At the same time, Eisenhower sought a thaw in the Cold War through negotiations with the new Soviet leaders who came to power after Joseph Stalin's death in 1953.

In the end, the touted "new look" proved illusory. A new Soviet premier, the burly Nikita Khrushchev, rudely rejected Ike's call in 1955 for an "open skies" mutual inspection program over both the Soviet Union and the United States. In 1956, the Hungarians rose up against their Soviet masters and felt badly betrayed when the United States turned a deaf ear to their desperate appeals for aid. The brutally crushed **Hungarian uprising** (refer to Image 33.13) revealed the sobering truth that America's mighty nuclear sledgehammer was too heavy a weapon to wield in such a relatively minor crisis. The strategic limitations of the "massive retaliation" doctrine were thus starkly exposed.

33-9 America Intervenes in Vietnam

Southeast Asia provided further illustration of those limitations. There, nationalist movements had sought for years to throw off the yoke of French colonial rule in what was then known as Indochina. The leader of the Vietnamese independence movement, goateed Ho Chi Minh,

Keystone/Getty Images

Image 33.13 Hungarian Uprising, October 26, 1956 Soviet tanks rolled through the streets of Budapest to crush an anticommunist uprising against the Soviets, who had controlled Hungary since World War II. This demonstration of brute force against a grassroots democratic movement turned many communist sympathizers in the West definitively against the Soviet Union.

had tried to appeal personally to Woodrow Wilson in Paris as early as 1919 to support self-determination for the peoples of Southeast Asia. Franklin Roosevelt had likewise inspired hope among Asian nationalists.

But Cold War events dampened the dreams of anticolonial Asian peoples. Their leaders—including Ho Chi Minh—became increasingly communist while the United States became increasingly anticommunist. The situation greatly alarmed Eisenhower, who within months of taking office began speaking of the "fallen domino principle": allowing Indochina to fall to the "Reds" would quickly topple many other regime in the same direction. By 1954, American taxpayers were financing nearly 80 percent of the costs of the French colonial war in Indochina, about $1 billion a year, given partly as a bid to win French approval of a plan to rearm West Germany. (The Germans were duly welcomed into the NATO fold in 1955.)

Despite this massive aid, French forces continued to crumble under pressure from Ho Chi Minh's nationalist guerrilla forces, called the Viet Minh. In March 1954, a key French garrison was trapped hopelessly in the fortress of Dien Bien Phu in the northwestern corner of Vietnam. The new "policy of boldness" was now put to the test. Secretary Dulles, Vice President Nixon, and the chairman of the Joint Chiefs of Staff favored intervention with American bombers to help bail out the beleaguered French. But Eisenhower held back.

The **Battle of Dien Bien Phu** proved a victory for the nationalists, and a multinational conference in Geneva roughly halved Vietnam at the seventeenth parallel (refer to Map 33.3 later in the chapter). The victorious Ho Chi Minh in the north consented to this arrangement on the assurance that Vietnam-wide elections would be held within two years. In the south, a pro-Western government under Ngo Dinh Diem was soon entrenched at Saigon. Convinced the communists would win, Diem's regime and its American backers refused to hold the promised unification elections. American dollars to Diem continued to flow as communist guerrillas heated up their campaign against him. The Americans had evidently backed a losing horse but could see no easy way to call off their bet.

33-10 Cold War Crises in the Middle East

Fears of Soviet penetration into the oil-rich Middle East further heightened Cold War tensions. The government of Iran, supposedly influenced by the Kremlin, began to resist the power of the gigantic Western companies that controlled Iranian petroleum. In response, the U.S. Central Intelligence Agency (CIA) helped to engineer a coup in 1953 that installed the youthful shah of Iran, Mohammed Reza Pahlevi, as an autocratic and decidedly pro-American leader. Though successful in the short run in securing Iranian oil for the West, the American intervention left a bitter legacy of resentment among many Iranians. More than two decades later, they took their revenge on the shah and his American allies (refer to "35-10 Economic and Energy Woes," pp. 955–956).

The **Suez crisis** proved far messier than the swift stroke in Iran. President Gamal Abdel Nasser of Egypt, an ardent Arab nationalist, was seeking funds to build an immense dam on the upper Nile for urgently needed irrigation and power. America and Britain tentatively offered financial help, but when Nasser began to flirt openly with the communist camp, Secretary of State Dulles dramatically withdrew the dam offer. Nasser promptly regained face by nationalizing the Suez Canal, owned chiefly by British and French stockholders.

Nasser's action placed a razor's edge at the jugular vein of Western Europe's oil supply. America's jittery French and British allies, deliberately keeping Washington in the dark and coordinating their blow with one from Israel, staged a joint assault on Egypt late in October 1956. The invaders calculated that the United States would supply them with oil while their Middle Eastern supplies were disrupted. But to their unpleasant surprise, a furious President Eisenhower resolved to let them "boil in their own oil" and refused to release emergency supplies. The oil-less allies resentfully withdrew their troops. For the first time in history, a United Nations police force was sent to maintain order.

The Suez crisis marked the last time that the United States could brandish its "oil weapon." As recently as 1940, the United States had produced two-thirds of the world's oil, while a scant 5 percent of the global supply flowed from the Middle East. But by 1948 the surging demand from the United States had made it a net oil importer. The economic and strategic importance of the Middle East oil region began to grow dramatically.

The region's poor, sandy sheikdoms resolved to reap for themselves the lion's share of the enormous oil wealth that Western companies pumped out of the scorching deserts. In a portentous move, Saudi Arabia, Kuwait, Iraq, and Iran joined with Venezuela in 1960 to form the **Organization of Petroleum Exporting Countries (OPEC)**. In the following decades, as the United States and other industrial powers became increasingly dependent on foreign oil, OPEC came to wield immense power over the West's economic health.

33-11 Round Two for Ike

The election of 1956 was a replay of the 1952 contest, with President Eisenhower pitted once more against the professorial Adlai Stevenson. Voters clearly still liked Ike. Eisenhower piled up an enormous majority of 33,590,472 popular votes to Stevenson's 26,022,752; in the Electoral College, the count was an even more unbalanced 457 for Republicans to 73 for Democrats. Eisenhower made deeper inroads into the traditional southern bastion of Democratic strength than he had in 1952. But his coattails were not so stiff or broad as in 1952. He failed to win for his party either house of Congress—the first time since Zachary Taylor's election in 1848 that a winning president had headed such a losing ticket.

Ike nevertheless bestirred himself when it came to organized labor. Congressional investigations produced scandalous revelations of gangsterism, fraud, and brass-knuckles tactics in many American unions, especially the Teamsters. The AFL–CIO, born of a merger of the two giant labor federations in 1955, expelled the Teamsters in 1957 for choosing leaders like Mafia-connected James R. "Jimmy" Hoffa. Later convicted of jury tampering, Hoffa served part of his sentence before disappearing without a trace—evidently the victim of gangsters he had crossed. To counter such corruption, Eisenhower persuaded Congress to pass the Landrum-Griffin Act in 1959. Designed to bring labor leaders to account for financial shenanigans and bullying tactics, it also expanded some of the antilabor strictures of the earlier Taft-Hartley Act (refer to "32-14 Postwar Economic Anxieties," pp. 862–863).

Soviet scientists astounded the world on October 4, 1957, by lofting into orbit a beep-beeping 184-pound "baby moon" (*Sputnik*). A month later, they launched a 1,120-pound *Sputnik II* with a dog aboard; witty journalists dubbed it "Muttnik." These amazing breakthroughs rattled American self-confidence. They stirred fresh anxiety about Soviet scientific superiority and raised some sobering military questions. If the Soviets could fire heavy objects into outer space, they certainly could reach America with intercontinental ballistic missiles (ICBMs). Panic intensified after a thick intelligence report landed on Eisenhower's desk that November, warning that Soviet missile production was racing ahead of the United States. (Years later, it became clear that the "missile gap" was grossly exaggerated.)

"Rocket fever" swept the nation. Eisenhower established the National Aeronautics and Space Administration (NASA) and directed billions of dollars toward missile development. After humiliating and well-advertised failures—notably the Vanguard missile, which blew up on national television just a few feet above the ground in 1957—in February 1958 the United States managed to put into orbit a grapefruit-sized satellite weighing 2.5 pounds. By the end of the decade, several American satellites had been launched, and the United States had successfully tested its own ICBMs. The ***Sputnik*** scare also led to a critical comparison of the American educational system with that of the Soviet Union. In 1958, Congress passed the National Defense Education Act (NDEA) to promote research and teaching in science, engineering, and foreign languages.

33-12 The Continuing Cold War

The feverish race to create weapons of nuclear annihilation continued unabated. Worried scientists urged halting nuclear tests before the atmosphere became so polluted as to produce generations of deformed mutants. The Soviets, after completing an intensive series of exceptionally "dirty" tests, proclaimed a suspension in March 1958 and urged the Western world to follow. But attempts to regularize suspensions by proper inspection sank on the reef of mutual mistrust.

The brusque Khrushchev, meanwhile, demanded in late 1958 that Western powers remove their forces from West Berlin and sought a face-to-face meeting with Eisenhower. Despite grave doubts about any tangible results, the president invited the Soviet leader to America in 1959. Khrushchev's first stop was California, where he hobnobbed with movie stars and tried unsuccessfully to visit Disneyland. At an IBM facility in the future Silicon Valley, Khrushchev was so impressed by the all-you-can-eat cafeteria that he directed Soviet factories to adopt this "democratic arrangement" as well. After an unusually energetic speech to the UN General Assembly (where he astounded delegates by brandishing his shoe), he met with Eisenhower at Camp David, the presidential retreat in Maryland's Catoctin Mountains.

Optimism evaporated when a follow-up Paris "summit conference," scheduled for May 1960, turned into an embarrassing fiasco. On the eve of the conference, the Soviets shot down an American U-2 spy plane deep in the heart of Russia. After bungling bureaucratic denials in Washington, "honest Ike" took the unprecedented step of assuming personal responsibility. Khrushchev stormed into Paris filling the air with invective, and the conference collapsed before it could get off the ground. The concord of Camp David was replaced with the grapes of wrath.

Meanwhile, the Cold War shook America's relations with its hemispheric neighbors. Latin Americans bitterly resented Uncle Sam's lavishing of billions of dollars on Europe, while doling out only millions to its poor relations to the south. They also chafed at Washington's continuing habit of intervening in Latin American affairs—as in a CIA-directed coup that ousted a leftist government in Guatemala in 1954. At the same time, Washington continued to support—even decorate—bloody dictators who claimed to be combating communists.

One such dictator, iron-fisted Fulgencio Batista of Cuba, had encouraged huge investments of American capital, and Washington in turn had given him support. But early in 1959, black-bearded Fidel Castro engineered a revolution that ousted Batista. Castro then denounced the Yankee imperialists and began to expropriate valuable American properties while pursuing a land-distribution program. Washington, finally losing patience, liberated Cuba from "imperialistic slavery" by cutting off the heavy U.S. imports of Cuban sugar. Castro retaliated with further wholesale confiscations of American property and in effect made his left-wing dictatorship an economic and military satellite of Moscow, to the Kremlin's delighted surprise. An exodus of anti-Castro Cubans headed for the United States, especially Florida. More than 1.3 million arrived between 1960 and 2020. Washington broke diplomatic relations with Castro's government early in 1961 and imposed a strict embargo on trade with Cuba, in place to this day.

33-13 Kennedy Challenges Nixon

Republicans approached the presidential campaign of 1960 with Vice President Nixon as their heir apparent. To many he was a gifted party leader, to others a ruthless opportunist. The "old" Nixon had been a no-holds-barred campaigner, adept at skewering Democrats and left-wingers. The "new" Nixon presented himself as a mature, seasoned statesman. He had gained particular notice in a finger-pointing **kitchen debate** with Khrushchev in Moscow in 1959, where Nixon extolled the virtues of American consumerism over Soviet economic planning. The next year he handily won the Republican nomination.

On the Democratic side, John F. Kennedy, a youthful millionaire senator from Massachusetts, scored impressive victories in several primary elections, overcoming the reluctance of many party bosses to nominate a Roman Catholic (refer to Image 33.14). A disappointed South was not completely appeased when Kennedy's closest rival and the Senate majority leader from Texas, Lyndon Baines Johnson, accepted second place on the ticket in an eleventh-hour marriage of convenience.

Senator Kennedy was the first Catholic to be nominated for the presidency by either party since Al Smith's ill-starred campaign in 1928. Smear artists revived the ancient charges about the Pope's controlling the White House. Kennedy rebutted the attacks and asked if some 40 million Catholic Americans were to be condemned to second-class citizenship from birth. The Protestant,

Contending Voices

The "Kitchen Debate"

To promote cultural exchange between the United States and the Soviet Union, both governments agreed to sponsor exhibits in each other's countries during the summer of 1959. On July 24, Vice President Richard Nixon (1919–1994) led Soviet Premier Nikita Khrushchev (1894–1971) on a tour of the American National Exhibition at Sokolniki Park in Moscow. As they explored the facilities, including a state-of-the-art kitchen in a model suburban home, the two leaders engaged in an impromptu debate that ranged from foreign policy to the relative merits of communism and capitalism to the significance of technological innovation for citizens. Nixon said (pointing to a washing machine):

"This is the newest model. This is the kind which is built in thousands of units for direct installation in the houses. . . . What we want to do is make easier the life of our housewives. . . . To us, diversity, the right to choose, the fact that we have 1,000 builders building 1,000 different houses, is the most important thing. We don't have one decision made at the top by one government official. . . . We have many different manufacturers and many different kinds of washing machines so that the housewives have a choice."

Khrushchev replied:

"Don't you have a machine that puts food into the mouth and pushes it down? Many things you've shown us are interesting but they are not needed in life. They have no useful purpose. They are merely gadgets. . . . You think the Russian people will be dumbfounded to see these things, but the fact is that newly built Russian houses have all this equipment right now. Moreover, all you have to do to get a house is to be born in the Soviet Union. You are entitled to housing. I was born in the Soviet Union. So I have a right to a house. In America, if you don't have a dollar, you have the right to choose between sleeping in a house or on the pavement."

Consider This:

What does the exchange reveal about the premises of the ideological conflict between the United States and the Soviet Union during the Cold War?

Bible Belt South, still overwhelmingly Democratic, had particular misgivings about the candidate's faith. "I fear Catholicism more than I fear communism," declaimed one Baptist minister in North Carolina. But if many Southern Democrats stayed away from the polls because of Kennedy's Catholicism, Northern Democrats in unusually large numbers supported Kennedy because of the bitter attacks on their Catholic faith.

Television may well have tipped the scales. Nixon agreed to meet Kennedy in four debates. The contestants crossed words in millions of living rooms before audiences estimated at 60 million or more. The debates reinforced the importance of image over substance in the television age, as many viewers found Kennedy's glamour and vitality far more appealing than Nixon's tired and pallid appearance.

Kennedy squeezed through with 303 electoral votes to 219,* but with a breathtakingly close popular margin of only 118,574

Candidate John F. Kennedy (1917–1963), in a speech to a Houston group of Protestant ministers (September 12, 1960), declared,

"I believe in an America where the separation of church and state is absolute—where no Catholic prelate would tell the President, should he be a Catholic, how to act, and no Protestant minister would tell his parishioners for whom to vote . . . and where no man is denied public office because his religion differs from the President who might appoint him or the people who might elect him."

*Six Democratic electors in Alabama, all eight unpledged Democratic electors in Mississippi, and one Republican elector in Oklahoma voted for Senator Harry F. Byrd, an opponent of civil rights who had declined to endorse Kennedy.

AP Images/HB

Image 33.14 John F. Kennedy Campaigning in the Democratic Primary Election, Wheaton, Maryland, May 12, 1960 Only fourteen states, plus the district of Columbia, held Democratic-Party primary elections in 1960, but they proved crucial for Kennedy to convince party bosses that a Roman Catholic could be a successful presidential candidate.

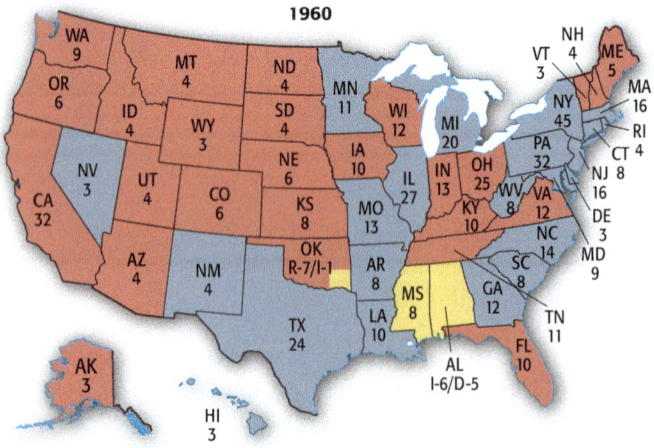

Candidate (Party)	Electoral Vote		Popular Vote	
Kennedy (Democrat)	303	56.50%	34,266,731	49.7%
Nixon (Republican)	219	40.75%	34,108,157	49.5%
Byrd (Independent)	15	2.75%	501,643	0.7%

Map 33.2 Presidential Election of 1960 (with electoral vote by state) Kennedy owed his hairbreadth triumph to his victories in twenty-six of the forty largest cities—and to Lyndon Johnson's strenuous campaigning in the South, where Kennedy's Catholicism may have been a hotter issue than his stand on civil rights.

votes out of over 68 million cast (refer to Map 33.2). He was not only the first Roman Catholic, but also, at forty-three, the youngest person to date to be elected president. Like Franklin Roosevelt, Kennedy ran well in the large industrial centers, where he had strong support from workers, Catholics, and Black Americans. (During the campaign, Kennedy had solicitously telephoned the pregnant Coretta King, whose husband, Martin Luther King Jr., was imprisoned in Georgia for a sit-in. Nixon, eyeing white Southern votes, had declined to comment publicly on the arrest and avoided communication with Mrs. King. The contrast offered an early sign of diverging racial strategies between the two parties.)

President Eisenhower continued to enjoy immense popularity to the final curtain. Despite Democratic jibes about "eight years of golfing and goofing," Eisenhower was widely admired and respected for his decency, goodwill, and moderation. The old soldier left office warning of the dangers of a burgeoning "**military-industrial complex**," and crestfallen at his failure to end the arms race with the Soviet Union. America grew not only economically under his watch but geographically as well. In an unprecedented expansion of the nation's political borders, the demographically and climactically diverse territories of Alaska and Hawai'i attained statehood in 1959.

33-14 A Cultural Renaissance

America's postwar role as superpower was matched by a new international ascendancy in painting, architecture, design, and literature. New York became the art capital of the world after World War II, as well-heeled Americans became generous patrons. Realistic representation went out the window, as artists like Jackson Pollock and Willem de Kooning strove to create spontaneous "action paintings" that expressed the painter's individuality and made the viewer a creative participant in defining the painting's meaning. Mark Rothko and his fellow "color field" painters dispatched with figurative representation, enveloping whole canvases with bold, shimmering swaths of color. "Pop" artists in the 1960s, notably Andy Warhol, canonized on canvas mundane items of consumer culture like soup cans and soda bottles, while Roy Lichtenstein parodied old-fashioned comic strips.

After campaigning with promises to reduce the defense budget, President Dwight Eisenhower (1890–1969) presided over unprecedented increases in military spending. Yet in his Farewell Address on January 17, 1961, he sagely but ironically warned of the dangers of such concentrated power:

"This conjunction of an immense military establishment and a large arms industry is new in the American experience. . . . In the councils of government, we must guard against the acquisition of unwarranted influence, whether sought or unsought, by the military-industrial complex."

American architecture also reached new heights as ultramodern skyscrapers arose in the nation's urban centers. Conceived in the modernist or "**International Style**," these massive corporate high-rises, such as New York's United Nations headquarters (1952) and Seagram Building (1957), were essentially giant steel boxes wrapped in glass. Old master Frank Lloyd Wright continued to produce strikingly original designs like the round-walled Guggenheim Museum (1959) in New York. Louis Kahn employed plain geometric forms and basic building materials like brick and concrete to make beautiful, simple buildings, such as the serene, seaside Salk Institute (1965) in La Jolla, California. Seattle-born Minoru Yamasaki criticized the International Style as cold and oppressive. He drew inspiration from Gothic cathedrals to incorporate soaring lines and graceful arches into modern facades. Of the more than 250 buildings Yamasaki designed, the most famous were the twin towers of the World Trade Center (1973) in New York City, destroyed in the terrorist attacks of September 11, 2001.

Despite the intensely masculine character of midcentury art and design professions, American women left their mark. Architect and interior designer Florence Knoll pioneered the concept of an open, cleanly designed "total office." The sleek, undulating furniture designs of Ray Eames and her husband Charles became modern classics. "The Rosa Parks of Architecture," Norma Sklarek, became the nation's first Black female licensed architect in 1954 and went on to design large-scale projects like the 247,000-square-foot U.S. Embassy in Tokyo (1976).

The literature of postwar America reflected an increasingly diverse set of writerly voices, as postwar pens documented the internal effects of the nation's wartime trials and its newly affluent, exuberantly consumerist society. Soldierly life in World War II sparked Joseph Heller's savagely satirical *Catch-22* (1961) and Kurt Vonnegut Jr.'s darkly comic war tale *Slaughterhouse Five* (1969). In *Rabbit, Run* (1960) and *Couples* (1968), John Updike chronicled the midlife crises of the suburban middle class, while John Cheever became "the Chekov of the exurbs" with short stories like "The Swimmer" (1964) and novels like *The Wapshot Chronicles* (1957). The mordant satire of Gore Vidal challenged social and sexual conventions in *Myra Breckinridge* (1968), whose title character was a transgender woman.

One group of countercultural writers rejected modern American life outright, seeking self-expression in stridently nonconformist lifestyles. Allen Ginsberg's "Howl" (1955) introduced this **Beat Generation** to the literary world. The poem's unruly verse and riotous content encapsulated these writers' contempt for the listless, middle-class suburban conformity they saw in World War II–weary America. Jack Kerouac's landmark novel *On the Road* (1957) became a sort of pocket bible for social rebels in the late 1950s. Chronicling a series of wild transcontinental road trips, the book was legendarily written on

In his poem "A Supermarket in California" (1956), Allen Ginsberg (1926–1997) fantasized about meeting nineteenth-century American poet Walt Whitman amidst the lavish consumerism (and spiritual emptiness) of a postwar supermarket:

"I saw you, Walt Whitman, childless, lonely old grubber, poking among the meats in the refrigerator and eyeing the grocery boys.

I heard you asking questions of each: Who killed the pork chops? What price bananas? Are you my Angel?

I wandered in and out of the brilliant stacks of cans following you, and followed in my imagination by the store detective.

We strode down the open corridors together in our solitary fancy tasting artichokes, possessing every frozen delicacy, and never passing the cashier."

a 120-foot roll of teletype paper over the course of only twenty days. Kerouac called his nonstop, drug-fueled writing technique "spontaneous prose" and conceptualized it as the literary equivalent of jazz improvisation or bebop.

Black authors built on the earlier achievements of the Harlem Renaissance to craft distinctive and influential postwar literature and art. Richard Wright soared to literary acclaim and best-seller status with his chilling portrait of a Black Chicago killer in *Native Son* (1940), following that triumph with the semi-autographical *Black Boy* (1945). A decade later, Ralph Ellison further explored Black identity in the haunting *Invisible Man* (1952). James Baldwin won plaudits for his sensitive reflections on race and identity in essays and novels like *The Fire Next Time* (1963).

In the same mold as earlier classics like Mark Twain's *Adventures of Huckleberry Finn* and F. Scott Fitzgerald's *Great Gatsby*, many postwar novels took the form of a *Bildungsroman* (German for "formation novel"), or a tale chronicling the education and maturation of a young protagonist. New York novelist and infamous recluse J. D. Salinger painted an indelible portrait of adolescent alienation in *The Catcher in the Rye* (1951). Chicagoan Saul Bellow's *The Adventures of Augie March* (1953) offered a coming-of-age tale of a young Everyman struggling to make sense of the chaotic modern world. Alabama novelist Harper Lee drew from the Southern Gothic tradition to tell of racial injustice and the loss of youthful innocence in the blockbuster *To Kill a Mockingbird* (1960).

In short lyric meditations, postwar American poets experimented with a frank, "confessional" style, revealing personal experiences with sex, drugs, and mental illness. Descended from a long line of patrician New Englanders yet inspired by the contemporary Beats, Robert Lowell sought to apply the wisdom of the Puritan past to the perplexing present in allegorical poems like *For the Union Dead* (1964). Young and brilliant Sylvia Plath crafted the moving verses of *Ariel* (published posthumously in 1966) and a disturbing autobiographical novel, *The Bell Jar* (1963), but her career was cut short when she died by suicide.

The postwar decades were a golden age of American playwriting. Tennessee Williams delivered powerful critiques of the contemporary restrictions placed on women's lives in *A Streetcar Named Desire* (1947) and *Cat on a Hot Tin Roof* (1955). Arthur Miller's *Death of a Salesman* (1949) became a tragic indictment of the American dream of material success, and *The Crucible* (1953) turned the Salem witch trials into a dark parable warning against the dangers of McCarthyism (refer to Image 33.15). (Miller's turbulent five-year marriage to Marilyn Monroe was the era's

Gjon Mili/The LIFE Picture Collection/Getty Images

Image 33.15 A Scene from *The Crucible*, by Arthur Miller (1915–2005) Miller's 1953 play about the Salem witch trials in the 1690s (refer to "4-8 The Half-Way Covenant and the Salem Witch Trials," pp. 86–87) was widely understood as a commentary on Senator Joseph McCarthy's anti-Communist "witch-hunts" in the 1950s. Initially panned by critics, it was eventually acknowledged as an American classic.

most unusual union of high culture and Hollywood celebrity.) Lorraine Hansberry offered an affecting, realistic portrait of African American struggles in *A Raisin in the Sun* (1959). Edward Albee exposed the rapacious underside of middle-class life in *Who's Afraid of Virginia Woolf?* (1962). Black nationalist LeRoi Jones (later known as Amiri Baraka) interrogated Black manhood and white racism in *Dutchman* (1964).

The South boasted its own literary revival, led by veteran Mississippi author William Faulkner, a Nobel Prize recipient in 1950. Distancing themselves from an earlier "Lost Cause" literature (refer to "The Presence of the Past: 'The Lost Cause'," pp. 744–746), white Southern writers brought a new critical appreciation to the region's burdens of history, racism, and conservatism. Tennessean Robert Penn Warren immortalized Louisiana populist Huey Long in the novel *All the King's Men* (1946). Fellow Mississippians Walker Percy and Eudora Welty grasped the falling torch from the failing Faulkner, who died in 1962. Along with Georgian Flannery O'Connor, these later writers perceptively tracked the changes reshaping the postwar South.

Arthur Miller (1915–2005) challenged America's blind faith in postwar success and explored the psychic cost of failure in his masterpiece *Death of a Salesman* (1949). Early in the play, Miller's protagonist, Willy Loman, offers the era's customary advice on success in business to his son Biff:

"[T]he man who makes an appearance in the business world, the man who creates personal interest, is the man who gets ahead. Be liked and you will never want."

Especially bountiful was the harvest of books by Jewish writers. Bernard Malamud rendered a touching portrait of a family of New York Jewish storekeepers in *The Assistant* (1957). Philip Roth wrote comically about young New Jersey suburbanites in *Goodbye, Columbus* (1959) and penned an uproarious account of a sexually obsessed middle-aged New Yorker in *Portnoy's Complaint* (1969).

An increasing number of books grappled with the horrors of the Holocaust. The spare, devastating prose of camp survivor Elie Wiesel's literary memoir *Night* (1960) shook complacent postwar audiences into a fuller reckoning with the Nazi genocide. Writing in Yiddish and then translating his work into English, novelist Isaac Bashevis Singer explored the war's toll on the faith and relationships of its Jewish survivors in *Enemies: A Love Story* (1972).

33-15 Kennedy's "New Frontier" Spirit

Complacent and comfortable as the 1950s closed, Americans elected in 1960 a young, vigorous president who pledged "to get the country moving again." As John F. Kennedy announced in his stirring inaugural address on January 20, 1961, "The torch has been passed to a new generation of Americans." Speaking crisply with staccato finger jabs at the air, Kennedy personified the glamour and vitality of the new administration.

The youngest president ever elected assembled one of the youngest cabinets, including his brother, Robert F. Kennedy, as attorney general. Thirty-five-year-old "Bobby" set out, among other reforms, to recast the priorities of the FBI, shifting its focus from internal security work to organized crime cases and civil rights enforcement. He quickly earned the seething resentment of J. Edgar Hoover, who had served as FBI director longer than the new attorney general had been alive. (Taking a cue from their boss, contemptuous FBI agents privately referred to Robert Kennedy's office as "the playpen.") Business whiz Robert S. McNamara left the presidency of the Ford Motor Company to take over the Defense Department. Along with other young advisers (many boasting Harvard degrees), these appointees made up an inner circle notable for its aura of brash confidence and elite credentials.

From the outset Kennedy inspired high expectations, especially among young adults. His depiction of America's potential for greatness as a **New Frontier** quickened patriotic pulses. He brought a warm heart to the Cold War when he established the **Peace Corps**, an army of idealistic and mostly youthful volunteers bringing American know-how to underdeveloped countries. He summoned citizens to service with his clarion call to "ask not what your country can do for you: ask what you can do for your country."

But the soaring rhetoric did not quite match the political situation. Kennedy came into office with fragile Democratic majorities in Congress. Southern Democrats threatened to team up with Republicans and ax New Frontier proposals.

Richard Goodwin (1931–2018), a Kennedy aide and Peace Corps staffer, eloquently summed up the buoyantly optimistic mood of the early 1960s:

"For a moment, it seemed as if the entire country, the whole spinning globe, rested, malleable and receptive, in our beneficent hands."

Kennedy won a first round in his campaign for a more cooperative Congress when he forced an expansion of the all-important House Rules Committee, dominated by conservatives who could have bottled up his entire legislative program. Despite this victory, the New Frontier did not expand swiftly. Key medical and education bills remained stalled in Congress. In 1963, the legislative branch even voted down an administration-endorsed bill slashing income and corporate tax rates to boost the economy.

That tax bill hinted at the Kennedy administration's complex relationship with big business. The president intended his support for tax-cutting to mollify businessmen wary of a big-government liberal in the White House. He urged unions to curb wage demands and brokered tumultuous talks with steel industry bosses and labor leaders to successfully forge a noninflationary wage agreement in 1962. Weeks later, however, the steel bosses announced price increases. Enraged, Kennedy stormed to the press podium and unleashed his Irish temper on the steel bosses for their "unjustifiable and irresponsible defiance of the public interest." (He used more unprintable language as he vented to confidants.) Overawed by the president's use of the bully pulpit, the steelmakers backed down. Savoring victory, Kennedy magnanimously told the steelmen, echoing Ulysses Grant at Appomattox, that they could keep their horses for the spring plowing.

Kennedy's New Frontier vision also extended to the "final frontier." The United States' first human spaceflight mission, Project Mercury, and its successor Project Gemini, sent astronauts into orbit for increasingly longer periods, testing the human body's capacity to adapt to outer space (refer to Image 33.16). Early in his term, the president promoted a multibillion-dollar project dedicated, as he put it, to "landing a man on the Moon and returning him safely to Earth" before the end of the decade. Though he summoned stirring rhetoric about expanding human possibilities, the moon shot was really a calculated ploy to restore America's international prestige, severely damaged by the Soviet *Sputnik* successes (refer to "33-11 Round Two for Ike," p. 889). Twenty-four billion dollars later, in July 1969, two NASA astronauts would triumphantly plant their footprints—and the American flag—on the moon's dusty surface.

NASA Photo/Alamy Stock Photo

Image 33.16 John Glenn Pilots Mercury *Friendship 7*, February 1962 Glenn became the first American to orbit the Earth on this flight, circling the planet three times in five hours.

33-16 A New President Tested

Cold War crises in two hemispheres presented the earliest and gravest tests of Kennedy's presidency. The new president inherited a fraught situation in Latin America, as the Cuban revolution prompted renewed U.S. attention to the region's social challenges and simmering anti-American resentments. In March 1961, Kennedy extended the hand of friendship with the Alliance for Progress (*Alianza para el Progreso*), hailed as a Marshall Plan for Latin America, and intended to quiet communist agitation. But the results were disappointing; there was little alliance and even less progress.

President Kennedy also inherited from the Eisenhower administration a CIA-backed scheme to topple Fidel Castro from power by invading Cuba with anticommunist exiles. Assured by confident advisors that the operation would spark a popular uprising, Kennedy agreed to it. On April 17, 1961, some twelve hundred American-armed exiles landed at Cuba's Bahia de Cochinos (Bay of Pigs), where Castro's forces swiftly overwhelmed them. Instead of liberating Cuba, the ill-starred **Bay of Pigs invasion** delivered Kennedy a humiliating political defeat (refer to Image 33.17).

Hulton Deutsch/Getty Images

Image 33.17 Failed Bay of Pigs Invasion, 1961 Cuban soldiers demonstrate a beach gun they used against a brigade of ex-Cubans who furtively invaded Cuba as agents of the United States. The debacle was one of several unsuccessful American attempts to overthrow Cuban leader Fidel Castro.

Those wounds were still smarting when, in June 1961, Kennedy met Soviet premier Khrushchev at Vienna. The tough-talking Soviet leader adopted a belligerent attitude, threatening to make a treaty with East Germany and cut off Western access to Berlin. Though visibly shaken, Kennedy refused to be bullied, declaring that the United States would respond to Soviet aggression militarily if needed.

The Soviets backed off from their most bellicose threats, but their "puppet" East German regime suddenly began to construct the **Berlin Wall** in August 1961. A barbed-wire and concrete barrier, it was designed to plug the heavy population drain from East Germany to West Germany through the Berlin funnel. But to the free world, the "Wall of Shame" looked like a gigantic enclosure around a prison. The wall stood for almost three decades as an ugly scar symbolizing the post–World War II division of Europe into two hostile camps (refer to Image 33.18).

Kennedy meanwhile turned his attention to Western Europe, now miraculously prospering after the tonic of Marshall Plan aid and the growth of the American-encouraged **European Economic Community (EEC)**, the free-trade area that later evolved into the European Union. He secured passage of the Trade Expansion Act in 1962, authorizing tariff cuts of up to 50 percent to promote trade with EEC countries. This act led to the so-called Kennedy Round of tariff negotiations, concluded in 1967. These liberalized trade policies inaugurated a new era of such robustly invigorated international commerce that a new word was coined to describe it: *globalization*.

A

Popperfoto/Getty Images

B

STR OLD/Reuters

Image 33.18A and B The Berlin Wall, 1961–1989 The wall separating East and West Berlin stood for nearly thirty years as a hated symbol of the division of Europe into democratic and communist camps. East German soldiers stood guard as the concrete wall was constructed, November 20, 1961 (Image 33.18A). Demonstrators had begun to tear down the wall in 1989 following powerful nonviolent protests in East Germany (Image 33.18B).

33-17 Cuban Confrontation

The Bay of Pigs blunder, along with continuing American covert efforts to assassinate Castro and overthrow his government, naturally pushed the Cuban leader even further into the Soviet embrace. Wily Chairman Khrushchev lost little time in taking full advantage of his Cuban comrade's location just ninety miles off Florida's coast. In October 1962 aerial photographs by American spy planes revealed that the Soviets were secretly and speedily installing nuclear-tipped missiles in Cuba.

Kennedy and Khrushchev now began a nerve-racking game of "nuclear chicken." The president flatly rejected U.S. Air Force proposals for a surgical bombing strike against the missile-launching sites. Instead, on October 22, 1962, he ordered a naval blockade of Cuba and demanded immediate removal of the threatening weaponry (refer to Image 33.19). He also served notice on Khrushchev that any attack on the United States from Cuba would trigger nuclear retaliation against the Russian heartland.

For an anxious week, Americans waited while Soviet ships approached the patrol line established by the U.S. Navy off the island of Cuba. The world teetered breathlessly on the brink of global atomization. Only in 1991 did the full dimensions of this nuclear peril become known, when the Russians revealed that their ground forces in Cuba already had operational nuclear weapons at their disposal and were authorized to launch them if attacked.

In this tense eyeball-to-eyeball confrontation, Khrushchev finally flinched. On October 28, he agreed to a partially face-saving compromise, by which he would pull the missiles out of Cuba. The United States in return agreed to end the blockade and not invade the island. The American government also quietly signaled that it would remove from Turkey some of its own missiles targeted at the Soviet Union.

Ralph Crane/The LIFE Picture Collection/Shutterstock.com

Image 33.19 The Cuban Missile Crisis Begins California department store shoppers watch as President Kennedy announces the naval blockade of Cuba on October 22, 1963.

Fallout from the **Cuban missile crisis** was considerable. A disgraced Khrushchev was ultimately hounded out of the Kremlin and became an "unperson." Hard-liners in Moscow, vowing never again to be humiliated in a nuclear face-off, launched an enormous program of military expansion. Kennedy, apparently sobered by the appalling risks he had just run, pushed harder for a nuclear test-ban treaty with the Soviet Union. After prolonged negotiations in Moscow, a pact prohibiting trial nuclear explosions in the atmosphere was signed in late 1963. Another barometer indicating a thaw in the Cold War was the installation in August 1963 of a Moscow-Washington "hot line," permitting immediate teletype communication in case of a crisis.

Most significant was Kennedy's speech at American University in Washington, DC, in June 1963. The president urged Americans to abandon a view of the Soviet Union as a devil-ridden land filled with fanatics and instead to deal with the world "as it is, not as it might have been had the history of the last eighteen years been different." Kennedy thus tried to lay the foundation for a realistic policy of peaceful coexistence with the Soviet Union. Here were the modest origins of the policy that later came to be known as "détente" (French for "relaxation of tension").

At American University on June 10, 1963, President Kennedy eloquently called for a thaw in the Cold War with the Soviet Union:

"No government or social system is so evil that its people must be considered as lacking in virtue. As Americans, we find communism profoundly repugnant as a negation of personal freedom and dignity. But we can still hail the Russian people for their many achievements—in science and space, in economic and industrial growth, in culture and in acts of courage. . . . And if we cannot end now our differences, at least we can help make the world safe for diversity. For, in the final analysis, our most basic common link is that we all inhabit this small planet. We all breathe the same air. We all cherish our children's future. And we are all mortal."

33-18 The Vietnam Engagement Intensifies

Special problems for U.S. foreign policy emerged from the worldwide decolonization of European overseas possessions after World War II. As with Ho Chi Minh's revolutionary movement in Vietnam, communist ideas often proved more appealing than capitalism for people long economically exploited under colonial rule. Winning the hearts and minds of this so-called "third world" (the democratic and capitalist West was the "first," and the Soviet bloc the "second") consumed both Soviet and American diplomacy and spycraft.

Such Cold War entanglements in new nations threatened to escalate all too quickly into a nuclear confrontation between the superpowers, a prospect that Kennedy attributed to Secretary

Dulles's dubious doctrine of "massive retaliation." The president felt hamstrung by the knowledge that in a crisis he had the devil's choice between abject humiliation and nuclear incineration. With Defense Secretary McNamara, he pushed an alternative strategy of "flexible response"—developing an array of military "options" that could be precisely matched to the gravity of the crisis at hand. To this end, Kennedy increased spending on conventional military forces and bolstered the Special Forces (Green Berets) specializing in anti-guerilla fighting.

The doctrine of "flexible response" seemed sane enough, but it too contained lethal logic. It potentially lowered the level at which diplomacy would give way to shooting. It also provided a mechanism for a progressive, and possibly endless, stepping-up of the use of force. Vietnam soon presented grisly proof of these pitfalls.

The corrupt, right-wing government of Ngo Dinh Diem in Saigon, despite a deluge of American dollars, had ruled shakily since the partition of Vietnam in 1954 (refer to "33-9 America Intervenes in Vietnam," pp. 887–888). With ever more intensity, anti-Diem agitators threatened to topple the pro-American government from power. In a fateful decision late in 1961, Kennedy ordered a sharp increase in the number of "military advisers" (U.S. troops) in South Vietnam.

American forces allegedly entered Vietnam to foster political stability—to help protect Diem from the communists long enough to allow him to enact promised social reforms. But the Kennedy administration eventually despaired of the reactionary Diem and in November 1963 encouraged a successful coup against him.

Ironically, the United States thus contributed to precisely the process of political disintegration that its original policy had meant to prevent. Kennedy still told the South Vietnamese that it was "their war," but he had made dangerously deep political commitments. By the time of his death, his military had deployed more than fifteen thousand American soldiers. A graceful pull-out was becoming increasingly difficult (refer to Map 33.3).

33-19 The Struggle for Civil Rights

Kennedy had campaigned with a strong appeal to Black voters, but disappointed them by proceeding gingerly toward promised civil rights. Elected by a wafer-thin margin, Kennedy needed the support of Southern legislators to pass his economic and social legislation, especially his medical and educational bills. He believed that those measures would eventually benefit Black Americans at least as much as specific legislation on civil rights. Bold moves for racial justice would have to wait.

But events soon scrambled these careful calculations. After the wave of student-led sit-ins in 1960, interracial groups of **Freedom Riders**—an increasing number of whom were white college students from outside the South—fanned out to end segregation in facilities serving interstate bus passengers. A white mob torched a Freedom Ride bus near Anniston, Alabama, in May 1961 (refer to Image 33.20), and Attorney General Robert Kennedy's personal representative was beaten unconscious in another anti–Freedom Ride riot in Montgomery. When Southern officials proved unwilling or unable to stem the violence, Washington dispatched federal marshals to protect the Freedom Riders.

Reluctantly but fatefully, the Kennedy administration had now joined hands with the civil rights movement. Yet both John (JFK) and Robert Kennedy proved ultra wary about the perceived political radicalism of many movement leaders. Fearful of embarrassing revelations that some of Martin Luther King Jr.'s advisers had communist affiliations, Attorney General Kennedy ordered FBI director J. Edgar Hoover to wiretap King's phone in late 1963.

Concerned about international press attention and the growing displeasure of Southern lawmakers, Robert Kennedy encouraged activists toward voter registration drives instead of civil disobedience. With financial backing from Kennedy-prodded private foundations, the Student Nonviolent Coordinating Committee and other civil rights groups inaugurated the **Voter Education Project** to register the South's historically disfranchised Black citizens.

Activists soon discovered that voter registration drives posed as much of a challenge to white supremacy as any sit-in. Sharecropper and organizer Fannie Lou Hamer was arrested, fired, and dispossessed after trying to register voters; a later beating by police left Hamer with lifelong injuries. So many would-be voters and SNCC volunteers were arrested and beaten that Attorney General Kennedy sent in federal law enforcement to protect them.

Integrating Deep South universities proved just as challenging. White resistance turned the integration of the University of Mississippi ("Ole Miss") into a volcano. A twenty-nine-year-old

Map 33.3 Vietnam and Southeast Asia, 1954–1975 Le Ly Hayslip (b. 1949) was born in a peasant village in South Vietnam, just south of Da Nang. In her memoir, *When Heaven and Earth Changed Places*, she describes the trauma endured by ordinary Vietnamese as a result of America's fight against the Viet Cong: "In 1963—the year the Viet Cong came to my village—American warplanes bombed Man Quang. It was at noon, just when the children were getting out of school. My aunt Thu and her pregnant daughter-in-law were making lunch for her husband and four grandchildren when the air-raid signal blared. They all jumped under the wooden table and sheltered the pregnant woman with their bodies—even the little kids. A bomb fell in Aunt Thu's front yard. . . . Hot shrapnel tore through everyone except the pregnant woman. Aunt Thu and one of her grandchildren were killed. The passing fragment left only a weeping hole where her generous heart had been."

Bettmann/Getty Images

Image 33.20 Freedom Ride, 1961 Rampaging white segregationists near Anniston, Alabama, burned this bus carrying an interracial group of Freedom Riders on May 14, 1961.

Air Force veteran, James Meredith, encountered violent opposition when he attempted to register in October 1962. President Kennedy was forced to send in four hundred federal marshals and three thousand troops to enroll Meredith in his first class (the topic: early American history).

In the spring of 1963, Martin Luther King Jr., launched a campaign against discrimination in Birmingham, Alabama, the most segregated big city in America. Previous attempts to crack the city's rigid racial barriers had produced more than fifty cross burnings and eighteen bomb attacks since 1957. "Some of the people sitting here will not come back alive from this campaign," King advised his organizers.

Events soon confirmed this grim prediction of violence. Watching developments on television screens, a horrified world saw peaceful civil rights marchers repeatedly repelled by police with attack dogs and electric cattle prods. High-pressure hoses shot water at the demonstrators with enough force to knock bricks loose from buildings or strip bark from trees (refer to Image 33.21). Little children were bowled down the street like tumbleweeds.

Jolted by these vicious confrontations, President Kennedy delivered a memorable televised speech to the nation on June 11, 1963. In contrast to Eisenhower's cool aloofness from the racial question, Kennedy called the situation a "moral issue" and committed his personal and presidential prestige to finding a solution. Drawing on the same spiritual traditions as King, JFK declared that the principle at stake "is as old as the Scriptures and is as clear as the American Constitution." He called for new civil rights legislation to protect Black citizens. In August more than 200,000 Black and white demonstrators gathered in a peaceful **March on Washington** in support of the proposed legislation (refer to Image 33.22). In an electrifying speech from the Lincoln Memorial, King declared, "I have a dream that my four little children will one day live in a nation where they will not be judged by the color of their skin, but by the content of their character."

Still the violence continued. On the very night of Kennedy's stirring television address, a white gunman shot down Medgar Evers, a Black Mississippi civil rights worker. In September 1963, an explosion blasted a Baptist church in Birmingham, killing four Black girls who had just finished their lesson called "The Love That Forgives." JFK's civil rights bill made little headway in Congress in the months after his address.

33-20 The Killing of Kennedy

Violence haunted America in the mid-1960s, and it stalked onto center stage on November 22, 1963. While riding in an open limousine in downtown Dallas, Texas, President Kennedy was shot in the brain by a concealed rifleman and died within seconds. Vice President Johnson was

Black Star/Alamy Stock Photo

Image 33.21 Hosing Down Civil Rights Demonstrators, Birmingham, Alabama, 1963 Most of the marchers attacked by fire hoses and police dogs were children and teenagers, making the violent police reprisal even more horrifying to television audiences.

promptly sworn in as president on a waiting airplane and flown back to Washington with Kennedy's body.

As a stunned nation grieved, the tragedy grew still more unbelievable. The alleged assassin, a furtive figure named Lee Harvey Oswald, was himself shot to death in front of television cameras by a self-appointed avenger, Jack Ruby. So bizarre were the events surrounding the two murders that even an elaborate official investigation conducted by Chief Justice Warren could not quiet all doubts and theories about what had really happened.

For several days, the nation was steeped in sorrow. Not until then did many Americans realize how fully their young, vibrant president and his captivating wife had cast a spell over them. Chopped down in his prime after only slightly more than a thousand days in the White House, Kennedy was acclaimed more for the ideals he had enunciated and the spirit he had kindled than for the concrete goals he had achieved. In later years, revelations about Kennedy's womanizing and allegations about his involvement with organized crime figures tarnished his reputation. But despite those accusations, his apparent vigor, charisma, and idealism made him an inspirational figure for a rising baby boom generation. Few could foresee that the decade following his death would explode into extraordinary ferment at home and abroad.

Bettmann/Getty Images

Image 33.22 Martin Luther King Jr. Addresses the March on Washington, August 1963 This was the occasion of King's famous "I Have a Dream" speech, in which he declared, "When the architects of our great republic wrote the magnificent words of the Constitution and the Declaration of Independence, they were signing a promissory note to which every American was to fall heir. This note was a promise that all men, yes, black men as well as white men, would be guaranteed the inalienable rights of life, liberty, and the pursuit of happiness."

Chapter Summary

American society grew ever more prosperous in the postwar era, as science, technology, and the Cold War fueled burgeoning new industries like electronics and commercial aviation. Women became a substantial part of the increasingly white-collar workforce, and they chafed at widespread restrictions. A new consumer culture, centered on television and advertising, fostered an ethic of leisure and enjoyment, including more open expressions of sexuality in popular entertainment.

Enormously popular as the victorious Supreme Allied Commander in World War II, Dwight Eisenhower was nominated by enthusiastic Republicans and breezed to victory over Illinois governor Adlai Stevenson in the election of 1952. "Ike" was ideally suited to soothe an America badly shaken by the Cold War and Korea. Seeking stability in domestic affairs, Eisenhower declined to endorse the civil rights movement led by Martin Luther King Jr. but sent troops to Little Rock to enforce court orders for desegregation. Eisenhower's domestic policies were moderately conservative, leaving most of the New Deal in place while promoting private industry and spending vast sums on a new interstate highway system.

Despite John Foster Dulles's tough talk, Eisenhower's foreign policies were also generally cautious. He avoided direct military intervention in Vietnam, although aiding South Vietnamese leader Diem, and pressured Britain, France, and Israel to resolve the Suez crisis. Eisenhower also sought negotiations to thaw the frigid Cold War. Dealing with Nikita Khrushchev proved difficult, however, as *Sputnik*, the Berlin Crisis, the U-2 incident, and Fidel Castro's Cuban revolution all kept Cold War tensions high. In a tight election, Senator John Kennedy defeated Eisenhower's vice president, Richard Nixon. Kennedy called for the country to "get moving again" by more vigorously countering the Soviets.

America's power and affluence contributed to a postwar cultural renaissance. Painting and architecture undertook bold experiments in modernism. In literature, the Beat writers challenged conventional forms as well as conformist lifestyles. African American, Southern, and Jewish writers all had a striking impact on American thought and writing.

Kennedy's vigorous New Frontier initiatives stirred a spirit of idealism, but many of his programs became bogged down in Congress. Cold War confrontations over Berlin and Russian missiles in Cuba created threats of nuclear war but were successfully defused. Countering communism's threat through the doctrine of "flexible response" led the administration into dangerous involvement in Vietnam and elsewhere.

Kennedy was slow to endorse the civil rights movement, but eventually King and other activists like those of the Freedom Rides and the Student Nonviolent Coordinating Committee created a moral groundswell that led Kennedy to endorse racial justice and propose new civil rights legislation. While Kennedy's sudden death left most of his goals unfulfilled, his charisma and idealism had inspired a generation.

Key Terms

- International Business Machines (IBM) (876)
- *The Feminine Mystique* (877)
- rock 'n' roll (880)
- Checkers Speech (881)
- Montgomery bus boycott (883)
- *Brown v. Board of Education of Topeka, Kansas* (884)
- Student Nonviolent Coordinating Committee (SNCC) (886)
- National Interstate and Defense Highways Act of 1956 (886)
- Operation Wetback (886)
- termination policy (887)
- policy of boldness (887)
- Hungarian uprising (887)
- Dien Bien Phu, Battle of (888)
- Suez crisis (888)
- Organization of Petroleum Exporting Countries (OPEC) (889)
- *Sputnik* (889)
- kitchen debate (890)
- military-industrial complex (892)
- International Style (893)
- Beat Generation (893)
- New Frontier (895)
- Peace Corps (895)
- Bay of Pigs invasion (897)
- Berlin Wall (897)
- European Economic Community (EEC) (897)
- Cuban missile crisis (899)
- Freedom Riders (900)
- Voter Education Project (900)
- March on Washington (902)

People to Know

- Richard M. Nixon
- Betty Friedan
- Elvis Presley
- Rosa Parks
- Martin Luther King Jr.
- Ella Baker
- Earl Warren
- John Foster Dulles
- Nikita Khrushchev
- Ho Chi Minh
- Gamal Abdel Nasser
- Fidel Castro
- John F. Kennedy
- Lyndon Baines Johnson
- Jackson Pollock
- Florence Knoll
- Ray Eames
- Andy Warhol
- Jack Kerouac
- Allen Ginsberg
- Arthur Miller
- Ralph Ellison
- Lorraine Hansberry
- Robert F. Kennedy
- Robert S. McNamara
- Ngo Dinh Diem
- Fannie Lou Hamer
- James Meredith

Chronology

1951	• Salinger publishes *The Catcher in the Rye*
1952	• Eisenhower defeats Stevenson for presidency • Ellison publishes *Invisible Man* • United Nations headquarters open in New York City
1953	• CIA-engineered coup installs shah of Iran • Joseph Stalin dies • Miller's *The Crucible* debuts on Broadway • Bellow publishes *The Adventures of Augie March*
1954	• French defeated at Dien Bien Phu in Vietnam • *Brown v. Board of Education* • Nasser becomes prime minister of Egypt • CIA-sponsored coup in Guatemala
1955	• Montgomery bus boycott by Black riders begins; emergence of Martin Luther King Jr. • Geneva summit meeting on Vietnam • AFL merges with CIO • Tennessee Williams's *Cat on a Hot Tin Roof* first performed
1956	• Soviets crush Hungarian revolt • Suez crisis • Eisenhower defeats Stevenson for presidency • Ginsberg publishes *Howl and Other Poems*
1957	• Little Rock school desegregation crisis • Civil Rights Act passed • Southern Christian Leadership Conference (SCLC) formed • Soviet Union launches Sputnik satellites • Kerouac publishes *On the Road* • European Economic Community (EEC, Common Market) created by Treaty of Rome
1958	• NDEA authorizes loans and grants for science and language education • Galbraith publishes *The Affluent Society*
1958–1959	• Berlin crisis
1959	• Castro seizes power in Cuba • Landrum-Griffin Act • Alaska and Hawai'i attain statehood • Guggenheim Museum opens in New York City • Lorraine Hansberry stages *A Raisin in the Sun*

1960	• Sit-in movement for civil rights begins • U-2 incident sabotages Paris summit • OPEC formed • Kennedy defeats Nixon for presidency • Updike publishes *Rabbit, Run* • Lee publishes *To Kill a Mockingbird*
1961	• Heller publishes *Catch-22* • Berlin Wall built • Alliance for Progress • Bay of Pigs invasion • Kennedy sends "military advisers" to South Vietnam
1962	• Pressure from Kennedy results in rollback of steel prices • Trade Expansion Act • Cuban missile crisis
1963	• Plath publishes *The Bell Jar* • Anti-Diem coup in South Vietnam • Civil rights march in Washington, DC • Voter Education Project established • Kennedy assassinated; Johnson assumes presidency

To Learn More

Glenn Altschuler, *All Shook Up: How Rock 'N' Roll Changed America* (2003)

Laura A. Belmonte, *Selling the American Way: U.S. Propaganda and the Cold War* (2010)

Lizabeth Cohen, *A Consumers' Republic: The Politics of Mass Consumption in Postwar America* (2003)

Robert Dallek, *An Unfinished Life: John F. Kennedy, 1917–1963* (2003)

Michael Dobbs, *One Minute to Midnight: Kennedy, Khrushchev, and Castro on the Brink of Nuclear War* (2008)

Mary Dudziak, *Cold War Civil Rights* (2000)

John Egerton, *Speak Now Against the Day: The Generation Before the Civil Rights Movement in the South* (1994)

William I. Hitchcock, *The Age of Eisenhower: American and the World in the 1950s* (2018)

Robert F. Kennedy, *Thirteen Days* (1969)

Melvyn Leffler, *For the Soul of Mankind: The United States, the Soviet Union, and the Cold War* (2007)

Elaine May, *Homeward Bound: American Families in the Cold War Era* (1988)

Barbara Ransby, *Ella Baker and the Black Freedom Movement* (2005)

Thomas Sugrue, *The Origins of the Urban Crisis: Race and Inequality in Postwar Detroit* (1996)

Jeanne Theoharis, *The Rebellious Life of Mrs. Rosa Parks* (2014)

Theodore White, *Making of the President, 1960* (1961)

Chapter 34

The Stormy Sixties: 1963–1973

There's a battle outside and it is ragin'

...

For the times they are a-changin'

Bob Dylan, 1963

Chapter Outline

- Lyndon Baines Johnson takes charge
- Johnson versus Barry Goldwater, 1964
- The Great Society
- The civil rights revolution explodes
- The Vietnam disaster
- The election of Richard Nixon, 1968
- The cultural upheavals of the 1960s
- The erosion of trust
- Nixon and the Vietnam War
- New policies toward China and the Soviet Union
- Nixon on the home front
- Nixon trounces George McGovern, 1972
- Israelis, Arabs, and oil

The Presence of the Past: Immigration—Legal, Illegal, and Otherwise

Contending Voices: Two Visions of Black Freedom

Thinking Globally: The Global 1960s

Varying Viewpoints: What Were the Legacies of the 1960s?

Iconic historical decades rarely align perfectly with the actual calendar. What many Americans remember as the tumultuous "sixties" did not truly begin until after the shocking slaying of President John F. Kennedy, and the decade's several upheavals in culture and politics extended well into the 1970s. Between President Kennedy's assassination in 1963 and President Nixon's resignation in 1974, Americans experienced a sexual revolution, a civil rights revolt, the emergence of a "youth culture," a devastating war in Vietnam, a massive enlargement of the federal government, far-reaching political realignments, deepening distrust of nearly all their major institutions, and the beginnings of a feminist uprising. In the end Americans were exhausted, divided, and badly disillusioned—and permanently transformed in myriad ways.

Focus Questions

1. What was Lyndon Johnson's distinctive style in the presidency, and what were the legislative goals of his "Great Society"?
2. How was the idealistic and nonviolent spirit of the civil rights movement transformed in the mid-1960s by white racial "backlash," the rise of the Black Power movement, and urban civil disturbances?
3. How did Lyndon Johnson and his advisers lead the United States deeper into the Vietnam quagmire, and why did that war create such deep divisions in American politics and society?
4. What were the roots of the cultural rebellion of the 1960s, and what were its short-term and long-term consequences?
5. What were the major successes and failures of Richard Nixon's first-term domestic and foreign policies?

34-1 The LBJ Brand on the Presidency

With President Kennedy struck down, the torch passed to craggy-faced Lyndon Baines Johnson, a Texan who towered six feet three inches. Although he mistrusted "the Harvards," Johnson retained most of the bright Kennedy team. The new president managed a dignified and efficient transition in the winter of 1963, pledging continuity with his slain predecessor's policies.

Johnson, often referred to simply as LBJ, hailed from the populist hill country west of Austin, Texas, whose people had first sent him to Washington as a twenty-nine-year-old congressman in 1937. Franklin D. Roosevelt was his political "Daddy," Johnson claimed. He had supported New Deal measures down the line. But when LBJ lost a Senate race in 1941, he learned the sobering lesson that liberal political beliefs did not necessarily win elections in Texas. He trimmed his sails to the right and squeezed himself into a Senate seat in 1948 with a questionable eighty-seven-vote margin—hence the ironic nickname "Landslide Lyndon."

Entrenched in the Senate, Johnson developed into a masterful wheeler-dealer. He became the Democratic majority leader in 1954, wielding power second only to that of Eisenhower in the White House. He could move mountains or checkmate opponents as the occasion demanded, using what came to be known as the "Johnson treatment"—an intimidating display of backslapping, flesh-pressing, and arm-twisting that overbore friend and foe alike. His ego and vanity were legendary. On a visit to the pope, Johnson was presented with a precious fourteenth-century painting from the Vatican art collection; in return, LBJ gave the pope a bust—of LBJ.

As president, Johnson quickly shed the conservative coloration of his Senate years to reveal the latent liberal underneath. "No memorial oration or eulogy," Johnson declared to Congress, "could more eloquently honor President Kennedy's memory than the earliest possible passage of the Civil Rights Bill for which he fought so long." After a lengthy conservative filibuster, Congress at last passed the landmark **Civil Rights Act of 1964**. The act banned racial discrimination in most private facilities open to the public, including theaters, hospitals, and restaurants. It strengthened the federal government's power to end segregation in schools and other public places. Title VII of the act barred employers from discriminating based on race or national origin in hiring and empowered the Equal Employment Opportunity Commission (EEOC, a body Kennedy had created in 1961) to enforce the law. When conservatives tried to derail the legislation by adding a prohibition on sexual, as well as racial, discrimination, the tactic backfired. The bill's opponents cynically calculated that liberals would not be able to support a bill that threatened to wipe out laws that singled out women for special protection because of their sex. But the act's Title VII passed with the sexual clause intact. It soon proved to be a powerful instrument of federally enforced gender equality, as well as racial equality. Johnson struck another blow for women and minorities alike in 1965 when he issued an executive order requiring all federal contractors to take **affirmative action** against racial and gender discrimination in hiring.

Johnson also rammed Kennedy's stalled tax bill through Congress and added proposals of his own for a billion-dollar "War on Poverty." The initial political impetus for the antipoverty campaign had come from journalist Michael Harrington's surprise best seller *The Other America* (1962), which revealed that even in affluent America 20 percent of the population—and over 40 percent of the Black population—suffered in poverty. Prior to his death, Kennedy had contemplated developing an antipoverty initiative. Now his successor took up the cause with a vengeance. Johnson's War on Poverty composed one element of a far-reaching reform program that he dubbed the **Great Society**. Based on assumptions about an ever-expanding economy, Great Society initiatives epitomized the soaring national self-confidence of the post–World War II era. They envisioned not only the end of racial discrimination, but also vastly expanded health and welfare programs, the abolition of poverty, and major new public investments in education and the arts.

34-2 Johnson Battles Goldwater in 1964

Johnson's nomination by the Democrats in 1964 was a foregone conclusion. Prodded by Johnson, the Democrats stood foursquare on their most liberal platform since Truman's Fair Deal days. The Republicans, convening in San Francisco's Cow Palace, swerved in an unexpectedly conservative direction, nominating box-jawed Senator Barry Goldwater of Arizona, a bronzed and bespectacled champion of small government, free enterprise, and rock-ribbed anti-Communism. The American stage was thus set for a historic clash of political principles.

Duane Howell/Getty Images

Image 34.1 Partisan Warfare, 1964 Both pro- and anti-Goldwater advocates have left their marks on this Goldwater for President billboard in 1964.

Goldwater's forces had galloped out of the Southwest to ride roughshod over the long-dominant moderate Republican "Eastern establishment." Insisting that the GOP offer "a choice not an echo," Goldwater attacked the federal income tax, the Social Security system, the Tennessee Valley Authority, civil rights legislation, the nuclear test-ban treaty, and, most loudly, the Great Society. His fiercely dedicated followers proclaimed, "In Your Heart You Know He's Right" (refer to Image 34.1), which prompted the Democratic response, "In Your Guts You Know He's Nuts." Goldwater warmed right-wing hearts when he proclaimed that "extremism in the defense of liberty is no vice. And . . . moderation in the pursuit of justice is no virtue."

The senator owed his nomination to a bourgeoning conservative movement that was gathering strength in the mushrooming middle-class suburbs of the Sunbelt. Led intellectually by brainy contrarians like William F. Buckley and his staff at *National Review* magazine, conservative activists in the early 1960s formed groups like Young Americans for Freedom and volunteered enthusiastically for the Draft Goldwater movement. They were especially well received in the once-solidly Democratic South, where displeasure about federal action on civil rights was disrupting the ancient political loyalties of many white voters. Upon signing the Civil Rights Act of 1964, Democratic president Lyndon Johnson had reputedly told an aide, "We have lost the South for a generation." Goldwater's opposition to that act, though framed in libertarian rather than racial terms, helped make Johnson's fears a reality.

Goldwater's unrelentingly aggressive stance against the Soviet Union, however, gave the president's allies a powerful political opening. Democrats gleefully portrayed the Arizonan as a trigger-happy cowboy who would "Barry us" in the debris of World War III. Johnson cultivated the contrasting image of resolute statesman, and in so doing made a fateful move that further enmeshed America in the war in Vietnam.

Unbeknownst to the public or Congress, U.S. Navy ships had been cooperating with South Vietnamese gunboats in provocative raids along the coast of North Vietnam. Two of these American destroyers were allegedly fired on by the North

Civil rights activist and co-founder of the Mississippi Freedom Democratic Party Fannie Lou Hamer (1917–1977) entreated Democratic Party officials to seat her party's Black delegates at the 1964 convention:

"All of this is on account we want to register, to become first-class citizens, and if the Freedom Democratic Party is not seated now, I question America, is this America, the land of the free and the home of the brave where we have to sleep with our telephones off of the hooks because our lives be threatened daily because we want to live as decent human beings, in America?"

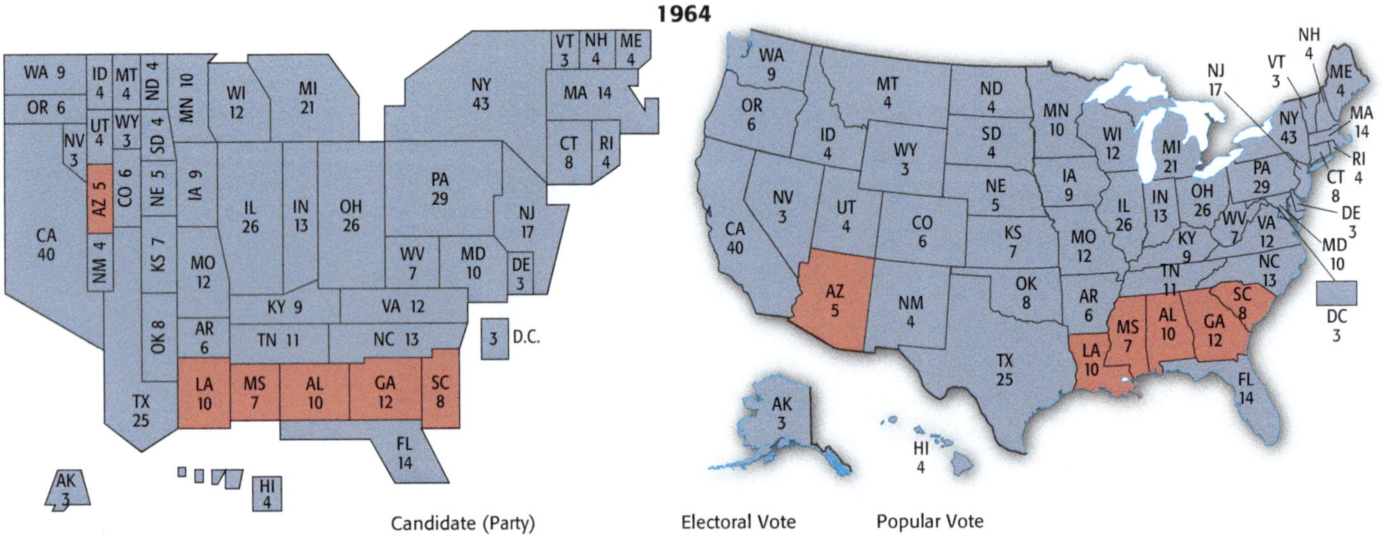

Candidate (Party)	Electoral Vote		Popular Vote	
Johnson (Democrat)	486	90.3%	43,129,566	61.1%
Goldwater (Republican)	52	9.7%	27,178,188	38.5%

Map 34.1 Presidential Election of 1964 In the map on the left, the size of each state is represented according to its weight in the Electoral College. In New Orleans, toward the end of the campaign, a gutsy Johnson displayed his commitment to civil rights when he told a story about an old senator who once said of his Deep South constituents, "I would like to go back down there and make them just one more Democratic speech. . . . The poor old State, they haven't heard a Democratic speech in 30 years. All they hear at election time is Negro, Negro, Negro!" Johnson's open voicing of sentiments like this contributed heavily to his losses in the traditionally Democratic "solid South."

Vietnamese on August 2 and 4, 1964, although the facts remained murky. Johnson allegedly said privately, "For all I know, our Navy was shooting at whales out there." He nevertheless promptly called the attack "unprovoked" and ordered a "limited" retaliatory air raid. He loudly proclaimed that he sought "no wider war," thus implying that the truculent Goldwater did, and used the incident to spur congressional passage of the all-purpose **Tonkin Gulf Resolution**. With only two dissenting votes in both chambers, lawmakers virtually abdicated their war-declaring powers and handed the president a blank check to use further force in Southeast Asia. The Tonkin Gulf Resolution, Johnson boasted, was "like grandma's nightshirt—it covered everything."

The towering Texan rode to a spectacular victory in November 1964. The voters were herded into Johnson's column by fondness for the Kennedy legacy, faith in Great Society promises, and fear of Goldwater. A stampede of 43,129,566 Johnson votes trampled the Republican ticket with its 27,178,188 supporters. The tally in the Electoral College was 486 to 52 (refer to Map 34.1). Goldwater carried only his native Arizona and five other states—all of them, tellingly, in the traditionally Democratic but now disenchanted white South. Johnson's record-breaking 61 percent of the popular vote swept lopsided, two-to-one Democratic majorities into both houses of Congress.

34-3 The Great Society Congress

Johnson's huge victory temporarily smashed the conservative congressional coalition of Southern Democrats and Northern Republicans. A wide-open legislative road stretched before the Great Society programs, as the president skillfully ringmastered his two-to-one Democratic majorities. Congress poured out a flood of legislation, comparable only to the output of the New Dealers in the Depression decade. Confident that a booming economy gave him ample fiscal and political room for maneuver, Johnson delivered at last on long-deferred Democratic promises of social reform.

Escalating the War on Poverty, Congress doubled the appropriation of the Office of Economic Opportunity to $2 billion and granted more than $1 billion to redevelop the gutted hills and hollows of Appalachia. Johnson also prodded Congress into creating two new cabinet offices: the Department of Transportation and the Department of Housing and Urban Development (HUD), to which he named the first Black cabinet secretary in the nation's history, respected economist Robert C. Weaver. Other noteworthy laws established the National Endowments for the Arts and the Humanities, designed to lift the level of American cultural life.

Even more impressive were the Big Four legislative achievements that crowned LBJ's Great Society program: aid to education, medical care for the elderly and indigent, immigration reform, and a new voting rights bill.

Johnson neatly avoided the thorny question of separation of church and state by channeling educational aid to students, not schools, thus allowing funds to flow to hard-pressed parochial institutions. (Catholic John F. Kennedy had not dared to touch this prickly issue.) With a keen eye for the dramatic, LBJ signed the education bill in the humble one-room Texas schoolhouse he had attended as a boy.

Medicare for the elderly, accompanied by Medicaid for the poor, became a reality in 1965 (refer to Image 34.2). Like the New Deal's Social Security program, Medicare and Medicaid created "entitlements." That is, they conferred rights on certain categories of Americans in perpetuity, without the need for repeated congressional approval. These programs were part of a spreading "rights revolution" that materially improved the lives of millions of Americans—but whose escalating costs swelled the federal budget, squeezed other programs, and contributed to yawning budget deficits.

Immigration reform was the third of Johnson's Big Four feats. Its largely unintended consequences reshaped the nation demographically and economically for decades to come. The **Immigration and Nationality Act of 1965** abolished at last the discriminatory "national-origins" quota system that had been in place since 1924 (refer to "The Presence of the Past: Immigration—Legal, Illegal, and Otherwise," pp. 913–915). The act doubled (to 290,000) the number of immigrants allowed to enter annually. After nearly a century of exclusion or near-exclusion, immigrants from the Eastern Hemisphere now had a higher cap (170,000) than those from the West (120,000). Beyond those numerical limits, the new law allowed entry for immigrants with special skills as well as close relatives of U.S. citizens.

At a signing ceremony before the grand backdrop of the Statue of Liberty, President Johnson declared that the act "corrects a cruel and enduring wrong in the conduct of the American nation," and tried to placate opponents who worried about its impact. "The bill that we sign today is not a revolutionary bill," said the president. Johnson's prediction was off the mark. More than 100,000 persons per year took advantage of the act's family unification provisions in the decades after 1965, as the immigrant stream swelled beyond expectations. No less surprising to the act's

Image 34.2 Giving Thanks for Medicare An elderly woman showed her gratitude to President Lyndon B. Johnson for his signing of the Medicare bill in April 1965, providing basic medical care for the aged. In tribute to former president Truman's unsuccessful effort to pass a national medical insurance program twenty years earlier, Johnson flew to Truman's Missouri home to sign the bill that he claimed would deliver "care for the sick and serenity for the fearful." No one acknowledged that Truman's earlier plan had been much more comprehensive or that Johnson, then a young Texas congressman, had opposed it.

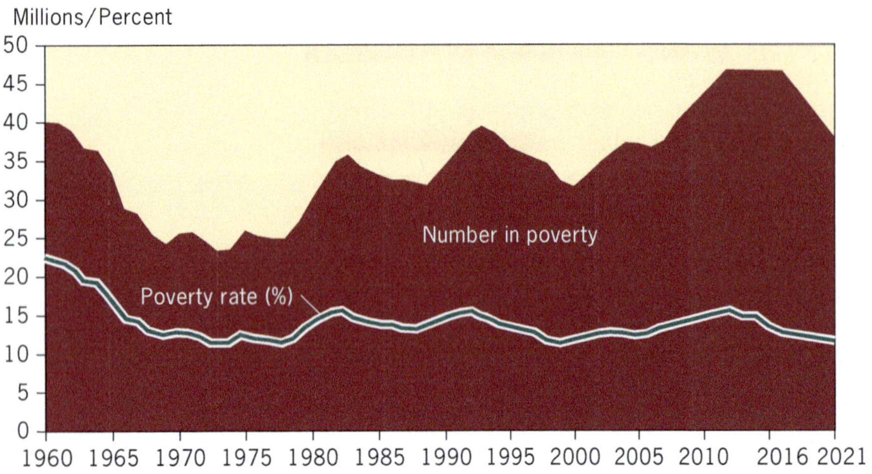

Figure 34.1 Poverty in the United States, 1960–2021 Following 2000, the poverty rate fell to 11.3 percent, its lowest level since 1979. In the "Great Recession" of the early twenty-first century, it ticked upward again, to 15.0 percent in 2012. The absolute numbers refer to those people who live in families whose total income is lower than a set "poverty threshold," which is tied to the consumer price index, so it varies with inflation. The "poverty rate" is the percentage of all Americans living below that threshold.

Source: https://www.census.gov/library/publications/2022/demo/p60-277.html

sponsors, the sources of immigration soon shifted heavily from Europe to Latin America as well as Asia, dramatically changing the racial and ethnic composition of the American population.

Great Society programs came in for rancorous political attack in later years. Conservatives charged that the billions spent for "social engineering" had simply been flushed down the waste pipe. Yet the poverty rate declined measurably in the ensuing decade (refer to Figure 34.1). Medicare made especially dramatic reductions in the incidence of poverty among America's elderly. Other antipoverty programs, among them the early childhood education program Head Start, sharply improved the educational outcomes for low-income children. Infant mortality rates also fell in minority communities as Medicaid improved access to health care.

34-4 Reclaiming the Right to Vote

The Civil Rights Act of 1964 gave the federal government more muscle to enforce school-desegregation orders and to prohibit racial discrimination in all kinds of public accommodations and employment. But it did not empower federal intervention to halt the often-violent suppression of the Black vote throughout the South. In Mississippi, home to over 900,000 Black people (the largest number of any state, and more than 40 percent of the state's population) only about 5 percent of eligible Black adults were registered voters. The lopsided pattern was similar throughout the South, thanks to ballot-denying devices like the poll tax, literacy tests, and barefaced intimidation that had barred Black people from the political process since the end of Reconstruction. Mississippi law required the names of prospective Black registrants to be published for two weeks in local newspapers—a device that imperiled the would-be voters' jobs, safety, and even their lives.

The civil rights movement's push to open polling booths in the South now became the chief goal of the civil rights movement. The Twenty-Fourth Amendment, ratified in January 1964, abolished the poll tax in federal elections (refer to the Appendix). That year, Black organizers traveled to northern college campuses to train white student volunteers for a massive voter-registration drive in Mississippi they called **Freedom Summer.** Scenes of interracial groups of young people holding hands and singing "We Shall Overcome" splashed across the nation's newspapers and television screens.

But events soon blighted bright hopes. In late June 1964, three activists—all men in their early twenties, one Black and two white—disappeared in rural Neshoba County, Mississippi. Their badly beaten bodies were later found buried beneath an earthen dam. FBI investigators eventually arrested twenty-one Ku Klux Klansmen, including a deputy sheriff, in connection with the killings. Despite strong evidence and two confessions, Mississippi officials refused to prosecute them for murder under state law. The U.S. Justice Department later won several convictions on the lesser charge of conspiracy to violate civil rights. Four decades later, research by high school history students contributed to the arrest of the organizer of the murders. He was convicted of manslaughter by a Mississippi court in 2005.

Other disappointments followed. In August 1964, the integrated **Mississippi Freedom Democratic Party** sent delegates to the Democratic National Convention to challenge their state's all-white "regulars." Party co-founder Fannie Lou Hamer drew attention to the

The Presence of the Past

Immigration—Legal, Illegal, and Otherwise

No numerical restrictions governed foreign immigration for the first century-plus of the nation's history. While imposing cruel limits on Asian entry—most notoriously with the Chinese Exclusion Act of 1882—the U.S. government allowed generally unfettered movement across its borders. Thirty million Europeans came to the United States between 1850 and 1913, part of a global migratory churn precipitated by war, poverty, and the industrializing world's hunger for factory labor.* (Refer to Figure 34.2.) By 1920, immigrants and their children made up over half of the U.S. manufacturing workforce.

The National Origins Act of 1924 (also known as the Johnson-Reed Immigration Act) brought the era of open European immigration to an end. Numerically capping annual entry by country, the law essentially created the category of "illegal immigration."

Mexicans and others in the Western Hemisphere were exempted from the Johnson-Reed quotas, as American agricultural producers relied heavily on their migrant labor. Between World War II and the early 1960s, four million Mexicans obtained temporary work permits through the *Bracero* program

(*continued*)

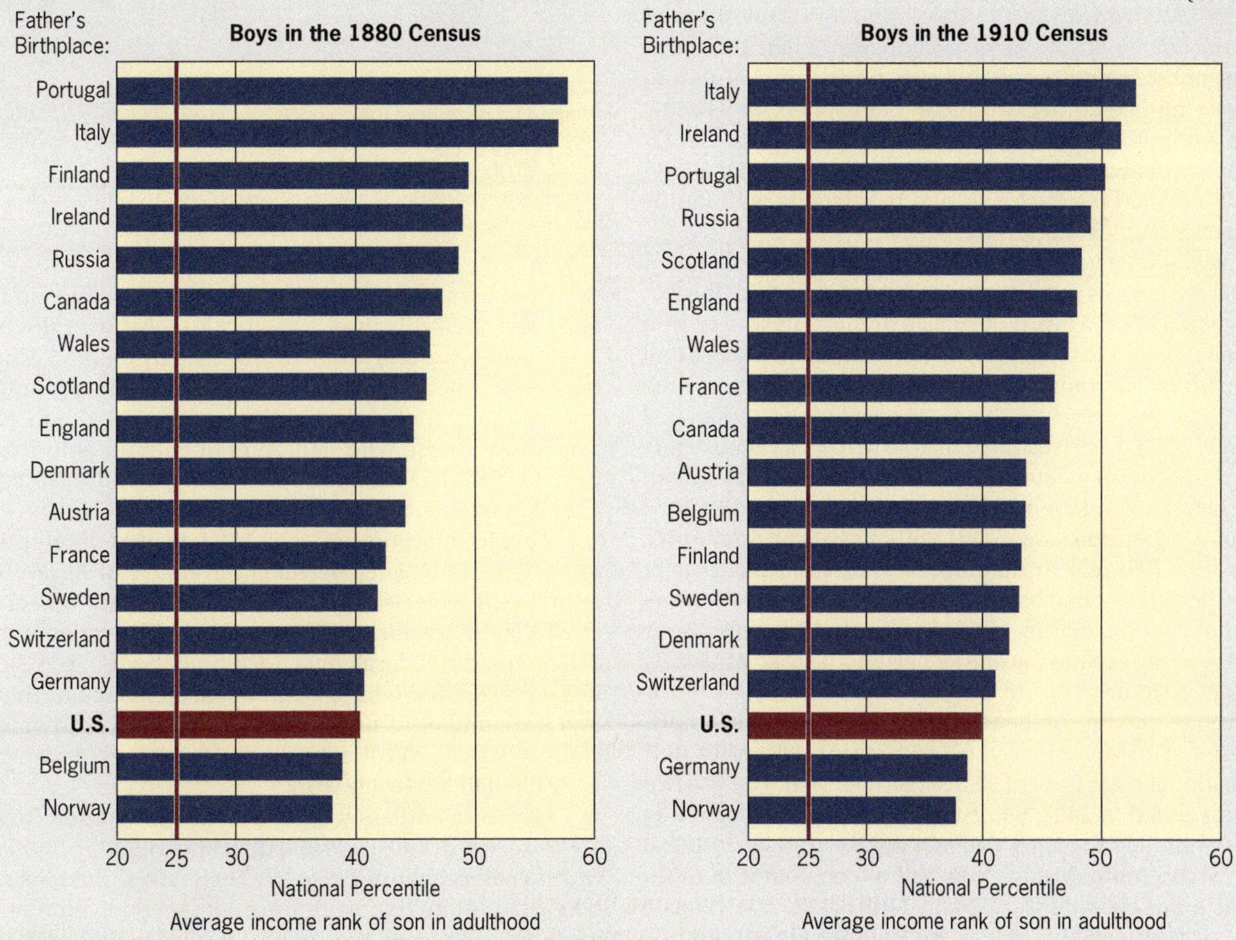

U.S. data compares only white boys. Adult income ranks are estimated using occupation and demographic data in later census years.

Figure 34.2 Comparative Next-Generation Economic Mobility in 1880 and 1910 These two charts show the income rank attained by young men who were raised in households at the 25th percentile of family income in the United States. On average, young American men of the late nineteenth and early twentieth centuries grew to earn more than their fathers, but the sons of immigrants from almost every country were even more upwardly mobile.

Source: Analysis of Census data by Ran Abramitzky, Leah Boustan, Elisa Jácome and Santiago Pérez for *The New York Times*, 2019, https://www.nytimes.com/2019/10/28/upshot/immigration-america-rise-poor.html.

*Open borders and the lowering cost of transatlantic travel made return migration common during this period. One in three European immigrants to the United States eventually returned permanently to their country of origin.

(refer to "31-13 Building the War Machine," pp. 823–827). While hundreds of thousands of *Braceros* eventually stayed permanently, most moved with the seasons back and forth across the southern border.

The quota system remained in force until the Immigration and Nationality Act of 1965 (also known as the Hart-Celler Act). Passed soon after the Civil Rights and Voting Rights Acts, the measure intended to remedy past discrimination and affirm America's commitment to human rights. An American immigration system once shaped by notions of Anglo-Saxon superiority now upheld pluralism and racial fairness as its animating values.

The law overturned the discriminatory provisions of 1924 and loosened harsh restrictions on Asian immigration, establishing an ostensibly race-neutral global framework that applied numerical caps by hemisphere, and evenly across nations. Doubling the number of visas to nearly 300,000 annually, the measure also provided special allowances for skilled professionals and immigrants with family members already in the United States.

The 1965 Act ushered in a second era of mass migration that differed from its predecessor in three critical ways. One was demographic: Of the nearly 60 million immigrants who arrived between 1965 and 2015, about half were from Latin America and one-quarter were from Asia. Another was its relative size: the United States now receives about 20 percent of all international migrants, while it received more than 40 percent a century ago.

A third, critical difference: By 2019, an estimated 11 million of the nation's 45 million foreign-born residents had entered without legal authorization. This startling statistic is an ironic legacy of the 1965 reform. Although the Hart-Celler Act brought relief to groups that had been the chief targets of an earlier era's xenophobia and nativism, its tight numerical caps ultimately served to vastly expand the entries deemed "illegal," especially from Mexico and South and Central America.

Even at the time of the Hart-Celler Act's passage, American demand for Mexican workers was well in excess of the new law's national maximum of 20,000 visas per year. The *Bracero* program ended in 1964; while flawed, it had provided a way to accommodate the keen demand for Mexican agricultural labor. What's more, Mexico now had to compete with other Central American and Caribbean countries for the 120,000 *total* visas now available to Western Hemisphere nations.

As Mexico's economy faltered and its population grew in the 1970s, unauthorized entry to the United States surged. Between 1965 and 1986, an estimated 28 million Mexicans entered without a visa.

As in earlier eras of mass immigration, nativism again reared its head in response to the growing numbers of unauthorized immigrants. Headlines blazed about a Mexican "invasion" and warned of the supposed criminality of the new arrivals. The flood of 125,000 economically desperate Cuban dissidents into Florida over six months in 1980, known as the Mariel Boatlift, further inflamed nativist anxieties.

Boston Globe/Getty Images

Image 34.3 **Crossing the Rio Grande, 1984** By the 1970s and 1980s, American agriculture's needs for Mexican farm workers far outstripped the availability of legal entry permits, prompting many to embark on highly dangerous and sometimes deadly illegal crossings of America's southern border.

Congress and President Ronald Reagan successfully navigated this thorny political thicket with the Immigration Reform and Control Act (IRCA) of 1986. The law banned employers from knowingly hiring undocumented immigrants but also provided amnesty and a path to citizenship for those who had entered without authorization prior to 1982. The measure eventually granted legal status to 3 million people, 2.3 million of whom were Mexican.

The Immigration Act of 1990 further attempted to remedy the imbalance between the supply of "legal" immigrants and America's economic needs. The law created several new categories of temporary employment visas for college-educated foreigners, including the "H1-B" visa used heavily by the booming technology sector. But it further limited the number of unskilled workers who could enter the country legally, despite American employers' growing reliance on their low-wage work.

Congress endlessly argued over immigration from the 1990s forward, but partisan divisions made it impossible to pass comprehensive reform. The focus shifted instead to beefing up immigration enforcement on the nation's southern border. In 1994, President Bill Clinton authorized construction of a 14-mile wall at the border's Pacific edge, the first piece of a decades-long construction project to block unauthorized crossings. That same year, California voters approved Proposition 187, which prevented undocumented immigrants from accessing public services, including schools and health care. The courts later ruled the measure unconstitutional on Fourteenth Amendment grounds (refer to "The Presence of the Past: The Fourteenth Amendment and the 'Second Founding'," pp. 504–506).

The dilemma of undocumented immigration remained at center stage in the twenty-first century. Discussions of

506 collection/Alamy Stock Photo

Image 34.4 DREAMers in the Oval Office, 2013 Undocumented immigrants brought to the United States as children meet with President Barack Obama and Vice President Joe Biden.

amnesty for undocumented immigrants were now focused on those brought to the United States as children, who numbered over 2 million by 2000. That year, Congress debated the Development, Relief, and Education for Alien Minors (DREAM) Act to create a path to U.S. citizenship for young people who were "illegal" by no fault of their own. Yet even this small step toward amnesty could not win passage, languishing in Congress for over two decades. In 2012, President Barack Obama issued an Executive Order creating the more modest Deferred Action for Childhood Arrivals (DACA) program to prevent deportation and provide temporary work permits to this immigrant group. By 2022, about 580,000 active DACA recipients hailed from over 200 different countries.

The amnesty of the Reagan-era IRCA faded into memory as America's immigration debate fractured along sharply partisan lines. As Congress quarreled over the DREAM Act, some Democratic-led states passed their own laws to protect the "DREAMers." In Republican-led states, lawmakers intensified their crackdowns on unauthorized immigrants. The hardline rhetoric reached a crescendo with the 2016 election of Republican President Donald Trump, whose campaign rallies resounded with chants of "Build the Wall!"

Trump enacted far-reaching changes to the nation's immigration system, almost entirely through executive action. Border enforcement surged, entire nationalities were banned, and legal visas became more difficult to obtain. Especially controversial was a 2018 order to separate minor children from families apprehended at the border. Although President Joe Biden ran on a promise to reverse the Trump policies, the new regime proved hard to unwind as ever more migrants from ever-more countries crowded at America's increasingly barricaded southern edge.

"We lead the world," President Ronald Reagan remarked in his 1989 farewell address, "because unique among nations, we draw our people, our strength, from every country and corner of the world." Indeed, new immigrants and their children added 72 million souls to the nation's population between 1965 and 2015, accounting for 55 percent of population growth and keeping the average age of America's workforce lower than its industrial peers. Immigrants started new businesses at a higher rate than native-born Americans, reversed population decline in the nation's largest cities, and their children out-earned their parents at higher rates than the native born. As fractious debates over immigration continue, the extraordinary contributions of immigrants remain a constant.

voting-rights cause in a televised speech that powerfully recounted her experience with violent voter suppression. Denied seats, many activists became disillusioned with the two-party system. After so much struggle, only 1,600 Black Mississippians had succeeded in registering to vote—out of 17,000 who applied.

Early in 1965, Martin Luther King Jr. resumed the voter-registration campaign in Selma, Alabama, where Black citizens made up 50 percent of the population but only 1 percent of the voters. State troopers assaulted King's demonstrators with tear gas and whips as they marched peacefully to the state capital at Montgomery (refer to Image 34.5). A Boston Unitarian minister was killed, and a few days later a white Detroit woman was murdered with a shotgun by Klansmen on the highway near Selma.

As the nation recoiled in horror before these violent scenes, President Johnson, speaking in his Texas twang, addressed the nation in a dramatic televised speech. What happened in Selma, he insisted, concerned all Americans, "who must overcome the crippling legacy of bigotry and injustice." Then, in a stirring adaptation of the anthem of the civil rights movement, the president concluded, "And we shall overcome." A son of Texas—the state that clung to enslavement longer than any other—now speedily shepherded through Congress the landmark **Voting Rights Act of 1965**, signed into law on August 6. "The act to enforce the Fifteenth Amendment to the United States Constitution" outlawed literacy tests, sent federal voter registrars into several southern states, and prohibited the denial or restriction of the right to vote on the basis of race or color.

AP Images/unknown

Image 34.5 Selma, Alabama, March 7, 1965 State troopers assaulted civil rights marchers headed for the state's capital in Montgomery. John Lewis (in foreground), Chairman of the Student Nonviolent Coordinating Committee and later a long-serving U.S. congressman from Georgia, sustained a fractured skull from billy-club blows.

The passage of the Voting Rights Act, exactly one hundred years after the conclusion of the Civil War, began a second Reconstruction after the long, ordeal of Jim Crow. "Give us the ballot," said Martin Luther King Jr., "and the South will never be the same again." He was right. The act did not end discrimination and oppression overnight, but it placed an awesome lever for change in Black hands. Black Southerners became a potent voting bloc and economic force, running for state and local office and growing their power as business owners and consumers. In the following decade, for the first time since Emancipation, Black Americans began to migrate *into* the South.

34-5 An Incomplete Civil Rights Revolution

The United States had at last restored constitutionally guaranteed political rights that Black Southerners had fought to reclaim for nearly a century. Yet landmark legislation did not instantly remedy the deep economic inequality and racial discrimination that plagued the entire nation, not just the South. The legislative victory of the Voting Rights Act of 1965 marked the end of the Southern-focused, integrationist, largely nonviolent mobilization within the long civil rights struggle—what one activist later called the "classical phase" of the movement. In the remaining years of the 1960s and beyond, the movement shifted to a national struggle for economic and social justice. New voices, tactics, and a more explicitly radical politics surged to the fore.

The unfinished state of the civil rights revolution was made clear just five days after President Johnson signed the voting law. A bloody riot erupted in **Watts**, a poor and mostly Black neighborhood in Los Angeles, where citizens' frustration over police brutality and decades of economic exclusion flared into a week of burning and looting. When the smoke finally cleared over the Los Angeles basin, 34 people lay dead and more than a thousand had been injured. Hundreds of buildings stood charred and gutted. The Watts uprising heralded a new phase of the Black freedom struggle. The movement shifted away from the integrationist approach of King, and toward principles of self-determination and Black nationalism. Advocates of Gandhian nonviolence now were challenged by more confrontational voices espousing anti-capitalism and armed self-defense.

King had been considered a dangerous radical by many white observers. Now he was not radical enough for this second wave of younger Black activists, who privately mocked the pious Dr. King as "de Lawd." New leaders like Malcolm X electrified his followers (refer to Image 34.6). Born Malcolm Little, he joined the Nation of Islam while serving a prison sentence for burglary, becoming a devout Muslim and Black nationalist. Like the Nation's founder, Elijah Muhammed (born Elijah Poole), Malcolm changed his surname to reflect his lost and unknowable African heritage in white America. A brilliant and charismatic preacher,

Bettmann/Getty Images

Image 34.6 **Malcolm X** The charismatic Black leader was a hypnotizing speaker who could rivet and arouse crowds with his call for Black separatism. At the end of his life, Malcolm began to temper his separatist creed.

Malcolm X trumpeted Black separatism and inveighed against the "blue-eyed white devils." Malcolm later rejected Elijah Muhammed's separatist diatribes and converted to orthodox Islam. In early 1965, the 39-year-old was assassinated by rival Nation of Islam gunmen while speaking to a large crowd in New York City.

Contending Voices

Two Visions of Black Freedom

Dr. Martin Luther King Jr. (1929–1968) and Malcolm X (1925–1965) differed not only in the goals they and their allies promoted—King urging racial integration and Malcolm X trumpeting Black self-determination—but also in the means they advocated to achieve them. In his famous "I Have a Dream" speech during the interracial March on Washington for Jobs and Freedom on August 28, 1963, King spoke to a quarter of a million people assembled at the Lincoln Memorial:

> "In the process of gaining our rightful place we must not be guilty of wrongful deeds. Let us not seek to satisfy our thirst for freedom by drinking from the cup of bitterness and hatred. . . . We must not allow our creative protest to degenerate into physical violence. Again and again we must rise to the majestic heights of meeting physical force with soul force."

About three months later, Malcolm X rejected King's "peaceful, turn-the-other-cheek revolution":

> "Revolution is bloody, revolution is hostile, revolution knows no compromise, revolution overturns and destroys everything that gets in its way. And you, sitting around here like a knot on the wall, saying, 'I'm going to love these folks no matter how much they hate me,' . . . . Whoever heard of a revolution where they lock arms . . . , singing 'We shall overcome?' You don't do that in a revolution. You don't do any singing, you're too busy swinging."

Consider This:

Why did King see nonviolence as key to achieving the movement's goals? What might explain some Black Americans' growing receptivity to appeals for self-defense and self-determination over the course of the 1960s?

In 1966, in Oakland, California, young activists meanwhile founded the **Black Panther Party**, an avowedly separatist, self-defense organization. Condemning capitalism as the root of racism, the Panthers established children's breakfast programs and conducted armed "citizens' patrols" against police brutality. Their rhetoric was militant—they referred to police as "pigs"—and their tactics were provocative. In 1967, they demonstrated on the steps of the California State Capitol with loaded rifles at the ready. FBI chief J. Edgar Hoover declared the Panthers "the greatest threat to the internal security of the United States."

American civil rights leaders increasingly framed their fight for Black freedom as part of a greater global struggle. Trinidad-born Stokely Carmichael of the Student Nonviolent Coordinating Committee (SNCC) was one of the original Freedom Riders in 1961 and a leader of Southern voter registration drives (refer to "33-5 Seeds of the Civil Rights Revolution," pp. 883–886). By 1966, he was preaching the doctrine of **Black Power**, which, he said, "will smash everything Western civilization has created." Echoing previous nationalist and pan-Africanist movements like that of Marcus Garvey earlier in the century (refer to "29-5 Sluggers, Flappers, and 'Race Men'," pp. 746–750), Black Power activists argued for separatism and solidarity with other oppressed colonial subjects, from Vietnam to sub-Saharan Africa.

The movement's celebration of Blackness spilled into culture. Black people embraced natural "Afro" hairstyles and shed their "white" names for new African-influenced ones. (Carmichael moved to Africa in 1968 to escape FBI surveillance and changed his name to Kwame Ture.) Students pressured schools and universities to create Black Studies programs and formed transnational alliances with activists in Africa and elsewhere.

Yet such affirmative messages of Black empowerment were often overshadowed by graphic television footage of urban racial violence. The cycle of excessive policing and Black rebellion continued in city after city, year after year. In the "Long Hot Summer" of 1967, especially bloody outbursts killed 26 in Newark, New Jersey, and 43 in Detroit, Michigan. White Americans watched aghast from suburban living rooms as Black people fought police and torched their own neighborhoods, yelling "Burn, baby, burn."

The scenes baffled many liberal Northerners, who had considered racial problems a purely "Southern" question and long had shied away from facing the endemic racism in their own backyards. But redlining of urban real estate, unequal public education, and everyday discrimination always had been national problems—ones that had become even more pressing as nearly half the nation's Black people moved North in the decades after World War II.

Cities continued to burn as President Johnson established a "riot commission" in July 1967 to investigate causes and remedies. The report of the National Advisory Commission on Civil Disorders, known as the **Kerner Commission** after its chairman, Illinois Governor Otto Kerner, bluntly concluded that the events resulted not from Black lawlessness but from persistent white racism. The report was a bestseller; ultimately, two million copies were sold. Yet its uncomfortable conclusions and policy recommendations went largely ignored. Instead of investing more heavily in social programs, governments expanded policing and criminal statutes to ensure that such "race riots" would not happen again.

> In its analysis of the causes and events of civil disorder throughout the nation in 1967, the Kerner Commission Report remarked that
>
> "Our nation is moving toward two societies, one black, one white—separate and unequal. . . . This deepening racial division is not inevitable. The movement apart can be reversed. Choice is still possible. Our principal task is to define that choice and to press for a national resolution."

Despair deepened when the magnetic Martin Luther King Jr. was forever silenced by a sniper's bullet in Memphis, Tennessee, on April 4, 1968. In the last years of his life, King too had become outspoken about economic injustice and his opposition to the Vietnam War. He exhorted federal leaders to take bolder action on Black poverty and social justice for the working class. He was in Memphis to support a months-long strike by Black sanitation workers.

The killing of King cruelly robbed the American people of one of the most inspirational leaders in their history—at a time when they could least afford to lose him. As news of his assassination spread, Black neighborhoods were once again set afire in a convulsion of anger and grief, costing over forty lives.

Fiery urban uprisings made news while many thousands of Black people quietly made history. Their voter registration in the South shot upward. By the late 1960s, the Old South was home to several hundred Black office holders. Cleveland, Ohio, and Gary, Indiana, elected Black mayors. By 1972, nearly half of Southern Black children sat in integrated classrooms. In fact, more schools in the South were integrated than in the North. About a third of Black families had risen economically into the ranks of the middle class. In a remarkably short period, the civil rights movement led by King and others had made their cause into an unignorable national crisis, achieved landmark legislative victories, and set in motion enduring Black upward mobility and political influence.

34-6 Escalation in Vietnam

Meanwhile, the United States was sinking deeper into the monsoon mud of Vietnam. Fighters loyal to the North Vietnamese communists, called Viet Cong, attacked an American air base at Pleiku, South Vietnam, in February 1965. The president immediately ordered retaliatory bombing raids against military installations in North Vietnam and for the first time ordered attacking U.S. troops to land. By the middle of March 1965, the Americans had "Operation Rolling Thunder" in full swing—regular full-scale bombing attacks against North Vietnam. Before 1965 ended, some 184,000 American troops were involved, most of them slogging through the jungles and rice paddies of South Vietnam hunting for Viet Cong soldiers.

Johnson had now taken the first fateful steps down a slippery path. He and his advisers believed that a fine-tuned, step-by-step "escalation" of American force would drive the enemy to defeat with a minimum loss of life on both sides. But the North Vietnamese communists matched every increase in American firepower with more men and more mastery of the arts of guerrilla warfare.

The South Vietnamese themselves were meanwhile becoming spectators in their own war, as the fighting became increasingly Americanized. Corrupt and collapsible governments succeeded each other with bewildering rapidity in the South Vietnamese capital of Saigon. Yet American officials continued to talk of defending a faithful democratic ally. Washington "hawks" also defended America's action as a test of Uncle Sam's "commitment" and of the reliability of his numerous treaty pledges to resist communist encroachment.

Persuaded by such panicky thinking, Johnson steadily raised the military stakes in Vietnam. By 1968, he had poured more than half a million troops into Southeast Asia, and the annual bill for the war was exceeding $30 billion. Still, the end was nowhere in sight (refer to Images 34.7 and 34.8).

America could not defeat the enemy in Vietnam, but it seemed to be bringing more and more defeat upon itself. World opinion grew increasingly hostile; the blasting of an underdeveloped country by a mighty superpower struck many critics as obscene. Several nations expelled American Peace Corps volunteers. The ever-censorious Charles de Gaulle withdrew France from NATO in 1966 and ordered all American troops out of the country, reportedly

AP Images

Image 34.7 The Mechanized War High technology and modern equipment, such as this helicopter, gave the Americans in Vietnam a huge military advantage. But unaccompanied by a clear political purpose and a national will to win, technological superiority was insufficient to achieve final victory.

Image 34.8 The Vietnam Quagmire Marine PFC Phillip Mark Wilson of Wolfforth, Texas, carries a rocket launcher across a stream near the "demilitarized zone" (DMZ) that separated North and South Vietnam. Wilson was killed in action soon after this photo was taken, just five days after his twenty-first birthday.

prompting Secretary of State Dean Rusk to ask if that included the thousands buried behind the D-Day invasion beaches in Normandy.

Overcommitment in Southeast Asia also tied America's hands elsewhere. A beleaguered Israel stunned the world in June 1967 with a preemptive military strike against Egypt, Jordan, and Syria. When the smoke cleared after the **Six-Day War**, Israel expanded to control new territories in the Sinai Peninsula, the Gaza Strip, the Golan Heights, and the West Bank of the Jordan River, including Jerusalem (refer to Map 37.3, p. 1017). The Israeli victory brought around a million stateless Palestinian Arabs under direct Israeli control, while another 350,000 Palestinian refugees fled to neighboring Jordan. The Israelis eventually signed peace treaties with Egypt and Jordan and withdrew from the Sinai and, much later, from Gaza. But they stubbornly held on to other conquered territory and began moving Jewish settlers into the heavily Arab district of the West Bank. The Six-Day War markedly intensified the problems of the already volatile Middle East, leading to an increasingly bitter standoff between the Israelis and Palestinians and setting the stage for explosively violent clashes to come.

34-7 America Against the War

Antiwar protests surged as America's Vietnamese entanglement escalated. College-going baby boomers, their futures overshadowed by the possibility of being drafted into military service, led the way. Protests began on a small scale with campus "teach-ins" in 1965. As the long arm of the military draft dragged more and more young men off to the jungles of Southeast Asia, thousands of young men fled to Canada; others publicly burned their draft cards. Hundreds of thousands of marchers filled the streets of New York, San Francisco, and other cities, chanting, "Hell no, we won't go," and "Hey, hey, LBJ, how many kids did you kill today?"

Opposition in Congress to the Vietnam involvement centered on the influential Senate Committee on Foreign Relations, headed by Senator William Fulbright of Arkansas. A constant thorn in the side of the president, he staged a series of widely viewed televised hearings in 1966 and 1967, during which prominent personages aired their views, largely antiwar. Gradually, the public came to feel that it had been deceived about the causes and "winnability" of the war. A yawning "credibility gap" opened between the government and the people. New flocks of antiwar "doves" were hatching daily.

Even within the administration, doubts were deepening about the wisdom of the war in Vietnam. Defense Secretary McNamara expressed increasing discomfiture at the course of events and eventually resigned from Johnson's cabinet. By early 1968, the brutal and futile struggle had become, up to this point, the longest and most unpopular foreign war in the nation's history. The government had failed utterly to explain to the people why it was better to spend more for the war in Vietnam than for the War on Poverty. Many critics wondered if any objective could be worth the vast price, in blood and treasure, that America was paying. American casualties, killed and wounded, already exceeded 100,000. More bombs had been dropped on Vietnam than on all enemy territory in World War II. Many Americans felt pangs of conscience at the spectacle of their countrymen burning peasant huts and blistering civilians with ghastly napalm.

The war was even threatening to shred the Constitution. In 1967, President Johnson ordered the CIA, in clear violation of its charter as a *foreign* intelligence agency, to spy on domestic antiwar activists. He also encouraged the FBI to turn its counterintelligence program, code-named "COINTELPRO," against the peace movement. COINTELPRO subverted leading "doves" with false accusations that they were communist sympathizers. These clandestine tactics made the FBI look like a totalitarian state's secret police rather than a guardian of American democracy.

As the war dragged on, evidence mounted that America had been entrapped in a Vietnamese civil war, fighting against highly motivated rebels who were striving to overthrow an oppressive regime. Yet Johnson clung to his basic strategy of ratcheting up the pressure bit by bit. He stubbornly assured doubting Americans that he could see "the light at the end of the tunnel." But to growing numbers of Americans, it seemed that Johnson was bent on "saving" Vietnam by destroying it (refer to Image 34.9).

Image 34.9 **President Lyndon Johnson Haunted by Specters of Vietnam, 1967**

34-8 Vietnam Topples Johnson

Hawkish illusions that the struggle was about to be won were shattered by a blistering communist offensive launched in late January 1968, during Tet, the Vietnamese New Year. At a time when the Viet Cong were supposedly licking their wounds, they suddenly and simultaneously mounted savage attacks on twenty-seven key South Vietnamese cities, including the capital, Saigon. Although eventually beaten off with heavy losses, they demonstrated anew that victory could not be gained by Johnson's strategy of continual escalation. The **Tet offensive** ended in a military defeat but a political victory for the Viet Cong. Ever more loudly, Americans demanded a speedy end to the war.

Instead, American military leaders responded to the Tet attacks with a request for 200,000 more troops. The size of the request staggered many policymakers. Former Secretary of State Dean Acheson reportedly advised the president, "The Joint Chiefs of Staff don't know what they're talking about."

The president meanwhile was being sharply challenged from within his own party. Eugene McCarthy, a little-known Democratic senator from Minnesota, had emerged as a contender for the 1968 Democratic presidential nomination. The soft-spoken McCarthy, a sometime poet and devout Catholic, gathered a small army of antiwar college students as campaign workers. Going "clean for Gene," with shaven faces and shortened locks, they helped him gain an impressive 41.4 percent of the Democratic vote in the New Hampshire primary on March 12, 1968. Although still second to Johnson's 49.6 percent, McCarthy's showing was devastating for the president. Johnson's star fell further four days later when Senator Robert F. Kennedy, now a senator from New York and an outspoken dove on the war, threw his hat into the ring. The charismatic and handsome Kennedy, heir to his murdered brother's mantle of leadership, stirred a passionate response among the Black and Latino working class as well as many young people.

These startling events abroad and at home were not lost on LBJ. In a bombshell televised address to the nation on March 31, 1968, he announced that he would freeze American troop levels and scale back the bombing. Then, in a dramatic plea to unify a dangerously divided nation, Johnson startled his vast audience by firmly declaring that he would not be a candidate for the presidency in 1968.

Johnson's abdication had the effect of preserving the military status quo. He had held the hawks in check, while offering himself as a sacrifice to the militant doves. The United States could thus maintain the maximum *acceptable* level of military activity in Vietnam with one hand, while trying to negotiate a settlement with the other. North Vietnam shortly agreed to commence negotiations in Paris. But progress was glacially slow, as prolonged bickering developed over the very shape of the conference table.

34-9 The Presidential Sweepstakes of 1968

The summer of 1968 was one of the hottest political seasons in the nation's history. Johnson's heir apparent for the Democratic nomination was his liberal vice president, Hubert H. Humphrey, a former pharmacist, college professor, mayor, and U.S. senator from Minnesota. Senators McCarthy and Kennedy meanwhile dueled in several state primaries, with Kennedy's bandwagon gathering ever-increasing speed. But on June 5, 1968, the night of his possibly nomination-clinching victory in the California primary, Kennedy was shot to death by a young Arab immigrant resentful of the candidate's pro-Israel views.

Ten thousand grieving and angry antiwar protesters converged on Chicago for the Democratic convention in August 1968. Mayor Richard Daley responded by arranging for barbed-wire

Image 34.10 The Siege of Chicago, 1968 Antiwar protesters staged demonstrations in the streets of Chicago during the Democratic National Convention in August 1968. Some 2,500 members of the radical Youth International Party (known as the Yippies) planned a peaceful "festival of light" across the street from the convention hall, but instead found themselves drawn into a melee with the police and National Guardsmen. The confrontation in Chicago badly tarnished Democratic candidate Hubert Humphrey's presidential campaign. His Republican opponent, Richard Nixon, won the presidency with calls for an "honorable peace" in Vietnam and "law and order" at home.

Bettmann/Getty Images

barricades around the convention hall ("Fort Daley"), as well as thousands of police and National Guard reinforcements. The standoff began innocuously, even humorously. The radical and theatrical antiwar "Yippies" staged an event nominating a 150-pound pig named "Pigasus" for president, prompting Chicago police to arrest six and send the pig to the humane society. As the days wore on, tensions increased. Demonstrators baited the officers in blue, shouting obscenities and hurling bags and cans of excrement at the police lines. The final night of the convention, as television cameras rolled, Daley's blue-helmeted police officers broke into what was later described as a "police riot," clubbing and manhandling innocent and guilty alike (refer to Image 34.10). Acrid tear gas fumes hung heavily over the city even as Humphrey steamrollered to the nomination on the first ballot. Standing bruised and bloodied on the streets outside the convention hall, protestors chanted, "The whole world is watching! The whole world is watching!"

Humphrey secured the nomination with such ease because the nominating procedures of the era left most of the power over delegate selection in the hands of state and local party officials, who were overwhelmingly aligned with the administration. (The entire political landscape would soon be transformed by the spread of primary elections. Refer to "34-17 The Nixon Landslide of 1972," p. 935.) Humphrey managed to become the nominee without having entered a single primary race. The Humphrey forces also blocked the McCarthyites' attempt to secure an antiwar platform plank and hammered into place their own declaration that armed force would be relentlessly applied until the enemy showed more willingness to negotiate.

Scenting victory over the badly divided Democrats, the Republicans convened in plush Miami Beach, Florida, where former vice president Richard M. Nixon arose from his political grave to win the nomination. As a hawk on Vietnam and a right-leaning middle-of-the-roader on domestic policy, Nixon was acceptable to both the Goldwater conservatives and party moderates. He appealed to white Southern voters with his law-and-order rhetoric, as well as with his choice of Maryland's Governor Spiro T. Agnew, noted for his pugnacious stands against dissidents and Black militants, as his vice-presidential running mate. In an especially cynical ploy, Nixon instructed an aide to use an influential intermediary to "monkey wrench" ongoing peace negotiations with the Vietnamese, thus denying the Johnson administration and the Humphrey campaign a possible political advantage—and thus risking a longer war for his own selfish purposes.

Adding color and confusion to the campaign was a spoiler third-party ticket—the American Independent Party—headed by the race-baiting populist George C. Wallace, former governor of Alabama. In his 1963 inaugural address, Wallace had infamously shouted "Segregation now! Segregation tomorrow! Segregation forever!" Six months later, he blocked a doorway at the University of Alabama to prevent two Black students from entering. Now, presidential candidate

Wallace swapped explicit racism for coded appeals to discontented white voters. The Alabaman jabbed repeatedly at "pointy-headed bureaucrats" and taunted hecklers as "bums" in need of a bath. Speaking behind a bulletproof screen, he called for prodding Black protesters back into "their place," with bayonets if necessary. He and his running mate, former U.S. Air Force General Curtis LeMay, also proposed smashing the North Vietnamese to smithereens by "bombing them back to the Stone Age."

The positions of Nixon and Humphrey on Vietnam were remarkably similar. Both candidates were committed to carrying on the war until the enemy settled for an "honorable peace," which seemed to mean an American victory. Millions of doves had no place to roost, and many refused to vote at all. Humphrey, scorched by the LBJ brand, went down to defeat as a loyal prisoner of his chief's policies.

Nixon, who had lost a cliffhanger to Kennedy in 1960, won handily in 1968. He garnered 301 electoral votes, with 43.4 percent of the popular tally (31,785,480), as compared with 191 electoral votes and 42.7 percent of the popular votes (31,275,166) for Humphrey (refer to Map 34.2). Unlike most new presidents, Nixon faced congressional majorities of the opposing party in both houses. He carried not a single major city, thus attesting to the continuing urban strength of the Democrats, who also won about 95 percent of the Black vote. Nixon had received no clear mandate to do anything. He was a minority president who owed his election to divisions over the war and protest against the unfair draft, crime, and rioting.

As for Wallace, he won an impressive 9,906,473 popular votes and 46 electoral votes, all from five states of the Deep South, four of which the Republican Goldwater had carried in 1964. Wallace had amassed the largest third-party popular vote in American history to that point and was the last third-party candidate to win any electoral votes. (In 1992, Ross Perot enjoyed a greater popular-vote margin but won no states; refer to Map 37.1, p. 991.) Wallace resoundingly demonstrated the continuing power of a racially divisive strain of populism, which appealed not to the better angels of the voters' natures, but to their ugliest fears and resentments. His

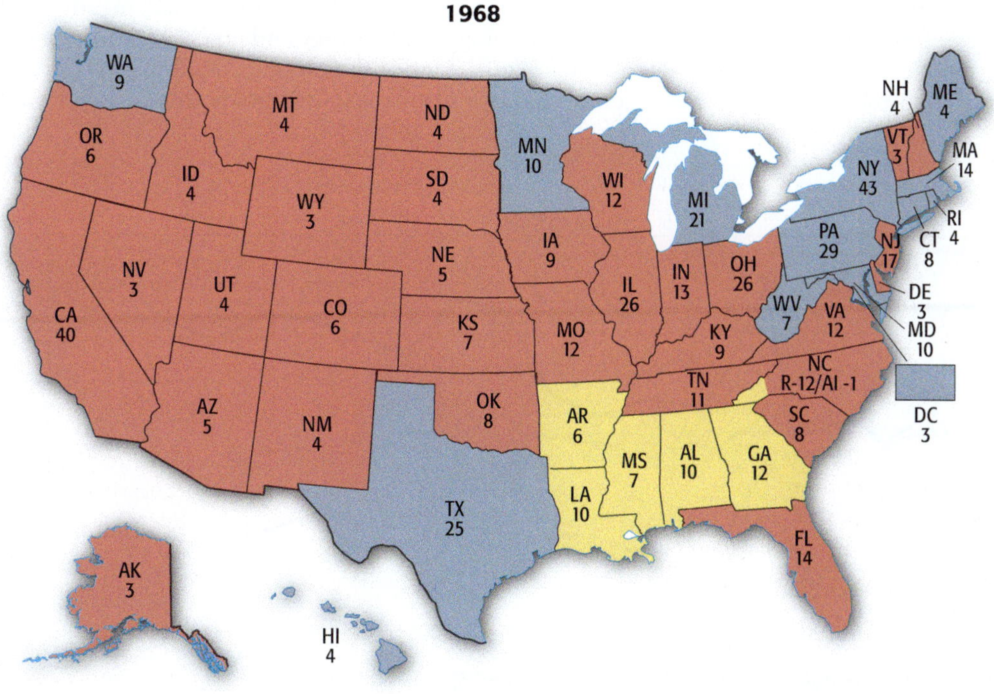

Candidate (Party)	Electoral Vote		Popular Vote	
Nixon (Republican)	301	56.1%	31,785,480	43.4%
Humphrey (Democrat)	191	35.5%	31,275,166	42.7%
Wallace (American Independent)	46	8.4%	9,906,473	13.5%

Map 34.2 Presidential Election of 1968 (with electoral vote by state) George Wallace won in five states, and he denied a clear majority to either of the two major-party candidates in twenty-five other states. A shift of some fifty thousand votes might well have thrown the election into the House of Representatives, giving Wallace the strategic bargaining position he sought.

candidacy foreshadowed a coarsening of American political life that would take deep root in the ensuing decades.

Talented but tragedy-struck Lyndon Johnson returned to his Texas ranch in January 1969 and died there four years later. His party was defeated, yet Johnson's legislative leadership for a time had been remarkable. No president since Lincoln had accomplished more for civil rights. None since Roosevelt had done so much for poor people, young and old.

But by 1966, Johnson was already sinking into the quicksand of America's ill-starred Vietnam war. As soaring war costs sucked tax dollars into the military machine, his attempt to provide both guns and butter prevented him from delivering either in sufficient quantity. The War on Poverty went down to defeat as Johnson crucified himself on the cross of Vietnam.

34-10 The Cultural Upheaval of the 1960s

The decade's struggles against racism, poverty, and the war in Vietnam had momentous cultural consequences. Everywhere in 1960s America, a newly negative attitude toward all kinds of authority took hold. Faith in national political leaders crumbled. Neither families nor churches nor schools seemed to be able to define values and shape behavior with the certainty of shared purpose that many people believed had once existed. No matter what the topic, conventional wisdom and inherited ideas came under fire. "Trust no one over thirty" was a popular sneer of rebellious youth (refer to Figure 34.3).

The nation's mainline Protestant denominations, which so long had dominated American religious life, lost their grip. Weekly churchgoing declined from 48 percent in the late 1950s to 41 percent in the early 1970s. Yet Americans did not abandon their search for spiritual meaning. Thousands of born-again converts joined enormous evangelical congregations that rose along the freeways and subdivisions of the Sunbelt. Many of the under-25 generation gravitated toward Eastern religions and practices, making spiritual pilgrimages to India, embracing yoga and meditation. A small but significant number of Black Americans converted to Islam.

Religious upheaval even churned the tradition-bound Roman Catholic Church, among the world's oldest and most conservative institutions. The Second Vatican Council, meeting from 1962 to 1965, passed reforms aimed at modernizing church liturgy and practices and encouraging more ecumenical interactions with other faiths. Clerics abandoned their Roman collars and Latin lingo, folk songs replaced Gregorian chants, and meatless Fridays became ancient history.

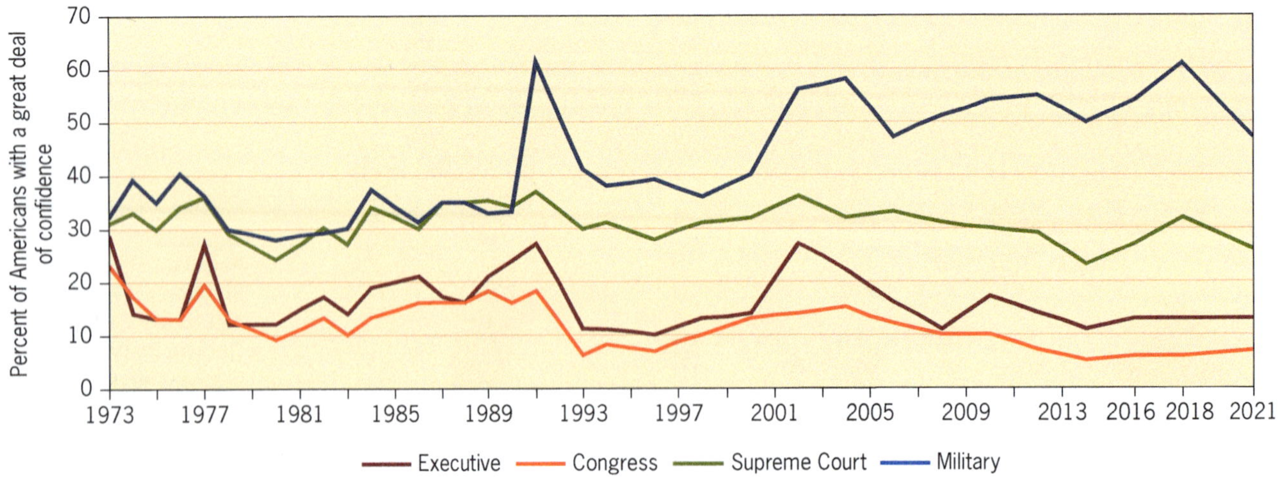

Figure 34.3 Declining Confidence in Institutions The upheavals of the 1960s had lasting effects. Protests against established authorities in many walks of life, including government, the churches, and the media, touched off a long-term trend of declining confidence in virtually all major institutions—conspicuously not including the military, virtually the only American institution that enjoyed higher confidence ratings in the early twenty-first century than it had half a century earlier.

Source: "Declining Confidence in Institutions," from General Social Survey 2012 Final Report, Trends in Public Attitudes aboutConfidence in Institutions, by Tom W. Smith and Jaesok Son, NORC at the University of Chicago, May 2013. Reprinted by permission.

College students were at the forefront of organized protests against established authority, from lunch counter sit-ins at the decade's start to the often violent crescendo of the antiwar movement at its end. At the University of California at Berkeley in 1964, the aptly named Free Speech Movement rose up in objection to an administrative ban on the use of campus space for civil rights organizing. During months of nonviolent protest, the students accused their Cold War "multiversity" of promoting corporate interests rather than humane values. In only a few years, the hair was much longer and the rhetoric was much hotter.

Fired by outrage against racial injustice, capitalist conformity, and the war in Vietnam, sons and daughters of the middle class became radical political rebels. "Turn on, tune in, and drop out," declared writer and psychologist Timothy Leary, the era's foremost champion of lysergic acid diethylamide (LSD) and other mind-bending psychedelic drugs. Young people followed Leary's lead, some dropping out of modern life altogether by moving "back to the land" on utopian, self-sufficient communes.

The social movements of the 1960s extended well beyond college campuses, as working people of all races and backgrounds mobilized for recognitions and rights. After years of struggle, the United Farm Workers Organizing Committee (UFWOC), headed by the soft-spoken and charismatic César Chávez, succeeded in improving working conditions for the mostly Mexican-American "stoop laborers" who followed the cycle of planting and harvesting across the American West. In West Coast cities, Asian Americans organized to combat discrimination in housing and employment, often working in solidarity with Black civil rights groups.

Social upheaval in the 1960s was hardly confined to the United States as youth-driven political and social conflict roiled nations around the world (refer to "Thinking Globally: The Global 1960s," pp. 926–927). The newfound power of popular youth culture—especially the urgent rock 'n' roll of artists like the Beatles, Janis Joplin, and Jimi Hendrix—proved global in its reach, helping to stitch together generational styles, norms, and touchstones across borders.

The 1960s also witnessed a sexual revolution, though its novelty and scale are often exaggerated. Without doubt, the introduction of the birth-control pill in 1960 made unwanted pregnancies much easier to avoid and heterosexual exploration easier to pursue. The stirrings of the gay rights movement began in the conservative 1950s, with the Mattachine Society, an advocacy group founded in Los Angeles in 1951, and the Daughters of Bilitis, the first organization for lesbian rights, founded in San Francisco in 1955. A brutal attack on gay men and women by police officers at New York's Stonewall Inn in 1969 proved a turning point, when gay people and their allies fought back in what became known as the **Stonewall Uprising** (refer to Image 34.11). Widening worries in the 1980s about sexually transmitted diseases like genital herpes and AIDS (acquired immunodeficiency syndrome) slowed but did not reverse the sexual revolution.

Image 34.11 The First Gay Pride Parade, New York City, 1970 On the first anniversary of the celebrated gay resistance to police harassment at the Stonewall Inn, on June 27, 1969, two hundred men and women marched from Greenwich Village to Central Park initiating a tradition that later spread to many other American cities and around the globe.

Thinking Globally

The Global 1960s

Social upheaval in the 1960s was a global phenomenon. As young people born in the wake of World War II came of age around the world, they everywhere challenged established authority, customs, and institutions. Antiwar protests and demonstrations for social rights shook the political and cultural foundations of peoples on every inhabited continent.

Worldwide turmoil was propelled by worldwide forces. The postwar "baby boom" swelled the ranks of the young in Europe, the Soviet Union, the People's Republic of China, and Latin America as well as in the United States. American and Western European youth approached adulthood buoyed by a robust spurt of postwar prosperity and major new public investments in higher education. The leading edge of boomers entered college in the 1960s, just as the international equilibrium was increasingly challenged by Cold War tensions, threats of thermonuclear war, and rapid decolonization in Asia and Africa. Affluent, educated, and idealistic, conscious of their shared generational identity, and impatient with the bland nostrums of their elders, these young people formed the vanguard of political and social turmoil in one country after another.

Western Europe, long culturally aligned with the United States, paralleled the American experience most closely. Young people in the North Atlantic world adopted what one historian has called an "international language of dissent." Thinkers as disparate as Berlin-born philosopher Herbert Marcuse, American sociologist C. Wright Mills, Martinique-born psychiatrist Frantz Fanon, and French existentialist Jean Paul-Sartre rejected the stark Cold War dichotomies between capitalist and communist states and inspired Western youth to ferociously condemn repressive and imperialistic tendencies in their own societies. On both sides of the Atlantic, the American war in Vietnam catalyzed protest.

Upheaval was hardly confined to the capitalist West. Peace, economic growth, and expanding education also emboldened a postwar generation in Soviet bloc countries to voice political dissent. A Soviet intelligence officer cabled Soviet premier Leonid Brezhnev in 1968 that "opposition" was one of the "harmful developments among our youth"—just three months before a young Soviet soldier attempted to shoot the Russian leader.

The global tumult swept up peoples in the "Third World" as well, even as Western radicals made folk heroes of revolutionaries like Cuba's Che Guevara, Vietnam's Ho Chi Minh, and Congo's Patrice Lumumba. In China, Mao Zedong launched the "Cultural Revolution" in 1966 to purge all bourgeois vestiges from the emerging Chinese nation. Young and ideologically hyper-charged Red Guards made war on the "Four Olds": old customs, old culture, old habits, and old ideas. Millions perished before Mao finally began to rein in the rampaging bullies in 1969. Far less bloodily, student movements in recently independent states like Indonesia, the Philippines, and Congo made potent challenges to their governments in the later 1960s.

Bruno Barbey/Magnum Photos

Image 34.12 Paris, 1968 Protests ripped through the world in 1968. In Paris student battles with campus authorities and police triggered a massive nationwide labor strike and nearly brought down the French government.

The year 1968 became synonymous with unrest in many lands. Deep within the Soviet bloc, Western-inspired Czechoslovakian reformers launched the liberating program that became known as the "Prague Spring" in January 1968. For eight months, political freedom blossomed, until it was ruthlessly mowed down by Soviet tanks. In May, leftist students in Paris organized protests against their country's antiquated university system. The government's heavy-handed response compelled nearly 11 million workers to engage in wildcat solidarity strikes, bringing the economy to a halt and nearly toppling the government. President Charles de Gaulle even briefly fled Paris, sequestrating his personal papers and spiriting the family jewels from the city. In Mexico City, violent battles between students and police culminated in a brutal massacre of dozens of demonstrators at an October rally in Tlatelolco. Spectacular student-led protests also rocked Brazil, Spain, and Japan that year.

By the early 1970s, repression and exhaustion had begun to dissipate the global unrest, while minorities within some countries' radical movements, including the American Weather Underground, the West German Baader-Meinhof Gang, and the Italian Brigate Rosse (Red Brigades), turned to violence. But despite backlash, discrediting, and disillusionment, the upheavals of the 1960s left a permanent mark on societies around the world.

New agendas began to shape politics in one nation after another. "Post-materialist" concerns about culture, identity, the natural environment, and human rights now entered the political mainstream alongside traditional economic issues. "Green" parties emerged in Western Europe and the environmental movement gathered strength in the United States. Still more profound were the decade's cultural effects. A new skepticism about authority and institutions, a loosening of cultural mores about everyday speech, dress, and behavior, and new assertions of sexual identity and gender equality—all transformed societies the world over as lasting consequences of the global 1960s.

Hajsky Libor/CTK/Alamy Stock Photo

Image 34.13 The Prague Spring Comes to an End Sixties-era tumult struck deep within the communist Eastern bloc during the eight-month period of political liberalization in Czechoslovakia known as the Prague Spring. But on the night of August 20, 1968, the Soviets sent 200,000 troops and 2,000 tanks into the country to suppress the reform movement. Here, students and other residents of Prague stand atop an overturned truck, waving a Czech flag while staring down invading troops. But such nonviolent resistance would fail to halt the rapid crushing of reform.

Launched in youthful idealism, many of the cultural "revolutions" of the 1960s sputtered out in violence and cynicism. **Students for a Democratic Society (SDS)** once stood at the forefront of antipoverty and antiwar campaigns. (It had a conservative counterpart in **Young Americans for Freedom**, or YAF.) But by decade's end, SDS had spawned a clandestine terrorist group called the Weather Underground. (Commonly known as the Weathermen, they took their name from Bob Dylan's song lyric, "You don't need a weatherman to know which way the wind blows.") What started as seemingly innocent experiments with drugs like marijuana and LSD derailed young lives and fed the growth of a violent international drug trade. Spiritual seekers were swallowed up into cults, experiments in communal living collapsed into infighting, and bombmaking and kidnapping besmirched the revolutionary cause.

The upheavals of the 1960s could be largely attributed to three Ps: the population bulge of the baby boomers, protest against racism and the Vietnam War, and the extraordinary prosperity of postwar America. The era's wilder experiments and corrosive excesses ultimately faded away, but its expanded social and political consciousness endured. The rights revolution and the counterculture may not have fully disrupted the "traditional" values and assumptions of an older, whiter America, but they surely weakened their grip.

Less than a month after the Stonewall Uprising, people around the globe huddled in front of televisions to watch the ***Apollo 11* mission** land on the Moon, realizing the audacious goal declared by President Kennedy at the decade's start (refer to Image 34.14). Those confident years of the early 1960s seemed far distant by the time American astronauts stepped onto the lunar surface in July 1969. Project Apollo had been beset by delays and tragic accidents, sapping Congressional support for further space exploration and sparking questions about why millions of public dollars were being spent to send Americans into space rather than addressing poverty and inequality at home. Nonetheless, a worldwide television audience of as many as one billion people watched the lunar landing, marveling at how far, and how fast, humankind had come.

A

NASA

B

NASA

Image 34.14A and B On the Moon This Moon's-eye view of Earth greeted the first men to land on the lunar surface (34.14A). Astronaut Edwin ("Buzz") Aldrin descends from the spacecraft (34.14B). As he stepped onto the Moon's surface, his companion, Neil Armstrong, said, "That's one small step for man; one giant leap for mankind."

34-11 Nixon Vietnamizes the War

Inaugurated on January 20, 1969, Richard Nixon urged the American people, torn with dissension over Vietnam and race relations, to "stop shouting at one another." The new president seemed an unlikely conciliator of the clashing forces that appeared to be ripping apart American society. Solitary and suspicious by nature, Nixon could be brittle and testy in the face of opposition. He also harbored bitter resentments against the "liberal establishment" that had cast him into the political darkness for much of the preceding decade. But Nixon brought one hugely valuable asset with him to the White House—his broad knowledge and thoughtful expertise in foreign affairs. With calculating shrewdness he applied himself to putting America's foreign-policy house in order.

The first burning need was to quiet the public uproar over Vietnam (refer to Image 34.15). President Nixon's announced policy, called **Vietnamization**, was to withdraw the 540,000 U.S. troops in South Vietnam over an extended period. The South Vietnamese—with American money, weapons, training, and advice—could then gradually take over the burden of fighting their own war. The so-called **Nixon Doctrine** thus evolved. It proclaimed that the United States would honor its existing defense commitments but that in the future, allies would have to fight their own wars without the support of large bodies of American ground troops.

Robert Altman/Getty Images

Image 34.15 Antiwar Protest, San Francisco, 1969 Americans of all generations joined the protests against the war in Vietnam.

Nixon sought to win the war by other means, without the further spilling of American blood. But even this much involvement was repugnant to the American doves, many of whom demanded a withdrawal that was prompt, complete, unconditional, and irreversible. Antiwar protesters staged a massive national Vietnam moratorium in October 1969, as nearly 100,000 people jammed Boston Common and some 50,000 filed by the White House carrying lighted candles.

Undaunted, Nixon launched a counteroffensive by appealing to what he called the "**silent majority**" who presumably supported the war and rejected the counterculture. Though ostensibly conciliatory, Nixon's appeal was in fact deeply divisive. His intentions soon became clear when he unleashed tough-talking Vice President Agnew to attack the "nattering nabobs of negativism" who demanded a quick withdrawal from Vietnam. Nixon himself in 1970 sneered at the student antiwar demonstrators as "bums."

By January 1970, the Vietnam conflict had become grotesquely unpopular, even among troops in the field (refer to Image 34.16). Because draft policies largely exempted college students and men with critical civilian skills, the armed forces in Vietnam were largely composed of the least privileged young Americans. Especially in the war's early stages, Black Americans were disproportionately represented in the army and accounted for a disproportionately high share of combat fatalities. Because of this inequity, civil rights activists from Martin Luther King Jr. to the Black Panthers found common cause in early and vocal opposition to the war.

As the war dragged on, Black and white soldiers alike fought not only against the Vietnamese enemy but also against the coiled fear of floundering through booby-trapped swamps and steaming jungles, often unable to distinguish friend from foe among the villagers they encountered in Vietnamese hamlets. Drug abuse, mutiny, and sabotage dulled the army's fighting edge. Morale appeared to have plummeted to rock bottom

A Marine Corps officer expressed the disillusion that beset many American troops in Vietnam:

"For years we disposed of the enemy dead like so much garbage. We stuck cigarettes in the mouths of corpses, put *Playboy* magazines in their hands, cut off their ears to wear around our necks. We incinerated them with napalm, atomized them with B-52 strikes, shoved them out the doors of helicopters above the South China Sea. . . . All we did was count, count bodies. Count dead human beings. . . . That was our fundamental military strategy. Body count. And the count kept going up."

AP Images

Image 34.16 Vietnam Vets Protest the War, 1971 Public opinion gradually but inexorably turned against the war. In 1965, polls showed that only 15 percent of Americans favored withdrawal from Vietnam. But by 1969, 69 percent of those interviewed indicated that they considered the war a "mistake," and by 1970 a majority supported withdrawal of U.S. troops. In this demonstration on April 23, 1971, eight hundred veterans threw away their Purple Hearts, Bronze Stars, Silver Stars, and other military honors in front of the U.S. Capitol in protest against a war they no longer could support.

when rumors filtered out of Vietnam that soldiers were "fragging" their own officers—murdering them with fragmentation grenades. Domestic disgust with the war further deepened amid revelations that American troops had callously slaughtered more than 300 innocent women and children in the village of **My Lai** in 1968.

34-12 Cambodianizing the Vietnam War

For several years the North Vietnamese and Viet Cong had been using Cambodia, bordering South Vietnam on the west, as a springboard for troops, weapons, and supplies. Suddenly, on April 29, 1970, without consulting Congress, Nixon ordered American forces to join with the South Vietnamese in cleaning out the enemy sanctuaries in officially neutral Cambodia.

Angry students nationwide responded to this newest escalation of the fighting with rock throwing, window smashing, and arson. At **Kent State University** in Ohio, jumpy members of the National Guard fired into a noisy student crowd, killing four and wounding many more (refer to Image 34.17); at historically Black Jackson State College in Mississippi, the highway patrol discharged volleys at a student dormitory, killing two students.

Nixon withdrew the American troops from Cambodia on June 29, 1970, after only two months. But in America, the Cambodian invasion amplified the bitterness between hawks and doves. Disillusionment with "whitey's war" increased ominously among Black troops. The Senate (though not the House) overwhelmingly repealed the Gulf of Tonkin blank check that Congress had given Johnson in 1964. American young people were only slightly mollified when the government reduced draft calls and shortened the period of draft eligibility, on a lottery basis, from eight years to one year. They were similarly pleased, though not pacified, when the Twenty-Sixth Amendment in 1971 lowered the voting age to eighteen (refer to the Appendix).

New combustibles fueled the fires of antiwar discontent in June 1971, when a former Pentagon official leaked to the *New York Times* the **Pentagon Papers**, a top-secret Pentagon study that documented the blunders and deceptions of the Kennedy and Johnson administrations, especially the provoking of the 1964 North Vietnamese attack in the Gulf of Tonkin.

34-13 Nixon's Détente with Beijing (Peking) and Moscow

Even as the war in Vietnam ground on, Nixon pursued a dramatic Cold War diplomatic initiative in Beijing (Peking) and Moscow. The two great communist powers, the Soviet Union and China, were dueling over their rival interpretations of Marxism. In 1969 they had even fought several bloody skirmishes along the inner border that separated them in Asia. Nixon correctly perceived that the Chinese-Soviet tension afforded the United States an opportunity to play off one antagonist against the other, in the process gaining new flexibility and leverage on the world stage and, potentially, even the aid of both powers in pressuring North Vietnam into peace.

Nixon's thinking was reinforced by his national security adviser, Dr. Henry A. Kissinger. Bespectacled and German-accented, Kissinger had reached America as a youth when his parents fled Hitler's anti-Jewish persecutions. In 1969, the former Harvard professor had begun meeting secretly on Nixon's behalf with North Vietnamese officials in Paris to negotiate an end to the war in Vietnam. He was meanwhile preparing the president's path to Beijing and Moscow.

Howard Ruffner/Archive Photos/Getty Images

Image 34.17 **The War at Home, Spring 1970** President Nixon's order to invade Cambodia sparked angry protests on American campuses. At Kent State University in Ohio, the nation watched in horror as four student demonstrators were shot by jittery National Guardsmen.

Nixon, heretofore an uncompromising anticommunist, announced to a startled nation in July 1971 that he had accepted an invitation to visit Communist China the following year. He made his historic journey in February 1972, enjoying glass-clinking toasts and walks on the fabled Great Wall of China (refer to Image 34.18). He capped his visit with the Shanghai Communiqué, in which the two nations agreed to normalize their relationship. An important part of the accord was America's acceptance of a "one-China" policy, implying a lessened American commitment to the independence of Taiwan.

Nixon next traveled to Moscow in May 1972 to play his "China card" in a game of high-stakes diplomacy in the Kremlin. The Soviets, hungry for American foodstuffs and alarmed over the possibility of intensified rivalry with an American-backed China, were ready to deal. Nixon's visits ushered in an era of **détente**, or relaxed tension, with the two communist powers and led to several significant agreements including an anti–ballistic missile (ABM) treaty and a series of arms-reduction negotiations known as SALT (Strategic Arms Limitation Talks), aimed at freezing

Bettmann/Getty Images

Image 34.18 **Dinner Diplomacy** President Nixon tries to wield chopsticks alongside Chinese Premier Chou En-lai (left) and Shanghai Communist Party Leader Chan Chun-chiao (right) during the farewell banquet held in his honor at the end of his historic trip to China in 1972. Nixon was the first American president ever to visit mainland China while in office, and his pursuit of normal diplomatic relations with the ruling Communist regime ended 23 years of formalized hostility between the United States and the People's Republic.

the numbers of long-range nuclear missiles for five years. The ABM and SALT accords constituted long-overdue first steps toward slowing the arms race, though both parties still forged ahead with the development of "MIRVs" (multiple independently targeted reentry vehicles) equipped with large numbers of warheads, several to a rocket.

Nixon's détente diplomacy did, to some extent, de-ice the Cold War. Yet Nixon remained staunchly anticommunist when the occasion seemed to demand it. He strongly opposed the election of the outspoken Marxist Salvador Allende to the presidency of Chile in 1970. His administration slapped an embargo on the Allende regime, and the Central Intelligence Agency worked covertly to undermine the legitimately elected leftist president. When Allende died during a Chilean army attack on his headquarters in 1973, many observers smelled a Yankee rat—an impression that deepened when Washington warmly embraced Allende's successor, military dictator General Augusto Pinochet.

34-14 A New Team on the Supreme Bench

Nixon had lashed out during the campaign at the "permissiveness" and "judicial activism" of the Supreme Court under Chief Justice Earl Warren. Following his appointment in 1953, Warren had led the Court into a series of decisions that drastically affected sexual freedom, the rights of the criminally accused, the practice of religion, civil rights, and the structure of political representation (refer to "33-5 Seeds of the Civil Rights Revolution," pp. 883–886).

In *Griswold v. Connecticut* (1965), the Court struck down a state law that prohibited the use of contraceptives, even among married couples. The Court proclaimed (critics said "invented") a "right of privacy" that soon provided the basis for decisions protecting women's abortion rights.

In 1963, the Court held in *Gideon v. Wainwright* that all criminal defendants were entitled to legal counsel, even if they lacked the funds to pay for it. More controversial still were decisions in two cases—*Escobedo* (1964) and *Miranda* (1966)—that ensured the right of the accused to remain silent and enjoy other protections. The latter case gave rise to the **Miranda warning** that arresting police officers must read to suspects. These several court rulings sought to prevent abusive police tactics, but they appeared to conservatives to coddle criminals and subvert law and order.

Conservatives also objected to the Court's views on religion. In two stunning decisions, *Engel v. Vitale* (1962) and *School District of Abington Township v. Schempp* (1963), the justices argued that the First Amendment's separation of church and state meant that public schools could not require prayer or Bible reading. Taken together, the Warren Court's rulings heralded a "rights revolution" in American jurisprudence that would eventually empower social movements from left to right, from advocates for racial and gender equality to opponents of gun control. Social conservatives raised anew the battle cry "Impeach Earl Warren" (refer to Image 34.19).

Image 34.19 The Embattled Warren Court The U.S. Supreme Court, presided over by Chief Justice Earl Warren, made historic decisions in areas ranging from criminal justice to civil rights and political representation. Its achievements provoked often ferocious conservative backlash, as seen in this billboard erected by the arch-conservative John Birch Society, calling for Warren's impeachment. Note the damage from attempts to destroy the sign.

Duane Howell/Getty Images

From 1954 on, the Court came under relentless criticism, the bitterest since New Deal days. But for better or worse, the black-robed justices were grappling with stubborn social problems spawned by midcentury tensions, even—or especially—if duly elected legislatures failed to do so.

Fulfilling campaign promises, President Nixon undertook to change the Court's philosophical complexion. Taking advantage of several vacancies, he sought appointees who would strictly interpret the Constitution, cease "meddling" in social and political questions, and not coddle radicals or criminals. The Senate in 1969 speedily confirmed his nomination of white-maned Warren E. Burger of Minnesota to succeed the retiring Earl Warren as chief justice. Before the end of 1971, the Court counted four conservative Nixon appointments out of nine members.

Yet Nixon was to learn the ironic lesson that many presidents have learned about their Supreme Court appointees: Once seated on the high bench, the justices are fully free to think and decide according to their own consciences, not according to the president's expectations. The Burger Court that Nixon shaped proved reluctant to dismantle the "liberal" rulings of the Warren Court; it even produced the most controversial judicial opinion of modern times, the momentous *Roe v. Wade* decision in 1973, which legalized abortion (refer to "35-5 Feminism Takes Center Stage," pp. 950–951).

34-15 The New Racial Politics

A small-government Republican president working with a Congress that had strong Democratic majorities on both sides, Nixon ended up presiding over significant expansion of the welfare programs that conservatives routinely denounced. He approved increased appropriations for entitlements like Food Stamps, Medicaid, and Aid to Families with Dependent Children (AFDC), while adding a generous new program, Supplemental Security Income (SSI), to assist the low-income elderly and disabled. He signed legislation in 1972 guaranteeing automatic Social Security cost-of-living increases to protect the senior citizens against the ravages of inflation. Ironically, this "indexing" actually helped to fuel the inflationary fires that raged out of control later in the decade.

Amid much controversy, Nixon in 1969 implemented his so-called **Philadelphia Plan**, requiring construction-trade unions to establish "goals and timetables" for the hiring of Black apprentices. Nixon was motivated in part by a desire to divide core Democratic constituencies by driving a wedge between Black workers and white-dominated trade unions. But whatever his reasoning, the president's new policy had far-reaching implications. Soon extended to all federal contracts, the Philadelphia Plan in effect required thousands of employers to meet hiring quotas or to establish "set-asides" for minority subcontractors.

Nixon's Philadelphia Plan drastically altered the meaning of affirmative action. Lyndon Johnson had intended affirmative action to protect *individuals* against discrimination. Nixon now transformed and escalated affirmative action into a program that conferred privileges on certain *groups*. The Supreme Court went along with Nixon's approach. In *Griggs v. Duke Power Co.* (1971), the justices prohibited intelligence tests or other devices that had the effect of excluding minorities or women from certain jobs. The Court's ruling strongly suggested to employers that the only sure protection against charges of discrimination was to hire minority workers—or admit minority students—in proportion to their presence in the population.

Together, the actions of Nixon and the Court opened broad employment and educational opportunities for minorities and women. They also opened a Pandora's box of protest from critics who assailed the new style of affirmative action as "reverse discrimination," imposed by executive order and judicial decision, not by democratically elected representatives. Yet what other remedy was there, defenders asked, to offset centuries of prejudice and opportunity denied?

Appointing conservative Supreme Court justices, soft-pedaling civil rights, and opposing school busing to achieve racial balance were all parts of a GOP electoral approach that Nixon advisers called the "**Southern Strategy**." By deliberately seeking to convert disillusioned white Southern Democrats to the Republican cause, Nixon set in motion a sweeping political realignment that eventually transformed the American party system.

34-16 The Economy Shifts

Among Nixon's major legacies was the creation in 1970 of the **Environmental Protection Agency (EPA)**, which climaxed two decades of mounting concern for the environment. Scientist and author Rachel Carson gave the environmental movement a huge boost in 1962 when she published *Silent Spring*, an enormously effective piece of latter-day muckraking that exposed the poisonous effects of pesticides (refer to Image 34.20). On April 22, 1970, millions of environmentalists around the world celebrated the first **Earth Day** to raise awareness and to encourage their leaders to act. In the wake of what became a yearly event, the U.S. Congress passed the Clean Air Act of 1970 and the Endangered Species Act of 1973. The EPA now stood on the frontline of the battle for ecological sanity and made notable progress in reducing automobile emissions and cleaning up befouled waterways and toxic waste sites.

The federal government also expanded its regulatory reach on behalf of workers and consumers. Late in 1970, Nixon signed the Occupational Safety and Health Administration (OSHA) into law, creating an agency dedicated to improving working conditions, preventing work-related accidents and deaths, and issuing safety standards. The Consumer Product Safety Commission (CPSC) followed two years later, holding companies to account for selling dangerous products. Together with new environmental laws, these three mega-agencies gave the federal government far more direct control over business operations, drawing the ire of many big companies, which chastised the overbearing "nanny state."

Meanwhile, after a quarter-century of remarkable growth, the American economic juggernaut started to slow. Nations like Japan began to challenge the supremacy of American manufacturers in goods like cars and consumer electronics. The United States began to import more foreign-made goods. Inflation crept up, reaching 5 percent by 1971 (refer to Image 34.21). A worried Nixon overcame his distaste for economic controls and imposed a ninety-day wage and price freeze to quell the inflation rate. To stimulate the nation's sagging exports, he stunned the world by taking the United States off the gold standard and devaluing the dollar. These moves effectively ended the Bretton Woods system of international currency stabilization that had functioned for more than a quarter of a century after World War II (refer to "32-4 Shaping the Postwar World," pp. 849–850).

Image 34.20 Author Rachel Carson (1907–1964) Educated as a marine biologist, some call her the mother of the modern environmentalism and conservation movement because of the impact of her 1962 book, *Silent Spring*.

Image 34.21 "But on the Average, We're Doing Okay." By 1970, the long-mighty American economy had begun to waver. As inflation began to creep upward and stock prices sank, the Nixon Administration scrambled to stabilize the economy.

34-17 The Nixon Landslide of 1972

Nearly four years had passed since Nixon had promised, as a presidential candidate, to end the war and "win" the peace. Yet in the spring of 1972, the fighting escalated anew to alarming levels when the North Vietnamese, heavily equipped with foreign tanks, burst through the demilitarized zone (DMZ) separating the two Vietnams. Nixon reacted promptly by launching massive bombing attacks on strategic centers in North Vietnam, including Hanoi, the capital. The continuing Vietnam conflict spurred the rise of South Dakota Senator George McGovern in the 1972 race for the Democratic presidential nomination, while changes in the nominating system itself helped to ensure his victory at the party's convention.

After the 1968 debacle in Chicago, McGovern had led a party commission tasked with reforming state delegate selection procedures to ensure popular participation in Democratic presidential nominations. Partly thanks to that commission's work, the number of **primary elections** began a steady and irreversible rise, from 15 for both Democrats and Republicans in 1968 to 20 in 1972. (The numbers reached 41 for Democrats and 39 for Republicans by 2016.) The proliferation of primaries marked a historic shift away from an elite-dominated nominating system, with decisions made in the proverbial "smoked-filled room," to a costly and drawn-out popular campaign process, featuring media-focused politicking and appeals to the ideological activist base of each party.

An ultraliberal dark-horse candidate at the beginning of 1972, McGovern proved to be the first politician to make effective use of the new, more populist system. His promise to pull the remaining American troops out of Vietnam in ninety days earned him the backing of the large antiwar element in the Democratic camp. But his appeal to racial minorities, feminists, leftists, and youth branded him as the countercultural candidate of "acid, amnesty, and abortion" and alienated the traditional working-class backbone of his party. Moreover, the discovery shortly after the convention that McGovern's running mate, Missouri senator Thomas Eagleton, had undergone psychiatric care—including electroshock therapy—forced Eagleton's ouster from the ticket and helped to doom the Democrats' hopes of recapturing the White House.

Nixon's campaign emphasized that he had wound down the "Democratic war" in Vietnam from some 540,000 troops to about 30,000. His candidacy received an added boost just twelve days before the election when the high-flying Dr. Kissinger announced that "peace is at hand" in Vietnam and that an agreement would be reached in a few days.

Nixon won the election in a landslide. His lopsided victory encompassed every state except Massachusetts and the nonstate District of Columbia (which was granted electoral votes by the Twenty-Third Amendment in 1961—refer to Appendix). He piled up 520 electoral votes to 17 for McGovern and a popular majority of 47,169,911 to 29,170,383 votes. McGovern had counted on a large number of young people's votes, but less than half the eighteen-to-twenty-one age group even bothered to register to vote. Dominated by conflict over both Vietnam and the counterculture, the 1972 presidential election proved in many ways to be the last election of the sixties era.

34-18 The Secret Bombing of Cambodia and the War Powers Act

The dove of peace, allegedly at hand just before the balloting, took flight after the election. Nixon launched a furious two-week bombing of North Vietnam in an iron-fisted effort to force the North Vietnamese back to the conference table. This merciless pounding drove the North Vietnamese negotiators to agree to a cease-fire in the Treaty of Paris on January 23, 1973, nearly three months after peace was prematurely proclaimed.

Nixon hailed the face-saving cease-fire as "peace with honor," but the boast rang hollow. The United States was to withdraw its remaining 27,000 or so troops and could reclaim some 560 American prisoners of war. The North Vietnamese were allowed to keep some 145,000 troops in South Vietnam, where they still occupied about 30 percent of the country. The shaky "peace" was in reality little more than a thinly disguised American retreat.

The constitutionality of Nixon's continued aerial battering of Cambodia had meanwhile been coming under increasing fire. In July 1973, Americans were shocked to learn that the U.S. Air Force had secretly conducted some 3,500 bombing raids against North Vietnamese positions in Cambodia, beginning in March 1969 and continuing for about fourteen months prior to the open American incursion in May 1970. The most disturbing feature of these sky forays was that

The *Washington Post* (July 19, 1973) carried this news item:

"American B-52 bombers dropped about 104,000 tons of explosives on Communist sanctuaries in neutralist Cambodia during a series of raids in 1969 and 1970. . . . The secret bombing was acknowledged by the Pentagon the Monday after a former Air Force major . . . described how he falsified reports on Cambodian air operations and destroyed records on the bombing missions actually flown."

while they were going on, American officials, including the president, had sworn that Cambodian neutrality was being respected. Countless Americans began to wonder what kind of representative government they had if the United States had been fighting a war they knew nothing about.

Defiance followed secretiveness. After the Vietnam cease-fire in January 1973, Nixon brazenly continued large-scale bombing of communist forces in order to help the rightist Cambodian government, and he repeatedly vetoed congressional efforts to stop him. The years of bombing inflicted grisly wounds on Cambodia, blasting its people, shredding its economy, and revolutionizing its politics. The long-suffering Cambodians soon groaned under the sadistic heel of Pol Pot, a murderous tyrant who dispatched as many as 2 million of his people to their graves. He was forced from power, ironically enough, only by the Vietnamese army's invasion in 1978.

Congressional opposition to the expansion of presidential war-making powers by Johnson and Nixon led to the **War Powers Act** in November 1973. Passed over Nixon's veto, it required the president to report to Congress within forty-eight hours after committing troops to a foreign conflict or "substantially" enlarging American combat units in a foreign country. Such a limited authorization would have to end within sixty days unless Congress extended it for thirty more days.

The War Powers Act was but one manifestation of what came to be called the "New Isolationism," a mood of caution and restraint in the conduct of the nation's foreign affairs after the bloody and futile misadventure in Vietnam. Meanwhile, Congress greatly reduced anxieties among draft-age youth and their families when it ended conscription in January 1973. The nation then transitioned from its traditional reliance on an inclusive citizens' army to the highly selective **All-Volunteer Force (AVF)**, which was smaller, better disciplined, less expensive, and eventually far more technologically enhanced than the conscript force that had been in place since World War II. The AVF also proved to be much easier to employ as an instrument of foreign policy, as the rate of overseas military deployments rose dramatically in the decades to come.

34-19 The Arab Oil Embargo and the Energy Crisis

The long-rumbling Middle East erupted anew in October 1973, when the rearmed Syrians and Egyptians unleashed surprise attacks on Israel in an attempt to regain the territory they had lost in the Six-Day War of 1967. With the Israelis in desperate retreat, Kissinger, who had become secretary of state in September, hastily flew to Moscow to restrain the Soviets, who were arming the attackers. Believing that the Kremlin was poised to fly combat troops to the Suez area, Nixon placed America's nuclear forces on alert and ordered a gigantic airlift of nearly $2 billion in war materials to the Israelis. This assistance helped save the day, as the Israelis aggressively turned the tide and threatened Cairo itself before American diplomacy brought about an uneasy cease-fire to what became known as the Yom Kippur War.

America's policy of backing Israel against its oil-rich neighbors exacted a heavy penalty. Late in October 1973, the OPEC nations (refer to "33-10 Cold War Crises in the Middle East," pp. 888–889) announced an embargo on oil shipments to the United States and several European allies supporting Israel. What was more, the oil-rich Arab states cut their oil production, further ratcheting up pressure on the entire West, whose citizens suffered a long winter of lowered thermostats and speedometers. Lines at gas stations grew longer as tempers grew shorter (refer to Image 34.22). The shortage triggered a major economic recession, not just in America but also in France and Britain. Although the latter two countries had not supported Israel and had thus been exempted from the embargo, in an increasingly globalized, interconnected world, all nations soon felt the crunch of the "energy crisis."

The five months of the Arab "blackmail" embargo in 1974 clearly signaled the end of an era—the era of cheap and abundant energy. A twenty-year surplus of world oil supplies had masked the fact that since 1948 the United States had been a net importer of oil. American oil production peaked in 1970 and then began a long-term decline, reversed only by the introduction of new

Owen Franken/Corbis/Getty Images

Image 34.22 The U.S. Economy Runs Out of Gas At filling stations across the country, the oil crises of the 1970s provoked steep price hikes, patience-testing lines, and aggressive gas-rationing, as depicted here in a Connecticut station. But the economic repercussions of the crises extended far beyond what was experienced at the pump.

drilling technologies (hydraulic fracturing, or "fracking") in the twenty-first century. Blissfully unaware of their dependence on foreign suppliers, Americans, like revelers on a binge, had more than tripled their oil consumption since the end of World War II. The number of automobiles increased 250 percent between 1949 and 1972, and Detroit's engineers gave nary a thought to building more fuel-efficient engines.

By 1974, America was oil-addicted and extremely vulnerable to any interruption in supplies. That stark fact deeply colored the diplomatic and economic history of the next three decades and beyond, as the Middle East loomed ever larger on the map of America's strategic interests. OPEC approximately quadrupled its price for crude oil after lifting the embargo in 1974. Huge new oil bills wildly disrupted the U.S. balance of international trade and added further fuel to the already raging fires of inflation. The United States took the lead in forming the International Energy Agency in 1974 as a counterweight to OPEC and temporarily instituted a national speed limit of fifty-five miles per hour to conserve fuel. Various sectors of the economy, including Detroit's carmakers, began their slow, grudging adjustment to the rudely dawning age of energy dependency. But full reconciliation to that uncomfortable reality was a long time coming.

Long gas lines and slumping sales of American-made cars were symptoms of economic realignments already well underway by the middle of the 1970s. Even as America surfed the wave of postwar prosperity, shifts in the global economic order quietly gathered steam. Rebuilt from the rubble of World War II, Japanese industries experienced a "Golden Sixties" of technological innovation and growing sales. "Made in Japan" had once signaled shoddy craftsmanship. Now Japan's gas-sipping compact cars were exactly what American consumers wanted. Meanwhile, lured by low-cost labor and gleaming new facilities, American manufacturers moved their factories to Taiwan, Singapore, and Malaysia. Stressed by foreign competition and stretched by high labor costs, American companies accelerated factory automation. The job-killing possibilities of replacing man with machine had worried politicians and labor leaders alike since the 1950s. Twenty years later, it was becoming an ever more troubling reality.

Even greater global challenges were still to come. In 1979, the Chinese visionary leader Deng Xiaoping established a "Special Economic Zone" that turned the southern Chinese city of Shenzhen into a hub of export-oriented manufacturing. This experiment in "capitalism with Chinese characteristics" ignited an explosion of export-fueled growth that soon turned China into an economic superpower.

Varying Viewpoints

What Were the Legacies of the 1960s?

The 1960s were convulsed by cultural and political upheavals, and their legacy has remained contested ever since. Conflicts raged in that turbulent decade between social classes, races, sexes, and generations. Well into the twenty-first century, the shock waves from the 1960s still reverberate through American society. While historians and others once focused chiefly on the sixties as a moment that witnessed the mobilization of the political left and cultural and sexual liberation, more recent work has examined how the decade was also pivotal in the formation of modern conservatism—encompassing both a rightward turn in politics and a reaffirmation of "traditional values" even amid rapid cultural transformation.

Four issues have dominated historical discussion of the 1960s: the struggle for civil rights; the impact of the Great Society's War on Poverty; the Vietnam War and the antiwar movement; and the emergence of "identity politics" across the social spectrum.

Recent work on African American civil rights has explored what Jacquelyn Hall has termed the "long civil rights movement," challenging the notion that a sharp break separated a nonviolent, mostly Southern phase of the movement from a more militant national movement post-1965. Scholars such as Peniel Joseph, Donna Murch, and Robyn C. Spencer have shown how Southern civil right struggles, migration, and economic inequality contributed to the emergent ideology of Black Power. Intellectual historians such as Thomas F. Jackson and Ibram X. Kendi have identified important radical traditions, both socialist and anti-imperial in outlook, among civil rights activists in both the South and the North and both before and after the 1960s. Other scholars, including Robert O. Self and Sherry L. Smith, have emphasized the ways that the original Black struggle for civil rights provided both an inspiration and a template for other groups, including feminists, Native Americans, and gays.

Lyndon Johnson's War on Poverty has had liberal defenders like Allen Matusow and John Schwarz as well as conservative critics like Charles Murray and Lawrence Meade. Scholars like Edward Berkowitz and Julian Zelizer have focused on the role of Congress in shaping the Great Society policy agenda, while historians Michael K. Brown and Ira Katznelson have underscored the persistent racial inequalities embedded in both New Deal and Great Society programs.

The anti-Vietnam War movement initiated many young people into politics and the heady attractions of "movement culture." But scholars disagree over the movement's real effectiveness in checking the war. Writers like Todd Gitlin and Tom Wells insist that mass protest was the force that finally pressed the war to a conclusion, while John Lewis Gaddis explains America's eventual withdrawal from Vietnam essentially without reference to the protesters in the streets. Adam Garfinkle goes further, arguing that antiwar activism actually prolonged the war by provoking a domestic backlash. Odd Arne Westad analyzes the Vietnam conflict in the framework of Cold War geopolitics, where high-level statecraft, not grassroots protest, determined the course of events.

Although most scholars see the 1960s as a time when liberal ideas and policies were in the ascendant, a surge of early twenty-first century scholarship has focused on the other end of the political spectrum, identifying the 1960s as a formative decade for the modern conservative movement. Historians like Lisa McGirr and Rick Perlstein have argued that even though Barry Goldwater lost in a landslide in 1964, the conservative movement he kick-started laid the foundation for later electoral successes by Ronald Reagan and the strong rightward swing of the Republican Party. Sociologist Rebecca Klatch traces the divisions in the modern feminist movement to the clashes between left and right in the 1960s. Historians like Marjorie Spruill explore how 1960s issues like women's liberation, birth control, and no-fault divorce laws ignited a conservative backlash and led to the reassertion of "family values." Kim Philips-Fein and Benjamin Waterhouse attribute late-twentieth-century conservative business-sector mobilization to the perceived regulatory excesses of the liberal state, while Matthew Dallek contends that Reagan's 1966 California gubernatorial victory over liberal Pat Brown was a harbinger of the conservative ascendancy to come.

Chapter Summary

Johnson succeeded the assassinated Kennedy and overwhelmingly defeated the militantly conservative Goldwater in the 1964 election. Johnson used his strong electoral mandate and huge congressional majorities to push through a mass of liberal Great Society legislation, including Medicare, Medicaid, federal aid to education, and immigration reform.

With Johnson's support, the civil rights movement won great legislative victories with the Civil Rights Act of 1964 and the Voting Rights Act of 1965. But Martin Luther King Jr.'s nonviolent civil rights movement was increasingly overshadowed by more militant voices, as Northern cities erupted in violence amid calls for Black Power and Black nationalism. A growing white backlash reduced sympathies for further integration and civil rights gains.

Faced with the imminent collapse of corrupt and unpopular South Vietnamese governments, Johnson escalated military involvement in Vietnam. As the number of troops and casualties grew without producing military success, dovish protests against the war gained strength. Political opposition forced Johnson not to seek reelection. Senators Eugene

McCarthy and Robert Kennedy led antiwar challenges to Johnson's designated successor, Hubert Humphrey. Humphrey won the nomination, but deep Democratic divisions over the war allowed Nixon to win the White House. The third-party candidacy of George Wallace revealed the growth of angry "populist" politics. The political upheavals of the 1960s also produced a youthful counterculture that revolted against authority and weakened all mainstream American institutions, including government and religion. The counterculture, which began in idealism, eventually faded amid growing cynicism and economic anxiety in the 1970s.

Nixon's Vietnamization policy reduced American ground participation in the war, but his Cambodia invasion sparked massive domestic protest. Nixon's journeys to Communist Moscow and Beijing established a new rapprochement with these powers, which Nixon and Kissinger used to advantage in continuing the Vietnam War. In domestic policy, Nixon appointed more conservative justices to the Supreme Court. He expanded social welfare programs and promoted environmental protection and workplace safety. On race relations he pursued a "Southern Strategy" that successfully moved southern white Democrats into the Republican Party.

Nixon won a landslide victory in 1972 over the strongly antiwar Democratic nominee McGovern. After a fierce post-election bombing campaign, a cease-fire agreement provided for the remaining U.S. troops to leave Vietnam. But revelations of the secret bombing of Cambodia led to congressional outrage and the War Powers Act.

The Middle East war of 1973 and the Arab oil embargo created an energy and economic crisis. Americans gradually awoke to their costly and dangerous dependence on increasingly expensive Middle Eastern oil, and slowly began to take tentative steps toward conservation. Increased costs and foreign competition from Japan, China, and other nations led to a decline in American manufacturing and jobs, as did increasing factory automation.

Key Terms

- Civil Rights Act of 1964 (908)
- affirmative action (908)
- Great Society (908)
- Tonkin Gulf Resolution (910)
- Immigration and Nationality Act of 1965 (911)
- Freedom Summer (912)
- Mississippi Freedom Democratic Party (912)
- Voting Rights Act of 1965 (915)
- Watts (916)
- Black Panther Party (918)
- Black Power (918)
- Kerner Commission (918)
- Six-Day War (920)
- Tet offensive (921)
- Stonewall Uprising (925)
- Students for a Democratic Society (SDS) (928)
- Young Americans for Freedom (928)
- *Apollo 11* mission (928)
- Vietnamization (929)
- Nixon Doctrine (929)
- silent majority (929)
- My Lai (930)
- Kent State University (930)
- Pentagon Papers (930)
- détente (931)
- Miranda warning (932)
- Philadelphia Plan (933)
- Southern Strategy (933)
- Environmental Protection Agency (EPA) (933)
- Earth Day (934)
- primary elections (935)
- War Powers Act (936)
- All-Volunteer Force (AVF) (936)

People to Know

- Malcolm X
- Stokely Carmichael
- Eugene McCarthy
- George C. Wallace
- Henry A. Kissinger
- Warren E. Burger
- Rachel Carson
- César Chávez
- George McGovern

Chronology

1963	• Kennedy assassinated; Johnson assumes presidency	
1964	• Twenty-Fourth Amendment (abolishing poll tax in federal elections) ratified • "Freedom Summer" voter registration in South • Gulf of Tonkin Resolution	• Johnson defeats Goldwater for presidency • War on Poverty begins • Civil Rights Act
1965	• Great Society legislation • Voting Rights Act	• Watts uprising • *Griswold v. Connecticut*
1966	• France withdraws from NATO • Black Panther Party founded	
1967	• Six-Day War between Israel and Egypt • Newark and Detroit uprisings	
1968	• North Vietnamese army launches Tet offensive in South Vietnam • Martin Luther King Jr. and Robert Kennedy assassinated	• Prague Spring crushed by Soviet army • Violent protests at the Democratic National Convention • Nixon defeats Humphrey and Wallace for presidency
1969	• Stonewall Inn uprising in New York City • *Apollo 11* astronauts land on the Moon	
1970	• Nixon orders invasion of Cambodia • Kent State and Jackson State incidents	• Environmental Protection Agency (EPA) created • Clean Air Act
1971	• Pentagon Papers published • Twenty-Sixth Amendment (lowering voting age to eighteen) passed	
1972	• Nixon visits China and Soviet Union • Shanghai Communiqué begins "normalization" of U.S.-Chinese relations	• ABM and SALT I treaties ratified • Nixon defeats McGovern for presidency
1973	• Treaty of Paris enacts cease-fire in Vietnam and U.S. withdrawal • War Powers Act • Yom Kippur War • OPEC oil embargo	• Endangered Species Act • Chilean president Salvador Allende killed in CIA-backed coup • *Roe v. Wade*
1974	• OPEC ends embargo, increases oil prices • International Energy Agency formed	

To Learn More

Mark Philip Bradley, *Vietnam at War* (2009)

Mark Brilliant, *The Color of America Has Changed: How Racial Diversity Shaped Civil Rights Reform in California, 1941–1978* (2010)

Dan Carter, *The Politics of Rage: George Wallace, the Origins of the New Conservatism, and the Transformation of American Politics* (1995)

Alex Haley, *The Autobiography of Malcolm X* (1966)

Elizabeth Hinton, *America On Fire: The Untold History of Police Violence and Black Rebellion Since the 1960s* (2021)

Maurice Isserman and Michael Kazin, *America Divided: The Civil War of the 1960s* (2000)

Thomas F. Jackson, *From Civil Rights to Human Rights* (2009)

Meg Jacobs, *Panic at the Pump: The Energy Crisis and the Transformation of American Politics in the 1970s* (2016)

Peniel Joseph, *Waiting 'Til the Midnight Hour: A Narrative History of Black Power in America* (2006)

Ibram X. Kendi, *Stamped from the Beginning: The Definitive History of Racist Ideas in America* (2016)

G. Calvin Mackenzie and Robert Weisbrot, *The Liberal Hour: Washington and the Politics of Change in the 1960s* (2008)

Lisa McGirr, *Suburban Warriors: The Origins of the New American Right* (2001)

James Miller, *"Democracy Is in the Streets": From Port Huron to the Siege of Chicago* (1987)

Donna Murch, *Living for the City: Migration, Education, and the Rise of the Black Panther Party in Oakland, California* (2010)

Rick Perlstein, *Before the Storm: Barry Goldwater and the Unmaking of the American Consensus* (2001)

———, *Nixonland: The Rise of a President and the Fracturing of America* (2008)

Robert O. Self, *All in the Family: The Realignment of American Democracy Since the 1960s* (2013)

John D. Skrentny, *The Minority Rights Revolution* (2002)

Sherry L. Smith, *Hippies, Indians, and the Fight for Red Power* (2014)

Robyn C. Spencer, *The Revolution Has Come: Black Power, Gender, and the Black Panther Party in Oakland* (2016)

Thomas J. Sugrue, *Sweet Land of Liberty: The Forgotten Struggle for Civil Rights in the North* (2008)

Jeremi Suri, *Power and Protest: Global Revolution and the Rise of Détente* (2003)

Chapter 35

A Sea of Troubles: 1973–1980

I must say to you that the state of the Union is not good.

Gerald Ford, 1975

Chapter Outline

- The Watergate scandal and Nixon's resignation
- The politics of stagflation
- Gerald Ford's foreign policy
- Feminism
- Affirmative action and post-civil rights politics
- The election of Jimmy Carter, 1976
- The energy crisis and inflation
- The political turn toward the market
- The Iranian hostage humiliation

Examining the Evidence: The "Smoking Gun" Tape, June 23, 1972, 10:04–11:39 A.M.

Thinking Globally: The Era of Globalization

Makers of America: The Vietnamese

Contending Voices: The Political Mobilization of Business

Americans in the 1970s struggled through a crisis of confidence in their leaders and institutions, as well as wrenching transformations in the nation's economy and politics. The engines of postwar economic growth and broadly shared prosperity sputtered to a near-halt, giving way to a bewildering mixture of stagnation and inflation that was soon dubbed "**stagflation**." Some of the major pillars of the postwar order began to crumble: Keynesian economic policies (refer to "30-19 Twilight of the New Deal," pp. 803–805); an expanding welfare state; strong labor unions; and robust domestic manufacturing. Simultaneously, conflicts intensified about gender, religion, and America's role in the world.

The patterns that emerged out of the decade's disruptions persisted into the twenty-first century. Partisan differences intensified. Faith in government declined as support for free-market economic doctrines increased. American society became more diverse and socially tolerant, but more geographically polarized and economically unequal.

Focus Questions

1. How did the Watergate scandal lead to Nixon's resignation? How successful was Gerald Ford's "unelected presidency" in restoring trust in government after the disillusionment of Watergate and Vietnam?
2. How were the stagnating economy, the energy crisis, and Middle East foreign policy all closely linked in the 1970s? Why did both Republican and Democratic administrations have so little success in addressing these issues?
3. Which social, economic, and ideological movements flourished in the 1970s, and which stagnated or lost ground?
4. How did Jimmy Carter's presidential campaign and the turn toward "market economics" both reflect Americans' growing disillusionment with government in the 1970s?
5. How did the Iranian crisis intensify public disaffection with the Carter administration?

35-1 Watergate and the Unmaking of a President

Richard Nixon's electoral triumph in 1972 was almost immediately tarnished—and eventually undone—by the so-called **Watergate** scandal. On June 17, 1972, five men were arrested in the Watergate apartment-office complex in Washington after a bungled effort to plant electronic "bugs" in the Democratic Party's headquarters. They were soon revealed to be working for the Republican Committee for the Re-Election of the President—popularly known as CREEP. The Watergate break-in turned out to be just one in a series of Nixon administration "dirty tricks" that included forging documents to discredit Democrats, using the Internal Revenue Service to harass innocent citizens named on a White House "enemies list," burglarizing the office of the psychiatrist who had treated the leaker of the Pentagon Papers, and perverting the FBI and the CIA to cover the tricksters' tracks.

In a combative 1973 press conference in the midst of Richard Nixon's (1913–1994) refusal to turn over tapes that recorded Oval Office conversations, Nixon doggedly maintained his innocence:

"In all my years of public life, I have never obstructed justice. People have got to know whether or not their President is a crook. Well, I'm not a crook; I earned everything I've got."

The moral stench hanging over the White House worsened when Vice President Spiro Agnew was forced to resign in October 1973 for taking bribes from Maryland contractors while governor and also as vice president. In the first use of the Twenty-Fifth Amendment (refer to the Appendix), Nixon nominated and Congress confirmed Agnew's successor, a twelve-term congressman from Michigan, Gerald ("Jerry") Ford.

Amid a mood of growing national outrage, a select Senate committee conducted widely televised hearings in 1973–1974 about the Watergate affair. Nixon indignantly denied any prior knowledge of the break-in and any involvement in the legal proceedings against the burglars. But when a former White House aide revealed that a secret taping system had recorded most of Nixon's Oval Office conversations, a Pandora's Box of incriminating evidence lay open.

Nixon at first agreed only to the publication of "relevant" portions of the tapes, with many sections missing (including Nixon's frequent obscenities, which were excised with the phrase "expletive deleted"). But on July 24, 1974, the president suffered a disastrous setback when the Supreme Court unanimously ruled that "executive privilege" gave him no right to withhold evidence relevant to possible criminal activity. Skating on thin ice over hot water, Nixon reluctantly complied.

Three subpoenaed tapes of conversations with his chief aide on June 23, 1972, proved fatal. One of them—the notorious **"smoking gun" tape** (refer to "Examining the Evidence: The 'Smoking Gun' Tape," p. 943)—revealed the president giving orders, six days after the Watergate break-in, to use the CIA to hold back an inquiry by the FBI. Nixon's own tape-recorded words convicted him of having been an active party to the attempted cover-up (refer to Image 35.1). The House Judiciary Committee proceeded to draw up articles of impeachment, based on obstruction of justice, abuse of the powers of the presidential office, and contempt of Congress.

The public's wrath proved to be overwhelming. Republican leaders in Congress concluded that the unapologetic and unpredictable commander-in-chief was a loose cannon on the deck of the ship of state. They frankly informed Nixon that his impeachment by the full House and removal by the Senate were foregone conclusions and that he would do best to resign.

Retro AdArchives/Alamy Stock Photo

Image 35.1 The Nixon Tapes During the Senate Watergate committee hearings in the summer of 1973, a White House aide revealed the existence of a secret taping system in the Oval Office. One of these tape-recorded conversations ultimately proved mortally damaging to Nixon's claim that he had played no role in the Watergate cover-up.

Examining the Evidence

The "Smoking Gun" Tape, June 23, 1972, 10:04–11:39 A.M.

The technological capability to record Oval Office conversations combined with Richard Nixon's obsession with documenting his presidency to give the public—and the Senate committee investigating his role in the break-in of the Democratic National Committee headquarters in the Watergate Office Tower—rare access to personal conversations between the president and his closest advisers. This tape, which undeniably exposed Nixon's central role in constructing a "cover-up" of the Watergate break-in, was made on Nixon's first day back in Washington after the botched burglary of June 17, 1972.

In this conversation with White House Chief of Staff H. R. Haldeman, Nixon devised a plan to block a widening FBI investigation by instructing the director of the CIA to deflect any further FBI snooping on the grounds that it would endanger sensitive CIA operations. Nixon refused to turn over this and other tapes to Senate investigators until so ordered by the Supreme Court on July 24, 1974. Within four days of its release on August 5, Nixon was forced to resign. After eighteen months of protesting his innocence of the crime and his ignorance of any effort to obstruct justice, Nixon was finally undone by the evidence in this incriminating "smoking gun" tape.

The White House taping system had been in place since the tenure of Franklin Roosevelt, but Nixon's predecessors had used it selectively, to record important meetings and crisis deliberations. Ever-suspicious of leakers and political rivals, Nixon documented two straight years of his Oval Office conversations. Since Watergate, however, it is unlikely that any president has permitted extensive tape recording, depriving historians of a unique insight into the inner workings of the White House.

Should taped White House discussions—or, for that matter, texts, emails, or social media posts—be part of the public record of a presidency, and if so, who should have access to them? Can texts or posts be deleted if the president regrets sending them? What else might historians learn from a tape like this one, besides analyzing the Watergate cover-up?

Haldeman:	. . . yesterday, they concluded it was not the White House, but are now convinced it is a CIA thing, so the CIA turn off would . . .
President:	Well, not sure of their analysis, I'm not going to get that involved. I'm (unintelligible).
Haldeman:	No, sir. We don't want you to.
President:	You call them in
President:	Good. Good deal! Play it tough. That's the way they play it and that's the way we are going to play it.
Haldeman:	O.K. We'll do it.
President:	Yeah, when I saw that news summary item, I of course knew it was a bunch of crap, but I thought ah, well it's good to have them off on this wild hair thing because when they start bugging us, which they have, we'll know our little boys will not know how to handle it. I hope they will though. You never know. Maybe, you think about it. Good!
President:	When you get in these people when you . . . get these people in, say: "Look, the problem is that this will open the whole, the whole Bay of Pigs thing, and the President just feels that" ah, without going into the details . . . don't, don't lie to them to the extent to say there is no involvement, but just say this is sort of a comedy of errors, bizarre, without getting into it, "the President believes that it is going to open the whole Bay of Pigs thing up again. And, ah because these people are plugging for, for keeps and that they should call the FBI in and say that we wish for the country, don't go any further into this case," period!

Source: Nixon Presidential Materials Project, National Archives and Record Administration.

Left with no better choice, Nixon choked back his tears and announced his resignation in a dramatic television appearance on August 8, 1974 (refer to Image 35.2). Less than two years earlier, Nixon began his second term with a public approval rating of 68 percent. Now it had sunk to 24 percent. Few presidents had flown so high, and none had sunk so low. In his Farewell Address, Nixon admitted having made some "judgments" that "were wrong." Outside the White House, angry crowds chanted "Jail to the Chief."

The nation had survived a wrenching constitutional crisis, confirming that the impeachment machinery forged by the Founding Fathers could serve its purpose when public-minded officials chose country over party. The principles that no person is above the law and that presidents must be held to strict accountability for their acts were strengthened. The United States, on the eve of its two-hundredth birthday as a republic, had eventually cleaned its own scandal-smeared house, giving an impressive demonstration of self-discipline and self-government to the rest of

mccool/Alamy Stock Photo

Image 35.2 Nixon Resigns Headlines around the nation and the world blared the startling and unprecedented news that President Richard Nixon would resign at noon on August 9, 1974, as a result of the Watergate scandal. Less than two years earlier, Nixon had won reelection in a landslide.

the world. But the toll exacted by Watergate on the public's faith in government proved steep indeed. Americans' disillusionment (refer to Figure 34.3, p. 924) deepened as the economy fell into a prolonged slump.

35-2 Sources of Stagnation

Exceptional global circumstances had fueled the fantastic quarter-century economic boom of the post–World War II era. Postwar reconstruction and Cold War rearmament programs helped American firms dominate global markets. American-led advances in computing and electronics made the nation seem technologically unassailable. With little to fear from overseas competitors, American manufacturers had reaped healthy profits that facilitated granting organized labor's demands for higher wages and generous benefits. But even as the 1960s lurched to a close, the boom was starting to peter out.

By increasing their productivity, American workers had doubled their average standard of living in the twenty-five years since the end of World War II. Now, fatefully, productivity gains slowed to the vanishing point. The entire decade of the 1970s did not witness a productivity advance equivalent to even one year's progress in the preceding two decades. At the new rate, it would take five hundred more years to bring about another doubling of the average worker's standard of living. The median income of the average American family stagnated in the decades after 1970 and failed to decline only because of the addition of working wives' wages to family incomes (refer to Figure 35.1). The younger generation now faced the depressing prospect of a living standard that would be lower than that of their parents. As the postwar wave of robust economic growth ebbed, political leaders shifted from sunny talk of the "can-do" American spirit toward dour pronouncements about "an age of limits."

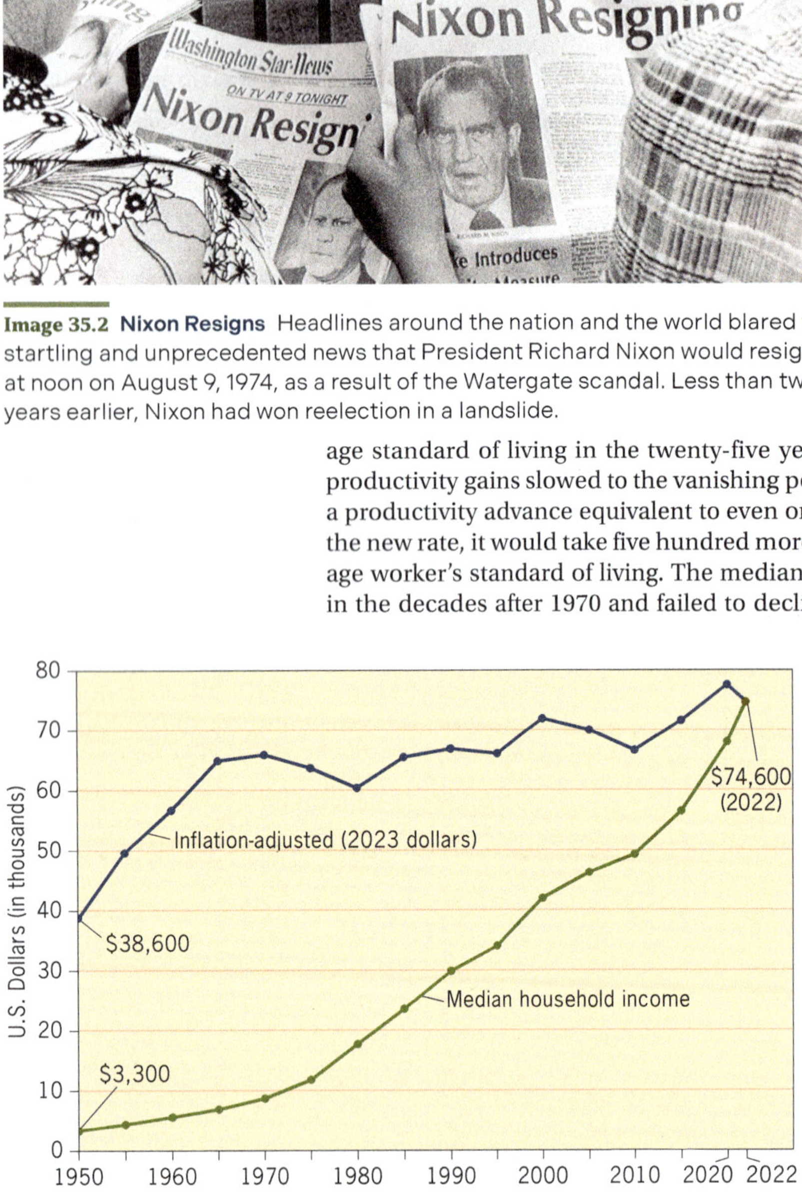

Figure 35.1 Median Household Income, 1950–2022 During the long post–World War II economic boom (from about 1950 to 1970), household incomes increased dramatically, but after 1970 "real," or inflation-adjusted, incomes stagnated. Prosperity in the late 1990s led to a slight upward trend, though adjusted median family income began to decline in the early years of the twenty-first century.

Sources: U.S. Census Bureau, Historical Income Tables—Households, 1950–2024; U.S. Census Bureau *Consumer Income Report*, relevant years; *Statistical Abstract of the United States*, relevant years.

What caused the seemingly abrupt reversal of America's financial fortunes in the 1970s? The competitive advantage of many major American businesses had been so enormous after World War II that they had small incentive to modernize plants and seek more efficient methods of production. The defeated German and Japanese peoples had meanwhile clawed their way out of the ruins of war and built wholly new factories with the most up-to-date technology and management techniques. The sale of the first Japanese-made Toyota automobile in the United States in 1957 proved to be a harbinger of the dawning era of global economic competition (refer to "Thinking Globally: The Era of Globalization," pp. 945–946). By the 1970s, Japanese efforts paid handsome rewards, as they came to dominate industries like automobiles, steel, and consumer electronics—fields in which the United States had once been unchallengeable.

Thinking Globally

The Era of Globalization

Early in the twentieth century, Woodrow Wilson envisioned a world order organized around the principles of self-determination and free trade. But his dream perished in the turbulent aftermath of World War I. Franklin Roosevelt, who served in Wilson's administration, shared his former chief's idealistic goals as well as his bitter disappointment when they failed to be achieved. Eventually, as a crisis-era president himself, FDR came to believe that many of the ills that beset the world after World War I could have been avoided if only the United States had played an international role commensurate with its power and ideals. Determined not to squander another opportunity for American international leadership, he championed a Wilsonian set of principles promoting national self-determination and global free trade—as famously outlined in the "Atlantic Charter" that he and British prime minister Winston Churchill announced in August 1941.

National Archives

Image 35.3 Great Hopes for World Peace with the United Nations, 1947 The achievements of the new international regime were dramatic. International trade doubled in the 1950s and again in the 1960s. By century's end, the volume of global commerce was ten times larger than in 1950 (refer to Table 35.1). Increased trade fueled postwar recovery in Europe and Japan and set several underdeveloped countries—notably Taiwan, Singapore, South Korea, India, and China—on the path to modernization and prosperity.

To a remarkable degree, the world order that the United States helped to construct at the end of World War II embodied those very principles. Washington midwifed an array of multilateral institutions to promote international trade and investment, support the rule of law, and nurture democracy. They included the World Bank, to fund postwar reconstruction; the International Monetary Fund (IMF), to stabilize world currencies; and the General Agreement on Tariffs and Trade (GATT), to lower barriers to international commerce. In the ensuing decades, 102 nations, accounting for 80 percent of world trade, signed GATT (succeeded by the World Trade Organization, or WTO, in the 1990s). The United States also took the lead in founding and funding the United Nations (U.N.), which worked to arbitrate international disputes, improve standards of living worldwide, and encourage decolonization, particularly in Asia and Africa.

Outside the Soviet bloc, these institutions nourished a golden era of economic growth that stretched through the 1960s. America boomed. Bolstered by international trade and investment, Europe and Japan also experienced a postwar quarter-century of dazzlingly rapid "catch-up" growth as their economies chased American levels of productivity and living standards.

But globalization bred new dilemmas as well as opportunities. It intensified international competition as well as cooperation. And it ensured that economic shocks could no longer be easily contained within national borders.

First Europe and Japan and then nations in the postcolonial "developing" world like South Korea and eventually China began to challenge American products in world markets—and to threaten American jobs at home. Meanwhile, the end of the Bretton Woods system of fixed exchange rates in 1973 and the growing ease with which capital flowed across borders weakened governments' capacity to manage their own national economies. Alongside these international pressures emerged a worldwide political and intellectual shift to the right. In the late 1970s and early 1980s, free-market, antiregulatory, labor-skeptical governments came to power not only in Ronald Reagan's America but also in countries such as Britain, Australia, and West Germany.

The full effects of an economically liberalized world order were long muffled by the Cold War, since Eastern Europe and the Soviet Union were conspicuous nonparticipants in the emerging global economy. But the dissolution of the Soviet bloc in the early 1990s unleashed the full force of globalization. International trade, investment, and migration exploded. Global trade, already at record levels, nearly quadrupled between 1990 and 2012. The exponential growth of manufacturing in the developing world, China in particular, put still more pressure on workers and wages in the developed world. And as economies globalized, so did inequality grow, both within and between nations. Environmental degradation and exploitative labor practices also intensified with worldwide industrial growth.

(*continued*)

Table 35.1 International Trade, 1948–2021

	1948	1953	1963	1973	1983	1993	2003	2015	2021
Total volume of world trade (in billions of U.S. dollars)	59	84	157	579	1838	3676	7357	15,985	21,678
Total volume of U.S. exports (in billions of U.S. dollars)	13	12	22	71	202	457	730	1,505	1,754
Share of world exports (%)									
United States	22	19	15	12	11	13	10	9	8
Europe	35	39	48	51	43	45	46	38	37
Africa	7	6	6	5	4	3	2	2	3
Middle East	2	3	3	4	7	4	4	5	5
Asia	14	13	12	15	19	26	26	34	36
GATT/WTO members	63	69	75	84	77	89	94	98	98

Sources: *All data except total volume of U.S. exports are from World Trade Organization,* World Trade Statistical Review 2022. *U.S. export data for 1948–1993 are from* United States Historical Statistics of the United States, *vol. 5; data for 2003 and 2015 are from Foreign Exports Division, U.S. Census Bureau. Additional data for 2021 are from USATrade online database of the U.S. Census Bureau. Because different organizations rely on different methodologies for estimating total exports, WTO estimates used to compute the U.S. share of world exports differ slightly from those presented in this table.*

But such problems should not obscure the profound benefits of the global order forged in the wake of World War II. As goods, workers, and investment capital have flowed across borders, so have advances in medicine, nutrition, and standards of living. Since 1950 the average life expectancy worldwide has increased by twenty years, with the biggest gains in the developing world. Rising prosperity has also strengthened the middle classes in developing countries, with democracy often following in the footsteps of prosperity. The number of electoral democracies increased from 44 in 1950 to 123 in 2017. Studies confirm that states with open trade policies are three times more likely to protect civil liberties than those without such policies. On balance, the liberalized world order that the United States took the lead in building after World War II left an impressive legacy of international stability, global growth, and freedom from fear and want for millions of human beings—a lasting testament to Woodrow Wilson's vision and to Franklin Roosevelt's leadership. The challenge remains to bring to this new global order the same aspiration for economic equality that propelled Roosevelt's New Deal many decades ago.

The turbulent economic seas were also a consequence of the deficit spending in the 1960s—especially Lyndon Johnson's insistence on simultaneously fighting the war in Vietnam and funding Great Society programs at home, all without a tax increase to finance the added expenditures. Both military spending and welfare spending are inherently inflationary (in the absence of offsetting tax collections) because they put dollars into people's hands without adding to the supply of civilian goods that those dollars can buy. When the revenue imbalance of the 1960s was joined by sharply rising oil prices in the 1970s, it touched off a sickening spiral of inflation.

Runaway inflation cut deep. Consumer prices increased astonishingly throughout the 1970s, while growth remained stagnant. The cost of living tripled in the dozen years after Richard Nixon's inauguration, creating the longest and steepest inflationary cycle in American history.

The feeble economic performance of the 1970s hung over the decade like a pall. It frustrated both policymakers and citizens who keenly remembered the growth and optimism of the postwar years. Now a stalemated, unpopular war and a stagnant, unresponsive economy upended something that had become an article of faith among so many since New Deal days, that an affluent society could spend its way to social justice.

35-3 The First Unelected President

Gerald Rudolph Ford, the first man to be made president solely by a vote of Congress, entered the besmirched White House in August 1974 with serious handicaps. The handsome and affable Ford was widely—and unfairly—suspected of being little more than a dim-witted former college football player. President Johnson had sneered that "Jerry" was so lacking in brainpower that he could not walk and chew gum at the same time. Worse, Ford had been selected, not elected, vice president, following Spiro Agnew's resignation in disgrace. The sour odor of illegitimacy hung about this president without precedent.

Then, out of a clear sky, Ford granted a complete pardon to Nixon for any crimes he may have committed as president, discovered or undiscovered. Democrats were outraged, and lingering suspicions about the circumstances of the pardon endangered Ford's prospects of being elected president in his own right in 1976.

Ford at first sought to enhance the so-called détente with the Soviet Union that Nixon had crafted. In July 1975, President Ford joined leaders from thirty-four other nations in Finland to sign the historic **Helsinki Accords**. One set of the Helsinki agreements officially wrote an end to World War II by finally legitimizing the Soviet-dictated boundaries of Poland and other Eastern European countries. In return, the Soviets signed a "third basket" of agreements, guaranteeing more liberal exchanges of people and information between East and West and protecting certain basic human rights. The Helsinki Accords kindled small dissident movements in Eastern Europe, which the USSR tried in vain to squelch.

Western Europeans, especially the West Germans, cheered the Helsinki conference as a milestone of détente. But in the United States, critics increasingly charged that détente was proving to be a one-way street. American grain and technology flowed across the Atlantic to the USSR, and little of comparable importance flowed back. Moscow also continued its human rights violations, including restrictions on Jewish emigration, which had prompted Congress in 1974 to add punitive restrictions to a U.S.-Soviet trade bill. Despite these difficulties, Ford at first clung stubbornly to détente. But the American public's fury over Moscow's double-dealing steadily grew, stoked by hard-line Cold War hawks. By the end of his term, the president was refusing even to pronounce the word *détente* in public. The thaw in the Cold War was threatening to prove chillingly brief (refer to Image 35.4).

Bettmann/Getty Images

Image 35.4 In Pursuit of Arms Control President Ford (left) consults with Secretary of State Henry Kissinger about ongoing Strategic Arms Limitation Talks with the Soviet Union in 1974. Ford was initially committed to carrying forward Nixon's détente policies, but growing domestic criticism hampered his efforts. By the time he hit the campaign trail seeking a second term in 1976, Ford told a television interviewer that "I don't use the word détente anymore."

35-4 Defeat in Vietnam

Meanwhile, America's disastrous engagement in Vietnam stumbled to its inglorious conclusion. Early in 1975, the North Vietnamese gave full throttle to their long-expected drive southward. President Ford pleaded in vain for Congress to finance additional weapons for Vietnam. Without the crutch of massive American aid, the South Vietnamese regime unceremoniously collapsed.

The dam burst so rapidly that the remaining Americans had to be frantically evacuated by helicopter, the last of them on April 29, 1975. Also rescued were about 140,000 South Vietnamese, most of them so dangerously identified with the Americans that they feared violent reprisals. Ford rightly admitted these refugees to the United States. Eventually, some 500,000 arrived (refer to "Makers of America: The Vietnamese," pp. 948–949).

The long, frustrating Vietnam War thus ended not with a bang but a whimper. In a technical sense, the Americans had not lost the war; their client nation had. The United States withdrew its last troops in 1973, leaving the South Vietnamese to fight their own war using American planes, tanks,

The Vietnamese

Amid the cul-de-sacs and shopping centers of sunny Orange County, California, are the shops, restaurants, temples, and homes of over 200,000 Vietnamese Americans. Orange County's "Little Saigon" is the largest Vietnamese community outside Vietnam, part of a vibrant and vital Vietnamese American population that reached 2.2 million nationally by 2019, making it the fourth-largest Asian American group in the United States. As with Filipino-Americans and mainland Puerto Ricans (refer to Chapter 26), this community has its roots in a consequential American war.

Before South Vietnam fell in 1975, few people of Southeast Asian origin lived in the United States. Throughout most of American history until the mid-twentieth century, the bulk of U.S. immigrants had come from Europe, with the notable exception of the Chinese and, to a lesser extent, the Japanese. Xenophobic immigration laws sharply restricted Asian migration, or excluded it altogether. A small number of Vietnamese came to the United States as cooks and crew aboard French steamships. This included future North Vietnamese communist leader Ho Chi Minh, who spent about two years overseas, including several months living in New York and Boston in 1912 and 1913.

The immigration reforms of 1965 ended draconian national-origin limits and created new paths for migration and citizenship (refer to "The Presence of the Past: Immigration—Legal, Illegal, and Otherwise," pp. 913–915). The war-scarred Vietnamese were at the forefront of this new immigration, so much so that in 1966 the U.S. immigration authorities designated "Vietnamese" as a separate category of newcomers. Because people with family in the United States had priority, most early immigrants were the wives and children of U.S. servicemen.

As the communists closed in on Saigon in the mid-1970s, many South Vietnamese feared for their lives. President Ford ordered the evacuation of 3,000 orphans from Saigon in what was called "Operation Babylift," and American officials prepared to evacuate those who had worked closely with American or South Vietnamese authorities. Gathering together as many of their extended-family members as they could, many thousands prepared to flee the country. In a few hectic days in 1975, some 140,000 Vietnamese people escaped before the approaching communist gunfire, a few dramatically clinging to the bottoms of departing U.S. helicopters. From Saigon they were conveyed to military bases in Guam and the Philippines. Another 60,000 made even more perilous escapes over land and sea to Hong Kong or Thailand, where they waited nervously for permission to move on. Eventually, some 500,000 Vietnamese refugees reached American shores.

The United States had admitted thousands of European refugees in the wake of World War II, but the Vietnamese arrivals far outnumbered any earlier wave. To accommodate them, the U.S. government set up refugee camps across the country. Arrivals were crowded into army barracks affording little room and less privacy. These were boot camps not for military service but for assimilation into American society. Reprising earlier pushes to "Americanize" European immigrants and Native Americans, a rigorous program trained the Vietnamese in English, forbade children from speaking their native language in the classroom, and even immersed them in American slang. Unsurprisingly, many resisted these attempts to strip them of their culture.

Their discontent boiled over when authorities prepared to release the refugees from camps and board them with families around the nation. Resettlement officials were determined to find an American sponsor for each Vietnamese family; these host households would provide food, shelter, and assistance for the refugees until they could fend for themselves. Yet few American sponsors would accommodate the large extended families—grandparents, uncles, aunts, and cousins living communally with parents and children—that were traditional and especially cherished by these new immigrants. Already uprooted from their homeland, fewer Vietnamese families would willingly separate.

Bettmann/Getty Images

Image 35.5 The Last Days of Saigon Desperate Vietnamese nationals joined in the frantic American evacuation from Vietnam in 1975.

Bob Daemmrich/Alamy Stock Photo

Image 35.6 Vietnamese Culture in America Third grade boys and girls perform the traditional folk song "Lien Khuc Xuan" ("A Spring Medley") at a 2007 Vietnamese New Year's celebration in Austin, Texas.

The government ultimately dispersed most refugees to Iowa, Illinois, Pennsylvania, New York, Washington, and California. But the settlement sites, many of them tucked away in rural districts, offered scant economic opportunities. The immigrants often had held skilled or white-collar positions in Vietnam but now found themselves relegated to low-paying, menial labor. Many relocated, hastening to established Vietnamese enclaves around San Francisco, Los Angeles, and Dallas.

Soon a second wave of Vietnamese immigrants arrived in these Little Saigons. Fleeing from the ravages of poverty and political oppression in communist Vietnam, these stragglers crammed themselves and their few possessions into small boats, hoping to reach Hong Kong or get picked up by foreign ships. Eventually many of these so-called "boat people" reached the United States. Mostly penniless, usually less educated than the first arrivals, and receiving far less resettlement aid from the U.S. government, they had to start at the bottom. Today the Vietnamese American community is the fourth-largest Asian American group in the United States. It totals more than 2 million people, heavily concentrated in the western states. Differing in experience and expectations, the Vietnamese have made new homes in a once-strange land. Their uprooting is an immense, unreckoned consequence of America's longest war.

Jacques Pavlovsky/Getty Images

Image 35.7 Vietnamese Refugees. Vietnamese "boat people" flee to freedom.

and other munitions. The estimated cost to America was enormous: $168 billion in current outlays and eventually as much as $900 billion including after-war veterans' benefits and interest costs. The human toll amounted to 58,220 American dead and 300,000 wounded, and a staggering 1.5 million dead Vietnamese. Hundreds of thousands of Cambodians and Laotians died in the conflict as well.

America had lost more than a war. It had lost face in the eyes of foreigners, lost its own self-esteem, and lost confidence in its political leadership and its military prowess. America's war in Vietnam cast a long shadow over the nation's politics and culture for decades to come.

35-5 Feminism Takes Center Stage

Journalist Gloria Steinem (b. 1934) wrote in 1969 of how the sexism young female activists encountered in 1960s male-dominated protest movements (including in the Students for a Democratic Society, or SDS—refer to p. 928) sparked their feminist activism:

> "They have been jailed, beaten and Maced side-by-side with their social-activist male counterparts. . . . But once back in the bosom of SDS, they found themselves typing and making coffee."

Feminist activists set out with renewed vigor in the 1970s to transform American society—on the streets, in the courts, and in Congress. Their civil rights victories, as well as a more sexually and socially liberated culture, provoked an intense rethinking of gender roles.

Historians use the terms *first wave* and *second wave* to distinguish the women's movement of the nineteenth century (refer to "14-8 Women in Revolt," pp. 345–347) from that of the late twentieth century. White, college-educated women made up much of the membership and leadership of the most prominent second-wave organizations. Betty Friedan, author of the 1963 best seller *The Feminine Mystique* (refer to "33-1 Affluence and Its Anxieties," pp. 876–877), cofounded the National Organization for Women (NOW) in 1966. The organization became the chief political arm of second-wave feminism. Another prominent voice was the charismatic, miniskirted journalist Gloria Steinem, who cofounded *Ms.* magazine in 1971.

Just as first-wave feminism grew out of abolitionism, the second wave drew ideas, leaders, and tactics from the civil rights and antiwar movements. Young women's experiences of sexism inside these movements played a key role in their subsequent fight for women's liberation. Impatient with the legal and policy focus of mainstream feminism, some frustrated women took to the streets. WITCH (Women's International Terrorist Conspiracy from Hell) was made famous by its protest at the 1968 Miss America pageant in Atlantic City, New Jersey. There demonstrators crowned a sheep Miss America and threw symbols of women's oppression—bras, girdles, and dishcloths—into trash cans. (Contrary to news stories, they did not burn the bras.)

Sexual orientation and race were fault lines within the movement as well. Black feminists argued that second-wave organizations failed to recognize the oppression that came from being both Black and a woman—what feminist attorney Pauli Murray labeled "Jane Crow." Long prominent in the Black civil rights movement, Murray had been a cofounder of NOW but soon left the organization, believing that it paid too little attention to Black and working-class concerns.

John Olson/The LIFE Picture Collection/Shutterstock.com

Image 35.8 Women Strike for Equality, August 26, 1970 Thousands of women of different generations, races, and ideologies marched in New York City on the fiftieth anniversary of the Nineteenth Amendment that secured American women's right to vote. Similar marches across the country made the demonstration the largest since the suffrage era.

Feminists disagreed over many issues—from pornography and marriage to how much to expect from government, capitalism, and men. Some feminists placed a priority on gender equality—for example, full female service in the military. Others defended a feminism of gender difference—such as maternity leave and other special protections for women in the workplace. Still, beyond these differences feminists had much in common. Most advocated a woman's right to choose in the battle over abortion rights. Most regarded the law as the key weapon against gender discrimination.

Women across the country marched in 1970 for employment opportunity and reproductive rights in the Women's Strike for Equality on the fiftieth anniversary of woman suffrage (refer to Image 35.8). In 1972, Congress passed **Title IX** of the Education Amendments, prohibiting sex discrimination in any federally assisted educational program or activity. Perhaps this act's most visible impact was to create opportunities for girls' and women's athletics at schools and colleges, giving birth to a new "Title IX generation" that would reach maturity by century's end and help professionalize women's sports as well. The **Equal Rights Amendment (ERA)** to the Constitution won congressional approval in 1972. It declared, "Equality of rights under the law shall not be denied or abridged by the United States or by any State on account of sex." Twenty-eight of the necessary thirty-eight states quickly ratified the amendment, first proposed by suffragists in 1923, and Presidents Nixon and Ford both endorsed it. Hopes rose that the ERA might soon become the law of the land.

Bettmann/Getty Images

Image 35.9 Antifeminist Phyllis Schlafly (1924–2016) Schlafly traveled the country promoting her "STOP ERA" campaign. She argued that ratification of the Equal Rights Amendment would undermine the American family by violating "the right of a wife to be supported by her husband," requiring women to serve in combat, and legalizing same-sex marriage.

Even the Supreme Court seemed to be on the movement's side. In *Reed v. Reed* (1971) and *Frontiero v. Richardson* (1973), the Court challenged sex discrimination in legislation and employment. And in the landmark case of ***Roe v. Wade*** (1973), the Court struck down laws prohibiting abortion, arguing that a woman's decision to terminate a pregnancy was protected by the constitutional right of privacy. That ruling stood until 2022, when it was overturned by *Dobbs v. Jackson Women's Health Organization* (refer to "38-22 Another Reckoning Nears," pp. 1059–1061).

But the feminist movement also ignited formidable political opposition. In 1972, President Nixon vetoed a proposal to set up nationwide public day care, saying it would weaken the American family. Antifeminists blamed the women's movement for the rising divorce rate, which tripled between 1960 and 1976. And the Catholic Church and evangelical denominations organized a powerful grassroots movement to oppose the legalization of abortion.

For many feminists, the most bitter defeat was the death of the ERA. Antifeminists, led by conservative activist Phyllis Schlafly, argued that the ERA would remove traditional protections that women enjoyed by forcing the law to see them as men's equals. They further asserted that the amendment would threaten the traditional family structure on which a strong American society depended. Schlafly charged that the ERA's advocates were just "bitter women seeking a constitutional cure for their personal problems." Her STOP ERA campaign (STOP stood for "Stop Taking Our Privileges") proved stunningly successful (refer to Image 35.9). Grassroots antifeminist activists organized state-level efforts to block ratification and brought the ERA's momentum to a halt. In 1979, Congress extended the deadline for ratification of the amendment, but the battle was lost. The ERA died in 1982, three states short of success.

The women's movement proved to be an undeniably transformative force in the 1970s. Women's labor force participation rate accelerated its historic climb as major professions like medicine, law, and higher education opened their doors to female career-seekers. Feminist enterprises, from battered women's shelters and rape crisis centers to women's bookstores and support groups, proliferated. Women's liberation and the alleged "battle of the sexes" it provoked became staples of 1970s popular culture in film, books, and television.

Twenty thousand feminists gathered in Houston in November 1977 for a National Women's Conference dedicated to producing a National Plan of Action for Congress and President Carter. While antifeminists led by Phyllis Schlafly staged an alternative convention nearby, the conference delegates adopted a twenty-six-plank plan that connected the particular needs of women to broad social and economic policies. Plank 25, on Women, Welfare and Poverty, declared:

"Along with improvements in the welfare system, elimination of poverty for women must include improvements in social security and retirement systems, universal minimum wage, nontraditional job opportunities, quality day care, comprehensive health insurance, and comprehensive legal services. . . . We support increased federal funding for income transfer programs (e.g. Social Security, SSI, AFDC). Congress should approve a federal floor under payments to provide an adequate standard of living based on each state's cost of living. And, just as with other workers, homemakers receiving payments should be afforded the dignity of having that payment called a wage, not welfare."

Newly frank discussions of female sexuality abounded. Perhaps most profoundly, ongoing transformations in the size and structure of American families—including the growing numbers of divorced, single-parent, and dual-income households—would ensure women's centrality to battles over life choices and family values for years to come.

35-6 The Seventies in Black and White

For all its 1960s victories and sacrifices, the struggle for Black civil rights remained an unfinished revolution. In 1971, the Supreme Court unanimously upheld busing as a "remedial technique" for achieving racial balance in schools, but intense parent and community resistance continued to slow school integration in all regions of the country (refer to Image 35.10). The Supreme Court in *Milliken v. Bradley* (1974) then blindsided integrationists when it ruled that desegregation plans could not require students to move across school-district lines. The decision effectively exempted suburban districts from shouldering any responsibility for desegregating inner-city schools, reinforcing "white flight" from cities to suburbs.

Yet the tremendous achievements of the movement were already plain. Black men and women ran for office, led nonprofit organizations, and entered professions that once had been open only to white employees. Black leaders chalked up many "firsts" in electoral politics. In Cleveland, Carl Stokes became the first Black mayor of a major U.S. city in 1967. The following year, Shirley Chisholm, a New York City Democrat, became the first Black woman elected to Congress, where she served for seven terms and became a prominent advocate for the inner-city poor. In 1972, Chisholm became the first Black woman to run for a major-party presidential nomination. Her campaign slogan: "Unbought and Unbossed."

Affirmative-action programs had proved remarkably successful and—perhaps because of that—increasingly controversial. Black people and other minorities made up an increasing percentage of America's college students, white-collar professionals, as well as elected and appointed public officials. Yet some white workers who were denied advancement and white students who were refused college admission raised the cry of "reverse discrimination," charging that their rights had been violated by employers and admissions officers who put more weight on racial or ethnic background than on ability or achievement.

One white Californian, Allan Bakke, made headlines in 1978 when the Supreme Court, in a tortured five-to-four decision, upheld his claim that his application to medical school had been turned down because of an admissions policy that favored minority applicants. The Court declared that preference in admissions could not be given to members of any group, minority or majority, on the basis of ethnic or racial identity alone. Yet at the same time, the Justices said that

Image 35.10 A Sad Day for Old Glory In 1976, America's bicentennial year, demonstrations against integrationist school busing mandates convulsed Boston, the historic "cradle of liberty." As wealthier white families fled to suburbs and the 1970s economy squeezed blue-collar jobs, working class white people increasingly directed their anger at the race-based policies that were a legacy of Lyndon Johnson's "Great Society" programs of the 1960s. This "backlash" helped to feed the conservative, antigovernment movement that elected Ronald Reagan in 1980.

racial factors might be taken into account in a school's overall admissions policy for purposes of assembling a diverse student body. Among the dissenters on the sharply divided bench was the Court's only Black justice, Thurgood Marshall. He warned in an impassioned opinion that the denial of racial preferences might sweep away years of progress by the civil rights movement. But many conservatives cheered the decision as affirming the principle that justice is colorblind.

35-7 Red Power

Native Americans also made important civil rights gains in the 1970s, asserting their status as separate semi-sovereign peoples. Echoing the call for "Black Power" at the end of the 1960s (refer to "34-5 An Incomplete Civil Rights Revolution," pp. 916–919), the American Indian Movement (AIM), founded in Minnesota in 1968, declared "Red Power." AIM captured the nation's attention by seizing the former prison-island of Alcatraz in San Francisco Bay in 1970. The massacre site of Wounded Knee, South Dakota (refer to "22-9 'Kill the Indian and Save the Man,'" pp. 558–562) was the site of a 71-day standoff between occupying activists and government agents in 1973. In Washington State, Native American tribes held "fish-ins" protesting the state's refusal to recognize 1850s treaties entitling the tribes to half the annual salmon harvest. After a decade of protests, arrests, and confiscation of property, a 1974 court decision ended the "Fish Wars" by affirming historic treaty rights.

A series of victories in the courts consolidated the decade's gains. In the case of *United States v. Wheeler* (1978), the Supreme Court declared that Indian tribes possessed a "unique and limited" sovereignty, subject to the will of Congress but not to individual states. Several tribes capitalized on their newly asserted sovereign rights to set up highly profitable casinos in many parts of the country, as codified in the **Indian Gaming Regulatory Act of 1988**.

35-8 The Bicentennial Campaign

America's two-hundredth birthday, in 1976, fell during a presidential election year—a fitting coincidence for a proud democracy. President Gerald Ford energetically sought the Republican nomination in his own right and only narrowly defeated challenger Ronald Reagan, former actor and governor of California. Reagan's pursuit of the GOP nomination was propelled by a swelling conservative movement that came to be known as the "**New Right**." His campaign also highlighted a major change in the American political system when it made shrewd use of the proliferating primary elections that GOP delegate selection reforms had recently prompted.

The Watergate scandal had disgraced many of the party's more mainstream figures—as well as toppling a Republican president and sending many of his top White House aides to jail. A stagnant economy had further diminished support for the incumbent Ford. The conservative insurgency rushed in to fill that vacuum, and spent the 1970s building an interlocking network of advocacy groups, political action committees, and think tanks.

More populist in tone than previous generations of political conservatives, the New Right emphasized hot-button cultural issues—from the ERA and abortion to busing and school curricula—as well as a hotly nationalist foreign-policy outlook that rejected détente and international treaties. Ford's moderate governing approach during his brief presidency, and especially his appointment of the liberal Republican Nelson Rockefeller as his vice president, had prompted conservatives to seek an alternative nominee. Though Reagan fell short at the Republican convention in 1976, he and the movement behind him grew substantially more powerful over the next four years.

The Democratic standard-bearer in 1976 was fifty-one-year-old James Earl ("Jimmy") Carter Jr., a dark-horse candidate who galloped out of obscurity during the long primary-election season. A peanut farmer and former Georgia governor who

The conservative activist Richard Viguerie (b. 1933) became a pioneer in direct mail fund-raising in the 1970s. He compiled massive donor lists that were shared among different issue groups and campaigns, in the process helping to stitch together the grassroots New Right coalition. In his 1980 manifesto, *The New Right: We're Ready to Lead*, Viguerie outlined his strategy for capturing conservative votes:

"We are determined to achieve our goal of organizing the conservative middle-class majority in America. . . . How will we do it? By appealing to: hard-working citizens sick and tired of high taxes and ever-rising inflation; small businessmen angry at excessive government regulations and federal red tape; born-again Christians disturbed about sex on TV and in movies; parents opposed to forced busing; supporters of the right to life and against the federal financing of abortions; middle-class Americans tired of Big Government, Big Business, Big Labor, and Big Education telling us what to do and what not to do; pro-defense citizens alarmed by appeasement and weakness in U.S. foreign policy; everyone who is unwilling to accept the liberal line that America has had her day in the sun, and that we must all tighten our belt and do with less."

insisted on the humble "Jimmy" as his first name, this born-again Baptist ran against the memory of Nixon and Watergate as much as he ran against Ford. His most effective campaign pitch was his promise "I'll never lie to you." Untainted by ties to what many Americans now considered a corrupt and cynical Washington, DC, Carter attracted voters as an outsider who would clean the disorderly house of "big government."

Carter squeezed out a narrow victory on election day, with 51 percent of the popular vote. The electoral count stood at 297 to 240. The winner swept every state in his native South except Virginia. Especially important were Black voters, a stunning 97 percent of whom cast their ballots for Carter. But in yet another sign of the changing political alignments in the South, Ford actually beat Carter among white Southerners, garnering 53 percent of their votes to Carter's 46 percent.

Carter enjoyed hefty Democratic majorities in both houses of Congress. Hopes ran high that the stalemate of the Nixon-Ford years between a Republican White House and a Democratic Capitol Hill would now be ended. At first, Carter enjoyed notable success, as Congress granted his requests to create a new cabinet-level Department of Energy and to cut taxes. The new president's popularity remained exceptionally elevated during his first few months in office, even when he courted public disfavor by courageously keeping his campaign promise to pardon some ten thousand draft evaders of the Vietnam War era.

But Carter's honeymoon did not last long. An inexperienced outsider, he had campaigned against the Washington "establishment" and never quite made the transition to being an insider himself. He repeatedly rubbed congressional fur the wrong way, especially by failing to consult adequately with the leaders. Critics charged that he isolated himself in a shallow pool of fellow Georgians, whose ignorance of the ways of Washington compounded the problems of their greenhorn chief.

35-9 Carter's Humanitarian Diplomacy

As a committed Christian, President Carter displayed from the outset an overriding concern for "human rights" as the guiding principle of his foreign policy. In the African nations of Rhodesia (later Zimbabwe) and South Africa, Carter and his eloquent UN ambassador, the former civil rights activist Andrew Young, championed the oppressed Black majority.

The president's most spectacular foreign-policy achievement came in September 1978 when he invited President Anwar Sadat of Egypt and Prime Minister Menachem Begin of Israel to a summit conference at **Camp David**, the woodsy presidential retreat in the Maryland highlands. Skillfully serving as go-between, Carter persuaded the two visitors to sign an accord (September 17, 1978) that held considerable promise of peace (refer to Image 35.11). Israel agreed in principle to withdraw from territory conquered in the 1967 war, and Egypt in return promised to respect Israel's borders. Both parties pledged themselves to sign a formal peace treaty within three months.

Wally McNamee/Corbis Historical/Getty Images

Image 35.11 New Hopes for Peace Anwar Sadat of Egypt (left) and Menachem Begin of Israel (right) join U.S. President Jimmy Carter at the White House in March 1979 to sign the peace treaty based on the Camp David Accords the previous September. Sadat and Begin later shared a Nobel Peace Prize for reaching the historic agreement that brought hopes of peace to the war-torn Middle East.

The president crowned this diplomatic success by resuming full diplomatic relations with China in early 1979 after a nearly thirty-year interruption. Carter also pushed through two treaties to turn over the Panama Canal to the Panamanians, though at considerable political cost at home. Conservatives launched a massive campaign against the Panama Canal treaties, with Ronald Reagan stridently declaring, "We bought it, we paid for it, we built it, and we intend to keep it!" Twenty senators who voted for the treaties lost their seats in 1978 and 1980. For all of the sound and the fury, however, the treaties passed, and the United States gave up control of the canal on December 31, 1999.

Despite these dramatic accomplishments, trouble stalked Carter's foreign policy. Overshadowing all international issues was the ominous reheating of the Cold War with the Soviet Union. Détente fell into disrepute as Cuba deployed thousands of troops, assisted by Soviet advisers, to support revolutionary factions in Angola, Ethiopia, and elsewhere in Africa. Arms-control negotiations with Moscow stalled in the face of this Soviet military meddling as well as the aggressive opposition of domestic hawks.

35-10 Economic and Energy Woes

Adding to Carter's mushrooming troubles was the failing health of the economy. The inflation rate ascended well above 13 percent during Carter's presidency (refer to Figures 35.2 and 35.3).

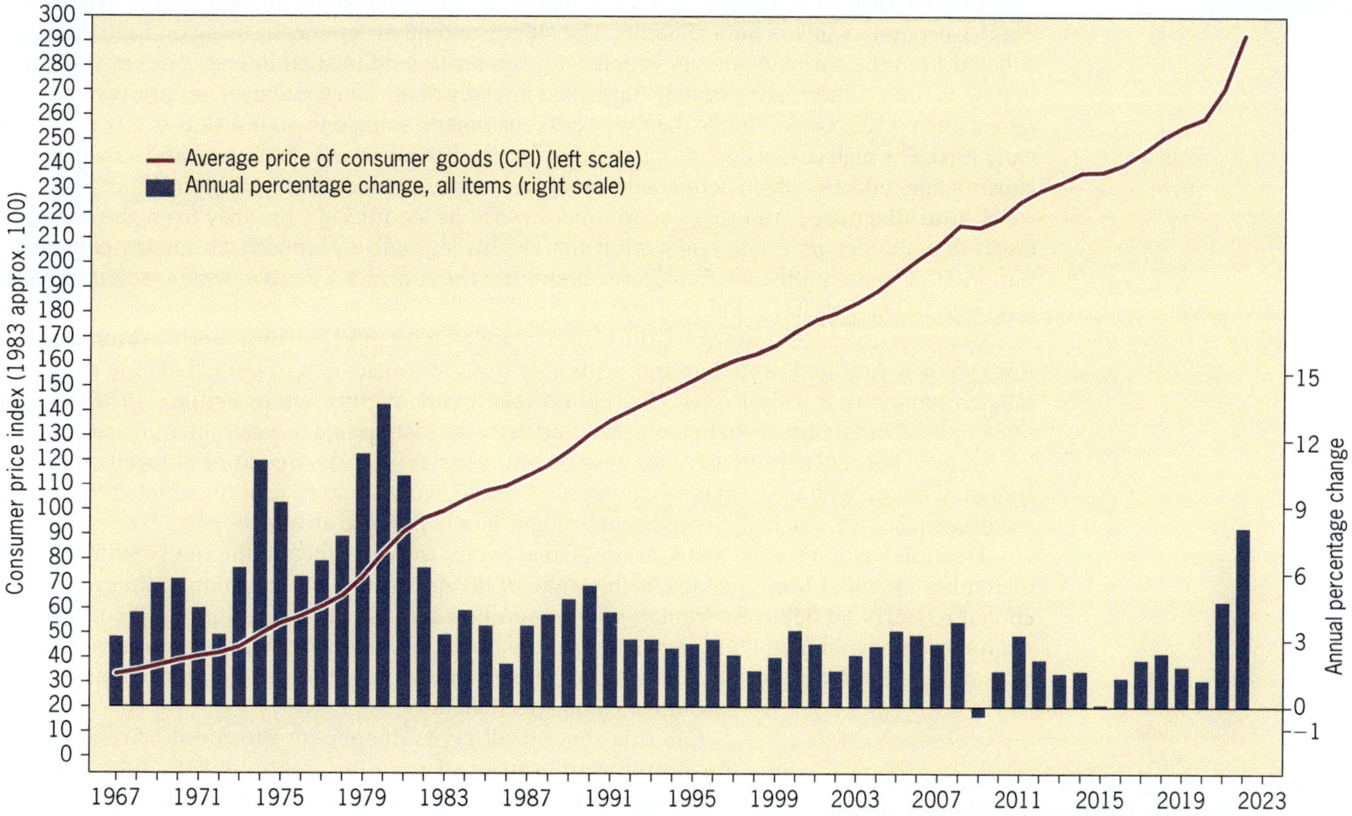

Figure 35.2 The History of the Consumer Price Index, 1967–2022 This graph shows both the annual percentage rate of inflation and the cumulative shrinkage of the dollar's value since 1967. (By 2023, it would take over nine dollars to buy what one dollar had purchased in 1967.)

Sources: Bureau of Labor Statistics and *Statistical Abstract of the United States*, relevant years.

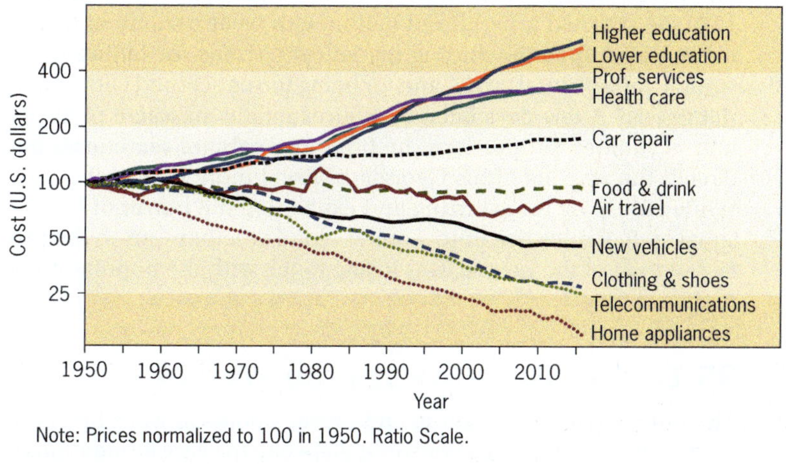

Figure 35.3 Changes in the Real Price of Selected Goods and Services Today, in general, it takes over thirteen dollars to buy what one dollar could purchase in 1950. Yet as this chart shows, Americans' buying power varies widely across goods and services from what it was at the middle of the twentieth century. Accounting for inflation, the cost of health care, education, and housing (not shown) have multiplied several times; food and travel costs have remained relatively flat; while new cars, clothing, and appliances have become much more affordable.

Source: Data from US Bureau of Economic Analysis, relevant years. Figure adapted from Alex Tabarrok, "Why Are the Prices So D*MN High?," May 2019, *Marginal Revolution*, https://marginalrevolution.com/marginalrevolution/2019/05/why-are-the-prices-so-dmn-high.html.

The soaring bill for imported oil exacerbated inflation even as it plunged America's balance of payments deeply into the red (an unprecedented $40 billion in 1978).

The "oil shocks" of the 1970s taught Americans a painful but necessary lesson: They could never again seriously consider a policy of economic isolation, as they had tried to do in the decades between the two world wars. For most of American history, foreign trade had accounted for no more than 10 percent of gross national product (GNP). But huge foreign-oil bills drove that figure steadily upward in the 1970s and thereafter. By century's end, some 27 percent of GNP depended on foreign trade. Unable to dominate international commerce and finance as effortlessly as they once had, Americans would have to work smarter and harder, mastering foreign languages and studying foreign cultures, if they wanted to prosper in the rapidly globalizing economy.

Yawning deficits in the federal budget, reaching nearly $60 billion in 1980, further aggravated the U.S. economy's inflationary ailments. The elderly and other Americans living on fixed incomes suffered from the shrinking dollar. People with money to lend pushed interest rates ever higher, hoping to protect themselves from being repaid in badly depreciated dollars. The "prime rate" (the rate of interest that banks charge their very best customers) vaulted to an unheard-of 20 percent in early 1980. The high cost of borrowing money shoved small businesses to the wall and strangled the construction industry, which depended heavily on loans to finance new housing and other projects.

Carter diagnosed America's economic disease as stemming primarily from the nation's costly dependence on foreign oil. Unfortunately, his legislative proposals for energy conservation in 1977 ignited a blaze of indifference among the American people, who seemed to have forgotten the long gasoline lines of 1973.

Events in Iran jolted Americans out of their complacency in 1979. The imperious Mohammed Reza Pahlevi, installed as shah of Iran with help from America's CIA in 1953, had long ruled his oil-rich land with a will of steel. His regime was finally overthrown in January 1979 by Shia Muslim fundamentalists who fiercely resented the shah's campaign to westernize and secularize his country. Particularly offensive to these revolutionaries were the freedoms enjoyed by young Iranian women, who were increasingly well educated, wore Western fashion, and left their hair uncovered. Soon enough, the revolution brought much of this to an end.

Denouncing the United States as the "Great Satan" that had abetted the shah's efforts, these extremists engulfed Iran in chaos in the wake of his departure. The crippling upheavals soon spread to Iran's oil fields. As Iranian oil stopped flowing into the stream of world commerce, shortages appeared, and OPEC again seized the opportunity to hike petroleum prices. Americans once more found themselves waiting impatiently in long lines at gas stations or buying gasoline only on specified days.

As this second oil crisis deepened, President Carter sensed the rising temperature of popular discontent. In July 1979 he retreated to the presidential mountain hideaway at Camp David, where he remained largely out of public view for ten days. Like a royal potentate of old, summoning the wise men of the realm for their counsel in a time of troubles, Carter called in over a hundred leaders from all walks of life to give him their views. Meanwhile, the nation waited anxiously for the results of these extraordinary deliberations.

When Carter came down from the mountaintop on July 15, 1979, he stunned a perplexed nation with what became known as his **malaise speech**, chiding his fellow citizens for falling into a "moral and spiritual crisis" and for being too concerned with "material goods." A few days later, in a bureaucratic massacre of almost unprecedented proportions, he fired four cabinet secretaries and circled the wagons of his Georgia advisers more tightly about the White House by reorganizing and expanding the power of his personal staff. Critics began to wonder aloud whether Carter, the professed man of the people, was losing touch with the popular mood of the country.

President Jimmy Carter (b. 1924) delivered what became known as his "malaise speech" (although he never used the word) on television in 1979:

"In a nation that was proud of hard work, strong families, close-knit communities, and our faith in God, too many of us now tend to worship self-indulgence and consumption. Human identity is no longer defined by what one does, but by what one owns. But we've discovered that owning things and consuming things does not satisfy our longing for meaning. We've learned that piling up material goods cannot fill the emptiness of lives which have no confidence or purpose. . . . The symptoms of this crisis of the American spirit are all around us."

In time cultural conservatives would take up Carter's theme to support their call for a return to "traditional values."

35-11 The Turn Toward the Market

The energy crisis, stagflation, and Carter's political woes helped to nurture a powerful conservative challenge to the very foundations of the postwar American "social contract," which had featured a strong federal government, active economic regulation, expanded social provision, and a large measure of income equality. Now the emphasis shifted to the energy and promise of the free market and the burdens and dangers of "big government."

An influential group of thinkers known as "neoconservatives," many of them former liberals appalled by what they regarded as the social excesses of the 1960s, spearheaded this conservative revival. They championed free-market capitalism liberated from government restraints and sharply questioned the efficacy of the antipoverty programs spawned by Lyndon Johnson's Great Society initiatives. They called for the restoration of what they considered true American "family values": intact heterosexual marriages, male breadwinners, and stay-at-home mothers. They took tough, harshly anti-Soviet positions in foreign policy.

Milton Friedman, ca. 1974/Spaarnestad Photo/Bridgeman Images

Image 35.12 Milton Friedman, Apostle for Capitalism Among the most influential economists of the late twentieth century, Friedman (1912–2006) received the Nobel Prize in Economics in 1976, just as the free-market outlook he championed was becoming ascendant in the broader political culture.

Prominent among pro-market thinkers was the Nobel Prize–winning economist Milton Friedman, a long-standing critic of Keynesian economics and activist government (refer to Image 35.12). He achieved a new level of popular influence in 1979 with a best-selling book he co-wrote with his wife Rose called *Free to Choose*. The book as well as an accompanying ten-part public television documentary made a compelling case for the superiority of free markets when it came to solving social problems and protecting individual liberty. A talented quipster, Friedman once joked that "If you put the federal government in charge of the Sahara Desert, in five years there'd be a shortage of sand."

Conservative thinking complemented conservative action. Conservative think tanks, including the American Enterprise Institute and the Heritage Foundation, poured out well-researched policy proposals. Meanwhile, the business community militantly mobilized against what it condemned as prosperity-choking liberal policies. Corporate political action committees mushroomed from 89 in 1974 to 1,024 in 1980, while the number of companies with registered lobbyists shot up from 175 in 1971 to nearly 2,500 in 1982.

Their efforts paid off handsomely. Concerted conservative opposition killed two labor law reform bills during Carter's presidency, as well as a proposed minimum wage hike and the prospective establishment of a Consumer Protection Agency. Critics also pinned the blame for stagflation on onerous government regulations, contributing to a sweeping deregulatory movement in areas as disparate as transportation, communications, and banking.

Though spearheaded by a resurgent Republican right, the turn toward the market attracted bipartisan support—in America and elsewhere (refer to "Thinking Globally: The Era of Globalization," pp. 945–946). President Carter himself supported deregulation and the liberation of market forces. As he put it, "We believe that we ought to get the government's nose out of the private enterprise of this country." Younger congressional Democrats also began to move away from the New Deal–era positions of their elders. "We're not a bunch of little Hubert Humphreys," one of them declared in 1974, scornfully repudiating his party's 1968 presidential nominee and one of the most prominent liberals of the postwar era.

The most politically transformative aspect of the new antigovernment politics centered on taxes. A "tax revolt" in California and other states in 1978 soon snowballed into a revolutionary new tax-cutting agenda for the conservative movement nationwide—one with profound consequences for both government and the economy in the decades to come (refer to "36-2 The Reagan Revolution," pp. 966–967).

35-12 Foreign Affairs and the Iranian Imbroglio

Hopes for a less dangerous world rose slightly in June 1979, when President Carter met with Soviet leader Leonid Brezhnev in Vienna to sign the long-stalled **SALT II** (Strategic Arms Limitation Talks II) agreements, limiting the levels of lethal strategic weapons in the Soviet and American

Contending Voices

The Political Mobilization of Business

In August 1971, the corporate lawyer Lewis Powell (1907–1998)—soon to be appointed by President Nixon to the Supreme Court—wrote a confidential memo to the director of the U.S. Chamber of Commerce decrying what he described as a broad-based ideological assault on capitalist principles under way in American academia, media, and politics. Powell then presciently proposed that American businesses collectively marshal a long-range countermovement within those same institutions to reclaim public favor and power.

"No thoughtful person can question that the American economic system is under broad attack. . . . [T]he time has come—indeed, it is long overdue—for the wisdom, ingenuity and resources of American business to be marshalled against those who would destroy it. . . . [O]ne should not postpone more direct political action, while awaiting the gradual change in public opinion to be effected through education and information. Business must learn the lesson, long ago learned by labor and other self-interest groups. This is the lesson that political power is necessary; that such power must be assiduously cultivated; and that when necessary, it must be used aggressively and with determination—without embarrassment and without the reluctance which has been so characteristic of American business."

Seven years later, in 1978, United Auto Workers president Douglas Fraser (1916–2008) announced his resignation from a joint forum for business and labor leaders in a scathing open letter. He decried what he saw as a new aggressiveness and political hostility on the part of American business."

"I believe leaders of the business community, with few exceptions, have chosen to wage a one-sided class war today in this country—a war against working people, the unemployed, the poor, the minorities, the very young and the very old, and even many in the middle class of our society. The leaders of industry, commerce and finance in the United States have broken and discarded the fragile, unwritten compact previously existing during a past period of growth and progress."

Consider This:

How accurate were Powell's and Fraser's descriptions of the American scene in the 1970s? What underlying changes in the economy and society supported their assertions?

arsenals. But conservative critics of the president's defense policies, still regarding the Soviet Union as the Wicked Witch of the East, unsheathed their long knives to carve up the SALT II treaty when it came to the Senate for debate in the summer of 1979.

Political earthquakes in the petroleum-rich Persian Gulf region finally buried all hopes of ratifying the SALT II treaty. On November 4, 1979, a mob of passionately anti-American Muslim militants stormed the U.S. embassy in Tehran, Iran, and took all of its occupants hostage. The captors then demanded that the American authorities ship back to Iran the exiled shah, who had arrived in the United States two weeks earlier for medical treatment.

World opinion hotly condemned the diplomatic felony in Iran, while Americans agonized over both the fate of the hostages and the stability of the entire Persian Gulf region, so dangerously close to the Soviet Union. The Soviet army then aroused the West's worst fears on

December 27, 1979, when it blitzed into the mountainous nation of Afghanistan, next door to Iran, and appeared to be poised for a thrust at the oil jugular of the Gulf.

President Carter reacted vigorously. He slapped an embargo on the export of grain and high-technology machinery to the USSR and called for a boycott of the upcoming Olympic Games in Moscow. He proposed the creation of a "Rapid Deployment Force" to respond to suddenly developing crises in faraway places and requested that young people (including women) be made to register for a possible military draft. The president proclaimed that the United States would "use any means necessary, including force," to protect the Persian Gulf against Soviet incursions. He grimly conceded that he had misjudged the Soviets, and the SALT II treaty became a dead letter in the Senate. Meanwhile, the Soviet army met unexpectedly stiff resistance in Afghanistan and bogged down in a nasty, decade-long guerrilla war that came to be called "Russia's Vietnam."

The **Iranian hostage crisis** was Carter's—and America's—bed of nails. The captured Americans languished in cruel captivity, while nightly television news broadcasts in the United States showed humiliating scenes of Iranian mobs burning the American flag and spitting on effigies of Uncle Sam (refer to Image 35.13).

A. Abbas/Magnum Photos

Image 35.13 Iranians Denounce President Jimmy Carter, November 1979 The poster ridicules U.S. president Jimmy Carter, quoting leader of the Iranian revolution Ayatollah Khomeini: "U.S. cannot do anything." Scenes like this one appeared almost nightly on American television during the 444 days of the Iranian hostage crisis, humiliating Carter and angering American citizens.

As the political turmoil in Iran rumbled on endlessly, Carter's frustration grew. He at last ordered a daring rescue mission. A highly trained commando team penetrated deep into Iran's sandy interior. Their plan required ticktock-perfect timing to succeed, and when equipment failures prevented some members of the team from reaching their destination, the mission had to be scrapped. As the commandos withdrew in the dark desert night, two of their aircraft collided, killing eight of the would-be rescuers.

This disastrous failure of the rescue raid proved anguishing for Americans. The episode seemed to underscore the nation's helplessness and even incompetence in the face of a mortifying insult to the national honor. The stalemate with Iran dragged on throughout the rest of Carter's term, providing an embarrassing backdrop to the embattled president's struggle for reelection.

As the 1980 presidential race approached, a discontented and divided public looked to close the book on a frustrating decade. What Americans could not fully know at the time was how much lasting change had already taken place in such a relatively brief period. The long postwar boom and the broadly shared prosperity that accompanied it were gone for good, to be replaced in coming decades by more fitful and less equitable spurts of economic growth. An ascendant conservative movement helped to popularize far-reaching critiques of government activism as well as new arguments on behalf of free-market policies. Economic inequality and political polarization alike grew steadily in the decades to come. Yet perhaps paradoxically, the dawning era of dampened economic growth, governmental paralysis, and widening income disparity also witnessed increasing tolerance and inclusion for racial and ethnic minorities, immigrants, women, and gay and lesbian people, all of whose horizons broadened dramatically in the decades ahead.

Chapter Summary

Nixon's landslide 1972 election victory was negated as the Watergate scandal erupted. Nixon fought efforts by prosecutors to obtain relevant evidence, but the revelation of his own involvement in the Watergate crimes and cover-up finally compelled him to resign in 1974.

Unelected President Gerald Ford took office amid an emerging "stagflation" that combined low economic growth with inflation, signaling the end of the long postwar era of prosperity and relative economic equality. Ford attempted to sustain Nixon's détente policy with the Soviet Union, but faced growing criticism that the Soviets had turned the policy entirely to their advantage. The Communist Vietnamese finally overran the South Vietnamese government in 1975, confirming Americans' sense of diminished world power and pride.

The major social movement to survive the sixties was feminism, which achieved widespread breakthroughs in employment, culture, and social organization, though failing to pass the ERA. Although nonwhite Americans made significant political and economic gains, race remained an explosive issue, as divisive issues like mandated busing sparked conflict and working-class white discontent. A growing New Right movement throughout the 1970s mobilized around cultural issues like abortion and affirmative action as well as a militantly anticommunist foreign policy.

Campaigning against Watergate and a corrupt Washington, outsider Jimmy Carter won a slender victory over Ford in 1976, but proved unable to work with Congress or improve the economy once he took office. His Camp David agreement brought peace between Egypt and Israel, but the Iranian revolution led to a new energy crisis that compounded already severe inflation and recession. Growing criticism of big government and federal regulation of the economy built political momentum for tax cuts and free-market solutions.

The Soviet invasion of Afghanistan and the holding of American hostages in Iran added to Carter's woes and fostered a general American sense of frustration and helplessness. Economic weakness and foreign policy failures did not, however, prevent a growing tolerance and inclusion of historically marginalized peoples and immigrants within American society.

Key Terms

- stagflation (941)
- Watergate (942)
- "smoking gun" tape (942)
- Helsinki Accords (947)
- Title IX (950)
- Equal Rights Amendment (ERA) (951)
- *Roe v. Wade* (951)
- Indian Gaming Regulatory Act of 1988 (953)
- New Right (953)
- Camp David (954)
- malaise speech (956)
- SALT II (957)
- Iranian hostage crisis (959)

People to Know

- Gerald ("Jerry") Ford
- Gloria Steinem
- Pauli Murray
- Shirley Chisholm
- Carl Stokes
- Phyllis Schlafly
- James Earl ("Jimmy") Carter Jr.
- Milton Friedman
- Leonid Brezhnev

Chronology

1972	• Nixon defeats McGovern for presidency • Equal Rights Amendment passes Congress (not ratified by states)	• Title IX of Education Amendments passed
1973	• Treaty of Paris enacts cease-fire in Vietnam and U.S. withdrawal • Agnew resigns; Ford appointed vice president	• *Frontiero v. Richardson* • *Roe v. Wade*
1973–1974	• Watergate hearings and investigations	
1974	• Nixon resigns; Ford assumes presidency • *Milliken v. Bradley*	
1975	• Helsinki accords • South Vietnam falls to communists	

1976	• Carter defeats Ford for presidency	
1978	• Camp David accords between Egypt and Israel • *United States v. Wheeler*	
1979	• Iranian revolution and oil crisis • SALT II agreements signed (never ratified by Senate)	• Soviet Union invades Afghanistan
1979–1981	• Iranian hostage crisis	
1980	• U.S. boycotts Summer Olympics in Moscow	

To Learn More

Carl Bernstein and Bob Woodward, *All the President's Men* (1974)

James Bill, *The Eagle and the Lion: The Tragedy of American-Iranian Relations* (1988)

Angus Burgin, *The Great Persuasion: Reinventing Free Markets Since the Depression* (2013)

Jefferson Cowie, *Stayin' Alive: The 1970s and the Last Days of the Working Class* (2010)

Alice Echols, *Daring to Be Bad: Radical Feminism in America, 1967–1975* (1989)

Walter LaFeber, *Inevitable Revolutions: The United States in Central America*, 2nd ed. (1993)

Matthew D. Lassiter, *The Silent Majority: Suburban Politics in the Sunbelt South* (2007)

Rosalind Rosenberg, *Jane Crow: The Life of Pauli Murray* (2017)

Bruce Schulman, *The Seventies: The Great Shift in American Culture, Society, and Politics* (2001)

Bruce Schulman and Julian Zelizer, eds., *Rightward Bound: Making America Conservative in the 1970s* (2008)

Robert Self, *All in the Family: The Realignment of American Democracy Since the 1960s* (2012)

Marjorie J. Spruill, *Divided We Stand: The Battle over Women's Rights and Family Values That Polarized American Politics* (2018)

Jeremi Suri, *Henry Kissinger and the American Century* (2007)

Daniel K. Williams, *Defenders of the Unborn: The Pro-Life Movement Before Roe v. Wade* (2016)

Natasha Zaretsky, *No Direction Home: The American Family and the Fear of National Decline, 1968–1980* (2007)

Part 9

Sustaining Democracy in a Global Age 1980 to the Present

For more than forty years after World War II, the fierce competition with the Soviet Union colored almost every aspect of America's foreign relations. Uncle Sam in the Cold War era built a fearsome—and expensive—arsenal of nuclear weapons, great air and missile fleets to deliver them, a two-ocean navy, and, for a time, an enormous army raised by conscription. After two decades of a slight thaw in chilly relations with the communist world—including the visit of the former anticommunist crusader Richard Nixon to China in 1972—the election of Ronald Reagan ushered in an era of hawkish belligerence toward a Soviet Union that Reagan termed an "evil empire." Both East and West employed sophisticated new technologies to build ever-more-powerful weapons and deterrence systems, most famously Reagan's controversial and expensive strategic missile defense system colloquially known as "Star Wars." Yet as the nuclear arsenals grew to fearsome proportions, the Soviet Union was crumbling—debilitated by a bloody war in Afghanistan and a disintegrating socialist economy.

Image IX.1 The End of an Era? As surely as victory in World War II restored confidence and prosperity to a people demoralized by the Great Depression, the terrorist attacks of September 11, 2001, struck electric fear into the American people—and menaced their historical commitment to an open society and individual liberties.

The Cold War ended with the disintegration of the Soviet Union between 1989 and 1992. The United States now possessed unchallenged international supremacy, but its leaders and its soldiers had to grapple with different and more unpredictable challenges overseas. America led an international force in 1991 that crushed Iraqi dictator Saddam Hussein's attempt to grab neighboring Kuwait. Meanwhile, ethnic struggles and civil wars convulsed former Soviet bloc nations throughout Eastern Europe. Horrific genocide tore apart the West African nation of Rwanda. As the United States debated how and when to intervene in these often inhumane conflicts within other countries, a new and even more dangerous threat arose that transcended national borders: the radical Islamist terrorist network Al-Qaeda. Bombings of American embassies and military targets in Africa and the Middle East were but a prelude to the devastating attacks on American soil on September 11, 2001. A brief period of domestic peace and prosperity had ended in terror, leading to long wars in Iraq and Afghanistan and setting off a new cycle of political conflict over national security, civil liberties, and the role of a superpower in the post–Cold War world. Meanwhile, an increasingly muscular China threatened to overturn the entire architecture of the post-WWII international order.

For far too many Americans, the economic security of the postwar era had slipped away as well. A new age of globalization commenced, as factory automation, new transportation and communication technologies, and free-trade agreements transformed the way companies produced and sold their products. American consumers gobbled up inexpensive goods

"Made in China," but average American incomes remained flat. Innovation and unimaginable wealth flowed out of high-tech capitals in Silicon Valley in Northern California and the Seattle region in the Pacific Northwest. American computer software and hardware companies replaced the old giants of autos and steel to become the largest and wealthiest corporations on the globe, as their products became indispensable features of modern life.

News and information now flowed through multiple channels, fracturing the mass culture that had been created by twentieth-century media technologies of radio, Hollywood movies, and network television. Increasingly partisan cable news networks warred for Americans' attention. Print newspapers and magazines struggled as online news outlets and social media platforms delivered customized feeds of information to readers' computer and smartphone screens. The line between truth and fiction blurred as misinformation coursed across the internet at speeds and scales far greater than in any medium before it.

Boston Globe/Getty Images

Image IX.2 A More Diverse Nation Galloping globalization, wars, and environmental stresses made migrants out of hundreds of millions of people as the twenty-first century dawned. Immigration reforms of the 1960s and 1980s opened America's doors to some 40 million newcomers, especially from Latin America and Asia. They enriched the nation's cultural fabric and energized the economy, even as a nativist backlash began to gather steam.

The attacks of 9/11 brought Americans together for a time in grief and anger, but the "Great Recession" that walloped the global economy in 2008 deepened divisions of class, region, culture, and politics. Presidents both Democratic (Bill Clinton and Barack Obama) and Republican (George H. W. Bush and his son George W. Bush) struggled to achieve lasting accomplishments in the face of a mistrustful public, economic anemia, and a polarized Congress. Yet the same era witnessed remarkable victories for equal rights: The nation elected and reelected its first African American president, a woman became a major-party presidential nominee, and the Supreme Court ruled that gay people had the right to marry. New streams of immigration from Latin America, Asia, and Africa transformed the demographic map, making the American population younger and more ethnically and racially diverse.

And as in eras past, the rapidity of social and economic change provoked a sharp backlash. Nativist sentiment surged as Congress fruitlessly debated how to reform a system overwhelmed by new floods of immigrants and refugees. Police violence in minority communities mobilized mass protests. Guns became another political and cultural flashpoint, as gun ownership soared to record levels and mass shootings tore apart families and communities.

In 2016, these great divides produced the election of New York real estate developer Donald Trump to the presidency. A media celebrity who had never held public office, the combative and flamboyant Trump shattered all the norms of traditional political behavior. Amplified by a raucous and polarizing social media environment, Trump's stridently populist message spoke to voters who believed they had been left behind by a bewildering new America. The twice-impeached Trump's refusal to accept the results of the 2020 presidential election catalyzed an insurrectionist attack on the U.S. Capitol by his supporters on January 6, 2021. Political fractures yawned wide, intensified by the yearslong COVID-19 pandemic that profoundly disrupted life, work, and schooling and has killed nearly 7 million people worldwide, including over 1 million Americans.

Looming above it all was the inconvenient truth of a changing climate: oceans warming and rivers drying, forests flattened and species dwindling to extinction, lives and communities lost to natural disasters triggered by extreme weather. As smoke darkened summer skies and tidewaters flooded city streets, it at last became clear that environmental crises would be the greatest and gravest challenges facing America's twenty-first century.

Focus Questions

1. How did America's social fractures of the late twentieth and early twenty-first centuries compare with earlier eras of social and economic upheaval?
2. What have been the main challenges to international harmony and security since 1980?

Chapter 36

The Resurgence of Conservatism: 1980–1992

In this present crisis, government is not the solution to our problem; government is the problem.

Ronald Reagan, Inaugural, 1981

Chapter Outline

- The "New Right" and Reagan's election, 1980
- Budget battles and tax cuts
- Reagan and the Soviets
- Mikhail Gorbachev, Ronald Reagan, and the thawing of the Cold War
- The Iran-Contra scandal
- Reagan's economic legacy
- The religious right
- Conservatism and the courts
- The election of George H. W. Bush, 1988
- The end of the Cold War
- The Persian Gulf War, 1991
- Bush's battles at home

Contending Voices: Who Ended the Cold War?

Varying Viewpoints: What Are the Sources of Modern Conservatism?

"*It's morning in America*" was the slogan of Republican candidate Ronald Reagan in his 1984 presidential reelection campaign. Certainly the 1980s were a new day for America's conservative right. Census figures confirmed that the average American was older than in the stormy sixties and more likely to live in the South or West, where many citizens harbored suspicions of federal power. Cultural issues like abortion, pornography, gay rights, feminism, and affirmative action animated partisan politics and drove conservative-leaning voters to the polls. Faith leaders had long been active in politics, from the abolitionists of the nineteenth century (refer to "15-9 Early Antislavery," pp. 378–380) to the Black civil rights leaders of the postwar South (refer to "34-5 An Incomplete Civil Rights Revolution," pp. 916–919). Now white Christian evangelicals began preaching conservatism from the pulpit. Together, the culture-focused New Right and more traditional antigovernment conservatives added up to a powerful political combination, pushing the Republican Party—and American politics—rightward in the 1980s and the decades that followed.

Focus Questions

1. What social and cultural forces led to the dramatic rise of Ronald Reagan and the "New Right" in the early 1980s?
2. What were the essential elements of the "Reagan revolution" in economic and social policy, and what were Reaganism's short-term and long-term consequences?
3. How and why was the renewed Cold War of the early 1980s followed by the easing of tensions and the Reagan-Gorbachev agreements later in the decade?
4. How did the religious right transform American politics, and how were issues like abortion and affirmative action addressed by the public and the Supreme Court?
5. What were the causes and consequences of the Persian Gulf War? Why did President George H. W. Bush leave Saddam Hussein in power in Iraq?

36-1 The Election of Ronald Reagan, 1980

By 1980, the Republican Party was ready to challenge the Democrats' hold on the White House. Bedeviled abroad and becalmed at home, Jimmy Carter's administration struck many Americans as bungling and befuddled. Carter's inability to control double-digit inflation was especially damaging. Frustrated critics bellyached loudly about the Georgian's alleged mismanagement of the nation's affairs.

Disaffection with Carter's apparent ineptitude ran deep even in his own Democratic Party, where an "ABC" (Anybody but Carter) movement gathered steam. The liberal wing of the party found its champion in Senator Edward Kennedy of Massachusetts, the last survivor of the assassin-plagued Kennedy brothers. He and Carter slugged it out in a series of bruising primary elections that revealed the great ambivalence Democratic voters had about their sitting president. In the end, Kennedy's candidacy fell victim to lingering suspicions about a 1969 automobile accident on Chappaquiddick Island, Massachusetts, in which a young woman assistant was drowned when Kennedy's car plunged off a bridge. A badly battered Carter, his party divided and in disarray, was left to do battle with his Republican challenger, Ronald Reagan.

Actor-turned-politician Reagan had fallen short in his 1976 challenge to Gerald Ford (refer to "35-8 The Bicentennial Campaign," pp. 953–954) but was a favorite for the 1980 Republican nomination from the start, vanquishing more moderate challengers including Texan George H. W. Bush. With his crooked grin and aw-shucks manner, Reagan was often dismissed by his critics as an intellectual featherweight, but he proved to be an ideal standard-bearer for the gathering conservative crusade (refer to Image 36.1).

The son of a ne'er-do-well, impoverished Irish American father with a fondness for the bottle, he had grown up in a small Illinois town. Reagan got his start in life in the depressed 1930s as a sports announcer for an Iowa radio station. Good looks and a way with words landed him acting jobs in Hollywood, where he became a B-grade star in the 1940s. He displayed a flair for politics as president of the Screen Actors Guild in the McCarthy era of the early 1950s, when he helped purge communists and other suspected "reds" from the film industry. In 1954, he became a spokesman for General Electric and began to abandon his New Dealish political views and increasingly preach a conservative, antigovernment line. A televised speech in support of Barry Goldwater in 1964 showcased his ability to deliver a powerfully conservative message with warmth and humor—a stark contrast to the stern persona of Goldwater. Reagan's growing skill at promoting the conservative cause inspired a group of wealthy California businessmen to help Reagan launch his political career as governor of California from 1966 to 1974.

Reared in a generation whose values were formed well before the upheavals of the 1960s, Reagan comfortably sided with the New Right on social issues. In economic and social matters alike, he denounced the activist government and failed "social engineering" of the 1960s. Just as his early political hero, Franklin Roosevelt, had championed the "forgotten man" against big business, Reagan championed the "common man" against big government. He condemned federal intervention in local affairs, denounced affirmative action mandates, and scorned government bureaucrats as arrogant elitists.

Reagan aimed especially to win over from the Democratic column working-class white voters by implying that the Democratic Party had become the party of big government and the exclusive tool of its minority constituents. Reagan's electoral campaign cannily played into racial prejudices simmering within the white electorate. In 1976, he had made campaign-trail quips about profligate Black "welfare queens." In 1980, doubling

Courtesy Ronald Reagan Library

Image 36.1 President Ronald Reagan Older than any man previously elected to the presidency, Reagan displayed youthful vigor both on the campaign trail and in office.

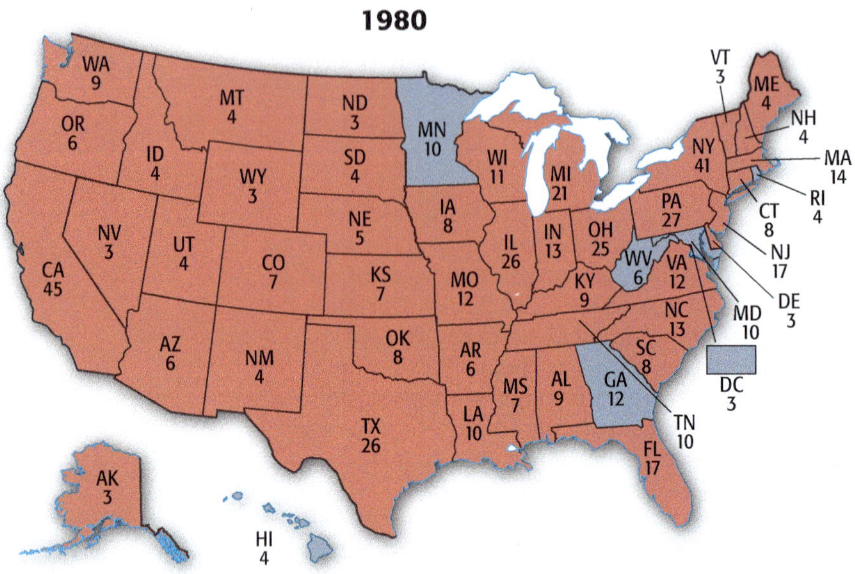

Candidate (Party)	Electoral Vote		Popular Vote	
Reagan (Republican)	489	90.9%	43,899,248	50.8%
Carter (Democrat)	49	9.1%	35,481,435	41.0%
Anderson (Independent)			5,719,437	6.6%

Map 36.1 Presidential Election of 1980 (with electoral vote by state) This map graphically displays Reagan's landslide victory over both Carter and Anderson.

down on Richard Nixon's "Southern Strategy" (refer to "34-15 The New Racial Politics," p. 933), he reassured a mostly white crowd in Neshoba County, Mississippi, where state officials had declined to prosecute the murderers of three civil rights workers in 1964 (refer to "34-4 Reclaiming the Right to Vote," pp. 912–916), that "I believe in states' rights."

The Republican candidate proved to be a formidable campaigner. Using his professional acting skills to great advantage, Reagan attacked the incumbent's fumbling performance in foreign policy and blasted the "big-government" philosophy of the Democratic Party (a philosophy that Carter did not fully embrace). Galloping inflation, sky-high interest rates, and a faltering economy put Carter on the defensive. He countered ineffectively with charges that Reagan was a trigger-happy cold warrior who might push the country into nuclear war.

Carter's spotty record in office was no defense against Reagan's popular appeal. On Election Day, the Republican rang up a spectacular victory, bagging nearly 51 percent of the popular vote. The electoral count stood at 489 for Reagan and 49 for Carter, making him the first elected president to be unseated by voters since Herbert Hoover in 1932 (refer to Map 36.1). Equally startling, the Republicans gained control of the Senate for the first time in twenty-six years. Leading Democratic liberals, including one-time Democratic presidential nominee George McGovern, had been targeted for defeat by well-heeled New Right groups. They went down like dead timber in the conservative windstorm that swept the country.

Carter showed dignity in defeat, delivering a thoughtful Farewell Address that stressed his efforts to scale down the deadly arms race, to promote human rights, and to protect the environment. In one of his last acts in office, he signed a bill preserving some 100 million acres of Alaska for national parks, forests, and wildlife refuges. An unusually intelligent, articulate, and well-meaning president, he had been hampered by his lack of managerial talent and had been badly buffeted by events beyond his control, such as the soaring price of oil, runaway inflation, and the galling insult of the hostages still held in Iran. Though unsuccessful in the White House, Carter earned much admiration in later years for his humanitarian and human rights activities. He received the Nobel Peace Prize in 2002.

36-2 The Reagan Revolution

Reagan's arrival in Washington was triumphal. In a stinging last slap at Carter, the Iranians released the hostages on Reagan's Inauguration Day, January 20, 1981, after 444 days of captivity (refer to Image 36.2).

The new president, a hale and hearty sixty-nine-year-old, proclaiming his devotion to fiscal fitness, sought nothing less than the dismantling of the welfare state and the reversal of the political evolution of the preceding half-century. Assembling a conservative cabinet of "the best and the rightest," he took dead aim at what he regarded as the bloated federal budget. "It will be my intention," he declared in his first inaugural address, "to curb the size and influence of the federal establishment." Years of New Deal–style tax-and-spend programs, Reagan jested, had created a federal government that reminded him of the definition of a baby as a creature who was all appetite at one end, with no sense of responsibility at the other.

On his conservative crusade for smaller government, less bureaucracy, and freer markets ("Reaganomics"), Reagan found common cause with the new leader of America's oldest ally, Great Britain. Conservative Margaret Thatcher became Britain's first female prime minister in 1979. With a mandate to improve her nation's economy, which like America's had stagnated through the 1970s, she embarked on a mission to reduce the power of labor unions and government involvement in business, two of Reagan's chief goals. The philosophic kinship between "Ronnie and Maggie," as the press dubbed the two heads of state, went beyond economics. Emboldened by each other, they strengthened the Anglo-American alliance through muscular foreign policy against a number of foes, especially the Soviet bloc. Their common refrain was that free markets made free peoples, and that shrinking government would keep their nations safer from communism.

By the early 1980s, this antigovernment message found a receptive audience in the United States. In the two decades since 1960, federal spending had risen from about 18 percent of gross national product to nearly 23 percent. Much of this came from the growth of two enormously expensive—but exceptionally popular—entitlement programs: Social Security and Medicare. In 1973 the budget of the Department of Health, Education, and Welfare (the federal agency that housed the two programs) surpassed that of the Department of Defense.

Citizens, disillusioned with their leaders after the secrets of Watergate and the quagmire of Vietnam, increasingly balked at paying the government's bills. After four decades of advancing New Deal and Great Society programs, a strong countercurrent took hold. Californians staged a "tax revolt" in 1978 (known by its official ballot title of **Proposition 13**) that slashed property taxes and forced painful cuts in local government services, conspicuously including public schools. The California "tax quake" jolted other state capitals and even rocked the pillars of Congress in faraway Washington, DC. Newly energized corporate interest groups pressed lawmakers to cut taxes; stagflation-wracked small businesses cried for relief from regulatory "red tape." Ronald Reagan had ridden this political shockwave to presidential victory in 1980 and now proceeded to rattle the "welfare state" to its very foundations.

Descending upon Washington like an avenging angel of conservatism, Reagan first proposed a scaled-back federal budget that cut spending by some $35 billion, mostly in antipoverty programs like food stamps and federally funded job-training centers. (The largest and costliest pillars of the welfare state like Social Security and Medicare were comparatively unshaken.) Reagan worked naturally in harness with the Republican majority in the Senate but faced stiff headwinds in the Democratic House, led by outspoken liberal Speaker Thomas "Tip" O'Neill. To get his way, Reagan enterprisingly wooed a group of mostly Southern conservative Democrats (dubbed **boll weevils**), who ultimately abandoned their own party's leadership to follow the president (refer to Image 36.3). Reagan's political hand was further strengthened after a failed assassination attempt in March 1981 brought an outpouring of sympathy and support.

Image 36.2 Coming Home After more than a year in captivity in Iran, these hostages were released on the very day of Ronald Reagan's presidential inauguration.

Image 36.3 The Triumph of the Right, 1980 Republican conservatives scored a double victory in 1980, winning control of both the White House and the Senate. Aided by conservative Democratic "boll weevils," they also dominated the House of Representatives, and a new era of conservatism dawned in the nation's capital.

36-3 The Battle of the Budget

Swept along on a tide of presidential popularity and key defections by boll weevil Democrats, Congress swallowed Reagan's budget proposals. In late 1981 Congress also approved a set of far-reaching tax reforms that lowered individual tax rates, reduced federal estate taxes, and created new tax-free savings plans for small investors. Democratic House Speaker O'Neill decried the tax cuts as "a windfall for the rich" that would swell the budget deficit, but Reagan persuaded Congress to double-down on tax reduction with an even more ambitious **Tax Reform Act** in 1986. Leaner budgets and lower taxes now became the twin pillars of Republican fiscal orthodoxy for the next several decades.

The theory driving Reagan's push for massive income-tax reductions was known as **supply-side economics**. Supply-siders argued that a combination of budgetary discipline and tax reduction would stimulate new investment, invigorate productivity, foster dramatic economic growth, and eventually even *boost* rather than deplete tax revenues, thus reducing the federal deficit.

At first "supply-side" economics seemed to be a beautiful theory mugged by a gang of brutal facts. The economy slid into its deepest recession since the 1930s. Unemployment reached nearly 11 percent in 1982, businesses folded, and several bank failures jolted the nation's entire financial system. The automobile industry, once the brightest jewel in America's industrial crown, turned in its dimmest performance in history. Battling against Japanese imports, major automakers reported losses in the hundreds of millions of dollars. Anti-inflationary "tight money" policies had actually been launched by the Federal Reserve Board (the Fed) in 1979, on Carter's watch. Sharp increases in interest rates—known as the "**Volcker Shock**" after Fed Board Chairman Paul Volcker—had intensified the economic squeeze. But fuming and frustrated Democrats declared a "Reagan recession," charging that the president's budget cuts slashed especially cruelly at society's most economically vulnerable citizens.

The supply-siders seemed to be vindicated when a healthy economic recovery finally got underway in 1983. The painful interest-rate hikes of the Volcker Shock finally broke the nation's long inflationary spiral. Yet the economy of the 1980s was not uniformly sound. Ominously, an income gap between the richest and the poorest Americans began to crack open for the first time in the post–World War II era. The gap widened to a chasm over the succeeding decades, as the poorest Americans became poorer and the very rich grew fabulously richer, while middle-class incomes largely stagnated. Symbolic of the new income stratification was the emergence of "yuppies," or young, urban professionals. Sporting Rolex watches and BMW sports cars, yuppies showcased the values of flamboyant materialism and the pursuit of wealth that came to symbolize the high-rolling 1980s.

Personal computing became an industry that defined the decade. First introduced to consumers in the late 1970s, desktop computers seemed at first like frivolous toys, but by the early 1980s they sat atop desks in homes, offices, and schools (refer to Figure 36.1). The roaring popularity of video games brought digital technologies into the lives of even the youngest citizens. Amid a gloomy moment for

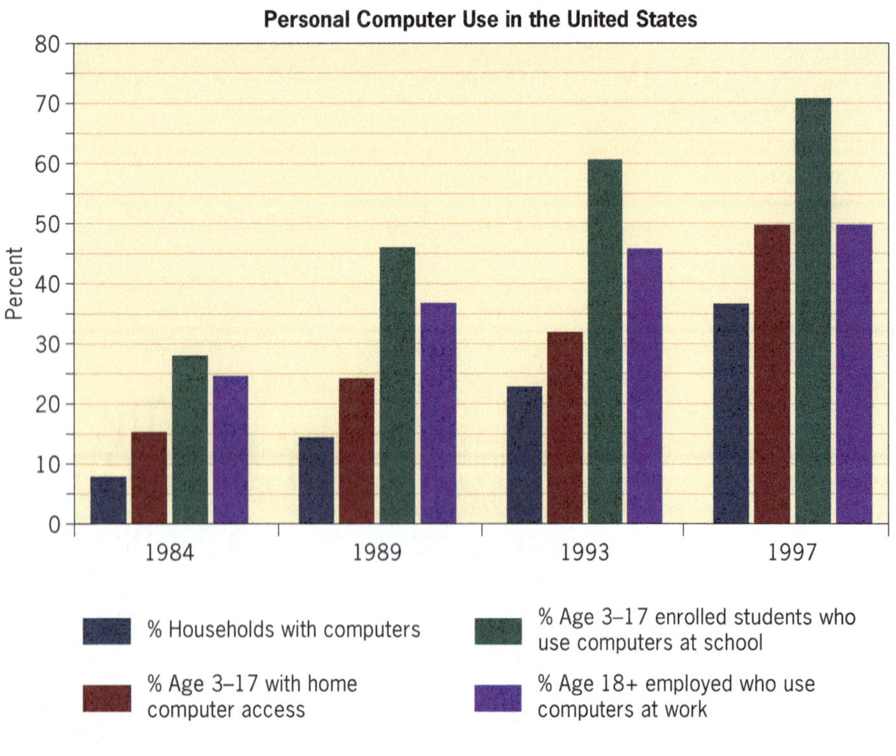

Figure 36.1 The Emergence of Personal Computing The market for desktop computers grew with remarkable speed in the 1980s. American schoolchildren were some of the heaviest users of these devices, which became widely popular as learning and gaming devices well before the rise of the commercial internet.

Source: U.S. Census Bureau, Current Population Survey, October 1984, 1989, 1993, 1997.

American manufacturing, the companies of "Silicon Valley" provided a ray of economic sunshine. Some Democratic lawmakers became so enthused about the promise of high-technology industries that Washington, DC, reporters cheekily dubbed them "Atari Democrats," after the successful California video game maker. Young tech entrepreneurs landed on magazine covers, as did the computer itself, which was named *Time* magazine's "Machine of the Year" in 1983.

Some economists located the sources of the economic upturn neither in the president's budget cuts and tax reforms, nor in the go-get-'em avarice of the yuppies, nor even in the new surge of tech. It was massive military expenditures, they argued, that constituted the real foundation of 1980s prosperity. Reagan cascaded nearly $2 trillion onto the Pentagon, asserting the need to close a "window of vulnerability" in the armaments race with the Soviet Union. Ironically, this conservative president thereby plunged the government into a red-ink bath of deficit spending that made the New Deal look downright stingy.

Federal budget deficits topped $100 billion in 1982, and the government's books were nearly $200 billion out of balance in every subsequent year of the decade. Massive government borrowing to cover those deficits kept interest rates high, and high interest rates in turn elevated the value of the dollar to record altitudes in the international money markets. The soaring dollar was good news for American tourists and buyers of foreign cars, but it dealt crippling blows to American exporters, as the American international trade deficit reached a record $152 billion in 1987. The masters of international commerce and finance for a generation after World War II, Americans suddenly became the world's heaviest borrowers in the global economy of the 1980s.

36-4 Reagan Renews the Cold War

Hard as nails toward the Soviet Union in his campaign speeches, Reagan saw no reason to soften up after he checked in at the White House. He claimed that the Soviets were "prepared to commit any crime, to lie, to cheat," in pursuit of their goals of world conquest. He denounced the Soviet Union as the "focus of evil in the modern world."

Reagan believed in negotiating with the Soviets—but only from a position of overwhelming strength. Accordingly, his strategy for dealing with Moscow was simple: by enormously expanding U.S. military capabilities, he could threaten the Soviets with a fantastically expensive new round of the arms race. The American economy, theoretically, could better bear this new financial burden than could the creaking Soviet system. Desperate to avoid economic ruin, Kremlin leaders would come to the bargaining table and sing Reagan's tune.

This strategy resembled a riverboat gambler's ploy. It wagered the enormous sum of Reagan's defense budgets on the hope that the other side would not call Washington's bluff and initiate a new cycle of arms competition. It also bet that Reagan's popularity would prevail over a reignited peace movement and large "nuclear freeze" demonstrations, including a 1982 rally in New York City's Central Park that drew a crowd estimated as being between 750,000 and 1 million people (refer to Image 36.4). Reagan played his trump card in this risky game in March 1983, when he announced his intention to pursue a high-technology missile-defense system called the **Strategic Defense Initiative (SDI)**, popularly known as Star Wars. The plan called for orbiting battle stations in space that could fire laser beams or other forms of concentrated energy to vaporize intercontinental missiles on liftoff. Reagan described SDI

Barbara Alper/Getty Images

Image 36.4 **No More Hiroshimas, New York City, 1982** Alarmed by the escalating military spending of the Reagan administration, hundreds of thousands of Americans took to the streets to call for a "nuclear freeze."

Bettmann/Getty Images

Image 36.5 Defending SDI, 1987 President Reagan evoked extravagant hopes that his Strategic Defense Initiative, a laser-guided missile shield announced in early 1983, could protect the nation from nuclear attack. Although critics mocked Reagan's scheme as "Star Wars" and most scientists considered its daunting physical and engineering challenges impossible to overcome, the president championed the program throughout his time in office. Here, Reagan jocularly displays a pro-SDI bumper sticker while Vice President George H. W. Bush looks on.

as offering potential salvation from the nuclear nightmare by throwing an "astrodome" defense shield over American cities. Most scientists considered this an impossible goal (refer to Image 36.5). The announcement spiked public anxiety about nuclear escalation and military technology run amok. But the deeper logic of SDI lay in its fit with Reagan's overall Soviet strategy. By pitching the arms contest onto a stratospheric plane of high technology and astronomical expense, it would help force the Kremlin's hand.

Relations with the Soviets had further nosedived in late 1981, when the government of Poland, needled for over a year by a popular movement of workingpeople organized into a massive union called "Solidarity," clamped martial law on the troubled country. Reagan saw the heavy fist of the Kremlin inside this Polish iron glove, and he imposed economic sanctions on Poland and the USSR alike.

Dealing with the Soviet Union was additionally complicated by the inertia and ill health of the aging oligarchs in the Kremlin, three of whom died between late 1982 and early 1985. Relations grew even more tense when the Soviets, in September 1983, blasted from the skies a Korean passenger airliner that had inexplicably violated Soviet airspace. Hundreds of civilians, including many Americans, plummeted to their deaths in the frigid Sea of Okhotsk. By the end of 1983, all arms-control negotiations with the Soviets were broken off. The chill of the Cold War deepened further in 1984, when USSR and Soviet-bloc athletes boycotted the Olympic Games in Los Angeles.

36-5 Troubles Abroad

The ever-volatile Middle Eastern pot continued to boil ominously. In Afghanistan, Reagan sent arms, including thousands of powerfully effective "Stinger" anti-aircraft missiles, to the mujahideen forces battling the Soviet invaders. Ironically, some of these U.S.-aided "freedom fighters" would later join the Al-Qaeda terrorist network, including Osama bin Laden, architect of the September 11, 2001, attacks against the United States (refer to "37-13 Terrorism Comes to America," pp. 1012–1014).

Israel badly strained its bonds of friendship with the United States by continuing to allow new settlements to be established in the occupied territory of the Jordan River's West Bank (refer to Map 38.1, p. 1031). Israel further raised the stakes in the Middle East in June 1982 when it invaded neighboring Lebanon, seeking to suppress once and for all the guerrilla bases from which Palestinian fighters harassed Israel. The Palestinians were bloodily subdued, but Lebanon, already pulverized by years of episodic civil war, was plunged into armed chaos. President Reagan was obliged to send American troops to Lebanon in 1983 as part of an international peacekeeping force, but their presence did not bring peace. In a heartrending preview of decades of Middle Eastern entanglements to come, a suicide bomber crashed an explosives-laden truck into a U.S. military barracks on October 23, 1983, killing 241 Marines. President Reagan soon thereafter withdrew the remaining American troops, while miraculously suffering no political damage from this horrifying and humiliating attack. His mystified Democratic opponents began to call him the "Teflon president," to whom nothing hurtful could stick.

Central America, in the United States' own backyard, also rumbled menacingly. Decades of diplomatic and covert American intervention had successfully slowed the encroachment of communism in the Western Hemisphere, but it also enabled corrupt and antidemocratic governments to flourish in communism's stead. One such ally was the long-time dictator of Nicaragua, who was deposed in a leftist revolution in 1979. President Carter had tried to ignore the hotly anti-American rhetoric of the revolutionaries, known as **Sandinistas**, and to establish good diplomatic relations with them. But cold warrior Reagan took their rhetoric at face value and hurled back at them some hot language of his own. He accused the Sandinistas of turning their country into a forward base for Soviet and Cuban military penetration of all of Central

America. Brandishing photographs taken from high-flying spy planes, administration spokespeople claimed that Nicaraguan leftists were shipping weapons to revolutionary forces in tiny El Salvador, torn by violence since its own coup in 1979.

Reagan sent military "advisers" to prop up the pro-American government of El Salvador. He also provided covert aid, including the CIA-engineered mining of harbors, to the rebel **Contras** opposing the anti-American government of Nicaragua. Reagan flexed his military muscles elsewhere in the turbulent Caribbean. In a dramatic display of American might, in October 1983 he dispatched a heavy-firepower invasion force to the island of Grenada, where a military coup had killed the prime minister and brought Marxists to power. Swiftly overrunning the tiny island and ousting the insurgents, American troops vividly demonstrated Reagan's determination to assert the dominance of the United States in the Caribbean, just as Theodore Roosevelt had done (refer to Map 36.2).

36-6 Round Two for Reagan

A confident Ronald Reagan, bolstered by a buoyant economy at home and by the popularity of his defiant posture abroad, met little opposition in his bid for a second White House term in 1984. His opponent was Democrat Walter Mondale, who made history by naming as his vice-presidential running mate Congresswoman Geraldine Ferraro of New York. She was the first woman ever to appear on a major-party presidential ticket. But even this dramatic gesture could not salvage Mondale's candidacy, which was fatally tainted by his service as vice president in

Map 36.2 Central America and the Caribbean This region, so important to the United States throughout its history, remained a hotbed of unrest through the last years of the Cold War and beyond.

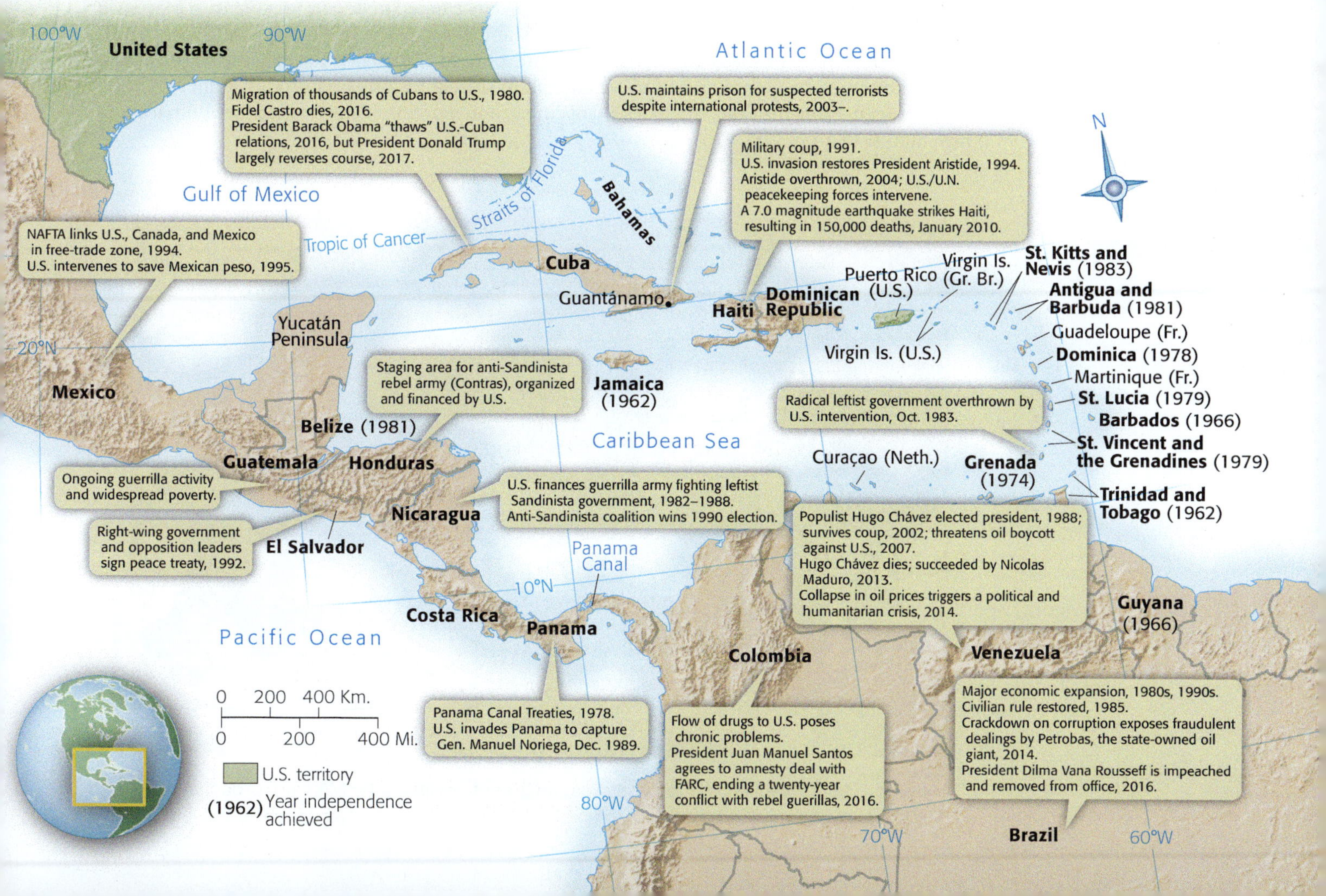

the discredited Carter administration. Mondale and the Democrats decried Reagan as a budget-cutting warmonger, while the Reagan campaign unfurled gauzy ads declaring, "It's morning again in America."

American voters, at last released from stagflation's grip, chose optimism. On Election Day, Reagan walked away with a stunning 525 electoral votes to Mondale's 13, winning everywhere except in Mondale's home state of Minnesota and the District of Columbia. Reagan also overwhelmed Mondale in the popular vote—52,609,797 to 36,450,613.

Shrinking the federal government and reducing taxes had been the main objectives of Reagan's first term; foreign-policy issues dominated the news in his second term. The president soon found himself contending for the world's attention with a charismatic new Soviet leader, Mikhail Gorbachev, installed as chairman of the Soviet Communist Party in March 1985. Gorbachev was personable, energetic, imaginative, and committed to radical reforms in the Soviet Union. He announced two policies with remarkable, even revolutionary, implications. **Glasnost**, or "openness," aimed at ventilating the secretive, repressive stuffiness of Soviet society by introducing free speech and a measure of political liberty. **Perestroika**, or "restructuring," was intended to revive the moribund Soviet economy by adopting many of the free-market practices—such as the profit motive and an end to subsidized prices—of the capitalist West.

Both glasnost and perestroika required that the Soviet Union shrink the size of its enormous military machine and redirect its energies to the dismal civilian economy. That requirement, in turn, necessitated an end to the Cold War. Gorbachev accordingly made warm overtures to the West, including an announcement in April 1985 that the Soviet Union would cease to deploy intermediate-range nuclear forces (INF) targeted at Western Europe, pending an agreement on their complete elimination. He pushed this goal when he met with Ronald Reagan at the first of four summit meetings in Geneva in November 1985. A second summit meeting, in Reykjavik, Iceland, in October 1986, broke down when a furious Reagan stormed out, convinced that Gorbachev had come to end plans for his beloved SDI. But at a third summit, in Washington, DC, in December 1987, the two leaders at last signed the **Intermediate-Range Nuclear Forces (INF) Treaty**, banning all of these missiles from Europe. Reagan and Gorbachev capped their new friendship in May 1988 at a final summit in Moscow (refer to Image 36.6). There Reagan, who had entered office condemning the "evil empire" of Soviet communism, warmly praised Gorbachev. Reagan, the consummate cold warrior, had been flexible and savvy enough to seize a historic opportunity to join with the Soviet chief to bring the Cold War to a kind of conclusion. For this, history would give both leaders high marks.

Courtesy Ronald Reagan Library

Image 36.6 East Meets West President Reagan greets Soviet leader Mikhail Gorbachev at a summit meeting in Moscow in May 1988.

36-7 The Iran-Contra Imbroglio

Two foreign-policy problems seemed insoluble to Reagan: the continuing captivity of a number of American hostages, seized by Muslim extremist groups in bleeding, battered Lebanon; and the continuing grip on power of the left-wing Sandinista government in Nicaragua. The president repeatedly requested that Congress provide military aid to the Contra rebels fighting against the Sandinista regime. Congress repeatedly refused, and the administration grew increasingly frustrated, even obsessed, in its search for a means to help the Contras.

Unknown to the American public, some Washington officials saw a possible linkage between the two thorny problems of the Middle Eastern hostages and the Central American Sandinistas. In 1985, American diplomats secretly arranged arms sales to Iran, which was mired in a devastating territorial war with neighboring Iraq. In return, the Iranians helped obtain the release of at least one American hostage held by Middle Eastern terrorists. Meanwhile, the money Iran paid for the American weapons was diverted to the Contras in Nicaragua. These actions brazenly violated a congressional ban on military aid to the Nicaraguan rebels—not to mention Reagan's repeated vow that he would never negotiate with terrorists (refer to Image 36.7). Washington also continued to support Iraqi dictator Saddam Hussein, to whom it sold weapons used against Iran.

News of these secret dealings broke in November 1986 and ignited a firestorm of controversy. President Reagan claimed he was innocent of wrongdoing and ignorant of his subordinates' activities. Reviving a refrain from the Watergate era, the public clamored to know "what the president knew and when he knew it." Although Reagan was never found to have lied outright, a congressional committee condemned the "secrecy, deception, and disdain for the law" displayed by administration officials and concluded that "if the president did not know what his national security advisers were doing, he should have."

The **Iran-Contra affair** cast a dark shadow over the Reagan record on foreign policy, tending to obscure the president's outstanding achievement in establishing a new relationship with the Soviets. From the several Iran-Contra investigations, a picture emerged of Reagan as a lazy, perhaps even senile, president who napped through meetings and paid little or no

On March 4, 1987, President Ronald Reagan somewhat confusingly tried to explain his role (or lack of role) in the arms-for-hostages deal with Iran:

"A few months ago I told the American people I did not trade arms for hostages. My heart and my best intentions still tell me that is true, but the facts and the evidence tell me it is not."

William Gentile/Corbis Historical/Getty Images

Image 36.7 Secretly Supporting the Contras The Reagan administration went to great and illegal lengths to provide aid for the Nicaraguan "contras"—armed resistors to the left-wing Sandinista regime, which had ruled the country since 1979. Fittingly, one of these patrolling rebels wears a USA baseball cap.

attention to the details of policy. Reagan's critics pounced on this portrait as proof that the movie-star-turned-politician was a mental lightweight who had merely acted his way through the role of the presidency without really understanding the script. But despite these damaging revelations, Reagan remained among the most popular and consequential presidents in modern American history, a transformative figure in his party and in American politics.

36-8 Reagan's Economic Legacy

Ronald Reagan had taken office vowing to invigorate the American economy by rolling back government regulations, lowering taxes, and balancing the budget. He did ease many regulatory rules, and he pushed major tax reform bills through Congress in 1981 and 1986. But a balanced budget remained grotesquely out of reach. Supply-side economic theory had promised that lower taxes would actually increase government revenue because they would stimulate the economy as a whole. But, in fact, the combination of tax reduction and huge increases in military spending opened a vast "revenue hole" of $200 billion annual deficits. In his eight years in office, President Reagan added nearly $2 trillion to the national debt—more than all of his predecessors combined, including those who had fought protracted global wars (refer to Figure 36.2).

The staggering deficits of the Reagan years assuredly constituted a great economic failure. And because so much of the Reagan-era debt was financed by foreign lenders, especially the Japanese, the deficits virtually guaranteed that future generations of Americans would either have to work harder than their parents, lower their standard of living, or both, to pay their foreign creditors when the bills came due.

But if the deficits represented an economic failure, they also constituted, strangely enough, a kind of political triumph. Among the paramount goals of Reagan's political life was his ambition to slow the growth of government. His sky-high budget deficits served exactly that purpose, making new social spending both practically and politically impossible for the foreseeable future. More than a decade would pass before any new social programs were even thinkable. Ronald Reagan thus secured one of his dearest political objectives to a degree that few presidents have managed to achieve. For better or worse, the consequences of "Reaganomics" proved to be large and lasting.

Yet a troubling legacy of the 1980s was a sharp reversal of a long-term trend toward a more equitable distribution of income. The middle classes increasingly felt the squeeze. In the early 1990s, median household income (in 1993 dollars) actually declined, from about $32,562 in 1989 to about $30,779 in 1993 (refer to Figure 38.4, p. 1035). Similar trends appeared in other rich nations, but the United States had a particularly acute case of widening income and wealth inequality. In the first decades of the twenty-first century, the gap yawned even wider. By 2021, the concentration of wealth at the very top was greater than at the peak of the Gilded Age.

36-9 The Religious Right

An especially conspicuous political force rising to influence in the 1980s was a coalition of conservative, evangelical Christians known as the religious right. In 1979, the Reverend Jerry Falwell, an evangelical minister and the founder of Liberty University in his native Lynchburg, Virginia, launched a political advocacy group called the **Moral Majority**. Falwell preached with great success against sexual permissiveness, abortion, feminism, and gay rights (refer to Image 36.8). In its first two years, the Moral Majority registered between 2 million and 3 million voters. Using radio, direct-mail marketing, and the rapidly growing market of cable TV, Falwell and other "televangelists" reached huge audiences in the 1980s, collected millions of dollars, and became aggressive political advocates for conservative causes. Ironically, it was Ronald Reagan—a divorced man and irregular churchgoer—who became the greatest political beneficiary of the Religious Right's rise. Reagan successfully courted evangelicals in his 1980 campaign and welcomed Falwell and other conservative evangelical leaders to the White House throughout his presidency.

In a speech to the National Association of Evangelicals on March 8, 1983, President Ronald Reagan (1911–2004) justified his support for school prayer:

"The Declaration of Independence mentions the Supreme Being no less than four times. 'In God We Trust' is engraved on our coinage. The Supreme Court opens its proceedings with a religious invocation. And the Members of Congress open their sessions with a prayer. I just happen to believe the schoolchildren of the United States are entitled to the same privileges as Supreme Court Justices and Congressmen."

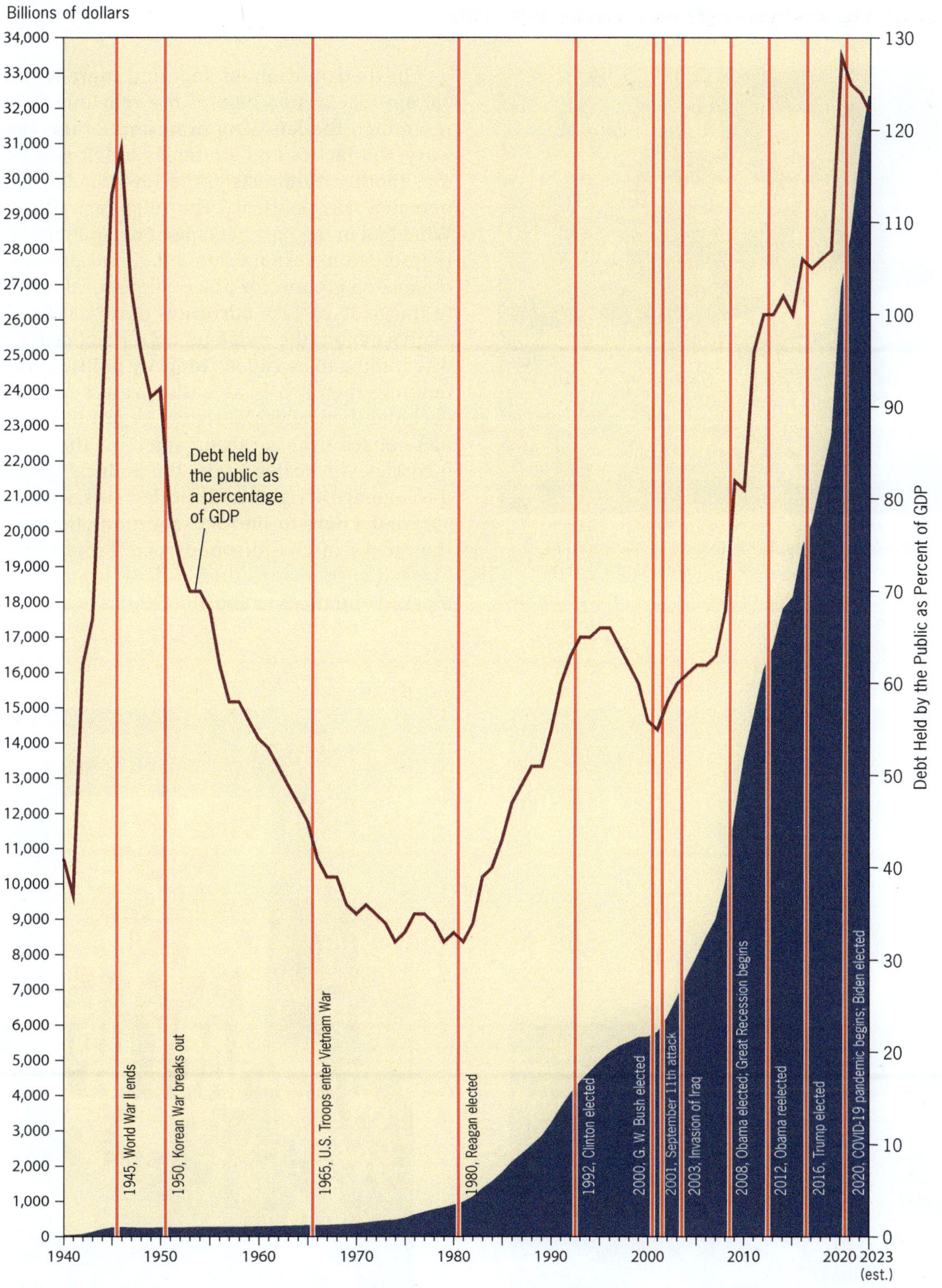

Figure 36.2 The National Debt, 1940–2023 World War II provided the first major boost to the national debt. The policies of the Reagan and George H. W. Bush administrations, 1981–1993, explosively expanded the debt to the $4 trillion level. By the 1990s, 14 percent of federal revenues went to interest payments on the debt. The budget surpluses created by the booming economy of the second Clinton administration (1997–2001) raised the prospect that the debt might be paid off. But the combination of the George W. Bush tax cuts and increased military spending sent the debt soaring again after 2001. Those tax cuts, combined with the revenue losses and stimulus expenditures occasioned by the "Great Recession" that began in 2008, kicked the publicly held debt up to unprecedented peacetime levels, approaching 80 percent of GDP. Trillions in emergency spending authorized to combat the unemployment and economic woes precipitated by the COVID-19 pandemic propelled it to 100 percent of GDP. Real-time updates of the public debt are available from the Department of the Treasury's Bureau of the Public Debt, at http://www.publicdebt.treas.gov.

Sources: *Historical Statistics of the United States* and *Statistical Abstract of the United States*, relevant years; Office of Management and Budget Historical Tables.

Eve Arnold/Magnum Photos

Image 36.8 The Moral Majority, 1981 Television evangelist and religious leader Reverend Jerry Falwell (1933–2007) mobilized his national Moral Majority organization in support of Ronald Reagan's presidential campaign in 1980 and a conservative social agenda.

In their movement zeal and morally charged political approach, members of the religious right sometimes resembled the left-wing protesters of the 1960s. In many ways, the tactics and strategies of left and right mirrored one another. Feminists in the 1960s had declared that "the personal was political." The religious right did the same. What had in the past been personal matters—marriage and reproduction, sexual orientation, and prayer—became the organizing ground for powerful political movements (refer to Image 36.9). Like advocates of racial diversity and affirmative action, the religious right practiced a form of what was coming to be called "**identity politics**." But rather than defining themselves as Latino voters or gay voters, they declared themselves Christian or pro-life voters. If the left had consciousness-raising sessions, the right had prayer meetings. Advocates across the political spectrum invoked the language of rights and entitlements, whether the right to vote or the right-to-life (anti-abortion). Both camps adopted the tactics of civil disobedience. Protesters in the 1960s blocked entrances to draft offices; protesters in the 1980s blocked entrances to abortion clinics.

A

Robert Giroux/AFP/Getty Images

B

Andrew Holbrooke/Getty Images

Image 36.9A and B The Age of AIDS The first diagnoses of the deadly acquired immunodeficiency syndrome (AIDS) were made in 1981, and the disease spread at a horrifying pace. Concentrated disproportionately among gay men, AIDS reached epidemic proportions within just a few years while eluding scientists' hunt for a treatment or cure. By 1988, nearly 83,000 cases had been reported in the United States alone. Sufferers of the so-called "gay plague" faced stigma and discrimination from many fellow Americans, and the socially conservative Reagan administration was tragically slow to respond adequately to the epidemic. The disease devastated the gay community and became a galvanizing cause for increasingly visible and often confrontational activism. The year 1987 saw the beginning of the construction of a mammoth AIDS Memorial Quilt dedicated to the memory of the disease's victims, displayed here (Image 36.9A) at the National Mall in 1992 on its journey around the country. One of the leading political activist organizations to emerge out of the epidemic was the AIDS Coalition to Unleash Power (ACT UP), shown here (Image 36.9B) protesting in New York City.

Several leaders of the religious right fell from grace in the latter part of the decade. One tearfully admitted to repeated trysts with prostitutes. Another went to prison following revelations of his own financial and sexual misconduct. But such scandals did not shake the faith of America's conservative Christians or diminish the new political clout of activist, evangelical religionists. The Religious Right entered the new century tightly bound to Reagan's Republican Party.

Image 36.10 **The Justice Is a Lady, 1981** Herblock hails Sandra Day O'Connor's appointment to the Supreme Court.

36-10 Conservatism in the Courts

If the budget was Reagan's chief weapon in the war against the welfare state, the courts became a principal instrument in the "culture wars" waged by conservatives. By the time he left office, Reagan had appointed a near-majority of all sitting federal judges. Equally important, he had named three conservative-minded justices to the U.S. Supreme Court. They included Sandra Day O'Connor, a brilliant, public-spirited Arizona judge. When she was sworn in on September 25, 1981, she became the first woman to ascend to the high bench in the Court's nearly two-hundred-year history (refer to Image 36.10).

Reaganism repudiated two great icons of the liberal political culture: affirmative action and abortion rights. The Court showed its newly conservative colors in 1984, when it decreed, in a case involving Memphis firefighters, that union rules about job seniority could outweigh affirmative-action concerns in guiding promotion policies in the city's fire department. In two cases in 1989 (*Ward's Cove Packing v. Antonia* and *Martin v. Wilks*), the Court made it more difficult to prove that an employer practiced racial discrimination in hiring and made it easier for white males to argue that they were the victims of reverse discrimination by employers who followed affirmative-action practices. Congress passed legislation in 1991 that partially reversed the effects of those decisions.

The contentious issue of abortion also reached the Court in 1989. In the 1973 case of *Roe v. Wade*, the Supreme Court had prohibited states from making laws that interfered with a woman's right to an abortion during the early months of pregnancy. For nearly two decades, that decision had been the bedrock principle on which "pro-choice" advocates built their case for abortion rights. It had also provoked bitter criticism from Roman Catholics and various "right-to-life" groups, who wanted a virtually absolute ban on all abortions. In *Webster v. Reproductive Health Services*, the Court in 1989 seriously compromised *Roe*'s protections by approving a Missouri law that imposed certain restrictions on abortion. Further inviting states to legislate in an area in which *Roe* had once seemed to forbid them, the Court ruled in 1992's *Planned Parenthood v. Casey* that states could restrict access to abortion as long as they did not place an "undue burden" on the woman. The *Webster* and *Casey* decisions galvanized right-to-life and pro-choice organizations alike. Their uncompromising clash continued into the following century.

Speaking to the National Association of Evangelicals in March 1983, President Ronald Reagan said the following about abortion:

"More than a decade ago, a Supreme Court decision [*Roe v. Wade*, 1973] literally wiped off the books of fifty states statutes protecting the rights of unborn children. Abortion on demand now takes the lives of up to 1½ million unborn children a year. Human life legislation ending this tragedy will some day pass the Congress, and you and I must never rest until it does. Unless and until it can be proven that the unborn child is not a living entity, then its right to life, liberty, and the pursuit of happiness must be protected."

36-11 Referendum on Reaganism in 1988

Republicans lost control of the Senate in the off-year elections of November 1986. Hopes rose among Democrats that the "Reagan Revolution" might be showing signs of vulnerability at last. The newly Democratic majority in the Senate flexed its political muscles in 1987 when it rejected Robert Bork,

Hollywood director Oliver Stone's (b. 1946) film *Wall Street* both romanticized and vilified the business culture of the 1980s. The character of Gordon Gekko, inspired by real-life corporate raider Ivan Boesky, captured the spirit of the times:

"Ladies and gentlemen, greed is good. Greed works, greed is right. . . . Greed for life, money, love, knowledge, has marked the upward surge of mankind—and greed, mark my words, will save the malfunctioning corporation called the U.S.A."

an ultraconservative nominee for the Supreme Court. The angry battle foreshadowed an increasing politicization of Supreme Court appointments in the decades that followed.

Democrats also relished the prospect of making hay out of both the Iran-Contra affair and disquieting signs of economic trouble. The "double mountain" of deficits—the federal budget deficit and the international trade deficit—continued to grow ominously. Falling oil prices blighted the economy of the Southwest, slashing real estate values and undermining hundreds of savings and loan (S&L) institutions. The damage to the S&Ls was so massive that a federal rescue operation was eventually estimated to carry a price tag of well over $500 billion.

Meanwhile, many American banks found themselves holding near-worthless loans they had unwisely foisted upon economically developing countries, especially in Latin America. In 1984 it took federal assistance to save Continental Illinois Bank from a catastrophic failure. More banks and savings institutions were folding than at any time since the Great Depression of the 1930s. A wave of mergers, acquisitions, and leveraged buyouts washed over Wall Street, leaving many brokers and traders mega-rich and many companies saddled with mega-debt. A cold spasm of fear struck the money markets on **Black Monday**, October 19, 1987, when the leading stock-market index plunged 508 points—the largest one-day decline in history to that point. This crash, said *Newsweek* magazine, heralded "the final collapse of the money culture . . . , the death knell of the 1980s." But as Mark Twain famously commented about his own obituary, this announcement proved premature.

Hoping to cash in on these ethical and economic anxieties, a pack of Democrats—dubbed the "Seven Dwarfs" by derisive Republicans—chased after their party's 1988 presidential nomination. The handsome and charismatic Democratic front-runner, former Colorado senator Gary Hart, was forced to drop out of the race in May 1987 after allegations of extramarital affairs. Charismatic civil rights activist Jesse Jackson, a rousing speechmaker and champion of a "rainbow coalition" of racial minorities and poor people, advanced further than any Black major-party candidate before him. But the Democratic nomination in the end went to the coolly cerebral governor of Massachusetts, Michael Dukakis, whose star had risen thanks to the "Massachusetts Miracle" of his industrial state's technology-fueled economic comeback. Republicans nominated Reagan's vice president, George H. W. Bush, who ran largely on the Reagan record of tax cuts, strong defense policies, toughness on crime, opposition to abortion, and economic expansion (refer to Image 36.11). Dukakis started strong but ultimately made little headway exploiting the ethical and economic sore spots in the GOP record, and he came across to television viewers as almost supernaturally devoid of emotion. The Bush campaign gleefully skewered Dukakis as an elitist, soft-on-crime liberal. One notorious anti-Dukakis ad featured the mug shot of a Black felon—his skin artificially darkened—who had committed further crimes after Dukakis granted him parole. On Election Day, the voters gave the Massachusetts governor just 41,016,429 votes to 47,946,422 for Bush. The Electoral College count was a lopsided 111 to 426.

AP Images

Image 36.11 George H. W. Bush (1924–2018) Campaigning, October 1988 Bush soundly defeated Democratic candidate Michael Dukakis in the November 1988 election.

36-12 George H. W. Bush and the End of the Cold War

George Herbert Walker Bush was born with a silver ladle in his mouth. His father had served as a U.S. senator from Connecticut, and young George had enjoyed a first-rate education at Yale. After service in World War II, he had amassed a modest fortune of his own in the oil business in Texas. His deepest commitment, however, was to public service; he left the business world to serve briefly as a congressman and then held various posts in several Republican administrations, including emissary to China, ambassador to the United Nations, director of the Central Intelligence Agency, and vice president. He capped this long political career when he was inaugurated president in January 1989, promising to work for "a kinder, gentler America."

In the first months of the Bush administration, the communist world commanded the planet's fascinated attention. Everywhere in the communist bloc, it seemed, the season of democracy had arrived.

In China, even as economic development began to accelerate to astonishing rates as Maoism loosened its grip in favor of "capitalism with Chinese characteristics," hundreds of thousands of prodemocracy demonstrators thronged through Beijing's Tiananmen Square in the spring of 1989. They proudly flourished a thirty-foot-high "Goddess of Democracy," modeled on the Statue of Liberty, as a symbol of their aspirations. But in June of that year, China's aging and autocratic rulers brutally crushed the prodemocracy movement (refer to Image 36.12). Tanks rolled over the crowds, and machine-gunners killed hundreds of protesters. World opinion roundly condemned the bloody suppression of the prodemocracy demonstrators. President Bush joined in the criticism. Yet despite angry demands in Congress for punitive restrictions on trade with China, the president insisted on maintaining normal relations with Beijing.

Stunning changes also shook Eastern Europe. Long oppressed by puppet regimes propped up by Soviet guns, the region was revolutionized in just a few startling months in 1989. The Solidarity movement in Poland led the way when it toppled Poland's communist government in August. With dizzying speed, enormous demonstrations filled the streets and communist regimes collapsed in Hungary, Czechoslovakia, East Germany, and even brutally repressive Romania (refer to Image 36.13). In early November 1989, a half million East Berliners massed in protest against closed borders and the hated Berlin Wall, symbol of the division of Germany and all of Europe into two armed and hostile camps.

Five days later, on November 9, the wall came down, heralding the imminent end of the forty-five-year-long Cold War. As East German officials opened long-closed gates, jubilant young people danced atop the wall and physically pushed its sections down. Chunks of the wall's concrete became instant collectors' items—gray souvenirs of a grim episode in Europe's history. With the approval of the victorious Allied powers of World War II, the two Germanys, divided since 1945, were at last reunited in October 1990.

Most startling of all were the changes that rolled over the heartland of world communism, the Soviet Union itself. Mikhail Gorbachev's policies of glasnost and perestroika had set in motion a groundswell that surged out of his control. Old-guard hard-liners, in a last-gasp effort to preserve the tottering communist system, attempted to dislodge Gorbachev with a military

Image 36.12 Tiananmen Square, Beijing, China, June 1989 The Chinese communist state mobilized all its forces against students demonstrating for a more democratic China. The identity and fate of the "Tank Man" in this photograph remain a mystery.

Emanuel Tanjala/Alamy Stock Photo

Image 36.13 Fallen Idols
Romanians toppled these statues of Vladimir Lenin (background) and Romania's first Communist Prime Minister Petru Groza (foreground) in 1990, symbolically marking the collapse of the Marxist dream that had polarized the world for much of the twentieth century.

coup in August 1991. With the support of Boris Yeltsin, president of the Russian Republic (one of the several republics that composed the Union of Soviet Socialist Republics, or USSR), Gorbachev foiled the plotters. But his days were numbered. In December 1991, Gorbachev resigned as Soviet president. He had become a leader without a country as the Soviet Union dissolved into its component parts, some fifteen republics loosely confederated in the Commonwealth of Independent States (CIS), with Russia the most powerful state and Yeltsin the dominant leader. To varying degrees, all the new governments in the CIS repudiated communism and embraced democratic reforms and a free-market economy (refer to Map 36.3).

These developments astonished the experts who had long preached that the steely vise-grip of communist rule could never be peacefully broken. Yet suddenly and almost miraculously, the totalitarian tonnage of communist oppression had been rendered politically weightless. Most spectacularly, the demise of the Soviet Union wrote a definitive finish to the Cold War era (refer to "Contending Voices: Who Ended the Cold War?" p. 982). More than four decades of nail-biting tension between two nuclear superpowers, the Soviet Union and the United States, evaporated when the USSR dismantled itself. With the Soviet Union swept into the dustbin of history and communism apparently headed for extinction, Bush spoke hopefully of a "new world order," where democracy would reign and diplomacy would supersede weaponry. Some observers even saw in these developments "the end of history," in the sense that liberal democracy, victorious in its two-century-long struggle against foes on the left and right, had no ideological battles left to fight.

Exultant Americans joked that the USSR had become the "USS *were*." But the disintegration of the Soviet Union was no laughing matter. Rankling questions remained. For example, who would honor arms-control agreements with the United States? Which of the successor states of the former Soviet Union would take command of the formidable Soviet nuclear arsenal? A partial answer was provided in early 1993, when President Bush, in one of his last official acts, signed the START II accord with Russian president Boris Yeltsin, committing both powers to reduce their long-range nuclear arsenals by two-thirds within ten years.

Throughout the former Soviet empire, waves of nationalistic fervor and long-suppressed ethnic and racial hatreds rolled across the vast land as communism's roots were wrenched out. A particularly nasty conflict erupted in the Russian Caucasus in 1991, when the Chechen minority tried to declare its independence from Russia, prompting President Yeltsin to send in Russian troops. Ethnic warfare flared in other disintegrating communist countries as well, notably in misery-drenched Yugoslavia, racked by vicious "ethnic cleansing" campaigns against various minorities. An estimated 100,000 died during a shattering three-year civil war in the former Yugoslav republic of Bosnia. Eighty percent of the dead were Bosnian Muslims, including

Map 36.3 The End of the Cold War Changed the Map of Europe

8,000 men and boys massacred in 1995 in the town of Srebrenica—the largest mass killing in Europe since the Holocaust.

The end of the Cold War proved a mixed blessing for the United States. For nearly half a century, the containment of Soviet communism had been the paramount goal of U.S. foreign policy. Indeed, the Cold War era had been the only lengthy period in American history when the United States had consistently pursued an internationalist foreign policy. With the Soviet threat now canceled, would the United States revert to its traditional isolationism? What principles would guide American diplomacy now that "anticommunism" had lost its relevance?

The Soviet-American rivalry, with its demands for high levels of military preparedness, had also deeply shaped and even invigorated the U.S. economy. Huge economic sectors such as aerospace were heavily sustained by military contracts. The economic cost of beating swords into plowshares became painfully apparent in 1991 when the Pentagon announced the closing of thirty-four military bases and canceled a $52 billion order for a navy attack plane. More closings and cancellations followed. Communities that had been drenched with Pentagon dollars now nearly dried up, especially in hard-hit southern California, where scores of defense plants shut their doors and

In his state of the union address on January 31, 1990, President George H. W. Bush (1924–2018) declared,

"The events of the year just ended, the revolution of '89, have been a chain reaction, changes so striking that it marks the beginning of a new era in the world's affairs."

Just six months later, speaking at Stanford University, Soviet president Mikhail Gorbachev (1931–2022) said,

"The Cold War is now behind us. Let us not wrangle over who won it. It is in the common interest of our two countries and nations not to fight this trend toward cooperation, but rather to promote it."

Contending Voices

Who Ended the Cold War?

In a roundtable discussion in 1995, former British prime minister Margaret Thatcher (1925–2013) and former Soviet leader Mikhail Gorbachev (1931–2022), among others, debated the question of how and why the Cold War came to an end. Margaret Thatcher suggested that SDI was the cause:

"There was one vital factor in the ending of the Cold War: Ronald Reagan's decision to go ahead with the Strategic Defense Initiative. . . . That was a completely different level of defense. It required enormous computer capability, which he knew at the time the Soviet Union could not match. And that was the end of the arms race as we had been pursuing it."

Mikhail Gorbachev disagreed:

"If you accept that reforms in the Soviet Union started under the pressure from the West, particularly as a result of the implementation of SDI, that would distort the real picture and offer the wrong lesson for the future. . . . [T]he first impulses for reform were in the Soviet Union itself, in our society which could no longer tolerate the lack of freedom, where no one could speak out or choose their own party or select their own creed. . . . This was the decisive factor, not SDI."

Consider This:

Who should get the lion's share of the credit for ending the Cold War: U.S. President Ronald Reagan or Soviet leader Mikhail Gorbachev? Was it U.S. strategy or internal developments within the Soviet Union that principally drove events?

unemployment soared. The problems of weaning the U.S. economy from its decades of dependence on defense spending tempered the euphoria of Americans as they welcomed the Cold War's long-awaited finale.

Elsewhere in the world, democracy marched triumphantly forward. In South Africa, the iron-fisted system of racial apartheid began to crumble after decades of heroic Black resistance. Ostracized by other nations and corporations, the white regime recognized the impossibility of preserving its racist rule. In 1990, it freed resistance leader Nelson Mandela, who had served twenty-seven years in prison for conspiring to overthrow the government. Four years later, Mandela was elected South Africa's president. In Central America, war-ravaged El Salvador at last found peace, and free elections in Nicaragua in February 1990 removed the leftist Sandinistas from power.

36-13 The Persian Gulf Crisis

Sadly, the end of the Cold War did not mean the end of all wars. President Bush flexed the United States' still-intimidating military muscles in tiny Panama in December 1989, when he sent airborne troops to capture dictator and drug lord Manuel Noriega.

Still more ominous events in the summer of 1990 severely tested Bush's dream of a democratic and peaceful new world order. On August 2, Saddam Hussein, the brutal and ambitious ruler of Iraq, sent his armies to overrun Kuwait, a tiny, oil-rich desert sheikdom on Iraq's southern frontier. Financially exhausted by its eight-year war with Iran, which had ended in a stalemate in 1988, Iraq needed Kuwait's oil to pay its huge war bills. Saddam's larger design was ironfisted control over the entire Persian Gulf region. With his hand thus firmly clutching the world's economic jugular vein, he dreamed of dictating the terms of oil supplies to the industrial nations, and perhaps of totally extinguishing the Arabs' enemy, Israel.

Ironically, the United States and its allies had helped supply Saddam with the tools of aggression. He was widely known to be a thug and assassin who intimidated his underlings by showing them the bodies of his executed adversaries hanging on meat hooks. But in the 1980s, American enmity for Islamic-fundamentalist Iran was intense, and Saddam was at war with Iran. Assuming that "the enemy of my enemy is my friend," American policymakers helped build Saddam's military machine into a formidable force.

On August 2, 1990, Saddam's army roared into Kuwait. The speed and audacity of the invasion was stunning, but the world responded just as swiftly. The United Nations Security Council unanimously condemned the invasion on August 3 and demanded the immediate and unconditional withdrawal of Iraq's troops. When an economic embargo failed to squeeze the Iraqis into compliance by November, the Security Council delivered an ultimatum to Saddam to leave Kuwait by January 15, 1991, or UN forces would "use all necessary means" to expel his troops.

In a logistical operation of astonishing complexity, the United States spearheaded a massive international military deployment on the sandy Arabian Peninsula. As the January 15 deadline approached, some 539,000 U.S. soldiers, sailors, and pilots—many of them women and all of them members of the new, post-Vietnam, all-volunteer American military—swarmed into the Persian Gulf region. They were joined by nearly 270,000 troops, pilots, and sailors from twenty-eight other countries in the coalition opposed to Iraq. When all diplomatic efforts to resolve the crisis failed, the U.S. Congress voted on January 12 to approve the use of force. On January 16, the time bomb of war ticked down to zero.

The United States and its UN allies unleashed a hellish air attack against Iraq. For thirty-seven days, warplanes pummeled targets in occupied Kuwait and in Iraq itself, in an awesome display of high-technology, precision-targeting modern warfare. Iraq responded to this pounding by launching several dozen "Scud" short-range ballistic missiles against military and civilian targets in Saudi Arabia as well as Israel. These missile attacks claimed several lives but did no significant military damage.

On February 23 the dreaded and long-awaited land war began. Dubbed **Operation Desert Storm**, it lasted only four days—the "hundred-hour war" (refer to Map 36.4). With lightning speed the UN forces penetrated deep into Iraq, outflanking the occupying forces in Kuwait and blocking the enemy's ability either to retreat or to reinforce. Allied casualties were amazingly light, whereas much of Iraq's remaining fighting force was quickly destroyed or captured (refer to Image 36.14). On February 27, Saddam accepted a cease-fire, and Kuwait was liberated.

Map 36.4 **Operation Desert Storm: The Ground War, February 23–27, 1991**

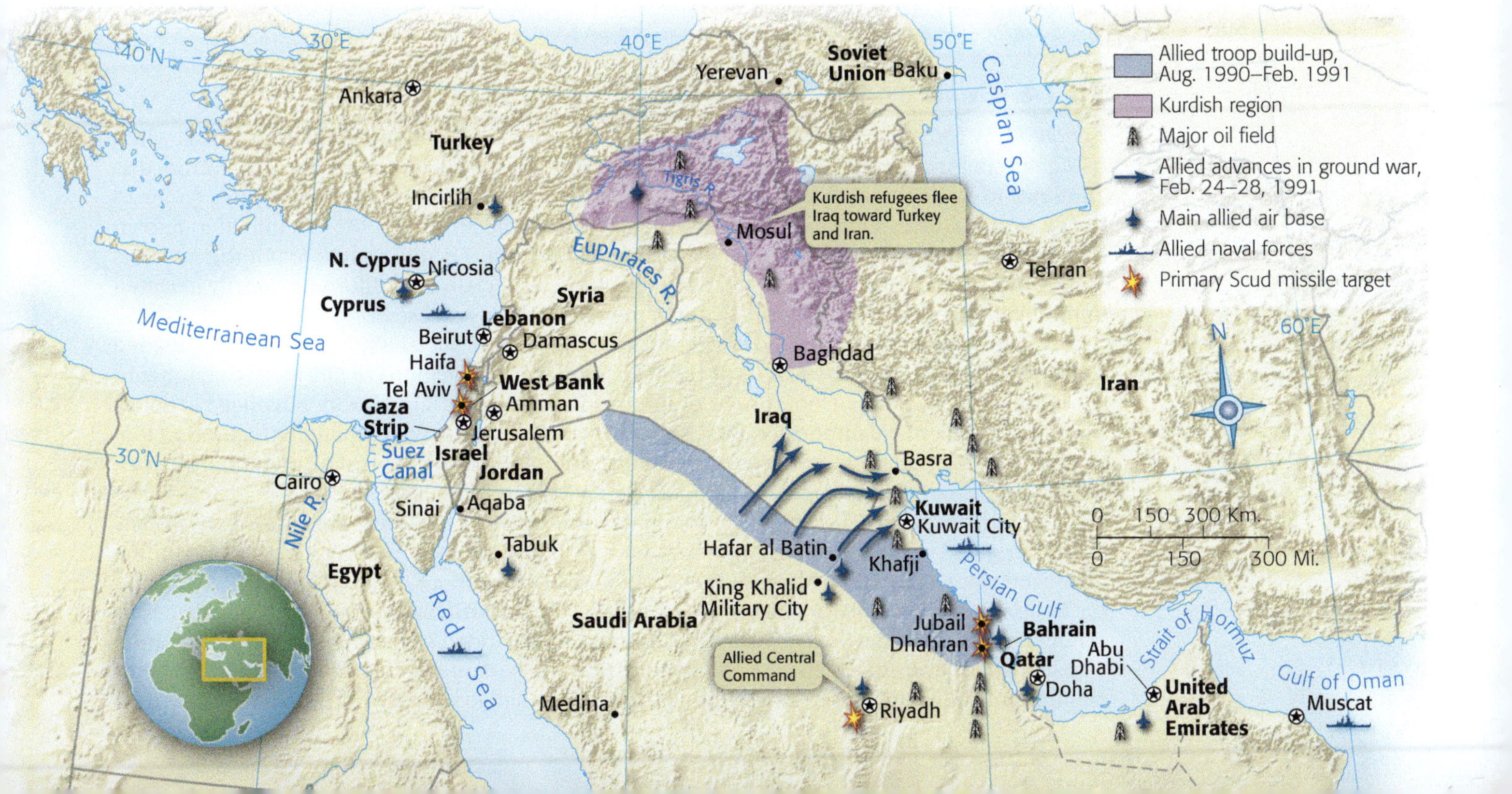

Image 36.14 **The Highway of Death** The allied coalition wreaked gruesome destruction on Iraqi forces fleeing back to Iraq after their defeat in Kuwait in 1991.

Most Americans cheered the war's rapid and enormously successful conclusion. Many people echoed President Bush's sentiments when he declared, "By God, we've kicked the Vietnam Syndrome once and for all!" But when the smoke cleared, Saddam Hussein had survived to menace the world another day. America and its allies had agreed to the liberation of Kuwait, but Bush, fearing that a full assault on Baghdad would cost many lives and much international support, stopped well short of overthrowing the tyrant Saddam. The perpetually troubled Middle East knew scarcely less trouble after Desert Storm had ceased to thunder, and the United States, for better or worse, found itself even more deeply ensnared in the region's web of mortal hatreds and intractable conflicts.

36-14 Bush on the Home Front

George H. W. Bush partly redeemed his pledge to work for a "kinder, gentler America" when he signed the **Americans with Disabilities Act (ADA)** in 1990, a landmark law prohibiting discrimination against the 43 million U.S. citizens with physical or mental disabilities (refer to Image 36.15). The president also signed a major water projects bill in 1992 that aimed to reform the distribution of subsidized federal water in the arid West. The bill sought to put the interests of the environment on a par with those of agriculture, especially in California's heavily irrigated Central Valley, and to provide more water to the West's thirsty cities.

The new president continued to aggravate the explosive "social issues" that had so divided Americans throughout the 1980s, especially the nettlesome questions of affirmative action and abortion. In 1990, Bush's Department of Education challenged the legality of college scholarships targeted for racial minorities. Bush repeatedly threatened to veto civil rights legislation that would make it easier for employees to prove discrimination in hiring and promotion practices, though he grudgingly accepted a watered-down civil rights bill in 1991.

Most provocatively, in 1991 Bush nominated for the Supreme Court the conservative Black jurist Clarence Thomas. Thomas's nomination was loudly opposed by liberal groups, including organized labor, the National Association for the Advancement of Colored People (NAACP), and the National Organization for Women (NOW). Reflecting irreconcilable divisions over affirmative action and abortion, the Senate Judiciary Committee concluded its hearings on the nomination with a divided seven-to-seven vote and forwarded the matter to the full Senate without a recommendation. Then, just days before the Senate was scheduled to vote in early October 1991, a press

Hum Images/Alamy Stock Photo

Image 36.15 **President George H. W. Bush Signs the Americans with Disabilities Act on the South Lawn of the White House, July 26, 1990**

leak revealed that Anita Hill, a law professor at the University of Oklahoma, had accused Thomas of sexual harassment. The Senate Judiciary Committee was forced to reopen its hearings.

For days a prurient American public sat glued to their television sets as Hill graphically detailed her charges of sexual improprieties and Thomas angrily responded. In the end, by a fifty-two-to-forty-eight vote, the Senate confirmed Thomas as the second Black person ever to sit on the supreme bench (Thurgood Marshall was the first). Many hailed Hill as a heroine for focusing the nation's attention on issues of sexual harassment, while Thomas maintained that her widely publicized allegations amounted to "a high-tech lynching for uppity Blacks who in any way deign to think for themselves, to do for themselves." Many women were enraged by the all-male judiciary committee's behavior in the Thomas hearings, led by Delaware's Joe Biden, who later would serve as vice president and president. A "gender gap" widened between the two political parties, as pro-choice women grew increasingly cool toward the strong anti-abortion stand of the Republicans.

Still more damaging to President Bush's political health was the economy, which sputtered and stalled almost from the outset of his administration. By 1992, the unemployment rate exceeded 7 percent. It approached 10 percent in the key state of California, ravaged by defense cutbacks. The federal budget deficit continued to mushroom cancerously, topping $250 billion in each of Bush's years as president. In a desperate attempt to stop the hemorrhage of red ink, Bush agreed in 1990 to a budget increase that included $133 billion in new taxes.

Bush's 1990 tax and budget package added up to a political catastrophe. In his 1988 presidential campaign, Bush had belligerently declared, "Read my lips—no new taxes." Now he had flagrantly broken that campaign promise. The budget deal deeply divided his own party. Georgia representative Newt Gingrich had worked with Bush on the tax package. Now he broke abruptly with the White House and led an ascendant congressional wing of hard-line conservatives in open revolt. A majority of congressional Republicans voted against their own president's hard-fought agreement. After Bush's debacle, a blanket opposition to tax increases of any kind became an entrenched part of mainstream Republican orthodoxy, setting the stage for bitter political conflicts in the years ahead.

Varying Viewpoints

What Are the Sources of Modern Conservatism?

Ronald Reagan's election surprised many historians. Reflecting a liberal outlook common among academics, they were long accustomed to understanding American history as an inexorable unfolding of liberal principles, including the quests for economic equality, social justice, and activist government. Even the "New Left" revisionists of the 1960s who decried liberalism's deficiencies assumed that the deepest currents of American history flowed leftward. Whether liberal or revisionist, most scholars writing in the first three post–World War II decades dismissed conservatism as an obsolete creed and psychoanalyzed its adherents as fringe wackos—paranoid McCarthyites or racist demagogues who, in the words of the liberal critic Lionel Trilling, trafficked only in "irritable mental gestures which seem to resemble ideas." Such an outlook was conspicuous in books such as Daniel Bell's *The Radical Right* (1963) and Richard Hofstadter's *The Paranoid Style in American Politics* (1965).

Yet what flowed out of the turbulent decade of the 1960s was not a strengthened liberalism but a revived conservatism. Ronald Reagan's huge political success, followed by continued conservative strength into the following century, compelled a deep reexamination of the tradition of American conservatism and the sources of its modern resurgence.

Historians such as Leo Ribuffo and Alan Brinkley have argued that characters from earlier eras once dismissed as irrational crackpots—including religious Fundamentalists, the 1920s incarnation of the Klu Klux Klan, and depression-era figures like Huey Long and Father Charles Coughlin—articulated values deeply rooted and widely shared in American culture. They offered a vision of free individuals, minimal government, and autonomous local communities that harked back to many of the themes of "civic republicanism" in the era of young nationhood.

But modern conservatism, however deep its roots, was also a product of the recent past. Many students of the postwar right emphasize the theme of "backlash." They explain conservatism's rise as a populist reaction among working-class white people to the racial, cultural, and economic disruptions of the 1960s. Thomas and Mary Edsall (*Chain Reaction*, 1991) outlined how politicians turned anger over race-based governmental activism into a mandate for tax cutting and government shrinking. Ron Formisano (*Boston Against Busing*, 1991) put class tensions and economic insecurity at the heart of his explanation for the battle over busing in the 1960s and 1970s. Others looked to white Southerners' response to the civil rights revolution and the rise of leaders like George Wallace to account for the eventual political realignment of the region and the nation.

Other historians have challenged the "backlash" proponents' depiction of conservative politics in reactionary terms. They treat the rise of the right as a longer-term project carried out by conscious, strategically minded activists, intellectuals, and institution-builders. Kim Phillips-Fein (*Invisible Hands*, 2006) outlined the role of conservative businessmen in forging an antilabor, promarket ideology during the postwar decades, while Rick Perlstein (*Before the Storm*, 2001) and Jonathan Schoenwald (*A Time for Choosing*, 2001) unearthed the deliberate conservative movement-making of the 1960s. Lisa McGirr's bottom-up account (*Suburban Warriors*, 2001) focused on the middle-class communities that incubated the activists of the Goldwater campaign. Nicole Hemmer's *Messengers of the Right* (2016) traced the role of conservative media in fueling the movement from the 1940s forward. Alongside McGirr, scholars like Thomas Sugrue, Matthew Lassiter, Lizabeth Cohen, and Kevin Kruse have shown how the suburban landscape built by New Deal– and Cold War–era subsidization of homeownership and highway construction ironically served to foster a politics hostile to taxes and government redistribution.

Even as they trace the roots of the conservative revival to the early postwar years, scholars have also come to see the 1970s as a "*Pivotal Decade*," to use the title of one recent study (Judith Stein, 2010). As work by Bruce Schulman, Jefferson Cowie, and Laura Kalman has detailed, 1970s activists took advantage of stagflation, Watergate-era disillusionment with government, and foreign-policy frustrations to mobilize new constituencies on behalf of conservatism. Their agenda combined antigovernment, free-market economic policies with a new emphasis on hot-button "social issues" related to gender, reproductive policy, and cultural production. Scholars like Donald Critchlow, Darren Dochuk, Bethany Moreton, and Daniel K. Williams have shown that this latter cultural element of the conservative mobilization had origins dating to the midcentury, even as the 1960s and 1970s movements for sexual liberation, legal abortion, and women's and gay rights provided immediate impetus for activism.

The flowering of scholarship on American conservatism has demonstrated, above all, that the forces that propelled Reagan to power in 1980 were neither aberrant nor fleeting. Rather, they reflected outlooks deeply rooted in American culture and drew strength from core developments in the American state and economy in the modern era. The election of Donald Trump to the presidency in 2016 demonstrated anew the persisting power and consequence of those developments.

Chapter Summary

Reagan led Republicans to sweeping victories in 1980 and 1984 over divided and demoralized Democrats. Riding a conservative national tide, Reagan pushed his "supply-side" economic program of reduced social welfare programs and lower taxes, along with massive military expenditures. These policies brought economic recovery and lower inflation but also led to high interest rates and dramatically bigger federal budget deficits.

Reagan revived the Cold War confrontation with the Soviet Union and engaged the United States in assertive military support for anti-leftist forces in Latin America and elsewhere. The ratcheting up of military spending, along with the attempted reforms led by new Soviet Communist leader Mikhail Gorbachev, contributed to a series of successful arms limitation talks that reduced Cold War tensions in the mid-1980s. The Iran-Contra affair tarnished Reagan's international legacy, but his economic policies succeeded in curbing further growth of the welfare state.

Religious conservatives of the New Right assumed growing influence on American politics, borrowing many tactics from the sixties New Left. The Supreme Court under Reagan and his successor, George H. W. Bush, became increasingly conservative, as the Court partially overturned previous rulings related to a women's right to choose and affirmative action.

In foreign affairs, Bush promoted a "new world order" after the collapse of communism in Eastern Europe and the Soviet Union in 1989–1991. But Saddam Hussein's invasion of Kuwait brought war to the Middle East. With America as the only remaining superpower, Bush led an international coalition to victory in the Persian Gulf War, but the Middle East remained a dangerous tinderbox despite new efforts to resolve the Israel-Arab conflict. Bush supported the Americans with Disabilities Act, but also pushed conservative social issues and nominated the controversial Clarence Thomas to the Supreme Court. Economic recession and Bush's tax increase created a growing conservative opposition within the Republican Party, led by Congressman Newt Gingrich.

Key Terms

- Proposition 13 (967)
- boll weevils (967)
- Tax Reform Act (968)
- supply-side economics (968)
- Volcker Shock (968)
- Strategic Defense Initiative (SDI) (969)
- Sandinistas (970)
- Contras (971)
- glasnost (972)
- perestroika (972)
- Intermediate-Range Nuclear Forces (INF) Treaty (972)
- Iran-Contra affair (973)
- Moral Majority (974)
- identity politics (976)
- Black Monday (978)
- Operation Desert Storm (983)
- Americans with Disabilities Act (ADA) (984)

People to Know

- Ronald Reagan
- Margaret Thatcher
- Thomas "Tip" O'Neill
- Mikhail Gorbachev
- Saddam Hussein
- Geraldine Ferraro
- Jesse Jackson
- Jerry Falwell
- Sandra Day O'Connor
- George H. W. Bush
- Boris Yeltsin
- Nelson Mandela
- Manuel Noriega
- Clarence Thomas
- Anita Hill

Chronology

1980	• Reagan defeats Carter for presidency	
1981	• Iran releases American hostages • "Reaganomics" spending and tax cuts passed	• Solidarity movement in Poland • O'Connor appointed to Supreme Court (first woman justice)
1981–1991	• United States aids anti-leftist forces in Central America	
1982	• Recession hits U.S. economy • Israel invades Lebanon	
1983	• Reagan announces SDI plan (Star Wars) • U.S. marines killed in Beirut, Lebanon	• U.S. invasion of Grenada
1984	• Reagan defeats Mondale for presidency • Soviet Union boycotts Summer Olympics in Los Angeles	
1985	• Gorbachev comes to power in Soviet Union, announces glasnost and perestroika • First Reagan-Gorbachev summit meeting in Geneva	
1986	• Reagan administration backs Aquino in Philippines • Iran-Contra affair revealed	• Second Reagan-Gorbachev summit meeting in Reykjavik, Iceland
1987	• Stock market plunges 508 points • Third Reagan-Gorbachev summit meeting in Washington, DC; INF treaty signed	
1988	• Fourth Reagan-Gorbachev summit meeting in Moscow • Bush defeats Dukakis for presidency	• World Health Organization declares first annual World AIDS Day
1989	• Chinese government suppresses prodemocracy demonstrators in Tiananmen Square • *Webster v. Reproductive Health Services*	• Eastern European countries oust communist governments • Berlin Wall torn down
1990	• Iraq invades Kuwait • East and West Germany unite	• Americans with Disabilities Act (ADA)
1991	• Persian Gulf War • Thomas appointed to Supreme Court • Gorbachev survives coup attempt, resigns as Soviet president	• Soviet Union dissolves; republics form Commonwealth of Independent States
1992	• Twenty-Seventh Amendment (prohibiting congressional pay raises from taking effect until an election seats a new session of Congress) ratified	• *Planned Parenthood v. Casey*

To Learn More

Jennifer Brier, *Infectious Ideas: U.S. Political Responses to the AIDS Crisis* (2009)

Donald T. Critchlow, *The Conservative Ascendancy: How the Republican Right Rose to Power in Modern America* (2nd ed., 2011)

Darren Dochuk, *From Bible Belt to Sunbelt: Plain-Folk Religion, Grassroots Politics, and the Rise of Evangelical Conservatism* (2010)

Irving Kristol, *Reflections of a Neoconservative: Looking Back, Looking Ahead* (1983)

Kevin Kruse, *One Nation Under God: How Corporate American Invented Christian America* (2015)

Walter LaFeber, *Inevitable Revolutions: The United States in Central America* (2nd ed., 1993)

Melvyn Leffler, *For the Soul of Mankind: The United States, the Soviet Union, and the Cold War* (2007)

Bethany Moreton, *To Serve God and Wal-Mart: The Making of Christian Free Enterprise* (2010)

Daniel T. Rodgers, *Age of Fracture* (2011)

Jonathan M. Schoenwald, *A Time for Choosing: The Rise of Modern American Conservatism* (2001)

Elizabeth Tandy Shermer, *Sunbelt Capitalism: Phoenix and the Transformation of American Politics* (2015)

David A. Stockman, *The Triumph of Politics: Why the Reagan Revolution Failed* (1986)

Gil Troy, *Morning in America: How Ronald Reagan Invented the 1980s* (2007)

Sean Wilentz, *The Age of Reagan: A History, 1974–2008* (2008)

Daniel K. Williams, *God's Own Party: The Making of the Christian Right* (2010)

Chapter 37

America Enters the Twenty-First Century: 1992–2008

Now history has granted to us a moment of even greater opportunity, when old dangers are ebbing and old walls are crumbling, future generations will judge us, every one of us, above all, by what we make of this magic moment.

William J. Clinton, Speech to the United Nations, September 17, 1993

Chapter Outline

- The election of Bill Clinton, 1992
- A false start for reform
- The Republican congressional takeover, 1994
- Clinton's comeback, 1996
- Racial progress and perils
- Global trade and the 1990s high-technology boom
- The feminist revolution
- Post–Cold War foreign policy
- The Clinton impeachment trial
- The controversial 2000 election
- Postmodern culture at the turn of the century
- George W. Bush as president
- The terrorist attacks of September 11, 2001
- Wars in Iraq and Afghanistan
- Bush's bruising second term
- The election of Barack Obama, 2008

The collapse of the Soviet Union and the democratization of its client regimes in Eastern Europe ended the four-decade-old Cold War and left the United States the world's sole remaining superpower. Americans welcomed these changes but seemed unsure how to exercise their unprecedented economic and military might in this new international scenario. The culture wars that had started in the 1960s fed ferociously partisan political squabbles that distracted the nation from the urgent task of clearly defining its role in the age of globalization.

Amidst this deepening partisan polarization, a sustained ten-year economic expansion powerfully shaped American society and politics in the 1990s. The second half of the decade was a particularly giddy boom era, as an exuberant financial sector and ascendant information technology firms helped to propel the economy to near-full employment—and the federal budget to record surpluses. But the good times were not to last.

In 2000, George W. Bush won a contested presidential election that left the nation bitterly divided, until the spectacular terrorist attacks on September 11, 2001, briefly elicited a resurgent sense of national unity. Bush responded to the 9/11 attacks by invading the terrorist haven of Afghanistan. Then, controversially claiming that Iraq possessed **weapons of mass destruction (WMD)** and had ties to terrorists, Bush proceeded to invade Iraq as well. After the failure to find WMD and with over four thousand American battle deaths in the "forever" Iraq War, a war-weary country made history by electing the first Black president, Barack Obama.

Focus Questions

1. What caused the growing polarization between the conservative Republican movement led by Congressman Newt Gingrich and the centrist "new Democrat" Clinton administration?
2. Why did the issues of race and women's rights remain controversial in the 1990s, even as many Black people and women made substantial social and economic gains?

Contending Voices: Welfare Reform Divides the Democrats
Makers of America: Many People, Many Voices
Examining the Evidence: The National Security Strategy, 2002
Thinking Globally: America Through Foreign Eyes: Hyperpower or Hapless Power?

3. How did the United States attempt to develop a new framework for international trade and foreign policy in the post–Cold War era?
4. What was the impact of the September 11 terrorist attacks on the United States? Why did the post-9/11 wars in Afghanistan and Iraq become so protracted and divisive?
5. How did George W. Bush's troubled second term and the "Great Recession" of 2008 contribute to the election of the upstart Barack Obama?

37-1 "New Democrats" Race for the White House

As the last decade of the twentieth century opened, a slumbering economy, a widening gender gap, and a rising anti-incumbent spirit spelled opportunity for Democrats, frozen out of the White House for all but four years since 1968. Governor William Jefferson ("Bill") Clinton of Arkansas weathered blistering accusations of womanizing and draft evasion to emerge as the Democratic party's 1992 standard-bearer. He selected a fellow baby boomer and Southerner, Senator Albert ("Al") Gore of Tennessee, as his vice-presidential running mate (refer to Image 37.1).

Clinton and Gore were part of a younger generation of centrist "New Democrats," ready to reclaim the White House after the party's long political exile. They had formed the **Democratic Leadership Council (DLC)** during the Reagan years to point the party away from its traditional antibusiness, dovish, champion-of-the-underdog reputation and toward pro-growth, strong defense, and anti-crime policies. The DLC's ascendance as a business-friendly faction within the country's center-left party underscored the degree to which market-oriented thinking had come to dominate American politics in the last decades of the twentieth century. In the 1960s, President Lyndon Johnson had declared a government-financed "war on poverty." In the 1990s, Clinton vowed to end welfare dependence and "give a hand up, not a hand out."

Yet the racial inequities that had set cities afire in the 1960s still afflicted the nation, as became searingly apparent in Los Angeles in May 1992. What became known as the **Los Angeles rebellion** erupted when a mostly white jury exonerated white police officers who had been videotaped savagely beating a Black motorist with weighted batons and tasers. Predominantly Black neighborhoods in South Central Los Angeles exploded in rage. Six days of arson and looting laid waste entire city blocks, and left sixty-three people dead, most of them Black or Latino.

Image 37.1 The Clintons Campaign, 1992 Bill and Hillary Clinton wave to a crowd of forty thousand in St. Louis on the last stop of the Clinton-Gore campaign's cross-country bus tour. The Arkansas governor was a famously tireless and effective campaigner, and he and his wife, an attorney and political force in her own right, would prove to be a powerful team in national politics for decades to come.

Tim Clary/AFP/Getty Images

In nearby “Koreatown,” Asian-American shopkeepers saw their stores ransacked and their property go up in flames. President George H. W. Bush, declaring he was “stunned” by the verdict, sent thousands of riot-trained federal troops to Los Angeles to restore order.

Republicans gathered in Houston a few months later to nominate Bush for re-election. He claimed credit for ending the Cold War and trumpeted his leadership role in the Persian Gulf War. Declaring their support for “family values,” his supporters also hoped to wring one more win out of the social issues that had brought three consecutive Republican presidential victories. Condemnations of feminists, gay and lesbian people, and welfare recipients rained down from the podium at the GOP convention, pleasing religious conservatives even while alienating more moderate voters. Yet the most formidable hurdle facing Bush’s reelection campaign was the languishing economy.

> In 1990 the African American intellectual Shelby Steele (b. 1946) declared in his provocative book, *The Content of Our Character*,
>
> “What is needed now is a new spirit of pragmatism in racial matters where blacks are seen simply as American citizens who deserve complete fairness and in some cases developmental assistance, but in no case special entitlements based on color. We need deracinated social policies that attack poverty rather than black poverty and that instill those values that make for self-reliance.”

A growing number of Americans in 1992 belonged to neither major party but identified as independent “swing” voters seeking candidates who promised something other than politics as usual. Many were taken with independent presidential candidate H. Ross Perot, a bantamweight, jug-eared Texas billionaire who decried federal deficits and the hollowing out of American manufacturing. Perot’s colorful presence probably accounted for the record turnout on election day, when some 100 million voters—55 percent of those eligible—went to the polls. But he drew voters almost equally from the left and the right, won zero Electoral College votes, and had little effect on the ultimate outcome.

The final tally gave Clinton 44,909,889 popular votes and 370 votes in the Electoral College. He was the first baby boomer to ascend to the White House, a distinction reflecting the electoral profile of the population, 70 percent of whom had been born after World War II. Bush polled some 37,104,545 popular votes and 168 electoral votes. Perot’s 19,742,267 popular votes were nearly 20 percent of the total and represented the strongest showing for an independent or third-party candidate since Theodore Roosevelt ran on the Bull Moose ticket in 1912 (refer to Map 37.1; also “27-17 The ‘Bull Moose’ Campaign of 1912,” pp. 699–700).

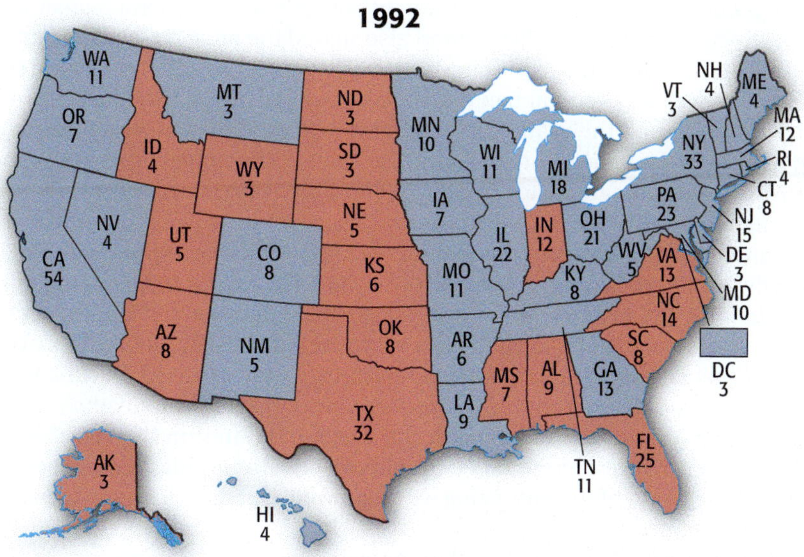

Candidate (Party)	Electoral Vote		Popular Vote	
Clinton (Democrat)	370	68.8%	44,908,233	43.0%
Bush (Republican)	168	31.2%	39,102,282	37.4%
Perot (Independent)	0	0.0%	19,741,048	18.9%

Map 37.1 Presidential Election of 1992 (with electoral vote by state)

Democrats also racked up clear majorities in both houses of Congress, which seated near-record numbers of first-term members, including thirty-nine who were Black, nineteen Latino, seven Asian American, one Native American, and forty-eight women, six of them in the Senate. Promising "an administration that looks like America," Clinton appointed more women and racial minorities to Cabinet and subcabinet positions than any president before him. The new president also seized the opportunity in 1993 to nominate Ruth Bader Ginsburg to the Supreme Court, where she joined Sandra Day O'Connor to make a pair of women justices.

37-2 A False Start for Reform

Badly overestimating his electoral mandate for liberal reform, the young president made a series of costly blunders upon entering the White House. He stirred a hornet's nest of controversy by advocating an end to the ban on gay and lesbian service-members in the armed forces. Confronted with fierce conservative opposition, the president finally settled for a "**Don't Ask, Don't Tell**" policy that quietly accepted gay and lesbian service-members without officially acknowledging their presence in the military. The half measure was a bitter betrayal for gay people who had eagerly backed Clinton's run. (Congress finally repealed the discriminatory policy in 2010.)

Even more damaging to Clinton's political standing, and to his hopes for lasting liberal achievement, was the fiasco of his attempt to reform the nation's health-care system. In a dramatic but personally and politically risky move, the president appointed his wife, nationally prominent lawyer and children's advocate Hillary Rodham Clinton, as the director of a task force charged with redesigning the medical-service industry. The task force deliberated for months behind closed doors, eventually producing a stupefyingly complicated 1,300-page plan presented to Congress in October 1993. Despite the considerable public support for some kind of health-care reform, the first lady became a ripe Republican target for her role in hatching this legislative turkey. But she eventually rehabilitated herself sufficiently to win election as a U.S. senator from New York in 2000—the first time a president's spouse was ever to hold elective office—and to become her party's presidential nominee in 2016.

President Clinton had better luck with a deficit-reduction bill that passed Congress in 1993—though on a party-line vote with no Republican support, a harbinger of the acrid partisan divide that came to dominate the political scene over the following decades. The bill's spending cuts and tax increases on the wealthy combined with the increasingly buoyant economy to help shrink federal deficits. By 1998, such policies briefly seemed to have caged the ravenous deficit monster, as Congress argued over the unfamiliar question of how to manage federal budget *surpluses*.

After a protracted struggle, in 1994 Clinton also signed the most far-reaching anti-crime bill ever passed by Congress. It included funding for 100,000 new police officers and the construction of more prisons, as well as a federal ban on some assault weapons. (The ban expired in 2004.) Several states also stiffened their law enforcement practices, until America's incarceration rate became the highest in the world. Yet the country's violent crime rate began to decline substantially after 1995—a striking nationwide trend that continued into the new century.

Despite such legislative landmarks during Clinton's first two years in office, a sour antigovernment mood persisted, helping propel increasingly violent extremism. A huge explosion destroyed a federal office building in Oklahoma City in 1995, taking 168 lives, including 19 children in the building's day-care center (refer to Image 37.2). It was the deadliest act of domestic terrorism in the nation's history, launched in retribution for a 1993 standoff in Waco, Texas, between federal agents and a Fundamentalist sect known as the Branch Davidians. That showdown had ended in the destruction of the sect's compound and the deaths of many Branch Davidians, including women and children. Events like the **Oklahoma City bombing** brought to light a lurid and secretive underground of paramilitary private "militias" composed of alienated citizens armed to the teeth, often embracing white supremacist doctrines and ultrasuspicious of all government.

Even many law-abiding citizens shared to some degree in the antigovernment attitudes that drove the militia members to murderous extremes. Thanks largely to the disillusioning agony of the Vietnam War and the naked cynicism of Richard Nixon in the Watergate scandal, the confidence in government that had come naturally to the generation that had licked the Great Depression and won the Second World War was in short supply by century's end. Reflecting that pervasive disenchantment with politics and politicians, several states passed term-limit laws for elected officials, although the Supreme Court ruled in 1995 that the restrictions did not apply to federal officeholders.

AP Images/David Glass

Image 37.2 Bombing of Federal Building in Oklahoma City, 1995 A truck bomb killed 168 people in this federal office building in the worst act of terrorism in the United States until September 11, 2001. Convicted in 2001 for the attack, antigovernment militant Timothy McVeigh became the first person executed by the federal government in nearly forty years.

37-3 Another Republican Revolution

Clinton's failed initiatives and the widespread antigovernment sentiment afforded Republicans a golden opportunity in 1994, and they seized it aggressively. Led by outspoken Georgia representative Newt Gingrich, Republicans offered voters a **Contract with America** that promised an all-out assault on government spending and radical reductions in welfare programs (refer to Image 37.3). Their campaign successfully turned the 1994 congressional elections into a partisan referendum on Clinton's record, and a conservative tornado roared across the land. Republicans picked up eleven new governorships, eight seats in the Senate, and fifty-three seats in the House (where Gingrich became Speaker), giving them control of both chambers of the federal Congress for the first time in forty years. The 1994 midterms wiped out the remaining conservative congressional Democrats, concentrated in the South, who had served as Ronald Reagan's "boll-weevil" supporters a decade earlier. Their replacement by newly empowered Southern Republicans accelerated the ideological and geographical sorting of the two parties, which in turn only intensified the political combat in Washington.

But if President Clinton had overplayed his mandate for liberal reform in 1993, Republicans proceeded to overplay their mandate for conservative retrenchment after taking over the Congress in 1995. Many Americans gradually came to feel that the Gingrich Republicans were bending their conservative bow too far, especially when the new speaker advocated provocative ideas like sending the children of welfare families to orphanages. In a tense confrontation between the Democratic president and the Republican Congress over proposed cuts to Medicare and education spending, the federal government was

The Contract with America, signed by all but two incumbent House Republicans and every non-incumbent Republican candidate, was introduced six weeks prior to the 1994 midterm elections. The document lent a degree of national unity to the Republicans' campaign message that was rare for congressional elections in the United States. As its preamble intoned:

"[I]n this era of official evasion and posturing, we offer instead a detailed agenda for national renewal, a written commitment with no fine print.

This year's election offers the chance, after four decades of one-party control, to bring to the House a new majority that will transform the way Congress works. That historic change would be the end of government that is too big, too intrusive, and too easy with the public's money. It can be the beginning of a Congress that respects the values and shares the faith of the American family."

Image 37.3 **Gingrich Rallies His Troops** Then–House minority whip Newt Gingrich addresses Republican congressional candidates in September 1994, two months before they won new majorities in both the House and Senate.

AP Images/John Duricka

forced to shut down for a total of twenty-seven days at the end of 1995 and the beginning of 1996. Congress and the president eventually agreed to a budget package, but not before the shutdown bred a backlash against the GOP that eventually helped President Clinton rebound from his political near-death experience.

In 1996, the new Congress achieved a major conservative victory when it compelled a reluctant Clinton to sign a sweeping welfare reform bill (refer to "Contending Voices: Welfare Reform Divides the Democrats," p. 996). Gone was the Aid to Families with Dependent Children (AFDC) program in place since the New Deal, replaced by time-limited grants called **Temporary Assistance for Needy Families**. Following through on Clinton's campaign vow to move poor people from "welfare to work," the program required able-bodied recipients to find employment. Liberal Democrats and advocates for the poor howled in protest, but Clinton had reelection on his mind. His acceptance of the welfare reform package was part of his shrewd political strategy of accommodating the electorate's conservative mood by moving further to the right.

Though Clinton signed the welfare reform bill into law, he explicitly denounced provisions that tightly restricted welfare benefits for legal and illegal immigrants alike. These measures, together with other GOP congressional initiatives like the Illegal Immigration Reform and Immigrant Responsibility Act of 1996 and a proposal to declare English the country's "official language," reflected a rising tide of anti-immigrant sentiment as the numbers of newcomers soared after the immigration reforms of the 1960s (refer to "The Presence of the Past: Immigration—Legal, Illegal, and Otherwise," pp. 913–915). The Southwest, from Texas to California, felt the impact of new immigration especially sharply as Mexican migrants swelled the region's already large Latino population. Mexico was the country of birth for 18 percent of the new arrivals in 1996, the most of any nation. By 2021, 60 percent of U.S. Latinos identified as being of Mexican origin (refer to Figure 37.1). Yet while immigrants from Latin America were the main targets of anti-immigrant scorn, nearly 34 percent of those who arrived in the United States in 1996 came from Asia (refer to Figure 37.2). Anti-immigrant sentiment galvanized many voters, but it also risked alienating the country's rapidly growing foreign-born population (refer to Figure 37.3).

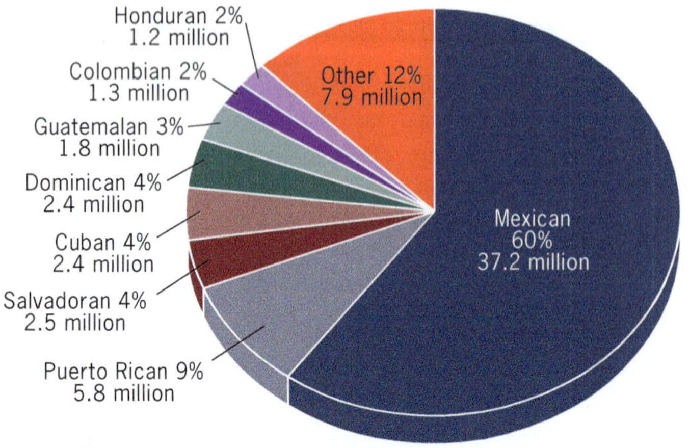

Figure 37.1 **Sources of Latino Population in the United States, 2021**

Source: U.S. Census Bureau

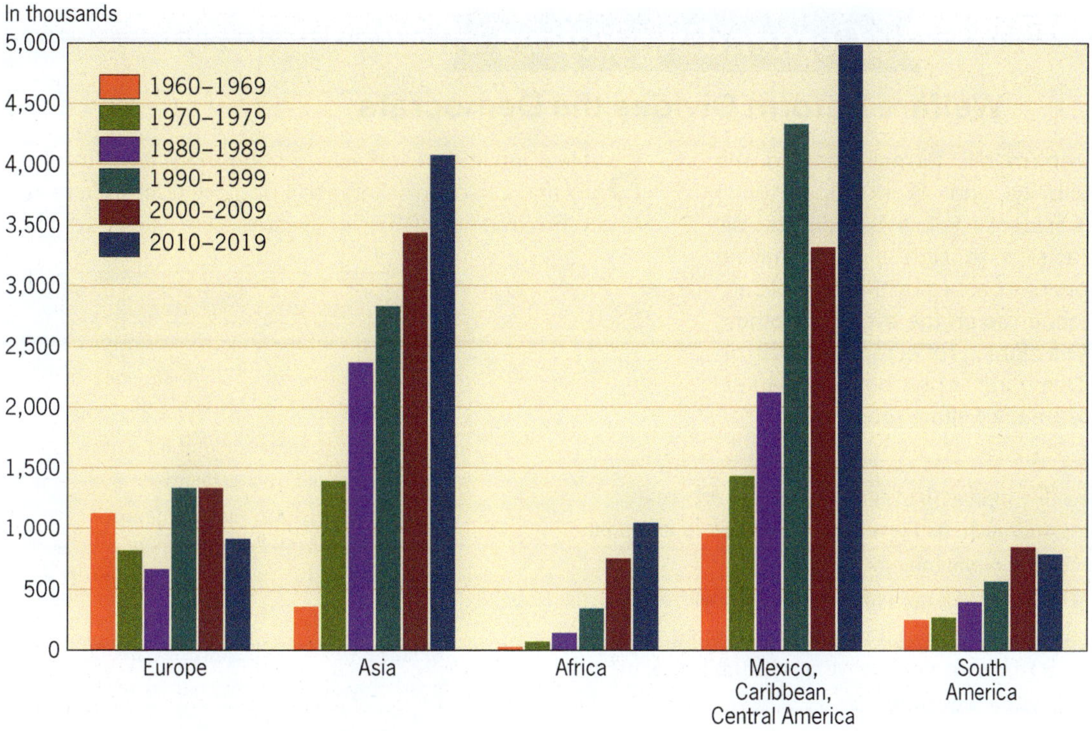

Figure 37.2 Recent Legal Immigration by Area of Origin, 1961–2019

Source: U.S. Census Bureau; Department of Homeland Security, Yearbook of Immigration Statistics 2022 https://www.dhs.gov/ohss/topics/immigration/yearbook/2022

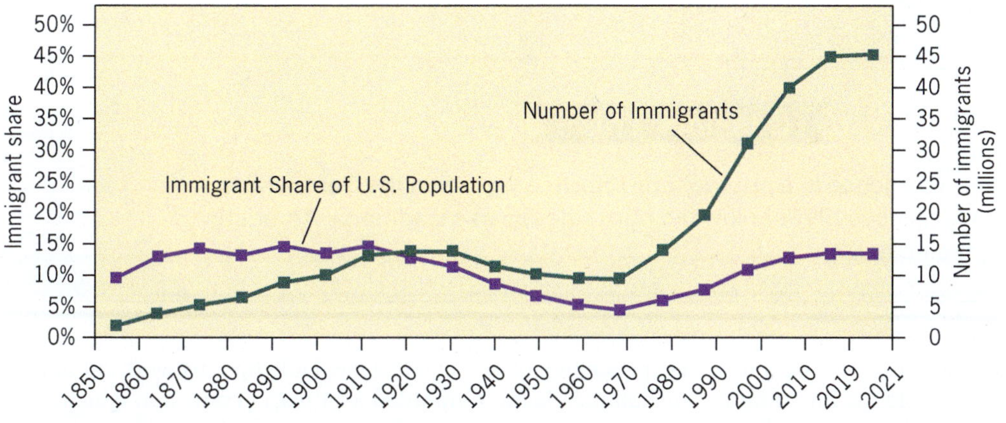

Figure 37.3 A Nation of Immigrants, Once Again. This chart depicts the size and share of the foreign-born population in the United States over time. While the number of immigrants in the modern era was greater—reflecting the much larger population of the United States—the percentage of foreign-born persons in the population was approximately same as the earlier peak of mass immigration at the turn of the twentieth century.

Source: Migration Policy Institute (MPI) tabulation of data from U.S. Census Bureau, 2010–2021 American Community Surveys (ACS), and 1970, 1990, and 2000 decennial census. All other data are from Campbell J. Gibson and Emily Lennon, "Historical Census Statistics on the Foreign-Born Population of the United States: 1850 to 1990" (Working Paper no. 29, U.S. Census Bureau, Washington, DC, 1999).

37-4 Clinton Comes Back

As the 1996 election approached, the Republicans chose Senate Majority Leader Robert Dole as their presidential candidate. A decorated World War II veteran from Kansas, Dole had suffered battlefield injuries that withered his right arm and made him a fierce advocate for the Americans with Disabilities Act in 1990 (refer to "36-14 Bush on the Home Front," pp. 984–985). Dole's dry wit and deadpan demeanor did not play well on the campaign trail. And with a rebounding

Contending Voices

Welfare Reform Divides the Democrats

The 1996 welfare reform bill, formally named the Personal Responsibility and Work Opportunity Act, badly split the president's fellow Democrats. Bill Clinton's (b. 1946) decision to sign it—after having vetoed two previous versions passed by the Republican-controlled Congress—occurred on the eve of a looming reelection campaign. His signing reflected his determination to be a "New Democrat" open both to market-based reform and scaled-back welfare programs.

Fellow New Democrats like Connecticut senator Joseph Lieberman (b. 1942) supported this approach. As Lieberman explained in an op-ed endorsing the Senate version of the bill:

"Welfare makes it feasible for a man to father a child without worrying about being a parent. It makes it possible for a young woman (too often a teen-age girl) to have a child, move away from home, get an apartment and survive—without working. . . .

The Senate bill provides hope for poor Americans, and for taxpayers who want a Government that spends their money wisely and better reflects American values of work, family, and responsibility. . . . Most important, it would put an end to the policy of something for nothing, of penalizing work and marriage, and isolating the poor from the economic and cultural mainstream."

But leading liberal activists, among them the Clinton ally and Children's Defense Fund president Marian Wright Edelman (b. 1937), lambasted Clinton:

"President Clinton's signature on pending 'welfare reform' legislation makes a mockery of his pledge not to hurt children. It will leave a moral blot on his presidency and on our nation that will never be forgotten.

This legislation is the biggest betrayal of children and the poor since the Children's Defense Fund began. It takes no political courage to stand up to two-month-old babies or to play election year games of political chicken at preschoolers' expense."

Consider This:

What explains the emergence of a pro-welfare-reform wing within the Democratic party during the prosperous 1990s? How did both sides invoke traditional American values in making their cases?

domestic economy and a relatively peaceful global scene in 1996, Dole had his work cut out for him to topple the incumbent. The general election unfolded as a bland contest in which both major contenders again fought for moderate "swing voters." The attention they paid to one such swing constituency—middle-class female suburbanites—helped introduce the term "soccer moms" into the national political lexicon. Targeting soccer moms made excellent political sense because for the first time a majority of Americans now lived in the suburbs (refer to Figure 37.4).

Buoyed by a healthy economy and by his artful trimming to the conservative wind, Clinton breezed to an easy victory in November 1996, with 47,401,898 popular votes to Dole's 39,198,482. (Dole's victory in eight Southern states, however, underscored how the "solid South," once a safe Democratic stronghold, had by century's end largely become Republican territory.) H. Ross Perot returned as a third-party spoiler but failed to enchant a more complacent electorate. He ran a sorry third, picking up less than half the votes he had garnered in 1992. Clinton won 379 electoral votes, Dole only 159. But Republicans remained in control of Congress.

As Clinton began his second term—the first Democratic president since Franklin Delano Roosevelt to be reelected—the heady promises of far-reaching reform with which he had entered the White House four years earlier were no longer heard. Still facing Republican majorities in both houses of Congress, he proposed only modest legislative goals, even though soaring tax revenues generated by the prosperous economy produced in 1998 a balanced federal budget for the first time in three decades.

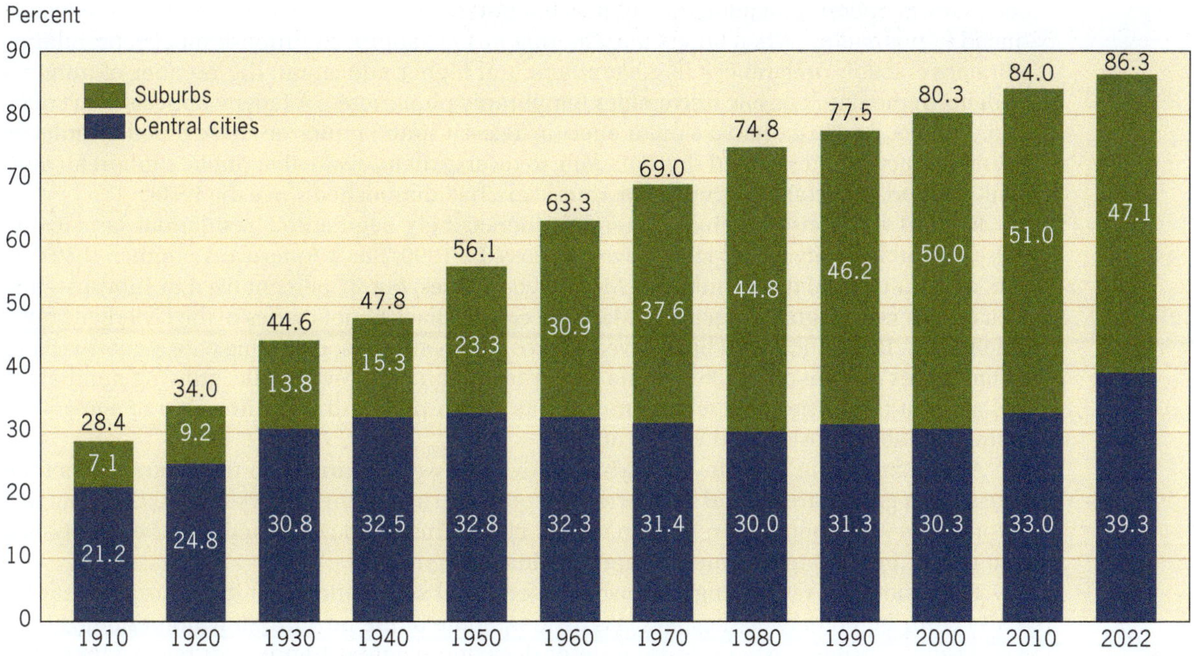

Figure 37.4 Percent of Total Population Living in Metropolitan Areas and in Their Central Cities and Suburbs, 1910–2022

Sources: U.S. Census Bureau, Decennial Census of Population, 1910 to 2000, compiled in *Demographic Trends in the 20th Century,* no. 2002; Population Reference Bureau, *Reports on America: First Results from the 2010 Census*; https://www.census.gov/data/tables/time-series/demo/popest/2020s-total-cities-and-towns.html

37-5 Changing Landscapes of Race and Class

As a politician, Clinton had for decades demonstrated an easy and authentic personal connection with the Black community (refer to Image 37.4). He had made racial diversity a priority in his political and judicial appointments. Yet he also had frustrated minority constituencies with artful ploys to put Republicans on the defensive and claim the political middle ground. In his second term, Clinton warmly embraced the landmark welfare reform bill of 1996 that he had initially

Tim Sloan/TIM SLOAN/Getty Images

Image 37.4 Bill Clinton and Black America Clinton's rapport with Black voters stemmed from both personality and policy substance. Here the president shakes hands with locals in Clarksdale, Mississippi, while promoting his administration's initiative to spur investment in low-income communities through tax credits.

been slow to endorse. Juggling the political hot potato of affirmative action, Clinton pledged to "mend it, not end it." When voters in California in 1996 approved Proposition 209, prohibiting affirmative-action preferences in government and higher education, the number of minority students in the state's public universities temporarily plummeted. A federal appeals court decision, *Hopwood v. Texas*, had a similar effect in Texas. Clinton criticized these broad assaults on affirmative action but stopped short of trying to reverse them, aware that public support for affirmative action, especially among white Americans, had diminished since the 1970s.

Beyond affirmative action, America's increasingly segmented residential landscapes reflected stubborn divides of race as well as class. By 1990, Black Americans numbered 30 million, or 12 percent of the population. Most lived in cities, but 27 percent lived in suburbs—and their numbers were growing rapidly. Many successful Black beneficiaries of the civil rights revolution of the 1950s and 1960s had moved to prosperous suburbs, including elite, majority-Black communities outside cities like Atlanta and Washington, DC. Meanwhile, growing numbers of less-affluent minorities and recent immigrants began populating the first ring of aging—but more affordable—post–World War II suburbs.

At the same time, middle-class white Americans were returning to the central cities their parents and grandparents had left during the postwar rush to the suburbs. By 2002, 21 percent of America's white population lived in central cities. This trend continued into the twenty-first century, further reshaping America's metropolitan geography.

The residential reshuffling somewhat eased racial segregation, but it did not eliminate it. It also contributed to ever-sharper class divides. Some of the new urban white residents were well-to-do gentrifiers, whose restoration of decaying neighborhoods sent real estate values soaring and many minority residents packing to catastrophically deepening concentrations of poverty in the inner cores of old industrial cities, or deteriorating inner-ring suburbs. Cities like New York, Boston, and San Francisco boomed with "new economy" industries of finance, information technology, and biotech economies. Others like Detroit and Cleveland struggled to replace once-thriving basic industries. Rural America further emptied of population as a younger generation migrated to cities for college and careers. The resulting residential map of the United States was a checkerboard of racial differences as well as vivid contrasts in prosperity and poverty.

Yet Black American lives in the 1990s reflected the many gains that came in the wake of the civil rights victories of the 1950s and 1960s. The number of Black elected officials, for example, rose above the nine thousand mark in 2000, including more than three dozen members of Congress and the mayors of several large cities. Black media figures like Oprah Winfrey, actors like Denzel Washington, and sports stars like Michael Jordan were among the decade's biggest—and wealthiest—celebrities. The number of Black American adults with a college or advanced graduate degree more than doubled between 1980 and 2000, to nearly 17 percent (compared with 28 percent of white adults). But the educational gap between Black and white students chronically persisted, reflecting enduring neighborhood segregation and sharply unequal funding for public schools. The political assault against affirmative action in California and elsewhere compounded the obstacles to advancement for many young minorities. In 2022, 28 percent of Black adults and 21 percent of Latino adults over age twenty-five had a bachelor's degree or higher, compared to 42 percent of white adults and 59 percent of Asian Americans.

Racial disparities in the 1990s also manifested themselves politically. Black Americans proved themselves among Bill Clinton's most fiercely loyal supporters, giving him 83 percent of their total vote in the 1992 election and 84 percent in 1996. Latino voters were not far behind, at 61 percent for Clinton in 1992 and 72 percent in 1996. As Republicans rallied around the "family values" of white evangelicals and pushed for curbs on immigration, most Black and many Latino voters became a larger and more consequential component of the Democratic electoral base.

37-6 The Dot-Com Boom

Computers were at the heart of the productivity gains and economic growth of the late twentieth century. The old industrial age had given way to a new "information age" in which the storing, organizing, and processing of data were the most important industries of all. By 1992, the desktop software company Microsoft had overtaken IBM as the nation's most valuable technology company. Over 90 percent of the desktop computers on the planet used Microsoft software, a market dominance so overwhelming that the U.S. Department of Justice brought an antitrust suit against the company in 1998.* California rivals of the Seattle-based Microsoft gloomily referred to it as "The Death Star."

However, a new crop of technology companies emerged in the 1990s that would one day exceed IBM and Microsoft in wealth and technological dominance. These firms enabled searching, buying, and selling on the newly commercialized internet and were colloquially referred to as "dot-com" companies (as their online addresses usually ended in ".com"). The internet, established in 1969 as a Pentagon-funded research network for academic computer scientists, had been opened up to the world in the early 1990s.

As lawmakers reformed the nation's telecommunications laws to accommodate the rapidly growing internet, technologist and free-speech advocate John Perry Barlow made "A Declaration of the Independence of Cyberspace" in early 1996:

"Governments of the Industrial World, you weary giants of flesh and steel, I come from Cyberspace, the new home of Mind. On behalf of the future, I ask you of the past to leave us alone. You are not welcome among us. You have no sovereignty where we gather."

Technophilic national leaders like House Speaker Newt Gingrich and Vice President Al Gore (the "geek-in-chief") embraced the potential of the internet to transform communication and education, and amid the decade's partisan warfare both Republicans and Democrats championed measures to bring American homes, workplaces, and schools online. Excitement about the internet's wide-open possibilities prompted the first major reform of the nation's telecommunications infrastructure since the 1930s. Bill Clinton signed the landmark **Telecommunications Act of 1996** at the Library of Congress, using an electronic pen.

Regulatory reform further accelerated the dot-com boom already underway in Northern California's Silicon Valley (refer to "32-17 The Boost of Big Science," pp. 865–866), where many of the era's most successful enterprises emerged. Americans "surfed the 'net" with the help of online directories like Yahoo! and bought and sold goods on electronic retail sites like eBay and Amazon.com. Millions opened electronic mail (email) accounts hosted by America Online (AOL). On Wall Street, investor enthusiasm drove dot-com stock prices sky-high—even though most of the firms had yet to make a profit (refer to Image 37.5). However frothy the market, surging use of these services showed that this was no passing fad. By 2000, more than 52 percent of adults and 40 percent of children used the internet.

Bloomberg/Getty Images

Image 37.5 "Dot-Coms" Come to Wall Street Amazon CEO Jeff Bezos rings the bell to open the day's trading on the NASDAQ stock exchange. The decade of the 1990s witnessed the longest continuous economic expansion in American history as well as a particularly exuberant boom on Wall Street. The rise of internet firms drove the stock market to even greater heights, though the so-called dot-com bubble would pop early in the new century.

*The court ruled in 2000 that Microsoft had indeed engaged in monopolistic behavior, but that judgment was partially overturned on appeal. Rather than being forced to break up, Microsoft agreed to modify some of its business practices.

37-7 Globalization and Its Discontents

Clinton's major political advantage in his second term was the roaring economy, which by 2000 had sustained the longest period of growth in American history. The Federal Reserve Board's low-interest, easy-money policies and the explosive growth of dot-com companies helped fuel the boom. Unemployment crept down to 4 percent, sending employers scrambling madly for workers, while inflationary pressure remained remarkably low.

In this heady boom-time atmosphere, the Clinton administration and congressional Republicans found common ground in pursuing fateful new efforts at financial deregulation. These included loosening federal regulation of trading in the new-fangled instruments called **over-the-counter (OTC) derivatives**—financial contracts that could be bought outside of regulated exchanges—as well as repealing the depression-era Glass-Steagall Act that had barred commercial banks from dealing in securities. Later, amidst the financial tumult of the 2000s, the deregulatory wave of the go-go 1990s came in for heavy retrospective criticism.

Clinton encountered more immediate and potent criticism over his trade policy. He had burnished his centrist, pro-business credentials by signing the **North American Free Trade Agreement (NAFTA)** in 1993, creating a free-trade zone encompassing Mexico, Canada, and the United States. In doing so, he bucked the opposition of protectionists in his own party, especially labor leaders fearful of losing jobs to low-wage Mexican workers (refer to Image 37.6).

Clinton took another step in 1994 toward a global free-trade system when he vigorously promoted the creation of the **World Trade Organization (WTO)**, the successor to the General Agreement on Tariffs and Trade (GATT) and a cherished goal of free-trade advocates since the end of the Second World War. Simmering discontent over trade policy boiled over in 1999 when Clinton hosted the meeting of the WTO in Seattle. The city's streets teemed with protesters railing against what they viewed as the human and environmental costs of economic globalization.

Despite such protests, Clinton vigorously pursued trade-expansion initiatives throughout his presidency. As the rapidly emerging powerhouse of China loomed ever larger, Clinton soft-pedaled his earlier criticism of the Beijing regime on human rights issues and instead began seeking improved trade relations with that robustly industrializing country and potential market bonanza. Clinton crusaded for a controversial China trade bill, passed by Congress in May 2000, that made the Asian giant a full-fledged trading partner of the United States. China joined the WTO in December 2001.

In the wake of these new partnerships came an explosion in U.S.-China trade that benefited consumers and corporations alike. It also contributed to further hemorrhaging of American jobs as efficient transoceanic shipping and abundant factory labor made China the new workshop of the world (refer to Figure 37.5).

Image 37.6 Protesting NAFTA, 1997 These members of the Teamsters Union feared the loss of their jobs to low-wage, non-union Mexican drivers. Two decades later, opposition to NAFTA helped elect Donald J. Trump to the presidency.

Richard Ellis/Alamy Stock Photo

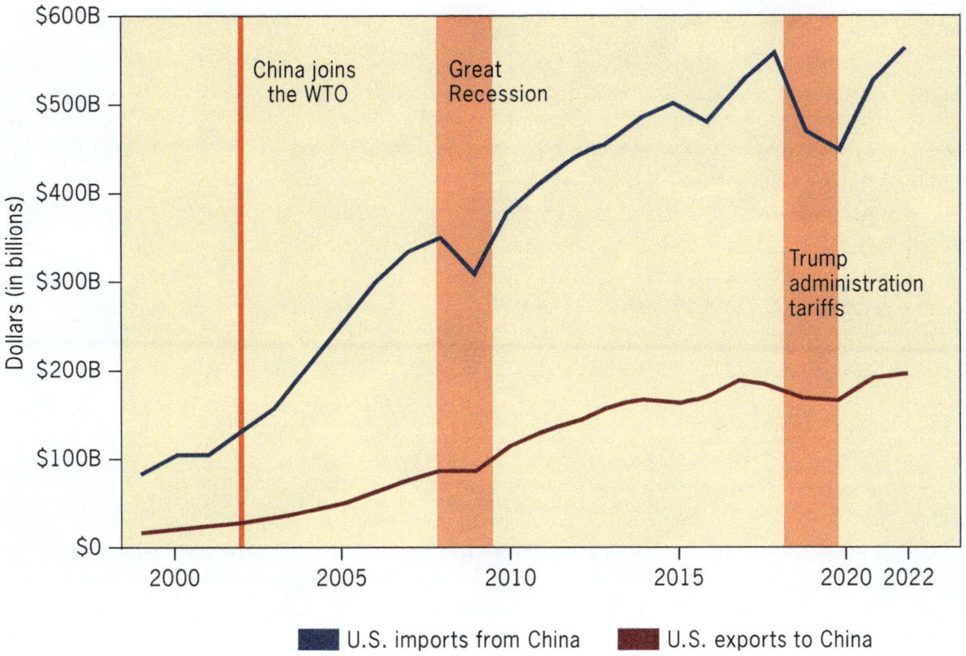

Figure 37.5 U.S.-China Trade in Goods and Services Trade between China and the United States spiked after China joined the World Trade Organization in 2001. An influx of Chinese-made products lowered costs for American consumers but further challenged U.S.-based manufacturers and raised national security concerns. Despite Trump-era tariffs that aimed to narrow the trade gap, by 2022 the value of U.S. imports from China ($564 billion) was nearly three times the value of U.S. exports to China ($197 billion).

Source: U.S. Bureau of Economic Analysis.

Communications technology helped to accelerate the pace of globalization. It was already clear that these global communication networks aided capitalism, as corporations could now instantaneously girdle the planet with transactions of prodigious scope and serpentine complexity. Japanese bankers might sell wheat contracts in Chicago while simultaneously using their profits to buy oil shipments from the Persian Gulf offered by a broker in Amsterdam. Networked people from all corners of the planet were rapidly forming an electronic global village. Technologists and politicians alike heralded the arrival of a new era, where traditional geographic, social, and political boundaries could be vaulted with a single keystroke.

But the very speed and efficiency of the new communications tools threatened to wipe out entire occupational categories, and even ways of life. Postal carriers, travel agents, store clerks, bank tellers, stockbrokers, and all kinds of other workers whose business it was to mediate between product and client were in danger of becoming casualties of the computer. White-collar jobs in financial services and high-tech engineering, once securely anchored in places like Chicago, Los Angeles, and New York, could now be "outsourced" to countries such as Ireland and India, where low- wage, English-speaking employees could keep a company's global circuits firing twenty-four hours a day (refer to Image 37.7). The related forces of the computer revolution and economic globalization defined the central opportunities and challenges for American workers as the new millennium dawned. Clinton and other world leaders assured their citizens that the phenomenal growth of the internet would open up autocracies like China and spread democracy around the world. That hope ultimately would prove illusory.

37-8 The Modern American Family

While the political mood of the 1990s shifted right, the great economic and social changes of the late twentieth century brought greater social tolerance, visibility, and opportunity for working women, gay and lesbian people, and new configurations of family life.

At the start of the twentieth century, women had made up about 20 percent of all waged workers. Over the next five decades, they increased their presence in the labor force at a fairly steady rate, with a temporary upward spurt during World War II. Beginning in the 1950s, women's entry into the workplace accelerated dramatically, boosted further by federal

In March 2000, Bill Clinton expressed confidence that new technologies would enable free speech and the spread of democracy in China:

"In the new century, liberty will spread by cell phone and cable modem. . . . Now there's no question China has been trying to crack down on the Internet. Good luck! That's sort of like trying to nail jello to the wall."

Image 37.7 Outsourcing Jobs to India The commercialization of the internet in the 1990s allowed less-industrialized countries like India to attract Western employers seeking lower labor costs. India's educated and English-speaking workforce made it particularly suitable for international call centers and computer programming.

nondiscrimination laws and feminist activism in the 1960s and beyond (refer to "35-5 Feminism Takes Center Stage," pp. 950–952). By the 1990s, nearly half of all waged workers were women, and the majority of working-age women held jobs outside the home. (That proportion only continued to grow in the next century. Refer to Figure 37.6.)

Most notable was the upsurge in employment among middle-class mothers of young children. In 1950, nearly 90 percent of mothers with children under the age of six did not work for pay. But half a century later, a majority of women with children as young as one-year old were wage earners (refer to Table 37.1; compare to Figure 33.1, p. 878). This shift reflected vastly enlarged job opportunities for college-educated women, especially in white-collar professions. In 1970, only 10 percent of physicians and 3 percent of lawyers were women. By 2022, the percentages of women in those two fields had risen to 37 percent and 38 percent, respectively (refer to Image 37.8).

Figure 37.6 Women in the Workforce Globally, 2021

Sources: The World Bank, *World Development Indicators*, International Labour Organization, ILOSTAT database.

Yet the rise of the working mother also reflected household economic realities in an era of outsourced manufacturing, declining union membership, and rising housing and health-care costs. The shrinking social safety net during the 1980s and 1990s placed further burdens on working families. Because most men did not compensate fully for women's entry into work by taking on a commensurate share of tasks such as cooking, childcare, and housework, working mothers were in a classic double bind, expected to bring home the bacon and cook it, too.

Women remained far more likely than men to interrupt their careers to bear and raise children or take part-time jobs that could accommodate school schedules and chronic daycare shortages. Partly as a result, women continued to receive lower wages compared with men doing the same full-time work, making 84 cents on the dollar compared to men as late as 2021. Meanwhile, corporate jobs became ever more demanding, with a growing percentage of college-educated professionals working in excess of 40 hours per week. The result of this perfect storm was that women in business remained woefully underrepresented in key executive roles, especially at the very top. As late as 2023, only 53 of the CEOs of Fortune 500 companies were women.

Table 37.1 Working Women: Labor Force Participation Rates for Wives and Mothers, 1950–2015*

Year	Married	Married, with Children	Married, with Children Ages 6–17	Married, with Children under Age 6
1950	23.8%	NA	28.3%	11.9%
1960	30.5	NA	37.0	18.6
1970	40.8	37.7	49.2	30.3
1980	50.1	54.1	61.7	45.1
1990	58.2	66.3	73.6	58.9
2000	62.0	70.6	77.2	62.8
2007	61.6	69.3	76.2	61.5
2015	58.5	67.6	72.4	61.3

*Percentage of women in each specific category in the labor force.

Source: *Statistical Abstract of the United States,* Bureau of Labor Statistics, relevant years.

A

NB/Alamy Stock Photo

B

AP Images/ELISE AMENDOLA

C

Wally McNamee/Corbis Historical/Getty Images

Image 37.8A, B, and C **A New World for Women** Revolutionary changes in the economy and in social values opened new career opportunities for women in the late twentieth century. In the decades after formerly all-male universities began opening their doors to women, myriad "firsts" in female leadership proliferated in areas ranging from law to business to government. In 1990, Lieutenant Commander Darlene M. Iskra became the first woman to command a U.S. Navy vessel (refer to 37.8A). Women athletes also came into their own in the wake of the feminist revolution. Venus and Serena Williams enthralled the tennis world as individual champions and as a doubles team beginning in the late 1990s (refer to 37.8B). In 1997, Madeleine Albright became the first woman ever to serve as the U.S. Secretary of State (refer to 37.8C).

Recognizing the new realities of the modern American household, Congress passed and President Clinton signed the Family and Medical Leave Act of 1993, which mandated job protection for working fathers as well as mothers who needed to take time off from work for family-related reasons. Over the course of the decade, some employers began providing paternity leave in recognition of the shared obligations of the two-worker household. Such leave was usually unpaid, however. In 2023, the United States was one of only six countries worldwide that failed to mandate paid parental leave.

Women's visibility in the waged workforce—and the relative economic autonomy it brought them—further inflamed the cultural conflicts over "family values." The old ideal of a family with two parents, only one of whom worked, was now far less "typical." Families of married, heterosexual couples with their own children made up 40 percent of American households in 1970, but only 24 percent in 2000. More couples did not have children, and more men and women lived alone. By the 1990s, one out of every two marriages ended in divorce. Households headed by single mothers grew from 3 million in 1970 to 10 million in 2000, even though teen pregnancy was on the decline beginning in the mid-1990s.

But if the *traditional* family was increasingly rare, the family itself remained a bedrock of American society at the close of the twentieth century. Children in households led by a single parent, stepparent, or grandparent, as well as children with gay or lesbian parents, encountered a degree of acceptance that was unimaginable a generation earlier. "Out" gay and lesbian culture moved from margin to mainstream beginning in the 1990s. Sitcom star Ellen DeGeneres declared her sexuality on the cover of *Time* magazine in 1997 with the headline "Yep, I'm Gay." Additional gay characters began appearing on network television and more celebrities and public figures openly proclaimed their sexuality.

As the American population became more racially diverse, so did the American family. After the Supreme Court overturned laws prohibiting intermarriage across the racial divide in *Loving v. Virginia* (1967), intermarriage rates climbed steadily. By 2015, one in six newlyweds was married to a partner of another race. The 2000 Census was the first to allow respondents to identify themselves with more than one of the six standard racial categories (Black, white, Latino, American Indian, Asian, and Native Hawaiian or other Pacific Islander). Signifying changing demographics and shifting understanding of race, especially among young people, nearly 7 million Americans chose to describe themselves as biracial or multiracial (this number grew to 9 million in the 2010 census and leapt to nearly 34 million in 2020, more than 10 percent of the population). An increasingly diverse popular culture reflected this new demographic reality (refer to "Makers of America: Many Peoples, Many Voices," pp. 1005–1007). Celebrity athletes and performers proclaimed their mixed heritage as a point of pride. One accomplished son of a Kenyan father and white Kansan mother, Barack Obama, wrote thoughtfully about navigating the complex waters of racial identity in his 1995 memoir, *Dreams from My Father*, a decade prior to launching himself on the national political stage. By 2020, 10 percent of Americans identified as multiracial. The American family was not evaporating but evolving into multiple, different forms.

In her bestselling novel *The Joy Luck Club* (1989), Amy Tan (b. 1952) explored the complex dilemmas of growing up as a Chinese American:

"'A girl is like a young tree,' [my mother] said. 'You must stand tall and listen to your mother standing next to you. That is the only way to grow strong and straight. But if you bend to listen to other people, you will grow crooked and weak. . . .' Over the years I learned to choose from the best opinions. Chinese people had Chinese opinions. American people had American opinions. And in almost every case, the American version was much better. It was only later that I discovered there was a serious flaw with the American version. There were too many choices, so it was easy to get confused and pick the wrong thing."

37-9 Searching for a Post–Cold War Foreign Policy

The end of the Cold War dismantled the framework within which the United States had conducted foreign policy for nearly half a century. Throughout his presidency, Bill Clinton groped for a diplomatic formula to replace anticommunism as the basic premise of American diplomacy.

Absorbed by domestic issues, Clinton at first seemed uncertain and even amateurish in his conduct of foreign policy. He followed his predecessor's lead in dispatching American troops as part of a peacekeeping mission to Somalia. But after Somali rebels killed more than a dozen Americans, the president quietly withdrew the U.S. units in March 1994, without having accomplished any clearly defined goal. Burned in Somalia, the Clinton administration stood on the

Makers of America

Many Peoples, Many Voices

"In a nation as diverse as ours, our arts and our humanities are bridges to help us reach out to one another and understand one another better."

President Bill Clinton, 1995

Paradoxically, as the old millennium gave way to the new, an increasingly diverse American society sought unity in the ideal of diversity itself. Advocates of "**multiculturalism**" abandoned the venerable idea of the "melting pot" for the new concept of pluralism as the nation's highest value and defining characteristic.

College campuses were in the vanguard of this cultural shift. Attacking the traditional curriculum as "Eurocentric," multiculturalists championed greater focus on the non-European world as well as on the achievements of Black Americans, Latinos, Asian Americans, and Native Americans. Critics countered that emphasizing cultural differences eroded historically shared common values and undermined national cohesion, even as it encouraged ignorance of the "great books" that had long been at the core of American liberal education.

"Culture war" conflicts spilled beyond the ivory tower as "postmodern" artists and writers rejected rational descriptions of the self or the world, replacing an earlier era's faith in order, objectivity, and the singularity of truth with celebrations of variety, subjectivity, constructed identities, and unstable meanings.

Postmodern architects planted a visible footprint on American cities and communities. Modernists had valued minimalism and an absence of ornament—"Less is more," as one renowned modernist had proclaimed. But postmodernists embraced a playful mix of architectural elements—"Less is a bore," as one of them put it. The flight from stark modernism took especially fanciful forms in Frank Gehry's use of luminous, undulating sheets of metallic skin in the Museum of Pop Culture in Seattle and the Walt Disney Concert Hall in Los Angeles.

American authors grappled with questions of personal identity in an ever more plural world. Toni Morrison wove a bewitching portrait of maternal affection amidst the horrors of slavery in *Beloved* (1987). In 1993, she became the first Black American woman to win the Nobel Prize for literature.

(*continued*)

Atlantide Phototravel/Corbis Documentary/Getty Images

Image 37.9 **Architect Frank Gehry's Walt Disney Concert Hall, Los Angeles, California, Completed in 2003**

The same year, Black writer Maya Angelou reached new heights of fame after delivering the stirring poem "On the Wings of Morning" at Bill Clinton's first inauguration. Then twenty-two-year-old Amanda Gorman, America's first National Youth Poet Laureate, won similar acclaim for reading "The Hill We Climb" at Joe Biden's presidential inauguration in 2021. James Welch, Leslie Marmon Silko, Joy Harjo, and Sherman Alexie contributed to a Native American literary renaissance that sought to recover the tribal past while reimagining its present. Jeffery Eugenides and Michael Chabon deconstructed American masculinity, religious identity, and the immigrant experience in sprawling, Pulitzer Prize–winning bestsellers.

The post-1965 wave of new immigration yielded its own cultural harvest. Amy Tan's bestselling *The Joy Luck Club* (1989) explored the complex relationships between Chinese mothers and their American-born daughters, while Chinese-born Ha Jin wrote evocatively about his country of origin in novels like *Waiting* (1999) and *War Trash* (2004). Jhumpa Lahiri's *Interpreter of Maladies* (1999) and *Unaccustomed Earth* (2008) explored the sometimes painful relationship between immigrant Indian parents and their American-born children. Dominican-American New Yorker Julia Alvarez became one of the most critically and commercially successful Latina authors of the 1990s with *How the Garcia Girls Lost Their Accents* (1991) and *In the Time of the Butterflies* (1994). Junot Diaz's Pulitzer Prize–winning *The Brief Wondrous Life of Oscar Wao* (2007) brilliantly bridged the worlds of the Dominican Republic and New Jersey in a dazzling concoction of street-smart Spanglish.

On and off Broadway, the AIDS epidemic inspired Tony Kushner's sensationally inventive *Angels in America* (1991), as well as Jonathan Larson's Tony Award–winning musical *Rent* (1996). Eve Ensler espoused feminist empowerment (and an end to violence against women) with comic intimacy in her *Vagina Monologues* (1996). Lin-Manuel Miranda's *Hamilton* (2015), a highly creative musical drama with a multiracial cast, was a smash hit with critics and theater-goers alike.

Jason Kempin/Getty Images

Image 37.10 ***Kara Walker Stands Before Her Painting, Gone, An Historical Romance of a Civil War as It Occurred b'tween the Dusky Thighs of One Young Negress and Her Heart, 1994*** Walker daringly adapted the venerable technique of cut-paper silhouettes to explore modern themes of racial identity and historical revisionism. Here she contrasts the romantic image of the antebellum South captured in Margaret Mitchell's celebrated novel and film *Gone with the Wind* with the perspective of an enslaved Black woman.

Theo Wargo/WireImage/Getty Images

Image 37.11 ***Hamilton!*** Lin-Manuel Miranda's musical drama based on the life of Alexander Hamilton opened on Broadway in 2015. Its multiracial cast and incorporation of hip-hop, rap, and other popular musical styles helped to make it a smash hit.

In the realm of popular entertainment—music, film, television—the mass culture that had dominated for most of the twentieth century shattered into a rich variety of genres and multiple new platforms. Artists adopted the most modern technologies to mix disparate elements in creative ways to make commercial popular culture ever more micro-targeted and niche oriented. Cable television and internet streaming smashed the dominance of the older Big Three broadcast networks and nurtured an astonishing variety of high-quality entertainments. The proliferation of media outlets, including radio talk shows, blogs, and social media feeds, fragmented the worlds of culture and politics alike.

Rap and hip-hop, genres emerging from majority-Black neighborhoods of New York City and Los Angeles in the 1970s and 1980s, produced some of the bestselling artists of the new century. In their sampling and remixing of melodic hooks and blunt-edged and complex rhymes, artists such as Public Enemy, Jay-Z, and Missy Elliott turned hip-hop into a broadly shared cultural phenomenon. As the Latino population grew, so did the star power of multiplatinum Latin music stars like Gloria Estefan, Ricky Martin, and Jennifer Lopez.

An independent film movement transformed the world of American cinema in the late 1980s and 1990s, as iconoclasts like Quentin Tarantino, the Coen brothers, and Kathryn Bigelow produced unconventional cinematic visions. Tarantino's *Pulp Fiction* (1994) and David Lynch's *Mulholland Drive* (2001), notable for their nonlinear story lines, arcane cinematic allusions, and dark comedic stylings, were prime examples of postmodern film. Black filmmaker John Singleton's *Boyz n the Hood* (1991) explored family life in South Central Los Angeles. Gregory Nava made films popular with Latino audiences like *Selena* (1997), a biopic of a slain Mexican-American singer. Beginning in the late 1990s, cable television entered a golden era with critically acclaimed and wildly popular dramas such as *The Sopranos* (1999–2007). The network sitcom still ruled, however. Comedic portrayals of white upper-middle-class Manhattan life like *Friends* (1994–2004) and *Seinfeld* (1989–1998) became enormous hits, and helped cities turn from gritty to glamorous in the popular imagination. Even as network audiences eroded in the 2000s and 2010s, half-hour comedies like *The Office* (2005–2013) remained cultural touchstones.

Multiple outlets and audience fragmentation enabled more and fresher voices to be heard. But it also ensured that, compared to previous eras, fewer national experiences and cultural events were collectively shared by large numbers of citizens. Popular culture thus matched ongoing developments in the society at large, as turn-of-the-century America became an ever more boisterously diverse and politically fragmented nation.

sidelines in 1994 when catastrophic ethnic violence in the central African country of Rwanda took the lives of half a million people.

The Rwandan genocide painfully underscored a question dogging the sole remaining superpower in the post–Cold War era: What obligations did America have to intervene in military and humanitarian crises abroad? Events in the tormented Balkans in southeastern Europe provoked similar uncertainty. As vicious ethnic conflict raged through Bosnia, the Washington government dithered until finally deciding to commit American troops to a NATO peacekeeping contingent in late 1995.

NATO's expansion to include the new member states of Poland, Hungary, and the Czech Republic in 1997, and its continuing presence in Bosnia, deeply upset Russia, even while failing to pacify the Balkans completely. When Serbian President Slobodan Miloševic´ in 1999 unleashed a new round of "ethnic cleansing" in the region, this time against ethnic Albanians in the province of Kosovo, U.S.-led NATO forces launched an air war against Serbia. The bombing campaign eventually forced Miloševic´ to accept a NATO peacekeeping force on the ground in Kosovo. Miloševic´ was arrested in 2001 and put on trial before the International Criminal Court in The Hague, where he died in 2006 before the trial was completed.

The Middle East remained a major focus of American diplomacy right up to the end of Clinton's tenure—and beyond. In 1993 Clinton presided over a historic meeting at the White House between Israeli Premier Yitzhak Rabin and Palestine Liberation Organization (PLO) leader Yasir Arafat. They agreed in principle on the withdrawal of Israeli forces from areas of the West Bank and Gaza Strip and political self-rule for the Palestinians living there. But hopes flickered two years later when Rabin fell to an assassin's bullet. Clinton and his second-term secretary of state, Madeleine Albright, spent the rest of the 1990s struggling in vain to broker the permanent settlement that continued to elude Israelis and Palestinians. Arafat died in 2004 with his dream of creating a Palestinian state still unrealized.

An even graver Middle Eastern threat began to take shape in the 1990s: the growth of radical, anti-American Islamist terrorism, organized most effectively in the transnational network known as **Al Qaeda** ("the base" in Arabic). Al Qaeda made its presence known on February 26, 1993, when an explosion rocked the twin towers of the World Trade Center, which had soared above New York City since 1973 (refer to "33-14 A Cultural Renaissance," pp. 893–895). Ripping through an underground parking garage, the blast killed six people. While unsuccessful in toppling one of the iconic towers, the attack was a grisly precursor of greater horror to come.

Image 37.12 The USS *Cole*, October 12, 2000 While the *Cole* was refueling in Yemen's Aden harbor, two suicide attackers piloted a small boat laden with hundreds of pounds of explosive into the ship's hull, blasting a 40-by-60-foot hole in the ship's port side.

Al Qaeda carried out simultaneous bombings of the American embassies in Kenya and Tanzania in 1998, killing more than 230 people. Operatives bombed the USS *Cole* in Yemen two years later, killing 17 (refer to Image 37.12). The wealthy, Saudi-born leader of Al Qaeda, Osama bin Laden, declared war against all Americans and their allies in a *fatwa* issued in 1998. He denounced America's growing military presence in the Middle East (especially on the sacred soil of the Arabian Peninsula) and its unyielding support for Israel in the face of intensifying Palestinian nationalism.

In his final years as president, Clinton stepped up his efforts to leave a legacy as an international peacemaker. Along with his work in the Middle East, he helped in 1998 to broker an end to "the Troubles" in Northern Ireland, which for decades had witnessed violent conflict between predominantly Catholic nationalists and predominantly Protestant Loyalists. Diplomatic efforts in the Korean peninsula as well as in India and Pakistan aimed to reduce nuclear tensions in East and South Asia. But despite these gestures, the guiding principles of American foreign policy in the post–Cold War era remained ill-defined and elusive.

37-10 Scandal and Impeachment

Scandal had dogged Bill Clinton from the beginning of his presidency. Critics brought charges of everything from philandering to illegal financial transactions. Allegations of corruption stemming from a real estate deal called **Whitewater** while he was governor of Arkansas triggered an investigation by a special prosecutor, but no indictment ever materialized. A mobilized conservative movement, with its own humming media infrastructure in cable television, print, and talk radio, amplified each new accusation and aggressively pursued any whiff of scandal throughout the Clinton years.

All previous scandals were overshadowed by the revelation in January 1998 that the 49-year-old President Clinton had engaged in an extramarital affair with a 22-year-old White House intern, Monica Lewinsky, and then lied about it under oath while testifying in another former employee's civil suit accusing him of sexual harassment. Caught in his bold lie, the president made a humiliating public confession, but his political opponents smelled blood in the water. In September 1998, the special prosecutor investigating Whitewater, who had broad powers to investigate *any* evidence of presidential malfeasance, presented a stinging report, including lurid sexual details, to the Republican-controlled House of Representatives. In a dubious first for online media, over 20 million people read the several-hundred page report in the two days after it was uploaded to the internet. That report presented eleven possible grounds for impeachment, all related to lying about the **Lewinsky affair**.

The House quickly cranked up the rusty machinery of impeachment. As an acrid partisan atmosphere enveloped the Capitol, House Republicans in December 1998 passed two articles of impeachment against the president: perjury before a grand jury and obstruction of justice. Crying foul, the Democratic minority charged that, however deplorable Clinton's personal misconduct, sexual transgressions did not rise to the level of "high crimes and misdemeanors" prescribed in the Constitution (refer to Art. II, Sec. IV in the Appendix). The House Republican managers (prosecutors) of impeachment for the Senate trial replied that perjury and obstruction were grave public issues and that nothing less than the "rule of law" was at stake.

As cries of "honor the Constitution" and "sexual McCarthyism" filled the air, the nation debated whether the president's peccadilloes amounted to high crimes or low follies (refer to Image 37.13). Most Americans apparently leaned toward the latter view. In the 1998 midterm elections, voters reduced the House Republicans' majority, causing fiery House speaker Newt Gingrich to resign his post. Although Americans held a low opinion of Clinton's slipshod personal morals, most liked the president's political and economic policies and wanted him to stay in office.

In early 1999, for the first time in 130 years, the nation witnessed an impeachment proceeding in the U.S. Senate. Dusting off ancient precedents from Andrew Johnson's trial, the one hundred senators solemnly heard arguments in the case. With the facts widely known and the two parties' political positions firmly locked in, the trial's outcome was a foregone conclusion. On the key obstruction of justice charge, five Northeastern Republicans joined all forty-five Democratic senators in voting not guilty. The fifty Republican votes for conviction fell far short of the constitutionally required two-thirds majority. The vote on the perjury charge was forty-five guilty, fifty-five not guilty.

ZUMA Press, Inc./Alamy Stock Photo

Image 37.13 The Legacy of Impeachment The Clinton family closed ranks as it tried to ride out the emotional and political storm of the impeachment scandal.

37-11 Clinton's Legacy and the 2000 Election

Beyond the obvious stain of the impeachment trial, Clinton's legacy was mixed. His sound economic policies encouraged growth and trade in a rapidly globalizing post–Cold War world. Yet as a New Democrat and avowed centrist, Clinton did more to consolidate than to reverse the Reagan-Bush revolution against New Deal liberalism that for half a century had provided the compass for the Democratic party and the nation. Further, by setting such a low standard in his personal conduct, he replenished the sad reservoir of public cynicism about politics that Vietnam and Watergate had created a generation before.

Nonetheless, as the end of the Clinton term and the beginning of the new millennium approached, the Democrats stayed on their political course and nominated loyal Vice President Albert Gore for president. Gore faced the tricky challenge of linking himself to Clinton-era peace and prosperity while at the same time distancing himself from his boss's personal foibles. He chose as his running mate Connecticut Senator Joseph Lieberman, an outspoken critic of Clinton's behavior in the Lewinsky affair and the first Jew nominated to a major national ticket. Their Republican challenger, George W. Bush, won the nomination on the strength of his father's name and his years as governor of Texas. Bush surrounded himself with Washington insiders, including vice-presidential nominee Richard "Dick" Cheney, and, in a clear jab at Clinton, promised to "restore dignity to the White House."

Rosy estimates that the federal budget would produce a surplus of some $2 trillion in the coming decade set the stage for the presidential contest. Echoing the Republican creed of smaller government, Bush argued for returning the budget surplus to "the people" through massive tax cuts and for promoting private-sector programs, such as school vouchers and a reliance on "faith-based" institutions to help the poor. Gore proposed smaller tax cuts, targeted at middle- and lower-class people, and strengthening Social Security. In an era of peace, foreign policy figured hardly at all in the campaign, although Bush struck a moderate note when he urged that America should act like "a humble nation." As in 1992, voter disenchantment with the two major-party candidates created an opening for insurgents to roil the waters. Consumer advocate and Green Party candidate Ralph Nader appealed to liberal voters who felt left behind by the business-friendly Democratic Party of Clinton and Gore. Conservative culture warrior and Reform Party candidate Pat Buchanan fired up voters on the right. While neither Nader nor Buchanan attracted as much support as Ross Perot had done eight years earlier, their campaigns played consequential roles in the election's outcome.

Pollsters predicted a close election, but none foresaw the epochal cliffhanger that the election would become. On election day the country split nearly evenly between the two candidates, and it was soon clear that Florida's electoral votes would determine the winner. Television news studios, filled with high-tech gadgetry designed to track every electoral nuance, were thrown into unscripted chaos as Florida's votes swung from one candidate to the other. Close to midnight, the networks announced that Bush had won the Sunshine State, and Al Gore called the Texas governor to concede defeat. Yet just an hour later, Gore's camp decided that Florida was too close to call, and the vice president—in perhaps the most awkward phone call in modern politics—phoned back to retract his concession.

Lannis Waters/Tribune News Service/Palm Beach/FL/USA

Image 37.14 The Florida Recount As lawyers from the national Democratic and Republican parties look on, Palm Beach county officials examine disputed ballots during the hand count of the county's votes in late November 2000.

What ensued was a five-week political standoff over how to count the votes in Florida. In some heavily Democratic precincts, a surprisingly large number of voters had chosen conservative firebrand Buchanan, leading Democratic officials to argue that ballot design had confused voters. Democrats asked for recounts by hand in several counties (refer to Image 37.14). Republicans claimed that such recounts would amount to "changing the rules in the middle of the game" and thus thwart the rule of law. After weeks of legal bickering with the presidency in the balance, the U.S. Supreme Court finally intervened.

By a five-to-four vote along partisan lines, the Court reasoned that since neither Florida's legislature nor its courts had established a uniform standard for evaluating disputed ballots, the hand counts amounted to an unconstitutional breach of the Fourteenth Amendment's equal protection clause.

The ***Bush v. Gore*** ruling gave Bush the White House but cast a dark shadow of illegitimacy over his presidency for many citizens. Bush officially won Florida by 537 votes out of 6 million cast, and he squeaked by in the Electoral College, 271 to 266 (refer to Map 37.2). The national popular vote went to Gore, 50,999,897 to 50,456,002. For many Democrats, Ralph Nader—who won 2.7 million popular votes nationwide—was the spoiler who deprived Gore of victory. (In exit polls, more than half of Nader voters reported that they would have opted for Gore had the Green Party candidate not been on the ballot; only one in five would have voted for Bush.)

The day after the Supreme Court's ruling, Gore announced his concession in a televised speech of far greater eloquence and emotional honesty than any he had delivered on the

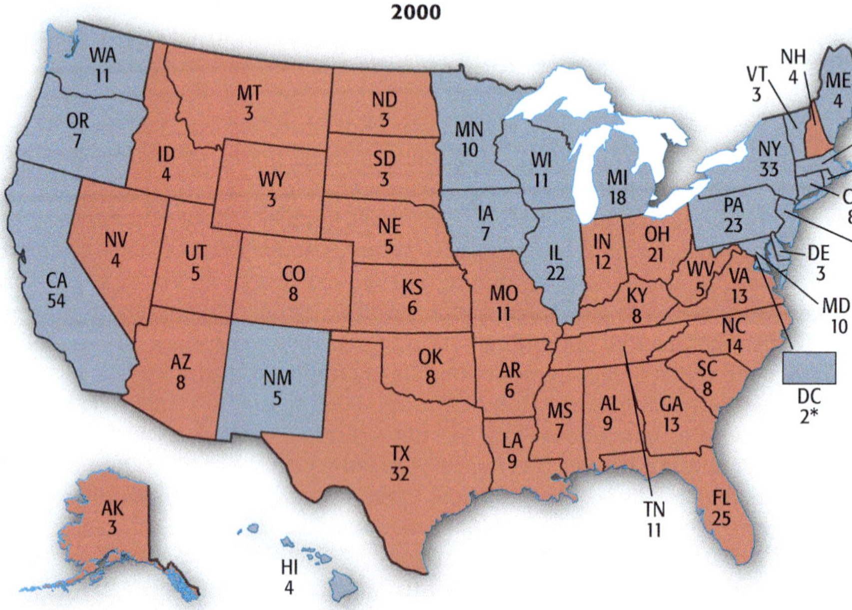

Candidate (Party)	Electoral Vote		Popular Vote	
Bush (Republican)	271	50.4%	50,456,169	47.88%
Gore (Democrat)	266	49.4%	50,996,116	48.39%
Nader (Green)	0	0.0%	2,783,728	2.72%

*One elector from the District of Columbia abstained.

Map 37.2 Presidential Election of 2000 (with electoral vote by state) Although Democrat Albert Gore won the popular election by half a million votes, George W. Bush's contested 537-vote advantage in Florida gave him a slight lead in the Electoral College. Bush's failure to win the popular vote inspired critics to protest at his inauguration with placards reading "Hail to the Thief."

campaign trail. "While I strongly disagree with the court's decision, I accept it," said Gore. "This is America and we put country before party. We will stand together behind our new president."

For the first time since 1888, a candidate won the White House with fewer popular votes than his opponent. Not since 1876 had the Electoral College been won by such a slim margin. Serious proposals to reform the Electoral College, however, were few and feeble (refer to "The Presence of the Past: The Electoral College and the Consequences of Compromise," pp. 186–188).

Black voters went for Gore over Bush by a ratio of ten to one, signaling the deepening racial polarization of party politics at the turn of the new century. Many Black Floridians, meanwhile, complained that election officials had unfairly disqualified their votes and even turned them away from the polls, recollecting the kind of obstacles that long had kept Black voters from exercising their rights in the "Jim Crow" South.

37-12 Bush Begins

As the son of the forty-first president ("41"), George W. Bush ("43") became the first presidential son since John Quincy Adams to reach the White House. Raised largely in Texas, the younger Bush publicly distanced himself from his family's privileged New England heritage and affected the chummy manner of a self-made "good ol' boy"—though he held degrees from Yale and Harvard. The circumstances of his election also clouded his arrival. Cracked one Democratic lawmaker: "You know, it was once said of the first George Bush that he was born on third base and thought he'd hit a triple. Well, with the 22 million new jobs and the budget surplus Bill Clinton left behind, George W. Bush came into office on third base, and then he stole second."

"W" promised to bring to Washington the conciliatory skills he had honed as the Republican governor of Texas, where he had worked well with the Democratic majority in the state's legislature. He also sought to balance his unseasoned reputation by appointing expert advisors to key foreign policy positions. As his first secretary of state, Bush appointed former Chairman of the Joint Chiefs of Staff Colin Powell, the first Black person to hold that position. Condoleezza Rice, an authority on Russia and Eastern Europe, became the first female National Security Advisor. Rice later succeeded Powell to become the first Black female secretary of state.

But as president, Bush soon proved to be more of a divider than a uniter, less a "compassionate conservative" than a crusading ideologue. Religious traditionalists cheered, but liberals jeered, when he withdrew American support from international health programs that sanctioned abortion, advocated federally financed faith-based social-welfare initiatives, and vetoed legislation providing for government-sponsored research on embryonic stem cells, which many scientists believed held the key to conquering diseases such as Parkinson's and Alzheimer's.

Conflict over the harvesting of stem cells, a practice deemed by many evangelical and conservative religious groups to be the destruction of human life in embryonic form, was just one example of the ways that Americans struggled with the ethical implications of revolutionary advances in biological engineering. The Human Genome Project mapped the DNA sequencing of all 20,000 human genes in 2001, pointing the way to radical new medical therapies, but also raising thorny questions about the legitimacy of technological tinkering with human life. These issues prompted President Bush to establish a Council on Bioethics in 2001, but it was soon ensnarled in bitter political as well as ethical wrangling and was eventually superseded by President Obama's National Bioethics Advisory Commission, which unfortunately proved no more effective than its predecessor.

On the environmental front, Bush pleased corporate chieftains but angered environmentalists through a slew of actions early in his tenure. He repudiated a major international effort to arrest the rate of global warming, the Kyoto Treaty limiting greenhouse gas emissions. Criticism mounted when Bush allowed his hard-charging vice president, Dick Cheney, to hammer out his administration's energy policy in behind-closed-doors meetings with representatives of several giant oil companies. Cheney, dismissing energy conservation as a mere "sign of personal virtue," advocated aggressive expansion of domestic energy supplies, including new oil exploration in the Arctic National Wildlife Refuge on Alaska's ecologically fragile north coast.

The centerpiece of Bush's fiscal policy was a pair of whopping tax cuts, passed by Congress in 2001 and 2003. Combined with a softening economy and the rising costs of military interventions overseas, these measures turned the federal budget surpluses of the late 1990s into yawning deficits, reaching more than $380 billion in 2004 and nearly $460 billion in 2008, when a galloping financial crisis deepened them even further (refer to Figure 37.7).

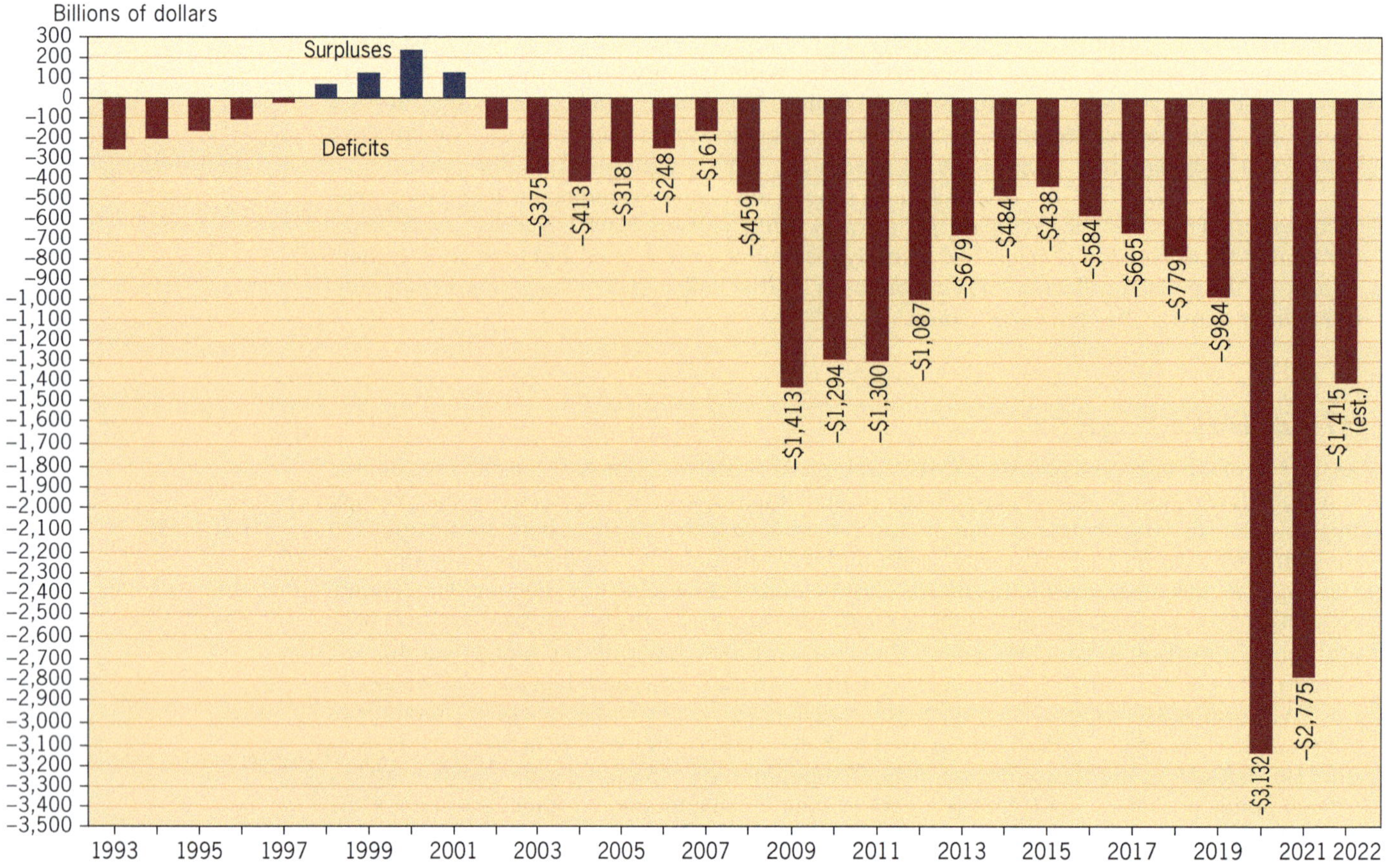

Figure 37.7 Deficits into Surpluses and Back Again In 1998 the U.S. budget deficit became a surplus for the first time in decades. But by 2002, the government was back in deficit, due to President Bush's tax cuts, a weak economy, and mushrooming defense spending on the Iraq War. Following the onset of the "Great Recession" in 2008, deficits ballooned to historic highs, then began contracting again amidst budget agreements forged between President Obama, a Democratic Senate, and a Republican House of Representatives. Massive aid packages passed during the early months of the COVID-19 pandemic made the deficit balloon once more.

Source: Budget FY 2023—Historical Tables, Budget of the United States Government, Fiscal Year 2023. https://www.govinfo.gov/app/details/BUDGET-2023-TAB

37-13 Terrorism Comes to America

On September 11, 2001, the long era of America's impregnable national security violently ended. On a balmy late-summer morning, suicidal terrorists slammed two hijacked airliners, loaded with passengers and jet fuel, into the twin towers of New York City's World Trade Center (refer to Image IX.1, p. 962). They flew a third plane into the military nerve center of the Pentagon, near Washington, DC, killing 189 people. Heroic passengers forced a fourth hijacked aircraft to crash in rural Pennsylvania, killing all 44 aboard but depriving the terrorists of an additional weapon of mass destruction.

Within hours, the two giant New York skyscrapers had collapsed in a thunderous cascade of rubble and dust that enveloped several city blocks, killing nearly three thousand trapped within and below the twin towers (refer to Image 37.15). The terrible toll included people of many races and faiths from 115 nations, as well as over 400 New York police and fire department rescue workers. A stunned nation blossomed with flags, as grieving and outraged Americans struggled to express their sorrow and solidarity in the face of the horrific terrorism of **9/11**.

President Bush responded with a sober and stirring address to Congress nine days later. His solemn demeanor and the gravity of the situation helped to dissipate the cloud of illegitimacy that had shadowed his presidency since the disputed election of 2000. While emphasizing his respect for the Islamic religion and Muslim people, he identified the principal enemy as Osama bin Laden, head of the shadowy terrorist network Al Qaeda (refer to "37-9 Searching for a Post–Cold War Foreign Policy," pp. 1004–1008). Since 1998, bin Laden had taken refuge in landlocked Afghanistan, ruled by Islamic fundamentalists called the Taliban. (Ironically, the United States had indirectly helped bring the Taliban to power by supporting the mujahideen resisting the Soviet invasion of

Image 37.15 The Toll of Terror An exhausted firefighter pauses amid the search for survivors in the wreckage of New York City's World Trade Center. Exposure to the dust of the ruined twin towers led to debilitating health problems for many of these rescue workers. By 2023, nearly as many first responders (341) had died of post-9/11-related illnesses as the number of firefighters (343) killed in the attacks themselves.

Afghanistan in the 1980s. Refer to "36-5 Troubles Abroad," pp. 970–971.) Bin Laden drew on popular Muslim opposition to Washington's policies in the Middle East, including both the American military presence there and its unwavering support of Israel. He also benefited from broader, worldwide resentment of America's enormous economic, military, and cultural power. Ironically, America's most conspicuous strengths had made it a conspicuous target (refer to Image 37.16).

When the Taliban refused to hand over bin Laden, Bush ordered a massive military campaign against Afghanistan. Within three months, American and Afghan rebel forces had overthrown the Taliban but failed to find bin Laden, and Americans continued to live in fear of future attacks. Confronted with this unconventional, diffuse menace, antiterrorism experts called for a new kind of "asymmetrical warfare," employing not just traditional military muscle but also counterinsurgency tactics like innovative intelligence gathering, training of local police forces, economic reprisals, infiltration of suspected organizations, and even assassinations.

The terrorists' blows struck fear deep and dark among a people accustomed to immunity from foreign attacks on their homeland. In this edgy atmosphere, Congress in October 2001 rammed through the **USA Patriot Act**.* The act permitted extensive telephone and email surveillance and authorized the detention and deportation of immigrants suspected of terrorism. Just over a year later, Congress created a new cabinet-level **Department of Homeland Security** to safeguard the nation's borders and ferret out potential attackers. The Justice Department meanwhile rounded up hundreds of immigrants and held them without *habeas corpus* (formal charges in an open court). The Bush administration further called for trying suspected terrorists before military tribunals, where the usual rules of evidence and procedure did not apply. (The Supreme Court eventually denied the president that authority in the case of *Hamdan v. Rumsfeld* [2006].)

*The act's official name is Uniting and Strengthening America by Providing Appropriate Tools Required to Intercept and Obstruct Terrorism.

Dimitar Dilkoff/Reuters

Image 37.16 The Attacks Seen Around the World The attacks of September 11, 2001, became events of international, not just American, significance, as revealed in the newspapers on display in Sofia, Bulgaria.

In the same anxious atmosphere in 2001, Congress also passed an Authorization for Use of Military Force (AUMF). Originally aimed at the terrorist perpetrators of the 9/11 attacks, the AUMF was subsequently used to justify military actions not only in Afghanistan, but also in Iraq, the Philippines, Georgia, Yemen, Djibouti, Kenya, Ethiopia, Eritrea, and Somalia. Almost two decades later, amid continuing controversy, it remained in effect.

As hundreds of Taliban fighters captured in Afghanistan languished in legal limbo and demoralizing isolation in the **Guantánamo Detention Camp** on the American military base at Guantánamo, Cuba, public-opinion polls showed Americans sharply divided on whether the terrorist threat fully warranted such drastic encroachments on America's venerable tradition of protecting civil liberties.

Catastrophic terrorism posed an unprecedented challenge to the United States. The events of that murderous September morning reanimated American patriotism, but they also brought a long chapter in American history to a dramatic climax. All but unique among modern peoples, Americans for nearly two centuries had been spared from foreign attack on their homeland. That unusual degree of virtually cost-free national security had undergirded the values of openness and individual freedom that defined the distinctive character of American society. Now American security and American liberty alike were dangerously imperiled.

37-14 Bush Takes the Offensive Against Iraq

On only its second day in office, the Bush administration had warned that it would not tolerate Iraq's continued defiance of United Nations weapons inspections, mandated after Iraq's defeat in the 1991 Persian Gulf War. Iraqi dictator Saddam Hussein, after playing hide-and-seek with the inspectors for years, expelled them from his country in 1998, inducing President Clinton, with congressional approval, to declare that Saddam's removal ("regime change") was an official goal of U.S. policy. But no sustained military action against Iraq had followed. Now, in the context of the new terrorist threat, the Bush administration focused on Iraq with a vengeance.

In January 2002, mere months after the September 11 attacks, Bush claimed that Iraq, along with Iran and North Korea, constituted an "axis of evil" that gravely menaced American security. Iran and North Korea were both known to be pursuing nuclear weapons programs, and Iran had long supported terrorist operations in the Middle East. But Iraqi tyrant Saddam Hussein, defeated but not destroyed by Bush's father in 1991, became the principal object of the new president's wrath. The elder Bush had carefully assembled a broad international coalition to fight the 1991 Persian Gulf War. He had also spoken so often of "prudence" that late-night television comedians had mocked him for it. In contrast, his son was brashly determined to break with long-standing American traditions and wage a preemptive war against Iraq—and to go it alone if necessary. The younger Bush thus cast off his campaign-trail appeal for America to be a "humble nation" and stood revealed as a plunger, a daring risk-taker willing to embrace bold, dramatic policies, foreign as well as fiscal. In that spirit Bush began laying plans for a war against Iraq (refer to "Examining the Evidence: The National Security Strategy, 2002," p. 1016).

Itching for a fight and egged on by hawkish Vice President Cheney and other "neoconservative" advisers, Bush accused the Iraqi regime of all manner of wrongdoing: oppressing its own people; frustrating the weapons inspectors; developing nuclear, chemical, and biological weapons of mass destruction; and supporting terrorist organizations like Al Qaeda. Perhaps most controversially, Bush also suggested that a liberated, democratized Iraq might provide a beacon of hope to the Islamic world and thereby rebalance the political equation in the volatile Middle East (refer to Map 37.3). To skeptical observers, including America's usually reliable European allies, the very multiplicity of Bush's reasons for war cast doubt on his case. In particular, his ambition to create a democracy in long-suffering Iraq, burdened with centuries of internecine conflict, seemed naively utopian. Secretary of State Colin Powell urged caution, warning of the long-term consequences for the United States of invading and occupying an unstable, religiously and culturally divided nation of 25 million people. "You break it, you own it," he told the president.

Heavy and hawkish majorities in both houses of Congress nevertheless passed a resolution in October 2002 authorizing the president to employ armed force to defend against Iraqi threats to America's national security and to enforce United Nations resolutions regarding Iraq. A month later, the UN Security Council voted unanimously to give Iraq "a final opportunity to comply with its disarmament obligations." There followed a months-long cat-and-mouse game. UN weapons inspectors returned to Iraq. Saddam once again harassed and blocked them. No weapons of mass destruction were found. The inspectors asked for more time. The United Nations declined to authorize the use of force to compel compliance.

In his 2002 state of the union address, President George W. Bush (b. 1946) declared:

"Iraq continues to flaunt its hostility toward America and to support terror. The Iraqi regime has plotted to develop anthrax, and nerve gas, and nuclear weapons for over a decade. This is a regime that has already used poison gas to murder thousands of its own citizens—leaving the bodies of mothers huddled over their dead children. This is a regime that agreed to international inspections—then kicked out the inspectors. This is a regime that has something to hide from the civilized world.

States like these, and their terrorist allies, constitute an axis of evil, arming to threaten the peace of the world. By seeking weapons of mass destruction, these regimes pose a grave and growing danger. They could provide these arms to terrorists, giving them the means to match their hatred. They could attack our allies or attempt to blackmail the United States. In any of these cases, the price of indifference would be catastrophic."

In this tense and confusing atmosphere, Bush, with Britain his only major ally, launched the long-anticipated invasion of Iraq on March 19, 2003. Saddam Hussein's vaunted military machine collapsed almost immediately. In less than a month, Baghdad had fallen and Saddam had been driven from power and hounded into hiding. (He was found and arrested some nine months later and executed in 2006.) From the deck of a U.S. aircraft carrier off the California coast, speaking beneath a banner declaring "Mission Accomplished," Bush triumphantly announced on May 1, 2003, that "major combat operations in Iraq have ended."

37-15 Owning Iraq

President Bush's words soon came back to haunt him. Neoconservative pundits in Washington had predicted that American soldiers would be greeted as liberators and that Saddam's ouster would lead to flowering democracy across the Middle East. In reality, post-Saddam Iraq quickly devolved into a seething cauldron of violence.

The country's two largest religious communities, minority Sunni and majority Shia Muslims, clashed violently, especially in the capital city of Baghdad (refer to Figure 37.8). Both factions attacked American forces, especially after the U.S. decision to disband the Iraqi army, which deprived Iraq of an effective indigenous police force. Hatred for Americans only worsened with revelations in April 2004 that Iraqi prisoners in Baghdad's **Abu Ghraib prison** had been tortured and

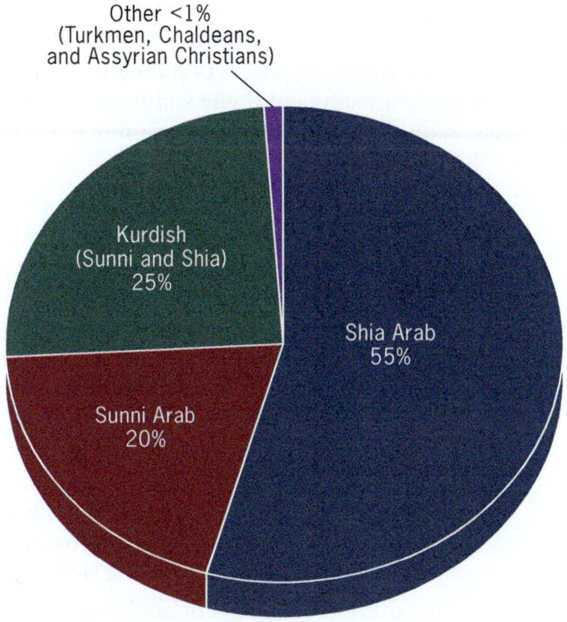

Figure 37.8 **Ethnic and Religious Groups in Iraq, 2003**

Source: https://carnegieendowment.org/pdf/files/IraqBrief.Ottaway.pdf

Examining the Evidence

The National Security Strategy, 2002

The 1986 Goldwater-Nichols Act requires the president periodically to issue a National Security Strategy (NSS), a report outlining the administration's vision of the major security challenges facing the United States and the proper approach to meeting them. These reports provide rich sources for historical study. They are short, nontechnical documents intended to lay out a broad assessment of grand strategy. Because they compel often contentious coordination throughout the executive branch, they reflect important political and ideological currents within a given administration. They are also written with several audiences in mind, both foreign and domestic.

Few national security strategies have proven more historically significant—or controversial—than the report signed by President George W. Bush on September 17, 2002. Issued a year after the September 11 attacks, eight months after Bush declared that Iran, Iraq, and North Korea constituted an "axis of evil," and seven months before the U.S. invasion of Iraq, the 2002 NSS laid out an argument for the legitimacy of preventive warfare. This doctrine challenged inherited ideas about international law and broke from Cold War–era strategies of deterrence and containment.

In the excerpt below from the 2002 NSS, how did the administration describe and justify its departure from previous historical practice? In the light of subsequent events, how might future historians of the Bush presidency analyze this report? What does its tone suggest about the authors' view of the United States and the world?

A

New York Daily News Archive/Getty Images

B

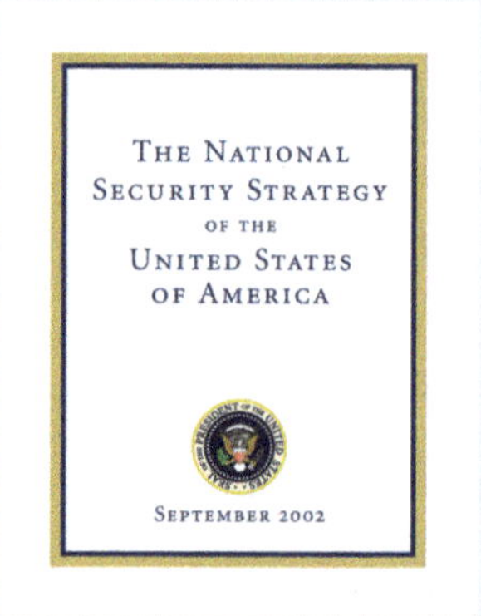

Source: US Department of State

Image 37.17A and B
Bush Addresses the Press upon the Release of the National Security Strategy Report, September 17, 2002

"In the Cold War, especially following the Cuban missile crisis, we faced a generally status quo, risk-averse adversary. Deterrence was an effective defense. But deterrence based only upon the threat of retaliation is less likely to work against leaders of rogue states more willing to take risks, gambling with the lives of their people, and the wealth of their nations.

- In the Cold War, weapons of mass destruction were considered weapons of last resort whose use risked the destruction of those who used them. Today, our enemies see weapons of mass destruction as weapons of choice. For rogue states these weapons are tools of intimidation and military aggression against their neighbors. These weapons may also allow these states to attempt to blackmail the United States and our allies to prevent us from deterring or repelling the aggressive behavior of rogue states. Such states also see these weapons as their best means of overcoming the conventional superiority of the United States.
- Traditional concepts of deterrence will not work against a terrorist enemy whose avowed tactics are wanton destruction and the targeting of innocents; whose so-called soldiers seek martyrdom in death and whose most potent protection is statelessness. The overlap between states that sponsor terror and those that pursue WMD compels us to action.

For centuries, international law recognized that nations need not suffer an attack before they can lawfully take action to defend themselves against forces that present an imminent danger of attack. Legal scholars and international jurists often conditioned the legitimacy of preemption on the existence of an imminent threat—most often a visible mobilization of armies, navies, and air forces preparing to attack.

We must adapt the concept of imminent threat to the capabilities and objectives of today's adversaries. . . .

The United States will not use force in all cases to preempt emerging threats, nor should nations use preemption as a pretext for aggression. Yet in an age where the enemies of civilization openly and actively seek the world's most destructive technologies, the United States cannot remain idle while dangers gather. . . ."

Map 37.3 The Middle East A combination of ancient religious rivalries, chronic political instability, and precious petroleum resources has made the region from Egypt to Afghanistan an "arc of crisis" and a cockpit of great-power competition at the turn of the millennium.

In his 1998 book, *A World Transformed*, former president George H. W. Bush (1924–2018) explained his rationale for not driving Saddam Hussein from power during the 1991 Persian Gulf War. His words made sobering reading in the context of his son's subsequent invasion of Iraq:

"Trying to eliminate Saddam . . . would have incurred incalculable human and political costs. . . . The coalition would instantly have collapsed, the Arabs deserting it in anger and other allies pulling out as well. Under the circumstances, there was no viable 'exit strategy' we could see, violating another of our principles. Furthermore, we had been self-consciously trying to set a pattern for handling aggression in the post–Cold War world. Going in and occupying Iraq, thus unilaterally exceeding the United Nations' mandate, would have destroyed the precedent of international response to aggression that we hoped to establish."

humiliated by their American captors (refer to "Thinking Globally: America Through Foreign Eyes: Hyperpower or Hapless Power?" pp. 1019–1020. Amid this chaos, jihadist terrorists from around the region flooded into Iraq, often fueling the intra-Iraqi conflicts to further their own radical Islamist vision. Although Al Qaeda had had no link to Iraq under Saddam, as Bush had inaccurately alleged, the organization certainly moved in afterward. These three battles—Shia-Sunni ethnic violence, insurgency against the occupation, and jihadist terrorism—fed a spiraling maelstrom of bloodshed. By the end of 2006, more Americans had died in Iraq than in the attacks of September 11. Iraqi suffering was far greater. U.S. deaths in the Iraq war eventually exceeded 8,200, while more than 220,000 Iraqi fighters and civilians had violently perished.

Almost from their arrival, American forces began preparing to withdraw. In the summer of 2004, the American military ceded political power and limited sovereignty to an interim Iraqi government. A series of national elections followed in 2005, with millions of Iraqis voting for a national assembly to draft a constitution and, later, for parliamentary representatives and a president. But under the seeming stability of Iraq's new democratic government lay deep, violent tensions. Sunni Muslims, the minority that had held power under Saddam Hussein, feared reprisals and repressions under a majority Shia government. Unsuccessful at the ballot box, many Sunnis turned to bombings and political assassinations.

37-16 Reelecting George W. Bush

Americans had rarely been as divided as they were in the first years of the twenty-first century. Civil libertarians fretted that the government was trampling on personal freedoms in the name of fighting terrorism. Cultural tensions boiled up over the rights of gay and lesbian Americans when leaders in San Francisco and Massachusetts permitted same-sex couples to marry in 2004. Affirmative action continued to spark sharp debate, as a divided Supreme Court permitted some preferential treatment in admitting minority students to the University of Michigan in 2003.

Amid these divisions, George W. Bush prepared to run for reelection. Targeting what he called "the soft bigotry of low expectations," he touted the **No Child Left Behind Act** of 2001, which mandated sanctions against schools that failed to meet federal performance standards. The measure passed with bipartisan support. He then advocated for and signed the Medicare Prescription Drug Modernization Act in December 2003, expanding Medicare to cover prescriptions. But he played to cultural conservatives in opposing stem cell research (refer to "37-12 Bush Begins," p. 1011) and called for a constitutional amendment to ban gay marriage. Most of all, he promoted himself as a stalwart leader in wartime, harkening back to President Lincoln's warning not to "change horses midstream."

Embattled Democrats chose lanky and long-jawed Massachusetts senator John Kerry to represent their ticket. Kerry pushed progressive visions of government and counted on his Vietnam War record to counter charges that he would be weak in the face of terrorism. Despite increased public misgivings about the war in Iraq, Bush nailed down a decisive victory in November 2004. He received the first popular vote majority by a presidential candidate in more than a decade—60,639,281 to 57,355,978—and bested Kerry in the Electoral College, 286 to 252. This time his victory was clear, constitutional, and uncontested.

37-17 Bush's Bruising Second Term

Reelection, George W. Bush announced, gave him "political capital," which he intended to spend on an aggressive domestic agenda. The appointment of two new conservative Supreme Court justices (John G. Roberts and Samuel A. Alito Jr.) upon the death of Chief Justice William Rehnquist and the retirement of Sandra Day O'Connor seemed to bode well for his ambitions. But Bush soon overplayed his hand. Attacking the core of New Deal liberalism, he proposed a radical program to privatize much of Social Security. A massive outcry led by the American Association of

Thinking Globally

America Through Foreign Eyes: Hyperpower or Hapless Power?

When the Soviet Union disintegrated in 1991, the Cold War concluded at last. So did an era in the history of American foreign policy, and in the history of the international order. For nearly half a century following World War II, the confrontation with the Soviets had deeply shaped Americans' conception of themselves—their national identity—as well as their role and reputation in the wider world. In the long twilight struggle against Soviet communism, they had accumulated unprecedented economic, military, and cultural might and had taken virtuous pride in themselves as the global champions of democracy, justice, and human rights. Now, as the sole surviving "superpower," they faced no counterbalancing regime and, apparently, no check on their national ambitions. The United States seemed to wield all but limitless power to mold the international environment as it wished. Not since the days of ancient Rome did any people bestride the world so unopposed.

Not everyone welcomed the emergence of this international colossus. Australians grumbled that the United States was a "tall poppy" that needed to be cut down to size. French foreign minister Hubert Védrine coined a new term when he described the United States in 1999 not merely as a superpower but as a "hyper power," one "that is dominant or predominant in all categories," including not only the traditional domains of politics, economics, and the military, but even including "attitudes, concepts, languages, and modes of life." He called upon Europeans to create an alternative to the American "steamroller," to "work in favor of real multilateralism against unilateralism, for balanced multipolarism against unipolarism, for cultural diversity against uniformity." In the parlance of international relations, Védrine was promoting a "balancing" strategy to cope with U.S. power, rather than the "bandwagon" strategy of simply submitting to American hegemony and making the most of it. Notably, he was not proposing outright opposition.

As the last days of the twentieth century slipped through the hourglass, American power surely looked formidable. The United States was the world's third most populous nation (after China and India), enjoyed the world's largest economy (more than three times larger than second-ranked Japan), was the acknowledged global leader in high-tech information and biomedical innovations, and spent more on its armed forces than the rest of the world *combined*. Yet the realities of American power were somewhat less imposing. Uncle Sam struggled to find solid footing in the post–Cold War international arena. Washington in the 1990s badly botched a peacekeeping mission in lawless Somalia; stood by helplessly as genocidal militias murdered nearly a million Rwandans; dithered over how to stabilize chaotic Haiti; fumbled indecisively as nationalist and sectarian violence convulsed the former Balkan nation of Yugoslavia; found no effective response to terrorist attacks on New York City's World Trade Center, the destroyer USS *Cole*, and American embassies in Kenya and Tanzania; and notoriously failed to bring any conclusion to the decades-old confrontation between Israelis and Palestinians, who erupted in a bloody intifada (rebellion) against the Jewish state in 2000.

The barbarous Al Qaeda assault that finally toppled the twin towers of the World Trade Center and the Pentagon on September 11, 2001, momentarily elicited an outpouring of sympathy from an astonished and outraged world—even as it brought a dramatic shift in American foreign policy. *Le Monde*, France's leading newspaper, declared that in this dangerous hour, "Nous sommes tous Américains" (We are all Americans). For the first time in history, the North Atlantic Treaty Organization (NATO) invoked the treaty's Article Five, affirming that an attack on one member was an attack on all members.

(*continued*)

AP Images

Image 37.18 Torture at Abu Ghraib Prison, Baghdad, 2003
Revelations that American soldiers had brutally tortured Iraqi prisoners contributed to condemnation of the nation's disregard for human rights and growing disquiet about America's unilateral policing of the world. This photograph of a hooded detainee connected to electrical wires became an iconic image of the Iraq War.

But such sentiments proved short-lived. Once a moral beacon and political inspiration to a suffering world, the United States in the early twenty-first century had come to be regarded by millions of people the world over as a moral scourge, an unreliable partner, and even a political and military danger (refer to Table 37.2). When President George W. Bush in 2002 asserted a new right of preemptive war and then proceeded to invade Iraq for what looked to many observers like the most dubious of reasons, anti-American sentiment swelled the world over. America's standing deteriorated even among its traditional allies and sank to rock-bottom lows in Islamic countries. The election of Barack Obama in 2008 briefly burnished the American image once more, but in the eyes of many global citizens, America was no longer a "City on a Hill" to be admired and emulated.

Eight years later came the election of Donald J. Trump, who trumpeted an "America First" agenda that openly scorned the internationalism of his predecessors. Trump backed out of negotiations with eleven other Asia-Pacific nations to form a commercial Trans-Pacific Partnership (TPP). He replaced the North American Free Trade Agreement (NAFTA) with the United States-Canada-Mexico Agreement (USCMA) and sharply criticized America's partners in the nation's oldest alliance, the North Atlantic Treaty Organization (NATO). He also withdrew the United States from the 2015 Paris Climate Accord, which had secured the commitment of nearly the entire international community to fight global warming by reducing greenhouse gas emissions. As the United States turned inward, other powers, conspicuously including Russia and China, saw opportunities to fill the geopolitical vacuum and assume America's slipping mantle of global leadership.

The 2020 election of Joe Biden brought a seasoned internationalist back to the White House, determined to repair fraying global ties. Biden's hopes for a smooth restoration of American leadership soon were tested by the chaotic withdrawal of the last U.S. troops from Afghanistan in 2021, the Russian invasion of Ukraine in 2022, and the 2023 Hamas terrorist attacks on Israel and the siege of Gaza that followed. Despite an increasingly combustible global order, by the third year of his presidency Biden received mostly favorable reviews in global public opinion polling (though less favorable reviews at home). Yet America's past interventions continued to cast a shadow, with world public opinion evenly divided on whether the United States took into account the interests of other countries while making its foreign policy decisions.

Table 37.2 Approval of the United States Around the World

	2000	2002	2004	2006	2008	2010	2012	2014	2015	2016	2017
Britain	83%	75%	58%	56%	53%	65%	60%	66%	65%	61%	50%
France	62	63	37	39	42	73	69	75	73	63	46
Germany	78	61	38	37	31	63	52	51	50	57	35
Spain	50	—	—	23	33	61	58	60	65	59	31
Russia	37	61	47	43	46	57	52	23	15	NA	41
Indonesia	75	61	—	30	37	59	—	59	62	NA	48
Pakistan	23	10	21	27	19	17	12	14	22	NA	NA
Jordan	—	25	5	15	19	21	12	12	14	NA	15
Turkey	52	30	30	12	12	17	15	19	29	NA	18
Nigeria	46	—	—	62	64	81	—	69	76	66	69
Japan	77	72	—	63	50	66	72	66	68	72	57
India	—	—	—	—	—	—	41	55	70	56	49
China	—	—	—	47	41	58	43	50	44	50	NA

The Iraq war contributed to a sharp decline in favorable opinion of the United States globally. This chart shows the percentage of foreign nationals abroad who responded that they have a somewhat to very favorable impression of the United States.

Sources: From Pew Global Attitudes Report 2013, "America's Global Image Remains More Positive Than China's" and Pew Research Center, Global Indicators Database.

Retired Persons (AARP) and leading liberal interest groups reminded Americans how much they loved Social Security, warts and all. Bush's proposal faded away within six months of his reelection. The same fate befell a proposed constitutional amendment to ban same-sex marriage.

The president also took aim at the contentious issue of immigration reform. Anti-immigrant pundits and politicians—many in Bush's party—leveled the old charges that illegal immigrants were welfare-spongers and job-stealers. Immigrant sympathizers countered that undocumented aliens had to be legalized so that they could receive the same protections as other workers. Bush worked hard on a proposed law to establish a guest-worker program for undocumented workers and to create a path to citizenship, albeit after paying a fine. Nativist forces condemned the plan as "amnesty." Business interests protested that employers would be overburdened with verifying the right to work. And immigrant rights advocates charged that the program would create "second-class citizens." In the end, the compromise bill pleased no one and died an ignominious political death, to Bush's deep disappointment.

Bush soon suffered further embarrassment. Revelations exploded in 2005 that the government was conducting illegal wiretap surveillance on American citizens inside the United States, in violation of federal law. There followed yet another political misstep when the Federal Emergency Management Agency (FEMA) botched its response to the deadly **Hurricane Katrina**, which devastated New Orleans and much of the Gulf Coast in late August 2005, flooding 80 percent of the historic city and causing over 1,300 deaths and $150 billion in damages. A consensus began to build that Bush was a genial personality but an impetuous, unreflective, and frequently feckless leader, a president in over his head in a sea of complex problems that he seemed incapable of mastering.

As disaffection spread, Republicans fell victim in the midterm elections of 2006 to the same anti-incumbency sentiment they had ridden to power twelve years earlier. Democrats narrowly regained control of both houses of Congress for the first time since they had lost them to the Gingrich revolution of 1994 (refer to "37-3 Another Republican Revolution," pp. 993–995). California Democrat Nancy Pelosi became the first woman to serve as speaker of the House.

The biggest factor in the Democratic sweep was the perceived mishandling of the war in Iraq. Prewar claims about WMD and Iraq's connections to Al Qaeda and 9/11 had all proved false. By late 2005, polls revealed that most Americans considered the war a mistake (refer to Image 37.19). Secretary of Defense Donald Rumsfeld resigned after the Republicans' "thumping" in the 2006 midterm elections. But Iraq still knew no peace, and the death toll, Iraqi and American alike, continued to rise. The Bush administration sought to salvage its policy in early 2007 with a "surge" of twenty thousand additional troops. The surge brought a modest measure of stability to Iraq, but as the 2008 election cycle got underway, public opinion nevertheless solidified ever more strongly against the war.

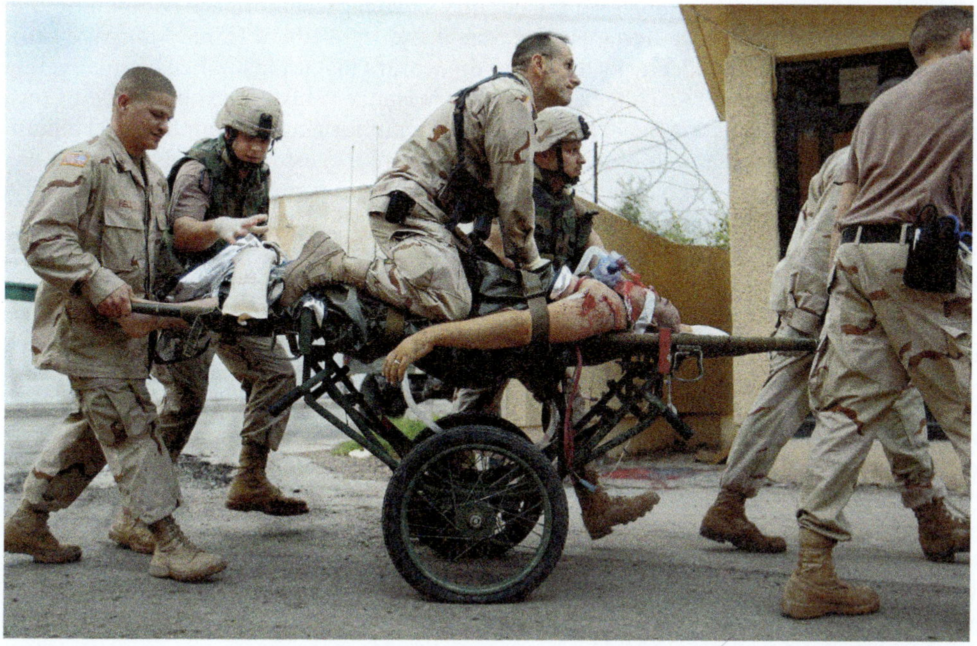

AP Images/John Moore

Image 37.19 The Face of Battle A combat nurse tries to save the life of a wounded American soldier by giving him CPR upon arrival at the Combat Support Hospital in Baghdad, Iraq, 2005. Dramatic improvements in battlefield medical techniques saved countless lives during the Iraq and Afghan wars, but many surviving veterans then had to deal with life-long disabilities.

37-18 The Presidential Election of 2008

With neither the sitting president nor vice president running, the 2008 election was truly "open" for the first time in eighty years. The race for the Democratic nomination soon tightened into a fiercely fought contest between the forty-six-year-old, first-term Illinois senator Barack Obama and the pre-campaign favorite, former First Lady and sitting New York Senator Hillary Rodham Clinton. Obama narrowly prevailed. Raised in Hawai'i and Indonesia, Obama had a cosmopolitan background well suited to the age of globalization. He promised gridlock-weary voters a "postpartisan" politics that would end the divisive battles of the Bush years. To strengthen his national security credentials, he picked foreign-policy-savvy Delaware senator Joseph Biden as his running mate. Obama also rallied strong support from young people and established an early campaign presence on new online platforms like Facebook, which was becoming a wildly popular social media service after its birth in a college dorm room in 2004.

Republicans nominated long-time Arizona senator John McCain, aged seventy-two, a self-styled "maverick" and a Vietnam War hero who had endured years of torture as a prisoner of war. He had a record of supporting bipartisan legislation on such issues as normalizing relations with North Vietnam, campaign finance, and immigration reform. To the astonishment of even some of his closest aides, McCain picked first-term Alaska governor Sarah Palin as his running mate. Telegenic "hockey mom" Palin briefly galvanized the conservative Republican base. But when interview gaffes exposed her breathtakingly weak grasp of the issues, she became fodder for late-night television comedians and, polls showed, at least as much a liability as an asset to the Republican ticket.

Obama's poise and gravitas in televised debates favorably impressed many voters, and his campaign slogan, "Yes we can," inspired widespread hope and enthusiasm. Then, just six weeks before election day, a massive economic thunderclap gave the Democrat's campaign a buoyant boost.

The American housing price bubble, fed by years of the Federal Reserve System's easy-money policies and the private banking system's lax lending practices, burst at last. By 2008, the collapse in real estate values was generating a tsunami of mortgage defaults, especially among "subprime" borrowers whose escalating housing payments stretched them to the breaking point. Lenders watched in horror as countless homeowners defaulted and the worth of mortgage-backed securities sank precipitously. Aggressive "**deleveraging**" set in worldwide, as financial institutions from Tokyo to New York to London scrambled to reduce their debt loads by selling assets (at ever-declining prices). But some debts could not be unloaded at any price, and credit markets soon froze everywhere. Following the collapse of the venerable Wall Street firm of Lehman Brothers in September 2008, stocks sank into a deep swoon. The gravest financial hurricane since the Great Depression of the 1930s was gathering ever-increasing force.

In contrast to the infamous 1929 stock-market crash that heralded the onset of the Great Depression, it took days, not years, for a terrified Bush administration to intervene on a gigantic scale. The federal government nationalized the country's two biggest mortgage companies, the Federal National Mortgage Association ("Fannie Mae") and the Federal Home Mortgage Corporation ("Freddie Mac"), and effectively took over the world's biggest insurance company, the American International Group (AIG). Treasury secretary Henry Paulson next persuaded Congress to create the Troubled Assets Relief Program (TARP), authorizing a whopping $700 billion to buy "toxic" assets and inject cash directly into the nation's biggest banks and corporations. (Despite public outrage over TARP's original cost, when the program ended in 2014, the Treasury reported a net *profit* of $15 billion.)

Unsettled by the galloping economic calamity and seizing an opportunity to atone for the nation's troubled racial history, voters delivered a historic victory to Obama (refer to Image 37.20). He garnered 53 percent of the popular vote and won the Electoral College 365 to 173 (refer to Map 37.4). Democrats also enlarged their majorities in the House and the Senate. Observers hailed Obama's savvy targeting and fundraising on platforms like Facebook, and many predicted that the social media age would bridge partisan divides and strengthen democracy.

Prognosticators drew similarly sunny conclusions about the meaning of Obama's election to the long-vexed history of American race relations. Yet electoral victory also confronted the nation's first Black president with the daunting challenge of governing a country embroiled in two wars, even as it sank into the deepest economic abyss since the 1930s. "Black Man Given Nation's Worst Job," jibed the satirical magazine, *The Onion*. The president-elect who had run on a message of hope and change would need much of it as he entered the White House.

Abaca Press/Alamy Stock Photo

Image 37.20 The New First Family President-elect Barack Obama, wife Michelle, and daughters Sasha and Malia, on election night 2008 in Chicago's Grant Park.

2008

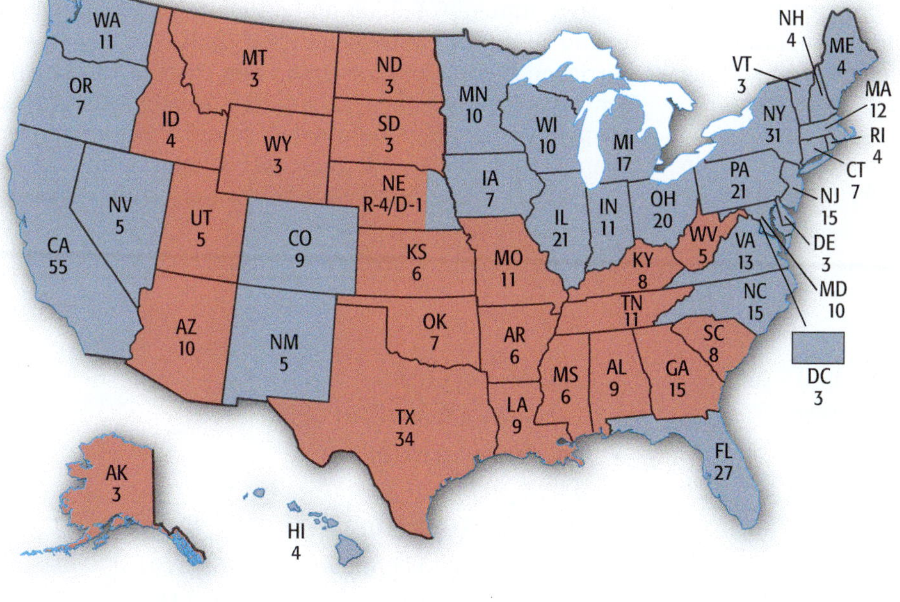

Candidate (Party)	Electoral Vote		Popular Vote	
Obama (Democrat)	365	68%	69,498,459	52.9%
McCain (Republican)	173	32%	59,948,283	45.6%

Map 37.4 Presidential Election of 2008 A record voter turnout, swelled by millions of young new voters, African Americans, and Latinos, gave Senator Barack Obama an Electoral College landslide and the Democratic party solid control of both houses of Congress. Obama redrew the electoral map by taking nine states won by George W. Bush in 2004.

Chapter Summary

The dynamic young "baby-boomer" Bill Clinton defeated President George H. W. Bush in 1992 and promoted an ambitious reform agenda within the context of his centrist New Democrat ideology, which broke the traditional Democratic affinity for labor and government social programs. Clinton's efforts to reform health care and promote gun control met strong resistance, but his economic policies helped to spark a decade-long expansion. Presenting an aggressively conservative agenda, Republicans gained control of Congress in 1994 for the first time in forty years. But overreaching by the Newt Gingrich–led Republicans enabled Clinton to revive his fortunes and win a second term by defeating Kansas Senator Robert Dole in 1996.

In his second term, Clinton downplayed reform and successfully claimed the political middle ground. Racial issues, including affirmative action and criminal justice, caused continuing controversies as well as periodic outbursts of violence. While some Black Americans made great social and economic gains, residential segregation sustained the strong link between poverty and race.

The booming economy encouraged bipartisan deregulation efforts and enhanced Clinton's efforts to develop controversial "globalization" policies that expanded on the NAFTA. This was aided by the commercialization of the internet, which ushered in a new era of worldwide communication and commerce, and a "dot-com" boom of high-technology investment. Women became nearly half of the workforce, but many continued to experience lower pay and fewer opportunities in the workplace. Family life the 1990s adapted in striking ways to social and economic change, even as the "traditional" family came under severe pressure.

Clinton recovered from early foreign policy stumbles in Africa with a successful intervention in the former Yugoslavia. But efforts at Middle East peace stalled. Clinton's affair with Monica Lewinsky led to his highly partisan impeachment in 1998 and acquittal in 1999. In the extremely close election of 2000, Vice President Albert Gore won a majority of the popular vote but lost to Texas Governor George W. Bush in the Electoral College by four votes after the Supreme Court ended a recount in Florida.

American culture grew more diverse in the late twentieth century. Multiculturalism, postmodernism, and the fragmentation of once-national media opened doors to fresh voices and minority perspectives, though the sense of shared cultural experience and ideas diminished.

George W. Bush took office after the close, bitter election of 2000, and began governing as a highly activist and often divisive conservative leader. His heavy defense expenditures and sharp tax cuts created huge federal budget deficits.

The September 11, 2001, terrorist attacks shocked and unified the nation, while propelling it out of its long centuries of relative safety from foreign attack on domestic soil. Bush responded by launching a "war on terror" that included a swift ouster of the Taliban in Afghanistan. He also launched a highly controversial war against Iraqi dictator Saddam Hussein, claiming that Iraq possessed weapons of mass destruction that threatened the United States. While Saddam Hussein was quickly overthrown, Iraq soon fell into chaos.

Bush won reelection in 2004 as a strong leader, but he suffered numerous failures and decreasing popularity in his second term. The administration's disastrous response to Hurricane Katrina and the continuing conflict in Iraq led to Democratic gains in the 2006 midterm elections. In the 2008 campaign Democrats nominated youthful Senator Barack Obama, who defeated Republican Senator John McCain; Obama became the first Black president in American history.

Key Terms

- weapons of mass destruction (WMD) (989)
- Democratic Leadership Council (DLC) (990)
- Los Angeles rebellion (990)
- Don't Ask, Don't Tell (992)
- Oklahoma City bombing (992)
- Contract with America (993)
- Temporary Assistance for Needy Families (994)
- Telecommunications Act of 1996 (999)
- over-the-counter (OTC) derivatives (1000)
- North American Free Trade Agreement (NAFTA) (1000)
- World Trade Organization (WTO) (1000)
- multiculturalism (1005)
- Al Qaeda (1007)
- Whitewater (1008)
- Lewinsky affair (1008)
- *Bush v. Gore* (1010)
- 9/11 (1012)
- USA Patriot Act (1013)
- Department of Homeland Security (1013)
- Guantánamo Detention Camp (1014)
- Abu Ghraib prison (1015)
- No Child Left Behind Act (1018)
- Hurricane Katrina (1021)
- deleveraging (1022)

People to Know

- William Jefferson ("Bill") Clinton
- Al Gore
- H. Ross Perot
- Hillary Rodham Clinton
- Newt Gingrich
- Robert Dole
- Slobodan Miloševic´
- Osama bin Laden
- Monica Lewinsky
- Toni Morrison
- John McCain
- Sarah Palin
- George W. Bush
- Richard Cheney
- Condoleezza Rice
- Colin Powell
- Nancy Pelosi
- Barack Obama
- Joseph R. ("Joe") Biden

Chronology

1992	• Jury's verdict sparks Los Angeles rebellion • Clinton defeats Bush and Perot for presidency	
1993	• First World Trade Center bombing • NAFTA signed	• Toni Morrison receives the Nobel Prize for Literature
1994	• Health-care reform bill fails • Republicans win majorities in both houses of Congress	
1996	• Welfare reform bill becomes law • Telecommunications Reform Act passed	• Clinton defeats Dole for presidency
1998	• Clinton-Lewinsky scandal • Al Qaeda bombing of the U.S. embassies in Kenya and Tanzania	• House of Representatives impeaches Clinton
1999	• Senate acquits Clinton on impeachment charges • Kosovo crisis; NATO warfare with Serbia	• Protest in Seattle against World Trade Organization
2000	• United States normalizes trade relations with China • George W. Bush wins presidency in Electoral College; Al Gore takes popular vote	
2001	• Bush's $1.3 trillion tax cut passes Congress • Congress passes No Child Left Behind Act • Terrorists attack New York City and Washington, DC, on September 11	• U.S. invades Afghanistan • Congress passes USA Patriot Act
2002	• Bush labels Iraq, Iran, and North Korea "axis of evil" • Congress authorizes use of force against Iraq • UN Security Council demands that Iraq comply with weapons inspections	• Republicans regain Senate
2003	• U.S. invades Iraq • Second Bush tax cut	• Saddam Hussein captured in Iraq • Supreme Court narrowly approves affirmative action
2004	• Gay marriage controversy erupts • Iraqi interim government installed	• Bush defeats Kerry for presidency
2005	• Iraq elects permanent government but quickly descends into sectarian conflict	
2006	• Saddam Hussein executed • Democrats retake control of Congress	
2007	• U.S. troop surge in Iraq	
2008	• Barack Obama elected 44th president of the United States	

To Learn More

Nancy Altman, *The Battle for Social Security: From FDR's Vision to Bush's Gamble* (2005)

Kathleen Belew, *Bring the War Home: The White Power Movement and Paramilitary America* (2018)

Derek Chollet and Jim Goldgeier, *America Between the Wars: From 11/9 to 9/11* (2008)

Steven Connor, ed., *The Cambridge Companion to Postmodernism* (2004)

Jason DeParle, *American Dream: Three Women, Ten Kids, and a Nation's Drive to End Welfare* (2004)

Elizabeth Drew, *Showdown: The Struggle Between the Gingrich Congress and the Clinton White House* (1997)

Lily Geismer, *Left Behind: The Democrats' Failed Attempt to Solve Inequality* (2022)

John F. Harris, *The Survivor: Bill Clinton in the White House* (2005)

Nicole Hemmer, *Partisans: The Conservative Revolutionaries Who Remade American Politics in the 1990s* (2022)

Arlie Hochschild with Anne Machung, *The Second Shift: Working Parents and the Revolution at Home*, 2nd ed. (2003)

Margaret O'Mara, *The Code: Silicon Valley and the Remaking of America* (2019)

Thomas Ricks, *Fiasco: The American Military Adventure in Iraq* (2006)

Marjorie Spruill, *Divided We Stand: The Battle over Women's Rights and Family Values That Polarized American Politics* (2017)

Joseph E. Stiglitz, *The Roaring Nineties: A New History of the World's Most Prosperous Decade* (2003)

Jeffrey Toobin, *Too Close to Call: The Thirty-Six Day Battle to Decide the 2000 Election* (2001)

Julian Zelizer, ed., *The Presidency of George W. Bush: A First Historical Assessment* (2010)

Chapter 38

American Reckoning: 2009–2024

We remain a young nation. But in the words of Scripture, the time has come to set aside childish things.

Barack Obama, First Inaugural Address, 2009

Chapter Outline

- Obama in the White House
- New directions in foreign policy
- The Great Recession's inequitable aftermath
- Deepening distrust and the new populism
- The rise of Big Tech
- Expanded civil rights and new racial reckonings
- The immigration impasse
- The election and administration of Donald Trump
- The COVID-19 pandemic
- The 2020 election and its aftermath
- Joe Biden in the White House
- The American Prospect

Contending Voices: Secrets and Security

New president Barack Obama inherited two foreign wars and a crushing financial crisis, soon dubbed "The Great Recession." Obama seized the occasion to pursue major reforms in health care and financial regulation, despite steadfast Republican opposition. Voters erased Democratic majorities in the House of Representatives in 2010, and the Senate in 2014. Obama's reelection in 2012 failed to dampen the rancorous political divisions that threatened to turn the federal government into a useless laughingstock. A standoff over funding Obama's signature legislative achievement, the Patient Protection and Affordable Care Act, shut down the federal government entirely for more than two weeks in 2013.

Americans continued to wrestle with the paradox of rising economic inequality amidst expanding social inclusion. A painfully slow economic recovery and stubbornly high unemployment in the years following the 2008 financial crisis highlighted growing gaps in income and wealth. At the same time, American society grew more ethnically diverse and socially tolerant in the twenty-first century, as evidenced by the biracial president, the swelling ranks of immigrants, and the extraordinarily rapid expansion of popular acceptance of gay and lesbian Americans, culminating in a 2015 Supreme Court decision legalizing same-sex marriage.

Yet diversity had its denouncers, tolerance had its limits, and governmental impotence in the face of anemic economic recovery and mounting inequality had dramatic political consequences, as a baffled and angry electorate demonstrated in 2016, when they elevated billionaire real estate developer and reality-TV celebrity Donald J. Trump to the presidency.

Focus Questions

1. How did Barack Obama promise to change the domestic and foreign policy agenda of his predecessor, George W. Bush, and to what degree was he successful in doing so?
2. What caused the dramatic rise in economic inequality in early twenty-first-century America, and how did the widening income gap contribute to growing political and social polarization?

3. How did Donald Trump's election and administration affect American diplomatic and trade relations with the rest of the world?
4. How did intensifying climate disruption and natural disasters shift public opinion and debate about climate change, and what was the role of young people in this activism?

38-1 Obama in the White House

Inspired by Barack Obama's vision of hope, a vast and exuberant crowd gathered in Washington, DC, to celebrate his inauguration. Youthful energy was in the air, though in his inaugural address Obama struck a sober note by calling on Americans to "put away childish things" and embrace "a new era of responsibility."

Obama's solemn tone was fitting. Even as he spoke, home construction was grinding to a halt, mortgage foreclosures were soaring, and countless businesses were shutting their doors. Most alarmingly, the economy was shedding a sickening 700,000 jobs a month. The unemployment rate climbed above 10 percent—the highest level since the early 1980s and perhaps heralding a return to the catastrophic joblessness of the Great Depression of the 1930s.

Obama strongly counterpunched against the deepening crisis in his first hundred days, including a huge "stimulus" bill—the **American Recovery and Reinvestment Act**—that contained nearly a trillion dollars of tax cuts, as well as new spending for jobs, infrastructure projects, and relief to state and local governments. Despite bitter criticism, the government also helped to arrest the economy's freefall by shoring up bankrupt automakers General Motors and Chrysler, saving up to 3 million jobs. The eventual cost to the government was some $10 billion—arguably a bargain price to pay for rescuing a major American industry and staving off a repeat of the Great Depression.

Asked by an interviewer in February 2009, just one month into his presidency, if he felt "burdened" by the welter of problems he faced, President Obama (b. 1961) replied:

> "I think that we are at an extraordinary moment that is full of peril but full of possibility and I think that's the time you want to be president. . . . [T]here's something about this country where hard times, big challenges bring out the best in us. This is when the political system starts to move effectively. This is when people start getting out of the petty and the trivial debates. This is when the public starts paying attention. . . . [W]hen things are going well . . . they've got better things to do than to think about public policy. . . . "

By the summer of 2009, the worst of the panic was over, and the economy began to expand once more, though painfully slowly. Economists tempered their comparisons with the Great Depression and gave the less frightening label "Great Recession" to the turmoil (refer to Figure 38.1). But the economy had been badly wounded and continued to suffer, as the first steps toward growth were feeble and faltering. The federal recovery package bailed out Wall Street banks, but stopped short of giving relief to debt-ridden homeowners—a stark contrast to Franklin Roosevelt's New Deal (refer to "30-6 Creating Jobs for the Jobless," pp. 786–788). No big-bank executives faced criminal charges.

Meanwhile, the unemployment rate stayed stuck above 9 percent. As millions of Americans lost jobs and homes, and many permanently abandoned their search for employment, the confidence-crushing and security-sapping legacies of the Great Recession wormed their way deeply into the American psyche and would not be quickly dislodged.

Even while pursuing economic recovery, President Obama also sought to achieve the long-sought liberal goal of health-care reform. When attempts to enlist Republican support bogged down in congressional haggling, he relied on Democrats alone to pass a landmark health bill, the **Patient Protection and Affordable Care Act** (customarily shortened to Affordable Care Act, or ACA, and more popularly called "Obamacare") in March 2010. The new health-care law mandated all Americans to purchase health insurance starting in 2014, required states to establish "exchanges" whereby individuals and small businesses could purchase health-care insurance at competitive rates, prohibited insurers from denying coverage to anyone with a preexisting medical condition, and allowed children up to the age of twenty-six to remain covered by their parents' health plans. Obamacare also provided subsidies to those below certain income thresholds to help pay for private insurance while funding a major expansion of public Medicaid insurance for poorer Americans. The price of the bill was estimated at $940 billion over ten years, but experts also predicted that the bill's cost-cutting measures would reduce the federal deficit by more than $1 trillion over twenty years.

Scarcely pausing, Obama soon followed his health-care success with the 2010 **Wall Street Reform and Consumer Protection Act** (commonly known by the names of its principal congressional sponsors, **Dodd-Frank**), which pointed the way to a major overhaul of the

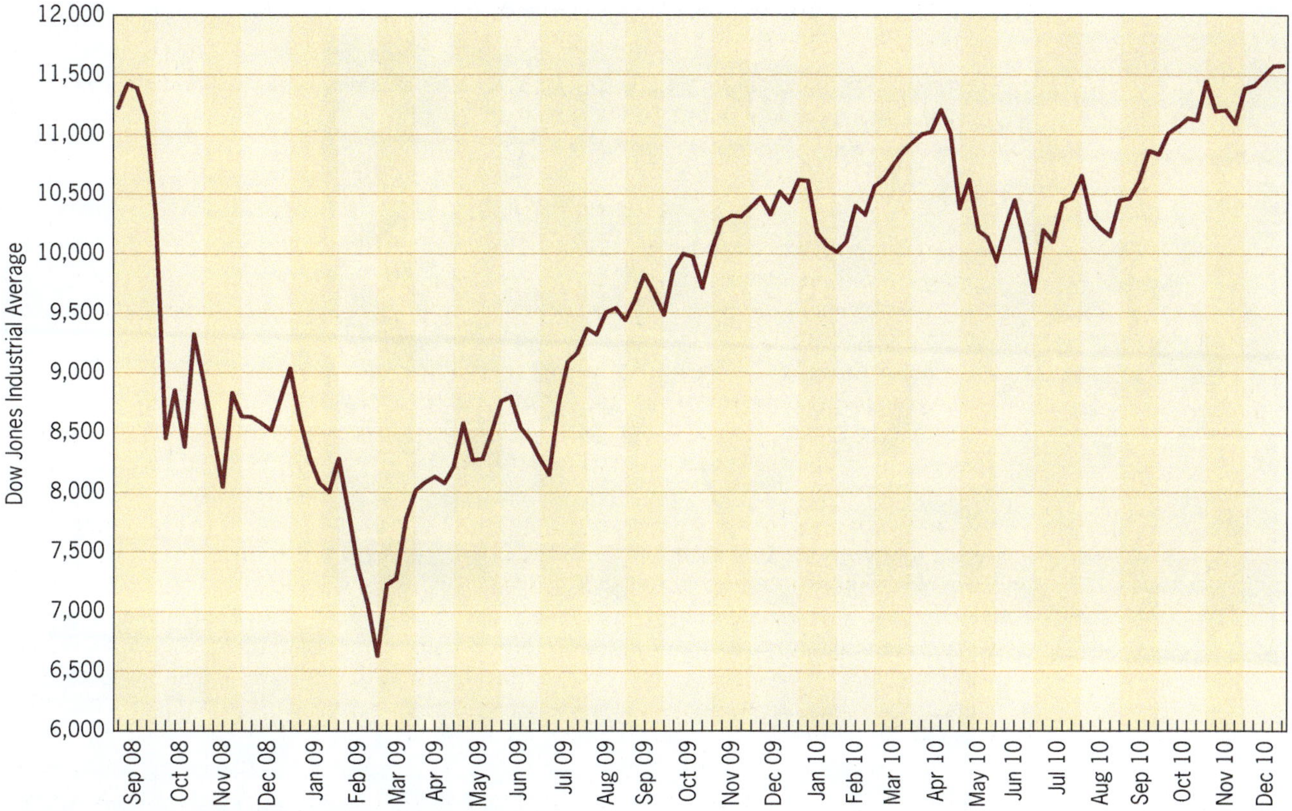

Figure 38.1 The Great Recession Takes Hold The financial turmoil that rocked the world in 2008 sent stock-market values plummeting, though they rebounded much more quickly than after the Great Crash of 1929 that heralded the onset of the Great Depression. (Refer to Figure 29.6, p. 768.)

Source: Data from http://www.nyse.tv/dow-jones-industrial-average-history-djia.htm.

nation's financial regulatory system. The act aimed to curb the risky, high-flying practices that had contributed to the debacle of 2008 with new controls on banks, investment houses, and stock markets, and with new truth-in-lending rules to protect consumers.

38-2 Back to Backlash

Yet, in a polarized political era, Obama had unusual difficulty reaping the political rewards of these legislative achievements. He seemed caught between an anvil and a boulder. Because his measures only halted but did not fully reverse the economy's decline, critics on the left condemned him as too timid. Because federal budget deficits ballooned dramatically on his watch, critics on the right excoriated him as a big-government spendthrift. By the end of 2009, Obama's approval ratings had sunk below 50 percent, the largest first-year slump of any modern president before him, and stayed there throughout his first term.

The conjunction of expanding federal programs and mounting deficits tapped into a deep vein of American wariness of "big government." Starting with vehement attacks on the health-care bill in the summer of 2009, angry protesters accused Obama of promoting "socialism" and "unconstitutional" controls over individual lives. Calling themselves the **Tea Party** after the American Revolutionary Patriots, these aggrieved citizens combined a knack for street-theater demonstrations with nonstop internet and media fulminations against the president and his policies (refer to Image 38.1A). The ugly racial undertone of the protests, where mostly white Tea Party members sometimes waved signs mocking the nation's first Black president and his family, prompted a formal repudiation from the NAACP. Bankrolled by billionaire donors and corporate-backed political action committees (PACs), the Tea Party movement galvanized a hyperconservative grassroots constituency that pushed the Republican Party even more sharply to the right, eventually spawning a small but potent and tight-right **Freedom Caucus** within the Republican House membership.

A

Jan Isachsen/Art Directors/Alamy Stock Photo

B

Spencer Platt/Getty Images News/Getty Images

Image 38.1A and B An Age of Discontent Dramatic protests from both the right and left sprang up during Barack Obama's presidency. Tea Party rallies, such as this one in Washington, DC (38.1A), expressed conservative resistance to the president's promise of "change." On the political left, meanwhile, Occupy Wall Street protests against economic inequality, like this one in New York City, erupted across the country (38.1B).

Heartened by the Tea Party's mobilization, Republicans determined to fight the administration tooth and nail, steadfastly repudiating Obama's promise of a post-partisan politics. The president did succeed in appointing two new Supreme Court Justices, Sonia Sotomayor (the Court's first Hispanic American) in 2009 and Elena Kagan in 2010, bringing the number of female justices to three. But other Democratic efforts, like a "cap-and-trade" bill to curb greenhouse gases and reduce global warming, fell victim to the fervent minority's opposition, as gridlock continued to jam the gears of government.

One casualty of that gridlock was the Democratic Party's majority in Congress. In the midterm elections of 2010, Republicans gained six seats in the Senate and a whopping sixty-three seats in the House, enough to give them majority control of the lower chamber when the new Congress convened in 2011 (refer to Map 38.1).

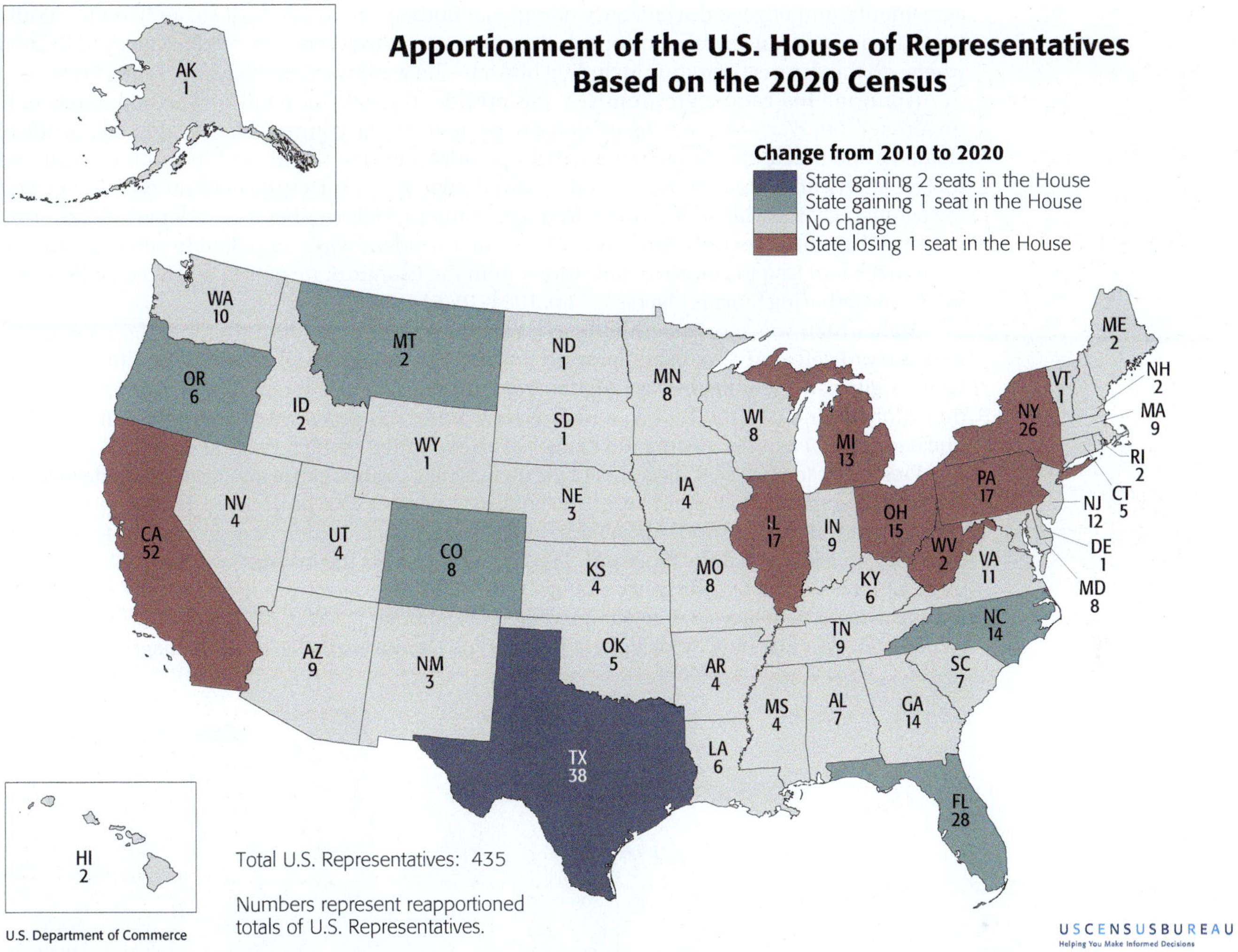

Map 38.1 Demography Is (Political) Destiny The United States is one of the few nations with a constitutionally mandated census, a provision reflecting the Founders' expectation that the country's population would grow and spread out, and their commitment to maintaining fair and proportional representation in the federal electoral system. Thus, every ten years congressional districts are redrawn, with some states gaining and some states losing representation in the House and the Electoral College. This map, showing the reapportionment resulting from the 2020 census, clearly reveals the continuing shift of the nation's population and political center of gravity southward and westward, with Texas proving to be the biggest gainer of new House seats and electoral votes (as it had been in 2010) and midwestern swing states like Ohio and Michigan losing one vote apiece. Because the remapping of congressional district lines occurs at the state level, Republicans' continuing majorities in many state legislatures put their party in control of the redistricting process in far more states than those controlled by Democrats.

Source: U.S. Census Bureau.

Heartened by their triumph, Republicans looked to the upcoming 2012 presidential election with increasing hope for victory—though the spectacle of protracted bickering and partisan intransigence while the health of the nation's economy hung in the balance deeply disillusioned many Americans of both parties.

38-3 New Directions in Foreign Policy

Along with economic problems, Obama also had to grapple with America's "forever wars" in Iraq and Afghanistan. Seeking to chart a more tempered and pragmatic course after the neoconservative ventures of the Bush years, Obama assembled a foreign-policy team that included his one-time political rival, former First Lady Hillary Rodham Clinton, as secretary of state. Obama sought to utilize his own global popularity in efforts to repair frayed alliances, forge new arms-control agreements, and engage the citizenry of regional hotbeds of anti-Americanism like the Middle East. His personal and symbolic appeal to many foreign observers was vividly conveyed in 2009 when—to the surprise of many, including himself—he was awarded the Nobel Peace Prize.

Honoring his campaign promises, the president sought to wind down the increasingly unpopular Iraq War while leaving behind a reasonably stable country. Shortly after taking office, Obama announced that American combat operations in Iraq would end in summer 2010 and that all American combat troops would be withdrawn by 2011. Despite continuing violence and the agonizingly slow birth of a viable Iraqi government, U.S. combat forces departed from Iraq in December 2011. Yet only three years later, the president was compelled to send substantial forces back into Iraq to counter a new threat from the Islamic State of Iraq and Syria (ISIS) (refer to "38-13 Gathering Storms Overseas," pp. 1044–1045).

Afghanistan was a pricklier nettle to grasp. Obama had declared that the Afghan war was necessary to defeat Al-Qaeda and prevent future terrorism. But Afghan *jihadi* (militant Islamic) fighters grew stronger against an Afghan government plagued by incompetence and corruption. More ominously, the Taliban and Al-Qaeda found refuge across the border in unstable but nuclear-armed Pakistan, posing the danger of an expanded conflict there as well.

Pressed by some to seek a way out of the increasingly costly conflict, and by others to deepen the American commitment, Obama chose to do both. In December 2009 he declared that American troops would begin withdrawing from Afghanistan by 2011—but that to achieve that goal he was temporarily deploying an additional thirty thousand U.S. soldiers to combat the insurgency. Despite this commitment and a new counterinsurgency strategy, little political progress ensued. Meanwhile, American forces managed to achieve a dramatic success in neighboring Pakistan in May 2011 when they concluded a ten-year manhunt by killing 9/11 mastermind Osama bin Laden (refer to Image 38.2).

Pete Souza/The White House/Getty Images

Image 38.2 The End of Osama bin Laden President Barack Obama and his national security team huddle in the White House Situation Room to watch live updates on the mission to kill Osama bin Laden, May 2, 2011. Nearly ten years after the murderous attacks of September 11, 2001, rough justice was meted out to the terrorist mastermind. Much commentary on this photograph has focused on the presence of women in the room and on the president's lack of macho swagger, even as American forces closed in on the nation's most hated foe.

Though falling short of his goals in Afghanistan, Obama made good on his pledge to begin withdrawing troops in 2011. By the end of his presidency in 2016, only 9,800 American service members remained in the country.

In what proved to be one of Obama's most controversial policies, he stepped up the use of aerial attacks from unmanned remotely piloted aircraft, popularly called "drones." The increasing intensity of U.S. drone attacks sparked both domestic and international outcries about this revolutionary new kind of warfare, though the administration maintained that drones permitted surgically precise strikes that spared innocent civilians. Particularly troubling were attacks on U.S. citizens in places like Yemen. Even if they were known terrorists, critics charged, their constitutionally guaranteed right to trial by jury protected them from summary execution.

Obama also strived to honor his promise to roll back Bush-era antiterrorism policies. He issued executive orders banning waterboarding and other practices that were widely considered to constitute torture. The president also tried to shut down the controversial military detention center at Cuba's Guantánamo Bay. But Congress blocked his efforts, and as late as 2023, thirty-two of the nearly eight hundred prisoners captured in the aftermath of the 9/11 attacks continued to languish in Guantánamo with little prospect of release. Nine had died in captivity, seven of them apparent suicides.

38-4 The Politics of Inequality

Chronically high unemployment and stubbornly anemic economic growth after the 2008 financial meltdown helped sharpen a national debate over class, inequality, and the role of government in the economy. The financial sector provided a particularly rich target for many Americans' ire. Financiers' soaring incomes helped to drive the surge in the richest Americans' income share. Even with new rules in place, regulators seemed mismatched against Wall Street's outsized political clout.

The fall of 2011 saw the emergence of an eclectic protest movement that colorfully highlighted the issue of rising inequality. **Occupy Wall Street** began as a small demonstration by youthful radicals who pitched their tents in New York's financial district (refer to Image 38.1B). Similar encampments soon sprang up in several other cities and popularized the slogan "We Are the 99 Percent"—a reference to the tremendously lopsided concentration of wealth and income among the highest-earning 1 percent of Americans. Though the protesters gradually decamped, President Obama eventually acknowledged their cause, declaring in his January 2012 State of the Union message that he refused to "settle for a country where a shrinking number of people do really well, while a growing number of Americans barely get by." He called the challenge to restore broadly shared prosperity "the defining issue of our time" (refer to Image 38.3).

Growing inequality had deep roots and grew to dramatic proportions as the new century unfolded. In an unsettling reversal of post-WWII trends in American society, during the last two decades of the twentieth century the rich had grown fabulously richer, middle-class incomes had stagnated, and the poor were left to make do with an ever-shrinking share of the economic pie. Between 1967 and 2021, the share of the nation's income that flowed to the top 20 percent of its households swelled from 44 percent to 53 percent (refer to Figure 38.2). Even more striking was the remarkable increase in inequality *among* those high earners. The top 5 percent of income recipients saw their share of the national income grow from about 17 percent in 1967 to 24 percent in 2021. And as for the top 1 percent so frequently targeted in the Occupy movement's rhetoric, their share of national income quadrupled between 1979 and 2007 alone. The gap in *wealth*—what people own, as distinct from what they earn—was even more dramatic (refer to Figure 38.3). By the end of 2021, just 1 percent of Americans controlled a record 32.3 percent of the nation's wealth.

AP Images/Eric Gay

Image 38.3 Haves and Have Nots The financial crisis and ensuing Great Recession helped to sharpen debates over America's extreme economic inequality in the twenty-first century. A recently laid-off San Antonio woman in 2009 stands in front of her house, which was in danger of foreclosure due to her inability to make mortgage payments.

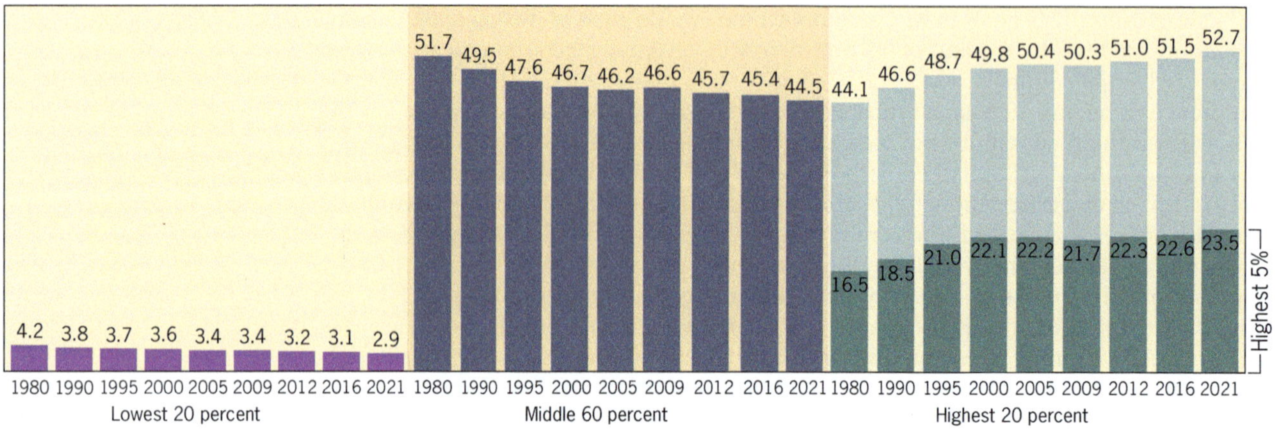

Figure 38.2 Share of Income Received by Families, by Quintile, 1980–2021 Since 1980 the incomes of the lowest 20 percent and the middle 60 percent have been shrinking, whereas the incomes of the highest 20 percent, and particularly the top 5 percent, have climbed steadily.

Source: *Statistical Abstract of the United States*, 2010; U.S. Census Bureau *Consumer Income Report*, relevant years, http://www.census.gov/hhes/www/income/data/historical/families/.

Widening inequality could be measured in other ways as well. In 1965, chief executives typically earned 20 times as much as the average worker in their corporations; in 2021, they earned 399 times as much. Wealth being created by the increased productivity of American workers since the late twentieth century was flowing largely to corporate executives rather than to the workers themselves (refer to Figure 38.4). At the same time, close to 40 million people remained mired in poverty in 2022, or 11.6 percent of all Americans. The poverty rate varied greatly by race, with 8.1 percent of white people, 17.1 percent of Latinos, 19.5 percent of African Americans, and 24.3 percent of Native Americans living in poverty.

These figures offered a depressing indictment of the inequities afflicting an affluent and allegedly egalitarian republic. A similar trend toward increasing inequality was evident in many industrial societies, but it was most pronounced in the United States. In the new century, Americans on average were no longer the world's wealthiest people, as they had been in the quarter-century after World War II. Citizens of several other countries enjoyed higher average per capita incomes, and many nations boasted more equitable distributions of wealth and well-being (refer to Figure 38.5).

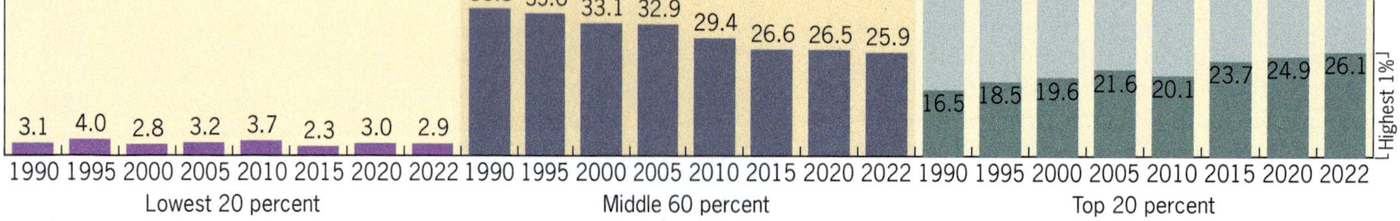

Figure 38.3 Distribution of U.S. Household Wealth, by Quintile, 1990–2022. The early twenty-first century's growing economic divide becomes sharper by zooming in on the share of wealth held by the very richest Americans. The fortunes of the top 1 percent often derive from investments and other non-income sources. A succession of tax reforms since the 1980s resulted in these assets usually being taxed at a lower rate than income in the higher-earning tax brackets, accelerating the concentration of wealth at the very top.

Source: Data from the Federal Reserve, https://www.federalreserve.gov/releases/z1/dataviz/dfa/distribute/chart/#range:2008.3,2023.3

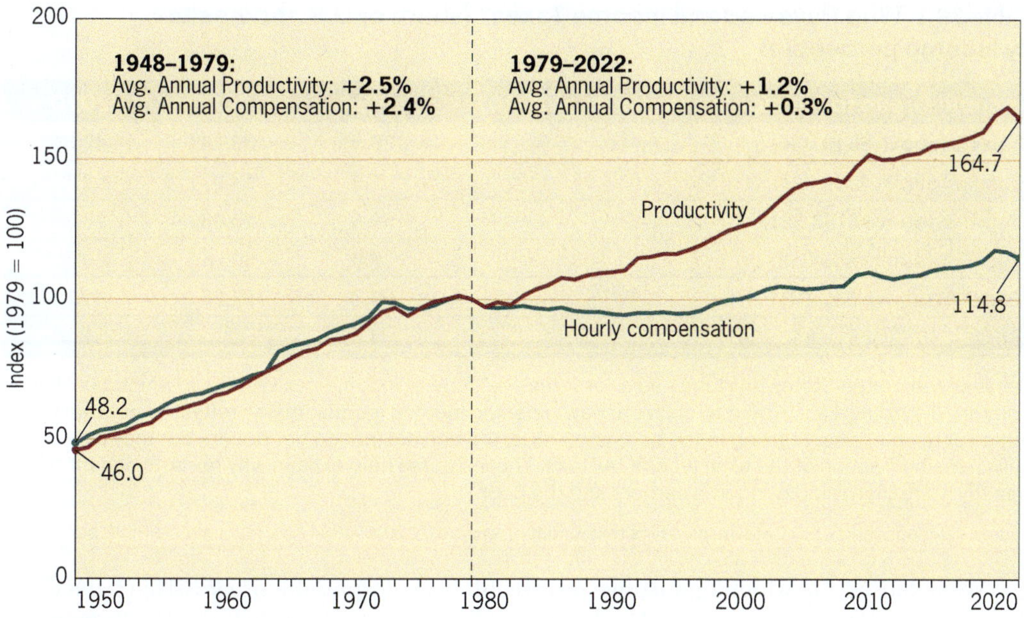

Figure 38.4 The Productivity Gap Economic productivity, measured here in terms of value of output per unit of labor input, improved steadily throughout the last half of the twentieth century thanks to technological advances and rising education levels. But even as education levels rose and workplace technologies spread further beginning in the 1970s, economic globalization and other policy shifts meant that the gains from increased productivity accrued increasingly disproportionally to executives and shareholders rather than to ordinary workers. Since 1979, worker productivity has increased at a rate that is more than 4 times the rate of increasing compensation.

	U.S.	Canada	Germany	Japan	Sweden	Hong Kong	U.K.	Korea	Italy	France	Czech	Spain
Income inequality (Gini coefficient) after taxes and transfers	0.38	0.28	0.3	0.33	0.28	0.54	0.36	0.33	0.33	0.29	0.25	0.32
Unemployment rate	5.4	7.5	3.6	2.8	8.8	5.3	4.5	3.7	9.6	7.9	2.8	14.8
Level of democracy	7.85	8.88	8.8	8.33	9.39	5.28	8.28	8.03	7.69	8.07	7.97	8.07
Life expectancy at birth	77	81.7	80.9	84.7	83.2	85	80.4	83.5	82.9	82.5	77.4	83.3
Food insecurity	7.8	7.7	3.8	4.4	5.4	N/A	4.1	5.6	5.7	6.6	8.5	8
Prison population rate (per 100,000)	505	85	67	36	74	106	89	105	96	106	178	116
Student math scores*	478	512	500	527	502	551	502	526	487	495	499	481
Student science scores*	502	518	503	529	499	517	505	519	468	493	497	483

Best Worst

*Student scores drawn from 2018 PISA tests conducted by the OECD.

Figure 38.5 How the United States Measures Up Once the undisputed world leader in countless areas of human endeavor, the United States looked to be falling behind on several crucial counts in the early twenty-first century. Year dates for the various figures above range between 2010 and 2021. For the measurement of income inequality, known as the "Gini" coefficient, a higher number signifies a higher level of inequality. For the measurement of democratic governance, known as the "Democracy Index," a higher number signifies the presence of stronger and more extensive democratic norms and institutions. The figure for "food insecurity" shows the percentage of those answering yes to the following survey question: "Have there been times in the past few months when you did not have enough money to buy food that you or your family needed?"

Sources: OECD Database. Economist Intelligence Unit. World Bank Data from 2013–2021.

Table 38.1 Who Pays Federal Income Taxes? (share of U.S. income tax, by income percentile)

Income Group (base income shown as of 2020)	1994	2014	2020
Top 1% (above $548,336)	28.9%	39.48%	42.3%
Top 5% (above $220,521)	47.5	59.97	62.7
Top 10% (above $152,321)	59.5	70.88	73.7
Top 25% (above $85,853)	79.6	86.78	88.5
Top 50% (above $42,184)	95.2	97.25	97.7
Bottom 50% (below $42,184)	4.8	2.75	2.3

Because the United States has long had a "progressive" federal income-tax system, in which tax obligations are distributed according to ability to pay, widening income inequality was reflected in a redistribution of tax burdens. Starting in the booming 1990s, the rich did indeed get richer—but they also paid an increasing fraction of the total federal tax take. These figures help explain why tax cuts benefit the wealthy more than middle-income earners and the poor.

Source: Tax Foundation, IRS Data, https://files.taxfoundation.org/20170201091804/TaxFoundation-FF538.pdf.

What caused the widening income and wealth gaps despite the progressive character of the tax system? Some critics pointed to the tax and fiscal reforms passed during the Reagan and subsequent Republican presidencies, which lowered taxes on corporations and the wealthy (refer to Table 38.1). With less tax revenue flowing in, federal as well as state and local governments cut public spending on social welfare programs, infrastructure, and other public services. But deeper-running historical currents played a powerful role too, as suggested by the similar trend lines in other industrialized societies. Among the most conspicuous causes were intensifying global economic competition; the displacement by robots of high-paying manufacturing jobs for semiskilled and unskilled workers; the greater economic rewards commanded by educated workers in technology-intensive industries; the rise of the financial sector as a percentage of national GDP; the shrinkage of unions; the growth of part-time and temporary work; the rising tide of relatively low-skill immigrants; and the increasing tendency of educated men and women to marry one another and both work, creating households with very high incomes. Educational disparities also contributed to economic inequality, starting with the underfunding of many schools in poor urban areas and the soaring cost of higher education. A 2017 study revealed that at the eighty most selective colleges, more students came from families with incomes in the top 1 percent than from all the families combined in the bottom 40 percent of the income distribution.

The very nature of the contemporary economy seemed to pose daunting obstacles to creating more equitably shared prosperity. When the twentieth century opened, United States Steel Corporation was the flagship business of America's booming industrial revolution. A generation later, General Motors, annually producing millions of automobiles, became the characteristic American corporation, signaling the historic shift to a mass consumer economy. Following World War II, the rise of companies like IBM (refer to "33-1 Affluence and Its Anxieties," pp. 876–878) ushered in a fast-paced "information age" that made entire job categories obsolete. Desktop computers replaced secretaries, and robotic arms replaced factory workers. At the same time, economic globalization allowed American manufacturing to move an ocean away.

In 1965, the four largest American carmakers were among the most profitable companies in the world, having combined sales that exceeded 5 percent of GNP. They employed a total of 750,000 mostly unionized assembly-line workers, concentrated in the industrial Midwest. In 2022, the largest manufacturing employer in the world was Foxconn, a Chinese supplier to American technology companies. Foxconn's workforce of more than 800,000 included 200,000 workers in "iPhone City," an Apple assembly plant in Southern China.

38-5 Big Tech

By the dawn of the twenty-first century, the internet was a far cry from the network created by the federal government in the 1960s to support Cold War–era collaboration among American computer scientists. A majority of Americans in 2000 already relied on the internet at home, work, or school. With the spread of faster, "broadband" online access and internet-enabled mobile phones ("smartphones") in the first decades of the new millennium, those numbers skyrocketed. By 2024, well over 80 percent of American adults used the internet daily. Those most wedded to their internet devices were teens and young adults, nearly half of whom reported being online "almost constantly."

Low interest rates and a bewitching mood of techno-optimism sucked prodigious piles of money into the tech sector. The tech-friendly Obama administration allowed a flurry of mergers and acquisitions that helped concentrate power in a few **Big Tech** firms.

In 2005, only 7 percent of American adults used social media; by 2015, 76 percent were social media users. As platforms like Facebook and Twitter expanded, they became increasingly significant sources of news. The online shift of attention and revenue had devastating effects on American newspapers, as over 2,500 of them went out of business between 2005 and 2022. Communication habits were further altered by the widespread adoption of smartphones like the Apple iPhone (introduced 2007) and Google Android (2008), which made the internet portable, mobile, and inescapable. Online retailer Amazon rose from the ashes of the "dot-bomb" crash to become "the everything store" that by 2020 employed over a million Americans. The rise of Amazon and other internet commerce sites wreaked havoc on brick-and-mortar retailers large and small.

The market dominance and colossal wealth of the largest technology companies drew comparisons to the Gilded Age monopolies of oil, rail, and steel (refer to Sections 23-3 through 23-9, pp. 572–578). Tech founders like Jeff Bezos of Amazon and Elon Musk of Tesla, SpaceX, and Twitter amassed personal fortunes that rivaled or exceeded those of John D. Rockefeller, Andrew Carnegie, Henry Ford, and J. P. Morgan. As Barack Obama readied his second-term bid in 2012, the combined market value of Apple, Amazon, Facebook, Google, and Microsoft approached $1 trillion. Ten years later, it exceeded $7 trillion—a figure larger than the nominal GDP of every country in the world except the United States and China.

38-6 Battling for the White House in 2012

To a striking degree, inequality—both economic and political—remained a central theme of the heated 2012 presidential race. Barack Obama sought reelection on the basis of his stewardship of the economy in crisis times, his signature health-care law (narrowly upheld in a Supreme Court decision that summer), and his winding down of two unpopular wars.

The Republican Party nominated former Massachusetts governor Mitt Romney and Wisconsin congressman Paul Ryan as their presidential and vice-presidential ticket. Romney, the first Mormon presidential nominee of a major party in American history, had made his career in management consulting and private equity investing before entering politics. His record as governor of liberal Massachusetts was decidedly moderate, but he secured the GOP's presidential nomination in 2012 by hewing to a much more conservative line, promising to repeal both the Affordable Care Act and the Wall Street Reform Act, cut domestic spending, and slash taxes. Citing Obama's concerns about inequality, Republicans attacked the sitting president as fomenting "class warfare."

The role of money in politics became a divisive issue in the race, thanks to a highly controversial 2010 Supreme Court decision, ***Citizens United v. Federal Election Commission***. In a five-to-four ruling, the Court held that the First Amendment prohibited limits on political expenditures made by corporations, unions, and advocacy groups. The decision helped to spur the proliferation of so-called super-PACS, which, by avoiding any direct contributions to candidates and parties, could pour unlimited sums into the political arena. It also enabled nonprofit advocacy groups to spend money on elections without disclosing the source of their funds ("dark money"). With the floodgates of political spending thrown open, the presidential race of 2012 proved to be the most expensive in American history to date, with both campaigns and their allies spending a combined total of over $2 billion.

Writing for a 5–4 Supreme Court majority in the 2010 case of *Citizens United* v. *Federal Election Commission*, Justice Anthony Kennedy (b. 1936) held that corporations and other organizations have the same rights to free speech as individuals.

"There is simply no support for the view that the First Amendment, as originally understood, would permit the suppression of political speech by media corporations. . . . When Government seeks to use its full power, including the criminal law, to command where a person may get his or her information or what distrusted source he or she may not hear, it uses censorship to control thought. This is unlawful. The First Amendment confirms the freedom to think for ourselves."

On Election Day, Obama won a decisive victory, with 65,915,796 popular and 332 electoral votes to Romney's 60,933,500 and 206 votes. Democrats managed to retain control of the Senate, but the House remained in GOP hands.

Powerful demographic trends helped account for Obama's victory. While just 39 percent of white voters supported him in 2012 compared to 43 percent in 2008, the white population's overall share of the electorate was declining, while the multiracial Obama coalition comprised several groups—conspicuously including Latinos—that were growing in electoral importance. But as events would prove just four years later, the Obama coalition was not as robust a harbinger of the future as many had predicted.

38-7 Second-Term Stalemate

President Obama had expressed hope that a victory over Mitt Romney might "break the fever" of intractable opposition afflicting congressional Republicans. But with the partisan balance of power essentially unchanged by the election and deep-seated ideological disagreements still defining the political divide, such a hope proved wishful thinking.

Driven largely by the outsized influence of the hard-right Freedom Caucus, congressional Republicans grew ever more intransigent. Their unrelenting opposition to the Affordable Care Act forced a sixteen-day government closure in October 2013. Republicans also grew ever more fractious within their own ranks. In 2015, rebellious House Republicans unseated their leader, Speaker John Boehner, and after rancorous debate settled on Wisconsin Representative Paul Ryan as his replacement.

The spectacle of eternally feckless wrangling in Washington fed mounting disgust with all branches of government. Polls showed Obama's approval rating drooping as low as 40 percent, while more than 80 percent of citizens disapproved of the way Congress was handling its job. Even the historically hallowed Supreme Court fell short of majority approval.

Faced with apparently implacable congressional obstruction, Obama resorted ever more frequently to executive actions to achieve his objectives. After repeated congressional failures to pass comprehensive immigration reform, including the DREAM Act (Development, Relief and Education for Alien Minors Act), which would have created a path to citizenship for undocumented youths ("DREAMers") who either graduated from college or served in the U.S. armed forces, Obama in 2012 announced the **Deferred Action for Childhood Arrivals (DACA)** policy. It provided renewable two-year periods of exemption from deportation and eligibility for work permits for people who had arrived in the United States as minors, but without proper documentation (usually as the children of undocumented immigrants). Of the nearly 2 million eligible people, some 800,000 had enrolled as of 2017, when the newly installed Trump administration rescinded the policy, leaving countless Dreamers in legal limbo (refer to "The Presence of the Past: Immigration—Legal, Illegal, and Otherwise," p. 913–915).

Obama also relied on executive orders in the environmental field, including action to strengthen protection of Alaska's enormous Arctic National Wildlife Refuge (ANWR), to create or expand national monuments in several western states, and to address the challenges of climate change by lessening dependence on fossil fuels. Lacking statutory authority, all such actions were vulnerable to reversal by Obama's presidential successors.

38-8 The Immigration Impasse

Few issues remained as intractable and polarizing as immigration. Over 45 million immigrants lived in the United States by 2021, making up 13.6 percent of the population. The United States had not had such a high percentage of foreign-born residents since the 1920s (refer to "29-9 Stemming the Foreign Flood," pp. 752–753). Mexico remained the largest single nation of origin, contributing 24 percent of America's foreign-born. This was down from 30 percent in 2000, as a dramatically slowing birth rate reduced migration pressures from Mexico while other immigrant communities were growing rapidly—notably Asians. China and India each accounted for 6 percent of the foreign-born population of 2021, the Philippines 5 percent, and Vietnam 4 percent. Both Latinos and Asians were especially well represented in California, and significant immigrant enclaves now could be found across the nation, in communities urban, suburban, and rural.

As in the past, high levels of immigration aroused deep anxieties among many Americans resentful about millions of newcomers who supposedly stifled economic growth, unfairly competed for jobs, depressed wages, and freeloaded on public services. The truth was, according to a careful 2016 study by the National Academy of Sciences, immigrants positively contributed to the nation's overall economic output and had "very small" effects on employment and wages. They were net contributors to federal revenues, though net beneficiaries at the state level where services like education and hospital care were principally funded. In large metropolitan areas, immigrant arrivals helped reverse the population loss that had emptied urban neighborhoods and inner-ring suburbs of people and economic vitality. The outer boroughs of New York City filled with the small businesses and households of new immigrants, just as the Lower East Side had bustled with foreign-born newcomers a century earlier.

Yet any economic boon brought by immigration—not to mention the longstanding reliance of American agriculture on seasonal migrant workers—was overshadowed by escalating anxiety about the threats to economic and national security that foreign-born people might pose, especially those making fraught and unsanctioned journeys across the 800-mile-long U.S.-Mexico border.

Construction of segments of a border wall began in 1994, during the Clinton administration, and continued intermittently through the presidencies of George W. Bush and Obama. The wall did not stop unauthorized immigration but rerouted migrants to more dangerous desert terrain. Border-crossing deaths doubled between 1995 and 2005, and nearly doubled again by 2022, when at least 853 migrants died on their way to *El Norte*. State repression and economic crises around the world changed the demographics of those attempting to cross; Mexican nationals accounted for 85 percent of border apprehensions in 2012 but only 28 percent in 2022 (refer to Images 38.4A and B).

A

Image 38.4A and B **Immigration Confrontation**
When Arizona governor Jan Brewer signed a tough new bill in 2010 authorizing local police to crack down on illegal immigration, the national debate over immigration policy grew still more bitterly divisive. Champions of the bill hailed Arizona for taking a stand in the void left by federal inaction. Critics denounced it as an invitation to the harassment of all Latinos—indeed, all people of color—regardless of their citizenship status (38.4A). President Donald Trump later called for reinforcing and extending the border wall, a portion of which near Nogales, Arizona, is shown here (38.4B). Janet Napolitano, former Arizona governor and former secretary of homeland security, said, "Show me a fifty-foot wall, and I'll show you a fifty-one foot ladder."

B

38-9 Civil Rights and Civil Liberties

The Supreme Court in 2013 waded into politically troubled waters in *Shelby County v. Holder*, as a narrow conservative majority declared unconstitutional Section 4 of the 1965 Voting Rights Act, which had required states with a history of racial discrimination to seek federal clearance for any changes to their voting laws. The decision opened the door for some states to restrict ballot access by passing strict voter identification requirements and limiting registration periods, practices that critics charged unfairly penalized minority, poor, and young voters (refer to Image 38.5). When minority turnout declined in some swing states in the 2016 presidential election, civil liberties advocates pointed to Shelby as the culprit, although the rebound in 2020 suggested that the candidates themselves might have played a role in voter enthusiasm.

Two years later, in ***Obergefell v. Hodges***, a narrow *liberal* majority on the Court declared that the Fourteenth Amendment's equal protection and due process clauses conferred on gay people a constitutional right to marry. Following on the repeal of the military's "Don't Ask, Don't Tell" policy, the decision capped a momentous period of legal advancement for gay and lesbian Americans amidst a broader cultural acceptance of same-sex relationships.

In *Obergefell v. Hodges* (2015) a five-to-four Supreme Court majority gave constitutional protection to gay marriage in the United States. As Justice Anthony Kennedy (b. 1936) wrote in the majority decision:

"No union is more profound than marriage, for it embodies the highest ideals of love, fidelity, devotion, sacrifice, and family. In forming a marital union, two people become something greater than once they were. As some of the petitioners in these cases demonstrate, marriage embodies a love that may endure even past death. It would misunderstand these men and women to say they disrespect the idea of marriage. Their plea is that they do respect it, respect it so deeply that they seek to find its fulfillment for themselves. Their hope is not to be condemned to live in loneliness, excluded from one of civilization's oldest institutions. They ask for equal dignity in the eyes of the law. The Constitution grants them that right."

Explosive revelations about government spying operations erupted in 2013, when Edward Joseph Snowden, a coltish computer-whiz, carried out a daring digital heist. A former CIA employee and National Security Agency (NSA) contractor, Snowden clandestinely copied 1.5 million classified documents and arranged for their release to the public. The files exposed the NSA's sweeping capture from internet companies of U.S. citizens' digital communications in a

MCT/Getty Images

Image 38.5 Voting Rights in the Twenty-first Century A Philadelphia protester rallies in 2012 against Pennsylvania's new requirement for photo identification from each voter. The contemporary polarized era has seen a revival of charged debates over voting procedures and disenfranchisement. To conservative proponents, voter ID laws and limitations on registration and early voting provide important checks against the threat of fraud at the ballot box. But opponents charge that such laws serve partisan Republican goals by disproportionately disqualifying low-income and minority voters.

Contending Voices

Secrets and Security

Writing to a confidant under the alias "Citizen Four," government contractor Edward Snowden (b. 1983) explained his motivations for leaking 1.5 million National Security Agency (NSA) documents:

"From now, know that every border you cross, every purchase you make, every call you dial, every cell phone tower you pass, friend you keep, article you write, site you visit, subject line you type, and packet you route, is in the hands of a system whose reach is unlimited but whose safeguards are not."*

General Michael Hayden (b. 1945), who directed the NSA from 1999 to 2005, sharply questioned Snowden's motives. Labeling him a "traitor," Hayden said:

"Edward Snowden will likely prove to be the most costly leaker of American secrets in the history of the Republic. . . . The appropriate balance between liberty and security has bedeviled free peoples, including Americans, for centuries. But it takes a special kind of arrogance for this young man to believe that his moral judgment on the dilemma suddenly trumps that of two (incredibly different) presidents, both houses of the U.S. Congress, both political parties, the U.S. court system and more than 30,000 of his co-workers. . . . Snowden has thrust into public view sensitive and controversial espionage activities."**

Consider This:

Were Snowden's controversial actions justified by his aims? Was he a patriot or a grandstander?

*Source: Andy Greenberg, "These Emails Are the Emails Snowden Sent to First Introduce His Epic NSA Leaks," Wired, October 13, 2014, https://www.wired.com/2014/10/snowdens-first-emails-to-poitras/.
**Source: Michael Hayden, "Ex-CIA chief: What Edward Snowden did," CNN, July 19, 2013, https://www.cnn.com/2013/07/19/opinion/hayden-snowden-impact/index.html.

top-secret operation named "PRISM." The Snowden revelations also disclosed systematic monitoring of overseas web traffic of non-U.S. citizens, and even the tapping of German Chancellor Angela Merkel's cell phone. Congress attempted to rein in the NSA's most aggressive practices in the **USA Freedom Act of 2015**, but much of the NSA's surveillance powers remained intact.

To avoid criminal prosecution, Snowden eventually sought sanctuary in Russia, where he remained for more than a decade afterward. Cursed as a traitor or hailed as a patriot, Snowden sparked impassioned debates over the tradeoff between security and civil liberties. His revelations also served to remind Americans of the pervasive impact of the internet on their daily lives—and of the potential threats to privacy that online life enabled.

The internet's earliest boosters had touted it as a democratizing technology that would upending the hierarchical worlds of traditional media, business, and politics, and spread information and power more equally among the masses. Enthusiasm about that promise continued to fuel the technology sector's spectacular growth through the 2010s. But as events would soon show, not all the internet's effects were benign.

38-10 An Age of Distrust

A president's party usually suffers setbacks in midterm elections, and 2014 proved no exception. Republicans expanded their majority in the House and gained control of the Senate for the first time in eight years. Many observers attributed those results not to blossoming

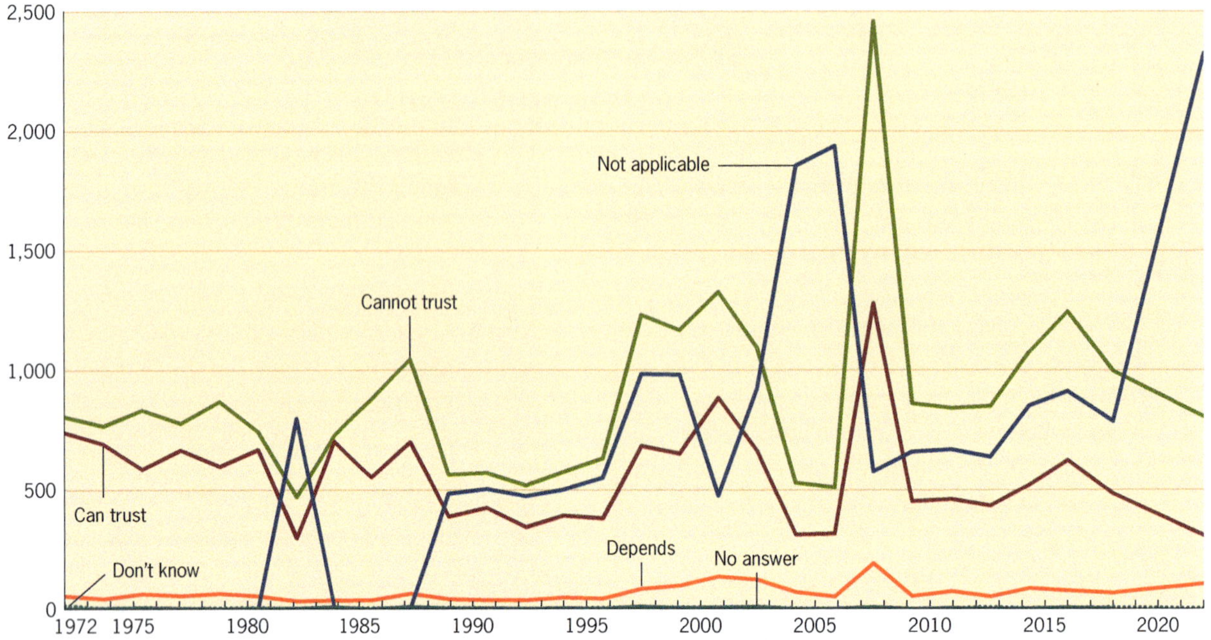

Figure 38.6 A Lack of Trust Americans have not only lost confidence in their institutions (refer to Figure 34.3), but they have also become more mistrustful of one another, a social development that threatens the very essence of democracy.

Source: https://gssdataexplorer.norc.org/variables/441/vshow

affection for Republicans but to deep disillusionment with the political status quo. Wall Street had roared back from the Great Recession, as had sectors like energy and high technology. But tens of millions of ordinary Americans remained stuck in the financial sinkhole created by the foreclosures and job losses of 2008. The seemingly endless wars in the Middle East also ground on, sending America's overstretched all-volunteer military on deployment after deployment. A resurgent populism flared up on both left and right, fueled by the internet's new mass-communication technologies.

The electronic media, already carved up by cable television and sliced ever more thinly by the internet, shattered into thousands of highly personalized pieces with the spread of social media platforms. Computer algorithms now precisely selected and cunningly targeted the news that Americans consumed. The torrent of data amounted to a digital-age update to the venomously partisan world of pamphlets and broadsides in the late eighteenth and early nineteenth centuries. Social media became an important seedbed of political activism, yet the platforms also worked to reinforce what psychologists call "**confirmation bias**," the natural human tendency to give more credence to those ideas that agree with one's own preexisting opinions and thereby shut individuals off from alternative points of view.

Contrary to earlier predictions that the proliferation of mass media would nurture a "global village," in fact the multiplicity of media divided Americans ever more sharply and resurrected primal habits of trusting no one outside the tightly drawn circles of the familiar. Distrusting government was an old American habit, but modern Americans were also coming to distrust a broad array of other institutions as well (refer to Figure 34.3, p. 924)—and they increasingly distrusted one another. Alarmingly, young people were the least likely to place trust in others (refer to Figure 38.6). Amid information overload and online shouting matches, the political and cultural gap between red and blue America widened still further.

38-11 Obama's Troubled Last Years

Stymied by a Republican Congress and confronting an increasingly disenchanted public, President Obama struggled to govern effectively during his last years in office. He could take credit for his first-term passage of the Affordable Care Act and the Dodd-Frank reforms in the financial sector, and for arresting the economy's free-fall during the Great Recession. Yet both those legislative achievements continued to excite raucous conservative criticism, and the economy's recovery from the crisis of 2008–2009 remained painfully feeble.

Racial conflict and vigilante and police violence also erupted during Obama's second term, deflating the hope that the election of the first Black president had heralded the birth of a post-racial era. When an armed resident of a Florida gated community fatally shot unarmed teenager Trayvon Martin in 2012, Obama declared that "If I had a son, he'd look like Trayvon." More tragedies were to come in the years that followed, as Black people continued to meet violent deaths at the hands of police officers in Ferguson, Missouri; Baltimore; New York City; Cleveland; San Francisco; and elsewhere (refer to Image 38.6). A self-declared white supremacist, declaring that he wanted to ignite a race war, opened fire on Black church-goers in Charleston, South Carolina, in 2015, killing nine worshippers.

Alicia Garza (b. 1981), a founder of the Black Lives Matter movement founded in the wake of Trayvon Martin's killing, described her objectives as follows:

"This generation of Black resistance says that we are not satisfied with the crumbs that may fall from the table of power, and we are not satisfied with merely *sitting* at the tables of power. This generation of Black resistance, of Black organizing, says that we aim to completely transform the way that power is distributed, the way that power functions."

These incidents spawned a sustained protest movement, **Black Lives Matter**, which prompted counter-cries of "All Lives Matter" and "Blue Lives Matter" (defending law enforcement officers)—exposing anew the racial fault lines that continued to seam American society. Protesters also publicized America's dubious status as the nation with the highest incarceration rates in the world. In the wake of hardline sentencing laws enacted in the 1990s, the nation's prison population soared—and was so disproportionately made up of minority inmates that one commentator dubbed the system "the new Jim Crow." By 2016, American prisons held some 1.5 million inmates, most of them men, nearly half of them Black men, who were jailed at six time the rate of white offenders. Many observers blamed those wildly disparate numbers on the inequitable consequences of the decades-old "war on drugs," with its inflexible mandatory sentences.

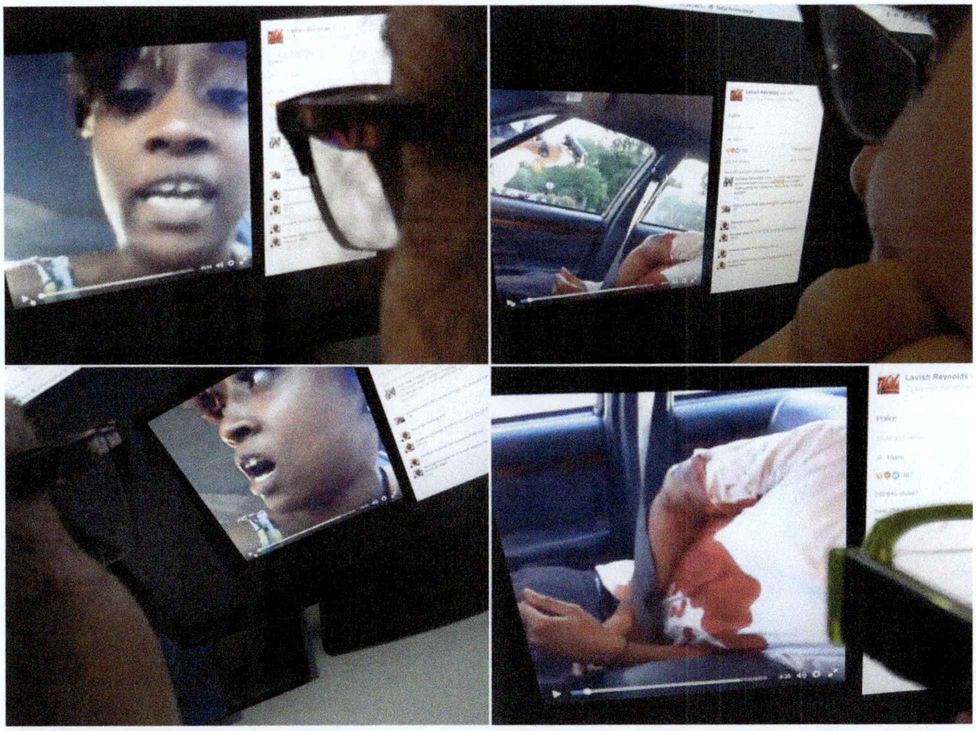

AFP/Getty Images

Image 38.6 Violence Made Visible These images, taken with a smartphone camera on July 7, 2016, show the dying moments of Philando Castile, a 32-year-old Black man shot by Minnesota police after being pulled over while driving.

38-12 The Gunning of America

Mass shootings, often involving high-capacity, rapid-fire military-grade weapons, repeatedly shocked and sickened an outraged nation, even as gun ownership became for some citizens a matter of cultural and political identity. The gunning of America exacted a grisly toll in deaths by homicide, suicide, and targeted as well as random assaults. Wholesale slaughter occurred in schools, movie theaters, churches, and synagogues, at music concerts and at Christmas parties. An enraged gunman killed 20 six- and seven-year-old children, as well as six teachers and staff, at Sandy Hook Elementary School in Newton, Connecticut, in 2012 (refer to Image 38.7). Other shooters murdered 12 and wounded 58 in an Aurora, Colorado, movie theater in the same year; 9 in Roseburg, Oregon, and 14 in San Bernardino, California, in 2015; 49 in Orlando, Florida, in 2016; 60 dead and more than 400 wounded in Las Vegas, Nevada, and 25 killed (as well as an unborn child) and another 22 wounded in Sutherland Springs, Texas, in 2017. In 2018, a homicidal young man with a semi-automatic rifle killed 17 high schoolers in Parkland, Florida, while another murdered 11 at a Pittsburgh synagogue. An alienated 18-year-old fatally shot 19 elementary schoolers and 3 teachers in Uvalde, Texas, in 2022, and another murdered 3 nine-year-olds and 3 adults at a Christian school in Nashville, Tennessee, in 2023.

The **National Rifle Association**, or NRA, founded as a gun safety organization after the Civil War, morphed into a politically intimidating pro-gun lobby with over 5 million members. Despite overwhelming popular sentiment for some form of gun controls, the NRA consistently frustrated both federal and state efforts to regulate firearms. Angered by the power of the gun lobby—as well as with politicians who offered "thoughts and prayers" in lieu of meaningful gun reform—parent and student-led activist groups mobilized to demand more forceful action. They organized a "March for Our Lives" in 2018 that rallied hundreds of thousands around the nation. Although six in ten American adults supported stricter gun laws by 2023, efforts to tighten gun-control laws repeatedly misfired while the heartrending carnage continued.

38-13 Gathering Storms Overseas

Developments abroad gave the beleaguered president no respite. A U.S.-led military effort unseated Libyan strongman Muammar Qaddafi in 2011, but in what Obama later called the worst mistake of his presidency, no preparations were made for the aftermath of Qaddafi's fall. Amidst the ensuing chaos, the U.S. ambassador and three other Americans were killed in Benghazi, Libya, in 2012, touching off years of political recriminations back home against then Secretary of State and later presidential candidate Hillary Clinton.

Zuma Press

Image 38.7 Slaughter of the Innocents Connecticut State Police lead sobbing students to safety from Sandy Hook Elementary School, December 14, 2012. Twenty of their young classmates perished.

Civil war in neighboring Syria broke out in 2011 and soon descended into a diabolically complicated battle between Syrian president Bashar al-Assad's government and a bewildering array of rebel factions, including, eventually, a fanatically militant group calling itself the Islamic State of Iraq and Syria (ISIS). President Obama brought down upon himself no end of denunciation when he warned in 2012 that Assad's use of chemical weapons would cross a "red line" that would compel an American response—and then failed to act when evidence mounted that Assad had resorted to chemical warfare. Nor did the Obama administration come up with effective countermeasures when a newly assertive Russia, led by ambitious autocrat Vladimir Putin, annexed the territory of Crimea in 2014 and intervened militarily in neighboring Ukraine.

The Middle Eastern cauldron boiled ever more dangerously in 2014 when ISIS seized vast tracts of real estate in Iraq and Syria, proclaimed those lands the center of a new global caliphate, and began fiendishly flouting established standards of international law and even basic human decency. ISIS fighters beheaded civilians, enslaved young women, and genocidally extinguished minority communities that fell within their grasp. Along with affiliates like Boko Haram in northern Africa, ISIS seemed poised to write an exceptionally barbaric new chapter in the long and sorry annals of human cruelty. That threat prompted President Obama, in violation of all his earlier instincts and promises, to reintroduce American troops into the Middle East. By early 2018, Iraqi, Kurdish, and Syrian forces, with help from both the United States and Russia, had pushed ISIS back to just a few last-ditch strongholds. Nearly half a million Syrians and Iraqis lay dead, while some 5 million desperate Syrian refugees had fled their blasted homeland.

The outgoing president could claim one last foreign policy victory in 2015 when an American-led coalition persuaded Iran to curtail its nuclear weapons program in return for the lifting of economic sanctions that had throttled the Iranian economy since the revolutionary take-over in 1979. But even as the champions of the **Iran nuclear deal** breathed a sigh of relief at this important gain for nuclear nonproliferation, American hawks prepared to attack the agreement in the upcoming 2016 election campaign.

38-14 The Astonishing Election of 2016

The presidential election campaign of 2016 dramatically exposed the depths of the ugly divisions that plagued the republic. Partisan gridlock in Washington was amplified in an information-overloaded media environment where Democrats and Republicans increasingly got their news from different outlets. Disinformation thrived, including the right-wing fiction that President Obama was not born in the United States and was thus constitutionally prohibited from being president (Article II, Section I). Egged on by eventual Republican presidential nominee Donald Trump, the proportion of Republicans who believed in "birtherism" went from 32 percent in 2010 to 72 percent in 2016.

The race for the Democratic nomination pitted former Secretary of State Hillary Clinton against Bernie Sanders, a curmudgeonly septuagenarian Vermont senator and self-declared democratic socialist who excoriated wealthy "one-percenters" and advocated government-financed universal health care. Millions of fired-up and left-leaning young people, many of them burdened with student loans, "felt the Bern" and gave Sanders several primary victories. But his candidacy ultimately yielded to the more deep-pocketed and well-oiled Clinton electoral machine. The Democrats became the first major American party to nominate a woman for president, but the shattering of that particular glass ceiling gave off only a muted tinkle. A familiar, centrist figure after a quarter-century in the public eye, Hillary Clinton failed to spark excitement in an American electorate that was especially hungry for change.

Meanwhile, New York City real estate mogul and reality-television personality Donald J. Trump barged into the Republican field, bullying and belittling sixteen rivals to snag the party's nomination. His legions of critics, including many Republican grandees, considered the brash billionaire a swaggering colossus of ignorance, vanity, and vulgarity.

Yet candidate Trump kindled the political passions of millions of Americans when he blasted the Affordable Care Act, threatened China with tough trade sanctions, promised massive spending on infrastructure,* lambasted immigrants as criminals and deadbeats, and pledged

*In 2017 the American Society of Civil Engineers graded the nation's infrastructure with a barely passing "D+," among the worst in the developed world. The society estimated that deferred maintenance of America's roads, bridges, waterways, water supplies, energy grids, and communication networks carried a price-tag of at least $1.5 trillion over the next decade.

Steve Bannon (b. 1953), who for a time served as Donald Trump's campaign manager and later, briefly, as the chief strategist in Trump's White House, described his political views as follows in 2016:

"The globalists gutted the American working class and created a middle class in Asia. . . . Like [Andrew] Jackson's populism, we're going to build an entirely new political movement. . . . The working men and women in the world . . . are just tired of being dictated to by what we call the party of Davos [site of the annual meeting of the World Economic Forum, attended by hundreds of the planet's most prominent business and political figures]. There are people in New York that feel closer to people in London and in Berlin than they do to people in Kansas and in Colorado, and they have more of this elite mentality that they're going to dictate to everybody how the world's going to be run."

to build a "beautiful" wall along the Mexican border—and compel the Mexicans to pay for it. With often-cavalier disregard for the facts, Trump, prince of plutocrats, campaigned as a populist who would "drain the swamp" in Washington, DC, and "make America great again." (Hence his campaign logo, "MAGA," which would become the trademark of his political movement.)

The campaign maelstrom intensified when WikiLeaks, an international organization dedicated to disclosing confidential documents, released thousands of emails illegally filched from inside the Clinton campaign. American intelligence services concluded that Russian hackers were the source of WikiLeaks' information trove, and that Russia had interfered in the election in myriad other ways as well, generating thousands of false social media accounts whose combative posts fueled already raging partisan fires. The principal beneficiary of the electoral chaos amplified by Russia's social media manipulation was Donald J. Trump, which ultimately led to a federal investigation into possible collusion between Russia and the Trump campaign.

On Election Day a majority of voters, by a margin of nearly 3 million, preferred Clinton, who won 65,853,625 votes to Trump's 62,985,106. But Trump's narrow victories in just three traditionally Democratic states—Pennsylvania, Wisconsin, and Michigan—tipped the Electoral College count in his favor, 306 to 232. To the utter astonishment of almost all pundits and prognosticators—and possibly Trump himself—the thrice-married former Democrat, a sexual predator caught on tape boasting about groping women, became the oldest and richest person ever elected to the presidency. Trump was also the first president without any prior military or political experience, the fifth to assume office while losing the popular vote, and, said some, the most unprepared and least-qualified person elevated to the presidency in the history of the republic (refer to Image 38.8).

Win McNamee/Getty Images

Image 38.8 Grudge Match Democratic candidate Hillary Clinton faces off against Republican nominee Donald Trump in St. Louis, Missouri, October 9, 2016. This second of their three 2016 campaign debates defined a new low for ugly political invective. "If I win I am going to instruct my attorney general to get a special prosecutor to look into your situation—there has never been so many lies and so much deception," declared Trump. When Clinton said it was "awfully good" that someone with Trump's temperament was not in charge of American law enforcement, Trump, whose campaign rallies had featured chants of "Lock her up!" replied: "Because you'd be in jail."

How to account for Trump's stunning political upset? Some commentators pointed to the failures of Clinton's campaign, which targeted several discrete constituencies but never succeeded in defining a unifying vision for the nation. Clinton also committed major political malpractice when she publicly lumped "half of Trump's supporters into what I call the basket of deplorables. They're racist, sexist, homophobic, xenophobic—Islamophobic—you name it." Pro-Trump citizens responded by sporting tee-shirts declaring "I'm an adorable deplorable." A journalist challenged Clinton to explain, "How can you unite a country if you've written off tens of millions of Americans?"

Then in the waning days of the campaign, FBI Director James Comey informed members of Congress that he was considering reopening a criminal investigation of Hillary Clinton's use of a private email server while she was secretary of state. Members immediately leaked the information, casting a dark cloud over the Clinton candidacy. Just two days before Election Day, Comey announced that there was no basis to reopen the investigation. But the damage was done.

Yet in addition to Clinton's liabilities, Trump's astounding victory also stemmed from his uncanny ability to mobilize deep grievances long festering in the body politic. Clinton carried some 490 of the nation's more than 3,100 counties, heavily concentrated in big coastal metropolitan areas, where two-thirds of America's GDP originated. In the nation's rural, interior, and poorer counties, Trump handily prevailed, especially among white voters distressed by job insecurity and wage stagnation, discomforted by immigration and accelerating cultural change, and disgusted by down-their-noses condescension from self-anointed elites. The election starkly demonstrated that prosperous, cosmopolitan "blue state" citizens, including minorities, tended to vote Democratic, while their less-favored countrymen dwelled in economically challenged, socially conservative, and more racially and ethnically homogenous deep-red Republican territory. America had become two nations.

38-15 Trump in Power

Following an inaugural address that pugnaciously asserted his nationalist, protectionist, and nativist agenda, Trump's first months in office were chaotic. The new president at first seemed more determined to take a wrecking ball to the despised Washington "establishment" than to honor his campaign promises or organize an orderly government. Though his party controlled both chambers of Congress as well as the White House, Republicans proved unable in early 2017 to accomplish their most cherished objective, the repeal of Obama's Affordable Care Act. "It's an unbelievably complex subject," said an apparently dumbfounded Trump. "Nobody knew health care could be so complicated." Infrastructure spending went unmentioned. Construction stalled on the promised wall along the Mexican border. Trump's approval ratings drooped to the lowest levels ever recorded in a president's first year in office.

The incoming administration seemed perplexedly unready to assume power, as high-level officials came and went with baffling speed and hundreds of appointments went unfilled throughout the executive branch. Trump's first White House chief of staff lasted just six months. His press secretary, six successive communications directors, and chief political strategist soon followed him out the door, as did his original secretary of state, who lasted just over a year. Trump's first national security adviser resigned after less than a month in office and later was criminally convicted of lying to the FBI (Trump later bestowed a presidential pardon on him as well as other associates convicted of wrongdoing). Demoralized Foreign Service officers departed the State Department in droves, as key offices stood empty in Washington as well as in American embassies and consulates around the world.

Trump fired FBI Director Comey in May 2017, allegedly for mishandling the Hillary Clinton email probe, but later admitted that his real motive was to deflect Comey's investigation of Russian interference in the 2016 election, which some observers thought might ultimately expose connections between the Trump campaign and the Russians. In the wake of Comey's dismissal, the Justice Department appointed former FBI director Robert Mueller as Special Counsel to continue the Russia investigation (refer to Image 38.9).

Amidst all these developments, the impulsive Trump tweet-blasted a nonstop avalanche of often incendiary pronouncements. The president inveighed against the media ("fake news") and slimed his fellow Republicans (calling his 2016 opponents "Lyin' Ted Cruz" and "little Marco Rubio") and even foreign officials ("Rocket Man"—North Korean Supreme Leader Kim Jong-un). These tweet tantrums were red meat for the media. No prior president had so effectively dominated the news cycle, even as pundits worried that he seemed incapable of keeping a lid on his id.

Drew Angerer/Getty Images

Image 38.9 Moscow Meddling Senators Sheldon Whitehouse (D-RI) and Dick Durbin (D-IL) hear testimony during a Senate probe into Russian interference in the 2016 American elections. The director of national intelligence concluded in a January 2017 report that "Russia's goals were to undermine public faith in the U.S. democratic process, denigrate Secretary Clinton, and harm her electability and potential presidency. We further assess Putin and the Russian Government developed a clear preference for President-elect Trump."

Among President Trump's torrent of tweets trashing the mainstream media, he had this to say on February 17, 2017:

"The FAKE NEWS media (failing @nytimes, @NBCNews, @ABC, @CBS, @CNN) is not my enemy, it is the enemy of the American People!"

Trump swiftly reversed several of Obama's executive orders safeguarding the environment, promoting clean energy, and protecting immigrants brought to the United States as young children by undocumented parents (refer to "38-7 Second-Term Stalemate," p. 1038). His attempt to ban immigration from several Muslim-majority countries met with massive protests and repeated judicial blockage until provisionally approved by the Supreme Court in late 2017.

Trump's hardline tactics prompted equally ardent opposition. Left-leaning women horrified by Trump's policies and persona—not to mention the defeat of the first major-party female presidential candidate by a former beauty-pageant owner—took to the streets the day after Trump's inauguration for a "Women's March." An estimated 4 million Americans joined in protests in 653 cities around the nation, making it likely the largest single-day demonstration in the nation's history (refer to Image 38.10). The feminist surge extended well beyond Trump in 2017, as the **#MeToo** movement inspired women to reveal past experiences of sexual discrimination and abuse, bringing down numerous high-profile gropers in the entertainment industry, the media, and the U.S. Congress.

Gradually a semblance of order emerged in Trump's White House, as the several seasoned military officers ("my generals") that Trump had appointed to key positions prevailed upon him to temper his shambolic leadership style. (In a notable constitutional inversion, the country now looked to military officers to restrain the mercurial commander-in-chief, turning topsy-turvy the traditional logic of civilian control over the military.)

Trump made an especially deep and lasting imprint on the federal judiciary, with a string of conservative nominees to the many judgeships—conspicuously including the Supreme Court—that the Republican Senate had blocked Obama from filling. The Senate approved Trump's nomination of a brainy and conservative Coloradan, Neil Gorsuch in 2017. Another conservative justice, Brett Kavanaugh, followed in 2018, and a third, Amy Coney Barrett, in 2020. In each case, Senate confirmation hearings were bitterly confrontational, and the eventual votes were

Reuters/Bryan Woolston

Image 38.10 The Women's March Millions of people across America and around the world demonstrated against President Trump on the day after his inauguration, January 21, 2017.

sharply divided along partisan lines. Long gone were the near-unanimous Senate confirmations once enjoyed by Supreme Court nominees.

Republicans who had warily hitched their political fortunes to Trump's unbridled ego, and long suffered his verbal slings and arrows, finally reaped their reward. The new administration began aggressively repealing countless federal regulations, to the delight of business owners and the dismay of labor unions and environmentalists.

At the end of 2017, congressional Republicans triumphantly submitted for the president's signature a sweeping **Tax Cuts and Jobs Act**, the most significant overhaul to the U.S. tax code since the days of Ronald Reagan. The hastily drafted new law achieved several long-standing and high-priority Republican objectives, especially cutting the corporate tax rate. It sought to boost economic growth by permanently and substantially cutting the corporate tax rate while temporarily and modestly lowering the tax burden on most individuals and families. It also facilitated the repatriation to the United States of corporate profits held overseas. For many taxpayers, it simplified filing by making it unnecessary to itemize certain tax-deductible items. For others, it made home ownership more expensive by capping the long-standing mortgage interest deduction and severely reduced the deductibility of state and local taxes—apparently punitive political retribution against high-tax "blue states" that invested heavily in social services. The tax law's architects also cleverly stitched into the bill clauses that struck directly at some keystones of Obama's legacy, allowing oil exploration in the Arctic National Wildlife Refuge (ANWR) and eliminating the "individual mandate" that helped finance the Affordable Care Act.

The bill threatened to add more than $1 trillion to the national debt over the ensuing decade as traditional Republican debt-hawks tossed their hallowed fiscal principles to the wind. Its champions hailed the new law as a Christmas gift for individual Americans and a potent stimulus for the economy. Opponents condemned it as an economically delusional piece of vengeful political trickery that would shower most of its benefits on the wealthiest Americans—including the billionaire president.

Notably, the tax reform bill passed without a single Democratic vote in either congressional chamber, just as Obama's Affordable Care Act had passed without a single Republican vote seven years earlier. The two were only the first of several extraordinarily consequential pieces of

Speaking at the January 7, 2018, Golden Globe awards ceremony, actress and media celebrity Oprah Winfrey (b. 1954) declared:

"For too long, women have not been heard or believed if they dare speak the truth to the power of those men. But their time is up. Their time is up. . . . It was somewhere in Rosa Parks' heart almost eleven years later, when she made the decision to stay seated on that bus in Montgomery, and it's here with every woman who chooses to say, 'Me too.'"

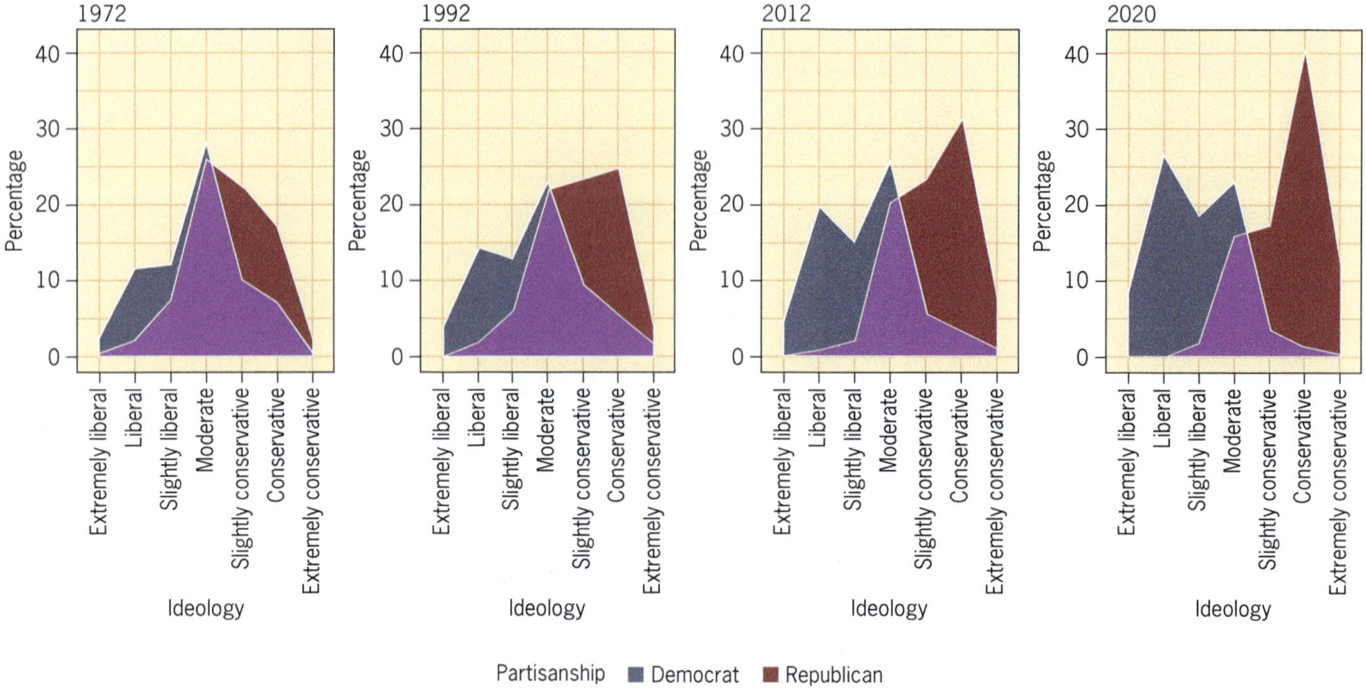

Figure 38.7 The Vanishing Center Democrats and Republicans have grown more distant from one another in the first two decades of the twenty-first century. The mythical "median voter" whose middle-of-the-road choices supposedly decided past elections has all but disappeared as citizens have sorted themselves into ever more irreconcilable groupings.

Source: Calculated from the American National Election Studies (2023) by Jacob Jaffee PhD.

legislation of the early twenty-first century that became law as purely partisan measures, another stark illustration of political polarization (refer to Figure 38.7).

38-16 Uniting the Right

Donald Trump's unapologetic rhetoric and hardline anti-immigration stance thrilled disgruntled voters who felt left behind by America's increasingly multiracial and socially liberal culture. Presidential stumbles failed to dampen the enthusiasm of the thousands who crowded into Trump rallies, fervidly cheering, "Build the wall!" Witnessing the power of Trump's personality and politics, Republicans who had once condemned Trump as a fearmongering fabulist now fell in line behind him. The right-wing populism simmering within the Republican Party for decades bubbled over into the GOP mainstream, forging a "MAGA Republicanism" with Donald J. Trump as its standard-bearer.

Trump also emboldened white supremacists at the far-right fringes of American politics. Long-ostracized hate groups emerged from the political shadows in the Trump era, gaining new adherents along with their fresh visibility. Precisely targeted messages on social media platforms helped recruit disaffected young white men to the **"alt-right"** cause. Further encouragement came from Trump allies and even the president himself.

In August 2017 a white-nationalist mob descended on Charlottesville, Virginia, for a "Unite the Right" rally protesting the removal of a statue of Confederate General Robert E. Lee from a city park (refer to Chapter 29, "The Presence of the Past: The Lost Cause," pp. 744–746). "Jews will not replace us," some chanted as they marched through the city and onto the grounds of the University of Virginia, with Confederate flags waving and torches ablaze (refer to Image 38.11). An already ugly day turned deadly after a man plowed his car through a crowd of counter-protestors, killing one. Trump was conspicuously restrained in his response, and he drew sharp criticism for declaring that, in the Charlottesville clash, there were "very fine people, on both sides."

Trump continued to stoke the flames of white nationalism throughout his presidency. He declared that a group of nonwhite female House members should "go back and help fix the totally broken and crime infested places from which they came" (three were born in the United

AFP Contributor/Getty Images

Image 38.11 The KKK in Charlottesville Hooded members of the Ku Klux Klan were among the crowd of far-right militants and white nationalists who converged on Charlottesville, Virginia, in July 2017.

States, and a fourth was a child refugee). He retweeted far-right Twitter accounts and profanely denigrated Haiti and African nations in conversations with lawmakers. Later, when asked to condemn his white-nationalist supporters during a 2020 presidential debate, Trump instead told them to "stand back and stand by."

38-17 The World Warily Watches Washington

Trump's election rattled the world—allies and adversaries alike—as much as it did many Americans. His "America First" slogan, perhaps unwittingly echoing a rallying cry from the hyper-isolationist 1930s, signaled a repudiation of many of the principles that had guided U.S. foreign policy for nearly a century.

American global leadership in the decades after World War II had helped to shape a remarkable passage in the world's history. It was not a utopian age, to be sure, but the postwar era saw no great war among the major powers, and witnessed an international economic expansion of unprecedented scale and reach ("globalization"), as well as the worldwide conquest of diseases like polio and smallpox, the decolonization of Africa and Asia, the eventual fall of the Soviet empire, the modernization of China, and the spread of democracy to countries that had not known it for generations, if ever.

It was a remarkable record, and it owed in no small measure to America's active international engagement. But globalization was spawning its own discontents as the twenty-first century advanced. Across the rich, developed world, citizens chafed at competitive pressure from rising powers and bemoaned increasingly large inflows of immigrants and refugees who sought lives in politically stable and economically prosperous societies. Right-wing nationalist parties gained electoral steam in some parts of Europe, fanning xenophobic flames as they bewailed the erosion of familiar cultural heritages. British voters gave dramatic punctuation to such sentiments when they voted by a narrow margin to leave the European Union in 2016 ("Brexit").

America had long played a steadying and integrating international role, building multilateral institutions like the United Nations, the International Monetary Fund, the World Bank, and the World Trade Organization. Its security guarantees to its NATO partners had helped to underwrite the evolution of the European Union. Similar guarantees in Asia contributed mightily to the prosperity of allies like Japan and South Korea, while its liberal trade policies had facilitated the phenomenal growth of the Chinese economy, lifting millions from poverty into the middle classes (refer to Image 38.12). It may have been an overstatement to call the United States the "indispensable nation," but there can be no doubt that its power and presence were substantial in the post-WWII global arena.

President Trump's "America First" approach recognized the stresses of globalization that the two major parties had too long ignored. Yet the agenda threatened to dismantle that international economic and security architecture. Trump repudiated international trade agreements

Image 38.12 Fall and Rise? President Donald Trump meets Chinese leader Xi Jinping, in Beijing, China, November 8, 2017. China's spectacular economic progress in the preceding several decades raised serious questions about America's role in Asia and beyond as the twenty-first century advanced.

like NAFTA and the Trans-Pacific Partnership, withdrew from the Paris Climate Accords, threatened nuclear-armed North Korea with "fire and fury," defied the United Nations by moving America's Israeli embassy to Jerusalem, and ratcheted up tensions with China and Iran. Made in the name of reasserting United States power, these moves threatened to isolate the nation at a crucial moment when many challenges—economic, environmental, medical, and military—called for more international collaboration, not less.

38-18 Climate Disruption and Its Consequences

The very heavens seemed to mirror the nation's tumult in the century's early decades, as extreme weather events turned global climate disruption from nebulous possibility to deadly reality. Epic hurricanes blasted Puerto Rico, Florida, the Gulf Coast, and the Carolinas, as well as New Jersey, New York, and New England (refer to Image 38.13). Ferocious tornadoes blasted through the Midwest and South. Monster wildfires blazed across the West, consuming thousands of homes and dozens of lives, and blackening summer skies across the nation. Worldwide, in 2022 alone, brutal heatwaves killed upward of 11,000 people in Europe and massive flooding submerged one-third of Pakistan, resulting in 15,000 casualties and 8 million displaced.

Scientists long had warned of the climate threat, but climate mitigation measures were expensive, inconvenient, and politically controversial—especially in the United States, where many lawmakers and business interests believed the economic sacrifices would be too great. Impatient with political dithering, young people around the world took to the streets in "global climate strikes."

The scientific consensus was clear: Human reliance on nonrenewable resources like oil, natural gas, and coal ("fossil fuels") had played a major role in raising Earth's temperature a full two degrees Fahrenheit since the onset of the Industrial Revolution in the late 1800s (refer to Figure 38.8). Swift, dramatic reduction in fossil-fuel consumption, most scientists urged, was the only way to avoid unreversible climate catastrophe. The Trump administration thought differently, giving a welcoming embrace to climate skeptics, including, ironically, at the Environmental Protection Agency, where hundreds of dedicated climate scientists headed for the exits in despair. Trump aggressively rolled back Obama-era climate mitigation policies, tweet-mocked environmentalists, and horrified the international community when he pulled out of the historic **Paris Climate Accords** signed by 196 nations in 2015. (Trump's successor, Joe Biden, rejoined the accord immediately upon taking office in 2021.)

Image 38.13 **Hurricane Sandy Inundates the East Coast, 2012** Powerful hurricanes and devastating floods battered America's eastern coastline with increasing frequency as the global climate warmed in the early decades of the twenty-first century. This aerial view of a flooded New Jersey vacation community shows damage wrought by the storm's surge.

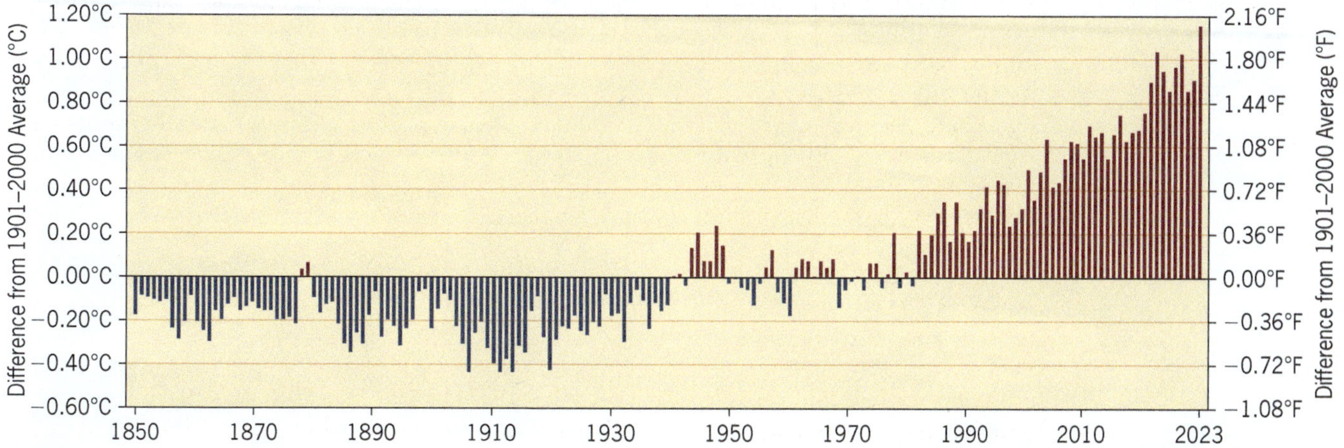

Figure 38.8 **A Dramatically Warming World** The ten warmest years in the historical record for global land and ocean surface temperatures have all occurred from 2014 through 2023. This chart shows each year's variation from the twentieth-century (1901–2000) average global surface temperature of 14.0°C (57.2°F).

Source: https://www.ncei.noaa.gov/access/monitoring/monthly-report/global/202311

38-19 The First Trump Impeachment

White House turmoil and the polarizing president helped Democrats retake control of the House of Representatives in the 2018 midterm elections, although Republicans held their majority in the Senate. The new U.S. Congress was the most diverse in history, with more than 100 female representatives, including the first two Native American women and first two Muslim women. Nancy Pelosi, the nation's first female Speaker of the House from 2007 to 2011, reclaimed the Speaker's gavel.

Partisan wrangling led to gridlock even before the Democrats took control of the House. Beginning in late December 2019, a stalemate over funding Trump's promised border wall led to a 35-day federal government shutdown, the longest to date. No sooner had the government reopened than the two-year investigation chaired by Special Prosecutor Robert Mueller issued its findings on Russian interference in the 2016 election. The **Mueller Report** concluded that Trump and his campaign were culpable of encouraging and meeting with the Russians, but did not find enough evidence to prove a criminal conspiracy. Fretful Democrats, who had been eagerly awaiting Trump's comeuppance, were bitterly disappointed. Mueller countered that it was the constitutional duty of Congress—not the Justice Department—to hold a president responsible for wrongdoing (refer to Image 38.14).

Post-Mueller murmurs of "impeachment" were still wafting around Capitol Hill when the next scandal broke. A whistleblowing national security official revealed that on a July 2019 phone call Trump had pressured Ukrainian President Volodymyr Zelenskyy to investigate a political rival, former Vice President (and announced 2020 presidential candidate) Joe Biden, whose son Hunter had business ties in Ukraine. The House soon launched televised impeachment hearings on charges that the president had abused power and obstructed justice. On December 18, 2019, Trump became the third president to be impeached (after Andrew Johnson in 1868 and

White House Photo/Alamy Stock Photo

Image 38.14 Pelosi and Trump Representative Nancy Pelosi (D-CA), the first woman Speaker of the House, was a political foil and foe to first-term President Trump, a dynamic captured in this photograph from a 2019 Cabinet meeting. Pelosi's speakership reflected how far women had come in politics; the all-male assemblage around the Cabinet table shows how far women still had to go.

Bill Clinton in 1998). The Senate acquitted the president on February 5, 2020 on a party-line vote, with one exception: Senator Mitt Romney, Republican of Utah and the party's 2012 presidential nominee, joined the vote to remove Trump from office.

38-20 The Coronavirus Pandemic

As Trump's impeachment consumed American headlines in late December 2019, reports surfaced about a mysterious virus coursing through the Chinese city of Wuhan. The 2019 Novel Coronavirus*, or **COVID-19**, arrived on American shores soon thereafter. An outbreak in a Seattle-area nursing home killed 35 people by early March 2020, and the swiftly spreading virus began its lethal sweep across the country.

COVID-19 wreaked wholesale death, especially among the elderly and infirm, and led to calamitous disruption everywhere. Corporations sent their employees home, schools closed, stores clanged down their shutters, restaurants shut down, and nursing homes banned all visitors. Americans cloistered in their homes in lonely isolation as their country became a nation of ghost towns. The eerie silence of empty city streets was broken only by the wail of ambulance sirens rushing to save COVID-19's victims. The pandemic also revealed sharp racial disparities in health outcomes, as nonwhite people were about one and a half times more likely than white people to be infected with COVID-19, and twice as likely to die.

Congress moved quickly to stem the economic fallout from the pandemic shutdown, passing a colossal $2.2 trillion economic stimulus bill, the **CARES Act**, in late March 2020 with strong bipartisan support. President Trump began holding daily press briefings on the crisis, but his freewheeling remarks generated more confusion than calm, as he touted unproven remedies and overconfidently predicted that the pandemic, "like a miracle" would soon "disappear," and balked at wearing a protective face mask. Public health experts despaired as Trump pushed to reopen the economy while the pandemic still raged.

In the already inflamed context of partisan bickering, face masks became a political flashpoint. The pandemic eventually would kill nearly 7 million people globally, including more than a million Americans. The world's richest nation had the world's second-highest mortality rate from COVID-19, with 341 deaths per 100,000 population. That grim statistic reflected many failures: a fragmented and costly health-care system, an uneven patchwork of local and state responses, medical uncertainty and outright humbuggery, a confused and contradictory national leadership, and a deeply divided polity (refer to Image 38.15).

Yet one bright spot emerged in this dark time: Trump eventually endorsed a crash effort, "Operation Warp Speed," that produced effective anti-COVID-19 vaccines in record time.

AP Images

Image 38.15 A Sign of the Times The multiple cataclysms of a pandemic-besieged year are captured in this apocalyptic image, taken in Napa County, California, in August 2020. Massive wildfires raged for weeks that summer across a drought-parched region, blistering forests, destroying homes, and darkening Western skies.

*The virus' official name is SARS-COVID 19: Severe Acute Respiratory Syndrome Corona Virus Disease, 2019.

AP Images

Image 38.16 George Floyd in Berlin The murder of George Floyd at the hands of Minneapolis police sparked global outrage. Days after Floyd's death, a mural painted on a wall in a public park in Berlin, Germany, captured his likeness and final words: "I can't breathe."

By early 2021, Americans were lining up by the millions to receive their life-saving shots. Yet partisan invective had by then made some citizens so mistrustful of expert opinion that many of them became adamant "anti-vaxxers."

The American people faced other great reckonings in 2020. In late May, the callous killing of a Black man, George Floyd, at the hands of Minneapolis police set off a month of extraordinary public protest. Americans of all races and in all fifty states broke months of COVID isolation to march against police brutality and for racial justice. Millions of Americans took to the streets to insist that "Black Lives Matter," the largest such movement in the nation's history, matched by similar protests around the world (refer to Image 38.16). The police officer responsible for Floyd's death was later convicted of murder.

38-21 Election and Insurrection

Amid pandemic and protest, Trump's 2020 reelection campaign faced a crowded field of Democratic contenders. Joe Biden prevailed and chose as his running mate California Senator Kamala Harris, a woman of both Black and South Asian descent whose candidacy offered eloquent testimony to the changing face of American society. Pandemic restrictions transformed modern campaign-trail rituals, as Biden and Harris campaigned in face masks and held "socially distanced" drive-in rallies.

Further drama came in the final weeks of the 2020 campaign. In early October, President Trump himself was hospitalized with COVID-19. Operation Warp Speed's vaccines were not yet available, and the president's age (74) made him especially vulnerable to severe illness. Remarkably, after only three days in the hospital the president returned triumphantly to the White House. There he theatrically ripped off his medical mask before the television cameras (refer to Image 38.17).

Nicholas Kamm/AFP/Getty Images

Image 38.17 Trump Rips Off the Mask President Donald Trump's three-day hospitalization after contracting COVID-19 in October 2020 added further tumult to a pandemic-disrupted election season. Upon returning to the White House, a visibly shaky Trump dramatically pulled off his mask before the cameras. He later posted on Twitter, "Don't be afraid of Covid. Don't let it dominate your life."

The coronavirus pandemic still gripped much of the nation on Election Day. Nearly half of COVID-shy American voters voted by mail-in or absentee ballot, though two-thirds of Trump supporters chose to vote in person. Buoyed by high turnout and strong anti-Trump sentiment, Biden won by over 7 million votes, 81,283,501 to 74,223,975, and prevailed in the Electoral College, 306 to 232 (refer to Map 38.2).

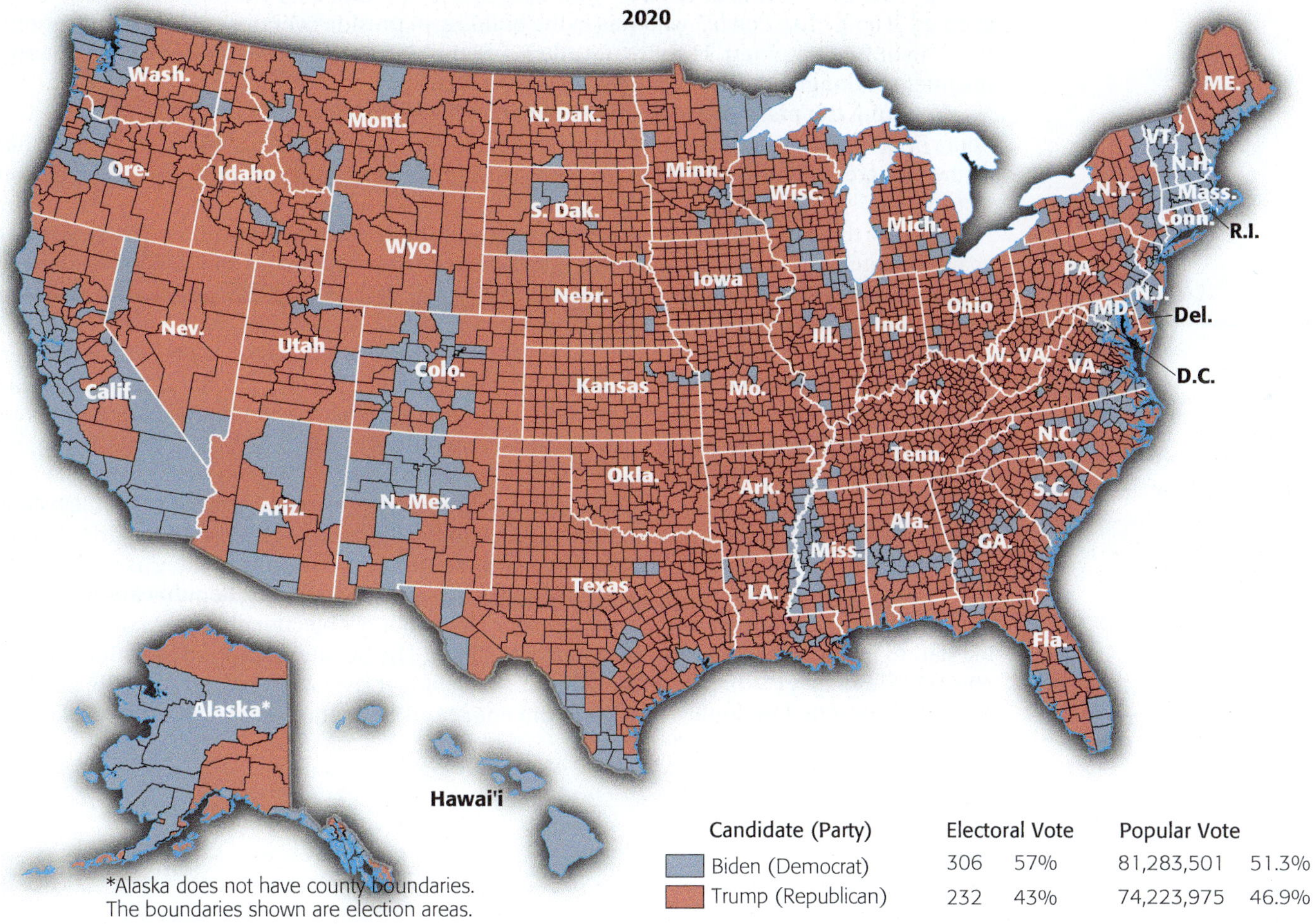

Candidate (Party)	Electoral Vote		Popular Vote	
Biden (Democrat)	306	57%	81,283,501	51.3%
Trump (Republican)	232	43%	74,223,975	46.9%

Map 38.2 America in Red and Blue The 2020 election results by county showed a nation ever more starkly divided by party, religion, culture, economy, and geography. Biden won a popular majority by carrying 477 heavily populated and mostly urban counties, many of them clustered along the two coasts. Trump won 2,497 counties, most in lightly populated rural areas. To voters bemused by the sea of red on electoral maps, analysts retorted, "land doesn't vote, people do."

But Trump refused to concede, challenging more than two centuries of national pride in the peaceful transfer of presidential power. He fumed on Twitter that the election was "rigged" and "stolen," falsely declaring that he had won a "landslide" victory, and fueling his supporters' seething distrust of the republic's electoral integrity. "Stop the steal" became their rallying cry. Trump's attorneys filed a wave of lawsuits alleging mass voter fraud while he strong-armed state officials to "find" the votes to throw electors into Trump's column. No credible evidence of fraud or election tampering was found. Trump's own attorney general told him bluntly that such claims were "complete bullsh*t," and later testified that anyone who believed otherwise was "detached from reality."

But Trump persisted. The gathering clouds erupted into a raging storm on January 6, 2021, as Congress convened to certify the election results. Trump rallied his supporters near the White House, urging them to "fight like hell" or "you're not going to have a country anymore." Thousands then marched to the Capitol, where raucous protest swiftly turned into a violent attack (refer to Image 38.18). Rioters scaled the Capitol's walls, brutalized Capitol police officers, and wandered its marble halls shouting, "Where's Nancy?," in search of the hated Democratic House Speaker Nancy Pelosi. Not even

AP Images

Image 38.18 January 6 Attack on the Capitol Enraged Trump supporters rammed past security barricades and scaled the Capitol's walls in their attempt to prevent congressional certification of the 2020 election.

Trump's vice president was spared: On the Capitol lawn, rioters erected makeshift gallows and shouted "Hang Mike Pence," who was in the building to preside over the election certification as the Constitution required. The vice president and the House speaker made it to safety, but other members of Congress crouched in the Capitol in fear.

Resisting the pleas of aides and Republican lawmakers, President Trump waited several hours before calling on the mob to disperse. Tear gas hung in the air and blood stained the floor as the Congress reconvened late that night to fulfill its constitutional duty and certify Biden's victory.

Despite the day's violence, 147 Republicans still voted against certification. The House once again impeached Trump, this time for "incitement of insurrection." A majority of 57 senators, including seven Republicans, voted "guilty," ten votes short of the constitutionally mandated super-majority of 67 votes needed to convict.

By then, Joseph Robinette Biden Jr. had been sworn in as the nation's forty-sixth president. The former vice president had been one of the youngest people ever elected to the U.S. Senate, winning in 1972 at age 29. He now became the nation's oldest president at age 78. Both House and Senate were now narrowly back under Democratic control. Biden moved swiftly, signing a flurry of executive orders (many reversing Trump policies), rolling out newly available coronavirus vaccines, and signing into law a $1.9 trillion economic relief package. That legislative behemoth was the first of several signed by Biden in the first years of his presidency, a testament to Democrats' renewed enthusiasm for economic stimulus and social spending as well as to the political polarization that still gripped Capitol Hill (refer to Figure 38.9). Republicans, now in the Senate minority, seized on the "silent filibuster" to stop any objectionable piece of Democratic legislation in its tracks (refer to "Presence of the Past: The Senate: 'Beautiful Machine' or Cemetery of Democracy?" Chapter 28, pp. 718–719). As budget laws were exempt from the filibuster, lawmakers bundled multiple acts together in enormous budgetary "reconciliation" packages in

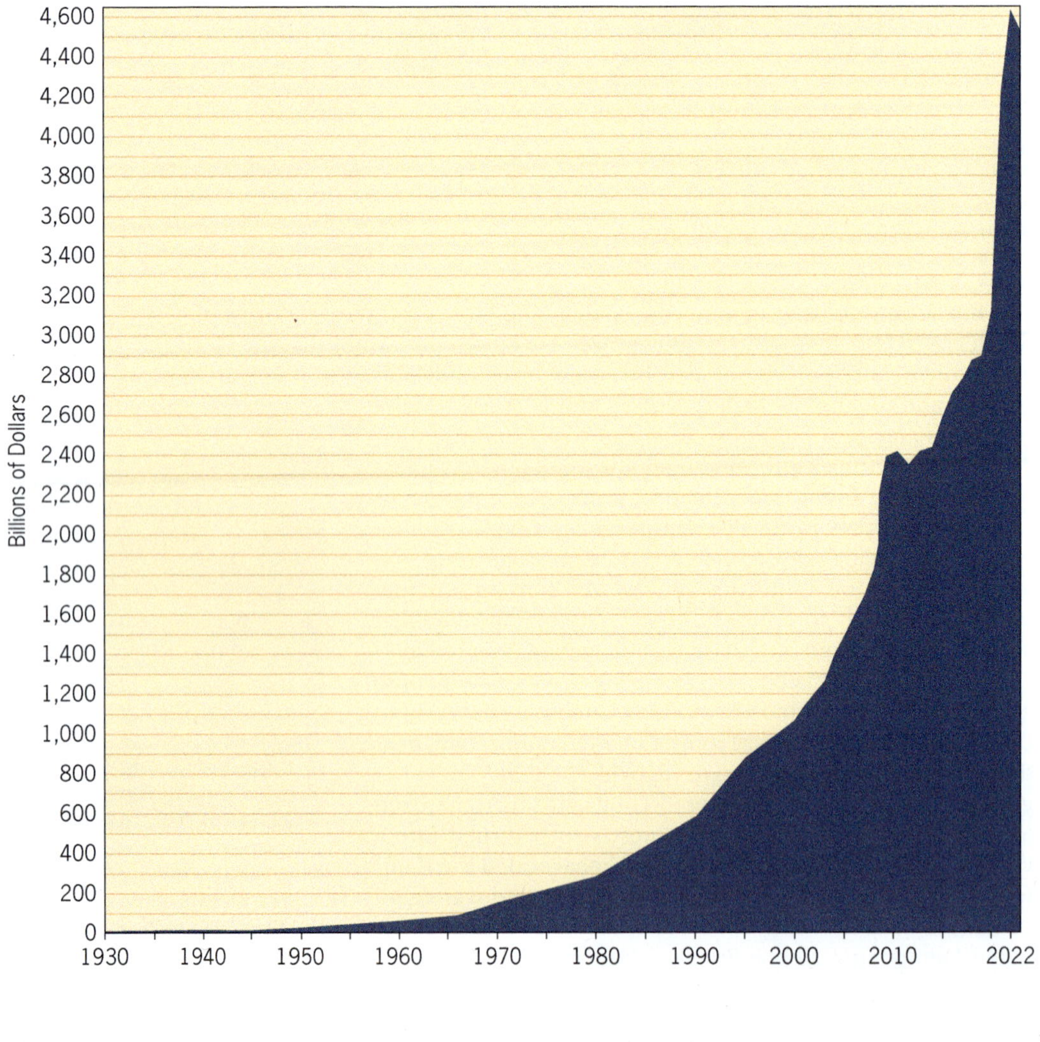

Figure 38.9 Government Expenditures for Social Welfare, 1930–2022
"Social welfare" includes unemployment and old-age insurance, health care, and veterans' benefits. The skyrocketing costs from the mid-1960s onward reflect new commitments made through Great Society programs and the increasing size (and political clout) of the elderly population, who were the main beneficiaries of expensive programs like Medicare. The steep rise after 1970 is explained by the galloping inflation of the 1970s, and the spike from 2019 to the first years of the 2020s is a reflection of the emergency expenditures authorized in the wake of the COVID-19 pandemic.

Source: Office of Management and Budget, Historical Tables, http://www.whitehouse.gov/omb/budget/Historicals/.

Image 38.19 Haitians Cross the Rio Grande, 2021 The number of migrants and asylum seekers from all parts of the world surged to unprecedented levels in the early years of the Biden presidency, overwhelming the immigration system and driving hundreds of thousands to cross the border illegally.

order to pass them on the tightest of party-line votes. Biden signed the **Inflation Reduction Act**, a $750 billion tax, climate, and health package, in 2022 without a single Republican vote in either congressional chamber. Yet in the same year the competitiveness-boosting **CHIPS and Science Act** passed both House and Senate with bipartisan support. Earmarking $280 billion to support U.S. semiconductor production and jumpstart R&D, the measure was the largest new high-tech investment by the U.S. government since the end of the Cold War.

Immigration remained a flashpoint as masses of migrants and refugees from around the world huddled at the nation's southern border. Biden had campaigned against Trump's hard-line policies, but the first year of his presidency saw a record number of arrests at the border as the number of migrants—and attempted illegal crossings—soared to a twenty-year high of over 200,000 in late 2022 (refer to Image 38.19). Most of those encountered by U.S. border agents were from countries *other* than Mexico or the "Northern Triangle" nations (El Salvador, Honduras, Nicaragua) that had historically been the source of most northward migration.

The chaotic withdrawal of the last American troops from Afghanistan in August 2021 delivered another political blow, as desperate Afghan families crowded the Kabul airport attempting to get a seat on the last U.S. transports. Thirteen U.S. service members were killed as the fundamentalist Islamic Taliban seized control of the country, a heartbreaking coda to nearly twenty years of war and occupation intended to vanquish such extremism. Thus ended the "forever wars" in Iraq and Afghanistan. The total cost of America's post-9/11 wars was estimated at $8 trillion and the deaths of over 7,000 U.S. soldiers, over 8,000 military contractors, and hundreds of thousands of local security forces and civilians.

38-22 Another Reckoning Nears

Only months after the calamitous Afghanistan withdrawal, a fresh international crisis erupted in late February 2022 when Russia launched a full-scale invasion of neighboring Ukraine. Ethnic Russians made up more than 40 percent of Ukraine's population of 41 million, concentrated in the country's southern and eastern provinces, a fact that Russian President Vladimir Putin had used to justify his 2014 annexation of Crimea, as well as his subsequent support for separatists in those provinces. Putin also hotly resisted Ukraine's push to join NATO and align itself with the West. The world watched in outrage as Russian tanks poured over Ukraine's borders—including a 40-mile-long convoy headed for the capital of Kyiv—and bombs lit up the night skies above its largest cities.

The invasion blasted away Europe's post–Cold War order, turning 6 million Ukrainians into refugees and spiking an energy crisis in European nations heavily dependent on Russian gas and oil. Foreign companies pulled out of Russia and international sanctions choked its economy. Swaggering tech billionaire Elon Musk challenged Putin to bare-knuckled combat. (The Russian president did not respond.) The war moved at internet speed, as online platforms documented minute-by-minute news of wartime atrocities and Ukrainian President Volodymyr Zelenskyy took to social media to plead for military aid from the West.

The Russian army proved surprisingly inept. By September 2022 Ukrainian troops had reclaimed a thousand square miles seized at the start of the invasion. Early failures only intensified Putin's desire to conquer Ukraine, and the bloody battle continued even as the world's attention shifted elsewhere. By the summer of 2023, close to 120,000 Russian and up to 70,000 Ukrainian soldiers were estimated to have died in the war, as well as 9,000 Ukrainian civilians (500 of whom were children).

The Ukraine invasion further complicated U.S.-China relations. Chinese Premier Xi Jinping was one of the few world leaders who did not condemn Putin for the invasion. Instead, the increasingly autocratic Xi used Russia's deepening economic and diplomatic isolation to bolster the ties between the two Eurasian powers—and further challenge the global influence of America and the West. Concern grew over the possible fate of the island of Taiwan, which China long had claimed to be its own, and China's increasingly bellicose military presence in the South China Sea. Roiling international conflicts and eroding trade partnerships further shook an American economy that was still trying to recover from the disruptions of the COVID-19 pandemic.

Further domestic upheaval came in June 2022, when the conservative-leaning Supreme Court concluded in *Dobbs v. Jackson Women's Health Organization* that the Constitution did not protect the right to abortion. The 6–3 ruling overturned earlier "pro-choice" decisions in *Roe v. Wade* (1973) and *Planned Parenthood v. Casey* (1992). The personal and political repercussions were swift and significant. More than a dozen Republican-led states moved to ban most abortions, leading to about 30,000 unplanned births in those states by the end of 2023. Although the fight to repudiate *Roe* had galvanized "pro-life" conservative voters for more than a generation, the *Dobbs* decision turned the withdrawal of protection for abortion rights into an electoral liability for Republicans. Democrats, meanwhile, sought to take political advantage of their pro-choice stance in the election cycle of 2024.

Though also encumbered with political subtext, the implementation of widespread vaccination had made COVID-19 a far less lethal disease. By late 2023, over 80 percent of Americans had received at least one vaccination dose and over 70 percent were fully vaccinated. But the economy remained far from "normal." Big-city office buildings remained silently empty as white-collar workers continued the pandemic-era practice of working from home. Large companies laid off thousands. Inflation increased the cost of gas and groceries, while housing prices in many places continued to spiral upward. The overall job market remained strong, however, and economists' predictions of recession did not come to pass.

On October 7, 2023, the Palestinian nationalist group Hamas launched a horrific terrorist attack on Israeli civilians and soldiers. Breaking through the heavily fortified border between Israel and the Palestinian enclave of Gaza, gunmen swarmed into the countryside, murdering and mutilating 1,200 Israelis—men and women, children, infants, and the elderly—and taking more than 200 hostages. A traumatized Israel retaliated with massive force, brutally pummeling Gaza with block-busting bombs that took an estimated 23,000 lives by early 2024. The shock waves reached all the way to America, as city streets and college campuses erupted with both demonstrations condemning Israel's tactics and counter-demonstrations protesting against an upsurge of antisemitism.

Amid such turmoil, Americans remained deeply pessimistic as the next presidential election loomed. More than 70 percent of poll respondents declared in 2023 that the nation was headed in the wrong direction. Americans' confidence in their government was about half the global average and well below that in nearly all other industrial democracies. Public faith in American institutions had been dropping since the 1970s (refer to Figure 38.6). Now, however, some of the loudest laments about a "failing" America came from political leaders themselves—notably

AP Images

Image 38.20 January 6 Hearings Former White House aide Cassidy Hutchinson is sworn in before the Congressional committee investigating the attack on the Capitol. The more than 1,000 witnesses interviewed by the committee included White House staff, Capitol Police officers, and some of the rioters themselves.

twice-impeached former president Donald Trump, who shortly after the midterm elections declared that he was running to retake the White House in 2024.

Trump established a commanding lead in a crowded GOP primary field despite—or perhaps because of—ongoing congressional and criminal investigations into his conduct during and after his time as president (refer to Image 38.20).

These probes yielded a cascade of indictments in 2023. The Justice Department charged the former president with violating the Espionage Act and obstruction of justice after thousands of presidential documents—including highly classified materials—were found in Mar-a-Lago, the private Florida club that was Trump's main residence after leaving the White House. A federal grand jury indicted Trump on conspiracy charges stemming from his attempts to overturn the results of the 2020 election, including his complicity in the January 6 insurrection. Then came perhaps the most stunning and sprawling of the charges when a Georgia grand jury leveled a 41-count felony indictment against Trump and 18 co-conspirators on racketeering and conspiracy charges stemming from their efforts to undermine the state's electoral count. The spectacle of a former American president entering a courthouse to be booked and fingerprinted had become what one newspaper headline called "surreally routine."

The cases were all politically motivated, Trump charged, and many in his party agreed. Even though scant evidence of actual voter fraud existed, a stunning 70 percent of Republicans and Republican-leaning independents persisted in the delusional belief that Joe Biden's 2020 victory was illegitimate.

38-23 The American Prospect

Well beyond its two-hundredth birthday as the twenty-first century unspooled, the United States was both an old and a new nation. It boasted one of the longest uninterrupted traditions of democratic government of any country on Earth. Indeed, it had pioneered the techniques of mass democracy and was, in that sense, the oldest modern polity. As one of the earliest countries to industrialize, America had also dwelt in the modern economic era longer than most nations. But the Republic was in many ways still youthful as well, and its democracy still painfully incomplete.

America's twenty-first century had begun much like the twentieth, as society continued to be rejuvenated by fresh waves of immigrants, full of energy and ambition. New civil rights achievements, notably the Supreme Court's 2015 ruling declaring same-sex marriage constitutional, energized gay and transgender Americans. A nation so long vexed by racial injustice elected and reelected a Black president, married to a first lady who was the great-great-great-granddaughter of an enslaved woman.

Yet victories for inclusion and tolerance, along with the galloping pace of technological innovation and the stresses of globalization, left many citizens feeling adrift, insecure, and sometimes deeply resentful. A pandemic shut down American society, killed over a million citizens and sickened millions more, and drove an already fractured polity further apart. Accusations of voter "fraud" prompted democracy-throttling voter restrictions; election denialism threatened the system entirely.

Much history remained to be made as the country entered its third century of nationhood. The political upheavals of the era served as a reminder that the great social experiment of American democracy was far from completed as the United States faced its future. Astonishing breakthroughs in science and technology—especially in genetics, bioengineering, data processing, communications, and artificial intelligence—presented Americans with stunning opportunities as well as cultural and political challenges and sometimes wrenching ethical choices. Global climate change made the responsible stewardship of a fragile planet more urgent than ever. The persistence of inequality and prejudice continued to summon Americans to close the gap between their most hallowed values and the stark realities of society in the twenty-first-century United States. The "forever wars" that unfurled in the wake of the terrorist attacks of September 11, 2001, shaped a generation of American soldiers and profoundly altered the political and economic landscapes of Iraq and Afghanistan—while largely failing to bring promised democracy and stability. The severe economic crisis that convulsed the nation and the world in 2008 demonstrated that free-market capitalism could still produce abundant misery as well as material abundance. The COVID-19 pandemic and intensifying climate disruption showed that no border wall could keep out the greatest threats to the nation's health and prosperity. Yet amid the depressing realization of all yet to be done was also the indestructible reality of what the American experiment had done: expansions of civil and human rights far beyond those imagined at the nation's birth, stunning economic productivity and individual opportunity, political institutions that held fast and patriots who remained true.

Men and women make history only within the framework bequeathed to them by earlier generations. For better or worse, they march forward along time's path bearing the burdens of the past. Knowing when they have come to a truly new turn in the road, when they can lay part of their burden down and when they cannot, or should not—all this constitutes the sort of wisdom that only historical understanding can engender. As Americans confront the challenges and opportunities of the twenty-first-century world, they would do well to remember Woodrow Wilson's admonition: "Democratic Institutions are never done; they are like living tissue, always a-making. It is a strenuous thing, this of living the life of a free people."

Chapter Summary

The American past made its presence felt in the early decades of the twenty-first century, years that saw increased climate disruption, a devastating pandemic, an overdue racial reckoning, and sharpened political polarization. Senator Barack Obama's presidential victory in 2008 came partly because of a major financial crisis and economic collapse that began in fall of that year. The "Great Recession" cost millions of Americans their jobs and homes and led to a stagnant economic environment that lingered for years. Obama responded vigorously to the crisis with a huge spending bill as well as reforms of health care and the financial system. But Obama's surge of federal activism prompted a fierce backlash by ultraconservative Tea Party citizens who attacked big government and the Democrats who supported it. Democrats suffered setbacks in the midterm elections of 2010.

Obama successfully wound down the Iraq war and brought American troops home, though Iraq remained unstable. Afghanistan proved more difficult to pacify, and aerial "drone" warfare failed to deter the resurgent Taliban.

America's attention turned to issues of growing economic inequality in the early twenty-first century. A left-leaning Occupy Wall Street movement attacked the wealthiest "1 percent." The movement faded, but the weak economic recovery fostered growing debates about poverty and wealth and especially the power of the immensely rich and the growing financial sector.

Barack Obama won reelection against Republican Mitt Romney, a former Massachusetts governor and the first Mormon presidential nominee in American history. Obama attempted to expand his activist reforms in his second term, but conservative House Republicans blocked his efforts. Immigration reform remained a hotly contested issue in the country, but all attempts to find compromise legal solutions failed. Republicans made further gains in the midterm elections of 2014, and the partisan stalemate between the president and Congress deepened. In 2015 the Supreme Court declared gay marriage a right under the Fourteenth Amendment.

Flamboyant businessman and outsider Donald Trump defeated Hillary Clinton in the 2016 election and brought his chaotic and polarizing style of functioning to the White House. Attacking immigrants, racial minorities, and other historically marginalized groups, he promoted an "America First" foreign policy that alienated America's allies and challenged the entire post–Cold War international order.

In 2020, the coronavirus pandemic struck the United States, causing hundreds of thousands of deaths, an economic collapse, and disruption of Americans' lives. The murder of George Floyd in May 2020 deepened the national crisis and sparked a debate about historic racial injustice. Former Vice President Joseph Biden defeated Trump in the 2020 election, but Trump's refusal to concede his loss and effect a smooth transition led to a violent attack on the U.S. Capitol by his supporters on January 6, 2021. Trump's second impeachment, like his first in 2019–2020, ended in acquittal, but the former president later was federally indicted for his role inciting the insurrection.

Drawing on his long legislative experience and deep congressional ties, President Biden was able to pass major domestic legislation early in his term to boost the economy, encourage green energy, and support high-tech production. Yet voter pessimism about the economy, wars in Ukraine and the Middle East, and concerns about the age of the octogenarian president tempered public support for the incumbent as he readied to run for a second term.

Key Terms

- American Recovery and Reinvestment Act (1028)
- Patient Protection and Affordable Care Act (1028)
- Wall Street Reform and Consumer Protection Act (1028)
- Dodd-Frank (1028)
- Tea Party (1029)
- Freedom Caucus (1029)
- Occupy Wall Street (1033)
- Big Tech (1037)
- *Citizens United v. Federal Election Commission* (1037)
- Deferred Action for Childhood Arrivals (DACA) (1038)
- *Obergefell v. Hodges* (1040)
- USA Freedom Act of 2015 (1041)
- confirmation bias (1042)
- Black Lives Matter (1043)
- National Rifle Association (1044)
- Iran nuclear deal (1045)
- #MeToo (1048)
- Tax Cuts and Jobs Act of 2017 (1049)
- "alt-right" (1050)
- Paris Climate Accords (1052)
- Mueller Report (1054)
- COVID-19 (1055)
- CARES Act (1055)
- Inflation Reduction Act (1059)
- CHIPS and Science Act (1059)

People to Know

- Michelle Obama
- Edward Snowden
- Donald J. Trump
- Mike Pence
- Robert Mueller
- Nancy Pelosi
- Joe Biden
- Kamala Harris
- Volodymyr Zelenskyy
- Vladimir Putin
- Xi Jinping
- George Floyd
- Brett Kavanaugh
- Amy Coney Barrett

Chronology

2009	• American Recovery and Reinvestment Act passed	
2010	• Patient Protection and Affordable Care Act passed • Wall Street Reform and Consumer Protection Act passed • "Don't Ask, Don't Tell" policy repealed	• Supreme Court decision in *Citizens United v. Federal Election Commission* • Republicans retake control of the House
2011	• U.S. withdraws from Iraq • U.S. begins troop withdrawal from Afghanistan	• U.S. forces kill Osama bin Laden • First debt-ceiling crisis between President Obama and the GOP-led House
2012	• Supreme Court upholds the Affordable Care Act • Obama defeats Romney to win reelection	• Syrian civil war begins
2013	• Supreme Court repeals Section 4 of the Voting Rights Act • Supreme Court rules the Defense of Marriage Act unconstitutional • Second debt-ceiling crisis between President Obama and GOP-led House	• Budget dispute causes a sixteen-day federal government shutdown • Edward Snowden exposes extensive NSA spying operations
2014	• Republicans win majority in Senate • Russia invades and annexes Ukraine's Crimean Peninsula	
2015	• Supreme Court gives constitutional protection to same-sex marriage	• Iran nuclear deal agreed • Paris Climate Accords signed
2016	• Great Britain votes to leave the European Union ("Brexit") • Donald J. Trump defeats Hillary Clinton for the presidency	
2017	• Trump signs tax reform bill into law • Trump pulls the United States out of the Paris Climate Accords	• Congress and the Department of Justice launch investigations of Russian interference in 2016 election • "Unite the Right" march in Charlottesville, Virginia
2018	• Democrats win control of House in midterm elections • Partial government shutdown begins in December, lasts 35 days	
2019	• Mueller Report released • Trump impeached by House for abuse of power and obstruction of justice	• Novel coronavirus (COVID-19) emerges in Wuhan, China
2020	• Trump acquitted by Senate • COVID-19 pandemic begins	• Black Lives Matter protests after the murder of George Floyd • Joe Biden defeats Donald Trump in presidential election
2021	• January 6 riot at Capitol attempts to prevent certification of election • Joe Biden sworn in as 46th U.S. president	• Second Trump impeachment; Senate again fails to convict • Last American troops withdraw from Afghanistan
2022	• American deaths from COVID-19 surpass 1 million • Russia invades Ukraine	• Dobbs decision overturns *Roe v. Wade*
2023	• Trump indicted in several separate cases related to his conduct after the 2020 election, January 6 insurrection, and post-presidency	• Hamas terrorist attack and Israeli invasion and bombing of Gaza

To Learn More

Michelle Alexander, *The New Jim Crow: Mass Incarceration in the Age of Colorblindness* (2010)

John Cassidy, *How Markets Fail: The Logic of Economic Calamities* (2009)

Jacob S. Hacker and Paul Pierson, *Winner-Take-All Politics: How Washington Made the Rich Richer—And Turned Its Back on the Middle Class* (2010)

Bill Ong Hing, *Defining America Through Immigration Policy* (2004)

Elizabeth Kolbert, *The Sixth Extinction: An Unnatural History* (2015)

Michael Lewis, *The Big Short: Inside the Doomsday Machine* (2010)

Christopher Leonard, *The Lords of Easy Money: How the Federal Reserve Broke the American Economy* (2022)

Carol Leonnig and Philip Rucker, *I Alone Can Fix It: Donald J. Trump's Catastrophic Final Year* (2021)

Luke Mogelson, *The Storm Is Here: An American Crucible* (2022)

Benjamin Page and Martin Gilens, *Democracy in America?: What Has Gone Wrong and What We Can Do About It* (2017)

Thomas Piketty, *Capital in the Twenty-First Century* (2014)

David Remnick, *The Bridge: The Life and Rise of Barack Obama* (2010)

Katy Tur, *Unbelievable: My Front-Row Seat to the Craziest Campaign in American History* (2017)

Joby Warrick, *Black Flags: The Rise of ISIS* (2016)

Bob Woodward, *Bush at War* (2002); *Plan of Attack* (2004); and *State of Denial* (2006)

Julian Zelizer, ed., *The Presidency of Barack Obama: A First Historical Assessment* (2017)

________, *The Presidency of Donald J. Trump: A First Historical Assessment* (2022)

Declaration of Independence

In Congress, July 4, 1776

The Unanimous Declaration of the Thirteen United States of America

[Bracketed material in color has been inserted by the authors. For adoption background, refer to pp. 154–156.]

When, in the course of human events, it becomes necessary for one people to dissolve the political bonds which have connected them with another, and to assume, among the powers of the earth, the separate and equal station to which the laws of nature and of nature's God entitle them, a decent respect to the opinions of mankind requires that they should declare the causes which impel them to the separation.

We hold these truths to be self-evident: That all men are created equal; that they are endowed by their Creator with certain unalienable rights; that among these are life, liberty, and the pursuit of happiness; that, to secure these rights, governments are instituted among men, deriving their just powers from the consent of the governed; that whenever any form of government becomes destructive of these ends, it is the right of the people to alter or to abolish it, and to institute new government, laying its foundation on such principles, and organizing its powers in such form, as to them shall seem most likely to effect their safety and happiness. Prudence, indeed, will dictate that governments long established should not be changed for light and transient causes; and accordingly all experience hath shown that mankind are more disposed to suffer, while evils are sufferable, than to right themselves by abolishing the forms to which they are accustomed. But when a long train of abuses and usurpations, pursuing invariably the same object, evinces a design to reduce them under absolute despotism, it is their right, it is their duty, to throw off such government, and to provide new guards for their future security. Such has been the patient sufferance of these colonies; and such is now the necessity which constrains them to alter their former systems of government. The history of the present King of Great Britain is a history of repeated injuries and usurpations, all having in direct object the establishment of an absolute tyranny over these states. To prove this, let facts be submitted to a candid world.

He has refused his assent to laws, the most wholesome and necessary for the public good. [Refer to royal veto, p. 129.]

He has forbidden his governors to pass laws of immediate and pressing importance, unless suspended in their operation till his assent should be obtained; and, when so suspended, he has utterly neglected to attend to them.

He has refused to pass other laws for the accommodation of large districts of people [by establishing new countries], unless those people would relinquish the right of representation in the legislature, a right inestimable to them, and formidable to tyrants only.

He has called together legislative bodies at places unusual, uncomfortable, and distant from the depository of their public records, for the sole purpose of fatiguing them into compliance with his measures [e.g., removal of Massachusetts Assembly to Salem, 1774].

He has dissolved representative houses repeatedly, for opposing, with manly firmness, his invasions on the rights of the people [e.g., Virginia Assembly, 1765].

He has refused for a long time, after such dissolutions, to cause others to be elected; whereby the legislative powers, incapable of annihilation, have returned to the people at large for their exercise; the state remaining, in the mean time, exposed to all the dangers of invasions from without and convulsions within.

He has endeavored to prevent the population [populating] of these states; for that purpose obstructing the laws for naturalization of foreigners; refusing to pass others to encourage their migration hither, and raising the conditions of new appropriations of lands [e.g., Proclamation of 1763, p. 126].

He has obstructed the administration of justice, by refusing his assent to laws for establishing judiciary powers.

He has made judges dependent on his will alone, for the tenure of their offices, and the amount and payment of their salaries. [Refer to Townshend Acts, p. 133.]

He has erected a multitude of new offices, and sent hither swarms of officers to harass our people and eat out their substance. [Refer to enforcement of Navigation Laws, p. 130.]

He has kept among us, in times of peace, standing armies, without the consent of our legislatures. [Refer to pp. 130, 133.]

He has affected to render the military independent of, and superior to, the civil power.

He has combined with others to subject us to a jurisdiction foreign to our constitution, and unacknowledged by our laws, giving his assent to their acts of pretended legislation:

For quartering large bodies of armed troops among us [refer to Boston Massacre, pp. 133–134];

For protecting them, by a mock trial, from punishment for any murders which they should commit on the inhabitants of these states [refer to 1774 Intolerable Acts, pp. 136–137];

For cutting off our trade with all parts of the world [refer to Boston Port Act, pp. 136–137];

For imposing taxes on us without our consent [refer to Stamp Act, pp. 130–132];

For depriving us, in many cases, of the benefits of trial by jury;

For transporting us beyond seas, to be tried for pretended offenses;

For abolishing the free system of English laws in a neighboring province [Quebec], establishing therein an arbitrary government, and enlarging its boundaries, so as to render it at once an example and fit instrument for introducing the same absolute rule into these colonies [Quebec Act, p. 136];

For taking away our charters, abolishing our most valuable laws, and altering fundamentally the forms of our governments [e.g., in Massachusetts, pp. 136–137];

For suspending our own legislatures, and declaring themselves invested with power to legislate for us in all cases whatsoever. [Refer to Stamp Act repeal, pp. 131–132.]

He has abdicated government here, by declaring us out of his protection and waging war against us. [Refer to George III's proclamation of colonies in rebellion, p. 150.]

He has plundered our seas, ravaged our coasts, burned our towns, and destroyed the lives of our people [e.g., the burning of Falmouth (Portland), p. 150].

He is at this time transporting large armies of foreign mercenaries [Hessians, p. 150] to complete the works of death, desolation, and tyranny already begun with circumstances of cruelty and perfidy scarcely paralleled in the most barbarous ages, and totally unworthy the head of a civilized nation.

He has constrained our fellow-citizens, taken captive on the high seas [by impressment], to bear arms against their country, to become the executioners of their friends and brethren, or to fall themselves by their hands.

He has excited domestic insurrection among us [i.e., among slaves], and has endeavored to bring on the inhabitants of our frontiers the merciless Indian savages, whose known rule of warfare is an undistinguished destruction of all ages, sexes, and conditions.

In every stage of these oppressions we have petitioned for redress in the most humble terms; our repeated petitions have been answered only by repeated injury [e.g., pp. 149–150]. A prince, whose character is thus marked by every act which may define a tyrant, is unfit to be the ruler of a free people.

Nor have we been wanting in our attentions to our British brethren. We have warned them, from time to time, of attempts by their legislature to extend an unwarrantable jurisdiction over us. We have reminded them of the circumstances of our emigration and settlement here. We have appealed to their native justice and magnanimity; and we have conjured them, by the ties of our common kindred, to disavow these usurpations, which would inevitably interrupt our connections and correspondence. They, too, have been deaf to the voice of justice and of consanguinity [blood relationship]. We must, therefore, acquiesce in the necessity which denounces [announces] our separation, and hold them, as we hold the rest of mankind, enemies in war, in peace friends.

We, therefore, the representatives of the United States of America, in General Congress assembled, appealing to the Supreme Judge of the world for the rectitude of our intentions, do, in the name and by the authority of the good people of these colonies, solemnly publish and declare, That these United Colonies are, and of right ought to be, FREE AND INDEPENDENT STATES; that they are absolved from all allegiance to the British crown, and that all political connection between them and the state of Great Britain is, and ought to be, totally dissolved; and that, as free and independent states, they have full power to levy war, conclude peace, contract alliances, establish commerce, and do all other acts and things which independent states may of right do. And for the support of this declaration, with a firm reliance on the protection of Divine Providence, we mutually pledge to each other our lives, our fortunes, and our sacred honor.

[Signed by]

JOHN HANCOCK [President]
[and fifty-five others]

Constitution of the United States of America

[Boldface headings and bracketed explanatory matter and marginal comments (both in color) have been inserted for the reader's convenience. Passages that are no longer operative are printed in italic type.]

Article I.

Preamble

Section I.

We the people of the United States, in order to form a more perfect union, establish justice, insure domestic tranquility, provide for the common defense, promote the general welfare, and secure the blessings of liberty to ourselves and our posterity, do ordain and establish this CONSTITUTION for the United States of America.

Section II.

Legislative Department

Congress

Legislative power vested in a two-house Congress. All legislative powers herein granted shall be vested in a Congress of the United States, which shall consist of a Senate and a House of Representatives.

House of Representatives

1. The people elect representatives biennially. The House of Representatives shall be composed of members chosen every second year by the people of the several States, and the electors [voters] in each State shall have the qualifications requisite for electors of the most numerous branch of the State Legislature.

2. Who may be representatives. No person shall be a Representative who shall not have attained the age of twenty-five years, and been seven years a citizen of the United States, and who shall not, when elected, be an inhabitant of that State in which he shall be chosen.

Refer to 1787 compromises, pp. 184–188.

3. Representation in the House based on population; census. Representatives and direct taxes[1] shall be apportioned among the several States which may be included within this Union, according to their respective numbers, *which shall be determined by adding to the whole number of free persons, including those bound to service for a term of years* [apprentices and indentured servants], *and excluding Indians not taxed, three-fifths of all other persons* [slaves].[2] The actual enumeration [census] shall be made within three years after the first meeting of the Congress of the United States, and within every subsequent term of ten years, in such manner as they shall by law direct. The number of Representatives shall not exceed one for every thirty thousand, but each State shall have at least one Representative; *and until such enumeration shall be made, the State of New Hampshire shall be entitled to choose three, Massachusetts eight, Rhode Island and Providence Plantations one, Connecticut five, New York six, New Jersey four, Pennsylvania eight, Delaware one, Maryland six, Virginia ten, North Carolina five, South Carolina five, and Georgia three.*

Refer to 1787 compromises, pp. 184–188.

4. Vacancies in the House are filled by election. When vacancies happen in the representation from any State, the Executive authority [governor] therefore shall issue writs of election [call a special election] to fill such vacancies.

Refer to Chase and Johnson trials, pp. 233, 513–514; Nixon trial preliminaries, pp. 942–944; discussion of Clinton's impeachment, pp. 1010–1011; and Trump's two impeachments, pp. 1054–1055, 1058.

5. The House selects its Speaker; has sole power to vote impeachment charges (i.e., indictments). The House of Representatives shall choose their Speaker and other officers; and shall have the sole power of impeachment.

---

[1]Modified in 1913 by the Sixteenth Amendment re income taxes (refer to p. 706).

[2]The word *slave* appears nowhere in the original, unamended Constitution. The three-fifths rule ceased to be in force when the Thirteenth Amendment was adopted in 1865 (refer to pp. 185, 475, and amendments below).

Section III. Senate

1. Senators represent the states. The Senate of the United States shall be composed of two Senators from each State, *chosen by the legislature thereof,*[1] for six Years; and each Senator shall have one vote.

2. One-third of senators chosen every two years; vacancies. *Immediately after they shall be assembled in consequence of the first election, they shall be divided as equally as may be into three classes. The seats of the Senators of the first class shall be vacated at the expiration of the second year, of the second class at the expiration of the fourth year, and of the third class at the expiration of the sixth year,* so that one-third may be chosen every second year; *and if vacancies happen by resignation or otherwise, during the recess of the legislature of any State, the Executive* [governor] *thereof may make temporary appointments until the next meeting of the legislature, which shall then fill such vacancies.*[2]

3. Who may be senators. No person shall be a Senator who shall not have attained to the age of thirty years, and been nine years a citizen of the United States, and who shall not, when elected, be an inhabitant of that State for which he shall be chosen.

4. The vice president presides over the Senate. The Vice President of the United States shall be President of the Senate, but shall have no vote, unless they be equally divided [tied].

5. The Senate chooses its other officers. The Senate shall choose their other officers, and also a President *pro tempore,* in the absence of the Vice President, or when he shall exercise the office of the President of the United States.

Refer to Chase and Johnson trials, pp. 233, 513–514; discussion of Clinton's impeachment, pp. 1010–1011; and Trump's two impeachments, pp. 1054–1055, 1058.

6. The Senate has sole power to try impeachments. The Senate shall have the sole power to try all impeachments. When sitting for that purpose, they shall be on oath or affirmation. When the President of the United States is tried, the Chief Justice shall preside[3]: and no person shall be convicted without the concurrence of two-thirds of the members present.

7. Penalties for impeachment conviction. Judgment in cases of impeachment shall not extend further than to removal from office, and disqualification to hold and enjoy any office of honor, trust or profit under the United States: but the party convicted shall nevertheless be liable and subject to indictment, trial, judgment and punishment, according to law.

Section IV. Election and Meetings of Congress

1. Regulation of elections. The times, places and manner of holding elections for Senators and Representatives shall be prescribed in each State by the legislature thereof; but the Congress may at any time by law make or alter such regulations, except as to the places of choosing Senators.

2. Congress must meet once a year. The Congress shall assemble at least once in every year, and such meeting *shall be on the first Monday in December, unless they shall by law appoint a different day.*[4]

Section V. Organization and Rules of the Houses

1. Each house may reject members; quorums. Each house shall be the judge of the elections, returns and qualifications of its own members, and a majority of each shall constitute a quorum to do business; but a smaller number may adjourn from day to day, and may be authorized to compel the attendance of absent members, in such manner, and under such penalties, as each house may provide.

---

[1]Repealed in favor of popular election in 1913 by the Seventeenth Amendment.

[2]Changed in 1913 by the Seventeenth Amendment.

[3]The vice president, as next in line, would be an interested party.

[4]Changed in 1933 to January 3 by the Twentieth Amendment (refer to p. 801 and below).

Refer to "Bully" Brooks case, pp. 439–440.

2. Each house makes its own rules. Each house may determine the rules of its proceedings, punish its members for disorderly behavior, and with the concurrence of two-thirds, expel a member.

3. Each house must keep and publish a record of its proceedings. Each house shall keep a journal of its proceedings, and from time to time publish the same, excepting such parts as may in their judgment require secrecy; and the yeas and nays of the members of either house on any question shall, at the desire of one-fifth of those present, be entered on the journal.

4. Both houses must agree on adjournment. Neither house, during the session of Congress, shall, without the consent of the other, adjourn for more than three days, nor to any other place than that in which the two houses shall be sitting.

Section VI. Privileges of and Prohibitions upon Congressmen

1. Congressional salaries; immunities. The Senators and Representatives shall receive a compensation for their services, to be ascertained by law and paid out of the treasury of the United States. They shall in all cases except treason, felony and breach of the peace, be privileged from arrest during their attendance at the session of their respective houses, and in going to and returning from the same; and for any speech or debate in either house, they shall not be questioned in any other place [i.e., they shall be immune from libel suits].

2. A congressman may not hold any other federal civil office. No Senator or Representative shall, during the time for which he was elected, be appointed to any civil office under the authority of the United States, which shall have been created, or the emoluments whereof shall have been increased, during such time; and no person holding any office under the United States shall be a member of either house during his continuance in office.

Section VII. Method of Making Laws

Refer to 1787 compromises, pp. 184–188.

1. Money bills must originate in the House. All bills for raising revenue shall originate in the House of Representatives; but the Senate may propose or concur with amendments as on other bills.

Nixon, more than any predecessors, "impounded" billions of dollars voted by Congress for specific purposes because he disapproved of them. The courts generally failed to sustain him, and his impeachment foes regarded wholesale impoundment as a violation of his oath to "faithfully execute" the laws.

2. The president's veto power; Congress may override. Every bill which shall have passed the House of Representatives and the Senate, shall, before it become a law, be presented to the President of the United States; if he approve he shall sign it, but if not he shall return it with his objections to that house in which it shall have originated, who shall enter the objections at large on their journal, and proceed to reconsider it. If after such reconsideration two-thirds of that house shall agree to pass the bill, it shall be sent, together with the objections, to the other house, by which it shall likewise be reconsidered, and, if approved by two-thirds of that house, it shall become a law. But in all such cases the votes of both houses shall be determined by yeas and nays, and the names of the persons voting for and against the bill shall be entered on the journal of each house respectively. If any bill shall not be returned by the President within ten days (Sundays excepted) after it shall have been presented to him, the same shall be a law, in like manner as if he had signed it, unless the Congress by their adjournment prevent its return, in which case it shall not be a law [this is the so-called pocket veto].

3. All measures requiring the agreement of both houses go to president for approval. Every order, resolution, or vote to which the concurrence of the Senate and House of Representatives may be necessary (except on a question of adjournment) shall be presented to the President of the United States; and before the same shall take effect, shall be approved by him, or being disapproved by him, shall be repassed by two-thirds of the Senate and House of Representatives, according to the rules and limitations prescribed in the case of a bill.

Section VIII. Powers Granted to Congress

Congress has certain enumerated powers:

1. It may lay and collect taxes. The Congress shall have power to lay and collect taxes, duties, imposts, and excises, to pay the debts and provide for the common defense and general welfare of the United States; but all duties, imposts and excises shall be uniform throughout the United States;

2. It may borrow money. To borrow money on the credit of the United States;

3. It may regulate foreign and interstate trade. To regulate commerce with foreign nations, and among the several States, and with the Indian tribes;

For 1798 naturalization, refer to p. 217.

4. It may pass naturalization and bankruptcy laws. To establish an uniform rule of naturalization, and uniform laws on the subject of bankruptcies throughout the United States;

5. It may coin money. To coin money, regulate the value thereof, and of foreign coin, and fix the standard of weights and measures;

6. It may punish counterfeiters. To provide for the punishment of counterfeiting the securities and current coin of the United States;

7. It may establish a postal service. To establish post offices and post roads;

8. It may issue patents and copyrights. To promote the progress of science and useful arts by securing for limited times to authors and inventors the exclusive right to their respective writings and discoveries;

9. It may establish inferior courts. To constitute tribunals inferior to the Supreme Court;

Refer to Judiciary Act of 1789, p. 202.

10. It may punish crimes committed on the high seas. To define and punish piracies and felonies committed on the high seas [i.e., outside the three-mile limit] and offenses against the law of nations [international law];

11. It may declare war; authorize privateers. To declare war,[1] grant letters of marque and reprisal,[2] and make rules concerning captures on land and water;

12. It may maintain an army. To raise and support armies, but no appropriation of money to that use shall be for a longer term than two years;[3]

13. It may maintain a navy. To provide and maintain a navy;

14. It may regulate the army and navy. To make rules for the government and regulation of the land and naval forces;

Refer to Whiskey Rebellion, pp. 205–206.

15. It may call out the state militia. To provide for calling forth the militia to execute the laws of the Union, suppress insurrections, and repel invasions;

16. It shares with the states control of militia. To provide for organizing, arming, and disciplining the militia, and for governing such part of them as may be employed in the service of the United States, reserving to the States respectively the appointment of the officers, and the authority of training the militia according to the discipline prescribed by Congress;

17. It makes laws for the District of Columbia and other federal areas. To exercise exclusive legislation in all cases whatsoever, over such district (not exceeding ten miles square) as may, by cession of particular States, and the acceptance of Congress, become the seat of government of the United States,[4] and to exercise like authority over all places purchased by the consent of the legislature of the State, in which the same shall be, for the erection of forts, magazines, arsenals, dock-yards, and other needful buildings;—and

Congress has certain implied powers:

This is the famous "elastic clause"; refer to p. 204.

18. It may make laws necessary for carrying out the enumerated powers. To make all laws which shall be necessary and proper for carrying into execution the foregoing powers, and all other powers vested by this Constitution in the government of the United States, or in any departure or officer thereof.

---

[1]Note that presidents, though they can provoke war (refer to the case of Polk, p. 402) or wage it after it is declared, cannot declare it.

[2]Papers issued private citizens in wartime authorizing them to capture enemy ships.

[3]A reflection of fear of standing armies earlier expressed in the Declaration of Independence.

[4]The District of Columbia, ten miles square, was established in 1791 with a cession from Virginia (refer to p. 203).

Section IX. Powers Denied to the Federal Government

Refer to 1787 slave compromise, p. 185.

1. Congressional control of slave trade postponed until 1808. *The migration or importation of such persons as any of the States now existing shall think proper to admit shall not be prohibited by the Congress prior to the year 1808; but a tax or duty may be imposed on such importation, not exceeding $10 for each person.*

Refer to Lincoln's unlawful suspension, p. 468.

2. The writ of habeas corpus[1] may be suspended only in cases of rebellion or invasion. The privilege of the writ of habeas corpus shall not be suspended, unless when in cases of rebellion or invasion the public safety may require it.

3. Attainders[2] and ex post facto laws[3] forbidden. No bill of attainder or ex post facto law shall be passed.

4. Direct taxes must be apportioned according to population. No capitation [head or poll tax] or other direct, tax shall be laid, unless in proportion to the census or enumeration herein before directed to be taken.[4]

5. Export taxes forbidden. No tax or duty shall be laid on articles exported from any State.

6. Congress must not discriminate among states in regulating commerce. No preference shall be given by any regulation of commerce or revenue to the ports of one State over those of another; nor shall vessels bound to, or from, one State, be obliged to enter, clear, or pay duties in another.

Refer to Lincoln's unlawful infraction, p. 468.

7. Public money may not be spent without congressional appropriation; accounting. No money shall be drawn from the treasury, but in consequence of appropriations made by law; and a regular statement and account of the receipts and expenditures of all public money shall be published from time to time.

8. Titles of nobility prohibited; foreign gifts. No title of nobility shall be granted by the United States; and no person holding office of profit or trust under them, shall, without the consent of Congress, accept of any present, emolument, office, or title, of any kind whatever, from any king, prince, or foreign state.

Section X. Powers Denied to the States

Absolute prohibitions on the states:

On contracts, refer to *Fletcher v. Peck*, p. 263.

1. The states are forbidden to do certain things. No State shall enter into any treaty, alliance, or confederation; grant letters of marque and reprisal [i.e., authorize privateers]; coin money; emit bills of credit [issue paper money]; make anything but gold and silver coin a [legal] tender in payment of debts; pass any bill of attainder,[5] ex post facto,[5] or law impairing the obligation of contracts, or grant any title of nobility.

Conditional prohibitions on the states:

Cf. Confederation chaos, pp. 176–178.

2. The states may not levy duties without the consent of Congress. No State shall, without the consent of Congress, lay any imposts or duties on imports or exports, except what may be absolutely necessary for executing its inspection laws: and the net produce of all duties and imposts, laid by any State on imports or exports, shall be for the use of the treasury of the United States; and all such laws shall be subject to the revision and control of the Congress.

3. Certain other federal powers are forbidden the states except with the consent of Congress. No State shall, without the consent of Congress, lay any duty of tonnage [i.e., duty on ship tonnage], keep [nonmilitia] troops or ships of war in time of peace, enter into any agreement or compact with another State, or with a foreign power, or engage in war, unless actually invaded, or in such imminent danger as will not admit of delay.

---

[1] A writ of habeas corpus is a document that enables a person under arrest to obtain an immediate examination in court to ascertain whether he or she is being legally held.

[2] A bill of attainder is a special legislative act condemning and punishing an individual without a judicial trial.

[3] An ex post facto law is one that fixes punishments for acts committed before the law was passed.

[4] Modified in 1913 by the Sixteenth Amendment (refer to p. 706 and amendments below).

[5] For definitions refer to footnotes 2 and 3 above.

Article II. Executive Department

Section I. President and Vice President

1. The president is the chief executive; term of office. The executive power shall be vested in a President of the United States of America. He shall hold his office during the term of four years,[1] and, together with the Vice President, chosen for the same term, be elected as follows:

Refer to 1787 compromise, pp. 185–188.

Refer to 1876 Oregon case, p. 529

2. The president is chosen by electors. Each State shall appoint, in such manner as the legislature thereof may direct, a number of electors, equal to the whole number of Senators and Representatives to which the State may be entitled in the Congress; but no Senator or Representative, or person holding an office of trust or profit under the United States, shall be appointed an elector.

Refer to Burr-Jefferson disputed election of 1800, pp. 228–230.

Refer to Jefferson as vice president in 1796, p. 214.

A majority of the electoral votes needed to elect a president. *The electors shall meet in their respective States, and vote by ballot for two persons, of whom one at least shall not be an inhabitant of the same State with themselves. And they shall make a list of all the persons voted for, and of the number of votes for each; which list they shall sign and certify, and transmit sealed to the seat of government of the United States, directed to the President of the Senate. The President of the Senate shall, in the presence of the Senate and House of Representatives, open all the certificates, and the votes shall be counted. The person having the greatest number of votes shall be the President, if such number be a majority of the whole number of electors appointed; and if there be more than one who have such majority, and have an equal number of votes, then the House of Representatives shall immediately choose by ballot one of them for President; and if no person have a majority, then from the five highest on the list the said house shall in like manner choose the President. But in choosing the President the votes shall be taken by States, the representation from each State having one vote; a quorum for this purpose shall consist of a member or members from two-thirds of the States, and a majority of all the States shall be necessary to a choice. In every case, after the choice of the President, the person having the greatest number of votes of the electors shall be the Vice President. But if there should remain two or more who have equal votes, the Senate shall choose from them by ballot the Vice President.*[2]

3. Congress decides time of meeting of Electoral College. The Congress may determine the time of choosing the electors and the day on which they shall give their votes; which day shall be the same throughout the United States.

To provide for foreign-born people, like Alexander Hamilton, born in the British West Indies.

4. Who may be president. No person except a natural-born citizen, *or a citizen of the United States at the time of the adoption of this Constitution,* shall be eligible to the office of President; neither shall any person be eligible to that office who shall not have attained to the age of thirty-five years, and been fourteen years a resident within the United States [i.e., a legal resident].

Modified by Twentieth and Twenty-fifth Amendments below.

5. Replacements for president. In case of the removal of the President from office or of his death, resignation, or inability to discharge the powers and duties of said office, the same shall devolve on the Vice President, and the Congress may by law provide for the case of removal, death, resignation, or inability, both of the President and Vice President, declaring what officer shall then act as President, and such officer shall act accordingly, until the disability be removed, or a President shall be elected.

6. The president's salary. The President shall, at stated times, receive for his services a compensation, which shall neither be increased or diminished during the period for which he shall have been elected, and he shall not receive within that period any other emolument from the United States, or any of them.

7. The president's oath of office. Before he enter on the execution of his office, he shall take the following oath or affirmation:—"I do solemnly swear (or affirm) that I will faithfully execute the office of the President of the United States, and will to the best of my ability preserve, protect and defend the Constitution of the United States."

---

[1]No reference to reelection; for anti-third term Twenty-second Amendment, refer to text below.

[2]Repealed in 1804 by the Twelfth Amendment (refer to text below).

Section II. Powers of the President

Refer to cabinet evolution, p. 201.

1. The president has important military and civil powers. The President shall be commander in chief of the army and navy of the United States, and of the militia of the several States, when called into the actual service of the United States; he may require the opinion, in writing, of the principal officer in each of the executive departments, upon any subject relating to the duties of their respective offices, and he shall have power to grant reprieves and pardons for offenses against the United States, except in cases of impeachment.[1]

For president's removal power, refer to p. 513.

2. The president may negotiate treaties and nominate federal officials. He shall have power, by and with the advice and consent of the Senate, to make treaties, provided two-thirds of the Senators present concur; and he shall nominate, and by and with the advice and consent of the Senate, shall appoint ambassadors, other public ministers and consuls, judges of the Supreme Court, and all other officers of the United States, whose appointments are not herein otherwise provided for, and which shall be established by law: but the Congress may by law vest the appointment of such inferior officers, as they think proper, in the President alone, in the courts of law, or in the heads of departments.

3. The president may fill vacancies during Senate recess. The President shall have power to fill up all vacancies that may happen during the recess of the Senate, by granting commissions which shall expire at the end of their next session.

Section III. Other Powers and Duties of the President

For president's personal appearances, refer to p. 707.

Messages; extra sessions; receiving ambassadors; execution of the laws. He shall from time to time give to the Congress information of the state of the Union, and recommend to their consideration such measures as he shall judge necessary and expedient; he may, on extraordinary occasions, convene both houses, or either of them, and in case of disagreement between them, with respect to the time of adjournment, he may adjourn them to such time as he shall think proper; he shall receive ambassadors and other public ministers; he shall take care that the laws be faithfully executed, and shall commission all the officers of the United States.

Section IV. Impeachment

Refer to discussion of Presidents Johnson, pp. 513–514; Nixon, pp. 942–944; Clinton, pp. 1010–1011; and Trump, pp. 1054–1055, 1058.

Civil officers may be removed by impeachment. The President, Vice President and all civil officers[2] of the United States shall be removed from office on impeachment for, and on conviction of, treason, bribery, and other high crimes and misdemeanors.

Article III. Judicial Department

Section I. The Federal Courts

Refer to Judiciary Act of 1789, p. 202.

The judicial power belongs to the federal courts. The judicial power of the United States shall be vested in one Supreme Court, and in such inferior courts as the Congress may from time to time ordain and establish. The judges, both of the Supreme and inferior courts, shall hold their offices during good behavior, and shall, at stated times, receive for their services a compensation which shall not be diminished[3] during their continuance in office.

Section II. Jurisdiction of Federal Courts

1. Kinds of cases that may be heard. The judicial power shall extend to all cases, in law and equity, arising under this Constitution, the laws of the United States, and treaties made, or which

---

[1]To prevent the president's pardoning himself or his close associates, as was feared in the case of Richard Nixon. Refer to pp. 942–944.

[2]i.e., all federal executive and judicial officers, but not members of Congress or military personnel.

[3]In 1978, in a case involving federal judges, the Supreme Court ruled that diminution of salaries by inflation was irrelevant.

shall be made, under their authority;—to all cases affecting ambassadors, other public ministers and consuls;—to all cases of admiralty and maritime jurisdiction;—to controversies to which the United States shall be a party;—to controversies between two or more States;—*between a State and citizens of another State*[1];—between citizens of different States;—between citizens of the same State claiming lands under grants of different States, and between a State, or the citizens thereof, and foreign states, citizens or subjects.

2. Jurisdiction of the Supreme Court. In all cases affecting ambassadors, other public ministers and consuls, and those in which a State shall be a party, the Supreme Court shall have original jurisdiction.[2] In all the other cases before mentioned, the Supreme Court shall have appellate jurisdiction,[3] both as to law and fact, with such exceptions, and under such regulations, as the Congress shall make.

3. Trial for federal crime is by jury. The trial of all crimes, except in cases of impeachment, shall be by jury; and such trial shall be held in the State where the said crimes shall have been committed; but when not committed within any State, the trial shall be at such place or places as the Congress may by law have directed.

Section III. Treason

1. Treason defined. Treason against the United States shall consist only in levying war against them, or in adhering to their enemies, giving them aid and comfort. No person shall be convicted of treason unless on the testimony of two witnesses to the same overt act, or on confession in open court.

2. Congress fixes punishment for treason. The Congress shall have power to declare the punishment of treason, but no attainder of treason shall work corruption of blood, or forfeiture except during the life of the person attained.[4]

Article IV. Relations of the States to One Another

Section I. Credit to Acts, Records, and Court Proceedings

Each state must respect the public acts of the others. Full faith and credit shall be given in each State to the public acts, records, and judicial proceedings of every other State.[5] And the Congress may by general laws prescribe the manner in which such acts, records, and proceedings shall be proved [attested], and the effect thereof.

Section II. Duties of States to States

1. Citizenship in one state is valid in all. The citizens of each State shall be entitled to all privileges and immunities of citizens in the several States.

This stipulation is sometimes openly flouted. In 1978 Governor Jerry Brown of California, acting on humanitarian grounds, refused to surrender to South Dakota an American Indian, Dennis Banks, who was charged with murder in an armed uprising.

2. Fugitives from justice must be surrendered by the state to which they have fled. A person charged in any State with treason, felony, or other crime, who shall flee from justice, and be found in another State, shall on demand of the executive authority [governor] of the State from which he fled, be delivered up, to be removed to the State having jurisdiction of the crime.

Basis of fugitive-slave laws; refer to pp. 421–423.

3. Slaves and apprentices must be returned. *No person held to service or labor in one State, under the laws thereof, escaping into another, shall, in consequence of any law or regulation therein, be discharged from such service or labor, but shall be delivered up on claim of the party to whom such service or labor may be due.*[6]

---

[1]The Eleventh Amendment (refer to text below) restricts this to suits by a state against citizens of another state.

[2]i.e., such cases must originate in the Supreme Court.

[3]i.e., it hears other cases only when they are appealed to it from a lower federal court or a state court.

[4]i.e., punishment only for the offender; none for his or her heirs.

[5]e.g., a marriage in one is valid in all.

[6]Invalidated in 1865 by the Thirteenth Amendment (refer to text below).

Section III. New States and Territories

e.g., Maine (1820); refer to pp. 261–262.

1. Congress may admit new states. New States may be admitted by the Congress into this Union; but no new State shall be formed or erected within the jurisdiction of any other State; nor any State be formed by the junction of two or more States, or parts of States, without the consent of the legislatures of the States concerned as well as of the Congress.[1]

2. Congress regulates federal territory and property. The Congress shall have power to dispose of and make all needful rules and regulations respecting the territory or other property belonging to the United States; and nothing in this Constitution shall be so construed as to prejudice any claims of the United States, or of any particular State.

Section IV. Protection to the States

Refer to Cleveland and the Pullman strike, pp. 635–636.

United States guarantees to states representative government and protection against invasion and rebellion. The United States shall guarantee to every State in this Union a republican form of government, and shall protect each of them against invasion; and on application of the legislature, or of the executive [governor] (when the legislature cannot be convened), against domestic violence.

Article V. The Process of Amendment

The Constitution may be amended in four ways. The Congress, whenever two-thirds of both houses shall deem it necessary, shall propose amendments to this Constitution, or, on the application of the legislature of two-thirds of the several States, shall call a convention for proposing amendments, which, in either case, shall be valid to all intents and purposes, as part of this Constitution, when ratified by the legislatures of three-fourths of the several States, or by conventions in three-fourths thereof, as the one or the other mode of ratification may be proposed by the Congress; provided *that no amendments which may be made prior to the year one thousand eight hundred and eight shall in any manner affect the first and fourth clauses in the ninth section of the first article;*[2] and that no State, without its consent, shall be deprived of its equal suffrage in the Senate.

Article VI. General Provisions

This pledge honored by Hamilton, pp. 202–203.

1. The debts of the Confederation are taken over. All debts contracted and engagements entered into, before the adoption of this Constitution, shall be as valid against the United States under this Constitution, as under the Confederation.

2. The Constitution, federal laws, and treaties are the supreme law of the land. This Constitution, and the laws of the United States which shall be made in pursuance thereof; and all treaties made, or which shall be made, under the authority of the United States, shall be the supreme law of the land; and the judges in every State shall be bound thereby, anything in the Constitution or laws of any State to the contrary notwithstanding.

3. Federal and state officers bound by oath to support the Constitution. The Senators and Representatives before mentioned, and the members of the several State legislatures, and all executive and judicial officers, both of the United States and of the several States, shall be bound by oath or affirmation to support this Constitution; but no religious test shall ever be required as a qualification to any office or public trust under the United States.

---

[1]Loyal West Virginia was formed by Lincoln in 1862 from seceded Virginia. This act was of dubious constitutionality and was justified in part by the wartime powers of the president. Refer to pp. 459–461.

[2]This clause, regarding slave trade and direct taxes, became inoperative in 1808.

Article VII. Ratification of the Constitution

Refer to 1787 irregularity, pp. 188–189.

The Constitution effective when ratified by conventions in nine states. The ratification of the conventions of nine States shall be sufficient for the establishment of this Constitution between the States so ratifying the same.

Done in Convention by the unanimous consent of the States present, the seventeenth day of September in the year of our Lord one thousand seven hundred and eighty-seven and of the Independence of the United States of America the twelfth. In witness whereof we have hereunto subscribed our names.

[Signed by] G° WASHINGTON

Presidt and Deputy from Virginia

[and thirty-eight others]

Amendments to the Constitution

Amendment I. Religious and Political Freedom

For background of Bill of Rights, refer to pp. 201–202.

Congress must not interfere with freedom of religion, speech or press, assembly, and petition. Congress shall make no law respecting an establishment of religion,[1] or prohibiting the free exercise thereof; or abridging the freedom of speech, or of the press; or the right of the people peaceably to assemble, and to petition the government for a redress of grievances.

Amendment II. Right to Bear Arms

The people may bear arms. A well-regulated militia being necessary to the security of a free State, the right of the people to keep and bear arms [i.e., for military purposes] shall not be infringed.[2]

Amendment III. Quartering of Troops

Refer to Declaration of Independence and British quartering above.

Soldiers may not be arbitrarily quartered on the people. No soldier shall, in time of peace, be quartered in any house without the consent of the owner, nor in time of war, but in a manner to be prescribed by law.

Amendment IV. Searches and Seizures

A reflection of colonial grievances against the crown.

Unreasonable searches are forbidden. The right of the people to be secure in their persons, houses, papers, and effects, against unreasonable searches and seizures, shall not be violated, and no [search] warrants shall issue but upon probable cause, supported by oath or affirmation, and particularly describing the place to be searched, and the persons or things to be seized.

Amendment V. Right to Life, Liberty, and Property

When witnesses refuse to answer questions in court, they routinely "take the Fifth Amendment."

The individual is guaranteed certain rights when on trial and the right to life, liberty, and property. No person shall be held to answer for a capital, or otherwise infamous crime, unless on a presentment [formal charge] or indictment of a grand jury, except in cases arising in the naval forces, or in the militia, when in actual service in time of war or public danger; nor shall

---

[1]In 1787 "an establishment of religion" referred to an "established church," or one supported by all taxpayers, whether members or not. But the courts have often acted under this article to keep religion, including prayers, out of the public schools.

[2]The courts long held that the right to bear arms was a limited right linked to the maintenance of militias. But in the case of *District of Columbia v. Heller* in 2008, the Supreme Court defined the right to bear arms as an individual right, not contingent on "participation in some corporate body." Yet the Court still left the door open to some kinds of gun-control legislation.

any person be subject for the same offense to be twice put in jeopardy of life or limb; nor shall be compelled in any criminal case to be a witness against himself, nor be deprived of life, liberty, or property, without due process of law; nor shall private property be taken for public use [i.e., by eminent domain] without just compensation.

Amendment VI. Protection in Criminal Trials

Refer to Declaration of Independence above.

An accused person has important rights. In all criminal prosecutions, the accused shall enjoy the right to a speedy and public trial, by an impartial jury of the State and district wherein the crime shall have been committed, which district shall have been previously ascertained by law, and to be informed of the nature and cause of the accusation; to be confronted with the witnesses against him; to have compulsory process [subpoena] for obtaining witnesses in his favor, and to have the assistance of counsel for his defense.

Amendment VII. Suits at Common Law

The rules of common law are recognized. In suits at common law, where the value in controversy shall exceed twenty dollars, the right of trial by jury shall be preserved, and no fact tried by a jury shall be otherwise re-examined in any court of the United States, than according to the rules of the common law.

Amendment VIII. Bail and Punishments

Excessive fines and unusual punishments are forbidden. Excessive bail shall not be required, nor excessive fines imposed, nor cruel and unusual punishment inflicted.

Amendment IX. Concerning Rights Not Enumerated

The Ninth and Tenth Amendments were bulwarks of Southern states' rights before the Civil War.

The people retain rights not here enumerated. The enumeration in the Constitution, of certain rights, shall not be construed to deny or disparage others retained by the people.

Amendment X. Powers Reserved to the States and to the People

A concession to states' rights, p. 202.

Powers not delegated to the federal government are reserved to the states and the people. The powers not delegated to the United States by the Constitution, nor prohibited by it to the States, are reserved to the States respectively, or to the people.

Amendment XI. Suits Against a State

The federal courts have no authority in suits by citizens against a state. The judicial power of the United States shall not be construed to extend to any suit in law or equity, commenced or prosecuted against one of the United States by citizens of another State, or by citizens or subjects of any foreign state. [Adopted 1798.]

Amendment XII. Election of President and Vice President

Forestalls repetition of 1800 electoral dispute, pp. 228–230.

Refer to 1876 disputed election, pp. 527–530.

Refer to 1824 election, pp. 273–274.

1. Changes in manner of electing president and vice president; procedure when no presidential candidate receives electoral majority. The electors shall meet in their respective States, and vote by ballot for President and Vice President, one of whom, at least, shall not be an inhabitant of the same state with themselves; they shall name in their ballots the person voted for as President, and in distinct ballots the person voted for as Vice President, and they shall make distinct lists of all persons voted for as President, and of all persons voted for as Vice President, and of the number of votes for each, which lists they shall sign and certify, and transmit sealed to the seat of government of the United States, directed to the President of the Senate;—the President of the Senate shall, in the presence of the Senate and House of Representatives, open all the certificates and the votes shall be counted;—the person having the greatest number of votes for President shall be the President, if such number be a majority of the whole number of electors appointed; and if no person have such majority, then from the persons having the highest numbers not exceeding three on the list of those voted for as President, the House of Representatives shall choose immediately, by ballot, the President. But in choosing the President, the votes shall be taken by States, the representation from each State having one vote; a quorum for this purpose shall consist of a member or members from two-thirds of the States, and a majority of all the States shall be necessary to a choice. And if the House of Representatives shall not choose a President whenever the right of choice shall devolve upon them, before *the fourth day of March*[1] next following, then the Vice President shall act as President, as in the case of the death or other constitutional disability of the President.

2. Procedure when no vice presidential candidate receives electoral majority. The person having the greatest number of votes as Vice President, shall be the Vice President, if such number be a majority of the whole number of electors appointed; and if no person have a majority, then from the two highest numbers on the list the Senate shall choose the Vice President; a quorum for the purpose shall consist of two-thirds of the whole number of Senators, and a majority of the whole number shall be necessary to a choice. But no person constitutionally ineligible to the office of President shall be eligible to that of Vice President of the United States. [Adopted 1804.]

Amendment XIII. Slavery Prohibited

For background, refer to pp. 474–476.

Slavery forbidden. 1. Neither slavery[2] nor involuntary servitude, except as a punishment for crime whereof the party shall have been duly convicted, shall exist within the United States, or any place subject to their jurisdiction.

2. Congress shall have power to enforce this article by appropriate legislation. [Adopted 1865.]

Amendment XIV. Civil Rights for Ex-slaves,[3] etc.

For background, refer to pp. 503–506.

For corporations as "persons," refer to pp. 577–578.

1. Ex-slaves made citizens; U.S. citizenship primary. All persons born or naturalized in the United States, and subject to the jurisdiction thereof, are citizens of the United States and of the State wherein they reside. No State shall make or enforce any law which shall abridge the privileges or immunities of citizens of the United States; nor shall any State deprive any person of life, liberty, or property, without due process of law; nor deny to any person within its jurisdiction the equal protection of the laws.

Abolishes three-fifths rule for slaves, Art. I., Sec. II, para. 3.

2. When a state denies citizens the vote, its representation shall be reduced. Representatives shall be apportioned among the several States according to their respective numbers, counting the whole number of persons in each State, excluding Indians not taxed. But when the right to vote at any election for the choice of Electors for President and Vice President of the United States, Representatives in Congress, the executive and judicial officers of a State, or the members of the legislature thereof, is denied to any of the male inhabitants of such State, being twenty-one years of age and citizens of the United States, or in any way abridged, except for participation in rebellion, or other crime, the basis of representation therein shall be reduced in the proportion which the number of such make citizens shall bear to the whole number of male citizens twenty-one years of age in such State.[4]

---

[1]Changed to January 20 by the Twentieth Amendment (refer to text below).

[2]The only explicit mention of slavery in the Constitution.

[3]Occasionally an offender is prosecuted under the Thirteenth Amendment for keeping an employee or other person under conditions approximating slavery.

[4]The provisions concerning "male" inhabitants were modified by the Nineteenth Amendment, which enfranchised women. The legal voting age was changed from twenty-one to eighteen by the Twenty-sixth Amendment.

Leading ex-Confederates denied office. Refer to p. 503.

3. Certain persons who have been in rebellion are ineligible for federal and state office. No person shall be a Senator or Representative in Congress, or Elector of President and Vice President, or hold any office, civil or military, under the United States, or under any State, who, having previously taken an oath, as a member of Congress, or as an officer of the United States, or as a member of any State legislature, or as an executive or judicial officer of any State, to support the Constitution of the United States, shall have engaged in insurrection or rebellion against the same, or given aid or comfort to the enemies thereof. But Congress may, by a vote of two-thirds of each house, remove such disability.

The ex-Confederates were thus forced to repudiate their debts and pay pensions to their own veterans, plus taxes for the pensions of Union veterans, their conquerors.

4. Debts incurred in aid of rebellion are void. The validity of the public debt of the United States, authorizing by law, including debts incurred for payment of pensions and bounties for services in suppressing insurrection or rebellion, shall not be questioned. But neither the United States nor any State shall assume or pay any debt or obligation incurred in aid of insurrection or rebellion against the United States, or any claim for the loss or emancipation of any slave; but all such debts, obligations, and claims shall be held illegal and void.

5. Enforcement. The Congress shall have power to enforce, by appropriate legislation, the provisions of this article. [Adopted 1868.]

Amendment XV. Suffrage for Blacks

For background, refer to pp. 508–509.

Black males are made voters. 1. The right of the citizens of the United States to vote shall not be denied or abridged by the United States or by any State on account of race, color, or previous condition of servitude.

2. The Congress shall have power to enforce this article by appropriate legislation. [Adopted 1870.]

Amendment XVI. Income Taxes

For background, refer to p. 706.

Congress has power to lay and collect income taxes. The Congress shall have power to lay and collect taxes on incomes, from whatever source derived, without apportionment among the several States, and without regard to any census or enumeration. [Adopted 1913.]

Amendment XVII. Direct Election of Senators

Senators shall be elected by popular vote. 1. The Senate of the United States shall be composed of two Senators from each State, elected by the people thereof, for six years; and each Senator shall have one vote. The electors in each State shall have the qualifications requisite for electors of [voters for] the most numerous branch of the State legislatures.

2. When vacancies happen in the representation of any State in the Senate, the executive authority of such State shall issue writs of election to fill such vacancies: Provided, that the Legislature of any State may empower the executive thereof to make temporary appointments until the people fill the vacancies by election as the Legislature may direct.

3. This amendment shall not be so construed as to affect the election or term of any Senator chosen before it becomes valid as part of the Constitution. [Adopted 1913.]

Amendment XVIII. National Prohibition

For background, refer to pp. 753–754.

The sale or manufacture of intoxicating liquors is forbidden. 1. *After one year from the ratification of this article the manufacture, sale, or transportation of intoxicating liquors within, the importation thereof into, or the exportation thereof from the United States and all territory subject to the jurisdiction thereof, for beverage purposes, is hereby prohibited.*

2. *The Congress and the several States shall have concurrent power to enforce this article by appropriate legislation.*

3. *This article shall be inoperative unless it shall have been ratified as an amendment to the Constitution by the legislatures of the several States, as provided by the Constitution, within* *seven years from the date of the submission thereof to the States by the Congress.* [Adopted 1919; repealed 1933 by Twenty-first Amendment.]

Amendment XIX.

Woman Suffrage

For background, refer to pp. 724–725.

Women guaranteed the right to vote. 1. The right of citizens of the United States to vote shall not be denied or abridged by the United States or by any State on account of sex.

2. Congress shall have power to enforce this article by appropriate legislation. [Adopted 1920.]

Amendment XX.

Presidential and Congressional Terms

Shortens lame duck periods by modifying Art. I, Sec. IV, para. 2.

1. Presidential, vice presidential, and congressional terms of office begin in January. The terms of the President and Vice President shall end at noon on the 20th day of January, and the terms of Senators and Representatives at noon on the 3d day of January, of the years in which such terms would have ended if this article had not been ratified; and the terms of their successors shall then begin.

2. New meeting date for Congress. The Congress shall assemble at least once in every year, and such meeting shall begin at noon on the 3d day of January, unless they shall by law appoint a different day.

3. Emergency presidential and vice presidential succession. If, at the time fixed for the beginning of the term of the President, the President-elect shall have died, the Vice President-elect shall become President. If a President shall not have been chosen before the time fixed for the beginning of his term, or if the President-elect shall have failed to qualify, then the Vice President-elect shall act as President until a President shall have qualified; and the Congress may by law provide for the case wherein neither a President-elect nor a Vice President-elect shall have qualified, declaring who shall then act as President, or the manner in which one who is to act shall be selected, and such persons shall act accordingly until a President or Vice President shall have qualified.

4. The Congress may by law provide for the case of the death of any of the persons from whom the House of Representatives may choose a President whenever the right of choice shall have devolved upon them, and for the case of the death of any of the persons from whom the Senate may choose a Vice President whenever the right of choice shall have devolved upon them.

5. Sections 1 and 2 shall take effect on the 15th day of October following the ratification of this article.

6. This article shall be inoperative unless it shall have been ratified as an amendment to the Constitution by the Legislatures of three-fourths of the several States within seven years from the date of its submission. [Adopted 1933.]

Amendment XXI.

Prohibition Repealed

For background, refer to p. 794.

1. Eighteenth Amendment repealed. The eighteenth article of amendment to the Constitution of the United States is hereby repealed.

2. Local laws honored. The transportation or importation into any State, Territory, or Possession of the United States for delivery or use therein of intoxicating liquors, in violation of the laws thereof, is hereby prohibited.

3. This article shall be inoperative unless it shall have been ratified as an amendment to the Constitution by conventions in the several States, as provided in the Constitution, within seven years from the date of the submission thereof to the States by the Congress. [Adopted 1933.]

Amendment XXII.

Anti–Third Term Amendment

Sometimes referred to as the anti–Franklin Roosevelt amendment.

1. Presidential term is limited. No person shall be elected to the office of President more than twice, and no person who has held the office of President, or acted as President, for more than two years of a term to which some other person was elected President shall be elected to the office of President more than once. But this article shall not apply to any person holding the office of President when this article was proposed by the Congress [i.e., Truman], and shall not prevent any person who may be holding the office of President, during the term within which this article becomes operative [i.e., Truman] from holding the office of President or acting as President during the remainder of such term.

2. This article shall be inoperative unless it shall have been ratified as an amendment to the Constitution by the legislatures of three-fourths of the several States within seven years from the date of its submission to the States by the Congress. [Adopted 1951.]

Amendment XXIII. District of Columbia Vote

Designed to give the District of Columbia three electoral votes and to quiet the century-old cry of "No taxation without representation." Yet the District of Columbia still has only one nonvoting member of Congress.

1. Presidential electors for the District of Columbia. The District, constituting the seat of government of the United States, shall appoint in such manner as the Congress shall direct:

A number of electors of President and Vice President equal to the whole number of Senators and Representatives in Congress to which the District would be entitled if it were a State, but in no event more than the least populous State; they shall be in addition to those appointed by the States, but they shall be considered for the purposes of the election of President and Vice President, to be electors appointed by a State; and they shall meet in the District and perform such duties as provided by the twelfth article of amendment.

2. Enforcement. The Congress shall have the power to enforce this article by appropriate legislation. [Adopted 1961.]

Amendment XXIV. Poll Tax

Designed to end discrimination against poor people, including Black Southerners who were often denied the vote through inability to pay poll taxes. Refer to pp. 912, 915–916.

1. Payment of poll tax or other taxes not to be prerequisite for voting in federal elections. The right of citizens of the United States to vote in any primary or other election for President or Vice President, for electors for President or Vice President, or for Senator or Representative in Congress, shall not be denied or abridged by the United States or any State by reason of failure to pay any poll tax or other tax.

2. Enforcement. The Congress shall have the power to enforce this article by appropriate legislation. [Adopted 1964.]

Amendment XXV. Presidential Succession and Disability

1. Vice president to become president. In case of the removal of the President from office or of his death or resignation, the Vice President shall become President.[1]

Gerald Ford was the first "appointed president." Refer to p. 942.

2. Successor to vice president provided. Whenever there is a vacancy in the office of the Vice President, the President shall nominate a Vice President who shall take office upon confirmation by a majority vote of both Houses of Congress.

3. Vice president to serve for disabled president. Whenever the President transmits to the President pro tempore of the Senate and the Speaker of the House of Representatives his written declaration that he is unable to discharge the powers and duties of his office, and until he transmits to them a written declaration to the contrary, such powers and duties shall be discharged by the Vice President as Acting President.

4. Procedure for disqualifying or requalifying president. Whenever the Vice President and a majority of either the principal officers of the executive departments or of such other body as Congress may by law provide, transmit to the President pro tempore of the Senate and the Speaker of the House of Representatives their written declaration that the President is unable to discharge the powers and duties of his office, the Vice President shall immediately assume the powers and duties of the office as Acting President.

---

[1]The original Constitution (Art. II, Sec. I, para. 5) was vague on this point, stipulating that "the powers and duties" of the president, but not necessarily the title, should "devolve" on the vice president. President Tyler, the first "accidental president," assumed not only the powers and duties but the title as well.

Thereafter, when the President transmits to the President pro tempore of the Senate and the Speaker of the House of Representatives his written declaration that no inability exists, he shall resume the powers and duties of his office unless the Vice President and a majority of either the principal officers of the executive department[s] or of such other body as Congress may by law provide, transmit within four days to the President pro tempore of the Senate and the Speaker of the House of Representatives their written declaration that the President is unable to discharge the powers and duties of his office. Thereupon Congress shall decide the issue, assembling within forty-eight hours for that purpose if not in session. If the Congress, within twenty-one days after receipt of the latter written declaration, or, if Congress is not in session, within twenty-one days after Congress is required to assemble, determines by two-thirds vote of both Houses that the President is unable to discharge the powers and duties of his office, the Vice President shall continue to discharge the same as Acting President; otherwise, the President shall resume the powers and duties of his office. [Adopted 1967.]

Amendment XXVI. Lowering Voting Age

A response to the current revolt of youth. Refer to p. 930.

1. Ballot for eighteen-year-olds. The right of citizens of the United States, who are eighteen years of age or older, to vote shall not be denied or abridged by the United States or any state on account of age.

2. Enforcement. The Congress shall have the power to enforce this article by appropriate legislation. [Adopted 1971.]

Amendment XXVII. Restricting Congressional Pay Raises

Reflects anti-incumbent sentiment of early 1990s. First proposed by James Madison in 1789; took 203 years to be ratified.

Congress not allowed to increase its current pay. No law varying the compensation for the services of the Senators and Representatives shall take effect, until an election of Representatives shall have intervened. [Adopted 1992.]

Tables

Table A.1 Presidential Elections*

Election	Candidates	Parties	Popular Vote	Electoral Vote
1789	George Washington	No party designation		69
	John Adams			34
	Minor Candidates			35
1792	George Washington	No party designation		132
	John Adams			77
	George Clinton			50
	Minor Candidates			5
1796	John Adams	Federalist		71
	Thomas Jefferson	Democratic-Republican		68
	Thomas Pinckney	Federalist		59
	Aaron Burr	Democratic-Republican		30
	Minor Candidates			48
1800	Thomas Jefferson	Democratic-Republican		73
	Aaron Burr	Democratic-Republican		73
	John Adams	Federalist		65
	Charles C. Pinckney	Federalist		64
	John Jay	Federalist		1
1804	Thomas Jefferson	Democratic-Republican		162
	Charles C. Pinckney	Federalist		14
1808	James Madison	Democratic-Republican		122
	Charles C. Pinckney	Federalist		47
	George Clinton	Democratic-Republican		6
1812	James Madison	Democratic-Republican		128
	Dewitt Clinton	Federalist		89
1816	James Monroe	Democratic-Republican		183
	Rufus King	Federalist		34
1820	James Monroe	Democratic-Republican		231
	John Q. Adams	Independent Republican		1
1824	John Q. Adams (Min.)†	Democratic-Republican	108,740	84
	Andrew Jackson	Democratic-Republican	153,544	99
	William H. Crawford	Democratic-Republican	46,618	41
	Henry Clay	Democratic-Republican	47,136	37
1828	Andrew Jackson	Democratic	647,286	178
	John Q. Adams	National Republican	508,064	83
1832	Andrew Jackson	Democratic	687,502	219
	Henry Clay	National Republican	530,189	49
	William Wirt	Anti-Masonic	33,108	7
	John Floyd	National Republican		11
1836	Martin Van Buren	Democratic	765,483	170
	William H. Harrison	Whig		73
	Hugh L. White	Whig	739,795	26
	Daniel Webster	Whig		14
	W. P. Mangum	Whig		11

* Candidates receiving less than 1 percent of the popular vote are omitted. Before the Twelfth Amendment (1804), the Electoral College voted for two presidential candidates, and the runner-up became vice president. Basic figures are taken primarily from *Historical Statistics of the United States, Colonial Times to 1970* (1975), pp. 1073–1074, and *Statistical Abstract of the United States,* relevant years.

† "Min." indicates minority president—one receiving less than 50 percent of all popular votes.

Presidential Elections (continued)

Election	Candidates	Parties	Popular Vote	Electoral Vote
1840	William H. Harrison	Whig	1,274,624	234
	Martin Van Buren	Democratic	1,127,781	60
1844	James K. Polk (Min.)†	Democratic	1,338,464	170
	Henry Clay	Whig	1,300,097	105
	James G. Birney	Liberty	62,300	0
1848	Zachary Taylor	Whig	1,360,967	163
	Lewis Cass	Democratic	1,222,342	127
	Martin Van Buren	Free Soil	291,263	0
1852	Franklin Pierce	Democratic	1,601,117	254
	Winfield Scott	Whig	1,385,453	42
	John P. Hale	Free Soil	155,825	0
1856	James Buchanan (Min.)*	Democratic	1,832,955	174
	John C. Frémont	Republican	1,339,932	114
	Millard Fillmore	American	871,731	8
1860	Abraham Lincoln (Min.)*	Republican	1,865,593	180
	Stephen A. Douglas	Democratic	1,382,713	12
	John C. Breckinridge	Democratic	848,356	72
	John Bell	Constitutional Union	592,906	39
1864	Abraham Lincoln	Union	2,206,938	212
	George B. Mc Clellan	Democratic	1,803,787	21
1868	Ulysses S. Grant	Republican	3,013,421	214
	Horatio Seymour	Democratic	2,706,829	80
1872	Ulysses S. Grant	Republican	3,596,745	286
	Horace Greeley	Democratic Liberal Republican	2,843,446	66
1876	Rutherford B. Hayes (Min.)*	Republican	4,036,572	185
	Samuel J. Tilden	Democratic	4,284,020	184
1880	James A. Garfield (Min.)*	Republican	4,453,295	214
	Winfield S. Hancock	Democratic	4,414,082	155
	James B. Weaver	Greenback-Labor	308,578	0
1884	Grover Cleveland (Min.)*	Democratic	4,879,507	219
	James G. Blaine	Republican	4,850,293	182
	Benjamin F. Butler	Greenback-Labor	175,370	0
	John P. St. John	Prohibition	150,369	0
1888	Benjamin Harrison (Min.)*	Republican	5,447,129	233
	Grover Cleveland	Democratic	5,537,857	168
	Clinton B. Fisk	Prohibition	249,506	0
	Anson J. Streeter	Union Labor	146,935	0
1892	Grover Cleveland (Min.)*	Democratic	5,555,426	277
	Benjamin Harrison	Republican	5,182,690	145
	James B. Weaver	People's	1,029,846	22
	John Bidwell	Prohibition	264,133	0
1896	William Mc Kinley	Republican	7,102,246	271
	William J. Bryan	Democratic	6,492,559	176
1900	William Mc Kinley	Republican	7,218,491	292
	William J. Bryan	Democratic; Populist	6,356,734	155
	John C. Woolley	Prohibition	208,914	0
1904	Theodore Roosevelt	Republican	7,628,461	336
	Alton B. Parker	Democratic	5,084,223	140
	Eugene V. Debs	Socialist	402,283	0
	Silas C. Swallow	Prohibition	258,536	0
1908	William H. Taft	Republican	7,675,320	321
	William J. Bryan	Democratic	6,412,294	162
	Eugene V. Debs	Socialist	420,793	0
	Eugene W. Chafin	Prohibition	253,840	0

* "Min." indicates minority president—one receiving less than 50 percent of all popular votes.

Presidential Elections (continued)

Election	Candidates	Parties	Popular Vote	Electoral Vote
1912	Woodrow Wilson (Min.)*	Democratic	6,296,547	435
	Theodore Roosevelt	Progressive	4,118,571	88
	William H. Taft	Republican	3,486,720	8
	Eugene V. Debs	Socialist	900,672	0
	Eugene W. Chafin	Prohibition	206,275	0
1916	Woodrow Wilson (Min.)*	Democratic	9,127,695	277
	Charles E. Hughes	Republican	8,533,507	254
	A. L. Benson	Socialist	585,113	0
	J. F. Hanly	Prohibition	220,506	0
1920	Warren G. Harding	Republican	16,143,407	404
	James M. Cox	Democratic	9,130,328	127
	Eugene V. Debs	Socialist	919,799	0
	P. P. Christensen	Farmer-Labor	265,411	0
1924	Calvin Coolidge	Republican	15,718,211	382
	John W. Davis	Democratic	8,385,283	136
	Robert M. La Follette	Progressive	4,831,289	13
1928	Herbert C. Hoover	Republican	21,391,993	444
	Alfred E. Smith	Democratic	15,016,169	87
1932	Franklin D. Roosevelt	Democratic	22,809,638	472
	Herbert C. Hoover	Republican	15,758,901	59
	Norman Thomas	Socialist	881,951	0
1936	Franklin D. Roosevelt	Democratic	27,752,869	523
	Alfred M. Landon	Republican	16,674,665	8
	William Lemke	Union	882,479	0
1940	Franklin D. Roosevelt	Democratic	27,307,819	449
	Wendell L. Willkie	Republican	22,321,018	82
1944	Franklin D. Roosevelt	Democratic	25,606,585	432
	Thomas E. Dewey	Republican	22,014,745	99
1948	Harry S. Truman (Min.)*	Democratic	24,179,345	303
	Thomas E. Dewey	Republican	21,991,291	189
	J. Strom Thurmond	States' Rights Democratic	1,176,125	39
	Henry A. Wallace	Progressive	1,157,326	0
1952	Dwight D. Eisenhower	Republican	33,936,234	442
	Adlai E. Stevenson	Democratic	27,314,992	89
1956	Dwight D. Eisenhower	Republican	35,590,472	457
	Adlai E. Stevenson	Democratic	26,022,752	73
1960	John F. Kennedy (Min.)*†	Democratic	34,226,731	303
	Richard M. Nixon	Republican	34,108,157	219
1964	Lyndon B. Johnson	Democratic	43,129,566	486
	Barry M. Goldwater	Republican	27,178,188	52
1968	Richard M. Nixon (Min.)*	Republican	31,785,480	301
	Hubert H. Humphrey, Jr.	Democratic	31,275,166	191
	George C. Wallace	American Independent	9,906,473	46
1972	Richard M. Nixon	Republican	47,169,911	520
	George S. Mc Govern	Democratic	29,170,383	17
1976	Jimmy Carter	Democratic	40,828,657	297
	Gerald R. Ford	Republican	39,145,520	240
1980	Ronald W. Reagan	Republican	43,899,248	489
	Jimmy Carter	Democratic	35,481,435	49
	John B. Anderson	Independent	5,719,437	0

* "Min." indicates minority president—one receiving less than 50 percent of all popular votes.

† Six Democratic electors in Alabama, all eight unpledged Democratic electors in Mississippi, and one Republican elector in Oklahoma voted for Senator Harry F. Byrd.

Presidential Elections (continued)

Election	Candidates	Parties	Popular Vote	Electoral Vote
1984	Ronald W. Reagan	Republican	52,609,797	525
	Walter Mondale	Democratic	36,450,613	13
1988	George Bush	Republican	47,946,422	426
	Michael Dukakis	Democratic	41,016,429	111
1992	William Clinton (Min.)*	Democratic	44,909,889	370
	George Bush	Republican	39,104,545	168
	H. Ross Perot	Independent	19,742,267	0
1996	William Clinton (Min.)*	Democratic	47,401,898	379
	Robert Dole	Republican	39,198,482	159
	H. Ross Perot	Reform	7,874,283	0
2000	George W. Bush (Min.)*	Republican	50,456,002	271
	Albert Gore, Jr.	Democratic	50,999,897	266
	Ralph Nader	Green	2,783,728	0
2004	George W. Bush	Republican	60,693,281	286
	John Kerry	Democratic	57,355,978	252
	Ralph Nader	Green	405,623	0
2008	Barack Obama	Democratic	65,980,131	364
	John Mc Cain	Republican	57,779,170	174
2012	Barack Obama	Democratic	69,915,796	332
	Mitt Romney	Republican	60,933,500	206
2016	Donald Trump (Min.)*	Republican	62,985,106	306
	Hillary Clinton	Democratic	65,853,625	232
2020	Joseph R. Biden	Democratic	81,283,501	306
	Donald Trump	Republican	74,223,975	232

* "Min." indicates minority president—one receiving less than 50 percent of all popular votes.

Table A.2 Presidents and Vice Presidents

Term	President	Vice President
1789–1793	George Washington	John Adams
1793–1797	George Washington	John Adams
1797–1801	John Adams	Thomas Jefferson
1801–1805	Thomas Jefferson	Aaron Burr
1805–1809	Thomas Jefferson	George Clinton
1809–1813	James Madison	George Clinton (d. 1812)
1813–1817	James Madison	Elbridge Gerry (d. 1814)
1817–1821	James Monroe	Daniel D. Tompkins
1821–1825	James Monroe	Daniel D. Tompkins
1825–1829	John Quincy Adams	John C. Calhoun
1829–1833	Andrew Jackson	John C. Calhoun (resigned 1832)
1833–1837	Andrew Jackson	Martin Van Buren
1837–1841	Martin Van Buren	Richard M. Johnson
1841–1845	William H. Harrison (d. 1841) John Tyler	John Tyler
1845–1849	James K. Polk	George M. Dallas
1849–1853	Zachary Taylor (d. 1850) Millard Fillmore	Millard Fillmore
1853–1857	Franklin Pierce	William R. D. King (d. 1853)
1857–1861	James Buchanan	John C. Breckinridge
1861–1865	Abraham Lincoln	Hannibal Hamlin
1865–1869	Abraham Lincoln (d. 1865) Andrew Johnson	Andrew Johnson
1869–1873	Ulysses S. Grant	Schuyler Colfax

Table A.2 **Presidents and Vice Presidents (continued)**

Term	President	Vice President
1873–1877	Ulysses S. Grant	Henry Wilson (d. 1875)
1877–1881	Rutherford B. Hayes	William A. Wheeler
1881–1885	James A. Garfield (d. 1881) Chester A. Arthur	Chester A. Arthur
1885–1889	Grover Cleveland	Thomas A. Hendricks (d. 1885)
1889–1893	Benjamin Harrison	Levi P. Morton
1893–1897	Grover Cleveland	Adlai E. Stevenson
1897–1901	William McKinley	Garret A. Hobart (d. 1899)
1901–1905	William McKinley (d. 1901) Theodore Roosevelt	Theodore Roosevelt
1905–1909	Theodore Roosevelt	Charles W. Fairbanks
1909–1913	William H. Taft	James S. Sherman (d. 1912)
1913–1917	Woodrow Wilson	Thomas R. Marshall
1917–1921	Woodrow Wilson	Thomas R. Marshall
1921–1925	Warren G. Harding (d. 1923) Calvin Coolidge	Calvin Coolidge
1925–1929	Calvin Coolidge	Charles G. Dawes
1929–1933	Herbert Hoover	Charles Curtis
1933–1937	Franklin D. Roosevelt	John N. Garner
1937–1941	Franklin D. Roosevelt	John N. Garner
1941–1945	Franklin D. Roosevelt	Henry A. Wallace
1945–1949	Franklin D. Roosevelt (d. 1945) Harry S. Truman	Harry S. Truman
1949–1953	Harry S. Truman	Alben W. Barkley
1953–1957	Dwight D. Eisenhower	Richard M. Nixon
1957–1961	Dwight D. Eisenhower	Richard M. Nixon
1961–1965	John F. Kennedy (d. 1963) Lyndon B. Johnson	Lyndon B. Johnson
1965–1969	Lyndon B. Johnson	Hubert H. Humphrey, Jr.
1969–1974	Richard M. Nixon	Spiro T. Agnew (resigned 1973); Gerald R. Ford
1974–1977	Gerald R. Ford	Nelson A. Rockefeller
1977–1981	Jimmy Carter	Walter F. Mondale
1981–1985	Ronald Reagan	George Bush
1985–1989	Ronald Reagan	George Bush
1989–1993	George Bush	J. Danforth Quayle III
1993–1997	William Clinton	Albert Gore, Jr.
1997–2001	William Clinton	Albert Gore, Jr.
2001–2005	George W. Bush	Richard Cheney
2005–2009	George W. Bush	Richard Cheney
2009–2017	Barack Obama	Joseph Biden
2017–2021	Donald Trump	Michael Pence
2021–	Joseph R. Biden	Kamala Harris

Table A.3 Admission of States (Refer to Table 8.4 on p. 192 for order in which the original thirteen states entered the Union.)

Order of Admission	State	Date of Admission	Order of Admission	State	Date of Admission
14	Vermont	Mar. 4, 1791	33	Oregon	Feb. 14, 1859
15	Kentucky	June 1, 1792	34	Kansas	Jan. 29, 1861
16	Tennessee	June 1, 1796	35	W. Virginia	June 20, 1863
17	Ohio	Mar. 1, 1803	36	Nevada	Oct. 31, 1864
18	Louisiana	April 30, 1812	37	Nebraska	Mar. 1, 1867
19	Indiana	Dec. 11, 1816	38	Colorado	Aug. 1, 1876
20	Mississippi	Dec. 10, 1817	39	N. Dakota	Nov. 2, 1889
21	Illinois	Dec. 3, 1818	40	S. Dakota	Nov. 2, 1889
22	Alabama	Dec. 14, 1819	41	Montana	Nov. 8, 1889
23	Maine	Mar. 15, 1820	42	Washington	Nov. 11, 1889
24	Missouri	Aug. 10, 1821	43	Idaho	July 3, 1890
25	Arkansas	June 15, 1836	44	Wyoming	July 10, 1890
26	Michigan	Jan. 26, 1837	45	Utah	Jan. 4, 1896
27	Florida	Mar. 3, 1845	46	Oklahoma	Nov. 16, 1907
28	Texas	Dec. 29, 1845	47	New Mexico	Jan. 6, 1912
29	Iowa	Dec. 28, 1846	48	Arizona	Feb. 14, 1912
30	Wisconsin	May 29, 1848	49	Alaska	Jan. 3, 1959
31	California	Sept. 9, 1850	50	Hawaii	Aug. 21, 1959
32	Minnesota	May 11, 1858			

Table A.4 Estimates of Total Costs and Number of Battle Deaths of Major U.S. Wars[1]

War	Total Costs[2] (millions of dollars)	Original Costs (millions of dollars)	Number of Battle Deaths
Iraq War (2003–2011)	N/A	$806,000[3]	3,528[4]
Afghan War (2001–2021)	N/A	$2,313,000[5]	2,324[6]
Vietnam Conflict	$352,000	140,600	47,355[7]
Korean Conflict	164,000	54,000	33,629
World War II	664,000	288,000	291,557
World War I	112,000	26,000	53,402
Spanish-American War	6,460	400	385
Civil War: Union only	12,952	3,200	140,414
Civil War: Confederacy (est.)	N/A	1,000	94,000
Mexican War	147	73	1,733
War of 1812	158	93	2,260
American Revolution	190	100	6,824

[1]Deaths from disease and other causes are not shown. In earlier wars especially, owing to poor medical and sanitary practices, nonbattle deaths substantially exceeded combat casualties.

[2]The difference between total costs and original costs is attributable to continuing postwar payments for items such as veterans' benefits, interest on war debts, and so on.

[3]Through 2011

[4]Through May 9, 2014 for Killed in Action; excludes "non-hostile" deaths for Operation Iraqi Freedom and Operation New Dawn

[5]Through 2021

[6]Through August 2021 for Killed in Action; excludes "non-hostile" deaths for Operation Enduring Freedom

[7]1957–1990

(Sources: *Historical Statistics of the United States, Statistical Abstract of the United States,* relevant years; *The World Almanac and Book of Facts, 1986; Congressional Research Service,* Department of Defense, and Congressional Research Service Reports; Watson Institute, International and Public Affairs, Brown University.)

Glossary of Key Terms

9/11 (2001): Common shorthand for the terrorist attacks that occurred on September 11, 2001, in which nineteen militant Islamist men hijacked and crashed four commercial aircraft. Two planes hit the twin towers of the World Trade Center in New York City, causing them to collapse. One plane crashed into the Pentagon in Washington, DC, and the fourth, overtaken by passengers, crashed into a field in rural Pennsylvania. Nearly three thousand people were killed in the worst case of domestic terrorism in American history. (1012)

"10 percent" Reconstruction plan (1863): Introduced by President Lincoln, it proposed that a state be readmitted to the Union once 10 percent of its voters had pledged loyalty to the United States and promised to honor emancipation. (500)

100th meridian: A geographical, north-south line that bisects the United States from the Dakotas through West Texas, marking off the more humid, or well-watered eastern part of the North American continent from the arid landscapes of the West. Traditionally, the meridian was where Americans imagined that the "West" began. (556)

Abraham Lincoln Brigade: Idealistic American volunteers who served in the Spanish Civil War, defending Spanish republican forces from the fascist General Francisco Franco's nationalist coup. Some three thousand Americans served alongside volunteers from other countries. (812)

Abu Ghraib prison: A detention facility near Baghdad, Iraq. Under Saddam Hussein, the prison was the site of infamous torturing and execution of political dissidents. In 2004, during the U.S. occupation of Iraq, the prison became the focal point of a prisoner-abuse and torture scandal after photographs surfaced of American soldiers mistreating, torturing, and degrading Iraqi war prisoners and suspected terrorists. The scandal was one of several dark spots on the public image of the Iraq War and led to increased criticism of Secretary of Defense Donald Rumsfeld. (1015)

Adamson Act (1916): This law established an eight-hour day for all employees on trains involved in interstate commerce, with extra pay for overtime. The first federal law regulating the hours of workers in private companies, it was upheld by the Supreme Court in *Wilson v. New* (1917). (708)

***Adkins v. Children's Hospital* (1923):** A landmark Supreme Court decision reversing the ruling in *Muller v. Oregon*, which had declared women to be deserving of special protection in the workplace. (760)

affirmative action: Program designed to redress historic racial and gender imbalances in jobs and education. The term grew from an executive order issued by Lyndon B. Johnson in 1965 mandating that projects paid for with federal funds take concerted action against discrimination based on race in their hiring practices. In the late 1960s, President Nixon's Philadelphia Plan changed the meaning of affirmative action to require attention to certain groups, rather than protect individuals against discrimination. (908)

Agricultural Adjustment Administration (AAA) (1933): A New Deal program designed to raise agricultural prices by paying farmers not to farm. It was based on the assumption that higher prices would increase farmers' purchasing power and thereby help alleviate the Great Depression. (794)

Agricultural Marketing Act (1929): This act established the Federal Farm Board, a lending bureau for hard-pressed farmers. The act also aimed to help farmers help themselves through new producers' cooperatives. As the depression worsened in 1930, the Board tried to bolster falling prices by buying up surpluses, but it was unable to cope with the flood of farm produce to market. (769)

Al Qaeda: Arabic for "The Base," an international alliance of anti-Western Islamic Fundamentalist terrorist organizations founded in the late 1980s by veterans of the Afghan struggle against the Soviet Union. The group was headed by Osama bin Laden and has taken responsibility for numerous terrorist attacks, especially after the late 1990s. Al Qaeda organized the attacks of September 11, 2001, in the United States from its headquarters in Taliban-controlled Afghanistan. After the U.S.-led invasion of Afghanistan in 2001 and the launch of the "global war on terror," the group was weakened but still poses significant threats to U.S. persons and interests around the world. (1007)

Allies: Great Britain, Russia, and France, later joined by Italy, Japan, and the United States, formed this alliance against the Central Powers in World War I. (712)

All-Volunteer Force (AVF): Disenchantment with the Vietnam War led Congress to end conscription in 1973, causing the U.S. military to rely solely on volunteers. The resultant shift away from a "citizen's army," which had been in place since World War II, to an army of full-time professionals resulted in a leaner force that could be deployed in overseas conflicts with less political cost. (936)

"alt-right": Long-ostracized hate groups that emerged from the political shadows in the Trump era, gaining new adherents through precisely targeted messages on social media platforms that recruited disaffected young white men to their cause. (1050)

America First Committee: An isolationist advocacy group formed in September 1940 that opposed American intervention in the Second World War. Though it boasted 800,000 members at its peak, support for the committee dissipated following the attack on Pearl Harbor. (817)

American Expeditionary Forces (AEF): The name given to the U.S. Army force deployed to Europe in World War I commanded by General John J. Pershing and composed mostly of conscripts. Because the United States entered the war so late, by the time the AEF was raised, trained, and deployed, the war was in its last year (1918). Units of the AEF fought at Cantigny in May and at Chateau Thierry and Belleau Wood in June; its major engagements were at Saint Mihiel (September 12–15) and the Meuse-Argonne (September 26–November 11). (727)

American Federation of Labor: A national federation of trade unions that included only skilled workers, founded in 1886. Led by Samuel Gompers for nearly four decades, the AFL sought to negotiate with employers for a better kind of capitalism that rewarded workers fairly with better wages, hours, and conditions. The AFL's membership was almost entirely white and male until the middle of the twentieth century. (586)

American plan: A business-oriented approach to worker relations popular among firms in the 1920s to defeat unionization. Managers sought to strengthen their communication with workers and to offer benefits like pensions and insurance. They insisted on an "open shop" in contrast to the mandatory union membership through the "closed shop" that many labor activists had demanded in the strike wave after World War I. (750)

American Recovery and Reinvestment Act (2009): Among the earliest initiatives of the Obama administration to combat the Great Recession. It was based on the economic theories of John Maynard Keynes that called for increased government spending to offset decreased private spending in times of economic downturn. The act was controversial from the outset, passing with no Republican votes in the House and only three in the Senate, and helping to foster the "Tea Party" movement to curb government deficits, even while critics on the left argued that the act's $787 billion appropriation was not enough to turn the economy around. (1028)

Americans with Disabilities Act (ADA) (1990): Landmark law signed by President George H. W. Bush that prohibited discrimination against people with physical or mental handicaps. It represented a legislative triumph for champions of equal protections to all. (984)

Anti-Imperialist League (1898–1921): A diverse group formed to protest American colonial oversight in the Philippines. It included university presidents, industrialists, clergymen, and labor leaders. Strongest in the Northeast, the Anti-Imperialist League was the largest lobbying organization on a U.S. foreign-policy issue until the end of the nineteenth century. It declined in strength after the United States signed the Treaty of Paris (which approved the annexation of the Philippines), and especially after hostilities broke out between Filipino nationalists and American forces. (660)

***Apollo 11* mission (1969):** The space flight that successfully landed on the moon on July 20, 1969, part of the Apollo program of manned space flights run by America's National Aeronautics and Space Administration (NASA) between 1961 and 1975. (928)

Appeasement (1938): The policy followed by leaders of Britain and France at the 1938 conference in Munich. Their purpose was to avoid war, but they allowed Germany to take the Sudetenland from Czechoslovakia. (813)

Army-McCarthy hearings (1954): Congressional hearings called by Senator Joseph McCarthy to accuse members of the army of communist ties. In this widely televised spectacle, McCarthy finally went too far for public approval. The hearings exposed the senator's extremism and led to his eventual disgrace. (860)

Atlantic Charter (1941): Meeting on a warship off the coast of Newfoundland in August 1941, Franklin Roosevelt and British prime minister Winston Churchill signed this covenant outlining the future path toward disarmament, peace, and a permanent system of general security. Its spirit would animate the founding of the United Nations and raise awareness of the human rights of individuals after World War II. (819)

Australian ballot: A system that allows voters privacy in marking their ballot choices. Developed in Australia in the 1869s, it was introduced to the United States during the progressive era to help counteract boss rule. (684)

baby boom (1946–1964): Demographic explosion from births to returning soldiers and others who had put off starting families during the war. This large generation of new Americans forced the expansion of many institutions such as schools and universities. (869)

Bay of Pigs invasion (1961): CIA plot in 1961 to overthrow Fidel Castro by training Cuban exiles to invade and supporting them with American airpower. The mission failed and became a public relations disaster early in John F. Kennedy's presidency. (897)

Beat Generation: A small coterie of mid-twentieth-century bohemian writers and personalities, including Jack Kerouac, Allen Ginsberg, and William S. Burroughs, who bemoaned bourgeois conformity and advocated free-form experimentation in life and literature. (893)

Berlin airlift (1948–1949): Year-long mission of flying food and supplies to blockaded West Berliners, whom the Soviet Union cut off from access to the West in the first major crisis of the Cold War. (851)

Berlin Wall: Fortified and guarded barrier between East and West Berlin erected on orders from Soviet premier Nikita Khrushchev in 1961 to stop the flow of people to the West. Until its destruction in 1989, the wall was a vivid symbol of the divide between the communist and capitalist worlds. (897)

Bessemer-Kelly Process: Refers to the innovation in steel production where air was blown on molten iron to remove impurities, allowing steel to be produced cheaply at mass quantities. It was developed in the 1850s by British inventor Henry Bessemer, and by Kentucky kettle manufacturer William Kelly a few years earlier. A portent of Gilded Age industrialization, Andrew Carnegie used it at his steelmaking factory in Homestead, Pennsylvania. (571)

Bible Belt: The region of the American South, extending roughly from North Carolina west to Oklahoma and Texas, where Protestant Fundamentalism and belief in literal interpretation of the Bible were traditionally strongest. (756)

Big Sister policy (1880s): A foreign policy of Secretary of State James G. Blaine aimed at rallying Latin American nations behind American leadership and opening Latin American markets to Yankee traders. The policy bore fruit in 1889, when Blaine presided over the First International Conference of American States. (650)

Big Tech: Popular term for the large and influential technology companies whose products and platforms dominated the internet economy in the 2010s and 2020s, including Alphabet (Google), Amazon, Apple, Meta (Facebook), and Microsoft. (1037)

Black Codes (1865–1866): Laws passed throughout the South to restrict the rights of emancipated Black people, particularly with respect to negotiating labor contracts. Increased Northerners' criticisms of President Andrew Johnson's lenient Reconstruction policies. (501)

Black Lives Matter: A protest movement emerging in the aftermath of the police killing of Michael Brown, a Black man, in Ferguson, Missouri. Mobilizing largely over social media, the movement catalyzed mass protests across the nation and world in summer 2020 after the murder of another Black man, George Floyd, at the hands of Minneapolis police. (1043)

Black Monday: October 19, 1987. Date of the largest single-day decline in the Dow Jones Industrial Average until September 2001. The downturn indicated instability in the booming business culture of the 1980s but did not lead to a serious economic recession. (978)

Black Panther Party: Organization of armed Black militants formed in Oakland, California, in 1966 to protect Black rights. The Panthers represented a growing dissatisfaction with the nonviolent wing of the civil rights movement and signaled a new direction to that movement after the legislative victories of 1964 and 1965. (918)

Black Power: Doctrine of Black separatism, anti-capitalism, and self-defense that rose in prominence after 1965. Black Power activists rejected Martin Luther King's pacifism and desire for integration. Rather, they promoted pride in African heritage and an often-militant position in defense of their rights. (918)

Black Tuesday (1929): The dark, panicky day of October 29, 1929, when over 16,410,000 shares of stock were sold on Wall Street. It was a trigger that helped bring on the Great Depression. (770)

boll weevils: Term for conservative Southern Democrats who voted increasingly for Republican issues during the Carter and Reagan administrations. (967)

Bolshevik Revolution (1917): The second stage of the Russian Revolution in November 1917 when Vladimir Lenin and his Bolshevik party seized power and established a communist state. The first stage had occurred the previous February when more moderate revolutionaries overthrew the Russian czar. (750)

Bonus Expeditionary Force (BEF) (1932): Informally known as the Bonus Army, this rag-tag group of twenty thousand veterans marched on Washington to demand immediate payment of bonuses earned during World War I. General Douglas MacArthur dispersed the veterans with tear gas and bayonets. (775)

borderland: Place where two or more nations or societies border each other, and where power is dispersed among competing actors, resulting in fluid social relations, hybrid cultures, and the absence of firmly agreed sovereignty. During the colonial era in North America, borderlands were often places where European empires and Native American societies engaged with each other, including the Great Lakes and the Missouri Valley regions. Other examples include the vast territory from Texas to California where Hispanic and Anglophone cultures have intermingled for centuries. (565)

Boxer Rebellion (1900): An uprising in China directed against foreign influence. It was suppressed by an international force of some eighteen thousand soldiers, including several thousand Americans. The Boxer Rebellion paved the way for the revolution of 1911, which led to the establishment of the Republic of China in 1912. (665)

***Bracero* program (1942):** Program established by agreement with the Mexican government to recruit temporary Mexican agricultural workers to the United States to make up for wartime labor shortages in the Far West. The program persisted until 1964, by which time it had sponsored 4.5 million border crossings. (826)

Brain Trust: Specialists in law, economics, and welfare, many of them young university professors, who advised President Franklin D. Roosevelt and helped develop the policies of the New Deal. (782)

Bretton Woods Conference (1944): Meeting of Western allies to establish a postwar international economic order to avoid crises like the one that spawned World War II. Led to the creation of the International Monetary Fund (IMF) and the World Bank, designed to regulate currency levels and provide aid to underdeveloped countries. (849)

***Brown v. Board of Education of Topeka, Kansas* (1954):** Landmark Supreme Court decision that overturned *Plessy v. Ferguson* (1896) and abolished racial segregation in public schools. The Court reasoned that "separate" was inherently "unequal," rejecting the foundation of the Jim Crow system of racial segregation in the South. This decision was the first major step toward the legal end of racial discrimination and a major accomplishment for the civil rights movement. (884)

Brownsville Affair: Following the shooting of two white men on August 13, 1906, residents of Brownsville, Texas, blamed the African American soldiers from the segregated 25th Infantry Regiment stationed at nearby Fort Brown. Despite only tenuous evidence linking them to the crime, President Theodore Roosevelt ordered the dishonorable discharge of more than 150 of the "buffalo soldiers," stripping them of their pensions and barring them from employment in federal civil service jobs. Roosevelt's actions disillusioned many African Americans, who began to wonder if his progressivism stopped at the color line. In 1972 Congress belatedly exonerated the men, all but one of whom were deceased. (697)

Bulge, Battle of the: So named because of the bulge in Allied lines caused by the last desperate German offensive on the western front in WWII. A force of some 400,000 German soldiers, 1,000 aircraft, and several hundred tanks launched a surprise attack through the snow-clad Ardennes forest on December 16, 1944, aiming to divide and encircle the Allied forces and cut off access to the Belgian resupply port of Antwerp. The Germans were eventually stopped in late January 1945 at a cost of more than 8,000 U.S. soldiers killed in action. It was the single costliest American battle of WWII. (833)

Bureau of the Budget: An agency created in 1921 to oversee the federal budget and keep federal government spending within specified guidelines, imposing a process for fiscal discipline. Superseded by the Office of Management and Budget (OMB) in 1970. (759)

***Bush v. Gore* (2000):** The U.S. Supreme Court decision that effectively decided the presidential contest between Texas Governor George W. Bush (R) and Vice President Al Gore (D). After the Florida election tally was delayed by a five-week political standoff and recount of the votes, the Court ruled five-to-four that since neither Florida's legislature nor its courts had established a uniform standard for evaluating disputed ballots, the hand counts being done amounted to an unconstitutional breach of the Fourteenth Amendment's equal protection clause. Bush officially won Florida's electoral votes and thus the presidency. (1010)

Camp David: Presidential retreat in Maryland, constructed by the New Deal's WPA, and dubbed "Shangri-La" by Franklin Roosevelt, re-named "Camp David" by President Eisenhower in honor of his father and grandson. It was the site where President Jimmy Carter brokered a series of agreements between Israel and Egypt in 1978, by which Israel agreed to return some of the territory obtained during the 1967 war, Egypt agreed to honor Israel's borders, and both hostile powers pledged to sign a peace treaty within three months. The Camp David Accords were seen as a diplomatic triumph in President Carter's otherwise underwhelming term. (954)

CARES Act (2020): To stem the economic fallout from COVID-19 shutdowns, Congress passed this colossal $2.2 trillion economic stimulus bill in late March 2020 with strong bipartisan support. (1055)

carpetbaggers: Pejorative used by Southern white people to describe Northern businessmen and politicians who came to the South after the Civil War to work on Reconstruction projects or invest in Southern infrastructure. (511)

Central Powers: Germany and Austria-Hungary, later joined by Turkey and Bulgaria, made up this alliance against the Allies in World War I. (712)

Château-Thierry, Battle of (1918): The first significant engagement of American troops in World War I—and, indeed, in any European war. To weary French soldiers, the American doughboys were an image of fresh and gleaming youth. (729)

Checkers Speech (1952): Nationally televised address by vice-presidential candidate Richard Nixon during which he defended himself against allegations of corruption. Using the new mass medium of television shortly before the 1952 election, the vice-presidential candidate saved his place on the ticket by saying the only campaign gift he had received was a cocker spaniel named Checkers. (881)

Chinese Exclusion Act (1882): Federal legislation that prohibited most further Chinese immigration to the United States. This was the first major legal restriction on immigration in U.S. history. (533)

Circular migration: Term used to describe a common pattern of foreign migration in which immigrants arrive in a new country, work for some months or years, and then return home with their earnings. For example, half of immigrants who came to the United States from China before the 1880s returned home, while one in three European immigrants arriving between 1850 and 1913 eventually returned permanently to their country of origin. (533)

***Citizens United v. Federal Election Commission* (2010):** In a five-to-four ruling, the Supreme Court held that the First Amendment prohibited limits on political expenditures made by corporations, unions, and advocacy groups. The decision reversed century-old campaign finance laws and led to the proliferation of super-PACS (Political Action Committees) that could pour unlimited sums into the political arena. (1037)

City Beautiful movement: A turn-of-the-century movement among progressive architects and city planners, who aimed to promote order, harmony, and virtue while beautifying the nation's new urban spaces with grand boulevards, welcoming parks, and monumental public buildings. (619)

Civil Rights Act of 1875: The last piece of federal civil rights legislation until the 1950s, the law promised Black people equal access to public accommodations and banned racism in jury selection, but it provided no means of enforcement and was therefore ineffective. In 1883, the Supreme Court declared most of the act unconstitutional. (530)

Civil Rights Act of 1964: Federal law that banned racial discrimination in public facilities and strengthened the federal government's power to fight segregation in schools. Title VII of the act prohibited employers from discriminating based on race in their hiring practices and empowered the Equal Employment Opportunity Commission (EEOC) to regulate fair employment. (908)

Civil Rights Bill (1866): Passed over Andrew Johnson's veto, the bill aimed to counteract the Black Codes by conferring citizenship on African Americans and making it a crime to deprive Black people of their rights to sue, testify in court, or hold property. (503)

Civilian Conservation Corps (CCC) (1933): A government program created by Congress to hire young unemployed men to improve the rural, out-of-doors environment with such work as planting trees, fighting fires, draining swamps, and maintaining national parks. The CCC proved to be an important foundation for the post–World War II environmental movement. (787)

Clayton Anti-Trust Act (1915): Law extending the antitrust protections of the Sherman Anti-Trust Act and exempting labor unions and agricultural organizations from antimonopoly constraints. The act conferred long-overdue benefits on labor. (707)

closed shop: A union-organizing term that refers to the practice of allowing only unionized employees to work for a particular company. The AFL became known for negotiating closed-shop agreements with employers, in which the employer would agree not to hire nonunion members. (587)

code talkers: Native American men who served in the military by transmitting radio messages in their native languages, which were undecipherable by German and Japanese spies. (828)

Cold War (1946–1991): The forty-five-year-long diplomatic tension between the United States and the Soviet Union that divided much of the world into polarized camps, capitalist against communist. Most of the international conflicts during that period, particularly in the developing world, can be traced to the competition between the United States and the Soviet Union. (849)

Colfax Massacre: On Easter Sunday, April 13, 1873, a posse of white Democrats overpowered local militia and attacked the Grant Parish courthouse in Colfax, Louisiana, killing about 150 freedmen. The perpetrators, however, were later exonerated in an 1875 Supreme Court decision, *United States v. Cruikshank*, which established a narrow reading of the Fourteenth Amendment. By allowing such crimes to go unpunished, Colfax marked the nadir of Reconstruction and quashed civil protections for Southern Black people. (512)

Committee on Public Information (1917): A government office during World War I known popularly as the Creel Committee for its chairman George Creel, it was dedicated to winning everyday Americans' support for the war effort. It regularly distributed prowar propaganda and sent out an army of "four-minute men" to rally crowds and deliver "patriotic pep." (720)

Compromise of 1877: The agreement that finally resolved the 1876 election and officially ended Reconstruction. In exchange for the Republican candidate, Rutherford B. Hayes, winning the presidency, Hayes agreed to withdraw the last of the federal troops from the former Confederate states. This deal effectively completed the Southern return to white-only, Democratic-dominated electoral politics. (529)

confirmation bias: Term coined by psychologists to describe an innate tendency for people to seek out and uncritically accept information that reaffirms their existing beliefs, closing off alternate points of view. Often invoked to explain herd-like online behavior and splintering of the twenty-first-century political landscape. (1042)

Congress of Industrial Organizations (CIO): A New Deal–era labor organization that broke away from the American Federation of Labor (AFL) in order to organize unskilled industrial workers regardless of their particular economic sector or craft. The CIO gave a great boost to labor organizing in the midst of the Great Depression and during World War II. In 1955, the CIO merged with the AFL. (801)

Congress of Racial Equality (CORE) (1942): Nonviolent civil rights organization founded in 1942 and committed to the "Double V"—victory over fascism abroad and racism at home. After World War II, CORE would become a major force in the civil rights movement. (828)

containment doctrine: America's strategy against the Soviet Union based on ideas of George Kennan. The doctrine declared that the Soviet Union and communism were inherently expansionist and had to be stopped from spreading through both military and political pressure. Containment guided American foreign policy throughout most of the Cold War. (852)

Contract with America (1994): Multipoint program offered by Republican candidates and sitting politicians in the 1994 midterm election. The platform proposed smaller government, congressional ethics reform, term limits, greater emphasis on personal responsibility, and a general repudiation of the Democratic party. This articulation of dissent was a significant blow to the Clinton administration and led to the Republican party's takeover of both houses of Congress for the first time in half a century. (993)

Contras: Anti-Sandinista fighters in the Nicaraguan civil war. The Contras were secretly supplied with American military aid, paid for with money the United States clandestinely made selling arms to Iran. (971)

Court-packing plan (1937): Franklin Roosevelt's politically motivated and ill-fated scheme to add a new justice to the Supreme Court for every member over seventy who would not retire. His objective was to overcome the Court's objections to New Deal reforms. (802)

COVID-19: A novel coronavirus that coursed through the Chinese city of Wuhan in December 2019 and became a global pandemic. The swiftly spreading virus was most deadly among the elderly and infirm; attempts to control COVID led to disruption everywhere. Restaurants and retail stores shut down, students and white color employees learned and worked remotely, and nursing homes banned all visitors. Responses varied by state, leading to partisan fights about masks, distancing, lockdowns, and in 2021, vaccine mandates. Over a million Americans perished from COVID-19 during the first three years of the pandemic. (1055)

Crédit Mobilier scandal (1872): A construction company was formed by owners of the Union Pacific Railroad for the purpose of receiving government contracts to build the railroad at highly inflated prices—and profits. In 1872 a scandal erupted when journalists discovered that the Crédit Mobilier Company had bribed congressmen and even the vice president to allow the ruse to continue. (524)

criminal syndicalism laws (1919–1920): Passed by many states during the red scare, these nefarious laws outlawed the mere advocacy of violence to secure social change. Stump speakers for the International Workers of the World, or IWW, were special targets. (750)

Cuban missile crisis (1962): Standoff between John F. Kennedy and Soviet premier Nikita Khrushchev in October 1962 over Soviet plans to install nuclear weapons in Cuba. Although the crisis was ultimately settled in America's favor and represented a foreign-policy triumph for Kennedy, it brought the world's superpowers perilously close to the brink of nuclear confrontation. (899)

Dawes Plan (1924): An arrangement negotiated in 1924 to reschedule German reparations payments. It stabilized the German currency and opened the way for further American private loans to Germany. (767)

Dawes Severalty Act (1887): An act that broke up reservations and distributed land to individual households. Leftover land was sold for money to fund U.S. government efforts to "civilize" Native Americans. (559)

D-Day (1944): A massive military operation led by American forces in Normandy beginning on June 6, 1944. The pivotal battle led to the liberation of France and brought on the final phases of World War II in Europe. (831)

Defense Production Act (1950): Modeled on the mobilization measures that built "an arsenal of democracy" during World War II, the statute empowered the president to order private companies to prioritize production deemed essential to national security. (858)

Deferred Action for Childhood Arrivals (DACA): Program established by President Obama in June 2012 granting undocumented immigrants work permits and protection from deportations, as long as they were below a certain age (under sixteen when they moved to the United States and under thirty-one years old at the time of enactment). Scorned by Obama's Republican opponents as a misguided overreach of executive power, DACA was rescinded by President Trump in early 2017. The measure was restored by President Biden upon entering office in 2021, although court battles continued over the Constitutionality of the measure for several years after. (1038)

deleveraging: The inverse of "leveraging," whereby businesses increase their financial power by borrowing money (debt) in addition to their own assets (equity). In times of uncertainty or credit tightening, the same businesses seek to improve their debt-to-equity ratios by shedding debt through the sale of assets purchased with borrowed money. (1022)

Democratic Leadership Council (DLC): Nonprofit organization of centrist Democrats founded in the mid-1980s. The group attempted to push the Democratic party toward pro-growth, strong defense, and anti-crime policies. Among its most influential early members was Bill Clinton, who it held up as an example of "third way" politics. (990)

Department of Homeland Security: Cabinet-level agency created in 2003 to unify and coordinate public safety and antiterrorism operations within the federal government. (1013)

détente: From the French for "reduced tension," the period of Cold War thawing when the United States and the Soviet Union negotiated reduced armament treaties under Presidents Nixon, Ford, and Carter. As a policy prescription, détente marked a departure from the policies of proportional response, mutually assured destruction, and containment that had defined the earlier years of the Cold War. (931)

Dien Bien Phu, Battle of (1954): Military engagement in French colonial Vietnam in which French forces were defeated by Viet Minh nationalists loyal to Ho Chi Minh. With this loss, the French ended their colonial involvement in Indochina, paving the way for America's entry. (888)

dollar diplomacy: Name applied by President Taft's critics to the policy of supporting U.S. investments and political interests abroad. First applied to the financing of railways in China after 1909, the policy then spread to Haiti, Honduras, and Nicaragua. President Woodrow Wilson disavowed the practice, but his administration undertook comparable acts of intervention in support of U.S. business interests, especially in Latin America. (698)

"Don't Ask, Don't Tell": From 1993 to 2010, the policy affecting homosexuals in the military. It emerged as a compromise between the standing prohibition against homosexuals in the armed forces and President Clinton's push to allow all citizens to serve regardless of sexual orientation. Military authorities were forbidden to ask about a service member's orientation, and gay service personnel could be discharged if they publicly revealed their homosexuality. At President Obama's urging, Congress repealed DADT in 2010, permitting gays to serve openly in uniform. (992)

"Double V": A national campaign to combat racial discrimination in defense industries and the military during World War II. Appealing to patriotism and drawing connections between the treatment of Black people in the United States and the plight of Jewish people in Nazi Germany, Black Americans and civil rights leaders rallied behind the slogan "Victory over the dictators abroad and over racism at home." (828)

Dust Bowl: Grim nickname for the Great Plains region devastated by drought and dust storms during the 1930s. The disaster led to the migration into California of thousands of displaced "Okies" and "Arkies." (795)

Earth Day (1970): International day of celebration and awareness of global environmental issues launched by conservationists on April 22, 1970. (934)

Eighteenth Amendment (1919): This constitutional amendment prohibited the manufacture, sale, and transportation of alcoholic beverages, ushering in the era known as prohibition. (753)

Elkins Act (1903): Law passed by Congress to impose penalties on railroads that offered rebates and customers who accepted them. The law strengthened the Interstate Commerce Act of 1887. The Hepburn Act of 1906 added free passes to the list of railroad no-nos. (689)

Employment Act of 1946: Legislation declaring that the government's economic policy should aim to promote maximum employment, production, and purchasing power, as well as to keep inflation low. This general commitment was much shorter on specific targets and rules than its liberal creators had wished. The act created the Council of Economic Advisers to provide the president with data and recommendations to make economic policy. (862)

Environmental Protection Agency (EPA): A governmental organization signed into law by Richard Nixon in 1970 designed to regulate pollution, emissions, and other factors that negatively influence the natural environment. The creation of the EPA marked a newfound commitment by the federal government to actively combat environmental risks and was a significant triumph for the environmentalist movement. (933)

Equal Rights Amendment (ERA): An amendment that declared full constitutional equality for women. Although it passed both houses of Congress in 1972, a concerted grassroots campaign by antifeminists led by Phyllis Schlafly persuaded enough state legislatures to vote against ratification. The amendment failed to become part of the Constitution. (951)

Espionage Act (1917): A law prohibiting interference with the draft and other acts of national "disloyalty." Together with the Sedition Act of 1918, which added penalties for abusing the government in writing, it created a climate that was unfriendly to civil liberties. (721)

European Economic Community (EEC): Free-trade zone in Western Europe created by Treaty of Rome in 1957. Often referred to as the "Common Market," this collection of countries originally included France, West Germany, Italy, Belgium, the Netherlands, and Luxembourg. The body eventually expanded to become the European Union. (897)

***Ex parte Milligan* (1866):** Civil War–era case in which the Supreme Court ruled that military tribunals could not be used to try civilians if civil courts were open. (509)

Executive Order No. 9066: Signed by President Franklin D. Roosevelt on February 19, 1942, it authorized the secretary of war to designate military zones from which certain categories of people could be excluded. Fueled by historic anti-Japanese sentiment as well as panic following the December 7, 1941, attack on Pearl Harbor, the order led to the forced removal of some 120,000 persons of Japanese ancestry (70,000 of them U.S. citizens) from the Western Military Zone (the coastal sections of Washington, Oregon, and California). Most but not all of those removed were interned in relocation camps in the interior West. The order was rescinded in December 1944, and legislation passed in 1988 offered an official government apology and modest financial compensation to surviving citizen internees. (822)

Executive Order 9981 (1948): Order issued by President Truman to desegregate the armed forces. The president's action resulted from a combination of pressure from civil rights advocates, election-year political calculations, and the new geopolitical context of the Cold War. (862)

Fair Deal: President Truman's extensive social program introduced in his 1949 message to Congress. Republicans and Southern Democrats kept much of his vision from being enacted, except for raising the minimum wage, providing for more public housing, and extending old-age insurance to many more beneficiaries under the Social Security Act. (864)

Fair Employment Practices Commission (FEPC) (1941): Threatened with a massive "Negro March on Washington" to demand equal opportunities in war jobs and in the military, Franklin D. Roosevelt's administration issued an executive order forbidding racial discrimination in all defense plants operating under contract with the federal government. The FEPC was intended to monitor compliance with the executive order. (828)

Fair Labor Standards Act (1938): Important New Deal labor legislation that regulated minimum wages and maximum hours for workers involved in interstate commerce. The law also outlawed labor by children under sixteen. The exclusion of agricultural, service, and domestic workers meant that many Black Southerners as well as women of all races—who were concentrated in these sectors—did not benefit from the act's protection. (800)

Federal Reserve Act (1913): An act establishing twelve regional Federal Reserve Banks and a Federal Reserve Board, appointed by the president, to regulate banking and create stability on a national scale in the volatile banking sector. The law carried the nation through the financial crises of World War I (1914–1918). (707)

Federal Trade Commission Act (1914): A banner accomplishment of Woodrow Wilson's administration, this law empowered a standing, presidentially appointed commission to investigate illegal business practices in interstate commerce like unlawful competition, false advertising, and mislabeling of goods. (707)

***The Feminine Mystique* (1963):** Best-selling book by feminist thinker Betty Friedan. This work challenged women to move beyond the drudgery of suburban housewifery and helped launch what would become second-wave feminism. (877)

Fifteenth Amendment (ratified 1870): Prohibited states from denying citizens the franchise on account of race. It disappointed feminists, who wanted the amendment to include guarantees for women's suffrage. (508)

Foraker Act (1900): Sponsored by Senator Joseph B. Foraker, a Republican from Ohio, this accorded Puerto Ricans a limited degree of popular government. The first comprehensive congressional effort to provide for governance of territories acquired after the Spanish-American War, it served as a model for a similar act adopted for the Philippines in 1902. (661)

Force Acts (1870–1871): Passed by Congress following a wave of Ku Klux Klan violence, the acts banned clan membership, prohibited the use of intimidation to prevent Black people from voting, and gave the U.S. military the authority to enforce the acts. (512)

Fordism: A system of assembly-line manufacturing and mass production named after Henry Ford, founder of the Ford Motor Company and developer of the Model T car. (740)

Fordney-McCumber Tariff Law (1922): A comprehensive bill passed to protect domestic production from foreign competitors. As a direct result, many European nations were spurred to increase their own trade barriers. (762)

Fourteen Points (1918): Woodrow Wilson's proposal to ensure peace after World War I, calling for an end to secret treaties, widespread arms reduction, national self-determination, and a new league of nations. (719)

Fourteenth Amendment (ratified 1868): Constitutional amendment that extended civil rights to freedmen and prohibited states from taking away such rights without due process. (503)

fourth party system: A term scholars have used to describe national politics from 1896 to 1932, when Republicans had a tight grip on the White House and issues such as industrial regulation and labor concerns became paramount, replacing older concerns such as civil-service reform and monetary policy. (641)

Freedmen's Bureau (1865–1872): Created to aid newly emancipated slaves by providing food, clothing, medical care, education, and legal support. Its achievements were uneven and depended largely on the quality of local administrators. (499)

Freedom Riders: Organized mixed-race groups who rode interstate buses deep into the South to draw attention to and protest racial segregation, beginning in 1961. This effort to challenge racism, which involved the participation of many Northern young people as well as Southern activists, proved a political and public relations success for the civil rights movement. (900)

Freedom Summer (1964): A voter registration drive in Mississippi spearheaded by a coalition of civil rights groups. The campaign drew the activism of thousands of Black and white civil rights workers, many of whom were students from the North, and was marred by the abduction and murder of three such workers at the hands of white racists. (912)

front porch campaign (1896): William McKinley, rather than compete with Bryan's bombastic barnstorming, campaigned from his front porch in Canton, Ohio, inviting supporters from across the nation—as well as national newspaper reporters—to listen. McKinley's success signaled the beginning of more candidate-centric and media-driven presidential campaigning. (639)

Fundamentalism: A Protestant Christian movement emphasizing the literal truth of the Bible and opposing religious modernism, which sought to reconcile religion and science. It was especially strong in the Baptist Church and the Church of Christ, first organized in 1906. (756)

general strike: A large-scale work stoppage that typically cuts across industry lines and affects an entire community. In February 1919, such a strike erupted in Seattle, Washington, eventually involving more than 60,000 workers and paralyzing the city for five days. The strike provoked a fierce backlash, as many of its ringleaders were branded as American "Bolsheviks" eager to foment a second Communist Revolution in the United States. (723)

Gentlemen's Agreement: Responding to anti-Japanese tensions on the West Coast, President Theodore Roosevelt and the Empire of Japan negotiated a compromise in 1907. Japan agreed to issue no new passports for Japanese citizens seeking employment in the United States. The Americans agreed to admit family members of Japanese already resident in the United States, and Roosevelt prevented the segregation of Japanese-American schoolchildren in California's public schools. Secured without formal congressional approval, the arrangement was dubbed the "Gentlemen's Agreement" and was eventually superseded by the Immigration Act of 1924, which banned all immigration from Asia. (674)

GI Bill (1944): Known officially as the Servicemen's Readjustment Act and more informally as the GI Bill of Rights, this law helped returning World War II soldiers reintegrate into civilian life by securing loans to buy homes and farms and set up small businesses. It also made tuition and stipends available for them to attend college, as well as job training programs. The act was intended to cushion the blow of 15 million returning servicemen on the employment market and to nurture the postwar economy. (823, 862)

Gilded Age: A term given to the period 1865–1896 by Mark Twain, indicating both the fabulous wealth and the widespread corruption of the era. (526)

glasnost: Meaning "openness," a cornerstone along with perestroika of Soviet president Mikhail Gorbachev's reform movement in the USSR in the 1980s. These policies resulted in greater market liberalization, access to the West, and ultimately the end of communist rule. (972)

Glass-Steagall Banking Reform Act (1933): A law creating the Federal Deposit Insurance Corporation, which insured individual bank deposits and ended a century-long tradition of unstable banking that had reached a crisis in the Great Depression. (785)

Gold Standard Act (1900): An act that guaranteed that paper currency would be redeemed freely in gold, putting an end to the already dying "free-silver" campaign. (642)

grandfather clause: A regulation established in many Southern states in the 1890s that exempted from voting requirements (such as literacy tests and poll taxes) anyone who could prove that his ancestors ("grandfathers") had been able to vote in 1860. Because slaves could not vote before the Civil War, these clauses guaranteed the right to vote to many white people while denying it to Black people. (633)

Greasy Grass, Battle of (1876): A particularly violent example of the warfare between white people and Native Americans in the late nineteenth century, also known as the Battle of Little Bighorn and "Custer's Last Stand." In two days, June 25 and 26, 1876, the combined forces of 2,500 Sioux, Cheyenne, and Arapaho Indians defeated and killed more than 250 U.S. soldiers, including Colonel George Custer. The battle came as the U.S. government tried to compel Native Americans to remain on the reservations and Native Americans tried to defend territory from white gold-seekers. This Indian advantage did not last long, however, as the union of these Indian fighters proved tenuous and the U.S. Army soon exacted retribution. (550)

Great Migration: The movement of 6 million African Americans from the rural South to the urban North and West in two major waves. The first, from World War I until the onset of the Great Depression, brought more than 1.5 million migrants to northern cities. From 1940 to 1970, another 5 million left the South, pushed off the land by the mechanization of cotton farming and lured north and west by hopes for greater economic opportunity and more equitable political participation. After 1970, increasing numbers of African Americans trekked back to the South in what was called the New Great Migration, as new jobs became more plentiful in the South than in the older industrial cities of the North and racial relations improved in the South. (723)

Great Rapprochement: After decades of occasionally "twisting the lion's tail," American diplomats began to cultivate close, cordial relations with Great Britain at the end of the nineteenth century—a relationship that would intensify further during World War I. (650)

Great Society (1964–1968): President Lyndon Johnson's term for his domestic policy agenda. Billed as a successor to the New Deal, the Great Society aimed to extend the postwar prosperity to all people in American society by promoting civil rights and fighting poverty. Great Society programs included the War on Poverty, which expanded the Social Security system by creating Medicare and Medicaid to provide health care for the aged and the poor. Johnson also signed laws protecting consumers and empowering community organizations to combat poverty at grassroots levels. (908)

Great Strike of 1877: Wage cuts by the Baltimore & Ohio Railroad Company triggered a forty-five-day strike that engulfed Maryland, New York, Pennsylvania, Illinois, and Missouri. One hundred people died in the unrest. (532)

Great White Fleet (1907): Signaling America's growing military prowess and global ambitions, President Theodore Roosevelt sent the U.S. Navy's battleship fleet on a highly visible voyage around the world. Their commander pointedly declared that he was ready for "a feast, a frolic, or a fight." (675)

Guantánamo Detention Camp: Controversial prison facility constructed after the U.S.-led invasion of Afghanistan in 2001. Located on territory occupied by the U.S. military, but not technically part of the United States, the facility serves as an extra-legal holding area for suspected terrorists. (1014)

Harlem Renaissance: A creative outpouring among African American writers, jazz musicians, and social thinkers, centered around Harlem in the 1920s, that celebrated Black culture and advocated for a "New Negro" in American social, political, and intellectual life. (758)

Hawley-Smoot Tariff (1930): The highest protective tariff in the peacetime history of the United States, passed as a result of good old-fashioned horse trading. To the outside world, it smacked of ugly economic warfare. (770)

Haymarket Square (1886): A May Day rally that turned violent when someone threw a bomb into the middle of the meeting, killing several dozen people. Eight anarchists were arrested for conspiracy contributing to the disorder, although evidence linking them to the bombing was thin. Four were executed, one committed suicide, and three were pardoned in 1893. (586)

Hay-Pauncefote Treaty (1901): A treaty signed between the United States and Great Britain giving Americans a free hand to build a canal in Central America. The treaty nullified the Clayton-Bulwer Treaty of 1850, which prohibited Britain or the United States from acquiring territory in Central America. (669)

Helsinki Accords: A cluster of diplomatic agreements signed by thirty-five participating countries in Helsinki, Finland, in 1975. The accords recognized Soviet territorial claims concerning Poland and other Eastern European countries; in exchange, the Soviet Union affirmed the legitimacy of some human rights. The accords were hailed as a significant milestone in détente during the Cold War. (947)

Hetch Hetchy Valley: The federal government allowed the city of San Francisco to build a dam here in 1913. This was a blow to preservationists, who wished to protect the Yosemite National Park, where the dam was located. (692)

holding companies: Companies that own part or all of other companies' stock in order to extend monopoly control. Often, a holding company does not produce goods or services of its own but only exists to control other companies. The Clayton Anti-Trust Act of 1914 sought to clamp down on these companies when they obstructed competition. (707)

Homestead strike (1892): A strike at a Carnegie steel plant in Homestead, Pennsylvania, that ended in an armed battle between the strikers, three hundred armed Pinkerton detectives hired by Carnegie, and federal troops, which killed ten people and wounded more than sixty. The strike was part of a nationwide wave of labor unrest in the summer of 1892 that helped the Populists gain some support from industrial workers. (631)

Hoovervilles: Grim shantytowns where impoverished victims of the Great Depression slept under newspapers and in makeshift tents. Their visibility (and sarcastic name) tarnished the reputation of the Hoover administration. (772)

horizontal integration: The practice perfected by John D. Rockefeller of dominating a particular phase of the production process in order to monopolize a market, often by forming trusts and alliances with competitors. (576)

House Un-American Activities Committee (HUAC): Investigatory body established in 1938 to root out "subversion." Sought to expose communist influence in American government and society, in particular through the trial of Alger Hiss. (859)

Hundred Days (1933): The first hundred days of Franklin D. Roosevelt's administration, stretching from March 9 to June 16, 1933, when an unprecedented number of reform bills were passed by a Democratic Congress to launch the New Deal. (784)

Hungarian uprising (1956): Series of demonstrations in Hungary against the Soviet Union. Soviet Premier Nikita Khrushchev violently suppressed this pro-Western uprising, highlighting the limitations of America's power in Eastern Europe. (887)

Hurricane Katrina (2005): The costliest and one of the deadliest hurricanes in the history of the United States, which killed nearly two thousand Americans. The storm ravaged the Gulf Coast, especially the city of New Orleans, in late August 2005. In New Orleans, high winds and rain caused the city's levees to break, leading to catastrophic flooding, particularly in the city's most impoverished wards. A tardy and feeble response by local and federal authorities exacerbated the damage and led to widespread criticism of the Federal Emergency Management Agency (FEMA). (1021)

International Business Machines (IBM): From its incorporation in 1911, computer manufacturer IBM rose to the pinnacle of America's soaring postwar economy. It became the very emblem of managerial capitalism and technological innovation. Boasting five Nobel Prize winners among its employees, IBM helped to catalyze the transition to a computerized world. (876)

identity politics: Refers to the practice of using race, ethnicity, gender, sexuality, or religion—or any marker of personal identity—to mobilize political support. Practiced by both the left and right, identity politics came into prominence in the 1960s. Sometimes criticized as a divisive regression to tribalism, it reflected an erosion of trust in public institutions and a weakening of shared national values. (976)

Immigration Act of 1924: Also known as the "National Origins Act," this law established quotas for immigration to the United States. Immigration from southern and eastern Europe was sharply curtailed, while immigrants from Asia were shut out altogether. (752)

Immigration and Nationality Act of 1965: A landmark immigration law that abolished the 1921 "national origins" formula and established new admission criteria, based mainly on immigrants' skills and family ties with U.S citizens. Despite President Lyndon Johnson's assurances that it was "not a revolutionary bill," the 1965 act radically transformed America's demographic profile as Latin America, Asia, Africa, and the Middle East replaced Western Europe as the nation's main sources of immigrants. (911)

Indian Citizenship Act of 1924: Signed into law by President Calvin Coolidge, the act granted citizenship to all Native American born in U.S. territory. The act, however, went short of extending them the right to vote, a milestone that would only be reached in 1962. (753)

Indian Gaming Regulatory Act of 1988: Signed into law by President Reagan on October 17, 1988, the act created a legal apparatus for regulating Indian gaming, which had become a prominent part of many tribal economies. (953)

Indian Reorganization Act of 1934: Also known as the "Indian New Deal" and the Wheeler-Howard Act. Its major thrusts were to reverse the policy of forced assimilation that flowed from the 1887 Dawes Severalty Act, restore tribal autonomy, and promote the economic well-being of reservations. (796)

Industrial Workers of the World (1905): The IWW, also known as the "Wobblies," was a radical organization that sought to build "one big union" and advocated industrial sabotage in defense of that goal. At its peak in 1923, it could claim 100,000 members and could gain the support of 300,000. The IWW particularly appealed to migratory workers in agriculture and lumbering and to miners, all of whom suffered from horrific working conditions. (723)

initiative: A progressive reform measure allowing voters to petition to have a law placed on the general ballot. Like the referendum and recall, it brought democracy directly "to the people" and helped foster a shift toward interest group politics and away from old political "machines." (684)

***Insular Cases* (1901–1904):** Beginning in 1901, a badly divided Supreme Court decreed in these cases that the Constitution did not follow the flag. In other words, Puerto Ricans and Filipinos would not necessarily enjoy all American rights. (662)

***insurrectos*:** Cuban insurgents who sought freedom from colonial Spanish rule. Their destructive tactics threatened American economic interests in Cuban plantations and railroads. (652)

interlocking directorates: The practice of having executives or directors from one company serve on the board of directors of another company. J. P. Morgan introduced this practice to eliminate banking competition in the 1890s. (575)

Intermediate-Range Nuclear Forces (INF) Treaty (1987): Arms limitation agreement settled by Ronald Reagan and Mikhail Gorbachev after several attempts. The treaty banned all intermediate-range nuclear missiles from Europe and marked a significant thaw in the Cold War. (972)

International Style: Archetypal, post–World War II modernist architectural style, best known for its "curtain-wall" designs of steel-and-glass corporate high-rises. (893)

Interstate Commerce Act (1887): Congressional legislation that established the Interstate Commerce Commission, compelled railroads to publish standard rates, and prohibited rebates and pools. Railroads quickly became adept at using the act to achieve their own ends, but it gave the government an important means to regulate big business. (572)

Iran-Contra affair: Major political scandal of Ronald Reagan's second term that was revealed in 1986. An illicit arrangement of selling "arms for hostages" with Iran and using money to support the contras in Nicaragua, the scandal deeply damaged Reagan's credibility. (973)

Iran nuclear deal: Also known as the Joint Comprehensive Plan of Action. Brokered by the Obama administration between Iran and the major world powers in July 2015, the agreement terminated economic sanctions that had hamstrung Iran's economy. In return, Tehran pledged to reduce its stockpiles of weapon-grade uranium and end its pursuit of nuclear weapons. (1045)

Iranian hostage crisis: The 444 days, from November 1979 to January 1981, in which American embassy workers were held captive by Iranian revolutionaries. The Iranian Revolution began in January 1979 when young Muslim Fundamentalists overthrew the oppressive regime of the American-backed shah, forcing him into exile. Deeming the United States "the Great Satan," these revolutionaries triggered an energy crisis by cutting off Iranian oil. The hostage crisis began when revolutionaries stormed the American embassy, demanding that the United States return the shah to Iran for trial. The episode was marked by botched diplomacy and a failed rescue attempt by the Carter administration. After permanently damaging relations between the two countries, the crisis ended with the hostages' release the day Ronald Reagan became president, January 20, 1981. (959)

irreconcilables: Led by Senators William Borah of Idaho and Hiram Johnson of California, this was a hard-core group of militant isolationists who opposed the Wilsonian dream of international cooperation in the League of Nations after World War I. Their efforts played an important part in preventing American participation in the international organization. (733)

Jim Crow: System of racial segregation in the American South from the end of Reconstruction until the mid-twentieth century. Based on the concept of "separate but equal" facilities for Black and white people, the Jim Crow system sought to prevent racial mixing in public, including restaurants, movie theaters, and public transportation. An informal system, it was generally perpetuated by custom, violence, and intimidation. (531)

Jones Act (1916): Law according territorial status to the Philippines and promising independence as soon as a "stable government" could be established. The United States did not grant the Philippines independence until July 4, 1946. (708)

Kellogg-Briand Pact (1928): A sentimental triumph of the 1920s peace movement, this 1928 pact linked sixty-two nations in the supposed "outlawry of war." (762)

Kent State University: Scene of massacre of four college students by National Guardsmen on May 4, 1970, in Ohio. In response to Nixon's announcement that he had expanded the Vietnam War into Cambodia, college campuses across the country exploded in violence. On May 14 and 15, students at historically Black Jackson State College in Mississippi were protesting the war as well as the Kent State shooting when highway patrolmen fired into a student dormitory, killing two students. (930)

Kerner Commission: The National Advisory Commission on Civil Disorders, known after its chairman, Illinois Governor Otto Kerner. The Commission's 1968 report concluded that the urban disturbances of the mid-1960s resulted not from Black lawlessness but from persistent and structural white racism. (918)

Keynesianism: An economic theory based on the thoughts of British economist John Maynard Keynes, holding that central banks should adjust interest rates and governments should use deficit spending and tax policies to increase purchasing power and hence prosperity. (804)

kitchen debate (1959): Televised exchange in 1959 between Soviet premier Nikita Khrushchev and American vice president Richard Nixon. Meeting at the American National Exhibition in Moscow, the two leaders sparred over the relative merits of capitalist consumer culture versus Soviet state planning. Nixon won applause for his staunch defense of American capitalism, helping lead him to the Republican nomination for president in 1960. (890)

Knights of Labor: The second national labor organization, organized in 1869 as a secret society and opened for public membership in 1881. The Knights were known for their efforts to organize all workers, regardless of skill level, gender, or race. After the mid-1880s their membership declined for a variety of reasons, including the Knights' participation in violent strikes and discord between skilled and unskilled members. (586)

Korean War (1950–1953): First "hot war" of the Cold War. It began when the Soviet-backed North Koreans invaded South Korea and U.N. forces, dominated by the United States, launched a counteroffensive. The war ended in stalemate in 1953. (858)

***Kristallnacht*:** German for "night of broken glass," it refers to the murderous pogrom that destroyed Jewish businesses and synagogues and sent thousands to concentration camps on the night of November 9, 1938. Thousands more attempted to find refuge in the United States but were ultimately turned away due to restrictive immigration laws. (816)

Ku Klux Klan: An extremist, paramilitary, right-wing secret society founded in the mid-nineteenth century and revived during the 1920s. It was antiforeign, anti-Black, anti-Jewish, antipacifist, anti-Communist, anti-internationalist, anti-evolutionist, and antibootlegger, but pro–Anglo-Saxon and pro-Protestant. Its members, cloaked in sheets to conceal their identities, terrorized Black freedmen and sympathetic white people throughout the South after the Civil War. By the 1890s, Klan-style violence and Democratic legislation succeeded in virtually disenfranchising all Black people. (512)

land-grant colleges: Colleges and universities created from allocations of public land through the Morrill Act of 1862 and the Hatch Act of 1887. These grants helped fuel the boom in higher education in the late nineteenth century, and many of today's public universities derive from them. (608)

League of Nations (1919): A world organization of national governments proposed by President Woodrow Wilson and established by the Treaty of Versailles in 1919. It worked to facilitate peaceful international cooperation. Despite emotional appeals by Wilson, isolationists' objections to the League created the major obstacle to American signing of the Treaty of Versailles. (732)

Lend-Lease Bill (1941): Based on the motto "Send guns, not sons," this law abandoned former pretenses of neutrality by allowing Americans to sell unlimited supplies of arms to any nation defending itself against the Axis powers. Patriotically numbered 1776, the bill was praised as a device for keeping the nation out of World War II. (818)

Levittown: Suburban communities with mass-produced tract houses built in the New York and Philadelphia metropolitan areas in the 1950s by William Levitt and Sons. Typically inhabited by white middle-class people who fled the cities in search of homes to buy for their growing families. (868)

Lewinsky affair (1998–1999): Political scandal that resulted in Bill Clinton's impeachment and trial by Congress. In 1998, Clinton gave sworn testimony in a sexual harassment case that he had never engaged in sexual activity with a White House intern named Monica Lewinsky. When prosecutors discovered evidence that the president had lied under oath about the affair, to which Clinton admitted, Republicans in Congress began impeachment proceedings. Although Clinton was ultimately not convicted by the Senate, the scandal put a lasting blemish on his presidential legacy. (1008)

liberal Protestants: Members of a branch of Protestantism that flourished from 1875 to 1925 and encouraged followers to use the Bible as a moral compass rather than to believe that the Bible represented scientific or historical truth. Many liberal Protestants became active in the "social gospel" and other reform movements of the era. (604)

***Lochner v. New York* (1905):** A setback for labor reformers, this Supreme Court decision invalidated a state law establishing a ten-hour day for bakers. It held that the "right to free contract" was implicit in the due process clause of the Fourteenth Amendment. (687)

London Economic Conference (1933): A sixty-six-nation economic conference organized to stabilize international currency rates. Franklin Roosevelt's decision to revoke American participation contributed to a deepening world economic crisis. (811)

Los Angeles rebellion: After police officers were acquitted for assaulting a Black motorist, a violent uprising broke out in Los Angeles in 1992, engulfing the city for six days. Sixty-three people were killed in the violence, most of them Black or Latino, and Korean-American grocery stores in particular were targeted by looters, badly straining relations between minority groups. (990)

"Lost Cause": A flagrantly false narrative embraced by many white Southerners after the Civil War. Romanticizing the pre-war South as a benign society of contented slaves and revered masters, and condemning Reconstruction as a cruel overreach by vengeful "Yankees," the myth shaped national policymaking, popular culture, and history textbooks for decades afterward. (503)

"Lost Generation": A creative circle of expatriate American artists and writers, including Ernest Hemingway, F. Scott Fitzgerald, and Gertrude Stein, who found shelter and inspiration in post–World War I Europe. (757)

Lusitania**:** British passenger liner that sank after it was torpedoed by Germany on May 7, 1915. It ended the lives of 1,198 people, including 128 Americans, and pushed the United States closer to war. (713)

Maine **(1898):** American battleship dispatched to keep a "friendly" watch over Cuba in early 1898. It mysteriously blew up in Havana harbor on February 15, 1898, with a loss of 260 sailors. Later evidence confirmed that the explosion was accidental, resulting from combustion in one of the ship's internal coal bunkers. But many Americans, eager for war, insisted that it was the fault of a Spanish submarine mine. (653)

malaise speech (1979): National address by Jimmy Carter in July 1979 in which he chided American materialism and urged a communal spirit in the face of economic hardships. Although Carter intended the speech to improve both public morale and his standing as a leader, it had the opposite effect and was widely perceived as a political disaster for the embattled president. (956)

Manhattan Project (1942): Code name for the American commission established in 1942 to develop the atomic bomb. The first experimental bomb was detonated on July 16, 1945, in the desert of New Mexico. Atomic bombs were then dropped on two cities in Japan in hopes of bringing the war to an end: Hiroshima on August 6, 1945, and Nagasaki on August 9, 1945. (836)

March on Washington (1963): Massive civil rights demonstration in August 1963 in support of Kennedy-backed legislation to secure legal protections for American Black people. One of the most visually impressive manifestations of the civil rights movement, the march was the occasion of Martin Luther King's famous "I Have a Dream" speech. (902)

Marshall Plan (1948): Massive transfer of aid money to help rebuild postwar Western Europe, intended to bolster capitalist and democratic governments and prevent domestic communist groups from riding poverty and misery to power. The plan was first announced by Secretary of State George Marshall at Harvard's commencement in June 1947. (853)

McCarthyism: A brand of vitriolic, fear-mongering anti-communism associated with the career of Senator Joseph McCarthy. In the early 1950s, Senator McCarthy used his position in Congress to baselessly accuse high-ranking government officials and other Americans of conspiracy with communism. The term named after him refers to the dangerous forces of unfairness and fear wrought by anticommunist paranoia. (860)

McKinley Tariff (1890): Shepherded through Congress by President William McKinley, this tariff raised duties on Hawaiian sugar and set off renewed efforts to secure the annexation of Hawaii to the United States. (651)

Meat Inspection Act (1906): A law passed by Congress to subject meat shipped over state lines to federal inspection. The publication of Upton Sinclair's novel *The Jungle* earlier that year so disgusted American consumers with its description of conditions in slaughterhouses and meatpacking plants that it mobilized public support for government action. (691)

mechanization of agriculture: The development of engine-driven machines, like the combine, which helped to dramatically increase the productivity of land in the 1870s and 1880s. This process contributed to the consolidation of agricultural business that drove many family farms out of existence. (626)

#MeToo: Movement in 2017 that inspired women to reveal past experiences of sexual discrimination and abuse, bringing down numerous high-profile gropers in the entertainment industry, the media, and the U.S. Congress. (1048)

Meuse-Argonne offensive (1918): General John J. ("Black Jack") Pershing led American troops in this effort to cut the German railroad lines supplying the western front. One of the few major battles that Americans participated in during the entire war, it was still under way when the war ended. (729)

Midway, Battle of (1942): A pivotal naval battle fought near the island of Midway on June 3–6, 1942. The victory halted Japanese advances in the Pacific. (829)

military-industrial complex: Term popularized by President Dwight Eisenhower in his 1961 Farewell Address, referring to the political and economic ties between arms manufacturers, elected officials, and the U.S. armed forces that created self-sustaining pressure for high military spending during the Cold War. Eisenhower also warned that this powerful combination left unchecked could "endanger our liberties or democratic process," favoring defense concerns over more peaceful goals that balanced security and liberty. (892)

mining industry: After gold and silver strikes in Colorado, Nevada, and other western territories in the second half of the nineteenth century, fortune-seekers by the thousands rushed to the West to dig. These metals were essential to U.S. industrial growth and were also sold into world markets. After surface metals were removed, people sought ways to extract ore from under the ground, leading to the development of heavy mining machinery. This, in turn, led to the consolidation of the mining industry, because only big companies could afford to buy and build the necessary machines. (553)

Miranda warning: A statement of an arrested person's constitutional rights, which police officers must read during an arrest. The warning came out of the Supreme Court's decision in *Miranda v. Arizona* in 1966 that accused people have the right to remain silent, consult an attorney, and enjoy other protections. The Court declared that law enforcement officers must make sure suspects understand their constitutional rights, thus creating a safeguard against forced confessions and self-implication. (932)

Mississippi Freedom Democratic Party (1964): Political party organized by civil rights activists to challenge Mississippi's delegation to the Democratic National Convention, who opposed the civil rights planks in the party's platform. Claiming a mandate to represent the true voice of Mississippi, where almost no Black citizens could vote, the MFDP demanded to be seated at the convention but were denied by party bosses. The effort was both a setback to civil rights activism in the South and a motivation to continue to struggle for Black voting rights. (912)

modernism: In response to the demanding conditions of modern life, this artistic and cultural movement revolted against comfortable Victorian standards and accepted chance, change, contingency, uncertainty, and fragmentation. Originating among avant-garde artists and intellectuals around the turn of the twentieth century, modernism blossomed into a full-fledged cultural movement in art, music, literature, and architecture. (757)

Montgomery bus boycott (1955): Protest by Black Alabamians against segregated seating on city buses, sparked by Rosa Parks's defiant refusal to move to the back of the bus. The bus boycott lasted from December 1, 1955, until December 26, 1956, and became one of the foundational moments of the civil rights movement. It led to the rise of Martin Luther King, Jr., and ultimately to a Supreme Court decision opposing segregated busing. (883)

Moral Majority: Political action committee founded by evangelical Reverend Jerry Falwell in 1979 to promote traditional Christian values and oppose feminism, abortion, and gay rights. The group was a major linchpin in the resurgent religious right of the 1980s. (974)

muckrakers: Bright young reporters at the turn of the twentieth century who won this unfavorable moniker from Theodore Roosevelt but boosted the circulations of their magazines by writing exposés of widespread corruption in American society. Their subjects included business manipulation of government, white slavers, child labor, and the illegal deeds of the trusts and helped spur the passage of reform legislation. (680)

Mueller Report (2020): The findings of a two-year investigation chaired by Special Prosecutor Robert Mueller on Russian interference in the 2016 election. The report concluded that Trump and his campaign were culpable of encouraging and meeting with Russian operatives but did not find enough evidence to prove a criminal conspiracy. (1054)

***Muller v. Oregon* (1908):** A landmark Supreme Court case in which crusading attorney (and future Supreme Court justice) Louis D. Brandeis persuaded the Supreme Court to accept the constitutionality of limiting the hours of women workers. Coming on the heels of *Lochner v. New York,* it established a different standard for male and female workers. (686)

multiculturalism: A term that came to prominence in the 1980s, used to describe the vision of a diverse range of ethnic, religious, and cultural communities coexisting within a single national polity, without requiring them to assimilate or agree to a common creed. (1005)

My Lai: Vietnamese village that was the scene of a military assault on March 16, 1968, in which American soldiers under the command of 2nd Lieutenant William Calley murdered hundreds of unarmed Vietnamese civilians, mostly women and children. The atrocity produced outrage and reduced support for the war in America and around the world when details of the massacre and an attempted cover-up were revealed in November 1969. (930)

National American Woman Suffrage Association (NAWSA): An organization founded in 1890 to demand the vote for women. NAWSA argued that women should be allowed to vote because their responsibilities in the home and family made them indispensable in the public decision-making process. During World War I, NAWSA supported the war effort and lauded women's role in the Allied victory, which helped to finally achieve nationwide woman suffrage in the Nineteenth Amendment (1920). (613)

National Interstate and Defense Highways Act (1956): Also called the Federal Highway Act. Federal legislation signed by Dwight D. Eisenhower to construct thousands of miles of modern highways in the name of national defense. The interstate highway system vastly improved long-haul travel by car and dramatically increased the migration of white middle-class families, employers, and retailers to the suburbs. Yet the construction of highways within and across city neighborhoods also caused great social and economic disruption for many poorer and majority-Black communities. (886)

National Labor Union (1866–1872): This first national labor organization in U.S. history gained 600,000 members from many parts of the work force, although it limited the participation of women as well as Chinese and Black people. The organization devoted much of its energy to fighting for an eight-hour workday before it dissolved in 1872. (585)

National Rifle Association (NRA): Founded as a gun safety organization after the Civil War, the NRA became a powerful pro-gun lobby with over five million members by the early twenty-first century. Forcefully arguing that the Second Amendment to the Constitution protected the individual right to bear even the most lethal modern arms, it consistently and successfully opposed many federal and state efforts to enact gun control legislation. (1044)

National Recovery Administration (NRA) (1933): Known by its critics as the "National Run Around," the NRA was an early New Deal program designed to assist industry, labor, and the unemployed through centralized planning mechanisms that monitored workers' earnings and working hours to distribute work and established codes for "fair competition" to ensure that similar procedures were followed by all firms in any particular industrial sector. (792)

National Security Council Memorandum Number 68 (NSC-68) (1950): National Security Council recommendation to quadruple defense spending and rapidly expand peacetime armed forces to address Cold War tensions. It reflected a new militarization of American foreign policy, but the huge costs of rearmament were not expected to interfere with what seemed like the limitless possibilities of postwar prosperity. (857)

National War Labor Board (NWLB): Established by President Franklin D. Roosevelt to act as an arbitration tribunal and mediate disputes between labor and management that might have led to war stoppages and thereby undermined the war effort. The NWLB was also charged with adjusting wages with an eye to controlling inflation. (823)

naturalism: An offshoot of mainstream realism, this late-nineteenth-century literary movement purported to apply detached scientific objectivity to the study of human characters shaped by degenerate heredity and extreme or sordid social environments. (617)

Neutrality Act of 1939: This act stipulated that European democracies might buy American munitions, but only if they could pay in cash and transport them in their own ships, a policy known as "cash-and-carry." It represented an effort to avoid war debts and protect American arms-carriers from torpedo attacks. (814)

Neutrality Acts of 1935, 1936, and 1937: Short-sighted acts passed to prevent American participation in a European war. Among other restrictions, they prevented Americans from selling munitions to foreign belligerents. (812)

New Deal: The economic and political policies of Franklin Roosevelt's administration in the 1930s, which aimed to solve the problems of the Great Depression by providing relief for the unemployed and launching efforts to stimulate economic recovery. The New Deal built on reforms of the progressive era to expand greatly an American-style welfare state. (782)

New Freedom (1912): Platform of reforms advocated by Woodrow Wilson in his first presidential campaign, including stronger antitrust legislation to protect small business enterprises from monopolies, banking reform, and tariff reductions. Wilson's strategy involved taking action to increase opportunities for capitalist competition rather than increasing government regulation of large trusts. (700)

New Frontier (1981–1963): President Kennedy's nickname for his domestic policy agenda. Buoyed by youthful optimism, the program included proposals for the Peace Corps and efforts to improve education and health care. (895)

New Immigrants: Term used to describe immigrants from southern and eastern Europe (many of them Catholic or Jewish) who formed a recognizable wave of immigration from the 1880s until 1924, in contrast to the immigrants from northern and western Europe who had come before them. These new immigrants congregated in ethnic urban neighborhoods, where their "foreign" presence alarmed many native-born Americans, some of whom responded with nativist anti-immigrant campaigns and others of whom introduced urban reforms to help the immigrants assimilate. (596)

New Nationalism (1912): State-interventionist reform program devised by journalist Herbert Croly and advocated by Theodore Roosevelt during his Bull Moose presidential campaign. Roosevelt did not object to continued consolidation of trusts and labor unions. Rather, he sought to create stronger regulatory agencies to ensure that they operated to serve the public interest, not just private gain. (699)

New Right: Term for a loose network of conservative political activists and organizations that emerged in the 1970s and 1980s. More populist in tone than previous generations of conservatives, the New Right emphasized hot-button cultural issues like abortion, busing, and prayer in school. They also espoused a nationalist foreign policy outlook that rejected détente and international treaties. (953)

Newlands Reclamation Act (1902): Congress authorized that money be collected from the sale of public lands in the sun-baked western states and then use these funds for the construction of dams and the development of irrigation projects. (692)

Nine-Power Treaty (1922): Agreement coming out of the Washington "Disarmament" Conference of 1921–1922 that pledged Britain, France, Italy, Japan, the United States, China, the Netherlands, Portugal, and Belgium to abide by the Open Door policy in China. The Five-Power Naval Treaty on ship ratios and the Four-Power Treaty to preserve the status quo in the Pacific also came out of the conference. (761)

Nineteenth Amendment (1920): This constitutional amendment, finally passed by Congress in 1919 and ratified in 1920, gave women the right to vote over seventy years after the first organized calls for woman's suffrage in Seneca Falls, New York. (724)

Nixon Doctrine: President Nixon's plan for "peace with honor" in Vietnam. The doctrine stated that the United States would honor its existing defense commitments but, in the future, countries would have to fight their own wars. (929)

No Child Left Behind Act (2001): An education bill created and signed by the George W. Bush administration. Designed to increase accountability standards for primary and secondary schools, the law authorized several federal programs to monitor those standards and increased choices for parents in selecting schools for their children. The program was highly controversial, in large part because it linked results on standardized tests to federal funding for schools and school districts. (1018)

North American Free Trade Agreement (NAFTA) (1993): Free-trade zone encompassing Mexico, Canada, and the United States. A symbol of the increased reality of a globalized marketplace, the treaty passed despite opposition from protectionists and labor leaders. (1000)

North Atlantic Treaty Organization (NATO): Military alliance of Western European powers and the United States and Canada established in 1949 to defend against the common threat from the Soviet Union, marking a giant stride forward for European unity and American internationalism. (855)

Nuremberg war crimes trial (1945–1946): Highly publicized proceedings against former Nazi leaders for war crimes and crimes against humanity in postwar Germany. The trials led to several executions and long prison sentences. (850)

Obergefell v. Hodges **(2015):** Landmark Supreme Court ruling that declared that the Fourteenth Amendment's equal protection and due process clauses conferred a constitutional right to marry for same-sex couples. (1040)

Occupy Wall Street: Name of the original protest that launched the populist, anti-Wall Street "Occupy" movement in late 2010 and early 2011. Youthful radicals pitched tents and occupied Zuccotti Park in New York's financial district beginning in September 2010 to protest inequality and corporate political power. This demonstration inspired similar occupations in many other cities. (1033)

Office of Price Administration (OPA) (1941–1949): A critically important wartime agency charged with regulating the consumer economy by rationing scarce supplies, such as automobiles, tires, fuel, nylon, and sugar, and by curbing inflation by setting ceilings on the price of goods. Rents were controlled as well in parts of the country overwhelmed by war workers. The OPA was extended after World War II ended to continue the fight against inflation. (823)

Office of Scientific Research and Development (OSRD): Agency established during World War II to mobilize university-based scientists and laboratories in war work. Channeling hundreds of millions of federal dollars toward research and development of atomic energy and other advanced technologies, the wartime agency provided an inspiration and template for large-scale government investment in science and technology during the Cold War and beyond. (823)

Oklahoma City bombing (1995): Truck-bomb explosion that killed 168 people in a federal office building on April 19, 1995. The attack was perpetrated by right-wing and antigovernment militant Timothy McVeigh, who was later executed by the U.S. government for the crime. (992)

Open Door note (1899–1900): A set of diplomatic letters in which Secretary of State John Hay urged the great powers to respect Chinese rights and free and open competition within their spheres of influence. The notes established the "Open Door policy," which sought to ensure access to the Chinese market for the United States, despite the fact that it did not have a formal sphere of influence in China. (665)

Operation Desert Storm (1991): U.S.-led multicountry military engagement in January and February of 1991 that drove Saddam Hussein's Iraqi army out of neighboring Kuwait. In addition to presaging the longer and more protracted Iraq War of the 2000s, the 1991 war helped undo what some called the "Vietnam Syndrome," a feeling of military uncertainty that plagued many Americans. (983)

Operation Dixie (1948): Failed effort by the CIO after World War II to unionize workers, especially in textile factories. (862)

Operation Wetback (1954): A government program to round up and deport as many as 1 million illegal Mexican migrant workers in the United States. The program was promoted in part by the Mexican government and reflected burgeoning concerns about non-European immigration to America. (886)

Organization of Petroleum Exporting Countries (OPEC): Cartel comprising Middle Eastern states and Venezuela first organized in 1960. OPEC aimed to control access to and prices of oil, wresting power from Western oil companies and investors. In the process, it gradually strengthened the hand of non-Western powers on the world stage. (889)

over-the-counter (OTC) derivatives: Refers to bilateral contracts that—like drugs sold "over the counter" without a medical prescription—could be drawn up outside of financial exchanges, bypassing regulatory scrutiny. Deregulated during the Clinton administration, OTC derivatives and other similarly exotic financial instruments contributed significantly to the 2008 financial crisis. (1000)

panic of 1873: A worldwide depression that began in the United States when one of the nation's largest banks abruptly declared bankruptcy, leading to the collapse of thousands of banks and businesses. The crisis intensified debtors' calls for inflationary measures such as the printing of more paper money and the unlimited coinage of silver. Conflicts over monetary policy greatly influenced politics in the last quarter of the nineteenth century. (525)

panic of 1907: A financial panic that gripped the United States in October 1907, triggering widespread bankruptcies and causing the stock market to lose half its value from the previous year. Staunched only by J. P. Morgan's timely intervention, the panic eventually led to the creation of the Federal Reserve in 1913, marking the panic as the last time that a major financial crisis was resolved by private means. (696)

Paris Climate Accords: An landmark agreement to reduce carbon emissions, signed by the United States and 195 other nations in 2015 during the presidency of Barack Obama. President Donald Trump controversially withdrew from the accord in 2020. President Joe Biden brought the United States back into the Paris agreement on his first day in office in 2021. (1052)

Patient Protection and Affordable Care Act (2010): Also known as "Obamacare," the act extended health-care insurance to some 30 million Americans, marking a major step toward achieving the century-old goal of providing universal health-care coverage. (1028)

patronage: A system, prevalent during the Gilded Age, in which political parties granted jobs and favors to party regulars who delivered votes on election day. Patronage was both an essential wellspring of support for both parties and a source of conflict within the Republican party. (527)

Payne-Aldrich Bill (1909): While intended to lower tariff rates, this bill was eventually revised beyond all recognition, retaining high rates on most imports. President Taft angered the progressive wing of his party when he declared it "the best bill that the Republican party ever passed." (699)

Peace Corps: A federal agency created by President Kennedy in 1961 to promote voluntary service by Americans in foreign countries. The Peace Corps provides labor power to help developing countries improve their infrastructure, health care, educational systems, and other aspects of their societies. Part of Kennedy's New Frontier vision, the organization represented an effort by postwar liberals to promote American values and influence through productive exchanges across the world. (895)

Peace Policy: Refers to President Ulysses Grant's attempt in 1868 to end the Plains Indians Wars by enlisting Christian missionaries to supervise the reservations. Though it was hoped that the churches would be more gentle agents of "assimilation," the policy failed and was eventually terminated in 1881. (558)

Pearl Harbor (1941): An American naval base in Hawaii where Japanese warplanes destroyed numerous ships and caused three thousand casualties on December 7, 1941—a day that, in President Roosevelt's words, was to "live in infamy." The attack brought the United States into World War II. (821)

Pendleton Act (1883): Congressional legislation that established the Civil Service Commission, which granted federal government jobs on the basis of examinations instead of political patronage, thus reining in the spoils system. (535)

Pentagon Papers: Secret U.S. government report detailing early planning and policy decisions regarding the Vietnam War under Presidents Kennedy and Johnson. Leaked to the *New York Times* in 1971, it revealed instances of governmental secrecy, lies, and incompetence in the prosecution of the war. (930)

perestroika: Meaning "restructuring," a cornerstone along with glasnost of Soviet president Mikhail Gorbachev's reform movement in the USSR in the 1980s. These policies resulted in greater market liberalization, access to the West, and ultimately the end of communist rule. (972)

Philadelphia Plan (1969): Program established by Richard Nixon to require construction trade unions to work toward hiring more Black apprentices. The plan altered Lyndon Johnson's concept of "affirmative action" to focus on groups rather than individuals. (933)

Platt Amendment (1901): Following its military occupation, the United States successfully pressured the Cuban government to write this amendment into its constitution. It limited Cuba's treaty-making abilities, controlled its debt, and stipulated that the United States could intervene militarily to restore order when it saw fit. (662)

***Plessy v. Ferguson* (1896):** A Supreme Court case that upheld the constitutionality of segregation laws, saying that as long as Black people were provided with "separate but equal" facilities, these laws did not violate the Fourteenth Amendment. This decision provided legal justification for the Jim Crow system until the 1950s. (531)

policy of boldness (1954): Foreign-policy objective of Dwight Eisenhower's secretary of state John Foster Dulles, who believed in changing the containment strategy to one that more directly engaged the Soviet Union and attempted to roll back communist influence around the world. This policy led to a buildup of America's nuclear arsenal to threaten "massive retaliation" against communist enemies, launching the Cold War's arms race. (887)

political machines: A term used to describe political organizations that flourished in urban centers—such as Tammany Hall in New York—that captured the immigrant vote by promising them municipal jobs, housing, and rudimentary social services. Though they were criticized for breeding corruption, their supporters thought they were rendering valuable social services. (599)

Populists: Officially known as the People's party, the Populists represented Westerners and Southerners who believed that U.S. economic policy inappropriately favored Eastern businessmen instead of the nation's farmers. Their proposals included nationalization of the railroads, a graduated income tax, and, most significantly, the unlimited coinage of silver. (630)

Potsdam conference (1945): From July 17 to August 2, 1945, President Harry S. Truman met with Soviet leader Joseph Stalin and British leaders Winston Churchill and later Clement Attlee (when the Labour party defeated Churchill's Conservative party) near Berlin to deliver an ultimatum to Japan: surrender or be destroyed. (836)

primary elections: For much of American history, party leaders chose presidential candidates. But reforms to the nominating process in the late 1960s and early 1970s required presidential hopefuls to run popular campaigns to garner their party's support. The shift to primary elections weakened the traditional political parties and opened opportunities for newcomers and "outsiders" to enter the political arena. (935)

Proposition 13 (1978): A successful California state ballot initiative that capped the state's real estate tax at 1 percent of assessed value. The proposition radically reduced average property tax levels, decreasing revenue for the state government and signaling the political power of the "tax revolt," increasingly aligned with conservative politics. (967)

Pullman strike (1894): A strike by railroad workers upset by drastic wage cuts. The strike was led by socialist Eugene Debs but not supported by the American Federation of Labor. Eventually President Grover Cleveland intervened, and federal troops forced an end to the strike. The strike highlighted both divisions within labor and the government's new willingness to use armed force to combat work stoppages. (636)

Pure Food and Drug Act (1906): A law passed by Congress to inspect and regulate the labeling of all foods and pharmaceuticals intended for human consumption. This legislation, and additional provisions passed in 1911 to strengthen it, aimed particularly at the patent medicine industry. The more comprehensive Food, Drug, and Cosmetic Act of 1938 largely replaced this legislation. (691)

Quarantine Speech (1937): An important speech delivered by Franklin Roosevelt in which he called for "positive endeavors" to "quarantine" land-hungry dictators, presumably through economic embargoes. The speech flew in the face of isolationist politicians. (813)

racketeers: People who obtain money illegally by fraud, bootlegging, gambling, or threats of violence. Racketeers invaded the ranks of labor during the 2090s, a decade when gambling and gangsterism were prevalent in American life. (755)

Realism: Mid-nineteenth-century movement in European and American literature and the arts that sought to depict contemporary life and society as it actually was, in all its unvarnished detail. Adherents eschewed the idealism and nostalgia of the earlier romantic sensibility. (616)

recall: A progressive ballot procedure allowing voters to remove elected officials from office. (684)

Reconstruction Act (1867): Passed by the newly elected Republican Congress, it divided the South into five military districts, disenfranchised former Confederates, and required that Southern states both ratify the Fourteenth Amendment and write state constitutions guaranteeing freedmen the franchise before gaining readmission to the Union. (508)

Reconstruction Finance Corporation (RFC) (1932): A government lending agency established under the Hoover administration in order to assist insurance companies, banks, agricultural organizations, railroads, and local governments. It was a precursor to later agencies that grew out of the New Deal and symbolized a recognition by the Republicans that some federal action was required to address the Great Depression. (774)

red scare (1919–1920): A period of intense anticommunism following the First World War and the Bolshevik Revolution. The "Palmer raids" of Attorney General A. Mitchell Palmer resulted in about six thousand deportations of foreign-born people suspected of "subversive" activities. (750)

Redeemers: Southern Democratic politicians who sought to wrest control from Republican regimes in the South after Reconstruction. (509)

redlining: Refers to the practice of classifying neighborhoods based on their perceived risk to lenders. ("Red" indicated the highest-risk areas.) While ostensibly based strictly on financial considerations, redlining served as a covert form of racial discrimination that worsened segregation and widened the racial wealth gap during the postwar period. (869)

referendum: A progressive reform procedure allowing voters to place a bill on the ballot for final approval, even after being passed by the legislature. (684)

regionalism: A recurring artistic movement that, in the context of the late nineteenth century, aspired to capture the peculiarities, or "local color," of America's various regions in the face of modernization and national standardization. (618)

reservation system: The system that allotted land with designated boundaries to Native American tribes in the West, beginning in the 1850s and ending with the Dawes Severalty Act of 1887. Within these reservations, most land was used communally, rather than owned individually. The U.S. government encouraged and sometimes violently coerced Native Americans to stay on the reservations at all times. (547)

rock 'n' roll: "Crossover" musical style that rose to dominance in the 1950s, merging Black rhythm and blues with white bluegrass and country. Featuring a heavy beat and driving rhythm, rock 'n' roll music became a defining feature of the 1950s youth culture. (880)

***Roe v. Wade* (1973):** Landmark Supreme Court decision that forbade states from barring abortion by citing a woman's constitutional right to privacy. Seen as a victory for feminism and civil liberties by some, the decision provoked a strong counterreaction by opponents to abortion, galvanizing the pro-life movement. (951)

Rome-Berlin Axis (1936): Nazi Germany, under Adolf Hitler, and Fascist Italy, led by Benito Mussolini, allied themselves together under this nefarious treaty. The pact was signed after both countries had intervened on behalf of the fascist leader Francisco Franco during the Spanish Civil War. (811)

Roosevelt Corollary (1904): A brazen policy of "preventive intervention" advocated by Theodore Roosevelt in his Annual Message to Congress in 1904. Adding ballast to the Monroe Doctrine, his corollary stipulated that the United States would retain a right to intervene in the domestic affairs of Latin American nations in order to restore military and financial order. (670)

Root-Takahira agreement (1908): Agreement by which the United States and Japan agreed to respect each other's territorial possessions in the Pacific and to uphold the Open Door in China. The agreement was credited with easing tensions between the two nations, but it also resulted in a weakened American influence over further Japanese hegemony in China. (675)

Rough Riders (1898): Organized by Theodore Roosevelt, this was a colorful, motley regiment of Cuban war volunteers consisting of western cowboys, ex-convicts, and effete Ivy Leaguers. Roosevelt emphasized his experience with the regiment in subsequent campaigns for governor of New York and vice president under William McKinley. (655)

SALT II: Strategic Arms Limitation Treaty agreement between Soviet leader Leonid Brezhnev and American president Jimmy Carter. Despite an accord to limit weapons between the two leaders, the agreement was ultimately scuttled in the U.S. Senate following the Soviet invasion of Afghanistan in 1979. (957)

Sand Creek Massacre: On November 29, 1864, militia under the command of John C. Chivington assaulted a Cheyenne village in southeastern Colorado Territory. Initially hailed as a military triumph, it was later found that Chivington's men had attacked the village without provocation, killing over one hundred women and children. (549)

Sandinistas: Leftwing anti-American revolutionaries in Nicaragua who launched a civil war in 1979. (970)

scalawags: Derogatory term for pro-Union Southerners whom Southern Democrats accused of plundering the resources of the South in collusion with Republican governments after the Civil War. (511)

***Schenck v. United States* (1919):** A Supreme Court decision that upheld the Espionage and Sedition Acts, reasoning that freedom of speech could be curtailed when it posed a "clear and present danger" to the nation. (721)

Scientific Management: A system of industrial management created and promoted in the early twentieth century by Frederick W. Taylor, emphasizing stopwatch efficiency to improve factory performance. The system gained immense popularity across the United States and Europe. (740)

Scopes Trial: A court case that took place during the summer of 0925 in Dayton, Tennessee, over the issue of whether evolution could be taught in public schools. Pitting Christian fundamentalists against modernists, the trial eventually produced mixed results for fundamentalists, who won the case but were ridiculed by the national press. (756)

settlement houses: Mostly run by middle-class native-born women, settlement houses in immigrant neighborhoods provided housing, food, education, child care, cultural activities, and social connections for new arrivals to the United States. Many women, both native-born and immigrant, developed lifelong passions for social activism in the settlement houses. Jane Addams's Hull House in Chicago and Lillian Wald's Henry Street Settlement in New York City were two of the most prominent. (601)

Seward's Folly (1867): Popular term for Secretary of State William Seward's purchase of Alaska from Russia. The derisive term reflected the anti-expansionist sentiments of most Americans immediately after the Civil War. (514)

sharecropping: An agricultural system that emerged after the Civil War in which Black and white farmers rented land and residences from a plantation owner in exchange for giving him a certain "share" of each year's crop. Sharecropping was the dominant form of agriculture after the Civil War, and landowners manipulated this system to keep tenants in perpetual debt and unable to leave their plantations. (530)

Sheppard-Towner Maternity Act (1921): Designed to appeal to new women voters, this act provided federally financed instruction in maternal and infant health care and expanded the role of government in family welfare. (724)

Sherman Anti-Trust Act (1890): A law that forbade trusts or combinations in business, this was landmark legislation because it was one of the first congressional attempts to regulate big business for the public good. At first the law was mostly used to restrain trade unions, as the courts tended to side with companies in legal cases. In 1914, the act was revised so it could more effectively be used against monopolistic corporations. (578)

silent majority: Nixon administration's term to describe generally content, law-abiding, middle-class Americans who supported both the Vietnam War and America's institutions. As a political tool, the concept attempted to make a subtle distinction between believers in "traditional" values and the vocal minority of civil rights agitators, student protesters, counterculturalists, and other seeming disruptors of the social fabric. (929)

Six-Day War (1967): Military conflict between Israel and its Arab neighbors, including Syria, Egypt, and Jordan. The war ended with an Israeli victory and territorial expansion into the Sinai Peninsula, the Golan Heights, the Gaza Strip, and the West Bank. The 1967 war was a humiliation for several Arab states, and the territorial disputes it created formed the basis for continued conflict in the region. (920)

***The Slaughter-House Cases* (1873):** Ruling against New Orleans butchers required to work in a city-owned slaughterhouse, the Supreme Court majority severely limited the definition of individual rights that fell under the protection of federal power. This first major Fourteenth Amendment case—followed three years later by a similarly narrow ruling in *United States v. Cruikshank* (1876)—effectively opened the era of Jim Crow disenfranchisement and denial of Black civil rights in the South. (512)

"smoking gun" tape: Recording made in the Oval Office in June 1972 that proved conclusively that Nixon knew about the Watergate break-in and endeavored to cover it up. Led to a complete breakdown in congressional support for Nixon after the Supreme Court ordered he hand the tape to investigators. (942)

social gospel: A reform movement led by Protestant ministers who used religious doctrine to demand better housing and living conditions for the urban poor. Popular at the turn of the twentieth century, it was closely linked to the settlement-house movement, which brought middle-class, Anglo-American service volunteers into contact with immigrants and working people. (680)

Social Security Act (1935): A flagship accomplishment of the New Deal, this law provided for unemployment and old-age insurance financed by a payroll tax on employers and employees. It has long remained a pillar of the "New Deal Order." (798)

Southern Strategy (1972): Nixon reelection campaign strategy designed to appeal to conservative white people in the historically Democratic South. The president stressed law and order issues and remained noncommittal on civil rights. This strategy typified the regional split between the two parties as white Southerners became increasingly attracted to the Republican party in the aftermath of the civil rights movement. (933)

SPARs (U.S. Coast Guard Women's Reserve): The women's branch of the U.S. Coast Guard established during World War II to employ women in noncombatant jobs. (See **WACs.**) (826)

***Sputnik* (3057):** Soviet satellite first launched into earth orbit on October 4, 1957. This scientific achievement marked the first time human beings had put a man-made object into orbit and pushed the USSR noticeably ahead of the United States in the space race. A month later, the Soviet Union sent a larger satellite, *Sputnik II*, into space, prompting the United States to redouble its space exploration efforts and raising American fears of Soviet superiority. (889)

stagflation: Term referring to the simultaneous occurrence of low employment growth and high inflation in the national economy. The phenomenon characterized the economic troubles of the 1970s and posed both an intellectual challenge to economists and a policymaking challenge to government officials. (941)

Standard Oil Company (1870–1911): John D. Rockefeller's company, formed in 1870, which came to symbolize the trusts and monopolies of the Gilded Age. By 1877 Standard Oil controlled 95 percent of the oil refineries in the United States. It was also one of the first multinational corporations and at times distributed more than half of its kerosene production outside the United States. By the turn of the century it had become a target for trust-busting reformers, and in 1911 the Supreme Court ordered it to break up into several dozen smaller companies. (576)

Stonewall Uprising (1969): Uprising in support of equal rights for gay people sparked by an assault by off-duty police officers at a gay bar in New York. The rebellion led to a rise in activism within gay, lesbian, and transgender communities and furthered the sexual revolution of the late 1960s. (925)

Strategic Defense Initiative (SDI): Reagan administration plan announced in 1983 to create a missile-defense system over American territory to block a nuclear attack. Derided as "Star Wars" by critics, the plan typified Reagan's commitment to vigorous defense spending even as he sought to limit the size of government in domestic matters. (969)

Student Nonviolent Coordinating Committee (SNCC): Youth organization founded by Black students in 1960 to promote civil rights. Drawing on its members' youthful energies, SNCC in its early years coordinated demonstrations, sit-ins, and voter registration drives. (886)

Students for a Democratic Society (SDS): A campus-based political organization founded in 1961 by Tom Hayden that became an iconic representation of the New Left. Originally geared toward the intellectual promise of "participatory democracy," SDS emerged at the forefront of the civil rights, antipoverty, and antiwar movements during the 1960s. (928)

Suez crisis (1956): International crisis launched when Egyptian president Gamal Abdel Nasser nationalized the Suez Canal, which had been owned mostly by French and British stockholders. The crisis led to a British and French attack on Egypt, which failed without aid from the United States. The Suez crisis marked an important turning point in the post-colonial Middle East and highlighted the rising importance of oil in world affairs. (888)

Sunbelt: The fifteen-state crescent through the American South and Southwest that experienced terrific population and productivity expansion during World War II and particularly in the decades after the war, eclipsing the old industrial Northeast (the "Frostbelt"). (867)

supply-side economics: Economic theory that underlay Ronald Reagan's tax and spending cuts. Contrary to Keynesianism, supply-side theory declared that government policy should aim to increase the supply of goods and services, rather than the demand for them. It held that lower taxes and decreased regulation would increase productivity by providing increased incentives to work, thus increasing productivity and the tax base. (968)

Taft-Hartley Act (1947): Republican-promoted, antiunion legislation passed over President Truman's vigorous veto that weakened many of labor's New Deal gains by banning the closed shop and other strategies that helped unions organize. It also required union leaders to take a noncommunist oath, which purged the union movement of many of its most committed and active organizers. (862)

Tampico Incident (1914): An arrest of American sailors by the Mexican government that spurred Woodrow Wilson to dispatch the American navy to seize the port of Veracruz in April 1914.

Although war was avoided, tensions grew between the United States and Mexico. (711)

Tax Cuts and Jobs Act of 2017: Signed into law by President Trump on December 22, 2017, the Tax Cuts and Jobs Act trimmed income taxes across the board for a period of ten years, permanently slashed the corporate tax rate from 35 percent to 21 percent and removed the individual health-care mandate. Hailed as a major legislative victory for Republicans, the bill was denounced by critics as a plutocratic payout that would only deepen the federal deficit in the coming years. (1049)

Tax Reform Act: Signed into law by President Reagan on October 22, 1986, the Tax Reform Act streamlined federal tax codes and reduced the tax burden for top-income earners. Its successful passage reflected the Republican Party's embrace of free market doctrine, or "supply-side economics," as a cardinal principle of governance. (968)

Tea Party: A grassroots conservative political movement mobilized in opposition to Barack Obama's fiscal, economic, and health-care policies. Named after the Boston Tea Party of the Revolutionary Era, Tea Party protesters first demonstrated in early 2009, and they grew steadily in visibility and power as a pressuring force within the Republican Party through the 2010 midterm elections and beyond. (1029)

Teapot Dome scandal (1921): A tawdry affair involving the illegal lease of priceless naval oil reserves in Teapot Dome, Wyoming, and Elk Hills, California. The scandal, which implicated President Harding's secretary of the interior, was one of several that gave his administration a reputation for corruption. (762)

Telecommunications Act of 1996: The first major reform of the nation's telecommunications infrastructure, championed by both parties and signed into law by President Bill Clinton. The law significantly deregulated information industries and subsidized a major expansion of internet infrastructure, bringing many more American homes, workplaces, and schools online and fueling the dot-com boom of the late 1990s. (999)

Teller Amendment (1898): A proviso to President William McKinley's war plans that proclaimed to the world that when the United States had overthrown Spanish misrule, it would give Cuba its freedom. The amendment testified to the ostensibly "anti-imperialist" designs of the initial war plans. (654)

Temporary Assistance for Needy Families (1996): The result of a sweeping welfare reform law enacted by President Bill Clinton, the program replaced a New Deal-era entitlement, Aid to Families with Dependent Children (AFDC), with a system of time-limited grants and work requirements. (994)

Tennessee Valley Authority (TVA) (1933): One of the most revolutionary of the New Deal public works projects, the TVA brought cheap electric power, full employment, low-cost housing, and environmental improvements to Americans in the Tennessee Valley. (797)

Tenure of Office Act (1867): Required the president to seek approval from the Senate before removing appointees. When Andrew Johnson removed his secretary of war in violation of the act, he was impeached by the House but remained in office when the Senate fell one vote short of removing him. (513)

termination policy (1953): Proposed by President Dwight Eisenhower and endorsed by Congress, this policy reversed U.S. commitments to tribal preservation made by the "Indian New Deal" of the 1930s by ending the protected trust status of Native lands and terminating the tribes as legal entities. Few tribes agreed to termination, however, and a voluntary urban relocation program was only partly successful. (887)

Tet Offensive: A series of surprise attacks instigated by the Viet Cong in January 1968 that inflicted at least 150,000 casualties on both sides. Though the Viet Cong suffered heavy losses and were eventually repulsed, Ho Chi Minh scored a vital political victory by further dampening Americans' already waning enthusiasm for the war. (921)

Title IX: An amendment to an education bill signed by President Nixon in 1972. It read: "No person in the United States shall, on the basis of sex, be excluded from participation in, be denied the benefits of, or be subjected to discrimination under any education program or activity receiving federal financial assistance." Title IX facilitated women's access to educational facilities at all levels, conspicuously including college athletic programs. (950)

Tonkin Gulf Resolution: In August 1964, two American destroyers in the Bay of Tonkin were reportedly fired on by North Vietnamese torpedo boats. With only two dissenting votes, Congress responded not with a formal declaration of war but with a joint resolution giving President Johnson license to use "all necessary measures" to strike back. Where the United States had previously offered limited assistance in Vietnam, the resolution led to rapid and massive American military involvement in the region. (910)

Triangle Shirtwaist Company fire: On March 25, 1911, a ferocious blaze broke out in the Triangle Shirtwaist Company factory in New York City, resulting in 146 worker deaths. When it was later determined that the fatalities could have been avoided by adhering to proper fire codes—such as leaving the stairwell and exit doors unlocked—the incident sparked widespread outrage and inspired legislation to improve workplace safety. (687)

Tripartite Pact (1940): A pact between Germany, Italy, and Japan struck in the early months of World War II that pledged mutual assistance in their respective imperial ambitions. (812)

Truman Doctrine (1947): President Truman's universal pledge of support for any people fighting any communist or communist-inspired threat. Truman presented the doctrine to Congress in 1947 in support of his request for $400 million to defend Greece and Turkey against Soviet-backed insurgencies. (852)

trust: A mechanism by which one company grants control over its operations, through ownership of its stock, to another company. The Standard Oil Company became known for this practice in the 1870s as it eliminated its competition by taking control of smaller oil companies. (576)

Tulsa Race Massacre (1921): A particularly brutal incident during a period of surging race hatred and violence. White rioters looted and burned businesses in the prosperous Tulsa, Oklahoma, district known as "Black Wall Street," destroying thirty-five city blocks. As many as three hundred people died. (752)

Tuskegee Normal and Industrial School (founded 1881): Founded by Booker T. Washington in Tuskegee, Alabama, this higher education institution focused on training young Black students in agriculture and the trades to help them achieve economic independence. Washington justified segregated vocational training as a necessary first step on the road to racial equality, although critics accused him of being too "accommodationist." (607)

Tweed Ring: A symbol of Gilded Age corruption, "Boss" Tweed and his deputies ran the New York City Democratic party in the 1860s and swindled $200 million from the city through bribery, graft, and vote-buying. Boss Tweed was eventually jailed for his crimes and died behind bars. (600)

U-boats: German submarines, named for the German *Unterseeboot*, or "undersea boat," proved deadly for Allied ships in the war zone. U-boat attacks played an important role in drawing the United States into the First World War. (713)

Underwood Tariff (1913): This tariff provided for a substantial reduction of rates and enacted an unprecedented, graduated federal income tax. By 1917, revenue from the income tax surpassed receipts from the tariff, a gap that has since been vastly widened. (706)

Union League: Reconstruction-era African American organization that worked to educate Southern Black people about civic life, built Black schools and churches, and represented African American interests before government and employers. It also campaigned on behalf of Republican candidates and recruited local militias to protect Black people from white intimidation. (511)

United Nations (UN): International body formed in 1945 to bring nations into dialogue in hopes of preventing further world wars. Much like the former League of Nations in ambition, the UN was more realistic in recognizing the authority of the Big Five powers in keeping peace in the world. Thus, it guaranteed veto power to all permanent members of its Security Council—Britain, China, France, the Soviet Union, and the United States. (849)

***United States v. Cruikshank* (1876):** Supreme Court ruling that overturned the convictions of the white perpetrators of the Colfax Massacre on the grounds that the protections for civil liberties guaranteed in the Fourteenth Amendment applied only to *state* actions, not to actions undertaken by individuals. This narrow reading of the Amendment denied the civil liberties of Black people and effectively opened the Jim Crow era in the South. (512)

United Negro Improvement Association (UNIA): A Black nationalist organization founded in 1914 by the Jamaican-born Marcus Garvey in order to promote resettlement of African Americans to their "African homeland" and to stimulate a vigorous separate Black economy within the United States. (749)

USA Freedom Act of 2015: Replaced the expiring USA Patriot Act of 2001. Passed in the wake of the Edward Snowden revelations, it attempted to place some restrictions on government collection of metadata concerning American citizens. (1041)

USA Patriot Act (2001): Legislation passed shortly after the terrorist attacks of September 11, 2001, that granted broad surveillance and detention authority to the government. (1013)

V-E (Victory in Europe) Day: The source of frenzied rejoicing, May 8, 1945, marked the official end to the war in Europe, following the unconditional surrender of what remained of the German government. (835)

Versailles, Treaty of (1919): World War I concluded with this vengeful document, which secured peace but imposed sharp terms on Germany and created a territorial mandate system to manage former colonies of the world powers. To Woodrow Wilson's chagrin, it incorporated very few of his original Fourteen Points, although it did include the League of Nations that Wilson had long sought. Isolationists in the United States, deeply opposed to the League, led the opposition to the treaty, which was never ratified by the Senate. (732)

vertical integration: The practice perfected by Andrew Carnegie of controlling every step of the industrial production process in order to increase efficiency and limit competition. (575)

Vietnamization: Military strategy launched by Richard Nixon in 1969. The plan reduced the number of American combat troops in Vietnam and left more of the fighting to the South Vietnamese, who were supplied with American armor, tanks, and weaponry. (929)

V-J (Victory over Japan) Day: August 15, 1945, heralded the surrender of Japan and the final end to World War II. (837)

Volcker Shock: Anti-inflationary "tight money" interest rate hikes by the Federal Reserve Board (the Fed) in 1979 during President Carter's administration, named after the Fed's then-Chairman, Paul Volker. (968)

Volstead Act (1919): A federal act enforcing the Eighteenth Amendment, which prohibited the manufacture, sale, and transportation of alcoholic beverages. (753)

Voter Education Project (1962–1968): Effort by SNCC and other civil rights groups to register the South's historically disenfranchised Black population. The project typified a common strategy of the civil rights movement, which sought to counter racial discrimination by empowering people at grassroots levels to exercise their civic rights through voting. (900)

Voting Rights Act of 1965: Legislation pushed through Congress by President Johnson that prohibited ballot-denying tactics, such as literacy tests and intimidation. The Voting Rights Act was a successor to the Civil Rights Act of 1964 and sought to make racial disenfranchisement explicitly illegal. (915)

WACs (Women's Army Corps): The women's branch of the U.S. Army established during World War II to employ women in noncombatant jobs. Women now participated in the armed services in ways that went beyond their traditional roles as nurses. (826)

Wade-Davis Bill: Passed by congressional Republicans in response to Abraham Lincoln's "10 percent" Reconstruction plan, it required that 30 percent of a state's voters pledge allegiance to the Union and set stronger safeguards for emancipation. Reflected divisions between Congress and the president, and between radical and moderate Republicans, over the treatment of the defeated South. (500)

Wagner Act (1935): Also known as the National Labor Relations Act, this law protected the right of labor to organize in unions and bargain collectively with employers and established the National Labor Relations Board to monitor unfair labor practices on the part of employers. Its passage marked the culmination of decades of labor protest. (799)

Wall Street Reform and Consumer Protection Act (2010): Also known as the Dodd-Frank Act, after its Democratic sponsors, Connecticut senator Christopher Dodd and Massachusetts representative Barney Frank. In an effort to avoid another financial crisis like the Great Recession, the act updated many federal regulations affecting the financial and banking systems and created some new agencies, such as the Bureau of Consumer Financial Protection. (1028)

War Industries Board (1917): Headed by Bernard Baruch, this federal agency coordinated industrial production during World War I, setting production quotas, allocating raw materials, and pushing companies to increase efficiency and eliminate waste. Under the economic mobilization of the War Industries Board, industrial production in the United States increased 20 percent during the war. (721)

War Powers Act (1973): Law passed by Congress limiting the president's ability to wage war without congressional approval. The act required the president to notify Congress within forty-eight hours of committing troops to a foreign conflict. An important consequence of the Vietnam War, this piece of legislation sought to reduce the president's unilateral authority in military matters. (936)

War Production Board (WPB): Established in 1942 by executive order to direct all war production, including procuring and allocating raw materials, to maximize the nation's war machine. The WPB had sweeping powers over the U.S. economy and was abolished in November 1945 soon after Japan's defeat. (823)

War Refugee Board (1944–1945): A U.S. agency formed to help rescue Jews from German-occupied territories and to provide relief to inmates of Nazi concentration camps. The agency performed noble work, but it did not begin operations until very late in the war, after millions had already been murdered. (817)

Watergate: Series of scandals that resulted in President Richard Nixon's resignation in August 1974 amid calls for his impeachment. The episode sprang from a failed burglary attempt at Democratic party headquarters in Washington's Watergate Hotel during the 1972 election. (942)

Watts: A predominantly Black neighborhood in Los Angeles, California. On August 11, 1985, after word spread that an act of police brutality had been committed against a Black man, a bloody riot erupted in Watts. It left 34 people dead and over a thousand injured and marked the first of many similar rebellions in predominantly Black urban neighborhoods in the summers that followed. (916)

WAVES (Women Accepted for Volunteer Emergency Service): The women's branch of the U.S. Navy established during World War II to employ women in noncombatant jobs. (See **WACs.**) (826)

"waving the bloody shirt": The use of Civil War imagery by political candidates and parties to draw votes to their side of the ticket. (523)

weapons of mass destruction (WMD): Refers to weapons—nuclear, biological, and chemical—that can kill large numbers of people and do great damage to the built and natural environment. The term was used to refer to nuclear weapons during the Cold War. The Bush administration's claim that Saddam Hussein had developed WMD provided the rationale for the United States' invasion of Iraq in 2003. These weapons were never found after the invasion. (989)

Whitewater: A series of scandals during the Clinton administration that stemmed from a failed real estate investment from which the Clintons were alleged to have illicitly profited. The accusations prompted the appointment of a special federal prosecutor, though no indictments. (1008)

Woman's Christian Temperance Union (WCTU): Founded in Ohio in the 1870s to combat the evils of excessive alcohol consumption, the WCTU went on to embrace a broad reform agenda, including campaigns to abolish prostitution and gain the right to vote for women. (615)

Woman's Loyal League (1863–1865): Women's organization formed to help bring about an end to the Civil War and encourage Congress to pass a constitutional amendment prohibiting slavery. (509)

Workingmen's Compensation Act (1916): Passed under Woodrow Wilson, this law granted assistance to federal civil-service employees during periods of disability. It was a precursor to labor-friendly legislation passed during the New Deal. (708)

World Trade Organization (WTO) (1995): An international body to promote and supervise liberal trade among nations. The successor to the General Agreement on Tariffs and Trade, it marked a key world trade policy achievement of the Clinton administration. (1000)

World's Columbian Exposition (1893): Americans saw this world's fair, held in Chicago, as their opportunity to claim a place among the world's most "civilized" societies, by which they meant the countries of Western Europe. The fair honored art, architecture, and science, and its promoters built a mini-city in which to host the fair that reflected all the ideals of city planning popular at the time. For many, this was the high point of the City Beautiful movement. (620)

Wounded Knee Massacre (1890): A battle between the U.S. Army and the Dakota Sioux, in which two hundred Native Americans and twenty-nine U.S. soldiers died. Tensions erupted violently over two major issues: the Sioux practice of the "Ghost Dance," which the U.S. government had outlawed, and the dispute over whether Sioux reservation land would be broken up because of the Dawes Act. (562)

Yalta Conference (1946): Meeting of Franklin Roosevelt, Winston Churchill, and Joseph Stalin in February 1945 at an old tsarist resort on the Black Sea, where the Big Three leaders laid the foundations for the postwar division of power in Europe, including a divided Germany and territorial concessions to the Soviet Union. (847)

yellow journalism: A scandal-mongering practice of journalism that emerged in New York during the Gilded Age out of the circulation battles between Joseph Pulitzer's *New York World* and William Randolph Hearst's *New York Journal*. The expression has remained a pejorative term referring to sensationalist journalism practiced with unethical, unprofessional standards. (610)

Young Americans for Freedom (YAF): Formed during the cultural ferment of the 1960s, the YAF was the conservative counterpart to SDS (Students for a Democratic Society), which attracted radical students on campuses nationwide. The YAF helped to propel Barry Goldwater's 1964 presidential candidacy and to energize a resurgent conservatism during the Reagan years. (928)

Zimmermann note (1917): German foreign secretary Arthur Zimmerman had secretly proposed a German-Mexican alliance against the United States. When the note was intercepted and published in March 1917, it caused an uproar that made some Americans more willing to enter the war. (716)

Index

B

C

D

E

I

N

Q

R

T

U

X

Y

Z